Troubleshooting Campus Networks

Practical Analysis of Cisco and LAN Protocols

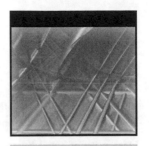

Troubleshooting
Campus Networks

Practical Analysis of Cisco
and LAN Protocols

Priscilla Oppenheimer
Joseph Bardwell

Wiley Publishing, Inc.

Publisher: Robert Ipsen
Editor: Carol Long
Developmental Editor: Adaobi Obi
Managing Editor: Micheline Frederick
Text Design & Composition: Wiley Composition Services

This book is printed on acid-free paper. ∞

Published by Wiley Publishing, Inc., Indianapolis, Indiana

Published simultaneously in Canada

For general information on our other products and services please contact our Customer Care Department within the United States at (800) 762-2974, outside the United States at (317) 572-3993 or fax (317) 572-4002.

Wiley also publishes its books in a variety of electronic formats. Some content that appears in print may not be available in electronic books.

Library of Congress Cataloging-in-Publication Data:

ISBN: 0-471-21013-7

Printed in the United States of America

10 9 8 7 6 5 4 3 2 1

Contents

Acknowledgments   **xvii**

Chapter 1   Introduction   **1**
 Why We Wrote This Book   1
  Guaranteed Not to Rust, Bust, or Collect Dust   2
 Audience and Scope   3
  Cisco Certifications   3
  The NAX Certification Program   4
 Organization   5
 Our Web Site   6

Chapter 2   Troubleshooting Methods   **7**
 Challenges in Today's Networking Environment   7
 Using a Systematic Troubleshooting Method   9
  Using the OSI Model for Troubleshooting   10
  Generic Problem-Solving Models   12
   Fundamental Network Troubleshooting Considerations   13
  Cisco's Troubleshooting Method   14
   Define the Problem   15
   Gather Facts   15
   Consider Possibilities   16
   Create an Action Plan   16
   Implement the Action Plan and Observe the Results   16
   Document the Results   17
 Proactive Troubleshooting and Baselining   17
  Documenting Your Network   18
   Documenting Network Names and Addresses   19
   Tools for Network Documentation   20
   Documenting Switched Networks   21
   The Cisco Discovery Protocol   22

Protocol Analysis   23
    WildPackets Protocol Analyzers   24
    Using a Protocol Analyzer in a Switched Network   24
Understanding Network Traffic   27
    Reliable Versus Unreliable Protocols   27
    Terminal/Host Traffic   28
    Peer-to-Peer Traffic   29
    Client/Server Traffic   30
    Server-to-Server Traffic   32
    Distributed Computing Traffic   32
Statistical Monitoring   32
    Simple Network Management Protocol and
        Remote Monitoring   34
    WildPackets Statistical Tools   35
Simulation and Modeling   35
Active and Reactive Troubleshooting   36
    Tools for Troubleshooting the Physical Layer   36
    Tools for Troubleshooting Above the Physical Layer   37
        Ping   37
        Trace-Route   41
    Other Troubleshooting Commands   45
        Cisco IOS Show Commands   45
        Cisco IOS Debug Commands   48
Summary   50

Chapter 3   **Troubleshooting and Analyzing Ethernet Networks**   **53**
Ethernet History and Architecture   53
    Ethernet Topologies   54
Ethernet Physical Layer   56
    Protocol Analyzers and Ethernet Media   59
    Signal Encoding   59
        Manchester Encoding   59
        MLT-3 Encoding   60
        Other Signal Encoding Methods on Ethernet Networks   62
    Clock Synchronization   62
Ethernet MAC Layer   63
    Carrier Sense Multiple Access with Collision Detection   63
    Collision Domains   65
        Bit Length and Measurement of a Collision Domain   65
        Collision Domains in 100-Mbps Ethernet   66
        Collisions on Networks with Hubs and Switches   67
    Full-Duplex Operations   68
        Full-Duplex Protocol Analysis   69
        Autonegotiation   70
        Flow Control on Full-Duplex Links   72
    Enhancements to Ethernet Media Access Control
        for Gigabit Ethernet   73

Ethernet Frames   75
    Fields in an Ethernet II or IEEE 802.3 Frame Header   76
        Destination Address   76
        Source Address   78
        Length or EtherType   78
        Logical Link Control Frame Formats   80
        Ethernet or IEEE 802.3 Frame Footer   83
    Ethernet Frame Sizes   84
        Configuring and Troubleshooting Ethernet Frame Sizes   85
        Maximum Transmission Unit   87
        Tunneling and Frame Lengths   87
        VLAN Tagging and Baby Giants   88
Collecting and Understanding Ethernet Performance Data   88
    Remote Monitoring   88
    The Cisco Show Interface Ethernet Command   89
        Bandwidth   90
        Delay   91
        Utilization   92
        Reliability   93
        Collision Rate   94
    Frame Corruption   95
    Broadcast and Multicast Rates   96
        Cisco's Broadcast Suppression Feature   97
    Summary   98

**Chapter 4   Troubleshooting and Analyzing IEEE 802.11
              Wireless Networks   99**
Chapter Scope and Depth   99
    Things That Are Beyond the Scope of This Chapter   100
A Primer on Wireless Networking   102
    Wireless Networking Fundamentals   102
    What Is a Wireless Network?   103
    The Challenge of Wireless Network Design   103
    Protocol Analysis in Wireless Networks   105
Wireless Networking Technologies   105
    Narrowband Radio Transmission (Radio LAN)   106
    Frequency Hopping Spread Spectrum (FHSS)   106
    Direct Sequence Spread Spectrum (DSSS)   106
    Infrared (IR)   107
    Bluetooth and the Personal Area Network (PAN)   107
        Conflicts between Bluetooth and 802.11 Networks   108
    Other Wireless Standards   108
Organization of the WLAN Environment   109
    The Basic Service Set (BSS)   109
    The Extended Service Set (ESS)   110
    The Timing Synchronization Function (TSF)   112

Station Initialization Behavior   112
    Channel Selection   113
    Authentication   115
    Association to the BSS   115
    Analysis of the Initialization Process   115
        Packet Acknowledgment   116
802.11 Media Access Control   117
    Interframe Spacing   117
    The Network Allocation Vector (NAV)   118
    The Request to Send/Clear to Send Mechanism   119
    Synopsis of the 802.11 Environment   119
Radio Frequency Transmission   120
    Frequency Allocation   121
    Mathematics for RF Engineering   122
        The Decibel Unit of Measurement   123
        A Synopsis without Any Complicated Math   123
        Understanding Decibels   124
        Important Things to Remember about Decibels   126
    Specifications Involving Gain or Loss   126
        The dB Milliwatt   127
        Relationships between Metrics   127
        The Wonder of Logarithmic Calculations   128
        Applying the Principle of Logarithmic Subtraction   129
        Concluding Thoughts on Logarithmic Subtraction   130
    Application of dB and dBm Measurements   130
        Free Space Propagation   130
        Multiplying Logarithms Is Like Exponentiation   131
        Free Space Path Loss Conclusions   133
Environmental Factors That Affect 802.11 Transmission   133
    Reflection   134
    Absorption   134
    Refraction   134
    Diffraction   134
Concepts for Site Survey Troubleshooting   134
    Clear Channel Power Assessment   135
    Limitations on RF Signal Transmission   136
    Shannon's Channel Capacity Theorem   136
    Gaussian Noise   137
    Multipath Transmission   137
    Real-World Path Loss   138
        Calculating Real-World Path Loss   138
    Antenna Positioning for Maximum Coverage   139
    Protocol Analyzer Reporting of Signal Strength   140
Determining the Significance of Vendor Specifications   141
    Output Power   142
    Receiver Sensitivity   143

The Impact of Environmental Noise   143
  Network Utilization   145
  Signal Strength, Bad Packets, and Network Utilization 145
    Checksum Errors   146
Site Survey Techniques for WLAN Troubleshooting   146
  Estimating Effective Range   146
  AP Placement Considerations   147
Troubleshooting Network Design Problems   148
  Large Packets and Collisions   149
  Numerous Simultaneous Users and Collisions   149
    Practical Limits on User Community Size   149
  Configuration Settings   151
    IP Address   151
    ESSID   151
    Fragmentation Threshold   151
    Request to Send (RTS) Threshold   151
    Authentication Type   152
    Wired Equivalent Privacy (WEP) Key and Passphrase 152
Understanding the 802.11 Packet Decode   152
Summary   154

Chapter 5   Troubleshooting and Analyzing the Spanning Tree Protocol   157
Poetic Interoperations   157
Transparent Bridging   158
  Bridging Tasks   162
  Bridging Loops   162
STP Behavior   165
  Bridge Protocol Data Units   166
    Protocol Analysis of BPDUs   166
  STP Convergence   172
    Electing the Root Bridge   172
    Electing Root Ports   174
    Electing Designated Ports   174
    Selecting Bridge Ports for the Spanning Tree 175
    Port States   176
    The Topology Change Process   177
Proactive Troubleshooting of STP   180
  Documenting Your Switched Network   182
  Monitoring STP   182
    Logging STP Events on Cisco Switches   184
    Logging STP Events on Cisco Routers   185
Reactive Troubleshooting of STP   186
  One-Way Connectivity   188
  Reducing Startup Delay on Cisco Switch Ports   188
    Cisco's Portfast Feature   189

	Optimizing Spanning Tree Implementations	192
	Uplink Fast and Backbone Fast	192
	Load Sharing	193
	Selecting the Root Bridge Deterministically	194
	Configuring Bridge Priority	197
	Summary	197
Chapter 6	**Troubleshooting and Analyzing Virtual LANs**	**199**
	VLAN Frameworks	199
	VLAN Definitions	200
	VLANs and Non-VLANs	200
	The Design of a VLAN	201
	Interconnected Switches	202
	Protocol Analysis in a VLAN Environment	202
	VLAN Memberships	204
	Configuring VLANs	204
	Assigning a VTP Domain	205
	Creating a VLAN	206
	Assigning Ports to VLANs	207
	Verifying VLAN Configuration	208
	VLAN Trunks	210
	ISL and 802.1Q Comparison	212
	Routers and VLAN Trunks	213
	Cisco's Inter-Switch Link	217
	Dynamic Inter-Switch Link Protocol	218
	DISL Frames	220
	IEEE 802.1Q	222
	Configuring 802.1Q	224
	Per-VLAN Spanning Trees	224
	Troubleshooting Cisco's VTP	227
	VTP Names and Passwords	228
	VTP Pruning	228
	Analyzing and Monitoring VTP	229
	Summary	235
Chapter 7	**Troubleshooting and Analyzing Campus IP Networks**	**237**
	TCP/IP History	237
	The TCP/IP Protocol Stack	238
	The Internet Protocol	241
	IP Protocol Analysis	241
	The IP Type of Service or DS Field	243
	IP Fragmentation and Reassembly	246
	IP Time to Live	252
	The IP Protocol Field	254
	IP Options	254
	IP Addressing	260
	Moving the Prefix Boundary to the Right (Subnetting)	261
	Claude Shannon and Boolean Logic	264

Moving the Prefix Boundary to the Left (Supernetting)   265
Address Resolution Protocol (ARP)   268
    Proxy ARP   269
    Reverse Address Resolution Protocol (RARP)   270
Dynamic Host Configuration Protocol   270
    DHCP and Routers   273
    Monitoring and Troubleshooting DHCP   276
Private IP Addresses   277
    Network Address Translation (NAT)   278
IP Multicast Addresses   279
    The Internet Group Management Protocol (IGMP)   280
    Multicast Routing Protocols   281
IPv6   282
    IPv6 Protocol Analysis   284
        IPv6 Extensions   285
    IPv6 Autoconfiguration   286
Summary   287

**Chapter 8   Troubleshooting and Analyzing Campus IP
Routing Protocols   289**
Host Routing   289
    The Hot Standby Router Protocol   292
    Monitoring and Troubleshooting Host Routing   292
Static and Default Routing   293
    Monitoring and Troubleshooting Static and Default Routes 294
Dynamic Routing   295
    Distance-Vector Versus Link-State Routing   298
        Distance-Vector Routing Protocols   298
        Link-State Routing Protocols   300
    Using Multiple Routing Protocols   301
        Integrated Routing and Bridging   302
General Comments on Troubleshooting IP Routing   303
Sample Network Used in Protocol Analysis Examples   304
Routing Information Protocol (RIP)   305
    RIP Protocol Analysis   306
    RIP Timers   309
    RIPv2   310
    Cisco Show and Debug Commands for RIP   311
Interior Gateway Routing Protocol (IGRP)   312
    IGRP Protocol Analysis   313
    IGRP Triggered Updates and Poison Reverse   315
    Cisco Show and Debug Commands for IGRP   318
Enhanced IGRP   319
    EIGRP Protocol Analysis   320
        EIGRP Queries   325
    Cisco Show and Debug Commands for EIGRP   327

Open Shortest Path First (OSPF)   329
  OSPF Network Architectures   330
  OSPF Protocol Analysis   331
    Building an Adjacency   333
  Cisco Show and Debug Commands for OSPF   338
Border Gateway Protocol (BGP)   340
  BGP Protocol Analysis   340
  Cisco Show and Debug Commands for BGP   343
Summary   344

**Chapter 9   Troubleshooting and Analyzing TCP, UDP, and
               Upper-Layer IP Protocols   345**
Upper-Layer IP Protocol Analysis   346
Transmission Control Protocol   346
  TCP Protocol Analysis   347
    TCP Port Numbers   348
    TCP Connection Establishment   350
    TCP Reliable Delivery and Flow Control   354
    TCP Delayed Acknowledgments   358
    TCP Slow Start   359
    TCP Window Size Analysis   359
    Identifying TCP Performance Problems   362
    TCP Connection Termination   364
    TCP Checksum   365
User Datagram Protocol   366
  UDP Protocol Analysis   367
    UDP Port Numbers   368
Application-Layer Protocols   368
  Domain Name System   369
    DNS Protocol Analysis   371
  Service Location Protocol   375
  Hypertext Transfer Protocol   377
    HTTP Proxy Servers   378
    HTTP Protocol Analysis   379
  File Transfer Protocol   381
    FTP File Types and Structures   382
    FTP Protocol Analysis   383
    FTP Active Versus Passive Mode   387
  Protocols for Electronic Mail   392
    SMTP Protocol Analysis   393
    POP3 Protocol Analysis   395
Summary   396

Chapter 10   Troubleshooting and Analyzing Campus IPX Networks   399
Novell NetWare Concepts   400
  IPX Addressing   401
  IPX Packets   403
    Ethernet Frames in IPX Environments   406

NetWare Core Protocol   409
Watchdog Spoofing   412
IPX Service Advertising Protocol   414
SAP Filters   417
Get Nearest Server   419
Cisco Routers and Get Nearest Server   420
IPX Routing   421
IPX Routing Information Protocol   422
Enhanced Interior Gateway Routing Protocol for IPX   424
NetWare Link Services Protocol   427
IPX Networks in Transition   430
Troubleshooting IPX   433
Applying Your Protocol Analyzer   434
IPX Ping and Trace   434
Show IPX Route   435
Show IPX Servers   436
Show IPX Interface   436
Show IPX Traffic   437
Show IPX EIGRP   438
Show IPX NLSP   439
Debug IPX Packet   439
Debug IPX Routing   439
Debug IPX SAP   439
Summary   440

**Chapter 11 Troubleshooting and Analyzing Campus
AppleTalk Networks   441**
AppleTalk Concepts   441
AppleTalk Architectures   442
AppleTalk Layering   443
AppleTalk Addressing   446
AppleTalk Addresses on a Cisco Router   447
AppleTalk Address Resolution Protocol (AARP)   448
Dynamic Addressing   448
Datagram Delivery Protocol (DDP)   452
Name Binding Protocol (NBP)   454
Apple Filing Protocol (AFP)   455
AFP over TCP   457
AppleTalk Routing   459
Routing Table Maintenance Protocol (RTMP)   460
End-Node Routing   463
Zone Information Protocol   464
AppleTalk Update-Based Routing Protocol   465
EIGRP for AppleTalk   468
Controlling AppleTalk Traffic   473
Static Routes   473

	AppleTalk Access Lists	474
	Filtering Cable Ranges	474
	Filtering Zones	475
	Macintosh Networks in Transition	475
	Mac OS X	476
	WebDAV	478
	Service Location Protocol (SLP)	478
	Mac OS X Initialization Traffic	478
	Mac OS X Server Network Management Tools	480
	Troubleshooting AppleTalk	480
	AppleTalk Ping (Echo)	482
	Cisco AppleTalk NBP Testing	483
	Cisco IOS Show Commands for AppleTalk	484
	Cisco IOS Debug Commands for AppleTalk	486
	Summary	487
Chapter 12	**Troubleshooting and Analyzing Windows Networking**	**489**
	Windows Networking Concepts	489
	The NetBIOS Basis for Windows Networking	491
	The History of NetBIOS	491
	NetBIOS Function Calls	491
	The Importance of NetBIOS	492
	NetBIOS Consistency across Different Implementations	494
	NetBIOS Naming Conventions	494
	Qualifier Byte = 0x00	495
	Qualifier Byte = 0x03	495
	Qualifier Byte = 0x05	495
	Qualifier Byte = 0x06	496
	Qualifier Byte = 0x1B	496
	Qualifier Byte = 0x1C	496
	Qualifier Byte = 0x1D	496
	Qualifier Byte = 0x1E	496
	Qualifier Byte = 0x1F	497
	Qualifier Byte = 0x20	497
	Qualifier Byte = 0x21	497
	The 0x0102_MSBROWSE_0x0201 Name	497
	The Significance of NetBIOS Naming	498
	NetBIOS Implementation Differences	499
	A Windows Internet Name Service Query Carried on UDP	500
	A TCP NetBIOS Session Setup Request	501
	TCP NetBIOS Data	502
	NetBEUI Data Exchange (A Browse Packet)	504
	IPX Name Query	506
	IPX NetBIOS Data	507
	Concluding Thoughts on NetBIOS Terminology	508

NetBIOS Name Management Mechanisms   508
  Name Registration   508
  Name Resolution   509
  Name Refresh   510
  Name Release   510
  Management of NetBIOS Names with NetBIOS/TCP   510
  Troubleshooting NetBIOS Naming Problems   512
NetBIOS Data Movement   513
  Session Behavior with NetBIOS/TCP   514
  Reliable Data Transport with NetBIOS   515
The Workgroup Model and the Domain Model   518
  Analysis of a Workgroup Authentication Operation   518
  Authentication in the Windows NT Domain Model   521
  NT Registry Parameters Controlling Replication   522
  The Browse Protocol   522
    Maintaining the Browse List   523
    Browsing with Multiple Protocols   524
The Windows 2000 Model   525
Summary   527

Chapter 13 WAN Troubleshooting for LAN Engineers   529
WAN Concepts   529
  WAN Standards   530
    Understanding WANs from a LAN Management Perspective 532
  WAN Components   532
  End-to-End WAN Considerations   533
    Troubleshooting WANs from a LAN Perspective 534
  Troubleshooting WANs from a Router Interface Perspective 536
  Provisioning WAN Capacity   537
WAN Technologies   539
  Leased Lines   539
  High-Level Data Link Control (HDLC)   539
    Troubleshooting Cisco's HDLC Implementation 540
  Point-to-Point Protocol (PPP)   541
    Troubleshooting PPP   543
  Frame Relay   544
    Frame Relay Virtual Circuits   544
    Frame Relay Congestion Control   545
    Frame Relay Inverse ARP   546
    Frame Relay Local Management Interface   547
    Troubleshooting Frame Relay   547
  Integrated Services Digital Network   551
    ISDN Layer 1   552
    ISDN Layer 2   553
    ISDN Layer 3   555
    Troubleshooting ISDN BRI Problems   556

Asynchronous Transfer Mode (ATM)   557
ATM Virtual Circuits and Adaptation Layers   558
Mapping a Protocol Address to an ATM PVC   559
ATM Quality of Service Specifications   560
Troubleshooting ATM   561
Chapter and Book Summary   562

References   **565**
Standards Documents   565
Web Sites and White Papers   567
Books   568
Books on LANs   568
Books on WANs   568
Books on TCP/IP   568
Books on Network Technology, Design, and Troubleshooting   569

Index   **571**

Acknowledgments

We would like to thank the professionals at Wiley who helped make this book a reality, especially Carol A. Long, Executive Acquisitions Editor, Adaobi Obi Tulton, Assistant Developmental Editor, and Micheline Frederick, Associate Managing Editor. In addition, each of us has many other people to acknowledge.

Priscilla Oppenheimer: I would like to thank the many protocol experts with whom I have worked over the years. Thanks to Howard Berkowitz, a helpful and wise computer networking wizard, and Marty Adkins, a CCIE who is always ready with a comprehensible answer. Thanks also go to my colleagues on the Group Study mailing list who have answered numerous technical questions, including Paul Borghese (the moderator), Chuck Larrieu, Leigh Anne Chisholm, David Madland (MADMAN), Pamela Forsyth, Jenny McLeod, John Neiberger, Rita Puzmanova, Paul Werner, Karen Young, and many others. Special thanks to Kevin Cullimore and Brant Stevens for their Novell NetWare expertise.

I would like to acknowledge my colleagues from the Network General days who inspired my love for protocol analysis, including Naheed Ferguson, Anita Lenk, Barbara Sandacz, Margo Lindenmayer, Don Prefontaine, Todd Perkins, Merilee Ford, Larry Young, Alex Cannara, Sean Finn, Tim Blackburn, Michelle Coomes, and many more.

And finally, thanks to Alan Oppenheimer, who is not only a protocol expert but also a terrific husband.

Joseph Bardwell: My own journey through the jungle of protocol-level communication has been a wonderful experience. Larry Denburg of the University of Delaware opened my eyes to the world of comparative programming languages in the 1970s, and many Saturday mornings found me standing at the counter of the local Radio Shack store programming the TRS Model I computer. I'm pleased to see that my son, Joshua, has followed in my footsteps as a protocol analysis engineer and teacher. With good fortune, this book will serve as a reference for him as well as for the rest of the networking community. I echo Priscilla's acknowledgment of our colleagues from the early days at Network General, and a very special thanks goes out to Naheed Ferguson for keeping me focused in the midst of confusion. Finally, I would like to thank my associates at WildPackets, Inc., who have worked diligently to create the EtherPeek NX and AiroPeek NX analyzers. There's a little bit of all of us in that software, and that means there's a little bit of me in there too.

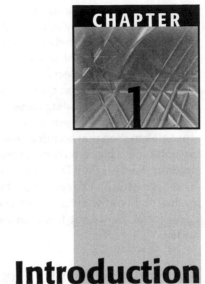

CHAPTER 1

Introduction

The turn of the century brings us into an era of exciting advancements in computer applications. New and innovative ways of integrating computer network technology into business, education, government, and even private homes have shifted focus from the underlying engineering that allows computer systems to talk to each other. And yet, when the systems don't talk to each other, the first thing people say is, "The network is having problems!" This book discusses methods for addressing those problems and explains how networks really work. Cisco and industry-standard troubleshooting methods for analyzing, diagnosing, and fixing problems are described in detail. The book also covers techniques for using protocol analyzers, such as the WildPackets EtherPeek and AiroPeek products, to recognize and isolate faulty network behavior.

Why We Wrote This Book

We wrote this book to provide technical people with technical information that they can apply to production environments and day-to-day network configuration, support, and troubleshooting. During the 1980s and 1990s, we worked with many experts in the computer industry, some very closely, some only in passing. It became clear who the experts were, because they all knew how networks really function. None of these people said "TCIP," and they all knew that a bridge operates at Layer 2 and a router at Layer 3. They also knew lots of other things.

Many people in the computer industry were not experts, however. They thought they understood many things, but they lacked certain fundamental knowledge. Lacking formal computer network education, and forced to use, implement, support, and maintain complex systems, they drew many erroneous conclusions and sometimes taught these to their peers.

This book focuses on many of the technology and engineering issues that are often misunderstood. In reading these pages you may encounter concepts that seem to contradict what others have told you. We have attempted to put down on paper some of the core information that is critical to successful troubleshooting and protocol analysis. This information is based on documents from renowned standards organizations such as the Internet Engineering Task Force (IETF) and the Institute of Electrical and Electronics Engineers (IEEE). Of more importance, the information is based on many years of analyzing real-world, diverse, and complex networks. This book has a unique protocol-level focus that is not found in most of the volumes of technical literature available today.

Guaranteed Not to Rust, Bust, or Collect Dust

Computer networks are like used cars, and, just as when you go to a used-car lot, you have to be careful not to get a lemon. The following can be said of both networks and used cars:

- They can be made to look good when you first examine them, but they sometimes have parts that are ready to fail when you need them most.

- An inexperienced technician can tinker with them and patch up the obvious problems, leading to the incorrect conclusion that the technician is an expert.

- Some problems have deceptive symptoms and only a true expert can discern the real causes.

- Even though the basic systems and technologies that make them work have not changed much over the years, they both incorporate whatever engineering schemes were popular at the time they were designed.

We were taught to pump the brakes if a car skids on an icy road, but this rule doesn't apply when using anti-lock breaking. We were taught to turn into a skid, but this doesn't apply when the car has front-wheel drive. Changes in automotive technology completely change the way we think about some of the fundamental aspects of driving.

We were taught that there are three Internet Protocol (IP) address classes (A, B, and C) that are used for unique host identification, but this doesn't apply when classless addressing is implemented. We often hear that network utilization shouldn't exceed 40 percent on Ethernet networks. However, this is no longer true on full-duplex Ethernet links. Changes in computer network technology change the way we think about fundamental methods of design and troubleshooting.

Whether you're inspecting a used car or troubleshooting a computer network, you have to be on guard for hidden problems, advice from inexperienced helpers, confusing symptoms, and the fact that design evolution brings with it changes in terminology and function.

Audience and Scope

The audience for this book is network engineers, administrators, and technicians who manage Cisco and multivendor campus networks. A campus network is a network that spans buildings and consists of wired and wireless technologies that connect clients and servers. Although the word *campus* often refers to colleges or universities, and this book is perfectly matched to the needs of college network administrators, the book is not just for college network administrators but for any administrator who manages a campus network based on the following technologies:

- 10-, 100-, and 1000-Mbps Ethernet connectivity.
- 802.11 wireless communication.
- Switched connections between machines within a single network.
- Virtual Local Area Networks (VLANs) that segregate networks in a mesh topology.
- Routed connections between networks in a campus environment.
- Wide Area Network (WAN) connections between campus networks. (Although this book focuses on Local Area Networks [LANs], WAN information is also provided.)
- Upper-layer protocols from the Transmission Control Protocol (TCP)/Internet Protocol (IP), AppleTalk, Novell NetWare, and Windows networking protocol families.

This book isn't about figuring out if a cable is disconnected in a simple LAN; rather, it is about troubleshooting complex internetworks with tens, hundreds, or even thousands of users. This book is for network engineers who manage and configure internetworking devices. Although it doesn't cover workstation or server configuration, some of the information in this book will help desktop support personnel and server administrators also.

Finally, this book is also written for certification candidates, in particular, candidates for Cisco certifications and the vendor-neutral Network Analysis Expert (NAX) certification program sponsored by WildPackets Academy.

Cisco Certifications

In the Cisco arena, this book focuses on the Cisco Certified Network Professional (CCNP) and the Cisco Certified Internetwork Expert (CCIE) certifications.

The CCNP certification indicates advanced or journeyman knowledge of networks. Having the CCNP certification denotes to employers that you can install, configure, operate, and troubleshoot multiprotocol LAN, WAN, and dial-access services for organizations with networks from 100 to more than 500 nodes. To achieve CCNP status, you must pass five tests. This book focuses on the most advanced test, which is the Support Test. All the topics in Cisco's list of topics for the Support Test are covered.

This book is also for CCIE candidates. To achieve CCIE status, you must pass both a qualification written exam and a hands-on lab exam. This book will help you with the following CCIE Routing and Switching Qualification Exam topics:

- Cisco device operation
- General networking theory
- LAN addressing
- 10-, 100-, and 1000-Mbps Ethernet encapsulation, media access control, topologies, errors, and limitations
- Logical Link Control (LLC) 802.2
- Bridging and LAN switching
- TCP/IP
- IP routing protocols
- Desktop protocols including Novell NetWare and Windows networking
- Performance management
- WAN addressing, signaling, and framing

Because this book focuses on troubleshooting, it will also prepare you for the CCIE lab test. Now that Cisco has moved from a two-day lab test to a one-day lab test, applying efficient troubleshooting methods is even more important than it once was. The methods taught in this book will help you isolate and fix problems that appear in your lab network as you perform the difficult tasks required of the CCIE lab test-taker.

Please see www.cisco.com/warp/public/10/wwtraining for more information about Cisco certification programs.

The NAX Certification Program

The NAX certification program is an industry-standard, vendor-neutral program sponsored by the WildPackets Academy. Since 1990, WildPackets has been developing user-friendly and affordable tools for designing, maintaining, troubleshooting, and optimizing computer networks. WildPackets products include EtherPeek for Ethernet network analysis and AiroPeek for 802.11 wireless network analysis. Both of these products include NetSense real-time expert system technology for automated problem analysis. The TokenPeek analyzer addresses the needs of 802.5 Token Ring users.

To pass the NAX certification tests, a candidate can use WildPackets or other industry-recognized protocol analyzers. The candidate downloads an analyzer trace file and answers questions about real-world network problems. The exams test a candidate's understanding of protocols and ability to apply protocol analysis techniques to typical network problems. Achieving NAX certification involves three steps:

1. The Applied Analysis Technician (AATech) certification.
2. The Protocol Analyzer Specialist (PAS) certification.
3. The NAX certification.

These certifications require passing knowledge exams and practical skills exams. The knowledge exams require a candidate to demonstrate solid understanding of protocol analysis concepts and detailed knowledge of the Open System Interconnection (OSI) Reference Model and the protocols that operate at the various layers of the model. The practical skills tests require a candidate to demonstrate proficiency with a protocol analyzer. To achieve NAX certification, a candidate must also write a dissertation (white paper) on a topic selected from a list of topics approved by WildPackets Academy. This book will help with all of the knowledge exams in the NAX certification program as well as provide a solid foundation for the protocol-related aspects of many other industry certifications.

Please go to www.nax2000.com and download the Pre-Test Study Guide and Test-Taking Instructions document for complete details on the NAX certification program.

Organization

This book is organized in a bottom-up fashion. After an essential chapter on troubleshooting methods, the book works its way up the OSI Reference Model, starting with physical and data link layer concerns and ending with upper-layer concerns. The chapters are grouped as follows:

- Chapter 2 covers methods and tools for problem isolation, including Cisco and industry-standard troubleshooting procedures and protocol analysis with WildPackets or other analyzers. Chapter 2 also covers the OSI Reference Model and the Internet Control Message Protocol (ICMP).

- Chapters 3 and 4 explain how Ethernet and 802.11 wireless networks work and how to troubleshoot them when they don't work. Chapter 3 also addresses 802.2 LLC.

- Chapters 5 and 6 remain at the data link layer and address the Spanning Tree Protocol, which is used on bridged and switched networks, and the configuration and troubleshooting of VLANs.

- Chapters 7 through 8 move up to the network layer and beyond, and cover IP addressing, IP routing protocols, a detailed analysis of TCP, and an overview of upper-layer TCP/IP protocols.

- Chapters 9 through 12 teach troubleshooting and protocol analysis for the most popular desktop protocols—Novell NetWare, AppleTalk, and Windows networking.

■ Chapter 13 discusses WAN technology and troubleshooting from the perspective of the LAN-oriented network engineer.

Our Web Site

We have set up a Web site, which we hope you will visit often. The Web site will include updates as new information about troubleshooting becomes available. It also includes links to practice tests to help you study for certification exams, and suggestions for exercises you can try in a lab network to strengthen your troubleshooting skills. The address of the companion Web site is www.troubleshootingnetworks.com.

Troubleshooting Methods

Computer networking isn't new. Organizations have connected computers for many years to distribute information, exchange messages, back up data, and share peripherals, such as printers and modems. Compared to those early networks, however, modern networks are complex and indispensable. Applications today include controlling space-station robots, providing medical images to surgeons, selling products, and managing manufacturing resources. Users depend on their networks for daily operations, research and development, and strategic planning. As a network support engineer, you are probably aware of increasing requirements for application support and reliability. This chapter teaches practical methods you can use to troubleshoot network problems, regardless of the newness of applications or the high level of service expectations.

Challenges in Today's Networking Environment

In the early 1980s, a large Personal Computer (PC)-based network consisted of possibly 20 workstations connected so users could share a printer and high-capacity hard disk (possibly as large as 5 Megabytes!) Typically, the network administrator was someone who had the intelligence and motivation to tinker with desktop computers. A staff of dedicated support engineers responsible for maintaining the network was little more than fantasy.

By the early 1990s, networks had changed dramatically. Twisted-pair cabling replaced the old coaxial Ethernet cabling. Switches started replacing hubs, and all large networks had dedicated teams of support people. The single file server with a handful of users sharing a disk drive evolved to a campus network that connected departments and buildings into a multiprotocol and multivendor resource critical to meeting productivity goals. However, global connectivity and the integration of voice, video, and data were little more than fantasy.

With the creation of the World Wide Web in the mid-1990s, a new epoch of networking was entered. Connectivity options for geographically separated campus networks expanded and large internetworks that provided access to employees, business partners, and customers became common. The final few years of the decade were focused on solving the Y2K problem. While the uninitiated smiled smugly on January 1, 2000, when almost none of the prophesied Y2K problems actually happened, the many unsung heroes of the software development community and the exhausted network support engineers knew that it was their hard work that caused the prophets of doom to be wrong.

Y2K came and went. With fervor, the networking industry redoubled its push to evolve. Today, global Wide Area Networks (WANs) connect campus networks composed of Ethernet and wireless devices, real and Virtual Local Area Networks (VLANs), switches and routers, Windows and UNIX servers, and a myriad of other technologies, both old and new, that must work together seamlessly and reliably. Those of us responsible for designing, implementing, supporting, troubleshooting, and repairing contemporary networks are faced with challenges on many levels. We must keep pace with accelerating technological and business changes while maintaining and troubleshooting a mission-critical production environment that was built on technologies that were developed 20 or 30 years ago.

The core engineering technologies that were invented in the 1960s and 1970s are still with us. Ethernet Version II, which was a direct evolution from the 1970s creation of Ethernet Version I, was standardized in 1982. Ethernet II frames remain typical for most Internet Protocol (IP) campus network traffic today. IP itself has not changed much since it was first created more than 20 years ago. Of course it has been repaired, and new services such as the Dynamic Host Configuration Protocol (DHCP) have augmented its functionality. But the issues of aggregating and segregating machines into reachable locations challenge the campus network designer, engineer, and administrator in much the same way as when the protocol was first created. Ethernet and IP are two of many implementations that have been with us for 15, 20, or 30 years. Today's network expert must have a solid understanding of the core engineering technologies that underlie contemporary networking.

Essentially all campus networks today implement the TCP/IP protocol, but many large networks also include AppleTalk and Novell NetWare in the mix. In business and educational environments, the desktop computer is typically based on Microsoft Windows or Mac OS, and the UNIX/Linux proponents will just have to keep on promoting the benefits of their solutions while the Bill Gates juggernaut drives the industry. Servers, on the other hand, are based on both Microsoft Windows and UNIX/Linux as well as Mac OS.

Putting all of these pieces together requires the development of a solid, effective troubleshooting methodology. It's not enough to simply "swap till you drop" and hope the problem goes away. (*Swap till you drop* is a phrase often used in the United States to mean a method of troubleshooting that involves replacing network components until you get so tired that you drop to the ground.) The significance of a good methodology will become even more evident as the present gives way to a faster, increasingly automated, and more sophisticated future.

Using a Systematic Troubleshooting Method

Network engineers who are experts in their field use a systematic process when troubleshooting problems. These experts may not be able to explain the process, but they can intuitively apply it when problems occur. Other experts evangelize their systematic methods, sometimes to the point of irrational criticism of different methods that work just as well. All the experts' methods, whether articulated or not, boil down to a logical set of steps for eliminating the causes of a problem. Experts use methods that are rational, efficient, practical, and applicable to most situations. They document the network architecture and device configurations before, during, and after making changes. They test the changes they make while troubleshooting to ensure the problem is fixed and no new problems have been introduced.

A systematic troubleshooting method is measurably different from the methods used by novices in the networking field. Novices often use random methods with no planning, no documentation, and no testing. Their methods often fail to find the actual problem in the quick time frame demanded by network users, and their efforts often leave the condition changed but still broken. An expert, on the other hand, can narrow down possibilities quickly, isolate the problem, fix the problem, and test the fix in a reasonably short time.

An expert can either intuitively or consciously define the following terms and use them to increase efficiency. These definitions are based on definitions in the online version of *Merriam-Webster's Collegiate Dictionary*:

Component.   A constituent part or ingredient of a whole.

Function.   The action for which a thing is specially fitted or used.

System.   A regularly interacting or interdependent group of components forming a unified whole.

Troubleshoot.   To locate trouble and make repairs in machinery and technical equipment; to anticipate and solve problems.

Upgrade.   To raise the quality of.

Systems, including network systems, are made up of interrelated components. Systems and components can be described by what functions they carry out. Troubleshooting and upgrading a system involves considering the components of the system, their functions, and how they affect the whole system. Malfunction of any component may cause the whole system to fail. Many newcomers to the networking field have not considered these basic concepts. Without any understanding of systems, components, and their functions, a newcomer has a difficult time troubleshooting. Going to the next step—from thinking about systems to using systematic methods—is also difficult for novices, especially in the current environment where networks have become quite complex and the interrelation of network components is not as clear as it once was.

One factor that distinguishes an expert from a novice is that the expert has researched how protocols work. Using a protocol analyzer, the expert has studied frame formats, protocol behavior, connection establishment, reliability mechanisms, routing protocols, and so on. It is not possible to learn all protocols and how they fit together, however. Protocol design engineers introduce new protocols and new ways of using old protocols on a regular basis. By the time a network engineer figures out one protocol, there's a new protocol, or, a new way of using an old protocol, to confuse the issue. Considering network behavior and troubleshooting from a higher level is a necessity in the crazy mix-and-match world of today's network protocols.

Using the OSI Model for Troubleshooting

An effective method for troubleshooting and understanding protocols is to use the International Organization for Standardization (ISO) Open System Interconnection (OSI) Reference Model as a guide. Figure 2.1 shows the OSI model.

The OSI model has seven layers. Each layer communicates with its peer running on another system. The layer doesn't do this directly, however. With the exception of the bottom layer, a layer passes its data to the layer below for further processing. Each layer provides services to the layer above. Table 2.1 describes the services provided by each layer of the model.

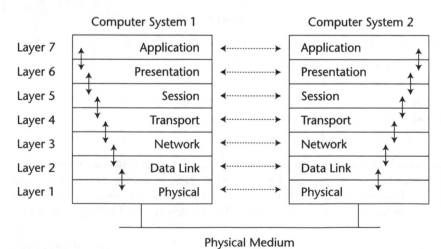

Physical Medium

Figure 2.1   The OSI model.

Table 2.1 Services Provided by the OSI Layers

LAYER	SERVICES
Application	Handles file and message transfer, directory lookups, naming, authentication, and other services required by applications
Presentation	Ensures that information sent by one system will be readable by the application layer of another system
Session	Establishes, manages, and terminates sessions between applications
Transport	Provides end-to-end communication, error recovery, and flow control
Network	Provides connectivity and path selection between networks
Data Link	Provides transit of data across a physical link
Physical	Defines the electrical and mechanical specifications for physical links between systems

It's important to understand the services offered by each layer of the OSI model and typical problems at each layer. When isolating the cause of a problem, you should work your way up from the bottom to the top layer. Starting at the bottom layer, check cabling and physical interfaces first. Next check encapsulation options at the data link layer and any problems with media access control. Move up the layers to routing protocol problems and network-layer addressing issues. At the upper layers, check for problems with buffer exhaustion, software bugs, naming, encryption, compression, data presentation, and user errors. The rest of the chapters provide more detail on these suggestions.

Newcomers to the field of networking faithfully memorize the OSI model and its functions. As the newcomers learn more about networking, they learn that many protocols were designed without reference to the model and do not fit the model perfectly. Some protocols do not fit into a linear stack at all, but rather sit outside the main list in a management or control plane. Despite these caveats, the model does a good job of explaining the typical functions required of a networking protocol and makes a good guidepost when troubleshooting.

The OSI model provides a skeleton for understanding both existing and future protocol behavior. When experts see the progression of addressing in a packet (from data link, through network, to the transport layer), they can apply an understanding of the OSI model to extract the meaning and function of the packet. Associating network devices with OSI layers (switch at Layer 2, router at Layer 3, file server at Layer 4 and above), engineers can correlate network symptoms with potential sources of network problems. Symptoms at the network layer may indicate a misconfigured routing protocol on a router. Retransmissions at the transport layer may indicate a problem with a shortage of memory or computing power on a file server. This kind of thinking can be extrapolated for numerous networking problems.

ANOTHER CAR ANALOGY

An expert protocol analyst is similar to an expert auto mechanic. You and I know that the gas goes in a hole on the outside of the car. Then the gas sort of mixes up in the cylinders in the motor, where the spark plugs explode the gas, and that makes the motor turn. Then the transmission connects the motor to the wheels, and so on. When we hear a funny noise we say, "Hmm...that sounds like I'm running out of gas," or "Sounds like I have a flat tire." We're not expert auto mechanics.

Trained mechanics, however, understand the nuances and relationships of the car's fuel system, ignition system, drive train, brakes, electrical system, and so forth. Although different makes of cars are different in many ways, mechanics can probably figure out many systems of cars they may not normally work on. So, too, with the OSI Reference Model and networking experts. Experts understand flow control, message encoding, acknowledgments, routing, and so on, whether they are working with Ethernet, Asynchronous Transfer Mode (ATM), TCP/IP, or some new protocol just out of the Internet Engineering Task Force (IETF).

The OSI model helps network engineers understand that protocol design is modular. Each layer of the model operates semi-independently and offers a service interface for a layer above it. When the OSI concept of independent layers isn't followed, problems arise. Take the case of the File Transfer Protocol (FTP), which has a 32-bit IP address encoded into the application layer, which causes challenges for Network Address Translation (NAT). Chapters 7 and 9 discuss NAT and FTP in more detail.

Because the OSI layers are semi-independent, protocols can be stacked in creative ways. For example, many companies route Systems Network Architecture (SNA) traffic over an IP network. The result is that the SNA traffic, which previously resided only on a Token Ring network, is now encapsulated in Logical Link Control (LLC) and Token Ring headers, encapsulated again in TCP/IP headers, and finally encapsulated again in another data link layer for traversal across the IP internetwork. An expert who understands the OSI model is not surprised to encounter this sort of creative layering when troubleshooting protocol behavior.

Although some network specialists scoff at the idea of using the OSI model for troubleshooting, anyone who claims to be an expert at troubleshooting and protocol analysis understands and uses the model. This book uses the model extensively and will help you, the reader, use the model to become an expert protocol analyst.

Generic Problem-Solving Models

Generic problem-solving models are a topic for research in the engineering, information science, business, and psychology fields. A generic model allows you to solve unstructured and complex problems of any sort. The study of problem-solving methods is important for both practical and theoretical reasons. Problems do not only occur in the technological realm. Learning problem-solving skills helps a person cope psychologically and cognitively.

Many high school and college classes, including the Cisco Networking Academy classes, teach the generic Dartmouth Problem-Solving and Design Method, developed by the Thayer School of Engineering at Dartmouth College. The Dartmouth model is definitely applicable to network troubleshooting. The Dartmouth approach solves problems by proceeding through a problem-solving cycle, step by step, carefully documenting each step in the process. If users of the model discover that a solution they are working on is not viable, they examine their paper trail and move back only as far as necessary—perhaps only a single step. The steps in the Dartmouth method are as follows:

1. State the problem after examining it carefully.

2. Redefine the problem to eliminate any bias of the customer reporting the problem or any preconceived notions about the ideal solution.

3. Identify any constraints on potential solutions and outline general specifications and goals for the solution.

4. Identify alternative solutions using brainstorming techniques that are structured by the constraints and goals identified in the previous step.

5. Analyze the alternatives, weighing the advantages and disadvantages of each.

6. Select and test the most viable alternative.

7. Iterate the cycle until you find the right solution.

The Dartmouth model is one of many generic models for problem solving. Generic models share important characteristics. All require the user to define and redefine the problem and to analyze and plan possible solutions. The generic models include a set of steps that are applied iteratively. The models are heuristic and incorporate knowledge gained from the testing of real-world conditions into the next step. The models are not random. They are not similar to the typical methods used by networking novices, which have just one iterated step: Make changes, without documenting them, until the problem seems to go away.

Fundamental Network Troubleshooting Considerations

Whatever troubleshooting method or model a networking professional develops, there are two fundamental questions that must be answered in every case:

What is the problem that needs to be solved?   Without carefully considering what is actually wrong, there is no way to know whether a particular piece of evidence relates to a solution. Typically, a complex network has many inefficiencies and possibly quite a few minor problems. The complaint that stimulated a call to action must be quantified completely or else initial research into the cause of the problem may turn up other unrelated problems. Fixing the unrelated problems won't address the complaint.

What is the impact of the problem on the end-user community?   Troubleshooting tools may identify numerous network anomalies. You need to ask yourself whether these anomalies are really affecting user productivity and satisfaction.

For example, if a large file transfer takes 130 seconds on Monday and 140 seconds on Friday, it is unlikely that any user will notice the difference. If a user is working on the Web and the response time goes from 4 seconds to 14 seconds, then there's going to be a complaint. Simply tabulating various network statistics has little meaning unless the statistics are correlated to the activities of the end-user community. This implies that the person doing the troubleshooting must have a reasonable understanding of the needs and expectations of the users of the computing system.

Cisco's Troubleshooting Method

For the Cisco Internetwork Troubleshooting (CIT) class, Cisco developed a troubleshooting method based on generic problem-solving models. In the CIT course materials, Cisco acknowledges that many systematic methods work for troubleshooting computer networks. Engineers are not expected to use the Cisco model simply because they use Cisco equipment. To pass the Cisco Support Test, however, you should learn the troubleshooting method verbatim. One purpose of this book is to help you pass Cisco tests, so this section describes the Cisco troubleshooting method, which is shown in Figure 2.2.

The Cisco troubleshooting method is a practical process that shares characteristics with any systematic method. The initial goal is that you have a clear and sufficient definition of the problem. After defining the problem, you should gather more facts and consider possible causes for the problem. Next, create an action plan for how you will test your theories about possible causes. Then, implement the plan and observe the results. If the symptoms don't stop, develop and try another action plan. It may be necessary to gather more facts at this point. If the symptoms stop, document how you resolved the problem. The following sections describe these steps in more detail.

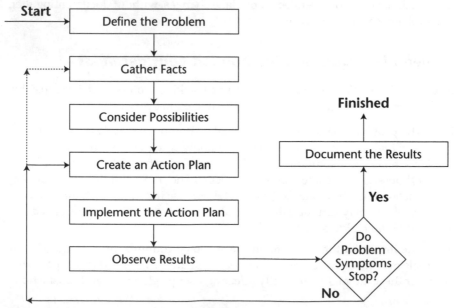

Figure 2.2   Cisco's troubleshooting method.

THE IMPORTANCE OF DEFINING THE PROBLEM TO BE SOLVED

A large metal parts fabrication company on the East Coast of the United States hired one of the authors as a protocol analyst to help with complaints of slow network performance. While walking around with the network administrator, the consultant noticed that users were literally leaning back in their chairs waiting for the company's database server to respond to their queries. The response time was in the neighborhood of 20 to 30 seconds! Back in the network administrator's office the consultant pointed out the evidence of slow response time that had been observed. The network administrator said, "Oh, I know, but please don't say anything to any of the users. They think that's normal and nobody is complaining. We're budgeted to upgrade the server next quarter. The problem I need help with is that our users in remote offices are getting over 60-second delays using the database." Had the consultant not stumbled onto a quantification of the complaint, there could have been many wasted hours tracking down the wrong problem.

Define the Problem

The first step is to define the problem. Writing a description of the problem and its symptoms is often a valuable step that will save time later. Writing may seem like a bureaucratic requirement, but it has practical value in that it helps you clarify the situation and requires you to analyze symptoms and possible causes. In some cases, writing about the problem causes you to realize the solution immediately, greatly reducing the amount of work in the following steps. When writing about the problem, form your observations with reference to the baseline you established for your network. You should have a good idea of what is normal for your network in terms of errors, throughput, response time, and efficiency. Describe to what extent the current situation deviates from normal.

In this first step, focus on symptoms and what might cause them. Many ideas may arise, but concentrate on those that could be major contributors to the problem. Focus on users' reports of the problem, but, at the same time, be somewhat skeptical of user reports. Users don't always tell the whole truth about the problem because they are afraid of looking dumb. Also, as mentioned in the *Generic Problem-Solving Models* section, users sometimes incorporate bias and preconceived notions about the solution into their descriptions of the problem. Proceed from your own knowledge of the problem and your understanding of the internetwork topology and typical network performance.

Gather Facts

Gather additional facts from affected users, network administrators, managers, and any key people involved with the network. Collect data from network management systems, protocol analyzers, router and switch diagnostic commands, software release notes, software bug reports, and documentation about changes made to the network. Check records that you kept (hopefully!) on the configuration of hosts, servers, switches, routers, and any other configurable network devices. Compare current configurations with saved configurations to see if anything has changed. Determine answers to the following questions:

- How often does the problem happen?
- When did the problem first occur?
- What changes were made right before the problem started happening?
- Is the problem reproducible?

Consider Possibilities

Using the data you gathered and previous knowledge you gained from proactive network monitoring, set some boundaries to help you effectively isolate causes for the problem. Consider probable possibilities and set aside details that seem irrelevant. Analyze symptoms to determine which possibilities are unlikely. For example, if local stations can communicate with each other but not with remote stations, you know that the Network Interface Cards (NICs) in the stations are operational. A likely possibility is that the problem lies above the physical and data link layers. Document possibilities and list them in order of most likely to least likely.

Create an Action Plan

Develop a plan for how you will test the most likely causes of the problem. Plan to change just one variable at a time; otherwise you won't know which change resulted in the fix. It often helps to use a *divide-and-conquer* approach whereby you partition your troubleshooting domain into discrete areas that are logically or physically isolated from each other. This approach will help you pinpoint the cause(s) of the problem. A *testing-outward* approach also helps in many cases. For example, from a source station, plan to test local communications first. Then create a plan to test reachability to each network along a path to a remote network until the problem occurs.

Document your action plans. Each plan should describe a set of steps to be executed. In addition, it is important to have a backout plan in case your actions make matters worse. For example, in your action plan, include an initial step of saving existing configurations. If problems occur, you can go back to a known state with the saved configurations.

Implement the Action Plan and Observe the Results

Follow the steps that you created in your action plan and observe the results. Make sure you document which plan you are currently trying; otherwise it is too easy to repeat yourself. Test all fixes that you make. Be sure you do not make the problem worse or introduce new problems. Try to limit as much as possible the invasive impact of your actions on network users. Also, minimize the extent and duration of any security lapses that could occur while implementing your action plan. If necessary, execute the backout plan if it appears that your actions are detrimental to security or network operations.

After manipulating a single variable based on your action plan, gather data to determine whether your action has fixed the problem. Ask users to try their applications again and to let you know if the problem is cured. If you determine that you have solved the problem, document the results and any changes you made. If you have not yet fixed the problem, repeat the problem-solving process. Implement another action plan, and, if necessary, gather more facts.

Document the Results

When you have resolved the problem, you have one more important step remaining— documenting the results. You may have tried many action plans. Be sure to complete the job by recording which plan worked and why (if you know why). Documenting the resolution will help you in the future when a similar problem occurs. Also, if you determine later that your fix unexpectedly caused another problem, you will have a paper trail of what has changed. In addition to documenting the resolution, be sure to save any configuration changes you made. If necessary, update your network map(s).

NOTE In the Cisco Certified Internetwork Expert (CCIE) lab test, the proctor will check that you document your work.

Proactive Troubleshooting and Baselining

How can you know something is wrong if you haven't defined the opposite of wrong? A *baseline* of your network defines normal performance and typical protocol behavior when no problems are occurring. With a baseline of your network, you can more efficiently troubleshoot problems. Instead of simply relying on user reports, you can check statistics and configurations to see what is different from the baseline. You can capture data with a protocol analyzer and compare the results to data you captured before. With a baseline, you have a basis for comparison so that problems can be more easily identified.

The online version of *Merriam-Webster's Collegiate Dictionary* defines a troubleshooter as "a person skilled at solving or anticipating problems or difficulties." According to this definition a troubleshooter must be able to *anticipate* problems. In the computer networking world, you may have encountered those eccentric, experienced experts who can seemingly foresee problems and their causes. They can immediately recognize when a problem is about to happen and often correctly guess the cause of the problem. They are like a mother who can recognize her child's cry in a nursery room filled with crying children and can accurately guess why her child is crying.

Experts are aware of the nuances of the networks they manage, including the networks' frailties and nonoptimal portions, and they can anticipate when something is going to break. This isn't magic. The experts can do this because they have worked on the network for a long time and because they spend time proactively monitoring it. Instead of using troubleshooting tools only to react to problems as they occur, experts use the tools to proactively develop a baseline for normal network behavior and performance. When problems occur, these experts can compare current problems with the baseline.

THE IMPORTANCE OF NETWORK DOCUMENTATION

One of the authors was hired by a major aerospace company to do protocol analysis. After examining network statistics and trace files, the author asked the network manager to check some configurations on the FS01 file server. The network manager replied, "Oh, FS01....Yeah, we know that one's acting up, but we don't know where it is anymore." The FS01 file server was somewhere on the company's campus—probably in some wiring closet—but nobody remembered where it was located!

Documenting Your Network

One goal of proactive network management is to document your network's logical and physical topology. Documenting a complex, ever changing network is challenging, but the benefits of having detailed network topology and configuration information make the effort worthwhile. Learning and documenting the locations of major hosts and servers, interconnection devices, and network segments is a good way to develop a basis for future troubleshooting and optimization. Coupled with data on the performance characteristics of network segments, location information gives you insight into where users are concentrated and the level of traffic a network must support. Network maps are important for both proactive and reactive network management. If a protocol analyzer or other management tool identifies that a device—for example, a file server—is misbehaving, you need to find that server. The map should help with this task.

Network managers often resist documenting their networks because they are so busy handling day-to-day operations and planning enhancements to the network. To overcome this resistance, consider the fact that good documentation is directly related to money. Your company has probably invested in many troubleshooting and network management tools. Perhaps you have an umbrella management system, such as Cisco Works, or protocol analysis equipment, such as WildPackets EtherPeek or AiroPeek. Your network may implement Remote Monitoring (RMON) probes and use a centralized RMON or Simple Network Management Protocol (SNMP) console to alert you to problems and provide ongoing statistical reporting. These are all useful tools, but don't forget that these tools identify numeric Ethernet, IP, AppleTalk, NetWare, DECnet, and other types of addresses. If you have no idea of the actual physical location of these addresses, then your troubleshooting capabilities are impaired and the investment you made in all the clever tools may be wasted.

Your goal should be to develop a map or set of maps that include the following information:

- Geographical information, such as a country, state, province, city, or campus name
- Buildings and floors, and possibly conference rooms, offices, and cubicles
- WAN and LAN connections between buildings
- An indication of the data link layer technology for WANs and LANs
- The name of the service provider for WANs
- Circuit IDs for WANs

- Network-layer addresses and names for LANs, WANs, and major devices
- The location of the Main Distribution Frame (MDF) and Intermediate Distribution Frame (IDF) wiring closets
- The location of routers and switches, though not necessarily every hub
- The location and extent of VLANs
- The location and extent of Virtual Private Networks (VPNs)
- The location of remote-access servers
- The location of major file, print, database, application, and Web servers
- The location of mainframes
- The location of major Network Management Stations (NMSs)
- The location of firewalls or other security management systems
- The location and topology of demilitarized zones for computers outside the firewall
- Some indication of where workstations reside, though not necessarily the explicit location of each workstation
- A depiction of the logical topology or architecture of the network

Networking experts use both logical topological diagrams and physical topological diagrams. *Logical topologies* refer to broad categories of devices, logical interconnections, and the flow of information in a network. *Physical topologies* refer to actual devices, ports, cables, connections, and the physical layout of a network. Both types of diagrams are helpful.

When documenting the network infrastructure, take a step back from the diagrams you develop and try to characterize the logical topology of the network as well as the physical components. The logical topology illustrates the architecture of the network, which can be hierarchical, flat, structured, unstructured, layered, bus, ring, star, and so on. The logical topology can affect your ability to upgrade a network. For example, a flat topology of devices all in the same subnet connected with switches and hubs does not scale as well as a hierarchical topology that makes use of routers.

In addition to documenting network topologies, many network documentation tools enable you to save detailed information about network resources. Documentation tools often include a device object library that contains detailed information about network objects, such as their configuration, serial number, make and model, software and hardware version, software license number, and so on. Of utmost importance is the name and network-layer address for the object, as discussed in the next section.

Documenting Network Names and Addresses

When drawing detailed network maps, you should include the names of major sites, routers, switches, network segments, and servers. Also document any standards for naming network elements. For example, some network engineers name sites using airport codes (Atlanta = ATL, Boston = BOS, and so on). Some engineers suffix names with an alias that describes the type of device (for example, rtr for router).

You should also document network-layer addresses and any standard policies for assigning addresses. Addressing information will be extremely valuable when looking at protocol analyzer packet data when troubleshooting. An understanding of the addressing policies will help you know which areas may have problems when you upgrade or optimize the network. The addressing policy (or lack of any policy) can make it difficult to upgrade. For example, current IP subnet masking may limit the number of nodes in a LAN or VLAN. Poorly designed addressing architectures might limit the use of *route summarization*. Route summarization reduces the number of routes in routing tables and minimizes routing table update traffic and overall router overhead. Route summarization also improves network stability and availability, because problems in one part of a network are less likely to affect the whole internetwork. Summarization works best if addresses have been assigned in a consistent and contiguous manner.

Tools for Network Documentation

To develop good network documentation, you should invest in good network diagramming tools. Although some smaller campus networks are documented with generic drawing tools such as CorelDRAW and PowerPoint, for larger campus networks you should use a tool that includes icons for typical devices, an object library for detailed data, and support for *autodiscovery*. With autodiscovery, a tool can learn about devices and topologies automatically by listening to traffic and sending queries and analyzing the results. Good diagramming tools also support printing large network diagrams on plotters. They also support conversion to the HTML and GIF formats for posting the data on a Web server so other network engineers and users can share the data.

> **CAUTION** If you store your network maps on a server to which many engineers have write access, be sure to have a change control process in place. When making a change, an engineer should check the map out. Other engineers should be unable to make a change until the first engineer checks the map in again.

The Microsoft Visio product line is highly recommended for network diagramming. The product line includes Visio Standard, Visio Professional, and Visio Enterprise Network Tools. You can check Microsoft marketing material to determine which tool is best for your needs. All Visio products share a common file format, which means you can share diagrams with other Visio users, regardless of which product you choose.

Many network engineers recommend the netViz products from netViz Corporation. netViz is an information management tool that allows you to visualize and work with complex data systems such as internetworks. Designed to deal with large amounts of information, netViz integrates graphics and data to create a visual database, making it easy for you to see system components, their unique characteristics, and their relationships to each other.

For large campus networks and service providers, Visionael Corporation offers client/server network documentation products that have network inventory, troubleshooting, and change management features. Visionael products support network planning, design, deployment, provisioning, validation, and daily operations. Vision-ael products provide detailed data about the physical topology as well as the logical topology.

For smaller networks that are managed by engineers who prefer Mac OS, a popular application is InterMapper from Dartware, LLC. With InterMapper you can quickly develop maps and see the state of your network at a glance. InterMapper also provides detailed information about devices, servers, and links. Another popular product in the Macintosh community is LANSurveyor from Neon Software.

For an overall view of Internet and TCP/IP measurement and diagramming tools, check the information collected by the Cooperative Association for Internet Data Analysis (CAIDA). CAIDA categorizes tools with respect to their intent and provides a summary along with Web page pointers to more detailed information. Review comments are also included when available. For more information on the CAIDA catalog, go to www.caida.org/tools/taxonomy/.

Documenting Switched Networks

Automated network mapping tools that use autodiscovery to locate network devices may not identify bridges or switches. A Layer 2 switch or bridge is transparent at the data link layer. This means that, by design, packets that are forwarded through the switch or bridge do not carry with them any evidence of the switch or bridge being present. Unless a Layer 2 interconnect device is configured to make its presence known to an autodiscovery tool, there is no consistent way to detect its presence. It's true that Layer 2 devices typically implement the Spanning Tree Algorithm to prevent loops in the network topology, and the Spanning Tree Algorithm uses periodic transmission of Bridge Protocol Data Unit (BPDU) packets, per the IEEE 802.1D standard. All of the ports on a switch don't send BPDU packets, however, and the port that does send them may change if the network topology changes. The only way to consistently identify the presence of a Layer 2 device in a network is to configure the device to announce its presence or to configure the device to respond to queries. The Cisco Discovery Protocol (CDP), covered in the next section, is one way to configure a Cisco switch to announce its presence.

A switch can be configured with an IP address in which case the switch is reachable via management tools such as ping, SNMP, and Telnet. If the switch implements VLANs, however, you can only reach it from devices that are in the same VLAN or are across a router interface that is in the same VLAN. By default, Cisco switches place management functions, such as ping and SNMP, in VLAN 1. The management VLAN can be changed, however. You should make sure any connected router or management ports are also in the management VLAN to ensure you can reach the switch for troubleshooting and remote configuration.

In general, VLANs make network documentation more challenging. In the old routed world, managers documented the network-layer addresses of network segments and major devices such as routers and servers. In a switched VLAN world, you may need to add much more detailed, Layer 2 documentation in order to understand your network. You should document the names and numbers of each VLAN and which ports are associated with the VLANs. You should also keep track of the Media Access Control (MAC) addresses that the switches use for management functions.

Cisco switches use multiple addresses for the Dynamic Inter-Switch Link (DISL), the Virtual Trunk Protocol (VTP), BPDUs, and other management and control functions. You will learn more about VLANs in Chapter 6.

The Cisco Discovery Protocol

CDP is a simple tool for basic network documentation that is built into every Cisco switch and router. CDP specifies a method for Cisco routers and switches to send configuration information to each other on a regular basis. Analyzing CDP data can help you learn about your network's structure and configuration. You can use the show cdp neighbors detail command to display detailed information about neighboring routers and switches, including which protocols are enabled, network addresses for enabled protocols, the number and types of interfaces, the type of platform and its capabilities, and the version of Cisco Internetwork Operating System (IOS) software running on the neighbor.

In the following example, a network engineer used CDP on the Charlotte router to confirm her suspicions that the network map that showed Charlotte connected to the Boston router's serial 1 interface was wrong. The CDP information confirmed that the connecting interface on Boston was serial 0, not serial 1. The outgoing serial 0 port on Charlotte connects to Boston's serial 0 interface.

```
charlotte#show cdp neighbors detail
-------------------------
Device ID: Boston
Entry address(es):
  IP address: 172.16.40.1
  Novell address: 100.4afc.4afc.4afc
Platform: cisco CSC4,  Capabilities: Router
Interface: Serial0,  Port ID (outgoing port): Serial0
Holdtime : 156 sec
Version :
Cisco Internetwork Operating System Software
IOS (tm) GS Software (GS3-AK-M), Version 11.0(5), RELEASE SOFTWARE (fc1)
Copyright (c) 1986-1996 by cisco Systems, Inc.
Compiled Mon 05-Feb-96 22:05 by hochan
```

CDP frames are sent to the Cisco multicast address 01-00-0C-CC-CC-CC. CDP frames are sent every 60 seconds by default, although you can change this with the cdp timer command. CDP frames are sent with a *holdtime* of 180 seconds by default. Holdtime specifies the amount of time a receiving device should hold the information before discarding it. When an interface is shut down, CDP sends a frame with the holdtime set to zero. You can configure holdtime with the cdp holdtime command.

CDP is enabled by default on all routers and switches. To disable CDP and later reenable it, use the no cdp run and cdp run commands. These commands can be entered in global configuration mode to affect all interfaces or in interface configuration mode to affect a single interface.

If you wish to reset CDP traffic counters to zero, use the clear cdp counters command. The clear cdp table command is also helpful when you wish to delete the CDP table of information about neighbors. The most useful CDP command, however, is show cdp. Arguments to this command let you see detailed or summary data, information about a particular neighbor, or information about a particular interface.

Protocol Analysis

To proactively learn about traffic on your network and to troubleshoot problems, you should use a *protocol analyzer*. A protocol analyzer records, interprets, and analyzes network traffic. It operates by placing its NIC into *promiscuous mode.* This means that the NIC accepts all packets without regard for the destination address. A protocol analyzer provides detailed information about packets and communication sessions. It decodes the various protocol layers and fields in each packet, and presents the layers and fields as readable text. When necessary, the analyzer decodes the meaning of each byte (or bit, for bit-oriented protocols). Relationships between packets may also be analyzed.

A protocol analyzer connects to a network and captures packets as they travel across the network. Throughout this book, we use terms such as *captured packets, capture results, capture rate*, and so on. We assume that you have a protocol analyzer and understand that to capture packets means to connect the analyzer to a network and configure it to start accepting packets into its buffer as the packets are read by the NIC in the analyzer.

An analyzer captures packets into a software buffer. In capture mode, *filters* can be set to save only traffic that meets certain criteria. For example, if a particular device is suspected of causing network problems, then a filter can be configured that captures all traffic to and from that device and ignores other packets. The analyzer also *timestamps* each packet as it arrives. Timestamps can be extremely important when analyzing protocol operation and performance. They can also be helpful when determining response times by measuring the delta time between packets. Once data is captured, the analyzer allows the user to save the data as a *trace file*. The trace file can be loaded later for continued analysis.

Most analyzers show packet data in three formats: a summary, detail, and hexadecimal view. In the summary view, an analyzer shows one line for each packet, with a configurable amount of data displayed for each packet. This view can be helpful when tracking multiple-packet communication sessions. In the detail view, the analyzer shows the meaning of layers, fields, bytes, and bits for each packet. In the hexadecimal (hex) view, the analyzer shows the raw packet. Figure 2.3 shows an example of a summary view. Figure 2.4, later in this chapter, shows an example of a detail view.

Packet	Source	Destination	Size	Time-Stamp	Protocol
1	IP-172.16.10.1	IP-224.0.0.10	78	14:05:54.892000	EIGRP Hello
2	IP-172.16.10.1	IP-224.0.0.5	82	14:05:56.800000	OSPF Hlo
3	IP-172.16.10.1	IP-224.0.0.10	78	14:05:59.893000	EIGRP Hello
4	00:00:0C:05:3E:80	00:00:0C:05:3E:80	64	14:06:00.416000	Loopback
5	IP-172.16.10.1	IP-224.0.0.10	78	14:06:04.893000	EIGRP Hello
6	IP-172.16.10.1	IP-224.0.0.5	82	14:06:06.801000	OSPF Hlo
7	IP-172.16.10.1	IP-224.0.0.10	78	14:06:09.894000	EIGRP Hello
8	00:00:0C:05:3E:80	00:00:0C:05:3E:80	64	14:06:10.417000	Loopback
9	00:00:0C:05:3E:80	01:00:0C:CC:CC:CC	300	14:06:13.423000	Discovery
10	IP-172.16.10.1	IP-224.0.0.10	78	14:06:14.894000	EIGRP Hello

Figure 2.3 Protocol analyzer summary view.

WildPackets Protocol Analyzers

We recommend the WildPackets protocol analyzers because they are easy to use, accurately decode hundreds of protocols, and are affordable. The WildPackets EtherPeek analyzer is available as a no-cost demo download from www.wildpackets.com. The demo version can't save files, print, or capture for extended periods, but it is fully functional and can provide a glimpse into the traffic on your network.

In the WildPackets EtherPeek and AiroPeek products, a real-time expert system analysis engine called NetSense runs during capture time and provides automated analysis of common network problems. NetSense can also provide limited modeling and simulation capabilities by allowing the user to change various parameters and pose "what-if" questions. NetSense also provides application response time and throughput analysis.

The iNetTools suite is part of EtherPeek and provides common network troubleshooting utilities from within EtherPeek. These utilities include ping, trace-route, whois, ping scan, port scan, finger, and a throughput measurement tool.

On his Ethernet Web site, Charles Spurgeon, the renowned author of *Ethernet: The Definitive Guide* and other books, maintains a list of protocol analyzers, including EtherPeek and others. (See the Web site at www.ethermanage.com/ethernet/software .html.) If you don't already have an analyzer, try one that is free or that has a free demo version. With an analyzer, you can reproduce the packet capture examples in this book and enhance your retention of the concepts discussed here.

Using a Protocol Analyzer in a Switched Network

When attached to a shared network, such as a set of cables and devices connected via hubs, an analyzer sees all traffic and can capture and decode all packets. When connected to a switched network, an analyzer sees broadcast, multicast, and flooded traffic. The analyzer also sees any traffic addressed to devices reachable via the same port to which the analyzer is attached. This may not be much traffic if the analyzer is the only device on that port, however. If other devices share the port—for example, if a hub is connected to the port—then the analyzer sees more data.

As discussed in more detail in Chapters 3 through 5, a switch forwards frames based on the destination MAC address in a frame. Switches filter frames that do not need to exit a particular port. Switches also forward broadcast and multicast frames, and frames for which the switch has not yet identified the location of the destination MAC address in the frame. Switches initially flood all traffic, but by examining the source address in each packet, the switch quickly learns which addresses are reachable from which port and then forwards frames selectively. This is a problem for protocol analysis, although a good thing for network performance.

There is a solution to this problem. Most switch vendors support *mirroring* traffic. With mirroring, a switch copies (mirrors) selected traffic to a monitor port. Enabling the mirroring feature tells a switch to copy traffic forwarded to the mirrored ports to an additional monitor port where an analyzer is attached. Some Cisco documentation calls the monitor port where the analyzer is attached the *Switched Port Analyzer* (SPAN) port. You can configure a single port as the monitor port and also configure which traffic should be sent to the monitor port. You can mirror traffic destined to an individual port or to multiple ports, or traffic for one or more VLANs.

LEARNING PROTOCOL ANALYSIS

In one sense, protocol analysis is the study of the language of network communication. Unfortunately, there's no way to grow up learning the language of protocols the way children grow up learning their native languages. One way to approach protocol analysis can be likened to an adult learning a foreign language for the first time. Of course, if the language uses foreign symbols, then the student will need to learn how to pronounce the symbols properly. English, Japanese, Greek, Arabic, and Hebrew all use different symbols to represent the sounds of words. So, too, the protocol analysis student will need to learn to recognize and "pronounce" binary and hexadecimal numbers, ASCII encoding, EBCDIC encoding, Manchester signal encoding, and even Reversible Half-ASCII in the NetBIOS arena. As for an American learning Japanese, there will be a learning curve just to get the basic symbols in mind.

In addition to teaching symbols and pronunciation, foreign language classes explain noun endings and possessives, verb tenses and voices, and whether or not adjectives precede or follow the nouns they modify. The students learn the structure and organization of the language. There is structure and organization in the protocol world as well. The OSI model, shown in Figure 2.1 on page 14, defines relationships between the components of network communication. In the same way that fluent speakers don't diagram sentences before they talk, or think about whether they're using the future perfect tense, the expert protocol analyst also knows how pieces of protocol languages fit together. This knowledge starts with a basic understanding of the layers in each protocol as outlined by the OSI model.

It's said that as people become fluent in a new language, there's a point when they can think in that language. When network professionals can think in TCP/IP or AppleTalk, they become intuitive problem solvers. The fluent speaker also becomes a fluent reader. You may have had the experience of reading a famous book in the native language of the author and gleaning nuances of meaning that were lost in a translation. When experienced protocol analysts "read" an analyzer trace file, they also glean the subtle behaviors expressed by the communicators. They can identify problems and performance degradation, and they can anticipate future events that may be showing early manifestations in the protocol interactions.

On Cisco switches that use the CatOS command line interface, use the `set span` command to specify which ports are mirrored and which port is the monitor (SPAN) port. Be careful with the syntax of this command. It is very similar to the `set spantree` command used by the Spanning Tree Protocol, which Chapter 5 discusses in more detail. Because Cisco lets you abbreviate commands, you might end up configuring SPAN when you meant to configure the Spanning Tree Protocol.

On most Cisco switches that use the Cisco IOS command line interface, the command to configure mirroring is `port monitor`. On some IOS switches, the command is `monitor-port`. You should first enter the command to enable the monitoring feature and then configure two parameters—the port where the analyzer resides and the ports that will be monitored.

NOTE Some Cisco switches disable the forwarding of unknown (flooded) unicast traffic and unregistered multicast traffic to the monitor port. The goal is to protect the network from problems associated with this traffic exiting an additional port. For example, a Cisco Catalyst 1900 switch automatically adds the `port block unicast` and `port block multicast` commands to the monitor port. This can make troubleshooting difficult. The workaround is to upgrade to a higher-end switch.

The following output shows a common mistake that is made with the `monitor-port` command. The user assumed that port monitoring was working, but in fact it was not working because only the parameters had been configured. The port monitoring feature had not been enabled. The user had a protocol analyzer connected to switch port 0/11. The user expected the analyzer to see the ping packets that traveled from switch port 0/12 to an external network, but the analyzer did not see the packets.

```
(config)#monitor-port ?
  monitored  Set monitored port
  port       Set monitor port
  <cr>
(config)#monitor-port monitored 0/12
(config)#monitor-port port 0/11
(config)#exit
#ping 172.16.50.1
Sending 5, 100-byte ICMP Echos to 172.16.50.1, time out is 2 seconds:
!!!!!
Success rate is 100 percent (5/5), round-trip min/avg/max 40/40/40/ ms
```

The analyzer did not see the five ping packets that the switch sent when the `ping 172.16.50.1` command was entered. Using the `show port monitor` command (note that the show command reverses the words *port* and *monitor* and leaves out the hyphen), the user discovered that port monitoring was not enabled. After enabling the feature, the analyzer did see the ping commands.

```
#show port monitor
Port monitoring state: Disabled
Monitor port: Ethernet 0/11
Ports being monitored: Ethernet 0/12
#config t
Enter configuration commands, one per line.  End with CNTL/Z
(config)#monitor-port
(config)#exit
#ping 172.16.50.1
Sending 5, 100-byte ICMP Echos to 172.16.50.1, time out is 2 seconds:
!!!!!
Success rate is 100 percent (5/5), round-trip min/avg/max 40/42/50/ ms
#
```

CAUTION   Be careful with port monitoring. Port monitoring sends traffic in two directions—to the destined port and to the monitor port. If the monitor port connects more than just a protocol analyzer, this extra forwarding of traffic can cause problems and may result in network loops. We recommend that you use the port monitoring feature only after you have visually verified that nothing other than an analyzer is connected to the monitor (SPAN) port. To avoid loops, some Cisco switches ensure that the monitor port does not participate in the Spanning Tree Algorithm, but don't count on this feature being available on all switches.

Understanding Network Traffic

As part of your proactive network management, you should use a protocol analyzer to gain an understanding of the day-to-day traffic on your network. Most networks carry user traffic, including terminal/host, client/server, and peer-to-peer application traffic. They also carry background traffic including network management data, exchanges of router topology information, switch and bridge configuration traffic, and polling between servers and devices such as printers.

In today's switched network environments, it is difficult to get a view of network-wide traffic, but as a first step, you should at least study traffic for a typical user and traffic to and from a typical busy file server. First, capture the traffic related to a single workstation as it is booted and as a user logs in and accesses representative applications. Include characteristic user activities in the capture session such as Web browsing, checking e-mail, and printing. This trace file will provide insight into the protocols and configurations that are in use. Second, capture traffic to and from a busy file server. This trace file will provide insight into the mix of protocols that are in use as well as the range of response times experienced by multiple client machines.

Reliable Versus Unreliable Protocols

As you study your network protocols, you will learn that protocols can be reliable or unreliable. A related characteristic is that they can be connection oriented versus connectionless. A reliable protocol is a protocol that has error correction and Positive Acknowledgment with Retransmission (PAR). PAR means that when a device sends data, it expects positive affirmation that the data was received. The device retransmits if it does not receive the affirmation. Senders sequence packets (or bytes, in the case of TCP) so that the recipient can identify which packets (bytes) have been received and which ones are missing. Errors related to lost packets are corrected.

A reliable protocol supports *flow control*, which is a process for adjusting the flow of data from one device to another to ensure that the receiving device can handle all of the incoming data. Flow control is beneficial when a sending device is capable of sending data more quickly than the receiving device can receive the data. With some types of flow control—for example, TCP flow control—the receiver specifies how much data it is able to accept by stating its current *receive window size*.

Unreliable protocols do not have acknowledgments, retransmissions, or flow control. They may have error detection, but no error correction. Unreliable protocols have the advantage of being efficient and easy to implement. They have the obvious disadvantage that they offer only a best-effort service that does not guarantee delivery of data. Unreliable protocols depend on higher-layer protocols to provide reliability.

A connectionless protocol allows a device to transmit data to another device in an unplanned fashion and without prior coordination. Each packet, which is also called a *datagram*, is transmitted independently of previous and subsequent packets. A connection-oriented protocol, on the other hand, has some method for connection establishment and termination. A logical association, or *connection*, is established between devices before any data is transferred. Depending on the protocol, session establishment might be the job of a specific type of device. In some protocols, either side can initiate the session.

When troubleshooting reliable, connection-oriented protocols, verify that sequence numbers, acknowledgments, window sizes, and other parameters associated with this type of traffic are appropriate and are being incremented and managed correctly. If there are multiple retransmissions of segments of data, determine why. Are packets getting lost due to errors, buffer overflows, queuing delays, or other types of congestion? Later chapters will help you answer such questions.

> **NOTE** Most connection-oriented protocols are reliable, and most connectionless protocols are unreliable, but there are exceptions. For example, Frame Relay is a connection-oriented protocol that does not guarantee packet delivery. Frame Relay requires a virtual circuit to be established before data can be sent, but Frame Relay does not have any reliability mechanisms. In like manner, Open Shortest Path First (OSPF) is connectionless but uses acknowledgments. When a router running OSPF sends link state updates, it sends them as multicast packets in a connectionless fashion, yet it expects acknowledgments from its neighbors.

In addition to characterizing whether a protocol is unreliable or reliable and connectionless or connection-oriented, it is helpful to classify protocols as supporting one of a few fundamental types of traffic, including terminal/host, peer-to-peer, client/server, server-to-server, and distributed computing network traffic. The next few sections explain these terms to help you gain an understanding of traffic on your network. Subsequent chapters provide more detail on traffic types.

Terminal/Host Traffic

Terminal/host traffic is network traffic caused by a user typing at a terminal or using a terminal emulation program designed to send text-oriented data to a host such as a mainframe or server. The terminal side has little intelligence. The actual application and data are stored on the host. Terminal/host traffic is usually connection oriented. Before data can be sent, a session is established. The amount of data sent by either side of the connection is usually asymmetrical. The terminal sends a few characters and the host sends many characters.

NOTE Terminal/host traffic could be traffic to a mainframe or traffic to any device, including a router, that supports text-oriented data entered into a simple terminal application. The term *host* sometimes refers to a powerful computing device, such as a mainframe. Networking professionals also use the term *host* in a generic fashion to mean a network device, node, or station. The IP community started this trend of referring to network devices as hosts many years ago.

Telnet is an example of an application that generates terminal/host traffic. The default behavior for Telnet is that the terminal (user) side sends each character the user types in a single packet. The host returns multiple characters, depending on what the user typed. With some full-screen terminal applications, such as IBM 3270-based terminal applications, the terminal sends characters typed by the user and the host returns data to repaint the screen. The amount of data transferred from the host to the terminal equals the size of the screen plus commands and attribute bytes. Attribute bytes specify the color and highlighting of characters on the screen.

Peer-to-Peer Traffic

Peer-to-peer traffic is generated on networks in which each workstation or process has equivalent capabilities and responsibilities. This differs from client/server architectures, in which some computers are dedicated to serving others. With peer-to-peer traffic, traffic flow is often symmetrical. Communicating entities transmit approximately equal amounts of protocol and application information. There is no hierarchy. Each device is considered as important as each other device, and no device stores substantially more data than any other device.

True peer-to-peer architectures are uncommon. A true peer-to-peer conversation involves the exchange of data in a bidirectional conversation between two machines running peer applications. For example, in a DECnet environment using Network Services Protocol (NSP), two DEC VAX computers might function as protocol-level peers, perhaps in a DEC Local Area VAX Cluster (LAVC) architecture.

In most cases, including the cases that follow, when the term *peer-to-peer* is used, it actually refers to *back-to-back client/server traffic*. With back-to-back client/server traffic, users share resources (files, printers, and so on) from their own machines. The users' machines now play the role of a server. Another user accesses these resources, playing the role of a client. Because any user could be both sharing resources with the network community and using the resources provided by some other member of the network, each machine is both a client and server. Because machines play the same role (both client and server at the same time), they function on an equal basis and are therefore *peers* in the communication environment. When analyzing the traffic with a protocol analyzer, file Input/Output (I/O) protocols would be seen between the machines, but the role of client and the role of server would be played by both machines. To understand the protocols, you should analyze the traffic as two separate client/server conversations.

In small LAN environments, network administrators often set up PCs in a peer-to-peer configuration so that all group members can access each other's data and printers.

There is no central file or print server. On larger networks, peer-to-peer communication is discouraged because it is hard to manage and may result in security problems as users have access to each other's hard drives.

Recently peer-to-peer applications for downloading music, videos, and software have gained popularity. Each user publishes music or other material and allows other users on the Internet to download the data. This is considered peer-to-peer traffic because every user acts as both a distributor and a consumer of data. There is no hierarchy. This type of peer-to-peer traffic should be discouraged on campus networks for two reasons. First, it can cause an inordinate amount of traffic, and, second, the published material is often copyrighted by someone other than the person publishing it. In other words, the person publishing the material is breaking United States copyright law.

Client/Server Traffic

Client/server traffic is generated by a network architecture in which each computer or process on the network is either a client or a server. Servers are powerful computers or processes dedicated to managing disk drives, printers, or other network resources. Clients are PCs or workstations on which users run applications. Clients rely on servers for resources, such as files, peripherals, application software, and processing power. Clients send queries and requests to the server. The server responds with data or permission for the client to send data.

With a client/server architecture, application software runs on the user's machine, which reads and writes data to the disk subsystem in the server. When analyzing client/server traffic, you should observe file I/O commands, replies, and data moving across the network. Client/server protocols include Server Message Block (SMB), Network File System (NFS), Apple Filing Protocol (AFP), NetWare Core Protocol (NCP), and other file I/O protocols.

Client/server protocols are generally reliable and connection oriented. Most modern client/server protocols also include some form of flow control whereby each side of the connection can specify how much data it can receive before the other side should stop and wait for an acknowledgment. Client/server protocols also have methods for a station to temporarily halt data transfer when a recipient experiences congestion.

In a TCP/IP environment, many applications are implemented in a client/server fashion, although the applications were invented before the client/server model was invented. For example, FTP has a client (user) side and a server side. X Windows is an example of a TCP/IP server (the screen manager) that actually runs on the user's machine. This can lead to a lot of traffic in both directions, such as when the user enables a blinking cursor or ticking clock that needs continual updating across the network, even when the user isn't present.

These days, Hypertext Transfer Protocol (HTTP) is probably the most widely used client/server protocol. Clients use a Web browser application, such as Internet Explorer, to talk to Web servers. Each session often lasts just a few seconds because users tend to jump from one Web site to another. Traffic volume is asymmetrical. Clients send small queries and the server responds with large amounts of text and multimedia data. To maximize perceived performance, some Web servers do not send full-sized packets. Packet sizes in the 400- to 600-byte range are typical.

Wireless Clients

When Ethernet connectivity is replaced with wireless connectivity, a *wireless client* is created. A wireless client doesn't know that it's wireless. Applications and upper-layer protocols operate in exactly the same manner as if the client were connected to an Ethernet network. IP still locates a default gateway by sending an Address Resolution Protocol (ARP) broadcast for the gateway's configured address. TCP still enacts a three-way handshake for session setup, sequences and acknowledges data, and provides flow control through the window-size parameter. In fact, the wireless client continues to construct Ethernet frames for carrying Layer 3 protocols. These frames are encapsulated in an 802.11 frame and transmitted through the air via radio frequency (RF) signals. The good news is that using a wireless analyzer, such as WildPackets' AiroPeek, requires the same skills needed for the wired LAN. Analysts must expand their methods and knowledge, however, to include 802.11 protocol behavior and RF signal propagation.

Wireless clients may talk directly to each other (peer-to-peer connectivity) as users share files between notebook computers, for example. Alternately, a wireless client may communicate with a server that is connected to the wired Ethernet using an *access point*. An access point is essentially a Layer 2 bridge between the wired Ethernet and the wireless network. Analyzing wireless network traffic is discussed in full detail in Chapter 4.

Thin Clients

A thin client is designed to be especially simple and to work in an environment where the bulk of data processing occurs on a server. Although the term *thin client* usually refers to software, it is also used for small hardware devices that don't have hard drives. With thin client technology (also known as *server-based computing*), user applications originate on a central server. In some cases, the application runs on the central server; in other cases, the software is installed on the server and is downloaded into the client machine for execution. Microsoft provides thin client solutions with its Windows NT Terminal Server Edition and Windows 2000 with Terminal Services products. Citrix Metaframe is another popular thin client server system. The Citrix solution uses memory in the server to create memory partitions for each client. Software applications run entirely in the Citrix server in the user's partition. The user accesses the software in a terminal/host mode.

An *information appliance* or *computing appliance* is a thin client designed to perform a particular set of dedicated tasks. The promise of computing appliances lies in the concept that dedicated functionality means a system can be easy to use and manage. A computing appliance could be a cash register, a dedicated e-mail machine, or a database retrieval device. Computing appliances often run the Linux operating system and a Java-enhanced Internet browser.

The main advantage of thin client technology is lower support costs. Information Technology (IT) managers can have a centralized base of applications that are managed, configured, and upgraded once, with no need to individually configure each user's machine. In addition, because applications are controlled from the central server, security and intrusion detection can be simplified. Thin client technology is not applicable to every computing application, however, because users may need computers capable of operating without constant connection to a central server.

Server-to-Server Traffic

Server-to-server network traffic includes transmissions between servers and transmissions from servers to NMSs. Servers talk to other servers to implement directory services, to cache heavily used data, to mirror data for load balancing and redundancy, to back up data, and to announce service availability. Servers talk to management applications for some of the same reasons, but also to enforce security policies and to update network management data. Server-to-server traffic may be either connectionless or connection oriented. Flow control may be supported. Traffic volume may be symmetrical or asymmetrical.

Distributed Computing Traffic

Distributed computing attempts to solve a difficult problem by giving small parts of the problem to many computers and then combining the solutions for the parts into a solution for the overall problem. Some complex tasks cannot be accomplished in a reasonable time unless multiple computers process data and run algorithms simultaneously. To make animated movies, for example, designers use multiple computers to speed up graphics rendering. Distributed computing is also used in the semiconductor industry for microchip design and verification, and in the defense industry for military simulations. An unfortunate use of distributed computing is *distributed denial of service* attacks where a hacker marshals many computers to attack a target. The attacker first gains control of many computers by surreptitiously installing a virus or *Trojan horse* via an e-mail attachment or downloaded software. Then, when the time comes to attack the target, the attacker can direct the infected computers to send large amounts of traffic to the target.

Recently, distributed computing projects that make use of computers on the Internet have become popular. Volunteers agree to download software that works in the background, usually when the user isn't doing anything anyway, to help solve a difficult scientific problem. Volunteers all over the world are helping to identify extraterrestrial radio signals, for example. The volunteers' computers accept periodic downloads of data, analyze the data, and send results back to the server on a regular basis. Other Internet distributed computing projects are looking for million-digit prime numbers and helping analyze data in an attempt to fight the AIDS virus. Usually, the Internet computers involved in these projects are home computers. Most campus network engineers discourage participation in these projects at work because of the extra network traffic and the risk that the downloaded software has a virus, Trojan horse, or software bug that may disable the computer or cause network problems.

Statistical Monitoring

In addition to learning about typical protocol behavior, proactive network management involves collecting statistics about network performance. The combined effect of user activity and background traffic results in a particular set of performance statistics on a network. When user activity or background traffic changes, the statistics also change. By monitoring performance statistics, you can establish a baseline of normal behavior. Changes in the measurements may indicate that there are problems occurring. Problems often show signs of their presence weeks or even months before they impact end users. Statistical monitoring will help you be that experienced guru that we mentioned before who appears to have psychic forewarning about problems.

The following list describes the types of statistical data that you should gather. Many of these terms (such as *bandwidth* and *utilization*) are often misused when discussing network statistics. A goal of this book is to teach you to use these terms correctly:

Bandwidth.   The data-carrying capacity of a circuit or network, usually measured in bits per second (bps).

Utilization.   The percent of available bandwidth in use.

Throughput.   The quantity of error-free data successfully transferred between stations per unit of time (usually seconds).

Accuracy.   The amount of useful traffic that is correctly transmitted, relative to total traffic.

Error rate.   The number of bad frames or bits compared to good frames or bits, or the number of bad frames in a time period.

Size distribution.   A count of frames of different sizes.

Efficiency.   A measurement of how much overhead is required to produce a certain amount of data throughput.

Delay (latency).   The time between a frame being ready for transmission from a node and delivery of the frame elsewhere in the network.

Delay variation.   The extent to which measured delay deviates from average delay.

Response time.   The amount of time between a request for some network service and a response to the request.

Active stations.   The average number of stations transmitting in a given time period.

Most active stations.   A list of the stations that transmit and receive the most data.

When you make statistical measurements, use the data to establish a baseline, to tune your understanding of the network, and to focus troubleshooting efforts. For example, if you assumed that File Server 1 was the most active station, but it turns out that File Server 2 is the most active, then you can avoid wasting time and money trying to optimize and troubleshoot the wrong machine. If it turns out that User 22 is actually the most active station, then perhaps you have a problem. Users may be playing graphics-intensive network games, downloading music or videos, or testing a new nonoptimized piece of software that probably should be tested in the lab first rather than on your operational network.

Analyze the statistics you gather with respect to the network maps and device configurations you also gathered. Understanding the structure of your network and the architecture of devices within the network can help you make sense of the statistics. For example, if you place a 10-Mbps Ethernet protocol analyzer on one port of a switch and configure the switch to mirror traffic for multiple 10-Mbps ports, don't be surprised if the analyzer reports that utilization is 100 percent. The analyzer is simply computing bits per second received and comparing the rate to 10 Mbps. It has no knowledge of the switch mirroring configuration or switch architecture. A statistic of 100 percent utilization does not mean that your network or your switch backplane are about to go into meltdown, as some novices have been known to report. It's helpful to remember the famous quote attributed to the Victorian-era statesman Benjamin Disraeli: "There are three kinds of lies: lies, damned lies, and statistics."

You should calculate more than a simple mean (average) for some types of statistics. Network performance data is often bimodal or heavily skewed from the mean. For example, response time from a server is often bimodal, if the server sometimes retrieves data from speedy Random Access Memory (RAM) cache and sometimes gets the data from a slow mechanical disk drive. When network performance data is bimodal, multimodal, or skewed from the mean, you should document a standard deviation with any measurements of the mean. Standard deviation is a measurement of how widely data disperses from the mean.

Simple Network Management Protocol and Remote Monitoring

One method for capturing statistical and troubleshooting data is to use a standard network management protocol such as SNMP. SNMP is a language for retrieving data from a managed device and setting configuration options on the device. An *SNMP agent* is software that resides in a managed device that keeps a database of management information in the device. SNMP uses the term *Management Information Base* (MIB) for a database of management data. An SNMP NMS polls the agent and runs applications to display management data.

The RMON MIB was developed by the IETF in the early 1990s to address shortcomings in the standard SNMP MIBs, which lacked statistics on data link and physical-layer parameters. The IETF originally developed the RMON MIB to provide Ethernet traffic statistics and fault diagnosis. In 1994, Token Ring statistics were added. Chapter 3 discusses Ethernet RMON in more detail.

SNMPv2, which is defined in Request for Comments (RFC) 1905, describes seven types of packets used for retrieving management data and setting parameters on SNMP and RMON agents:

- *Get Request.* Sent by an NMS to an agent to collect a management parameter.

- *Get-Next Request.* Sent by an NMS to collect the next parameter in a list or table of parameters.

- *Get-Bulk Request.* Sent by an NMS to retrieve large blocks of data, such as multiple rows in a table (not in SNMPv1).

- *Response.* Sent by an agent to an NMS in response to a request.

- *Set Request.* Sent by an NMS to an agent to configure a parameter on a managed device.

- *Trap.* Sent autonomously (not in response to a request) by an agent to an NMS to notify the NMS of an event.

- *Inform.* Sent by an NMS to notify another NMS of information in a MIB. Supports Managers of Managers (MoM) architectures (not in SNMPv1).

WildPackets Statistical Tools

On many campus networks, devices are not configured to use SNMP or RMON. In these cases, and in situations where SNMP and RMON do not provide the desired data in an easy-to-use fashion, a portable protocol analyzer is a better option. WildPackets' EtherPeek and AiroPeek products are best known for their packet capture and protocol analysis features, but they are also valuable tools for statistical monitoring. EtherPeek captures global statistics based on all network traffic from the moment the NIC is chosen. It also captures statistics based only on the unhidden packets in the capture buffer or on a user-controlled sample of network traffic.

EtherPeek and AiroPeek display real-time packet counts and traffic volume for the network as a whole and for each node on the network. In addition, the Protocol Statistics window shows network traffic volume broken down by protocol and subprotocol, which is essential information when learning about and optimizing a network. The Conversation Statistics window shows traffic statistics aggregated by source/destination node pairs, and by protocol. The Network Statistics window displays a real-time utilization percentage and a packets-per-second rate. The Error Statistics window shows error counts, and the Size Statistics window shows the distribution of packet sizes.

WildPackets also provides useful tools for application-layer statistical monitoring. The WebStats Analysis Module, for example, adds Web site management tools to the EtherPeek program. It collects data on TCP-based protocols, including HTTP and FTP data streams, and displays the results in EtherPeek.

Simulation and Modeling

Simulation and modeling software is another ingredient in a toolbox of proactive network management applications. This type of software typically uses object-oriented data structures to help you predict the performance of a network after a planned reconfiguration or redesign or to help you stress-test a model of your current network. Simulation and modeling tools let you select objects that represent network topology, protocols, traffic levels, and routing algorithms to simulate the operation of a network. The output provides network performance predictions, including response times, throughput measurements, network utilization, and packets dropped by routers.

For a simulation tool to be effective, it must be developed by software engineers who understand computer networking in addition to statistical analysis and modeling techniques. Because performance problems on networks often arise from the complex interaction of media access methods, switch and router architectures, server architectures, and software implementations of buffers and queuing on these devices, modeling network behavior can be challenging. One solution to this problem is that a simulation tool can incorporate measurements of actual network traffic, rather than relying solely on device libraries that model theoretical behavior. This approach not only solves the problem of modeling complex devices, but also allows the tool to calibrate assumptions made about traffic load and characteristics. There is less reliance on the user of the tool to accurately predict traffic load, and more reliance on real measurements. A recommended tool that uses this calibrated approach is NetPredictor from a company called NetPredict.

Active and Reactive Troubleshooting

No matter how much proactive monitoring and optimization you do, your network is going to experience failures at times, requiring you to react to problems. Using a systematic method, such as the Cisco troubleshooting method or some other orderly process, you will need to define, isolate, and fix the problem. There are a variety of tools to use when reacting to problems. In addition to some of the tools already mentioned, which can be used for both proactive and reactive troubleshooting, you can also use the tools described in the next few sections.

Tools for Troubleshooting the Physical Layer

Many tools are available for troubleshooting at the physical layer. Volt-ohm meters and digital multimeters are low-end devices that can provide basic troubleshooting information. These devices measure electrical indicators such as alternating current (AC) and direct current (DC) voltage, current, resistance, capacitance, and cable continuity. Although you may be asked a question about these basic tools on the Cisco Support Test, in actual field practice most network support engineers test with more sophisticated tools.

Cable testers (also sometimes called *scanners*) are useful tools for testing cables and checking physical connectivity. Cable testers are available for Shielded Twisted Pair (STP), Unshielded Twisted Pair (UTP), and coaxial and twinax cables. These testers can test and report cable conditions including Near-End Crosstalk (NEXT), attenuation, and noise. Some of the tools also have a Time-Domain Reflectometer (TDR) function, wire-mapping features, and traffic-monitoring capabilities. Some testers display MAC-level information about network utilization, error rates, and collisions. Some tools also allow for limited protocol testing—for example, sending IP pings.

Similar tools exist for fiber optic cabling. Because of the relatively high cost of fiber optic cable and its installation, it is recommended that fiber optic cable be tested before installation (also called *on-the-reel testing*) and after installation. Continuity testing of the fiber requires either a visible light source or a reflectometer. Light sources capable of providing light at the three predominant wavelengths—850, 1300, and 1550 nm—are used with power meters that test attenuation and return loss in the fiber.

A TDR locates kinks, sharp bends, shorts, opens, impedance mismatches, and other defects in copper cables. Optical TDRs (OTDRs) work on fiber optic cabling. A TDR works by bouncing a signal off the end of the cable, much like radar. Opens, shorts, and other problems reflect the signal back at different amplitudes, depending on the problem. A TDR measures how much time it takes for the signal to reflect. Together with knowledge of the speed at which a signal travels in a cable, a measurement of how much time it takes for the signal to reflect gives the TDR an estimate of the distance to the problem. TDRs can also be used to measure the length of a cable. When a signal reaches the end of a cable, it reflects at a very low amplitude.

When troubleshooting physical-layer interfaces, it sometimes helps to measure digital signals that are present. A breakout box is often attached at a data communications interface—for example, between a computer and a modem or between a router and a Channel Service Unit (CSU). A breakout box monitors interface signals and displays information using Light-Emitting Diodes (LEDs). For example, an EIA/TIA-232 breakout box might contain 25 LEDs, 1 for each signal on the DB-25 EIA/TIA-232 connector. A positive voltage might cause the LED for a signal to light; a negative voltage might cause it to turn off. The user can monitor the LEDs to troubleshoot control signals.

Some testing tools have the capability to perform a Bit Error Rate Test (BERT). With BERT, a known pattern of 1s and 0s is continually transmitted across a link so that proper reception can be measured at the other end. If 1000 bits are transmitted and two bit errors are detected, for example, the bit error rate for that circuit is 0.002. Another measure of reliability, the Block Error Rate Test (BLERT), measures the ability of a link to pass entire blocks of data rather than just bits. When using most modern protocols, a BLERT test may be more indicative of actual reliability, because protocols retransmit a whole block of data if a single bit error occurs.

Tools for Troubleshooting Above the Physical Layer

This section focuses on commands and tools you can use to quickly test reachability to a remote device or network, determine the path to a remote device, determine name-to-address mapping, and efficiently test other upper-layer functions. Theoretically, these tools should be used after the physical-layer tools mentioned in the previous section have verified that the physical layer is functioning correctly. In actual field practice, however, these tools are usually used before testing at the physical layer. If the tools indicate a problem, then the troubleshooter reverts to a check of the physical cabling and interfaces before deciding that the problem lies at a higher layer. Troubleshooting is an iterative process that migrates between OSI layers as the troubleshooter gathers facts about the problem.

Ping

The *Packet Internet Groper (ping)* utility is a popular and effective tool for testing reachability to a remote device. Ping sends a command to a remote station that causes the station to respond, somewhat like a Ping-Pong ball returns when it is sent across a net to a partner. Ping is usually used to test reachability to an individual device. *Ping scan* sends to a range of addresses. The intended purpose of ping scan is to discover active nodes on a network during a network reconfiguration when new machines are being added or removed from the network. Ping scan is sometimes misused by hackers.

Although ping originated in the TCP/IP community, Cisco allows the use of the Cisco IOS ping command to test reachability to devices running the following protocols:

- Apollo
- Connectionless Network Service (CLNS)
- DECnet
- Banyan Virtual Integrated Network Service (VINES)
- Xerox Network System (XNS)
- IP
- AppleTalk
- Novell Internetwork Packet Exchange (IPX)
- SNA

The SNA ping requires you to type the whole command sna ping. (For the other pings, you type ping followed by enter and then select the protocol.) The SNA ping initiates an Advanced Program to Program (APPC) session. The AppleTalk ping is an AppleTalk Echo Protocol (AEP) packet and is covered in more detail in Chapter 11. The IPX ping frame format depends on configuration parameters and is covered in more detail in Chapter 10. The IP ping is actually an Internet Control Message Protocol (ICMP) echo packet. A detailed view of a packet capture of an IP ping (echo) reply is shown in Figure 2.4.

When in privileged mode on a Cisco IOS router, there are many options for the ping command. Enter ping with no parameters and immediately press enter to see the options. One useful option is the selection of the source address for use in the ping packet. Because a router has potentially many IP addresses, setting the source address for the packet is a useful troubleshooting feature. If you don't set the source IP address, the router uses by default the address of the outgoing interface used to reach the device you are trying to ping. When routing problems are occurring, however, the router can be confused regarding which outgoing interface to use. In this case, being able to explicitly configure the source address is helpful. The following example shows the use of ping options.

```
Charlotte# ping
Protocol [ip]:
Target IP address: 172.16.40.2
Repeat count [5]:
Datagram size [100]:
Timeout in seconds [2]:
Extended commands [n]: yes
Source address: 172.16.10.1
Type of service [0]:
Set DF bit in IP header? [no]:
Data pattern [0xABCD]:
Loose, Strict, Record, Timestamp, Verbose[none]:
Sweep range of sizes [n]:
Type escape sequence to abort.
Sending 5, 100-byte ICMP Echos to 172.16.40.2, timeout is 2 seconds:
!!!!!
Success rate is 100 percent, round-trip min/avg/max = 40/40/40 ms
```

When pinging on a Cisco router or switch, the default is to send five ping packets. The router displays five characters, one for the result of each ping. The five exclamation points in the example indicate that five pings were successfully sent and a reply was received for each one.

A ping, which is really an ICMP echo packet, results in an ICMP echo reply when there are no problems. If there is a problem, the result is often an ICMP error message. The error message can come from a router en route to the destination or from the destination itself. ICMP packets have a type field and a code field. The combination of the type and code provides the significance of the message. Table 2.2 lists ICMP types and codes relevant to ping and to trace-route, which is covered in the next section.

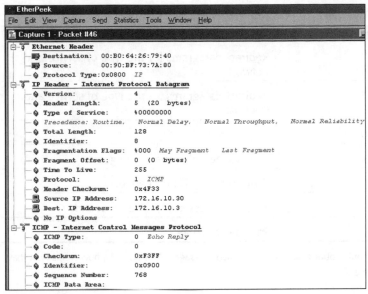

Figure 2.4 A Ping reply packet.

Table 2.2 ICMP Types and Codes

TYPE	CODE	MEANING
0	0	Echo reply (ping reply).
3	x	Destination unreachable (generic category).
3	0	Network unreachable.
3	1	Host unreachable.
3	2	Protocol unreachable.
3	3	Port unreachable.
3	4	Fragmentation was needed and the Don't Fragment (DF) bit was set.
3	5	Source route failed.
3	13	Packet administratively prohibited.
4	0	Source quench.*
5	x	Redirect (generic category).
5	0	Redirect datagrams for the network.
5	1	Redirect datagrams for the host.

(continues)

Table 2.2   ICMP Types and Codes *(Continued)*

TYPE	CODE	MEANING
5	2	Redirect datagrams for the type of service and network.
5	3	Redirect datagrams for the type of service and the host.
8	0	Echo (ping).
11	x	Time exceeded (generic category).
11	0	Time-to-Live (TTL) exceeded.
11	1	Fragment reassembly time exceeded.
12	0	Parameter problem.

*Per RFC 1812, a router should not originate source quench messages. Per RFC 1122, however, a host may send source quench messages.

Cisco routers and switches output a character code that represents the received message and the result of the ping. Table 2.3 shows the character codes for ping. Cisco IOS software does not provide detailed information on the ICMP error message received when using ping. In most cases, if there is a problem, Cisco IOS software simply outputs a period, meaning there was no response, or a U, meaning an ICMP destination unreachable message was received. Cisco IOS software does not distinguish between network unreachable, host unreachable, or protocol unreachable when using ping.

Table 2.3   Cisco IOS Ping Result Codes

RESULT CODE	MEANING
!	Each exclamation point indicates receipt of an ICMP echo reply.
.	Each period indicates the router timed out while waiting for a reply.
U	A destination unreachable message was received.
Q	A source quench message was received.
M	A fragmentation needed and DF bit set message was received.
?	An unknown packet was received.
C	A packet was received with the congestion-experienced bit set.*

* See RFC 2481, an experimental protocol that adds explicit congestion notification to IP.

To prevent an errant packet stream from impacting router performance, Cisco routers limit the rate at which they send ICMP destination unreachable messages. So when a problem with pinging occurs, you probably won't see UUUUU in a network with Cisco routers. You will most likely see U.U.U. Every other ping times out without an explicit error. In Cisco IOS version 12.1 and later, the rate limiting is configurable with the `ip icmp rate-limit unreachable` command.

Trace-Route

Cisco IOS software and most operating systems have a *trace-route* facility for investigating the routing path to a destination device. Trace-route displays the sequence of hops a packet traverses to get from a given source to a destination. Trace-route originated in the TCP/IP community, but Cisco lets you use the tool for other protocols also, including AppleTalk, CLNS, Novell IPX, and Banyan VINES.

The results provided by trace-route are a measurement of the round-trip time to each router in the path to a destination and also a measurement of the round-trip time to the actual destination. The timing measurements account for processing time at the recipients in addition to propagation delay. Trace-route can be used as a rough estimate of delays on a network. It is most useful, however, as a method for determining the path to a remote destination.

With UNIX and Cisco IOS operating systems, an IP trace-route packet is a User Datagram Protocol (UDP) *probe* sent to a high UDP port number, usually in the 33,000 to 43,000 range. Trace-route works by taking advantage of the ICMP error message a router generates when a packet exceeds its TTL value. TTL is a field in the IP header of an IP packet.

Trace-route starts by sending a UDP probe packet with a TTL of 1. This causes the first router in the path to discard the probe and send back a TTL exceeded message. One of the first things a router does when forwarding IP packets is decrement the TTL (which is essentially a hop count value). If the decrement causes the TTL to reach 0, then the packet is dead (discarded) and a TTL exceeded message is sent.

The trace-route command sends several probes, increasing the TTL by 1 after sending three packets at each TTL value. For example, trace-route sends three packets with TTL equal to 1, then three packets with TTL equal to 2, then three packets with TTL equal to 3, and so on, until the destination host is reached or a configured maximum number of tries (usually 30) is reached.

Each router in the path decrements the TTL. The router that decrements the TTL to 0 sends back the TTL exceeded message. The final destination host sends back a port unreachable ICMP message, because the high UDP port number is not a well-known port number. This process allows a user to see a message from every router in the path to the destination, and a message from the destination.

NOTE When executing a trace-route to a Cisco router, keep in mind that the sending of port unreachable messages may be rate limited.

The trace-route facility in Microsoft operating systems sends a ping rather than a UDP packet. The trace-route command makes use of the IP TTL feature and router behavior

Table 2.4   Cisco IOS Trace Result Codes

RESULT CODE	MEANING
.	Each period indicates the router timed out while waiting for a reply.
?	An unknown packet was received.
Q	A source quench message was received.
A	An administratively prohibited message was received, probably due to an access list.
H	A host unreachable message was received.
N	A network unreachable message was received.
P	A protocol unreachable message was received.

with respect to TTL, but the packet is an ICMP echo instead of a UDP probe. The only real difference is that when the message reaches the final destination, the destination normally responds to the ping, rather than sending a port unreachable message.

When using the `trace` command with Cisco IOS software, the results are more detailed than the results for the `ping` command. In addition to reporting the amount of time that elapses until receipt of each message, the software also reports errors. Table 2.4 shows the character codes for trace results.

Unfortunately, trace-route is not dependable. Some non-Cisco routers do not send TTL exceeded messages. Other non-Cisco routers incorrectly use the TTL of the incoming packet to send the TTL exceeded message, which does not work. Some service providers purposely change the results of trace-route to hide internal hops. Also, some end systems do not send the port unreachable message, which means that trace-route waits for a long time before timing out. It is important to realize that trace-route shows the path *to* a remote station. It does not show the path *from* a remote station. Sometimes the problem exists on the return path. For IP networks, you can use the *record route* option in an IP header to learn more about return paths. Chapter 7 discusses record route in more detail.

Trace-Route Example

This section describes an example of the trace command being used on a Cisco router to track the path to a PC running Windows 98. Figure 2.5 shows the topology of the network, which was learned using CDP.

The router output shows the results of the Charlotte router executing a trace-route to a Windows 98 PC whose address is 172.16.10.2. Notice that the PC did not respond. Two routers in the path sent ICMP TTL exceeded messages. In the first case, 172.16.40.1 sent TTL exceeded messages in response to messages it received when Charlotte sent three UDP packets with the TTL set to 1. In the second case, the next router, 172.16.20.1, sent TTL exceeded messages when Charlotte sent three UDP packets with the TTL set to 2. Charlotte then increased the TTL until it reached 30, and then gave up.

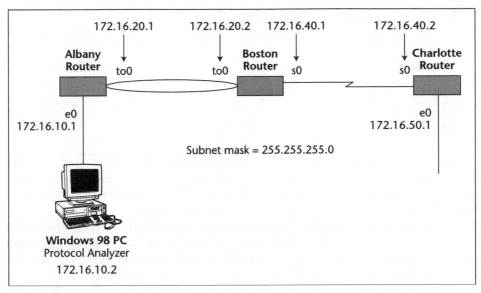

Figure 2.5   Network topology in trace-route example.

```
charlotte#trace 172.16.10.2
Type escape sequence to abort.
Tracing the route to 172.16.10.2
  1 172.16.40.1 24 msec 24 msec 24 msec
  2 172.16.20.1 28 msec 28 msec 24 msec
  3  *  *  *
  4  *  *  *
  5  *  *  *
  6  *  *  *
  7  *  *  *
  8  *  *  *
  9  *  *  *
 10  *  *  *
 11  *  *  *
 12  *  *  *
 13  *  *  *
 14  *  *  *
 15  *  *  *
 16  *  *  *
 17  *  *  *
 18  *  *  *
 19  *  *  *
 20  *  *  *
 21  *  *  *
 22  *  *  *
```

```
23   *   *   *
24   *   *   *
25   *   *   *
26   *   *   *
27   *   *   *
28   *   *   *
29   *   *   *
30   *   *   *
charlotte#
```

In the example, the Charlotte router continued to send UDP packets, increasing the TTL after three packets at each level. Figure 2.6 shows the final packet that the Charlotte router sent. Notice that in the final packet, the TTL is 28 from the recipient's point of view. The recipient was the Windows 98 PC, which was also where the protocol analyzer software was running. The TTL is 28 because it has already been decremented by the two routers in the path. The Windows 98 PC should have sent a port unreachable message to end the process, but it did not. This is an example of where trace-route gives unreliable results. The PC is definitely reachable, but it did not react to the trace-route process, resulting in a false view that the PC was not reachable. Note that a ping to 172.16.10.2 succeeded.

```
charlotte#ping 172.16.10.2
Type escape sequence to abort.
Sending 5, 100-byte ICMP Echos to 172.16.10.2, timeout is 2 seconds:
!!!!!
Success rate is 100 percent, round-trip min/avg/max = 40/40/40 ms
```

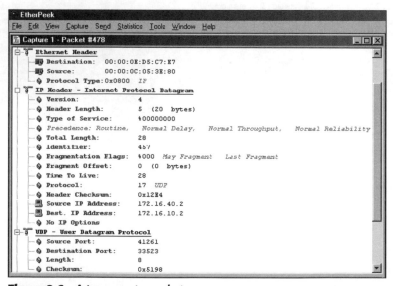

Figure 2.6 A trace-route packet.

Other Troubleshooting Commands

Many operating systems and third-party troubleshooting products include tools beyond just ping and trace-route to aid in isolating network problems. A requirement that often comes up when troubleshooting is the need to match a host or domain name to an IP address. A *name lookup* tool lets you resolve a host name to an IP address or an IP address to a host name. A *name scan* tool performs a name lookup for each address in a specified range of IP addresses.

UNIX operating systems have the *nslookup* utility. Some troubleshooting tools that run on operating systems besides UNIX provide the same sort of functionality, which is the ability to tailor queries to retrieve any of the information kept by Domain Name System (DNS) servers on the Internet, including host names, IP addresses, the class of an address, pointer records, mail exchange records, and the name of the server that is the best source of information for data within a domain (the *start-of-authority* record).

Some troubleshooting tools support a function known as *port scan*. With a port scan, you can query a specified range of ports on a host, searching for available services. Although hackers are the biggest users of port scan utilities, port scan is also useful for legitimate reasons. Many versions of UNIX, Windows, and other operating systems activate multiple ports by default on installation. A good use for port scan is to test for open ports so they may be explicitly closed to protect the host. Closing ports can be accomplished with a *software firewall* on the host.

The *finger* tool, available on UNIX and in some third-party tools, queries Remote User Information Protocol (RUIP) servers for information about users who may be logged on to a particular host. You can also get more detail on a particular user by specifying the user name and host in the same form as an e-mail address—for example, username@domain.dom.

The whois command queries Whois servers—for example, the *whois.internic.net* server—for Internet directory information. You can ask a Whois server for information about the owner of a domain name and the addresses of the DNS servers that hold authoritative information for the name. Internet names in the .com, .org, and .net domains may be registered with registrars other than the InterNIC. If you can't find information at the whois.internic.net server, you can find pointers to other registrars at www.internic.net. You can also find pointers to the registrars and Whois servers for the .edu, .gov, .mil, and other domain spaces at that site.

On both UNIX and Windows machines, a useful tool for monitoring network performance on an individual computer is the netstat command. Depending on the arguments supplied with the command, you can use the tool to determine which ports are open and their status, the number of packets in and out of the interface card, the local routing table, and statistics for IP, ICMP, UDP, and TCP. Figure 2.7 shows a printout of the options for netstat on a Windows 98 machine.

Cisco IOS Show Commands

The Cisco *show commands* are among the most important tools for understanding the status of a router, detecting neighbor routers, displaying routing tables, monitoring

TELNET TCP PORT PROBING

Cisco IOS doesn't support a user running a port scan, which is a good thing from a security point of view, but you can test access to a single TCP port from a Cisco IOS router using *Telnet TCP port probing*. For example, perhaps you just configured a new access list on a router to block HTTP, FTP, Secure Sockets Layer (SSL), or some other TCP-based application. Perhaps the only troubleshooting tool available is another router. Although routers make poor troubleshooting tools, sometimes they are the most convenient tool because you are already doing router configuration when you need to test or troubleshoot. Also, for a network engineer, access to routers may be more readily available than access to hosts running the application you are testing.

A simple technique you can use on a Cisco IOS router is Telnet TCP port probing. The Cisco IOS Telnet command allows you to specify a port other than the default Telnet port, port 23. (Other operating systems support this also; it is not unique to Cisco IOS Telnet.) The result is an attempt to open a TCP session at the specified port. For example, the `telnet 172.16.50.1 80` command tests the capability to open an HTTP (Port 80) session on the 172.16.50.1 device. The `telnet 172.16.50.1 443` command attempts to connect to the SSL port on the device. These commands can be used to test an access list or other security measure that is designed to deny HTTP or SSL traffic.

You can specify from which interface you want to Telnet using the `ip telnet source-interface` global configuration command followed by an interface. This command is useful when you wish to test the path through a particular interface on a router.

The Telnet testing technique has limitations. Only TCP ports can be probed, for one thing; UDP probing is not supported. Also, it can be time consuming to check a large number of ports in this manner. To test many ports, port scanning software is more appropriate.

interfaces, and troubleshooting and isolating problems in general. Throughout this book, we will recommend the use of show commands specific to the topic being discussed. This chapter mentioned show cdp, for example, when discussing network documentation. Chapter 3 covers show interface ethernet; Chapters 7, 8, and 9 cover the show ip commands; Chapter 10 covers the show ipx commands; and Chapter 11 covers the show appletalk commands.

Outside the realm of show commands for specific protocols are some useful show commands for monitoring the performance of a router and troubleshooting problems related to high Central Processing Unit (CPU) utilization, memory leaks, or crashes on a router. Table 2.5 gives a brief description of some show commands that you should use on your Cisco IOS routers and switches to proactively and reactively troubleshoot problems. Many of the commands have optional arguments not shown. The arguments can be used to retrieve additional information. Press the spacebar and question mark key (?) after typing the command to see the possible arguments.

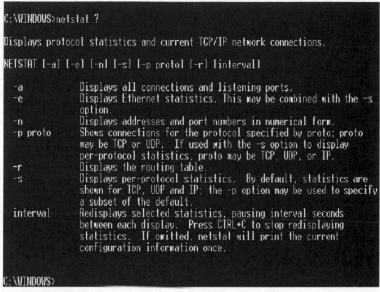

```
C:\WINDOWS>netstat ?

Displays protocol statistics and current TCP/IP network connections.

NETSTAT [-a] [-e] [-n] [-s] [-p proto] [-r] [interval]

  -a        Displays all connections and listening ports.
  -e        Displays Ethernet statistics. This may be combined with the -s
            option.
  -n        Displays addresses and port numbers in numerical form.
  -p proto  Shows connections for the protocol specified by proto; proto
            may be TCP or UDP. If used with the -s option to display
            per-protocol statistics, proto may be TCP, UDP, or IP.
  -r        Displays the routing table.
  -s        Displays per-protocol statistics. By default, statistics are
            shown for TCP, UDP and IP; the -p option may be used to specify
            a subset of the default.
  interval  Redisplays selected statistics, pausing interval seconds
            between each display. Press CTRL+C to stop redisplaying
            statistics. If omitted, netstat will print the current
            configuration information once.

C:\WINDOWS>
```

Figure 2.7   Netstat options on a Windows 98 machine.

Table 2.5   Cisco Show Commands

SHOW COMMAND	USE
show version	Displays software version and features, the names and sources of configuration files, the boot images, the configuration register, router uptime, and the reason for the last reboot.
show running-config	Displays the router's configuration stored in memory and currently in use.
show startup-config	Displays the configuration the router will use on the next reboot.
show memory	Displays statistics about system memory, including total bytes, used bytes, and free bytes. Also shows detailed information about memory blocks.
show buffers	Displays statistics for memory buffer pools, which Cisco technical support can use when helping you troubleshoot.
show processes	Displays information about active processes and CPU utilization for the last 5 seconds, 1 minute, and 5 minutes, and percentage of CPU power used by interrupt routines.

(continues)

Table 2.5   Cisco Show Commands *(Continued)*

SHOW COMMAND	USE
show interface	Displays interface status and counts of packets in interface queues and the number of packets dropped from queues.
show protocols	Displays a list of Layer 3 protocols that are configured and Layer 3 configuration information for each interface.
show environment	Displays temperature, voltage, and blower information on Cisco 7000 series, Cisco 7200 series, Cisco 7500 series routers, and Cisco 12000 series Gigabit Switch Routers.
show debug	Displays the status of debugging options. Because debug commands tax a router's CPU, use this command to check whether unnecessary debug options are enabled.
show tech-support	Displays the output of several commands of interest to Cisco technical support.

Cisco IOS Debug Commands

A Cisco router includes debugging software to aid in troubleshooting problems internal to the router and general network problems. The debug commands display text on the router console (by default) as events and packets occur. The amount and format of the output depends on the command that is used. There are hundreds of debug commands, some of which result in a lot of output and should not be used on an operational router. The router can get so busy outputting text that it falls behind doing its real jobs—forwarding packets and learning the network topology. The following paragraphs describe the debug feature in general. Refer to the *Cisco IOS Debug Command Reference* manual for complete information regarding debug commands. Throughout this book, we will recommend particular debug commands that can help you troubleshoot specific problems.

WARNING Cisco routers give high priority to debugging output. For this reason, debugging commands should be turned on only for troubleshooting specific problems or during troubleshooting sessions with Cisco technical support personnel. Excessive debugging output can render a router inoperable. Use debug commands with care on operational networks or restrict your use of debug commands to routers in a lab environment.

Use the debug ? command (debug followed by a space and question mark) to determine which debug commands are supported on your router. Using the question mark causes the router to display a list and brief description of all the debug command options. Debug commands come in all shapes and sizes. Some of them display events; some display hardware status; some act as a poor man's protocol analyzer and display information about each packet in a protocol family. For example, to display information about Novell IPX packets received, sent, and forwarded, you could use the debug ipx packet command. Using the debug commands as an analyzer has the following disadvantages, however, and is not recommended:

- The packets are only partially decoded—that is, they are not displayed in plain language as a real protocol analyzer would display them.

- The router's performance can be severely degraded by the task of capturing, decoding, and displaying packets.

- To debug protocol packets, you may need to configure the router to *process-switch* the protocol. Process switching is the slowest possible method of forwarding packets. By default, many packets are *fast-switched* rather than process-switched, in which case the debug commands do not have access to the packets.

- The router displays debug packets while you are typing, interleaving characters with the commands you are trying to type, which makes it hard to do any configuration or testing while debugging.

In order to generate debugging output, a protocol-specific debug command for the desired output must be enabled. To enable a protocol-specific debug command, use the debug protocol command, where protocol is one or more words that specify what kind of debugging you wish to enable. For example, to display routing neighbors as they are discovered by the Enhanced Interior Gateway Routing Protocol (EIGRP), use the debug eigrp neighbors command. To analyze EIGRP packets, use the debug eigrp packet command.

To disable a debug command, use the no form of the command—for example, no debug eigrp packet. Use the no debug all command to turn off all debugging. The undebug all command also works.

NOTE You should avoid the debug all command. Because debugging output takes priority over processing network traffic, and because the debug all command generates more output than any other debug command, it can severely diminish the performance of the router or even render it unusable. Use a specific debug command rather than the debug all command, unless you are working in a lab environment.

By default, a router sends the output from debug commands to the console, which requires the most CPU power of any of the options for output. You can redirect debug output using the logging global configuration command. Possible destinations include the console, virtual terminals running Telnet, an internal buffer, and UNIX hosts running a *syslog server*. The syslog format is compatible with 4.3 Berkeley Standard Distribution (BSD) UNIX and its derivatives. Logging to the console causes very high overhead, whereas logging to a virtual terminal causes less overhead. Logging to a syslog server causes even less overhead, and logging to an internal buffer causes the least overhead of any method. Use the show logging command to view the current logging output method and status. The show logging command also displays the actual log where logging is output to a buffer.

It is recommended that you configure timestamping of debug messages. Timestamping enhances real-time debugging by providing the relative timing of logged events. To enable timestamping of debug messages, use the service timestamps debug command in global configuration mode.

Normally, a router generates debugging messages for every interface, resulting in a large number of messages. The large number of messages consumes system resources and can affect your ability to find the specific information you need. When the *conditionally-triggered debugging* feature is enabled, the router generates debugging messages for packets entering or leaving the router on a specified interface or interfaces. The router does not generate debugging output for packets entering or leaving through different interfaces. To enable debugging messages for specific interfaces, use the debug condition interface command. Repeat the command for each interface for which you wish to see debugging information.

Summary

This chapter has covered troubleshooting methods that have proven efficacy when solving problems that arise on typical campus networks. We have discussed using the OSI model for troubleshooting, Cisco's troubleshooting method, and a variety of tools to document, monitor, and troubleshoot campus networks. Both proactive network troubleshooting and reactive troubleshooting have been covered. Many of the tools discussed can be used for both.

The main theme of this chapter is the importance of being systematic when troubleshooting. Systematic methods provide quick resolution to problems and prepare the troubleshooter for future problems. The use of systematic methods helps network engineers meet increasing demands for reliability and application support. Users count on network support staff to keep their networks running so that daily operations, strategic planning, education, and other activities are not impacted. To meet network users' goals, network support engineers must use orderly processes and have a solid understanding of the core engineering technologies that underlie contemporary networking.

Another major theme of this chapter is the importance of proactive network management. Use the Cisco IOS ping, trace, show, and debug commands to monitor your network even when no problems are occurring. Be careful with the debug command, however, because it causes high CPU usage on routers. Instead of looking at packets with a debug command, we recommend using a protocol analyzer to record, interpret, and analyze network traffic. An analyzer provides detailed information about packets and communication sessions.

Don't let a troubleshooting situation be the first time in many weeks that you've loaded analyzer software and tried to use it. Build a baseline of network performance and behavior by using your analyzer on a regular basis on normally operating networks. If you don't know what your network looks like when it's healthy, then you can't know what it's going to look like when it's sick.

This chapter has described the challenges facing network engineers today and some typical network traffic types—for example, client/server and peer-to-peer traffic. Subsequent chapters provide more detail on actual protocol traffic found on campus networks and will help you develop a solid foundation for understanding how networks operate—and how to troubleshoot them when they do not operate correctly. Chapter 3 covers troubleshooting Ethernet networks, Chapter 4 covers troubleshooting wireless 802.11 networks, and later chapters migrate up the seven layers of the OSI model to cover routing and upper-layer problems.

CHAPTER

3

Troubleshooting and Analyzing Ethernet Networks

In this chapter, you will learn how Ethernet and associated IEEE 802 standards work—and what causes them not to work sometimes. An assumption is made that you have already read many simple descriptions of Ethernet behavior. The goal of this chapter is to introduce you to new ways of thinking about Ethernet that will help you troubleshoot common problems found on 10-, 100-, and 1000-Mbps Ethernet networks. The chapter provides suggestions on how to troubleshoot Ethernet problems using Cisco switch and router commands. It is highly recommended that you use a protocol analyzer to explore the aspects of Ethernet engineering that the chapter discusses.

Ethernet History and Architecture

Ethernet history began in the 1970s when the University of Hawaii created the Aloha radio frequency network to connect campuses spread out over four islands. The engineering challenge was to design a set of rules for sending data in an environment where multiple communicators could potentially conflict with each other. The Aloha developers created a mechanism for sharing the medium (the atmosphere) and handling communication collisions. These concepts and rules eventually evolved into what we know today as Ethernet.

The term *Ethernet* first appeared on May 22, 1973, when Dr. Robert M. Metcalfe of the Xerox Corporation circulated a memo to his colleagues proposing that they stop calling their prototype network the Alto Aloha Network. According to Metcalfe, the network should support other computers besides the Alto—for example, the Nova and PDP-11 minicomputers. In addition, the architecture was "beginning to look very much more beautiful than the Aloha Radio Network." The memo has a hand-written note that suggests alternatives to the term Ethernet, including *Lazy Susan, Parley, Bulletin Board,* and *Parliamentary Procedure.* Luckily none of those other possibilities caught on. Talking about the physical medium as ether was more adaptable to the technical requirements than referring to a parley, which nobody could define, or to a lazy Susan, which had the wrong connotation.

In 1980, Digital Equipment Corporation (DEC), Intel, and Xerox published the DIX V1.0 standard, which increased the speed of Ethernet from 2.94 Mbps to 10 Mbps. In 1982, the DIX V2.0 standard, also known as Ethernet II, was released. In February 1980, the Institute of Electrical and Electronics Engineers (IEEE) formed Project 802 with the goal of developing open Local Area Network (LAN) standards. Before long it became clear that the objective of a single standard was not achievable due to competing ideas from engineers representing different vendors. The 802 committee divided into working groups, each focusing on different technologies. Thus was the now-famous IEEE 802.3 Working Group founded.

While many of the core engineering standards embodied in the Ethernet II standard carried forward into the 802.3 standards, there are some minor differences in frame formats. The 802 committee provided a backward-compatible frame format, called the Subnetwork Access Protocol (SNAP) frame format, to allow Ethernet II frames to be converted to the newer 802.3 standard. In 1983, Novell, Inc. created its NetWare network operating system (OS), which introduced yet another frame format that differs slightly from the other three. When using a protocol analyzer to assess an Ethernet network, it is important to differentiate between these four frame formats. The similarities and differences are discussed later in this chapter in the *Ethernet Frames* section.

The original Xerox Ethernet specification supported many media. The goal was for the media to become ubiquitous, much like the rarefied ether substance that scientists in the 1800s believed filled all space and matter. When the IEEE 802.3 Working Group published "Carrier Sense Multiple Access with Collision Detection Access Method and Physical Layer Specifications" in December 1984, the authors stayed with an architecture that supported different media. The physical layer was distinguished from the data link layer using the International Organization for Standardization (ISO) Open System Interconnection (OSI) model as a reference. As shown in Figure 3.1, modern-day 802.3 standards use a layered architecture that has its roots in the original Ethernet goal for medium independence.

Ethernet Topologies

In the 1970s and 1980s, Ethernet networks were connected in a bus topology using coaxial cable. The coaxial cable provided a shared high-speed communications channel. During an exchange of data, devices could take advantage of the high capacity, but the devices did not need the capacity on a sustained basis. A properly designed shared Ethernet had more capacity than the sum of the steady-state communication needs of the attached stations. Different Physical-Medium Attachments (PMAs), also known as Medium Attachment Units (MAUs), or simply *transceivers*, connected stations to the shared channel, which was implemented as either a thick or thin coaxial cable.

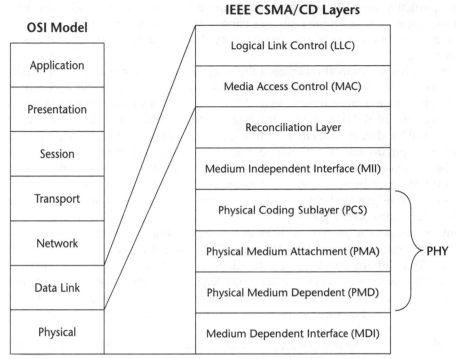

Figure 3.1   IEEE 802.3 architecture layers.

In the 1990s, with the standardization of 10BaseT, administrators started connecting stations to the shared channel in a star topology, using twisted-pair cabling and hubs. A hub relays all bits, allowing devices in a star topology to recognize when the shared channel is busy or free. A hub performs a repeating function by accepting an incoming signal from a port and sending the signal out all other ports. Star topologies were a welcome change to the challenges of properly installing and troubleshooting the older bus networks. Although the addition of a hub meant one more device to troubleshoot, cabling designs could be structured in a more logical fashion.

During the 1990s, computing power in LAN devices, especially personal computers, increased so much that network administrators became concerned that high-speed workstations could deplete the available bandwidth on shared Ethernet networks. It became difficult to achieve the original goal that the shared channel should generally be available when needed by a particular station. Whereas in the past the bottleneck on networks had been Central Processing Unit (CPU) capacity in the workstations, now the shared 10-Mbps channel became a bottleneck.

To improve performance on shared Ethernet networks, administrators used *bridges*. With bridges, the administrator could divide an overutilized LAN into multiple groupings of devices. The bridges allowed broadcast and multicast traffic to reach all members of the LAN but provided intelligent forwarding for directed traffic. Unlike hubs, which forward all bits out all ports, bridges forward frames based on the destination Media Access Control (MAC) address in a frame. Bridges filter frames that do not need to exit a particular port. Whereas a hub facilitates the sharing of bandwidth and simplifies cabling designs, a bridge segments bandwidth domains. The bandwidth available to users in one group is not consumed by directed traffic between stations in another group.

In 1991, Kalpana Corporation entered the bridge market, offering high-speed, low-cost bridges with support for numerous Ethernet ports operating simultaneously at full capacity. Kalpana called these bridges *LAN switches*, and a whole new market was born. Cisco bought Kalpana in 1994 and began actively selling switches as a way of providing full bandwidth capacity to individual computers. Switches quickly replaced hubs in many environments. Although placed into topologies at the same place as the old hubs, switches offer dedicated bandwidth on each port, rather than the shared bandwidth provided by hubs. Switches forward frames based on the destination MAC address in a frame, just like bridges. In fact, the term *switch* is just a marketing term for a high-speed, multiport bridge.

Many newcomers to the world of Ethernet confuse hubs, switches, and bridges. Hubs and switches physically look the same. They are both rectangular boxes with numerous RJ-45 Ethernet ports. They connect stations in a similar, star-wired fashion, and are often placed in wiring closets and racks together. But remember that a *hub* simplifies wiring designs for devices that share a channel in a star topology. A *switch* subdivides channels so that fewer stations are contending for the shared bandwidth. A switch is a fast *bridge*.

A distinction between bridges and switches is that switches support parallel forwarding, whereas bridges usually do not. When a typical bridge is forwarding a frame from one port to another, no other frame can be forwarded. There is only one forwarding path. A switch, on the other hand, allows multiple, parallel forwarding paths, which means a switch can handle a high volume of traffic more quickly than a bridge. At the same time that a switch is forwarding a frame from Port 1 to Port 5, for example, it can forward another frame from Port 2 to Port 6. High-end switches may support numerous simultaneous forwarding paths, depending on the structure of the switching fabric. (Manufacturers use the term *switching fabric* to describe the architecture of their switches.) Whereas the internal workings of a bridge are straightforward from an engineering and software standpoint, the internal workings of a switch are more complex.

Ethernet Physical Layer

It has been said that, given the right encoding, Ethernet can run on a coat hanger. In the realm of field consulting, you may come across networks where it seems like this statement is being tested. Because of the overall robustness of Ethernet's design, it is possible to construct a rickety Ethernet network and still push data across it. The IEEE, however, does not officially support coat hangers, and instead defines a set of standards for coaxial, Shielded Twisted Pair (STP), Unshielded Twisted Pair (UTP), and fiber optic cabling. The IEEE uses a designation for the standards that has the following three parts:

1. *Rate.* Indicates the data rate in megabits per second (Mbps).
2. *Signal.* Indicates either baseband or broadband.

3. *PHY.* Indicates the nature of the physical medium and, in earlier systems, the maximum length of a cable segment, rounded to the nearest 100 meters.

For example, 10Base2 is 10 Mbps, uses baseband signaling, and can span 185 meters (rounded up to 200 meters). Table 3.1 lists the different types of IEEE 802.3 media.

Table 3.1   IEEE 802.3 Media Standards

STANDARD	SPECIFICATION	MAXIMUM DISTANCE IN METERS
1Base5	1-pair UTP, also known as StarLAN	500
10Base5	1 thick coaxial cable	500
10Base2	1 thin coaxial cable, also known as Cheapernet	185
10Broad36	3 channels (each direction) of a private CATV system	3600
10BaseT	2 pairs Category 3 or better UTP	100
10BaseF	Generic name for 10-Mbps fiber optic standards	NA
10BaseFL	2 multimode optical fibers with asynchronous active hub	2000
10BaseFB	2 multimode optical fibers with synchronous active hubs	2000
10BaseFP	2 multimode optical fibers with passive hub	1000
100BaseT	Generic name for 100-Mbps standards	NA
100BaseX	Generic name for 100BaseT standards using 4B/5B encoding	NA
100BaseTX	2 pairs Category 5 UTP, uses 4B/5B	100
100BaseFX	2 multimode optical fibers, uses 4B/5B	2000
100BaseT4	4 pairs Category 3 (or better) UTP, uses 8B/6T	100
100BaseT2	2 pairs Category 3 (or better) UTP, uses Pulse Amplitude Modulation 5 (PAM 5)	100
1000BaseX	Generic name for 1000-Mbps standards using 8B/10B encoding	NA

(continues)

Table 3.1   IEEE 802.3 Media Standards *(Continued)*

STANDARD	SPECIFICATION	MAXIMUM DISTANCE IN METERS
1000BaseCX	2 pairs 150-Ω STP, uses 8B/10B	25
1000BaseSX	2 multimode optical fibers using shortwave laser optics, uses 8B/10B	550
1000BaseLX	2 multimode or single-mode optical fibers using longwave laser optics, uses 8B/10B	550 multimode, 5000 single-mode
1000BaseT	4 pairs Category 5 UTP, uses PAM 5	100

In the original DIX and 802.3 standards, an Ethernet controller on an adapter or Net-work Interface Card (NIC) connected to a transceiver using an Attachment Unit Inter-face (AUI).

The AUI is a 15-pin D-subminiature connector that carries transmit, receive, colli-sion presence, and power signals. The AUI connector is still present on many Cisco routers and switches that support 10-Mbps Ethernet. To use UTP cabling with an AUI connector, you need a transceiver that provides an RJ-45 receptacle.

Some Cisco routers—for example the Cisco 4500, 4700, and 3600 series routers—support network modules that provide both AUI and RJ-45 interfaces, but you can use only one or the other. The router can usually determine which interface is connected to a network if you use the *autoselect* option. However, from a troubleshooting point of view, it is important to realize that some Cisco IOS releases default to AUI or 10BaseT rather than autoselect. (Some Cisco IOS releases default to AUI even on routers that only support 10BaseT.) In interface configuration mode, you can use the following command to choose autoselect or to manually configure the interface correctly:

```
media-type {10Baset | aui | auto-select}
```

The developers of the 100-Mbps Ethernet standards developed a new Medium-Independent Interface (MII) for connecting controllers with transceivers. The MII architecture is more sophisticated than the AUI architecture because it needs to sup-port 10-Mbps and 100-Mbps transceivers and work with different physical layer implementations that use various encoding schemes. The MII is a 40-pin, high-density D-connector that carries transmit data, transmit clock, transmit enable, transmit error, receive data, receive clock, carrier sense, collision detect, management, and power sig-nals. The Gigabit MII (GMII) is based on the 100-Mbps MII design and allows a Giga-bit Ethernet controller to connect to transceivers that support 1000BaseX or 1000BaseT.

On some Cisco routers, the 100-Mbps Ethernet interface is equipped with either an MII receptacle or an RJ-45 receptacle. You need to choose one or the other. For 100-Mbps Ethernet, the media-type interface command supports two additional options:

1. *100basex.* Specifies an RJ-45 100BaseX physical connection.

2. *mii.* Specifies a media-independent interface.

Protocol Analyzers and Ethernet Media

When attaching a protocol analyzer to an Ethernet network, the physical connection is no different than it is with any other device. Whether an analyzer is connected to a 10-, 100-, or 1000-Mbps Ethernet, the analyzer needs to have the correct hardware interface to allow packet capture. Protocol-analyzer users should ask their analyzer vendors which NIC or other hardware is required for attachment and how to configure the analyzer software for proper hardware use. When capturing data with an analyzer and saving the trace file for future assessment, it is important to document exactly how the analyzer was attached to the network. Otherwise statistics may be misleading and cause unnecessary troubleshooting. When viewing a trace file on an analyzer configured for 10-Mbps Ethernet, for example, if the trace file has been captured from a Gigabit Ethernet segment, bandwidth utilization and other statistics will be misleading.

Signal Encoding

To receive data correctly on a high-speed network, a receiving controller on a NIC must synchronize its clock with the frequency and phase of the clock used to transmit the bitstream. Otherwise, the receiver will be unable to determine when a bit starts and ends. With LAN technologies, clocking information is not sent separately from data, as that requires an additional communications channel and a method for dealing with timing skew. Instead, clock and data information are encoded in a single signal in which the encoding itself provides timing information. The receiving adapter recovers the clock signal from the bitstream and thereby coordinates its understanding of when bits begin and end with the transmitter's view.

Because the signal encoding and clock recovery aspects of data transmission and reception are handled in the hardware of an Ethernet controller, the nuances of encoding are not discernible to a protocol analyzer. An electronics engineer in the 1970s may have used an oscilloscope to analyze early Ethernet networks and gather direct data about signal encoding. Today's engineer, however, uses a protocol analyzer that acquires fully formed packets that are passed to the device driver from the Ethernet adapter. A protocol analyzer provides only indirect information about signaling. One reason to understand the internal operation of Ethernet signal encoding is so that reasonable conclusions can be drawn about how a protocol-level event may have been caused by a signal-level issue.

Manchester Encoding

The original 10-Mbps Ethernet II and 802.3 standards use *Manchester encoding* for all media types. Manchester encoding specifies that a bit period is divided into two equal intervals and there is always a transition from either high to low or low to high in the middle of the bit period. A binary 0 is high first and then low. A binary 1 is low first and then high. Figure 3.2 shows a representation of 1s and 0s encoded with the Manchester method.

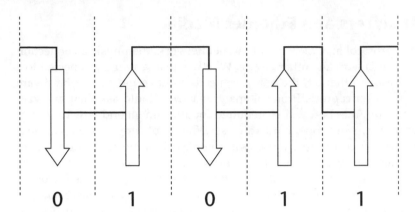

Figure 3.2   Manchester encoding.

With Manchester encoding, the transition in the middle of each bit period is the clock signal. If an alternating series of binary 1s and 0s is transmitted, then only clock signal is required. If, on the other hand, a series of repeating 1s and 0s is transmitted, then an additional signal transition is required at the beginning of the bit period in order to set up the clock for the high-to-low or low-to-high transition in the middle of the bit period. Notice the extra transition required to transmit binary 11 at the end of the data in Figure 3.2.

Manchester encoding has some advantages. For example, it is well balanced for direct current (DC) and transmission through transformers. The amount of time in the high state is the same as the amount of time in the low state, even during a long string of 1s or 0s. The net DC voltage is zero. If you put an oscilloscope on an Ethernet network, you should see a flat line (depending on the measuring time frame and the oscilloscope screen resolution). If, on the other hand, you see your favorite AM radio station, then you know there's a problem; perhaps the cables are poorly shielded or not properly terminated.

The disadvantage of Manchester encoding is that it requires up to two cycles per bit. Using Manchester encoding, a 10-Mbps signal generates up to 20 million transitions per second (20 MBaud) on the medium. The bandwidth required, measured in cycles per second, is twice that needed if data is transmitted unencoded. The potential for two cycles is due to the fact that repeated 1s or 0s require that the signal level be pulled up or down at the beginning of the bit period in preparation for the low-to-high or high-to-low clock pulse in the middle of the bit period, as shown in the transmission of binary 11 in Figure 3.2.

MLT-3 Encoding

A particular conductive medium, such as copper wire, has a specific upper limit on how many signal transitions per second it can handle. There is a point, depending on twisting, shielding, and wire type and size, where the signal can no longer be transmitted properly as frequency increases. Electronics engineers developed methods for transmitting 20 MBaud signals on standard twisted-pair network cable. If Manchester encoding were used in a 100-Mbps Ethernet, however, it would be necessary to carry 200 MBaud over the medium, which was determined to be impractical. For 100-Mbps Ethernet, therefore, a different encoding method was needed.

When 100-Mbps Ethernet was developed, the FDDI standards had already documented methods for transmitting data at 100 Mbps. Instead of designing a new solution, the 100BaseX developers adopted techniques used by FDDI on fiber optic cabling and copper UTP cabling. 100BaseFX uses Non Return to Zero, Invert on One (NRZI), as does FDDI. 100BaseTX uses a variation of NRZI that reduces the cycles per second for UTP cabling. The 100BaseTX scheme is called *Multiple Level Transition-3* (MLT-3).

MLT-3 encodes bits as transitions, as do NRZI and Manchester encoding. What makes MLT-3 different is that the base waveform is a three-state alternating wave. Rather than alternating between low and high, as in Manchester and NRZI encoding, MLT-3 alternates from low to middle to high, back to middle, then back to low. A change from one level to the next means a logical 1. A halt in the back-and-forth progression means a logical 0.

With MLT-3, there is no longer a maximum 2:1 ratio between signal transitions and bits, as there is with Manchester encoding. Instead, many bits can be transmitted without requiring a signal transition. For example, a change in level from high to middle encodes a binary 1 and a continued change from middle to low encodes a second binary 1. There is one overall signal transition from high through middle to low, but 2 bits are transmitted. The signal does not change direction and 2 bits are sent.

A disadvantage of NRZI and MLT-3 is that a steady stream of 0s—not uncommon in data—is represented as no transition, which is indistinguishable from no signal or a dead link. With no transitions, the circuitry that the receiving station uses to recover the clock can drift. If enough drift is introduced, the station cannot accurately receive data. To avoid this problem, the Physical Coding Sublayer (PCS) first encodes data using a technique called *4B/5B translation*. With 4B/5B translation, each possible 4-bit pattern is assigned a 5-bit code. Every 5-bit code has at least two transitions to ensure proper clocking.

Figure 3.3 shows the transmission of the hexadecimal byte 0x0E using MLT-3 encoding and 4B/5B translation. First, the byte was broken into the 4-bit nibbles 0x0 and 0xE. Then, each nibble was looked up in the 4B/5B translation table to find the code associated with that number. The code for 0x0 is binary 11110. The code for 0xE is binary 11100. Table 3.2 shows the 4B/5B Translation Table.

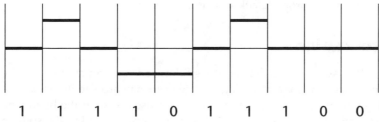

Figure 3.3 MLT-3 encoding.

Table 3.2 Data Codes in the 4B/5B Translation Table

HEX	BINARY	5B CODE	HEX	BINARY	5B CODE
0	0000	11110	8	1000	10010
1	0001	01001	9	1001	10011
2	0010	10100	A	1010	10110
3	0011	10101	B	1011	10111
4	0100	01010	C	1100	11010
5	0101	01011	D	1101	11011
6	0110	01110	E	1110	11100
7	0111	01111	F	1111	11101

In addition to data codes, the 4B/5B translation table includes a transmit error code, an idle code, and control codes used to form delimiters. Repeaters use the transmit error code to propagate received errors. The idle code is a 4B/5B pattern of all transitions. When no data is transmitted, stations continually synchronize to each other using the idle code. Unlike other implementations of Ethernet, 100BaseTX and 100BaseFX are never quiet; there is always at least an idle code being transmitted.

With MLT-3 and 4B/5B encoding, the efficiency is 80 percent. The 125-MBaud physical channel supports a 100-Mbps data rate. The 125-MBaud signal transition rate means that 100BaseTX requires cabling that can handle high-frequency signaling. It is important to use UTP cabling that meets or exceeds Category 5 specifications to handle the high frequency of the MLT-3 ternary signaling.

Other Signal Encoding Methods on Ethernet Networks

100BaseT2 is a newer, but less commonly used, standard than 100BaseTX. 100BaseT2 supports two pairs of Category 3 (or better) UTP cabling and requires Ethernet stations to have special Digital Signal Processors (DSPs) that support the advanced encoding method called PAM 5. 1000BaseT, which is the IEEE standard for Gigabit Ethernet over four pairs of Category 5 cabling, also uses PAM 5. 1000BaseX, which includes 1000BaseCX, LX, and SX, uses *8B/10B encoding*. 8B/10B was developed for Fibre Channel (ANSI94) and patented by IBM. As you can guess, 8B/10B encodes each 8-bit byte of data into a 10-bit code. Like 4B/5B, 8B/10B provides guaranteed ones density in the transmitted signal to allow for proper clock synchronization.

Clock Synchronization

From the previous discussion of the details of signal encoding, you should get the impression that it can take time for a receiving controller to synchronize its clock with the frequency and phase of the clock that the transmitter used to send the bitstream. How does Ethernet deal with the possibility that synchronization could take so long that the recipient misunderstands the first few data bits? That's what the *preamble* is all about. Ethernet stations are not synchronized to a master clock. They resynchronize to the timing information contained in the preamble of each frame.

The preamble of an Ethernet frame is a 64-bit sequence of alternating 1s and 0s, starting with a 1 and ending with binary 11. The preamble precedes the start of every frame. The receiving controller synchronizes its clock and begins moving bits into its frame buffer after receiving the binary 11 at the end of the 64-bit preamble. Repeaters and hubs regenerate a received preamble to avoid the preamble getting shorter as it goes through each repeater that uses some bits for synchronization.

Most collisions on Ethernet networks occur in the preamble. (Collisions are discussed in more detail in the *Ethernet MAC Layer* section.) Depending on the protocol analyzer and Ethernet adapter, you can sometimes see evidence of the collider's preamble when looking at damaged frames. Protocol analyzers show data in hexadecimal form, so you see 0xAA (binary 10101010), or 0x55 (binary 01010101), if the bits have gotten skewed. This information helps you determine if the frame was damaged by a collision, which is usually a normal event, or by a problem such as electrical noise or faulty hardware.

With shared 100BaseX networks, a colliding preamble may also leave behind its telltale 10101010 pattern. The 4B/5B interpretation of this pattern shows up at the end of the damaged frame as a series of 0x43 or 0x34 bytes. The protocol analyzer adapter looks in the 4B/5B translation table for 10101 and finds 0011, which is 0x3 in hexadecimal. A bit sequence of 01010 is also possible and translates to 0100, or 0x4 in hexadecimal. (If you are wondering how 10101 becomes 0011 and 01010 becomes 0100, refer to the 4B/5B translation chart in Table 3.2.)

Ethernet MAC Layer

The DIX Ethernet II standard describes a physical layer and data link layer corresponding to the two lowest levels in the OSI model. The IEEE, on the other hand, describes a physical layer and a data link layer that is divided into two sublayers—the MAC and the Logical Link Control (LLC) sublayers. (Refer to the right side of Figure 3.1 for a view of the IEEE sublayers.) The job of the MAC sublayer is to make a best effort to acquire the medium and transfer a serial stream of bits to the physical layer. The MAC sublayer also provides frame transmission and reception services for the LLC sublayer. The LLC sublayer, which is defined by the IEEE 802.2 working group, provides an interface between the network layer and the IEEE MAC sublayer. For more information on LLC, see the IEEE 802.2 standard and the *Logical Link Control Frame Formats* section on page 80 in this chapter.

Carrier Sense Multiple Access with Collision Detection

This section describes the Carrier Sense Multiple Access with Collision Detection (CSMA/CD) used by traditional Ethernet controllers and modifications to CSMA/CD for newer Ethernet controllers. CSMA/CD is one of the most important jobs of the Ethernet II data link layer and the IEEE 802.3 MAC sublayer. You have probably heard CSMA/CD described before, but stay tuned to learn new ways of looking at CSMA/CD.

A 10-Mbps Ethernet station wishing to send data determines if Manchester clocking can be detected on the channel, which is an indication that another station is already sending. If another station is already sending, the station defers sending its data. As soon as the channel becomes idle, the station continues to defer until the Interframe Gap (IFG) time expires, which is a minimum of 96 bit times (9.6 µs on 10-Mbps Ethernet). If the cable appears to still be idle, the station starts transmitting while observing its collision detect circuitry. If no collisions are detected after 512 bit times (not counting the preamble), the station has acquired the channel and other stations should defer. The 512-bit-time period is also called the *slot time*. It is equal to 51.2 µs on 10 Mbps.

The slot time is set to the round-trip propagation delay on a network of maximum size, plus the length of the jam signal (described in the next paragraph), plus a few extra bits to bring the number to a multiple of 32 because programmers like to deal in multiples of 32. The maximum round-trip propagation delay is 464 bit times and the jam signal is 32 bit times.

If a transmitting station detects a collision while sending bits, the transmitter continues to send the preamble (if the preamble has not completed), and also sends 32 additional bits, which are called a *jam signal*. The jam signal extends the duration of the collision event to ensure that other participants hear the collision. The contents of the jam can be any pattern that is not intentionally equal to the 32-bit Cyclic Redundancy Check (CRC) value corresponding to the (partial) frame already transmitted. Most implementations send all 1s. Sending the complete preamble and the jam signal guarantees that a signal stays on the media long enough for all transmitting stations involved in the collision to recognize the collision and respond to the result.

After the collision, the transmitting station backs off from retransmitting using a backoff algorithm called the *binary exponential backoff algorithm*. The backoff algorithm requires each transmitter to wait an integer multiple of the slot time. The integer r is determined by the equation:

$$0 \leq r < 2^k \text{ where } k = \min (n, 10)$$

The variable k is the number of collisions that have occurred, although after 10 collisions the value of k does not increase. The value of r is determined by a random process. As the number of consecutive collisions increases up to 10, the top of the range of possible integer values for r increases exponentially. Successive backoff times could increase or decrease, but the amount of time to backoff is chosen from a range of values that are always larger, so that stations probabilistically back off for longer amounts of times with each successive collision. After the backoff time expires, the station returns to its original state, senses the carrier, and waits for the IFG. A station can retry 16 times before giving up and reporting the problem to the attached system. (On normally operating networks, stations never need to retry that many times. Even in heavily loaded Ethernet networks, three or four retries is typically sufficient to finally gain access to the medium and transmit a frame.)

When two stations transmit at the same time, their signals intermix on the network, causing a Manchester code violation on 10-Mbps Ethernet. (Environmental noise can also cause a Manchester code violation, which is why it is important to use a protocol analyzer to distinguish these two causes of frame corruption.) If a transmitting station detects a Manchester code violation, it assumes a collision has occurred. On coaxial-cable transceivers, circuitry that detects the DC level of the signal on the cable determines if a collision has occurred. On fiber optic and twisted-pair interfaces with separate receive and transmit circuitry, a collision is detected by the simultaneous receiving and transmitting of data.

A collision that happens beyond the first 512 bits (64 bytes) of a frame, not counting the preamble, is a *late collision.* Late collisions are illegal. Ethernet networks that are too large experience late collisions because sending stations do not detect bits from other stations within the allowed time frame. The extra propagation delay caused by the excessive size of the network causes late collisions between the most widely separated stations. Faulty repeaters and NICs can also cause late collisions.

Collision Domains

A *collision domain* is defined as a single CSMA/CD network in which a collision occurs if two devices attached to the network transmit at the same time. An Ethernet network composed of a single segment or multiple segments linked with repeaters (hubs) is a single collision domain. A switch or router port bounds a collision domain. In other words, stations reachable from different switch or router ports can transmit at the same time without a collision occurring. Each switch or router port provides a separate collision domain.

An important configuration rule for Ethernet is that the round-trip propagation delay in one collision domain must not exceed the time it takes a sender to transmit 512 bits, which is 51.2 μs for 10-Mbps Ethernet. This time limit is also known as the slot time, as mentioned in the previous section. A single collision domain must be limited in size so that a station sending a minimum-sized frame (64 bytes or 512 bits) can detect a collision and jam signal reflecting back from the opposite side of the network while the station is still sending the frame. If the collision domain is too large, the station will be finished sending and not listening for a collision, thus losing the efficiency of Ethernet in detecting collisions and quickly retransmitting the frames involved. For a higher layer to notice that a frame needs retransmitting takes much more time. Ethernet retransmissions occur within microseconds.

A popular topology rule for explaining propagation delay on 10-Mbps Ethernet networks is the *5-4-3 rule.* With a 5-4-3 topology, you can have up to five Ethernet segments in series and up to four repeaters or hubs. No more than three of the segments can be *mixing segments.* A mixing segment is a segment with more than one attachment—for example, a coaxial cable that connects multiple stations. If three mixing segments are used, then the remaining two segments must be *link segments.* A link segment is a point-to-point connection—for example, a coaxial or fiber optic link between two repeaters. A connection from a 10BaseT hub port to a single end station is also a link segment. Other topologies besides the 5-4-3 topology are possible as long as round-trip delay does not exceed the time to send 512 bits.

Bit Length and Measurement of a Collision Domain

When troubleshooting problems with late collisions or excessive delay, a natural question that arises is, "Does this collision domain meet the 512-bit round-trip propagation delay requirement?" A starting point for answering this question is the determination of the length of a bit. A signal in a cable propagates at roughly two-thirds the speed of light in a vacuum. The value 0.59c is used for twisted-pair cabling, where c stands for the speed of light in a vacuum, which is 300,000 km/s or 186,282 mi/s. To start the bit-length calculation, determine how far a signal can travel in 1 second, using the following equation:

$$300{,}000 \text{ km/s} * 0.59 = 177{,}000 \text{ km/s}$$

In 1 second, a signal can propagate 177,000 kilometers. In that same second, there can be 10 million bits on a 10-Mbps Ethernet network. Hence, the electrical energy associated with a single bit stretches out 0.0177 kilometers or 17.7 meters. A single bit is a very long thing on a cable. The mental image that many of us have of bits looking like numerous little boxcars in a railroad train, moving along a cable, is not very accurate. The 100-meter cable between a workstation and a wiring closet, for example, contains only about five discrete bits.

Determining the length of a bit allows a calculation whereby cable length can be converted to bit length. Simply divide the number of meters of cable by 17.7 to arrive at the number of bits in the path. To calculate the cable propagation delay in a collision domain, calculate the bit length for each cable in the path between the most distant devices in the network. That's not the end of the story, however. You must account for hubs in the collision domain also.

A switch, bridge, or router forms the end of a collision domain. Hubs, on the other hand, extend a collision domain. A hub requires a certain amount of time to recover the preamble from a received Ethernet frame and then regenerate the preamble on the other side. The time required for the hub circuitry to recover the preamble and pass a bit from one side to the other is the propagation delay associated with the hub. This time may be in the range of 4 to 20 bit times, or more for some hubs. Some hardware vendors can provide specifications for the propagation delay through their hubs; in other cases, it is necessary to measure the time or to guess. If it's not possible to determine the measured propagation delay through a hub, then it is probably safe to use 20 bit times as a reasonable estimate.

With the knowledge of bit times for cables and hubs, you can simply add up the numbers for the path that connects the farthest ends of a collision domain to confirm that the end-to-end propagation delay is within the 512-bit round trip limit. In practice, it is not likely that a contemporary network will exceed the 256-bit one-way propagation delay limit.

NOTE Switches, which form the end of a collision domain, are replacing hubs in the core of most networks.

The likelihood of finding 256 bits worth of cable and hubs hanging off a switch port is small. On the other hand, if a large infrastructure is based on a series of hierarchical, cascaded hubs, then it may be possible to exceed the limit.

Collision Domains in 100-Mbps Ethernet

With some exceptions, 100-Mbps Ethernet is simply standard Ethernet, just 10 times faster. Therefore, in most cases, delay parameters for 100-Mbps Ethernet are simply 10 times smaller than those for the 10-Mbps version. As mentioned before, the round-trip propagation delay in one Ethernet collision domain must not exceed the time it takes a sender to transmit 512 bits, which is only 5.12 µs on 100-Mbps Ethernet. To make 100-Mbps Ethernet work, there are more severe distance limitations than those required for 10-Mbps Ethernet. Distance limitations for shared 100-Mbps Ethernet depend on the type of repeaters (hubs) that are used. In the IEEE 100BaseT specification, two types of repeaters are defined:

- Class I repeaters have a latency of 0.7 µs or less. Only one repeater hop is allowed.

- Class II repeaters have a latency of 0.46 µs or less. One or two repeater hops are allowed.

When troubleshooting late collisions and possible propagation delay problems on 100BaseT networks, check the path between two communicating stations to determine that the path delay does not exceed 512 bit times by adding up the cable and repeater delays as described earlier.

The IEEE specifications concerning 100-Mbps repeaters are often moot. A common design is to attach a single Class 1 repeater to a switch port, in which case there are no occurrences of a 100-Mbps repeater attached directly to another 100-Mbps repeater. Each repeater is attached to a switch. Moreover, it is very common to find that no repeaters are in use at all, but that all stations are attached directly to their own switch ports. Because the use of multiple repeaters in a 100-Mbps environment is limited, there is little general discussion in the field regarding the two classes of repeaters.

Collisions on Networks with Hubs and Switches

A hub is a repeater that simplifies cabling designs, permitting a star configuration with a hub at the center, like the hub in an old hub-and-spoke wheel. Repeaters and hubs have a few other important jobs and characteristics also. Signals going through a repeater are retimed using the repeater's timing circuitry to prevent the accumulation of signal jitter. A repeater also regenerates the signal to the proper amplitude and symmetry. Another job of a repeater is to rebuild a received preamble to avoid preambles getting shorter as they go through repeaters' timing circuits. Repeaters also extend any fragments that have resulted from frames that collided and were cut short. The repeater extends the signal so that the total number of bits output equals 96 bits. Fragment extension ensures that short collision fragments survive a trip through a maximum-size network in the correct time frame. Stations receiving the extended fragment discard it and also defer sending until the collision event is over.

One of the most important tasks of a repeater is to enforce collisions on each connected segment. Repeaters enforce collisions by transmitting a collision-enforcement jam signal. Upon detecting a collision on one segment, a repeater transmits a collision enforcement jam signal on that segment and all other connected segments. This ensures that any station trying to send at that moment hears the collision. In this way, a repeater makes sure all stations are in the same collision domain and can react to collisions correctly. When a repeater detects a collision, it sends a 96-bit jam composed of alternating 1s and 0s.

Switches are replacing hubs in large campus networks. It is a common misconception that switches don't need to know about CSMA/CD and that collisions don't occur on switched networks. In fact, each switch port implements the CSMA/CD standard. When sending a frame, a half-duplex switch port senses carrier, defers if necessary, detects collisions, backs off, and retransmits. Whether a collision might occur or not depends on what is connected to the switched port. If a shared medium is connected to the switch, collisions may occur.

Ethernet troubleshooters often wonder about cut-through switches and collisions. A cut-through switch outputs bits as soon as the destination address has been received and the destination port determined. What if there is a collision on that port? Should the switch send a collision enforcement jam on the port that received the frame so the original sender knows to try again? Or has the switch cached the frame so that it can do the retransmitting? Some troubleshooters assume that cut-through processing means that the frame was not cached. Vendor implementations may vary, but Cisco cut-through switches cache all frames, even when in cut-through mode. In this way, each port can handle CSMA/CD duties for that port and no other port. A switch retransmits if a collision occurs and does not notify the original sender in any way. Each port truly delimits a collision domain.

Full-Duplex Operations

A point-to-point Ethernet link can support simultaneous transmitting and receiving, which is called *full-duplex Ethernet.* When troubleshooting problems associated with a slow server that supports many users, determine if the server could benefit from a full-duplex link to a switch. With full-duplex, the switch can transmit the next user request at the same time the server is sending a response to a previous request. First determine if the CPUs and software applications on the server and user machines are the bottlenecks. If they aren't, a significant improvement can be made by setting the switch port and server interface to full-duplex.

CAUTION **If a server is overloaded, but medium contention has limited the rate at which transactions are hitting it, simply replacing a hub with a switch could sufficiently overload the server to crash it.**

The IEEE defines full-duplex operations in its 802.3x standard. Full-duplex Ethernet isn't CSMA/CD. There are only two stations that can send and each station has its own private transmit channel. So it's not multiple access (MA). There's no need for a station to sense the carrier to see if someone else is sending on its transmit channel. There isn't anyone else. So it's not carrier sense (CS). There are no collisions. Both stations sending at the same time is normal. Receiving while sending is normal. So there is no collision detection (CD) either.

Full-duplex operation requires the cabling to dedicate one wire pair for transmitting and another for receiving. Full-duplex operation does not work on cables with only one path (for example, coaxial cable). Full-duplex also does not work with 100BaseT4 (100-Mbps Ethernet on four pairs of Category 3 UTP). 100BaseT4 uses three pairs for transmit/receive and one pair for collision detection.

Full-Duplex Protocol Analysis

A question that often arises during troubleshooting is whether a protocol analyzer can support full-duplex operation. The illogical but optimistic troubleshooter harbors hope that more data can be pumped into the analyzer by configuring full-duplex on the switch mirror port that connects the analyzer. Unfortunately, it doesn't work that way. The analyzer is a passive device that simply collects data on its receive pair. Unless the analyzer user sends data (for example, pings or other test traffic), the transmit pair from the analyzer device is idle.

The question of full-duplex operations on an analyzer also comes up when a troubleshooter wishes to tap into a full-duplex switch-to-switch or switch-to-server link, which should be a good place to capture rich data. Usually this requirement must be accomplished by inserting a hub between the switches and reconfiguring the switch ports to half-duplex, which reduces performance on the network. Some protocol analyzer vendors offer specialized hardware *taps*, also known as *pods*, to meet this need.

When purchasing a protocol analyzer for use in a full-duplex environment, carefully consider the capabilities and drawbacks of the available options. Some questions to pose to analyzer vendors regarding their full-duplex solutions are as follows:

- Does the full-duplex pod properly sequence and timestamp frames that cross paths in the middle of the cable? Because a client can send a frame to a server at the same time a server sends a frame to the client, there may be two frames crossing through the full-duplex pod at the same time. Will the analyzer software exhibit problems if the frames arrive in the analyzer's buffer out of order? What time resolution does the analyzer support? Can it accurately timestamp the client and server frames? (A time resolution of 10 nanoseconds is considered outstanding.)

- Can the pod be left in place, inserted between switches and servers, at all times? Does it introduce latency into the path? Does the pod require external power? If it loses power, does it bring down the switch-to-switch or switch-to-server link? Must it be connected to an uninterruptible power supply to ensure resiliency of the network?

- How expensive is the pod? If pods were inexpensive, you could buy numerous pods and leave them inserted in many places in a network. Most pods are expensive, however, which means that users do not leave them inserted at all times. Users disconnect a full-duplex link and insert the pod at the time of analysis, which disrupts traffic for the time it takes to do this.

- Does the pod buffer frames or are frames sent directly to the analyzer? If an analyzer has a single 100-Mbps Ethernet interface, then the maximum traffic it can capture is 100 Mbps. The analyzer can't acquire frames any faster than its own Ethernet interface allows. If a full-duplex Ethernet is at 60 percent utilization on each of the two transmit/receive channels, that is 120 Mbps of aggregate traffic. Some of that traffic will be dropped if the pod sends directly to an analyzer with a 100-Mbps receive capability. By buffering frames in the pod, it is possible to provide full-rate capture, but only until the buffer memory in the pod is exhausted. Buffering adds cost to pods.

Autonegotiation

Full-duplex sounds simple, but what happens if both sides of the link are not config-ured for full-duplex? A station configured for half-duplex reports a collision every time it senses the other side sending while it is also sending. With UTP and fiber optic cabling, sensing data on the receive channel while sending data on the transmit chan-nel means a collision has occurred in shared (half-duplex) Ethernet. A station config-ured for full-duplex, however, sends whenever it has data, without regard for whether the other side is sending. So collisions naturally occur. As a troubleshooter, you may notice a high rate of collisions, including late collisions, on a link that has functional hardware and cabling and presumably dedicated transmit channels for each of the two partners sharing the link. Both partners on a link must be correctly configured for half- or full-duplex (as well as speed) to avoid problems. Autonegotiation of parameters should help.

Clause 28 of the *IEEE 802.3 2000 Edition* describes an autonegotiation function for 10-, 100-, and 1000-Mbps Ethernet on twisted-pair cabling. Autonegotiation is not sup-ported on fiber optic cabling because the various Ethernet systems using optical fibers are so different in their signaling and clocking techniques that they cannot negotiate. With fiber optic Ethernet, you must manually configure the proper mode of operation on each device.

With autonegotiation, an interface advertises its abilities and detects the abilities of the device on the other end of the cable, called the *link partner*. The partners exchange their information in a reliable, acknowledged fashion. Autonegotiation compares the two sets of abilities and decides which technology to use, based on a standard priority for technologies. Once the highest-performance common mode is determined, autone-gotiation relinquishes control to the appropriate technology and becomes transparent until the connection is broken or reset.

Autonegotiation is most useful if it is configured at both ends of the link, because then both ends speak the same language at startup and can exchange useful informa-tion. Autonegotiation is also designed to work if only one end of the link supports it. Faulty implementations may mean that errors occur, however, when one partner is hard-coded for speed and duplex mode and the other partner uses autonegotiation, even though the protocol was designed to handle this situation. Setting both partners to use autonegotiation solves the problem sometimes. With other implementations, hard-coding both partners for speed and duplex mode is the solution.

The IEEE 802.3 autonegotiation standard specifies that an interface advertises its abilities in link pulses that encode a 16-bit word of information known as the Link Code Word (LCW). An interface sends a series of link pulses called a Fast Link Pulse (FLP) burst. An FLP burst is a sequence of 10BaseT Normal Link Pulses (NLPs). Each FLP is composed of 33 pulse positions, with the 17 odd-numbered positions corre-sponding to clock pulses and the 16 even-numbered positions corresponding to data pulses. All clock positions must contain a link pulse, although data positions do not need to contain a link pulse. The presence of a link pulse in a data position represents a logical 1 and the lack of a link pulse represents a logical 0.

To ensure flexibility, the LCW has a Selector Field that allows 32 different definitions of the Technology Ability Field. Currently, Selector Field values are defined for IEEE 802.3, 802.5, and 802.9. The Technology Ability Field is defined relative to the Selector Field. For 802.3, a device advertises its abilities as one of the following:

1. 1000BaseT full-duplex
2. 1000BaseT half-duplex
3. 100BaseT2 full-duplex
4. 100BaseTX full-duplex
5. 100BaseT2 half-duplex
6. 100BaseT4 half-duplex
7. 100BaseTX half-duplex
8. 10BaseT full-duplex
9. 10BaseT half-duplex

The technology abilities list also defines the priority hierarchy for resolving multiple common abilities. For example, if both devices support 10BaseT and 100BaseTX, autonegotiation causes the devices to use 100BaseTX instead of 10BaseT because 100BaseTX has a better priority.

Advantages and Disadvantages of Autonegotiation

A disadvantage of not using autonegotiation is that you need to manually configure ports, which is time consuming and also risky. It is quite common for technicians to manually set the speed and duplex on one link partner and forget to configure the other partner, or to set the parameters differently on the partners, resulting in a mismatch. On the other hand, the disadvantage of using autonegotiation is that it may not work, causing annoying and often serious problems. Until recently, most engineers have recommended avoiding autonegotiation. Improvements in the interoperability of autonegotiation and the maturity of the technology may mean it is safe to start using autonegotiation again, but opinions vary.

Autonegotiation problems can result from hardware incompatibilities and old or defective Ethernet software drivers. Some vendors' NICs or switches do not conform exactly to the IEEE 802.3u specification, which results in incompatibilities. Hardware incompatibility may also occur when vendors add advanced features, such as autopolarity, that are not in the IEEE 802.3u specification. (Autopolarity corrects reversed polarity on the transmit and receive twisted pairs.)

Negotiating the speed of the connection usually proceeds correctly. If the speed doesn't negotiate correctly, the interface does not work and the administrator hopefully notices and corrects the problem immediately. Duplex negotiation happens after the speed is set. Problems with duplex negotiation are harder to detect because any performance impact is dependent on the link partners transmitting at the same time. A workstation user who doesn't send much traffic may not notice a problem, whereas a server could be severely impacted by a duplex mismatch.

Sometimes problems with negotiation occur because configuration changes are made in software without any hardware change. For example, perhaps a switch is set for autonegotiation and the partner is a desktop manually configured for half-duplex 10BaseT. If the devices also support full-duplex 100BaseT, the user or network administrator might decide to upgrade to the faster capability. If the change is made in software, without pulling the cable or rebooting, negotiation link pulses may produce enough signal in the frequency band of the 10BaseT link pulses that the partners never see a loss of signal and don't detect that there is a reason to renegotiate. The problem can also occur if a desktop OS changes the configuration while booting, but after the initial negotiation. The fix is to have the OS driver momentarily drop signal whenever speed or duplex is modified. If the OS doesn't have that behavior, a workaround to the problem is to pull the cable momentarily or to reset the port, but network users don't usually think to use such simple workarounds.

As mentioned earlier, most engineers recommend that you carefully and manually configure interfaces to avoid the potential for problems with autonegotiation. To override autonegotiation with static configurations, the commands on Catalyst® 4000-, 5000-, and 6000-series switches are as follows:

```
set port speed mod_num/port_num {10 | 100 | auto}
set port duplex mod_num/port_num {full | half}
```

The *auto* keyword tells the port to autonegotiate both speed and duplex mode. Note that Gigabit Ethernet ports have a fixed speed. To verify the configuration, use the `show port` command.

On Cisco IOS switches, the configuration commands are as follows:

```
speed {auto | 10 | 100}
duplex {auto | full | half}
```

To verify your configuration when using Cisco IOS software, use the `show interface` command.

Flow Control on Full-Duplex Links

For those of us who have worked with Ethernet for years, the idea of Ethernet providing flow control is strange. Higher layers seem better equipped to handle congestion, and MAC-layer flow control could confuse the operation of flow control at higher layers. Also, flow control may disrupt the normal buffering and queuing in switches, resulting in head-of-the-line blocking. Head-of-the-line blocking occurs when a switch cannot process incoming frames beyond the frame at the head of the line because the output port for that frame is busy or temporarily disabled. Nonetheless, the IEEE's 802.3x standard defines flow control for Fast and Gigabit full-duplex Ethernet devices.

Flow control allows a device that is overloaded to send a *pause* message to its link partner to temporarily reduce the amount of data the partner transmits. Flow control was designed to prevent switches and end systems from discarding frames when buffers overflow during brief overload conditions. It was not designed to handle the case where the steady-state traffic level exceeds that for which the device is designed; that's a design problem. It also does not provide end-to-end flow control, which is usually handled by Transmission Control Protocol (TCP) or an upper layer. IEEE 802.3x flow control operates only across a single full-duplex data link layer connection.

> **PAUSE FRAMES ON AN ANALYZER**
>
> Some protocol analyzers do not provide decode information for control frames such as the pause frame. Many analyzers simply report the presence of the frame, with addressing information in the Ethernet header properly decoded, but with no description of the frame.

Flow control can be either symmetrical or asymmetrical and negotiated with autonegotiation. When the traffic level is relatively identical in both directions and both devices have similar buffer memory constraints, symmetrical flow control makes most sense. For example, two switches operating in the backbone of a campus network might be good candidates for symmetrical flow control. In other circumstances, it may be better to allow one link partner to pause the other, but not vice versa. One partner may be a low-end switch operating on the edge of the network, and the other partner a backbone switch. A more obvious case is when one partner is an end station (user's machine) and the other partner a switch. The end station can pause the switch, but there may be no need for the switch to pause the end station.

The IEEE standard requires a device to respond to pause frames but not to initiate them. In actuality, some vendor devices are not capable of receiving or responding to pause messages because they do not yet support the standard. In addition, vendors have different thresholds for initiating a pause, and there are reports that some switches, which supposedly support the feature, never actually send a pause frame.

Many Cisco switches support flow control, mostly on Gigabit Ethernet ports. To enable transmit or receive flow control, and to monitor flow control, use the following commands:

```
set port flowcontrol {receive | send} [mod_num/port_num] {off | on |
desired}
show port flowcontrol
```

On Cisco IOS switches, use the following command in interface configuration mode:

```
flowcontrol [asymmetric | symmetric]
```

Enhancements to Ethernet Media Access Control for Gigabit Ethernet

In the development of Gigabit Ethernet, some changes were made to the MAC standards to support high-speed shared networks. A common misconception of Gigabit Ethernet is that the IEEE increased the minimum frame size, but that's not true from the point of view of upper layers. The Gigabit Ethernet chipset does add a carrier extension, however, so that a sender sends for a long time even if the upper layer has only a few bytes to send.

With shared 10- and 100-Mbps Ethernet, the minimum frame size is equal to the maximum round-trip propagation delay of the network. In other words, the minimum frame size = slot time = 512 bits. Using this rule with shared Gigabit Ethernet would have resulted in impracticably small networks. Instead, the minimum frame is maintained at 512 bits (64 bytes), but the slot time is defined as 4096 bit times (512 bytes). Frames that are shorter than the slot time are artificially extended by appending a carrier extension field so that the frames are exactly one slot time in length. By increasing the minimum time a station sends, the standards can support a larger maximum network topology.

From a network troubleshooting point of view, you should be wondering how badly this enhancement affects efficiency. Carrier extension adds substantial overhead to small frames. Let's say an upper layer wishes to send 512 bits. The frame ends up being 4096 bits long, preceded by a 64-bit preamble and followed by a 96-bit IFG. When considering efficiency, you may also wonder whether a receiver discards a frame if a collision happens in the carrier extension part of the frame even though the actual data part arrived without error. The receiver must discard the frame because the sender retransmits and Ethernet has no method for handling duplicate frames. If a collision occurs during any time from the beginning of the frame to the end of the extension field, the sender jams, aborts, backs off, and retransmits.

Carrier extension could cause performance degradation for some applications, although the developers included a workaround in the standards to avoid problems. Consider an application that is trying to output many small frames at a quick rate—for example, a Voice over Internet Protocol (VoIP) application. If the interface adds bits to reach 4096 bits, will the application be able to send at the proper rate? When the application is finished and releases control of the medium, will some other application jump in, causing the first application to defer? The Gigabit Ethernet designers addressed these problems. The IEEE 802.3z standard lets a sender send multiple frames! A station may choose to burst frames if there is a frame in its transmit queue when it has finished sending its first frame (plus extension, if one was necessary). The station may send again without contending for use of the channel. During the IFG, the station sends nondata symbols. Only the first frame requires a carrier extension. The station may start the transmission of frames for up to one burstLength. The IEEE defines the burstLength parameter as 8192 bytes.

Is the multiple-frame enhancement fair to other senders? Well, was Ethernet ever fair? It was fair from an access point of view, but senders of large frames could always use a greater portion of the bandwidth. The new bursting feature makes Ethernet fair from a bandwidth usage point of view. A station can send for up to the burstLength time (plus one frame) regardless of whether the frames are short or long. This is a major difference in philosophy that is similar to the difference between Cisco's priority queuing and custom queuing. With priority queuing, a router administrator can specify that frames of a certain type are always processed first. Priority queuing can starve other senders. With custom queuing, the administrator can specify an approximate amount of bandwidth each traffic type can use. Custom queuing is more fair than priority queuing in the same sense that Gigabit Ethernet bursting is more fair than standard Ethernet. (If these enhancements to CSMA/CD worry you, don't be too concerned, because shared Gigabit Ethernet is not common anyway. Gigabit Ethernet is usually used on a full-duplex link.)

Ethernet Frames

You have probably heard that there are two types of frames on Ethernet networks: Ethernet Version II and IEEE 802.3. Actually there are four types of frames common on Ethernet networks: Ethernet II, 802.3, SNAP, and Novell raw. (The documents that specify just two frame types probably count SNAP and Novell raw as subsets of the 802.3 frame format.) The frame formats are shown in Figure 3.4.

Two stations cannot communicate unless they share a common frame format, which is sometimes beneficial. For example, if you have two networks on a physical medium that you wish to keep separate for security reasons, you can configure the networks for different frame types and they won't communicate with each other. As another example, protocol developers sometimes change frame formats so that older versions cannot communicate with newer versions to avoid compatibility problems. For example, AppleTalk Phase 1 used Ethernet Version II, whereas AppleTalk Phase II uses SNAP.

Sometimes the fact that there are different frame types can be a problem, however. Because of a mismatch in configurations, you may have two stations that should be able to communicate but cannot. Troubleshooting frame format problems is difficult because vendors use different names for the frame types, as do troubleshooting tools. Table 3.3 shows some frame format names.

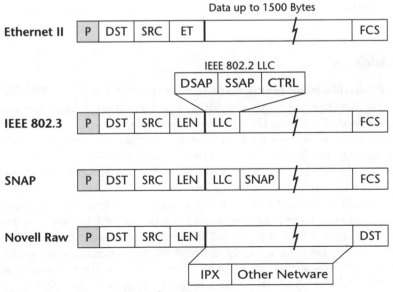

Figure 3.4 Ethernet frame formats.

Table 3.3   Different Names for Ethernet Frame Types

COMMON NAME	NETWORK ASSOCIATES SNIFFER	WILDPACKETS ETHERPEEK	NOVELL	CISCO
Ethernet II or V.2	Version II	Ethernet Type 2	ETHERNET_II	arpa
IEEE 802.3	IEEE 802.3	IEEE 802.3 LSAP	ETHERNET_802.2	sap
SNAP	IEEE 802.3 SNAP	IEEE 802.3 SNAP	ETHERNET_SNAP	snap
Novell Raw	Novell Proprietary	IEEE 802.3 IPX	ETHERNET_802.3	novell-ether

Fields in an Ethernet II or IEEE 802.3 Frame Header

An Ethernet II or IEEE 802.3 frame starts with a 64-bit preamble (labeled P in Figure 3.4). As discussed in the *Clock Synchronization* section, a receiving adapter uses the preamble to synchronize to the sender's clock. The adapter begins moving bits into its frame buffer after receiving the final 2 bits of the preamble, which are always binary 11. (To be precise, the Ethernet II standard calls all 64 bits the preamble. IEEE 802.3 divides the 64 bits into two fields: a 56-bit preamble consisting of alternating 1s and 0s, and an 8-bit start-frame sequence that has the 10101011 pattern.) Following the preamble, an Ethernet or 802.3 frame has a 14-byte header. The next three sections describe the fields in the header.

Destination Address

The first 6 bytes (48 bits) of a frame are the destination address (DST in Figure 3.4). The destination address identifies the hardware address of the Ethernet interface that should receive and process the frame. Hardware addresses, also known as physical or MAC addresses, are assigned by the manufacturer of the interface. The first 3 bytes are a vendor code assigned by the IEEE to manufacturers. The IEEE calls the vendor code an Organizationally Unique Identifier (OUI). The last 3 bytes are assigned by the manufacturer of the interface and uniquely identify the interface.

The first bit transmitted in the 48-bit destination address differentiates between frames that should go everywhere (broadcast and multicast) and frames that are addressed to a specific target (directed frames). The significance of using the first bit is that bridges and switches need to see only the first bit to immediately recognize whether they can simply forward the frame to all ports, as in broadcast or multicast frames, or whether they need to evaluate the destination address, as in directed frames.

If the first bit transmitted is a binary 1, then the frame is a broadcast or multicast frame. Otherwise the frame is a directed frame, also known as a *unicast frame*. A multicast frame is a frame that is intended for all stations in a predefined group, for example, the All Bridges or the All NetBIOS Stations group. A broadcast, which goes to the destination address FF:FF:FF:FF:FF:FF, is a special form of multicast. Broadcasts go to the group consisting of every station in the broadcast domain. A broadcast domain includes all devices in a switched or bridged network. A broadcast domain is bounded by a router port.

LITTLE-ENDIAN VERSUS BIG-ENDIAN TRANSMISSION

When looking at an Ethernet destination address, how do you determine which bit was transmitted first in order to distinguish multicast/broadcast frames from unicast frames? There are two schools of thought concerning how an 8-bit byte should be converted to a serial bitstream for transmission. On the one hand, the first bit transmitted could be the low-order bit (the rightmost bit at the 2^0 numeric position). Alternately, the first bit transmitted could be the high-order bit (the leftmost bit at the 2^7 numeric position). In the 1980s, there were major arguments regarding which way was better.

The arguments about bit order were taken to such extremes that the two sides were compared to the political factions described in Jonathan Swift's book *Gulliver's Travels*. In the book, Gulliver travels to the land of the Lilliputians where a law requires that eggs be opened by cracking the little end only. A civil war breaks out between those who want to crack their eggs on the big end and those who want the little end. The Big-Endians go to a nearby island and form their own kingdom, while the Little-Endians remain in Lilliput. The egg controversy is politically and ethically significant to the Lilliputians, but the reader sees the trivial nature of the issue. Swift's goal was to satirize religious wars. Whereas *Gulliver's Travels* targets the struggle between the Protestant Church of England and the Catholic Church of France, the terms *Big-Endian* and *Little-Endian* are best known in the computer industry as the two schools of thought about the correct way to transmit and interpret a byte.

Big-Endian transmission, which is used on 802.5 Token Ring and FDDI networks, sends the big end (the high-order bit) first. Little-Endian transmission, which is used on 802.3 and Ethernet networks, sends the little end (the low-order bit) first. For example, if a hexadecimal byte with a value of 0x71 is in system memory, then the first bit that an Ethernet adapter transmits is a binary 1. The binary value of 0x71, which is 01110001, is transmitted from right to left, with the low-order (the 2^0 or ones-place) bit sent first.

The protocol analysis implication of this discussion is that when viewing Ethernet addresses, to recognize the first bit transmitted, you must look at the low-order bit. If that bit is a 1, then the frame is a broadcast or multicast.

A shortcut for recognizing broadcast and multicast frames is that the first byte of the destination Ethernet address is always numerically odd for broadcasts and multicasts. Addresses are displayed using two digits for each byte. To determine if an address is a multicast address, check the second digit, which displays the low-order 4 bits of the byte, including the first bit transmitted. Multicast frames have a 1, 3, 5, 7, 9, B, D, or F in the second digit. They are all odd because the 2^0 or ones-place bit is a 1. For example, Cisco sends Cisco Discovery Protocol (CDP) frames to the multicast address 01:00:0C:CC:CC:CC. This is a multicast address because the second digit is odd—it is 0x1—which means that the first bit transmitted is a 1.

Source Address

The source address (SRC in Figure 3.4) follows the destination address in an Ethernet II or 802.3 frame. The source address is the 6-byte (48-bit) hardware address of the interface that generated the Ethernet frame. The first bit transmitted in an Ethernet source address is always assumed by the recipient to be a binary 0. Even if an errant device driver sets the bit to a 1—which does happen occasionally—the recipient station assumes that it is a 0, because a source address can never be a multicast or broadcast. A frame always comes from a particular source and never from a group.

Length or EtherType

Following the destination and source address is the length or EtherType (LEN and ET, respectively, in Figure 3.4) 2-byte field. A recipient station differentiates frame formats through an assessment of these 2 bytes. If the value of the field is between 0x0000 and 0x05DC, then the frame is an IEEE 802.3 frame and the 2 bytes are an 802.3 length field. In decimal, 0x5DC is 1500, which is the maximum length of an Ethernet frame, not counting the preamble, header, tags, footer, or IFG. The length field indicates the number of bytes in the data portion of the frame.

If the 2 bytes following the source address are greater than 0x05DC, then the frame is an Ethernet II frame and the field is an EtherType field. The EtherType specifies the type of protocol being carried in the frame. The smallest EtherType value is 0x0600 (used for the Xerox Network Services [XNS] protocol). When the 802.3 standards were created, there were a few protocols used by the Palo Alto Research Center (PARC) that had EtherType values less than 0x05DC. The PARC Universal Packet (PUP) and others had to be assigned new EtherType values to make the differentiation between a length and EtherType field possible.

Protocol Identifiers

At each protocol layer, there is typically a numerical identifier to tell the recipient protocol handler what is coming next. The recipient uses the identifier to decide which process should receive the frame. The Internet Protocol (IP) has a field called the Protocol Type that differentiates between User Datagram Protocol (UDP), TCP, and other protocols carried in an IP header. TCP has a port number that differentiates between Telnet, Mail, Web access, and other applications. Ethernet II uses the EtherType for protocol identification. IEEE 802.3 uses an 802.2 Service Access Point (SAP).

The 802.2 SAP field is just 1 byte long, which caused the IEEE to become concerned about running out of SAPs in the late 1980s. Newer protocols were never assigned a SAP. Instead, these protocols use a SNAP header. The LLC SAP is set to 0xAA to identify SNAP. Inside the SNAP header, the protocol can place a protocol identifier. SAP and SNAP are discussed in more detail in the *Logical Link Control Frame Formats* section later in this chapter.

Think of the EtherType or SAP as a hole in the ceiling. A frame comes into the Ethernet adapter at floor level. The software driver for the adapter checks the protocol identifier and pushes the frame into the correct ceiling hole based on the value of the EtherType or SAP. Using the holes, the adapter can place frames into the correct buffer for collection by the network layers implemented in the attached system. A sending station also uses the holes. Software programs, residing on the second floor, push frames down through the holes to arrive at the adapter, which encodes the ceiling hole number as an EtherType or SAP. Chapter 7 revisits the concept of holes in the ceiling. IP protocol types and TCP and UDP port numbers can also be explained with ceiling holes.

To be a good troubleshooter, you should learn the EtherTypes, SAPs, and default frame types for typical protocol implementations. When you see a protocol use a different implementation than expected, you should recognize the abnormal situation. Look at the MAC or network-layer address of the sending station, find the station, and check its configuration. For example, a Cisco router can be configured to send Address Resolution Protocol (ARP) frames using SNAP as well as EtherType 0x0806. Sending ARPs in a SNAP format is atypical and causes extra traffic. (The router sends ARPs twice, once in each format, if the first ARP isn't answered.) In some cases, a SNAP ARP is necessary to support workstations that require it, but in other cases it is simply a misconfiguration. Table 3.4 documents typical EtherTypes and SAPs to help you learn what to expect.

Table 3.4 Typical EtherTypes and SAPs

PROTOCOL	DEFAULT FRAME TYPE	TYPE	SAP
IPv4	Ethernet Version II	0x0800	0x06
IPv6	Ethernet Version II	0x86DD	0x06
IP ARP	Ethernet Version II	0x0806	0xAA
SNAP	SNAP	NA	0xAA
AppleTalk Phase 2	SNAP	0x809B	0xAA
AppleTalk ARP	SNAP	0x80F3	0xAA
Novell NetWare	Novell Raw	0x8137	0xEO
NetBEUI	802.3	NA	0xF0
SNA	802.3	NA	0x04, 0x05, 0x08, 0x0C
IS-IS	802.3	NA	0xFE
BPDU	802.3	NA	0x42
CDP	SNAP	0x2000	0xAA

IPV6 AND ETHERTYPES

Theoretically, IPv6 could have used the same EtherType as IPv4. Many vocal participants of the Internet Engineering Task Force (IETF) insisted that this was the right thing to do. Unfortunately, it was discovered that some vendors' bridges and switches, which theoretically should not look into frames past the data link layer, do in fact look into frames past the data link layer. For example, some switches look into the network layer to add advanced features such as IP fragmentation and reassembly. These devices do not look at the IP version number in the first 4 bits of the IP header. So, to avoid confusing these devices, a new EtherType (0x86DD) was assigned to IPv6.

Logical Link Control Frame Formats

When an IEEE 802.3 frame header is used, it is usually followed by an IEEE 802.2 Logical Link Control (LLC) header. (The Novell raw frame format is the only exception; it has only an 802.3 header.) The LLC header has three fields:

1. *Destination SAP (DSAP).* The DSAP identifies the service to which the frame is destined.

2. *Source SAP (SSAP).* The SSAP identifies the sending service, which is almost always the same as the destination service.

3. *Control.* The Control field identifies the type of frame as information transfer, supervisory, or an unnumbered command or response. The format of the Control field depends on the mode of communication service. With connection-oriented communication, the control field is 2 bytes to accommodate an acknowledgment number. With connectionless service, the control field is just 1 byte.

LLC supports three modes of service. Connectionless mode, also known as *datagram service* and *LLC Type 1*, is a simple service that does not use sequence numbers or acknowledgments and does not require a connection to be established before data can be exchanged. *LLC Type 2* is a connection-oriented service that guarantees delivery of data using sequence numbers and acknowledgments. The third mode of service, *LLC Type 3*, is acknowledged, but connectionless. LLC Type 3 lets network layers exchange data that is acknowledged at the LLC layer without establishing a connection first. LLC Type 3 is not common and is not covered in this book.

LLC Type 1 Frame Format

The following example shows protocol analyzer output for an LLC Type 1 header. Because LLC Type 1 is connectionless, there is little analysis required.

```
LLC: ----- LLC Header -----
LLC:
LLC: DSAP Address = E0, DSAP IG Bit = 00 (Individual Address)
LLC: SSAP Address = E0, SSAP CR Bit = 00 (Command)
LLC: Unnumbered frame: UI
```

The Individual/Group (IG) bit in the DSAP is 0 in this example, which means that the frame is destined to an individual SAP. A frame addressed to a group SAP is destined to more than one process in the receiving system. If you see the IG bit set to Group, you should find out which station is setting the bit and why. The use of a group SAP is a possible misconfiguration or bug that could lead to communication problems in recipient devices.

The Command/Response (CR) bit in the SSAP is 0 in the example, which means that the frame is a command. An LLC command designation simply means that the frame was not in response to a previous frame; that is, it was originated spontaneously by the sending station. When a station responds, it sets the CR bit to 1 to designate a response.

The Control field for the frame in the example specifies an Unnumbered Information (UI) frame. This means that there is essentially no processing at the LLC layer. LLC moves the incoming data into the specified SAP without any special attention.

LLC Type 2 Frame Format

NetBEUI and Systems Network Architecture (SNA) use LLC Type 2. NetBEUI is an implementation of the NetBIOS session layer running directly over a data link layer, without a network or transport layer. SNA is a complex architecture and set of protocols developed by IBM in the early 1970s. SNA originally ran on serial links and later on Token Ring and Ethernet LANs.

Because SNA and NetBEUI are becoming less common, the use of LLC Type 2 is diminishing. However, it is still important to learn LLC Type 2 because it shares many characteristics with the quintessential High-Level Data Link Control (HDLC) family of WAN protocols. HDLC influenced the development of LLC Type 2, IBM's Synchronous Data Link Control (SDLC), and the X.25 Link Access Procedure (LAP) protocols. The LAP on the D Channel (LAPD) protocol, also known as ITU-T Q.921, is still very common on ISDN circuits. So a quick explanation of LLC Type 2 is warranted because it will help you troubleshoot WANs as well as legacy Ethernet networks that still use LLC Type 2.

NOTE Cisco's HDLC is a customized version of HDLC and is not similar to LLC Type 2. Cisco's HDLC is connectionless and is similar to LLC Type 1.

Because LLC Type 2 is connection oriented, a connection setup must precede the transmission of data. A connection teardown process occurs at the end of an LLC session. During a session, each frame is numbered and acknowledged. The session setup follows this sequence:

```
1. Station A -> Station B LLC C DSAP=F0 SSAP=F0 SABME P
2. Station B -> Station A LLC R DSAP=F0 SSAP=F0 UA F
3. Station A -> Station B LLC C DSAP=F0 SSAP=F0 RR NR=0 P
4. Station B -> Station A LLC R DSAP=F0 SSAP=F0 RR NR=0 F
```

In Frame 1, Station A tells Station B to Set Asynchronous Balanced Mode Extended (SABME), which means that either side can initiate a conversation and send data without permission from the other side. In the old days of mainframes and terminals, a lowly device like a terminal could not send data until it was polled. With the advent of mini- and microcomputers, communication became more democratic. Station authority was more balanced, and either station could send asynchronously with respect to the other. The original Asynchronous Balanced Mode allowed the transmission of 8 frames without an acknowledgment. To improve performance, the 8 frames were later extended to 128 frames. The extension to 128 frames is called Asynchronous Balanced Mode Extended.

When Station A in the example makes the SABME request, it also sets the poll bit (that's the letter P at the end of the line in Frame 1). The poll bit has nothing to do with polling terminals. It simply means, "Answer immediately; don't wait until I've sent the full 128 frames that are possible." Station B replies to the SABME with an Unnumbered Acknowledgment (UA) in Frame 2. The final bit (F) is set to indicate that this response is complying with the request to answer immediately.

Following the SABME and UA, Station A says in Frame 3 that its Receiver is Ready (RR) and that it expects to receive protocol data unit #0 from Station B. Next Receive (NR) = 0. In Frame 4, Station B says its receiver is also ready and that it expects to receive protocol data unit #0 from Station A.

After the session establishment, analysis of LLC Type 2 is simply a matter of following the conversation from the SABME to the Disconnect Mode (DM), the last frame in a normal LLC session. You can track the sequence numbers and acknowledgments by viewing the Now Sending (NS) sequence number and the NR acknowledgment number for each side of the conversation. There are two error commands that might occur:

Reject (REJ).   A station sends a REJ when it receives an unexpected sequence number.

Frame Reject (FRMR).   A station sends an FRMR when it receives an invalid frame or sequence number.

REJs are normal; they simply ask for retransmission when a frame is lost. An LLC connection spans hubs, switches, and possibly routers. (To reduce the chance of LLC timeouts, you can optionally terminate an LLC connection at a router.) A frame could get lost as the result of congestion in switches, routers, or hosts, or on shared network segments. A recipient can send an REJ frame to indicate that there's a missing sequence number so that the sender retransmits. FRMRs, on the other hand, are abnormal and probably indicate a bug in a device driver or other serious problem with system memory or processing in the device to which the FRMR is sent. The FRMR could also be the result of an error in the station sending the FRMR.

Subnetwork Access Protocol

Figure 3.4 and Table 3.4 showed that some protocols use a SNAP header in addition to an LLC and 802.3 header. The IEEE adopted SNAP in order to identify protocols that were not assigned a SAP due to concern about running out of SAP numbers, as already mentioned. SNAP was also invented for backward compatibility with protocols that used an EtherType—in particular, IP. The SNAP header embeds the 2-byte EtherType value from Ethernet II. The presence of 0xAA as a SAP identifier signals the fact that a SNAP header follows the LLC header. The SNAP header is 5 bytes that consist of two fields:

1. *Vendor code.* A 3-byte field that is the same as the vendor code or OUI in an Ethernet hardware address. You may see the vendor code set to all 0s. To ease the porting of frames from Ethernet to IEEE 802.3 format, the IEEE allowed vendors to not include a vendor code for protocols that previously used Ethernet II frames.

2. *Type.* The type field is a protocol identifier. It identifies the next layer being carried in the frame. When the vendor code is all 0s, the type field contains an Ethernet II EtherType. When the vendor code contains a specific vendor number, then the last 2 bytes can be a specialized value defining a vendor-specific protocol. For example, in CDP frames, the vendor code is one of Cisco's codes, and the type is 2000, which is not an EtherType.

Ethernet or IEEE 802.3 Frame Footer

Now that we have traveled through the gory details of the Ethernet, 802.3, LLC, and SNAP headers, it is time to close the discussion of frame formats with a quick mention of the end of an Ethernet or IEEE 802.3 frame. A frame ends with a 4-byte Frame Check Sequence (FCS), which is used for error detection. The sending Ethernet chip calculates a CRC based on the bits in the frame and places the result in the FCS field. The recipient recalculates the CRC and, in most cases, drops frames with a result that differs from the value in the frame. A difference means that one or more bits were changed or dropped during transmission, resulting in a corrupted frame. When troubleshooting with a protocol analyzer, it is often helpful to look at corrupted frames to see if there is evidence of what caused the problem. Capturing corrupted frames may require a special NIC or driver, however. Check with your protocol analyzer vendor to determine if your analyzer can capture corrupted frames.

APPLETALK SNAP FRAMES AND THE VENDOR CODE

AppleTalk Phase 1 used Ethernet II frames and had two EtherTypes, one for AppleTalk (0x809B) and one for AppleTalk ARP (0x80F3). AppleTalk Phase II uses an IEEE 802.3 SNAP frame format. The AppleTalk developers took a literal interpretation of the IEEE recommendations that said the SNAP field could carry an EtherType with no vendor code for protocols ported unchanged from Ethernet II. When AppleTalk went from using Ethernet II to IEEE 802.3 SNAP framing, it also went through many upper-layer changes, because this was the same time that the change from AppleTalk Phase 1 to AppleTalk Phase II happened. Hence, AppleTalk Phase 2 frames have a vendor code. AppleTalk ARP frames do not have a vendor code because the frames remained unchanged when ported to IEEE 802.3 SNAP format.

   The following protocol analyzer output shows the LLC and SNAP headers for an AppleTalk frame. The analyzer does not break out SNAP, but you can see the vendor code (0x080007 for Apple Computer) and type (0x809B for AppleTalk) in the Protocol field.

```
802.3 Header
  Destination:   09:00:07:FF:FF:FF  ATalk Ph2 Multicast
  Source:        08:00:07:4F:FC:EC
  Length:        52
802.2 Logical Link Control (LLC) Header
  Dest. SAP:     0xAA  SNAP
  Source SAP:    0xAA  SNAP
  Command:       0x03  Unnumbered Information
  Protocol:      0x080007809B  AppleTalk
```

> **IS A PAD MERELY A PLACE TO REST?**
>
> Most protocol analyzers show the value of the Ethernet padding in the hexadecimal view. Why should you care what is in the padding? In some cases, you will be surprised at the contents of the padding. An older version of a popular database application had an interesting problem related to padding. In the short acknowledgment frames that followed the encrypted login phase, the application placed the user's unencrypted password in the padding. The resolution to the problem was a bug fix from the database vendor.

NOTE Some protocol analyzers don't capture the FCS field. Not being able to see the value of the CRC in the FCS field is not a problem unless you have the job of troubleshooting the Ethernet chip logic that calculates the CRC.

Ethernet Frame Sizes

The minimum size of an Ethernet frame is 64 bytes, counting the 14-byte header and 4-byte FCS, but not counting the preamble, which is used for clock synchronization. The 64 bytes also do not count the IFG, which provides a short recovery time between frames so that receiving stations can get ready for the next frame. A frame that is less than 64 bytes is illegal and is called a *runt*. As discussed previously, the minimum frame size is based on the maximum size of a shared network, which is 256 bit lengths, or 512 round-trip bit lengths. When a protocol such as IP or ARP passes a frame to the Ethernet driver, the protocol may pad short frames to 64 bytes. Another option is for the protocol to request the Ethernet driver to pad the frame.

The maximum frame size for Ethernet is 1518 bytes, counting the header and FCS but not the preamble, IFG, or any specialized tags. The maximum frame size was somewhat arbitrarily decided, based on four goals:

1. *Fairness.* No device should hold control of the medium for too long.
2. *Buffers.* The maximum frame size bounds the size of buffers that receivers must maintain.
3. *Low overhead.* Frames should carry more user data (payload) than header (overhead) information.
4. *Efficiency.* If a frame is damaged, it should not require too much bandwidth to retransmit it.

Large frames have more bits and thus are more likely to have bit errors. If network media were perfect and there were no possibility of errors, an infinitely large frame would be the most efficient (although not the most fair to other senders). If a frame has a bit error, then it must be retransmitted, which wastes time and effort and reduces efficiency. The larger the frame, the more bandwidth is wasted in retransmission. So, because networks experience errors, frame sizes are limited to maximize efficiency (and provide fairness). The maximum frame size is not minimized too much, however, because another important goal for efficiency is that the amount of user data (payload) compared to header bytes should be maximized.

Configuring and Troubleshooting Ethernet Frame Sizes

When applications and protocols are configured to send large amounts of data per frame, the number of frames and round-trip delays required for an action to take place on a network are minimized, which improves performance. The number of frames per action can also be minimized if the receiver is configured with a large receive window, allowing it to accept multiple frames before it must send an acknowledgment. The goal is to maximize the number of data bytes compared to the number of bytes in headers and in acknowledgment packets. When monitoring your network's performance, you can use a protocol analyzer or Remote Monitoring (RMON) probe to examine the frame sizes on your network. Many protocol analyzers let you output a chart such as the one in Figure 3.5 that documents how many frames fall into standard categories for frame sizes.

Figure 3.5 shows frame sizes at an Internet Service Provider (ISP). Many of the frames were 64-byte acknowledgments. Most of the traffic was Hypertext Transfer Protocol (HTTP), with some e-mail packets mixed in. The Web servers sent most data in 500- or 600-byte packets, which is typical. If many Web-hosting customers had been transferring pages to a Web server using a file transfer or file-sharing protocol, there would have been many more 1500-byte frames.

A simple way to determine an average frame size is to divide the total number of megabytes seen on a segment by the total number of frames in a specific time frame. Cisco teaches this method in some of its training classes. The average frame size is not a very meaningful piece of information, however. On most networks, there are many small acknowledgment frames that skew the average. A frame size distribution chart, such as the one in Figure 3.5, is a better way to analyze frame sizes.

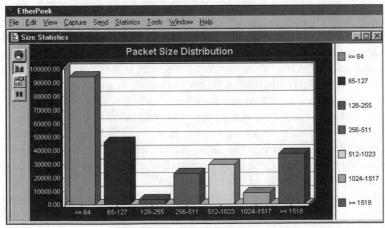

Figure 3.5 Bar graph of frame sizes on an Ethernet network.

In general, there are six broad categories of frame sizes. An analyzer may break down frame sizes into fewer or more categories, but, as a general starting point for network analysis, you should check for frames that are runts, tiny, small, medium, large, or giants:

1. *Runt frames.* These frames are less than 64 bytes and are illegal.

2. *Tiny frames.* These frames are 64 bytes. They may contain application data that is less than 64 bytes, padded to the minimum 64-byte frame size, or they may be frames used by background activities or acknowledgments. For example, when a TCP connection is idle, a communicator eventually enters a *keepalive* mode where it sends periodic 64-byte acknowledgments just to see if the other side is still active and connected. Bridge Protocol Data Unit (BPDU) frames, used in the Spanning Tree Algorithm, also use 64 bytes. Many periodic background activities that are always present in a network use tiny frames.

3. *Small frames.* These frames are between 64 and 300 bytes. Terminal/host traffic often uses small frames.

4. *Medium-sized frames.* These frames are between 400 and 800 bytes. Database and Web access produces medium-sized frames.

5. *Large frames.* These frames are more than 1000 bytes. Large frames are typical of file transfer activities. Saving files, executing applications, loading word processing documents, and uploading Web pages to a Web server, are all file transfer activities that use large frames.

6. *Giant frames.* These frames are more than 1518 bytes, counting the header and FCS. In most cases, giant frames are illegal, but sometimes extra tags that are legal cause giant frames. See the *VLAN Tagging and Baby Giants* section for more information on legal giants.

These size approximations are not rules or concrete guidelines; they are a starting point for network assessment. Using a frame size distribution graph, such as the one in Figure 3.5, you can do an initial assessment to see if frame sizes are as expected considering your network applications and traffic types. If the graph is weighted to the left (small frames), and your network's purpose is transferring files, you should wonder about this unexpected result. On the other hand, if the graph is weighted to the right (large frames), and the network is idle (it's 2 A.M., for example), or most of the applications are host/terminal applications, those results may also be cause for concern. Just because reality doesn't fit with the frame size suggestions provided here doesn't mean that anyone has to stay late to troubleshoot a problem, however. It simply draws attention to a potential source of inefficiency in the network. Analysis of individual conversations may demonstrate that some terminal applications use full-screen displays and some file transfers involve small blocks of data.

Analyzing frame sizes can help you diagnose the health of a network as well as its efficiency. For example, an excessive number of Ethernet runt frames can indicate too many collisions. Typically, collisions increase with utilization when many stations are contending for bandwidth access at the same time. If collisions and runt frames increase even when utilization does not increase, or even when only a few nodes are transmitting, there could be a hardware problem, such as a bad hub or NIC, or most likely, a duplex mismatch.

Maximum Transmission Unit

On Cisco routers you can configure the maximum packet size used on Ethernet inter-faces, which is also known as the *Maximum Transmission Unit* (MTU), using the mtu interface configuration command. There is usually no reason to change the MTU from the default of 1500 bytes, however. Some network applications and OSs also support changing the MTU, which is not necessary unless the default is smaller than 1500 bytes.

Cisco IOS software also has an ip mtu configuration command. If you configure the ip mtu command after the mtu command, the IP value can differ from the inter-face value. Generally it is not a good idea to specify an IP value that is greater than 1500 bytes, however. If the value is greater than 1500 bytes, and the interface MTU is 1500 bytes or less, then the router must fragment packets, using the IP fragmentation process. IP fragmentation slows down packet forwarding and uses extra CPU cycles and should be avoided. Use the show processes cpu command to check the *ip input* value. If the value is high, it could be due to IP fragmentation.

Tunneling and Frame Lengths

Before leaving the discussion of MTU, there is another consideration to take into account, which is tunnels. In some networks, data is encapsulated in tunnels. In fact, it is not uncommon to encapsulate IP in IP, perhaps to route through areas of a network with addresses that are inconsistent with the rest of the network, to implement secu-rity, or to provide Virtual Private Networking.

Cisco tunnels are often implemented using the Generic Route Encapsulation (GRE) feature, which adds a 24-byte header to each frame. Problems can occur when the extra header causes frames to be larger than the MTU, especially in cases where an applica-tion sets the Don't Fragment (DF) bit and Internet Control Message Protocol (ICMP) packets are filtered. A typical symptom of this problem is that users can ping and Tel-net but not use HTTP or the File Transfer Protocol (FTP).

When a 1500-byte packet arrives at a router tunnel interface, the router tries to encapsulate the packet into a tunnel packet, which it cannot do if there are only 1476 bytes available after the 24-byte GRE header is applied. In this situation, the router sends an ICMP Destination Unreachable (Type 3), Fragmentation Needed and DF Bit Set (Code 4) message to the originator of the packet. The ICMP message contains the MTU that the originator should use. You can view the ICMP message with a protocol analyzer or with the Cisco IOS debug ip icmp command.

CISCO'S MOBILE NETWORKING AND TUNNELING

A modern example of IP encapsulated in IP is Cisco's mobile networking. The IP/IP tunneling enables a router on a user's home subnet to intercept and transparently forward IP packets to users who roam to an 802.11 wireless network or cellular network. Routers acting as home agents, located on the mobile node's home network, tunnel the mobile node's packets to the node while it is away. Routers acting as foreign agents remove data from the tunnel. An outer IP header is used to route the packet to the foreign agent router. The inner IP header contains the actual node's static IP address. (If Dynamic Host Configuration Protocol [DHCP] is used instead of static IP addresses, then this feature is not necessary.)

If the ICMP message is blocked by access lists or other filters, communication is impacted. If possible, and if it won't negatively affect security measures, find out where along the path the ICMP message is blocked and unblock it. You can also change the MTU on affected servers and clients, although this can be impractical if it involves a large number of devices.

VLAN Tagging and Baby Giants

In networks with multiple Virtual LANs (VLANs), switches need some method of identifying the VLAN to which a frame belongs. The IEEE 802.1Q specification defines a standard way to mark Ethernet frames with a VLAN identifier, called a *tag*. Cisco also has a proprietary VLAN tagging protocol called Inter-Switch Link (ISL). ISL adds bytes to the beginning and end of the original frame, which is called *double-tagging* or *two-level tagging*. IEEE 802.1Q adds bytes inside the frame, which is called *single-tagging* or *one-level tagging*.

Switches use VLAN tags to determine where to forward frames. End stations and switches that don't support VLANs should not receive tagged frames. If a misconfiguration or poor network design results in such a device receiving a tagged frame, the device should drop the frame. The device may also report an error. A device that doesn't support ISL drops ISL frames because the first 48 bits appear to be a multicast address that the station does not recognize. A device that doesn't support 802.1Q drops 802.1Q frames because the 2 bytes after the destination and source addresses appear as a nonsupported EtherType (0x8100). In actuality they are a Tag Protocol Identifier (TPID).

IEEE 802.1Q inserts 4 bytes into an Ethernet frame, including the TPID, a priority field, a canonical format indicator, and the VLAN ID. If 4 bytes are added to a frame that was already the maximum size of 1518 bytes, the result is an oversized frame. A receiving station that does not support 802.1Q reports these frames as giants or baby giants to distinguish them from frames that are truly oversized. To support IEEE 802.1Q and avoid the need to drop and report baby giants, the IEEE 802.3ac VLAN Tag Task Force (that's a mouthful!) received approval in September 1998 for extending the Ethernet maximum frame size to 1522 bytes.

Collecting and Understanding Ethernet Performance Data

Using protocol analyzers, RMON, and Cisco IOS diagnostic commands, you can determine the normal state of your Ethernet networks and troubleshoot problems when conditions deviate from the norm. There are no absolute right values for the data you gather. Each network is different. By collecting data on a regular basis, you can recognize which values are right for your networks.

Remote Monitoring

RMON can provide useful information about the health and performance of an Ethernet segment on which an RMON agent resides. Many Cisco switches and routers can act as RMON agents. RMON provides a view of the health of the whole segment, rather than the device-specific information that many SNMP agents provide. RMONv1 (RFC 1757) provides data link layer statistics. RMONv2 (RFC 2021) allows network behavior to be observed above the data link layer, providing data beyond the scope of this chapter, which covers Ethernet data link and physical layer troubleshooting.

RMONv1 Ethernet agents gather statistics on CRC errors, collisions, packet sizes, the number of packets and bytes in and out, the rate of broadcast packets, and the number of runts and giants. The RMON alarm group lets a network administrator set thresholds for performance parameters and configure agents to deliver alerts to a network management station. RMON also supports capturing packets (with filters if desired) and sending the captured packets to a network management station for protocol analysis. If you plan to do a lot of packet capturing (which is recommended for learning if for no other reason), capturing with a standalone protocol analyzer is much more efficient than using RMON.

The Hosts and Host Top N RMON groups provide useful tables of information on active stations, including packets and bytes in and out, multicast and broadcast packets in and out, and error counts. The Matrix group is helpful when analyzing traffic flows. The Matrix group provides the amount of traffic and number of errors occurring between pairs of stations on a segment.

The Cisco Show Interface Ethernet Command

The best command to use when collecting Ethernet performance data on a Cisco router or switch is the show interface ethernet command. (Use show port on non-IOS Cisco switches.) Below is output from the show interface ethernet command. The following sections describe the output and how to compare Cisco results to protocol analyzer results.

```
Albany#show interface ethernet 0
Ethernet0 is up, line protocol is up
  Hardware is MCI Ethernet, address is 0000.0c05.3e80 (bia
0000.0c05.3e80)
  Internet address is 172.16.10.1 255.255.255.0
  MTU 1500 bytes, BW 10000 Kbit, DLY 1000 usec, rely 255/255, load 2/255
  Encapsulation ARPA, loopback not set, keepalive set (10 sec)
  ARP type: ARPA, ARP Timeout 4:00:00
  Last input 0:00:02, output 0:00:01, output hang never
  Last clearing of "show interface" counters never
  Output queue 0/40, 0 drops; input queue 0/75, 0 drops
  5 minute input rate 6000 bits/sec, 17 packets/sec
  5 minute output rate 82000 bits/sec, 17 packets/sec
     6471 packets input, 388476 bytes, 0 no buffer
     Received 7 broadcasts, 0 runts, 0 giants
     0 input errors, 0 CRC, 0 frame, 0 overrun, 0 ignored, 0 abort
     0 input packets with dribble condition detected
     6722 packets output, 3583669 bytes, 0 underruns
     0 output errors, 0 collisions, 4 interface resets, 0 restarts
     0 output buffer failures, 0 output buffers swapped out
```

When troubleshooting with the show interface ethernet command, the first line to view is the one that says Ethernet is up, down, or administratively down, and line protocol is up or down. The interface is administratively down if the administrator has never entered the no shut command to open the interface. (Some interfaces default to no shut, which you would think would be the default for all interfaces, but it's not.) The interface is up if the hardware has been activated. Note that this is a hardware test, not a link integrity test. The interface can be up even if no cable is attached. With some types of interfaces, you should also check that the link integrity light is green at the router, switch, hub, and/or workstation end. If the light is not green, check for a speed mismatch or other configuration error. Also, examine the cable and make sure the right pairs are in use. Make sure the cross-connect between transmit and receive is handled correctly. For example, be sure to use straight-through cables between a router and hub or switch, and crossover cables to connect two routers or switches back-to-back.

NOTE Cisco Ethernet interfaces differ from serial and Token Ring interfaces in that they can be "up" even when they can't really be up, such as when no cable is attached. You can also cause the line protocol to come up, even with no cable attached, by configuring the no keepalive command.

If the interface is up, then the line protocol can be up or down. A Cisco interface tests the line protocol by sending a keepalive frame to itself every 10 seconds. The first time you see these frames with a protocol analyzer, you may be surprised. Especially in a lab environment, where not much else is happening on the network, you may get a false impression that the router wastes an awful lot of bandwidth testing itself. (The keepalives don't really use much bandwidth.) The keepalive frame format is also surprising to some old-timers because it is actually a loopback frame (EtherType 0x9000) from the "Ethernet Configuration Testing Protocol" section of the Ethernet II standard, which was never widely adopted (except by Cisco). A capture of a keepalive frame is shown here:

```
Flags:          0x00
  Status:         0x00
  Packet Length:64
  Timestamp:      14:42:20.319000 04/26/2001
Ethernet Header
  Destination:  00:00:0C:05:3E:80
  Source:       00:00:0C:05:3E:80
  Protocol Type:0x9000
  Packet Data: 46 bytes (all zeros)
```

Bandwidth

In the show interface ethernet display earlier, you can see that the bandwidth (BW) for the network attached to the interface is 10,000 kbps or 10 Mbps. Bandwidth is a measure of the data-carrying capacity of a circuit or network, usually measured in bits per second (bps). The mystery that many troubleshooters don't realize about Cisco's BW value is that it has nothing to do with the physical or data link layers. Cisco's Interior Gateway Routing Protocol (IGRP) and Enhanced IGRP (EIGRP) use the BW parameter for computing their composite routing protocol metrics. The bandwidth portion of the composite metric is the lowest bandwidth of any interface in the path to a network in the routing table. Cisco's implementation of Open Shortest Path First (OSPF) also uses the BW parameter in its routing protocol metric, which is referred to as *cost*. The default OSPF cost for an interface is 100,000,000 divided by BW. You can change an interface's bandwidth with the `bandwidth` command to effect changes in routing protocol metrics. The change has no affect on the physical or data link layers, however, and in fact does not need to match the actual capacity for the connected network.

Delay

In addition to bandwidth, IGRP and EIGRP also use the *delay* parameter displayed by the `show interface ethernet` command in their composite routing protocol metric. Delay is inversely proportional to bandwidth. The delay metric is a sum of all delays for outgoing interfaces on the path to a network. Delay is a static or configured value. People assume that IGRP and EIGRP keep track of actual measured delay, but they do not.

Outside the specialized Cisco IGRP and EIGRP view of delay is a whole realm of factors that affect delay on networks. Academic papers on Ethernet use the term *delay* to mean the time it takes to send a packet, measured from the time a station first wishes to acquire the channel. Because that type of delay is hard to measure, most troubleshooters measure round-trip delay, not counting the time to acquire the channel, using the ping or trace-route command. Round-trip delay is affected by the following factors:

Propagation delay.   Network signals experience propagation delay resulting from the finite speed of light, which is 300,000 km/s or 186,282 mi/s. These values are for light traveling in a vacuum. A signal in a cable or optical fiber travels at approximately two-thirds the speed of light in a vacuum.

Serialization delay.   Another fundamental cause for delay is the time to put digital data onto a transmission line, which depends on the data volume and the speed of the line. Serialization delay is a major factor for low-speed serial lines. It is not much of an issue on fast LANs.

Packet-switching delay.   Packet-switching delay refers to the latency accrued when bridges, switches, and routers forward data. The latency depends on the speed of the internal circuitry and CPU and the switching architecture of an internetworking device. The delay can be as small as 10 to 20 µs for 64-byte Ethernet frames crossing high-end switches or routers that have hardware ASICs that handle the forwarding of frames.

Queuing delay.   Packet-switching delay may include queuing delay when a packet switch needs to queue data because an output buffer or interface is busy. The number of packets in a queue on a packet-switching device increases exponentially as utilization on an output port increases.

EXPONENTIAL AVERAGES

Cisco uses the vague phrase "exponential average over 5 minutes" when describing load, reliability, 5-minute input and output rates, and 5-minute packets per second statistics. Actually, the software calculates a sample every 5 seconds and provides a moving average over a 5-minute period. A moving average incorporates feedback from previous samples into the current result. The most recent sample is weighted slightly more than previous samples, but because there are so many more previous samples, they contribute heavily to the result also. The weighting decays exponentially for each previous sample, but in 5 minuets there are 60 previous samples, so they are still significant. The goal is to avoid skewing the result too much if the 5-second sample happens to take place when someone is downloading a huge MP3 file, for example, or when nobody was doing anything on the network for whatever reason. The details of the exponential average calculation are buried in a Cisco document titled "Definition of 'bits/sec' from 'sh int.'" The URL for the document is www.cisco.com/warp/public/66/3.html.

Utilization

Utilization is a measure of how much bandwidth is used during a time period. Utilization is specified as a percentage of bandwidth. Network analysis tools use varying methods for measuring bandwidth usage and averaging the usage over elapsed time. Usage can be averaged every millisecond, every second, every minute, every hour, and so on. Some tools use a weighted average whereby more recent samples are weighted more prominently than older samples.

Cisco displays utilization in the Load field of the output of the `show interface ethernet` command. Load on an interface is expressed as a fraction of 255 and is calculated as an exponential average over 5 minutes. A value of 255/255 is a saturated link. IGRP and EIGRP can use the dynamically calculated load in their composite metric if the `metric weights` command is configured. Troubleshooters can also use the load value to monitor network utilization.

You have probably heard the rule that a shared Ethernet segment should not exceed 37 percent utilization. Allegedly, beyond this limit, the collision rate becomes excessive. This rule is a myth. Consider the case of an Ethernet segment that is shared by only two stations—a client that sends requests and a server that responds after receiving requests. In this case, it is not a problem if network utilization exceeds 37 percent. There are no collisions because the server and client never try to send at the same time, so the 37 percent rule, which is concerned with collisions, does not apply. The load should be almost 100 percent unless the client or server are slow.

The 37 percent number was first reported by Metcalfe and Boggs in a 1976 paper that described the original 2.94-Mbps Ethernet. The paper describes a simple model that was not meant to resemble real-world networks. The 37 percent limit was also discussed in studies done by the IEEE comparing CSMA/CD to token passing. Token passing makes a node wait for a token before sending. At modest loads, this wait means that token passing results in more delay than CSMA/CD. However, at around 37 percent utilization on a medium shared by 50 stations using 128-byte frames, Ethernet frames experience more delay than Token Ring frames. After many years of hearing the "37 percent rule," Boggs and two other researchers published a 1988 paper called "Measured Capacity of an Ethernet: Myths and Reality." The paper is available at www.research.digital.com/wrl/publications/abstracts/88.4.html.

Instead of slavishly obeying a rule about utilization thresholds, you should track other reliability indicators on your network, as described in the next section. You should also use a protocol analyzer and RMON matrix data to gain an understanding of traffic flow on your network. Coupled with your network map that documents a logical and physical topology, you should have a feel for which networks can support high utilization and which need to be kept at a low utilization. In addition, apply some common sense. Your main concern should be whether users are justifiably complaining about the network being slow.

Reliability

From a Cisco standpoint, the reliability of an interface is displayed as *rely* and is expressed as a fraction of 255, calculated as an exponential average over 5 minutes. A reliability of 255/255 is 100 percent reliability. IGRP and EIGRP can use reliability in their composite metric if the `metric weights` command is configured. Troubleshooters can also use the reliability statistic to determine if an interface and the connected Ethernet segment are stable. The rely statistic documents the fraction of frames that arrived without input errors. It also takes into account the number of collisions encountered while sending. Low reliability on an Ethernet segment with low load and few collisions is usually the result of a hardware problem, such as a bad cable, bad connection, faulty NIC, or external electrical noise. Low reliability on an Ethernet segment with collisions is the result of oversubscribing the network or misconfiguring the duplex mode. Table 3.5 describes reliability indicators that are displayed with the `show interface ethernet` command.

Table 3.5 Errors Displayed with the `show interface ethernet` Command

ERROR	EXPLANATION
runts	Number of frames that were discarded because they were smaller than 64 bytes. Runts are usually the result of a collision.
giants	Number of frames that were discarded because they were larger than 1518 bytes. Giants are usually caused by a nonstandard Ethernet driver. Baby giants can result from VLAN tagging.
input error	Includes runts, giants, no buffer, CRC, frame, overrun, and ignored counts. The number of input errors may not equal the sum of the other errors because frames may have more than one error. Also, frames may have errors that do not fall into any of the specific categories.

(continues)

Table 3.5 Errors Displayed with the `show interface ethernet` Command *(Continued)*

ERROR	EXPLANATION
CRC	Number of frames received where the CRC generated a checksum that did not match the checksum calculated by the originating station.
frame	Number of frames received having a CRC error and a noninteger number of octets. This is usually the result of a collision and is referred to as an *alignment error* by some troubleshooting tools.
overrun	Number of times the receiver hardware was unable to hand received data to a hardware buffer because the input rate exceeded the receiver's ability to handle the data.
ignored	Number of received frames ignored by the interface because the interface hardware ran low on internal buffers.
input packets with dribble condition	The dribble bit error indicates that a frame is slightly too long. This counter is informational only; the router accepts the frame. The Ethernet and IEEE 802.3 specifications state that when the last bit is transmitted, the station does not simply turn off the signal. The station gradually tapers the signal to zero, which may result in dribble bits.
underruns	Number of times the transmitter ran faster than the interface could handle.
output errors	Sum of all errors that prevented the final transmission of frames. The number of output errors may not equal the sum of the other errors because frames may have more than one error. Also, some frames may have errors that do not fall into any of the specific categories.
collisions	Number of messages retransmitted due to an Ethernet collision. A frame that collides is counted only once in output frames.

Collision Rate

According to Cisco documentation, the total number of collisions with respect to the total number of output frames should be 0.1 percent or less. This number may seem terribly low, but keep in mind that the collision rate that Cisco reports is only from the transmitter's point of view. The collision counter increases each time the Ethernet interface on the Cisco device hears another station sending while the interface is also sending. Many protocol analyzer and RMON probes, on the other hand, report all collisions for a connected segment. Some analyzers report collisions in the preamble, in addition to collisions inside a frame. The threshold for an acceptable rate of collisions depends on the number of stations sharing the bandwidth, their traffic loads and sending patterns, and how the collision rate is measured.

Because Cisco interfaces report only collisions that occur while the interface is transmitting, it is important to also look at input errors to analyze the collision rate. From a receiving point of view, frames that encountered a collision en route to the interface in question will probably be runts and have a CRC or frame error.

Keep in mind that collisions should not occur on a full-duplex link. If you see collisions on a link that you think is configured for full-duplex mode, you have likely been bitten by an autonegotiation problem. Probably one side failed to autonegotiate and is using half-duplex mode, as discussed previously in the *Advantages and Disadvantages of Autonegotiation* section.

Frame Corruption

Noise, faulty hardware, or a collision with another frame can cause bits in a frame to get changed or dropped, resulting in an error condition that is often referred to as *frame corruption*. After receiving a valid preamble, an adapter buffers incoming bits until it detects loss of clock or an out-of-range voltage condition indicating that the frame has ended. If the frame is addressed to the receiver, or if it is addressed to the broadcast address or to a multicast group to which the receiver belongs, then error checking begins. The frame must include a minimum of 64 bytes. It must have a valid 802.3 length, if it is an 802.3 frame. Finally, the frame must have a valid CRC. If a recipient adapter detects that a frame has an error, then the frame is discarded.

A protocol analyzer operates by placing its Ethernet adapter into *promiscuous mode*. This means that the adapter accepts all frames without regard for the destination address. Some adapters also support error frame capture. It's important to determine if your analyzer is using a NIC that supports error capture. If it is not, then no error statistics will be available and the error counts in the analyzer will always be zero.

Because almost all corrupted frames have a bad CRC, it is also important to know how a particular analyzer categorizes corrupted frames. Does the analyzer categorize corrupted frames as CRC errors and also runts, alignment errors, and so on? Or does the analyzer categorize errors on the basis of a predominant fault, in which case a corrupted frame less than 64 bytes long would probably be called a fragment or runt, but not a CRC error? Analyzer users need to understand the rules for statistical reporting of corrupted frames as implemented by their analyzer vendor.

When deciding whether CRC errors are excessive, it helps to consider the de facto standards for bit error rates on standard cabling. Fiber optic cabling should not experience more than one bit error per 10^{11} bits. Copper cabling should not experience more than one bit error per 10^6 bits. If you determine that the rate of CRC errors on your Ethernet segments is too high, try to determine the cause. First, distinguish CRC errors that are related to collisions from CRC errors caused by hardware problems. Next determine if the collisions are a normal part of CSMA/CD or the result of a duplex mismatch. When considering error rates, it is helpful to classify the basic causes of frame corruption in an Ethernet network into the following four classes:

1. *Excessive propagation delay.* As discussed in the *Ethernet MAC Layer* section, every station on shared Ethernet senses the carrier for a signal from another station before sending. Propagation delay causes stations not to sense each other's signals right away, resulting in two stations sending simultaneously and collisions. Excessive delay caused by illegally long segments or too many

repeaters can cause excessive collisions and late collisions. A late collision occurs past the first 512 bits (64 bytes) in a frame, not counting the preamble. When viewing collision frames with a protocol analyzer, you can sometimes see the collision damage in the form of another station's preamble at the end of the corrupted frame. Look for repeated patterns of 0xAA and 0x55.

2. *Faulty hardware.* Bad hardware can cause frame corruption. A station with faulty receive hardware, for example, may not accurately sense the carrier before sending. The result can be abnormal collisions, including late collisions. A rare (but always discussed) fault is with the transmit hardware, causing a station to jabber. Isolating a jabbering station requires physically segmenting the network until the faulty transceiver is found. Unfortunately, a jabbering station doesn't send a correct source address, so looking at source addresses with a protocol analyzer doesn't help isolate the station, though it can be useful to see that instead of a preamble at the end of corrupted frames, which would indicate a collision, you see long strings of 1s or 0s. Most transceivers have jabber control circuitry, so jabbering is not a common problem.

3. *Electrical noise.* Noise caused by power grids, fluorescent lighting, x-ray machines, and other sources disrupts the clock and pattern of a signal and can destroy one or more bits. The presence of CRC errors in many frames of various sizes, along with a low rate of collisions, is an indication of excessive noise. Bad installation practices can be involved, such as using lighting fixtures as a physical support for media cables, maximizing the distance over which signals can couple over parallel cables.

4. *Signal reflection.* In coaxial cable, badly spaced taps, unterminated segments, cables with mismatched impedance, and breaks or kinks in the cable can cause the signal to reflect back to the sender. The reflection may be reported as a collision by the sending station. The characteristic of signal reflection is very short frames (typically less than 16 to 32 bytes) of approximately the same size. The frames are uniformly cut off where the reflection occurs. (Although theoretically you could have signal reflection problems on twisted-pair cabling, it is not common. Signal reflection was more common in the old days of coaxial cable.)

Broadcast and Multicast Rates

The final performance statistic this chapter covers is the rate of broadcast or multicast traffic. A broadcast frame goes to all network stations on a LAN. At the data link layer, the destination of a broadcast frame is FF:FF:FF:FF:FF:FF (all 1s in binary). A multicast frame goes to a subset of stations. For example, a frame destined to 01:00:0C:CC:CC:CC goes to all Cisco routers and switches that use CDP.

Protocols use broadcasts and multicasts for such important functions as dynamic address assignment, address and name resolution, service location, and service advertisement. ARP, DHCP, CDP, Routing Information Protocol (RIP), EIGRP, OSPF, Internet Group Management Protocol (IGMP), and NetBIOS are some of the many protocols that make use of broadcasts and multicasts. It is a common misconception that broadcasts use a lot of bandwidth. Actually, individual broadcast frames don't use much bandwidth. Broadcast frames are usually short. Also, most normal applications don't broadcast thousands of times in a second. For a station to use up most of 100 Mbps with 64-byte broadcast frames, it would need to send approximately 200,000 times per second, which is obviously abnormal.

Bridges and switches forward broadcast and multicast frames out all ports, unless configured to do otherwise. The forwarding of broadcast and multicast frames can result in performance problems in large, flat (switched or bridged) networks. Broadcasts can cause problems because they disturb every device in the broadcast domain. The network interface at a station passes broadcasts and relevant multicasts to the CPU of the station. (Some interfaces pass all multicasts to the CPU, even when the multicasts are not relevant, because the interfaces do not have driver software that is more selective.) The CPUs on network stations can get overwhelmed when processing high levels of broadcasts and multicasts. A general guideline that Cisco and some protocol analyzer vendors preach is that if more than 20 percent of the network traffic on a segment is broadcasts or multicasts, than the network needs to be segmented using routers or VLANs.

A *broadcast storm* is an abnormal event on a network. A broadcast storm occurs when bugs in a protocol stack implementation or in a network configuration cause a station to send hundreds or thousands of broadcasts per second. In the worst case, the broadcasts from one station result in other stations also sending broadcasts, much like a storm that builds upon itself. On slow CPUs, broadcast storms can be a serious problem. Broadcast storms can wreak havoc on 100-Mbps Ethernet LANs with slow computers, because misbehaving devices have an opportunity to send broadcasts really quickly at 100 Mbps.

Broadcast storms are readily detectable with a protocol analyzer. Typically, the analyzer provides statistical displays that show the number of broadcast and multicast frames. Moreover, the frames themselves can be viewed in a summary display window. When more than 10 percent of the frames are broadcast or multicast, it's time to determine whether the network is operating normally (with a high number of normal broadcasts) or whether a storm is in progress. If the broadcasts appear repetitive, and if they don't appear to be performing anything useful, then scrolling back in the analyzer's summary display to the point where the broadcast storm began may disclose the cause of the problem.

Cisco's Broadcast Suppression Feature

Cisco switches support a feature called *broadcast suppression*. New network engineers have been known to configure the broadcast suppression threshold so low that normal network operations are negatively affected. The goal of the broadcast suppression feature is to prevent broadcast storms, not broadcasts in general. Cisco implements broadcast suppression in software or hardware, depending on the switch platform. Software broadcast suppression uses a packet-based method. Hardware broadcast suppression uses a bandwidth-based method.

When a packet-based method is used to measure broadcast activity, the threshold parameter is the number of broadcasts or multicasts received over a 1-second time period. When a bandwidth-based method is used, the threshold parameter is the percentage of total available bandwidth used by broadcasts or multicasts. In either case, if the threshold is reached, the switch port filters broadcast and multicast frames for the rest of that second. Because frame sizes vary, a bandwidth-based measurement is more accurate than a packet-based measurement. The proper setting for the threshold depends on your applications and traffic types. Be sure not to set the threshold so low that the switch filters normal broadcast activity.

Summary

This chapter has discussed Ethernet and IEEE 802.3 architectures, topologies, and configurations. We have provided background information on physical layer concerns, such as signal encoding and clock synchronization as well as information on media access control concerns, such as collision detection, full-duplex mode, autonegotiation, and frame formats. The chapter has also presented troubleshooting commands and methods that will help you recognize the differences between normal and abnormal conditions on typical Ethernet networks.

There is no substitute for real-world experience and practice in mastering Cisco commands and interpreting the output from a protocol analyzer. By using a combination of Cisco diagnostic commands, performance statistics, and protocol analyzer packet captures, you can develop the skills to keep your Ethernet networks reasonably trouble free. Using the tools and commands discussed in this chapter, you can help ensure that your networks are unaffected by frame corruption or misconfiguration.

Many campus network engineers are migrating portions of their wired Ethernet networks to the new IEEE 802.11 wireless standard. The next chapter provides information on physical layer and data link layer concerns for 802.11 networks. The chapter provides engineering-level background information on radio frequency transmission, antenna types, signal encoding, and propagation delay and attenuation problems.

CHAPTER

4

Troubleshooting and Analyzing IEEE 802.11 Wireless Networks

In the 1990s, networking professionals saw the emergence of twisted-pair Ethernet, 100-Mbps Ethernet, and the switched network infrastructure. On the heels of these new technologies came the World Wide Web, wide-scale integration of Internet protocols, and Gigabit Ethernet. By the wayside fell 802.5 Token-Ring networking, FDDI fiber optic networks, and the 300-Baud modem. Today we watch as the continued integration of data, voice, and video communication moves these historically disparate worlds together toward a single worldwide infrastructure. There's little question that we'll look back on the first decade of the new millennium and reflect on the excitement, opportunities, challenges, and dangers of Wireless Local Area Network (WLAN) integration, as it, too, moves to center stage.

Chapter Scope and Depth

This chapter sets forth the basic aspects of 802.11 WLAN technology. The focus is on how a WLAN can be analyzed using a wireless protocol analyzer, such as WildPackets AiroPeek. The analyzer captures packets using a promiscuous radio receiver (one that captures all packets) and allows a network engineer to assess network behavior and performance. Interpreting the results requires that the engineer's knowledge expand into a realm that is different in many ways from the realm of Ethernet engineering. This chapter provides the springboard for understanding and troubleshooting 802.11 wireless network operation and design.

Three general categories of people are typically involved in supporting wireless networks. Some individuals may be relatively new to networking. Some engineers may come from an Ethernet and TCP/IP background (or another networking environment) and may have significant experience outside the wireless world. Finally, some people may already be involved in the design, installation, support, and maintenance of WLANs today.

If you are new to networking, we hope this chapter will provide a solid foundation for your understanding of the engineering issues and technological basis for the rapidly growing wireless network marketplace. If you are an experienced Ethernet person, then you will need to learn some new fundamental engineering concepts because 802.11 is based on radio frequency (RF) transmission. This chapter will explain those concepts. Unlike the somewhat invisible Manchester or ternary bit encoding that underlies 10- and 100-Mbps Ethernet, the impact of RF issues on day-to-day troubleshooting cannot be treated lightly. If you are already immersed in the 802.11 wireless world, then this chapter will provide you with operational details related to wireless protocol analysis that you won't find consolidated in too many other sources.

Many technologies come under the umbrella of *wireless networking*. This chapter focuses on the implementation of the Institute of Electrical and Electronics Engineers (IEEE) 802.11 standard. After a general description of wireless technologies, the chapter describes the organization of an 802.11 WLAN and the behavior of wireless stations as they initialize and access the medium (air) to send data. Following those sections is a discussion of RF transmission that will help you understand vendor specifications and perform a site survey to determine if an environment is suitable for wireless networking.

Things That Are Beyond the Scope of This Chapter

Networking professionals responsible for WLAN design, implementation, or troubleshooting are assumed to be well versed in the classic Local Area Network (LAN) aspects of their networks. The WLAN replaces the Ethernet as a data link through which otherwise normal upper-layer protocols (such as those in the TCP/IP, AppleTalk, or NetWare families) are transmitted. See other chapters for information on upper-layer protocols.

There are two additional areas of study that are beyond the scope of this chapter. This chapter will not expound on every detail of the IEEE 802.11 standard. The focus will be on topics that are relevant to an engineer using a wireless protocol analyzer. This chapter will also not explain everything about RF engineering. There are many excellent books available that cover this topic in exhaustive detail.

If you are serious about learning how a WLAN operates in the context of the IEEE 802.11 standards, then you should download copies of the standards documents from the IEEE home page. They are now available for free download in PDF format at www.standards.ieee.org/getieee802/. Every detail of behavior and operation of an 802.11 network is completely described in the documents. After you have read and studied this chapter, you will have the technical foundation to read and understand the standards.

If you search the Cisco Web site (www.cisco.com) for occurrences of *802.11*, you'll find many papers that provide solid technical information on the 802.11 standards. In addition, a search for *802.11* at www.intel.com produces some excellent reference material. Intersil Corporation, a chipset manufacturer, also has many superb papers available on the Web that delve into relevant technical topics. The index to these papers is located at www.intersil.com/design/prism/wirelessb.asp.

In a WLAN, a radio transmitter sends data and a radio receiver acquires electromagnetic energy and converts it into bits. Some level of understanding of RF transmission is fundamental to working with a WLAN. Understanding RF transmission in depth is an entire career path in itself, however. There are many excellent texts that discuss RF transmission. Network engineers who want to learn about the transmission of electromagnetic energy from the perspective of the physicist could start by learning about Maxwell's wave equations. The following equation is one of Maxwell's basic laws of electromagnetism.

$$\oint \overline{H} \bullet d\overline{s} = I_{total}$$

The equation is one of the four basic laws of electromagnetism in its simplified integral form. The figure shows that the vectors representing the magnetic intensity H measured in amps per meter and the resulting total electric current I can be calculated for a specific distance (the closed interval of the integration). The amount of energy present at a particular receiving station is affected by many factors in a real-world environment. The *vector dot* product in the equation, the integration across the closed interval, and a strong background in mathematics could make for some late-night entertainment if someone were so inclined! This is not what you'll learn in this chapter, but you should remember that wireless networking is based on the physical properties of electromagnetic wave propagation in space—it's not Ethernet anymore! If you were doing a Web search, or if you were at your favorite bookstore or library, and you wanted to learn more about the physics of wave propagation and data transmission as it relates to 802.11, you might study some of the following topics:

- Frequency Hopping Spread Spectrum (FHSS)
- Direct Sequenced Spread Spectrum (DSSS)
- Antenna gain
- Free space path loss
- Shannon's theorems
- Maxwell's wave equations

To learn detailed RF information, take advantage of the many technical papers available from various wireless equipment vendors, including Cisco Systems and WildPackets, Inc., in particular the *Technical Compendium* at www.wildpackets.com/compendium. A technically comprehensive overview of the 802.11 RF environment is available from Intersil Corporation on the Web at www.intersil.com/data/an/an9/an9829/an9829.pdf.

A Primer on Wireless Networking

Removing the wires that connect clients, servers, switches, and routers in a network is an interesting and attractive option. Users don't need a place to plug in and they can move around without having to depend on a network administrator to reconfigure a router or Dynamic Host Configuration Protocol (DHCP) server. Wireless networking may improve user productivity and reduce the technical complexities that users often encounter in the wired LAN experience. Plus, there's no reasonable way to run wires across a four-lane highway (unless you have a big budget and an environmental impact statement!). Sure, there's line-of-sight microwave, but that is generally perceived as a less attractive option in today's marketplace. Only time will tell the ease with which wireless technology becomes integrated into the mainstream of network connectivity. There doesn't appear to be any question that, in the same way that coaxial Ethernet has become an antiquated technology, wired networks will be seen as turn-of-the-century engineering, and we'll look back on the days when you had to plug in to the wall to access the Internet.

Consequently, whether a network engineer is currently involved with a wireless network implementation, or whether a networking professional simply wants to keep up with the trends in communication technology, there's a whole new realm of information and methodology to learn. This section starts that journey with an introduction to wireless networking.

Wireless Networking Fundamentals

A wireless network is composed of client machines that use an RF link to communicate with a server. The server is usually located on a wired Ethernet LAN. The client machines communicate in a normal manner (using TCP/IP, AppleTalk, Windows networking, NetWare, or some other family of higher-layer protocols). Instead of creating an Ethernet frame, however, the clients transmit higher-layer protocols inside an 802.11 frame. Stations take turns accessing the WLAN using the rules of an access method called *Carrier Sense Multiple Access with Collision Avoidance* (CSMA/CA).

An 802.11 network can be configured as an *infrastructure* or *ad hoc* network. An infrastructure network is based on an *access point* (AP; also sometimes called a *master base station*). An AP is a small device with an antenna that provides synchronization between stations. An AP may provide connection from the wireless network to a wired medium, in which case it is technically called a *portal*. An ad-hoc network is based on an elected controlling station providing synchronization. An ad hoc network is typically created spontaneously and does not require an AP.

When powering on or rebooting, a wireless device must initialize itself and become part of the local WLAN. The device locates an AP, if one is present, and then goes through a process of authenticating and associating itself with the AP. These behaviors are visible in a trace file taken with a WLAN analyzer and will serve as the starting point for WLAN protocol analysis.

RF signals carry the bits that senders transmit through the air. DSSS is a signal scheme used in 802.11 to transmit the RF energy. An alternative to DSSS is FHSS. FHSS is more complicated to engineer than DSSS, which is why DSSS was deployed in the wireless marketplace before FHSS. FHSS is able to sustain higher speeds than DSSS, however. The issues related to environmental problems, signal degradation, and measurement are similar for both technologies.

The transmission of RF signals can be affected by environmental factors. When dealing with an RF environment, a support engineer needs to understand how RF signals are transmitted, how they are measured, and what environmental factors impact their transmission. The basic units used in the measurement of RF signals and antennas are the decibel (dB) and the dB milliwatt (dBm). This chapter completely explains these metrics and their significance in different situations.

What Is a Wireless Network?

The term *wireless network* is quite broad. It's worthwhile to consider a definition for the term and then quantify that definition to bound a discussion of specific technology. A network, defined with a protocol analysis spin, can be thought of as a group of communicating machines bounded by routers. This is, perhaps, an atypical way to define the term; however, there's a subtle aspect of the network concept that's embodied in the definition. When thinking about machines being bounded by routers, it can be seen that if a packet is transmitted onto a particular physical medium and then that packet is never forwarded by a router (operating at Layer 3 of the OSI Reference Model), then that packet remains in the same network. When a packet does cross a router, then it's in a different network. The whole realm of IP subnetting revolves around the aggregation of machines into locations (networks). The geographic location of, and topological relationship between, these locations is then exchanged between routers, making the routers aware of the next hop to which to forward a packet to reach the intended target location.

Closely bound to the concept of an aggregate of communicating machines bounded by routers is the concept of a broadcast domain. Given the fact that a Layer 2 switch forwards data-link broadcast frames, but a router does not forward broadcasts, it can be seen that the location that we're calling a network also defines the realm in which a particular broadcast (or multicast) packet travels. All stations in a broadcast domain have access to all broadcast or multicast packets.

The Challenge of Wireless Network Design

Having defined and considered the meaning of the word *network*, it seems like a simple extension of the concept to define a wireless network. "Isn't it just a network, but without wires?" you may suggest. The answer to that question, and the ramifications of the answer, form a core concept in the realm of wireless network engineering. Imagine, if you will, a simple situation in which a central router has only two ports active. A switch is attached to each of these two ports, and a client is attached to each switch. The clients are sharing files in a peer-to-peer architecture, as shown in Figure 4.1.

A basic understanding of IP routing will immediately bring out the fact that the two hosts (the two clients sharing their files) are on different networks. When the client on the left wishes to contact the client on the right, it doesn't send an Address Resolution Protocol (ARP) frame for the client on the right. Instead, it sends to its default gateway.

Now consider the situation when the wires between the clients and their respective switches are replaced with a wireless AP and each client is equipped with a WLAN adapter card, as shown in Figure 4.2.

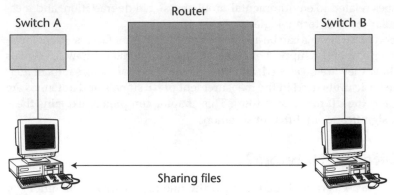

Figure 4.1 Clients in a peer-to-peer architecture.

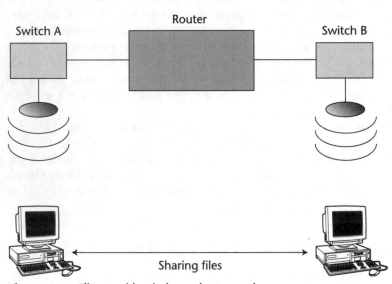

Figure 4.2 Clients with wireless adapter cards.

Nothing appears to have changed except the medium through which the client's data is transmitted. It used to be sent on a wire; now it's sent through the air. There would be no change except for the fact that now the two clients have the possibility of actually communicating with each other directly through the air. The RF energy being transmitted by one client could simply be received by the other client. It's as if they were now attached directly with a mystical piece of Ethernet crossover cable.

The fact that all wireless clients that are within transmission range of each other have the capability of communicating directly presents a challenge when designing, implementing, configuring, or troubleshooting a WLAN. The constraints of a network, bounded by routers, in which there are clear boundaries to the broadcast domain, have been relaxed. Should these two clients now be configured to appear as part of the same network? What happens if this network was originally a wired Ethernet and now a migration is taking place to a wireless environment? Perhaps the router/switch infrastructure used to divide floors in a building, or buildings in a campus network. Now, however, machines have the capability of hearing each other.

To complicate things even more, there are security concerns. Previously, an unauthorized intruder into the network had to come in and physically plug in to a switch in order to bypass firewall security. Now there's a possibility that the intruder can simply sit in a car in the parking lot and listen or connect to a previously secure network.

These are some of the engineering challenges that were met by the IEEE in the establishment of the 802.11 standards. A protocol mechanism called *association* allows a host device to map itself to a specific AP. This allows the wireless connection to have a behavior that is analogous to a wired Ethernet. A protocol mechanism called *authentication* allows the confirmation of the identity of a station and ensures that the station is allowed to associate with a particular AP. Finally, the data being transmitted can be encrypted using a mechanism called Wired Equivalent Privacy (WEP) to make it more difficult for the intruder in the parking lot to see traffic or gain access to the wireless network.

Protocol Analysis in Wireless Networks

Using a protocol analyzer in the wireless network environment is fundamentally no different than using an analyzer in a wired network. Data is captured from the air and placed in the analyzer's buffer. If the data is WEP-encrypted, then it looks meaningless to the analyzer, unless the analyzer has been configured with the special WEP Keys selected by the network administrator in a particular location. This is also true if other encryption methods are in use, such as Cisco's Lightweight Extensible Authentication Protocol (LEAP). The traffic seen with a wireless protocol analyzer is identical to that which would have been seen on the Ethernet itself, with the exception that additional traffic is present related to the operation of the WLAN. This traffic includes the packets related to association and authentication. Also, there are packets (called *beacon frames*) used as part of the process of locating an AP and determining when it's time to switch to a different AP (because a machine has physically moved too far away from the one to which it's currently associated).

Wireless Networking Technologies

There are three fundamental standards documents associated with 802.11 wireless networking. The core IEEE 802.11 standard discusses media access and framing issues, as well as FHSS, DSSS, and infrared (IR) transmission at 1- and 2-Mbps data rates. The

802.11b standard, the next to be released, describes DSSS at 5.5 and 11 Mbps. Finally, 802.11a defines FHSS at 54 Mbps. In addition to FHSS, DSSS, and IR, wireless networks can be implemented using *narrowband radio transmission* (radio LAN) or *Bluetooth*. This section describes the technologies used by 802.11 and other standards that are relevant to understanding and troubleshooting WLANs.

Narrowband Radio Transmission (Radio LAN)

In a narrowband radio transmission communication environment, the two devices talking to each other share a common, single radio frequency. This is loosely analogous to a portable radio (walkie-talkie or CB radio) where the two people talking to each other need to be on the same channel. Narrowband channels are similar to the bands used by standard broadcast radio stations. That is, transmitters constrain their range of transmitted signal to a narrow band and each band is separated from adjacent bands so there's no conflict between stations. When you tune your car radio to your favorite station, you hope that other stations aren't going to distort a good song.

It's very important to realize that 802.11 does not use narrowband channel assignments in the same way that broadcast radio does. A common point of confusion arises when people try to understand 802.11 channels on the basis of broadcast radio or television channels. Narrowband radio LANs are not part of the 802.11 standard.

Frequency Hopping Spread Spectrum (FHSS)

Communicators transmitting using FHSS actually send narrowband signals on discrete channels. However, they do not restrict themselves to a single channel. Instead, they use a series of channels and they alternate between the channels using a pattern of hopping that is known to both the sender and the receiver. The synchronization between sender and receiver creates, in effect, a logical channel of communication that functions as a single pipeline between the two stations. The transmitter sends data on the narrowband channel at a prespecified data rate for a prespecified amount of time, known as the *dwell time*. This may be enough time to send more than one data bit. The dwell time is variable but is never more than 400 milliseconds.

There is some confusion when talking about FHSS channels because the actual narrowband frequency ranges used to implement FHSS are also called channels. An FHSS channel consists of a number of narrowband RF channels that are alternated between according to the FHSS hopping scheme. If there's a conflict in a particular frequency range, or if there's noise in the environment, there's a chance that the conflict or noise will impact only one of the narrowband RF channels, leaving the others without error.

Direct Sequence Spread Spectrum (DSSS)

In both FHSS and DSSS, the transmitting station uses more than one narrowband RF channel to send information. In FHSS, the transmitter sends data on a narrowband channel and then hops to the next channel in accordance with the rules for hopping. In DSSS, the transmitter sends each bit on all channels. Consequently, DSSS provides redundancy (because each individual bit is actually transmitted in more than one narrowband RF channel). Moreover, the bits themselves are not simply sent as a 1 signal or a 0 signal. A special coded RF signal, called a *chipping code*, is what's actually transmitted into the air. There's a chipping code that represents a binary 1, and another chipping code that represents a binary 0. It's possible for a station to vary the length of the chipping code, chipping for a longer or shorter time, if the environmental factors that might corrupt the RF signal require it. Of course, sending 1s and 0s with long chipping code strings makes for an overall reduction in data throughput, but DSSS can maintain reliability as a trade-off. It's reasonable to think about implementing DSSS in a noisy environment where users demand high data reliability but are not too concerned about consistent throughput. The initial deployment of 802.11 wireless networks was based exclusively on DSSS technology. FHSS arrived shortly thereafter.

Infrared (IR)

IR communication is part of the 802.11 standard; however, due to the very high frequency and low power used by IR transmitters, this technology is only effective over relatively short distances. As a result, there's no implementation of IR for truly mobile users.

Bluetooth and the Personal Area Network (PAN)

Bluetooth is a standard for supporting a radio transmitter that is built into a single, small, integrated circuit and is designed to be embedded in a hand-held device, such as a personal data assistant or cellular telephone. This creates what's known as a PAN, with a data rate of 721 kbps or 1 Mbps. Today's networking engineers need to add the acronym PAN to the growing list of acronyms that define communication systems.

A group called the Bluetooth Special Interest Group (SIG) created the Bluetooth standards. Erickson, IBM, Intel, Nokia, and Toshiba were the founding companies. Microsoft, 3Com, Motorola, and Lucent Technologies joined the SIG later. To provide a perspective on where Bluetooth fits into the wireless networking picture, consider these proposed applications for embedded Bluetooth technology:

- Dialing the Internet using a cell phone that is connected to a notebook computer via a wireless Bluetooth link rather than a cable.

- Sending a digital photo from your camera to your cell phone and then transmitting the photo to a friend. Your friend transfers the photo from a Bluetooth AP to a notebook computer.

- Connecting your cell phone and your cellular headset via a Bluetooth audio link, rather than a cable.

Bluetooth operates in the 2.4-GHz transmission band, which is the same band used by 802.11 and by some cordless telephones. With Bluetooth, the range of transmission is limited to roughly 30 feet. (Throughout this chapter, most distance measurements are given in feet. Divide feet by 3.28 to arrive at the measurements in meters. One meter = 3.28 feet.)

In one sense, Bluetooth is loosely analogous to IR but without the requirement for line-of-sight connectivity. They both are designed for relatively low-power use and relatively short distances. They both implement a data rate that is lower than a typical Ethernet LAN, and typically lower than what would be expected with 802.11.

When a machine connects to a network through a Bluetooth link, it does so in much the same way it would create a dial-up connection through a phone line. This is distinct from the mechanism in 802.11 where a station connects through an AP in much the same way it would connect through an Ethernet Network Interface Card (NIC).

Conflicts between Bluetooth and 802.11 Networks

It's reasonable to consider a business, school, or even home environment having both Bluetooth and 802.11 networks implemented in their buildings. Because both technologies operate in the same frequency range, it's likely that they will conflict with each other. When Bluetooth and 802.11 are implemented in the same space, it is important to consider the possible performance implications.

Experiments have shown that an 802.11 receiving device that is less than 65 feet from an AP (in unobstructed space) typically receives an 802.11 signal that is strong enough to overcome that of a Bluetooth transmitter, if the Bluetooth transmitter is more than 30 feet from the 802.11 receiving device. When the Bluetooth transmitter is less than 30 feet from the 802.11 receiving device, then the potential for interference begins. There is roughly a 20 percent chance that a transmission from an 802.11 device will conflict with one from a Bluetooth device in an environment where both technologies are in heavy, continuous use.

Obviously, the amount of traffic present in the two environments plays a role in whether the conflict is noticeable by the end user. In a home environment, where only a few transmitting devices are present, the impact is much less than in a business office where 802.11 wireless connections are being used for data transfer and Bluetooth is being used for voice telephone calls, for example.

A Bluetooth conflict causes 802.11 packet corruption. If a conflict is suspected, then it's time to bring out your wireless 802.11 protocol analyzer and look for the presence of Cyclic Redundancy Check (CRC) errors. If there are no CRC errors, then there is no conflict. If corruption is present, then experimentally turn off the Bluetooth transmitters. If the corruption goes away, then you have isolated the problem. If a conflict is found, you might try changing the 802.11 channel on which the WLAN is operating and performing the experiment again. The spread spectrum signaling used in 802.11 is often able to overcome the influence of Bluetooth transmission in the space.

Other Wireless Standards

The standards and technologies just presented don't stand alone in the wireless marketplace. The HomeRF and OpenAir standards are just two examples of other choices in the wireless networking marketplace.

The HomeRF standard is being promoted by Siemens and provides an FHSS implementation in the 2400-MHz band. It supports a 1- or 2-Mbps data rate, with expectations for development of 10- and 20-Mbps rates in the future. One of the benefits associated with HomeRF is the mechanism built into the standard to facilitate interfacing to the phone company for voice integration.

OpenAir was conceived as an alternative to 802.11. It was designed by a multivendor forum called the Wireless LAN Interoperability (WLI) Forum in the late 1990s. OpenAir defined a 2.4-GHz FHSS technology with different rules for association, authorization, and encryption than those found in 802.11.

The point to be realized from these descriptions is that 802.11 is not the only show in town. It just happens to be the one that the IEEE has standardized. Proponents of other wireless technologies will extol the virtues of their particular favorite, and there's no question that the competing technologies have their specific niches in the marketplace.

Organization of the WLAN Environment

Understanding 802.11 architecture and station interaction begins with an understanding of the mechanisms by which stations are configured to be members of a common communicating group called a *Basic Service Set* (BSS). Two types of BSSs can be created, one using an AP (also called a *master base station*) and the other without an AP. An AP is a small device with an antenna that interconnects BSSs.

Multiple BSSs are interconnected to form an *Extended Service Set* (ESS). Stations in an ESS communicate with each other through APs. Each BSS in an ESS has an AP, and the APs may serve as portals into an Ethernet LAN that connects the APs together. A wireless client has a BSS identifier value, and, optionally, an ESS identifier value that specifies the aggregate group in which the client is a member. A standalone BSS, or an interconnected BSS group forming an ESS, operates as a single, flat broadcast domain and thus is viewed as a network. Communication from one ESS to another requires the services of a router operating at Layer 3.

A wireless client must locate an AP for the BSS in which it will be a member, and must then synchronize itself with the AP. The client then associates itself to that AP and authenticates to the BSS. After that, the client is ready to send user or operating system data through the air. The next sections describe this process in more detail.

The Basic Service Set (BSS)

The term Basic Service Set refers to an administrative grouping of 802.11 stations that interoperate and communicate as a fully interconnected network. The grouping is administrative because a parameter called the *Basic Service Set Identification* (BSSID) is configured into the individual stations and the stations form a network based on this identification. The stations are a network from the standpoint that they share a common logical broadcast domain. The broadcast domain is logical, as opposed to physical, because many BSSs may coexist in a single physical location and thus the physical manifestations of transmitted packets (the RF signals) are receivable by all stations in range of the transmitting device. Stations only accept packets in which the transmitter is in the same BSS.

A term that is occasionally applied to a BSS is a *cell*. The term *cell* is defined as a bounded space, and the boundary of the BSS cell is the logical boundary formed because stations that have the same configured BSSID form a logical group. All of the stations that are members of the same cell share a synchronized microsecond counting clock coordinated through the Timing Synchronization Function (TSF), discussed later in this section.

The Extended Service Set (ESS)

A station can only communicate directly with other stations in the same BSS. To extend the range of portability or mobility, a group of BSSs can be interconnected forming an ESS. An Extended Service Set Identification (ESSID) configuration parameter is employed to identify the group. The architectural system that provides the connectivity between BSSs in the ESS is called the *Distribution System* (DS). Stations in an ESS can communicate to each other transparently at the Logical Link Control (LLC) layer. That is, the elements of the protocol stack that underlie LLC, which include the Medium Access Control (MAC) layer and its sublayers, provide transparent communication between BSSs in an ESS so a station neither knows nor needs to know to which BSS it is currently associated.

This architecture implies that there is some type of connectivity between the BSSs in the ESS. This could be through a wired Ethernet, a fiber optic repeater link, or a wireless repeater link. The term *Wireless Medium* (WM) is used to refer to the atmosphere that is the transmission medium within a BSS. The term *Distribution System Medium* (DSM) is used to refer to the medium that interconnects BSSs. The distinction is important. The rules and specifications in the 802.11 standard define behaviors, capabilities, and expectations that relate to the logical implementation of the WM or DSM. This is said to be a *logical* implementation because the actual physical mechanism employed to provide connectivity is transparent to the communicators. There is an element of the communication stack called the *Physical Medium Dependent* (PMD) sublayer that is aware of the physical media type, but the MAC layer doesn't know or care whether packets are being encoded across the air, through a fiber link, or on an Ethernet. The DS treats the WM and the DSM as two separate logical elements.

The question now arises as to whether the actual data packets need to undergo a translation as they move through the DS. If the WM and the DSM are the same (both 802.11 compliant), then no translation takes place. If the WM is an 802.11 network and the DSM consists of an Ethernet that interconnects APs, then 802.11 packets need to be translated into 802.3 Ethernet packets, and then back to 802.11 as they enter the target BSS.

This distinction explains two terms used to refer to the AP. To be technically correct, an AP can connect the WM to the DSM if no translation is involved. When the WM and the DSM are different, then the AP is called a portal. A typical AP is, in all probability, actually functioning as a portal. Although the unit itself is called an AP by the vendor, the fact that it has an antenna and an RJ-45 Ethernet connector categorizes the unit as a portal, and not, technically, as an AP. In common discussion, however, the term *access point* is commonly used even though the 802.11 standard would refer to the unit as a portal.

In Figure 4.3 you see three portals. They are portals by virtue of the fact that they connect the WM to the wired Ethernet and thus must translate between 802.11 packets and 802.3 packets. In practice, however, these portals would typically be referred to as APs and the technical distinction between a portal and an AP would be ignored.

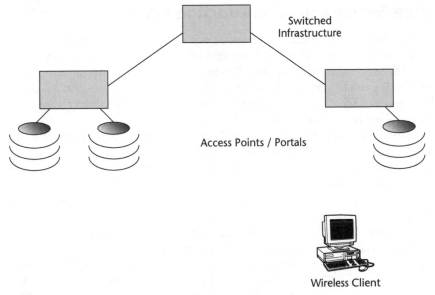

Figure 4.3   A wireless network with three portals.

Assume that the wireless client is mobile and that it moves from right to left across the network in Figure 4.3. There is a point at which the signal strength from the AP on the right, to which the client initially associated, will become weak, and the next AP's signal will dominate. At this point, the client will disassociate from the first AP and reassociate to the next one. This implies that the forwarding of packets destined to the wireless client will have to follow a different path through the DS medium (through the switches in this case). The distribution services will have to take the responsibility of making sure the packets are delivered properly.

There is a glaring absence in the 802.11 standard of the specific mechanism to provide distribution services. Remember that the 802.11 standard refers to the DSM as a logical medium. The standard sets down the rules, expectations, and capabilities that must be provided by the DSM in order to provide a transparent LLC path between communicators in the ESS, but it doesn't force a designer or manufacturer into providing these services in any particular way. The implementation (and, thus, the configuration) of the components that make up the DSM are always vendor specific.

At issue is the method by which a mobile client's location is known to the DSM when it moves out of range of one AP and reassociates to a different AP. How will the switches in Figure 4.3 know that the client has moved? Will the APs send some type of notification or dummy traffic back onto the Ethernet to cause the switches to update their forwarding tables?

As a networking professional responsible for the design, implementation, maintenance, or troubleshooting of 802.11 networks, it's critical to understand the mechanism for management of the DSM that is being used by your vendor's equipment. The only way to know how a particular vendor accomplishes the task of reassociation across the DS that connects APs in an ESS is to ask the vendor.

The Timing Synchronization Function (TSF)

Stations in a BSS maintain a synchronized time clock. This synchronization refers to a numerical microsecond count value that is kept the same for all stations in a BSS. That's a different kind of synchronization than Ethernet's Manchester or ternary signal encoding in which a clock pulse synchronizes the transmitter and receiver at the signal level. Each station in a BSS cell has an internal 64-bit counter that constantly goes up in 1-µs increments. This counter is called the TSF timer.

There are two mechanisms by which the TSF timers are synchronized in a cell. The mechanism used depends on whether there is an AP in the BSS cell. When an AP is present, it provides the master time clock for the entire BSS. The AP sends the TSF timer value (the master value) periodically in packets called *Beacons*.

When no AP is present, the network is said to be an Independent Basic Service Set (IBSS) or, simply, an ad hoc network. An ad hoc network is created when two or more users decide to share files between their wireless notebook computers and they aren't in range of a usable AP. In an IBSS, the station that happens to have the fastest-running clock counter is viewed as the master clock and all other stations set their TSF timers to the fastest counter. In an IBSS ad hoc network, all stations send Beacons. When a Beacon is received, a recipient adjusts its own TSF timer forward (ahead), if necessary. That is, the station with the fastest-running internal clock becomes the master time source because its clock is always ahead of everyone else's clock. If a TSF timer value is received in a Beacon packet and the value is less than the one currently held by the recipient, the Beacon is ignored and the recipient does not update its own TSF timer.

A sophisticated algorithm controls each station's transmission of Beacon packets and introduces randomized time delays so that all stations don't end up constantly sending Beacon packets. A very broad generalization of the algorithmic approach would be to say that if a client hears someone else send a viable Beacon packet, then the client doesn't send its own Beacon packets. The protocol analysis implication of this is that an IBSS ad hoc 802.11 network may manifest apparently confusing Beacon traffic. While an analyst may choose to spend many hours attempting to decipher each step-wise behavior related to Beacons (and *Probes* and *Probe Responses*), it's more important to realize that the Beacon process in an ad hoc network should not cause all stations to send Beacons all the time.

The underlying need for TSF timer synchronization relates to FHSS and not directly to DSSS. In an FHSS implementation, a station hops from one frequency (one narrow-band channel) to another in a preset pattern. Stations use the TSF timer to determine the hopping pattern and thus are able to acquire each other's transmissions.

Station Initialization Behavior

There are several initial behaviors that take place within the hardware of the wireless NIC and under the control of the microcode onboard the NIC. Other behaviors are controlled by the device driver software that is resident in the host computer. A station manifests the following behaviors as it initializes:

- Attempts to locate an AP with a sufficiently strong signal
- Synchronizes the TSF timer

- Authenticates itself as being an authorized participant in the WLAN
- Associates itself to the AP so that one specific AP knows to transmit packets destined for the station, as opposed to some other AP transmitting those packets

For the sake of discussion, let's assume that either an AP in a BSS, or an existing station in an IBSS, is sending Beacon packets. These packets are typically sent at 100 millisecond intervals, so capturing a trace file with a wireless analyzer (such as AiroPeek) shows constant Beacons. Note that once the fundamental behavior of a wireless network is confirmed to be working properly, it may be wise to set a filter to eliminate Beacon packets from wireless captures, just to keep the analyzer's buffer a little less cluttered.

As a first step, the new, initializing station attempts to update its TSF timer so it is synchronized with the rest of the BSS. There are two configurable behaviors that may be used to accomplish this task: *Passive Scanning Mode* and *Active Scanning Mode*.

In Passive Scanning Mode, the initializing station simply waits to hear Beacon packets and, when it does, it sets the TSF timer accordingly. In Active Scanning Mode, the initializing station sends *Probe Frames* and listens for *Probe Responses*. If the station is unsuccessful in either receiving appropriate Beacon packets (with the right BSSID and other parameters), or if no Probe Response is returned for the Probe Frames, then, according to the 802.11 standard, the station (typically and under configurable control) starts its own IBSS and begins sending Beacon frames. In this way, an environment always has either an AP or an ad hoc station sending Beacon frames. It's important to note that in practice you'll probably discover that a vendor's device driver for the wireless adapter offers a configuration parameter whereby a choice between infrastructure and ad hoc mode is preselected. If this is the case, then the default 802.11 behavior is overridden by the vendor's configuration and the device operates only in one mode or the other. The end result of scanning is that the station synchronizes its TSF timer with the rest of the BSS (or creates a new IBSS in which it is the master).

Channel Selection

The process of synchronizing to the BSS is called *scanning* because the initializing NIC moves from one 802.11 channel to another in accordance with a configurable list of allowable channels and with an internal timer that determines how long the NIC attempts to locate Beacons (or send Probes) on each channel.

802.11 defines 14 different transmission channels for DSSS, the first 11 of which are in use in the United States. It's very important not to think of these channels in the same way you think of television channels. The details of RF transmission, using spread spectrum technology, are explained in a later section; however, some discussion of general principles is called for now.

Each 802.11 transmitter uses a range of individual frequencies that spread out from the central frequency. There are two ways to use this spread spectrum of frequencies. In one case, the transmitted signal hops around from frequency to frequency using an algorithm based on the current value of the TSF timer. This is called FHSS. In the other case, the signal is transmitted directly onto all the spread frequencies, but with a stronger transmission on the center frequencies and weaker transmission on the lower and higher sides of the center frequency. This is called DSSS. The most common implementation in the initial deployment of 802.11b was DSSS. It's easier to implement, but it's more prone to noise corruption than FHSS. The FHSS and DSSS market segments continue to coexist and compete with each other.

One potentially confusing aspect of DSSS is the use of the term *channel* when describing the transmission of a signal. Each of the transmission channels used for DSSS consists of a series of contiguous RF narrowband channel frequencies over which the signal is transmitted. A station transmitting on Channel 6 would actually be sending RF energy out at a frequency that is also part of the range defined for adjacent channels. The channel number in a DSSS environment refers to the group of adjacent narrowband channels over which the sender's signal is spread. It should be noted that Channels 1, 6, and 11 do not in any way overlap each other.

When a station is initializing, it either looks for Beacon packets (in Passive Scanning Mode) or sends Probe packets (in Active Scanning Mode) on one channel after the other, moving sequentially through the list. The allowable channels that a station can use are configurable in the NIC device driver, typically using utility configuration software provided by the card manufacturer. Using a WLAN analyzer, the channel number used by an AP appears as a field in the decode of a Beacon packet.

In a case where more than one Beacon or Probe Response source is identified with the correct BSSID (or ESSID, depending on which configuration parameter is present), the station selects the first observed channel on which the received packets have a signal strength that is above a lowest allowable value set by the hardware manufacturer. The initializing station has now completed two of its required tasks: synchronizing to the BSS and selecting a channel for transmission.

PROTOCOL ANALYZER CHANNEL SCANNING

An interesting effect is observed when using a protocol analyzer to scan multiple channels in an 802.11 environment. Even though a single AP may be present, configured on Channel 6, the protocol analyzer may show traffic on other channels. In fact, if the analyzer is close enough to the AP, the traffic may show up on all channels! This effect is referred to as *bleedover*, and is the combined result of the nature of spread spectrum transmission and the fact that 802.11 receivers are not able to block frequencies to which they are not tuned, if those frequencies are transmitted with sufficient energy.

Channels 1, 6, and 11 have no overlapping transmission frequencies (in the spread spectrum of frequencies that are defined by a channel number). To minimize bleedover, it's recommended that adjacent APs be configured, when possible, to use these nonoverlapping channels. Even when nonoverlapping channels are used, however, expect to see some bleedover when capturing with your wireless analyzer.

There is an implication of the bleedover effect that should be taken into consideration when using a protocol analyzer's channel scanning features. In the example, where a single AP is present on Channel 6 but the analyzer shows traffic on, say, Channels 5 and 7, a careful assessment must be made. It will probably be found that the traffic captured from Channel 5 or 7 is not at 100 percent signal strength. Perhaps this traffic will show up at 80 percent strength. If bleedover occurred into Channels 4 and 8, then you might expect the signal strength to be indicated as even a smaller value, perhaps 30 percent.

If you're trying to make a determination as to what APs and what channels are in use in a particular environment, and you're looking at the results of a channel scan, never forget that the traffic that you see may simply be the result of bleedover and may not actually be indicative of a different AP operating on a different channel.

Authentication

In a wired Ethernet, it's necessary to physically plug into the network in order to communicate. This may seem obvious, and rightly so. However, this fundamental feature of a wired Ethernet is not present in the realm of RF transmission in an atmospheric medium. There is nothing to plug in; stations are simply present. *Authentication* is the process by which the basic physical security afforded by a wired network (requiring someone to physically plug in to communicate) is emulated in the 802.11 WLAN. After synchronization and channel selection, the authentication process must take place. Authentication is accomplished when the client sends an *Authentication Request* to the AP and receives an *Authentication Reply* with a positive success indicator. There are two forms of Authentication: *Open System* and *Shared Key*. With Open System authentication, the client is always authenticated as long as the AP has been configured to allow Open System authentication. This is the default mode for most systems. Open System authentication can be thought of as *null authentication*. The client asks to be authenticated and the AP says, "OK." With Shared Key authentication, a WEP shared key must be properly configured in both the client and AP.

Association to the BSS

The final initialization behavior is called *association*. Through association, the AP records the client's address and thereby becomes the AP through which packets will be forwarded to the client (as opposed to having some other AP be responsible for forwarding to the client).

Technically, the 802.11 standard defines an AP as "Any entity that has station functionality and provides access to the distribution services, via the WM for associated stations." The distribution services are those mechanisms by which a station communicates in the WLAN environment, and an associated station is one that has become part of a particular BSS. The act of association is somewhat analogous to some of the behavior associated with a Layer 2 switch or bridge in a wired LAN. A switch learns which station is connected to which port by looking at the source Ethernet address of any frame received. Suppose a switch receives a frame from a particular station on Port 5. The switch now knows that Port 5 is the one to which frames should be sent if they are later destined for that particular station. The switch has *mapped* an Ethernet address to a port. Association is the process whereby a wireless station is mapped to an AP. Once associated, the AP knows that it is responsible for transmitting packets destined for the particular station. APs to which a particular station is not associated will not transmit that station's packets.

Analysis of the Initialization Process

The following AiroPeek trace file printout shows the behavior of a station initializing in an 802.11 BSS. At the beginning (Packets 1, 2, and 3) the AP was sending Beacons and the network was in all other respects idle (there was no end-station behavior). The client enters the picture in Packet 4. After sending Probe, Authentication, and Association packets (Packets 4, 8, and 12), and receiving the appropriate responses, the client's initialization behavior is finished. The packet trace shows that the network returns to its idle state, with the AP sending Beacons.

Packet Number	Source	Destination	Delta Time	Packet Summary
1	AP 20:1F	Broadcast		802.11 Beacon
2	AP 20:1F	Broadcast	0.102	802.11 Beacon
3	AP 20:1F	Broadcast	0.103	802.11 Beacon
4	Client B9:AA	Broadcast	0.029	802.11 Probe Req
5	AP 20:1F	Client B9:AA	0.001	802.11 Probe Rsp
6		AP 20:1F	0.000	802.11 ACK
7	AP 20:1F	Broadcast	0.072	802.11 Beacon
8	Client B9:AA	AP 20:1F	0.009	802.11 Auth
9		Client B9:AA	0.000	802.11 ACK
10	AP 20:1F	Client B9:AA	0.001	802.11 Auth
11		AP 20:1F	0.000	802.11 ACK
12	Client B9:AA	AP 20:1F	0.001	802.11 Assoc Req
13		Client B9:AA	0.000	802.11 ACK
14	AP 20:1F	Client B9:AA	0.001	802.11 Auth
15		AP 20:1F	0.000	802.11 ACK
16	AP 20:1F	Client B9:AA	0.001	802.11 Assoc Rsp
17		AP 20:1F	0.000	802.11 ACK
18	AP 20:1F	Broadcast	0.088	802.11 Beacon
19	AP 20:1F	Broadcast	0.103	802.11 Beacon
20	AP 20:1F	Broadcast	0.102	802.11 Beacon
21	AP 20:1F	Broadcast	0.103	802.11 Beacon

Packet Acknowledgment

It can be seen in the trace file printout that various packets are acknowledged with an *ACK* packet. Notice that both the client and the AP send ACKs to each other as necessary. An ACK packet is one of six special packets called *control frames*. All directed traffic (packets addressed to any nonbroadcast, nonmulticast destination) is positively acknowledged with an ACK packet. The reason this is necessary is to implement a retransmission mechanism not unlike the Ethernet retry process that occurs when a collision occurs. In a wired Ethernet, the transmitting station has the ability to detect collisions through the rules of Carrier Sense Multiple Access with Collision Detection (CSMA/CD), the method and rules used to access the physical Ethernet medium (the wire). With RF transmission, the choice of CSMA/CA as the access method does not depend on collision detection to operate. Instead, an ACK control frame is returned to a sender for each directed packet received. (The terms *frame* and *packet* are used interchangeably in this discussion to mean the same thing.) If a directed frame does not receive an ACK, then the frame is retransmitted.

It can be seen in the trace file that the ACK packet does not have a normal Source Address (the field is blank). There is only a Destination Address field in an ACK packet. No bytes are wasted, including any source identifier, and, of course, because acknowledging is done on a packet-by-packet basis there is no need for any sequence number or transaction identifier. Remember, too, that when a client sends a packet through its associated AP, it's the AP that sends back the ACK. The identity of the AP is moot. Just like a Layer 2 bridge or switch in a wired Ethernet actually has an Ethernet address for each port, an AP has an address too. Just like the address of an Ethernet switch is transparent during the forwarding of a packet, so too, the address of the AP is not relevant to packet forwarding. It's sufficient for the AP to simply say, "Your packet was received" (the ACK packet) in response to a received packet.

802.11 Media Access Control

An *access method* is the means stations use to take turns transmitting packets. In a wired Ethernet network, this is CSMA/CD. Wired Ethernet stations listen while they transmit, and if they detect another station transmitting at the same time (called a *collision event*), they go through a process whereby a random time interval is introduced between successive retries, thereby letting conflicting stations take turns. In an 802.11 WLAN, the access method is CSMA/CA. A transmitting station does not listen to attempt to detect a collision. Failure to successfully transmit a packet is determined by the absence of a required ACK packet and the lost packet is retransmitted. There is a prioritization mechanism inherent in the transmission of packets that allows those of greater significance to be sent ahead of those that can tolerate a momentary delay. This mechanism is based on the use of different waiting periods being specified for different activities. The waiting period is the amount of time that a station must see an idle RF environment prior to beginning transmission. The waiting period is referred to as the *interframe spacing*.

Interframe Spacing

The interframe spacing is the time interval between the end of one frame and the start of the next. In a 10-Mbps Ethernet network, this is 9.6 microseconds, and in a 100-Mbps Ethernet, it is 0.96 microseconds. In essence, when a station wants to transmit, it must confirm that no other station is currently transmitting. This idle state of the network must continue for the time interval of the interframe spacing. In an 802.11 WLAN, there are four possible values that can be used for interframe spacing. These are listed here in order, from shortest to longest time:

1. Short Interframe Space (SIFS).
2. Point Coordination Function Interframe Space (PIFS or PCF Interframe Space).
3. Distributed Coordination Function Interframe Space (DIFS or DCF Interframe Space).
4. Extended Interframe Space (EIFS).

Different types of packets (performing different functions) are transmitted using different interframe spacing values. In this way, a natural prioritization takes place when two stations want to transmit at the same time. The station currently using the shortest interframe space can begin transmission before another station that has a longer required interframe space. In this way, the architects of the 802.11 standards set up a scheme whereby operations that are considered more time sensitive can take precedence over those of a less time-critical nature. The transmission of an ACK packet, for example, always uses the SIFS interval. Consider this sequence of events:

1. Station 1 sends a data packet to Station 2. The data packet requires an ACK.

2. While Station 1's packet is being transmitted, Station 3 wants to send a data packet, but it must wait for the network to be idle. Hence, this new station (Station 3) is waiting for Station 1 to finish its transmission.

3. When Station 1 completes its transmission, Station 2 is now required to send back an ACK. At this moment, both Station 2 and Station 3 are now competing for use of the wireless media.

4. Because an ACK is transmitted after the SIFS, and data packets are not, Station 2 can begin transmitting ahead of Station 3. When Station 3 times out of the PIFS, DIFS, or EIFS interval, it sees that the network is busy (with Station 2's ACK) and waits its turn.

The interframe spacing is an internal function of the 802.11 protocol stack and is not something that can be configured or modified by a network administrator. The prioritization mechanism is solely for use by the stack itself and is not a way to improve or change application or operating system behavior on a network. It operates below the level (and below the awareness) of the LLC, TCP/IP, AppleTalk, NetWare, or Windows protocols that may be using the WLAN for communication.

Complete details regarding the internal behavior of the 802.11 MAC layer with regard to interframe spacing may be found in the 1999 IEEE 802.11 standard, Section 9.2.3, "Interframe Space."

The Network Allocation Vector (NAV)

In an effort to minimize the possibility of two (or more) stations transmitting their packets at the same time (resulting in a collision and the accompanying corruption of both packets), the carrier sense mechanism is augmented with a numerical value called the *Network Allocation Vector* (NAV). The NAV is, in essence, a way that a station can predict future use of the medium (the atmosphere) and, hence, avoid collisions. Consider the following AiroPeek decode of a MAC header. This happens to be the header in a Probe Response packet, but the issue being discussed is identical for any packet carrying data. Of interest here is the *Duration* field.

```
802.11 MAC Header
  Version:              0
  Type:                 %00  Management
  Subtype:              %0101  Probe Response
  To DS:                0
  From DS:              0
  More Frag.:           0
  Retry:                0
  Power Mgmt:           0
  More Data:            0
  WEP:                  0
  Order:                0
  Duration:             218  Microseconds
  Destination:          00:A0:F8:9B:B9:AA  Client B9:AA
  Source:               00:A0:F8:8B:20:1F  AP 20:1F
  BSSID:                00:A0:F8:8B:20:1F  AP 20:1F
```

```
Seq. Number:        3095
Frag. Number:       0
```

The CSMA/CA process involves having a station wait a random amount of time before it transmits. The hope is that two stations will wait different amounts of time and one will then be able to see that the other one is already transmitting, avoiding a collision. Every station examines the MAC header in every packet on the channel. The Duration field is used to extend the random interval so as to help ensure that the random timer won't expire while a transmission is already in progress. The Duration field is set by a transmitter and represents the amount of time that the transmitter believes will be necessary to complete its transmission. The NAV is part of what's referred to as *virtual carrier sense* because a station can predict that the network is going to be busy for some specific time into the future using the Duration information.

The Request to Send/Clear to Send Mechanism

In the most common 802.11 implementation, stations take turns transmitting as per the rules of CSMA/CA. There is another mechanism that can be employed, called the *contention-free mode*, in which no collisions occur normally. In this mode, a station wishing to transmit must first send a *Request to Send* (RTS) packet and receive a *Clear to Send* (CTS) response. The overhead added to the network is minimized by the fact that the RTS and CTS packets are very small. In a case where large data packets are being sent without fragmentation, the loss of a single packet necessitates a long retransmission. In this environment, the use of RTS/CTS might improve performance by attempting to guarantee a contention-free environment.

Synopsis of the 802.11 Environment

The behaviors that have been discussed thus far are the ones that you can observe with a protocol analyzer. You can capture and analyze the initialization behavior. You can observe disassociation and reassociation with a protocol analyzer. After completing your analysis of the 802.11-specific behavior, the analysis of client/server and upper-layer protocol communication in a WLAN is identical to that in its wired counterpart. TCP/IP clients still broadcast an ARP frame to locate their default gateway. Subnet masking issues remain the same (albeit with additional complexities related to mobile users). AppleTalk Macintosh clients use the Name Binding Protocol and the AppleTalk ARP just as if they were on a wired Ethernet. In summary, the fact that 802.11 specifies that the mechanism by which the LLC path is established and maintained through a WLAN be transparent to the users of LLC means that the higher-layer protocols operate exactly as they would in a wired network. The analysis and troubleshooting of the higher-layer protocols also remain the same.

When troubleshooting a network (or, for that matter, when troubleshooting anything!), there is a healthy portion of basic common sense and intuition that goes into problem solving. Troubleshooters obtain various pieces of information and then make sense out of that information on the basis of their training, expertise, and experience. It is through understanding the technology that underlies the troubleshooting scenario that common sense and intuition can work.

FUEL FOR THE INTELLECTUAL FURNACE

There was a time in history when the medical community understood in a vague way that sickness was somehow related to blood. Doctors employed their common sense and intuition on the basis of their knowledge and experience and used leeches to drain a sick person's blood. Oops. As doctors began to understand the details of how body chemistry worked, they were able to fine-tune their common sense and fuel their intuition and they realized that their original concepts needed to be updated.

Today, when a doctor is thumping your knee or looking in your ears, he or she is probably not thinking about the chemical composition of hydrocarbons or about any number of detailed technical concepts he or she learned in many years of schooling. Rather, these technical details have formed the basis for an internalized understanding of how the body works. Unless doctors are involved in some specialized research, they aren't directly using all of their technical knowledge on a daily basis. Protocol analysis and network troubleshooting are like medicine in this regard. It's necessary to understand the internal workings of a technology in order to fine-tune your common sense and feed the intuitive process so that solutions to problems can be determined. On that basis, the engineering details of the 802.11 WLAN environment are critical to the networking professional. The place to start is with an understanding of the signaling and framing that are used to convey data through the atmosphere.

Radio Frequency Transmission

When an electromagnetic signal in a wire becomes strong enough, the energy leaves the wire and propagates (radiates) into the air. Sometimes the purpose for this signal propagation is to send your favorite radio program to your car radio; other times it's to carry a television program to an antenna. In the 802.11 environment, the RF energy carries the bits that make up the frames (or packets) that manifest the behaviors of the WLAN. There are many ways of generating electromagnetic energy into the atmosphere and many ways of representing information. In every case, however, the energy must increase and decrease in strength, and that is where the term *frequency* is used.

When the increasing and decreasing of the energy level of a signal occurs more slowly (when the frequency is lower), the physical distance traveled during one oscillation is greater and the signal is said to have a longer *wavelength*. When the frequency increases, the distance traveled decreases and the wavelength is said to be shorter, as illustrated in Figure 4.4.

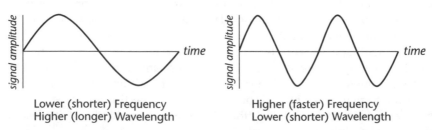

Lower (shorter) Frequency
Higher (longer) Wavelength

Higher (faster) Frequency
Lower (shorter) Wavelength

Figure 4.4 Frequency and wavelength.

The Greek letter lambda (λ) is used to represent wavelength measured in meters. Frequency is the number of cycles per second that the signal varies, and the unit of measurement is hertz (Hz). The symbol used by engineers for frequency is the Greek letter nu (ν). Because signals that are of interest vary many thousands of times per second, the typical unit is megahertz (MHz), or millions of cycles per second. In 802.11, the signals vary millions of times per second, and the unit is gigahertz (GHz), or billions of cycles per second—that's a lot of cycles! 802.11 operates in a range of frequencies that is referred to as the 2.4-GHz band.

The relationship between the measured wavelength and frequency is dependent on the speed with which the signal travels. The signal travels at the speed of light in the medium. The unit c is used to represent the speed of light (186,282.4 mi/s or 300,000 km/s, if traveling in a vacuum). This value may also be represented in meters as $3 * 10^8$ m/s. The wavelength is equal to the speed of light divided by the frequency (and the frequency is equal to the speed of light divided by the wavelength).

$$\nu = c / \lambda$$

So, how does this information prove useful at two o'clock in the morning when you're trying to figure out why users on the first floor are losing their wireless connections to the server? It can be seen from the equation that if the speed of propagation changes, then either the frequency or the wavelength has to change. An AP transmits on specific frequencies and a receiving station expects the signal to comply with the standard. If the signal must pass through a concrete wall, or a warehouse full of metal shelving, or through some other medium in which the speed of propagation varies, then the signal is affected. The signal loses some of its energy and is perhaps changed to the point where it can no longer be properly received. It is for this reason that one of the steps in designing a wireless network is to perform a site survey. In the site survey, the strength and quality of the signal in different locations is determined. Strength can be determined with a protocol analyzer. AiroPeek, for example, presents the signal strength seen for each frame received.

An AP typically sends Beacon packets every 100 milliseconds. By dividing the area being surveyed into a grid, AiroPeek can be moved from grid point to grid point and the signal strength of the Beacon packets can be plotted on a diagram. Signal quality can be indirectly ascertained by determining whether or not packets are being lost in transmission. If AiroPeek is capturing relatively close to the AP and a mobile client is pinging a server through the AP onto the wired Ethernet, then it can be determined whether the ping packets are all being seen. Each ping packet has a sequence number inside it; if the observed sequence is 1,2,3,5, then packet 4 was lost. As the wireless client is moved around in the area being surveyed, a determination can be made about the quality of reception by the AP.

Frequency Allocation

Various governmental bodies oversee the assignment of different ranges of frequencies to different users. This is necessary to prevent conflicts whereby two organizations might use the same frequency, the result being garbage for both. Because the strength of a signal decreases as the distance from the transmission point increases, it's possible to assign the same range of frequencies to multiple organizations as long as they are sufficiently far away from each other. In the United States, the Federal

Communications Commission (FCC) allocates frequencies. In Europe, the European Radio-Communications Committee (ERC) maintains that responsibility. Because many countries around the world have their own regulatory bodies, there can be potential conflicts when implementing equipment intended for use in a different country.

A particular range (band) of frequencies, called the Industrial, Scientific, and Medical (ISM) band, has been accepted almost universally by many countries. This band uses frequencies near 2.4 GHz and so is called the *2.4-GHz band*. 802.11 operates in this band.

There are other users of the 2.4-GHz band in addition to 802.11 WLAN users. Some portable telephones and microwave ovens can interfere with 2.4-GHz signals. The network engineer who is troubleshooting or designing in the 802.11 environment must be aware of possible frequency conflicts within the network. A protocol analyzer, such as WildPackets' AiroPeek, is not an oscilloscope, nor is it an RF spectrum analyzer tool. Capturing packets with an analyzer will disclose corrupted or retransmitted packets, but will not directly show a conflict in the RF signal space. When these types of signal corruption-related events are observed with an analyzer, it's up to the engineer to be reasonably intuitive in determining what in the environment may be the cause of such corruption.

Mathematics for RF Engineering

Every specification that you encounter describing an RF aspect of 802.11 engineering will include references to measurements using decibels (dB) or dB milliwatts (dBm). You'll see many complicated-looking calculations relating to the transmission of RF energy. This section presents the mathematical foundation for understanding these calculations and metrics. In order to understand the 802.11 standard, and to understand the significance of vendors' specifications for transmitters, receivers, and antennas, you must be comfortable with the topics presented here.

BIOLOGICAL HAZARDS ASSOCIATED WITH RF TRANSMISSIONS

The FCC Office of Engineering and Technology (OET) has published an informative and technically detailed report on the potential and real hazards associated with the presence of RF energy in the environment. The complete text of the report may be found on the Web at www.fcc.gov/Bureaus/Engineering_Technology/Documents/bulletins/oet56/oet56e4.pdf.

When passing through various substances (including the human body), RF energy raises the energy level of the molecules that make up the substance, causing heating. This is referred to as a *thermal effect*. In the presence of high-power RF energy, the human body can experience damaging thermal effects. Fortunately the energy levels found in 802.11 transmitters have been shown to be below the level necessary to bring about any thermal effects in human tissues. There is speculation that there may be nonthermal effects that have not yet been experimentally isolated. Federal government and international organizations are actively studying the issues related to the increased use of RF equipment by the general population. Normal installation guidelines appear to be sufficient to provide a safe RF environment for the user community.

The Decibel Unit of Measurement

Networking professionals won't proceed very far in their work with 802.11 WLANs before they encounter specifications and standards using two basic units of measurement, the decibel (dB) and the dB milliwatt (dBm). The decibel is a unit for expressing the ratio between two values for signal strength, which is an important concept when designing and troubleshooting 802.11 networks. The decibel milliwatt is a unit of measure that represents power, which is also an important concept. While there is no question that some engineers have both the math and technical background to interpret these units of measurement with complete comprehension, the majority may experience some confusion. In fact, it's not uncommon to encounter networking professionals who believe that they understand dB and dBm measurements only to discover that they have deficits in their comprehension of which they aren't even aware!

So, if you feel that you completely understand dB and dBm measurements, you are encouraged to read this section carefully to confirm that your knowledge is sound. If you are uncertain as to exactly what these measurements mean, then this section will provide a valuable foundation for your interpretation of a wide variety of measurements related to 802.11.

You may refer to the 802.11 standard and encounter a statement like the following: "The frame error ratio (FER) shall be less than $8 * 10^{-2}$ at a PSDU length of 1024 octets for an input level of -76 dBm measured at the antenna connector." In another case, a vendor's hardware may include a specification indicating that the "Receiver Noise Floor = -111 dBm + 7 dB = -104 dBm." (In case you're wondering, there's no typographic error in the previous formula; the -111-dBm value and the 7-dB value are being added together, yielding a result measured in dBm.) Whether the 802.11 standard is being consulted, or a vendor's product spec is being evaluated, or an antenna is being selected, applying and understanding the dB and dBm measurement mechanism is a fundamental skill.

A Synopsis without Any Complicated Math

dB measurements are based on the mathematical principles of *logarithms*. A logarithm is a special way to represent a number that uses powers of 10 (10^1, 10^2, and so on) and positive and negative fractional powers of 10 ($10^{1.123}$, $10^{-1.123}$, and so on) to take the place of original values. The decibel number is actually the power (exponent) to which 10 is raised. This can appear very complicated and confusing to networking professionals without a reasonably strong background in mathematics. An engineer who is seeking professional certification as a wireless expert should learn the details of the underlying mathematics, but a person with a purely field-oriented interest in decibel measurement can draw valid conclusions with only a superficial understanding of the unit. If you feel that this section is beyond your desire to learn in detail, the most fundamental points to remember are:

- A dB measurement is a ratio (a fraction, like a percentage) that refers to the change in a signal.

- The dB milliwatt (dBm) is a unit of measure used to represent the number of milliwatts of power.

- A dB measurement can be subtracted from a dBm measurement, resulting in a new dBm value. Even though the units are different, the underlying mathematics allows the mixed-unit calculation to work properly.

- If one signal is 3 dB stronger than another, then it's twice as strong. (If you choose to not accept this fact at face value, you'll find a complete explanation in the text of this chapter.)

- If a signal changes by -3 dB, its strength is halved.

- When a signal *gain* value is positive, it means the signal gets stronger, but you may see references to *negative gain*, meaning the signal gets weaker.

- A signal *loss* is always a positive number, but it means that the signal gets weaker. A loss is exactly the same as a negative gain, and both terms are used to refer to the condition when a signal gets weaker.

Understanding Decibels

A decibel is 1/10 of a bel. The bel, named after Alexander Graham Bell, is a unit that represents a ratio between two numbers. When bels were used as the unit of measurement in practical applications, the result was often a very small decimal number. Instead of dealing with the whole bel unit, the common unit of measurement was arrived at by multiplying the bel result by 10, producing the decibel unit. Ten decibels is 1 bel, or, to put it another way, a decibel is 1/10 of a bel. If a calculation results in an answer equal to 0.123 bels, then the answer is represented as 1.23 dB, a simple multiplication by 10.

To understand the bel, and hence the decibel, it's necessary to understand logarithms. If you have a mathematics background, the logarithms should be familiar to you. To lay the groundwork for understanding logarithms, consider Table 4.1 of exponential powers of 10.

Mathematicians tell us that any number raised to the 0 power is equal to 1, and any number raised to the first power is equal to the number itself. The logarithmic representation of a value involves using the exponent, instead of the number itself, when referring to the number. We say that 2 is the logarithm of 100 because 10 raised to the second power equals 100. When 10 is used as the base for the logarithm, it's said to be a *common logarithm*. There are other types of logarithms (*natural logarithms*, for example) that don't use 10 as the base, but they are not going to be encountered in the realm of 802.11 specifications. Table 4.2 shows how a logarithm appears in an equation.

Table 4.1   Exponential Powers of 10

EXPONENTIAL POWER	RESULTING VALUE
10^0	1
10^1	10
10^2	100
10^3	1,000
10^4	10,000

Table 4.2 Logarithm Representation in an Equation

LOGARITHMIC REPRESENTATION	RESULTING VALUE
log 1	0
log 10	1
log 100	2
log 1000	3
log 10000	4

It should be easy to see that if log 1 = 0 and log 10 = 1, then computing log 5 (a number between 1 and 10) should yield a result that is somewhere between 0 and 1 (as you know that log 1 = 0 and log 10 = 1 and that the number 5 lies between 1 and 10). You can use the log function on a scientific calculator to compute log 5 = 0.69897. (In this text you'll find fractional results truncated at the fifth decimal place without rounding for the sake of convenience.) You can see that 0.69897 lies between 0 and 1, as expected. The implication of the logarithmic calculation is that $10^{0.69897} = 5$. (In this text you'll find the equals sign used in cases where the result is perhaps not exactly equal, but is sufficiently close for the purposes of discussion. Actually $10^{0.69897} = 4.99999$, but we'll just call it 5.)

Now we're ready to understand the bel. It's quite simple. Consider any situation where two values are being represented as a ratio. For example, an 802.11 AP transmits a signal with a strength of 100 milliwatts (mw). At some distance from the AP it is determined that the signal strength has decreased to a value of 1 mw. The ratio of original power to measured power is 100/1. When the fractional ratio is converted to a decimal and then represented as a logarithm, the unit is a bel.

$$\log (100/1) = 2 \text{ bel}$$

You may recall that log 100 = 2. That was an easy example. Suppose that the 100-mw signal decreases to 2 mw at some distance. Now the calculation requires a calculator and is as follows:

The ratio is 100/2, which equals the decimal value 50
log 50 = 1.69897
The answer is 1.69897 bels

It turns out that many measurements involve two values that are much closer together than 100 and 2. Consider the calculation where the 100-mw signal is decreased to 78 mw:

100/78 = 1.28205
log 1.28205 = 0.10790
The answer is 0.10790 bels

Because the common unit of measurement is the decibel, the answer in bels is simply multiplied by 10 resulting in decibels.

$$0.10790 \text{ bel} = 1.0790 \text{ dB}$$

That is a complete explanation of the mathematical meaning of a decibel. When two power levels P_1 and P_2 are being compared, the following formula can be applied to determine the ratio measured in dB:

The ratio $P_1{:}P_2$ measured in dB = 10 log (P_1/P_2)

Thus far we've examined examples where the numerator in the ratio was larger than the denominator, resulting in a quotient greater than 1. By inference we could deduce that because log 1 = 0 then log x (where $x < 1$) would result in a logarithm that was less than 0—a negative log. And that is exactly what would be shown with a calculator. Consider the following examples using the formula previously defined.

$$dB = 10 \log (P_1/P_2)$$

Assume: $P_1 = 10$ mw *and* $P_2 = 100$ mw
$$(10/100) = 0.1$$
$$\log 0.1 = -1.0 \ (because\ 10\text{p}^{-1} = 0.1)$$
$$10 \log (P_1/P_2) = 10 * -1.0 = -10 \text{ dB}$$

Assume: $P_1 = 78$ mw *and* $P_2 = 100$ mw
$$(78/100) = 0.78$$
$$\log 0.78 = -0.107905 \ (because\ 10^{-0.107905} = 0.78)$$
$$10 \log (P_1/P_2) = 10 * -0.107905 = -10.7905 \text{ dB}$$

Important Things to Remember about Decibels

As a networking professional involved with 802.11 you will regularly encounter decibel measurements. Remember that a decibel is 10 times the logarithm of the ratio between two values. A positive decibel value implies that the ratio is greater than one, and a negative decibel value implies a ratio that is less than one. Remember, too, that a decibel does not represent any particular physical quantity (like a milliwatt); it represents a ratio between two values.

Specifications Involving Gain or Loss

It's important to pay attention to whether a particular dB measurement is stated as a gain, as a loss, or simply as the change from one value to another. In the previous example, we could imagine that an 802.11 AP was generating the initial 100-mw signal and, at some location in the area, the signal strength was measured (using an RF signal strength meter) at 78 mw. This would be a -10.7905-dB change in the signal strength.

Now things get confusing and require a certain degree of intuition for proper interpretation. Intuition should tell you that there was a loss in signal strength (and that's correct) as the signal went from 100 mw to 78 mw. This would be represented as a positive 10.7905-dB loss. The change in signal strength was negative 10.7905 dB. In fact, sometimes this is referred to as a negative 10.7905 gain. When gain measurements are represented as negative dB values, it implies that the ratio was less than one and there was a decrease. On the other hand, when a loss measurement is represented with a positive dB value, it, too, implies a decrease. Reread this explanation carefully until it makes sense. It is a fundamental concept for interpreting dB measurements.

The dB Milliwatt

Another common metric that will be encountered is the decibel-milliwatt (dBm). Unlike the dB (which is only a ratio, and not a specific quantity of some thing), the dBm is a measurement of the number of milliwatts of power measured. The metric is quite simple if decibels are understood. When using dBm as the unit of measurement, the denominator (P_2) in the $10 \log (P_1/P_2)$ equation is simply assumed to be 1 milliwatt. The rest of the math remains the same. Instead of just being a ratio, the dBm is a direct measurement of the number of milliwatts of power present. Consider the previous example, where a 100-mw signal was first measured and then it experienced a 10.7905 loss and ended up as a 78-mw signal. To convert milliwatts to dBm, simply plug the milliwatt value into the equation as the numerator (P_1) and use 1 as the denominator (P_2).

$$10 \log (P_1 \text{ mw}/1 \text{ mw}) = 10 \log (78/1) = 10 \log 78 = 18.92094 \text{ dBm}$$

Instead of calling the measurement *78 milliwatts*, it is referred to as *18.92094 dBm* (pronounced by saying the three letters, d, b, m). The dBm unit is important and its significance will become clear as this explanation continues.

Relationships between Metrics

Assume you have a friend who lives 30 minutes away by car. Unfortunately, if you are forced to drive to your friend's house during rush hour, when traffic is heavy, it takes you 60 minutes to get there. It's obvious that the trip takes twice as long during rush hour. The relationship between the 30-minute metric and the 60-minute metric is perceived immediately. Decibels and dBm measurements are not as obvious, because they are logarithmic, and not linear. Consider the relationships in Table 4.3.

Notice that when the power doubles, the dBm value goes up by roughly 3 dBm. When two dBm values differ by roughly 3 dBm, then one of them is twice (or half) as great as the other. Another way to consider and confirm this is by straightforward mathematical exponentiation. Two values (a and b) are compared, and b is found to be twice as large as a.

$$2a = b$$

The ratio between a and b is 2. Using a scientific calculator, it's now a matter of finding the common logarithm of 2. The results would be as follows:

Table 4.3

VALUE IN MW	EQUIVALENT VALUE IN DBM
39 mw	15.91064 dBm
78 mw	18.92094 dBm
156 mw	21.93124 dBm

$$\log 2 = 0.30102$$

Remembering that a decibel is 1/10 of a bel, the log of the ratio must be multiplied by 10 to arrive at decibels.

$$0.30102 * 10 = 3.0102$$

If the decimal portion of the answer is ignored (for simplicity's sake), the answer is simply 3. A change of 3 dB means that the ratio is 2:1, which is to say, one value is twice as large as the other.

A similar confusion can arise when examining various ratios expressed in dB. You should be familiar with the meaning of dB metrics so you have an idea of just how much a particular value changes when the change is represented in decibels. Consider Table 4.4.

Table 4.4

CHANGE	RESULT
No change (ratio = 1/1)	0 dB
Change by a factor of 2 (ratio = 2/1)	3 dB
Change by a factor of 4 (ratio = 4/1)	6 dB
Change by a factor of 10 (ratio = 10/1)	10 dB
Change by a factor of 100 (ratio = 100/1)	20 dB
Change by a factor of 1000 (ratio = 1000/1)	30 dB

The Wonder of Logarithmic Calculations

There is a special mathematical aspect of logarithms that comes into play when performing an RF site survey, and this aspect is important to understand. When you add the logarithms of two numbers, it's like multiplying the two numbers together. When you subtract logarithms, it's like dividing.

$$\log (X * Y) = \log X + \log Y$$
$$\log (X/Y) = \log X - \log Y$$

This relationship can be easily seen if the examples only involve the number 10, as follows:

Given: $10 * 10 = 100$
Calculate: $\log 10 = 1$
Add logarithms: $\log 10 + \log 10 = 1 + 1 = 2$
Calculate: $10^2 = 100$ (...same as calculating $\log 100 = 2$)

Given: $10 * 100 = 1000$
Calculate: $\log 10 = 1$ and $\log 100 = 2$
Add logarithms: $\log 10 + \log 100 = 1 + 2 = 3$
Calculate: $10^3 = 1000$ (...same as calculating $\log 1000 = 3$)

A calculator will demonstrate that this rule is true for all numbers. Let's pick two numbers at random for this example: 925 and 541.

Problem: Calculate 925/541 using logarithms
Calculate: $\log 925 = 2.96614$ and $\log 541 = 2.73319$
Subtract logarithms to divide: $2.96614 - 2.73319 = 0.23295$
Calculate the quotient: $10^{0.23295} = 1.70981$
Problem solved: $925/541 = 1.70979$

The error beyond the fourth decimal place is due to rounding, but it can be seen that adding logs is like multiplying, and subtracting logs is like dividing.

Applying the Principle of Logarithmic Subtraction

To apply this mathematical principle, consider a situation in which an AP that is transmitting a 100-mw signal experiences a 13-dB loss. The 100-mw power level can be represented as 20 dBm. Because one value is represented in milliwatts and the other is a dimensionless decibel ratio, it's difficult to immediately see the real-world power levels that are being represented. By converting milliwatts to dBm, the units can be subtracted, and, because logarithmic subtraction is really division, the reduced power level can be determined. The following example will make this principle clear.

We've assumed that there is a 13-dB loss experienced between a 100-mw AP and a point of measurement. Watch how these numbers work out:

Calculate: 100 mw = 20 dBm
Subtract: 20 dBm − 13 dB = 7 dBm

You may think, "How can a valueless ratio (dB) be subtracted from a value metric (dBm)? Isn't that like subtracting apples from oranges?" Herein lies the wonder of the logarithmic system. Remember that subtracting logarithms is like dividing the original numbers. Because both dBm and dB are logarithmic, the subtraction is mathematically the same as dividing one result by the other! The explanation progresses as follows:

Given: 20 dBm = 100 mw because $10^2 = 100$

Remember, 20 dBm = 10 log (100/1), so 20 is divided by 10 when it's used as the exponent of 10 to convert back to the original value.

Calculate the ratio represented by 13 dB: $10^{1.3} = 19.95262$

Again, 13 is divided by 10 yielding the exponent of 1.3.

The original 100 mw is being divided by 19.95262 (because subtracting the logarithms is the same as dividing the original numbers), so the result is:

Calculate: 100 mw/19.95262 = 5.01187 mw

Now, we'll convert 5.01187 mw back into dBm:

Convert the result to dBm: 10 log (5.01187/1 mw) = 6.99999 dBm

The result of the division of the milliwatt values (6.99999) and the result of the subtraction of the dBm and dB values (7) are the same (with recognition of the rounding errors that result during the calculations).

Concluding Thoughts on Logarithmic Subtraction

When performing a wireless site survey, there are calculations (which will be presented later) that begin with the AP output power and then subtract the loss associated with propagation and noise. It's sufficient to simply subtract the dB loss values from the original dBm power level to arrive at the resulting dBm power for a particular location. By understanding the mathematical foundation of the measurements, a networking professional can appreciate that subtraction of a dB loss implies reduction of the power level by some ratio (expressed in dB). When dB is subtracted from dBm, the mathematical result is to multiply the dBm value by a fraction, expressed as a dB ratio. The calculation looks like a subtraction problem (and it works out like one, too), and the underlying foundation is that it's actually a division problem.

When referring to the 802.11 standard, an antenna specification, or a vendor's product spec, if dB or dBm measurements are encountered, the meaning of the measurements and the relationship between them can be ascertained from the underlying logarithmic operations.

Application of dB and dBm Measurements

Power output in 802.11 is measured in dBm. When a station transmits a signal, the strength of the signal decreases with distance. The ratio of the received signal to the original signal is measured in dB. This is said to be the *attenuation* of the signal.

The 802.11 standard specifies that a receiving station must be able to properly acquire 1024-byte packets at 11 Mbps with a signal level as low as –76 dBm measured at the antenna connector. This value can be converted into milliwatts as follows:

$$10^{(-76/10)} = 0.000,000,025,118 \text{ mw}$$

At first glance, this doesn't seem to be a very large value (and it's not!). However, this can be compared to the transmit power level of, say, a typical AP to put it into perspective. An AP may typically transmit at either 100 mw or 500 mw.

Free Space Propagation

The design of a WLAN involves two separate aspects of site planning. First, a design plan must be drafted based on reasonable technical and engineering assumptions. This is typically in the form of a floor plan on which APs have been located. The second aspect of the design is the site survey, during which the assumptions made in the initial plan are tested to confirm proper signal propagation and strength. The blueprint (floor plan) aspect of design, and the site survey aspect, may be combined in many different ways.

In order to make intelligent decisions regarding the placement of APs, it's necessary to calculate and estimate the signal loss that will be experienced between an AP and the potential users of that AP. The starting point for this type of calculation and estimation is to consider how a signal would experience loss in the vacuum of space, without any obstructions or other interference. This is called the free space path loss L_f and it's measured in dB.

Physicists apply the inverse-square law of signal propagation, which states that the strength of a signal varies inversely with the square of the distance from the source. Put simply, when you get two times further away from a source, the signal gets four times weaker. When you are three times further away, then the signal is nine times weaker. When you square the ratio of distance, you arrive at the ratio of signal loss. The actual formula used to calculate free space path loss is:

$$L_0 = 10 \log (4\pi d/\lambda)^2$$

where

L_0 = the free space path loss measured in dB

d = distance between transmitter and receiver in meters (Note: The variable d does not stand for diameter. In fact, d, being the distance from the transmitter to the receiver, is the radius of a sphere of propagation outward from the transmitter.)

λ = the wavelength of the transmitted signal measured in meters

Bear in mind that L_0 is a *loss* metric and, hence, the formula indicates that the value of the loss increases with the square of the distance. That's why the distance variable d is in the numerator of the equation. The 4π multiplier produces the area of the surface of a sphere, since the formula assumes that the radiated signal travels outward in all directions from the source. A shorter wavelength (hence, a higher frequency) results in a higher energy and, hence, the loss decreases in inverse proportion to the wavelength.

Multiplying Logarithms Is Like Exponentiation

Recall that adding the logarithms of two numbers and using the result as an exponent is the same as multiplying the two numbers. In like fashion, multiplying the logarithm of a number is the same as raising the number to the power of the multiplier, as shown in the following equation:

$$\log (x^n) = n \log x$$

Consider the following examples for clarity:

Given: $x = 10$ *and* $\log x = 1$
Problem: Determine the result if 10 is raised to the third power ($n = 3$)
Calculate: $3 * (\log 10) = 3 * 1 = 3$ *and* $10^3 = 1000$
This is the same as: $10^3 = 1000$
Given: $x = 4$ *and* $\log x = 0.602059$
Problem: Determine the result when 4 is raised to the second power
Calculate: $2 * (\log 4) = 2 * 0.602059 = 1.204118$ and $10^{1.204118} = 15.99992$
This is the same as: $4^2 = 16$

Knowing that exponentiation is equal to logarithmic multiplication allows the free space path loss calculation to be rewritten as follows:

$$L_0 = 20 \log (4\pi d/\lambda)$$

The exponent (2) becomes a multiplier for the logarithmic representation and, hence, it's mathematically the same as the original exponentiation operation. This equation can be simplified even more in the 802.11 realm, since the only calculations being considered are those related to 2.4-GHz transmissions.

Notice that the inverse-square law is what led to the use of 2 as the exponent in the free space path loss equation. If you're mathematically inclined, you may wonder why the equation puts the circumference of the sphere of propagation ($4\pi d$) as the numerator in the fraction. That is, with the circumference in the numerator, the value L_0 gets larger as the circumference gets larger, and we're stipulating that the inverse-square law says that the signal gets smaller. This is because L_0 is the loss and the loss increases in proportion to the decrease in gain. In case you're awake at three in the morning thinking about these things, you'll now be able to get back to a restful night's sleep.

As we've said, the Greek letter lambda (λ) represents wavelength in meters, and the Greek letter nu (ν) represents frequency, which is the number of cycles per second (Hz) by which a signal varies. Frequency is also typically written simply as f, as in the following example. Wavelength and frequency are related to the speed of light by the following equation:

$$\lambda = c/f$$

where c = the speed of light ($3 * 10^8$ m/s) and f = frequency in hertz. The wavelength in the 2.4-GHz band used by 802.11 can be calculated as follows:

$$\lambda = c/f$$
$$\lambda = 3 * 10^8/2.4 \text{ GHz} = 0.125 \text{ m}$$
where
λ = the wavelength of the transmitted signal measured in meters
c = speed of light (300,000,000 meters per second)
f = signal frequency in Hertz

Therefore it can be calculated that λ for 802.11 at 2.4 GHz is 0.125 meters. Substituting the value of λ in the equation, the result is:

$$L_0 = 20 \log (4\pi d/0.125)$$

The exponential value 2 is used in the theoretical application of the free space path loss equation. In practice, the loss is much greater inside a building, for example. Some schools of thought suggest that a value of 3.5 be used instead of 2. The implication is that path loss in an obstructed environment is much greater than in free space. If 3.5 were used, then the equation would look like this:

$$L_0 = 35 \log (4\pi d/0.125)$$

In vendors' white papers and technical literature you may encounter many forms of the path loss formula with many different multipliers used in the equation. If you are a math hobbyist, it's an interesting exercise to transform a particular equation back to the basic free space path loss form, but for those of us working in the field, it's sufficient to remember that the various forms of the equation used in the real world simply substitute different estimates for the factor. It should also be realized that the denominator of the fraction (0.125) can be divided into 4π, yielding 100.53096. The transformation of the equation would then become:

$$Given: L_0 = 35 \log (100.53096d)$$
$$Apply\ the\ rule: \log (a * b) = \log a + \log b$$
$$Result: L_0 = 35 (\log 100.53096 + \log d)$$
$$Calculate: \log 100.53096 = 2.00229$$
$$Substitute: L_0 = 35 (2.00229 + \log d)$$
$$Simplify: L_0 = (35 * 2.00229) + 35 \log d = 70.08049 + 35 \log d$$

The point of this exercise is to make you aware of some of the many ways you may see a path loss calculation represented in different vendors' and authors' writings. The following two representations are essentially mathematically identical:

$$L_0 = 35 \log (4\pi d/0.125)$$

$$L_0 = 35 \log d + 70$$

Free Space Path Loss Conclusions

Accurately calculating the expected power level for any particular distance from an AP is an exceptionally complex process. The design of the transmitting antenna, the frequency of the transmitted signal, the medium through which the signal is passing, and the various types of obstructions in the environment that may cause attenuation, reflection, or dispersion of the signal must all be taken into account. Pursuit of the details of the physics and mathematics will quickly result in being faced with complex calculations with esoteric-sounding names like the Fresnel-Kirchoff diffraction parameter, Snell's Law, Brewster's angle, Gaussian variables, the Longley-Rice model, Okumura model, and more. To become well versed in the engineering and physics details of wave propagation, get a masters degree in physics! As a networking professional, be aware that the technology involved in making an 802.11 wireless network work introduces a variety of complexities that are simply not part of the wired Ethernet world.

The free space path loss for a single frequency (2.4 GHz) in a vacuum does not take into account the fact that the actual signal is transmitted on a group of narrowband frequencies in the spread spectrum mode. It also does not take into consideration any of the ways that the signal could be affected by factors in the environment. It does indicate, however, that the effective range of a 100-mw AP using an omnidirectional antenna is not going to be greater than 628 meters.

Environmental Factors that Affect 802.11 Transmission

The reality is that free space path loss only provides a starting point for determining the anticipated signal level at some distance from a transmitter. The RF signal must pass through much more than a vacuum! The signal may be affected in any one or more of the following ways.

Reflection

Reflection causes the signal to bounce back on itself. The reflected signal may either interfere with itself in the air or affect the receiver's ability to discriminate between the signal and noise in the environment. Reflection is caused by metal surfaces such as steel girders, metal scaffolding, metal shelving units, or metal doors.

Absorption

When passing through certain objects, some of the electromagnetic energy of the signal is absorbed by the material in the object, resulting in a reduced power level beyond the object. Water has great absorption properties, and while it's not assumed that an 802.11 receiver is going to be at the bottom of a swimming pool, it's reasonable to think that other absorbent materials such as trees or thick wooden structures may be between an AP and a recipient.

Refraction

When an RF signal passes from a medium with a particular density into a medium with another density, the signal can be bent, much like light passing through a prism. This means that, as with a reflected signal, there can be interference between the refracted portion of the RF signal and the nonrefracted signal passing to the other side of the object. For example, a water tank not only introduces absorption, but the difference in density between the atmosphere and the water can bend the RF signal almost as if it were a lens.

Diffraction

Diffraction, which is similar to refraction, results when a region through which it is easy for the RF signal to pass is adjacent to a region in which reflective obstructions exist. As with refraction, the RF signal is bent around the edge of the diffractive region and can then interfere with that part of the RF signal that is not bent.

The designers of 802.11 transmitting devices attempt to compensate for variable environmental factors that may cause reflection, absorption, refraction, or diffraction by boosting the power level above that which would be required if free space path loss (and other measurable characteristics) were the only consideration. The additional power added to a transmission is called the *fade margin*.

Concepts for Site Survey Troubleshooting

A *site survey* is the process whereby a network engineer measures the RF characteristics and the data-carrying capabilities of a particular site. This could be done prior to network installation or at any time a problem appears to be causing packet loss.

The complexities of the mathematics underlying RF engineering should not be underestimated. In this section you'll encounter a variety of formulae and calculations that are presented for your perspective and education. The text does not attempt to provide mathematical proofs or derivations for many of the calculations, as these would be lengthy and beyond the scope of the topic. Many of the calculations have logarithmic operations as their basis and, as we've seen, adding logarithms is akin to multiplication; subtracting them is like dividing; and multiplying them is like raising a number to an exponential power.

To determine whether or not a particular design is feasible, and to initially make assumptions about where to place APs, it's necessary to have a reasonable scale drawing of the building (or other area) in which the WLAN will be implemented. Using reasonable intuition, a mark is placed on the drawing to represent an AP. By reasonable intuition it's meant that an AP shouldn't be placed behind a floor-to-ceiling metal storage rack or in the farthest corner of a large room. A location in the center of the desired coverage area is best. Next, some basic calculations are done to see if the placement meets the requirements for proper signal propagation.

One important aspect of design that must not be overlooked is the fact that the RF signal propagates outward in all directions from a typical AP. While there are specialized antennas that can increase signal strength in a particular direction, a simple mast antenna (as found on most typical APs) can be initially assumed to be *isotropic* (that is, radiating in all directions). As such, placing an AP in an exterior corner of a room means that some of the signal may radiate strongly outside the building, where an unauthorized user sitting in the parking lot can easily receive it. An AP in one room may be able to propagate through the wall (and probably will) to potentially interfere with an AP in the next room. Don't forget that walls only attenuate (decrease) the strength of the signal; they don't block it completely.

The goal, in the RF realm, is to have a transmitting device that is capable of generating a sufficiently strong and properly formed signal in a manner whereby the intended receivers can recover the intended bit stream without undue error. There are three important basics to be considered:

1. How powerful (measured in milliwatts) is the transmitting device?

2. At what speed will the data be transmitted (1 Mbps, 5 Mbps, 11 Mbps)?

3. What is the desired degree of reliability? (How many bits are allowed to be lost?)

Clear Channel Power Assessment

The 802.11 standard requires that compliant receivers be able to properly detect a signal at a specific power level and then extract bits from the received signal with a specified minimum bit loss. A checklist is provided in the standard that hardware designers or equipment manufacturers can use to confirm that their equipment meets the 802.11 requirements. There are several pages of checklist items relating to a wide variety of constraints and minimum acceptable levels of performance. The weakest signal that must be properly received is –85 dBm, but only a 70 percent probability of detection is required at that level. The standard uses –75 dBm as the receiver sensitivity level required for 2-Mbps transmissions.

For field engineers, there is a great likelihood that determinations regarding signal strength made during a site survey are going to include various measurement errors. The real world and the laboratory are very different. It's reasonable to assume that when the signal level that is calculated for a 100-mw (20-dBm) AP during WLAN design is determined to be –65 dBm or less, then the reasonable useful range of transmission has been found. For APs with rated output power greater than 100 mw, the –65-dBm lower limit can be further reduced by 1/2 dB for every dB of output power above 20 dB. Hence, the signal transmitted from a 500-mw AP (26 dBm) could be as low as –68 dBm before its signal would be considered unusable.

To arrive at the theoretical range for an AP, it's necessary to take a number of factors into consideration. There are physical limitations on how many bits per second can be transmitted at a particular frequency, and there are various environmental factors that cause signal loss. An initial design and accompanying site survey must take these factors into account for you to make reasonable decisions concerning placement of APs. Additional information about clear channel power assessment can be found from Intersil Corporation at www.intersil.com/data/an/an9/an9804/an9804.pdf.

Limitations on RF Signal Transmission

There is a physical upper limit on the ability of a receiver to differentiate between the valid signal and the background noise present in the environment. This is referred to as the *signal-to-noise ratio*. There is a point at which the noise energy becomes sufficiently large so as to make recovery of the valid data signal impossible. When you're driving in your car and you're going away from your favorite radio station, the signal you receive gets weaker with distance. In addition to hearing your favorite song, you also hear noise and static. There is a point at which the noise and static becomes too distracting and you can't hear enough of the song to sing along. The signal-to-noise ratio has reached the point where the intended signal can no longer be extracted from the noise. In the RF data transmission world, the fastest data rate that can be extracted from the background noise can be calculated using Shannon's Channel Capacity Theorem.

Shannon's Channel Capacity Theorem

The theorem is stated as follows:

$$C = B * \log 2 (1 + S/N)$$
$$where$$
$$C = \text{channel capacity (bps)}$$
$$B = \text{channel bandwidth (Hz)}$$
$$S = \text{signal strength (watts)}$$
$$N = \text{noise power (watts)}$$

In an 802.11 WLAN, there may be many users transmitting 11-Mbps data at the same time. Shannon's theorem shows that there is a maximum number of users (maximum channel capacity) that can transmit without an appreciable *Bit Error Rate* (BER). Because the frequency range is a constant (2.4 GHz), and because the signal strength varies inversely with the square of the distance from the transmitter, it can be seen that the noise variable becomes the most significant unknown in determining real-world channel capacity.

Gaussian Noise

Heat, as you probably learned in school, causes molecules to vibrate. One of the effects of this process is the generation of RF energy. The energy is random in nature and follows a known type of randomization known as a *Gaussian distribution*. The energy contributed to a system as a result of *Gaussian noise* can be calculated based on the temperature of the system. The formula for calculating Gaussian noise is:

$$N = kTB$$
where
N = noise power (watts)
k = Boltzman's constant ($1.38 * 10^{-23}$ Joules/K, where K is degrees Kelvin)
T = system temperature in degrees Kelvin (relative to absolute zero)
B = channel bandwidth (Hz)

Room temperature, measured in degrees Kelvin, is about 290K. Examining this equation it can be seen that, for a particular environment (where T is a constant), there will be more noise present in a channel with a higher bandwidth capacity. Hence, an 11-Mbps data transmission is subject to more noise than a 1-Mbps transmission. As a result, when Shannon's theorem and the Gaussian noise calculations are considered together, it can be seen that a lower-bandwidth transmission could overcome environmental noise effects that could not be overcome with a higher-bandwidth transmission.

An 802.11 transmitter uses the 1-Mbps data rate to perform certain critical communication functions and then attempts to send data at the highest rate feasible in the environment. Consequently, when analyzing a WLAN, it's normal to see a transmitter switching data rates during communication activities. The data rate used in the transmission of each packet can be observed using a protocol analyzer. If data is consistently being transmitted at a rate lower than expected (less than 11 Mbps, for example), then an examination of the environment to attempt to isolate the cause is warranted.

Multipath Transmission

When the RF signal radiates outward from the antenna on an AP, it travels in all directions. Consider the problem that occurs when the signal going north bounces off a wall, window, or metal object and is reflected back across the path of the signal going east. There is interference between the two signals, and, in some parts of a room, the multiple paths taken by the RF energy can actually cancel each other out completely. This is referred to as *multipath transmission,* and an extra amount of transmission power is needed to overcome the effects of signals that would diminish, cancel, or distort each other. The extra power that is designed into a transmitting device is called the fade margin. Multipath loss can account for as much as a 20- to 30-dB reduction in overall signal strength. When hardware design engineers want to make 70 dBm of output power available, they may add a fade margin of 30 dB to produce a 20-dBm (100 mw) transmitter.

Because the effects of multipath interference are dependent on the size, shape, construction, and contents of the environment, the impact can be reduced by placing multiple antennas in a location, each operating on a different channel. By configuring two APs to operate on different channels, the chances are increased that a station can locate and associate to an AP with a sufficiently strong signal. Because the APs operate on different channels, the chance of interference between the two transmitters is reduced. It's important, however, to realize that simply populating a space with multiple APs is not a cure-all. As a general rule, the effective transmission radius of an AP should not overlap with more than two other APs. That is, if a circle is drawn on a floor plan around each AP (representing the area in which the signal strength is assumed to be greater than –65 dBm), then there should be no location that is covered by more than three circles.

Real-World Path Loss

Recall that free space path loss was calculated in a vacuum, without taking real-world factors into consideration. In a building, where walls and metal obstructions impact the signal, the loss can be significantly greater than that which would be calculated in a vacuum. Equipment vendors and others have performed a variety of practical experiments in a attempt to see how real-world signal loss compares to the theoretical inverse-square law. Whereas the inverse-square law uses an exponent of 2 to express signal attenuation, the rate of loss in the real world is often significantly greater. A real-world signal may decrease by an exponential factor of 3 or 4, or more. (Hence, with a factor of 4, moving twice as far away from a transmitter would result in 2^4 or 16 times less power.)

Not only does the material used in the construction of walls and floors affect signal loss, but also the presence of furniture, bookshelves, in-wall plumbing, windows, and even people in the environment can impact the RF energy transmission. It's not unreasonable to consider the potential impact that might result if a large area with a relatively low ceiling was surveyed when it was empty but was occupied by 100 people when in use.

In the real world, it can be assumed that a 2 × 4-inch wood stud wall, with sheetrock on both sides, introduces roughly a 6-dB loss as a signal passes through it. The basic inverse-square law holds true for roughly the first 20 feet of unobstructed space around an AP. Beyond that, the combined effects of environmental factors cause the loss ratio to increase dramatically. A general guideline that may be applied in a typical office environment is to assume a 30-dB loss for every 100 feet. Two factors that may increase the loss are the presence of metal objects (such as metal wall studs, doors, shelving units, and scaffolding) and the presence of numerous objects with a high water content (such as plants, trees, or large aquariums). When an environment contains objects that are known to cause RF signal loss, the degree of diligence that must be applied to the site survey increases.

Calculating Real-World Path Loss

This discussion is targeted at field engineers. The equipment being installed or tested presumably meets the requirements of the 802.11 standard. Consequently, it should be possible to develop some general guidelines for placing APs, based on the actual path loss encountered in a real-world environment.

A 100-mw AP transmits at 20 dBm and a 500-mw AP transmits at 26 dBm. Assume that a receiver is 75 feet away from the AP and that it is necessary to go through five walls to get to the receiver. This results in the following loss figures:

- 75 feet unobstructed free space loss @ 30-dB loss per 100 feet = 22.5-dB loss
- Five walls @ 6 dB per wall = 30 dB
- Fade margin: 30 dB
- Total: 82.5-dB loss

With a 100-mw AP (starting with 20 dBm), the result at 75 feet would be a –62.5-dBm signal level. If –65 dBm is used as the lower limit of acceptability, then that limit has just about been reached.

The conclusion is that, in a typical environment, reliable, consistent operation at 11 Mbps should not be assumed much beyond the 50- to 75-foot range. A 1-Mbps transmission may be received at the upper boundary of this range, and perhaps beyond the upper boundary, but not much beyond it.

Outdoors, the operating range is not impacted by multipath transmission in the same way as it is in a building's interior. Line-of-sight outdoor range may be as much as 300 feet, and the theoretical limit can be shown to be upward of 1000 feet in some situations.

Antenna Positioning for Maximum Coverage

The most common type of antenna found on many APs is the *omnidirectional antenna*. An omnidirectional antenna is usually a 4- to 6-in transmitting element, often attached to a rotating or positionable pivot. The signal propagating from an omnidirectional antenna is strongest in a direction perpendicular to the antenna shaft and weakest in the same direction as the antenna shaft. If you imagine taking a doughnut or a tire inner tube and placing it down over the antenna, then you get an idea of what the signal pattern looks like.

Using this guideline, and remembering that when an omnidirectional antenna is pointing straight up the signal is being sent out to the sides in all directions, can help you position your antennas for maximum coverage. APs may often be mounted or positioned in either a horizontal or a vertical position. It's important to make sure that the antenna elements are always pointing straight up, however.

SURPRISING TEST RESULTS

An engineer reported to the authors that during his testing of 802.11 equipment for an important military application, he was able to receive the signal from an AP 15 miles away! Although this report was never verified, it should be realized that there are unique environments that may be quite different from a normal 802.11 environment. That's why, after doing the theoretical calculations, a real-world site survey must be performed to validate the calculations.

Protocol Analyzer Reporting of Signal Strength

A fundamental value reported by a protocol analyzer using an appropriate 802.11 interface card is the *signal strength*. There are two mechanisms by which utility and protocol analysis software report this value, and neither purports to provide the accuracy that would be obtained using a spectrum analyzer or RF signal strength meter.

The method used by some utility programs (and not used by true protocol analyzers) is to compare the number of Beacon frames seen to the number of Beacon frames expected, and to use the ratio as a representation of signal strength. The idea is that when the signal is poor, more Beacon frames are lost. Because a Beacon frame has a field called the *Beacon Interval* that reports the configured interval between Beacon packets, a receiving station knows what to expect. The problem with this method is that RF energy is not actually being measured. The actual signal strength could be quite high, but in a very noisy RF environment, Beacon frames may be corrupted or lost. A utility that uses the Beacon Interval as a basis for reporting signal strength would report a low value when, in fact, the actual energy level was high.

The other method, used by true protocol analyzer tools, is to receive information directly from the wireless NIC where the actual power level is being measured. The signal strength is then reported for each packet. This value is typically reported as a percentage, and the natural question arises, "A percentage of what?" The 802.11 standard explains that a value called the *Receive Signal Strength Indicator* (RSSI) measures the energy observed at the receiving antenna during receipt of a single packet. The RSSI is intended to be used in a relative manner and does not reflect a particular dBm value. Furthermore, the required degree of accuracy of the RSSI is not specified.

The key concept in understanding the percentage metric reported by an analyzer after acquiring the RSSI value is that the 802.11 standard specifies that this metric is *relative*. Of course, it makes sense that a percentage metric is a relative numeric value. If a student receives a score of 82 percent on a test, the score says nothing about how many questions were answered correctly or how many total questions there were on the test. The actual quantity to which a relative measurement refers is not implied by the measurement itself.

In the case of the signal strength percentage reported by a protocol analyzer, the RSSI value is passed up from the wireless NIC and the analyzer software converts it into a percentage. This value ranges from zero to an upper bound no greater than 255, determined by the hardware manufacturer of the wireless chipset. In fact, the NIC itself uses the RSSI value to determine when the wireless medium is clear, implementing a function called the *Clear Channel Assessment* (CCA). When the RSSI value falls below an internal parameter called the *energy detect threshold*, then the communication channel is assumed to be idle.

You may be tempted to ask, "But what dBm power level is associated with a particular RSSI value, and why is this so mysterious?" The answer to the mystery lies in the fact that an 802.11 communicator can, and typically will, change speeds in the course of using a particular channel. Some packets (Request To Send and Clear To Send, for example) are always transmitted at 1 Mbps in order to ensure that the sender is most capable of overcoming any noise in the environment. The individual bits of information are encoded by shifting the phase of the signal using schemes called *Binary Phase Shift Keying* (BPSK), *Differential Binary Phase Shift Keying* (DBPSK), and *Complementary Code Keying* (CCK). With BPSK, the phase of the transmitted signal is shifted into two different patterns. DBPSK uses four phase shifts during bit encoding. The signaling for both BPSK and DBPSK is fundamentally sinusoidal (a sine wave signal) and the energy carried is calculated using a system called *root mean square* (rms), which is not a matter of simple addition and subtraction. To add to the complexity of the RF signal transmission, the signal is spread over a series of frequencies (spread spectrum transmission), using either Direct Sequence Spread Spectrum (DSSS) or Frequency Hopping Spread Spectrum (FHSS) techniques.

Additional information about CCK as used in 11-Mbps 802.11 transmission is available from Intersil Corporation on the Web at:

www.intersil.com/data/an/an9/an9850/an9850.pdf.

It is not possible (outside an engineering and design laboratory) to accurately and directly convert the RSSI value into a specific dBm power level that conveys any meaning in the real world. In part, this is why the 802.11 standard does not specify the required accuracy of the RSSI value; it is simply stated as a relative measure of energy. A frequency analyzer would be able to show dBm levels at each particular frequency band within a spread spectrum transmission, but that information would not be directly useful for determining whether data can be successfully transmitted. This is because the instantaneous dBm power measured at any moment is a measurement of the power manifested by the type of RF signal being acquired. The type, structure, and phase of the signal stream used to encode the bits changes within the band of frequencies used in the spread spectrum transmission. Indicating that a particular dBm power level is associated with a particular packet would be a strange average at best, and it would have questionable meaning because the encoding and waveform are changing. It would be analogous to asking, "What is the average amount of food consumed by a group consisting of five computer engineers, three bamboo trees, and eight million bacteria cells?" Asking about the average amount of food consumed by any member of this group has no meaning. The way that the measurement would be made in each case, and the aspects of what would be measured, are vastly different. The designers of 802.11 hardware implement the RSSI metric as a catchall value that represents the power over a set of otherwise disparate metrics.

The RSSI value is presented to the user of a protocol analyzer as a percentage value. It is the percentage by which the RSSI value has ranged from the lowest allowable threshold (indicating that no usable signal is present) to the maximum value specified by the hardware, called the *RSSI_Max*. Different vendors use different values for RSSI_Max. The RSSI value passed up to the driver from the NIC is converted into a percentage for display in the analyzer. That implies that using two vendors' wireless NIC cards may produce different power percentages with two analyzers both capturing side by side in the same environment.

Determining the Significance of Vendor Specifications

The thing that's important is not signal strength, noise, receiver sensitivity, or any other particular metric. What's important is that data can be successfully transmitted and received at the required speed. Consequently, a decision must be made about the speed necessary to serve the end-user community. A voice application may be quite successful with a 1-Mbps data rate, whereas a complex database application may seem slow and unresponsive unless a full 11 Mbps is available. It's also important to identify those locations at a site where coverage will not be required. There's no point in adding APs to provide proper data transfer capabilities when nobody is going to be there to do any transferring!

Having defined the data transmission requirements, it's now time to install an AP and do some real-world measuring. Vendors and manufacturers of wireless NICs provide utilities that come with the card and offer access to signal-level information. Typically, this information is not replicated inside a protocol analyzer, so it is very important that you learn how to apply the tools that your vendor supplied.

Being able to receive data properly is a complex combination of many factors. Many of these factors are often misunderstood and, as a result, decisions are sometimes made that are based on false assumptions. Two ratings that are often misunderstood are output power and receiver sensitivity.

Output Power

A wireless NIC or an AP has a particular rated output power. This may be 100 mw, 500 mw, or some other value. There have been few comprehensive test results released to the public concerning the effectiveness of increased power. People generally assume that more power is better. One way to increase rated output power is to use sophisticated high-gain antennas. Experiments have indicated that doubling the output power of an AP indoors may only result in a 7 to 10 percent increase in range. While range increases may be dramatic in an unobstructed outdoor environment with high-gain antennas or higher-power APs, the indoor improvements are not guaranteed to be significant. This is why a site survey is so important.

CISCO'S AIRONET CLIENT UTILITY

Cisco 802.11 NICs ship with the Cisco Aironet Client Utility (ACU), which is a graphical tool for configuring, monitoring, and managing the NIC and its wireless environment. The utility reports a signal-to-noise ratio, measured in dB, and displays signal strength and noise level, measured in dBm. Signal strength can also be displayed as a percentage. The utility reports numerous statistics, including CRC errors, data rate mismatches, missing ACKs, and retry counters. The utility lets the user configure the transmit output power, set the data rate or choose automatic rate selection, and configure the channel for ad hoc mode. The utility also includes client settings such as the Service Set Identifier (SSID), authentication method, WEP key, and type of network (infrastructure or ad hoc).

ACU also includes a Site Survey Tool and a Link Test Tool. The Site Survey Tool operates at the RF level. The Link Test Tool sends IP pings to assess the performance of the RF link. The results from both tools include information on whether association has completed successfully, the name of the AP, current signal strength as a percentage or dBm value, the percentage of Beacon packets received versus those expected to be received, and so on. Because the Link Test Tool operates above the RF level, it also checks the status of wired sections of the network and verifies that IP has been configured correctly.

Receiver Sensitivity

One vendor may claim that its wireless NIC can extract data at a signal level as low as –85 dBm, another claims –95 dBm, and yet another vendor may only provide –75 dBm. The reality is that the 802.11 standard demands only –76 dBm, and so, while it's nice that vendors go beyond the specs, it may not make a big difference in a particular network. Experiments conducted by WildPackets, Inc. showed that two different vendors' NIC cards (with different receiver sensitivity) began dropping packets at different ranges from an AP. The first vendor's NIC began dropping packets at roughly 60 feet and the second vendor's NIC began dropping packets at roughly 75 feet. The conclusion was that the differences were minor in the big scheme of things. In both cases, during the test, engineers had to leave the building and walk outward across the parking lot before they reached the point where packets were lost. Because the AP being tested was for use inside the building, the fact that one card performed differently than the other was moot.

The Impact of Environmental Noise

A powerful signal (high signal strength) in the presence of a lot of environmental noise or significant multipath reflection may not be able to properly carry data. A very weak signal (low signal strength) in an environment without such detriments may carry data quite well. The fact is that dBm measurements of signal strength are not sufficient, by themselves, to determine whether data can be properly exchanged in a wireless environment. The noise must also be taken into consideration.

There are sophisticated tools in the category of spectrum analyzers and meters that can measure Gaussian noise in the environment. Armed with such tools, and using Shannon's Channel Capacity Theorem, some calculations could be made to indicate whether or not data could theoretically be carried in some particular environment. The signal strength percentage, presented by a protocol analyzer, can also be used if interpreted accurately and carefully.

There are two statistics that you must evaluate along with signal strength to get a reasonable assessment of environmental suitability. The CRC error count and the retry packet count both reflect situations where packets were corrupted in transit.

Each 802.11 packet (including control and data packets) ends with a frame check sequence, or CRC field. When bits have been corrupted, the CRC is bad. The transmitter initially calculates the CRC value carried at the end of the packet. The receiver calculates the CRC value for the received bits. If the CRC value calculated on receipt doesn't match the CRC value calculated by the transmitter (and carried at the end of the packet), then the checksum is bad and the packet is discarded.

When packets are sent requiring an ACK, and the sender receives no ACK, then the packet is retransmitted by the 802.11 MAC layer. Consider the following 802.11 MAC header.

```
802.11 MAC Header
  Version:              0
  Type:                 %10   Data
  Subtype:              %0000   Data Only
  To DS:                1
```

```
From DS:              0
More Frag.:           0
Retry:                0
Power Mgmt:           0
More Data:            0
WEP:                  0
Order:                0
Duration:             314  Microseconds
BSSID:                00:A0:F8:8B:20:1F  AP 20:1F
Source:               00:A0:F8:9B:B9:AA  Client B9:AA
Destination:          00:90:27:44:B1:FF
Seq. Number:          328
Frag. Number:         0
```

Notice that the Retry bit is set to 0. This bit is set to 1 when the MAC layer is retransmitting a packet. The implication of a retry packet is that the original packet (or the ACK for that packet) was corrupted.

Both the CRC error count and the retry count are indicative of the presence of corrupted packets. Collectively we'll simply refer to both of these as *bad packets*.

By calculating the percentage of bad packets to total packets, a metric can be created that is an indication of the quality of the transmission. It may come as quite a surprise to find that some networks have as many as 30 percent bad packets and continue to operate normally (albeit more slowly than they would if there were no bad packets). Determining the percentage of bad packets is more important than simply measuring signal strength.

A network with less than 10 percent bad packets is operating well. A network with more than 30 percent bad packets is in need of some attention.

Consider the following packet summary decode printout.

Packet	Source	Destination	Access Point	Data Rate	Signal Strength	Protocol Type
8	IP-192.168.0.1	IP-192.168.0.5	AP 20:1F	11	94%	TCP TELNET
9		Client B9:AA		1	65%	802.11 ACK
11	IP-192.168.0.5	IP-192.168.0.1	AP 20:1F	11	61%	TCP TELNET
12		AP 20:1F		1	94%	802.11 ACK
14	IP-192.168.0.1	IP-192.168.0.5	AP 20:1F	11	65%	TCP TELNET
15		Client B9:AA		1	52%	802.11 ACK
17	IP-192.168.0.5	IP-192.168.0.1	AP 20:1F	11	48%	TCP TELNET
18		AP 20:1F		1	65%	802.11 ACK
19	IP-192.168.0.1	IP-192.168.0.5	AP 20:1F	11	65%	TCP TELNET
20		Client B9:AA		1	52%	802.11 ACK

Notice that in Packet 8, an 11-Mbps data transmission (some Telnet data) is sent from 192.168.0.1 to 192.168.0.5. In Packet 9, the recipient (192.168.0.5) sends back an 801.11 ACK packet. This packet originates at the MAC layer in the station and, hence, does not have a source address. Notice, too, that the ACK, as with all 802.11 control and management packets, is transmitted at 1 Mbps. This printout is representative of normal behavior. It can also be inferred that the analyzer is located closer to the AP than to the client machine itself. Notice how the Telnet packets (coming from the AP) have almost consistently higher signal strengths.

If we assume that the Retry Count statistic observed with the analyzer remained at zero during this capture, then we could conclude that this environment would be suitable with signal strengths as low as 48 percent. By itself, this conclusion is meaningless. If, however, at some point in the future, it was observed that a high rate of errors were present and the signal strength were still 48 percent or better, then it's clear that signal strength alone is not a specific cause of the newly observed errors. By measuring signal strength in a normally operating network, you develop a baseline of performance that can then be used as a point of comparison if the network later experiences problems. The key thing that was meaningful in this capture is the fact that each data packet was met with an 802.11 ACK, and that the conversation proceeded with an 11-Mbps data rate for user data. All is good.

Network Utilization

When a station transmits data, it generates a certain amount of RF signal energy into the space surrounding its antenna. The signal frequency being transmitted spreads across several narrow channel bands both above and below the one on which the station is transmitting. This is the essence of spread spectrum transmission. If two stations attempt to transmit at the same time on the same channel, the result is that the two signals interfere with each other and probably destroy the bit pattern being transmitted by the other station. This is referred to as a *collision*, and it's very similar to the way that Ethernet stations can experience collisions on a shared-medium Ethernet (such as 10Base2 coaxial ThinNet).

A good approximation of the RF signal density can be obtained by ascertaining the number of bits that are actually transmitted in a particular environment. Remember that Shannon's Channel Capacity Theorem sets an upper bound on how many bits can be successfully recovered from a particular environment, and the upper bound is based on the noise present (given a fixed 2.4-GHz band transmission).

Signal Strength, Bad Packets, and Network Utilization

Assume that you are evaluating a particular network operating at an average 40 percent bandwidth utilization and you discover that the typical signal strength shown by your analyzer is between 60 and 100 percent. You look at the packet statistics and find that 20 percent of the packets at 11 Mbps are bad. On a different network, also operating at about 40 percent utilization, you find that the typical signal strength is between 25 and 40 percent, but on this network, too, there are about 20 percent bad 11-Mbps packets. Please realize that both of these networks are currently operating with essentially the same performance characteristics. They are equally good and equally bad. The fact that the signal strength varies may be due to a difference in noise level, multipath reflection, or other environmental factors. The fact that both networks are able to carry 11 Mbps with the same packet loss rate means that, from the perspective of the user community, both networks provide the same performance.

The most important characteristic of a WLAN is its ability to carry data. When evaluating the various metrics that are provided by a WLAN analyzer, the first assessment must be relative to packet corruption, and not simply to the raw measurement of signal strength.

Checksum Errors

Packets may be captured that show a CRC (checksum) error. This would be the result of some type of packet corruption and could be caused by environmental noise or collisions between packets. A packet with a CRC error is discarded by a normal client machine and it's just as if it were never sent. You can see it with your WLAN analyzer, however. In some extreme cases, it may be discovered that as many as 30 percent of all packets experience CRC errors and must be retransmitted by the upper-layer protocol stack in the originating machine. Of course, in an extreme case like this, the throughput observed by the user would only be 70 percent of what's expected. The data rate may continue at 11 Mbps, but the CRC errors will reduce the overall effective throughput.

Site Survey Techniques for WLAN Troubleshooting

There are three distinct phases to the site survey process: initial design of the survey process and the network, field measurement, and validation. The initial design begins with a scale drawing of the site and an assessment of the building construction and awareness of potential factors that may degrade an 802.11 transmission. Next, a preliminary location selection for AP placement is made (or, if the network is already installed, the actual locations are used), marking each location on the drawing. A circle is drawn around each AP showing the anticipated and expected coverage area. Now the drawing is taken into the field and an AP is put into position. Measurements are made based on the Beacon packets transmitted every 100 milliseconds by the AP, and an initial signal strength assessment is made. If everything looks good, then it's time to validate the findings by actually transmitting data through the network to confirm that the desired data rate will be supported.

Estimating Effective Range

Based on the building construction (or outdoor environment factors), the radius of predicted transmission must be established. Do you think an AP will cover a 50-foot radius, a 100-foot radius, or a 1000-foot radius? Some value must be selected. One way to experimentally select a radius for expected transmission range is to simply set up an AP and measure the signal using Beacon packets for the test. There is a specific lower limit of raw signal strength at which a particular vendor's NIC enters the roaming mode and attempts to locate alternative APs to which it can associate. You can find out from your card vendor what this lower limit is, or simply use 25 percent as a reasonable guess. Use a signal strength that is 10 percent higher than the roaming limit as the minimum acceptable level for the range experiment.

Place an AP in a reasonable location at the site and begin capturing Beacon packets with your analyzer. Examine the real-time signal strength indication. Move to each of the four corners of the area being tested and confirm that the unobstructed signal strength remains above the minimum level (35 percent in our example). Now move outside the area being tested (and close the door if you're inside a building). Measure the signal strength on the far side of each wall of the area under test. Try to pick a worst-case location, perhaps behind a concrete fire wall or through a room filled with metal shelving units. At some point you'll reach the 35 percent minimum signal strength level and then you'll have a benchmark range to use in your initial network design.

AP Placement Considerations

Let's assume that you discover that 100 feet is the radius for expected transmission range for your environment. Also, assume that the building is of consistent construction. If one part of the building is plaster on lath dating from the 1940s, and a new section is poured concrete with steel reinforcing rod, then you'll have to develop a range value for each section. Go to your scale drawing of the site and mark the intended location of your APs. Don't forget the following important considerations when selecting AP locations:

- An AP located on the exterior wall of a building not only transmits into the building, but also makes the network accessible from the exterior of the building.

- No single point on the site map should be covered by more than two APs.

- When two or three APs cover the same area, they should be configured to transmit on different channels. When possible, use Channels 1, 6, and 11. This guideline is somewhat vendor specific. Some vendors require that all APs in a network be configured on the same channel. Read your AP documentation carefully.

- Channels 1, 6, and 11 use completely separate frequency ranges and thus do not conflict with each other in the electromagnetic spectrum. A station transmitting on one of these three channels does not corrupt the transmission on either of the other two. Remember that some vendors require single-channel operation and, in that case, there may be more collisions.

Using these guidelines, draw circles on the site map to indicate the area of coverage for each AP. Table 4.5 shows transmission range (radius) and the area of the space covered.

COMPARING CRC ERRORS TO SIGNAL STRENGTH

There are no universal rules for setting the threshold of acceptable performance relative to CRC errors or signal strength. The two metrics must be compared to see if CRC errors are present even in the presence of a strong signal. To provide a starting point for determining what's good and what's bad, we can make several general assumptions:

- ◆ Signal strength over 75 percent is strong.

- ◆ Signal strength under 25 percent is weak.

- ◆ If more than 10 percent of all packets experience CRC errors, that's cause for concern.

Table 4.5   Transmission Range and Area

RADIUS	AREA
50 ft	7,854 ft^2
100 ft	31,415 ft^2
150 ft	70,685 ft^2
200 ft	125,663 ft^2

An open warehouse 100 feet long and 250 feet wide is 25,000 sq. feet. That's a big space, but it may be possible to provide 802.11 wireless access using a single AP in the middle. In a school or office building (with more signal attenuation through the walls), you may be able to cover four rooms (or more) with a single AP located in the inside corner where the four rooms join.

Troubleshooting Network Design Problems

Some thought must be given to the criticality of the site survey being performed. If a network is going to be extended through a single warehouse building, the design is perhaps much less critical than a master plan that is going to be used to install APs in corporate offices or school buildings across the country. It may be sufficient to do very simple field testing of the proposed design, or it may be critical to carefully measure real-world performance. As long as you follow the guideline about two or three APs with overlapping coverage being configured to transmit on different channels, then you can't have too many APs. If cost is not a major consideration, and if the channel and overlap requirements for AP coverage are followed, then the more APs you have, the better your network will be.

If a design is going to be replicated in many locations, then it may be wise to perform an elaborate field verification. On the other hand, if the design is simple, then a simple verification may suffice. Let's consider an elaborate verification for a business network design. The building being tested contains offices to the left and right of a central corridor. To prove the design, you place a client computer in all of the offices within range of a single AP and start all of the client computers transferring files from a LAN-based server. Using a macro command, DOS batch file, or other automated operation, the client machines can be made to continuously transfer data.

Having created an extreme real-world traffic scenario, it's now a matter of confirming the ratio of CRC errors and retry packets to total data. Using your wireless analyzer, you can determine the impact of multiple transmitters in the environment at the same time. Once the viability of the design for a single AP coverage area has been established, it's reasonable to extrapolate those findings to other APs in similar environments in the design. If this office building had 20 floors, it would be reasonable to perform a detailed site survey on only one floor and extrapolate those results to the other floors.

The key consideration in the validation phase of the site survey is to determine whether the interaction between active users in the real-world network environment will have a detrimental impact on performance. There are some detailed engineering foundations to this assessment, but, in general, it requires an experimental trial to ascertain the threshold of degradation. Some factors that should be taken into consideration are the average packet size anticipated in the network and the number of users who will be simultaneously transmitting data. Both of these are often difficult to predict.

Large Packets and Collisions

With file transfer or database applications (as opposed to host/terminal applications), the average packet size tends to be large. Even though the CSMA/CA algorithm is relatively effective at preventing unduly high rates of collisions, there is an upper boundary to the available bandwidth. The *fragmentation threshold* (a configurable parameter in an AP and wireless NIC) can be lowered, causing large Ethernet packets to be broken into smaller groups of 802.11 packets. Because each packet is smaller, other stations may be able to jump into the WM and take turns without as many collisions. The fragmentation threshold defines the threshold above which the MAC layer will fragment packets into a series of smaller packets.

Large packets tend to result in a statistically higher probability of collisions occurring between two or more stations that are waiting for the large packet transmission to end. When the large-packet transmission is finished, all of the stations that were waiting have more chance of colliding with each other. Because a larger (and therefore longer in terms of time) packet introduces a higher probability of having more than one station waiting to transmit, longer average packet lengths result in higher collision probability. This is why the fragmentation process and the fragmentation threshold exist. In an environment where the average packet size (as measured with your protocol analyzer) is above 800 bytes, it may be advantageous to experimentally lower the fragmentation threshold to 1024 bytes and see if performance improves. Performance can be measured by transferring a single large file (1 GB, for example) and timing how long it takes for the transfer to complete. Try it with different values for the fragmentation threshold and compare the results.

Numerous Simultaneous Users and Collisions

The more people who are using the WLAN, the more chance there is that two of them are going to transmit at essentially the same time and cause a collision. Also, when more people are accessing the WLAN, the time that any one of them may have to wait before taking a turn sending a packet increases. Each AP manufacturer specifies the maximum number of associations that its hardware supports. Don't exceed that number! In general, three or fewer simultaneous users usually experience essentially no interference, but beyond that number, the probability of collisions goes up.

Practical Limits on User Community Size

The actual number of users that can operate in any particular environment depends on the type of user activity, the type of data, and the underlying data rate. Imagine a site where each floor of a building has two parallel hallways, with rooms on both sides, for a total of 16 rooms, such as the site illustrated in Figure 4.5.

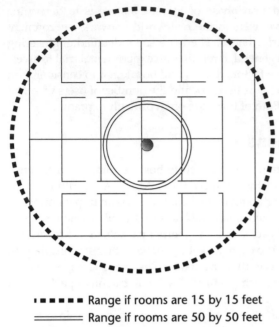

▪▪▪▪▪ Range if rooms are 15 by 15 feet
══════ Range if rooms are 50 by 50 feet

Figure 4.5   A building floor with two hallways and rooms on both sides.

If each room is a single-person office, then the radius of required transmission range for a single AP is probably less than 100 feet (assuming the offices are approximately 15 square feet each). There are only 16 users within range of the AP, and this isn't going to create a problem.

If each room is a classroom in a school building, then perhaps the rooms are each 50 square feet and there may be 25 or 30 users in each room simultaneously accessing the network. Notice in Figure 4.5 how the coverage of the AP is clearly good enough for one of these rooms but may not quite be good enough to cover four adjacent rooms. For the sake of discussion, let's assume that the coverage is quite good and four rooms can be completely covered by one centrally located AP. Now there are perhaps over 100 users attempting to associate to the single AP. Some vendors' APs won't support association by 100 simultaneous users. In that case, more APs will be required. The interesting fact, though, is that the students in the classroom may not require the same high (11-Mbps) data rate that would be expected by the business user in an office. Some degradation due to collisions would probably be more acceptable in a classroom than in a business office.

In the first scenario, it seems reasonable that one AP per floor would work, and in the second scenario one AP in the center of each room may be required. This is where validation of the network design in the real world defines the requirements for the installation. It is interesting to note, however, that a network with more potential users associating to a single AP is often a good candidate for tolerance of some performance degradation, as in the school classroom example.

Configuration Settings

A wireless NIC and AP have various configuration option settings, some of which can affect network performance. This section describes some of the typical configuration option settings.

IP Address

An AP probably has a default IP address that is used to log into and manage the AP across an Ethernet network. If an AP is shipped with a default IP address of 192.168.1.250, for example, then it is necessary to change the IP address of a client machine on the network so that it is also in network 192.168.1.0, thus allowing direct access (via an ARP) to the AP. Once you are able to access the AP, the first thing you should do is set the IP address in the AP to an address that is consistent with the IP addressing scheme in use on the network to which the AP is attached. Remember that as soon as you change the IP address of the AP, you'll no longer be able to communicate with it until you return the IP address of your configuration machine back to one that is also consistent with the network. Now, your station and the AP both have valid addresses and configuration can proceed.

ESSID

The Extended Service Set ID (ESSID) is a text string that is a unique name shared among all APs in the ESS. It is case sensitive.

Fragmentation Threshold

This is the Ethernet packet size above which the wireless transmitter fragments the packet into a series of smaller packets. Leave this value at the manufacturer's default setting unless you are experiencing performance degradation. Then reduce it to 1024 bytes and check throughput again. Raise (and lower) the value in 100-byte jumps and continue to monitor performance. You want the value to be as high as possible. As you increase the value, continue to test throughput. Attempt to determine the value at which throughput is maximized. Obviously, your test data transmission must have packets larger than the fragmentation threshold in order to perform the experimental configuration.

Request to Send (RTS) Threshold

Some devices include this parameter. It is the packet size above which the *Clear to Send / Request To Send* (CTS/RTS) mechanism is invoked for packet transmission. In a network with many collisions, it may be helpful to reduce this value to 1024 (and then test experimentally for performance gains).

Authentication Type

You may need to specify Open System versus Shared Key authentication for the card or AP. Open System allows any station to associate with the AP. Shared Key requires WEP encryption.

Wired Equivalent Privacy (WEP) Key and Passphrase

When WEP packet encryption is used, then either one or four *WEP keys* are specified. As a way to make it easier to create the hex values used in the WEP keys, a *passphrase* may be input that is converted into the WEP key values.

Understanding the 802.11 Packet Decode

When a WLAN analyzer is used to capture and decode packets, you should see many fields relative to 802.11. This section briefly describes each of these fields. It's important to remember that some of the information disclosed by a packet analyzer goes beyond that which is critical and relevant to field network troubleshooting. Some fields simply come under the umbrella of information that is nice to know, as opposed to information that you need to know.

Here is an example (taken from the WildPackets AiroPeek analyzer) of an 802.11 MAC header. A brief description of each field follows.

```
802.11 MAC Header
  Version:           0
  Type:              %10    Data
  Subtype:           %0000  Data Only
  To DS:             1
  From DS:           0
  More Frag.:        0
  Retry:             0
  Power Mgmt:        0
  More Data:         0
  WEP:               0
  Order:             0
  Duration:          314    Microseconds
  BSSID:             00:A0:F8:8B:20:1F   AP 20:1F
  Source:            00:A0:F8:9B:B9:AA   Client B9:AA
  Destination:       00:90:27:44:B1:FF
  Seq. Number:       328
  Frag. Number:      0
```

Version   This two-bit field is set to binary 00 when the IEEE 802.11 standard is in use. All other values are reserved.

Type and Subtype   These fields identify the type of frame (data, control, or management) and the specific subtype of frame that is being sent. Subtypes include frames such as a simple Data Only frame, an RTS control frame, or an Authentication or Association Request management frame.

The following eight fields are each a single bit flag where 1 is the True condition.

- **To DS**   Indicates the frame was sent to the DS from a wireless end station.

- **From DS**   Indicates the frame was sent from the DS to a wireless end station.

- **More Frag**   Indicates that this frame is one of many fragments of a larger frame. When an Ethernet (or wireless frame queued for transmission) exceeds the length set in the fragmentation threshold configuration parameter, then it is broken into smaller pieces for transmission. Each piece is given a sequence number. When the last piece is received (as evidenced by the More Frag flag returning to 0), the resulting frames are reassembled into the original large one.

- **Retry**   This bit is set when a frame is the second or greater attempt to transmit. The original frame was sent, but no ACK frame was received in response, so a retry was initiated. The retry bit aids a receiver in discarding multiple copies of a retransmitted frame.

- **Power Mgmt**   This bit indicates the power save mode in which the station will be after the successful completion of the current frame exchange sequence. A value of 1 indicates that the station will be in power save mode. This bit is somewhat subtle in its meaning. To understand the bit, remember that a current frame may be part of a series of frames making up a fragmented data block. Or, a station may have transmitted a frame and is now waiting for an ACK. Therefore, there are situations where a station will have completed its current data exchange process after some number of additional frames. The power management bit is set to a 1 to indicate that the station is going to enter the power save mode after completion of the data exchange activity in which it is currently involved.

- **More Data**   This field is closely related to the Power Mgmt field. When a station receives a frame with the More Data bit set, it knows that the transmitter has more data pending, beyond the currently received frame. The receiving station postpones entering the power save mode because it realizes that the sender has more data pending that will be sent in subsequent frames. If a station sends a frame with the Power Mgmt bit set, the recipient may send back a frame with the More Data bit set. The result is that the power save mode is not entered when the first station completes its data exchange.

■ **WEP**   The WEP bit indicates that the frame body has been encrypted using the WEP algorithm.

■ **Order**   This bit is set to 1 when a frame is sent using a special class of transmission service called the strictly ordered service class.

Duration   This is the predicted number of microseconds that a transmitter believes the network will be busy with the current frame, any required acknowledgment, and the associated interframe gaps. It is used by the CSMA/CA algorithm to allow stations to predict when the network media will be idle, and thereby minimize collisions.

BSSID   This is the physical MAC address of the AP to which a station has associated or from which the frame has been sent.

Source   This is the Ethernet source address of the station that originally sent the frame.

Destination   This is the Ethernet destination address of the station to which the frame is intended.

Receiver   This is the physical address on the WM to which a frame is addressed, when such addressing is being used. This is not present in the example printout.

Transmitter   This is the physical address on the WM from which a frame was transmitted, when such addressing is being used. This is not present in the example printout.

Seq. Number   Each frame contains a sequence number (modulo 4096) that uniquely identifies it.

Frag. Number   When a frame is one of many in a fragmented data block, this number is the sequence of the fragment. All fragments of a frame carry the same Seq. Number and are differentiated by the incremental Frag. Number value.

Summary

This chapter has provided a basis for your further in-depth study of 802.11 WLAN engineering. Armed with the IEEE standards and a good WLAN analyzer, you will be able to explore the details and nuances of this growing technology. The steps that a wireless device goes through as it initializes and participates in a WLAN may vary from one implementation to another, but the basic principles of RF engineering and 802.11 behavior presented in this chapter remain fairly consistent.

There is no better source for additional information than the IEEE 802.11 standard itself. There is no better way to learn how to recognize and understand the protocol behaviors present in a WLAN than to capture packets with a WLAN analyzer and study them.

Because the history of the wireless marketplace is much shorter than that of the Ethernet world, and because the collective experience of the engineering experts doesn't stretch back over 30 years, there are sure to be some surprises. The guidelines for proper operation will be solidified as more diverse real-world implementations are examined. The integration of 802.11, Bluetooth, and other wireless technologies will surely provide technical challenges that continue long past the useful life of this book. The technical foundation presented here, though, will continue to serve as a springboard to understanding and troubleshooting many types of complex wireless networks.

In the next two chapters, we will continue to explore the lower levels of network operation and troubleshooting. You will be introduced to the Spanning Tree Algorithm that switches use to prevent loops and to Virtual LANs (VLANs), which might be used to segregate stations and APs into separate logical groups. The upcoming topics have relevance in the wired world of Ethernet and in the integrated WLAN/LAN environment.

Troubleshooting and Analyzing the Spanning Tree Protocol

The Spanning Tree Protocol (STP), also known as the Spanning Tree Algorithm, is one of the most important technologies in a campus network. STP allows bridges that are physically connected in a redundant topology to dynamically discover a tree topology that spans the bridged network but has no loops. Because an Ethernet switch is fundamentally a high-speed transparent bridge, STP has gained prominence as a major protocol running on campus networks. In the past, little time was spent troubleshooting STP because it operated on a few bridges in a mostly routed network and it did its job without intervention. In today's campus networks, which have numerous switches connected in redundant topologies, a network engineer may spend a lot of time optimizing and troubleshooting STP. This chapter will help you understand how STP works, how to examine its behavior with a protocol analyzer, and how to enhance its performance using Cisco switch commands. The chapter also covers the basic behavior of transparent bridges, and what to expect when analyzing packets that cross a transparent bridge.

Poetic Interoperations

This chapter discusses the classic bridge and its evolution into today's version, which is called a *switch*. In fact, the interconnect box that is mounted in the rack in the wiring closet may be called a router, but some of its functionality may actually be that of a switch. It's amazing that when three marketing people go out to lunch with one engineer, they come back with terminology that doesn't always reflect the way something actually works. In every case, however, the field engineer must be aware of how the actual engineering technology is implemented, and that's how troubleshooting becomes successful. Joseph Bardwell put it this way:

> *Making The Connection*
> *Sometimes it amazes me*
> *that routers work at Layer 3*
> *when switches very well could do*
> *the job at simply Layer 2*
> *But switches work at Layer 3*
> *Oh, how confusing this can be*
> *When bridges work at Layer 2*
> *and routers can be bridges too!*
> *And when you hope there'd be no more*
> *you find a switch at Layer 4*
> *So Layer 4, and 2, and 3*
> *imply OSI conformity*
> *But these are simply building blocks*
> *in what we'll call an "Interconnect Box"*

Transparent Bridging

STP is documented in the Institute of Electrical and Electronics Engineers (IEEE) 802.1D standard, which describes the behavior of Media Access Control (MAC) transparent bridges. A transparent bridge creates an interconnection of stations attached to separate Local Area Network (LAN) segments and allows the stations to communicate as if they were attached to a single LAN segment. The bridge is transparent to protocols operating above the MAC layer. Before you can understand the details of STP, you should learn the basics of transparent bridging, as discussed in this section.

Transparent bridges were first developed at Digital Equipment Corporation (DEC) in the early 1980s. DEC submitted its work to the IEEE, which incorporated the work into the IEEE 802.1D standard. Transparent bridges are common in Ethernet/IEEE 802.3 networks, especially on campus networks built around Layer 2 switches. A Layer 2 Ethernet switch is, in essence, a high-speed transparent bridge. In the historical perspective, bridges came first. They allowed multiple network segments to be interconnected, but only one frame could be forwarded across the bridge at a time. The basic concept that sets a switch apart from a bridge is the fact that a switch allows multiple frames to participate in the forwarding process simultaneously. At the same time that Client 1's frame is being forwarded to Server 1, for example, Client 2's frame can be forwarded to Server 2. There are many varieties of switch design, but the fundamental aspect of simultaneous frame forwarding is inherent to all. Throughout this chapter, we use the term *bridge* when discussing fundamental technology, because that is the term used in formal specifications, such as IEEE 802.1D. Throughout the chapter, you can substitute the term *switch* for *bridge*.

TROUBLESHOOTING SOMETHING THAT IS TRANSPARENT CAN BE DIFFICULT

Because the contents of a frame passing through a bridge in an Ethernet network are not changed in any way, there is no way for a protocol analysis tool to determine whether a bridge forwarded a frame. The bridge is truly transparent. As a result, issues related to bridging topology may be hidden from the engineer performing analysis. One of the authors saw an extreme example of this in the late 1980s, when the industry's collective awareness of bridging issues in large networks was less complete than it is today. A multinational company had a manufacturing facility located on a Caribbean island. The company's data center was located one mile down the road from the manufacturing facility, with a private T1 link between the two sites. The company was experiencing extremely slow communication between the two sites, and the network engineers called for a consultant to fly down to the Caribbean and help troubleshoot the problem. It was a tough job, but somebody had to do it.

After a careful analysis of the network architecture, the consultant found the source of the performance degradation. The company had a flat, bridged network, including Wide Area Network (WAN) bridges linking various sites. The consultant discovered that frames were being bridged from the data center, through a satellite link to a site in Virginia, through land lines to a second site in Texas, and then through a second satellite link back to the manufacturing facility, one mile down the road. With an understanding of bridging technology, the problem was solvable.

Transparent bridges are so named because their presence and operation are transparent to network hosts. Transparent bridges are also invisible from a protocol analysis and network management point of view, with some exceptions. When a bridge sends Bridge Protocol Data Unit (BPDU) frames or other control frames, such as Cisco Discovery Protocol (CDP) or VLAN Trunk Protocol (VTP) frames, an analyzer learns a MAC address for the bridge. When a host sends a frame through a bridge, however, there is no evidence in the frame of the bridge having forwarded the frame. The bridge's address does not appear in the frame.

Bridges are transparent. Routers are not. Consider the network in Figure 5.1. Assume a protocol analyzer is attached to a hub port on Segment B. What MAC and Internet Protocol (IP) addresses will the analyzer see if the interconnect device is a bridge versus a router?

We'll take the bridge case first. In the first example, assume that the subnet mask is 255.255.0.0 and that both Host A and Host B are in network 172.16.0.0. When Host A wishes to send IP traffic to Host B, Host A sends an Address Resolution Protocol (ARP) broadcast frame to find the MAC address for Host B. The bridge forwards the frame. As a side effect of this process, the bridge also learns that Host A's MAC address is reachable via the interface on which Host A's frame arrived. In this example, the bridge learns that Host A's MAC address is reachable via Ethernet interface 0/1 (*e 0/1* in the figure). The bridge stores this information in its bridging table. The bridging table is also sometimes called the MAC address table, the station cache, or Content Addressable Memory (CAM).

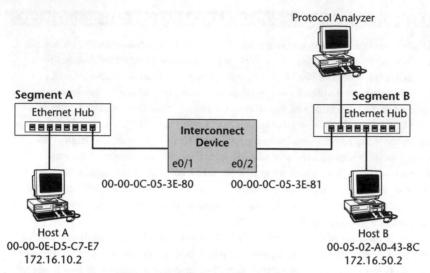

Figure 5.1   An interconnect device with two hosts.

When Host B responds to the ARP frame, Host A learns the MAC address to use for Host B. In addition, the bridge learns which of its interfaces connects to Host B and stores this information in its bridging table. The bridging table is a list of MAC addresses and the interface number to use to reach each address. For example, the following output shows the bridging table on a Cisco Catalyst 1900 switch. Notice that the switch has learned that Host A (0000.0ED5.C7E7) is reachable via Ethernet interface 0/1 and Host B (0005.02A0.438C) is reachable via Ethernet interface 0/2.

```
SwitchA#show mac-address-table
Number of permanent addresses : 0
Number of restricted static addresses : 0
Number of dynamic addresses : 2
Address             Dest Interface    Type         Source
Interface List
-------------------------------------------------
0000.0ED5.C7E7      Ethernet 0/1      Dynamic      All
0005.02A0.438C      Ethernet 0/2      Dynamic      All
```

After learning the MAC address for Host B, Host A sends an IP packet to Host B. Host A places its own MAC and IP addresses in the source address fields and Host B's MAC and IP addresses in the destination address fields. Host A is unaware that Host B is on the other side of a bridge. The bridge is transparent. The bridge forwards the packet without changing it. The bridge does not insert its own addresses in to the frame. A protocol analyzer residing on Segment B sees the packet from Host A and records the source MAC and IP addresses as those of Host A. The analyzer records the destination MAC and IP addresses as those of Host B. The MAC address of the bridge is irrelevant. Following is protocol analyzer output for the IP packet sent by Host A.

```
Ethernet Header
  Destination:  00:05:02:A0:43:8C
  Source:       00:00:0E:D5:C7:E7
  Protocol Type:0x0800  IP
IP Header - Internet Protocol Datagram
  Version:              4
  Header Length:        5  (20  bytes)
  Type of Service:      %00000000
  Precedence: Routine, Normal Delay, Throughput, Reliability
  Total Length:         48
  Identifier:           14610
  Fragmentation Flags:  %010  Do Not Fragment   Last Fragment
  Fragment Offset:      0  (0  bytes)
  Time To Live:         128
  Protocol:             6  TCP
  Header Checksum:      0x8006
  Source IP Address:    172.16.10.2
  Dest. IP Address:     172.16.50.2
```

Now, let's consider the case where the interconnect device is a router. Assume for this part of the example that the subnet mask is 255.255.255.0 and that Host A is configured with the router as its default gateway. In this case, Host A sends an ARP for the router because Host A can tell from the subnet mask that it cannot reach Host B directly. Host A must depend on its default gateway (router). After learning the MAC address of the router's local Ethernet interface, Host A sends its IP packet to Host B. At the data link layer, Host A sends the packet to the router. At the IP layer, Host A sends the packet to Host B.

The router receives the packet, strips the data link layer header, and examines IP configuration and routing data in Random Access Memory (RAM) to determine how to forward the packet. The router determines that the packet should exit Ethernet interface 0/2 and should contain Host B's MAC address as the destination MAC address. The router checks its ARP cache to determine if it knows a MAC address for Host B. If it does not, the router sends an ARP broadcast to get the MAC address. The router then encapsulates the frame in a new data link layer header and sends the frame out Ethernet interface 0/2. Following is protocol analyzer output for the IP packet sent by Host A. The analyzer is connected to the hub on Segment B and sees the frame after the router has forwarded it. Notice that the source MAC address belongs to the router. The source and destination IP addresses belong to the hosts.

```
Ethernet Header
  Destination:  00:05:02:A0:43:8C
  Source:       00:00:0C:05:3E:81
  Protocol Type:0x0800  IP
IP Header - Internet Protocol Datagram
  Version:              4
  Header Length:        5  (20  bytes)
  Type of Service:      %00000000
  Precedence: Routine, Normal Delay, Throughput, Reliability
  Total Length:         48
  Identifier:           25696
```

```
Fragmentation Flags:   %010  Do Not Fragment    Last Fragment
Fragment Offset:       0  (0  bytes)
Time To Live:          128
Protocol:              6  TCP
Header Checksum:       0xD5BB
Source IP Address:     172.16.10.2
Dest. IP Address:      172.16.50.2
```

Bridging Tasks

From the previous section, you can see that a bridge is a simpler device than a router and that a bridge has just a few jobs. A bridge listens promiscuously to every frame transmitted on all its connected interfaces. A bridge learns where MAC addresses reside and maintains a bridging table. A bridge forwards frames. Notice that a bridge forwards frames, not bits. A repeater (hub) forwards bits without regard for traffic already existing on the output medium. A repeater increases the size of an Ethernet collision domain, as discussed in Chapter 3. A bridge, on the other hand, segments collision domains. A bridge forwards a frame onto a medium after sensing the carrier and making sure no other device is already sending on the attached medium.

For each frame received, a bridge examines its bridging table to determine if the destination address is in the table with information on which interface to use for the address. If the address is found in the table, the bridge forwards the frame out only that interface. If the interface in the table is the same as the interface on which the frame arrived, however, the bridge drops the frame. This dropping of frames that don't need forwarding is called *filtering*.

If the destination address is not found in the bridging table, the bridge forwards the frame out all interfaces except the one on which it was received. This forwarding of frames where the interface cannot be determined is called *flooding unknown destinations* or *flooding unknown unicasts*. A bridge also floods broadcast and multicast frames.

Bridging Loops

To increase the resiliency of their campus networks, most network engineers design their switched networks with redundancy. For example, Cisco recommends that each end-user switch in an Intermediate Distribution Frame (IDF) wiring closet be connected to two high-end switches in the Main Distribution Frame (MDF) wiring closet of a building. For a large campus network, MDF switches may also be connected redundantly to high-end core (backbone) switches. The core switches may connect servers. Figure 5.2 shows a typical campus network design per Cisco recommendations. A design such as this offers high availability. Without STP, however, the loops in the topology cause problems.

There are three problems with loops in a bridged network. First, a host may receive more than one copy of a frame. Second, a bridge may become confused regarding where MAC addresses reside. Third, the flooding of broadcast, multicast, and unknown destination frames causes the frames to loop endlessly, resulting in excessive bandwidth utilization and high CPU utilization at the stations receiving the frames. To explain these situations, Figure 5.2 has been simplified to a network that contains two bridges and two hosts. The simplified network is shown in Figure 5.3.

UNKNOWN DESTINATIONS

In theory, once a network has stabilized and bridges have stopped flooding unknown unicast frames, unicast frames moving between a particular client and server should not be visible in any part of the interconnected network except on the bridging path between the client and the server. However, if bridging tables overflow (because of the sheer quantity of traffic), then the destination address in some of the frames will be treated as an unknown destination. Capturing traffic with a protocol analyzer will reveal these frames in parts of the network that are not on the bridging path between the client and the server. Sometimes an analyst's initial assessment is that STP is not working properly (because frames are appearing in locations where they obviously don't belong). The reality may be simply that bridges are performing their normal forwarding process for unknown destinations. Of course, this may be indicative of a need to further troubleshoot the loading of the network and the capacity of the bridges.

One of the authors was called in to troubleshoot a hospital campus network consisting of several buildings star-connected back to a central data center with fiber optic Ethernet repeater links. Each remote building had an edge switch with a fiber connection. In the data center it was found that entire bidirectional conversations between clients in remote buildings and servers in the same remote building were visible on the data center backbone. At first it was thought that the forwarding path between a client and server was extending through the data center somehow, which was not the intent of the network design. Upon further analysis, it was discovered that the switches used in the remote buildings only supported 256 MAC addresses in the bridging tables. Consequently, with over 500 users in each remote building, it was common for many addresses to become unknown. The recommendation was made to replace the remote building switches with ones having greater capacity, thereby eliminating the unnecessary traffic on the data center backbone.

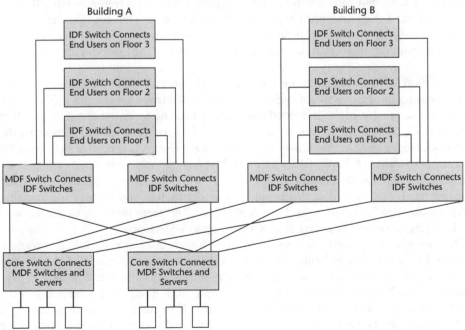

Figure 5.2 A redundant campus network design that offers high availability.

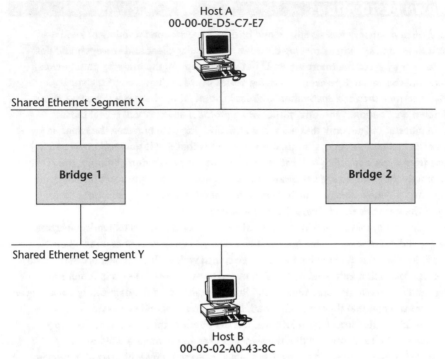

Figure 5.3   A simple bridged network with a loop.

Consider what happens when Host A in Figure 5.3 sends a frame to Host B. Both bridges forward the frame onto Segment Y. Host B receives two copies of the frame. Many upper-layer protocols can deal with this error and simply drop the duplicate. Some upper-layer protocols, however, may be confused by the reception of a duplicate frame.

In addition to the duplicate frame, a second problem occurs. Both bridges forward the frame, causing the bridges to see each other's forwarded frames on Segment Y. Because the bridges see each other's forwarded frames, they become confused about the position of Host A. On Bridge 1, the forwarded frame from Bridge 2 on Segment Y contains the source address of Host A. Previously, Bridge 1 thought Host A was reachable through its interface on Segment X. Now, Bridge 1 thinks Host A is reachable through its interface on Segment Y. Bridge 2 is also confused in the same way because it sees the forwarded frame from Bridge 1. A symptom of this problem is evident when you display the bridging (CAM) table. The information for Host A goes back and forth between two interfaces. The bridging table becomes corrupted when a network has loops.

The result of both switches forwarding the frames may not be looping frames. Assume for now that both bridges have learned the position of Host B. The bridging tables for both bridges state that Host B resides on the interface that connects to Segment Y. When Bridge 1 hears the forwarded frame from Bridge 2, Bridge 1 filters the frame and does not forward it back onto Segment Y or forward it onto Segment X. Bridge 2 also filters the frame it receives from Bridge 1. As mentioned earlier, if the entry in the bridging table for a destination address specifies the interface on which the frame arrived, the bridge drops (filters) the frame.

Now consider the case where the bridges have not yet learned which interface to use for Host B. There's no entry in the bridging table for Host B. When Host A sends the frame, both bridges forward the frame onto Segment Y. Both switches see each other's forwarded frames. The bridges look into their bridging tables, and, not finding Host B, send the frame back onto Segment X. On Segment X, the bridges see each other's forwarded frames, and forward them onto Segment Y. This forwarding of the frame continues forever, until the switches are rebooted, and then it starts again. With unknown unicast, multicast, and broadcast frames, the third problem occurs—the frames loop forever.

Let's consider broadcasts and multicasts in a bit more detail. The normal behavior for handling broadcasts is to send the broadcast out all ports. If there's a loop in the network, the frames get forwarded endlessly. This is typical behavior for multicasts also, unless the switch has advanced software to learn where multicast frames should go. Cisco's Web site contains information on the Cisco Group Management Protocol (CGMP) and the Internet Group Management Protocol (IGMP) Snooping features, which are methods for making switches smarter about the forwarding of multicast frames. See this URL: www.cisco.com/warp/public/473/22.html.

Because of these three problems (duplicate frames, bridging table corruption, and looping frames), it is necessary that some bridge interfaces be blocked from forwarding frames when a bridged network is constructed in a redundant fashion. The looped mesh network must be reduced to a simple tree topology. STP handles that requirement, as the next section describes.

STP Behavior

A tree is more than just a woody perennial plant with few limbs on its lower part. A tree is also a mathematical concept. A tree is a diagram or graph that branches from a single stem without forming loops or polygons. A computer network is usually not physically constructed as a tree because of the requirements to provide redundancy and avoid any single points of failure. STP prunes the physical topology of a bridged network into a logical tree topology.

Topology is more than just a word that Cisco and other vendors throw around when discussing network design. Topology is a branch of mathematics concerned with those properties of geometric configurations that are unaltered by elastic deformations such as stretching or twisting. (For example, did you know that according to topology principles, a doughnut is the same shape as a coffee cup? Think about it!)

To understand a tree topology, think about a document outline, a table of contents, a hierarchical org chart, cluster diagrams used in brainstorming, and genealogy charts. These are all trees. Unless brothers and sisters or cousins marry (which does happen sometimes), there is a single path between any two people in a genealogical tree. In a bridged or switched computer network, STP ensures that there is a single path between LANs. STP allows bridges to discover a loop-free, tree-shaped subset of the physical topology that spans the bridged network. In other words, STP produces a *spanning tree*.

> **NOTE** With networking, as with mathematics, the tree is usually drawn upside down. The root is placed at the top of the drawing.

Bridge Protocol Data Units

To develop the spanning tree, bridges transmit Bridge Protocol Data Unit (BPDU) messages to each other. In some cases these messages are referred to as *BPDU frames*, and in other cases (WildPackets EtherPeek, for example) they are called *802.1 Bridge Spanning Tree frames*. There are two types of BPDUs: topology change notification and configuration BPDUs. Bridges send topology change notification BPDUs when bridge ports change state. Bridges send configuration BPDUs continuously. A bridge uses configuration BPDUs to accomplish the following four tasks:

1. Participate with other bridges in the election of a single bridge as the Root Bridge.

2. Calculate the distance of the shortest path to the Root Bridge and choose a port (known as the *Root Port*) that provides the shortest path to the Root Bridge.

3. For each LAN segment, elect a *Designated Bridge* and a *Designated Port* on that bridge. The Designated Port is a port on the LAN segment that is closest to the Root Bridge. (All ports on the Root Bridge are Designated Ports.)

4. Select bridge ports to be included in the spanning tree. The ports selected are the Root Ports and Designated Ports. These ports forward traffic. Other ports block traffic.

Protocol Analysis of BPDUs

Using a protocol analyzer, you can analyze BPDU messages to help you troubleshoot problems with STP. This section describes the fields in a BPDU message per the IEEE 802.1D specification. In the *STP Convergence* section that follows, additional material is provided to help you understand BPDUs better. Figure 5.4 shows a configuration BPDU captured with the WildPackets EtherPeek analyzer.

By default, bridges send configuration BPDUs every 2 seconds, so it's easy to capture them with an analyzer. In fact, when troubleshooting non-STP problems, you may want to set a capture filter so that you don't capture BPDUs. Their quick arrival rate can be annoying when you are trying to troubleshoot an upper-layer problem. From a network performance point of view, however, it's beneficial that BPDUs are sent so often. Their frequency allows bridges to learn about topology changes quickly. BPDU frames are very short (64 bytes) and don't use a lot of bandwidth.

BPDU messages are sent to a multicast address for all bridges. The multicast address is 01:80:C2:00:00:00. The source address in a BPDU message is the MAC address of the port on the bridge that is transmitting the configuration message. (IEEE requires a bridge to have a distinct MAC address for each port.)

MULTIPLE VERSIONS OF THE SPANNING TREE

There are multiple versions of the STP. The two that are most common are the IEEE and DEC versions. This book covers the IEEE version. Most Cisco switches support only the IEEE version. Cisco routers configured to act as bridges support many varieties. Be careful not to use a non-IEEE version if you intend Cisco routers to interoperate with Cisco switches.

Each implementation uses a different multicast (or broadcast, in the case of DEC) address for sending BPDU frames. Imagine that a large, meshed, switched network topology was mistakenly configured so that some switches used IEEE spanning tree and others used DEC. The DEC-configured switches would not recognize that the IEEE BPDUs were anything other than normal multicasts, and the IEEE BPDUs would be forwarded everywhere. The same would be true in reverse for the DEC BPDUs when encountered by the IEEE-configured switches. It is possible to construct a topology in which these two overlapping spanning trees create a loop for user broadcast traffic. This could be disastrous.

When analyzing a network, note the destination address used for spanning tree frames. Wherever you insert your analyzer in a particular broadcast domain, you should always see the same destination address being used for spanning tree frames. If you see more than one destination address, then one or more switches are misconfigured.

Notice in Figure 5.4 that the Ethernet frame format for BPDUs is 802.3 with 802.2, also known as *IEEE 802.3 LSAP, ETHERNET_802.2*, or just plain *sap* in Cisco lingo. See Table 3.3 on page 76 for more information on the different names and types of Ethernet frames.

Figure 5.4   Protocol analysis of a configuration BPDU.

BPDU messages use a Logical Link Control (LLC) Service Access Point (SAP) of 0x42. In her terrific book, *Interconnections: Bridges, Routers, Switches, and Internetworking Protocols*, Radia Perlman, the primary inventor of STP, implies that the IEEE developers chose 42 because it is the meaning of life, at least if you adhere to Douglas Adams' philosophy. (Be sure to read Perlman's book as well as Adams' book, *The Hitchhiker's Guide to the Galaxy*, if you haven't already.) Perlman also notes that the SAP value of 0x42 is 01000010 in binary, which is the same forward and backward, which was important in the days of the Little Endian/Big Endian battles about bit order. (See the "Ethernet Frames" section of Chapter 3 of this book for more information on those battles.)

A Protocol Identifier is encoded in the first 2 bytes of all BPDUs. The IEEE 802.1D standard reserves a single Protocol Identifier value of 0x0000. The standard places no further restriction on the structure, encoding, or use by other protocols of BPDUs with different values for the Protocol Identifier field. The Protocol Version number follows the Protocol Identifier. The Protocol Version is 1 byte and is set to 0x00. The BPDU Type field follows and is 1 byte, with two possible values:

1. 0x00 for configuration BPDUs.
2. 0x80 for topology change notification BPDUs.

Topology change notification BPDUs have only the Protocol Identifier, Protocol Version, and BPDU Type fields, as shown in Figure 5.5. Configuration BPDUs have additional fields, which are described in the next sections.

Flags

The Flags field in a configuration BPDU is 1 byte. Figure 5.6 breaks down the bits in the Flags field. The least significant bit of the Flags field is the *topology change flag*. If set, the topology change flag bit indicates that the receiving bridge should use the *Forward Delay* parameter for aging the bridging table rather than the aging timer that is normally used. (The normal aging timer is 300 seconds. Forward Delay is 20 seconds by default.) The Root Bridge sets the topology change flag in configuration BPDUs when it gets notification that the topology has changed.

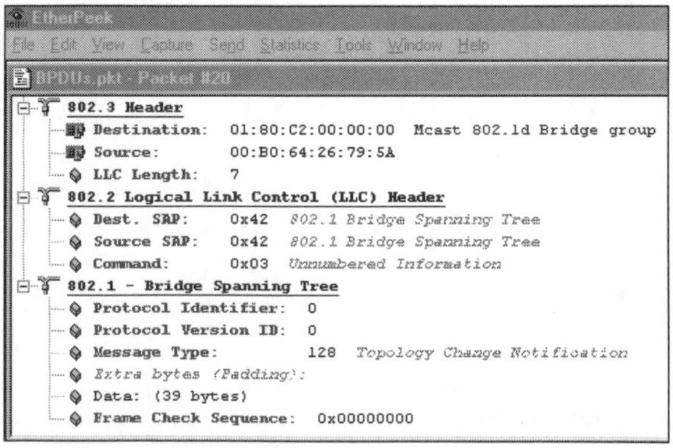

Figure 5.5 Protocol analysis of a topology change notification BPDU.

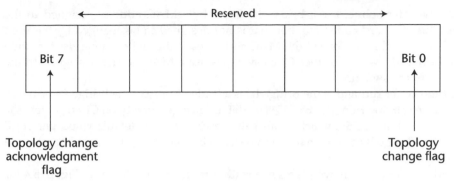

Figure 5.6   Format of the Flags field in a configuration BPDU.

The most significant bit of the Flags field is a *topology change acknowledgment flag*. A bridge sets this bit in configuration BPDUs to confirm receipt of a topology change notification BPDU. Bridges receiving a frame with this bit set no longer need to inform the upstream parent bridge that a topology change has occurred. The parent bridge will take responsibility for informing the Root Bridge of the topology change. Once the Root Bridge finally figures out that a change has occurred, it sets the topology change flag in its configuration message.

Notice that with STP, bad news travels uphill from the branches toward the root in the upside-down tree. A bridge that notices a problem sends *topology change notifications* until its upstream parent acknowledges them by setting the topology change acknowledgment flag in configuration BPDUs. The parent sends notifications upstream to its parent. Finally the root hears the news and sets the topology change flag in configuration BPDUs. See the *The Topology Change Process* section later in this chapter for more details on this process.

Bridge IDs

As mentioned earlier, a bridge has a unique address on each port. A bridge also has an overall *Bridge ID*. The Bridge ID is an important component of STP. The Root Bridge is the bridge with the lowest Bridge ID. A Bridge ID is an 8-byte field that is composed of two subfields, the *Bridge Priority* field and the MAC address of the bridge. Figure 5.7 illustrates the format of the Bridge ID field.

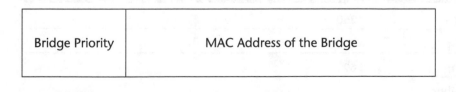

Figure 5.7   Format of a Bridge ID.

The low-order subfield of a Bridge ID is a 6-byte MAC address assigned to the bridge. This is a hard-coded number that is not designed to be changed by the user. Some Cisco switches use one of the MAC addresses of the switch supervisor module for the Bridge ID, whereas other Cisco switches use a MAC address assigned to the backplane of the switch.

The high-order subfield of the Bridge ID is a Bridge Priority. The Bridge Priority is a 2-byte value ranging from 0 to 65,535. The default Bridge Priority on Cisco switches is the middle value, 32,768, which is also the recommended default value per IEEE 802.1D. The Bridge ID can be changed in order to influence which bridge becomes the Root Bridge.

A Bridge ID appears in two places in a configuration BPDU. (Refer to Figure 5.4 for an example of a configuration BPDU.) First, the transmitting bridge specifies the Bridge ID of the bridge that it assumes is the Root Bridge. The EtherPeek analyzer that captured the frame in Figure 5.4 calls this field the *Root Priority/ID* field. The MAC address portion of the field probably looks familiar because it is in the traditional format used for MAC addresses. The Bridge Priority field may look unfamiliar because it is in hexadecimal format. The Bridge Priority for the Root Bridge is 0x8000, which is 32,768 in decimal (the Cisco and IEEE default value).

In addition to sending the Bridge ID of the Root Bridge, a bridge also sends its own Bridge ID. EtherPeek calls this field the *Bridge Priority/ID* field. In the example in Figure 5.4, this value is 0x8000/00:B0:64:26:79:42. Note that the bridge sending this BPDU does not think it is the Root Bridge. The transmitter's Bridge ID is not the same as the Root Bridge ID.

Cost of Path to Root

Bridges use the concept of *cost* to evaluate how close they are to the Root Bridge. Each LAN segment (link) has a cost. The total path cost to the Root Bridge is a 4-byte value that is the sum of the link costs to the Root Bridge. A link cost is based on the speed of the network. Table 5.1 shows the cost values for links with different speeds according to the 1998 version of the IEEE 802.1D specification. Note that some Cisco switches do not use these values yet. IEEE used to define the cost as 1000 divided by link speed. For example, a 100-Mbps interface had a cost of 10. Figure 5.4 shows a Cisco switch that specifies a cost of 0x0000000A (10 in decimal). The switch is not yet using the 1998 version of cost values.

Table 5.1   IEEE 802.1D Cost Values

LINK SPEED	RECOMMENDED COST VALUE
4 Mbps	250
10 Mbps	100
16 Mbps	62
100 Mbps	19
1 Gbps	4
10 Gbps	2

Port ID

In addition to having an overall Bridge ID, a bridge also has an ID associated with each port. The Port ID contains a priority field followed by a port number that identifies a physical port on a switch or bridge. In Figure 5.4, EtherPeek shows that the port priority is 0x0A (10 in decimal), which is not the default. The default value for port priority is 128 in decimal. (See the "Per-VLAN Spanning Trees" section of Chapter 6 for an explanation of why the default priority is not in use.) EtherPeek shows that the Port ID is 0x1B. The sending port was Fast Ethernet interface 0/27 on a Catalyst 1900 switch. Note that decimal 27 is 0x1B in hexadecimal.

Message Age

Message Age is the estimated time, in 1/256ths of a second, since the Root Bridge transmitted the configuration BPDU. The Root Bridge starts the sending of configuration BPDUs with a Message Age of zero. Other bridges propagate the BPDUs and add time to the Message Age. Although the IEEE allows bridges to add exact time, in practice, bridges add 1 second to the Message Age, so the Message Age acts like a hop count. Using an analyzer, you can estimate the logical size (number of hops) in your switched network's spanning tree by looking at Message Age values.

During normal operation, configuration BPDUs are refreshed quickly (every 2 seconds, by default), and Message Age is not used by the bridges. If connectivity to the Root Bridge fails, the Message Age field is used to track the age of any stale BPDUs that are currently saved or that arrive during the outage.

Maximum Age

Maximum Age is the time, in 1/256ths of a second, at which a configuration BPDU should be deleted. The Maximum Age timer controls the maximum length of time that a bridge port saves configuration BPDU information. The default Maximum Age value is 20 seconds. The Maximum Age can be configured at the Root Bridge. The other bridges learn the value from the Root Bridge. On Cisco switches, use either the `set spantree maxage` or the `spantree-template (max-age)` command to configure the Maximum Age timer.

Hello Time

Hello Time is the time, in 1/256ths of a second, between the generation of configuration BPDUs by the Root Bridge. The Hello Time also controls how often topology change notification BPDUs are re-sent until acknowledgment is received. The default Hello Time value is 2 seconds. Hello Time can be configured at the Root Bridge. On Cisco switches, use either the `set spantree hello` or the `spantree-template (hello-time)` command to configure the Hello Time.

Forward Delay

Forward Delay is the length of time, in 1/256ths of a second, that a bridge port should wait before changing its state from listening to learning and from learning to forwarding. A port starts in the blocking state. While in the blocking state, a port is not part of the spanning tree. The port listens to BPDUs but does not send BPDUs or forward user traffic. A port that becomes part of the active spanning tree topology transitions to the listening and learning states and then finally to a forwarding state. In the forwarding state, the port finally starts forwarding user traffic. See the *Port States* section later for more detail on these states.

The Forward Delay timer specifies how long a port waits in the listening state and also how long it waits in the learning state. The Forward Delay timer is also used as a timer for aging entries in the bridging table when the topology changes. The default value for Forward Delay is 15 seconds. The Forward Delay timer can be configured at the Root Bridge. On Cisco switches, use either the `set spantree fwddelay` or the `spantree-template (forwarding-time)` command to configure the Forward Delay timer.

> **CAUTION** If you are careful and know what you are doing, you can change STP timers such as *Maximum Age, Hello Time,* and *Forward Delay* by configuring the timer values at the Root Bridge. Changing the values is risky and not recommended in most cases. Avoid the frustration of changing the timers at a bridge that is not the Root Bridge. The timer changes only take effect if they are changed on the Root Bridge. If you change the timers on the Root Bridge, you should also change them on the bridge most likely to become the root if the primary Root Bridge fails.

STP Convergence

This section describes how the Spanning Tree Algorithm uses BPDUs to converge on a loop-free tree topology with a single root and multiple branches. STP convergence occurs in four steps. These are the same steps that were mentioned at the beginning of the *Bridge Protocol Data Units* section:

1. Elect a single bridge as the Root Bridge.

2. Elect a port on each bridge (known as the Root Port) that provides the shortest (lowest-cost) path to the Root Bridge.

3. For each LAN segment, elect a Designated Bridge and a Designated Port on that bridge. The Designated Port is a port on the LAN segment that is closest to the Root Bridge. The Designated Port forwards frames from the LAN segment toward the Root Bridge. (All ports on the Root Bridge are Designated Ports.)

4. Select bridge ports to be included in the active spanning tree topology. The ports selected are the Root Ports and Designated Ports. These ports forward traffic. Other ports block traffic.

Electing the Root Bridge

When first booted, bridges assume that they are the root and transmit configuration BPDUs on each port with their ID in the Root Bridge field. The bridges set the cost to the root to zero. In addition to sending BPDUs, each bridge receives BPDUs on each of its ports. A bridge saves only the best BPDU for each port. The bridge determines which message is best by evaluating BPDUs received on the port as well as the BPDU that it would send on the port. If the new BPDU (or the locally generated BPDU) is better, the old message is replaced. To determine the best BPDU, the bridge checks four criteria in the following order:

1. Lowest Root Bridge ID.
2. Lowest path cost to the Root Bridge.
3. Lowest sender Bridge ID.
4. Lowest Port ID.

For example, if a bridge accepts a BPDU that contains a lower Root Bridge ID, then the bridge replaces that BPDU with the saved one. If the Root Bridge ID is the same as the one in the stored BPDU, then the bridge checks the path cost. If the path cost is lower than the path cost in the saved BPDU, then the bridge replaces the saved BPDU. If there's a tie, it checks the next criterion, and so on. In addition to saving the best BPDU, a bridge eventually stops sending BPDUs on a port if it receives a better BPDU on the port. The end result is that the bridges agree on the identity of the Root Bridge and bridge ports are pruned from the active spanning tree topology. The four criteria are also used in the selection of Root and Designated Ports. For the following discussion of an actual network going through this process, refer to Figure 5.8.

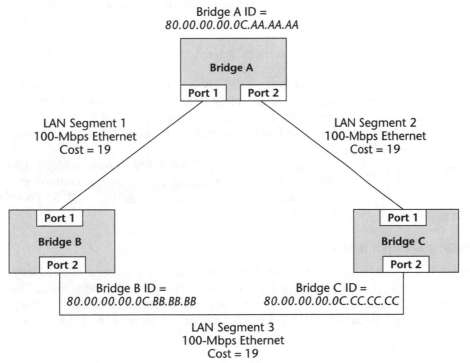

Figure 5.8   A simple network with three bridges.

Suppose that Bridge B in Figure 5.8 boots first and starts sending BPDUs announcing itself as the Root Bridge. A few minutes later, Bridge C boots and declares that it is the Root Bridge. When messages from Bridge C arrive at Bridge B, Bridge B discards them because Bridge B has a lower Root Bridge ID saved. (It has its own Bridge ID saved as the identity of the root.) Within a few seconds, Bridge C learns that it cannot be the root and gives up the job to Bridge B.

Now, suppose Bridge A boots. Bridge A declares itself to be the root. As soon as Bridge A's BPDUs arrive at Bridge B and Bridge C, these bridges agree that Bridge A should be the root. Note that all the bridges are set to the default bridge priority (0x8000 or decimal 32,768), so it is the lowest MAC address that wins. Bridge A's MAC address is 00 00 0C AA AA AA, which is quite low and, in fact, is lower than the other bridges. If Bridge A happened to be the slowest bridge on your network, you could make sure that it did not win the root contest by increasing its default priority. Remember, it's the lowest ID that wins. In the logic of STP, low means better.

Electing Root Ports

After the root has been determined, each non-Root Bridge determines which of its ports is closest to the Root Bridge. That port becomes the Root Port. As mentioned earlier, bridges use the concept of cost to judge closeness to the root. Bridges track a cumulative cost of all links to the Root Bridge. Referring to Figure 5.8, when Bridge A sends BPDUs, it announces a cost to the root that is 0 because Bridge A is the root. When Bridge B receives these messages on Port 1, it adds 19 to the cost because 19 is the default cost for the 100-Mbps LAN segment between Bridge B and Bridge A. (See Table 5.1 for default cost values.) Bridge B sends BPDUs out Port 2 stating that the cost to reach the root is 19.

When Bridge C receives the BPDUs from Bridge B, it increases the cost to 38 because the LAN segment between Bridge B and Bridge C is a 100-Mbps link, which has a default cost of 19. Bridge C is also receiving BPDUs from the Root Bridge with a cost of 0. Bridge C has an easy choice. Even after adding 19 to the received cost on Port 1, the total cost is still less than the cost associated with Port 2. The cost on Port 1 is 19, whereas the cost on Port 2 is 38. Port 1 is obviously closer to the root. So Port 1 becomes the Root Port on Bridge C.

Back on Bridge B, there is a similar story. Bridge B hears BPDUs from Bridge C that state a cost of 19. Bridge B adds 19 to the received value and determines that the cumulative cost for that path to the root is more than the cost if Port 1 is used. So Port 1 becomes the Root Port on Bridge B.

Electing Designated Ports

Each LAN segment in a bridged network has one Designated Bridge and one Designated Port on the Designated Bridge. The Designated Port forwards traffic toward the Root Bridge. The goal is to ensure that only one port handles traffic for the LAN segment so that loops are avoided. The Designated Port is chosen based on the list of four criteria (Root Bridge ID, cumulative cost to the root, Bridge ID, and Port ID) just like the Root Bridge and Root Ports are selected.

Using Figure 5.8, take a look at LAN Segment 1, the segment between Bridge A and Bridge B. There are two bridge ports on the segment, one on Bridge A and one on Bridge B. Both bridge ports agree that Bridge A is the root. Port 1 on Bridge A has a root path cost of zero because Bridge A is the Root Bridge. Port 1 on Bridge B has a root path cost of 19. Because Port 1 on Bridge A has a lower cost, it becomes the Designated Port for this link and Bridge A is the Designated Bridge for the link.

Now, take a look at LAN Segment 2, the segment between Bridge A and Bridge C. Once again, the port on Bridge A wins. Bridge A becomes the Designated Bridge. This is expected. Every active port on a Root Bridge becomes a Designated Port. The only exception to this rule is if a Layer 1 physical loop connects two ports on the Root Bridge. For example, you could connect two ports on the bridge with a hub or crossover cable, in which case only one of those ports is a Designated Port.

Now, take a look at LAN Segment 3, the link between Bridge B and Bridge C. Both ports on this segment have a root path cost of 19. (The ports didn't save the BPDUs that resulted in a cost of 38; they saved the BPDUs that they send that specify a cost of 19.) There is a tie between Port 2 on Bridge B and Port 2 on Bridge C. In this case, the next criterion must be examined. Both bridge ports are in agreement that Bridge A is the Root Bridge. Both ports have a cost to the root of 19. So, the next item in the list is the lowest Bridge ID. Bridge B has a lower ID than Bridge C, so Bridge B becomes the Designated Bridge and Port 2 on Bridge B becomes the Designated Port.

Selecting Bridge Ports for the Spanning Tree

The final step in STP convergence is easy. This is the step that at last creates the spanning tree and specifies which ports forward traffic and which ports block traffic. This step is easy because the other steps did all the work. All Root and Designated Ports become part of the tree and have the job of forwarding traffic. All other ports block traffic. Figure 5.9 shows the final result of the STP convergence for the small network in our example. Notice that Port 2 on Bridge C is blocking traffic, so the loop is broken.

Once the logical tree has been formed, BPDU traffic continues endlessly. The Root Bridge sends configuration BPDUs out all its ports every Hello Timer interval, which is every 2 seconds by default. Configuration BPDUs arrive at the Root Ports on bridges downstream from the root. These bridges send configuration BPDUs on their Designated Ports. A few rules to keep in mind are summarized in the following list:

- Configuration BPDUs flow away from the Root Bridge.
- Root Ports receive BPDUs.
- Root Ports do not send BPDUs.
- Blocking ports do not send BPDUs.
- Designated Bridges propagate BPDUs out their Designated Ports.

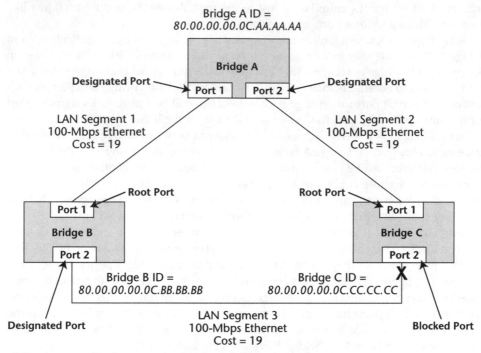

Figure 5.9 A simple network with three bridges in a spanning tree.

Port States

The chapter has mentioned that ports can be in a forwarding or blocking state. Although these are the only two states commonly seen in a stable network, Table 5.2 illustrates that there are actually five STP states.

Table 5.2 STP Port States

STATE	BEHAVIOR
Forwarding	Send and receive user data
Learning	Build bridging table
Listening	Build spanning tree
Blocking	Receive BPDUs only
Disabled	Administratively down

Bridge ports start at the bottom of the list of states as disabled or blocking and work their way up to forwarding. The disabled state allows network administrators to manually shut down a port. The disabled state is not really part of the STP convergence process. After initialization, a port that is not shut down begins in the blocking state, where it listens for BPDUs. The bridge does not learn MAC addresses or send or receive user frames in the blocking state.

A bridge port transitions to listening after expiration of a short timer or receipt of a configuration BPDU on this port or another port. While in the listening state, the port is still not sending any user data or building the bridging table, but it is sending and receiving BPDUs in an effort to build the spanning tree. While in this state, the port may determine that it really isn't a Designated or Root Port and revert to the blocking state.

Ports that remain Designated or Root Ports after 15 seconds (the default Forward Delay timer) progress into the learning state, where the bridge starts building its bridging table. If the bridge supports Virtual LANs (VLANs), it may also learn VLAN information during this time. User data is still not being passed, however. Learning lasts for another 15 seconds (the default Forward Delay timer). The learning state reduces the amount of flooding required when data forwarding begins.

If a port is still a Designated or Root Port at the end of the learning state period, the port transitions into the forwarding state. At this point, the port finally starts sending and receiving user data frames. Note that over 30 seconds have elapsed. The exact amount of time depends on how much time elapses before a port transitions from blocking to listening, which depends on the bridge's capabilities and configuration. The *Optimizing Spanning Tree Implementations* section later in this chapter discusses methods for reducing the amount of time that elapses before a port finally forwards frames. It is not a good idea to reduce the time if the port connects another switch, but if the port connects a workstation or server, then it is a good idea.

You may wonder why the IEEE decided to incorporate so much waiting into the algorithm. The goal of the IEEE STP designers was to avoid loops or duplicated frames during the time that a network is undergoing changes. Because there are propagation delays in passing information throughout a bridged LAN, a sharp transition from one active topology to another should be avoided. According to the IEEE 802.1D 1998 document, "to move a bridge port directly from nonparticipation in the active topology to the forwarding state would be to risk having temporary data loops and the duplication and misordering of frames. It is also desirable to allow other bridges time to reply to inferior protocol information before starting to forward frames. Bridge ports must therefore wait for new topology information to propagate throughout the Bridged LAN, and for the frame lifetime of any frames forwarded using the old active topology to expire, before forwarding frames."

The Topology Change Process

A goal of STP is to adapt to physical-layer problems and reconfigurations as quickly as possible without introducing any loops. There are many possible failures and reconfigurations. Some result in traffic being disrupted for 30 seconds (Forward Delay timer × 2) and some result in traffic being disrupted for 50 seconds (Maximum Age timer +

Forward Delay timer × 2). Remember from the previous discussions that the Maximum Age timer controls the maximum length of time that a bridge port saves configuration BPDU information. The default value of Maximum Age is 20 seconds. Forward Delay determines how long a port remains in the listening state as well as how long a port remains in the learning state. The default value for Forward Delay is 15 seconds.

If the Root Bridge fails, another bridge waits until its Maximum Age timer expires and then starts the process of taking over as the Root Bridge. If the Root Bridge doesn't fail, but a path to the Root Bridge fails, if an alternate path exists, a blocking port on a downstream bridge transitions to listening, learning, and forwarding after its Maximum Age timer expires. If a Root Port fails, another port on the bridge where the failure occurred may transition directly into the listening and learning states without waiting for the Maximum Age timer to expire.

As an example, let's go back to the simple network with three bridges shown in Figures 5.8 and 5.9. Assume that LAN Segment 3 in the example is a shared LAN with users who expect the network to keep running despite problems. Now assume that the janitor runs over the cable that connects Port 2 on Bridge B to LAN Segment 3, causing the port to be disabled. Figure 5.10 shows the network with Port 2 on Bridge 2 missing its connection. Assume that Bridge C does not notice a problem right away because its physical connection is still working.

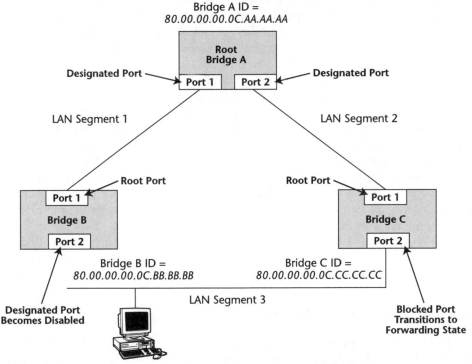

Figure 5.10   A simple network with a problem on Port 2 at Bridge B.

Port 2 on Bridge C was originally in the blocking state because it lost the contest to become a Designated Port. Although a port in the blocking state does not forward traffic, it does listen to BPDUs. Bridge C should notice that it is not receiving BPDUs on Port 2.

Port 2 on Bridge C waits until the Maximum Age timer expires before purging the stale BPDUs that list Bridge B as the Designated Bridge for LAN Segment 3. After Maximum Age expires, Port 2 on Bridge C goes into the listening state in an effort to become the Designated Port. It eventually achieves that goal and transitions into the learning and finally into the forwarding state. The users can start sending data again. Note that the amount of time that elapsed is 50 seconds, however, so some annoying users have probably already started ringing your beeper. The amount of time to recovery is Maximum Age (20 seconds by default) plus the times in the listening and learning states, which are both 15 seconds by default (the default value of the Forward Delay timer).

The example illustrated just one of many possible failures. What if Port 1 on Bridge B fails instead of Port 2? Bridge B stops receiving configuration BPDUs. After its Maximum Age timer expires, Bridge B starts the process of becoming the Root Bridge, but eventually gives up on that goal as Bridge C starts announcing that Bridge A is the root. Port 2 on Bridge C eventually transitions to the forwarding state and traffic starts flowing from LAN Segment 3 again after 50 seconds. What if Port 1 on Bridge C fails? In this case, Bridge C can immediately transition Port 2 into the listening and then learning states, so recovery takes only 30 seconds.

There is bad news and good news when considering how much time it takes before traffic is forwarded again when bridges or bridge ports fail or are disabled by management. The bad news is that it may take 30 to 50 seconds, which may be longer than upper-layer session timeout values. End stations may need to reconnect to their servers or host applications.

The good news is that, in some topologies, the entire network of bridges is not affected. Many descriptions of STP make it sound like the whole network has to reconverge when a bridge or bridge port fails or is disabled. The truth is that topology change notifications travel upstream to the Root Bridge. The Root Bridge does not forward them. Also, a bridge saves only the best configuration BPDU for each port. The bridge determines which message is best by evaluating BPDUs received on the port as well as the BPDU that it would send on the port. If a new BPDU isn't better, then the old message is not replaced. So, if a bridge announces itself as the Root Bridge, for example, the other bridges don't believe this information if it is worse than the information they already saved. Therefore there may be whole branches of the tree that do not hear the information and do not need to reconverge. The Root Bridge does, however, tell all bridges to flush their bridging tables more quickly than they normally do, as explained in the next section.

Bridging Table Timeout

When the spanning tree changes, the direction of traffic flow may need to change also. Bridges may need to forward traffic to end stations using different ports than they used before. The bridging table becomes unreliable during topology changes. For example, if Port 1 or Port 2 on Bridge B fails in our sample network in Figure 5.10, then Bridge A needs to update its bridging table. Bridge A will now reach Host A on LAN Segment 3 via Bridge A's Port 2 rather than Bridge A's Port 1. As you can imagine, topology change notification BPDUs play a role in this process, as do configuration BPDUs. The process has already been alluded to in the discussion of the Flags field in a configuration BPDU.

A bridge sends topology change notification BPDUs when a port goes into the forwarding state and when a port reverts to the blocking state. These situations mean that the Root Bridge, the mother of all topologies, must be told that the active topology is changing. Assuming that a bridge is not the root itself, a bridge sends topology change notifications out its Root Port. The bridge continues sending the notifications until a notification is acknowledged by the parent bridge setting the topology change acknowledgment flag in a configuration BPDU. The timeout between sending the notifications is set by the local configuration of the Hello Time timer (which may be different than the Hello Time timer being advertised by the Root Bridge, and is sometimes referred to as the *Notification Timer*).

The parent bridge should receive notifications on its Designated Port and propagate them out its Root Port. This process continues until the Root Bridge receives notification that the topology is changing. The Root Bridge then sets the topology change acknowledgment and the topology change flags in the next configuration BPDU it sends.

The Root Bridge continues to set the topology change flag in all configuration BPDUs until it sends for a total of Forward Delay + Maximum Age seconds, which is also sometimes called the *Topology Change Timer* and has a default value of 35 seconds (15 seconds for Forward Delay and 20 seconds for Maximum Age). The topology change flag instructs bridges to shorten the time for aging their bridging tables from the default value of 300 seconds to the Forward Delay value. This process helps speed up the time it takes until all traffic is correctly forwarded again in the new spanning tree.

Proactive Troubleshooting of STP

Whether considering STP or some other protocol, the most fundamental axiom of troubleshooting is that a proactive approach is best. Design your network with a goal that it won't fail, but also assume that the network will fail at times and monitor it to watch for impending problems. One proactive step you can take is to make sure your network design is simple, layered, redundant, and hierarchical. Figure 5.11 shows a hierarchical, layered design that is redundant but also simple.

Cisco engineers and network design experts in general recommend that both routed and switched networks be designed in a layered, hierarchical fashion, using a *core*, *distribution*, and *access* layer. These layers have the following functions:

- The *core layer* is the high-speed backbone of the network. The core layer should be highly reliable and should adapt to changes quickly. Because the core layer is critical for connectivity, you should design it in a redundant fashion. The core layer should have a limited diameter, however, and a balanced topology to ensure predictable performance and ease of troubleshooting. When configuring switches in the core layer, you should use features that optimize throughput.

Avoid packet filters or other features that slow down the forwarding of frames. You should optimize the core layer for low latency and good manageability.

- The *distribution layer* is the demarcation point between the access and core layers. The distribution layer has many roles, including controlling access to resources for security reasons and controlling how much traffic traverses the core layer for performance reasons. The distribution layer is often the layer that delineates broadcast domains and implements VLANs.

- The *access layer* provides users on local segments access to the network. The access layer can include routers, switches, bridges, and shared-media hubs, but it is usually implemented with low-end (low-cost) switches.

Remember to keep the network hierarchical. It will be tempting to add a direct link between switches in a layer. For example, you might think you can increase redundancy by adding a link to connect Switch A and Switch C in the core layer in Figure 5.11. Don't fall for this temptation. The extra link between switches or routers at a particular layer is sometimes called a *backdoor*. Backdoors should be avoided because they cause traffic to flow in unexpected ways and they make network documentation and troubleshooting more difficult.

Backdoors between switches in a redundant campus network cause STP to put additional ports into the blocking state. When a port leaves the blocking state and enters the forwarding state, it sends topology change notification BPDUs and causes bridges upstream from it to reconverge the spanning tree. Reconverging the spanning tree can disrupt traffic for 30 to 50 seconds. You should reduce the number of ports that are blocking in case the ports correctly or incorrectly transition into the forwarding state frequently. This goal can be accomplished by using a network design that is simple, layered, and hierarchical.

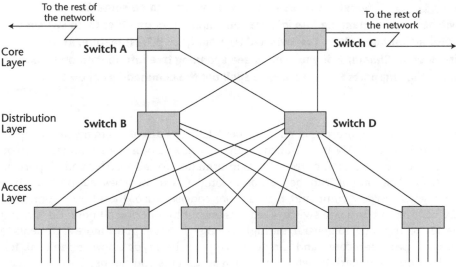

Figure 5.11   A hierarchical switched network.

Documenting Your Switched Network

As discussed in Chapter 2, understanding and documenting your network is of utmost importance. This is a principle that network engineers tend to forget when working with bridged (switched) networks. The assumption is that bridged networks are so basic that documentation isn't necessary. In fact, with the abundance of switches in modern campus networks, the importance of understanding your network's bridged structure has increased, as has the difficulty in achieving the goal of accurate documentation. Before you ever have to troubleshoot an STP problem, you should use a protocol analyzer and Cisco switch commands to make sure you know the following facts about your switched network:

- The physical topology of the switched network
- The logical topology of the spanning tree
- The identity and location of the bridge most likely to become the Root Bridge
- The identity and location of the bridge most likely to become the Root Bridge if the usual Root Bridge fails
- The location of blocked ports under normal operation

Monitoring STP

Probably the easiest way to start documenting your bridged network is to use the show spantree command on your Cisco switches. On Cisco routers with bridging enabled, use the show span command. These commands will help you with both proactive monitoring and reactive troubleshooting when problems occur.

CAUTION Although show span on Cisco routers and on some Cisco switches shows spanning tree information, show span on other Cisco switches shows information about the Switched Port Analyzer (SPAN) feature, as discussed in Chapter 2. If you want to see spanning tree information on a Cisco switch that supports SPAN, be sure to spell out the command as show spantree.

Because Cisco supports a spanning tree per VLAN, as discussed in the next chapter, you can include a VLAN ID argument with the show spantree command. If you leave out the argument, the output shows information for all VLANs and all ports in all VLANs. The output can be verbose. Some Cisco switches support a show spantree summary command that is more concise. Also, the show spantree active command on some switches reduces output by filtering all ports that are not connected to anything. In general, the higher-end switches support more arguments to the show spantree command. On your own switches, type show spantree followed by a question mark to determine which arguments you can use.

Most of the output from the show spantree command should look familiar if you have read this chapter so far. You can see items such as the bridge's Bridge ID, including the priority and MAC subfields of the Bridge ID. You can see the priority and MAC address for the Root Bridge, the identity of ports that are acting as Root and Designated Ports, and information about various timers. The output displays information for the bridge as a whole and for each VLAN and each port. Following is output on a Catalyst 1900 switch for VLAN 1. The Fast Ethernet 0/26 and 0/27 ports are in VLAN 1.

```
SwitchA#show spantree 1
VLAN1 is executing the IEEE compatible Spanning Tree Protocol
    Bridge Identifier has priority 32768, address 00B0.6426.7942
    Configured hello time 2, max age 20, forward delay 15
    Current root has priority 32768, address 0090.BF73.7A82
    Root port is FastEthernet 0/26, cost of root path is 10
    Topology change flag not set, detected flag not set
    Topology changes 2, last topology change occured 0d00h11m16s ago
    Times:  hold 1, topology change 8960
            hello 2, max age 20, forward delay 15
    Timers: hello 2, topology change 35, notification 2
Port FastEthernet 0/26 of VLAN1 is Forwarding
    Port path cost 10, Port priority 10
    Designated root has priority 32768, address 0090.BF73.7A82
    Designated bridge has priority 32768, address 0090.BF73.7A82
    Designated port is FastEthernet 0/26, path cost 0
    Timers: message age 20, forward delay 15, hold 1
Port FastEthernet 0/27 of VLAN1 is Blocking
    Port path cost 10, Port priority 10
    Designated root has priority 32768, address 0090.BF73.7A82
    Designated bridge has priority 32768, address 0090.BF73.7A82
    Designated port is FastEthernet 0/27, path cost 0
    Timers: message age 20, forward delay 15, hold 1
```

On this switch, the network has settled down and there have been no changes for 11 minutes and 16 seconds. The switch is not setting the topology change flag and is not receiving frames with the flag set. (See Topology change flag not set, detected flag not set in the output.)

For the various timers, the output shows the configured value first, for example, Configured hello time 2, max age 20, forward delay 15. The output also shows the timer value for each port, based on BPDUs from the Root Bridge. Near the top of the output, you can also see how much time has elapsed for some of the timers:

```
Times:  hold 1, topology change 8960
        hello 2, max age 20, forward delay 15
```

In the example, all the timers have reached their maximum value, which is normal after convergence has completed. The Topology Change timer is the length of time a Root Bridge sends BPDUs with the topology change flag set after a change in the spanning tree, which by default is Maximum Age (20) + Forward Delay (15) = 35 seconds. In the Times output, the switch shows the elapsed value in 1/256ths of a second. (256 * 35 = 8960.)

So far, we haven't discussed the mysterious *Hold Time* that you can see in the output, because Hold Time is not transmitted in BPDUs and is not configurable. Hold Time is the minimum time period that can elapse between transmissions of configuration BPDUs out a given port. IEEE fixes this parameter at 1 second. The timer ensures that configuration BPDUs are not transmitted too frequently out any bridge port, especially during reconfigurations when multiple bridges may consider themselves the root and be emitting configuration BPDUs that are propagated. Unlike Hold Time, Hello Time is configurable. The minimum value for Hello Time is 1 second because of the Hold Time restriction.

One other important timer is the amount of time that a switch holds an address in its bridging table before removing it upon not hearing from the address. The show spantree command doesn't display that timer, but you can use the show mac aging-time command instead, as shown in the following output.

```
SwitchA#show mac aging-time
Aging time in seconds : 300
```

Logging STP Events on Cisco Switches

When monitoring STP behavior or troubleshooting STP problems, if you find yourself without a protocol analyzer, you can still log STP events on high-end Cisco switches. To receive real-time feedback about STP behavior, use the set logging level spantree 7 command. The 7 parameter tells the switch to display debugging information. The debugging information is somewhat similar to data displayed by some of the simpler router debug commands.

Early versions of the set logging level spantree 7 command showed limited information, such as when ports entered or left the forwarding or blocking states. Later versions show all transitions (including listening and learning). The output from the command can be helpful when isolating the cause of a port taking a long time to start forwarding frames. The long delay before a port forwards frames can be a serious problem for some types of hosts, as discussed in the *Reducing Startup Delay on Cisco Switch Ports* section later. Using the show time command with the set logging level spantree 7 command can help you understand the delay, as shown in the following output. The output documents the events that occurred after a port on a Catalyst 5000 switch was enabled.

```
SwitchA> (enable) show time
Fri Aug 24 2001, 12:20:17
SwitchA> (enable) set port enable 2/1
Port 2/1 enabled.
SwitchA> (enable)
2001 Aug 24 12:20:39 %PAGP-5-PORTTOSTP:Port 2/1 joined bridge port 2/1
2001 Aug 24 12:20:39 %SPANTREE-6-PORTBLK: port 2/1 state in vlan 1
changed to blocking.
2001 Aug 24 12:20:39 %SPANTREE-6-PORTLISTEN: port 2/1 state in vlane 1
changed to Listening.
2001 Aug 24 12:20:53 %SPANTREE-6-PORTLEARN: port 2/1 state in vlan 1
changed to Learning.
2001 Aug 24 12:21:08 %SPANTREE-6-PORTFWD: port 2/1 state in vlan 1
changed to forwarding.
```

Notice from the output that it took about 22 seconds (12:20:17 to 12:20:39) for the port to start the STP process by entering the blocking state. The time before this was spent joining the bridge group and participating in Cisco's Port Aggregation Protocol (PAgP). (PAgP automates the creation of Fast EtherChannel groups, which are multiple Fast Ethernet links acting as a single logical link to another switch, router, or server.)

After blocking, the port went immediately into the listening state. The listening state lasted approximately 14 seconds (12:20:39 to 12:20:53). The learning state lasted approximately 15 seconds (12:20:53 to 12:21:08). The total time before the port actually became functional for traffic was about 51 seconds (12:20:17 to 12:21:08).

NOTE Both the listening and learning states should have lasted 15 seconds, which is how the Forward Delay parameter is set for this VLAN. The clock on the switch probably does not display precise times, which is not a serious problem.

Logging STP Events on Cisco Routers

When monitoring or troubleshooting STP on Cisco routers configured as bridges, you can use the debug span command. Depending on the version of Cisco IOS software on the router, there are many variations of this command. One of the most useful variations is the debug span events command. This command displays a line of information when relevant events, such as topology changes, occur. Its use is illustrated in the following example.

```
Albany# debug span events
Spanning Tree event debugging is on
Albany#
ST: Topology Change rcvd on Ethernet0
ST: Topology Change rcvd on Ethernet1
ST: Topology Change rcvd on Ethernet0
ST: Topology Change rcvd on Ethernet1
```

Some versions of the Cisco IOS software support a debug span tree command that shows every BPDU frame sent and received. This variety of the command is not recommended for two reasons. First, BPDUs are sent and received every 2 seconds, so a router needs to spend an awful lot of CPU cycles displaying BPDU frames when the command is enabled. Second, the display is not very usable, as shown in the following output. It's just a dump of the frame that you can only understand if you have IEEE documentation handy (or memorized in your head) or if you use an analyzer. Table 5.3 explains what each letter below the output means.

```
Albany# debug span tree
02:35:22: ST: Data
0000000000800000002167632420000000778000001 00D958400804202001 40002000F00
02:35:22: ST: FastEthernet0/0
0000000000800000002167632420000000778000001 00D958400804202001 40002000F00
02:35:24: ST: Data
0000000000800000002167632420000000778000001 00D958400804202001 40002000F00
02:35:24: ST: FastEthernet0/0
0000000000800000002167632420000000778000001 00D958400804202001 40002000F00
A  B C D  E    F        G      H   I          J K L   M     N     O
```

Table 5.3 Explanation of the `debug span tree` Output

FIELD	VALUE	MEANING
A	0000	Indicates that this is an IEEE BPDU packet
B	00	BPDU protocol version
C	00	BPDU type (00 = configuration BPDU; 80 = topology change notification BPDU)
D	00	BPDU flags
E	8000	Root priority
F	000216763242	Root ID
G	00000077	Root path cost
H	8000	Bridge priority
I	00100D958400	Bridge ID
J	80	Port priority
K	42	Port ID
L	0200	Message age in 1/256ths of a second
M	1400	Maximum age in 1/256ths of a second
N	0200	Hello time in 1/256ths of a second
O	0F00	Forward delay in 1/256ths of a second

Reactive Troubleshooting of STP

No matter how much proactive management of your spanning tree you do, STP can fail at times, usually due to misconfigurations or physical-layer problems. In addition, some of the default STP behaviors and timers may not be appropriate for modern networks. STP was designed in the 1980s when networks, bridges, and end stations were much slower. The STP developers provided an excellent protocol that met reliability goals for the networks of the 1980s and 1990s. A bridged network could have physical redundancy but logical simplicity that was well matched to the simple Layer 2 protocols in use on LANs. Because some of those LAN protocols are still in use today, some STP behaviors are still required. Other behaviors can be tuned to better match today's fast switches and end stations.

The STP developers were challenged by the fact that LAN data link layers (Ethernet, 802.3, Token Ring, 802.5, and FDDI) do not have any method of recognizing duplicate or misordered frames. They also can't tell when a frame is looping around a bridged network. Unlike IP and other network layers, the data link layer does not have a maximum hop count or a Time-to-Live (TTL) function. With IP, a frame starts with a large

TTL such as 128 or 255. Each router decrements the TTL. If the TTL reaches zero, the router drops the frame. If a frame is looping around a network of routers, at some point the TTL reaches zero and a router drops the frame. Bridges that implement Ethernet, 802.3, and other data link layer protocols don't have such a feature. So frames loop forever, consuming bandwidth and CPU cycles on receiving stations. Loops must be avoided on bridged networks. STP usually does a good job of avoiding loops, although there are cases where it fails.

STP can fail if bridges don't receive BPDUs consistently. Usually the cause of inconsistent BPDU reception is a configuration error or a physical layer problem. The best advice regarding troubleshooting STP is to check first for the kinds of data link and physical layer problems that previous chapters have described. For example, BPDUs cannot be received correctly on an Ethernet link that has a duplex or speed mismatch or a high level of frame corruption. Chapter 3 discusses Ethernet errors.

Consider the problems that result when a bridge port that is hard-coded for full duplex is connected to a port on another bridge that is hard-coded for half duplex. A port configured for full duplex does not perform carrier sense when accessing the link. The port sends frames even if the other side is already using the link. The port on the other side of the link detects a collision and runs the backoff algorithm before attempting another transmission of its frame. If there is enough traffic, the result may be that all frames (including BPDUs) sent by the half duplex port are deferred and eventually dropped. From an STP point of view, because the other switch port is not receiving BPDUs, it misunderstands the spanning tree and unblocks ports that should be blocked, creating a loop.

Another cause for the inconsistent sending and receiving of BPDUs can be a switch that is so overloaded that it can't participate in the STP process correctly. Because STP is not very complicated, this problem is rare, but it can happen, especially on a switch with many VLANs and the Cisco per-VLAN spanning tree feature enabled. Use the `show processes cpu` command on Cisco IOS switches to check that a switch is not running low on CPU resources. The CPU utilization should be under about 80 percent. On a CatOS switch, look for the field RsrcErrors (resource errors) in the output of a `show inband` command. (On some CatOS switches, use the `show biga` command.) The resource error counter is incremented when the processor is too overloaded to perform some of its tasks.

If you suspect an unresolved loop on your network due to the inconsistent sending or receiving of BPDUs, use an analyzer to check traffic. When there is a loop, you will see much more traffic than normal, especially broadcast traffic. You can also use the `show mac` or `show interface` Cisco commands to check for overutilized switch ports.

Because loops can be catastrophic, it may not be wise to spend a lot of time analyzing loop conditions. Instead, focus on getting them fixed as soon as possible. Using your network map that you gathered as part of your proactive network management, identify the bridge ports that are supposed to be blocking. Pull the cables or disable in software the ports that should be blocking. Each time you disable a port, check if connectivity is restored in the network. Knowing which action stopped the loop will help you isolate the cause of the problem. You can conclude that the failure is located on a redundant path that included the port that you disabled right before the problem went away. If this port should have been blocking, you have probably found the link on which the failure to send or receive BPDUs occurred.

One-Way Connectivity

In her book *Interconnections: Bridges, Routers, Switches, and Internetworking Protocols*, Radia Perlman discusses a problem that can be deadly for STP and also tricky to troubleshoot—a *one-way connectivity* failure. Cisco documentation discusses this failure also and calls it a *unidirectional link*. With one-way connectivity, hardware fails in such a way that connectivity between two bridges works in only one direction. Bridge A can hear Bridge B, but Bridge B can't hear Bridge A. This situation can be caused by Bridge B's receiver being dead or weak, by Bridge A's transmitter being dead or weak, or by some other component, such as a repeater or cable, having problems transmitting or receiving. For example, a cable may be working at the physical layer (so the link is up) but be constructed incorrectly so that a switch port can transmit but not receive, even though its partner is unaware of the problem and can transmit and receive.

One-way connectivity may cause a loop in a bridged network. If a bridge port can't receive data, then it can't hear BPDUs, and it might go into the forwarding state when its partner is already forwarding. If a bridge port can't send data, then it can't send BPDUs, and its partner may be unaware of its existence. The IEEE doesn't say how to handle this situation, but vendors recognized the potential for a problem and offer fixes. Cisco provides the Unidirectional Link Detection (UDLD) protocol on high-end switches.

The UDLD protocol allows devices connected through fiber optic or copper Ethernet cables to monitor the physical configuration of the cables and detect when a unidirectional link exists. When a unidirectional link is detected, UDLD shuts down the affected port and alerts the user. UDLD is enabled by default on some types of ports on some high-end switches. To determine if it is enabled, use the `show udld` command. To enable UDLD, use the `set udld enable` command either on a global basis for the entire switch or on individual ports.

A switch port that is configured to use UDLD transmits UDLD messages periodically to neighbor devices. Devices on both ends of a link must support UDLD for the protocol to successfully identify and disable unidirectional links. When both autonegotiation and UDLD are enabled and working correctly, Layer 1 and Layer 2 detection mechanisms work together to prevent defective connections that can result in STP malfunctions.

Reducing Startup Delay on Cisco Switch Ports

Previous sections of this chapter have discussed the long delay that occurs before a switch port starts forwarding frames. The *Logging STP Events on Cisco Switches* section showed an example where a port took 51 seconds to start forwarding frames. Approximately 30 seconds elapsed in the listening and learning states. The rest of the time was used by Cisco-specific software features, including PAgP. This long amount of time is beneficial when ports connect to other switches, but it can be a serious problem for a port that connects a workstation or server. The problem can cause workstations or servers to be unable to join the network after a switch boots or reboots. This problem is unfortunately common and extremely disruptive to network operations, especially at sites that have recently migrated from a hub to a switch environment.

Problems due to switch port startup delay happen most often with workstations, but may affect servers also. Problems can occur on Windows 95/98/NT/XP, Novell NetWare, Banyan VINES, and AppleTalk clients. Problems can also occur on IBM NetVista Thin Clients. If the software on the clients is not persistent during the startup procedure, the clients give up trying to connect to the network before the switch port starts forwarding frames. The startup delay problem often becomes evident when errors appear as you boot a workstation. Following are several examples of problems and error messages you might encounter:

- A Microsoft networking client displays "No Domain Controllers Available."

- A Novell NetWare client does not have the Novell Login Screen upon bootup.

- A Dynamic Host Configuration Protocol (DHCP) client reports "No DHCP Servers Available."

- A DHCP client uses an address from the Automatic Private IP Addresses range (169.254.0.1 to 169.254.255.254) rather than an address assigned by a DHCP server.

- An AppleTalk client has problems displaying zones or connecting to servers.

- An AppleTalk client displays "Access to your AppleTalk network has been interrupted. To reestablish your connection, open and close the AppleTalk control panel."

- An IBM NetVista Thin Client displays one of the following messages:

  NSB83619—Address resolution failed.

  NSB83589—Failed to boot after 1 attempt.

  NSB70519—Failed to connect to a server.

On AppleTalk, the startup delay can result in a client using a dynamic network-layer address that is a duplicate of another station's address. This can cause serious problems for both the newly booted client and the client that was already using the address. In addition, a client may not hear from a router and decide that it is on a single LAN without a router. This will make it impossible for the client to communicate with any devices not on its LAN segment. The client's Chooser application may display an empty or incomplete zone list. The client may also see the error mentioned earlier about access to the AppleTalk network being interrupted.

On IP, the most serious problem with switch port startup delay is that a client may time out while waiting to receive an IP address from a DHCP server. With some implementations, if this happens, the client uses an address from the Automatic Private IP Addresses range. This address does not allow communication across a router. The first complaint you are likely to hear is that users can't reach Internet or corporate servers.

Cisco's Portfast Feature

If you are connecting a switch port to a workstation or server that has a single Network Interface Card (NIC), the risk that the connection will create a loop is minimal. Therefore, there is no need for the port to wait 30 seconds before entering the forwarding state. Cisco supports a feature called *Portfast* or *Fast-Start* that moves a port immediately to the forwarding state without going through the blocking, listening, and learning states. The port still listens for BPDUs and reacts correctly if a switch or bridge is connected to it. The feature does not disable STP; it simply causes STP to skip a few unnecessary steps when a switch port connects a workstation or server.

STP isn't the only process that causes delays. A switch port also spends time autonegotiating the link speed and duplex mode. It may also negotiate PAgP and VLAN trunking features. (VLAN trunking is described in the next chapter.) You probably don't want to disable autonegotiation because, even though it doesn't always work correctly, it's usually less risky to leave it enabled so that a port doesn't encounter a speed or duplex mismatch problem. A port that connects a workstation, however, does not need to negotiate PAgP or VLAN trunking features.

To enable Portfast on a Cisco switch that uses set commands, use the `set spantree portfast mod_num/port_num enable` command. To disable PAgP, use the `set port channel mod_num/port_num off` command. To disable the Dynamic Inter-Switch Link (DISL) and Dynamic Trunk Protocol (DTP) VLAN trunking protocols, use the `set trunk mod_num/port_num off` command.

> **NOTE** Switch software version 5.2 and later for Catalyst 4000/5000 switches has a `set port host` command, which is a macro that combines the commands necessary to speed up the startup of a port that connects a workstation.

To verify that Portfast is enabled for a port, issue the `show port spantree` command, which displays the Portfast (Fast-Start) mode and other information, as shown in the following example.

```
SwitchA> (enable) show port spantree 2/1
Port      Vlan Port-State      Cost   Priority Fast-Start Group-Method
--------  ---- -------------   -----  -------- ---------- ------------
 2/1      1    forwarding        19         32 enabled
```

To verify that PAgP is off, use the `show port channel` command. Be sure to specify the switch module number (2 in this case) so that the command displays the channel mode even if there is no channel formed. If you issue `show port channel` with no channels formed, the switch reports that there are no ports channeling and does not display the current channel mode, as illustrated in the following example.

```
SwitchA> (enable) show port channel
No ports channeling
SwitchA> (enable) show port channel 2
SwitchA> (enable) show port channel 2
Port  Status     Channel   Channel    Neighbor                  Neighbor
                 mode      status     device                    port
----- ---------- --------- ---------- ------------------------- ----------
 2/1  connected  off       not channel
 2/2  connected  off       not channel
```

To verify that trunking negotiation is off, use the show trunk command, as shown in the following example.

```
SwitchA> (enable) show trunk 2
Port      Mode         Encapsulation  Status        Native vlan
--------  -----------  -------------  ------------  -----------
  2/1     off          negotiate      not-trunking  1
  2/2     off          negotiate      not-trunking  1
```

To reduce startup delay on a Catalyst switch running the Cisco IOS command line interface, use the switchport mode access and spanning-tree portfast commands. To verify the configuration, use the show interface command. With Cisco IOS software, PAgP is not active until you add a port to an EtherChannel, so you do not need to turn it off.

To enable Portfast on a Catalyst 1900 or Catalyst 2820 switch, use the spantree start-forwarding command. Depending on the version of software running, these switches enable Portfast by default on 10-Mbps Ethernet ports. Portfast is disabled by default on the Fast Ethernet trunk ports. With some software versions, Portfast cannot be enabled on a trunk port.

To verify that Portfast is enabled on a Catalyst 1900 or Catalyst 2820 switch, use the show running-config command. If the display for a 10-Mbps Ethernet port shows nothing about Portfast, then Portfast is enabled. If a 10-Mbps Ethernet port reports no spantree start-forwarding in the configuration, then Portfast is disabled. On a Fast Ethernet (100-Mbps) port, the opposite case is true. For a Fast Ethernet port, Portfast is on only if the port shows spantree start-forwarding in the configuration.

In the following example, interface Ethernet 0/1 has Portfast disabled (you can see the command to disable it), interface Ethernet 0/2 has Portfast enabled (you see nothing, which means it is enabled), and interface Fast Ethernet 0/26 has Portfast enabled (you can see the command to enable it).

```
SwitchA# show running-config
Building configuration...
...
interface Ethernet 0/1
  no spantree start-forwarding
!
interface Ethernet 0/2
...
interface FastEthernet 0/26
  spantree start-forwarding
```

NOTE The easiest way to view the Portfast status on a Catalyst 1900 switch is to use the menu system. If you select (P) for Port Configuration from the main menu, then select a port; the output displays whether Portfast is enabled.

Optimizing Spanning Tree Implementations

STP was designed with conservative assumptions that may not be appropriate on modern networks. It was designed to avoid loops and the duplication and misordering of frames, even on large, slow-bridged networks where news of transitions travels slowly. Since the development of STP, faster bridges and high-speed links have become available. In addition, modern networks are designed with more structured approaches than was assumed in the original design of STP. Vendors also offer methods for reducing the size of a spanning tree—for example, Cisco's per-VLAN spanning tree feature. On small, speedy, structured switched networks, some of the original parameters associated with STP are no longer appropriate.

The IEEE recently published a new standard, 802.1W, "Media Access Control (MAC) Bridges, Amendment 2, Rapid Reconfiguration," that amends the 1998 version of 802.1D and defines the changes necessary in bridges to provide rapid reconfiguration. The goal of the 802.1W committee was to standardize an improved mode of bridge operation that reduces the time STP takes to reconfigure and restore service after link failures, while retaining the plug-and-play benefits of STP. The amendment will no doubt become one of the most important IEEE standards for campus networks. Until vendors start implementing it, there are numerous ways to tactically manipulate STP to achieve performance improvements, as described in the next few sections.

Cisco worked closely with the IEEE on the 802.1W amendment. As of this writing, 802.1W features are just starting to become available in Cisco products. Before 802.1W was approved by the IEEE Standards Board, Cisco engineers also developed numerous proprietary methods for speeding STP convergence after a failure. Due to lots of field experience because of Cisco's large installed base of switches, Cisco engineers have come to realize that in many typical topologies, STP does not need to go through its ordinary mechanisms to reinstate a spanning tree. In many cases, optimizations are possible.

Uplink Fast and Backbone Fast

Uplink Fast is a Cisco-specific feature that can be configured on access-layer switches. Uplink Fast improves the convergence time of STP in the event of a failure of a redundant uplink from an access-layer switch. An uplink is a connection from an access-layer switch to a higher-end switch in the distribution layer of a hierarchical network design. Figure 5.12 illustrates a typical redundant, hierarchical network design. Users are connected to Switch A in the access layer. The access-layer switch is attached to two distribution-layer switches. One of the uplinks is blocked by STP.

If the uplink to Switch B in Figure 5.12 fails, STP eventually unblocks the uplink to Switch C, thus restoring connectivity. With the default STP parameters, the recovery takes 30 to 50 seconds. The Uplink Fast feature is a Cisco proprietary technique that reduces the recovery time to the order of 1 second. The Uplink Fast feature is based on the definition of an *uplink group*. On a given switch, the uplink group consists of the Root Port and all the ports that provide an alternate connection to the Root Bridge. If the Root Port fails or the primary uplink fails, a port from the uplink group is selected to immediately replace the Root Port. For more information on Uplink Fast, see www.cisco.com/warp/public/473/51.html.

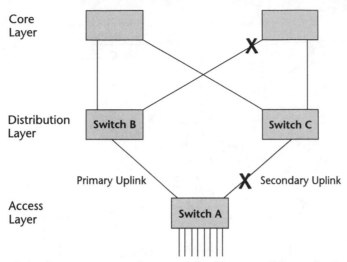

Figure 5.12 An access-layer switch with two uplinks to distribution-layer switches.

Cisco also supports a feature called *Backbone Fast*. Backbone Fast is a Cisco proprietary feature that can save a switch up to 20 seconds (Maximum Age) when recovering from an indirect link failure that occurs on a nonlocal port. Once enabled on all switches in a bridged network, Backbone Fast speeds up convergence after a failure by taking advantage of the fact that a bridge involved in a nonlocal failure may be able to move into the listening state immediately. In some topologies, it is not necessary for a switch to wait for the Maximum Age timer to lapse. The switch first checks with other switches to determine if its status is valid. The checking is accomplished with two Cisco proprietary Protocol Data Units (PDUs) called the *Root Link Query* (RLQ) and the *RLQ Response*. For more information on Backbone Fast, see www.cisco.com/warp/public/473/18.html.

Load Sharing

Because only one path in a redundant network design is active with STP, load balancing and load sharing are not supported. (Load balancing and load sharing enable the distribution of traffic across two or more network links. Processing load can also be distributed among switches. Load sharing is akin to load balancing, but is less precise. With load sharing, the share of traffic or processing might not be evenly balanced.) Some switch vendors, including Cisco, let you implement one spanning tree per VLAN. If you use VLANs in a campus network with Cisco switches, redundant links can offer load sharing in addition to fault tolerance. Figure 5.13 shows a redundant, hierarchical campus LAN that has VLANs.

Switch B in Figure 5.13 acts as the Root Bridge for VLANs 2, 4, and 6. (Switch D can become the Root Bridge for those VLANs if Switch B fails.) Switch D acts as the root bridge for VLANs 3, 5, and 7. (Switch B can become the Root Bridge for those VLANs if Switch D fails.) The result is that both links from an access-layer switch carry traffic, and failover to a new Root Bridge happens automatically if one of the distribution-layer switches fails. Both load sharing and fault tolerance are achieved. The next chapter describes how to configure load sharing.

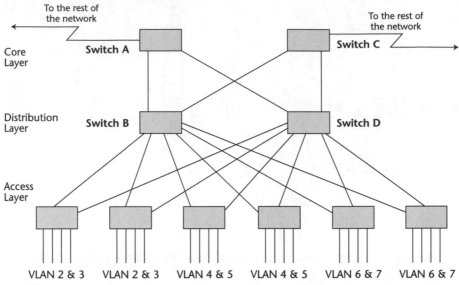

Figure 5.13   A campus network with VLANs that offers redundancy and load sharing.

Selecting the Root Bridge Deterministically

The final and perhaps most important optimization this chapter discusses is one that focuses on overall performance of a bridged network—deterministically selecting the Root Bridge. Selection of the Root Bridge can have a surprisingly strong effect on network throughput. Remember from previous discussions that the Root Bridge is the bridge with the lowest Bridge ID. The Bridge ID has two parts: the priority field and the MAC address of the bridge. If all priorities are left at their default value, the bridge with the lowest MAC address becomes the root. Most network engineers naively let this process happen automatically. The result can be an overall degradation of throughput on the bridged network.

Consider the redundant network in Figure 5.14. This network was designed properly using design templates from Cisco. Even the introduction of the test lab bridge at the bottom of the drawing is not necessarily a bad addition, although it could have unexpected, negative consequences.

NOTE Figure 5.14 illustrates a physical topology, showing bridges on each floor of the building in the IDF and MDF wiring closets. For this reason, it is upside down from the other drawings (that is, the access layer is at the top).

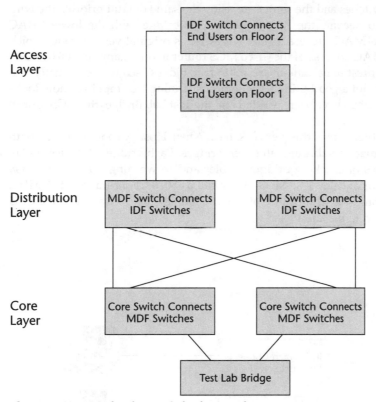

Figure 5.14   A redundant switched network.

Perhaps you have decided that you need to learn how to enable bridging on a Cisco router because you have heard that this skill is required to pass Cisco certification tests. So, you search through the closet and find an old Cisco MGS router that nobody is using and place it in the network topology between the core-layer switches shown in Figure 5.14. The Cisco router becomes the *Test Lab Bridge* shown in the figure. You quickly discover that it is easy to enable bridging on a router, using the following commands:

```
bridge 1 protocol ieee
interface ethernet 0
bridge-group 1
interface ethernet 1
bridge-group 1
```

Because all the switches and the router are using the same default priority, the winner in the contest to become the Root Bridge is the bridge with the lowest MAC address. Older Cisco MAC addresses start with Cisco's original vendor code, which was 00-00-0C. The MAC address of the Cisco MGS router in our example is 00 00 0C 05 3E 80. It wins the contest to become the root. (In fact, older Cisco routers usually win the contest, which is not a good thing.) The logical spanning tree topology now looks like Figure 5.15. The loops have been avoided and the Test Lab Bridge (the MGS router) is the Root Bridge.

Consider the problems that this network has. When Host A communicates with Host B, the traffic must pass through all seven bridges. Each bridge introduces delay related to the process of checking bridging tables and forwarding traffic. The MGS router introduces a lot of delay. The MGS router had a 68020 CPU running at 30 MHz. To help you understand the significance of this number, the 68020 was the same CPU that Macintoshes used in the late 1980s.

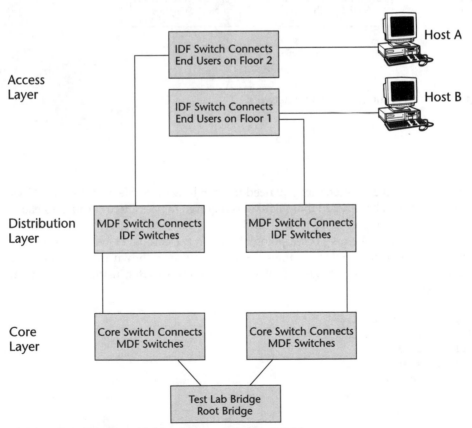

Figure 5.15 A low-end bridge becomes the Root Bridge.

CAUTION The lesson to learn is that if you let bridges elect the root on their own, without any intervention, you affect the direction in which traffic flows and the amount of packet forwarding delay in your network. If you aren't careful, a slow bridge can become the Root Bridge. Also, high-speed links can accidentally be removed from the spanning tree in deference to low-speed links that are closer to the Root Bridge.

Configuring Bridge Priority

Manually controlling selection of the Root Bridge is critical to maintaining high throughput on bridged networks. This can be accomplished by ensuring that a particular bridge has the lowest Bridge ID. It is not recommended (or even possible on some switches) to change the MAC address portion of a Bridge ID. Instead, to control the Bridge ID, set the bridge priority using the `set spantree priority` or the `spantree-template 1 priority` command. You should give a single, high-speed, centrally located switch the lowest priority so that it becomes the Root Bridge. You should also lower the priority on another high-speed, centrally located switch, so that it becomes the root if the primary root fails.

High-end switches also support the `set spantree root` macro. This macro causes the switch to look at the priority of the acting Root Bridge. If the priority at the existing Root Bridge is higher than 8192, the macro automatically sets the local priority to 8192. If the existing Root Bridge has a priority less than 8192, the macro sets the local priority to 1 less. To configure a backup root, use the `set spantree root secondary` macro.

Root Guard

Cisco also supports a feature called *Root Guard* that protects your network from a low-speed bridge highjacking the job of Root Bridge. Cisco's Root Guard feature is designed to provide a way to enforce a particular spanning tree topology on a redundant network. Root Guard is configured on a per-port basis. A port configured for Root Guard cannot become a Root Port. Instead the port becomes a Designated Port for its LAN segment. If there is a better BPDU received on the port, Root Guard disables the port, rather than taking the BPDU into account and starting the reelection of the Root Bridge. Root Guard needs to be enabled on all ports on all bridges that should not become the Root Bridge. It protects from the installation of rogue bridges, such as the Cisco MGS router that was added in Figure 5.15. For more information on this feature, see www.cisco.com/warp/public/473/74.html.

Summary

It's important to understand how a protocol behaves before you attempt to troubleshoot the protocol when it misbehaves. For this reason, this chapter has described in detail the functions and processes associated with STP. We have seen how bridges use

BPDUs to exchange information on priorities and path costs in order to build a spanning tree. The bridges elect a Root Bridge and then identify Root Ports and Designated Ports. The result is a spanning tree that is a loop-free subset of the physical topology. The tree spans the entire topology.

When troubleshooting STP problems, it's important to know which bridge is the Root Bridge, which bridge is most likely to become the root if the customary Root Bridge fails, and which ports are forwarding traffic. An analyzer that correctly decodes BPDUs, such as WildPackets EtherPeek, is a valuable tool for proactively and reactively monitoring a bridged (switched) network. Remember that all BPDU frames in a broadcast domain must use the same destination address, confirming that the same version of the Spanning Tree Algorithm is in use by all switches. The show spantree Cisco switch command is also helpful. In addition, there are many other Cisco commands for troubleshooting and optimizing STP, including the commands to enable Portfast, UDLD, Uplink Fast, Backbone Fast, and Root Guard.

This chapter has mentioned a few times that the spanning tree has a relationship with the configuration of VLANs in your campus network. Cisco supports one spanning tree per VLAN. To learn more about VLANs, keep reading. The next chapter presents general information on the definition and uses of VLANs. It also provides detailed information about configuring and troubleshooting VLANs implemented in Cisco switches.

CHAPTER

6

Troubleshooting and Analyzing Virtual LANs

This chapter provides information on common problems that occur as network administrators migrate their switched and routed networks to Virtual Local Area Networks (VLANs). A lot of confusion surrounds VLANs, which can make designing, implementing, and supporting VLANs troublesome. Trade journal articles and books present different interpretations of the technology. Switch designers have varied approaches to implementing VLANs, and management software offers different methods for an administrator to assign devices to a VLAN. VLANs have the potential to be used in many different ways. This chapter focuses on how they are used in typical campus Local Area Networks (LANs) with Cisco switches and includes a perspective on how protocol analysis can be applied to the assessment of a VLAN environment.

VLAN Frameworks

VLANs are used in switched networks. As discussed in Chapter 3, switches were originally intended to replace hubs and solve problems related to bandwidth contention and overutilization of shared capacity. In the mid- to late 1990s, network designers started replacing routers with switches because of the low cost and faster packet forwarding capabilities of switches. An expanded switched network, without routers, represented a large administrative and broadcast domain that was hard to manage. Network engineers needed a method to divide these large domains without buying expensive routers. VLANs solved that problem. VLANs brought with them other problems, however, due to their complexity and to confusion in the industry about how they should be deployed. This section attempts to simplify the complexity and remove some of the confusion.

In the early days of VLANs, there was a lot of talk about VLANs simplifying moves, adds, and changes in campus networks. In theory, with VLANs, network administrators can stay seated in their offices or in the wiring closet when an end user moves into a new office or cubicle. If a user in the marketing department, for example, moves to a new office that is physically located among engineers, the marketing person might not have the skills to configure the Network Control Panel for compatibility with the new location. Asking the engineers for help might not work because engineers don't like marketers, and asking the network administrator to come to the office and make the change might take a long time because administrators are so busy. Instead, the network administrator can configure the switch port for the moved device to be part of the marketing VLAN. Additional changes may be necessary to make sure the other switches learn that the marketing VLAN has expanded into a new area. No change is required on the marketer's PC or Macintosh.

In actuality, VLANs do not simplify network operations. VLANs complicate network designs, documentation, and troubleshooting, and they require more detailed data link layer configuration than networks with no VLANs. Although it's true that VLANs lessen the need for an administrator to walk to a user's cubicle to change network configurations, there is little need to do this anyway now that Dynamic Host Configuration Protocol (DHCP) is so common for Internet Protocol (IP) configurations. (There was never a need for individual end-user configurations for AppleTalk or Novell NetWare.) VLANs offer many advantages, but they do not simplify networks.

VLAN Definitions

A VLAN is a set of LAN devices that belong to an administrative group. Group membership is based on configuration parameters and administrative policies rather than physical location. Members of a VLAN communicate with each other as if they were on the same wire or hub, when in fact they may be located on different LAN segments. Members of a VLAN communicate with members in a different VLAN as if they were on different LAN segments, even when they are located in the same switch. Because VLANs are based on logical instead of physical connections, they are extremely flexible.

VLANs and Non-VLANs

To understand a VLAN, it's necessary to first provide a working definition for a network that is not virtual. A *network* is a group of communicating devices bounded by routers. A network is created through the configuration of individual communicating devices. When building a network, an identifier is used to represent a group and all stations in that group are configured with the appropriate group identifier. The group identifier is typically called the *network number* or *subnetwork number*. In the case of IP, for example, a network is formed by configuring the network and subnetwork portion of the IP address identically on all devices in a group. The boundary between the network/subnetwork and host portions of an IP address is indicated with a subnet mask or a prefix length parameter.

A station configured as a member of a particular network can communicate directly with any other members of that network. To communicate with a member of a different network requires the services of a router operating at Open System Interconnection (OSI) Layer 3. The router evaluates the network number portion of the destination Layer 3 address in a packet and makes an appropriate forwarding decision regarding that packet. Routers use protocols such as Enhanced Interior Gateway Routing Protocol (EIGRP), Routing Information Protocol (RIP), and Open Shortest Path First (OSPF) to exchange information on how to reach networks, thus making routers aware of how to forward packets to a specified group.

The reason the working definition of a network says that the group is bounded by routers is because when a router is crossed, a packet is in a different network. If no router is crossed, then a packet is in the same network as that in which it originated. If Station 1 wishes to talk to Station 2, for example, if the two stations are configured to be members of different networks, a router must be crossed to complete the communication path between the two stations.

A fundamental aspect of a network is that a broadcast or multicast frame sent by one member of a network is forwarded to all other members of that network. When a station broadcasts an Address Resolution Protocol (ARP) frame, for example, all other stations in the network receive a copy of the ARP frame. Broadcast and multicast traffic does not cross routers (unless special configuration options have been implemented in the routers, sometimes called *helper addresses*). A router forms the boundary of the network's broadcast domain. In addition, if a station sends a directed frame (to a unique, nonbroadcast destination) and a switch does not know where the destination address is located, then the frame is forwarded out all switch ports, exactly like a broadcast.

The Design of a VLAN

Imagine two switches that are not connected in any way. The switches form two separate networks. We'll call them Network A and Network B. There are some clients and servers in each network; we'll simply give them station numbers, as shown in Figure 6.1

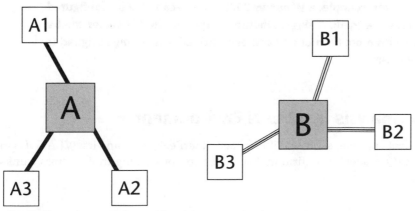

Figure 6.1 Two switches with stations attached.

It should be obvious that when A1 in Figure 6.1 sends a broadcast, A2 and A3 receive the broadcast, but none of the stations in Network B receive the broadcast, because the two switches are not connected. This same configuration can be implemented through configuration options in a single switch, with the result looking like Figure 6.2.

Through the configuration of the switch, there are now two VLANs implemented in a single switch instead of two separate physical LANs. This is the essence of the VLAN concept. The broadcast, multicast, and unknown-destination traffic originating with any member of VLAN A is forwarded to all other members of VLAN A, and never to a member of VLAN B. VLAN A has the same properties as a physically separate LAN bounded by routers. The protocol behavior in Figures 6.1 and 6.2 is exactly the same.

Interconnected Switches

Another aspect of VLAN implementation that is commonplace is the extension of a VLAN across multiple switches. In Figure 6.3, both switches contain stations that are members of VLAN A and VLAN B. This design introduces a special problem, the solution to which has been specified in the Institute of Electrical and Electronics Engineers (IEEE) 802.1Q standard and the Cisco proprietary Inter-Switch Link (ISL) protocol. The issue focuses on the forwarding of a broadcast, multicast, or unknown-destination frame from a member of a VLAN on one switch to the members of the same VLAN on the other switch.

As you can see in Figure 6.3, all frames coming from the switch on the left must take the same interconnection path to cross over to the switch on the right. The 802.1Q standard and Cisco's ISL protocol define a method for the switch on the right to recognize whether an incoming frame belongs to VLAN A or to VLAN B. As a frame leaves the switch on the left, a special header is added to the frame, called the *VLAN tag*. The VLAN tag contains a *VLAN identifier* (ID) that specifies to which VLAN the frame belongs. Because both switches have been configured to recognize VLAN A and VLAN B, they can exchange frames across the interconnection link, and the VLAN into which those frames should be sent can be determined by examining the VLAN tag. The link between the two switches is sometimes called a *tag domain*. In Cisco and IEEE terminology, the link is called a *trunk link* or simply *a trunk*.

> **NOTE** A trunk usually connects switches or possibly a switch and a router. A file server—for example, a Windows 2000 server—can also be configured to participate in a trunk. A single Ethernet adapter in the file server can be configured with more than one IP address, each address being assigned to a different VLAN.

Protocol Analysis in a VLAN Environment

Using a protocol analyzer, such as WildPackets' EtherPeek, you can view VLAN IDs in an ISL or 802.1Q header to confirm that switches are forwarding traffic across trunks correctly. In addition, you can mirror a nontrunk port to confirm that a switch has been correctly configured to separate traffic between VLANs. If you're mirroring a port that connects a server, for example, and that server is a member of VLAN 2 and VLAN 3, then you should not see broadcast or multicast frames intended for targets in VLAN 4. If you see broadcasts being sent incorrectly, then you know that the switch was improperly configured. The switch port for the server was probably placed into the wrong VLAN.

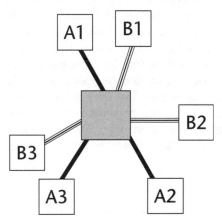

Figure 6.2   A single switch with stations from Network A and Network B attached.

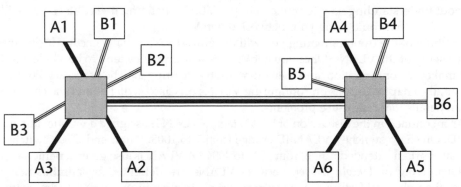

Figure 6.3   VLAN A and VLAN B span two switches.

VLAN Memberships

In theory, VLAN membership can be based on applications, protocols, policies, performance requirements, security requirements, traffic loads, or other characteristics of devices. In practice, there is often a one-to-one correspondence between VLANs and IP subnets or other network-layer subnetworks. Because a VLAN is a broadcast domain and because of the way network-layer protocols use broadcasts to find communication partners, a VLAN usually delimits subnetworks. A router is required for inter-VLAN communication just as it would be for intersubnet traffic. See the *Routers and VLAN Trunks* section later in this chapter for more information on this topic.

When deciding how many devices should be members of a VLAN, it's important to consider broadcast behavior. Within a VLAN, the same performance restrictions apply as with any single traditional LAN. Because a VLAN is a single broadcast domain, the number of hosts that can safely operate is limited by the tolerance of those hosts to broadcasts. Broadcasts are a normal part of network behavior, used in such necessary functions as dynamic address assignment, address and name resolution, service location, and service advertisement. If too many protocols send numerous broadcasts, devices in a VLAN become overwhelmed. Both end-user and internetworking devices slow down as their CPUs process many broadcasts. Users may complain about their personal computers acting sluggish. Cisco recommends that you include no more than about 200 devices in a VLAN, depending on the protocols in use and how many broadcasts the protocols send.

Configuring VLANs

Conceptually, VLANs are easy to understand, as you saw in the previous sections. A VLAN is a virtual wire or hub that may span multiple switches. A VLAN is a broadcast domain. Unfortunately, configuring VLANs on Cisco routers is not straightforward, as Cisco has added numerous features to the simple concept. These features benefit network performance, but they complicate configurations. A disadvantage of the advanced features is that you need to understand them even when implementing simple configurations. (For example, if you set up redundant trunks between switches without understanding how to implement per-VLAN spanning tree (PVST), you will cause a loop that could bring your network down.)

The bulk of the troubleshooting you will do with VLANs usually occurs during the initial setup of the VLANs. Once you get VLANs working, they tend to be stable, until you make a reconfiguration, and then more troubleshooting may be necessary. For this reason, the chapter focuses on configuring VLANs on Cisco switches and the configuration details that may cause problems.

As mentioned in the discussion of VLAN tags, a VLAN is assigned a unique numerical ID. On Cisco switches, VLAN IDs range from 1 to 1005. (High-end Cisco switches also support an extended range from 1025 to 4094.) A VLAN is also given a name, such as *Engineering* or *Lincoln_School*. Because VLANs are delimited by administrative rather than physical factors, try to use names that are meaningful from an administrative point of view. For example, use *Engineering* rather than *Building2_Floor5*. Using logical names will let you take advantage of the power of VLANs to allow engineers (or whomever) to be somewhere other than Building 2, Floor 5, but still communicate with their colleagues as if they were local.

Cisco requires one VLAN on a switch to be the *management VLAN*. The management VLAN is VLAN 1 by default, but it can be changed. Only one management VLAN can be active at a time. If you assign an IP address to a switch in order to communicate with it through network management software, the IP address is associated with the management VLAN. To avoid communication problems, make sure local network management devices are also in the management VLAN. For communication with nonlocal management devices, make sure the locally connected router interface is in the management VLAN.

Once you have created VLANs, to configure a switch port as a member of a specific VLAN, you can either statically configure the port or allow it to be dynamically configured based on the Media Access Control (MAC) address of the attached station. With dynamic VLANs, when a station connects to a switch port, the switch hears the MAC address of the station and consults a VLAN Membership Policy Server (VMPS) to determine the VLAN assignment. A workstation configured as a TFTP server can act as a VMPS server, or you can activate server functionality on a high-end Cisco switch, such as the Catalyst 5500 switch.

To tell a switch to retrieve VLAN membership information from a VMPS server, use the `vlan-membership server ip-address` command. Up to four server IP addresses can be supplied on most Cisco switches. The switch tries the servers in the order that you configure them. If the switch can't reach a server, it tries the next one. You can configure how many times the switch tries to reach a server with the `vmps retry` command. The default value for the retry counter is three.

Although the dynamic VMPS method might sound appealing, it is a less popular choice than static configuration. With static configuration, there is no need to work with MAC addresses. Instead, each switch port is assigned to a VLAN by configuring the switch rather than a list of MAC addresses at a server. Any MAC address that connects to the port becomes part of the configured VLAN. The next few sections provide more detail on typical methods for configuring VLAN memberships.

To implement VLANs, you should first do some planning to determine the grouping of devices into administrative domains, the names and IDs to use for VLANs, and which switch ports to assign to VLANs. After designing your network, you can configure VLANs on a Cisco switch using the following three steps:

1. Assign the switch to a VLAN Trunk Protocol (VTP) administrative domain.

2. Create the VLAN.

3. Associate switch ports with a VLAN.

Assigning a VTP Domain

Cisco developed VTP to facilitate the creation, deletion, and management of VLANs on Cisco switches. Switches in a single VTP domain share VLAN configuration information. VTP supports both server and client switches. When you create a VLAN on a VTP server switch, VTP client switches in the domain automatically learn about the VLAN and update their configurations.

NOTE Don't confuse VTP with VMPS. VMPS assigns MAC addresses to VLANs. VMPS is optional. VTP keeps track of VLAN IDs and names, but not port assignments. VTP is required on Cisco switches.

Cisco switches can be configured to be VTP servers or clients, or to be in *transparent mode*. Server mode is the default. In VTP server mode you can create, modify, and delete VLANs and specify other configuration parameters, such as the version of the VTP protocol to use. (There are currently two versions, V1 and V2.) VTP servers advertise their VLAN configurations to other switches in the VTP domain and synchronize VLAN configurations with other switches based on advertisements received. VTP servers save their VLAN configurations when they are powered down.

VTP clients exchange information with other VTP clients and servers, but you cannot create, change, or delete VLANs on a VTP client. You must do that on a VTP server. VTP clients do not save their VLAN configurations when powered down. Most switches should be clients.

A VTP transparent switch does not advertise its VLAN configuration and does not synchronize its VLAN configuration based on received advertisements. However, VTP transparent switches do forward received VTP advertisements to other switches. Transparent mode is suitable for small networks and cases where a switch must remain isolated due to security requirements.

In large switched networks, you can divide the network into multiple VTP domains. Dividing the network into multiple domains reduces the amount of VLAN information each switch must maintain. A switch accepts VLAN information only from switches in its domain. VTP domains are loosely analogous to autonomous systems in a routed network where a group of routers share common administrative policies. Multiple VTP domains are recommended on large networks. On medium-size and small networks, a single VLAN domain is sufficient and minimizes potential problems.

All switches in a VTP domain must be configured with the same VTP domain name. On a Catalyst 4xxx, 5xxx, or 6xxx switch, use the `set vtp domain` command to configure the domain name and VTP mode (server, client, or transparent). On Cisco IOS switches, use the `vtp name` and `vtp mode` commands. The VTP domain name is case sensitive. To avoid problems, type the name carefully and check your work.

Creating a VLAN

Once a switch belongs to a VTP domain, you can create a VLAN. To create VLANs on a Catalyst 4xxx, 5xxx, or 6xxx switch, use the `set vlan` command. The parameters to this command are the VLAN ID and the VLAN `name` keyword, followed by the VLAN name. On Cisco IOS switches, use the `vlan` command, followed by the VLAN ID and the keyword `name` and the VLAN name.

VLAN names can be between 1 and 32 characters long. Names must be unique and are case sensitive. (For example, *Lincoln_School* is different from *lincoln_school*.) Be careful to use the correct name when creating VLANs. If you are creating a VLAN on multiple switches, be sure to type the VLAN name exactly as you typed it on the other switches. To avoid problems caused by typing mistakes, you can use VTP, which allows you to type the VLAN name just once on a VTP server switch.

If you don't supply a VLAN name when creating a VLAN, the switch appends the VLAN ID (in four-digit format) to the word *VLAN*. For example, issuing the command `vlan 15` creates VLAN 15 with the default name *VLAN0015*.

The following example shows the creation of VLAN 2, which has been named *Lincoln_School,* on a Cisco Catalyst 5000 switch. Notice that the creation of VLAN 2 fails at first due to a syntax error. It fails a second time because the switch was not first assigned to a VTP domain, which for this example has been named *Ashland_School_District.* The creation of the VLAN finally succeeds and Ports 2/1-2/8 are added to the VLAN. Those ports were previously in VLAN 1, which is the default VLAN.

```
Console> (enable) set vlan 2 Lincoln_School
Usage: set vlan <vlan_num> [name <name>]
Console> (enable) set vlan 2 name Lincoln_School
Cannot add/modify VLANs on a VTP server without a domain name.
Console> (enable) set vtp domain Ashland_School_District
VTP domain Ashland_School_District modified
Console> (enable) set vlan 2 name Lincoln_School
Vlan 2 configuration successful
Console> (enable) set vlan 2 2/1-2/8
VLAN 2 modified.
VLAN 1 modified.
VLAN  Mod/Ports
--------------------------
2     2/1-8
```

Assigning Ports to VLANs

Once you have created a VLAN, you can use the set vlan command to specify the switch ports that are members of the VLAN, as shown in the previous example where ports 2/1-2/8 were added to the Lincoln_School VLAN. (On Cisco IOS switches, use the vlan-membership command to place a port in a VLAN.)

CAUTION A VLAN should be created before a port is assigned to it. If you assign a port to a VLAN before the VLAN has been created, the port is disabled. On some switches, the port Light-Emitting Diode (LED) changes from green to amber to indicate that the port is disabled. To avoid disrupting network communication, it is best to create, delete, and rename VLANs when the network is not in active use.

Some Cisco implementations allow multiple VLANs per switch port. A multi-VLAN port can belong to up to 250 VLANs. (Some models support only 64 VLANs.) Multiple VLANs are manually assigned to a port. You cannot use the dynamic VMPS method. Also, you cannot configure a multi-VLAN port when a trunk is configured on a switch. A trunk is a point-to-point link that connects two switches and carries data for multiple VLANs. VLAN traffic on a multi-VLAN port is not encapsulated in a VLAN trunking protocol such as the Cisco ISL or IEEE 802.1Q. (See the *VLAN Trunks* section for more information on this topic.)

Most Cisco switches associate a switch port with a single VLAN. Any device attached to the port belongs to the VLAN of the switch interface. Even if a shared hub attaches to the port, all stations on the hub belong to the same VLAN. Most network administrators associate switch ports with VLANs using the manual method (set vlan or vlan-membership), although, as mentioned earlier, port assignments can be accomplished with a VMPS server.

Verifying VLAN Configuration

To verify configuration of a VLAN, use the show vlan command. You can specify a particular VLAN by adding an argument that specifies the VLAN ID, for example show vlan id 10, or the VLAN name, such as show vlan name engineering. (The exact syntax for these commands depends on the switch platform.) If you don't supply an argument, the command displays detailed information for all VLANs. If you supply the brief argument on some switches—for example, show vlan brief— less information is displayed, which is usually what you want.

The following text shows typical output for the show vlan command. In addition to the default management VLAN 1, the Engineering and Accounting VLANs have been configured. The A and B ports, which are the Fast Ethernet trunk ports on a Catalyst 1900 switch, are in VLAN 1. Ports 1 through 6 and 12 are in VLAN 10 (Engineering). Ports 7 through 11 and the Attachment Unit Interface (AUI) port are in VLAN 50 (Accounting). The other VLANs were automatically created by the switch and are suspended (not in use). Table 6.1 describes the fields in the output from the show vlan command.

```
SwitchA#show vlan
VLAN Name               Status    Ports
-------------------------------------
1    default            Enabled   A, B
10   Engineering        Enabled   1-6, 12
50   Accounting         Enabled   7-11, AUI
1002 fddi-default       Suspended
1003 token-ring-defau   Suspended
1004 fddinet-default    Suspended
1005 trnet-default      Suspended
-------------------------------------

VLAN Type      SAID   MTU    Parent RingNo BridgeNo Stp  Trans1 Trans2
-----------------------------------------------------------------------
1    Ethernet  100001 1500   0      0      0        Unkn 1002   1003
10   Ethernet  100010 1500   0      0      0        Unkn 0      0
50   Ethernet  100050 1500   0      0      0        Unkn 0      0
1002 FDDI      101002 1500   0      0      0        Unkn 1      1003
1003 Token-Ring 101003 1500  1005   1      0        Unkn 1      1002
1004 FDDI-Net  101004 1500   0      0      1        IEEE 0      0
1005 Token-Ring 101005 1500  0      0      1        IEEE 0      0
-----------------------------------------------------------------------
```

Table 6.1   Fields Displayed in Output from the `show vlan` Command

FIELD	EXPLANATION
VLAN	The VLAN ID
Name	The name of the VLAN
Status	Status of the VLAN (enabled or suspended, active on some switches)
Ports	Ports that belong to the VLAN
Type	LAN type of the VLAN—for example, Ethernet
SAID	Security association ID value for the VLAN, used on 802.10 FDDI VLAN trunks
MTU	Maximum transmission unit size for the VLAN
Parent	Parent VLAN, if one exists
RingNo	Token Ring ring number for the VLAN, if applicable
BridgeNo	Token Ring bridge number for the VLAN, if applicable
Stp	Spanning Tree Protocol type used on the VLAN (IEEE or DEC)
Trans1	When translating from one type of VLAN to another, the address of the VLAN of the other type
Trans2	When translating from one type of VLAN to another, the address of the VLAN of the other type (two translations are allowed)

In addition to the `show vlan` command, the `show vlan-membership` command is useful for seeing which ports belong to VLANs. The following output is from the same Catalyst 1900 switch as was used in the previous example.

```
SwitchA#show vlan-membership
  Port   VLAN    Membership Type
   1      10        Static
   2      10        Static
   3      10        Static
   4      10        Static
   5      10        Static
   6      10        Static
   7      50        Static
   8      50        Static
   9      50        Static
   10     50        Static
```

```
11       50        Static
12       10        Static
AUI      50        Static
A         1        Static
B         1        Static
```

When troubleshooting VLANs, the show interface command can also provide information to help you isolate problems, as shown in the following example from a different Catalyst switch. Notice that Ethernet port 0/8 is *Disabled-no-vlan*. This output appears when a port has been assigned to a VLAN but the VLAN has not been created.

```
SwitchZ#show interface ethernet 0/8
Ethernet 0/8 is Disabled-no-vlan
Hardware is Built-in 10Base-T
Address is 00B0.64D1.F747
MTU 1500 bytes, BW 10000 Kbits
802.1d STP State:  Disabled       Forward Transitions:   1
Port monitoring: Disabled
Unknown unicast flooding: Enabled
Unregistered multicast flooding: Enabled
Description:
Duplex setting: Half duplex
Back pressure: Disabled
```

VLAN Trunks

Most campus networks consist of multiple switches connected via redundant links. On a network with multiple switches, administrators face the challenge of choosing the right technology to stitch together VLANs that span multiple switches. One approach, shown in Figure 6.4, is to dedicate a link between switches to each VLAN.

A link that is dedicated to a single VLAN is called an *access link*. Access links never carry traffic for more than one VLAN. These links work well on the edges of a network. You could also build a complete network with access links. The problem with this approach is that each access link uses a port on a switch and switch ports are expensive. Also, switch ports may be high speed (100 or 1000 Mbps) and can handle traffic for more than one VLAN, so dedicating a link to a single VLAN may not be necessary.

Using dedicated access links in a switched network is not a scalable solution. The network in Figure 6.4, for example, uses 7 links and 14 ports to connect the 4 switches (not counting the end-user ports). Imagine if there were 20 switches in the network and 15 VLANs. Purchasing the correct number of ports and cables to support such a solution would require a lot of money, not to mention the problem with the rat's nest of cables that would be created.

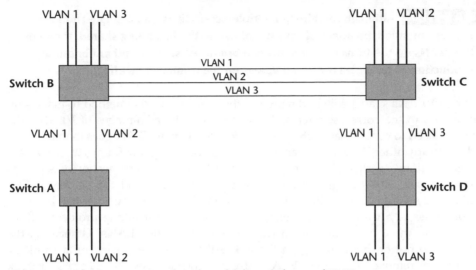

Figure 6.4   A campus network with multiple switches and VLANs.

Instead of dedicating links to single VLANs, you can enable *trunk links* between switches. A trunk link carries traffic for multiple VLANs. Trunks can also connect routers and servers to switched networks. In the past, Cisco allowed only Fast or Giga-bit Ethernet interfaces to act as trunks. Recently, however, Cisco has started to support trunks on 10-Mbps Ethernet interfaces as well. Trunks allow you to more easily scale your network. Figure 6.5 shows the same network as the network in Figure 6.4, but the network has been redesigned to use trunk links. Notice that with the redesign, only three links and six ports are required to interconnect the switches.

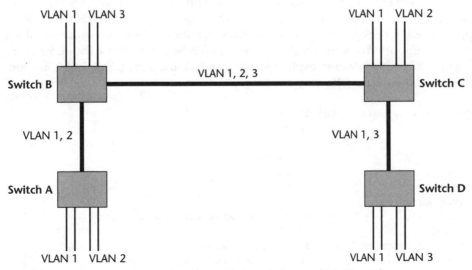

Figure 6.5   A campus network with multiple switches and VLAN trunks.

CAUTION Although combining multiple access links into a single trunk link is recommended, be aware of caveats related to the link being shared. If one of the VLANs on the trunk is experiencing a broadcast storm or other abnormal production of excessive traffic, all VLANs on the trunk will be affected.

When VLANs span a switched network, the switches need a method to make sure traffic goes to the correct segments. To benefit from the advantages of VLANs, the switches need to ensure that traffic destined for a particular VLAN goes to that VLAN and not to any other VLAN. This can be accomplished by tagging frames with a VLAN ID, as mentioned earlier in this chapter in the *VLAN Frameworks* section. Cisco supports two methods for tagging: the Cisco proprietary ISL and the standard IEEE 802.1Q. For mixed networks that have non-Cisco switches, you must use 802.1Q.

Both sides of a trunk must be configured for the same trunking protocol (ISL or 802.1Q) and must be configured to carry the same set of VLANs. Otherwise, the switches do not enable trunking on the link. All VLANs are carried on a trunk by default. To remove individual VLANs from a trunk, use the `clear trunk mod_num/port_num vlan_range` command on switches that use the Cat OS software. To restrict the traffic a trunk carries on Cisco IOS switches, use the `remove vlan-list` parameter when creating the trunk. On Catalyst 1900 switches, use the `trunk-vlan` command.

ISL and 802.1Q Comparison

Kalpana, Inc. developed ISL to carry VLAN information on 100-Mbps Ethernet switch-to-switch or switch-to-router links. After Cisco bought Kalpana, Cisco and Kalpana software engineers continued to develop and enhance ISL. Cisco also influenced the development of the IEEE 802.1Q standard, so conceptually the technologies are similar.

Some Cisco switches support only 802.1Q, some support only ISL, and some support both. Check Cisco's product catalog for information on which trunking method is supported on a switch. Also, on some switches, you can use the `show port capabilities` command to explicitly display which trunking technologies are supported, as shown in the following example.

```
cat5509 show port capabilities 3
Model                   WS-X5234
Port                    3/1
Type                    10/100BaseTX
Speed                   auto,10,100
Duplex                  half,full
Trunk encap type        802.1Q,ISL
Trunk mode              on,off,desirable,auto,nonegotiate
Channel                 3/1-2,3/1-4
Broadcast suppression   percentage(0-100)
Flow control            receive-(off,on),send-(off,on)
Security                yes
Membership              static,dynamic
```

```
Fast start              yes
QoS scheduling          rx-(none),tx-(1q4t)
CoS rewrite             yes
ToS rewrite             IP-Precedence
Rewrite                 yes
UDLD                    yes
AuxiliaryVlan           1..1000,untagged,dot1p,none
SPAN                    source,destination
```

Aside from differences in how they tag frames, which is discussed in more detail in the next few sections, the most important difference between ISL and 802.1Q is in their interaction with the Spanning Tree Protocol (STP). ISL allows one spanning tree per VLAN, which is also known as PVST, whereas 802.1Q puts all VLANs in one spanning tree.

With PVST, each VLAN can have its own Root Bridge and Designated Ports, which improves performance and makes troubleshooting easier. If one VLAN is having a problem with failing links, the problem is less likely to spread to another VLAN. As discussed in Chapter 5, reconverging the spanning tree can take a few minutes on a network with numerous switches. PVST means that reconvergence occurs on a subset of switches rather than all switches in a campus network, which speeds up the process.

802.1Q supports a single spanning tree for all VLANs in the campus network. This is sometimes called *Mono Spanning Tree* (MST). In a hybrid ISL/802.1Q environment where both MST and PVST are active, switches can become confused. In the past, the only solution was to force ISL to use MST, thus losing the benefits of PVST. To deal with this issue, Cisco developed PVST+, which tunnels PVST Bridge Protocol Data Units (BPDUs) through the 802.1Q MST, thus allowing each VLAN to maintain its own spanning tree. Cisco uses the multicast address 01-00-0C-CC-CC-CD for PVST+.

NOTE The IEEE is working on adding PVST support to 002.1Q.

Routers and VLAN Trunks

Before diving into more detail on tagging protocols used on trunks, it's important to answer the question of why a router should care about VLANs. The *Configuring VLANs* section mentioned that a router interface may be configured to belong to a VLAN, and this section mentioned that routers can participate in trunk protocols. Why should a Layer 3 router need Layer 2 VLAN information? The answer has to do with a topic touched on briefly in the *VLAN Frameworks* section at the beginning of the chapter. There is generally a one-to-one correspondence between a VLAN and a Layer 3 network segment. Because a VLAN is a broadcast domain and network-layer protocols use broadcasts to find communication partners, a VLAN usually delimits subnetworks. A router is required for inter-VLAN communication just as it would be for intersubnet traffic.

To use IP as an example, when an IP host needs to find the MAC address of another device in its subnet, the host sends an Address Resolution Protocol (ARP) broadcast.

The other host must be in the same VLAN (or on the same physical wire or hub) to hear the broadcast. When an IP host communicates with a device outside its subnet, the host sends an ARP broadcast for a router. The router's interface must be in the same VLAN for this to work. AppleTalk is similar, but uses the AppleTalk Address Resolution Protocol (AARP). Novell NetWare sends a GetNearestServer broadcast. When designing and troubleshooting VLANs, you must consider the broadcast behavior of network-layer protocols.

One method to support a router that connects multiple VLANs is to use multiple Ethernet interfaces on the router. Silly as it may sound, this is sometimes the only solution on older routers that don't understand tagging protocols such as ISL or 802.1Q. Figure 6.6 shows an example of a router that connects three VLANs and three IP subnets.

Recent versions of Cisco IOS software allow a router interface to participate in VLANs and to handle frames that are tagged using ISL or 802.1Q. Using a single physical interface, you can configure multiple IP subnets and multiple VLANs. This feature makes use of subinterfaces, a facility that Cisco has supported for many years. A subinterface is a logical subdivision of a single physical interface.

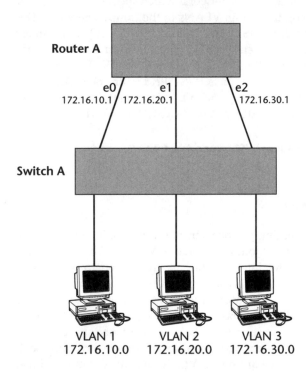

Figure 6.6 A campus network with a router that connects VLANs using multiple router ports.

Figure 6.7 shows the same network as Figure 6.6. The router has been upgraded to a Cisco IOS software version that supports ISL or 802.1Q. The network design shown in Figure 6.7 is sometimes called a *router on a stick* or a *one-armed router*. Traffic goes into the Fast Ethernet port and back out the same port when devices in one of the VLANs communicate with devices in one of the other VLANs.

There are a few things to point out about the configuration shown in Figure 6.7. One subinterface is used for each VLAN. In the `interface fastethernet 1/0.1` command, the `0.1` is a subinterface of the Fast Ethernet interface 1. The number used in the `encapsulation isl` command is the VLAN ID. The subinterface and the VLAN ID do not need to be the same, but it is recommended that you make them the same to simplify network management and documentation.

Notice that there is no IP address on the physical interface in Figure 6.7. Placing an IP address on the physical interface instead of on the subinterfaces causes no traffic to get routed through the interface. To avoid problems, be sure to place IP addresses on the subinterfaces. A `show ip interface brief` command should list each subinterface along with its IP address. You can also check that routes are being learned via subinterfaces with the `show ip route` command.

It's important to consider how traffic flows on a network with a one-armed router. To increase your troubleshooting efficiency and help you understand messages on troubleshooting tools, spend some time with your own network analyzing VLAN traffic and how it changes when a one-armed router is added to the network. Figure 6.8 shows an example.

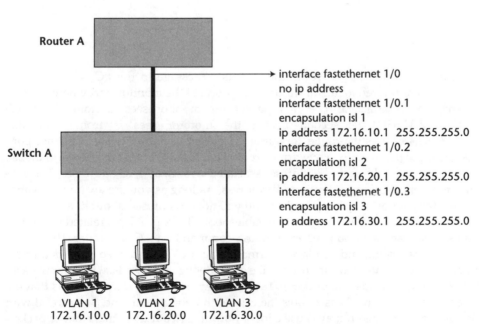

Figure 6.7 A campus network with a router that connects VLANs using a Fast Ethernet trunk port.

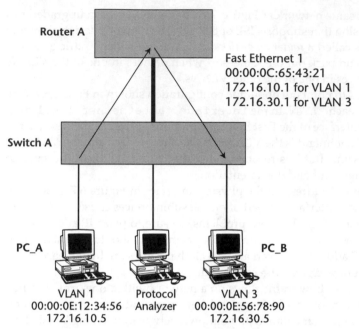

Figure 6.8   Traffic flow on a campus network with a router that connects VLANs.

In Figure 6.8, the PC_A workstation sends a message to the PC_B workstation. Switch A is configured to mirror traffic for all ports to the monitor port where a protocol analyzer is attached. The first packet the monitor sees is from 172.16.10.5 (00:00:0E:12:34:56). The second packet the monitor sees is from 172.16.10.5 (00:00:0C:65:43:21) as the router forwards the packet back out its Fast Ethernet port. This is normal behavior for a one-armed router, but it may confuse a protocol analyzer. The analyzer sees the same IP address associated with two MAC addresses. The analyzer may report this as a duplicate IP address. As long as you are aware in advance that this false report may happen, then you will not be confused about it.

In addition to using an analyzer to troubleshoot VLAN problems related to routers, you can also use the debug vlan packet command on a Cisco router. The debug vlan packet command displays information about VLAN-tagged packets that the router is not configured to support. Unlike some debug commands, which show packets the router forwards, the debug vlan packet command shows packets that the router cannot forward. As is always the case with debug commands, be careful with this command because it may cause a lot of output. Cisco routers make better packet-forwarding devices than troubleshooting tools, but if router CPU utilization is low and you don't have an analyzer handy, go ahead and try the debug vlan packet command. The command displays information about tagged packets the router cannot forward, as shown in the following example.

```
RouterA# debug vlan packet
vLAN: Received ISL encapsulated UNKNOWN packet bearing color ID 4
      on interface FastEthernet0/0.4 which is not configured to
      route or bridge this packet type.
vLAN: ISL packet received bearing color ID 1 on FastEthernet0/0
      which has no sub-interface configured to route or bridge ID 1.
```

In the first part of the output, subinterface 0.4 received an ISL packet for VLAN 4 but could not determine how to forward the packet because there was no routing or bridging configuration on the router for the type of packet. The router decoded the ISL header and went farther into the packet, where it encountered the problem. Don't be confused by the *color ID* terminology in the output. It just means VLAN ID. (Cisco often references VLANs with colors.) In the second part of the example, the router received an ISL packet on its main interface but had no subinterface configured for routing or bridging the packet for VLAN 1. The router could not forward the packet.

The debug vlan packet command shows information about packets that are dropped due to a problem. Although there is no debug command to show information about VLAN-tagged packets that are forwarded, the show vlan router command shows packet counts for VLANs.

Cisco's Inter-Switch Link

Cisco's Inter-Switch Link (ISL) protocol runs on switches (and routers) and has the job of placing a VLAN ID in frames that travel across a trunk. The VLAN ID is used by switches to determine which output ports should receive the frame. File servers and other application-layer servers can also use ISL to participate in multiple VLANs if Network Interface Cards (NICs) that support ISL are used.

When a Cisco switch that is configured for ISL sends a frame out a trunk port, it encapsulates the original frame in an ISL header and trailer. The frame maintains the ISL encapsulation as it travels across the switched network, until it is forwarded out an access link port to an end-user device. Before exiting the access link port, the switch strips the ISL information.

ISL encapsulates an Ethernet frame, adding a 26-byte ISL header to the front of the frame and a 4-byte Cyclic Redundancy Check (CRC) to the end of the frame. Because two tags are added to the Ethernet frame, ISL tagging is referred to as *two-level tagging* or *double-tagging*. Figure 6.9 shows the fields in the ISL header and trailer, and Table 6.2 describes these fields.

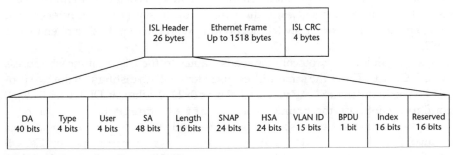

Figure 6.9 ISL header and trailer.

Table 6.2   Fields in the ISL Header and Trailer

FIELD	EXPLANATION
DA	A 40-bit multicast address (0x01-00-0C-00-00) indicating that the frame is an ISL-encapsulated frame.
Type	Type of the encapsulated LAN frame: 0000 = Ethernet, 0001 = Token Ring, 0010 = FDDI, 0011 = ATM.
User	Extension to the type field for Token Ring, or an Ethernet priority field (0000 = lowest priority, 0111 = highest priority).
SA	48-bit MAC address of the source switch.
Length	Length of the ISL header and encapsulated data (not including the DA, Type, User, SA, Length, or ISL CRC fields).
SNAP	Always set to 0xAA-AA-03, as it would be for a Logical Link Control (LLC) Subnetwork Access Protocol (SNAP) frame.
HSA	High-order bits (Organizational Unique ID) of the Source Address (SA) of the originating switch.
VLAN ID	15-bit field; however, only the lower 10 bits are used to identify the VLAN ID (1-1024). The other bits are reserved.
BPDU	A value of 1 in this field indicates the frame is a BPDU, Cisco Discovery Protocol (CDP), or VTP message destined for the switch, rather than an end-user device.
Index	Port ID of the transmitting port on the source switch.
Reserved	Used for additional information required to transport Token Ring and FDDI frames over an ISL link, for example source-routing route descriptors. Not used on Ethernet trunks.
ISL CRC	ISL calculates a 32-bit CRC for the header and user frame. This double-checks the integrity of the message as it crosses an ISL trunk. It does not replace the CRC of the encapsulated frame.

Dynamic Inter-Switch Link Protocol

Early versions of ISL had to be manually enabled at both ends of a link. In more recent versions of Cisco switching software, the Cisco proprietary Dynamic Inter-Switch Link (DISL) protocol supports a switch negotiating with the remote side to enable or disable ISL.

DISL is a data link layer protocol that sends frames to the Cisco multicast address 01-00-0C-CC-CC-CC. This is the same address used for CDP. To distinguish the two protocols, Cisco uses a different SNAP value. CDP uses 0x2000, whereas DISL uses 0x2004.

To configure DISL, use the `trunk {on | off | desirable | auto | nonegotiate}` command on Cisco IOS switches and the `set trunk mod_num /port_num {on | off | desirable | auto | nonegotiate}` on Cat OS switches. These commands enable ISL and choose the DISL mode. Table 6.3 describes the modes that are available when enabling DISL.

Table 6.3 DISL Modes

OPTION	DESCRIPTION
Off	Disables ISL trunking on the port and negotiates with the connected switch port to become a nontrunk port.
On	Sets the port to ISL trunk mode and negotiates with the connected switch port to enable trunking.
Desirable	Sets the port to ISL trunk mode if the connected port is set to the *on*, *auto*, or *desirable* state. If negotiation is unsuccessful, the port becomes a nontrunk port.
Auto	Sets the port to become an ISL trunk if the connected switch port initiates negotiation. The connected switch port must be set to the *on* or *desirable* state.
Nonegotiate	Sets the port to trunk mode. No negotiation takes place with the connected switch port.

You should use the off mode whenever you do not want the local interface to be a trunk, but you do want it to participate in DISL to inform the remote side of its configuration. Use the on mode when the remote side supports DISL, and when you want the local side to remain in trunk mode regardless of the remote side's mode.

The desirable mode causes a switch interface to inform the remote end of its intent to enable ISL, but does not actually enable ISL unless the remote side agrees to enable it. The remote side must be set to on, auto, or desirable for the link to use ISL. Do not use the desirable mode if the remote side doesn't support DISL, because receiving DISL frames may confuse the remote switch.

The auto mode means that the switch can receive a request to enable ISL and automatically enter into trunk mode. A switch configured in auto mode never initiates a request. The other side must be set to on or desirable. The nonegotiate mode enables trunking, but does not send any configuration requests to the remote device. Use this mode when connecting to a switch that does not support DISL.

CAUTION Switches default to auto mode when you enable trunking. You must change one of the switches to some other mode or ISL trunking will never be enabled. With one side left at the default auto mode, you must set the other end to either on or desirable.

DISL was supposed to make configuring ISL simpler. With all those options, however, it is easy to make a mistake, especially since some combinations are not legal and result in an *ISL mode mismatch*. If one side is trunking and the other side is not, then the switch ports won't understand each other's traffic. One side will be encapsulating frames in ISL, whereas the other side is not doing any encapsulation. Table 6.4 shows legal and illegal combinations.

Table 6.4 Combinations That Result in ISL Trunking Being On or Off

SWITCH CONFIGURATIONS	ON	OFF	AUTO	DESIRABLE	NONEGOTIATE
On	On	*	On	On	On
Off	*	Off	Off	Off	*
Auto	On	Off	Off	On	*
Desirable	On	Off	On	On	On
Nonegotiate	On	*	*	On	On

*This is a configuration mistake and ISL will not be enabled on the trunk.

Troubleshooting DISL problems can be tricky because the link might appear to be operational when it really is not. A show port or show interface command indicates that the port is connected. However, if the interface is sending many frames and not receiving frames, this could be an indication of a DISL negotiation problem. The most useful command when troubleshooting the status of a trunk is the show trunk command, as shown in the next example. Notice that the status is *trunking*, which means negotiation succeeded. If it had not succeeded, the status would be *off* and encapsulation would be *unknown*.

```
switch (enable) show trunk 1/1
Port    Mode          Encapsulation Status
------  -----------   ------------- ------------
1/1     desirable     isl           trunking
Port    Vlans allowed on trunk
------  -----------------------
1/1     1-100,250,500-1005
Port    Vlans allowed and active in management domain
------  --------------------------------------------------
1/1     1,521-524
Port    Vlans in spanning tree forwarding state and not pruned
------  ---------------------------------------------------------
1/1     1,521-524
```

DISL Frames

When troubleshooting DISL problems, it helps to view DISL frames with a protocol analyzer. Configure the switch to mirror traffic for the interface on which you wish to enable trunking and view the DISL frames to make sure the switches negotiate ISL as expected. Figure 6.10 shows a local switch, 00-B0-64-26-79-5A, sending a DISL frame. Note that the switch is configured for desirable mode but the trunk is not operational yet.

```
⊟ 🖪 DISL: ----- Cisco Dynamic Inter-Switch Link (DISL) Packet -----
  └ 📋 DISL:
    📋 DISL: Destination Address    = 01000CCCCCCC
    📋 DISL: Source Address         = 00B06426795A
    📋 DISL: Message length         = 19
    📋 DISL: ----- Pseudo LLC/SNAP Portion -----
    📋 DISL:
    📋 DISL: LLC                    = 0xAAAA03
    📋 DISL: SNAP Org ID            = 0x00000C (Cisco)
    📋 DISL:
    📋 DISL: HDLC Protocol Type     = 0x2004
    📋 DISL: Version                = 1
    📋 DISL:
    📋 DISL: Message type           = 0x0001 (Domain Name)
    📋 DISL: Message length         = 5
    📋 DISL: Management domain name = ""
    📋 DISL:
    📋 DISL: Message type           = 0x0002 (Status)
    📋 DISL: Message length         = 5
    📋 DISL: Status flag = 03
    📋 DISL:   0... .... = Operational state is not trunk
    📋 DISL:   .... .011  = Configured state: port would like to become trunk
    📋 DISL:
    📋 DISL: Message type           = 0x0000 (Unknown)
    📋 DISL: Message length         = 0
  └ 📋 DISL: Invalid message length, 23 uninterpreted bytes
```

Figure 6.10   DISL frame from switch set to desirable mode when trunk is not operational.

A few seconds later, the switch hears from its partner, whose MAC address is 00-90-BF-73-7A-9A. Figure 6.11 shows the DISL frame from the partner. The partner is set for auto mode. The auto/desirable combination should work. Notice that the partner is also set to be a VTP server, whereas the local switch is set as a VTP client. The clue that the partner is a VTP server is that it knows the VTP domain name. The VTP domain name is *Lab*.

```
⊟ 🖪 DISL: ----- Cisco Dynamic Inter-Switch Link (DISL) Packet -----
  └ 📋 DISL:
    📋 DISL: Destination Address    = 01000CCCCCCC
    📋 DISL: Source Address         = 0090BF737A9A
    📋 DISL: Message length         = 22
    📋 DISL: ----- Pseudo LLC/SNAP Portion -----
    📋 DISL:
    📋 DISL: LLC                    = 0xAAAA03
    📋 DISL: SNAP Org ID            = 0x00000C (Cisco)
    📋 DISL:
    📋 DISL: HDLC Protocol Type     = 0x2004
    📋 DISL: Version                = 1
    📋 DISL:
    📋 DISL: Message type           = 0x0001 (Domain Name)
    📋 DISL: Message length         = 8
    📋 DISL: Management domain name = "Lab"
    📋 DISL:
    📋 DISL: Message type           = 0x0002 (Status)
    📋 DISL: Message length         = 5
    📋 DISL: Status flag = 84
    📋 DISL:   1... .... = Operational state is trunk
    📋 DISL:   .... .100  = Configured state: port in default auto mode
    📋 DISL:
    📋 DISL: Message type           = 0x0000 (Unknown)
    📋 DISL: Message length         = 0
  └ 📋 DISL: Invalid message length, 20 uninterpreted bytes
```

Figure 6.11   DISL frame from switch set to auto mode.

Within a few seconds, the local switch figures out that ISL should be enabled and in its next DISL frame, we see that the trunk is operational, as shown in Figure 6.12. Notice that the switch has learned the VTP domain name also.

IEEE 802.1Q

The IEEE has defined a standard (nonproprietary) method for tagging frames with a VLAN ID. The method is published in the 1998 IEEE 802.1Q document, "Virtual Bridged Local Area Networks." With 802.1Q, a VLAN tag is added inside the frame. The frame is not encapsulated, as it is with ISL. 802.1Q adds a header that is inserted immediately following the destination and source MAC addresses (and source routing information, if present) of the frame to be transmitted. This is normally where an EtherType would reside for Ethernet II frames, or where the length field would reside for 802.3 frames. (See Chapter 3 for more information on Ethernet frame types.) The EtherType or length field from the original frame is pushed forward and follows the 802.1Q header, as shown in Figure 6.13. Figure 6.13 shows the fields in the 802.1Q header, and Table 6.5 describes the fields in the header.

The first 2 bytes of the 802.1Q header are the TPID. The TPID is set to 0x8100 for Ethernet and 802.3 frames. Because this number is bigger than the maximum size of an Ethernet frame, a recipient knows that the frame is not a standard 802.3 frame and that the field is not an 802.3 length field. If the recipient supports 802.1Q, it continues to process the rest of the header as an 802.1Q header. If the recipient does not support 802.1Q, it sees the two TPID bytes as an unsupported EtherType and drops the frame.

If the 4-byte 802.1Q header is added to a frame that was already the maximum Ethernet size of 1518 bytes, the result is an oversized frame. A receiving station that does not support 802.1Q reports these frames as giants or baby giants to distinguish them from frames that are truly oversized. To support IEEE 802.1Q and avoid the need to drop and report baby giants, the IEEE 802.3ac VLAN Tag Task Force received approval in September 1998 for extending the Ethernet maximum frame size to 1522 bytes.

```
DISL: ----- Cisco Dynamic Inter-Switch Link (DISL) Packet -----
  DISL:
  DISL: Destination Address    = 01000CCCCCCC
  DISL: Source Address         = 00B06426795A
  DISL: Message length         = 22
  DISL: ----- Pseudo LLC/SNAP Portion -----
  DISL:
  DISL: LLC                    = 0xAAAA03
  DISL: SNAP Org ID            = 0x00000C (Cisco)
  DISL:
  DISL: HDLC Protocol Type     = 0x2004
  DISL: Version                = 1
  DISL:
  DISL: Message type           = 0x0001 (Domain Name)
  DISL: Message length         = 8
  DISL: Management domain name = "Lab"
  DISL:
  DISL: Message type           = 0x0002 (Status)
  DISL: Message length         = 5
  DISL: Status flag = 83
  DISL:    1... ....  = Operational state is trunk
  DISL:    .... .011  = Configured state: port would like to become trunk
  DISL:
  DISL: Message type           = 0x0000 (Unknown)
  DISL: Message length         = 0
  DISL: Invalid message length, 20 uninterpreted bytes
```

Figure 6.12 DISL frame from switch set to desirable mode when trunk is operational.

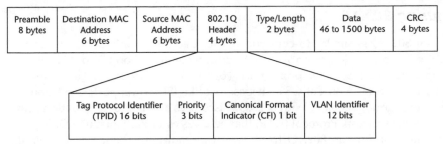

Preamble 8 bytes	Destination MAC Address 6 bytes	Source MAC Address 6 bytes	802.1Q Header 4 bytes	Type/Length 2 bytes	Data 46 to 1500 bytes	CRC 4 bytes

Tag Protocol Identifier (TPID) 16 bits	Priority 3 bits	Canonical Format Indicator (CFI) 1 bit	VLAN Identifier 12 bits

Figure 6.13   IEEE 802.1Q frame format.

Because 802.1Q changes an Ethernet/802.3 frame, rather than encapsulating the frame as ISL does, a switch must recompute the Frame Check Sequence (FCS) at the end of the frame, which is a minor disadvantage of 802.1Q compared to ISL. However, the CPUs on switches these days are so fast that recomputing the FCS does not take a significant amount of time.

If the value of the VLAN ID is zero, then the frame is actually not VLAN tagged. Instead, the 802.1Q header is used simply to transport priority information. The IEEE defines a method for prioritizing LAN traffic in the 802.1P document. If a LAN switch supports 802.1P, the switch can forward traffic flagged as high priority before it forwards other traffic. Eight priority levels are supported.

Table 6.5   Fields in the IEEE 802.1Q Header

FIELD	EXPLANATION
Tag Protocol Identifier (TPID)	Identifies the frame as a tagged frame, conforming to the tagging format described in the 802.1Q standard. For Ethernet, the TPID is 0x8100.
Priority	Allows the tagged frame to carry user priority information across bridged LANs in which individual LAN segments may be unable to signal priority information (for example, 802.3/Ethernet segments).
Canonical Format Indicator (CFI)*	Used in Token Ring and FDDI source-routed MAC methods to signal the bit order of address information carried in the encapsulated frame, and in 802.3/Ethernet and transparent FDDI MAC methods to signal the presence or absence of a Routing Information Field (RIF).
VLAN Identifier	Uniquely identifies the VLAN to which the frame belongs.

*Taken together, the priority and CFI fields are called the Tag Control Information (TCI) field.

Configuring 802.1Q

Configuring 802.1Q is similar to configuring ISL. Use the `trunk {on | off | desirable | auto | nonegotiate} dot1q` command on Cisco IOS switches and the `set trunk mod_num/port_num {on | off | desirable | auto | nonegotiate} dot1q` on Cat OS switches. Just like ISL, trunk ports can be on, off, desirable, auto, or nonegotiate. With 802.1Q, Cisco uses a new link negotiation protocol called Dynamic Trunk Protocol (DTP) that behaves essentially just like DISL.

When you configure an 802.1Q trunk, you can configure the *native VLAN*, also sometimes called the *default VLAN*. A trunk port configured with 802.1Q tagging can receive both tagged and untagged traffic. By default, the switch forwards untagged traffic in the native VLAN configured for the port. The native VLAN is VLAN 1 by default, but you can change it.

The native VLAN configured on each end of an 802.1Q trunk must be the same. A common mistake that engineers make is to change the native VLAN on one switch and not on another switch. Remember that a switch receiving a nontagged frame assigns the frame to the native VLAN of the trunk. If one end has been configured to define the native VLAN as VLAN 2, and the other end considers VLAN 2 an ordinary VLAN, traffic may flow where it was not intended to flow. This could compromise the goals you had for setting up VLANs in the first place.

Per-VLAN Spanning Trees

As discussed in Chapter 5, STP provides a method for a switch or bridge to dynamically work around loops in a network topology by creating a spanning tree. A spanning tree is a loop-free subset of the network topology. Switches exchange BPDU messages with other switches to detect loops, and then remove the loops by shutting down selected switch interfaces. Theoretically, you should not need to consider VLANs when configuring and troubleshooting STP, but you do. On Cisco switches with VLANs, if you configure and connect two trunks between switches, you will create a loop that STP does not automatically fix.

If you want to have redundant trunks, which is a good idea, you must configure the trunks to carry different VLANs. One trunk carries a set of VLANs that the other trunk does not carry unless a trunk fails. Not only does this avoid loops, but it also allows you to use both trunks. Whereas the generic Spanning Tree Algorithm would disable one of the trunks, Cisco's PVST feature allows both trunks to be active. PVST means that you can do *load sharing* across the redundant links. (It's not *load balancing* because the traffic may not be evenly balanced across the two links, but it is load sharing, which improves network throughput.)

Figure 6.14 shows part of a network at a medium-sized software engineering firm. Both Catalyst 1900 switches support VLAN 40 (Engineering) and VLAN 50 (Accounting). Both switches have two trunk ports, Fast Ethernet 0/26 and Fast Ethernet 0/27. Cisco abbreviates these interfaces as fa 0/26 and fa 0/27, and on Catalyst 1900 switches these interfaces are also known as Trunk A and Trunk B. The trunk ports connect Switch X and Switch Y. Both trunks are active and provide load sharing. Switch X connects to a router using two old-fashioned 10-Mbps nontrunk Ethernet links.

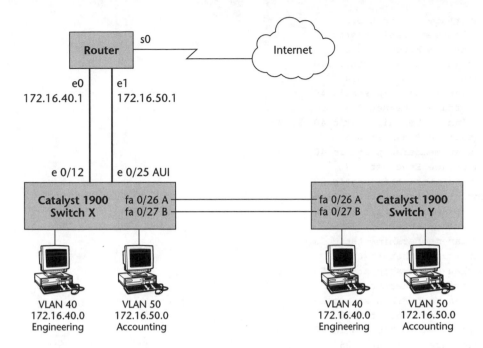

Figure 6.14 A switched network with redundant trunks that use PVST.

On both switches, Trunk A (fa 0/26) is configured to forward VLAN 40 as its first priority. If Trunk B goes down, then Trunk A also forwards traffic for VLAN 50. On both switches, Trunk B (fa 0/27) is configured to forward VLAN 50 as its first priority. If Trunk A goes down, then Trunk B also forwards traffic for VLAN 40. This sort of configuration enhances network performance (by offering load sharing) and facilitates network resiliency (by providing redundant links that take over for each other when a problem arises). A partial configuration for the switches follows.

```
SwitchX#show run
Building configuration...
Current configuration:
!
vtp domain "SoftwareWithPassion"
vtp client
!
vlan 40 name "Engineering" state Operational mtu 1500
vlan 50 name "Accounting" state Operational mtu 1500
!
hostname "SwitchX"
!
interface Ethernet 0/1
  vlan-membership static 40
```

```
interface Ethernet 0/2
  vlan-membership static 40
interface Ethernet 0/3
  vlan-membership static 40
interface Ethernet 0/4
  vlan-membership static 40
interface Ethernet 0/5
  vlan-membership static 40
interface Ethernet 0/6
  vlan-membership static 40
interface Ethernet 0/7
  vlan-membership static 50
interface Ethernet 0/8
  vlan-membership static 50
interface Ethernet 0/9
  vlan-membership static 50
interface Ethernet 0/10
  vlan-membership static 50
interface Ethernet 0/11
  vlan-membership static 50
interface Ethernet 0/12
  vlan-membership static 40
interface Ethernet 0/25
  vlan-membership static 50
interface FastEthernet 0/26
  trunk Desirable
  spantree-option 1 priority 10
  spantree-option 2 priority vlan 50
interface FastEthernet 0/27
  trunk Desirable
  spantree-option 1 priority 10
  spantree-option 2 priority vlan 40
```

Let's examine the trunk configuration on Fast Ethernet 0/26. The configuration is confusing in many ways, and it doesn't help that Cisco leaves out default values when displaying configurations. The `spantree-option 1 priority 10` command sets the port priority for the first option on the port to 10. Because 10 is lower than the default port priority of 128, this is the preferred option. For spanning tree configurations, a low priority is a better priority. (Port priority is a component of Port IDs, which are discussed in more detail in Chapter 5.) No VLANs are added to the end of the command, which means that all VLANs that are not explicitly configured elsewhere travel across this trunk. In other words, VLAN 40 crosses this trunk as a first priority. VLAN 50 is configured elsewhere, with the second option.

The `spantree-option 2 priority vlan 50` command on Fast Ethernet interface 0/26 states that the port priority for the second option for this port is the default value of 128. This trunk acts as a backup for VLAN 50. VLAN 50's first choice is to travel the other trunk, as specified in the configuration for Fast Ethernet 0/27.

The configuration for the first option on Fast Ethernet 0/27 has a low port priority (10) for all VLANs including VLAN 50. So VLAN 50 travels across Fast Ethernet 0/27 normally and uses the other trunk only if Fast Ethernet 0/27 fails. The `spantree-option`

2 priority vlan 40 command on Fast Ethernet 0/27 means that VLAN 40 travels this trunk as a backup when Fast Ethernet 0/26 is unavailable. As you can see, configuring PVST is convoluted, but you must do it if you have redundant trunks in a VLAN environment. Otherwise, loops result, despite the fact that STP should work around loops.

To finish the example, take a look at the configuration of Fast Ethernet 0/26 and Fast Ethernet 0/27 on the other switch, Switch Y. Notice that the trunk configurations on Switch Y are the same as they were for Switch X, with one exception. The trunks on Switch Y are set to auto mode, whereas the trunks on Switch X are set to desirable mode. See the *Dynamic Inter-Switch Link Protocol* section for more information on auto and desirable mode.

```
interface FastEthernet 0/26
  trunk Auto
  spantree-option 1 priority 10
  spantree-option 2 priority vlan 50
!
interface FastEthernet 0/27
  trunk Auto
  spantree-option 1 priority 10
  spantree-option 2 priority vlan 40
```

Troubleshooting Cisco's VTP

This brings us back around to a topic covered at the beginning of the chapter: VTP. A lot of Cisco documentation covers VTP with ISL and 802.1Q, but VTP is not similar to those protocols. Remember, a trunk is a link that carries traffic for multiple VLANs. The trunk may carry management traffic also, such as VTP, BPDU, and CDP frames. VTP is carried in the management VLAN on a trunk, but VTP is not a trunking protocol. It does not tag frames with a VLAN ID, which is the main job of ISL and 802.1Q.

VTP is a switch-to-switch VLAN management protocol that exchanges VLAN configuration changes as they are made to the network. VTP manages the creation, deletion, and renaming of VLANs across a campus network without requiring manual intervention at each switch. VTP also reduces manual configuration by automatically configuring a new switch or router with existing VLAN information when the new switch or router is added to the network.

As discussed earlier, Cisco switches can be configured to be VTP servers or clients, or to be in transparent mode. A switch in server mode sends VTP advertisements announcing VLAN names and IDs. You can configure VLANs on a VTP server. A switch in client mode also sends advertisements, but you cannot configure VLANs on a client switch. Clients do not save VLAN configurations when powered down. A switch in VTP transparent mode does not transmit or learn from advertisements. The switch does receive VTP advertisements, however, and forwards them on all trunk ports except the one on which the advertisement was received.

> **CAUTION** A switch automatically changes from VTP server mode to VTP client mode if it detects a failure while writing a configuration to Nonvolatile Random Access Memory (NVRAM). The switch cannot return to server mode until NVRAM is functioning again and you manually change the mode back to server.

VTP has many advantages, but it can also cause long nights of troubleshooting. VTP is required, so the solution is not to turn it off. Although you can place all switches in transparent mode, be careful with transparent mode. Transparent mode means that a switch is in its own world. A VTP transparent switch does not advertise its VLAN configuration and does not synchronize its VLAN configuration based on received advertisements. Starting in transparent mode and then changing to server or client mode should work but sometimes does not. The switch tends to remain isolated. Don't use transparent mode unless you are sure the switch will not need to share VLAN information with other switches.

Most problems with VTP are due to nonsystematic updating of VLAN data by novice network engineers. To avoid problems, it is recommended that you have no more than two servers per domain—one that holds the most up-to-date information and one that is a backup. Do not add changes to the backup server unless you are sure the primary server has failed and won't be operational for a long time. Also, make changes to servers that are communicating on the network to ensure that all switches synchronize to the latest information. Don't make changes while a server is offline.

VTP Names and Passwords

All switches in a VTP domain must share the same domain name. As mentioned earlier in the chapter, use the `set vtp domain` command to configure the domain name and VTP mode (server, client, or transparent). On Cisco IOS switches, use the `vtp name` and `vtp mode` commands. To avoid problems, type the VTP domain name carefully. Many network engineers have spent hours troubleshooting missing or inconsistent VLANs only to discover that the VTP domain name was not assigned exactly the same on all switches in the domain.

You can also optionally configure a password for VTP using either the `set vtp passwd` or the `vtp password` command. The VTP password can be 8 to 64 characters in length and it is case sensitive. If a password is configured, it needs to be configured on all switches in the VTP domain and it needs to be exactly the same on all switches. If some switches are not configured to use the password or have a different password, they will not learn VLAN information. The VTP password is translated into a 16-byte word using the MD5 algorithm, which results in an *MD5 digest value* that represents the password. VTP summary advertisements carry the MD5 digest, as shown in the protocol analyzer output of a VTP summary advertisement in the *Analyzing and Monitoring VTP* section later in the chapter.

VTP Pruning

VTP pruning is a method for reducing bandwidth utilization on trunks and on switch backplanes. Without VTP pruning, a switch floods broadcast, multicast, and unknown unicast traffic across all trunk links within a VTP domain even though receiving switches might discard them. VTP pruning blocks unneeded traffic for VLANs that are included in a *pruning-eligible list*. VTP pruning defines an additional VTP message type that announces VLAN membership. With this information, a switch can decide if flooded traffic should transit a trunk or not.

Consider the switched network in Figure 6.15. Without pruning, the switches don't know any better than to send flooded traffic from VLAN 10 to all the switches. With pruning, the switches can avoid wasting bandwidth on trunks and within switches that aren't participating in VLAN 10. Switch 5 and Switch 6 are configured to prune VLAN 10 when sending traffic on the trunks that don't need to receive traffic for VLAN 10.

Analyzing and Monitoring VTP

A VTP server or client sends a *summary advertisement* frame every 5 minutes. The summary advertisement contains a *Configuration Revision Number* (CFN). The CFN is used to make sure all switches have the most recent VLAN configuration. If a switch sees a higher number, indicating a more recent configuration, the switch should update its VLAN configuration. A VTP server also sends a summary advertisement whenever a change is made to its VLAN configuration.

If a VTP server or client receives an advertisement where the CFN is equal to the current CFN in memory, the switch ignores the data in the advertisement and floods the advertisement out all trunk ports. A switch in transparent mode also ignores the advertisement and floods it out all trunk ports. If a VTP server receives an advertisement where the CFN is less than the current CFN, the switch sends a summary advertisement back to the originating server so the originating server can be updated. A VTP client or switch in transparent mode ignores the advertisement and floods it out all trunk ports.

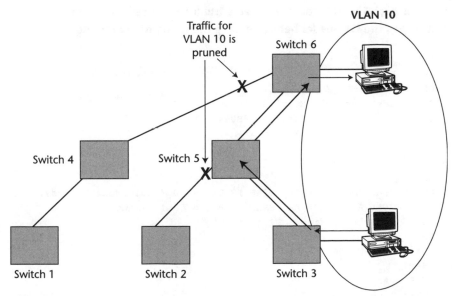

Figure 6.15   VTP pruning conserves bandwidth.

If a VTP server or client receives an advertisement where the received CFN is higher then the current CFN, the switch sends a request to the originating server for a *subset advertisement*. The switch then replaces its VLAN configuration with the contents of the subset advertisement. The switch floods the original summary advertisement out all trunk ports. A switch in transparent mode ignores the advertisement and floods it out all trunk ports.

Note that when a server or client receives a VTP subset advertisement, the switch erases its old VLAN configuration and replaces it with the new information from the advertising server. This behavior can result in problems. Consider the case where you have configured a switch offline before connecting it to a network. Now suppose you have configured the switch to be a VTP server and that you made many changes as you were working, resulting in a switch with a higher CFN than exists in the running network. When you connect the new switch to the network, its VLAN configuration replaces that of all the switches in the network. VTP does not add to existing configurations; it replaces them. So, you may have just wiped out numerous VLANs that already existed. Any ports that were in the deleted VLANs are now disabled. The network becomes unusable at this point! VTP is a powerful tool, but it must be used with care. To avoid problems, be sure to document the VLAN names and IDs that are in use, using network management software or an Excel spreadsheet.

When troubleshooting VTP, it helps to view VTP frames with a protocol analyzer to check for mismatches of VTP domain names or inconsistent VLAN information. Servers and clients send summary advertisements every 5 minutes to specify the CFN and domain name, so leave the analyzer capturing packets for at least 5 minutes. Summary advertisements contain the number of subset advertisements to follow, the VTP domain name, the CFN, the identity of the sender, the update timestamp, and the MD5 digest, as shown in the following output.

NOTE The VTP frames in this chapter were captured on an analyzer attached to a monitor port. The VTP frames crossed a trunk configured for ISL, but the switch stripped the ISL header before sending the frame to the monitor port.

```
DLC:    ----- DLC Header -----
        DLC:
        DLC:  Destination = Multicast 01000CCCCCCC
        DLC:  Source      = Station 00B06426795A
        DLC:  802.3 length = 83
        DLC:
LLC:    ----- LLC Header -----
        LLC:
        LLC:  DSAP Address = AA, DSAP IG Bit = 00 (Individual Address)
        LLC:  SSAP Address = AA, SSAP CR Bit = 00 (Command)
        LLC:  Unnumbered frame: UI
        LLC:
SNAP:   ----- SNAP Header -----
        SNAP:
        SNAP: Vendor ID = Cisco1
        SNAP: Type = 2003 (VTP)
        SNAP:
```

```
VTP: ----- Cisco Virtual Trunk Protocol (VTP) Packet -----
     VTP:
     VTP: Version                          = 1
     VTP: Message type                     = 0x01 (Summary-Advert)
     VTP: Number of Subset-Advert messages = 1
     VTP: Length of management domain name = 3
     VTP: Management domain name           = "Lab"
     VTP: Number of Padding bytes          = 29
     VTP: Configuration revision number    = 0x00000002
     VTP: Updater Identity IP address      = 172.16.10.3
     VTP: Update Timestamp                 = "000000000000"
     VTP: MD5 Digest value                 = 0xA8D8D7E57E0B98D7
     VTP:                                     0x3BE87AE8FE2EC4AB
```

From a troubleshooting point of view, you usually want to capture the subset advertisements rather than the summary advertisements. Despite their name (subset), these are the frames that have the detailed information that will help you troubleshoot. Subset advertisements contain information on the status of the VLAN. They also contain the VLAN type (Ethernet, Token Ring, FDDI, or other), the VLAN name and ID, the MTU, and the SAID value, if applicable. Following is partial output from an analyzer showing a VTP subset advertisement. The default Token Ring and FDDI VLAN information was removed for the sake of brevity.

```
DLC:  ----- DLC Header -----
      DLC:
      DLC:  Destination = Multicast 01000CCCCCCC
      DLC:  Source      = Station 00B06426795B
      DLC:  802.3 length = 284
      DLC:
LLC:  ----- LLC Header -----
      LLC:
      LLC:  DSAP Address = AA, DSAP IG Bit = 00 (Individual Address)
      LLC:  SSAP Address = AA, SSAP CR Bit = 00 (Command)
      LLC:  Unnumbered frame: UI
      LLC:
SNAP: ----- SNAP Header -----
      SNAP:
      SNAP: Vendor ID = Cisco1
      SNAP: Type = 2003 (VTP)
      SNAP:
VTP:  ----- Cisco Virtual Trunk Protocol (VTP) Packet -----
      VTP:
      VTP: Version                      = 1
      VTP: Message type                 = 0x02 (Subset-Advert)
      VTP: Sequence number              = 1
      VTP: Management Domain Name length = 3
      VTP: Management Domain Name       = "Lab"
      VTP: Number of Padding bytes      = 29
      VTP: Configuration revision number = 0x00000002
      VTP:
      VTP: VLAN Information Field # 1:
```

```
VTP: VLAN information field length    = 28
VTP: VLAN Status                      = 00 (Operational)
VTP: VLAN type                        = 1 (Ethernet)
VTP: Length of VLAN name              = 7
VTP: ISL VLAN-id                      = 1
VTP: MTU size                         = 1500
VTP: 802.10 SAID field                = 100001
VTP: VLAN Name                        = "default"
VTP: # padding bytes in VLAN Name     = 1
VTP: Reserved 8 bytes
VTP:
VTP: VLAN Information Field # 2:
VTP: VLAN information field length    = 24
VTP: VLAN Status                      = 00 (Operational)
VTP: VLAN type                        = 1 (Ethernet)
VTP: Length of VLAN name              = 11
VTP: ISL VLAN-id                      = 10
VTP: MTU size                         = 1500
VTP: 802.10 SAID field                = 100010
VTP: VLAN Name                        = "Engineering"
VTP: # padding bytes in VLAN Name     = 1
VTP:
VTP: VLAN Information Field # 3:
VTP: VLAN information field length    = 24
VTP: VLAN Status                      = 00 (Operational)
VTP: VLAN type                        = 1 (Ethernet)
VTP: Length of VLAN name              = 10
VTP: ISL VLAN-id                      = 50
VTP: MTU size                         = 1500
VTP: 802.10 SAID field                = 100050
VTP: VLAN Name                        = "Accounting"
VTP: # padding bytes in VLAN Name     = 2
```

In addition to using an analyzer to troubleshoot VTP, the Cisco show vtp command is helpful for learning general information about a VTP domain. You can add the keyword counters or status to adjust the output. The following is sample output from the show vtp counters command. Table 6.6 describes each field in the display.

```
Switch# show vtp counters
VTP statistics:
Summary advertisements received   : 38
Subset advertisements received    : 0
Request advertisements received   : 0
Summary advertisements transmitted : 13
Subset advertisements transmitted  : 3
Request advertisements transmitted : 0
Number of config revision errors  : 0
Number of config digest errors    : 0
Number of V1 summary errors       : 0

VTP pruning statistics:
```

```
Trunk            Join Transmitted Join Received   Summary
                                                  advts
                                                  received
                                                  from
                                                  non-pruning-
                                                  capable
                                                  device
---------------  ---------------- ---------------- -----------
Fa0/9                 827              824              0
Fa0/10                827              823              0
Fa0/11                827              823              0
```

Table 6.6 `show vtp counters` Field Descriptions

FIELD	DESCRIPTION
Summary advertisements received	Number of summary advertisements received by this switch on its trunk ports. Summary advertisements contain the domain name, MD5 digest, and other summarized information.
Subset advertisements received	Number of subset advertisements received by this switch on its trunk ports. Subset advertisements contain detailed information for one or more VLANs.
Request advertisements received	Number of advertisement requests received by this switch on its trunk ports. Advertisement requests normally request information on all VLANs. They can also request information on a subset of VLANs.
Summary advertisements transmitted	Number of summary advertisements sent by this switch on its trunk ports.
Subset advertisements transmitted	Number of subset advertisements sent by this switch on its trunk ports.
Request advertisements transmitted	Number of advertisement requests sent by this switch on its trunk ports.
Number of config revision errors	Number of configuration revision errors seen on this switch. Configuration revision errors increment when a switch receives a summary advertisement or subset advertisement where the CFN is smaller than the saved CFN.
Number of config digest errors	Number of MD5 digest errors. MD5 digest errors increment whenever the MD5 digest in a received summary advertisement does not match the locally calculated value of the MD5 digest. This error usually means that the VTP passwords in the two switches are different. To solve this problem, make sure the VTP passwords on all switches are the same.

(continues)

Table 6.6 `show vtp counters` Field Descriptions *(Continued)*

FIELD	DESCRIPTION
Number of V1 summary errors	Number of Version 1 summary errors. Version 1 summary errors increment whenever a switch in VTP Version 2 mode receives a VTP Version 1 frame. These errors mean that at least one neighboring switch is either running VTP Version 1 or VTP Version 2 with V2 mode disabled. If any switches run Version 1, then all switches should run Version 1. To fix the problem, reconfigure or upgrade the switches.
Join Transmitted	Number of VTP pruning messages transmitted on the trunk.
Join Received	Number of VTP pruning messages received on the trunk.
Summary Advts Received from non-pruning-capable device	Number of VTP summary advertisements received on the trunk from devices that do not support VTP pruning.

The following is sample output from the `show vtp status` command. Table 6.7 describes each field in the display.

```
Switch# show vtp status
VTP Version                     : 2
Configuration Revision          : 0
Maximum VLANs supported locally : 1005
Number of existing VLANs        : 5
VTP Operating Mode              : Server
VTP Domain Name                 :
VTP Pruning Mode                : Disabled
VTP V2 Mode                     : Disabled
VTP Traps Generation            : Disabled
MD5 digest                      : 0xBF 0x86 0x94 0x45 0xFC 0xDF 0xB5
0x70
Configuration last modified by 0.0.0.0 at 0-0-00 00:00:00
Local updater ID is 172.20.135.196 on interface Vl1 (lowest numbered
VLAN interface found)
```

Table 6.7 `show vtp status` Field Descriptions

FIELD	DESCRIPTION
VTP Version	Displays the VTP version operating on the switch, either 1 or 2.
Configuration Revision	Current CFN on this switch.

Table 6.7   *(Continued)*

FIELD	DESCRIPTION
Maximum VLANs Supported Locally	Maximum number of VLANs supported on this switch.
Number of Existing VLANs	Number of configured VLANs.
VTP Operating Mode	Displays the VTP operating mode, which can be server, client, or transparent.
VTP Domain Name	Name that identifies the VTP domain for the switch.
VTP Pruning Mode	Displays whether pruning is enabled or disabled. Enabling pruning on a VTP server enables pruning for the entire management domain. Pruning restricts flooded traffic to those trunk links that the traffic must use to access the appropriate network devices.
VTP V2 Mode	Displays if VTP Version 2 mode is enabled. All VTP Version 2 switches use VTP Version 1 by default, but this can be changed by configuring *V2 mode*. A network of VTP devices should be configured to use V2 mode only if all VTP switches in the network can operate in V2 mode.
VTP Traps Generation	Displays whether VTP traps are transmitted to a network management station.
MD5 Digest	A 16-byte digest of the VTP password.
Configuration Last Modified	Displays the date and time of the last configuration modification and the IP address of the switch that caused the configuration change to the database.

Summary

This chapter has covered troubleshooting switched VLAN networks in a Cisco environment. The chapter started with some definitions of VLANs and some caveats about the confusion in the industry regarding the use of VLANs. Next we talked about configuring Cisco switches for VLAN support by first configuring the VTP domain name, then creating VLANs, and then adding switch interfaces to VLANs. Much of the chapter has focused on configuring and troubleshooting trunks. A trunk is a point-to-point link between two switches. A trunk carries traffic for multiple VLANs. Each frame that crosses a trunk is tagged with a VLAN ID so that recipient switches know where to forward the frame. Two methods for tagging are supported on Cisco switches: the proprietary ISL and the standard IEEE 802.1Q.

Using a protocol analyzer, such as WildPackets' EtherPeek, you can mirror trunk traffic to confirm that switches are forwarding traffic across trunks correctly. In addition, you can mirror a nontrunk port and use an analyzer to confirm that a switch has been correctly configured to separate traffic between VLANs. Analyzers also come in handy when troubleshooting control protocols, such as DISL and VTP.

VTP is used to synchronize VLAN configurations across switches. The main message about VTP is to be careful and systematic when configuring and reconfiguring it. If you remember the following four rules, you should avoid problems:

1. Document the VLANs that are in use, using network management software or an Excel spreadsheet.

2. Configure no more than one or two switches per domain as VTP servers.

3. Don't configure VTP servers offline.

4. Remember that VTP replaces configurations; it doesn't add to them.

This chapter has also discussed the interaction of VLANs with the Spanning Tree Algorithm, which was covered in more detail in Chapter 5. In the following chapters, we will move beyond data link layer troubleshooting and travel up the layers of the OSI Reference Model. The next three chapters talk about the most common protocol suite in use today: Transmission Control Protocol (TCP)/Internet Protocol (IP). Chapters 7, 8, and 9 are some of the most important chapters in the book, providing information on IP addressing and routing, TCP reliability and flow control, and application layers, such as the Domain Name System (DNS) and the Hypertext Transfer Protocol (HTTP). Following Chapter 9, the book provides information on other upper layers, including Novell NetWare and AppleTalk.

CHAPTER

7

Troubleshooting and Analyzing Campus IP Networks

This chapter starts our journey up the layers of the Open System Interconnection (OSI) Reference Model and moves into the most common network layer protocol—the Internet Protocol (IP). In the past, many campus networks didn't use IP. Instead, they were based on simpler *desktop protocols*, such as the NetBIOS Extended User Interface (NetBEUI), AppleTalk, and Novell NetWare. Despite some of the advantages of these protocols, they are starting to fade into pockets of campus networks. The overall campus network of today is usually connected using IP and provides access to servers that run IP protocols. This chapter provides an overview of the IP protocol stack and then concentrates on two main topics: IP protocol analysis and IP addressing. The chapter finishes with a short introduction to IP version 6 (IPv6). Although IPv6 has not gained widespread acceptance in corporate and commercial networks, it is in use at many universities and colleges. Chapter 8 continues the discussion of campus IP networks and covers IP routing protocols. Chapter 9 discusses the upper layers of the IP protocol stack.

TCP/IP History

The Advanced Research Projects Agency (ARPA) of the United States government started working on networking protocols in the late 1960s with the help of a small company in Boston, Massachusetts, called Bolt, Beranek, and Newman, Inc. (BBN). The result of their work was the ARPANET, which was a packet-switched network of leased lines that connected government agencies and universities across the United States. In the 1970s, government and university researchers started working on a method to transmit packets across diverse networks, including the ARPANET and packet radio and satellite networks that had sprung up after the creation of the ARPANET. The researchers developed a new protocol, called the Transmission Control Protocol (TCP). In 1978, the protocol developers decided to optimize the efficiency of TCP by breaking it into two parts. The part of TCP used by gateways to connect dissimilar networks became IP. By the early 1980s, numerous networks were communicating with the TCP/IP protocols. The collection of networks gradually came to be called the *Internet*, borrowing the first word from *Internet Protocol*. The TCP/IP protocols were conceived and developed at a time when only an imaginative science fiction writer could have pictured what the Internet would become 20 years later. The design of the IP protocol stack was intended to provide solutions to the networking problems of the day. Many of these problems are different in both scope and depth from the problems facing today's networking professionals. Nonetheless, the core IP protocols (IP, TCP, and the User Datagram Protocol [UDP]) have the same packet format and fundamental behavior as when they were created. When using a protocol analyzer to examine the internal details of the protocols, one challenge that arises is the need to recognize when fields in the packets are either unused (because they are obsolete), are used in a manner that differs from their original intent, or have been resurrected from obsolescence to provide completely new functionality.

Today, the Internet is a decentralized internetwork composed of government, public, and commercial Internet Service Provider (ISP) networks connected in a global mesh topology. In the 1990s, the success of the Internet and the protocols used on the Internet led to the emergence of the *intranet*, which is an internal internetwork that uses TCP/IP protocols. Chapters 7 through 9 discuss the TCP/IP protocols mostly from the point of view of analyzing and troubleshooting a campus intranet composed of routers, servers, and workstations that run the TCP/IP protocols. Much of what you will learn applies to troubleshooting problems accessing the Internet as well.

In the late 1980s, many industry experts predicted that the TCP/IP protocols could not survive the requirements of new applications and would not be suitable to the capabilities of new high-speed equipment. In January 1988, *Data Communications* magazine published an article about progress in the development of upper-layer protocols for the International Organization for Standardization (ISO) set of OSI protocols. The lead-in to the article states, "Standards atop the OSI stack, once merely strange abstractions, are now showing up in carnival-like trade-show demonstrations. Can a thriving marketplace be far behind?" The thriving marketplace never happened. The staid, practical, and non-carnival-like methods of the Internet Engineering Task Force (IETF) won out. The IETF's method of publishing Request for Comments (RFCs) to standardize TCP/IP protocols worked, as did the protocols, which remain in wide use today.

The TCP/IP Protocol Stack

In addition to developing actual protocols, the ISO developed the OSI Reference Model, which Chapter 2 discussed in more detail. (See Figure 2.1 for a diagram of the model.) The TCP/IP protocols were developed without reference to the OSI model, although they do fit into a layered model that is similar to the OSI model. It's important to remember that, while protocol descriptions often refer to a TCP/IP protocol as operating at one or another OSI layer, the TCP/IP protocols do not manifest all the characteristics that the OSI model attributes to each layer. IP, for example, can be said to work at the network layer, but there are OSI network layer characteristics that are not implemented by IP (connection-oriented operation, for example), and there are IP functions that are not defined as part of the OSI network layer (the mechanism by which IP fragments and reassembles packets, for instance).

IP routing protocols can be said to work at the network layer. According to ISO documents, however, routing protocols stand outside the basic protocol stack in a management plane. Routing protocols provide management services for the network layer. (Chapter 13 discusses the management, control, and user planes of the OSI model in more detail. See Figure 13.1.) The original OSI model, defined in ISO 7498 and published in 1984, did not contain routing protocols. Routing protocol functionality was added later in a management annex. Routing protocols are also described in the *OSI Routeing Architecture* document. (Note the British spelling of *routing*.)

You will see various authors and lecturers present diagrams showing how different TCP/IP protocols fit into different layers of the OSI model. Some authors will use one representation, and some will use another. Don't get confused by the differences. There is no standard way to map between the OSI model and the layers developed by the creators of TCP/IP. Figure 7.1 shows the TCP/IP protocol stack with our attempt to map the TCP/IP layers to the OSI model.

Table 7.1 lists the major TCP/IP protocols and categorizes them according to the TCP/IP model for protocol layering. The table also explains the services offered by each of the protocols.

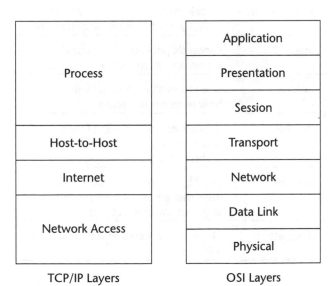

TCP/IP Layers   OSI Layers

Figure 7.1   The TCP/IP protocol stack.

Table 7.1 TCP/IP Protocols

PROTOCOL	LAYER	SERVICES
Telnet	Process	Transmits character-oriented terminal data
File Transfer Protocol (FTP)	Process	Provides reliable file transfer
Trivial File Transfer Protocol (TFTP)	Process	Provides simple file transfer
Network File System (NFS)	Process	Supports distributed file sharing
Simple Mail Transfer Protocol (SMTP)	Process	Provides reliable exchange of electronic messages
Simple Network Management Protocol (SNMP)	Process	Protocol for managing TCP/IP networks
Domain Name System (DNS)	Process	Distributed naming system and protocol for mapping names to addresses
Hypertext Transfer Protocol (HTTP)	Process	Used by Web servers to transfer text and graphics to Web clients
Transmission Control Protocol (TCP)	Host-to-Host	Connection-oriented, bytestream protocol for reliable end-to-end communication
User Datagram Protocol (UDP)	Host-to-Host	Simple connectionless, unreliable protocol for transmitting datagrams
Internet Protocol (IP)	Internet	Forwards packets (datagrams) across an internetwork
Routing protocols	Internet	Used to exchange information on how to reach networks
Internet Control Message Protocol (ICMP)	Internet	Reports errors in packet forwarding and supports testing connectivity (Echo or Ping)
Internet Group Management Protocol (IGMP)	Internet	Used by IP hosts to report their multicast group memberships to an adjacent multicast router
Address Resolution Protocol (ARP)	Internet	Maps IP addresses to data link layer addresses

The Internet Protocol

IP has the job of delivering packets across an internetwork, whether the internetwork is the Internet or a campus intranet. IP packets are called *datagrams* in the RFCs that describe IP, which include RFC 760 and RFC 791. IP transmits datagrams from sources to destinations, where sources and destinations are hosts identified by fixed-length, 32-bit IP addresses. TCP, UDP, ICMP, IGMP, and most routing protocols send their data in IP datagrams. Some routing protocols also use a TCP or UDP header.

IP is a *connectionless protocol*, which means that IP does not require that a connection be established before datagrams can flow between hosts and does not retain information on datagrams that it has transmitted. IP provides a best-effort delivery service that offers no guarantees that an IP datagram successfully got to its destination. When something goes wrong, such as when a router is unable to forward a datagram, IP drops the datagram and sends an ICMP message to the source to notify the source that there was a problem. From a protocol analysis perspective, the examination of these (and any) ICMP messages is fundamental to the process of troubleshooting routing-related problems.

IP has the job of fragmenting and reassembling datagrams that are too large to travel across a network. Fragmenting can happen at a router or at an end-station host. For example, an IP router may receive a 4500-byte packet on a Token Ring segment. From information in its IP routing table, the router may determine that the packet needs to be transmitted on an Ethernet segment. Because Ethernet supports a maximum frame size of 1500 bytes, not counting the Ethernet header and the Frame Check Sequence (FCS), the Token Ring frame must be fragmented. Fields in the IP header allow this process to happen and help the recipient host reassemble the fragments into the original datagram.

As another illustration, an upper-layer protocol (for example NFS) may pass a block of data as large as 8192 bytes down through the protocol stack for delivery by IP. In this case, IP fragments the block prior to initial transmission on the Ethernet segment. The individual fragments are forwarded across the internetwork to be reassembled by the destination host.

IP Protocol Analysis

From a protocol analysis point of view, because IP is a best-effort, connectionless protocol, you will not see any session establishment at the IP layer. You will also not see any flow control, sequence numbers, or acknowledgments. As will be explained, the number that identifies each IP datagram is not used for sequencing or reliability. Instead, it is used to identify the parts of a datagram when a datagram is divided into fragments for traversal across a network that supports small frame sizes.

Due to the connectionless nature of IP, you should not see any indication that IP maintains state information about datagrams that it has sent or will send. A new version of IP, IPv6, does offer a method for IP to identify a flow of datagrams so that a particular flow can receive special handling. IPv6 is discussed later in this chapter. In general, if you see the acronym IP in this book without a version, you should assume the discussion applies to IPv4, which is the version in use on the Internet and most intranets today. (There is no implementation of IP v1, v2, v3, v5, or anything beyond v6, so those can be ignored.)

An IP datagram starts with an IP header that is normally 20 bytes, unless options are present. Figure 7.2 shows the format of an IP header. The first bit is numbered 0 at the left, and the last bit of each 32-bit unit is numbered 31 on the right, which is the way the IP header is usually shown. Table 7.2 and the following sections describe the fields in an IP header.

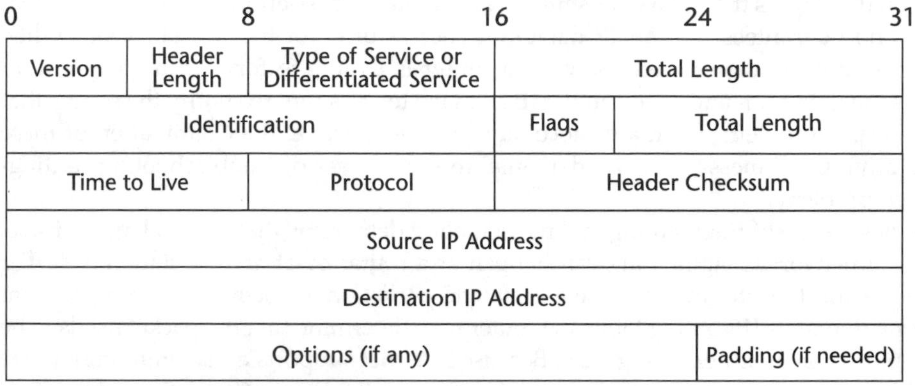

0	8	16	24	31
Version	Header Length	Type of Service or Differentiated Service	Total Length	
Identification			Flags	Total Length
Time to Live		Protocol	Header Checksum	
Source IP Address				
Destination IP Address				
Options (if any)			Padding (if needed)	

Figure 7.2   The IP header.

Table 7.2   Fields in an IP Header

FIELD	EXPLANATION
Version	The IP version being implemented (either 4 or 6).
Header Length	The length of the IP header in 32-bit units. If there are no IP options, the length is 5 to indicate a 20-byte header (five 32-bit or 4-byte units).
Type of Service or Differentiated Services (DS)	An 8-bit field that specifies the type of forwarding or any DS a datagram should receive. See the *The IP Type of Service or DS Field* section.
Total Length	The total length of the IP datagram in bytes. The recipient uses this field and the Header Length field to determine where the data starts and how long it is.
Identification	Identifies a datagram. See the *IP Fragmentation and Reassembly* section.
Flags	A 3-bit field where the 1st bit is not used, the 2nd bit tells routers not to fragment, and the 3rd bit is set when there are more fragments to arrive to complete a datagram. See the *IP Fragmentation and Reassembly* section.

Table 7.2   (Continued)

FIELD	EXPLANATION
Fragment Offset	A 13-bit field that indicates the position of a fragment relative to the beginning of a datagram. See the *IP Fragmentation and Reassembly* section.
Time-to-Live (TTL)	Sets an upper limit on the number of routers through which a datagram can travel. See the *IP Time to Live* section.
Protocol	Identifies the next-layer protocol in the packet—that is, the protocol that should receive the data in the datagram. See the *The IP Protocol Field* section.
Header Checksum	Contains the checksum for the IP header. Because some header fields change (for example, the Time to Live), the checksum is recomputed and verified at each point that the IP header is processed.
Source Address	The 32-bit address of the host that sent the datagram.
Destination Address	The 32-bit address of the host to whom the datagram is destined.
Options	A variable-length list of optional information. See the *IP Options* section.
Padding	Padding bytes with a value of 0 are added to the end of the IP options, if necessary, to ensure that the IP header has a multiple of 32 bits (as required by the Header Length field).

The IP Type of Service or DS Field

The third field of the IP header, after the Version and Header Length fields, has undergone many changes over the years. The field was originally called the *Type of Service* field, and that is what it is still called by many applications and reference materials. The field provides support for different levels of precedence and types of service in the handling of IP datagrams. Per RFC 2474, published in 1998, the field is now called the DS field. This section discusses the Type of Service field first, followed by a quick description of the DS field. Figure 7.3 shows the Type of Service field.

The IP Type of Service field specifies both precedence and type of service. Precedence helps a router determine which packet to send when several packets are queued for transmission to the same output interface. Type of service helps a router select a routing path when multiple paths to a particular destination are available.

The Type of Service field is divided into two subfields, which are followed by a bit that is always set to 0:

- The 3-bit Precedence subfield supports eight levels of priority.

- The 4-bit Type of Service subfield supports four types of service. (Note that the subfield has the same name as the major field, which can be confusing.)

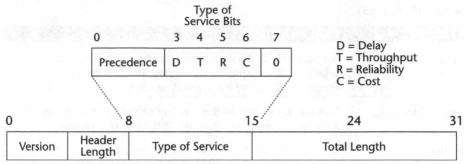

Figure 7.3　The IP Type of Service field.

The IP Precedence Subfield

An application can use the Precedence subfield to specify the importance of a packet. The importance can range from routine priority (the bits are set to 000) to high priority (the bits are set to 111).

Precedence values 6 and 7 are reserved for network and internetwork control packets. One of the original uses envisioned for the Precedence subfield was congestion control. By giving congestion-control packets a precedence of 7 (111 in binary), an application can specify that these packets are more important than data packets, thus facilitating the effectiveness of the congestion-control mechanism. Precedence values 0 through 5 can be used for applications and user data. Some service providers offer a premium service that uses the Precedence field to mark a customer's traffic as high-priority data. Cisco routers and some host applications support configuring the Precedence value. The Precedence value is typically set to 5 for Voice over IP (VoIP) and other real-time multimedia applications.

In the past, as protocol analyst consultants, we used to tell customers to be concerned if they saw any IP packets with a non-0 Precedence field. A non-0 Precedence value used to be an indication of an abnormal configuration or a bug, and a potential cause for problems, especially if the packet traversed or ended up at a device that didn't support the Precedence field. These days, the Precedence field is actually used, especially in voice and video applications.

The IP Type of Service Subfield

The goal of the Type of Service subfield is to help a router select a route from a set of routes to a particular destination, especially when the routes have different characteristics. Routing protocols attempt to determine the best route to a destination, but there are several definitions of *best*—cheapest, fastest, most reliable, least delayed, and so on.

According to RFC 1349, which clarified the use of the Type of Service byte (but is now obsolete), the Type of Service subfield contains 4 bits that specify the routing service an application wishes to receive from a router. An application or host can set 1 (and only 1) of the 4 bits:

1. The delay (D) bit tells routers to minimize delay.

2. The throughput (T) bit tells routers to maximize throughput.

3. The reliability (R) bit tells routers to maximize reliability.

4. The cost (C) bit tells routers to minimize monetary cost.

Setting the D bit is suitable for interactive applications, such as Telnet and Rlogin. When the D bit is set, a router should select a path that minimizes delay—for example, a dedicated high-speed leased line instead of a shared Frame Relay link. File transfer applications, or any applications that send bulk data, can set the T bit. Setting the T bit tells routers to select high-throughput links. Network management and mission-critical applications can set the R bit. Setting the R bit tells routers to select reliable paths. Applications for which delay, throughput, or reliability are not critical—but a low monetary cost is important—set the C bit. Some implementations of the Network News Transfer Protocol (NNTP), which reads UseNet news, set the C bit, presumably because reading news is not a critical activity and should not use a lot of monetary resources.

In practice, routing protocols and routers never had good methods for handling these bits. Selecting a path based on the setting of these bits proved to be impractical. Although early versions of the Open Shortest Path First (OSPF) and Border Gateway Protocol (BGP) routing protocols specified support for the bits, newer versions of OSPF and BGP specifications do not require support for routing based on the setting of the bits.

As a protocol analyst, you should not expect to see any of the Type of Service subfield bits set, unless you know that the bits are actually defining a DS, as discussed in the next section. If you see the bits in the Type of Service subfield set, you should find out which station is doing it and what the expectations are for service through the internetwork. It may be that some particular application or operating system is using these bits for a vendor-proprietary or experimental purpose, but it's likely that the routers in the network won't know how to correctly process the bits. The packets will be forwarded according to the standard rules for routing, and the intent of the Type of Service bits will be ignored.

The DS Field

RFC 1349 was declared obsolete with the publication of RFC 2474, "Definition of the Differentiated Services Field (DS Field) in the IPv4 and IPv6 Headers," and RFC 2475, "An Architecture for Differentiated Services." Per these newer RFCs, the Type of Service field became the DS field. The DS field has two Currently Unused (CU) bits at the end. The first 6 bits are called the Differentiated Services Codepoint (DSCP), as shown in Figure 7.4.

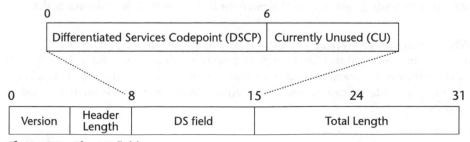

Figure 7.4 The DS field.

The DSCP has essentially the same goal as the Precedence field, which is to influence queuing and packet-dropping decisions for IP datagrams on an output interface of a router. RFC 2474 refers to these decisions as *Per-Hop Behaviors* (PHBs). The DSCP can have 1 of 64 possible values, each of which outlines a PHB. The DSCP field is backward compatible with the Precedence field. No attempt was made to retain compatibility with the Type of Service subfield, however.

The IETF has a DiffServ Working Group whose charter is to develop a set of building blocks for providing a Quality of Service (QoS) architecture for the Internet and intranets. The DS field is one of the building blocks that allows datagrams to be classified to receive a particular PHB on routers along the path to a destination. Setting the DSCP bits is often accomplished on a router at the edge of an internetwork. Setting the bits can cause routers inside the core of the internetwork to reserve resources so that datagrams for real-time or other high-priority applications can receive the high level of service that they require. For more information on the concepts behind the DS field, check RFC 2474, RFC 2475, and the Web pages of the DiffServ Working Group, starting at www.ietf.org/html.charters/diffserv-charter.html. For more information on implementing DSCP on Cisco routers, search for DSCP at Cisco's Web site, www.cisco.com.

IP Fragmentation and Reassembly

IP has the job of fragmenting and reassembling datagrams when necessary. RFC 791 specifies that all hosts and routers must be prepared to accept datagrams of up to 576 bytes. In practice, datagrams are often larger than 576 bytes. Datagram sizes vary depending on the message sizes used by applications and the Maximum Transmission Unit (MTU) supported by data link layers. Because Ethernet is so common, most applications send datagrams that fit into the Ethernet MTU of 1500 bytes, with some notable exceptions, such as many implementations of NFS. Also, applications running on Token Ring or FDDI networks may default to using an MTU that is much larger than 1500 bytes, typically around 4500 bytes.

CAUTION Unfortunately, simply setting the MTU to 1500 on hosts and routers does not guarantee that datagrams won't need to be fragmented. Packets may traverse tunnels, Virtual Private Networks (VPNs), Virtual Local Area Networks (VLANs), or encryption devices, all of which can increase the size of datagrams. See the *Configuring and Troubleshooting Ethernet Frame Sizes* section in Chapter 3 for some examples of situations where the Ethernet MTU was exceeded, resulting in the need for IP fragmentation and reassembly.

When a datagram arrives at an output interface, IP has the job of dividing the datagram into frames of legal size for the type of output interface, if necessary. The division of a datagram into fragments can happen at an end host or at a router. The Flags, Fragment Offset, and Identification fields are involved in the fragmentation and reassembly process.

Flags

The Flags field is 3 bits with the following format:

Bit 0.   This bit is reserved and must be 0.

Bit 1.   This bit is called the *Don't Fragment* (DF) bit and has two possible values: 0 = May Fragment, 1 = Don't Fragment. A host has the option of setting the DF bit. If the DF bit is set, then routers in the path to the destination may not fragment the datagram. This can result in problems if the router determines that the output interface requires the datagram to be divided into smaller frames. In this case, the router drops the datagram and sends an ICMP *destination unreachable* (ICMP Type 3), *Fragmentation was needed and the DF bit was set* (ICMP Code 4) message to the source. Some applications set the DF bit on initial packets to determine an optimal size to use to avoid fragmentation and reassembly for subsequent packets. This is called *MTU Discovery*.

Bit 2.   This bit is called the *More Fragments* (MF) bit and has two possible values: 0 = Last or Only Fragment, 1 = More Fragments. A 0 value is an indication that the packet either stands alone and is not part of a set of fragments, or the packet is the final fragment in a set of fragments. If the MF bit is set to 1, then the packet is part of a set of fragments and it is not the last fragment. There are more fragments to come.

Fragment Offset

The Fragment Offset field identifies the position of the fragment relative to the beginning of the data in the original datagram. For example, consider a case where an output interface supports a small MTU of 576 bytes, not counting the data link header. Twenty of the 576 bytes are the IP header itself, so the payload of each frame is 556 bytes. If an application sends 1500 bytes of data that must cross this interface, then IP has the job of dividing those 1500 bytes into three fragments. The fragment offset is 0 in the first fragment, 556 in the second fragment, and 1112 in the third fragment.

Identification

Each IP datagram has a number that is placed in the Identification field. Together with the Source Address, Destination Addresses, and Protocol fields, the identification number uniquely identifies a datagram. The number usually increases by 1 for each IP datagram sent by a host. The initial number that an IP implementation uses for the first datagram it sends depends on the operating system. UNIX, for example, initializes the value based on the time of day when the system was booted.

The Identification field identifies a complete datagram. When a datagram is divided into fragments, each fragment has the same Identification number. This helps the recipient put the fragments back into the correct datagram. Using the Identification and Fragment Offset fields, the recipient can put the bytes back together in the order that they were originally placed into the datagram by an upper layer. In general, the Identification field can be ignored, except when troubleshooting fragmentation and reassembly problems.

IP FRAGMENTATION IN AN 802.11 WIRELESS LAN

When a segment (probably the last segment in the forwarding path) of a route is a wireless segment, the issues related to fragmentation remain the same, but with some additional considerations. An 802.11 wireless network uses its own packet encapsulation and MTU size. The 802.11 basic header is 32 bytes, plus a 4-byte checksum field at the end and an optional 8-byte Wired Equivalent Privacy (WEP) field used for encryption. The body (data portion) of an 802.11 packet may contain up to 2312 bytes. The largest possible Ethernet frame can easily fit into a single 802.11 frame.

802.11 implements its own special form of fragmentation. A value, called the *fragmentation threshold*, is configured into each wireless driver. When a frame is received for transmission that is larger than the fragmentation threshold, the 802.11 data link breaks the frame into smaller pieces and reassembles them on the receiving end. This process behaves like IP fragmentation, but it takes place at the Media Access Control (MAC) sublayer of the data link layer. The purpose of 802.11 fragmentation is to reduce the likelihood of collisions that could result if two or more stations are waiting for a third station to complete the transmission of a long frame. The longer the frame, the greater the likelihood that more than one other station has data to transmit. Multiple stations could start to transmit at essentially the same time, after the long transmission ends.

These thoughts may lead you to believe that the behavior of an 802.11 data link can impact IP fragmentation. It can't. The behavior of the 802.11 transmission mechanism is completely transparent to the higher layers. A maximum-size Ethernet frame can be passed down to the 802.11 driver in its entirety (without requiring IP fragmentation). On the receiving end, the 802.11 driver will do whatever is necessary (MAC-layer reassembly, Cyclic Redundancy Checks [CRCs], 802.11 acknowledgment) to pass the identical frame up the stack. The fact that 802.11 can use packet lengths that are greater than those allowed in Ethernet is not perceptible by the Ethernet communicators using the wireless link.

Monitoring and Troubleshooting Fragmentation and Reassembly

Fragmentation and reassembly should be avoided if possible. When a sending host or a router must divide up packets, it takes extra time and can cause performance problems. A router may not be able to use its fastest packet-forwarding processes if it is required to fragment packets. Fragmentation can also tax the CPU of a router. On a Cisco router, use the show processes cpu command to determine if fragmentation may be causing high CPU usage. Check the *ip input* value.

Reassembly of fragments into a datagram occurs at the recipient, not at intermediate router hops. This can result in unnecessary inefficiencies. For example, perhaps a packet starts out large, gets divided into small fragments for traversal across a network that requires small packets, and then reenters a part of the internetwork that supports large packets. The packets remain fragmented even on the part of the internetwork that allows large packets. The recipient must reassemble the packets. The recipient could be an older PC that is noticeably slowed down by the need to reassemble IP datagrams. Also, the PC may be configured with firewall software that blocks IP fragments. Because of hacker techniques that send IP fragments, many firewalls default to not accepting IP fragments. This blocking of fragments can cause problems, especially in cases where IP datagrams have traversed tunnels or VPNs and fragmentation cannot be avoided.

When troubleshooting fragmentation and reassembly problems, it helps to use a protocol analyzer that fully decodes the bits in an IP header—for example, the Wild-Packets EtherPeek and AiroPeek products. Figure 7.5 shows EtherPeek's decoding of the first fragment that was sent during a troubleshooting session. In an attempt to reproduce a problem, the troubleshooter started some pings from the MS-DOS prompt on a PC running Windows 98. The ping utility reported that there were no replies. The pings were sent to the default gateway router, which was configured with the 172.16.10.1 address. The troubleshooter used the `ping -l 4096 172.16.10.1` command. The `-l 4096` option specifies that 4096 bytes of data should be sent in the ping. The PC was connected to an Ethernet network, so IP was required to fragment the 4096 bytes into three fragments.

Figure 7.5 shows the first fragment of the 4096-byte ping. Notice at the bottom of the figure that the first fragment includes 1472 bytes of data, not counting any headers. Where does 1472 come from? Before you continue reading, see if you can answer this question for yourself.

The total size of the frame is 1518 bytes, counting the Ethernet header and FCS. At the IP layer, notice that the Total Length field specifies 1500 bytes, which does not count the Ethernet header and FCS, because the total length is from the point of view of IP, not Ethernet. The IP header length is five 32-bit units (20 bytes). The ICMP header is 8 bytes. The ICMP header includes the ICMP Type, Code, Checksum, Identifier, and Sequence Number fields. (Each ICMP ping or echo has an identifier and sequence number that the recipient places into the reply so that the sender can match replies with requests.) If you subtract the 20-byte IP header and the 8-byte ICMP header from 1500 bytes, then there are 1472 bytes left for data.

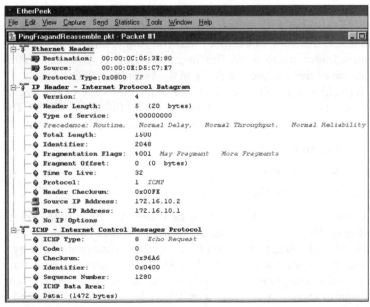

Figure 7.5   The first IP fragment when pinging with 4096 bytes of data.

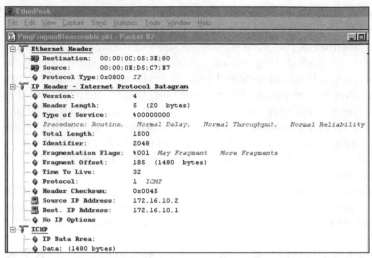

Figure 7.6   The second IP fragment when pinging with 4096 bytes of data.

In the IP header, notice that the DF bit in the Fragmentation Flags field is 0, which means May Fragment. In other words, routers in the path to the destination may fragment this packet even further. The MF bit is 1, which means that there are more fragments to come. The fragment offset is 0, which is expected as this is the first fragment. The IP identification (which EtherPeek calls the identifier) is 2048. We should expect to see that same identifier in all the fragments. Figure 7.6 shows the second fragment.

In the second IP fragment, there are 1480 bytes of data. Notice that the ICMP header is not repeated. This fragment just includes more data bytes that were sent as part of the original ping. The identifier is 2048, as expected. (It is the same as the first fragment.) The Flags field is also the same as the first fragment. Routers may fragment the packet and there are more fragments to come. The fragment offset, which is 1480 in this case, identifies the position of this fragment relative to the beginning of the data.

The Fragment Offset field is a 13-bit field. In the hexadecimal view of the packet (which is not shown), the 3-bit Flags and 13-bit Fragment Offset fields are 0x20B9. The first 4 bits are binary 0010 or 0x2. The first 3 bits signify the following information:

- The first bit is reserved and should always be 0.

- The second bit is 0, which means May Fragment.

- The third bit is 1, which means More Fragments.

In the detail view of the packet, EtherPeek shows the Fragment Offset field in decimal. The fragment offset is 185 in decimal. (Convert 0x0B9 to decimal by multiplying B, or 11, by 16 and adding 9.) The Fragment Offset field stipulates the number of 8-byte units past the beginning of the original data. Multiply 185 by 8 to get 1480. This fragment starts 1480 bytes into the datagram, which makes sense, as this is the second datagram and the first datagram included 1480 bytes of data (8 bytes of an ICMP header and 1472 bytes of ICMP data). The third fragment should be the final fragment, if all works as expected. Figure 7.7 shows the third fragment.

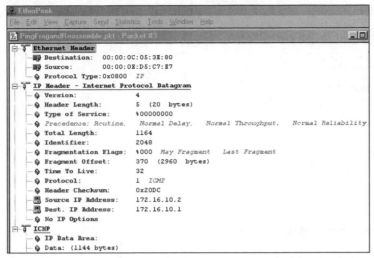

Figure 7.7 The third IP fragment when pinging with 4096 bytes of data.

The third fragment is similar to the other fragments with some differences. Notice that it has the same identifier, as expected. The MF bit is 0, which means that this is the last fragment for the datagram. Upon receipt of this fragment, the recipient can reassemble the fragments and allow IP to process the complete datagram and hand off the data to ICMP. The fragment offset is 370 in decimal. Multiply 370 by 8 to determine that the fragment offset is 2960 bytes, which makes sense as the first two fragments each had 1480 bytes, and 1480 doubled is 2960. This final fragment is smaller than the other two fragments. Before reading further, see if you can determine why this final fragment has only 1144 bytes of data.

The reason this fragment has 1144 bytes of data is because that's all that's left! The ping included 4096 bytes of data plus an 8-byte ICMP header, for a total of 4104 bytes. Subtract 2960 from 4104 and you get 1144 bytes. In summary, the 4096 bytes of data were sent in the three fragments shown in Table 7.3.

Figure 7.8 shows the first reply from the router that was being pinged. ICMP specifies that when an ICMP echo includes data, the reply should include the same data as the request. So, the router sent the same 4096 bytes back, divided into three fragments. Figure 7.8 shows the first fragment. Notice that the ICMP identifier and sequence number are the same as they were in the ICMP echo request shown in Figure 7.5. (The fact that the IP identifier is also the same is surprising. There is no requirement that this be the case. It wouldn't be the case if the destination were a non-Cisco device.)

Table 7.3 IP Fragments

FRAGMENT	IDENTIFIER	OFFSET	NUMBER OF BYTES
1	2048	0	1472 plus an 8-byte ICMP header
2	2048	1480	1480
3	2048	2960	1144

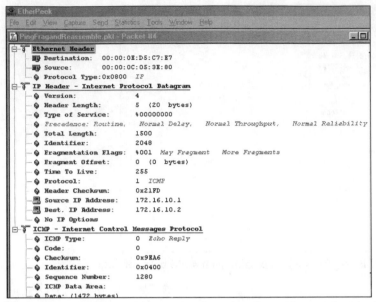

Figure 7.8   The first IP fragment reply to the ping with 4096 bytes of data.

The router sent the final two fragments and the troubleshooter verified that there was nothing wrong with any of the replies. Nonetheless, the MS-DOS ping utility reported that all four attempted pings timed out. EtherPeek running on the PC (which captured the frames shown in the figures) confirmed that the PC really did receive the replies. The problem turned out to be that the software firewall on the PC blocked the fragments and did not pass them to the ping application. The problems with ping and other applications were solved once this option was disabled on the firewall.

IP Time to Live

The IP Time to Live (TTL) field is set by the sender of an IP datagram. Each router along the path to the destination decrements the TTL field by one, which means that the TTL ends up being sort of a reverse hop count. In the original IP specifications, an option was provided for routers to track how many seconds they took to handle a datagram and to decrement the TTL by the number of seconds. For example, if a busy router had to queue a frame for 3 seconds, then the TTL would be decremented by three. Remember that the TTL field was designed in the 1960s. Today, if your router takes 3 seconds to forward a packet, then you should remove the router from the rack, attach a strong rope to it, and use it as a boat anchor! Today's router throughput is measured in thousands of packets per second. Routers take much less than a second to handle a datagram and do not track how much time they actually take. The routers simply decrement the TTL by one. In some troubleshooting tools, you may still see the TTL defined as the number of seconds or the number of router hops, but just ignore the seconds part.

Decrementing the TTL is one of the first tasks an IP router does upon arrival of an IP datagram. If the decrementing results in the TTL becoming zero, the router drops the datagram and sends an ICMP *TTL exceeded message* (ICMP Type 11, Code 0). As mentioned in Chapter 2, the trace-route facility makes use of the TTL and ICMP message.

Other than the creative use of TTL by trace-route, the main reason that TTL exists is to avoid packets living forever on a network that has a routing loop. Although routing protocols have other methods for avoiding loops, as will be discussed in Chapter 8, a misconfiguration or buggy implementation could cause a packet to go from a router to another and back again in a loop. Because each router decrements the TTL and drops the packet when the TTL reaches zero, the packet does not loop forever. At some point, the packet dies when its TTL expires.

As mentioned, the TTL is initially set by the sender. Because the field is just 1 byte, the sender cannot make the TTL larger than 255. Many operating systems set the TTL to a much smaller value. The story is told (although it may simply be a myth, but it makes for a good story anyway) that Microsoft selected 32 as the starting hop count for the TCP/IP stack in Windows 95 to focus on the fact that Windows 95 was a 32-bit operating system. Perhaps one engineer went out to lunch with three marketing people and came back with the idea.

Notice in Figures 7.5 through 7.7 that the Windows 98 sender set the TTL to 32. Windows 98 uses a TTL of 128 for most IP datagrams, but it uses 32 when sending a ping. The recipient, which was a Cisco router, set the TTL to 255, as shown in Figure 7.8. There is no requirement for both ends of a conversation to use the same starting value for the TTL field. The only issue is the implied diameter (measured in hops) of the internetwork that can be reached. An originator using 32 as its starting TTL could not reach a destination network that was more than 32 hops away.

Typically, in campus and even most corporate networks (as opposed to the Internet), it would be unusual for a packet to cross more than four or five router hops. Although the total number of routers on the internetwork may be large, they are usually arranged in a hierarchical topology so that the longest path from any station to another does not include numerous hops. When analyzing a trace file, if you see a TTL that makes you think a packet crossed more than about five hops, then you should explore the situation further. If you discover more than about 10 hops, then you should pay even more attention, because this would indeed be atypical. In all likelihood, routing is not acting as expected and the logical topology is different from what the administrator intended. If the true topology of a network is not known, then the decisions regarding configuration and modification of the network are made based on false presumptions.

NOTE Because the IP TTL is a reverse hop count (starts large and gets smaller), it's not a great troubleshooting tool. You can't tell how many routers a packet has gone through unless you know the starting TTL. In general, programmers work with rounded numbers and powers of 2, so you can make a scientific guess about the starting value. Windows 95 uses 32 in most cases. Newer versions of Windows use 128 in most cases. Many UNIX versions use 60. Cisco uses 255 for non-routing-protocol packets originated at the router. Instead of using the TTL to determine a hop count, you can use the trace-route utility, which Chapter 2 discussed, and the IP record-route option, which will be discussed later in this chapter.

The IP Protocol Field

In general, almost all protocols have a *type field* to tell the recipient what is coming next in a packet. The recipient uses the type field to decide which process should receive the frame. As discussed in Chapter 3, Ethernet II uses the EtherType field for this purpose. IEEE 802.3 uses an 802.2 Service Access Point (SAP). TCP has a port number that differentiates between Telnet, SMTP, HTTP, and other applications. UDP also has a port number that differentiates between DNS, SNMP, TFTP, and other applications that run on top of UDP. IP has a type field called the IP Protocol field that differentiates between TCP, UDP, and other protocols carried in an IP datagram.

Think of the IP Protocol field as similar in function to the EtherType or SAP fields. These protocol identifiers are like holes in the ceiling. A frame comes into the Ethernet adapter at floor level. The software driver for the adapter checks the protocol identifier and pushes the frame into the correct ceiling hole based on the value of the EtherType or SAP. Using the holes, the adapter can place a frame into the correct buffer for collection by IP at the network layer. IP processes the frame and pushes it upward into the right hole for the next layer. A sending host also uses the holes. Software programs, residing on the upper floors, push frames down through the holes to arrive at the correct layers.

To be a good troubleshooter, you should learn some of the typical IP protocol types you will see in an IP network. Table 7.4 documents typical protocol types to help you learn what to expect. For more information, see documents from the Internet Assigned Numbers Authority (IANA), in particular the "Protocol Numbers and Assignment Services" document at www.iana.org/numbers.html.

IP Options

The Options field follows the Destination Address field in an IP header and is not required. However, if a recipient receives a datagram with an Options field, the recipient is required to process the options per RFC 791. (Support for the field is not optional, despite its name.) The Options field is included primarily for network testing and debugging. Although most datagrams don't include any IP options, it is still a good idea to have some idea of what the options are used for, in case you see some while troubleshooting. Also, some of the options (loose source routing, strict source routing, and record-route) have some use in troubleshooting.

The length of the Options field varies depending on which options are present. When multiple options are present in a datagram, they appear contiguously. Each option starts with an Option Code byte, which may be followed by a 1-byte length field and a set of data bytes for the particular option. The Option Code byte is divided into three subfields, as shown in Figure 7.9.

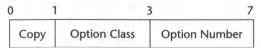

Figure 7.9   The Option Code byte in the IP Options field.

Table 7.4 Common IP Protocol Types

PROTOCOL	PROTOCOL TYPE IN HEX	PROTOCOL TYPE IN DECIMAL
ICMP	0x01	1
IGMP	0x02	2
IP (IP-in-IP tunneling)	0x04	4
TCP	0x06	6
Interior Gateway Routing Protocol (IGRP)	0x09	9
UDP	0x11	17
Generic Route Encapsulation (GRE)	0x2F	47
Enhanced Interior Gateway Routing Protocol (EIGRP)	0x58	88
OSPF	0x59	89

The Copy bit of the Option Code byte controls how routers treat options during fragmentation. When the Copy bit is set to 1, the option should be copied into all fragments. When the Copy bit is set to 0, the option should only be copied into the first fragment and not into all fragments.

The Option Class subfield specifies the general class of the option and can be either 0 (datagram or network control) or 2 (debugging and measurement). Option classes 1 and 3 are also possible and mean "reserved for future use." Table 7.5 lists the currently defined options, with their class and option number.

Table 7.5 IP Options

CLASS	NUMBER	LENGTH	DESCRIPTION
0	0	1	End of the options list. This option is used at the end of all options, not the end of each option, and need only be used if the end of the options would not otherwise coincide with the end of the IP header. It consists of just an Option Code byte.
0	1	1	No operation. This option may be used between options—for example, to align the beginning of a subsequent option on a 32-bit boundary. It consists of just an Option Code byte.

(continues)

Table 7.5 IP Options *(Continued)*

CLASS	NUMBER	LENGTH	DESCRIPTION
0	2	11	Security. Used to carry security information for obsolete military applications.
0	3	Varies	Loose source routing. Used to route the datagram based on partial information supplied by the source.
0	9	Varies	Strict source routing. Used to route the datagram based on exact information supplied by the source.
0	7	Varies	Record-route. Used to track the routers through which a datagram travels.
0	8	4	Stream ID. Used to carry a stream identifier for obsolete Application Program Interfaces (APIs) to TCP/IP.
2	4	Varies	Internet timestamp. Used with record-route to record timestamps along a route.

IP Source Routing

Under normal conditions, when a router receives an IP packet, it evaluates the destination IP address on the basis of information contained in the router's routing table and makes a decision on how to forward the packet. A particular destination, which could be a network/subnetwork or a host-specific target, is reachable either directly through one of the router's interfaces or by sending the packet on to the *next hop* (the IP address of the next router in the routing path). The IP address is resolved to a data link layer address using ARP, or a method similar to ARP for Wide Area Networks (WANs).

Options are available in IP to allow the source station to specify all or part of a routing path as an alternative to using routers to make the decisions about forwarding. These options, referred to as *IP Source Routing*, are in the realm of testing and troubleshooting and are not part of normal host-to-host data communication in a network.

NOTE The concept of a source station constructing a frame-forwarding path is also used in 802.5 Token Ring networks. However, with Token Ring, the source specifies data link layer bridge numbers and ring numbers. You may hear the term *source-route bridging*, or simply *source routing*, used in relationship to 802.5 Token Ring networks. Although the concept is similar to IP source routing, the implementation is completely different.

The goal of IP source routing is to allow a network engineer to test a path through IP routers to a remote destination. Rather than depending on dynamic routing to select the path, the engineer specifies the route. IP supports two forms of source routing:

1. *Strict source routing.* The sender specifies the exact path that the IP datagram must follow. The sender includes a list of IP addresses that indicate each router that must forward the datagram. If a router encounters an address in the list that isn't on a directly-connected network, the router drops the datagram and sends an *ICMP source route failed* (ICMP Type 3, Code 5) message to the originator of the datagram.

2. *Loose source routing.* The sender specifies a list of router IP addresses that the datagram must traverse, but the datagram can also pass through other routers between any two addresses in the list.

Figure 7.10 shows the format of the source routing option in an IP header. The sending host takes the list of router addresses from the application, removes the first entry, and uses that entry as the destination address of the datagram. Each router that handles the datagram checks whether it is the destination address in the datagram. If not, the datagram is forwarded as normal. (This would only happen if loose source routing was specified; otherwise the router shouldn't receive the datagram.) If the router is the destination, the next address in the list becomes the destination address of the new datagram. The router also replaces its own address in the list with the IP address of the outgoing interface. (Source routing also records the IP address for each router, much like the record-route option does.) The router increments the pointer field by four so that it points to the next address.

From a protocol analysis point of view, it is easy to get confused when looking at addresses in datagrams with the source routing option. With source routing, the destination IP address changes for each hop, which is not what you might expect. If a host pings 172.16.50.2, for example, and uses source routing to specify that the packet must go through a set of routers, you won't see the final 172.16.50.2 destination address unless your analyzer is on the network where the final destination resides. Instead, you will see a datagram addressed to the next hop to 172.16.50.2.

The list of addresses in the source routing option can also be confusing. The list must start out as a list of addresses used by incoming datagrams on routers in the path to the destination. The list ends up as a list of outgoing interfaces because each router replaces its address in the list with the address for the interface it uses when forwarding the datagram.

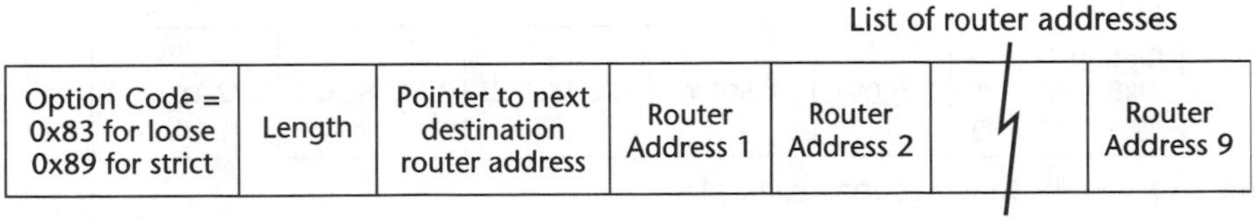

List of router addresses

Option Code = 0x83 for loose 0x89 for strict	Length	Pointer to next destination router address	Router Address 1	Router Address 2		Router Address 9

Figure 7.10 The format of the IP source routing option.

If you plan to use IP source routing for troubleshooting, you must know the address of each router hop to put into the datagram. Figure 7.11 shows an example if you were to send a datagram with strict source routing from 172.16.10.2 to 172.16.50.2. Because of the need to know router addresses, IP source routing is not used much for troubleshooting, although it is a helpful tool for campus network engineers who have good network documentation and can specify router addresses.

IP Record-Route

Record-route uses an Options field that is similar to the Options field for source routing; however, there is no need for the engineer to specify the address of each router. Instead, the engineer specifies how many blank spaces to leave for router addresses, and each router fills in its own address. Note that if you send a packet that requires a reply—such as a ping—each router en route to the destination fills in its address, and each router on the way back fills in its address. Figure 7.12 shows the use of the record-route option when doing a ping from the MS-DOS prompt on a Windows 98 PC. The PC was the 172.16.10.2 host shown on the left side of Figure 7.11. The PC pinged the 172.16.50.1 interface on the Charlotte router shown in Figure 7.11.

NOTE If you don't use a datagram that results in a reply, such as a ping, you have to monitor the results of the record-route option at the recipient to see the router addresses.

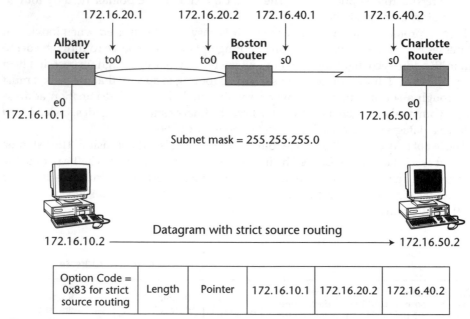

Figure 7.11   An IP source routing example.

```
C:\WINDOWS>ping -n 1 -r 9 172.16.50.1

Pinging 172.16.50.1 with 32 bytes of data:

Reply from 172.16.50.1: bytes=32 time=39ms TTL=253
    Route: 172.16.20.1 ->
           172.16.40.1 ->
           172.16.50.1 ->
           172.16.40.2 ->
           172.16.20.2 ->
           172.16.10.1

Ping statistics for 172.16.50.1:
    Packets: Sent = 1, Received = 1, Lost = 0 (0% loss),
Approximate round trip times in milli-seconds:
    Minimum = 39ms, Maximum =  39ms, Average =  39ms
```

Figure 7.12   Using the record-route option with MS-DOS Ping.

Many troubleshooters confuse record-route with trace-route, even though they are quite different. Record-route is the IP capability that uses the IP Options field to record the outgoing router interface addresses on the path to the destination and the outgoing router interfaces on the path from the destination, if there is a reply. Trace-route is a utility program that makes use of the TTL field, rather than the Options field, and relies on ICMP messages returning from each router.

The IP source address in an ICMP message sent by a router must be one of the IP addresses associated with the physical interface over which the ICMP message is transmitted, according to the Router Requirements RFC 1812. If the interface has no IP addresses associated with it, another address is used instead. (This could happen if *IP unnumbered* was used on a serial interface, for example.) From a troubleshooting perspective, it's important to realize that you may see different router addresses when using record-route versus trace-route. The ICMP messages come from the interfaces closest to you. The addresses in the Record Route fields are outgoing interfaces toward the destination.

Record-route has limited value on large internetworks because the space allocated for options in the IP header isn't large enough to handle more than nine router IP addresses. If you are looking at addresses both to and from a destination, then this limitation is even more of a problem.

The IP Options field also supports a timestamp option. The timestamp option is similar to the record-route option, but each router adds a timestamp with its address. The timestamp is 4 bytes, and its preferred value is the number of milliseconds past midnight. Given the limitations on the size of the Options field, the timestamp option is of little value. Assuming you are displaying addresses to and from a destination, you can only see two hops in each direction and their respective timestamps. Also, when viewing the timestamps, if you don't know how a router specifies the time, the results are not very useful.

IP Addressing

This book does not include a lot of detail about basic IP addressing concepts. Instead, we assume you have already read many descriptions of IP addressing and that you work with IP addresses on a regular basis. On the other hand, this book will help you look at IP addresses in a new way, without the old-fashioned constraints that divide addresses at strict boundaries.

Each interface on each IP host in an IP internetwork has a unique 32-bit (4-byte) IP address assigned to it. When a host sends a datagram, the host places the IP address of the output interface in the Source Address field. The host places the intended recipient's address in the Destination Address field. Because 32 is a large number of bits, IP addresses are usually written in *dotted-decimal notation*. Each 8-bit byte is converted to decimal and separated from the next byte by a dot. Table 7.6 shows some examples.

Although it's easiest to read IP addresses in dotted-decimal notation, when troubleshooting problems related to IP addressing, it's best to think of addresses in binary. It often helps to spell out an address in binary and not to worry about how the bits are divided into bytes during your initial analysis.

As shown in Figure 7.13, at the simplest level, a 32-bit IP address contains a *prefix* field and a *host* field. Routers use the prefix field to determine how to forward a datagram for a destination address that is not local and the host field to reach local hosts. The number of bits that belong in the prefix field and the host field are defined by a *prefix length* value. On modern networks, the prefix length is not fixed and can differ for each network segment in an internetwork. The engineer who designs an internetwork decides the value of the prefix and its length for each connected segment. Each host interface is configured with a prefix, prefix length, and host number. The prefix length is often configured as a *subnet mask*, as will be seen.

Originally, the boundary between the prefix and the host portions of an IP address was less flexible than it is today. Per RFC 760, the boundary was after the first byte. RFC 791 introduced address classes and stated that the boundary could be after either the first, second, or third byte. If the leftmost bit in an address was 0, the boundary was after the first byte and the address was a *Class A address*. If the leftmost 2 bits in an address were 10, the boundary was after the second byte and the address was a *Class B address*. If the leftmost 3 bits in an address were 110, the boundary was after the third byte and the address was a *Class C address*. Later RFCs also defined two additional classes, Class D and Class E. This information is summarized in Table 7.7.

Table 7.6 Dotted-Decimal Notation Examples

32-BIT BINARY ADDRESS	EQUIVALENT DOTTED-DECIMAL ADDRESS
00001010 00000010 00000000 00100101	10.2.0.37
10101100 00010000 00001010 00000001	172.16.10.1
10000001 00110100 00000110 00000001	129.52.6.1

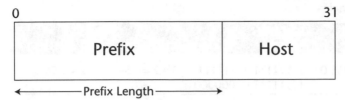

Figure 7.13   The two fields in an IP address.

Moving the Prefix Boundary to the Right (Subnetting)

In early IP implementations, IP hosts and routers understood only three prefix lengths: 8, 16, and 24. This became a limitation as networks grew, so *subnetting* was introduced in RFC 950, "Internet Standard Subnetting Procedure." With subnetting, a host or router can be configured to understand that the local prefix boundary has been moved to the right and that bits have been borrowed from the host portion to identify subnets. This configuration is accomplished with a subnet mask. A subnet mask is a 32-bit value that is used with an address to specify where the prefix boundary resides. For each 1 bit in the mask, the corresponding bit in the address is considered part of the prefix portion of the address. For each 0 bit in the mask, the corresponding bit in the address is considered part of the host portion of the address. The subnet mask is usually written in dotted-decimal notation. Table 7.8 shows some examples for the 172.16.0.0 network.

The *Subnets* column of Table 7.8 shows how many subnets are allowed when the specified subnet mask is used. The *Hosts Per Subnet* column shows how many hosts are allowed on each subnet. The table avoids using all 1s or all 0s for host or subnet numbers. A host number of all 1s means a broadcast. For some older operating systems, a host number of all 0s may also mean a broadcast. A host number of all 0s is also the common method for referring to an entire network or subnet. For example, Table 7.8 refers to the entire 172.16.0.0 network by using 0s in the host field.

Table 7.7   IP Address Classes

CLASS	FIRST FEW BITS	FIRST BYTE	PREFIX LENGTH	INTENT
A	0	1-126*	8	Very large networks
B	10	128-191	16	Large networks
C	110	192-223	24	Small networks
D	1110	224-239	NA	IP multicast addresses
E	1111	240-255	NA	Reserved for experimental use

*Addresses starting with 127 are reserved for IP traffic local to a host.

Table 7.8   Subnetting Examples

NETWORK	DECIMAL MASK	BINARY MASK	SUBNETS	HOSTS PER SUBNET
172.16.0.0	255.255.255.0	11111111 11111111 11111111 00000000	$2^8 - 2 = 254$	$2^8 - 2 = 254$
172.16.0.0	255.255.252.0	11111111 11111111 11111100 00000000	$2^6 - 2 = 62$	$2^{10} - 2 = 1022$
172.16.0.0	255.255.240.0	11111111 11111111 11110000 00000000	$2^4 - 2 = 14$	$2^{12} - 2 = 4094$

A subnet address of all 1s means all subnets and should be avoided. A subnet address of all 0s may actually be a legitimate subnet number depending on the operating system. With Cisco IOS software, you can use a subnet address of all 0s if you configure the `ip subnet-zero` command.

In the past, hosts and routers understood a prefix length that was no shorter than the class (A, B, or, C) for the address. Although the prefix boundary could be moved to the right, it could not be moved leftward beyond the class boundary. In modern practice, however, hosts and routers use *classless addressing*. In this system, the prefix length is not restricted by the class. This is especially helpful when aggregating network numbers for advertisement by a routing protocol, as will be discussed in the *Moving the Prefix Boundary to the Left (Supernetting)* section. Eliminating the need to assign addresses with the old class system also meant that the 32-bit IP address space could be used much more efficiently than before. Once classless addressing became the norm, many fewer addresses went to waste.

A new notation that has gained popularity in recent years for specifying the boundary between the prefix and host portion of an address indicates the prefix length with a length field, following a slash. For example, in the address 192.168.0.1/16, the 16 indicates that the prefix is 16 bits. So the 192.168.0.1/16 notation means network/subnet 192.168 and host 0.1. If you were to configure this address with a traditional subnet mask, you would use 255.255.0.0.

When a datagram arrives at a router, a router uses the subnet mask to determine which output interface to use. For example, a router may be on network 10.0.0.0, with each interface in a different subnet. Ethernet interface 0 (e0) may be on network 10.1.0.0. Ethernet interface 1 (e1) may be on network 10.2.0.0, and Token Ring interface 0 (to0) may be on network 10.3.0.0. When a datagram that is addressed to 10.3.0.1 arrives, the router uses the subnet mask to determine that the Token Ring interface should receive the datagram for forwarding.

End-station hosts also use subnet masks. A host uses a subnet mask to determine if a destination is local or on the other side of a router. When the IP layer at a host receives a datagram from an upper layer that is destined to a particular address, IP performs a Boolean AND operation with the subnet mask to determine if the datagram can be sent locally or not. You should be familiar with Boolean logic, which is illustrated in Table 7.9. Table 7.9 shows a table that is often referred to as a *Truth Table*, where 0 is false and 1 is true.

Table 7.9 Boolean Logic Truth Table

0 AND 0 = 0	0 OR 0 = 0
0 AND 1 = 0	0 OR 1 = 1
1 AND 0 = 0	1 OR 0 = 1
1 AND 1 = 1	1 OR 1 = 1

Consider the following example of how a host uses a subnet mask with the AND operation: A host that is assigned the IP address 10.6.15.3 and a subnet mask of 255.255.0.0 wishes to send a frame to 10.7.9.2. If 10.7.9.2 is on the same network as 10.6.15.3, then the host will broadcast an ARP frame to determine the data link layer address of the destination. The host will then send the frame directly to the destination. If 10.7.9.2 is on a different network, then the host must send the frame to a router for forwarding to the destination network. The dotted-decimal notation must be converted to the underlying 32-bit binary numbers to understand what is taking place, as shown in Table 7.10.

The source host performs a Boolean AND with its IP address and the mask, with the results shown in Table 7.11.

The source host performs a Boolean AND with the destination IP address and the mask, with the results shown in Table 7.12.

Table 7.10 Decimal and Binary Addresses

ELEMENT	DECIMAL	BINARY
Source host	10.6.15.3	00001010 00000110 00001111 00000011
Destination host	10.7.9.2	00001010 00000111 00001001 00000010
Mask	255.255.0.0	11111111 11111111 00000000 00000000

Table 7.11 Boolean AND of Source Address with Mask

ELEMENT	DECIMAL	BINARY
Source host	10.6.15.3	00001010 00000110 00001111 00000011
Mask	255.255.0.0	11111111 11111111 00000000 00000000
Result of AND	10.6.0.0	00001010 00000110 00000000 00000000

Table 7.12 Boolean AND of Destination Address with Mask

ELEMENT	DECIMAL	BINARY
Destination host	10.7.9.2	00001010 00000111 00001001 00000010
Mask	255.255.0.0	11111111 11111111 00000000 00000000
Result of AND	10.7.0.0	00001010 00000111 00000000 00000000

Because the results (10.6.0.0 and 10.7.0.0) are not equal, the source host concludes that the destination must be on a different network and sends the datagram to a router.

Claude Shannon and Boolean Logic

Students of networking often get confused when using Boolean logic, perhaps because it is an intangible concept and networking people like concrete, physical things, such as cables and routers. In actuality, Boolean logic is not ethereal, and, in fact, it was the basis for the original switches that were used to build computers. (In this case, we are not using the term *switch* to mean a data link layer interconnect device, but rather a device in an electrical circuit that is either closed, and thus allows current to flow, or is open and does not allow current to flow.)

Claude Shannon, who passed away in February 2001, had the cleanest and most practical way of describing Boolean logic of any method we have seen. This makes sense, as Shannon invented information theory and was the father of the Information Age. Shannon showed that multiple switches connected in circuits can carry out the operations of Boolean logic. If you line up two switches in series, they embody the Boolean AND operation. Current can flow through the circuit only if both switches are closed, as shown in Figure 7.14. Both values for circuit flow need to be 1 (true) for the result to be 1 (true).

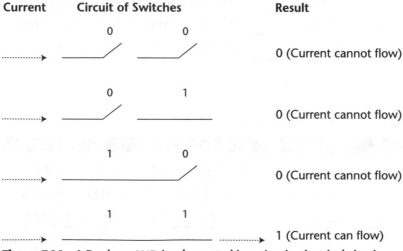

Figure 7.14 A Boolean AND implemented in a simple electrical circuit.

Current	Circuit of Switches		Result

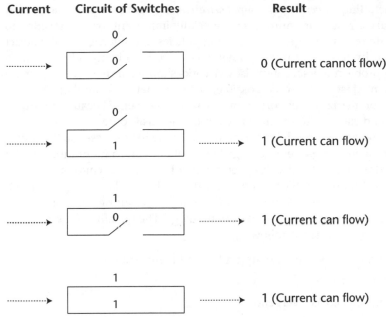

Figure 7.15 A Boolean OR implemented in a simple electrical circuit.

A circuit with two switches in parallel performs an OR operation, meaning that the current flows if either switch is closed, as shown in Figure 7.15. If either value for circuit flow is 1 (true), the result is 1 (true). For many network engineers who are graphically oriented, but require concrete examples, remembering these simple circuit diagrams is easier than memorizing a Truth Table.

In his 1937 master's degree thesis for the Massachusetts Institute of Technology (MIT), Shannon showed that any logical statement, no matter how complex, can be physically implemented as a network of simple switches. He later went on to show that switches could perform simple and complex mathematical operations and even make comparisons. These profound discoveries formed the foundation of digital computer design. Without Shannon, computer networking, Cisco Systems, and WildPackets would not exist, and we would probably all be plumbers instead of network engineers.

Moving the Prefix Boundary to the Left (Supernetting)

With subnetting, the prefix boundary is moved to the right so that more bits are used to define groups of hosts and fewer bits are used to identify each host within a group. There is also a process for moving the prefix boundary to the left, which sometimes goes by the name *supernetting*. Supernetting aggregates networks so that routing protocols can advertise them as a group rather than multiple individual networks.

In modern IP internetworking practices, it is important to advertise a group of networks (prefixes) together rather than separately. Grouping networks is known by many names, including *supernetting, summarization, aggregation,* and *hierarchical addressing.* Summarizing network numbers is especially important for a connection to the Internet. Despite recent changes in addressing policies, the Internet is still subject to problems caused by too many routes to networks (prefixes) being advertised. To avoid making this problem worse, enterprise networks should summarize (aggregate) network numbers into just a few—or, if possible, just one—network number. On large campus intranets, summarizing network numbers also makes sense because it reduces bandwidth usage and eases CPU and memory requirements at routers.

Hierarchical addressing is a model for applying structure to addresses so that numbers in the left part of an address refer to large blocks of networks and numbers in the right part of an address refer to individual networks or hosts. Hierarchical addressing facilitates hierarchical routing, which is a model for distributing knowledge of a network topology among internetwork routers. With hierarchical routing, no single router needs to understand the complete internetwork topology. The benefits of hierarchy in addressing and routing include the following:

- Support for easy troubleshooting, upgrades, and manageability
- Optimized performance
- Faster routing protocol convergence
- Scalability
- Stability
- Fewer network resources needed (CPU, memory, buffers, bandwidth, and so on)

Hierarchical addressing permits the summarization (aggregation) of network numbers. Summarization allows a router to group many network numbers when advertising its routing table. Summarization enhances network performance and stability. Hierarchical addressing also facilitates Variable-Length Subnet Masking (VLSM). With VLSM, a network can be divided into subnets of different sizes, which helps optimize available address space.

This section covers a route summarization example that is based on the network shown in Figure 7.16. Looking at Figure 7.16, you can see that a network engineer assigned network numbers 172.16.0.0 through 172.19.0.0 to networks in a branch office.

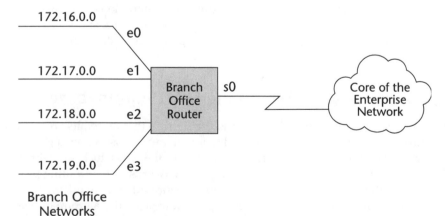

Figure 7.16 An example of hierarchical addressing.

The branch office router in Figure 7.16 can summarize its local network numbers and report that it has 172.16.0.0/14 behind it. By advertising this single route, the router is saying, "Route packets to me if the destination has the first 14 bits set to 172.16." The router is reporting a route to all networks where the first 14 bits are equal to 10101100 000100 in binary. The router has moved the prefix boundary to the left for the purpose of advertising routes. The router is supernetting.

To understand the summarization in this example, you should convert the number 172 to binary, which results in the binary number 10101100. You should also convert the numbers 16 through 19 to binary, as shown in Table 7.13.

Notice that the leftmost 6 bits for the numbers 16 through 19 are identical. This is what makes route summarization with a prefix length of 14 possible in this example. The first 8 bits for the networks are identical (all the networks have 172 for the first octet), and the next 6 bits are also identical. For route summarization to work correctly, the following requirements must be met:

- Multiple IP network numbers must share the same leftmost bits.

- Routers must base their routing decisions on a 32-bit IP address and prefix length that can be up to 32 bits. (A host-specific route has a 32-bit prefix.)

- Routing protocols must carry the prefix length with 32-bit network addresses. (Modern routing protocols do this, although older protocols do not.)

In many cases, hierarchical addressing and routing are new concepts for IP network engineers, but they are not complicated concepts. By spending some time analyzing network numbers (and converting the addresses to binary), you can see the simplicity and elegance of hierarchical addressing and route summarization. When you look at a block of subnets, you can determine if the addresses can be summarized by using the following rules:

- The number of subnets to be summarized must be a power of 2—for example, 2, 4, 8, 16, 32, and so on.

- The relevant octet in the first address in the block to be summarized must be a multiple of the number of subnets.

Table 7.13 Binary Numbers for Summarization Example

SECOND OCTET IN DECIMAL	SECOND OCTET IN BINARY
16	00010000
17	00010001
18	00010010
19	00010011

Let's consider one more example. The following network numbers are defined at a branch office. Can they be summarized?

- 10.108.48.0
- 10.108.49.0
- 10.108.50.0
- 10.108.51.0
- 10.108.52.0
- 10.108.53.0
- 10.108.54.0
- 10.108.55.0

The number of subnets is 8, which is a power of 2, so the first condition is met. The relevant octet (third in this case) is 48, which is a multiple of the number of subnets. So, the second condition is met. The subnets can be summarized as 10.108.48.0/21. (Convert the numbers to binary to understand the prefix length of 21.)

Address Resolution Protocol (ARP)

A station wishing to send frames to another station on its LAN segment must know the data link layer address of the Network Interface Card (NIC) that will receive the frames. A station must have some means of mapping a destination network layer address to the data link layer address of the destination NIC. ARP solves this problem on an IP network.

ARP is used by IP to associate network layer IP addresses with data link layer addresses. An IP host maintains a data structure called an *ARP cache*, which contains mappings of IP addresses to data link layer addresses. When a host wishes to send a message to an IP address, the station looks for the IP address in its ARP cache, finds the associated data link layer address, and then properly addresses the message. During a troubleshooting session, to view the ARP cache on a Cisco router, use the show arp command. To view the ARP cache on a UNIX or Windows (DOS) machine, use the arp -a command.

ARP frames come into play when a host wishes to communicate with a particular IP address, but does not have an entry for the IP address in its ARP cache. A host in this situation sends an ARP frame addressed to the data link layer broadcast address, so that all IP stations on the network segment receive the frame. The ARP broadcast says, "If you have the IP address I'm looking for, please respond and tell me your data link layer address." If a host on the network segment has the IP address in the ARP frame, it responds directly to the requesting host, which adds an entry to its ARP cache and then initiates a conversation. If no host responds, then the requesting host times out.

On a Cisco router, you will sometimes see that the router is waiting for an ARP response. When you view the ARP cache you see *Incomplete*, as shown in the following example.

```
Router#show arp
Protocol    Address     Age (min)  Hardware Addr   Type    Interface
Internet    100.0.0.4     2         0004.c059.c1a1  ARPA    Ethernet0/1
Internet    100.0.0.5     0         Incomplete      ARPA
Internet    100.0.0.1     6         0004.c059.c061  ARPA    Ethernet0/1
```

After a short period of time, this incomplete entry is purged from the ARP cache. When you can't successfully reach another host on a LAN segment, you can look at ARP caches and ARP traffic to determine what is wrong. On a Cisco router, you can use the debug arp command, which shows output similar to the following example.

```
Router4#ping 100.0.0.5
Type escape sequence to abort.
Sending 5, 100-byte ICMP Echos to 100.0.0.5, timeout is 2 seconds:
IP ARP: creating incomplete entry for IP address: 100.0.0.5
IP ARP: sent req src 100.0.0.4 0004.c059.c1a1,
              DST 100.0.0.5 0000.0000.0000 Ethernet0/1.
IP ARP: sent req src 100.0.0.4 0004.c059.c1a1,
              DST 100.0.0.5 0000.0000.0000 Ethernet0/1.
IP ARP: sent req src 100.0.0.4 0004.c059.c1a1,
              DST 100.0.0.5 0000.0000.0000 Ethernet0/1.
IP ARP: sent req src 100.0.0.4 0004.c059.c1a1,
              DST 100.0.0.5 0000.0000.0000 Ethernet0/1.
IP ARP: sent req src 100.0.0.4 0004.c059.c1a1,
              DST 100.0.0.5 0000.0000.0000 Ethernet0/1.
Success rate is 0 percent (0/5)
```

Because outputting debugging information taxes the CPU on a Cisco router, use the debug arp command with care. A better plan is to view ARP traffic with a protocol analyzer. To limit captured traffic to just ARP traffic, you can set a capture filter for just ARP traffic. A common mistake that novice protocol analysts make is to set a filter for IP traffic, assuming this will catch ARP traffic also. An ARP frame does not have an IP layer. An ARP frame carries IP addresses as data, but the frame is a data link layer frame. The following example shows a typical ARP frame that occurred when host 172.16.10.1 sent a broadcast trying to find the data link layer address of 172.16.10.10.

```
Ethernet Header
   Destination:  FF:FF:FF:FF:FF:FF  Ethernet Broadcast
   Source:       00:00:0C:05:3E:80
   Protocol Type:0x0806
ARP - Address Resolution Protocol
   Hardware:               1  Ethernet (10Mb)
   Protocol:               0x0800  IP
   Hardware Address Length: 6
   Protocol Address Length: 4
   Operation:              1 ARP Request
   Sender Hardware Address: 00:00:0C:05:3E:80
   Sender Internet Address: 172.16.10.1
   Target Hardware Address: 00:00:00:00:00:00
   Target Internet Address: 172.16.10.10
```

Proxy ARP

According to the original ARP specification, RFC 826, a host sends an ARP for local devices only. A host either sends an ARP for another host on its segment or for its default gateway to reach a host not on its segment. Depending on the operating system and version running on the host, some hosts ARP for nonlocal devices also. With some versions of the Windows OS, if you forget to configure the default gateway router address, the PC sends ARPs for all stations, both local and nonlocal. Also, with some versions of the Windows OS, if you configure your own address as the default gateway, the PC sends ARPs for all stations, both local and nonlocal. Due to the fact that people have misconfigured end stations in these ways for many years, Cisco started using a default configuration whereby the Cisco router responds to an ARP broadcast for a nonlocal device. This is called *proxy ARP*.

If a host sends an ARP for a station that the router knows how to reach (because the destination prefix is in its routing table), a Cisco router responds with its own data link layer address. The host can then use this address to get to the remote station. Because the router only responds if it has a route, this works. Note that proxy ARP is enabled by default on Cisco routers, which is usually beneficial. If you need to disable it, however, use the `no ip proxy-arp` command.

Reverse Address Resolution Protocol (RARP)

RARP is rarely used today. Despite what many basic networking books claim, RARP is not simply the opposite of ARP. RARP is not a simple method for finding the IP address of a station when you know its data link layer address; rather, it is used by a station to discover *its own* IP address from a RARP server. The RARP server is typically implemented on a UNIX machine. The RARP client is typically a diskless station that has no place to store a configured IP address. Instead, when the station boots, it broadcasts a RARP message asking for its configuration. A RARP server responds with a unicast message that gives the device its IP address. Some stations also ask for more information—for example, a boot file that can let the station continue booting. Once the station has an IP address, it can use TFTP to download more data to help it get started on the network. For RARP to work, the RARP server must have a list of data link layer addresses and the IP addresses that will be assigned to them, and typically a list of filenames also.

RARP uses the same frame format as ARP. In the ARP frame there is a field called the *Opcode* (operation code). A different Opcode is used to differentiate between an ARP Request (Opcode = 1), ARP Reply (Opcode = 2), RARP Request (Opcode = 3), and RARP Reply (Opcode = 4).

In modern networks, RARP is uncommon, having been replaced by BOOTP and then later the Dynamic Host Configuration Protocol (DHCP). The main advantage of BOOTP over RARP is that BOOTP returns more detailed information—for example, the address of the default gateway and 64 bytes of vendor-specific information. BOOTP evolved into DHCP, which has gained considerable popularity in the last decade.

Dynamic Host Configuration Protocol

DHCP is based on BOOTP, but DHCP adds many enhancements to BOOTP, including a much larger vendor-specific information field (called the *Options* field in DHCP) and the automatic reallocation of reusable IP addresses. BOOTP assumed that IP addresses were assigned permanently based on a list that mapped data link layer addresses to IP addresses. Remember that BOOTP evolved from RARP. DHCP does not require a network administrator to maintain such a list. Instead, the administrator can define a pool of IP addresses (also called a *scope*) that are assigned as each client requests an IP address.

DHCP uses a client/server model. Servers allocate IP addresses, save information about which addresses have been allocated, and provide other configuration parameters to clients. Clients dynamically request an IP address and, optionally, other configuration parameters from servers. With the so-called *manual allocation* method, a server can assign a permanent IP address to a data link layer client. In most campus networks, however, DHCP servers are configured to use *dynamic allocation* for most addresses, wherein the DHCP server assigns an IP address from the pool of addresses for use by the client for a limited period of time, called the *lease time*.

When a DHCP server gives out an IP address with a lease, the server guarantees not to reallocate the address to any other device within the lease time. The server also attempts to return the same IP address each time the client requests an address within the lease time. The client may extend its lease with subsequent requests to get an IP address. The client may also choose to relinquish its lease by sending a DHCP *Release Message* to the server.

The DHCP server can reuse an address if the lease for the address has expired. As a consistency check, the allocating server should probe the reused address before allocating it. The server can do this with an ICMP Echo Request (ping). The client should also probe any address it receives. The client can do this with an Echo Request or an ARP request.

When a DHCP client boots, the client/server conversation uses four DHCP message types. To remember the messages, it helps to use the mnemonic DORA:

1. The client sends a Discover (D) Message.

2. The server sends an Offer (O) Message.

3. The client sends a Request (R) Message.

4. The server sends an Acknowledgment (A) Message.

The first message that a client sends is the DHCP *Discover Message*. The client sends this message as a broadcast packet. A client that has previously received an address can include the address in the DHCP Discover Message to ask that it be used again. The client can put the requested IP address in the *ciaddr* field of the DHCP header. EtherPeek calls this simply the *IP Address Known By Client* field. Alternately, the client can place its requested IP address in the Options field of the DHCP message.

Each server that receives a Discover Message from a client responds to the request with an Offer Message that includes an available IP address in the *your address (yiaddr)* field of the DHCP header. (EtherPeek calls this the *Client IP Addr Given By Srvr* field.) The Offer Message can include additional configuration parameters in the Options field.

After the client receives DHCP Offer Messages from one or more servers, the client chooses one server from which to request configuration parameters. Generally, the client selects the server whose response arrived first. The client then broadcasts a DHCP *Request Message* that includes a *Server Identifier* field to indicate which server the client selected. The request is broadcast so that all nonselected DHCP servers can reclaim the IP address that they offered to the client. The server selected in the DHCP Request Message commits the configuration parameters for the client to persistent storage and responds with a DHCP ACK message, containing the configuration parameters for the requesting client.

The client can request many configuration options in the Request Message besides just an IP address. As shown in the following example, a client can request information about the subnet mask, Network Basic Input/Output System (NetBIOS) servers, DNS servers, and other configuration parameters.

```
Ethernet Header
  Destination:  FF:FF:FF:FF:FF:FF  Ethernet Broadcast
  Source:       00:00:0E:D5:C7:E7
  Protocol Type:0x0800  IP
IP Header - Internet Protocol Datagram
  Version:              4
  Header Length:        5  (20  bytes)
  Type of Service:      %00000000
  Precedence: Routine,   Normal Delay, Throughput, Reliability
  Total Length:         328
  Identifier:           256
  Fragmentation Flags:  %000  May Fragment   Last Fragment
  Fragment Offset:      0  (0  bytes)
  Time To Live:         128
  Protocol:             17  UDP
  Header Checksum:      0x38A6
  Source IP Address:    0.0.0.0
  Dest. IP Address:     255.255.255.255  IP Broadcast
  No IP Options
UDP - User Datagram Protocol
  Source Port:          68  Bootstrap (BOOTP Client)
  Destination Port:     67  Bootstrap Protocol Server
  Length:               308
  Checksum:             0x4B43
BootP - Bootstrap Protocol
  Operation:               1  Boot Request
  Hardware Address Type:   1  Ethernet (10Mb)
  Hardware Address Length: 6  bytes
  Hops:                    0
  Transaction ID:          406117751
  Seconds Since Boot Start: 2304
  Flags:                   0x0000
  IP Address Known By Client:  0.0.0.0
  Client IP Addr Given By Srvr: 10.6.4.17
  Server IP Address:       10.6.4.1
  Gateway IP Address:      0.0.0.0
  Client Hardware Address: 00:00:0E:D5:C7:E7
  Unused:                  0x00000000000000000000
  Server Host Name: 00 00 00 00 00 00 00 00 00 00 00 00 00 00 00 00
  Boot File Name:   00 00 00 00 00 00 00 00 00 00 00 00 00 00 00 00
DHCP - Dynamic Host Configuration Protocol
  DHCP Magic Cookie:         0x63825363
  Message Type DHCP Option
    Option Code:     53  Message Type
    Option Length:   1
```

```
      Message Type:        3  Request
Client Identifier DHCP Option
      Option Code:         61  Client Identifier
      Option Length:       7
      Hardware Type:       1
      Hardware Address:    00:00:0E:D5:C7:E7
Requested IP Address DHCP Option
      Option Code:         50  Requested IP Address
      Option Length:       4
      Address:             10.6.4.17
Host Name Address DHCP Option
      Option Code:         12  Host Name Address
      Option Length:       12
      String:              PRISCILLA03.
Parameter Request List DHCP Option
      Option Code:         55  Parameter Request List
      Option Length:       7
      Requested Option:    1  Subnet Mask
      Requested Option:    15  Domain Name
      Requested Option:    3  Routers
      Requested Option:    44  NetBIOS (TCP/IP) Name Servers
      Requested Option:    46  NetBIOS (TCP/IP) Node Type
      Requested Option:    47  NetBIOS (TCP/IP) Scope
      Requested Option:    6  Domain Name Servers
DHCP Option End
      Option Code:         255  End
```

If a client doesn't receive any DHCP Offer or DHCP ACK messages, the client times out and retransmits the DHCP Discover and Request messages. To avoid synchronicity and excessive network traffic, the client uses a randomized exponential backoff algorithm to determine the delay between retransmissions. The delay between retransmissions should be chosen to allow sufficient time for replies from the server, based on the characteristics of the network between the client and server. For example, on a 10-Mbps Ethernet network, the delay before the first retransmission should be 4 seconds, randomized by the value of a uniform random number chosen from the range –1 to +1. The delay before the next retransmission should be 8 seconds, randomized by the value of a uniform number chosen from the range –1 to +1. The retransmission delay should be doubled with subsequent retransmissions up to a maximum of 64 seconds.

DHCP and Routers

A router can act as a *DHCP relay agent*. This means that the router passes DHCP broadcast messages from clients to DHCP servers that are not on the same subnet as the clients. This avoids a requirement for a DHCP server to reside on each subnet with clients. With Cisco routers, you can use the `ip helper-address address` command on each router interface where clients reside to cause the router to become a DHCP relay agent. The `address` parameter for the command should point to the IP address of the DHCP server. (Alternately, the address could be a directed broadcast address so that the router broadcasts the DHCP Discover Message onto the specified network.)

CAUTION When you enable an IP helper address, Cisco routers forward numerous UDP broadcasts by default, including TFTP, DNS, NetBIOS, and TACACS broadcasts. To configure the router to be more discerning in its forwarding, use the `ip forward-protocol` command for the protocols that should be forwarded and the `no ip forward-protocol` command for the protocols that should not be forwarded. To make sure DHCP packets are forwarded, use the `ip forward-protocol udp 67` command. (DHCP Discover and Request messages use UDP destination port number 67, the port number reserved many years ago for BOOTP.)

When a router relays a Discover Message to another network or subnet, the router places the IP address for the interface on which the message arrived in the *gateway address (giaddr)* field of the DHCP header. (EtherPeek simply calls this the *Gateway IP Address* field.) The server can use the giaddr information to determine which scope the assigned address should come from.

In the following Cisco router configuration, notice the use of the IP helper address on Ethernet interface 1. Clients reside on the Ethernet LAN that connects to this interface. These clients need the router to forward DHCP requests to the DHCP server whose address is 10.10.0.1. The DHCP server resides on the LAN connected to the router's Ethernet interface 0.

```
charlotte#show run
hostname charlotte
interface Ethernet0
   ip address 10.10.0.2 255.255.255.0
interface Ethernet1
   ip address 172.16.1.1 255.255.255.0
   ip helper-address 10.10.0.1
interface Serial0
   ip address 192.168.40.2 255.255.255.0
router ospf 100
   network 192.168.0.0 0.0.255.255 area 2
   network 10.10.0.0 0.0.255.255 area 0
   network 172.16.0.0 0.0.255.255 area 2
```

A protocol analyzer was placed on the 10.10.0.0 LAN to capture the relayed DHCP requests from the router. The following output shows a relayed Discover Message.

```
Ethernet Header
    Destination:  00:00:0C:05:3E:80
    Source:       00:00:0C:00:2E:75
    Protocol Type:0x0800  IP
IP Header - Internet Protocol Datagram
    Version:              4
    Header Length:        5  (20  bytes)
    Type of Service:      %00000000
    Precedence: Routine, Normal Delay, Throughput, Reliability
    Total Length:         328
    Identifier:           12800
```

```
        Fragmentation Flags:   %000  May Fragment    Last Fragment
        Fragment Offset:       0  (0  bytes)
        Time To Live:          127
        Protocol:              17  UDP
        Header Checksum:       0xD998
        Source IP Address:     172.16.1.1
        Dest. IP Address:      10.10.0.1
        No IP Options
    UDP - User Datagram Protocol
        Source Port:           68  Bootstrap (BOOTP Client)
        Destination Port:      67  Bootstrap Protocol Server
        Length:                308
        Checksum:              0x3159
    BootP - Bootstrap Protocol
        Operation:                 1  Boot Request
        Hardware Address Type:     1  Ethernet (10Mb)
        Hardware Address Length:   6  bytes
        Hops:                      0
        Transaction ID:            678970121
        Seconds Since Boot Start:  0
        Flags:                     0x0000
        IP Address Known By Client:  0.0.0.0
        Client IP Addr Given By Srvr: 0.0.0.0
        Server IP Address:         0.0.0.0
        Gateway IP Address:        172.16.1.1
        Client Hardware Address:   00:E0:98:89:52:FA
        Unused:                    0x00000000000000000000
        Server Host Name: 00 00 00 00 00 00 00 00 00 00 00 00 00 00 00 00
        Boot File Name: 00 00 00 00 00 00 00 00 00 00 00 00 00 00 00 00
    DHCP - Dynamic Host Configuration Protocol
        DHCP Magic Cookie:         0x63825363
        Message TypeDHCP Option
          Option Code:         53  Message Type
          Option Length:       1
          Message Type:        1  Discover
        Client IdentifierDHCP Option
          Option Code:         61  Client Identifier
          Option Length:       7
          Hardware Type:       1
          Hardware Address:    00:E0:98:89:52:FA
        Requested IP AddressDHCP Option
          Option Code:         50  Requested IP Address
          Option Length:       4
          Address:             172.16.1.2
        Host Name AddressDHCP Option
          Option Code:         12  Host Name Address
          Option Length:       8
          String:              MACTEAM.
        Vendor Class IdentifierDHCP Option
          Option Code:         60  Vendor Class Identifier
          Option Length:       7
          Option Data:
```

```
MSFT 98            4D 53 46 54 20 39 38
Parameter Request ListDHCP Option
   Option Code:        55   Parameter Request List
   Option Length:      9
   Requested Option:   1    Subnet Mask
   Requested Option:   15   Domain Name
   Requested Option:   3    Routers
   Requested Option:   6    Domain Name Servers
   Requested Option:   44   NetBIOS (TCP/IP) Name Servers
   Requested Option:   46   NetBIOS (TCP/IP) Node Type
   Requested Option:   47   NetBIOS (TCP/IP) Scope
   Requested Option:   43   Vendor Specific Information
   Requested Option:   77   User Class Information
DHCP Option End
   Option Code:        255  End
```

Notice that the relayed DHCP packet is a unicast, rather than a broadcast. The client originally broadcast a DHCP Discover Message. The router relayed this as a unicast. Also, notice at the IP layer that the source address is the router, not the client's 0.0.0.0 address that you normally see with DHCP. The router also put its address in the *Gateway IP Address* field. The DHCP server needs to see this to know which subnet the client's request came from. Another interesting aspect of this DHCP Discover Message is that the client requested a specific address. See 172.16.1.2 under the *Requested IP Address* section of the DHCP Options field. This client was rebooting. It asked for the same address that it used before, which it had saved in nonvolatile memory. The operation would have worked even if the client didn't specify an address, however.

Monitoring and Troubleshooting DHCP

A client can fail to receive an address from a DHCP server for a variety of reasons. When troubleshooting problems, check for physical and data link layer problems first. A very common reason for a client not to receive an address is that the client is attached to a switch port that does not start forwarding frames right away due to the Spanning Tree Algorithm. See the *Reducing Startup Delay on Cisco Switch Ports* section in Chapter 5 for more information on this topic.

After verifying physical and data link layer connectivity, check network layer connectivity next. See if you can ping the DHCP server from the client. If the server is on the other side of a router, see if you can ping the router. Check the IP helper-address configuration at the router. On the DHCP client, try to renew the lease. Capture this communication with a protocol analyzer and determine whether there are any anomalies in the conversation. Make sure that there is a response and that it offers an IP address. If there is no response or a response with no address, check the configuration of the server to make sure it has not run out of IP addresses.

If a DHCP client appears to be missing some network configuration details, such as the address of the default gateway or DNS or NetBIOS servers (which should be returned if the client requested them), verify that these details have been configured at the server, particularly for the scope that the client is in. If your DHCP server is running a Microsoft operating system, check Microsoft's support pages for more details. For Windows 2000, a good place to start is www.microsoft.com/windows2000/en/server/help/.

If a DHCP client acquires the wrong IP address—in other words, an IP address that is not for the location (network or subnet) where the client resides—check your analyzer trace file to see which server actually responded. When routers are configured (or misconfigured) with helper addresses, sometimes DHCP requests go to networks that you didn't anticipate and unexpected servers hear the request and respond. Also, numerous devices these days can act as DHCP servers, including firewalls, Network Address Translation (NAT) gateways, wireless access points, and soon even your refrigerator or washing machine (just kidding, hopefully!). Try to maintain control over which devices actually act as a DHCP server in your campus network, and make sure that the servers have enough addresses to serve the end users.

On most networks, DHCP servers are Windows, Mac OS, UNIX, or Linux server machines. Cisco also supports turning a Cisco router into a DHCP server. Configuring a router as a DHCP server takes away resources from the router's main tasks of forwarding packets and learning the network topology. However, on small networks with low traffic loads, newer high-speed routers can handle all of these tasks. When a Cisco router acts as a DHCP server, you can use a variety of show ip dhcp commands to monitor DHCP performance.

Private IP Addresses

Private IP addresses are addresses that a network engineer assigns to internal networks and hosts without any coordination from an ISP or one of the regional addressing authorities such as the American Registry for Internet Numbers (ARIN), the Asia-Pacific Network Information Center (APNIC), or the Réseaux IP Européens (RIPE).

As a campus network engineer, you probably received a set of public IP addresses from a corporate numbering authority or from your ISP. The public IP addresses can be used to assign addresses to public services, such as Web servers or other servers that external users access. Public addresses are not necessary for internal hosts and networks, however. Internal hosts that need access to outside services can be handled by a NAT gateway. (NAT is covered later in this chapter.)

In RFC 1918, the IETF reserved the following numbers for addressing hosts on internal private networks:

- 10.0.0.0 through 10.255.255.255
- 172.16.0.0 through 172.31.255.255
- 192.168.0.0 through 192.168.255.255

One advantage of private network numbers is security. Private network numbers are not advertised to the Internet. In fact, private network numbers *must not* be advertised to the Internet because they are not globally unique. By not advertising private internal network numbers, a modicum of security is achieved. (Additional security measures, including firewalls, should also be used.)

Private addressing is also more flexible than public addressing. Using private addressing makes it easier to change to a different ISP for Internet connectivity in the future. If private addressing has been used, when moving to a new ISP, the only address changes required are in the router or firewall providing NAT services and in any public servers.

Another advantage of private network numbers is that a campus network can advertise just one network number, or a small block of network numbers, to the Internet. It is good practice to avoid advertising many network numbers to the Internet, as mentioned earlier. One of the goals of modern Internet practices is that Internet routers should not need to manage huge routing tables. As a campus network grows, the network engineer can assign private addresses to new networks, rather than requesting additional public network numbers from an ISP or the regional addressing authority. This avoids increasing the size of Internet routing tables.

Although the benefits of private addressing outweigh the disadvantages, it is important to be aware of the drawbacks. One drawback is that outsourcing network management is difficult. When a company delegates network management responsibility to an outside company, the outside company typically sets up network consoles at its own site that communicate with internetworking devices inside the client's network. With private addressing, however, the consoles cannot reach the client's devices, because no routes to internal networks are advertised to the outside. The outsourcing company might require that consoles and personnel be placed within the internal network, or that an out-of-band network management system be used, which could raise the price of network management.

Another drawback of private addressing is the difficulty of communicating with business partners, vendors, and suppliers. Because the partner companies are also probably using private addresses, communication becomes more difficult. Also, companies that merge with each other face a difficult chore of renumbering any duplicate addresses caused by both companies using the same private addresses.

One other caveat with private addresses is that it is easy to forget to use a hierarchical addressing model with private addresses. Campus network administrators, who were once starved for addresses that were carefully doled out by ISPs or the regional addressing authority, get excited when they move to private addressing and have all of network 10.0.0.0 at their disposal, for example. The excitement should not overshadow the need to assign the new address space in a structured, hierarchical fashion. Hierarchical addressing facilitates route summarization within the campus network, which decreases bandwidth consumption by routing protocols, reduces processing on routers, and enhances network resiliency.

Network Address Translation (NAT)

NAT, as described in RFC 3022, is a mechanism for converting IP addresses from an inside network to IP addresses that are appropriate for an outside network, and vice versa. NAT is useful when hosts that need access to Internet services have private addresses. NAT gateway functionality can be implemented in a router, firewall, server, or wireless access point.

A network engineer responsible for NAT configures a pool of outside addresses that can be used for translation. When an inside host sends a packet, the source address is translated dynamically to an address from the pool of outside addresses. NAT also has a provision for static addresses for servers that need a fixed address—for example, a Web or mail server that must always map to the same well-known address.

Some NAT products also offer *port address translation* for mapping several addresses to the same address. With port translation, all traffic from a network has the same address. Port numbers are used to distinguish separate conversations. Port translation reduces the number of required outside addresses.

Monitoring and Troubleshooting NAT

NAT can fail for a variety of reasons, the most common being a misconfiguration. After checking for physical, data link, and network layer problems that could cause devices not to be able to reach the NAT gateway, be sure to check the NAT configuration on the gateway. Cisco has numerous features for configuring, optimizing, and monitoring NAT gateway functionality on a Cisco router. Cisco's NAT features let you dynamically translate addresses, assign nondynamic static addresses to servers, and support overlapping IP addresses, in the case where you chose IP addresses that officially belong to another network and you need to communicate with that network. Cisco also supports port address translation, which Cisco calls *overloading*.

To monitor Cisco NAT implementations, use the show ip nat translations and show ip nat statistics commands. When troubleshooting Cisco's NAT implementation, it may become necessary to clear dynamic address translation entries from the NAT translation table. Use one of the clear ip nat translation commands to accomplish this task.

Another reason NAT can perform poorly is that the NAT gateway is not fast enough to provide service to the number of hosts it supports. NAT is sometimes implemented on a low-end PC or other device that was not intended to provide this service. When translating between private and public addresses, all traffic between a campus network and the Internet must go through the NAT gateway. For this reason, you should make sure the NAT gateway has superior throughput and low delay, particularly if campus network users depend on Internet applications to accomplish mission-critical tasks. The NAT gateway should have a reasonably fast processor that can examine and change packets quickly. Keep in mind that, in addition to modifying IP addresses, a NAT gateway must modify the IP, TCP, and UDP checksums. (The checksums for TCP and UDP cover a *pseudo header* that contains source and destination IP addresses.)

In many cases, NAT must also modify IP addresses that occur inside the data part of a packet. IP addresses can appear in ICMP, FTP, DNS, and other types of packets. Because NAT has the job of translating something so basic and ubiquitous as network-layer addresses, it can be tricky to guarantee correct behavior with all applications. A NAT gateway should be thoroughly tested in a pilot environment before it is generally deployed.

IP Multicast Addresses

IP supports sending data to a group of hosts, which is often called *IP multicasting*. IP multicasting uses *IP multicast addresses*, which are a special range of addresses used for sending to multiple destinations on a network. Multicasting saves bandwidth by sending a single traffic stream to a group of hosts rather than to each host individually. Multicasting also avoids the need to send the stream as broadcast packets, which would consume processing power on all devices in the broadcast domain. Some technologies that use IP multicasting are streaming video, streaming audio, and video conferencing. Multicasting enables such applications as distance learning, desktop management, collaborative software, electronic whiteboards, and real-time financial data delivery. IP multicast addresses are also used for more mundane purposes, such as service location and routing protocols.

IP multicasting uses a Class D IP address to identify a group. In dotted-decimal notation, Class D group addresses range from 224.0.0.0 to 239.255.255.255. IP hosts recognize an address as being a Class D address because the first 4 bits must be 1110 in binary. A multicast group is also identified by a MAC-layer multicast address, which is an address that is formatted such that the first bit transmitted is a 1. Using a MAC-layer multicast address theoretically improves host performance because a NIC can ignore data addressed to a group that the NIC has not joined.

IANA owns a block of MAC-layer addresses that are used for group multicast addresses. The range of addresses for Ethernet is 0x01:00:5E:00:00:00 through 0x01:00:5E:7F:FF:FF. When a host sends a frame to an IP group that is identified by a Class D address, the host inserts the low-order 23 bits of the Class D address into the low-order 23 bits of the MAC-layer destination address. The top 9 bits of the Class D address are not used. The top 25 bits of the MAC address are 0x01:00:5E followed by a 0 bit (00000001 00000000 01011110 0 in binary).

The Internet Group Management Protocol (IGMP)

IGMP allows a host to join a group and inform routers of the need to receive a multicast data stream. When a user (or system software) starts a process that requires the host to join a multicast group, the host transmits an IGMP *Membership Report* message to inform routers on the segment that traffic for the group should be multicast to the host's segment. Although it is possible that a router is already sending data for the group, the IGMP specification states that a host should send a Membership Report in case it is the first member of the group on the network segment.

In addition to allowing hosts to join groups, IGMP specifies that a multicast router should send an IGMP *Membership Query* out every interface at regular intervals to see if any hosts belong to a group. A host responds by sending a Membership Report for each group in which it is a member (based on the applications running on the host). To minimize the amount of bandwidth used by Membership Reports, hosts set a random timer before responding to queries. If the host sees another host respond for a group to which the host belongs, then the host cancels its response. The router does not need to know how many or which specific hosts on a segment belong to a group; it just needs to recognize that a group has at least one member on a segment so that it will forward group traffic to that segment using the IP and MAC multicast addresses for the group.

RFC 2236 defines a new version of IGMP: *IGMPv2*. The main feature of IGMPv2 is the ability for a router to more quickly learn that the last host has left a group, which is important if there are multicast groups that cause a lot of network traffic or undergo frequent changes to their membership list. IGMPv2 supports a new message, the *Leave Group* message, that a host can use to explicitly leave a group. The router can then send a Membership Query to determine if there are any remaining hosts on the segment that are group members for the particular multicast group.

By default, a data link layer switch floods multicast frames out every port. The Cisco Group Management Protocol (CGMP) and the IETF IGMP Snooping methods allow switches to participate in the process of determining which segments have hosts in a particular multicast group. CGMP is a Cisco proprietary method that lets a router send a message to switches to tell the switches about Membership Reports and Leaves occurring on their segments. IGMP Snooping is an IETF standard that causes no extra traffic, but allows a switch to learn from the IGMP messages sent to routers. Only high-end Cisco switches support IGMP Snooping. You cannot configure IGMP Snooping on a switch that is already configured to use CGMP. To determine which method is configured and to see other useful IGMP or CGMP information, use the `show cgmp statistics` or `show igmp statistics` switch commands.

On Cisco routers, you can use the `show ip igmp group` command to verify which multicast groups have been joined. The `show ip igmp interface` command is also helpful to verify that IGMP and CGMP are enabled or disabled on an interface and to determine which version of IGMP is in use.

Multicast Routing Protocols

In addition to determining which local network segments should receive traffic for particular multicast groups, a router must also learn how to route multicast traffic across an internetwork. Multicast routing protocols provide this function. Multicast routing protocols augment the services provided by standard routing protocols, which learn paths to destination networks, to include the capability of learning paths to multicast destination addresses.

The most common multicast routing protocol is the Protocol-Independent Multicast (PIM) protocol. PIM works in tandem with IGMP. It also works with unicast routing protocols, such as OSPF, the Routing Information Protocol (RIP), Cisco's Enhanced Interior Gateway Routing Protocol (EIGRP), and so on. In fact, from a troubleshooting point of view, keep in mind that PIM cannot work correctly unless unicast routing is also working correctly. Chapter 8 covers many details on troubleshooting unicast routing.

PIM has two modes: dense and sparse. The terms *dense* and *sparse* refer to the density of group members. Dense groups have many members. An example of a dense group might be employees at a corporation who listen to the company president's quarterly report when it is multicast on the corporate intranet in streaming video format. A sparse group might be a much smaller group of employees who have signed up for a streaming video class on how to reduce stress. These employees might be spread out across the campus internetwork in many different departments (except Network Operations, because network engineers don't have time for classes on stress reduction.)

Dense-mode PIM uses a Reverse-Path Forwarding (RPF) mechanism to compute the shortest (reverse) path between a source and all possible recipients of a multicast data stream. When a router running dense-mode PIM receives the first multicast packet for a group, it floods the packet out all dense-mode interfaces. After forwarding the first packet, the router then listens for *Prune* messages coming back from other routers. The Prune messages tell the router about network segments that don't have any receivers for a particular multicast data stream. The messages help routers develop a map of the internetwork that lets them send multicast packets only to those networks that should receive the packets. The Prune messages also let routers avoid loops that would cause more than one router to send a multicast packet to a segment.

Dense-mode PIM works best in environments with large multicast groups and a high likelihood that any given network segment has a group member, which limits the number of Prune messages. Because of the flooding of the first packet for a group, dense-mode PIM does not make sense in environments where a few sparsely located users wish to participate in a multicast application. In this case, sparse-mode PIM is a better solution.

Sparse-mode PIM defines a *rendezvous point,* which provides a registration service for a multicast group. Sparse-mode PIM relies on IGMP, which lets a host join a group by sending a Membership Report message and detach from a group by sending a Leave message. A *designated router* for a network segment tracks Membership Report and Leave messages on its segment and periodically sends PIM Join and Prune messages to the rendezvous point. The Join and Prune messages are processed by all the routers between the designated router and the rendezvous point. The result is a distribution tree that reaches all group members and is centered at the rendezvous point. The distribution tree for a multicast group is initially used for any source, but the sparse-mode PIM specification also provides a mechanism for the rendezvous point to develop source-specific trees, which further enhances the pruning of network traffic.

A useful Cisco command for troubleshooting PIM is the show ip pim neighbor command. It will help you determine if the router is learning about PIM neighbor routers and verify that the neighbors are in the correct PIM mode. Some sample output from the command follows:

```
router#show ip pim neighbor
PIM Neighbor Table
Neighbor Address   Interface        Uptime Expires   Mode
10.10.1.1          Serial0/0        1d8h   00:00:18   Dense
10.10.2.1          Serial0/1        1d8h   00:00:18   Dense
10.10.3.1          FastEthernet0/0  2d12h  00:00:40   Sparse
```

You can also use the show ip pim interface command to determine how many neighbors an interface has, the time interval for queries, the PIM mode of the interface, and whether there is a designated router present.

IPv6

IP is starting to show its age. Although it has been patched and updated to deal with scalability and security concerns, the IETF is hard at work on a new version that is more than just a set of interim fixes. This new version is version 6, which is also known as *IPv6* and *IP the next generation (IPng)*. IPv6 is already in use on parts of Internet2, which is an advanced, high-speed prototype network being deployed by a group of over 190 universities, working in partnership with industry and government. See www.internet2.edu/html/about.html for more information.

When the IETF developed IPv6, there was concern that the IPv4 address space was too small. When every possible 32-bit IPv4 address was given out, there could be no further growth of the Internet. The larger address space built into IPv6 was a solution to the problem. The developers of IPv6 originally assumed that the entire world would eventually migrate to IPv6. The advent of classless addressing made universal migration to IPv6 unnecessary, however. Classless addressing reduced the number of wasted addresses and made it possible to use more of the four billion addresses available in the 32-bit IPv4 address space. NAT also provided a solution to the potential problem of running out of IPv4 addresses. Prior to NAT, a campus network with several thousand nodes needed several thousand IPv4 Internet addresses. With NAT, several thousand private addresses can communicate to the Internet through a single IPv4 Internet address.

Nonetheless, the migration to an entirely new protocol and away from interim fixes such as NAT is compelling. As a network engineer responsible for a TCP/IP network, you shouldn't ignore IPv6. The IETF still expects many networks to migrate over time to IPv6 in order to take advantage of the scalability, security, ease-of-configuration, QoS, and network management features of IPv6.

RFC 1752 summarizes progress made in the early 1990s toward a new version of IP. Although this RFC is old (1995), it is still a good place to start to understand the goals and capabilities of IPv6. You should also peruse RFC 2460, which is the formal specification of IPv6. According to these two RFCs, the goals of IPv6 are as follows:

- *Expanded addressing capabilities*. IP addresses are increased from 32 bits to 128 bits, providing support for many more addressable nodes and more levels of addressing hierarchy. New addressing capabilities will also support autoconfiguration of addresses. The scalability of multicast routing is improved by adding a scope field to multicast addresses. Also, a new type of address called an *anycast address* is defined, used to send a packet to any one of a group of nodes.

- *Simplified header format*. Some IPv4 header fields have been dropped or made optional to reduce the common-case processing cost of packet handling and to keep the bandwidth overhead of the IPv6 header as low as possible, in spite of the increased size of addresses. Although IPv6 addresses are four times longer than IPv4 addresses, the IPv6 header is only twice the size of the IPv4 header.

- *Extension headers and options*. IPv6 options are placed in separate headers that are located in the packet between the IPv6 header and the transport-layer header. Because most IPv6 option headers are examined at the final destination and are not examined or processed by routers along a packet's delivery path, this organization facilitates a major improvement in packet-forwarding performance at routers. Another improvement is that IPv6 options can be of arbitrary length.

- *Flow labeling*. A new capability is added to enable the labeling of packets belonging to particular traffic flows so that the sender can request special handling for flows, such as nondefault QoS for real-time or other time-critical applications.

- *Authentication and privacy*. IPv6 includes the definition of an extension that provides support for authenticating the sender of a packet and encrypting the contents of a packet. This extension is included as a basic element of IPv6. Support for it is required in all implementations.

- *Autoconfiguration*. IPv6 supports multiple forms of autoconfiguration, from plug-and-play configuration of node addresses to the full-featured facilities offered by DHCP.

- *Source routing*. IPv6 includes the definition of an extension that supports source routing. The purpose is to support the source-initiated selection of routes to complement the route selection provided by routing protocols.

- *Simple, flexible, and low-cost transition from IPv4*. The transition to IPv6 must support incremental upgrades and deployment. Existing installed IPv4 hosts and routers may be upgraded to IPv6 at any time without being dependent on any other hosts or routers being upgraded. New IPv6 hosts and routers can be installed at any time without any stipulations regarding the rest of the network. When existing installed IPv4 hosts or routers are upgraded to IPv6, they may continue to use their existing addresses.

IPv6 Protocol Analysis

An IPv6 packet starts with a 40-byte IPv6 header. If extensions are present, they are added after the basic header. Figure 7.17 shows the format of an IPv6 header. Table 7.14 describes the fields in an IPv6 header.

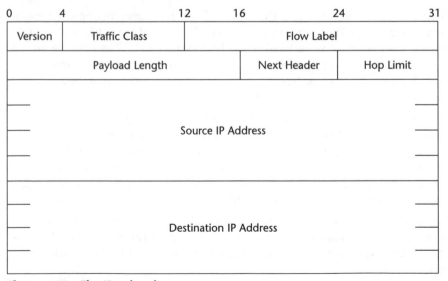

Figure 7.17   The IPv6 header.

Table 7.14 Fields in an IPv6 Header

FIELD	EXPLANATION
Version	The IP version, which is 6 for IPv6.
Traffic Class	8 bits. Available for use by originating nodes or forwarding routers to identify and distinguish between different classes or priorities of IPv6 packets. Intended to allow functionality that is similar to that of the IPv4 Type of Service field.
Flow Label	20 bits. May be used by a source to label sequences of packets for which it requests special handling by IPv6 routers, such as nondefault QoS.
Payload Length	Measures the length in bytes of the payload (that is, the balance of the IPv6 packet that follows the basic IPv6 header).
Next Header	Identifies the header immediately following the IPv6 header. Uses the same values as the IPv4 Protocol field—for example, 6 is TCP and 17 is UDP. Also identifies some of the IPv6 extensions—for example, 43 means a routing extension header follows, 44 means a fragmentation extension header follows, and 60 means destination options follow.
Hop Limit	Analogous to the IPv6 TTL field. Sets an upper limit on the number of routers through which a datagram can travel. The hop limit is decremented by one by each router that forwards the packet. When the hop limit reaches zero, the packet is discarded and an error message is returned.
Source Address	128-bit address of the host that sent the datagram.
Destination Address	128-bit address of the host to whom the datagram is destined.

IPv6 Extensions

One of the goals of IPv6 is to simplify the header so that the resources required to handle a basic packet are kept to a minimum. To achieve this goal, much of the optional data has been moved to extension headers. To further improve performance, IPv6 mandates a particular order for extension headers, moving information that is only important for the destination to the end of the extensions header. The following list describes the possible header extensions. They are listed in the order in which they should appear when multiple headers are included in a packet.

1. *Hop-by-Hop Options Header*. Carries optional information that must be examined by each router along a packet's delivery path. Includes a field to identify the next header and a set of variable-length options.

2. *Destination Options Header 1*. For options that are to be processed by the final destination and by destinations listed in the Routing Header. Includes a field to identify the next header and a set of variable-length options.

3. *Routing Header.* Lists one or more intermediate nodes (routers) that are visited on the path from the source to the destination. Includes a field to identify the next header and an ordered list of addresses. Replaces the source routing feature of IPv4.

4. *Fragment Header.* Used by an IPv6 source to send packets that are larger than would fit in the path MTU to the destination. Note that, unlike IPv4, fragmentation for IPv6 is only done at the source node, not at intermediate routers along the packet's delivery path. Includes fields to identify the next header, the fragment offset, identification, and a more fragments bit (M). If this is the last fragment, M=0. If there are more fragments, M=1.

5. *Authentication Header.* Provides integrity and data origin authentication for IP datagrams, plus optional protection against replays. See RFC 2406.

6. *Encapsulating Security Payload Header.* Provides confidentiality, data origin authentication, integrity, protection against replays, and limited traffic-flow confidentiality. See RFC 2406.

7. *Destination Options Header 2.* Contains options to be processed only by the final destination of the packet.

IPv6 Autoconfiguration

To reduce the complexities associated with deploying IPv6, the IETF has defined a set of autoconfiguration protocols and processes. The autoconfiguration features will help network engineers migrate IPv4 networks to IPv6 because they eliminate many of the requirements for human configuration of addresses and routing parameters. There are three methods for automatically obtaining configuration information: a stateful mechanism, a stateless mechanism, or both. (Stateful and stateless autoconfiguration may be used simultaneously.) The type of autoconfiguration in use on a LAN is specified in *Router Advertisement* messages.

In a stateful autoconfiguration model, hosts obtain addresses and other parameters from a server. The server stores a database containing the necessary information and maintains control over address assignments. (This should sound familiar. The stateful autoconfiguration model is defined in Internet draft proposals that describe DHCPv6.)

Stateless autoconfiguration requires no manual configuration of hosts, minimal (or no) configuration of routers, and no servers. For a network engineer who is not concerned about which addresses are used, as long as they are unique and routable, stateless autoconfiguration offers many benefits. Stateless autoconfiguration is discussed in RFC 2462. It is similar to AppleTalk dynamic addressing, which we will discuss in more detail in Chapter 11.

With stateless autoconfiguration, a host generates its own address using locally available information plus information advertised by routers. The process begins with the generation of a *link-local address* for an interface, which is generated by combining the well-known *link-local address prefix* (1111 1110 10) with a 64-bit *interface identifier*. The interface identifier is usually derived from the hardware address in ROM on the NIC.

The next step determines the uniqueness of the tentative address that has been derived by combining the link-local address prefix with the interface identifier. The host transmits a *Neighbor Solicitation* message with the tentative address as the target address. If another host is using this address, a *Neighbor Advertisement* is returned. In this event, autoconfiguration stops and some manual intervention is required. (Because the address is partially based on a NIC address, duplicates are very unlikely.) If no responses are returned, the tentative address is considered unique, and IP connectivity with local hosts is now possible.

> **NOTE** Before sending a Neighbor Solicitation message, an interface must join two groups: the *all-nodes multicast group* and the *solicited-node multicast group* for the tentative address. The former ensures that the node receives Neighbor Advertisements from other nodes, the latter that two nodes attempting to use the same address simultaneously detect each other's presence. To check an address, a node sends Neighbor Solicitations with the IP destination set to the solicited-node multicast address of the target address.

The final phase of the autoconfiguration process involves listening for Router Advertisement messages that routers periodically transmit. A host can also force an immediate Router Advertisement by transmitting a *Router Solicitation* message to the *all-routers multicast address*. Router advertisements contain zero or more prefix information options that contain information used by the host to generate a site-local address that has a scope that is limited to the local site. The router advertisements also include a global address with unlimited scope. The advertisement may also tell a host to use a stateful method to complete its autoconfiguration.

Summary

In this chapter we have moved beyond previous chapters that covered lower-layer problems and traveled into the network layer, discussing the most common network layer protocol—IP. The chapter started with a short history of IP. Learning about the history of IP will help you understand why IP behaves the way it does and why certain fields exist in the header, even though they are rarely used today and complicate header processing. The chapter finished with a short introduction to IPv6, which aims to simplify the job of processing IP headers.

After an overview of the IP protocol stack, the chapter concentrated on IP protocol analysis and addressing. Understanding the fields in an IP header will help you troubleshoot problems on campus networks and use your protocol analyzer effectively. Understanding IP addressing is a fundamental requirement for the effective management of campus networks. This chapter has provided basic information to help you with that task, including an introduction to modern techniques for managing IP addresses, such as DHCP and NAT.

IP's main jobs are the forwarding of datagrams across an internetwork, based on information in an IP header and the segregation and aggregation of hosts based on hierarchical addressing plans. The other main job that IP has is to learn how to forward packets based on information carried in IP routing protocols. Chapter 8 covers IP routing protocols. Chapter 9 finishes our discussion of campus IP networks with a discourse on the upper layers of the IP protocol stack, including TCP, UDP, and the most important application layer protocols.

Troubleshooting and Analyzing Campus IP Routing Protocols

An Internet Protocol (IP) router has two main jobs: forwarding traffic and learning how to reach networks. The process of learning how to reach networks is called *IP routing* and is accomplished through the use of an *IP routing protocol*. An IP routing protocol lets an IP router dynamically learn how to reach networks and exchange this information with other routers and hosts. Routing protocols learn and share network reachability information in a variety of ways. Some broadcast a routing table to all devices on the Local Area Network (LAN); others require routers to establish an adjacency with each other and then send periodic Hello packets to maintain their adjacent status. Some routing protocols include advanced information such as a prefix length or subnet mask with route information. Most routing protocols share dynamically learned information, but in some cases, static configuration information is more appropriate. Before getting into a general discussion of dynamic routing protocols, this chapter goes on a quick tangent to discuss two other important and related topics: host routing and static routing.

Host Routing

When considering routing, network administrators often assume that the only real troubleshooting concerns deal with the communication between routers. Actually, an end-station host needs some limited information about routing also. The section on

Address Resolution Protocol (ARP) in Chapter 7 talked about the fact that a host must have some method of communicating with nonlocal hosts through a router. A host can ARP for nonlocal hosts, which should work if *proxy ARP* is configured on routers. Usually a host does not ARP for nonlocal hosts, however, and instead ARPs for a *default gateway* and then sends all nonlocal traffic to the default gateway. Every host must be configured with the IP address of the default gateway (which is really a router, not a gateway). In the past, this configuration was a major cause of problems because it was so often misconfigured. These days, a Dynamic Host Configuration Protocol (DHCP) server usually provides the address of the default gateway, so the configuration is more controlled and less likely to be wrong.

Most network administrators know that a router maintains a routing table that lets the router know where packets should be sent to reach destinations. Many network administrators don't realize, however, that end-station hosts, including clients and servers, also maintain a routing table. The information in a host's routing table is fundamentally the same as that found in a router's routing table, although a host's routing table is usually much smaller than that of a router. On a Windows machine, the host routing table can be viewed from a DOS prompt by typing the `route print` command. Figure 8.1 shows an example for a host configured with the 10.10.0.3 IP address. The host's default gateway is configured as 10.10.0.1.

Notice in Figure 8.1 that the first entry in the host's routing table is 0.0.0.0 0.0.0.0, which points to the default gateway address 10.10.0.1. If you are familiar with Cisco routing tables, this should look familiar, because this is the same format that Cisco uses for displaying and configuring a default route. The meaning of the entry is that all nonlocal traffic should go to the router with the 10.10.0.1 IP address. The host will ARP for this address to get the data link layer address for the default gateway and use the data link layer address as the destination address for all nonlocal packets.

When a host initializes, it places the IP address of its default gateway in its routing table. When the host learns from the default gateway that there are other routers to which packets should be sent, the host places these router addresses in the local routing table also. The host learns this information from Internet Control Message Protocol (ICMP) Redirect messages. For example, consider a network in Chicago that has two routers on the LAN where hosts reside. One router has Wide Area Network (WAN) connectivity to the East Coast of the United States; the other router connects to points on the West Coast. One of these two routers must be selected as the default gateway when configuring hosts. Assume, for the purpose of discussion, that the West Coast router is the default gateway for a host. If the host wants to send a packet to a destination on the East Coast, it initially sends the packet to its default gateway (the West Coast router). The West Coast router then sends an ICMP Redirect that updates the host's routing table with the address of the East Coast router and the target network or host. The West Coast router forwards the packet to the East Coast router but, from then on, the host has the correct entry in its routing table, and subsequent packets for the East Coast are sent directly from the host to the East Coast router. The entry stays in the routing table while it is being used and generally for about 10 additional minutes, depending on the operating system in use.

```
C:\WINDOWS>route print

Active Routes:

 Network Address        Netmask    Gateway Address      Interface  Metric
        0.0.0.0         0.0.0.0         10.10.0.1       10.10.0.3      1
      10.10.0.0   255.255.255.0         10.10.0.3       10.10.0.3      1
      10.10.0.3 255.255.255.255         127.0.0.1       127.0.0.1      1
 10.255.255.255 255.255.255.255         10.10.0.3       10.10.0.3      1
      127.0.0.0       255.0.0.0         127.0.0.1       127.0.0.1      1
      224.0.0.0       224.0.0.0         10.10.0.3       10.10.0.3      1
255.255.255.255 255.255.255.255         10.10.0.3         0.0.0.0      1
```

Figure 8.1 A host routing table.

Because a host may not have enough information about prefix lengths (subnet masks) for nonlocal networks, the host may place a host-specific route in its local routing table, despite the fact that the default gateway sends an ICMP Redirect for an entire network. Figure 8.2 shows the routing table for the 10.10.0.3 host after it sent traffic to an East Coast host with the 192.168.30.1 address. Notice that the routing table specifies that to send to the 192.168.30.1 address, the host should send to the 10.10.0.2 router rather than the default gateway.

To avoid ICMP Redirects, an administrator can place static entries into the host routing table, but this is rarely done because of the amount of manual configuration required. Another option is to place two default gateways into the routing table—in other words, two entries for 0.0.0.0 0.0.0.0. The first entry is always used unless the router referenced in the first entry fails, in which case the second entry is used. This doesn't avoid the ICMP Redirect message, but it does provide some redundancy for the host-to-gateway link. The capability to place two default gateways into a host's routing table is not supported on all versions of Windows or other operating systems. For this reason, Cisco invented another method for configuring redundancy for the host-to-gateway link. That method, called the Hot Standby Router Protocol (HSRP), is described in the next section.

```
C:\WINDOWS>route print

Active Routes:

 Network Address        Netmask    Gateway Address      Interface  Metric
        0.0.0.0         0.0.0.0         10.10.0.1       10.10.0.3      1
      10.10.0.0   255.255.255.0         10.10.0.3       10.10.0.3      1
      10.10.0.3 255.255.255.255         127.0.0.1       127.0.0.1      1
 10.255.255.255 255.255.255.255         10.10.0.3       10.10.0.3      1
      127.0.0.0       255.0.0.0         127.0.0.1       127.0.0.1      1
   192.168.30.1 255.255.255.255         10.10.0.2       10.10.0.3      1
      224.0.0.0       224.0.0.0         10.10.0.3       10.10.0.3      1
255.255.255.255 255.255.255.255         10.10.0.3         0.0.0.0      1
```

Figure 8.2 A host routing table that has been updated by an ICMP Redirect message.

The Hot Standby Router Protocol

The link between a host and its default gateway is a critical link that must not fail if interconnectivity between hosts on different networks is required. Nonetheless, this link is often designed as a single point of failure on many networks. To ensure that it is not a single point of failure, Cisco invented HSRP. HSRP is not a routing protocol, even though some books incorrectly spell out the acronym with *Routing* in the middle instead of *Router*. It's the router (default gateway) that is on standby, not the routing protocol. HSRP provides a method for an IP host to keep communicating on an internetwork even if its default gateway has become unavailable. The Internet Engineering Task Force (IETF) has invented a similar, but less popular, protocol called the *Virtual Router Redundancy Protocol* (VRRP).

HSRP works by creating a *virtual router*, which is also called a *phantom router*. The virtual router, which is just a conceptual device and not an actual hardware box, has its own IP address and its own Media Access Control (MAC) address. Each host is configured to use the virtual router as its default gateway. When a host broadcasts an ARP frame to find its default gateway, the active HSRP router responds with the virtual router's MAC address. If the active router goes offline, a standby router takes over as the active router, continuing the delivery of the host's packets. The change is transparent to the host.

HSRP routers on a LAN communicate among themselves to designate an active and standby router. The active router sends periodic Hello messages, and the other HSRP routers listen for the Hello messages. If the active router fails, causing the other HSRP routers to stop receiving Hello messages, the standby router takes over and becomes the active router. Because the new active router assumes both the IP and MAC addresses of the virtual router, end-station hosts see no change. They continue to send packets to the virtual router's MAC address, and the new active router delivers those packets. The HSRP Hello timer should be short enough so that workstation applications and protocols do not drop connections before the standby router becomes active.

HSRP uses a priority scheme to determine which router should be the default active router. To configure a router as the active router, assign it a priority that is higher than the priority of all the other HSRP routers. The default priority is 100, so if you configure just one router to have a higher priority, that router will become the default active router.

Monitoring and Troubleshooting Host Routing

Problems with HSRP occur when HSRP routers cannot communicate with each other. When you suspect that this is the case, check for physical and data link layer problems first. Use the `show interface` and `show ip interface` commands to ensure that interfaces are up and correctly configured with a unique IP address for the subnet on which the interface resides.

Other problems occur because of misconfigurations of HSRP or other router features. Verify that the HSRP configuration is correct with the `show standby` command on each router. Also, verify that access lists configured on HSRP routers are not filtering the HSRP destination address or User Datagram Protocol (UDP) data using the `show access-list` command. Specifically, verify that the multicast address used to send traffic to all routers on a subnet (224.0.0.2) is not filtered. Also, verify that UDP traffic destined to port 1985 is not filtered. HSRP uses this address and port to send Hello messages.

A potential problem that you should monitor with HSRP is related to its security—or lack thereof. HSRP uses an authentication string that must be configured on all routers participating in HSRP. This string is transmitted unencrypted in HSRP messages. It's a simple task for a hacker who has gained access to your campus LAN to capture HSRP packets with a protocol analyzer and determine the string. The hacker's machine can then declare that it is the HSRP active router. The other routers consent as long as the hacker's machine announces a higher HSRP priority and has the right authentication string, and hosts on the LAN will start sending packets to the hacker's machine instead of the legitimate default gateway. This obviously disrupts network connectivity for hosts, and also allows the hacker to possibly see confidential data.

A workaround to the problem of a hacker taking over as the active HSRP router is to set up access lists that accept HSRP packets only from legitimate routers. For example, you could apply the following access list on the inbound router interface that receives HSRP packets. In this example, the router where the access list is applied is on a network where 192.168.1.2 is the only other legitimate sender of HSRP packets.

```
access-list 100 permit udp host 192.168.1.2 eq 1985 host 224.0.0.2 eq 1985
access-list 100 deny udp any eq 1985 any eq 1985
access-list 100 permit ip any any
```

One other caveat with HSRP is that HSRP can confuse network monitoring tools. A common problem is that *Duplicate IP Address* messages appear on network management consoles or when using a protocol analyzer with automated analysis capabilities, such as WildPackets' EtherPeek. In particular, when HSRP is in use, *Duplicate IP Address* messages appear in the Hewlett-Packard (HP) OpenView Network Node Manager (NNM) event browser. For more information on workarounds to this problem, see www.cisco.com/warp/public/477/GenNMS/23.html.

When analyzing an HSRP implementation, be ready to recognize the virtual HSRP IP address that a host uses when it sends ARP frames for its gateway and the virtual Ethernet address that a host uses when sending nonlocal traffic. Also, you will probably see the "real" Ethernet and IP addresses of the routers when the routers send management and HSRP Hello packets. Be sure that host conversations are not using the real addresses of HSRP-enabled routers. If they are, then the gateway configuration in the errant host is not properly set to the virtual HSRP address.

Static and Default Routing

On some campus networks, there is often no need to run a dynamic routing protocol. Instead, you can use static routing. A *static route* is a route that is manually configured and does not rely on updates from a routing protocol. A disadvantage of static routing is the amount of administration that may be required, especially on large networks.

However, static routes have many advantages on small (and even large) networks, and should not be overlooked when designing or upgrading a campus network. Static routes reduce bandwidth usage and are easy to troubleshoot. They allow you to use a route other than the one that dynamic routing would choose, which can be beneficial when you want traffic to follow a specific path. Static routes may also let you use a route that is more specific than the dynamic routing protocol permits. Static routes also facilitate security. With static routes, the campus network engineer has more control over which networks are reachable.

Most Internet Service Providers (ISPs) have numerous static routes in their routing tables. An ISP can use a static route to reach a customer's campus network. Traffic into the ISP from the Internet that has a destination address that matches the network address assigned to the customer goes in just one direction—to the router at the customer's site that connects to the Internet. There's no need for a routing protocol, which means that bandwidth on the link between the customer and the ISP is conserved and troubleshooting is simplified.

To configure a static route on a Cisco router, use the `ip route network mask address | interface` command. The `network` parameter identifies the network you want to reach. The `address | interface` parameter identifies the address of the peer router or the local router interface that can reach the network.

On Cisco routers, static routes take precedence over routes to the same destination that are learned via a routing protocol. Cisco Internetwork Operating System (IOS) software also supports a *floating static route,* which is a static route that has a higher *administrative distance* than dynamically learned routes and can thus be overridden by dynamically learned routes. One important application of floating static routes is to provide backup routes when no dynamic information is available.

A *default route* is used when there is no entry in the routing table for a destination network. A default route is also called the *route of last resort.* In some cases, a default route is all that is necessary. Let's look again at the example of the campus network connected to an ISP. At the campus side, it may not be necessary or practical to learn routes to all the networks on the Internet. If there's just one connection to the Internet (the link to the ISP), all Internet traffic has to go in that direction anyway. So, the campus network engineer can simply define a default route that points to the ISP's router. On a Cisco router, default routes are configured in the same way as static routes, although you use a network number and mask of all 0s. For example, to state that all nonlocal traffic that is not explicitly listed in the routing table should go to the ISP router, use the `ip route 0.0.0.0 0.0.0.0 address` command, where `address` is the address of the ISP router.

Monitoring and Troubleshooting Static and Default Routes

To monitor static and default IP routing, use the `show ip route` command. This command displays the routing table for a router. Static and default routes are listed after the *S* code. A default route is also listed after the "Gateway of last resort" comment, as shown in the following example:

```
Albany#show ip route
Codes: C - connected, S - static, I - IGRP, R - RIP, M - mobile, B - BGP
       D - EIGRP, EX - EIGRP external, O - OSPF, IA - OSPF inter area
       E1 - OSPF external type 1, E2 - OSPF external type 2, E - EGP
       i - IS-IS, L1 - IS-IS level-1, L2 - IS-IS level-2, * - candidate
default
Gateway of last resort is 172.16.10.2 to network 0.0.0.0
     172.16.0.0 255.255.255.0 is subnetted, 5 subnets
C       172.16.50.0 is directly connected, Ethernet1
D       172.16.40.0 [90/2195456] via 172.16.10.2, 00:02:33, Ethernet0
S       172.16.30.0 [1/0] via 172.16.10.2
C       172.16.20.0 is directly connected, TokenRing0
C       172.16.10.0 is directly connected, Ethernet0
S*      0.0.0.0 0.0.0.0 [1/0] via 172.16.10.2
```

When troubleshooting static and default routes, check for physical and data link layer problems first. Look for problems such as a bad cable, an incorrectly constructed cable that uses the wrong pin-outs, bad interfaces on routers or switches between routers, and incorrect speed or duplex settings. Next move up to the IP layer and check network numbers and subnets. Interfaces on the same network must have IP addresses that are within the same subnet to communicate directly. Check for duplicate IP addresses. IP addresses must be unique; that is, the network portion must be the same for all addresses in a subnet, but the host portion must be unique.

Although static and default routes reduce resource usage, including bandwidth and router CPU and memory resources, the trade-off is a loss of detailed information about routing. Routers with a default route always send traffic that is not local to a peer router. They have no way of knowing that the other router may have lost some of its routes. They also have no way of knowing if a destination is always unreachable—for example, when someone is doing a ping scan and sending multiple pings to numerous IP destination addresses. A router with a default route forwards these packets. It has no way of distinguishing destinations that it can't reach from destinations that no routers can reach. Default routing can also cause a router to use suboptimal paths. For many networks, dynamic routing, discussed in the following sections, is more appropriate.

Dynamic Routing

When it is not practical or desirable to rely on static and default routes, you should run a dynamic routing protocol. A dynamic routing protocol allows routers to exchange information about the network topology and learn from each other how to reach destination networks. The administrator doesn't need to configure routing information. Instead, the routers learn routing information on their own. They also learn if a route fails and automatically reroute around failures when possible, without intervention from an administrator.

When troubleshooting dynamic routing protocols, keep in mind that routing protocols differ in how they exchange network reachability information, how they measure the distance to a network (*metrics*), whether they support hierarchical addressing and summarization, and how quickly they agree on a new network topology (*convergence*). Routing protocols also differ in their applicability. Some are best suited for use on small intranets, whereas others are used to learn thousands of Internet routes. The first part of this section explains some criteria that can be used when comparing routing protocols.

Routing protocols use metrics to determine which route is preferable when more than one route to a remote network is available. Routing protocols vary on which metrics are supported. Traditional routing protocols, such as the Routing Information Protocol (RIP), used only one metric—a *hop count*. A route that used fewer router hops to get to a remote network was considered better than a route that used more router hops. Newer protocols can also take into account delay, bandwidth, reliability, and other factors that characterize a route to a remote network. Metrics can affect how large you can grow a network. For example, RIP supports only 15 hops. Metrics can also affect network performance. A router that only uses hop count for its metric misses the opportunity to select a route that has more hops but also more bandwidth than another route.

Routing protocols can be characterized by how quickly they converge. *Convergence* is the time it takes for routers to arrive at a consistent understanding of the internetwork topology during initialization or after a change takes place. Because packets may not be routed reliably to all destinations while convergence is taking place, it is important to monitor typical convergence times on your routed networks. The convergence process should be complete within a few seconds for time-sensitive applications, such as real-time applications and applications that are based on IBM's Systems Network Architecture (which is time sensitive). When these applications are transported across an IP internetwork, a fast-converging protocol such as Open Shortest Path First (OSPF) or Enhanced Interior Gateway Routing Protocol (EIGRP) should be used.

When comparing routing protocols, it's important to realize that some routing protocols do not support any sort of pecking order or hierarchy for routers. All routers have the same tasks, and every router is a peer of every other router. Routing protocols that support hierarchy, on the other hand, assign different tasks to routers and group routers in *areas*, *autonomous systems*, or *domains*. In a hierarchical arrangement, some routers communicate with local routers in the same area, and other routers have the job of connecting areas, domains, or autonomous systems. A pecking order for routers enhances stability and scalability. No single router needs to do all tasks.

NOTE A loose definition of an autonomous system is a set of routers and networks using the same routing policies. An autonomous system could be a single router that connects a local network to the Internet, a corporate network that links several local networks through a backbone, or a set of customer networks served by a single ISP.

Routing protocols can be characterized by where they are used. *Interior routing protocols*, such as RIP, OSPF, and Cisco's Interior Gateway Routing Protocol (IGRP) and EIGRP, are used by routers within the same enterprise or autonomous system. Exterior routing protocols, such as the Border Gateway Protocol (BGP), perform routing between multiple autonomous systems. BGP is used on the Internet by peer routers in different autonomous systems to maintain a consistent view of the Internet's routing table.

Another pair of terms that you may hear when comparing routing protocols is *classful* versus *classless* routing protocols. A classful routing protocol, such as RIP or IGRP, always considers the IP network class (Class A, B, or C). Address summarization is automatic by major network number. A classful routing protocol does not support Variable-Length Subnet Masking (VLSM). VLSM is a technique for using a different prefix length (subnet mask) on different parts of an internetwork. For example, on your LANs, you might use a subnet mask of 255.255.255.0, whereas on a point-to-point WAN that has only two devices (the routers that connect the WAN link), you might use a mask of 255.255.255.252. A single local router can understand this configuration, but remote routers may route incorrectly in this situation. With classful routing, a router does not know how the subnet mask is configured on any interface other than its own interfaces. The subnet mask is not carried in the routing protocol updates.

Classful routing protocols also do support a *discontiguous subnet*. A discontiguous subnet is one that is divided into parts that are distant from each other, as shown in Figure 8.3. With classful routing, traffic may not be correctly routed to the portions of the subnet.

Classless routing protocols, on the other hand, transmit prefix length or subnet mask information with IP network addresses. With classless routing protocols, the IP address space can be mapped so that discontiguous subnets and VLSM are supported. The IP address space should be mapped carefully so that most subnets are arranged in contiguous blocks, allowing route updates to be summarized at area boundaries.

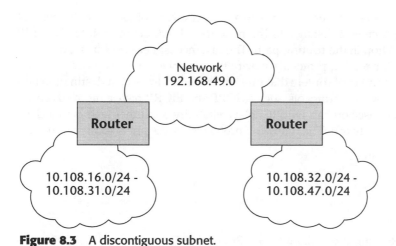

Figure 8.3 A discontiguous subnet.

Distance-Vector Versus Link-State Routing

Dynamic routing protocols fall into two major classes: *distance-vector* and *link-state*. These two routing mechanisms can be distinguished by the internal algorithms and data structures they use to determine which networks are reachable and which path to each network is best. The differences between the algorithms lie not so much in what kind of information is exchanged, but in how the routers process the information once they receive it. In both cases the routers exchange information about the topology of the network and can send detailed or partial information. For example, EIGRP, which is a distance-vector protocol, only sends updates. OSPF, which is a link-state protocol, generally just sends updates also. Sending a complete routing table is not necessary in either case.

A distance-vector routing protocol creates a consolidated list of all reachable destinations. If the list contains multiple entries for a destination (because there are multiple ways to reach the destination), the entries are sorted by metric and the one with the lowest metric is selected. A link-state routing protocol, on the other hand, creates a mathematical graph that depicts the network. A link-state protocol implements a sophisticated process, called the *Dijkstra algorithm*, to determine the shortest path to all points in the graph when the nodes and links in the graph are known.

Distance-Vector Routing Protocols

This chapter discusses distance-vector protocols first. To help you understand distance-vector routing protocols, consider the following definition of *vector* from the online version of *Merriam-Webster's Collegiate Dictionary*:

> **Vector.**   A quantity that has magnitude and direction and that is commonly represented by a directed line segment whose length represents the magnitude and whose orientation in space represents the direction.

So the term *distance vector* means a route to a network that points in the direction of the network and specifies a distance to the network. The direction pointer is the IP address of the next hop in the routing path. The distance is measured using a metric. Many distance-vector routing protocols specify the distance with a hop count. A hop count specifies the number of routers that must be traversed to reach a destination network. Some distance-vector protocols, such as IGRP and EIGRP, have a more advanced measure of distance based on bandwidth, delay, reliability, and other factors that characterize the path to a network. The following protocols are distance-vector protocols:

- RIP Versions 1 and 2
- IGRP
- EIGRP
- BGP
- AppleTalk Routing Table Maintenance Protocol (RTMP)
- Novell Internetwork Packet Exchange (IPX) RIP

A distance-vector routing protocol maintains a routing table that lists known networks and the distance to each network. Table 8.1 shows a typical distance-vector routing table.

Table 8.1   Distance-Vector Routing Table

NETWORK	DISTANCE (IN HOPS)	SEND TO (NEXT HOP)
10.0.0.0	0 (directly connected)	Interface 1
172.16.0.0	0 (directly connected)	Interface 2
172.17.0.0	1	172.16.0.2
172.18.0.0	2	172.16.0.2
192.168.1.0	1	10.0.0.2
192.168.2.0	2	10.0.0.2

Advanced Features of Distance-Vector Routing Protocols

With most distance-vector routing protocols, a router sends its routing table out each of its interfaces on a periodic basis. If the protocol supports the *split-horizon* technique, the router sends only routes that are reachable via other interfaces, which reduces the size of the update and improves the accuracy of routing information. With split horizon, a router does not tell another router information that is better learned locally.

Most distance-vector protocols also implement a *holddown* timer so that new information about an unstable route is not believed right away, in case the information is based on stale data. Holddown timers are a standard way to avoid loops that can happen during convergence. To understand the loop problem, consider the network shown in Figure 8.4.

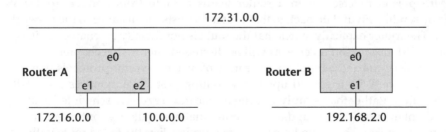

Figure 8.4   Distance-vector routing tables on Router A and Router B.

When distance-vector routing protocols send their routing tables, they simply send the Network and Distance columns of the table. They do not send the Send To (Next Hop) column, which is one of the causes of loops. The sequence of events that can lead to a routing loop is as follows:

1. Router A's connection to Network 172.16.0.0 fails.

2. Router A removes Network 172.16.0.0 from its routing table.

3. Based on previous announcements from Router A, Router B broadcasts its routing table saying that Router B can reach Network 172.16.0.0 and the distance is 1.

4. Router A adds Network 172.16.0.0 to its routing table with a Send To (Next Hop) value of Router B and a distance of 2.

5. Router A receives a packet for a host on Network 172.16.0.0.

6. Router A sends the packet to Router B.

7. Router B sends the packet to Router A.

8. The packet loops back and forth from Router A to Router B until its IP Time-To-Live (TTL) value expires.

To make matters worse, without split horizon, at some point Router A sends a route update saying it can get to Network 172.16.0.0, causing Router B to update the route in its table with a distance of 3. Both Router A and Router B continue to send route updates until finally the distance field reaches infinity. (Routing protocols arbitrarily define a distance that means infinity. For example, 16 means infinity for RIP.) When the distance reaches infinity, the routers remove the route. This problem is called the *count-to-infinity problem*. A holddown function tells a router not to add or update information for a route that has recently been removed until a holddown timer expires. In the example, if Router A uses holddown, it does not add the route for Network 172.16.0.0 that Router B sends. Split horizon also solves the problem in the example, because if Router B uses split horizon, it does not tell Router A about a route to 172.16.0.0.

Poison-reverse messages are another way of speeding convergence and avoiding loops. With poison reverse, when a router learns a route from another router, it responds by sending an update back to that router that lists the distance to the network as infinity. The router explicitly states that the route is not directly reachable via itself. IGRP and EIGRP use poison reverse, as will be discussed later in this chapter.

Triggered updates are another advanced feature of distance-vector protocols that can speed convergence. With triggered updates, a routing protocol announces route failures immediately. Rather than simply waiting for the next regularly scheduled routing update and not including in the update any routes that have failed, a router can immediately send an update. The immediate (triggered) update lists the failed route with the distance set to infinity.

Link-State Routing Protocols

A link-state routing protocol is a protocol that uses the Dijkstra algorithm to determine how to reach destination networks. The Dijkstra algorithm, which is named after Edsger Dijkstra, the computer scientist who invented it, solves the problem of finding the shortest path from a source point in a graph to a destination point. One of the beauties of the algorithm is that while finding the shortest path to one destination, a source can also find the shortest path to all points in the graph at the same time. This makes the algorithm a perfect fit for a routing protocol, although it does have other uses.

With link-state routing, routers establish a relationship (called an *adjacency*) with neighbor routers. Each router sends *Link State Advertisements* (LSAs) to each adjacent neighbor. The advertisements identify links and metrics. Each neighbor that receives an advertisement propagates the advertisement to its neighbors. The result is that every router ends up with an identical link-state database that describes the nodes and links in the internetwork graph. Using the Dijkstra algorithm, each router independently calculates its shortest path to each network and enters this information into its routing table.

Link-state routing requires more router CPU power and memory than distance-vector routing, and can be harder to troubleshoot. Link-state routing does have some advantages over distance-vector routing, however. In general, link-state routing was designed to use less bandwidth, be less prone to loops, and converge more quickly than distance-vector routing (although there are distance-vector protocols, such as EIGRP, that have those qualities also).

In the IP world, OSPF is a prevalent link-state routing protocol. The word *Open* in *OSPF* refers to the fact that the protocol is not proprietary. It is specified in Request for Comments (RFC) 2328, which is publicly available. Another link-state routing protocol is the Intermediate System-to-Intermediate System (IS-IS) protocol, which is not commonly used on typical campus IP networks, although many ISPs use IS-IS in their internal networks. In Novell environments, the NetWare Link Services Protocol (NLSP) is a link-state routing protocol, as will be discussed in Chapter 10.

Using Multiple Routing Protocols

Many campus internetworks use multiple routing protocols, perhaps because of the merger of departments or companies that were once separate. Also, multiple routing protocols often make sense because the criteria for selecting protocols are different for different parts of an internetwork. Simple distance-vector protocols, such as RIP or IGRP, work well at the access layer of a hierarchical topology, but are not appropriate for the distribution or core layers. OSPF or EIGRP should run at those layers because they converge more quickly and are less susceptible to loops.

When examining a network with a protocol analyzer, you should pay close attention to which routing protocols are present. If your policy is to support only EIGRP and OSPF, for example, then you should not see any RIP traffic on the network. If you don't use Novell's NLSP, then you should not see any NLSP traffic with your analyzer, of course.

Cisco has a technique called *redistribution* that allows a router to run more than one routing protocol and share routes among routing protocols. Implementing redistribution can be challenging because every routing protocol behaves differently and routing protocols cannot directly exchange information about routes, metrics, link states, and so on.

THE INCREDULOUS MANAGER

When one of the authors was working on site with a network engineer, a trace file showed the presence of a foreign routing protocol that was not supposed to be there. When the engineer called her manager over to show him, it was hard to convince him. When he saw that the protocol analyzer indicated the presence of the foreign routing protocol, his response was, "Well, the analyzer is wrong." Of course, the analyzer was simply displaying what was present on the cable, and the manager, who was so sure that his network couldn't possibly be configured incorrectly, refused to believe his eyes. As it turned out, the manager became a believer when, in an attempt to prove his position, he checked the configuration of the routers.

A network engineer configures redistribution by specifying which protocols should insert routing information into other protocols' routing tables. The configuration should be done with care to avoid *feedback*. Feedback happens when a routing protocol learns about routes from another protocol and then advertises these routes back to the other routing protocol. For example, if a router is configured to redistribute between IGRP and RIP, the router must filter any routes in its routing table that were inserted by RIP before sending them back into the RIP network. This avoids any problems caused by the differences in metrics used by different routing protocols.

When a router runs multiple routing protocols and learns about a destination via more than one protocol, the router must decide which information to use. Cisco assigns an *administrative distance* to routes learned from different sources. A lower administrative distance means that a route is preferred. For example, if a router learns about a route via both IGRP and RIP, the IGRP route is preferred because IGRP has a default administrative distance of 100 and RIP has a default administrative distance of 120. If a router also has a static route to the destination, then the static route is preferred, because the default administrative distance for a static route is 0 or 1 (depending on whether the static route is defined using a connected interface or the IP address of the next-hop router).

When troubleshooting multiple routing protocols, there may be a need to modify the administrative distance of a protocol so that it takes precedence. For example, if you want a router to select RIP-learned routes (default value 120) rather than IGRP-learned routes (default value 100) to the same destination, you must increase the administrative distance for IGRP to a number larger than 120. Table 8.2 shows the default values for administrative distances.

Integrated Routing and Bridging

In campus networks that have a requirement to merge bridged and routed networks, Cisco IOS software supports Integrated Routing and Bridging (IRB), which connects Virtual LANs (VLANs) and bridged networks to routed networks within the same router.

Table 8.2 Administrative Distance for Routing Protocols

SOURCE OF INFORMATION	DISTANCE
Connected interface	0
Static route	1
EIGRP summary route	5
External BGP route	20
Internal EIGRP route	90
IGRP route	100
OSPF route	110
IS-IS route	115
RIP route	120
Exterior Gateway Protocol (EGP) route	140
External EIGRP route	170
Internal BGP route	200
Route of unknown origin	255

An older Cisco IOS feature, called Concurrent Routing and Bridging (CRB), supported routing and bridging within the same router, but simply allowed you to connect bridged networks to other bridged networks and routed networks to other routed networks within the router. IRB extends CRB by providing the capability to forward packets between bridged and routed interfaces via a software-based interface called the Bridged Virtual Interface (BVI).

One advantage of IRB is that a bridged IP subnet or VLAN can span a router. This can be useful when there is a shortage of IP subnet numbers and it is not possible to assign a different subnet number to each interface on a router. It can also be useful during migration from a bridged environment to a routed environment. IRB-based networks can be difficult to understand, monitor, and troubleshoot, however. IRB may be necessary on some networks that are in transition, but it should be avoided if possible.

General Comments on Troubleshooting IP Routing

The remainder of this chapter covers specific campus IP routing protocols. Before we get to those sections, however, let's look at a general-purpose list of steps you should take when troubleshooting a problem that appears to be related to routing protocols. Troubleshooting efforts should focus on examining router configuration information and routing data that a router has in memory. You can also use a protocol analyzer to view routing protocol packets sent by routers, but this may not give you a complete picture of whether routing is working properly:

1. Use the show ip route command to display the routing table. Check that the networks you are trying to reach are listed in the table with a next-hop value that makes sense based on your knowledge of the network topology. For a summarized view of the routing table, use the show ip route summary command. If networks are missing or the table contains questionable information, proceed to the following steps.

2. Check for physical and data link layer problems with the show interface command. Check that interfaces are up and reliably sending and receiving frames. If they aren't, try to isolate any bad cables, incorrectly constructed cables, faulty interfaces on routers or switches between routers, and incorrect speed or duplex settings.

3. Check for a network-layer misconfiguration using the show ip interface command. Carefully check IP addresses and subnet masks.

4. Test reachability with the ping and trace utilities. For stubborn problems, do some advanced ping and trace testing by taking advantage of the IP source-routing and record-route options.

5. Use the show running-config and the show ip protocols commands to display configuration information, carefully checking all network statements and masks. Also check routing protocol configurations, especially timers. For most protocols, all routers should have the same timers for sending updates, removing routes from the routing table, sending Hello messages, and so on.

6. Use the show ip traffic command to display statistics that the router has gathered about its IP protocol processes.

7. Use the show access-lists command to ensure that no access lists are defined that could incorrectly inhibit routing protocols or traffic flow.

8. On a router with low CPU usage, some general-purpose debug commands that can help troubleshoot routing problems include debug ip routing, debug ip packet, debug ip icmp, and debug arp.

Sample Network Used in Protocol Analysis Examples

The following sections describe the most common campus IP routing protocols. To understand the examples of Cisco IOS and protocol analyzer output, refer to the network illustrated in Figure 8.5. The RIP, IGRP, and EIGRP configurations were tested on the network shown in Figure 8.5. The OSPF and BGP configurations were tested on the network that you will see later in Figure 8.6, which is based on the network shown in Figure 8.5.

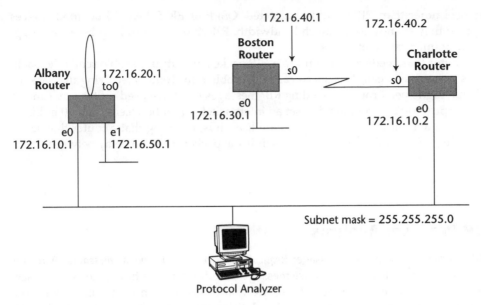

Figure 8.5 Campus network used in examples.

Routing Information Protocol (RIP)

RIP was the first standard routing protocol developed for TCP/IP internetworks. RIP was originally developed for the Xerox Network System (XNS) and was adopted by the IP community in the early 1980s. RIP is still commonly used as an interior routing protocol on campus networks, probably because it is easy to configure and it runs on routers from every major vendor. RIP version 1 (RIPv1) is documented in RFC 1058. RIP version 2 (RIPv2), documented in RFC 2453, is covered in the next section.

RIP is a distance-vector routing protocol that features simplicity and ease of troubleshooting. RIP is a classful routing protocol, which means it always summarizes on a network boundary and it does not support discontiguous subnets or VLSM. Troubleshooting RIP often involves hunting out any unintentional discontiguous subnets or VLSM configurations. When you display the RIP routing table with a show ip route command, if there are inaccurate or missing routes, check all network numbers and subnet masks to determine if there may be some discontiguous subnets or VLSM configurations.

RIP broadcasts its entire routing table (after applying the split horizon rule) every 30 seconds. RIP allows 25 routes per packet. On large internetworks, multiple packets are required to send the whole routing table. Because of the multiple packets and the 30-second update timer, bandwidth utilization by RIP can be an issue on large internetworks that include low-capacity links. If the links cannot be upgraded, then a routing protocol other than RIP should be selected. OSPF or EIGRP would be good choices because they do not use as much bandwidth. RIPv2 would also help because it supports summarization of routes.

A router that needs to send multiple RIP packets to output its table sends the packets as quickly as it can. This speed can be a problem for routers receiving the packets. When a high-speed router is sending RIP messages to a low-speed router, you can use the output-delay command to set an interpacket gap of between 8 and 50 milliseconds. The default interpacket gap is 0 milliseconds, meaning that a router that sends multiple packets for one route update sends the packets with no delay between them.

RIP Protocol Analysis

RIP defines two types of message: *Request messages* and *Response messages*. A router running RIP broadcasts a Response message containing its routing table every 30 seconds by default, as mentioned. These are gratuitous Responses not in answer to a Request. RIP sends its messages in UDP datagrams. Both the source and destination UDP ports are 520. The following text shows a RIP broadcast from the Charlotte router in Figure 8.5.

```
Ethernet Header
   Destination:   FF:FF:FF:FF:FF:FF   Ethernet Broadcast
   Source:        00:00:0C:00:2E:75
Protocol Type:0x0800   IP
IP Header - Internet Protocol Datagram
   Version:             4
   Header Length:       5   (20  bytes)
   Type of Service:     %00000000
   Precedence: Routine,   Normal Delay, Throughput, Reliability
   Total Length:        72
   Identifier:          0
   Fragmentation Flags: %000  May Fragment    Last Fragment
   Fragment Offset:     0  (0  bytes)
   Time To Live:        2
   Protocol:            17  UDP
   Header Checksum:     0x0294
   Source IP Address:   172.16.10.2 Charlotte
   Dest. IP Address:    255.255.255.255   IP Broadcast
   No IP Options
UDP - User Datagram Protocol
   Source Port:         520  RIP
   Destination Port:    520
   Length:              52
   Checksum:            0xA53A
RIP - Routing Information Protocol
   Command:                 2  Response containing network distance pairs
```

```
        Version:              1
        Zero:                 0x0000
Info on Net # 1
   Network Number:    2
   Zero:              0x0000
   Net Address:       172.16.40.0
   Zero:              0x0000000000000000
   Distance:          1
Info on Net # 2
   Network Number:    2
   Zero:              0x0000
   Net Address:       172.16.30.0
   Zero:              0x0000000000000000
   Distance:          2
```

RIP uses a single metric (hop count) to measure the distance to a destination network. A distance of 16 signifies an unreachable network whose distance is infinity; a distance of 1 means a network that is directly connected to the advertising router. In the preceding example, the Charlotte router is directly connected to Network 172.16.40.0. Notice that the distance is 1. Charlotte is two networks away from the 172.16.30.0 network using RIP's method of counting. Notice that the distance to 172.16.30.0 is 2.

The following output shows the results of the show ip route command on the Charlotte router. Directly connected networks are listed after the C code with no distance displayed. Routes learned through RIP are listed after the R code. Routes learned through RIP include the address of the router from which the route was learned (see *via 172.16.10.1*) and how much time has elapsed since the last update for the route in hours:minutes:seconds (see *00:00:13*). The final entry for the route identifies which interface can reach the route (see *Ethernet0*).

```
charlotte#show ip route
Codes: C - connected, S - static, I - IGRP, R - RIP, M - mobile, B - BGP
       D - EIGRP, EX - EIGRP external, O - OSPF, IA - OSPF inter area
       E1 - OSPF external type 1, E2 - OSPF external type 2, E - EGP
       i - IS-IS, L1 - IS-IS level-1, L2 - IS-IS level-2, * -candidate
default
Gateway of last resort is not set
     172.16.0.0 255.255.255.0 is subnetted, 5 subnets
R       172.16.50.0 [120/1] via 172.16.10.1, 00:00:13, Ethernet0
C       172.16.40.0 is directly connected, Serial0
R       172.16.30.0 [120/1] via 172.16.40.1, 00:00:14, Serial0
R       172.16.20.0 [120/1] via 172.16.10.1, 00:00:14, Ethernet0
C       172.16.10.0 is directly connected, Ethernet0
```

The output shows that the administrative distance is 120 and the hop-count distance is 1 for all routes learned by Charlotte. (See the *[120/1]* output.) Notice that the show ip route command displays a hop-count distance that is 1 less than the distance advertised in route updates. The show ip route output from Charlotte shows that the hop count for 172.16.30.0 is 1, but, as illustrated in the EtherPeek output, when sending a route update out the Ethernet interface, Charlotte announces that the distance to 172.16.30.0 is 2. Before sending the update, Charlotte adds the local metric, which states that locally connected networks have a distance of 1. This is a strange feature of RIP; most distance-vector protocols consider the locally connected network to have a distance of 0. When troubleshooting with both Cisco commands and a protocol analyzer, remember that RIP distances will vary by 1.

To avoid routing loops during convergence, most modern implementations of RIP, including Cisco implementations, support advanced features such as split horizon, a holddown timer, triggered updates, and poison reverse. In the preceding protocol analyzer output, the Charlotte router did not include its complete routing table because many of the entries in its routing table were learned on the Ethernet 0 interface to which it was sending its routing table. In other words, Charlotte applied the split-horizon rule.

Because of split horizon, the Albany router in Figure 8.5 should not advertise networks 172.16.40.0 or 172.16.30.0 in its update out its Ethernet 0 interface, because the Albany router learned about these routes on its Ethernet 0 interface. The following output displays an update from Albany that confirms this.

```
Ethernet Header
   Destination:  FF:FF:FF:FF:FF:FF   Ethernet Broadcast
   Source:       00:00:0C:05:3E:80
Protocol Type:0x0800   IP
IP Header - Internet Protocol Datagram
   Version:              4
   Header Length:        5  (20  bytes)
   Type of Service:      %00000000
   Precedence: Routine,   Normal Delay, Throughput, Reliability
   Total Length:         72
   Identifier:           0
   Fragmentation Flags:  %000  May Fragment    Last Fragment
   Fragment Offset:      0  (0  bytes)
   Time To Live:         2
   Protocol:             17  UDP
   Header Checksum:      0x0295
   Source IP Address:    172.16.10.1 Albany
   Dest. IP Address:     255.255.255.255   IP Broadcast
   No IP Options
UDP - User Datagram Protocol
   Source Port:          520  RIP
   Destination Port:     520
   Length:               52
   Checksum:             0xA53C
RIP - Routing Information Protocol
   Command:              2  Response containing network distance pairs
   Version:              1
   Zero:                 0x0000
Info on Net # 1
```

```
    Network Number:     2
    Zero:               0x0000
    Net Address:        172.16.50.0
    Zero:               0x0000000000000000
    Distance:           1
Info on Net # 2
    Network Number:     2
    Zero:               0x0000
    Net Address:        172.16.20.0
    Zero:               0x0000000000000000
    Distance:           1
```

The Albany router did not list all its routes in the update (because of split horizon), but a show ip route issued at the router shows that Albany does know about all routes:

```
Albany#show ip route
Codes: C - connected, S - static, I - IGRP, R - RIP, M - mobile, B - BGP
       D - EIGRP, EX - EIGRP external, O - OSPF, IA - OSPF inter area
       E1 - OSPF external type 1, E2 - OSPF external type 2, E - EGP
       i - IS-IS, L1 - IS-IS level-1, L2 - IS-IS level-2, * -candidate
default
Gateway of last resort is not set
     172.16.0.0 255.255.255.0 is subnetted, 5 subnets
C        172.16.50.0 is directly connected, Ethernet1
R        172.16.40.0 [120/1] via 172.16.10.2, 00:00:11, Ethernet0
R        172.16.30.0 [120/2] via 172.16.10.2, 00:00:11, Ethernet0
C        172.16.20.0 is directly connected, TokenRing0
C        172.16.10.0 is directly connected, Ethernet0
```

RIP Timers

RIP includes several timers that are configured on individual routers. The timers are not transmitted in RIP messages. The *update timer* specifies how often the routing table should be broadcast. The default value is 30 seconds, as mentioned earlier. Actually, Cisco routers add some jitter to the 30-second update timer. This is to avoid all routers on a network synchronizing their timers and sending updates at the same time, which can result in unnecessary taxing of bandwidth and CPU resources. When analyzing a RIP network, don't be surprised to see the interval between a router's updates being 25 to 30 seconds rather than exactly 30 seconds.

The *invalid timer* limits the time for which a route is considered valid in the case that advertising routers have stopped including the route in their updates. This timer is 180 seconds by default. After 180 seconds, a router continues to advertise the route in its messages, but states the distance as 16 (infinity). After another 60 seconds, the *flush timer* expires, and the route is removed from the router's routing table.

To avoid loops, Cisco's implementation of RIP also has a *holddown* timer. The holddown timer puts a route in holddown for 180 seconds whenever an update with a hop count higher than the recorded hop count arrives. During the holddown time, the router doesn't accept any updates about the route. This avoids loops and counting to infinity.

RIP timers can be changed with the `timers basic update invalid holddown flush` command, but changing them is not advisable due to risks that the changes may be misconfigured or not implemented identically on all routers. All routers on an internetwork should agree on the timer values. As mentioned, routers do not have any way of updating each other regarding timer values. The timer values are not carried in RIP messages. It's up to the network engineer to get them right.

RIPv2

RIPv2 is documented in RFC 2453. RIPv2 is a distance-vector protocol that behaves essentially just like RIPv1, but RIPv2 has some enhancements that make it perform better than RIPv1. For example, to avoid disturbing devices that don't speak RIP, RIPv2 sends its updates to a multicast address instead of a broadcast address. RIPv2 uses the 224.0.0.9 multicast address. RIPv2 also adds the following fields to route entries within a routing table:

Route tag.   Distinguishes internal routes that are within the RIP routing domain from external routes that have been imported from another routing protocol or a different autonomous system. Route tags facilitate merging RIP and non-RIP networks and help avoid redistribution feedback.

Subnet mask.   Contains the subnet mask or prefix length that is applied to the network number listed in the route entry. Inclusion of this field means that RIPv2 is a classless protocol and supports VLSM and discontiguous subnets.

Next hop.   Specifies a better next-hop address (if one exists) than the address of the advertising router. The next hop field indicates a next-hop address, on the same subnet, that is metrically closer to the destination than the advertising router. If the field is set to 0.0.0.0, then the address of the advertising router is the best next-hop address. This field is especially useful when RIP is not in use on all routers in an internetwork. See Appendix A of RFC 1723 for an example.

RIPv2 supports a simple authentication method to foil hackers sending route updates. The authentication scheme uses the space of a route entry, which means that there can be only 24 route entries in a message when authentication is used. Currently, the authentication methods supported on a Cisco router include a simple plaintext password and MD5 authentication. Non-Cisco routers may not support the MD5 method, so you may not be able to use it on multivendor networks. Whenever possible, however, you should use MD5 because it is much more secure than a plaintext password. Be careful when configuring authentication: Many network engineers have spent long nights troubleshooting problems related to misconfigured passwords, authentication modes, encryption keys, and key management parameters.

On a mixed network with both RIPv1 and RIPv2, you can tell a particular router interface to send RIPv1, RIPv2, or both types of messages with the `ip rip send version` command. You can also configure a RIP router to accept RIPv1, RIPv2, or both types of messages with the `ip rip receive version` command.

Cisco Show and Debug Commands for RIP

The main Cisco command to use when troubleshooting RIP is the show ip route command and all its varieties, such as show ip route summary, show ip route connected, and show ip route rip.

To display information about summarized RIP routes, use the show ip rip database command, which is a new command as of Cisco IOS version 12.0(6)T. Remember that RIPv1 automatically summarizes on a major network boundary. Summarization can be configured for RIPv2.

The main Cisco debug command to use when troubleshooting RIP is the debug ip rip command, which shows RIP updates sent and received, as seen in the following example from the Albany router:

```
Albany#debug ip rip
RIP protocol debugging is on
Albany#
RIP: sending update to 255.255.255.255 via Ethernet0 (172.16.10.1)
      subnet 172.16.50.0, metric 1
      subnet 172.16.20.0, metric 1
RIP: sending update to 255.255.255.255 via Ethernet1 (172.16.50.1)
      subnet 172.16.40.0, metric 2
      subnet 172.16.30.0, metric 3
      subnet 172.16.20.0, metric 1
      subnet 172.16.10.0, metric 1
RIP: sending update to 255.255.255.255 via TokenRing0 (172.16.20.1)
      subnet 172.16.50.0, metric 1
      subnet 172.16.40.0, metric 2
      subnet 172.16.30.0, metric 3
      subnet 172.16.10.0, metric 1
RIP: received update from 172.16.10.2 on Ethernet0
      172.16.40.0 in 1 hops
      172.16.30.0 in 2 hops
```

A variation of the debug ip rip command is the debug ip rip events command, which shows less output, as illustrated in the following example:

```
Albany#
RIP: received update from 172.16.10.2 on Ethernet0
RIP: Update contains 2 routes
RIP: sending update to 255.255.255.255 via Ethernet0 (172.16.10.1)
RIP: Update contains 2 routes
RIP: sending update to 255.255.255.255 via Ethernet1 (172.16.50.1)
RIP: Update contains 4 routes
RIP: sending update to 255.255.255.255 via TokenRing0 (172.16.20.1)
RIP: Update contains 4 routes
```

Using the debug ip rip events command can help identify problems, as illustrated in the following output from a network in Ashland, Oregon. This network had a mix of RIPv1 and RIPv2, and the 172.40.120.242 router was misconfigured for authentication.

```
Ashland#
RIP: ignored v1 packet from 172.30.120.241 (illegal version)
RIP: ignored v2 packet from 172.40.120.242 (invalid authentication)
```

Interior Gateway Routing Protocol (IGRP)

Cisco invented IGRP in the mid-1980s. Many of the company's customers migrated their RIP networks to IGRP to overcome RIP's 15-hop limitation and use of a single metric (hop count). Another reason customers preferred IGRP was its 90-second update timer for sending route updates, compared to RIP's 30-second update timer, which can cause significant bandwidth consumption on low-speed links. Today quite a few IGRP networks have been upgraded to EIGRP, which is covered in the next section. The original IGRP still makes sense for many campus networks, however, because it is less complex than EIGRP and it is very easy to configure and troubleshoot.

Like RIP, IGRP is a classful distance-vector protocol. It supports split horizon, triggered updates, and poison reverse. Like RIP, IGRP has several timers that can be changed with the `timers basic update invalid holddown flush` command. Changing the timers is usually not necessary or advisable. By default, IGRP's update timer is 90 seconds, its invalid timer is 270 seconds, its holddown timer is 280 seconds, and its flush timer is 630 seconds. (Incorrect IGRP routes stay in the routing table for a long time!) IGRP also supports a *sleeptime*, which is the amount of time for postponing routing updates after receiving a triggered update. The sleeptime should not be greater than the update time to avoid routing tables becoming unsynchronized. The default value for sleeptime is zero milliseconds.

Both IGRP and EIGRP have an advantage over RIP with regards to load sharing across multiple paths. RIP allows load sharing across paths with equal hop counts. IGRP allows load sharing over equal-metric and non-equal-metric paths. The IGRP *variance* feature means that if one path is three times better than another, the better path can be used three times more than the other path. (Only routes with metrics that are within a certain range of the best route can be used as multiple paths. See Cisco's configuration documentation for more information on variance.)

Both IGRP and EIGRP use a composite metric that is based on the following elements:

Bandwidth.   The bandwidth of the lowest-bandwidth segment on the path to a network. A network engineer can configure bandwidth at each interface or use the default value, which is based on the type of interface. Configuration is recommended for high-speed WAN interfaces if the default bandwidth value is less than the actual speed. It is also recommended on Frame Relay links to make sure that bandwidth matches the Committed Information Rate (CIR).

Delay.   A sum of all the delays for outgoing interfaces in the path to a network. Each delay is inversely proportional to the bandwidth of each outgoing interface. Delay is not dynamically calculated, contrary to popular beliefs about IGRP and EIGRP.

Reliability.   The worst reliability on any link. By default, reliability is not used unless the `metric weights` command is configured, in which case reliability is dynamically calculated based on the fraction of frames that arrive without input errors. It also takes into account the number of collisions encountered while sending on Ethernet networks. The reliability of an interface can be displayed with the `show interface` command.

Load.   The heaviest load on any link. By default, load is not used unless the `metric weights` command is configured, in which case load is dynamically calculated. The load on an interface can be displayed with the `show interface` command.

Although they are not used as part of the metric, two additional pieces of information are passed with the composite metric in IGRP and EIGRP routing updates: hop count and Maximum Transmission Unit (MTU). Hop count is the number of hops to the destination. An IGRP router advertises a directly connected network with a hop count of 0 (unlike RIP, which uses 1 for directly connected networks). Recipient routers add 1 to the hop count. Hop count is passed in the routing update packets but it is not used in the composite metric to decide which route is best when there are multiple routes to a network. It can be used to recognize a count-to-infinity problem, however, which results in a route being put in holddown.

MTU is the maximum packet size that can be sent along the entire path to a network without requiring fragmentation. (That is, it is the minimum of the MTUs of all the networks involved in the path.) Because IGRP routers include MTU information in their updates, a router could theoretically select paths based on MTU, but actually the MTU has never been used in the calculation of the metric.

> **NOTE** To pass Cisco tests, many people remember the IGRP and EIGRP composite metric with the mnemonic "Big Dogs Really Like Me." Big (B) is for Bandwidth. Dogs (D) is for Delay. Really (R) is for Reliability. Like (L) is for Load. Me (M) is for MTU. This is a great way to remember the metric, but keep in mind that MTU doesn't really fit into the list. Also, by default, reliability and load are not part of the composite metric unless the `metric weights` command is configured.

IGRP Protocol Analysis

When a Cisco router running IGRP boots, it broadcasts an IGRP *Request message*. It also broadcasts *Update messages* as each of its interfaces becomes operational. After all interfaces are operational, the router finally broadcasts an Update message that lists all routes not filtered by the split-horizon rule. Once in steady state, the router sends Updates every 90 seconds. The Updates list all routes not filtered by split horizon.

IGRP advertises three types of routes: interior, system, and exterior. Interior routes are routes between subnets. If the network attached to a router is not subnetted, IGRP does not advertise interior routes. System routes are routes to networks within the autonomous system. Exterior routes are routes to networks outside the autonomous system. The Cisco IOS software chooses a gateway of last resort from the list of exterior routes that IGRP provides. (Unlike RIP, IGRP automatically determines a gateway of last resort. This would have to be configured with a default route if RIP were used.)

In the following output, the Charlotte router (see Figure 8.5) broadcasts its routing table. Note that interface Serial 0 on the Charlotte router has a nonstandard MTU of 512 bytes, which means that all networks reachable via that interface (including Network 172.16.30.0) are listed as having an MTU of 512 also. Also note that the bandwidth for Serial 0 is 1.5 Mbps and that all networks reachable via that interface are listed as having a low bandwidth and high delay because of this. Even though Network 172.16.30.0 is an Ethernet segment, it is listed with a low bandwidth, low MTU, and high delay because it is reachable via the serial link between Charlotte and Boston.

```
Ethernet Header
   Destination:   FF:FF:FF:FF:FF:FF   Ethernet Broadcast
   Source:        00:00:0C:00:2E:75
   Protocol Type:0x0800  IP
IP Header - Internet Protocol Datagram
   Version:             4
   Header Length:       5  (20  bytes)
   Type of Service:     %00000000
   Precedence: Routine,   Normal Delay, Throughput, Reliability
   Total Length:        60
   Identifier:          0
   Fragmentation Flags: %000  May Fragment    Last Fragment
   Fragment Offset:     0  (0  bytes)
   Time To Live:        2
   Protocol:            9  IGP/IGRP
   Header Checksum:     0x02A8
   Source IP Address:   172.16.10.2  Charlotte
   Dest. IP Address:    255.255.255.255  IP Broadcast
   No IP Options
IGRP - Interior Gateway Routing Protocol
   Protocol Version:    1
   Opcode:              1  Update
   Edition:             6
   Autonomous System #: 100
   Interior Routes:     2
   System Routes:       0
   Exterior Routes:     0
   Checksum:            0x2214
InteriorRouting Entry #1
      Destination:           16.40.0
      Delay (microseconds):  20000
      Bandwidth (Kbit/sec):  6476
      Max. Transmission Unit: 512
      Reliability:           100%
      Load:                  0%
      Hop Count:             0
InteriorRouting Entry #2
```

```
Destination:            16.30.0
Delay (microseconds):   21000
Bandwidth (Kbit/sec):   6476
Max. Transmission Unit: 512
Reliability:            100%
Load:                   0%
Hop Count:              1
```

Notice in the output that IGRP uses only 3 bytes for the IP addresses that appear in routing entries. For example, 172.16.30.0 becomes 16.30.0. On modern networks, it seems silly to save 1 byte at the risk of confusing protocol analysts—not to mention other routers—but when IGRP was invented, bandwidth consumption was a bigger concern.

As it turns out, a destination is recognizable with only 3 bytes. For interior routes (the type of routes shown in the output), at least the first byte of the IP address is always known from the address of the interface on which the Update is received. System and exterior routes can also be carried in 3 bytes, because the last byte is always 0 for these types of routes.

Because the IGRP metric is a composite metric, when you issue a show ip route command, you won't see delay and bandwidth called out, but you can notice in the following output that the network reachable via the serial link has lower bandwidth and higher delay than the networks reachable via the Ethernet link. The metric is shown following the administrative distance, which is 100 for IGRP routes. For example, [100/1200] means administrative distance 100 and metric 1200.

```
charlotte#show ip route
Codes: C - connected, S - static, I - IGRP, R - RIP, M - mobile, B - BGP
       D - EIGRP, EX - EIGRP external, O - OSPF, IA - OSPF inter area
       E1 - OSPF external type 1, E2 - OSPF external type 2, E - EGP
       i - IS-IS, L1 - IS-IS level-1, L2 - IS-IS level-2, * - candidate
default
Gateway of last resort is not set
     172.16.0.0 255.255.255.0 is subnetted, 5 subnets
I       172.16.50.0 [100/1200] via 172.16.10.1, 00:00:52, Ethernet0
C       172.16.40.0 is directly connected, Serial0
I       172.16.30.0 [100/8576] via 172.16.40.1, 00:00:54, Serial0
I       172.16.20.0 [100/1163] via 172.16.10.1, 00:00:53, Ethernet0
C       172.16.10.0 is directly connected, Ethernet0
```

IGRP Triggered Updates and Poison Reverse

To reduce convergence time, IGRP supports triggered updates. A router sends a triggered update in response to a change—for example, the failure of an interface. Upon receipt of a triggered update, other routers also send triggered updates. A failure causes a wave of Update messages to propagate throughout the network, thus speeding convergence time and reducing the risk of loops.

In the following example, the Ethernet 1 interface on the Albany router became disabled when the Ethernet Attachment Unit Interface (AUI) fell out. (This may seem unlikely, but many routers do not have a locking AUI connector.) The Ethernet 1 interface was the interface that connected the 172.16.50.0 network. The Albany router took almost a full minute to figure out that there was a problem. Once Albany realized there was a problem, it broadcast a triggered update that announced that the delay to reach the 172.16.50.0 network was 0xFF FF FF (the maximum possible). In decimal, the delay is 167772150. The following output shows the triggered update.

```
Ethernet Header
  Destination:  FF:FF:FF:FF:FF:FF   Ethernet Broadcast
  Source:       00:00:0C:05:3E:80
  Protocol Type:0x0800   IP
IP Header - Internet Protocol Datagram
  Version:              4
  Header Length:        5  (20  bytes)
  Type of Service:      %00000000
  Precedence: Routine,   Normal Delay, Throughput, Reliability
  Total Length:         60
  Identifier:           0
  Fragmentation Flags:  %000  May Fragment    Last Fragment
  Fragment Offset:      0  (0  bytes)
  Time To Live:         2
  Protocol:             9  IGP/IGRP
  Header Checksum:      0x02A9
  Source IP Address:    172.16.10.1  Albany
  Dest. IP Address:     255.255.255.255   IP Broadcast
  No IP Options
IGRP - Interior Gateway Routing Protocol
  Protocol Version:     1
  Opcode:               1  Update
  Edition:              10
  Autonomous System #:  100
  Interior Routes:      1
  System Routes:        0
  Exterior Routes:      0
  Checksum:             0x49DD
InteriorRouting Entry #1
    Destination:           16.50.0
    Delay (microseconds):  167772150
    Bandwidth (Kbit/sec):  6648430
    Max. Transmission Unit: 25972
    Reliability:           19%
    Load:                  0%
    Hop Count:             4
```

Following the triggered update, Albany broadcast an IGRP Request message. The Charlotte router responded with an immediate unicast update. Obeying the laws of poison reverse, Charlotte included Network 172.16.50.0 in its update with a maximum delay of 0xFF FF FF. To avoid loops, Charlotte made sure Albany wouldn't try to send packets for the 172.16.50.0 network to Charlotte, whose only means of reaching the network is through Albany. The following output shows the poison reverse update from Charlotte.

```
Ethernet Header
  Destination:  00:00:0C:05:3E:80
  Source:       00:00:0C:00:2E:75
  Protocol Type:0x0800  IP
IP Header - Internet Protocol Datagram
  Version:              4
  Header Length:        5  (20  bytes)
  Type of Service:      %00000000
  Precedence: Routine,  Normal Delay,  Normal Throughput,  Normal
Reliability
  Total Length:         88
  Identifier:           0
  Fragmentation Flags:  %000  May Fragment   Last Fragment
  Fragment Offset:      0  (0  bytes)
  Time To Live:         2
  Protocol:             9  IGP/IGRP
  Header Checksum:      0x4C7A
  Source IP Address:    172.16.10.2  Charlotte
  Dest. IP Address:     172.16.10.1  Albany
  No IP Options
IGRP - Interior Gateway Routing Protocol
  Protocol Version:     1
  Opcode:               1  Update
  Edition:              6
  Autonomous System #:  100
  Interior Routes:      3
  System Routes:        0
  Exterior Routes:      0
  Checksum:             0xBC58
InteriorRouting Entry #1
  Destination:          16.50.0
  Delay (microseconds): 167772150
  Bandwidth (Kbit/sec): 1000
  Max. Transmission Unit: 1500
  Reliability:          100%
  Load:                 0%
  Hop Count:            1
InteriorRouting Entry #2
  Destination:          16.40.0
  Delay (microseconds): 20000
  Bandwidth (Kbit/sec): 6476
  Max. Transmission Unit: 1500
  Reliability:          100%
  Load:                 0%
  Hop Count:            0
```

```
InteriorRouting Entry #3
    Destination:            16.30.0
    Delay (microseconds):   21000
    Bandwidth (Kbit/sec):   6476
    Max. Transmission Unit: 1500
    Reliability:            100%
    Load:                   0%
    Hop Count:              1
```

Cisco Show and Debug Commands for IGRP

As was the case with RIP, the main show command to use when troubleshooting IGRP is the show ip route command and all its varieties, including show ip route summary and show ip route igrp. Also, be sure to use the show running-config command to check the configuration of IGRP timers and variance features.

Cisco supports two debugging commands for IGRP: debug ip igrp transactions and debug ip igrp events. The debug ip igrp transactions command displays information about each Update sent, including each network number and its metric. This command also displays information about each Update received, including the metric stored in the routing table and the metric advertised by the neighbor sending the information. "Metric... inaccessible" usually means that the neighbor router has put the destination in a holddown state.

The debug ip igrp events command displays summary information for IGRP routing messages. This command is particularly useful when there are many networks in the routing table. In this case, using debug ip igrp transactions could flood the console and make the router unusable. Use debug ip igrp events instead to display summary routing information. Following is sample output from the Charlotte router:

```
charlotte#debug ip igrp events
IGRP event debugging is on
charlotte#
IGRP: received update from 172.16.40.1 on Serial0
IGRP: Update contains 1 interior, 0 system, and 0 exterior routes.
IGRP: Total routes in update: 1
IGRP: sending update to 255.255.255.255 via Ethernet0 (172.16.10.2)
IGRP: Update contains 2 interior, 0 system, and 0 exterior routes.
IGRP: Total routes in update: 2
IGRP: sending update to 255.255.255.255 via Serial0 (172.16.40.2)
IGRP: Update contains 3 interior, 0 system, and 0 exterior routes.
IGRP: Total routes in update: 3
IGRP: received update from 172.16.10.1 on Ethernet0
IGRP: Update contains 2 interior, 0 system, and 0 exterior routes.
IGRP: Total routes in update: 2
```

Enhanced IGRP

Like IGRP, EIGRP is a distance-vector protocol, but it has many advanced features and behaviors not found with other distance-vector protocols. Although EIGRP still sends vectors with distance information, the updates are nonperiodic, partial, and bounded. *Nonperiodic* means that updates are sent only when a metric changes rather than at regular intervals. *Partial* means that updates include only routes that have changed, not every entry in the routing table. *Bounded* means that updates are sent only to affected routers. These behaviors mean that EIGRP uses very little bandwidth.

> **NOTE** EIGRP limits its consumption of bandwidth. By default, EIGRP uses no more than 50 percent of the bandwidth of a link. This ensures that regular traffic can get through even when EIGRP is sending information. In later Cisco IOS releases, this percentage can be changed with the `ip bandwidth-percent eigrp` command. From a troubleshooting point of view, if your routing protocol is using more than 50 percent of your bandwidth, something is probably wrong and the problem should be investigated.

Cisco developed EIGRP in the early 1990s to meet the needs of customers with large, complex, multiprotocol internetworks. To help customers migrate from IGRP to EIGRP, Cisco has provided an automatic redistribution mechanism to allow IGRP routes to be imported into EIGRP and vice versa. EIGRP can also redistribute routes for RIP, IS-IS, BGP, and OSPF. In addition, EIGRP offers support for AppleTalk and Novell routing and can redistribute AppleTalk RTMP routes, Novell RIP routes, and Novell Service Advertising Protocol (SAP) updates.

One of the main reasons for developing EIGRP was to improve the slow convergence of RIP and IGRP, especially on large networks. To meet this goal, Cisco adopted the *Diffusing-Update Algorithm* (DUAL) developed by Dr. J. J. Garcia-Luna-Aceves at SRI International. DUAL specifies a method for routers to store neighbors' routing information so that routers can switch to an alternate path very quickly. Routers can also query other routers to learn alternate routes.

A router using DUAL develops its routing knowledge using the concept of a *feasible successor*. A feasible successor is a neighbor router that also has a path to a destination. A router can become a feasible successor for a neighbor if its metric is less than the neighbor's metric for a destination. When a router detects that a link has failed, if a feasible successor has an alternate route, the router switches to the alternate route immediately, without causing any network traffic. If there is no successor, the router sends a Query to neighbors. The Query propagates across the network until a new route is found. Because of DUAL, EIGRP uses significantly less bandwidth than RIP or IGRP and converges much more quickly.

A router running EIGRP keeps track of its neighbors. (Use the `show ip eigrp neighbor` command to confirm a router's neighbors.) The router also develops a topology database that contains all destinations advertised by neighbors. (Use the show ip eigrp topology all-links command to see the database.) Each entry in the database contains a destination and a list of neighbors that have advertised the destination. For each neighbor, the entry includes the metric that the neighbor advertised for the destination.

After building neighbor and topology databases, a router runs the distance-vector algorithm to determine its best path to each remote network. These results are stored in the routing table, which can be displayed just like any routing table with the show ip route command. A router computes its own metric for a destination by using each neighbor's metric in combination with a local metric that the router uses to reach the neighbor. The router compares metrics and determines the lowest-metric path to a destination.

EIGRP uses the same composite metric that IGRP uses, combining bandwidth, delay, reliability, and load. Unlike IGRP, EIGRP multiplies the bandwidth and delay components by 256 to achieve a finer level of granularity. Like IGRP, reliability and load are not used unless the metric weights command is configured.

EIGRP Protocol Analysis

EIGRP sends both multicast and unicast traffic. When it sends multicast traffic, it sends to the 224.0.0.10 destination IP address. EIGRP runs directly above IP. The IP Protocol Type for EIGRP is 88. Many of the packets sent by EIGRP use reliable delivery, in which case packets include sequence numbers and are acknowledged. Some Cisco documents use the term *Reliable Transport Protocol* (RTP) for the elements of EIGRP that provide guaranteed delivery. This is unfortunate because to the rest of the world RTP means the Real-Time Transport Protocol. Protocol analyzers do not use the term RTP when displaying EIGRP packets.

Table 8.3 describes the different types of packets used by EIGRP. Each packet is identified by an Opcode field near the beginning of the EIGRP header. Table 8.3 shows the Opcode values.

The first task of a router running EIGRP is to learn about neighbors. On most networks, routers send Hello packets every 5 seconds to accomplish this task. On multipoint X.25, Frame Relay, and Asynchronous Transfer Mode (ATM) networks, with speeds of less than 1.5 Mbps, Hellos are unicast every 60 seconds. Hellos are also sent only every 60 seconds on ISDN Basic Rate Interface (BRI) links. Hellos are not acknowledged. In the Hello packet, a router specifies a *holdtime*, which does not have the same function as the holdtime used by RIP or IGRP. The EIGRP holdtime specifies the maximum time a router should wait to receive subsequent Hellos from a neighbor. If the holdtime timer expires, the neighbor is declared lost and DUAL is notified of the problem.

The rate at which EIGRP sends Hello packets is called the *hello interval*, and you can adjust it per interface with the ip hello-interval eigrp command. The holdtime is typically three times the hello interval (by default, 15 seconds on LAN interfaces). You can adjust the holdtime with the ip hold-time eigrp command.

Table 8.3 EIGRP Packets

PACKET	OPCODE	DESCRIPTION
Hello	5	Hellos are used by the neighbor discovery and recovery processes. Hello packets are multicast and use unreliable delivery. Although the EIGRP header in a Hello packet includes a sequence and acknowledgment number, the numbers are always 0. Hellos include data about EIGRP parameters and the version of Cisco IOS in use.
Acknowledgment (ACK)	5	ACKs are used to confirm receipt of Queries, Updates, and Replies. The ACK number in the packet is the 32-bit sequence number last heard from the neighbor to which the packet is being sent. ACKs look like Hello packets with no data and a non-0 ACK number. ACKs are unicast and use unreliable delivery.
Update	1	Updates convey route information. When Updates are required by a specific router, they are unicast. When Updates are required by multiple routers, such as upon a metric or topology change, they are multicast. Updates use reliable delivery.
Query	3	Queries are sent when a router needs to request route information from neighbors when no feasible successor exists for a route that has failed. Queries can be multicast or unicast. Queries use reliable delivery.
Reply	4	Replies are answers to Queries. They are unicast and use reliable delivery. Replies include an ACK number that is the sequence number last heard from the neighbor to which the packet is being sent.

CAUTION If you change the hello interval, the EIGRP holdtime is not automatically adjusted to account for this change. You must manually adjust the holdtime to reflect the configured hello interval.

Once a router has a neighbor, the router sends a unicast Update packet to the neighbor. On the sample network shown in Figure 8.5, both the Albany and Charlotte routers sent Hello multicast packets when they booted. The Charlotte router was the first one to notice that there was a neighbor, causing Charlotte to send the following unicast Update message to Albany. You can tell that this is an Update packet from the *Opcode = 1 (Update)* text in the EIGRP header. The purpose of the Update is to tell Albany that Charlotte can get to the 172.16.40.0 network, which you can see listed at the bottom of the packet.

```
DLC:  ----- DLC Header -----
      DLC:  Destination = Station Cisco1053E80
      DLC:  Source      = Station Cisco1002E75
      DLC:  Ethertype   = 0800 (IP)
 IP: ----- IP Header -----
      IP: Version = 4, header length = 20 bytes
      IP: Type of service = 00
      IP:        000. .... = routine
      IP:        ...0 .... = normal delay
      IP:        .... 0... = normal throughput
      IP:        .... .0.. = normal reliability
      IP: Total length   = 68 bytes
      IP: Identification  = 0
      IP: Flags          = 0X
      IP:        .0.. .... = may fragment
      IP:        ..0. .... = last fragment
      IP: Fragment offset = 0 bytes
      IP: Time to live   = 2 seconds/hops
      IP: Protocol       = 88 (EIGRP)
      IP: Header checksum = 4C3F (correct)
      IP: Source address      = [172.16.10.2] Charlotte
      IP: Destination address = [172.16.10.1] Albany
      IP: No options
EIGRP: ----- Enhanced IGRP Header -----
      EIGRP:
      EIGRP: Version       = 2
      EIGRP: Opcode        = 1 (Update)
      EIGRP: EIGRP Checksum = E17D (correct)
      EIGRP: Flags (unused) = 0000
      EIGRP: Flags         = 0001
      EIGRP:  .... .... .... ..0. = Conditionally receive mode is not
required
      EIGRP:  .... .... .... ...1 = Is an initial update packet
      EIGRP: Sequence number      = 1
      EIGRP: Acknowledgment number = 0
      EIGRP: Autonomous System number = 100
      EIGRP:
      EIGRP: Protocol ID       = 0x01 (IP)
      EIGRP: Type Code         = 0x0102 (IP Internal Routes)
      EIGRP: Field length      = 28
      EIGRP: Next hop address              = 0 (use source IP
addr)
      EIGRP: Time delay (10 msec/256)      = 512000
      EIGRP: Path bandwidth (2,560,000,000/kbps) = 1657856
```

```
EIGRP: Min/max transmission unit (MTU)    = 1500
EIGRP: Hop count                          = 0
EIGRP: Reliability (error percentage)     = 250
EIGRP: Load utilization percentage        = 1
EIGRP: Reserved
EIGRP: Prefix length in bits              = 24
EIGRP: IP Destination Address             = 0.172.16.40
```

Notice the sequence number in the EIGRP header of the Update packet. This is evidence of the reliable nature of EIGRP. The Albany router will unicast an ACK back to Charlotte, with the ACK number set to 1, which is the sequence number used by Charlotte. Also notice that a prefix length is sent with the network number in the Update from Charlotte. See *Prefix length in bits = 24* before the IP destination address for the network route. The sending of a prefix length is evidence that EIGRP is a classless protocol and thus supports discontiguous subnets and VLSM.

NOTE The IP address field in an EIGRP route entry varies in size, depending on the prefix length. The analyzer shows the address as 0.172.16.40 in the example, but in the hexadecimal view of the packet, it is clear that the address is really only 3 bytes (172.16.40), which makes sense as the prefix length is 24.

After acknowledging the Update from Charlotte and sending a few more Hellos, the Albany router sends its own Update as a unicast to Charlotte. After sending its first Update message, Albany does an interesting thing, which is to immediately send a multicast Update that lists 172.16.40.0 with a maximum delay. Because Albany has figured out that its only path to 172.16.40.0 is through Charlotte, Albany announces to all routers on the Ethernet segment that they should not use Albany as a feasible successor for the 172.16.40.0 network. If the route through Charlotte fails, then Albany can't get to the network either. Albany's metric to the 172.16.40.0 network is larger than Charlotte's metric, which means that by the rules of DUAL, Albany cannot be the feasible successor.

Sending the explicit notification that the 172.16.40.0 network has maximum delay and thus is unreachable is a form of poison reverse, although, because it's a multicast packet, technically it's not "reverse" (back to the sender). Shortly after sending the multicast packet, Albany also sent the same data that lists 172.16.40.0 as unreachable directly to Charlotte in a unicast packet. That packet can definitely be considered a poison reverse packet. The output that follows is the multicast packet from Albany that lists 172.16.40.0 as unreachable. Notice the maximum delay (0xFFFFFFFF).

```
DLC:  ----- DLC Header -----
      DLC:  Destination = Multicast 01005E00000A
      DLC:  Source      = Station Cisco1053E80
      DLC:  Ethertype   = 0800 (IP)
   IP: ----- IP Header -----
      IP: Version = 4, header length = 20 bytes
      IP: Type of service = 00
      IP:      000. ....   = routine
```

```
      IP:        ...0 .... = normal delay
      IP:        .... 0... = normal throughput
      IP:        .... .0.. = normal reliability
      IP: Total length    = 68 bytes
      IP: Identification   = 0
      IP: Flags           = 0X
      IP:        .0.. .... = may fragment
      IP:        ..0. .... = last fragment
      IP: Fragment offset = 0 bytes
      IP: Time to live    = 2 seconds/hops
      IP: Protocol        = 88 (IGRP/EIGRP)
      IP: Header checksum = 2247 (correct)
      IP: Source address    = [172.16.10.1] Albany
      IP: Destination address = [224.0.0.10]
      IP: No options
   EIGRP: ----- Enhanced IGRP Header -----
      EIGRP: Version       = 2
      EIGRP: Opcode        = 1 (Update)
      EIGRP: EIGRP Checksum = B182 (correct)
      EIGRP: Flags (unused) = 0000
      EIGRP: Flags         = 0002
      EIGRP:    .... ....  .... ..1. = Conditionally receive mode is
required
      EIGRP:    .... ....  .... ...0 = Is not an initial update packet
      EIGRP: Sequence number        = 2
      EIGRP: Acknowledgment number   = 0
      EIGRP: Autonomous System number = 100
      EIGRP:
      EIGRP: Protocol ID           = 0x01 (IP)
      EIGRP: Type Code             = 0x0102 (IP Internal Routes)
      EIGRP: Field length          = 28
      EIGRP: Next hop address              = 0 (use source IP
addr)
      EIGRP: Time delay                    = 0xFFFFFFFF (route
unreachable)
      EIGRP: Path bandwidth (2,560,000,000/kbps) = 1657856
      EIGRP: Min/max transmission unit (MTU) = 1500
      EIGRP: Hop count              = 1
      EIGRP: Reliability (error percentage) = 250
      EIGRP: Load utilization percentage  = 1
      EIGRP: Reserved
      EIGRP: Prefix length in bits        = 24
      EIGRP: IP Destination Address       = 0.172.16.40
```

After the preemptive poison reverse packets from Albany, the process of announcing networks continued at Albany and Charlotte, followed by additional multicast and unicast poison reverse packets. Although many packets went by, not much time elapsed (about 20 seconds) until both routers settled down and simply sent multicast Hellos every 5 seconds.

EIGRP Queries

When a router detects that a route has failed, if a feasible successor has an alternate route, the router starts using the alternate route immediately, without causing network traffic. If there is no successor, the router sends a Query. In the following example, the Charlotte router detected that its path to the 172.16.30.0 network was lost and sent a multicast Query. You can tell that this is a Query packet from the *Opcode = 3 (Query)* text in the EIGRP header.

```
DLC:   ----- DLC Header -----

       DLC:  Destination = Multicast 01005E00000A

       DLC:  Source      = Station Cisco1002E75
       DLC:  Ethertype   = 0800 (IP)
       DLC:
IP:  ----- IP Header -----
       IP: Version = 4, header length = 20 bytes
       IP: Type of service = 00
       IP:       000. .... = routine
       IP:       ...0 .... = normal delay
       IP:       .... 0... = normal throughput
       IP:       .... .0.. = normal reliability
       IP: Total length   = 68 bytes
       IP: Identification  = 0
       IP: Flags          = 0X
       IP:       .0.. .... = may fragment
       IP:       ..0. .... = last fragment
       IP: Fragment offset = 0 bytes
       IP: Time to live   = 2 seconds/hops
       IP: Protocol       = 88 (EIGRP)
       IP: Header checksum = 2246 (correct)
       IP: Source address      = [172.16.10.2] Charlotte
       IP: Destination address = [224.0.0.10]
       IP: No options
       IP:
EIGRP:  ----- Enhanced IGRP Header -----
       EIGRP: Version      = 2
       EIGRP: Opcode       = 3 (Query)
       EIGRP: EIGRP Checksum = 1095 (correct)
       EIGRP: Flags (unused) = 0000
       EIGRP: Flags         = 0000
       EIGRP:  .... .... .... ..0. = Conditionally receive mode is not
required
       EIGRP:  .... .... .... ...0 = Is not an initial update packet
       EIGRP: Sequence number       = 16
       EIGRP: Acknowledgment number = 0
       EIGRP: Autonomous System number = 100
       EIGRP:
```

```
         EIGRP: Protocol ID              = 0x01 (IP)
         EIGRP: Type Code                = 0x0102 (IP Internal Routes)
         EIGRP: Field length             = 28
         EIGRP: Next hop address                   = 0 (use source IP
addr)
         EIGRP: Time delay                         = 0xFFFFFFFF (route
unreachable)
         EIGRP: Path bandwidth (2,560,000,000/kbps) = 256000
         EIGRP: Min/max transmission unit (MTU)    = 1500
         EIGRP: Hop count                = 0
         EIGRP: Reliability (error percentage)     = 255
         EIGRP: Load utilization percentage        = 1
         EIGRP: Reserved
         EIGRP: Prefix length in bits    = 24
         EIGRP: IP Destination Address   = 0.172.16.30
```

Albany sent a unicast ACK back to Charlotte with the acknowledgment number set to 16, the same as the sequence number used by Charlotte. Albany also sent a Reply with the acknowledgment number set to 16. The Reply stated that the 172.16.30.0 network was unreachable from Albany also. Charlotte acknowledged the Reply. The routers also sent some unicast and multicast Updates to announce that the route was lost and then quickly went back to sending Hello packets every 5 seconds.

EIGRP Routes Stuck in Active

Sometimes it can take a long time for Queries to be answered. Remember that EIGRP routers propagate Queries to other routers if they can't provide an answer. If it takes too long to get a Reply, a router reports that a route is *Stuck in Active* (SIA). This state is evidenced by repeated messages on the router console of the form:

```
%DUAL-3-SIA: Route 172.16.30.0 stuck-in-active state in IP-EIGRP 100.
Cleaning up.
```

After a period of time, the router that issued the Query gives up and clears its connection to the router that isn't answering, effectively restarting the neighbor session. One solution to the stuck-in-active problem is to increase the amount of time a router waits after sending a Query before declaring a route SIA. This setting can be changed using the timers active-time command. The default value is 3 minutes, which is already very long. Instead of simply changing the timer, you should try to determine why it is taking a long time to get a Reply. Some possible explanations are:

- There may be too much propagation delay on the network. For example, when you run EIGRP on a network that includes satellite links, you may see this problem.
- A router may be too busy with other tasks to reply. Use the show processes command to determine the router's CPU utilization and the tasks that are using most of the router's resources.
- A router may be having memory problems and may be unable to allocate the memory to process the Query or build the Reply packet.

- There may be errors on the link between the two routers. Perhaps enough packets are getting through to maintain the neighbor relationship, but some Queries or Replies are getting lost between the routers.

- There is a unidirectional link, which is a link on which traffic can flow in only one direction because of a failure. Chapter 5 covered unidirectional links in more detail.

Cisco Show and Debug Commands for EIGRP

When troubleshooting EIGRP, you should use the following show commands, in addition to the generic show ip route command:

show ip eigrp traffic. Displays EIGRP traffic statistics, including how many Hellos, Updates, Queries, Replies, and ACKs have been sent and received.

show ip eigrp neighbors. Displays detailed information about neighbors, including which interface can reach the neighbor, holdtime, uptime, number of Queries from the neighbor, sequence number of the last packet from the neighbor, average amount of time it has been taking to receive ACKs from the neighbor (in milliseconds), and amount of time the router will wait before retransmitting packets to the neighbor (in milliseconds). The amount of time to wait before retransmitting is based on the average amount of time it has been taking to receive ACKs.

show ip eigrp topology. Displays information from the topology database about routes and successors. This command only displays feasible successors for a route. To display the entire topology database, use the show ip eigrp topology all-links command.

The show ip eigrp topology command and its varieties are helpful when troubleshooting, but can also be hard to parse. Following is an example. Table 8.4 explains the output.

```
Albany#show ip eigrp topology
IP-EIGRP Topology Table for process 100
Codes: P - Passive, A - Active, U - Update, Q - Query, R - Reply,
       r - Reply status
P 172.16.50.0 255.255.255.0, 1 successors, FD is 281600
        via Connected, Ethernet1
P 172.16.40.0 255.255.255.0, 1 successors, FD is 2195456
        via 172.16.10.2 (2195456/2169856), Ethernet0
P 172.16.30.0 255.255.255.0, 1 successors, FD is 2221056
        via 172.16.10.2 (2221056/2195456), Ethernet0
P 172.16.20.0 255.255.255.0, 1 successors, FD is 176128
        via Connected, TokenRing0
P 172.16.10.0 255.255.255.0, 1 successors, FD is 281600
        via Connected, Ethernet0
```

Table 8.4 Explanation of the `show ip eigrp topology` Command

OUTPUT	DESCRIPTION
P	Stands for *passive*, which means that no EIGRP computations are being performed for this destination. Routes are almost always in a passive state on stable networks.
A	Stands for *active*, which means that EIGRP computations are being performed for this destination.
U	Stands for *Update*, which indicates that an Update packet was sent to this destination and the router is awaiting an ACK.
Q	Stands for *Query*, which indicates that a Query packet was sent to this destination and the router is awaiting an ACK.
R	Stands for *Reply*, which indicates that a Reply packet was sent to this destination and the router is awaiting an ACK.
r	Stands for *reply status*, which is a flag that is set after the software has sent a Query and is waiting for a Reply.
172.16.50.0	Destination network number.
255.255.255.0	Destination subnet mask.
successors	Number of successors (or paths) available for this destination. If *successors* is capitalized, the route is in transition.
FD	Feasible distance, which is the best metric for the destination.
via 172.16.10.2	IP address of the neighbor that told this router about the destination.
(2195456/2169856)	The first number is the EIGRP metric for the destination. The second number is the EIGRP metric that the neighbor advertised.
Ethernet1	Interface from which this information was learned.

NOTE The output in the example is from a simple, stable network. On a complex, nonstable network, the output can get very complicated. Cisco's Technical Assistance Center (TAC) has attempted to explain what you might see with a White Paper at www.cisco.com/warp/public/103/eigrp12.html.

If routers do not have high CPU utilization, then you can use the following debug commands when troubleshooting EIGRP. Keep in mind that EIGRP is not specific to IP. EIGRP can be used on AppleTalk and Novell NetWare networks also. For that reason, some of the debug commands do not include the word *ip* in them.

debug eigrp neighbor.   Displays information about the neighbor discovery and recovery processes, and limited information about communication with neighbors.

debug eigrp fsm.   Displays detailed information about events taking place in the EIGRP Finite-State Machine (FSM). This command helps you observe EIGRP feasible successor activity and determine whether route updates are being installed and deleted by the routing process.

debug eigrp packets.   Outputs a line for every EIGRP packet sent and received. This can cause a lot of output on a LAN, where routers send Hello packets every 5 seconds. Its use is not recommended on an operational network unless it is used with the next command.

debug ip eigrp neighbor.   Used with the debug eigrp packets command, this command adds a filter to the data displayed. It tells the router to display only packets concerning the IP neighbor whose address is provided as a parameter to the command.

Open Shortest Path First (OSPF)

In the late 1980s, the IETF recognized the need to develop an interior link-state routing protocol to meet the needs of enterprise and campus networks engineers who were having problems scaling and troubleshooting RIP. OSPF is a result of that work. The current version of OSPF (version 2) is defined in RFC 2328.

OSPF has many advantages over other interior routing protocols. It is an open standard that is supported by many vendors, rather than being a proprietary protocol such as IGRP or EIGRP. It is a classless protocol, so it supports discontiguous subnets and VLSM. It converges quickly and does not use a lot of bandwidth. Its messages are sent as multicast or unicast messages, rather than broadcasts. To minimize bandwidth usage, it sends messages only when changes occur. Other network traffic is limited to database-synchronization traffic that occurs infrequently (every 30 minutes), and Hello packets that establish neighbor adjacencies.

Per RFC 2328, the metric for OSPF is a single dimensionless value called *cost*. A network administrator assigns an OSPF cost to each router interface on the path to a network. The lower the cost, the more likely the interface is to be used to forward data traffic. A cost is also associated with externally derived routes (for example, routes learned from a different routing protocol).

On a Cisco router, the cost of an interface defaults to 100,000,000 divided by the bandwidth for the interface. For example, a 100-Mbps Ethernet interface has a cost of 1. The cost can be manually configured. Both ends of a link should use the same cost. If a Cisco router is at one end of a link and a non-Cisco router is at the other end, you might need to manually configure the cost. Because RFC 2328 defines the cost metric so broadly, vendors are not required to agree on how the cost is defined.

> **NOTE** As of this writing, Cisco does not allow a cost of less than 1 for links with speeds over 100 Mbps. (The parameter for the `ip ospf cost` command is an integer between 1 and 65,535.) In an internetwork with high-speed links of 100 Mbps or higher, you can manually set the cost to 1 on the high-speed links and to an integer greater than 1 on slower links.

OSPF Network Architectures

OSPF allows sets of networks to be grouped into *areas*. The topology of an area is hidden from the rest of the autonomous system. By hiding the topology of an area, routing traffic is reduced. Routers within an area don't need to hear entire routing updates about other areas. Also, routing within an area is determined only by the area's own topology, providing the area protection from external routing data that may be inaccurate. By dividing routers into areas, the memory and CPU requirements for each router are limited.

A contiguous backbone area, called *Area 0*, is required when an OSPF network is divided into areas. Every other area connects to Area 0 via an *Area Border Router* (ABR), as shown in Figure 8.6. All traffic between areas must travel through Area 0. Area 0 should have high reliability, throughput, and bandwidth and should be easy to manage and troubleshoot. A set of routers and switches in a rack connected via a high-speed LAN makes a good Area 0.

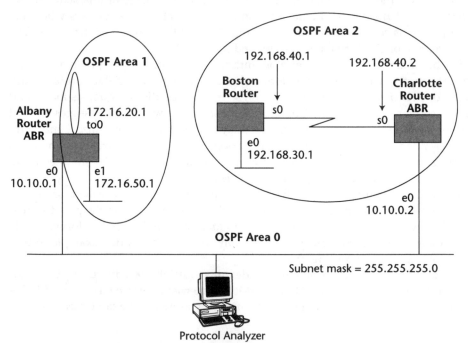

Figure 8.6 OSPF areas connected via ABRs.

In addition to ABRs, an OSPF network may include one or more Autonomous System Boundary Routers (ASBRs). An ASBR connects an OSPF network to a different autonomous system or to a network that uses a routing protocol other than OSPF. For example, an ASBR could connect an internal OSPF campus network to the Internet.

According to RFC 2328, a network that has only one connection to the rest of the internetwork is called a *stub network*. For an example, refer to Figure 8.6. With the exception of Network 10.10.0.0, all the LANs in Figure 8.6 are stub networks. An ABR that connects a stub network can be configured to inject a default route into the stub area for all external networks that are outside the autonomous system or that are learned from other routing protocols. The router can also be configured to inject a default route for routes to other areas within the autonomous system. If an ABR router injects a default route for both external and inter-area routes, Cisco calls the area a *totally stubby area*.

Cisco also supports *not-so-stubby areas* (NSSAs), which allows the redistribution of some external routes into an otherwise totally stubby area. (In most cases, you won't need to know about NSSAs. They are typically used on a stub network that includes a legacy link to another routing protocol or autonomous system that is different from the link used by the rest of the internetwork to reach the outside world.)

In addition to stub networks, OSPF defines five other categories of networks:

1. *Point-to-point networks.* These networks connect a single pair of routers, generally over a WAN link.

2. *Broadcast networks.* Examples are Ethernet, Token Ring, and FDDI. These are multiaccess networks that connect multiple devices that can hear each other's broadcast packets.

3. *Nonbroadcast Multiaccess (NBMA) networks.* These networks are capable of connecting more than two routers, but have no broadcast capability. This type of network includes X.25, Frame Relay, and ATM networks.

4. *Point-to-multipoint networks.* These are special configurations of the NBMA format in which the networks are treated as a collection of point-to-point networks. Frame Relay networks are often configured as point-to-multipoint networks.

5. *Virtual links.* These are special configurations that connect an area to the backbone Area 0 through another area. A virtual link is also used to connect two parts of a partitioned backbone Area 0 through a nonbackbone area. Virtual links should be avoided. Whenever possible, to simplify troubleshooting, an OSPF network topology should have at most two layers: the backbone Area 0 and other areas connected directly to the backbone.

OSPF Protocol Analysis

OSPF routers send Hello multicast packets out all interfaces. If two routers on a data link agree on certain parameters specified in their respective Hello packets, they become *neighbors*. To list a router's neighbors, use the show ip ospf neighbor command. The period between Hello packets is called the *hello interval*. Cisco uses a default hello interval of 10 seconds, although it can be changed with the ip ospf hello-interval command. If a router has not heard a Hello from a neighbor within a period of time called the *dead interval*, the router declares its neighbor unreachable. Cisco's default dead interval is four times the hello interval and can be changed with the `ip ospf dead-interval` command.

Adjacencies are formed between some neighbors. To avoid too many adjacencies, which require CPU and memory resources on routers, a router does not develop adjacencies with all its neighbors. The establishment of an adjacency is determined by the types of routers exchanging Hellos and the type of network over which the Hellos are exchanged.

On a LAN, an OSPF network has a *Designated Router* (DR) and a *Backup Designated Router* (BDR). The DR represents a multiaccess network to the rest of the area. All routers on a LAN form adjacencies with the DR and also the BDR. The DR and BDR also become adjacent with each other. Routers on the LAN do not become adjacent with any routers other than the DR and the BDR, however. On large LANs with many routers, this approach reduces the workload on most of the routers.

Each router sends Link State Advertisements (LSAs) over all adjacencies. The LSAs describe all of the router's links, or interfaces, and the state of the links. These links may be to stub networks, to other OSPF routers, to networks in other areas, or to external networks. OSPF defines multiple LSA types, as shown in Table 8.5.

Each router that receives an LSA from a neighbor records the LSA in its link-state database and sends a copy of the LSA to all of its other neighbors. By flooding LSAs throughout an area, all routers in an area build identical link-state databases. To view the link-state database, use the `show ip ospf database` command.

When the databases are complete, each router uses the Dijkstra Shortest-Path-First (SPF) algorithm to calculate a loop-free tree that describes the shortest (lowest-cost) path to every known destination in its area, with itself as the root of the tree. Each router builds its routing table from the SPF tree. As with any routing protocol, you can view the routing table with the `show ip route` command.

Table 8.5   LSA Types

TYPE NUMBER	TYPE NAME	FUNCTION
1	Router	Sent by all routers to advertise links
2	Network	Sent by the DR to advertise routers
3	ABR Summary	Sent by an ABR to advertise summarized routes to other areas
4	ASBR Summary	Sent by an ABR to advertise a route to an ASBR
5	External	Sent by an ASBR to advertise routes to external networks
6	Group	Used by Multicast OSPF
7	NSSA External	Sent by an ASBR into an NSSA

OSPF EXHIBITS SOME DISTANCE-VECTOR-LIKE BEHAVIOR

Network engineers often want to make a strict distinction between link-state and distance-vector protocols and categorize a particular routing protocol as being one or the other. Often this categorization is based on the type of information routers exchange. It may surprise you to learn that in many situations, the information exchanged between routers running a link-state protocol is very distance-vector-like.

With OSPF, Type 1 and Type 2 LSAs contain information about routers (nodes) and their respective interfaces (links). These LSAs are flooded throughout an area and provide sufficient information for all routers in the area to develop an accurate, detailed, and identical graph of the area topology. Routers piece together the information about individual routers and nodes, and, using the Dijkstra algorithm, derive intra-area IP reachability information.

Summary LSAs (Type 3 and Type 4), and External LSAs (Type 5 and Type 7), on the other hand, convey information about IP prefix reachability much like distance-vector protocols do. This information allows routers to learn which other routers to use to reach particular prefixes. A router takes into account the cost (distance) to a remote prefix and the direction (a vector via the ABR). It fact, the router acts like it's running a distance-vector protocol!

Building an Adjacency

Neighbors on point-to-point, point-to-multipoint, and virtual-link networks always become adjacent unless parameters in their Hellos don't match. On broadcast and NBMA networks, the DR and BDR become adjacent with all neighbors and with each other, but no adjacencies form between other routers. The process of building adjacencies uses Hello, Database Description, Link State Request, and Link State Update packets.

NOTE If you suspect that adjacencies are unstable and wish to keep track of their status, you can add the `ospf log-adjacency-changes` command to a router's OSPF configuration.

On the network shown in Figure 8.6, the Albany and Charlotte ABR routers started the process of finding neighbors and building adjacencies after the routers booted. Albany sent the Hello packet shown in the following EtherPeek output out its Ethernet 0 interface. Albany sends the Hello to the 224.0.0.5 multicast address. Notice from the packet that OSPF runs directly above IP and uses 89 in the IP Protocol field. Another interesting thing to notice is that OSPF uses the IP precedence bits. Notice that the bits are set to *Internetwork Control*.

```
Ethernet Header
  Destination:   01:00:5E:00:00:05
  Source:        00:00:0C:05:3E:80
  Protocol Type:0x0800  IP
IP Header - Internet Protocol Datagram
```

```
        Version:                4
        Header Length:          5  (20 bytes)
        Type of Service:        %11000000
        Precedence: Internetwork Control,    Normal Delay, Throughput,
    Reliability
        Total Length:           64
        Identifier:             0
        Fragmentation Flags:    %000  May Fragment   Last Fragment
        Fragment Offset:        0  (0 bytes)
        Time To Live:           1
        Protocol:               89  OSPF IGP
        Header Checksum:        0xCE95
        Source IP Address:      10.10.0.1 Albany
        Dest. IP Address:       224.0.0.5
        No IP Options
    OSPF - Open Shortest Path First Routing Protocol
        Version:                2
        Type:                   1 Hello
        Packet Length:          44
        Router IP Address:      172.16.50.1
        Area ID:                0.0.0.0
        Checksum:               0x1E8D
        Authentication Type:    0  No Authentication
        Authentication Data:
        ........        00 00 00 00 00 00 00 00
        Network Mask:           0xFFFFFF00
        Hello Interval:         10   seconds
        Options:                %00000010
        Router Priority:        1
        Dead Interval:          40   seconds
        Designated Router:      0.0.0.0  No Desgntd Rtr
        Backup Designated Router: 0.0.0.0  No Backup Desgntd Rtr
```

Notice in the IP layer of the previous output that Albany places the IP address for its Ethernet 0 interface in the IP header (10.10.0.1). From OSPF's point of view, Albany uses its numerically highest address, which is 172.16.50.1. The numerically highest address is called the *Router ID* and it is the IP address that you will see in OSPF headers. The Router ID for Albany is 172.16.50.1. The router ID for Charlotte is 192.168.40.2.

After booting, both the Charlotte and the Albany router sent multicast Hello packets every 10 seconds. After a few Hello packets, each router started listing an additional parameter at the end of the OSPF packet, which is the Router ID of the neighbor. Notice the neighbor parameter at the end of this Hello from Albany. For the sake of brevity, the first part of the packet has been left out.

```
    Source IP Address:      10.10.0.1 Albany
    Dest. IP Address:       224.0.0.5
        No IP Options
    OSPF - Open Shortest Path First Routing Protocol
        Version:                2
```

```
Type:                      1  Hello
Packet Length:             48
Router IP Address:         172.16.50.1
Area ID:                   0.0.0.0
Checksum:                  0x35DE
Authentication Type:       0  No Authentication
Authentication Data:
........          00 00 00 00 00 00 00 00
Network Mask:              0xFFFFFF00
Hello Interval:            10  seconds
Options:                   %00000010
Router Priority:           1
Dead Interval:             40  seconds
Designated Router:         0.0.0.0  No Desgntd Rtr
Backup Designated Router:  0.0.0.0  No Backup Desgntd Rtr
   Nghbr IP Add:           192.168.40.2
```

Following the Hello packets, the Albany and Charlotte router sent Database Description packets as unicast packets to each other. The OSPF Database Description exchange is reliable. It uses sequence numbers, and data is acknowledged. It is also a *master/slave* negotiation that goes through many states. The negotiation starts in the *ExStart* state. In this state, both routers claim to be the master. The neighbor with the lower Router ID becomes the slave and sends a Database Description packet with the Master/Slave bit set to 0 and the *DD Sequence Number* set to the master's sequence number. The Database Description packet carries a summary description of each LSA in the sender's link-state database. Following is the first Database Description packet from the Albany router, which became the slave partner. For the sake of brevity, the first part of the packet has been left out.

```
Source IP Address:     10.10.0.1 Albany
Dest. IP Address:      10.10.0.2 Charlotte
   No IP Options
OSPF - Open Shortest Path First Routing Protocol
   Version:                2
   Type:                   2  Database Description
   Packet Length:          92
   Router IP Address:      172.16.50.1
   Area ID:                0.0.0.0
   Checksum:               0x92E4
   Authentication Type:    0  No Authentication
   Authentication Data:
   ........          00 00 00 00 00 00 00 00
   Reserved:               0x0000
   Options:                %00000010
   Database Desc. Bits:    %00000010
         More Descriptions To Follow
   DD Sequence Number:     0x00000DF0
Link State Advertisement Header
   Age:                    39  seconds
```

```
        Options:                  %00000010
        Type:                     1  Router Links
        ID:                       172.16.50.1
        Advertising Router:       172.16.50.1
        Sequence Number:          0x80000002
        Checksum:                 0x67EB
        Link State Length:        36
    Link State Advertisement Header
        Age:                      23   seconds
        Options:                  %00000010
        Type:                     3  Summary Link (IP Network)
        ID:                       172.16.20.0
        Advertising Router:       172.16.50.1
        Sequence Number:          0x80000001
        Checksum:                 0x4D49
        Link State Length:        28
    Link State Advertisement Header
        Age:                      43   seconds
        Options:                  %00000010
        Type:                     3  Summary Link (IP Network)
        ID:                       172.16.50.0
        Advertising Router:       172.16.50.1
        Sequence Number:          0x80000001
        Checksum:                 0x2A4A
        Link State Length:        28
```

If a router receives an LSA that is not in its own link-state database, the router sends a Link State Request asking for a complete copy of the LSA in question. The router also sends a Link State Request if it receives an LSA that is more recent than the router's own entry. Each LSA has a sequence number that helps routers make sure they have the latest version of the LSA in their databases. (See *Sequence Number: 0x80000001* in the previous output.) Each time a router produces a new instance of the LSA, it increments the sequence number by one. Following is the Link State Request from Charlotte that occurred after Albany sent the initial Database Description packet.

```
    Source IP Address:    10.10.0.2 Charlotte
    Dest. IP Address:     10.10.0.1 Albany
      No IP Options
    OSPF - Open Shortest Path First Routing Protocol
      Version:              2
      Type:                 3  Link State Request
      Packet Length:        60
      Router IP Address:    192.168.40.2
      Area ID:              0.0.0.0
      Checksum:             0xFEA5
      Authentication Type:  0  No Authentication
      Authentication Data:
      ........         00 00 00 00 00 00 00 00
      Link State Type:      1
        Link State ID:      2886742529
```

```
          Advertising Router:     172.16.50.1
        Link State Type:          3
          Link State ID:          2886742528
          Advertising Router:     172.16.50.1
        Link State Type:          3
          Link State ID:          2886734848
          Advertising Router:     172.16.50.1
```

The Albany router responded with a Link State Update that has more details on the LSAs, as shown in the following output.

```
Source IP Address:      10.10.0.1 Albany
Dest. IP Address:       10.10.0.2 Charlotte
  No IP Options
OSPF - Open Shortest Path First Routing Protocol
  Version:                2
  Type:                   4  Link State Update
  Packet Length:          120
  Router IP Address:      172.16.50.1
  Area ID:                0.0.0.0
  Checksum:               0x978A
  Authentication Type:    0  No Authentication
  Authentication Data:
  ........                00 00 00 00 00 00 00 00
  # Of Advertisements:    3
Link State Advertisement Header
  Age:                    40  seconds
  Options:                %00000010
  Type:                   1  Router Links
  ID:                     172.16.50.1
  Advertising Router:     172.16.50.1
  Sequence Number:        0x80000002
  Checksum:               0x67EB
  Link State Length:      36
Router Link Advertisement
  Router Info:            %00000001
        Area Border Router
  Reserved:               %00000000
  Number of Links:        1
Link
  Link ID:                10.10.0.0
  Link Data:              0xFFFFFF00
  Type:                   3  Connectn To Stub Net
  Number of Metrics:      0
  Type Of Service 0 Metric: 10
Link State Advertisement Header
  Age:                    44  seconds
  Options:                %00000010
  Type:                   3  Summary Link (IP Network)
  ID:                     172.16.50.0
```

```
        Advertising Router:        172.16.50.1
        Sequence Number:           0x80000001
        Checksum:                  0x2A4A
        Link State Length:         28
  Summary Links Advertisement (IP Network)
      Network Mask:                0xFFFFFF00
      Type Of Service:             0
      Metric:                      0x00000A
  Link State Advertisement Header
      Age:                         24  seconds
      Options:                     %00000010
      Type:                        3  Summary Link (IP Network)
      ID:                          172.16.20.0
      Advertising Router:          172.16.50.1
      Sequence Number:             0x80000001
      Checksum:                    0x4D49
      Link State Length:           28
  Summary Links Advertisement (IP Network)
      Network Mask:                0xFFFFFF00
      Type Of Service:             0
      Metric:                      0x000006
```

After one or two minutes have passed following the initial Hello packets, all routers that wish to establish adjacency should have exchanged Database Description, Link Request, and Link State Update packets. The Link State Update packets are acknowledged with a packet that is sometimes called a *Link State Acknowledgment* (LSA). This is an unfortunate term because LSA usually refers to Link State Advertisement. After establishing adjacencies, the routers simply send Hello packets every 10 seconds unless a change occurs. In addition, every 30 minutes, the routers synchronize their databases by exchanging Link State Update packets. OSPF is a very quiet protocol.

If a change occurs—for example, a link becomes disabled—a router sends a Link State Update listing the network with a metric (cost) of FF FF FF. Depending on the type of network, this can be a multicast or unicast packet. Other routers acknowledge the packet and spread the word to their neighbors. On most networks, the change propagates within one or two minutes. OSPF converges very quickly on well-designed networks.

Cisco Show and Debug Commands for OSPF

When troubleshooting OSPF, the show running-config command, which displays the router's current configuration, is even more important than with other routing protocols, because OSPF is tricky to configure. When you configure an OSPF router, you specify the networks to include in an area with a mask parameter. This is not a subnet mask, even though it looks just like one; it's a mask that lets you include and exclude networks. See Cisco's configuration documentation for more information on this. You should also use the show running-config command to check interface addresses and subnet masks, protocol timers, authentication configuration, and any access lists that could be blocking OSPF. Following is partial output of the show running-config command for the Albany router that is configured as an ABR, per the network diagram in Figure 8.6.

```
Albany#show running-config
hostname Albany
interface Ethernet0
 ip address 10.10.0.1 255.255.255.0
interface Ethernet1
 ip address 172.16.50.1 255.255.255.0
interface TokenRing0
 ip address 172.16.20.1 255.255.255.0
 ring-speed 16
router ospf 100
 network 10.10.0.0 0.0.255.255 area 0
 network 172.16.0.0 0.0.255.255 area 1
end
```

When troubleshooting OSPF, as with any routing protocol, the show ip route command is helpful. Following is output for the Albany router:

```
Albany#show ip route
Codes: C - connected, S - static, I - IGRP, R - RIP, M - mobile, B - BGP
       D - EIGRP, EX - EIGRP external, O - OSPF, IA - OSPF inter area
       E1 - OSPF external type 1, E2 - OSPF external type 2, E - EGP
       i - IS-IS, L1 - IS-IS level-1, L2 - IS-IS level-2, * - candidate
default
Gateway of last resort is not set
     10.0.0.0 255.255.255.0 is subnetted, 1 subnets
C       10.10.0.0 is directly connected, Ethernet0
O IA 192.168.40.0 [110/74] via 10.10.0.2, 00:04:34, Ethernet0
O IA 192.168.30.0 [110/84] via 10.10.0.2, 00:04:34, Ethernet0
     172.16.0.0 255.255.255.0 is subnetted, 2 subnets
C       172.16.50.0 is directly connected, Ethernet1
C       172.16.20.0 is directly connected, TokenRing0
```

When you use the show ip route command on an OSPF network that connects to external networks, you may see *external type 1* (E1) and *external type 2* (E2) routes. An ASBR can inject external routes into an OSPF network. Inside the OSPF network, depending on router configurations, these external routes may be listed with a cost that adds all internal costs to the external cost advertised by the ASBR, or with a cost that just reflects the external cost advertised by the ASBR. In the first case, the route is listed as an E1 route; in the second case, the route is listed as an E2 route.

Other show commands to use when monitoring and troubleshooting OSPF are as follows:

show ip ospf.   Displays general information about OSPF routing processes, including the type of router (ABR, ASBR, and so on), the number of areas and networks that fall into the areas, and the number of times the Dijkstra SPF algorithm has run.

show ip ospf database.   Displays the link-state database.

show ip ospf neighbor.   Displays information about neighbors and their status.

show ip ospf interface.   Displays OSPF-related interface information, including the type of network, the cost metric, the identity of the DR and BDR, and a list of neighbors and their adjacency states.

On a router with low CPU usage, you can also use the following debug commands to troubleshoot OSPF problems:

debug ip ospf adjacency.   Outputs information about adjacency establishment processes for neighbors. Because it outputs a line for every Hello packet, it can cause a lot of output that can overwhelm both the router and the user of the command. See the earlier note about using the ospf log-adjacency-changes command instead.

debug ip ospf events.   Outputs information about OSPF-related events, such as adjacency establishment, sending Updates, selecting a DR, and SPF calculations.

Border Gateway Protocol (BGP)

The IETF developed BGP in the 1990s to replace EGP as the standard method for routing on the Internet. BGP solved problems that EGP had with reliability and scalability. BGP4, the current version of BGP, is specified in RFC 1771.

This book does not cover BGP in detail because BGP is not a campus routing protocol. However, a few comments are included because many campus networks connect to the Internet using BGP. When a campus network is *multihomed* (connected redundantly to the Internet via two ISPs), BGP is one way to make sure Internet routers correctly send traffic to the campus network. (It is a common misconception that multihoming requires BGP, but this is not true. Depending on your goals for multihoming and the flexibility of your ISPs' policies, you can multihome with other methods.)

BGP should be used on routers with a lot of memory and a high-bandwidth connection to the Internet. Running BGP can be challenging, not only because the protocol is complex, but also because a full Internet routing table contains over 100,000 routes, and is continually growing as the Internet expands and more companies use BGP to multihome. Even more troubling are the frequent updates and changes to the BGP routing table that require a lot of router processing power.

BGP Protocol Analysis

BGP allows routers to exchange information about paths to destination networks. Each BGP router maintains a routing table that lists all feasible paths to a particular network. BGP routers exchange routing information upon initial startup, and then send *Update messages* when changes occur. An Update specifies path attributes, which include the origin of the path information, a sequence of autonomous-system path segments, and next-hop information.

INTERNET WORMS AND BGP

At the time of this writing, the Internet BGP routing table was experiencing frequent changes. There seems to be a high correlation between Internet instability and worms, such as the Code Red and Nimbda worms. There are two theories about the correlation. First, the worms cause a lot of network traffic, resulting in congestion. BGP sessions, especially ones that are not configured correctly, can time out when network traffic is excessive. BGP messages should be considered high-priority traffic and should not be subject to congestion-related packet loss until the situation becomes dire. It is possible that network engineers are not routinely enabling this kind of prioritization, however.

The second hypothesis regarding the correlation between Internet instability and worms is that excessive worm traffic at the Internet's edge causes many network engineers at corporations and small ISPs to reboot or reconfigure their border routers. We may be seeing an "epidemic of sysadmin panic," according to James Cowie et. al. of Renesys Corporation. See their article at www.renesys.com/projects/bgp_instability/.

When a BGP router receives Updates from multiple autonomous systems that describe different paths to the same destination, the router must choose the single best path for reaching that destination. Once chosen, BGP propagates the best path to its neighbors. The decision is based on the value of attributes in the Update (such as next hop, administrative weights, local preference, the origin of the route, and path length) and other BGP-configurable factors.

BGP uses TCP for reliable delivery of BGP packets. BGP packets go to TCP port 179 (0x00 B3 in hexadecimal). When studying BGP routers as they boot, you can use a protocol analyzer to capture the TCP *three-way handshake* that establishes a connection between two BGP routers. Chapter 9 discusses TCP connection establishment in detail.

After establishing a TCP connection, both routers send BGP *Open messages*, which specify BGP parameters, an autonomous system number, and the router's *BGP Identifier*. The BGP Identifier is similar to the OSPF Router ID and is the numerically highest IP address on a Cisco router. Both routers send Update packets following the Open packets. After the routers have updated each other, they simply send BGP *Keepalive messages* to each other every 60 seconds. On a stable BGP link, you should expect to see only Keepalive packets.

Following is an Update packet from the Charlotte router, so you can get an idea of what one looks like. In this Update, Charlotte informed Albany about the 192.168.40.0/24 network.

```
DLC:    ----- DLC Header -----
   DLC:   Destination = Station Cisco1053E80
   DLC:   Source      = Station Cisco1002E75
   DLC:   Ethertype   = 0800 (IP)
   DLC:
```

```
IP: ----- IP Header -----
    IP: Version = 4, header length = 20 bytes
    IP: Type of service = C0
    IP:     110. ....  = internetwork control
    IP:     ...0 .... = normal delay
    IP:     .... 0... = normal throughput
    IP:     .... .0.. = normal reliability
    IP: Total length   = 92 bytes
    IP: Identification  = 5
    IP: Flags          = 0X
    IP:        .0.. .... = may fragment
    IP:        ..0. .... = last fragment
    IP: Fragment offset = 0 bytes
    IP: Time to live    = 1 seconds/hops
    IP: Protocol        = 6 (TCP)
    IP: Header checksum = A4C1 (correct)
    IP: Source address      = [10.10.0.2] Charlotte
    IP: Destination address = [10.10.0.1] Albany
    IP: No options
TCP: ----- TCP header -----
    TCP: Source port           = 11007
    TCP: Destination port      = 179 (BGP)
    TCP: Sequence number       = 747648577
    TCP: Acknowledgment number = 532057514
    TCP: Data offset           = 20 bytes
    TCP: Flags                 = 18
    TCP:              ..0. .... = (No urgent pointer)
    TCP:              ...1 .... = Acknowledgment
    TCP:              .... 1... = Push
    TCP:              .... .0.. = (No reset)
    TCP:              .... ..0. = (No SYN)
    TCP:              .... ...0 = (No FIN)
    TCP: Window                = 16317
    TCP: Checksum              = E7B8 (correct)
    TCP: No TCP options
    TCP: [52 Bytes of data]
BGP: ----- BGP Message -----
    BGP: 16 byte Marker (all 1's)
    BGP: Length        = 52
    BGP: BGP type      = 2 (Update)
    BGP: Unfeasible Routes Length    = 0
    BGP:    No Withdrawn Routes in this Update
    BGP: Path Attribute Length    = 25 bytes
    BGP: Attribute Flags = 4X
    BGP:        0... .... = Well-known
    BGP:        .1.. .... = Transitive
    BGP:        ..0. .... = Complete
    BGP:        ...0 .... = 1 byte Length
    BGP: Attribute type code    = 1 (Origin)
    BGP: Attribute Data Length  = 1
    BGP: Origin type            = 0 (IGP)
    BGP: Attribute Flags = 4X
```

```
BGP:        0... .... = Well-known
BGP:        .1.. .... = Transitive
BGP:        ..0. .... = Complete
BGP:        ...0 .... = 1 byte Length
BGP: Attribute type code      = 2 (AS Path)
BGP: Attribute Data Length    = 4
BGP: Path segment type = 2 (AS_SEQUENCE)
BGP: Path segment length = 1
BGP: AS Identifier            = 500
BGP: Attribute Flags = 4X
BGP:        0... .... = Well-known
BGP:        .1.. .... = Transitive
BGP:        ..0. .... = Complete
BGP:        ...0 .... = 1 byte Length
BGP: Attribute type code      = 3 (Next Hop)
BGP: Attribute Data Length    = 4
BGP: Next Hop                 = [10.10.0.2]
BGP: Attribute Flags = 8X
BGP:        1... .... = Optional
BGP:        .0.. .... = Non-transitive
BGP:        ..0. .... = Complete
BGP:        ...0 .... = 1 byte Length
BGP: Attribute type code      = 4 (Multi Exit Disc)
BGP: Attribute Data Length    = 4
BGP: Multi Exit Disc Attribute = 0
BGP:
BGP: Network Layer Reachability Information:
BGP:  IP Prefix Length = 24 bits, IP subnet mask [255.255.255.0]
BGP:    IP address [192.168.40.0]
```

Cisco Show and Debug Commands for BGP

When monitoring a BGP network, the following Cisco IOS commands are helpful:

show ip bgp.   Displays entries in the BGP routing table, including metrics, weights, paths, and status.

show ip bgp summary.   Displays the status of all BGP connections, including the version of routing tables, network entries in the routing table, the amount of memory used by network entries, and path attributes.

show ip bgp neighbors.   Displays information about the TCP and BGP connections to neighbors, including BGP Identifiers, neighbor capabilities, and the number of error messages received.

show ip bgp flap-statistics.   Displays BGP statistics about routes that are flapping (going down and up repeatedly), including the duration of the flapping.

debug ip bgp.   Displays information related to processing BGP packets. On a stable network, this command displays no data.

Summary

This chapter has provided information about the protocol behavior and packet formats of the major IP routing protocols, including RIP, RIPv2, IGRP, EIGRP, OSPF, and BGP. Despite the level of detail in the chapter, this is just the tip of the iceberg. For each protocol you use on your campus network, you should read vendor documentation on configuring and monitoring the protocol, and you should capture some routing protocol traffic from your own network with a protocol analyzer. We recommend that you capture traffic as routers boot and once they reach steady state. The capture files you save will act as a baseline of normal behavior when you are troubleshooting abnormal behavior.

This chapter has also discussed routing protocol behavior in general, including routing metrics, convergence, static versus dynamic routing, distance-vector versus link-state routing, and the methods that routers use to communicate. Routing protocols send broadcast, multicast, and unicast traffic to neighbor routers. Some routing protocols run above UDP, whereas others simply use IP. BGP takes advantage of TCP's reliability. In Chapter 9, you will learn more about UDP and TCP as well as application layer protocols that run on top of UDP and TCP, including application layer protocols that facilitate e-mail and Web browsing.

CHAPTER

9

Troubleshooting and Analyzing TCP, UDP, and Upper-Layer IP Protocols

This chapter is an overview of the transport layer and the most widely used upper-layer protocols in the Transmission Control Protocol (TCP)/ Internet Protocol (IP) protocol stack. At the transport layer, which the TCP/IP developers called the *host-to-host layer*, the TCP/IP protocol stack provides the connection-oriented TCP and the connection-less User Datagram Protocol (UDP). Both TCP and UDP pass their data down to IP for transmission across an internetwork. This data starts out as messages created by upper-layer protocols, including the following protocols, which are covered in this chapter:

Domain Name System (DNS).   A distributed naming system and protocol for mapping names to addresses.

Service Location Protocol (SLP).   A protocol for allowing network clients to discover and select network services.

Hypertext Transfer Protocol (HTTP).   A protocol used by Web servers to transfer text and graphics to Web clients, and by clients to request data from Web servers.

File Transfer Protocol (FTP).   A protocol that provides reliable file transfer between a client and a server.

Simple Mail Transfer Protocol (SMTP).   A protocol for sending e-mail messages to a server.

Post Office Protocol (POP).   A protocol for retrieving e-mail messages from a server.

Upper-Layer IP Protocol Analysis

Upper-layer protocols perform a variety of operations. From the perspective of their transport-layer protocols (TCP or UDP), they are all identical, however. This is true whether we are talking about the protocols covered in this chapter or other upper-layer protocols such as Telnet, Internet Message Access Protocol (IMAP), Simple Network Management Protocol (SNMP), or Remote Procedure Call (RPC) with Network File System (NFS). Whatever the purpose for an upper-layer protocol may be, the transport layer views it simply as a set of bytes. These bytes may mean something to the Telnet, NFS, or other upper-layer processes that are communicating, but the data is meaningless to the transport layer.

The transport layer is responsible for receiving data from an upper-layer sender and transporting the data to a recipient using the services of lower layers. An application-layer process associated with a TCP or UDP Destination Port number listens for data arriving at that port. The fact that TCP implements a sequence number and acknowledgment mechanism along with flow control and session management, whereas UDP includes none of these connection-oriented features, doesn't change the fundamental similarity between TCP and UDP: They both move data from a source port to a destination port.

With this in mind, there are two fundamental aspects to the analysis of any upper-layer protocol. First, the protocol has its own set of capabilities, expectations, and behaviors. Underlying the upper-layer behavior, however, is the transport-layer behavior. This is the second fundamental aspect to the analysis process (and, in some cases, it becomes the first and only aspect!). If an upper-layer protocol uses TCP, then it is possible to analyze the behavior of the TCP transport layer without knowing anything about the application or upper layer. Because TCP treats all data in exactly the same manner, the operation of the communication infrastructure can be evaluated apart from any specific knowledge of why the infrastructure is being used.

Consider a situation in which performance problems are reported with a custom Oracle database application. The upper layers, including the Oracle Transparent Network Substrate (TNS) protocol and Structured Query Language (SQL), are foreign to most network engineers. TNS uses TCP as its transport layer, however. If you analyze the TCP movement of data and find that TCP is working properly and efficiently, then you know that the communication infrastructure is not responsible for the reported inefficiencies with the Oracle application. You have isolated and described the problem and eliminated routers, WAN links, Ethernet segments, backbones, and other network elements from the list of potential problem makers. Your solid understanding of TCP will become the foundation for troubleshooting not only upper-layer protocols that you understand, but also upper-layer protocols that are foreign to you. (With UDP-based upper-layer protocols, there is no such luxury. Because UDP is connectionless, there is no expected behavior at the transport layer.)

Transmission Control Protocol

TCP provides a reliable bytestream transmission service to upper-layer applications. Applications pass an unstructured stream of bytes to TCP and expect TCP to guarantee delivery of the bytes to a recipient host. TCP sequences the bytes for transmission and packages them into packets, which TCP calls *segments*, per the Request for Comments (RFC) that describes TCP (RFC 793). When TCP sends segments, it maintains a timer and waits for an acknowledgment. If an acknowledgment isn't received in time, data is retransmitted. In this way, TCP offers a reliable data delivery service to upper layers. TCP also provides reliability by maintaining a checksum on its header and data and by making sure bytes are delivered to an upper-layer application in the correct order.

The TCP implementation on a host can send data for multiple applications running on the host, which is often called *multiplexing*. A Source Port number in the TCP header distinguishes the different applications. Upon receipt of segments, TCP determines which application should receive the data by examining the destination port in the TCP header. This process is often called *demultiplexing*.

The two hosts using TCP must establish a TCP connection with each other before exchanging application-layer data. Each side of the connection sequences the bytes that it sends and acknowledges the bytes that it receives. Each side stipulates to its partner how many bytes it is ready to receive, using a *Window Size* parameter. The other side complies, honoring the receiver-initiated flow control. As we study the fields in a TCP header in the next few sections, the mechanisms for flow control and reliability will become clearer.

TCP Protocol Analysis

The TCP header provides the fields necessary to offer the reliable service described in the previous paragraphs. The TCP header is typically 20 bytes, unless options are present. Figure 9.1 shows the format of a TCP header. Table 9.1 and the following sections describe the fields in a TCP header.

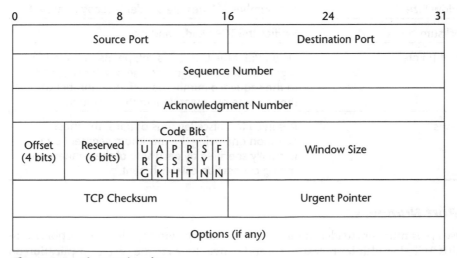

Figure 9.1   The TCP header.

Table 9.1 Fields in a TCP Header

FIELD	EXPLANATION
Source Port	A number that identifies the sending application in the sending host.
Destination Port	A number that identifies the recipient application in the destination host.
Sequence Number	The position in the sender's bytestream of the 1st byte of data in this segment.
Acknowledgment Number	The next byte that the sender expects to receive from its partner, which indicates that bytes up to this point have been received.
Offset	Identifies where the data starts, following the header. This field signifies the length of the TCP header in 32-bit units. If there are no TCP options, the length is 5 to indicate a 20-byte header (five 32-bit or 4-byte units).
Code Bits	A 6-bit field of 1-bit flags that have the following meanings if set: URG: The Urgent Pointer field is in use. ACK: The Acknowledgment Number field is in use. PSH: The receiver should pass the data to the application right away. RST: Reset the connection. SYN: Connection request. FIN: Connection termination.
Window Size	The number of bytes the sender is ready to accept.
Checksum	Verifies the TCP header and data.
Urgent Pointer	Only valid if the URG bit is set; points to the end of urgent data in the segment. The pointer is added to the sequence number to yield the number of the last byte of urgent data in the segment.
Options	Reserved for miscellaneous options, the most common one being the maximum segment size, normally specified by each side of the connection during connection establishment.

TCP Port Numbers

TCP uses port numbers to identify the sending and receiving application. A port number helps TCP demultiplex bytestreams and deliver bytes to the correct application on the recipient end. In this sense, the port number has the same function as the EtherType in Ethernet II frames, the Service Access Point (SAP) field in IEEE 802.2 frames, and the Protocol Type field in an IP header. The port number identifies the next layer up in a layered stack of protocols.

TCP ports can be semipermanent or ephemeral (short-lived). Servers listen on the semipermanent ports for clients wishing to access services. Clients use ephemeral ports to identify their end of a conversation. The client side is ephemeral (short-lived) and only lasts while the client is using a service, whereas a server port is usually open the entire time that a server is running.

TCP port numbers fall into three categories:

1. *Well-known port numbers* are used to identify standard services that run above TCP, including HTTP, Telnet, SMTP, and so on. Well-known port numbers are 0 to 1023.

2. *Registered port numbers* identify an application that has been registered with the Internet Assigned Numbers Authority (IANA). Registered port numbers are 1,024 to 49,151.

3. *Private port numbers* are unregistered and can be dynamically assigned to any application. Private port numbers are 49,152 to 65,535.

A registered port number is intended for use by only the registered application. For example, Microsoft SQL Server uses TCP ports 1,433 and 1,434; Oracle uses 1,525; and IBM uses 12,001 through 12,004 for Systems Network Architecture (SNA) implementations that run above TCP/IP. In the past, the Assigned Numbers RFC (RFC 1700) documented well-known and registered port numbers. Unfortunately, that RFC has not been updated since 1994. However, you can still get an up-to-date list of port numbers from IANA at www.iana.org/assignments/port-numbers.

When a client application opens a connection to a server, the TCP layer assigns an ephemeral port number to the connection and sets aside a block of memory for use by the client. The client places its ephemeral port number in the Source Port field of the TCP header and sends a connection request (SYN) packet to the server. The client places a port number in the Destination Port field that identifies the service that the user wishes to access. When the server responds, it places its port number in the Source Port field and the ephemeral port for the client in the Destination Port field. As we walk though a connection establishment example in the next section, these concepts will become more clear.

An application on a server can request that TCP listen on a particular port. For example, on a Web server, HTTP can request that TCP listen for data coming into the well-known port number for HTTP, which is 80. TCP reserves a block of memory for bytestreams that will be arriving for HTTP. TCP lets HTTP know where to pick up this data by giving HTTP the location of the memory block. When data arrives for Port 80, TCP drops off the data in the block of memory reserved for HTTP. HTTP picks up the data from that block.

Of course, the Web server also has data to send in addition to the data that it receives, so TCP also provides HTTP with a block of memory for sending data. HTTP places data in its memory block, which appears as an unstructured stream of bytes to TCP. TCP picks up the data and, knowing that the data came from HTTP, places a Source Port number of 80 in the segments it sends. This example used HTTP, but FTP, SMTP, POP, and other applications interact with TCP in the same fashion.

PORT NUMBERS FALL VICTIM TO ENTROPY (INCREASING CHAOS IN THE UNIVERSE)

A lot of confusion surrounds port numbers. This is partly because RFC 1700 wasn't kept up to date, and partly because of vague wording in the RFC regarding the use of registered port numbers. One confusing situation is that ephemeral (client-side) port numbers can fall anywhere between 1,024 and 65,535. This means that a client may use a number that is also registered as a port number for use by a service. This isn't a problem, but it can cause confusion when troubleshooting, especially if your protocol analyzer displays a service name with the port number. Another strange thing about registered port numbers is that IANA refused to police their use. Just because a company registers a port number doesn't mean that some other application won't also use it.

For example, if you are analyzing a conversation and your analyzer tells you that a particular conversation involves Microsoft SQL Server, and you know that your network doesn't implement Microsoft SQL Server, don't get too concerned. Your analyzer simply presents the service name that is associated with the port number in the analyzer's port number table.

Many analyzers allow user configuration of the port number table. If you find that the table includes port numbers for registered applications that you are not using on your network, you can remove the port numbers from the table. Conversely, if your network implements an application or service that regularly uses a registered or private number, you can add the service name and port number to the table.

NOTE On both the client and the server, the establishment of a TCP connection means that a communication buffer is reserved and a TCP process is spawned to manage the connection. This implies that there is a limit to the number of TCP connections that can be created at any one time and a point at which the collective work done by TCP could exceed available memory. To avoid problems, some operating systems let you configure the number of TCP connections that will be supported to stop TCP from consuming so much memory that other work can't get done.

To become a good troubleshooter, you should learn which standard services run above TCP (versus UDP) and the well-known port numbers that identify the services. Table 9.2 lists the most common services.

TCP Connection Establishment

The two end points in a TCP connection use a *three-way handshake* to establish the connection. The requesting end (usually the client) sends a segment with the SYN bit set, signifying a request to synchronize and establish a connection. The server responds with its SYN and ACK bits set. The client completes the three-way handshake by sending a segment with its ACK bit set. Figure 9.2 shows a graphical representation of the three-way handshake.

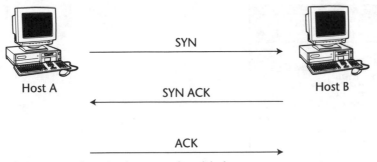

Figure 9.2   The TCP three-way handshake.

To understand TCP connection establishment, you should study TCP traffic with a protocol analyzer. To help you learn what to expect, the next few figures show some TCP packets captured with the Wild Packets EtherPeek analyzer. Figure 9.3 shows the TCP header for the first TCP packet that was generated when a client running a Web browser displayed a Web page from a Web server. The figure shows the first segment in the three-way handshake.

Table 9.2   TCP Port Numbers

SERVICE	PORT NUMBER IN DECIMAL
File Transfer Protocol (FTP)	21 for control, 20 for data
Telnet	23
Simple Mail Transfer Protocol (SMTP)	25
Domain Name System (DNS)	53*
Gopher	70
Finger	79
Hypertext Transfer Protocol (HTTP)	80
Post-Office Protocol (POP)	110
Network News Transfer Protocol (NNTP)	119
Network Basic Input/Output System (NetBIOS) Session	139
Border Gateway Protocol (BGP)	179
Lightweight Directory Access Protocol (LDAP)	389
Secure Sockets Layer (SSL)	443
NetWare Core Protocol (NCP)	524
Apple Filing Protocol (AFP)	548

* DNS uses TCP for large transfers, but otherwise uses UDP.

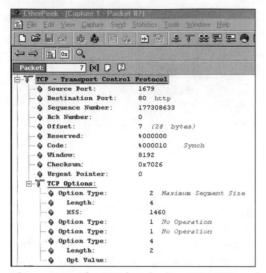

Figure 9.3   The TCP header in a TCP SYN packet.

Notice in Figure 9.3 that the source port (1679) is an ephemeral port, but the destination port is 80 for HTTP. The TCP implementation on the client obtained the Source Port number using an internal mechanism that picks a number greater than 1023. The TCP implementation on the server uses the destination port to recognize that it should pass the connection request to the HTTP Web server software.

Following the port numbers in the TCP header is the Sequence Number field. The client uses an initial sequence number of 177,308,633 in this example. You might think that the initial sequence number would be 1 or 0. However, most TCP implementations start with a random number rather than using a number that can be easily guessed by hackers. The ACK number in the packet is 0, because there isn't anything to acknowledge yet. The ACK bit in the Code Bits field is also not set. The SYN bit is the only bit that is set in the Code Bits field.

Looking at Figure 9.3, you can see that the client specifies a value of 8192 in the Window Size field. (EtherPeek shows the field as just *Window*.) The window size is used for flow control. Using the Window Size field, each side specifies how many bytes it is currently able to receive. The window size is specified in every packet. It is not a negotiated parameter as is sometimes suggested. Each side specifies its own Receive window size, and the sizes for the two sides do not need to match. In this example, the client says that it can receive 8192 bytes. In other words, the client tells the server that the server can send a burst of 8192 bytes, but then the server should cease sending temporarily to make sure that the client is keeping up with the flow. The 8192 bytes will probably be divided into separate segments, because 8192 is too big to fit into a typical packet, but the segments can be sent immediately following one another without requiring an acknowledgment, until all 8192 bytes are sent.

Notice in Figure 9.3 that the Offset field in the packet is 28. This field is somewhat misnamed: It probably should be called a *header-length field*. In most cases, the TCP header is 20 bytes. The first two segments in a TCP session usually include an 8-byte Options field, however, which makes the header longer.

The Options field in a SYN packet specifies the maximum segment size that the sender can accept. The maximum segment size refers to the amount of payload in individual packets that the host is able to receive. Don't confuse this with the window size, which is used for flow control and is usually much larger than a single segment. The maximum segment size is not used for flow control, but rather for controlling the size of individual packets that the other side will send. The maximum segment size is not a negotiated parameter, despite what some sources claim. Each side can specify a different size. In practice, both sides usually specify 1460. In our example, the client uses 1460 bytes. The packets on Ethernet will end up being 1518 bytes counting the 14-byte Ethernet header, 4-byte Ethernet FCS, 20-byte IP header, and 20-byte TCP header.

Figure 9.4 shows the TCP SYN packet that the Web server returned after receiving the SYN packet from the client. The Web server set the SYN and ACK bits to synchronize the connection and acknowledge the SYN from the client.

In Figure 9.4 we can see that the segment from the server comes from the well-known HTTP port 80 and goes to the client's ephemeral Port 1679. The server uses an initial sequence number of 479,744,360. There's no requirement that the server start with the same number as the client, which, as you may recall, started with 177,308,633. The server has a window size of 8760. There's no requirement that the server's Receive window be the same size as the client's, and usually servers use a larger size. Remember that the window size specifies how many bytes the sender can accept before the other side should stop and wait for an acknowledgment. The amount of bytes that a TCP host can receive depends on how much memory it has and also on the type of application. Perhaps this server software is smart enough to know that there's no need to specify a large Receive window size and allocate memory for a large window, because HTTP clients rarely send much data.

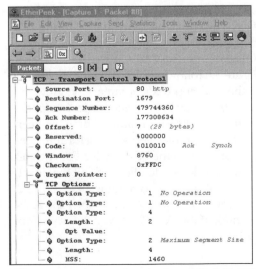

Figure 9.4   The TCP header in a TCP SYN ACK packet.

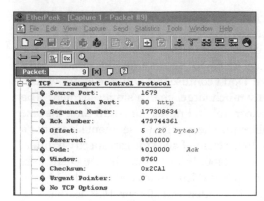

Figure 9.5 The TCP header in a TCP ACK packet.

As was the case with the client, the server uses the TCP Options field to specify its maximum segment size. Its maximum segment size is 1460, which is standard. Remember that this field specifies the largest payload the sender can accept in individual packets.

The three-way handshake completes with an ACK from the client. Figure 9.5 shows the Acknowledgment packet. Notice that this packet has a 20-byte header and that there are no options. Also, the client has increased its window size to 8760 bytes for some unknown reason.

TCP Reliable Delivery and Flow Control

When troubleshooting TCP problems, you may start with a quick analysis of the three-way handshake, using the techniques illustrated in the previous section. Most of your analysis will focus on the packets after the handshake, however. By analyzing sequence numbers and acknowledgments as clients and servers exchange data, you can troubleshoot performance problems that appear as repeated sequence numbers (retransmissions), missing acknowledgments, slow acknowledgments, and so on. During this phase of your troubleshooting you will see the beauty of using an analyzer such as Wild Packets' EtherPeek which automatically points out problems and summarizes the most relevant factors in the Summary window. Figure 9.6 follows the conversation between the PC client and the Web server. This figure shows EtherPeek's Summary window.

Let's examine Figure 9.6. The figure starts with Packet 7, because the first six packets were not TCP packets. The Delta Time column shows the amount of time between packets in seconds. The Summary column shows multiple pieces of useful information. The first set of characters shows the Code Bits field in the TCP header. For each bit that is not set, and is thus not relevant, EtherPeek displays a dot. For each bit that is set, EtherPeek outputs a letter that identifies the bit. If you see something like .A..S., then you know that the ACK and SYN bit are set. If you see .AP..., then the ACK and PSH bits are set. As described at the beginning of the *TCP Protocol Analysis* section, the Code Bits field includes the following six bits:

- URG (U)
- ACK (A)
- PSH (P)

- RST (R)
- SYN (S)
- FIN (F)

Following the Code Bits field, EtherPeek shows the sequence number (S = x), the length of the TCP payload (L = x), the ACK number (A = x), and the window size (W = x).

Packets 7 through 9 in Figure 9.6 represent the three-way handshake. Notice that the length in all these packets is zero (L = 0). There is no upper-layer data. Packet 10 is the first packet with any payload. In Packet 10, the client PC sends 366 bytes of payload (L = 366). The payload consists of HTTP commands to get data from the server, although you can't see this in the figure. (You would need to view the EtherPeek Detail window to see this.) In Packet 10, the client's bytes are sequenced with the numbers 177308634 through 177308999. You can see the sequence number of the first byte in the S = 177308634 field. To derive the sequence number of the last byte, add the length (366) and subtract one.

After the PC client sends HTTP commands to get data from the server in Packet 10, the server ACKs in Packet 11 and starts sending data in Packet 12. From a troubleshooting and optimization viewpoint, it's important to recognize that the server sent a quick TCP ACK to the client's request. The delta time for Packet 11 is 0.032 seconds. The server didn't start sending any HTTP data for another 0.5 seconds, however. The delta time for Packet 12 is 0.524 seconds. This means that the network is probably healthy and any performance problems reside at the server. If the user complains about slow performance, you have proof that the server responded quickly at the TCP and lower layers and that the response reached the client quickly. (The EtherPeek analyzer that captured this data was running on the client.) However, the Web server software did not respond quickly. How many times have you needed a tool to help you prove that the problem is with the application and not with your network? Here we have shown you how to use an analyzer as that tool!

Packet	Source	Destination	Size	Delta Time	Summary
7	PC	Server	66	00.000000	....S.,S= 177308633,L= 0,A= 0,W= 8192
8	Server	PC	66	00.070000	.A..S.,S= 479744360,L= 0,A= 177308634,W= 8760
9	PC	Server	64	00.001000	.A....,S= 177308634,L= 0,A= 479744361,W= 8760
10	PC	Server	424	00.000000	.AP...,S= 177308634,L= 366,A= 479744361,W= 8760
11	Server	PC	64	00.032000	.A....,S= 479744361,L= 0,A= 177309000,W= 8760
12	Server	PC	1518	00.524000	.A....,S= 479744361,L= 1460,A= 177309000,W= 8760
13	Server	PC	1518	00.008000	.AP...,S= 479745821,L= 1460,A= 177309000,W= 8760
14	PC	Server	64	00.000000	.A....,S= 177309000,L= 0,A= 479747281,W= 8760
15	Server	PC	1466	00.041000	.A....,S= 479747281,L= 1408,A= 177309000,W= 8760
16	Server	PC	1518	00.008000	.A....,S= 479748689,L= 1460,A= 177309000,W= 8760
17	PC	Server	64	00.000000	.A....,S= 177309000,L= 0,A= 479750149,W= 8760
18	Server	PC	1518	00.008000	.A....,S= 479750149,L= 1460,A= 177309000,W= 8760
19	Server	PC	1246	00.046000	.A....,S= 479751609,L= 1188,A= 177309000,W= 8760
20	PC	Server	64	00.000000	.A....,S= 177309000,L= 0,A= 479752797,W= 8760
21	Server	PC	1518	00.008000	.A....,S= 479752797,L= 1460,A= 177309000,W= 8760
22	Server	PC	1518	00.009000	.AP...,S= 479754257,L= 1460,A= 177309000,W= 8760
23	PC	Server	64	00.000000	.A....,S= 177309000,L= 0,A= 479755717,W= 8760

Figure 9.6   A TCP connection between a PC client and a Web server.

ORDINAL AND CARDINAL NUMBERS

When working with TCP sequence numbers and lengths, you need to be careful to avoid getting a result that is off by one. To derive the sequence number of the last byte in a segment, you should add the length of the payload to the sequence number of the first byte (which is specified in the Sequence Number field of the TCP header) and subtract one. The reason you need to subtract one is that the sequence numbers are ordinal numbers, whereas the length field is a cardinal number. Now you wish you had paid attention in your elementary-school math classes, right? Ordinal numbers identify an order, such as first, second, third. Cardinal numbers identify "how many." You need to be careful if you mix and match these types of numbers.

Try this trick. Hold up your hands in front of your face. The finger on your far left is your first finger. How many fingers do you have? Hopefully, ten. Add ten to one. Does that mean that your last finger, the one on the far right, is your eleventh finger? Of course not. This is an example of adding ordinal (sequence) numbers and cardinal (how-many) numbers. The result is off by one. Ordinal numbers identify a sequence, such as first and eleventh. In a TCP header they identify the progression of bytes in the sender's stream of bytes. Cardinal numbers identify a length.

If you were responsible for the Web server, your next step might be to examine the complexity of the data the server was returning, which could be the reason for the slowness. You should also try to determine if the data came from Random Access Memory (RAM) cache on the server or from the hard disk, and perhaps upgrade one or the other.

To help you learn techniques for analyzing and troubleshooting TCP behavior, Table 9.3 explains each packet shown in Figure 9.6, using the steps an expert protocol analyst might use as a first pass at studying any problems.

Table 9.3 TCP Packets in a Conversation between a PC and a Web Server

PACKET	EXPLANATION
7	The PC sends a SYN session-establishment segment to the server. The PC apparently starts with a random sequence number, which is good security practice. The PC has a Receive window of 8192 bytes, which is typical.
8	The server responds reasonably quickly (delta time is 0.070 seconds). The server apparently uses a random sequence number also. The server's Receive window size is 8760 bytes, which seems somewhat small for a server but is perhaps normal for HTTP. The ACK number is one more than the sequence number the PC used, which is normal, even though the length of the PC's payload was zero. (ACK numbers behave a little differently in the three-way handshake than they do during the session.)

Table 9.3 *(Continued)*

PACKET	EXPLANATION
9	The PC sends an ACK. The PC turnaround time is very quick (0.001 seconds). The PC increases its window size by a few bytes, which is a bit surprising but not really significant. The PC's ACK number is one more than the sequence number the server used, which is normal.
10	The PC sends a segment with 366 bytes of payload which contains HTTP commands (not shown) to get data from the Web server. The PC sets the PSH bit to ask TCP to send the commands to HTTP immediately. The sequence numbers for the PC's bytes are 177308634-177308999.
11	The server isn't ready to send any HTTP data, but it does acknowledge the TCP segment from the PC. The ACK number (177309000) is one more than the last byte of data sent by the PC. This indicates that the server got the bytes and is expecting sequence number 177309000 next from the PC.
12	After over 0.5 seconds (see the delta time), the server finally starts sending some HTTP data. The ACK number remains the same as it was in Packet 11, which is normal because the PC hasn't sent any new data. The server sends 1460 bytes of data. The sequence numbers for the server's bytes are 479744361-479745820.
13	The server sends 1460 more bytes of data. The sequence numbers for the server's bytes are 479745821-479747280. The server's ACK number remains the same because the PC hasn't sent any more data.
14	The PC ACKs the bytes that it has received and specifies that the next expected byte is numbered 479747281. The PC didn't really need to send this ACK, as the server has not yet filled the PC's Receive window. However, acknowledging after two segments is typical. (See the *TCP Delayed Acknowledgments* section.) The PC doesn't send any data (the payload length is 0), so the PC's sequence number does not change.
15	The server continues to send Web page data. The sequence numbers for the server's bytes are 479747281-479748688. There is no obvious reason for this segment containing only 1408 bytes of data instead of the 1460 bytes in other segments. A clue in the HTTP data indicates that there may have been a natural break in the data, as the last 2 bytes of the 1408 bytes are a carriage return and line feed. The server's ACK number remains the same because the PC hasn't sent any more data.
16	The server sends 1460 more bytes of data. The sequence numbers for the server's bytes are 479748689-479750148. The server's ACK number remains the same because the PC hasn't sent any more data.

(continues)

Table 9.3 TCP Packets in a Conversation between a PC and a Web Server *(Continued)*

PACKET	EXPLANATION
17	The PC ACKs the bytes received and specifies that the next expected byte is numbered 479750149. The PC doesn't send any data (the payload length is 0), so the PC's sequence number does not change.
18-23	The conversation between the PC and server continues, with the PC acknowledging data and the server sending more data.
24-200	Although not shown in Figure 9.6, in Packet 40, the PC temporarily slides its Receive window closed to 6485 bytes, but then quickly opens it back up to 8760 bytes. The PC also opens an additional TCP connection to download graphics. After about 200 packets and 10 seconds, the TCP server completes its download, and the user's screen displays the entire Web page.

TCP Delayed Acknowledgments

TCP is not required to send an ACK the instant it receives data. In fact, a host can reduce network overhead and increase efficiency by sending fewer ACKs. This is known as *delayed ACKs*. The Host Requirements RFC (RFC 1122) states that a TCP implementation should implement delayed ACKs, but an ACK should not be excessively delayed. In particular, the delay must be less than 0.5 seconds, and when receiving a stream of full-sized segments, there should be an ACK for at least every second segment. Most implementations do not wait a full 0.5 seconds, which would seem awfully long on modern networks. Upon receipt of a TCP segment, a host sets an ACK timer. When the timer elapses, the host acknowledges data received so far. A typical value for the ACK timer is 0.2 seconds.

One reason for delaying an ACK is that the host may have its own data to send in the same direction as the ACK. The data can be sent with the ACK, which avoids extra network traffic caused by so-called *empty ACKs*. An ACK that is sent with data is sometimes called a *piggyback ACK*. If an application has data to send before TCP's ACK timer expires, then TCP sends an ACK with the application-layer data. If the application is not ready to send data, however, TCP waits for the application to catch up and then sends an ACK after the ACK timer expires, with or without upper-layer data. In addition, per RFC 1122, TCP should send an ACK after receiving two full-sized segments. A full-sized segment is typically 1460 bytes. Bulk data-transfer applications, such as FTP and some HTTP implementations, send full-sized segments.

Delayed ACKs are criticized by many protocol experts who claim that they result in worse performance than if they were not used, especially on high-latency network segments such as satellite links. Nonetheless, they are the default behavior for most operating systems, including Windows operating systems.

TCP Slow Start

At the beginning of a session, a sender does not attempt to fill a receiver's window right away. Modern TCP implementations use a *slow start algorithm*. With older TCP implementations, a sender started traffic flow by transmitting multiple segments, up to the window size advertised by the receiver. While this worked well when the sender and receiver were on the same LAN, it resulted in problems when the hosts were separated by routers and slow links. An intermediate router could queue the packets and at some point run out of queue space and drop packets. The queuing and dropping of packets causes worse TCP performance than if the sender would simply slow down a bit. The slow start algorithm gives the sender a chance to determine how fast or slow it should transmit. The rate at which the sender should transmit is the rate at which acknowledgments are being returned by the other host.

Slow start adds another window, called the *Congestion window*, to the sender's TCP implementation. The sender can transmit up to the minimum of its Congestion window and the advertised Receive window of the other host. Think of the Congestion window as flow control imposed by the sender, based on the sender's assessment of network congestion. The advertised Receive window is flow control imposed by the receiver, based on the amount of available buffer space at the receiver.

When a new connection is established, the sender starts by transmitting one segment and waiting for the ACK. When the ACK is received, the Congestion window is incremented from 1 to 2, and two segments can be sent. When those two segments are acknowledged, the Congestion window is increased to 4. At some point the capacity of the internetwork is reached, and an intermediate router starts dropping packets and ACKs stop arriving. This tells the sender that its Congestion window has gotten too large and it should slow down.

The reason you should care about slow start, delayed ACKs, and other advanced protocol details is so that you don't waste time troubleshooting supposedly bad TCP implementations if you see them sending and acknowledging more slowly than they should considering the basic behavior of flow control. In general, you need to think past the basics when troubleshooting and develop an understanding of how the protocols have been enhanced over the years to improve performance.

TCP Window Size Analysis

As we discussed in previous sections, the Window Size field in the TCP header is a report of the size of the Receive window at the time a TCP frame is transmitted. You may observe several normal behaviors related to the window size, and one problematic behavior (a frequent window size of zero, which means no data can be received).

When a station initiates a TCP connection by transmitting the first SYN packet of the three-way handshake, the station determines how much communication buffer memory will be assigned to the conversation for bytes that are received. This memory is the Receive window in the initiating station. Its size is reported as the window size value. When the recipient station receives the SYN and replies, it determines and reports the size of its Receive window also. These sizes may be different.

As bytes are received into the Receive window, the window buffer must be constantly cleared to allow for a continuous receipt of bytes. Using your protocol analyzer, you can observe and analyze this process and determine whether it is proceeding properly and efficiently.

Consider a situation in which a station initially offers an 8-kbyte window. This station now begins to receive a steady stream of 1-kbyte data segments. Each of these segments contains bytes that must be acknowledged. Depending on the rate at which the segments are delivered, they may be acknowledged individually or in groups. If the sender is much faster than the receiver, the sender transmits eight segments and stops (because the 8-kbyte window has been filled, and the sender is not allowed to send bytes beyond the window). The key question is, "What is the size of the receiver's window when it sends an ACK?" Here are some examples and their significance.

The Sender Does Not Approach the Receiver's Capacity

When the sender does not approach the receiver's capacity to receive and process bytes, the receiver returns a window size (with an ACK) that is set to its original, maximum value. The receiver is able to clear its buffer just as fast as it is able to construct and send the ACK. When the window size doesn't change, it is an indication that the reporting station has sufficient communication resources to handle the task. If data packets are acknowledged individually, it indicates that the sending station is not transmitting data very aggressively. Perhaps the data cannot be constructed in large blocks (as in the case when individual data records are retrieved from a database). When the sender completely fills the receiver's window and then stops to wait for an acknowledgment, it can indicate one of two things: Either the sender has a large block of data queued for transmission (as with a file transfer), or the receiver is busy doing other tasks and can't get clock cycles for processing the received data and constructing the ACK.

The Sender Begins to Approach the Receiver's Capacity

In our example, the sender is sending 1-kbyte data segments into an 8-kbyte window. Imagine that an assessment of the window size in successive ACKs looks like this:

```
8192, 7168, 6144, 6656, 6144, 7168, 7680, 7680, 7168, 8192
```

Notice that the size of the window is reduced by the received data segments and the receiver is trying to clear the buffer and get the size of the window back to its original value. If you study the sequence of values, you can imagine the receiver struggling against the received data, as if it is a person running up the down escalator in a store. The receiver is working against the continuous stream of received data, and, although it is forced back sometimes, it ultimately manages to return to the fully open window (8192 kbytes).

This is normal behavior for the TCP sliding window. There is nothing wrong here. However, this is an indication that the sender is making the receiver work. In the next example, you'll see what happens when the receiver can't keep up with the sender.

The Sender Overloads the Receiver's Capacity

With the constant receipt of 1-kbyte segments into an initial 8-kbyte window, consider the following window size reports in successive ACKs:

```
8192, 7168, 6144, 6656, 6144, 7168, 7680, 7680, 7168, 6144, 5120, 4096,
3072, 2048, 1024, 1740, 1024, 0
```

As with the previous example, the receiver is trying to open the window and, periodically, it manages to make some progress. In the end, however, the size of the window is gradually dragged lower and lower, eventually reaching zero. A zero window condition indicates that the receiver is no longer able to receive any data and the sender must stop. Normally, if a zero window condition exists, you will see the window open again after 3 to 10 milliseconds. It is important to realize that when a sender detects a zero window condition it waits until the window is fully open—back to its maximum size—before it recommences transmission. You may see something like the following:

```
First ACK Packet: Window Size = 0
4 millisecond delta time
Second ACK Packet: Window Size = 6144
3 millisecond delta time
Third ACK Packet: Window Size = 8192
```

In this case, the total delay before the sender continues transmission is 7 milliseconds, plus the transmission time of the three ACK packets.

An occasional zero window condition is not a problem; it's a normal part of the memory management process of the TCP stack. However, when the size of the Receive window is reduced to zero more than once per megabyte of data received by a station, this indicates that the receiver is too slow (doesn't have enough CPU power), overloaded (has too many tasks running), or has insufficient communication buffer memory. (We use 1 Mbyte of data as a general guideline for measuring the frequency of errors. Problems should not occur more than once per megabyte of data.)

Zero Window at Conversation Start

A zero window condition sometimes occurs at the beginning of a new TCP connection, when a server sends a sudden burst of data without following the TCP slow start algorithm. For example, when FTP begins sending a file, it may blast out packets until the receiver's window is full, and then wait for an ACK. The receiver, which didn't know whether it was going to receive small or large quantities of data, must adjust its memory management mechanism to accommodate the received data rate. After the initial blast of data, the receiver may report that the size of its Receive window is zero. If the receiver immediately increases the size of the window, this is not a problem.

If the data rate in a conversation suddenly increases dramatically during the course of an established connection, this is another case where a zero window condition can occur. The difference between this normal situation and the zero window overload problem is in the way that the window is reduced to zero. When the window is slowly dragged down to zero, and you can see the recipient struggling to keep it open, that's a problem. When the window suddenly goes straight down to zero as the result of a sudden blast of data segments, and then you see continued transmissions working properly, this is normal memory management behavior. As with any zero window condition, you should be concerned if you observe this happening more than once per megabyte of data, however.

The Stuck Window Situation

When the size of the Receive window goes below its original maximum value, without reaching zero, and does not return to the maximum value in a timely manner, the window is considered stuck or frozen. WildPackets EtherPeek and AiroPeek expert systems call this a *stuck window,* while Network Associates SnifferPRO expert analyzers use the term *window frozen.* Other expert systems may use different terminology. (An expert system is artificial intelligence software that goes beyond ordinary protocol decoding software to automatically identify and diagnose problem symptoms on a network.)

If you see a stuck window or frozen window symptom with your expert system, you should go to the packet where the problem is reported and then work backward to identify the flow of sequence and acknowledgment numbers. Watch the shrinking and growing of the recipient's Receive window by looking at the Window Size field that the recipient reports. Determine whether the recipient is struggling to open the window (due to overload) or the window has suddenly decreased (due to memory management). Continue to examine the size of the window after the stuck window symptom report. You may see the window eventually return to full size, in which case the data flow is normal. On the other hand, you may see the window remain small for the remainder of the conversation, indicating that an overload is imminent (but not currently impacting the conversation). As long as the window is open (greater than zero), data can flow.

Identifying TCP Performance Problems

When users observe performance degradation on a network, the question often arises, "Is the problem with the network, or is it the application itself that's slow?" By comparing the response time for TCP acknowledgments with application response times, the source of degradation can be isolated.

When a host has a nonzero Receive window, its partner should send TCP segments as rapidly as the network and application allow, after getting past the slow start period. When data is received, the TCP recipient sends ACKs. The application program has its own requests and replies. For example, if a client sends an FTP RETR (retrieve) command or an SMTP HELO (hello) command, the server should send a positive reply. If a client sends a Read Request to a file server, the server should send a Read Reply. Application requests and replies may require that data be accessed from a server disk and processed in some manner by the client, which can slow down performance. When assessing performance, you should compare application response times to TCP ACK times to distinguish network and application problems.

Consider a situation where a client has just issued a Read Request. TCP must acknowledge the request segment, and the application must also process the request and send back a reply. One of these situations can occur:

- *The TCP ACK is carried with the application reply.* In this case, the application is able to respond just as quickly as TCP is able to acknowledge data. This means that the application is operating at its maximum level of performance. If there is a performance problem, it doesn't lie with the application.

- *The TCP ACK comes back immediately and the application reply is delayed.* This indicates that the network is not the cause of the observed performance problem but, rather, the application is at fault. Because the TCP ACK is able to come back immediately, it proves that the network is working properly.

- *The TCP ACK is delayed a long time.* In this situation, there is a long delay between the original transmission of the application request and the TCP ACK for the TCP segment that carried the request. The delay is longer than the ordinary delayed ACK timer. In this case, the network is suspect.

When analyzing sequence and ACK numbers, you need to know where your protocol analyzer is placed in the internetwork with respect to the placement of the client and server in the TCP conversation. If your analyzer resides on the LAN with the client, keep in mind that you may see ACKs that the server never sees. The client may be keeping up, but ACKs are getting dropped in the internetwork somewhere before reaching the server. If your analyzer resides on the LAN with the server, you may see transmissions from the server that never make it to the client.

On Cisco routers, you can use the show interface command to see whether routers are dropping packets. If the router seems fine, another possibility is that a WAN or LAN between the client and server is having problems. A WAN service provider could be dropping or inadvertently changing packets. A LAN could be experiencing a high level of collisions (Ethernet), could be beaconing (Token Ring or FDDI), or could be misconfigured for speed or duplex mode. If possible, move your analyzer to different parts of the internetwork or work with a partner who can place an analyzer on the opposite side of the internetwork where you are working.

TCP Poetry

The essence of TCP sequence and acknowledgment is embodied in the following attempt at poetry written by Joe Bardwell.

> *When sequence equals previous ACK,*
> > *the conversation is quite on track!*
> *Sequence number pulls ahead,*
> > *the lazy ACKer needs to get out of bed.*
> > > *If you're with the ACKer and he's keeping pace,*
> > > > *the network is slowing in some other place.*
> > > *If the network's tested, and everything's passed,*
> > > > *maybe it's just that the sender is fast.*
> *Sequence number cycles back*
> > *because he missed a required ACK,*
> > > *If you're with the ACKer and you see the ACK go,*
> > > > *the network is broken, error-prone, or slow.*
> > > *If you're with the sender and the ACK is plainly seen,*
> > > > *something is wrong with the sending machine.*
> > > *When subnets or hop counts say, "Routers are near,"*
> > > > *be wary of saying, "The problem is here."*

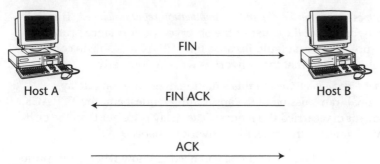

Figure 9.7   A TCP connection termination.

TCP Connection Termination

A TCP connection ends when one of the hosts sends a packet with the FIN bit set. The other host acknowledges the FIN by sending a segment with the ACK bit set. The host also sends a segment with its own FIN bit set and that segment is acknowledged. The session termination uses a four-way handshake in this case. Sometimes a single segment is used to send a FIN and acknowledge the other side's FIN, in which case the session termination uses a three-way handshake. When a host receives a FIN packet, the host notifies the application. The application closes any files, releases memory, and notifies the user if necessary. The application then tells TCP to send its FIN. If these events happen quickly enough, then the host's ACK and FIN travel in a single segment. Figure 9.7 shows a connection termination that uses three segments.

A TCP connection may also end when one of the hosts sends a segment with the RST bit set. In the past, sending a RST was reserved for abnormal conditions. Recently, some TCP implementations have started using RST to close a normal connection, presumably because it's faster than using a three- or four-way handshake. A host can send a RST and release memory and other resources for the connection immediately, rather than waiting for a FIN ACK from the other side and then acknowledging the FIN.

There are four connection termination patterns that are used in various network operating environments. Your own experience may show you only one or two of them, but they're all in use. They are:

1. Host A sends a FIN and Host B ACKs the FIN. Host B sends a FIN and Host A ACKs the FIN.

2. Host A sends a FIN and Host B sends a FIN that also ACKs Host A's FIN. Host A ACKs the FIN. (This is what Figure 9.7 shows.)

3. Host A sends a FIN and Host B sends a RST.

4. Host A sends a RST and no other packets are sent by either host.

You may also see a RST in response to a SYN to open a connection. This use of RST is not mentioned in RFC 793, but it is in wide use today nonetheless. Some hosts send a RST when they receive a SYN to a port that is not in the listening state. For example, if you try to open a Web page on a host that is not acting as a Web server, your SYN packet to Port 80 may result in a RST response. Security experts recommend that TCP/IP software developers avoid this use of RST, although their advice is not widely followed yet. In general, it's better for a host to ignore a SYN rather than send a RST. According to security experts, when a hacker is knocking on the door of many ports, the software should ignore the SYNs rather than send a RST or, even worse, open the connection part way and then send a RST.

According to RFC 793, as a general rule, a host must send a RST whenever a segment arrives that apparently is not intended for the current connection. The RFC discusses two specific situations when a host must send a RST:

1. If a connection does not exist, then a host must send a RST in response to any incoming segment, except another RST segment.

2. If a connection is in any nonsynchronized state, and the incoming segment acknowledges something not yet sent (the segment carries an unacceptable ACK number), a host must send a RST. A connection is in a nonsynchronized state when a host is listening or when a host has sent a SYN but not received an ACK yet. A connection is also in a nonsynchronized state when a host has received a SYN but has not yet sent a SYN ACK.

As you develop your protocol analysis skills, you will be able to apply intuition to determine whether the presence of RSTs in an analyzer trace file is cause for concern. The situations mentioned in RFC 793 should not happen and probably are reason for concern. What might cause a host to receive a segment for a connection that doesn't exist? One possibility is duplicate IP addresses. If two hosts are configured with the same IP address, a host can receive segments that are intended for a connection on the other host. What might cause a host to receive a segment with an ACK number that doesn't match anything already sent? This could be due to a software bug. It could also be evidence of a hacker rummaging around in your network. On the other hand, RSTs are often sent for legitimate reasons—for example, to close a connection or to disallow a connection establishment.

TCP Checksum

The TCP checksum is used to verify that a TCP segment arrived at the TCP layer intact. The checksum is the ones complement of the ones complement sum of all 16-bit words in the header and data. Luckily, as a network support engineer, there's no need to understand the exact mechanism for calculating the checksum. There are a few things you should know about the checksum, however.

The TCP checksum covers both the TCP header and data portion of the packet. Recall from Chapter 7 that the IP checksum covered only the IP header. The TCP checksum covers the entire segment. The sender runs the checksum algorithm against the header and data and places the results in the Checksum field of the TCP header. The recipient runs the same algorithm and drops the segment if the result doesn't match the field in the header. TCP does not acknowledge the segment, so the sender retransmits it.

Theoretically, TCP checksum errors should be very rare. Recall from Chapter 3 that Ethernet II and IEEE 802.3 also have a checksum. In fact, almost all data-link-layer protocols have a checksum. If a packet gets damaged in transit across a network, the recipient data-link layer drops the packet and TCP never sees it. It is possible, however, that software at the recipient host, or software within an intermediate router en route to the recipient host, could change or drop bits in the TCP header or data. TCP checksum errors should be infrequent, but if they do occur, they usually indicate a software problem or faulty memory chips within the recipient host or within routers on route to the recipient. It's also possible that software or memory problems reside at the sender, causing the sender to miscalculate the TCP checksum.

The TCP checksum actually covers the TCP header, data, and an extra 96 bits called the *pseudo header*. The pseudo header is a conceptual header that is added to the actual TCP header for the purpose of calculating the checksum. The pseudo header includes the length of the actual TCP header and data, which is a calculated number that is not transmitted. The pseudo header also borrows fields from the IP header, including the Source Address, Destination Address, and Protocol Type fields. (The protocol type for TCP is six.)

According to RFC 793, including the pseudo information in the TCP checksum calculation "gives TCP protection against misrouted segments." Although the authors of RFC 793 don't elaborate on how TCP could possibly receive misrouted segments, the one area where you may see problems is with Network Address Translation (NAT). NAT translates IP addresses, which means it must also recalculate the TCP checksum. If a NAT implementation doesn't do this correctly, you will see TCP checksum errors. If you see numerous TCP checksum errors and you are using NAT, start your troubleshooting by investigating any known bugs with the NAT software you are using.

User Datagram Protocol

UDP is a connectionless transport-layer alternative to TCP. From a protocol analysis and troubleshooting viewpoint, there's little need to examine UDP in detail. It is unlikely that UDP will cause problems or display symptoms of problems occurring at other layers. As you saw in the previous sections, TCP allows you to study sequence numbers, acknowledgment numbers, delta times, and window sizes to investigate dropped packets and performance problems. UDP, on the other hand, does not yield much troubleshooting data. You will generally just take a quick look at the UDP header to determine the sending and receiving application, and then refocus your troubleshooting on upper layers.

UDP provides a simple but unreliable communication service to upper layers. You may wonder why any software or protocol developer would choose to use UDP if it is unreliable. The answer is that the use of the term *unreliable* is not negative; it just means there are no guarantees when sending data with UDP. UDP does not sequence data, does not wait for an acknowledgment, and does not implement flow control. It does have many advantages, however. It is easy to implement, uses minimal network bandwidth, and requires minimal software to implement. UDP is perfect for applications that must fit into a small amount of memory. For example, SNMP runs above UDP because SNMP is often implemented in small hardware devices that don't have enough memory to store an entire implementation of TCP. If an upper layer implements reliability anyway, which SNMP does, there's no need to use TCP. UDP is sufficient.

0	16	31

Source Port	Destination Port
Length	Checksum

Figure 9.8   The UDP header.

UDP Protocol Analysis

The UDP header is always 8 bytes. There are no options. Figure 9.8 shows the format of a UDP header, and Table 9.4 describes the fields in a UDP header.

NOTE The RFC that defines UDP (RFC 768) implies that the UDP checksum is optional. The sender can simply place all 0s in the field. The Host Requirements RFC (RFC 1122) requires that the UDP checksum be enabled by default, however. In the 1980s, some computer vendors turned off the UDP checksum by default, to speed up their implementations of NFS, which uses RPC on top of UDP. While this worked on a single LAN because of the data link layer checksum, it resulted in problems on networks with faulty routers (non-Cisco, of course) that changed bits in forwarded packets, and on Serial Line Internet Protocol (SLIP) implementations that didn't use a data link layer checksum.

Table 9.4   Fields in a UDP Header

FIELD	EXPLANATION
Source Port	A number that identifies the sending application in the sending host.
Destination Port	A number that identifies the recipient application in the destination host.
Length	The length of the UDP header and data in bytes.
Checksum	Verifies the UDP header and data. As with TCP, the UDP checksum is based on the data, an actual header, and a pseudo header. The pseudo header includes the UDP length (again), the source and destination IP addresses, and the IP protocol type (17 for UDP). Because of the IP data in the pseudo header, NAT must recalculate the UDP checksum.

UDP Port Numbers

UDP uses port numbers to identify the sending and receiving application. Like TCP, UDP has two types of ports: well known and ephemeral. The well-known ports are used by standard services that run above UDP, including DNS, SNMP, and others. Servers listen on the well-known ports for clients wishing to access services. Clients use ephemeral ports on their end of a conversation. Unlike the case for TCP, the UDP Source Port number is optional. If a sending application doesn't need a reply, UDP is not required to identify the sending application and can place a 0 in the Source Port field.

To become a good troubleshooter, you should learn which standard services run above UDP (versus TCP) and the well-known port numbers that identify the services. Table 9.5 lists the most common services.

Application-Layer Protocols

The final sections in this chapter cover application-layer protocols. The Open System Interconnection (OSI) application layer, which the TCP/IP developers called the *process layer*, provides common services to application programs. Common services include file transfer, electronic message transfer, directory searching, name-to-address mapping, cryptographic key exchange, time-of-day exchange, and so on. The application layer should not be confused with the actual application programs that users see. For example, a Web browser is a program that a user sees. The program uses the application layer's capability to send messages—in this case, messages that follow the rules of HTTP and include text that is encoded with the Hypertext Markup Language (HTML).

There are numerous application-layer protocols in the TCP/IP world; this chapter covers only the most widely used. Subsequent chapters cover a few more application-layer protocols that are often found on a TCP/IP campus network, including NCP, AFP, and Microsoft's Server Message Block (SMB), all used for sharing files.

Many TCP/IP application-layer protocols, including HTTP, FTP, SMTP, and POP, use human-readable text to send their commands and replies. The commands and replies are sent as alphabetic characters encoded with the American Standard Code for Information Interchange (ASCII). This eases troubleshooting and testing because the tester can recognize the commands and replies without an extra level of decoding. The commands are designed to be used by both programmers and testers, although, as we will see with FTP, the user interface implementation often requires the user to type something slightly different from the command defined in the protocol specification.

To understand the benefits of ASCII commands, compare them to the method used by TCP to identify an operation. Instead of sending a text string that says SYN in human-readable format, TCP sets a bit that programmers and analysts must know stands for SYN. TCP is a bit-oriented protocol (individual bits have meaning). Other protocols use entire bytes to identify operations. For example, the routing protocols covered in Chapter 8 mostly use 1-byte numeric opcodes to identify operations. These opcodes are sent as numbers rather than ASCII characters.

Table 9.5 UDP Port Numbers

SERVICE	PORT NUMBER IN DECIMAL
Domain Name System(DNS)	53
Dynamic Host Configuration Protocol (DHCP)	67 for the DHCP server 68 for the DHCP client
Trivial File Transfer Protocol (TFTP)	69
Remote Procedure Call (RPC)	111
NetBIOS datagram	138
Simple Network Management Protocol (SNMP)	161
AppleTalk Update-Based Routing Protocol (AURP)	387
Service Location Protocol (SLP)	427
Routing Information Protocol (RIP)	520
NetWare Core Protocol (NCP)*	5x24

*NCP can use TCP or UDP.

The other feature that most application-layer protocols share, besides sending ASCII commands, is that they use a client/server architecture. The DNS architecture has both clients and servers (and servers that act as clients, as will be seen). The HTTP architecture includes clients that run Web browser software and servers that run Web server software that communicates with the clients. FTP was designed before the term *client/server* came in vogue, but it fits the architecture nonetheless, as do SMTP and POP.

Domain Name System

The first application-layer protocol we will cover is DNS. DNS is more than just a protocol; it is also a system of servers that provides naming on the Internet and on intranets. DNS servers manage a distributed database that maps between IP host names and IP addresses. It also provides e-mail routing information and can map between NetBIOS server names and IP addresses on Windows networks. The DNS database is called *distributed* because no single site knows all the information. A DNS server maintains resource records (RRs) for information in the server's *zone of authority*. Other systems act as clients and query the server for information. DNS defines the protocol that allows clients and servers to communicate with each other.

To facilitate the distributed nature of the DNS database, DNS names are hierarchical. A DNS name has multiple parts. For example, in the *cco.cisco.com* name, *cco* is a host within the cisco.com domain. At the highest level of the hierarchy, there is a small set of top-level domains. Table 9.6 shows some of the most common top-level domains.

Table 9.6   Top-Level DNS Domains

DOMAIN	DESCRIPTION
.edu	Educational institutions
.gov	Government agencies
.net	Network providers
.com	Commercial companies
.org	Nonprofit organizations

There are also many geographical top-level domains, for example .uk for the United Kingdom, and .de for Germany. Work is currently under way to develop some new top-level domains, such as .biz and .info. Increasing the options for top-level domains may help prevent the many disputes that occur over the right to use popular, sales-oriented names.

The Internet Corporation for Assigned Names and Numbers (ICANN) is a nonprofit corporation that has responsibility for overall DNS management and top-level domains. ICANN has accredited a set of competitive registrars that have authority over names under the top level. Each layer of the hierarchy can also delegate authority. For example, a registrar might delegate authority to a corporate IS department for a name such as *cisco.com*. The IS department can delegate authority to the engineering department for names in the *engineering.cisco.com* subdomain. Within the engineering department, there might be multiple hosts with names such as *frodo.engineering.cisco.com* and *gandalf.engineering.cisco.com*. Delegation of authority allows DNS to be autonomously managed at each layer, which increases scalability for the system.

DNS uses a client/server model. Each end-station client is configured with the IP address of a DNS server. An administrator can configure the address of the DNS server just once on a DHCP server to avoid the need to manually configure the address on each client. When a client asks the DHCP server for an IP address, the DHCP server can also return the IP address of the DNS server. When a client needs to send a packet to a named station, such as www.cisco.com, DNS *resolver software* on the client machine sends a query to the DNS server.

A DNS server may offer *recursion*, which allows the server to ask other servers for information not found in the local database or memory cache. Each server is configured with the IP address of one or more higher-level DNS servers that should have more extensive knowledge about other domains. When a DNS server receives a response from another server, it replies to the resolver client software that originally asked the question. The server also caches the information for future requests. The network administrator of the authoritative DNS server for a name defines the length of time that a nonauthoritative server may cache information. Long time intervals decrease network traffic but can also make it difficult to change a name. The old name might be cached on thousands of servers on the Internet.

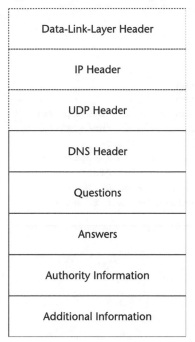

Figure 9.9 The DNS packet structure.

DNS Protocol Analysis

When a user accesses another host by name, the resolver software on the user's machine sends a query to the DNS server, with a question about a host name. Reverse DNS is also possible, where a client sends a query with a question about an IP address. The server should respond with a set of records that repeat the question and include an answer (if one is available). The reply may also include information about which server has the authoritative answer and possibly additional information. A DNS packet includes a UDP header, a DNS header, and a set of Question, Answer, Authority Information, and Additional Information records, as shown in Figure 9.9.

The following EtherPeek output shows a query from a PC. The user at the PC was trying to check the latest hockey scores. The DNS query is a request to find the Internet host address for the name www.nhl.com (the Web site of the National Hockey League).

```
Source IP Address:      PC
Dest. IP Address:       Local DNS Server
UDP - User Datagram Protocol
  Source Port:          1381
  Destination Port:     53  domain
```

```
         Length:              37
         Checksum:            0x5BBD
DNS - Domain Name System Protocol
         Identification:      0x0002
         Flags:               0x0100
                              0... .... .... ....  Request
                              .000 0... .... ....  Standard Query
                              .... .0.. .... ....  (Non-Authoritative Answer)
                              .... ..0. .... ....  (Message Not Truncated)
                              .... ...1 .... ....  Recursion Desired
                              .... .... 0... ....  (Recursion Not Available)
                              .... .... .0.. ....  (Unknown Flag Off)
                              .... .... ..0. ....  (Unknown Flag Off)
                              .... .... ...0 ....  (Packet Was Not Broadcast)
   Number of Questions:  1
   Number of Answers:    0
   Number of Authority:  0
   Number of Additional: 0
Question
   Domain Name:          www.nhl.com.
   Type:                 1  A - Host Address
   Class:                1  Internet
```

Notice in the Flags field in the EtherPeek output that the client PC says recursion is desired. In other words, the client asks the server to ask other servers if the answer is not available locally. Ignore the line that says `Recursion not available`, because it's not relevant on a packet from a client. Clients don't support recursion; servers do.

The DNS server to which the PC sent the query did not know the IP address for www.nhl.com. However, because the client requested recursion, the server asked another server. The following output shows the DNS query that was sent to one of the main Internet DNS servers at the 192.26.92.30 destination IP address. Notice that the server doesn't ask for additional recursion, as recursion of recursion is not necessary.

```
Source IP Address:    Local DNS Server
Dest. IP Address:     192.26.92.30 Remote DNS Server
UDP - User Datagram Protocol
   Source Port:          53  domain
   Destination Port:     53  domain
   Length:               37
   Checksum:             0x4AE4
DNS - Domain Name System Protocol
   Identification:       0x1BA5
   Flags:                0x0000
                         0... .... .... ....  Request
                         .000 0... .... ....  Standard Query
                         .... .0.. .... ....  (Non-Authoritative Answer)
                         .... ..0. .... ....  (Message Not Truncated)
                         .... ...0 .... ....  (Recursion Not Desired)
                         .... .... 0... ....  (Recursion Not Available)
```

```
                               .... .... .0.. ....  (Unknown Flag Off)
                               .... .... ..0. ....  (Unknown Flag Off)
                               .... .... ...0 ....  (Packet Was Not Broadcast)
    Number of Questions:   1
    Number of Answers:     0
    Number of Authority:   0
    Number of Additional:  0
Question
    Domain Name:           www.nhl.com.
    Type:                  1  A - Host Address
    Class:                 1  Internet
```

To continue with the example, the remote server at 192.26.92.30 had some information about the www.nhl.com name, but it was not the authority, so it did not have the IP address for the name. The following output shows the remote server's response sent to the local server.

```
Source IP Address:     192.26.92.30 Remote DNS Server
Dest. IP Address:      Local DNS Server
UDP - User Datagram Protocol
    Source Port:           53   domain
    Destination Port:      53   domain
    Length:                106
    Checksum:              0xE7F9
DNS - Domain Name System Protocol
    Identification:        0x1BA5
    Flags:                 0x8000
                           1... .... .... ....  Response
                           .000 0... .... ....  Standard Query
                           .... .0.. .... ....  (Non-Authoritative Answer)
                           .... ..0. .... ....  (Message Not Truncated)
                           .... ...0 .... ....  (Recursion Not Desired)
                           .... .... 0... ....  (Recursion Not Available)
                           .... .... .0.. ....  (Unknown Flag Off)
                           .... .... ..0. ....  (Unknown Flag Off)
                           .... .... ...0 ....  (Packet Was Not Broadcast)
                           .... .... .... 0000  No Error Response
    Number of Questions:   1
    Number of Answers:     0
    Number of Authority:   1
    Number of Additional:  1
Question
    Domain Name:           www.nhl.com.
    Type:                  1  A - Host Address
    Class:                 1  Internet
Authority
    Domain Name:           nhl.com.
    Type:                  2  NS - Authoritative Name Server
    Class:                 1  Internet
    Time to Live:          172800
```

```
       Data Length:          6
       Domain Name:          DNS.nhl.com.
    Additional
       Domain Name:          DNS.nhl.com.
       Type:                 1  A - Host Address
       Class:                1  Internet
       Time to Live:         172800
       Data Length:          4
       IP Address:           64.124.31.149
```

Notice from the ouptut that the most useful piece of information the remote server provided was that the authority for the www.nhl.com name belongs with DNS.nhl.com, and that the IP address for that server is 64.124.31.149. This caused the local server to send a query to 64.124.31.149, which isn't shown for the sake of brevity. The query looks like the other queries we have already seen. The DNS.nhl.com server responded with the following reply:

```
Source IP Address:     64.124.31.149 DNS.nhl.com
Dest. IP Address:      Local DNS Server
UDP - User Datagram Protocol
   Source Port:           53   domain
   Destination Port:      53   domain
   Length:                122
   Checksum:              0xB2BA
DNS - Domain Name System Protocol
   Identification:        0x1BA5
   Flags:                 0x8480
                          1... .... .... ....  Response
                          .000 0... .... ....  Standard Query
                          .... .1.. .... ....  Authoritative Answer
                          .... ..0. .... ....  (Message Not Truncated)
                          .... ...0 .... ....  (Recursion Not Desired)
                          .... .... 1... ....  Recursion Available
                          .... .... .0.. ....  (Unknown Flag Off)
                          .... .... ..0. ....  (Unknown Flag Off)
                          .... .... ...0 ....  (Packet Was Not Broadcast)
                          .... .... .... 0000  No Error Response
   Number of Questions:   1
   Number of Answers:     1
   Number of Authority:   0
   Number of Additional:  0
Question
   Domain Name:           www.nhl.com.
   Type:                  1  A - Host Address
   Class:                 1  Internet
Answer
   Domain Name:           www.nhl.com.
   Type:                  1  A - Host Address
   Class:                 1  Internet
   Time to Live:          28800
   Data Length:           4
   IP Address:            209.191.172.130
```

Notice that the DNS.nhl.com server told the local server it can cache the information it retrieved for 28,880 seconds. (See `Time to live: 28800`.) This is 8 hours. So the next time a client asks for the IP address for www.nhl.com, the local server can respond from memory if 8 hours have not elapsed.

The local DNS server finally sent a reply to the PC client and told the PC client to use the 209.191.172.130 address to get to www.nhl.com. The reply isn't shown as it looks essentially like the reply from the DNS.nhl.com server to the local server, shown in the previous output.

The amount of traffic to get an answer to a simple question might seem excessive, but the DNS traffic actually completed in just 0.365 seconds. After learning an IP address for www.nhl.com, the PC user was then able to pull up the www.nhl.com Web page and confirm that the San Jose Sharks are the best hockey team in the National Hockey League!

Service Location Protocol

SLP is a relatively new protocol that handles some of the same tasks as DNS. SLP allows users to locate servers by their names. It provides dynamic resource discovery and point-and-click access to services. SLP is currently supported by Apple Computer, Novell, Inc., Sun Microsystems, and other vendors. Although SLP has not caught on yet as a major IP protocol, it may still become an important service on campus IP networks. Many companies and universities that have an AppleTalk or Novell NetWare heritage are starting to implement SLP. RFC 2608 defines the current version of SLP, which is version 2 (SLPv2).

SLP uses the concept of a *scope*, which is similar to an AppleTalk zone. By configuring scopes, a network administrator can allow clients to search for services in a hierarchical manner. Services are grouped into scopes. A client is typically assigned to a scope, in which case the client can only discover a particular set of services. Alternatively, the client may be configured with no scope, in which case the client can discover any service available on the internetwork.

With SLP, client applications implement a *user agent* and servers advertise their services through a *service agent*. The user agent makes a *Service Request* on behalf of the client application, specifying the characteristics of the service that the client is trying to find. The user agent should receive a *Service Reply* specifying the location of services on the network that satisfy the request.

SLP supports dynamic naming services without the need for any centralized name server or other agent. User agents use IP multicast for this purpose. Service agents that receive a request for a service they offer send a unicast reply containing the service's location. To work across an internetwork, IP multicast requires the cooperation of IP routers. Most modern IP routers can support IP multicast, but it may not be enabled, thus limiting the effectiveness of SLP. (See Chapter 7 for more information about IP multicast addressing and routing.) In the absence of IP multicast support, SLP name lookups work only within the subnet on which they are performed.

SLP has an option for scaling service location through the use of name servers, also called *directory agents*. Service agents send *Register* messages to directory agents containing a list of the services they wish to advertise. The directory agents send acknowledgments in reply. The service advertisements are refreshed through additional messages sent to the directory agent at regular intervals. User agents send unicast requests to directory agents to find services.

User and service agents discover directory agents by sending multicast Service Requests for the directory agent service when they initialize. The directory agent also sends unsolicited advertisements infrequently, for which the user and service agents listen. In either case, the user and service agents receive a *Directory Agent Advertisement* (DAAdvert) message.

Directory agents minimize the requirement for routers to implement IP multicast routing. They can also result in much less network traffic compared to a distributed architecture that has no agents. Also, directory agents allow a network administrator to divide services into scopes. As SLP momentum builds, it is expected that more directory agent implementations will become available. As of today, you can implement a directory agent on Apple's Mac OS X Server platform and on Novell servers. Microsoft's Windows 2000 also supports a directory agent, although you have to implement Novell services for it to work.

The following EtherPeek output shows a Macintosh running Mac OS X that just booted and is trying to find an SLP directory agent. Notice the use of IP multicast and that SLP runs above UDP, using UDP port 427. SLP messages are multicast to the *administratively scoped SLP multicast address*, which is 239.255.255.253. (SLPv1 used 224.0.1.22 and 224.0.1.35.) The Ethernet destination address is also a multicast address. Chapter 7 discusses how an IP multicast address is manipulated into an Ethernet multicast address.

```
Ethernet Header
   Destination:             01:00:5E:7F:FF:FD
   Source:                  00:30:65:1A:91:90
   Protocol Type:           0x0800  IP
IP Header - Internet Protocol Datagram
   Version:                 4
   Header Length:           5  (20  bytes)
   Type of Service:         %00000000
                            000. .... Precedence: Routine,
                            ...0 .... Normal Delay,
                            .... 0... Normal Throughput,
                            .... .0.. Normal Reliability
                            .... ..0. ECT, transport protocol ignores CE
                            .... ...0 CE bit - no congestion
   Total Length:            77
   Identifier:              459
   Fragmentation Flags:     %000
                            0.. Reserved
                            .0. May Fragment
                            ..0 Last Fragment
   Fragment Offset:         0  (0  bytes)
   Time To Live:            255
   Protocol:                17  UDP - User Datagram Protocol
   Header Checksum:         0xA913
   Source IP Address:       208.1.80.194
   Dest. IP Address:        239.255.255.253
   No IP Options
UDP - User Datagram Protocol
   Source Port:             49159
```

```
        Destination Port:      427  svrloc
        Length:                57
        Checksum:              0xBA88
    Service Location Protocol
        Version:               2
        Function Id:           1      Service Request
        Length:                49
        Bits                   %001   Request Multicast
        Reserved:              0
        Next Extension Offset: 0
        XID:                   51107
        Language Tag Length:   2
        Language Tag:          en
    Service Request
        PRList Length:         0
        PRList:
        Service Type Length:   23
        Service Type:          service:directory-agent
        Scope List Length:     0
        Scope List:
        Predicate Length:      0
        Predicate:
        SLP SPI Length:        0
```

Hypertext Transfer Protocol

HTTP is the protocol that makes the World Wide Web (www) work. HTTP defines the structure of messages that Web servers and clients exchange, and the actions that servers and clients should take in response to various commands carried in the messages. When you enter a Uniform Resource Locator (URL) such as http://www.nhl .com in your Web browser, the HTTP implementation on your machine sends a command to the Web server directing it to retrieve and transmit the requested Web page. This happens after your machine has used DNS to get the IP address of the Web server and after TCP has set up a connection with the Web server.

Currently, most Web browsers and servers support HTTP version 1.1. One of the main features of HTTP 1.1 is support for *persistent connections*. This means that once a browser connects to a Web server, it can retrieve multiple files through the same connection. For example, if the HTML for the Web page refers to a graphics file, the client can request the graphics file without opening another TCP connection. With HTTP 1.0, the client was required to open another TCP connection.

The goal of persistent connections is to improve performance. Remember that each TCP connection establishment requires a TCP three-way handshake, which takes time. Also, most TCP connections begin by using the slow start algorithm. Each connection has low throughput at first, as the hosts ascertain how quickly they can send segments. With HTTP applications, the connections may be so short-lived that they never get out of slow start mode. It makes more sense to open a single TCP connection and download all data using that connection, as HTTP 1.1 specifies.

> **NOTE** Despite support for persistent connections in HTTP 1.1, many browsers that support the 1.1 version still open multiple TCP connections to download objects. Internet Explorer 5.0, for example, typically opens two connections to each Web server.

HTTP 1.1 also supports *pipelining*. Pipelining allows an HTTP client to have many HTTP requests open at the same time. If the HTML for a Web page refers to multiple objects, including graphics, video, or music files, the client can send simultaneous HTTP requests to download those objects without waiting for a response to the previous request. Because of the persistence of HTTP 1.1, these requests can be sent on a single TCP connection.

HTTP is a stateless protocol, which means that each command is executed independently, without any knowledge of the commands that came before it. The advantage of a stateless protocol is simplicity, but there are disadvantages also. Because of the stateless nature of HTTP, it is difficult to implement Web sites that react intelligently to user input. This shortcoming of HTTP is being addressed by more advanced technologies such as ActiveX, Java, JavaScript, and cookies. Troubleshooting these advanced techniques is outside the realm of this book.

HTTP Proxy Servers

To support users who access Web pages on the Internet, many campus network administrators install a *proxy Web server*. A proxy server is positioned between clients and the actual Internet Web servers, where it forwards requests on behalf of clients and relays responses from servers. Proxy servers offer several important services. Some administrators use them to enforce policies. Browser software on users' machines is directed to access the public Internet through the proxy, allowing the proxy to filter inappropriate material returning from the Internet. On the flip side, some administrators use proxies to make sure inappropriate information doesn't go out to the Internet to Web sites that gather personal information about clients. On some campus networks, proxy servers require a login. This brings with it a host of troubleshooting issues related to misconfigured authentication parameters and users who forget their usernames and passwords.

The most common use for a proxy server is caching. A proxy cache server improves Web performance by remembering the objects requested by clients, and, if an object is requested again (by the same client or a different client), the proxy server returns the object without requesting it from the original server. The proxy server does not transmit the request to the Internet, but instead returns data it saved earlier to RAM or its hard disk. This means that the client receives a response more quickly. It also reduces resource consumption at the original server, which improves server performance for other users.

HTTP 1.1 includes header information that tells proxy cache servers whether an object can be cached and, if so, how long it can be saved. Many Web server applications don't allow data to be cached, in which case the proxy server can't improve performance by returning the data itself. The proxy server must forward the request to the Internet. When analyzing HTTP performance on your network, set a filter for all traffic from the proxy server to determine if it is sending numerous requests to the Internet rather than replying itself.

One of the challenges with using proxy servers is the need to configure each user's Web browser with the address of the proxy server. Some organizations preconfigure browser software before distributing it to users. Users who download the latest browser software directly from the Internet can defeat this effort, however. Microsoft and other companies have proposed methods to make the proxy configuration more foolproof, including the Web Proxy Auto-Discovery Protocol (WPAD) and Proxy Auto Configuration (PAC) scripts, but these methods have not gained wide acceptance. For more information on methods for handling this problem, see RFC 3040, "Internet Web Replication and Caching Taxonomy."

HTTP Protocol Analysis

HTTP 1.1 is defined in RFC 2616. The RFC defines four basic commands, called GET, POST, PUT, and DELETE. The commands are sent as uppercase ASCII characters, which makes troubleshooting easy. You can look at an ASCII view of an HTTP packet and easily understand which command is being sent. The GET command is used by a client to retrieve an object from a server. Figure 9.10 shows a GET message that Internet Explorer generated when a Windows 98 PC tried to retrieve the Web page at www.wildpackets.com.

Notice in Figure 9.10 that EtherPeek uses the term *Uniform Resource Identifier* (URI) instead of the more common Uniform Resource Locator (URL). Technically, a URL is a specific type of URI that identifies a location. A URI is any formatted string that identifies a resource via its name, location, or other characteristics.

The significance of the single-slash (/) URI shown in Figure 9.10 is that the client is requesting a resource that is at the root of the file system on the server. If the client had attempted to reach an actual file on the server, then the URI would specify a path and file name. The example in RFC 2616 is GET /pub/WWW/TheProject.html. The host field for the example is www.w3.org.

> **NOTE** You can try this. Start your protocol analyzer capturing traffic and go to the Web site www.w3.org/pub/WWW/TheProject.html. You should capture a GET message that has the /pub/WWW/TheProject.html path and file name in the URI and www.w3.org in the host field of the HTTP header.

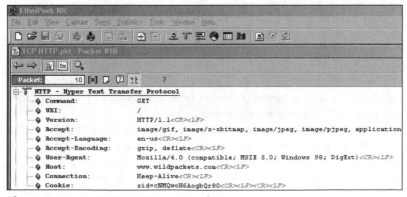

Figure 9.10 An HTTP GET command.

When the client issues a GET, the server replies with a status code that indicates whether the server was able to retrieve the resource. A status code of 200 means success. In addition, the server should start sending the resource, which in the case of a Web page consists of HTML that describes the Web page. The entire HTTP response will probably be divided into multiple TCP segments, unless the Web page is very small (1460 bytes or less). The *HTTP Replies* section discusses HTTP responses and status codes in more detail.

The HTTP POST command provides a method for clients to send information to servers. POST is most commonly used to send forms to Web servers. For example, when you shop on the Internet (and don't tell me you don't do this), the information for your name, mailing address, credit card, and so on is sent to the Web server with a POST command.

HTTP also supports a PUT command that allows the client to place a file on the Web server. The PUT command is not as common as the POST command because most Web servers don't support users placing files on them, but some applications do support this. An example is the terrific service offered by Blackboard, Inc. for teachers. Teachers use the Web server at www.blackboard.com to plan and implement their classes. The site lets students place homework assignments on the Web server for the teacher to pick up.

The technical difference between a POST and a PUT is in how the server interprets the URI. With a POST, the URI identifies an object on the server that can process the included data. The object is usually a software program or script. With a PUT, on the other hand, the URI identifies an object in which the server should place the data, usually a file.

The DELETE command gives clients a way to delete objects on servers. To use the Blackboard example, students may need a way to pull back homework assignments when they submit them by mistake. For example, a student may have forgotten to spell check and may need to delete the file before submitting a new one. The DELETE command provides this capability.

HTTP Advanced Commands

In addition to the basic HTTP commands (GET, POST, PUT, and DELETE), HTTP supports four other commands that are not the direct result of user actions but occur behind the scenes. These are the CONNECT, OPTIONS, HEAD, and TRACE commands.

Despite its important sounding name, the CONNECT command doesn't do anything. The RFC says only this about the CONNECT command: "This specification reserves the method name CONNECT for use with a proxy that can dynamically switch to being a tunnel." According to RFC 2616, a tunnel is an intermediary program that acts as a blind relay. The tunnel ceases to exist when both ends of the relayed connections are closed, which makes a tunnel different from a proxy. No HTTP implementations use the CONNECT command at this time.

The OPTIONS command is used by clients to discover the capabilities of a server. If the client includes a URI, the server responds with the options relevant to that object. If the client sends an asterisk (*) as the URI, the server returns the general options that apply to the entire server. A server should respond to an OPTIONS command with a status code of 200 and a message that includes the server's capabilities. The RFC does not specify exactly what the server must include in the response, but possible information includes the HTTP version, languages, plug-in applications, and encoding methods supported by the server.

The HEAD command is like a GET command, except that the server does not return the actual object requested. The server just returns a status code with no data. Clients can use a HEAD message to verify that an object exists. Programs that help Web developers test their Web pages send a HEAD message to ensure that links work.

The TRACE command is like an application-layer ping. Clients use this command to invoke a remote loopback of a request message. The final recipient of the TRACE message should reflect the message back to the client in the body of a reply with a status code of 200. TRACE allows the client to see what is being received at the other end and use that data for testing or diagnostic information.

TRACE is most useful when there are intermediate servers between the client and the ultimate server. For example, a proxy server could be in the path between the client and the final server. When an intermediate server receives a TRACE message, it modifies the request by inserting a *Via* option in the message. The Via option becomes part of the message that arrives at the destination server and is copied into the server's reply. When the client receives the reply, it can use the Via option to learn more about the path taken by HTTP messages.

HTTP Replies

An HTTP reply begins with a status line. The reply may also include headers and a message body. The status line includes the highest version of HTTP that the server supports; a status code, such as 200; and a reason phrase, such as OK. The headers include information such as the date, the brand of server software used by the server, encoding methods, and cookies.

> **NOTE** The most famous HTTP status code is 404, which means the server could not find the requested information. The term 404 has entered the vernacular to describe someone who doesn't have a clue.

The HTTP status codes can be helpful when troubleshooting a problem. The codes fall into five major categories, as described in Table 9.7. There are over 40 status codes. This book doesn't describe each individual code, but by knowing the broad category of the code, you can determine whether a request was successful, and if it wasn't, the reason for failure. See RFC 2616 for a description of individual codes.

File Transfer Protocol

FTP provides facilities for transferring files to and from remote computer systems. When using FTP, a user instructs the FTP software to copy an entire file from one system to another—for example, to upload new Web pages to a Web server or to upgrade configuration files on an internetwork device. This is different from the file-sharing protocols that we will discuss in future chapters, including NCP, AFP, and SMB, which can access portions of a file in a manner that is mostly transparent to the user.

Table 9.7   HTTP Status Code Categories

STATUS CODE	MEANING	DESCRIPTION
100-199	Informational	The server received the request but is still working on it.
200-299	Success	The request was successfully received, understood, and accepted.
300-399	Redirection	The client needs to take further action for the request to be fulfilled, usually because the URI moved.
400-499	Client error	The request cannot be fulfilled because of an error in the request, such as bad syntax or incorrect authorization.
500-599	Server error	The server failed to fulfill an apparently valid request.

FTP has a user and server side. FTP was invented before the client/server architecture, but you can think of these as being a client and server side. FTP client software is built into most operating systems. FTP server software is reserved for operating systems that run on servers. This may seem obvious, but many novices think they can use FTP to send a file to, or retrieve a file from, any system, which isn't true. You can only send or retrieve files from a system acting as an FTP server. A file-sharing protocol, on the other hand, is usually implemented so that any host can act as both a client and server.

Usually the user transferring a file with FTP needs authority to log in and access files on the server. The common facility known as *anonymous FTP* works via a special type of public guest account implemented on the server. The user supplies guest for the username and anything for the password. Netiquette states that users should send their e-mail address as the password so that the administrator has some way of identifying them.

CAUTION   FTP provides a false sense of security when anonymous FTP is not used, because the user must provide an actual username and password. The username and password are sent across the network as clear text and are easily visible with a protocol analyzer. This wouldn't be such a serious problem if it weren't for the fact that users tend to use this same username and password for accessing confidential data.

FTP File Types and Structures

FTP was designed to work with various types of computers that use different operating systems, file formats, and character sets. As specified in RFC 959, FTP handles these differences by supporting a limited set of files types and structures. Supported file types are as follows:

ASCII.   The file is transferred across the data connection in ASCII format with a carriage return and line feed at the end of each line.

EBCDIC.   The file is transferred across the data connection using Extended Binary Coded Decimal Interchange Code (EBCDIC), which was common on mainframes in the past.

Image.   The file is transferred as a contiguous stream of bits. The image type is also known as *binary* and is used to send executable programs, graphics, and other files that don't fit the ASCII or EBCDIC characteristics. This is the most common file type.

Local byte.   This is a way of transferring binary files between hosts with different byte sizes. The number of bits per byte is specified by the sender. (These days all hosts use an 8-bit byte, but that wasn't the case when FTP was invented in the 1970s.)

An FTP file structure can be one of the following:

File.   The file is considered a contiguous stream of bytes. There is no internal file structure. This is the most common structure.

Record.   The file consists of text-based records.

Page.   Each page is transmitted with a page number to let the receiver store the pages in a random order and later retrieve them in order. The Host Requirements RFC recommends against the use of this structure.

FTP Protocol Analysis

FTP uses two TCP connections, one for control information and one for the actual data. Analysis of an FTP session involves an examination of the FTP commands sent on the control connection and an assessment of the TCP segments sent on the data connection. The default behavior, which is called *normal* or *active FTP*, is for the control connection to be initiated by the client side and the data connection to be initiated by the server side. The fact that the data connection is initiated by an outside FTP server may go against security policies that do not allow incoming TCP connection establishments. To avoid problems, a user can specify that *passive FTP* be used, in which case the client side establishes the data connection. The *FTP Active versus Passive Mode* section discusses this topic in more detail.

An FTP server listens on the well-known TCP port number 21 for control connection requests. The choice of port numbers for the data connection depends on the commands issued on the control connection. With active FTP, the client sends a command that indicates the port number on which the client is prepared to accept an incoming data connection request. The server then sends a TCP SYN from the well-known TCP port number 20 (FTP data) to the port number specified by the client.

The FTP control connection carries FTP commands to specify the data port, transfer mode, file type, and file structure. The FTP control connection also carries the FTP commands that direct servers to store, retrieve, append, and delete files and directories. Typically, after administrative details are taken care of, a user asks for a directory listing. The client software sends the LIST command and then also sends a PORT command to tell the server the port number to use to open a data connection for sending the directory listing. Note that a data connection is used for both the actual files and directory listings that itemize files.

FTP Commands

FTP clients send FTP commands as ASCII strings that start with three or four uppercase ASCII characters, followed by optional parameters and a carriage return and line feed. Table 9.8 describes the FTP commands.

Table 9.8 FTP Commands

COMMAND	DESCRIPTION
ABOR	Tells the server to stop the transfer taking place on the data connection.
ACCT	Sends user account information. (Some systems associate user accounts with file system objects.)
ALLO	Allocates space for the file about to be sent. A parameter specifies the number of bytes to allocate. This command may be required by some servers to reserve sufficient storage to accommodate the new file to be transferred.
APPE	Appends data to an existing file.
CDUP	Changes to the parent directory on the server.
CWD	Changes the working directory on the server. The parameter is a path name of a directory.
DELE	Deletes a file on the server.
HELP	Asks the server to send help information, which could include a list of commands supported.
LIST	Asks the server to send a list of file names in the current directory.
MKD	Makes a directory.
MODE	Specifies the transfer mode. The default is stream. Other options are block or compressed. Some servers only recognize stream.
NLST	Asks the server to send the contents of a specified subdirectory, as opposed to simply listing the name of the subdirectory.
NOOP	Keeps the connection alive. The client specifies no operation other than a request that the server send an OK reply.
PASS	Sends the user's password.
PASV	Specifies that the server data transfer process is to listen for a connection request from the client data transfer process. See the *FTP Active versus Passive Mode* section for more details.

Table 9.8   *(Continued)*

COMMAND	DESCRIPTION
PORT	Specifies the client port number and IP address on which the client data transfer process is listening for a connection request from the server data transfer process. See the *FTP Active versus Passive Mode* section for more details.
PWD	Asks the server to return the current directory name.
QUIT	Ends the connection.
REIN	Asks the server to reinitialize the FTP connection. This terminates the user's session, flushing all I/O and account information, except to allow any transfer in progress to be completed. All parameters are reset to the default settings, and the control connection is left open. A new USER command is expected to follow.
REST	Restarts a transfer from a specified byte offset. Some servers do not support this command, even though it is in the RFC, and many client implementations try to use it.
RETR	Retrieves a file from the server.
RMD	Removes a directory on the server.
RNFR	Specifies the old path and file name of a file to be renamed.
RNTO	Specifies the new path and file name of a file to be renamed.
SITE	Asks the server to return a description of the server's site
SMNT	Supplies the path name of a new file system structure.
STAT	Asks the server to display the current configuration and operational status of the FTP session.
STOR	Stores a file on the server, overwriting the file if it already exists.
STOU	Stores a file on the server without overwriting a file if it already exists. The file is created in the current directory under a unique name. The server reply includes the file name used.
STRU	Specifies the structure of the file to be transferred. The default is *file*, which means no structure. Other options are *record* or *page*. Some servers only recognize file.
SYST	Asks the server to report its operating system type.
TYPE	Specifies the file type. The default is *image*, also known as *binary*. Other options are ASCII, EBCDIC, and Local Byte.
USER	Sends the username to the server.

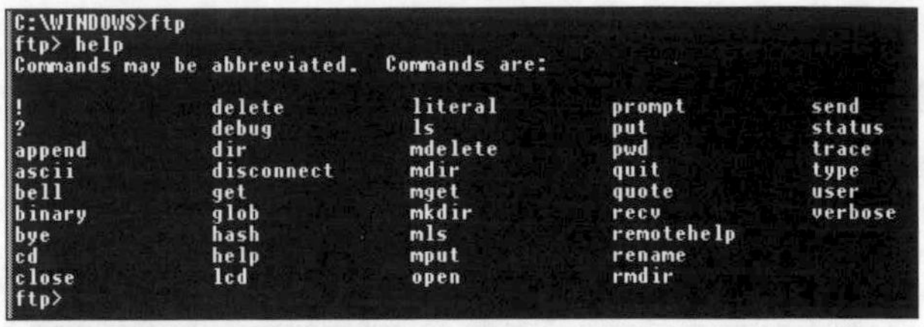

```
C:\WINDOWS>ftp
ftp> help
Commands may be abbreviated.  Commands are:

!              delete         literal        prompt         send
?              debug          ls             put            status
append         dir            mdelete        pwd            trace
ascii          disconnect     mdir           quit           type
bell           get            mget           quote          user
binary         glob           mkdir          recv           verbose
bye            hash           mls            remotehelp
cd             help           mput           rename
close          lcd            open           rmdir
ftp>
```

Figure 9.11   DOS FTP commands.

These days, FTP client software usually includes a graphical user interface (GUI). However, most operating systems also support the user typing text-oriented commands. One area for confusion with the text-oriented systems is that the commands a user types do not match the ASCII commands defined in the protocol specification. For example, the command in DOS or UNIX to cause the software to place a file on an FTP server is put, but the software actually sends the STOR command in the FTP message. The commands you see with a protocol analyzer are consistent with the RFCs that define a protocol, so you will see STOR in your analyzer for the DOS put command. Figure 9.11 shows the FTP commands available in the DOS operating system. UNIX commands closely resemble the DOS commands.

FTP Replies

FTP servers send FTP replies, which consist of a three-digit number (transmitted as three alphanumeric characters) followed by some text. The three-digit replies are similar to the HTTP replies we saw earlier. RFC 959 refers to the format of the replies as xyz. The first digit (x) denotes whether a response is good, bad, or incomplete. The second digit (y) specifies the type of reply. The third digit (z) provides finer gradation for the categories specified by the first two digits. Table 9.9 shows the five broad categories for replies.

Table 9.9   FTP Reply Code Categories

REPLY CODE	MEANING	DESCRIPTION
1yz	Positive preliminary reply	The server received the command but is still working on it. Expect another reply before sending another command.
2yz	Positive completion reply	The command completed successfully.
3yz	Positive intermediate reply	The client needs to take further action for the request to be fulfilled.
4yz	Transient negative completion reply	The requested action did not take place but can be retried.
5yz	Permanent negative completion reply	The requested action did not take place and should not be retried.

Table 9.10 FTP Reply Code Subcategories

REPLY CODE	MEANING	DESCRIPTION
x0z	Syntax	The command had a syntax error, is syntactically correct but doesn't fit any functional category, is superfluous, or is not implemented.
x1z	Information	Replies to requests for information, such as status or help.
x2z	Connections	Replies referring to the control and data connections.
x3z	Authentication and accounting	Replies for the login process and accounting procedures.
x4z	Unspecified	Reserved for future use.
x5z	File system status	Replies indicating the status of the server file system with regards to the requested transfer or other file system action.

Table 9.11 Typical FTP Reply Codes

REPLY CODE	MEANING
125	Data connection open, transfer starting
200	Command OK
331	Username OK, password required
452	Error writing to file
500	Syntax error or command not recognized

Table 9.10 shows the meaning of the second digit in an FTP reply.
Table 9.11 shows some typical replies.

FTP Active Versus Passive Mode

FTP has two modes of operation, active and passive. (Active mode is also sometimes called port mode). The troubleshooting and security concerns for these two modes are distinct, as is their behavior on the network. When investigating an FTP problem, one of the first questions you should ask is whether active or passive mode is in use. In the past, client implementations defaulted to active mode. These days, some client implementations default to passive mode due to security concerns with active mode.

The modes of operation determine whether the FTP server or client initiates the TCP connections that are used to send data. In active FTP, the client opens a control connection on the server, and, before data transfer occurs, the server opens a data connection on the client. The active mode of operation complicates the construction of firewalls, because the firewall must anticipate the connection from the FTP server back to the client. In passive FTP, the client opens the control and data connections. This is considered more secure and may work better with firewalls.

NOTE It can be difficult to configure an FTP application to use passive mode. If you are using an FTP program with its own GUI (as opposed to using FTP from within a Web browser or from a command prompt), then you should look for a checkbox that says something like "Use Passive Mode" or simply "PASV." This option is probably hidden in the Edit or File menu under Properties, Settings, or Options. It may be in a section related to using FTP with firewalls. If you can't find the option, check with the vendor of your FTP software to find out whether passive mode is supported and how to activate it.

FTP Active Mode

The steps for active FTP are described in the following list:

1. The client sends a TCP SYN to the well-known FTP control port (Port 21) on the server. The client uses an ephemeral port as its source port.

2. The server sends the client a SYN ACK from Port 21 to the ephemeral port on the client.

3. The client sends an ACK. The client uses this connection to send FTP commands and the server uses this connection to send FTP replies.

4. When the user requests a directory listing or initiates the sending or receiving of a file, the client software sends a PORT command that includes an ephemeral port number that the client wishes the server to use when opening the data connection. The PORT command also includes an IP address, which is usually the client's own IP address, although FTP also supports a *third-party mode* where a client can tell a server to send a file to a different host. (Third-party mode is rarely used.)

5. The server sends a SYN from Port 20 to the client's ephemeral port number, which was provided to the server in the client's PORT command.

6. The client sends a SYN ACK from its ephemeral port to Port 20.

7. The server sends an ACK.

8. The host that is sending data uses this new connection to send the data in TCP segments, which the other host ACKs. (With some commands, such as STOR, the client sends data. With other commands, such as RETR, the server sends data.)

9. After the data transfer is complete, the host sending data closes the data connection with a FIN, which the other host ACKs. The other host also sends its own FIN, which the sending host ACKs.

10. The client can send more commands on the control connection, which may cause additional data connections to be opened and then closed. At some point, when the user is finished, the client closes the control connection with a FIN. The server ACKs the client's FIN. The server also sends its own FIN, which the client ACKs.

The FTP PORT command causes problems for network support engineers in two ways. First, the encoding of the IP address and port number in a PORT message is not straightforward. Second, an application-layer protocol command theoretically shouldn't include network-layer information (an IP address). This breaks the principles of protocol layering and can cause problems, as will be discussed. Figure 9.12 shows an example of an FTP PORT command.

In the detail view of the packet shown in Figure 9.12, EtherPeek decodes the IP address parameter for the PORT command, but EtherPeek does not entirely decode the digits that follow. (See PORT 192,168,10,232,6,127.) The 6,127 portion becomes a port number by multiplying the first digit by 256 and adding the second digit. So the client specified a port number that is (6 * 256) + 127, which equals 1663. Figure 9.13 verifies that the server did indeed open a TCP connection from Port 20 to Port 1663.

Figure 9.12 An FTP PORT command from a client to a server.

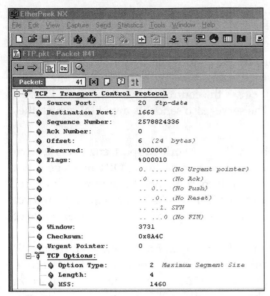

Figure 9.13   A server in active mode opens a TCP connection for data transfer.

If your network uses network address translation (NAT), as many campus networks do, the NAT gateway must track FTP sessions and be on the lookout for FTP PORT commands. NAT must translate the IP address in the FTP PORT command to the address assigned to the client. Then NAT must recalculate the TCP checksum, which is based on segment data as well as the TCP segment header. If the NAT software doesn't perform these operations correctly, FTP can fail.

FTP Passive Mode

The steps for passive FTP are described in the following list. Steps 1 through 3 are the same as the first three steps for active mode; steps 9 through 11 are the same as the last three steps for active mode.

1. The client sends a TCP SYN to the well-known FTP control port (Port 21) on the server. The client uses an ephemeral port as the source port.

2. The server sends the client a SYN ACK from Port 21 to the ephemeral port on the client.

3. The client sends an ACK. The client uses this connection to send FTP commands and the server uses the connection to send FTP replies.

4. When the user requests a directory listing or initiates the sending or receiving of a file, the client software sends a PASV command to the server indicating the desire to enter passive mode.

5. The server replies. The reply includes the IP address of the server and an ephemeral port number that the client should use when opening the connection for data transfer.

6. The client sends a SYN from a client-selected ephemeral port to the server's ephemeral port number, which was provided to the client in the reply to the client's PASV command.

7. The server sends a SYN ACK from its ephemeral port to the client's ephemeral port.

8. The client sends an ACK.

9. The host that is sending data uses this new connection to send the data in TCP segments, which the other host ACKs. (With some commands, such as STOR, the client sends data. With other commands, such as RETR, the server sends data.)

10. After the data transfer is complete, the host sending data closes the data connection with a FIN, which the other host ACKs. The other host also sends its own FIN, which the sending host ACKs.

11. The client can send more commands on the control session, which may cause additional data connections to be opened and then closed. At some point, when the user is finished, the client closes the control connection with a FIN. The server ACKs the client's FIN. The server also sends its own FIN, which the client ACKs.

Figure 9.14 shows a server's reply to a client's PASV command. The server tells the client that the server is listening on Port 5365. (See 192,168,179,100,20,24.5) To calculate the port number, multiply 20 times 256 and add 245. (20 * 256) + 245 = 5365.)

After receiving a reply to its PASV command, the client opens a TCP connection from an ephemeral port to the port number supplied by the server. Figure 9.15 shows the TCP connection establishment from the client. Notice that the destination port is 5365, as expected.

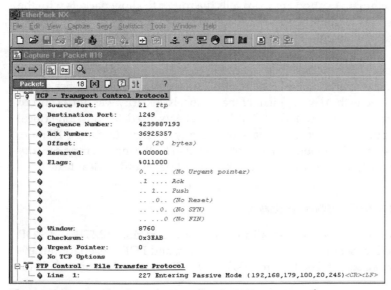

Figure 9.14   A server's reply to a client's PASV command.

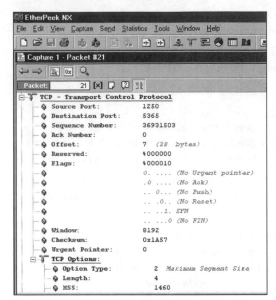

Figure 9.15   A client in passive mode opens a TCP connection for data transfer.

Most people assume that passive mode causes fewer problems for firewalls than active mode, but note that the client opens a connection to an ephemeral (not well-known) port when using passive mode. Some firewalls and Cisco access-list filters block this. Also, the response from the server comes from an ephemeral port and goes to an ephemeral port. Firewalls and Cisco access-list filters might block this also. On a Cisco router you can use the established keyword with an access list to avoid this second problem. The established keyword tells the router to allow packets with the ACK bit set. The SYN ACK from the server has the ACK bit set.

The overall message we would like to leave you with is that FTP is problematic in environments with NAT gateways, firewalls, and Cisco access lists, whether you use active or passive mode. FTP was designed in the 1970s. At that time, the Internet was a closed network connecting universities, research institutes, government agencies, and a few companies involved in the development of the protocols. Security was not a concern because the network was private. Today, FTP is mistakenly used for mission-critical applications on the public Internet. There have been many attempts to make FTP more secure, but they cause troubleshooting issues and also fail to fix the most glaring security problem with FTP, which is that it sends the username and password in clear text.

Protocols for Electronic Mail

On campus TCP/IP networks, two e-mail protocols are common: SMTP and POP. SMTP is usually used for sending mail to an e-mail server, and POP is used for retrieving mail from an e-mail server. The RFC for SMTP (RFC 2821) includes commands for sending mail to a server or sending mail directly to an end user, but SMTP is no longer used to send mail directly to an end user. On the Internet and intranets, e-mail is delivered via SMTP to a server that also supports POP. Users access the server and retrieve their mail using POP. The current version of POP is version 3, and you will often see POP referred to as *POP3*. POP3 is defined in RFC 1939.

POP3 is not intended to provide extensive manipulation of mail on a server. Typically, mail is downloaded and then deleted. RFC 2060 describes a more advanced and complex protocol for handling e-mail called the Internet Message Access Protocol, Version 4rev1 (IMAP4rev1). For more information about IMAP, see RFC 2060 and the Web site at www.imap.org.

Both SMTP and POP run on top of TCP. SMTP uses Port 25; POP3 uses port 110. Both SMTP and POP open a single TCP connection, rather than using two connections like FTP does. Simplicity was one of the major design goals for these protocols. and for that reason the protocols generally don't require much troubleshooting. (Configuring end user stations and servers to correctly handle e-mail messages, user accounts, attachments, and so on is rife with troubleshooting issues, but that is outside the realm of this book.)

SMTP Protocol Analysis

SMTP is a client/server protocol. After establishing a TCP connection, SMTP clients send commands as ASCII strings that start with four uppercase ASCII characters, followed by optional parameters and a carriage return and line feed. The server generates three-digit replies similar to FTP replies. The replies include a status code. A typical SMTP session includes the following steps:

1. The client sends a TCP SYN to the well-known SMTP port (Port 25) on the server. The client uses an ephemeral port as the source port.

2. The server sends the client a SYN ACK from Port 25 to the ephemeral port on the client.

3. The client sends an ACK. The client uses this connection to send SMTP commands and the server uses the connection to send SMTP replies.

4. The server sends a Welcome message in an unsolicited reply with a status code of 220.

5. The client sends an extended hello (EHLO) or hello (HELO) command that specifies the client's host name. (HELO is not a typo. Remember most SMTP commands are only four characters.) The EHLO command allows the client to specify whether it supports any SMTP extensions. The server replies to the EHLO or HELO command with a positive reply that has a status code of 250.

6. The client resets the mail session with a RSET command and the server replies with a 250 positive reply after resetting the mail session and flushing any old data. This RSET command may come as a surprise when you first analyze SMTP trace files, but it is normal.

7. The client sends a RCTP TO command that specifies the recipient's e-mail address for the message being sent. The server replies saying that it will forward the message. The status code is 250.

8. The client sends a DATA command and the server responds with `354 start your message`.

9. The client sends a message ID, the current date, some e-mail message header data, and finally the actual message, which is often divided into small 200- to 300-byte TCP segments. The server responds with `250 message received OK`.

10. The client sends a QUIT command, to which the server responds with `221 closing connection`.

11. The client closes the TCP connection with a FIN. The server ACKs the FIN and sends its own FIN, which the client ACKs.

SMTP Replies

SMTP servers send SMTP replies, which consist of a three-digit number (transmitted as three alphanumeric characters) followed by some text. The first digit (x) denotes whether a response is good, bad, or incomplete. The second digit (y) specifies the type of reply. The third digit (z) provides finer gradation for the categories specified by the first two digits. Table 9.12 shows the five broad categories for replies.

Table 9.13 shows the meaning of the second digit in an SMTP reply.

Table 9.12 SMTP Reply Code Categories

REPLY CODE	MEANING	DESCRIPTION
1yz	Positive preliminary reply	The server received the command but is still working on it. Expect another reply before sending another command.
2yz	Positive completion reply	The command was completed successfully.
3yz	Positive intermediate reply	The client needs to take further action for the request to be fulfilled.
4yz	Transient negative completion reply	The requested action did not take place but can be retried.
5yz	Permanent negative completion reply	The requested action did not take place and should not be retried.

Table 9.13   SMTP Reply Code Subcategories

REPLY CODE	MEANING	DESCRIPTION
x0z	Syntax	The command had a syntax error, is syntactically correct but doesn't fit any functional category, is superfluous, or is not implemented.
x1z	Information	Replies to requests for information, such as status or help.
x2z	Unspecified	Reserved for future use.
x3z	Unspecified	Reserved for future use.
x4z	Unspecified	Reserved for future use.
x5z	Mail system status	Replies indicating the status of the receiver mail system with regards to the requested transfer or other mail system action.

POP3 Protocol Analysis

POP was designed to overcome the challenges associated with requiring SMTP server software to reside on every system that might receive e-mail. A workstation system might have insufficient resources (disk space, CPU power, memory) to keep an SMTP server resident and continuously running. Despite this, it is useful to be able to manage mail on these smaller systems. The systems often support a user interface that allows them to handle e-mail, so it makes sense to have a client protocol that can retrieve e-mail without requiring local server software. POP was designed to permit a workstation to dynamically access mail stored on a server in a *maildrop* set aside for the workstation. Mail is delivered to the POP server via SMTP, and the workstation can pick up the mail from the server whenever the user desires.

POP3 commands are formatted as three or four ASCII characters that may be followed by one or more parameters. All commands are terminated by a carriage return and line feed. Each parameter may be up to 40 characters in length. POP3 commands are more similar to FTP commands than they are to SMTP commands. POP3 commands include USER, PASS, LIST, RETR, DELE, STAT, NOOP, and QUIT, which also occur in FTP. POP3 also supports a RSET command like SMTP does.

POP3 responses consist of a status indicator, possibly followed by additional information. All responses are terminated by a carriage return and line feed and may be up

to 512 characters long. Although more status indicators may be defined in future versions of POP, only two are defined currently: positive (+OK) and negative (-ERR).
A typical POP3 session includes the following steps:

1. The client sends a TCP SYN to the well-known POP3 port (port 110) on the server. The client uses an ephemeral port as the source port.

2. The server sends the client a SYN ACK from Port 110 to the ephemeral port on the client.

3. The client sends an ACK. The client uses this connection to send POP3 commands and the server uses the connection to send POP3 replies.

4. The server sends a Welcome message in an unsolicited +OK reply.

5. The client sends a username and password with the USER and PASS commands. The server responds with +OK replies.

6. The client sends a STAT command. The server responds with a +OK reply and the number of messages in the client's maildrop.

7. The client sends a LIST command. The server responds with a +OK reply and a *scan listing* for each message in the client's maildrop. The scan listing includes a message ID and the size of the message in bytes. The client can also send a separate LIST command for each message, for example LIST 1, LIST 2, LIST 3, and so on.

8. The client sends a RETR command for each message. The server replies with +OK and the text of the message, possibly divided into TCP segments. POP3 uses full-size TCP segments, unlike SMTP.

9. The client may send a DELE command if the client's software is configured to not leave messages on the server (which is the preferred configuration from the point of view of most e-mail server administrators). The server replies with +OK message will be deleted.

10. The client sends a QUIT command, to which the server responds with +OK closing connection.

11. The client closes the TCP connection with a FIN. The server ACKs the FIN and sends its own FIN, which the client ACKs.

Summary

This chapter has provided information to help you troubleshoot and analyze transport- and application-layer protocols that commonly run on campus TCP/IP networks. The goal is to help you understand protocol behavior on your network and correctly decode protocol packets. Many of the protocols covered are quite simple, such as HTTP, SMTP, and POP3. Troubleshooting efforts for these protocols will probably focus on server administration and user errors. Nonetheless, it's a good idea to understand typical network traffic when a user surfs the Web and sends and retrieves e-mail, so that you can contrast normal traffic with abnormal traffic when problems occur. FTP is an application-layer protocol that is more complex than the others, and we have provided some information on the issues with FTP in campus networks that implement NAT gateways and firewalls.

The most important protocol covered in the chapter is TCP. To pass either the Wild-Packets Network Analysis Expert (NAX) or Cisco certification tests, you must understand TCP behavior, including connection establishment, windows, delayed ACKs, and slow start. To become a proficient troubleshooter, you should also learn to use the techniques modeled in this chapter for studying sequence and ACK numbers and the delta time between packets. There's no substitute for actual practice. We recommend that you use your own analyzer to track some typical and atypical TCP sessions and learn to use the fields in the TCP header for performance management.

The next few chapters cover other protocol stacks besides TCP/IP, including Novell NetWare, AppleTalk, and Windows networking. Much of what you learned in this chapter and the previous chapters will help you understand these protocol stacks, which include a variety of protocols that behave in similar ways to UDP, TCP, DNS, and the routing protocols covered in Chapter 8.

CHAPTER

10

Troubleshooting and Analyzing Campus IPX Networks

Novell, Inc. developed the Internetwork Packet Exchange (IPX) protocol suite in the early 1980s. The suite is also called *Novell NetWare*. Since that time, Novell has made a name for itself by offering reliable multiprotocol server software and useful configuration and troubleshooting tools. Novell continues to make innovative and practical networking products, despite competitors' attempts to declare the company dead or irrelevant. Today, NetWare servers support several protocol stacks. They can act as Apple Filing Protocol (AFP) servers, IBM Systems Network Architecture (SNA) gateways, Internet Protocol (IP) Network File System (NFS) servers, and Internet Web servers. This chapter focuses on the native IPX stack that allows client PCs and servers to communicate using the NetWare Core Protocol (NCP), and on the Novell protocols for routing and service discovery. The goal of the chapter is to help you understand the behavior of the fundamental IPX protocols in a campus network. To learn about the other protocols supported by Novell servers, such as AppleTalk, IP, and Windows networking, please see the other chapters in this book that cover those topics. To learn more about administering Novell servers, please see Novell documentation.

Novell NetWare Concepts

When we started developing this chapter, the first thing we heard was, "You don't need to talk about IPX because NetWare doesn't use it anymore now that NetWare is IP-based." When we considered what we actually observe in real-world Novell networks, however, it was clear that IPX has not yet gone away. Although many Novell NetWare networks are migrating to pure IP, there are still numerous small and medium-sized companies and universities that use the native IPX protocols.

During the 1980s, Novell dominated the client/server market. Novell's influence still pervades the market and the original NetWare protocols refuse to die, despite some scalability, interoperability, and performance problems. Novell made some implementation choices in the 1980s that still cause confusion for network engineers and certification candidates alike. To become an effective campus network engineer, and to pass Cisco and WildPackets certification tests, you need to learn some details about the IPX protocol suite, and perhaps unlearn some of the myths you have heard about IPX.

One of the confusions that lives on after almost 20 years is the purpose of Novell's transport-layer Sequenced Packet Exchange (SPX) protocol. SPX behaves like Transmission Control Protocol (TCP), and people assume that its role is as important as the role played by TCP in IP networks. This is not the case. SPX is used for the RCONSOLE program, which allows remote server administration, and by some SNA gateways. Printing processes on a NetWare network may also use SPX, depending on the version of NetWare in use. The most common NetWare protocol, NCP, does not use SPX. Figure 10.1 shows the NetWare protocol stack. Note that NCP provides application-layer services (file and print sharing) and also implements some functions that could be considered part of the presentation, session, and transport layers. NCP runs directly above IPX.

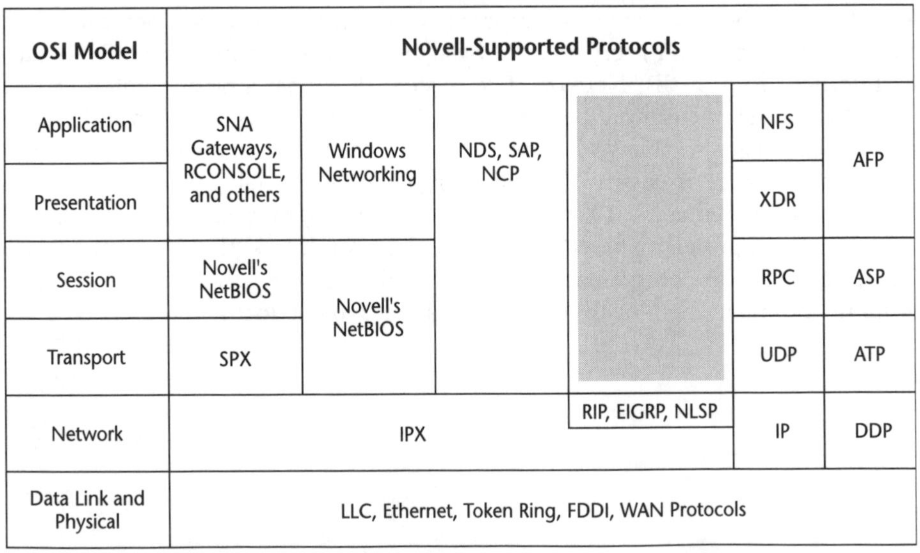

OSI Model	Novell-Supported Protocols						
Application	SNA Gateways, RCONSOLE, and others	Windows Networking	NDS, SAP, NCP		NFS	AFP
Presentation					XDR	
Session	Novell's NetBIOS	Novell's NetBIOS			RPC	ASP
Transport	SPX				UDP	ATP
Network	IPX			RIP, EIGRP, NLSP	IP	DDP
Data Link and Physical	LLC, Ethernet, Token Ring, FDDI, WAN Protocols						

Figure 10.1 The NetWare protocol suite.

IPX LAYERS

You will often hear this statement about Novell NetWare: "SPX provides a connection-oriented, reliable service and IPX provides a connectionless datagram service." The statement is true at face value; however, it implies that SPX and IPX are alternative peers in the communication stack. They aren't. SPX is reasonably consistent with the Open System Interconnection (OSI) definition of a transport-layer protocol and is carried on top of the IPX network layer.

IPX is based on the Internet Datagram Protocol (IDP) that Xerox designed as part of the Xerox Network Services (XNS) protocol suite in the 1970s. IPX, as a network-layer protocol, does in fact provide a connectionless datagram service, but this service carries many different upper-layer protocols across a NetWare internetwork, including SPX, NCP, and Novell's Network Basic Input/Output System (NetBIOS). There are some specialized applications that use IPX directly by implementing vendor-specific IPX sockets to carry their data. In these cases the connectionless datagram nature of IPX is more apparent.

In the XNS protocol stack, there are actually two Layer 4 protocols. The XNS Sequenced Packet Protocol (SPP) was the basis for Novell's SPX and is connection oriented. The XNS Packet Exchange Protocol (PEP) provides a semireliable packet delivery service for single packet exchanges. PEP is a request-response protocol that uses a packet ID to match responses to requests. A sending host sets the packet ID, then looks for PEP responses containing the same packet ID. The sender retransmits the packet if no response arrives. PEP formed the foundation for NCP. Although NCP does much more than PEP, the bottom sublayer of NCP resembles PEP. NCP—in particular the bottom sublayer of NCP—runs directly above IPX, and does not use SPX.

NetWare supports two native IPX routing protocols—the distance-vector Novell Routing Information Protocol (RIP) and the link-state NetWare Link Services Protocol (NLSP). On Cisco routers you can also use the Enhanced Interior Gateway Protocol (EIGRP) to accomplish routing on an IPX network. The routing protocols work with Novell's protocol for resource discovery and advertisement, which is the Service Advertising Protocol (SAP). Novell also supports a sophisticated directory service protocol called the NetWare Directory Services (NDS). NDS is a globally distributed network database that replaces the *bindery* mechanisms used in previous versions of NetWare. In an NDS-based network, a user logs into the entire network and can access all network services.

IPX Addressing

As is the case with most protocols that run on an internetwork, IPX assigns an identifier to each node and to each network. An IPX node ID is the same as the 6-byte data link layer address assigned to the Network Interface Card (NIC). This means there is no need for an Address Resolution Protocol (ARP) to map network-layer addresses to data link layer addresses. If a source knows the destination network-layer node address, then it also knows the destination data link layer address. The IPX header contains a Destination Node field and a Source Node field. When viewing an IPX packet with an Ethernet protocol analyzer, these fields should be the same as the destination and source addresses in the Ethernet header.

The IPX network number uniquely identifies each network. The network number serves as the basis for IPX packet forwarding, just like an IP subnet does in an IP network. An IPX network number is 4 bytes and is usually displayed and configured as a hexadecimal number. An IPX hexadecimal network number can contain up to eight digits, including zeros. Leading zeros are usually not displayed. For example, 0x12345678, 0xD7, and 0xCC1E are all valid network numbers. Many network administrators use a hexadecimal number that matches the IP subnet for the network; for example, subnet 172.16.10.0 becomes 0xAC.10.0A.00.

If a sending node sets the source network to 0x0, it means that the sending node does not know the local network to which it is connected. When a node first boots, for example, it does not know its own network number. When a sending node sets the destination network to 0x0, the destination node is assumed to be on the same network segment as the source node. If a router receives a packet with a destination network number of 0x0, the router assumes that the packet's source and destination nodes are attached to the same segment.

When assigning a network number to a network, whether on a NetWare server or a Cisco router, the number must agree with the number that other servers and routers use for that network. This may seem like an obvious statement, but administrators often make mistakes in this area. Some versions of NetWare can automatically detect the network number and data link frame type used on an IPX network. (The *Ethernet Frames in IPX Environments* section discusses data link frame types in more detail.) A NetWare server acting as a router can broadcast RIP request packets to the network. From the responses it receives, the server determines the network number and frame type it needs to use.

Older NetWare servers (running NetWare versions 3 and 4) have an additional identifier called an *internal network number*. This is a unique hexadecimal number between one and eight digits that is assigned to the server at installation. The internal network is a logical network that NetWare uses to advertise services and route IPX packets to the physical networks attached to the server. The internal network number was a workaround to some routing and connectivity challenges that were present in NetWare 2. In modern networks, an internal network is also used on routers running NLSP, as discussed in the *NetWare Link Services Protocol* section later.

CAUTION Servers should not be configured to use an internal network number that is the same as any other network in use on the internetwork. Many administrators assume that the choice of an internal network number doesn't matter. It does matter. The number must be unique on the internetwork. The number appears in routing updates and is used for forwarding packets.

IPX addresses also contain a socket number. The next section covers sockets in more detail, but suffice it to say at this point that the socket number is a 2-byte number that identifies the ultimate destination of an IPX packet within a node. This destination is a process, such as routing (RIP) or file sharing (NCP), that operates within the node.

You may see IPX addresses written as `network.node.socket`. For example, the address `C0FFEE.00000C3456B2.453` identifies the RIP process (Socket 453) on the `00000C3456B2` node, which resides on the `C0FFEE` network. The node seems to be associated with a Cisco NIC (notice the Cisco vendor code 00000C). The network administrator used a creative hexadecimal number for the network ID (C0FFEE), which is common practice on NetWare networks, although not a very good idea. It's better to use a network number that means something that relates to the network's purpose or will help you find the network when it's having problems. It's also good practice to use network numbers that can be aggregated (summarized) with other network numbers to reduce routing overhead. NLSP supports summarization, although RIP does not.

IPX Packets

IPX is a connectionless datagram protocol that delivers packets across an IPX internetwork and provides addressing services to IPX devices. As is the case with all connectionless protocols, each packet is treated individually and has no logical or sequential relation to any other packet. Nodes can send packets without establishing a connection first. There is also no guarantee or verification of successful delivery of datagrams. Protocols above IPX, such as NCP, provide reliability, if it is required.

IPX uses a 30-byte packet header. The minimum IPX packet size, excluding the data link header and trailer, is 30 bytes (a packet with just a header). IPX allows packet sizes up to 65,535 bytes. Historically, the maximum size of routed IPX packets was only 576 bytes, counting the IPX header and data. NetWare versions in use today (beginning with NetWare 386) support larger routed packet sizes. Be careful if you increase the packet size to be larger than the Maximum Transmission Unit (MTU) sizes in use on the routed network, however. Unlike IP, IPX does not support fragmentation and reassembly.

Figure 10.2 shows the structure of the IPX packet header. Table 10.1 explains the fields in the header.

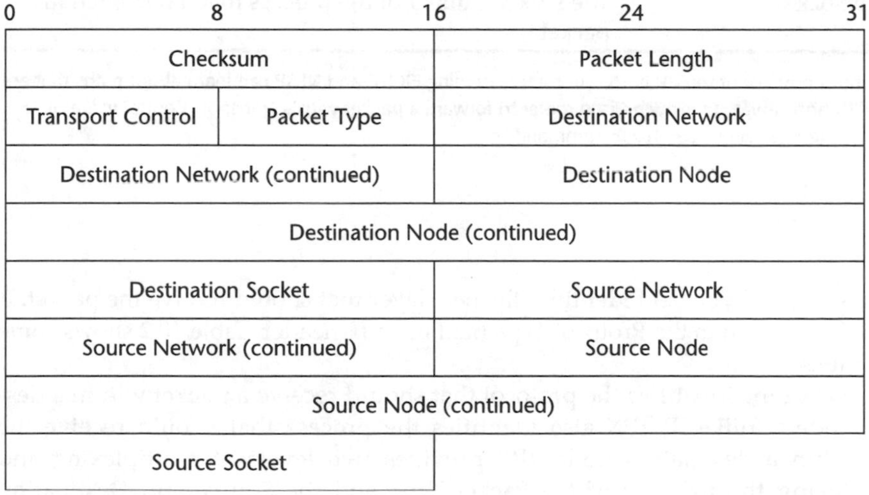

0	8	16	24	31
Checksum		Packet Length		
Transport Control	Packet Type	Destination Network		
Destination Network (continued)		Destination Node		
Destination Node (continued)				
Destination Socket		Source Network		
Source Network (continued)		Source Node		
Source Node (continued)				
Source Socket				

Figure 10.2   The IPX header.

Table 10.1 Fields in an IPX Header

FIELD	EXPLANATION
Checksum	Checks the integrity of the IPX packet. The checksum is not used in most versions of NetWare, in which case it is set to 0xFFFF.
Packet Length	Length, in bytes, of the complete packet, which is the length of the IPX header plus the length of the data.
Transport Control	The number of routers a packet has traversed on the way to its destination. Sending nodes set the Transport Control field to 0. When a router receives a packet that requires forwarding, it increments the field by 1. When this value reaches 16, the packet is discarded under the assumption that a routing loop might be occurring.*
Packet Type	Type of service offered or required by the packet. See Table 10.2 for a list of packet types.
Destination Network	The number of the network to which the destination node is attached.
Destination Node	The address of the destination node, which is the same as the data link address.
Destination Socket	The socket number of the destination process.
Source Network	The number of the network to which the source node is attached.
Source Node	The address of the source node, which is the same as the data link address.
Source Socket	The socket number of the process that transmitted the packet.

*The maximum hop count for RIP is 15, but routers running EIGRP and NLSP can learn about paths that are more than 15 hops away. To allow a Cisco router to forward a packet with a Transport Control value of 15 or more, use the `ipx maximum-hops` command.

The IPX Packet Type field identifies the next layer that should receive the packet. It is similar in function to the Protocol Type field in an IP header. Table 10.2 shows some typical values.

The packet type identifies the protocol that should receive a packet within a destination node. Unlike IP, IPX also identifies the process that should receive the packet within a destination node. IPX provides two levels of multiplexing and demultiplexing through use of the Packet Type and the Source and Destination Socket numbers.

Table 10.2   IPX Packet Types

TYPE	PROTOCOL
0x00	Novell (used by NLSP, older versions of SAP, EIGRP, and others)
0x01	RIP
0x04	SAP
0x05	SPX
0x11	NCP
0x14	Novell NetBIOS

The socket numbers are similar in function to the port numbers found in the TCP and User Datagram Protocol (UDP) transport-layer protocols in the IP protocol stack. A process that wishes to communicate on a network requests that the operating system assign a socket number to it. Any packets that IPX receives that are addressed to that socket are passed to the process. On a network of clients and servers, the server usually listens on a specific socket for service requests. In this case, the source socket is not necessarily the same or even significant.

Socket numbers between 0x4000 and 0x7FFF are dynamic sockets; these are used by clients to communicate with servers. Socket numbers between 0x8000 and 0xFFFF are well-known sockets; these are assigned by Novell to specific processes. Software developers who write NetWare applications can ask Novell to reserve a socket number and get on the list of well-known sockets. Novell also reserves several sockets for use in the NetWare environment. Table 10.3 is a partial list of NetWare socket numbers.

Table 10.3   IPX Socket Numbers and Processes

SOCKET	PROCESS
0x0002	Cisco IPX ping
0x0451	NCP server
0x0452	SAP
0x0453	RIP
0x0455	Novell NetBIOS
0x0456	Diagnostics
0x85BE	EIGRP
0x9001	NLSP
0x9004	IPXWAN
0x9086	Novell IPX ping

Ethernet Frames in IPX Environments

When Novell invented the NetWare protocols in the early 1980s, the Institute of Electrical and Electronics Engineers (IEEE) had not yet standardized 802.3 and 802.2. Novell guessed incorrectly about what would become the standard method for encapsulating upper layers in 802.3 packets. Novell encapsulated IPX in an 802.3 header without an 802.2 Logical Link Control (LLC) header, a frame structure that is not supported by IEEE. Novell realized its mistake a few years later and offered three standard encapsulation methods, in addition to the original method, which became known as *Novell raw*. This issue has confused network engineers for years.

Figure 10.3 shows the frame types supported by Novell on an Ethernet network. (The figure is essentially the same as Figure 3.4 because Ethernet frames were also discussed in Chapter 3, although Figure 10.3 shows Novell names for the frame types.) If you are analyzing a NetWare network, you must be able to differentiate between the frame types, and you should be aware of the features, statistics, and capabilities your analyzer has to help you understand which frames are present in a trace file.

The Ethernet_II frame type at the top of Figure 10.3 is a standard Ethernet II frame. (Ethernet II also goes by the following names: Ethernet 2, Ethernet V2, Version 2 Ethernet, Ethernet Type 2, and DIX.) The EtherType (ET in Figure 10.3) for Novell is 0x8137. When Novell developed the NetWare protocols, many vendors assumed that Ethernet II would disappear, as IEEE was busy working on the official 802.3 standard. Ethernet II is still here today, however, probably because the protocol that became most widespread (IP) uses Ethernet II frames.

On a Cisco router, to use Ethernet II frames for Novell packets on an IPX network, use the `ipx network {network} encapsulation arpa` command. The WildPackets EtherPeek protocol analyzer decodes these frames as simply Ethernet frames, with the Protocol Type (EtherType) decoded as Novell NetWare. The analyzer groups these packets under an Ethernet Type 2 outline header in its protocol statistics reports.

> **NOTE** For a list of the different names for the different frames types used on Ethernet networks, please see Table 3.3 in Chapter 3. The table includes names used by both Cisco and WildPackets.

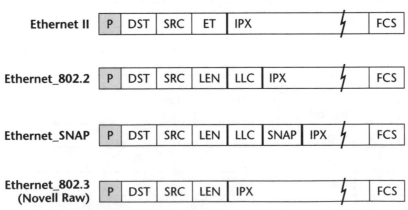

Figure 10.3 Novell Ethernet frame types.

THE MUCH MISUNDERSTOOD AND MALIGNED NOVELL RAW FRAME FORMAT

Many Cisco and other documents claim that the Novell raw (Ethernet_802.3 or novell-ether) frame format includes a 0xFFFF field at the data link layer that identifies the frame as an IPX frame. This is absolutely wrong. The 802.3 header in a Novell raw frame looks exactly like any other 802.3 header with a Destination Address, Source Address, and Length field. Recipients can only recognize the frame as being for IPX because they peek into the next layer where the IPX checksum is set to 0xFFFF. Recent versions of NetWare support IPX actually calculating a checksum, in which case the value of the checksum field is not 0xFFFF. If IPX is configured to use the checksum, then the Novell raw frame format cannot be used.

For years, network engineers explained the Novell raw frame format by calling Novell arrogant, saying that the company had no need to identify the protocol being carried by 802.3, because everyone would use IPX. (Remember Novell did almost corner the client/server market in the 1980s.) However, it's more likely that Novell simply envisioned a different method for demultiplexing packets. In Novell's vision, the software driver for the NIC receives a frame that does not identify the next layer. The driver, however, can pass the frame to the network operating system, which in this case would be NetWare. The network operating system can figure out what to do with the frame—process it as a native packet or give it to some other protocol, such as IP.

Recent versions of NetWare default to using the Ethernet_802.2 frame format, which is a good thing because then the frame has a protocol identifier (the DSAP of 0x0E). Older versions of NetWare are still quite prevalent, however. Older versions defaulted to the Ethernet_802.3 frame format. If possible, you should wean users from their old ways if they are running this frame format in a multiprotocol environment. The problem with the frame format is that when it arrives at a station configured to use 802.2, the 0xFFFF in the IPX header appears to be global (broadcast) SAPs. The checksum arrives in the same place in the packet where a DSAP and Source Service Access Point (SSAP) should be. This may cause a station to pass the frame to every process, which could result in performance problems.

The Ethernet_802.2 frame type illustrated in the next row in Figure 10.3 is a standard 802.3 and 802.2 frame. Most of the world would simply call this an 802.3 frame, but Novell calls it an 802.2 frame. The 802.2 LLC Service Access Point (SAP) for Novell is 0xE0. On a Cisco router, to use 802.2 frame formats for Novell packets, use the `ipx network {network} encapsulation sap` command. Notice that this SAP has nothing to do with the Novell application-layer Service Advertising Protocol which is also known as SAP. The networking industry unfortunately has many acronym collisions such as this.

The next row in Figure 10.3 shows the Subnetwork Access Protocol (SNAP) frame format. There's usually little reason to configure an Ethernet Novell network to use a SNAP frame format, but if there is a need, then Novell supports it, as does Cisco. On a Cisco router, to use SNAP frame formats for Novell packets, use the `ipx network {network} encapsulation snap` command.

The final row in Figure 10.3 shows the infamous Novell raw frame format, which Novell calls *Ethernet_802.3* and Cisco calls *novell-ether*. This is the encapsulation method that has caused so much controversy over the years. The technical problem with the format is that it has no way of specifying which network layer is carried in the frame. There isn't an EtherType field, a Destination Service Access Point (DSAP) field, or any other protocol identifier. As it turns out, multiprotocol applications, including routers and protocol analyzers, can recognize a Novell raw frame nonetheless because the first 2 bytes of the IPX header always start with the 0xFFFF checksum (for most versions and configurations of NetWare).

Configuring Multiple IPX Ethernet Frame Types on Cisco Routers

Although most IPX networks use a single Ethernet frame type, the need to use multiple types may arise. Cisco has two ways of handling this—*secondary addresses* and *subinterfaces*. Subinterfaces are the preferred method. Both methods allow networks that use different IPX Ethernet frame types to coexist on the same physical media. The router can route between the networks so that clients and servers configured with different frame types can communicate. To increase performance of the routing, make sure to configure the router to do *fast switching* in and out of the interface with the two networks, using the `ipx route-cache same-interface` command.

The following example shows a secondary address being added to interface Ethernet 0.

```
RouterA# config t
RouterA(config)# interface ethernet 0
RouterA(config-if)# ipx network 200 encapsulation arpa
RouterA(config-if)# ipx network 201 encapsulation novell-ether secondary
```

In this example, we created a second network that uses `novell-ether` encapsulation. The second network communicates on the same wire as the first network. You can create the networks in any order, but make sure the configuration for one of them includes the word *secondary*; otherwise, the second network number overwrites the first one. The outcome of the configuration in the example is that devices on Network 200 that use Ethernet II (`arpa`) frames can now communicate through the router with devices on Network 201 that use Novell raw (`novell-ether`) frames.

In the past, secondary addresses were quite common for both IPX and IP networks, but Cisco plans to discontinue support for them in future releases of the Cisco Internetwork Operating System (IOS) software. You should be familiar with secondary addresses and be able to recognize them when you see the commands, but do not plan to use them on your network.

The preferred method to support multiple frame types is to use subinterfaces. To create a subinterface, specify an actual interface number followed by a virtual (made-up) decimal number from 1 to 65,000, as shown in the following example:

```
RouterA# config t
RouterA(config)# interface ethernet 0
RouterA(config)# interface ethernet 0.200
```

```
RouterA(config-if)# ipx network 200 encapsulation arpa
RouterA(config)# interface ethernet 0.201
RouterA(config-if)# ipx network 201 encapsulation novell-ether
```

There's no requirement that the subinterface and IPX network number be the same, as shown in the example, but it's good practice to do it this way to simplify network documentation and understanding.

NOTE If a Cisco router receives IPX packets encapsulated with a frame type that the router has not been configured to support, you will see many format errors in the `show ipx traffic` command output. Format errors can also occur when the length of the received packet is smaller than 30 bytes or larger than the interface MTU, or when a router receives a packet with a corrupted header.

NetWare Core Protocol

NetWare Core Protocol (NCP) is the most widely used protocol in the IPX protocol stack. NCP is a connection-oriented, reliable client/server protocol that allows client software to manipulate files on a server using commands such as Open, Close, Read, Write, Create, Delete, and so on. NCP also provides print services to allow users to share printers and send print jobs to a print queue on a print server. Another job of NCP is security services to verify passwords, set access privileges on files and directories, and set file attributes.

In traditional IPX networks, NCP runs directly above IPX. In modern Novell networks, NCP can also run above UDP or TCP. The information in this section about the NCP header and functionality applies regardless of which transport and network layer protocols are in use. For more information about NCP with TCP/IP, see the *IPX Networks in Transition* section near the end of this chapter.

The following EtherPeek output shows a typical NCP packet. In the example, the client (node 00:01:83:A0:28:CD on Network 0x1) is reading from a file on the file server located on Network 0x00094301. The file server uses the node ID that is traditionally used by file services within a server, which is 00:00:00:00:00:01.

```
802.3 Header
  Destination:          00:80:5F:05:77:29
  Source:               00:01:83:A0:28:CD
  Length:               50
IPX - NetWare Protocol
  Checksum:             0xFFFF
  Length:               50
  Transport Control:
  Reserved:             %0000
```

```
         Hop Count:              %0000
         Packet Type:            17   NCP - Netware Core Protocol
         Destination Network:    0x00094301
         Destination Node:       00:00:00:00:00:01
         Destination Socket:     0x0451  NetWare Core Protocol
         Source Network:         0x00000001
         Source Node:            00:01:83:A0:28:CD
         Source Socket:          0x4003   IPX Ephemeral
      NCP - Netware Core Protocol
         Request Type:           0x2222   Request
         Sequence number:        209
         Low number:             123
         Task number:            20
         High number:            0
         Function Code:          72   Read File Data
      Read File Data Request
         Unused:                 0x00
         File Handle:            0x02004A030300
         Starting Byte Offset: 0
         Number of Bytes To Read:1436
```

There are a few things to recognize in the analyzer output. First, the client is using
an 802.3 (Novell raw) Ethernet frame. Notice that there is an 802.3 Destination
Address, Source Address, and Length field. Immediately following the 802.3 header is
the IPX header, which starts with a checksum value of 0xFFFF, which is typical. At the
NCP layer, notice that the client is sending a request. (See `Request Type 0x2222`
`Request`.) In requests, the NCP header also includes a Function Code, which in this
case is 72 for `Read File Data`. NetWare assigns a file handle to a file when a client
opens it. (See `File Handle: 0x02004A030300`.) The file handle allows the client to
use a number to refer to the file, instead of a potentially long path and file name. The
file handle appears in the data portion of the packet, following the NCP header. The
basic NCP header, as shown in Figure 10.4, is 6 bytes.

The first field in the NCP header is the Request Type field. Table 10.4 shows the possible values for the Request Type.

The second field in the NCP header is a sequence number to track packets between
the client and server. A request and reply should have the same sequence number. The
client increases the sequence number with each request. Traditional NCP is what we
call a request-response or Ping-Pong protocol, because each request from the client
results in a response from the server. Novell also supports the *Burst Mode* protocol,
which behaves more like TCP, allowing a server to send multiple packets until the
client's receive window is full. Without Burst Mode, NCP behaves like its ancestor protocol, XNS PEP. The NCP sequence number is essentially the same as a PEP packet ID.

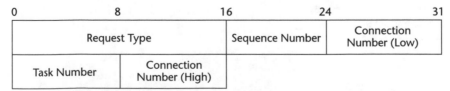

Figure 10.4   The NCP header format.

AVOIDING A PRINTER DISASTER

In addition to file sharing, NCP also provides print services to allow users to share printers and send print jobs to a print queue on a print server. A NetWare print server interrogates its print queue at periodic intervals to determine whether or not a document is waiting to be printed. When a printer is connected directly to a file server, the print server and the print queue both reside in the file server, so you don't see any network traffic associated with this polling process. The print queue is usually in the file server, but remote print servers are commonplace also. When a remote print server polls the queue, it can produce a tremendous amount of network traffic if you don't change the default polling timer.

By default, vendors of print servers (such as the JetDirect or NetPort print servers) set their default polling intervals to small values. A JetDirect polls the queue every 2 seconds unless it is reconfigured. A NetPort print server, using a zero polling time, sends a request to the server every 2/10 of a millisecond!

To determine a reasonable poll time for your print servers, consider how long it takes users to get up from their desks and walk over to the printer. As long as the activity light is blinking on the printer by the time they get there, everything's OK. Set the polling interval to a time that will make this happen. (20 seconds is often a good value.) Remember, if the polling interval is too long, then users will walk over to the printer, not see any activity, and go back to their desk and print the document a second time!

The *Low Number* and *High Number* fields in the NCP header are a connection identifier. When a client logs into a NetWare server, the server assigns the client a connection number, which is carried in two parts in the NCP header—in the Low Number and High Number fields. Novell added the High Number field to the header to support the 1000-user version of NetWare. The client and server interpret the two fields as a single 16-bit connection number. On a NetWare server statistics screen, you would not see the low-high format; you would see a single integer between 1 and 1000. The integer is derived by multiplying the high number by 256 and adding the low number. For example, if the low number = 3 and the high number = 2, then the actual connection number is 515 (because 2 * 256 = 512, and 512 + 3 = 515).

Table 10.4 NCP Request Types

TYPE	MEANING
1111	Create a service connection
2222	Service request
3333	Service reply
5555	Destroy a service connection
7777	Burst mode transfer
9999	Request being processed

NOTE When creating a protocol analyzer filter to select an NCP conversation on the basis of the connection number, remember that the Connection Number field is made up of two non-contiguous bytes. An advanced pattern match filter is needed to target the byte offsets associated with these two separate bytes.

Following the Low Number field in the NCP header is the Task Number field, which identifies the client task that is making the request. The server tracks these tasks and automatically deallocates resources when a task ends. With NCP requests, the basic header also includes an NCP *function code*. On replies, the header includes a *completion code* and *status flags*.

Watchdog Spoofing

NetWare file servers that support NCP can be configured to use Novell's *watchdog protocol* to check a client's connection periodically. When a client is logged into a server but has not transmitted a packet for some period of time (the default is 5 minutes), the server sends a watchdog packet to the client. If the client does not reply after 5 minutes, the server sends additional watchdog packets until 15 minutes have elapsed. If the client still has not replied, the server terminates the connection. This is a useful feature in environments where users have a tendency to forget to log out. Each client connection uses resources on a server. The goal of the watchdog protocol is to identify connections that are idle so resources for the connections can be released.

The watchdog frame consists of an IPX header followed by the connection number and a *signature character*. the signature character can be a question mark (?), the capital letter Y, or the capital letter N.

The exchange of watchdog packets can keep a network active. For networks that are billed based on the amount of connect time, administrators often have a goal to keep the network deactivated whenever possible. Many campus networks connect to other networks using Dial-on-Demand Routing (DDR) over ISDN, telephone, or serial links. A DDR link remains deactivated when nobody is using it. If there are multiple NCP clients and servers connected via the DDR link, the link may never deactivate if the watchdog protocol is in use. Depending on the telecommunications carrier, the bill can be quite a surprise!

You can avoid this problem by configuring your router to perform *watchdog spoofing*. This means that the router captures watchdog packets on their way to a client and responds on behalf of the client, without activating the DDR link. The command to configure this on a Cisco router is ipx watchdog-spoof. Figure 10.5 shows an example of a router doing NCP watchdog spoofing.

CAUTION When using IPX NCP watchdog spoofing, a client's connection remains active even if the user has gone home for the day. To avoid this problem, you may want to configure servers to execute a forced logout of all clients at a predetermined time (midnight, for example), so that all server connections are freed for the next day. Also, if you are using Cisco IOS 12.0(1)T or later, you can avoid the problem by setting the duration of IPX NCP watchdog spoofing. This way you can make sure the watchdog spoofing is disabled during certain periods, so that NetWare servers can clean up inactive connections.

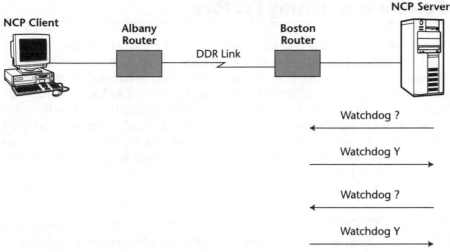

Figure 10.5 Watchdog spoofing for NCP.

Applications that use SPX, such as SNA gateways and RCONSOLE, have a similar feature, sometimes called *SPX keepalives* or *SPX watchdog.* The SPX watchdog protocol behaves a little differently than the NCP watchdog protocol. After a period of idleness, SPX software sends a keepalive packet with the same sequence number that it used in the last real packet that contained data. The sender expects an ACK to this keepalive. A router can be configured to send the ACK to avoid the need to send these packets over a DDR link. The command to configure this on a Cisco router is `ipx spx-spoof`. Figure 10.6 shows an example of a router doing SPX watchdog spoofing.

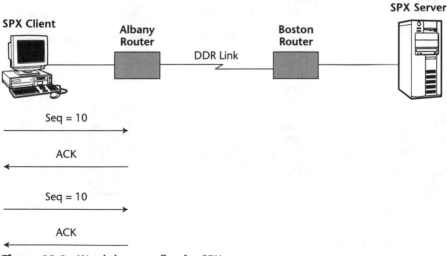

Figure 10.6 Watchdog spoofing for SPX.

IPX Service Advertising Protocol

Network resources, such as file and print servers, use SAP to advertise their services. Services are identified by a 2-byte hexadecimal Service Type number and a service name. Routers and servers listen to SAP packets from other servers and build a table of known services along with their network addresses. The routers and servers broadcast their SAP tables every 60 seconds out all interfaces except those blocked by the split-horizon rule. (Split horizon states that when sending information out an interface, a device should not announce information that was learned via the interface.) Cisco routers also send a SAP update when a change occurs, which is called a *flash update*. Novell clients can send a SAP query requesting information about file, print, or gateway services. The local router responds to the query with the network address of the requested service, and the client can then contact the service directly.

NOTE When talking about Novell NetWare, SAP stands for *Service Advertising Protocol*. For years, Cisco has spelled it out as *Service Advertisement Protocol*, but that is not how the creators of the protocol (Novell) spell it out. The most egregious spelling mistake that you will see in some documents is Novell's SAP spelled out as *Service Access Point*. From reading this book, you should know that a Service Access Point, in general terms, is a method for identifying the process that generated or should receive a packet. It's a protocol identifier, similar to a port number or the EtherType in an Ethernet II frame. In specific terms, *Service Access Point* is used in IEEE 802.2 to identify the sending and receiving processes. For example, as discussed earlier, Novell protocols can use an 802.2 frame format, in which case the DSAP and SSAP are both 0xE0.

Most SAP packets are sent as data link and network-layer broadcasts. Routers do not forward the broadcasts, although routers do build their own SAP tables and broadcast those. Figure 10.7 shows a router on Network 100 broadcasting a SAP packet that advertises a file server on Network 200.

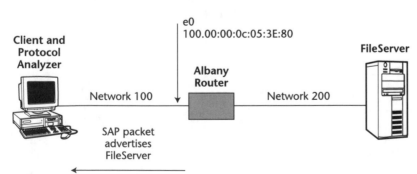

Figure 10.7 A router broadcasts a SAP packet that advertises a file server.

A SAP packet is encapsulated within an IPX header and includes a SAP header and data field that announces services and how to get to them. The following EtherPeek output shows the SAP packet that the router in Figure 10.7 sent to announce the availability of the file server on Network 200.

```
802.3 Header
  Destination:            FF:FF:FF:FF:FF:FF   Ethernet Broadcast
  Source:                 00:00:0c:05:3E:80
  Length:                 96
IPX - NetWare Protocol
  Checksum:               0xFFFF
  Length:                 96
  Transport Control:
  Reserved:               %0000
  Hop Count:              %0000
  Packet Type:            4   SAP
  Destination Network:    0x00000100
  Destination Node:       FF:FF:FF:FF:FF:FF
  Destination Socket:     0x0452   Service Advertising Protocol
  Source Network:         0x00000100
  Source Node:            00:00:0C:05:3E:80
  Source Socket:          0x0452   Service Advertising Protocol
SAP - Service Advertising Protocol
  Operation:              2   NetWare General Service Response
Service Advertising Set #1
  Service Type:           4   FILE SERVER
  Service Name: FileServer....................................
  Network:                512
  Node:                   00:00:00:00:00:01
  Socket:                 1105
  Inter networks/hops:    2
```

Notice that the router is configured to use the Ethernet_802.3 frame format on Network 100. (See the Destination Address, Source Address, and Length fields with no 802.2 header.) The IPX header immediately follows the 802.3 header. SAP packets are defined in the IPX header as Packet Type 4 and Socket Number 0x452. (Older versions of SAP used a Packet Type of 0.) The first 2 bytes of a SAP packet define an operation. Table 10.5 shows the possible values for the SAP operation.

Table 10.5 SAP Operations

OPERATION	MEANING
1	Request
2	Response
3	Get nearest server request
4	Get nearest server response

Table 10.6 SAP Service Types

TYPE	MEANING
0x0001	User
0x0002	User group
0x0003	Print queue
0x0004	File server
0x0005	Job server
0x0006	Gateway
0x0007	Print server
0x0009	Archive server
0x000A	Job queue
0x000B	Administrative object
0x0021	SNA gateway
0x0024	Remote bridge server
0x0027	TCP/IP gateway
0x0047	Advertising print server
0x8000-0x7FFF	Reserved
0xFFFF	Wildcard

The next 2 bytes in a SAP header define the service type, which can be one of the values shown in Table 10.6.

The service name is a 48-byte field. In the example, the name is *FileServer* followed by numerous null (0x00) characters. The file server resides on Network 0x200, which EtherPeek shows in decimal (512). The file server's node address is 0x00 00 00 00 00 01. The NCP file service process on the file server resides at Socket 0x0451, which EtherPeek shows in decimal (1105). See Table 10.3 for a list of sockets.

The final field shown in the SAP packet is the *Intervening Network Count* field, which EtherPeek calls the *Internetwork/Hops* field and some Novell documents call a *Hop Count*. The goal of the field is to let recipients know the distance to a service. We know from Figure 10.7 that the file server is connected to Network 0x200, which is directly connected to the router. Then why does the router claim that the server is two hops away? The router is really saying that there are two networks between users on Network 100 and the server on Network 200. The two networks are Network 100 and Network 200. It's a strange way of counting, but it's important to know that SAP counts this way. Understanding SAP (and RIP) counts will help you use SAP and RIP packets to draw a network map that accurately places networks and services.

SAP REFUSES TO DIE

We have worked on many networks where the administrator assured us that SAP was disabled when it really wasn't. We often discover numerous SAP packets coming from two sources—clients and printers. Clients often have the Novell protocol stack bound to the Ethernet card, even though IPX is not in use on the internetwork. This causes clients to send SAP Get Nearest Server queries repeatedly. HP JetDirect print servers also send SAPs to advertise their presence every 60 seconds by default, depending on the version and configuration of the print server software. To make matters worse, in both situations, the client and print server are often configured to send the SAP packets with all four frame types. Four frames are generated for each request or announcement!

Both of these situations should be fixed. Remember that a broadcast packet causes an interrupt on the Central Processing Unit (CPU) of every device in the broadcast domain. Older CPUs on large, fast switched networks are especially susceptible to performance degradation caused by numerous broadcasts. We have found that older CPUs seem to be prevalent in the types of networks where SAP is still running, whether by design, by mistake, or simply because older networks have a legacy that includes IPX.

Only seven services are allowed per SAP packet, so on some networks numerous SAP packets are sent, even though split horizon is used. When a router needs to send multiple SAP packets to output its entire SAP table, it sends the packets immediately following each other. This can cause problems for slow recipients. You can slow down the router by increasing the time between packets with the `ipx default-output-sap-delay` command. (You can also configure a router to send more than seven services per SAP with the `ipx sap-max-packetsize` command. Although this goes against Novell's specifications, it doesn't seem to cause any problems.)

SAP is pervasive on networks based on NetWare 3.11 and earlier, but is less frequently found on networks based on NetWare 4.0 and later. With those versions, clients can locate services by consulting an NDS server and by using the Internet Engineering Task Force (IETF) Service Location Protocol (SLP). With some versions, SAP is still required, however, so that clients can locate an NDS server. When analyzing a network that has been upgraded to NetWare 4.0 or later, don't be surprised to see a small amount of SAP traffic, even if you think you have disabled it. On the other hand, if you see a lot of SAP traffic, you should investigate where it is coming from and disable it.

SAP Filters

The amount of traffic caused by IPX SAP can be a problem for low-capacity circuits and routers with insufficient processing power and memory. SAP filters can mitigate the problem, although filters require CPU processing and so are not appropriate on a router that already has high CPU usage. Most large networks have routers that are capable of handling SAP filters, however, and the filters improve network performance by limiting bandwidth usage by SAPs. SAP filters also facilitate the implementation of security and access policies. If a service is filtered, then users who shouldn't get to it can't get to it.

A SAP filter is implemented with an access list numbered in the 1000 to 1099 range. Recent versions of the Cisco IOS software also support named SAP filters. To create a named SAP filter, use the `ipx access-list sap name` command, which puts you into access list configuration mode, where you enter the same parameters you would enter with a numbered access list. The command to configure a numbered access list is as follows:

```
access-list access-list-number
{deny | permit} network [.node]
[network-mask.node-mask]
[service-type[server-name]]
```

For example, to set up an access list to filter SAPs from a file server whose name is BadServer and whose address is 11.0000.0000.0001, you would use the following command:

```
access-list 1000 deny 11.0000.0000.0001 451 BadServer
```

As with any access list, keep these caveats in mind:

- A router scans the access list entries in the order that you enter them. The router uses the first matching entry. To improve performance, we recommend that you place the most commonly used entries near the beginning of the access list.

- An implicit "deny all" entry is defined at the end of an access list, unless you include an explicit permit at the end of the list.

- For numbered access lists, all new entries to an existing list are placed at the end of the list. You cannot add an entry to the middle of a list. The solution is to delete the access list and reenter it with the new entries.

- For named access lists, all new entries to an existing list are placed at the end of the list also. You cannot add entries to the middle of a list with named access lists either. However, you can remove specific entries using the `no deny` and `no permit` commands, rather than deleting the entire access list.

Once you have configured an access list, you must apply it to an interface. To apply SAP filters to an interface, use one of the following commands in interface configuration mode:

ipx input-sap-filter {access-list-number | name}. Filters incoming service advertisements.

ipx output-sap-filter {access-list-number | name}. Filters outgoing service advertisements.

ipx router-sap-filter {access-list-number | name}. Filters service advertisements received from a particular router.

Get Nearest Server

One of Novell's goals with NetWare was that clients shouldn't need much, if any, configuration. There is no requirement for a user or network administrator to configure an IPX client with either a network number or node ID. The client learns which network it is on when it boots and uses its NIC address for its network-layer node ID.

When an IPX client boots, it broadcasts a SAP Get Nearest Server request. Servers on the local LAN respond. If there are no servers on the local LAN, routers can respond. Because routers have a SAP table, they can tell a client how to get to a server. The response includes the network number where the nearest server resides, which may be the local LAN or a network on the other side of a router.

After discovering the nearest server, the client broadcasts a RIP request to find the network on which the nearest server resides. Routers or servers answer the RIP request and provide the client with a route to the nearest server. (Most NetWare servers also act as routers, so they can do this task as well as hardware routers.) The source network number in the IPX header of the RIP response is also useful, because the client can learn its own network number from that information. Once the client knows its own network number and the identity and location of a server, it can connect to the server and start the login process, using NCP packets. Figure 10.8 summarizes the client initialization process. The figure illustrates a case where a file server is not on the local LAN and a router responds to the SAP and RIP packets that the client sends.

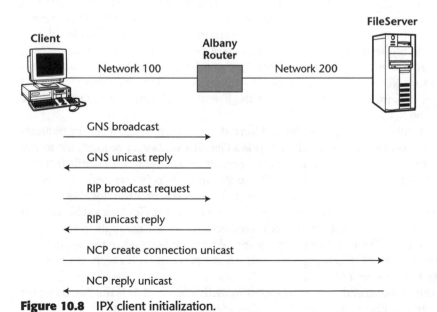

Figure 10.8   IPX client initialization.

Cisco Routers and Get Nearest Server

As mentioned, routers can help a client initialize by answering the Get Nearest Server and RIP requests. This is good news and bad news. Allowing a router to respond removes the need to have a server on every LAN where clients reside. The bad news is that routers may be too aggressive with their assistance. One problem that can occur is that a router responds before any servers have a chance to reply, and the router may not have the best information regarding the nearest server. On a Cisco router, you can configure a router's behavior with respect to Get Nearest Server requests. You can set the delay time in responding to the requests or you can disable the sending of responses altogether.

With older versions of Cisco IOS software, by default, routers always respond to Get Nearest Server requests and send the response immediately. To disable Get Nearest Server responses on a per-interface basis, use the `ipx gns-reply-disable` command in interface configuration mode. You can also configure a router to wait a short amount of time before responding, in case there are servers on the LAN that should respond first. Use the `ipx gns-response-delay` global configuration command to configure a router to wait before responding. The command is also supported as an interface configuration command. To override the global delay value for a specific interface, use the command in interface configuration mode.

With newer versions of IOS software, a router responds to Get Nearest Server requests only if appropriate. For example, if the router knows there are servers on the local LAN (from hearing their SAP packets), the router does not respond to Get Nearest Server requests on that LAN.

When there are no servers on the local LAN, the default method of responding to Get Nearest Server requests is to respond with the server whose availability was learned most recently. This can result in the server in the response becoming overwhelmed with NCP connection requests. To configure a router to respond with a different server each time, using a round-robin approach, use the `ipx gns-round-robin` global configuration command. Round-robin means that the router selects the next server in the list for each request, until it reaches the end of the list, at which time it goes back to the beginning of the list.

One tricky troubleshooting issue related to routers and Get Nearest Server requests has to do with access lists. When a client sends a Get Nearest Server request, the router may reply with a server which the client can't actually reach because of traffic filtering implemented with IPX access lists (in the 800 to 899 and 900 to 999 ranges). This leaves the client in a strange state, having learned about its nearest server but not able to reach it. The worst case is when the client receives a valid reply to the Get Nearest Server and RIP requests, but then cannot get its NCP connection request through to the server because of filters. NCP will continue trying for many minutes, giving the appearance to the PC user that the PC has hung. The mouse and keyboard won't work because the PC is waiting for network I/O.

To avoid the problem of the router responding with a server that is not reachable (or with a server that is inappropriate for any other reason), you can create filters that control which servers are included in the Get Nearest Server responses. First create a SAP filter access list and then apply a Get Nearest Server filter to an interface with the `ipx output-gns-filter` command.

IPX Routing

Novell NetWare networks have three options for routing—IPX RIP, NLSP, and EIGRP. NLSP is newer than RIP and is gaining limited popularity in large organizations that haven't migrated to pure IP yet. RIP is still common at many small and medium-size companies, and EIGRP is a good option for large IPX networks with Cisco routers. You can also use static and default routing in a NetWare network with the `ipx route` IOS command. IPX also has a concept of a *route of last resort*, in other words, a default route that a router uses if none of the other entries in the routing table match the destination network.

> **NOTE** Many of the features of IPX routing mirror the features discussed in Chapter 8. If you see a term in this chapter that you don't recognize, you may want to review Chapter 8, which covers general routing concepts.

When Novell invented NLSP, it reserved the 0xFFFFFFFE network number to mean the default route for both NLSP and RIP. Cisco adopted this standard. Original RIP implementations allowed the use of 0xFFFFFFFE to identify an actual network in an internetwork. You should make sure your IPX internetwork no longer uses 0xFFFFFFFE, or you could have problems with recent implementations of RIP or NLSP. If you must use 0xFFFFFFFE for some reason, you can disable the default handling of the network number with the `no ipx default-route` command.

When a Cisco router sends IPX routing packets, the source network address in the IPX header is the number for the network onto which the packet is being sent. On LANs, the node ID is the interface data link layer address. WAN serial interfaces don't have a data link layer address, however. You can configure the address that should be used on a serial interface when you enable IPX routing with the `ipx routing` command. If you do not specify the node ID, the IOS software uses the data link address of the first Ethernet, Token Ring, or FDDI interface. If there are no valid LAN interfaces, the software randomly assigns a node ID using a number based on the system clock. It's a good idea to know the node ID for a serial interface because then you can ping it.

> **CAUTION** If you use both DECnet and IPX routing on an interface, you should enable DECnet routing first, then enable IPX routing without specifying the optional node ID. If you enable DECnet routing after enabling IPX routing, routing for IPX stops working because DECnet forces a change in the data link layer address of an interface.

By default, Cisco IPX routing learns and uses only one path to a given IPX network. IPX routing doesn't do load sharing across multiple paths by default. You can use the `ipx maximum-paths` command on a Cisco router to permit load sharing on equal-cost paths. For example, to load-share over four equal-cost paths, use `ipx maximum-paths 4`. The behavior of IPX load-sharing depends on the switching mode the router uses for forwarding packets. Switching modes for IPX do not correspond exactly to switching modes for IP on the router. The three main switching modes for IPX are as follows:

> **Process switching.**   Load sharing is done packet by packet (like IP).
>
> **Fast switching.**   Load sharing is still done packet by packet (unlike IP).
>
> **Autonomous switching.**   Load sharing is done by destination (like IP).

IPX Routing Information Protocol

IPX RIP is similar to IP RIP but differs in minor ways. IPX RIP uses *ticks* for its main routing metric. One tick is approximately 1/18 of a second. Ticks specify the amount of delay on a path; however, they are not dynamically calculated. RIP considers a LAN to be one tick and a WAN to be six ticks by default. If two paths have an equal tick count, RIP uses hop count as a tie breaker. If two paths have both an equal tick count and an equal hop count, Cisco routers break the tie by looking at the local interface delay value. In most cases, the default tick values for LANs and WANs are accurate and there is no need to change them. In some cases—for example, an exceptionally fast or slow WAN interface—you may need to adjust an interface's default ticks value with the `ipx delay ticks` command.

RIP sends the entire routing table (after applying split horizon) every 60 seconds. Cisco's RIP implementation also sends immediate (flash) updates when a link fails or when a new network is enabled.

On large networks, the amount of traffic caused by RIP (and SAP) can cause problems. You can configure Cisco routers to send RIP and SAP updates less or more frequently than the 60 seconds dictated by Novell standards using the `ipx update interval {rip | sap} {value | changes-only}` command. This is risky, however. All routers in an internetwork must use the same timer to avoid problems with routes and services appearing and disappearing. Changing the update timer also affects the invalid and removal timers. A router marks an IPX route as invalid if no routing updates are heard for the route within three times the value of the update interval. A router removes an IPX route from the routing table if no routing updates are heard for the route within four times the value of the update interval. A router advertises an invalid route with a hop count of 16. (Surprisingly, the router doesn't adjust the ticks count when advertising invalid routes, just the hop count.)

Because of a limitation on the size of a RIP packet, only 50 routes are allowed per packet, so on large networks, multiple packets are sent. When a router needs to send multiple RIP packets to output its entire routing table, it sends the packets immediately following each other. This can cause problems for slow recipients. You can slow down the router by increasing the time between packets with the `ipx default-output-rip-delay` command.

Figure 10.9 shows an IPX network that we will use to illustrate a RIP packet. RIP packets look exactly like you would expect them to. They list networks with ticks and hop counts.

The following example is a RIP packet sent by the Charlotte router in Figure 10.9. Charlotte is advertising Network 0x400, which is directly connected to the router's serial port, and Network 0x500, which is on an Ethernet LAN on the other side of a router that connects to Charlotte's serial port. Charlotte is sending this packet onto the 0x100 Ethernet LAN.

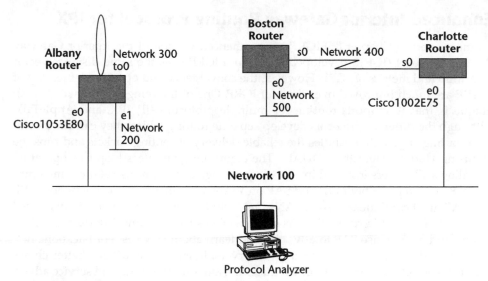

Figure 10.9   An IPX network using RIP.

```
802.3 Header
  Destination:           FF:FF:FF:FF:FF:FF   Ethernet Broadcast
  Source:                00:00:0C:00:2E:75
  Length:                48
IPX - NetWare Protocol
  Checksum:              0xFFFF
  Length:                48
  Transport Control:
  Reserved:              %0000
  Hop Count:             %0000
  Packet Type:           1  RIP
  Destination Network:   0x00000100
  Destination Node:      FF:FF:FF:FF:FF:FF   Ethernet Broadcast
  Destination Socket:    0x0453  Routing Information Protocol
  Source Network:        0x00000100
  Source Node:           00:00:0C:00:2E:75
  Source Socket:         0x0453  Routing Information Protocol
RIP - Routing Information Protocol
  Operation:             2  Response
Network Number Set # 1
  Network Number:        0x00000400
  Number of Hops:        1
  Number of Ticks:       1
Network Number Set # 2
  Network Number:        0x00000500
  Number of Hops:        2
  Number of Ticks:       7
```

Enhanced Interior Gateway Routing Protocol for IPX

As mentioned in Chapter 8, EIGRP is an enhanced version of the Interior Gateway Routing Protocol (IGRP) developed by Cisco. EIGRP uses the same distance-vector algorithm and metrics as IGRP. However, the convergence and operating efficiency of EIGRP are much improved over those of IGRP. One of the things that makes EIGRP unique is that it supports routing for multiple protocols—IP, IPX, and AppleTalk. Although the different protocols develop separate routing tables, they can use a common routing engine that handles the reliable delivery of routing packets and runs the Diffusing-Update Algorithm (DUAL). The algorithm guarantees loop-free operation and allows all routers involved in a topology change to synchronize at the same time.

EIGRP can replace both RIP and SAP on WAN and other backbone networks. RIP and SAP must continue to run on LANs that include clients and servers. As discussed in the *IPX Service Advertising Protocol* section, clients use SAP and RIP during initialization and servers use SAP to advertise and learn about services. For backbone networks that don't include any clients and servers, however, EIGRP is a better choice than RIP and SAP because it greatly reduces the amount of routing and service advertisement traffic that routers send and process. EIGRP sends updates only when changes occur, rather than every 60 seconds. Once EIGRP stabilizes, the only packets you should see are IPX EIGRP Hello packets. EIGRP also converges more quickly than RIP, usually within 1 second. (RIP convergence can take several seconds on small networks and several minutes on large networks.)

EIGRP automatically redistributes routes and services between itself and RIP and SAP. EIGRP tracks the RIP ticks metric as an external metric. An EIGRP backbone that connects RIP networks does not add to the tick metric. EIGRP also tracks hop count as an external metric. The backbone adds two hops. If the automatic redistribution of routes between EIGRP and RIP is not appropriate for your network, you can disable this feature with the `no redistribute` EIGRP routing protocol command. EIGRP does not automatically redistribute NLSP routes into EIGRP routes and vice versa. To configure this type of redistribution, use the `redistribute nlsp` command.

Figure 10.10 shows an IPX network that is using both IPX RIP and EIGRP. The routers are using the automatic redistribution between the two protocols.

In the following protocol analyzer output, the Charlotte router has recently booted and is sending the first EIGRP Update packet out Ethernet interface 0. Can you see a problem with the data in the packet? (See Figure 10.10 for a clue.)

```
DLC:   ----- DLC Header -----
   DLC:   Destination = Station Cisco1053E80
   DLC:   Source      = Station Cisco1002E75
   DLC:   802.3 length = 216
IPX:   ----- IPX Header -----
   IPX:   Checksum = 0xFFFF
   IPX:   Length = 216
   IPX:   Transport control = 00
   IPX:         0000 .... = Reserved
   IPX:         .... 0000 = Hop count
   IPX:   Packet type = 0 (Novell)
   IPX:   Dest   network.node = 100.00000C053E80, socket = 85BE
   IPX:   Source network.node = 100.00000C002E75, socket = 85BE
```

```
EIGRP: ----- Enhanced IGRP Header -----
       EIGRP: Version         = 2
       EIGRP: Opcode          = 1 (Update)
       EIGRP: EIGRP Checksum = CF29 (correct)
       EIGRP: Flags (unused) = 0000
       EIGRP: Flags           = 0001
       EIGRP:                      Conditionally receive mode not required
       EIGRP:                      Initial update packet
       EIGRP: Sequence number         = 1
       EIGRP: Acknowledgment number   = 0
       EIGRP: Autonomous System number = 100
       EIGRP:
       EIGRP: Protocol ID             = 0x03 (Novell IPX)
       EIGRP: Type Code               = 0x0303 (IPX External Routes)
       EIGRP: Field length            = 58
       EIGRP: Next hop address        = 0 (use received IPX header)
       EIGRP: Next hop host ID            = 000000000000
       EIGRP: Route ID                   = 00000C002E75
       EIGRP: AS number               = 0
       EIGRP: Arbitrary tag           = 0
       EIGRP: External protocol       = 3 (RIP)
       EIGRP: Reserved
       EIGRP: External metric         = 2
       EIGRP: External delay          = 1
       EIGRP: Time delay (10 msec/256)        = 1408000
       EIGRP: Path bandwidth (2,560,000,000/kbps) = 266496000
       EIGRP: Min/max transmission unit (MTU)    = 1500
       EIGRP: Hop count               = 0
       EIGRP: Reliability (error percentage) = 255
       EIGRP: Load utilization percentage   = 1
       EIGRP: Reserved
       EIGRP: IPX destination network number   = 00000200
       EIGRP: IPX destination network number   = 00000300
       EIGRP:
       EIGRP: Protocol ID             = 0x03 (Novell IPX)
       EIGRP: Type Code               = 0x0303 (IPX External Routes)
       EIGRP: Field length            = 54
       EIGRP: Next hop address        = 0 (use received IPX header)
       EIGRP: Next hop host ID            = 000000000000
       EIGRP: Route ID                   = 00000C002E75
       EIGRP: AS number               = 0
       EIGRP: Arbitrary tag           = 0
       EIGRP: External protocol       = 4 (Connected)
       EIGRP: Reserved
       EIGRP: External metric         = 0
       EIGRP: External delay          = 0
       EIGRP: Time delay (10 msec/256)        = 0
       EIGRP: Path bandwidth (2,560,000,000/kbps) = 266496000
       EIGRP: Min/max transmission unit (MTU)    = 1500
       EIGRP: Hop count               = 0
       EIGRP: Reliability (error percentage) = 255
       EIGRP: Load utilization percentage   = 1
```

```
EIGRP: Reserved
EIGRP: IPX destination network number      = 00000400
EIGRP:
EIGRP: Protocol ID                = 0x03 (Novell IPX)
EIGRP: Type Code                  = 0x0303 (IPX External Routes)
EIGRP: Field length               = 54
EIGRP: Next hop address           = 0 (use received IPX header)
EIGRP: Next hop host ID              = 000000000000
EIGRP: Route ID                      = 00000C002E75
EIGRP: AS number                     = 0
EIGRP: Arbitrary tag                 = 0
EIGRP: External protocol          = 3 (RIP)
EIGRP: Reserved
EIGRP: External metric            = 2
EIGRP: External delay             = 6
EIGRP: Time delay (10 msec/256)            = 8448000
EIGRP: Path bandwidth (2,560,000,000/kbps) = 266496000
EIGRP: Min/max transmission unit (MTU)     = 1500
EIGRP: Hop count                           = 0
EIGRP: Reliability (error percentage)      = 255
EIGRP: Load utilization percentage         = 1
EIGRP: Reserved
EIGRP: IPX destination network number      = 00000500
```

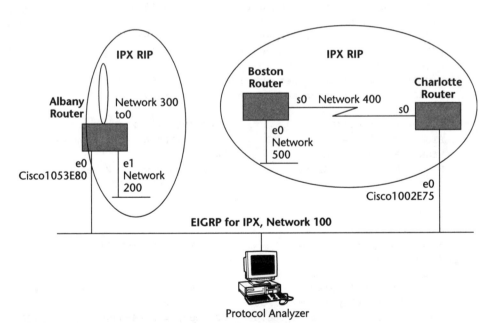

Figure 10.10   An IPX router running both IPX RIP and EIGRP for IPX.

The potential problem in the EIGRP Update packet is that the Charlotte router is telling the Albany router that Charlotte can get to Networks 200 and 300 and that the next hop to those networks is Charlotte! (See `Next hop address = 0 use received IPX header`.) From looking at the network drawing in Figure 10.10, you should be able to recognize the problem with this: It breaks the split-horizon rule! Charlotte learned about those networks from Albany and should not tell Albany about them. Luckily, in the next Update packet, Charlotte fixed the problem by listing Networks 200 and 300 with a maximum EIGRP delay of 0xFFFFFFFF (unreachable).

There was still a minor problem on the network, however. The protocol analyst discovered that, despite the fact that Network 100 was configured to use EIGRP, the routers on Network 100 (Charlotte and Albany) were still sending RIP and SAP updates every 60 seconds. One of the goals for using EIGRP was to reduce bandwidth usage by routing and service advertisement traffic. Configuring EIGRP, however, was not sufficient to achieve this goal because RIP was also enabled, so the router continued to send RIP and SAP packets every 60 seconds on every interface. This is a common problem. To fix it, use the `no network` RIP routing protocol command, as seen in the following Cisco router configuration session, which also displays the configuration of Charlotte.

```
charlotte#config t
charlotte(config)#ipx router rip
charlotte(config-ipx-router)#no network 100
charlotte(config-ipx-router)#end
charlotte#
charlotte#show running-config
hostname charlotte
ipx routing 0000.0c00.2e75
interface Ethernet0
 ipx network 100
interface Serial0
 ipx network 400
ipx router eigrp 100
 network 100
ipx router rip
 no network 100
end
```

NetWare Link Services Protocol

NLSP is a link-state routing protocol that is based on the OSI Intermediate System-to-Intermediate System (IS-IS) protocol. NLSP is a good option for reducing routing traffic in a large IPX network, although it is very complex and harder to troubleshoot than EIGRP and RIP. NLSP advertises routes and services incrementally rather than broadcasting a table on a regular basis. It also sends messages on LANs as multicast packets instead of broadcast packets. The multicast address for NLSP is 09:00:1B:FF:FF:FF.

NLSP is designed for use in a hierarchical routing environment where networks are grouped into routing areas. Routing areas can then be grouped into routing domains, and domains can be grouped into an internetwork. NLSP supports three levels of routers. A Level 1 router connects networks within a routing area; a Level 2 router connects areas and also acts as a Level 1 router within its own area; and a Level 3 router connects domains and also acts as a Level 2 router within its own domain.

Because NLSP is a link-state protocol, every router in a routing area maintains an identical copy of a link-state database. The database contains information about the topology of the area. Routers communicate with each other to keep their copies of the link-state database synchronized.

NLSP also keeps an adjacency database, which keeps track of the immediate neighbors of a router. Adjacencies are created upon receipt of periodic Hello packets. If a link or router goes down, adjacencies time out and are deleted from the database. Routers aggregate neighbor information from all other routers to learn about the connectivity of an entire routing area. This is accomplished through the use of Link-State Packets (LSPs), which contain lists of adjacencies. Every time a link state changes, routers flood LSPs to all other devices via a reliable flooding algorithm. LSPs are also refreshed every 2 hours. To keep the size of the link-state database reasonable, NLSP uses fictitious *pseudonodes*, which represent a LAN as a whole, and designated routers, which originate LSPs on behalf of the pseudonode.

Once a router has developed its adjacency and link-state databases, it calculates a routing table from the information in the databases using Dijkstra's Shortest-Path-First (SPF) algorithm. See Chapter 8 for more information on Dijkstra's algorithm.

To configure NLSP, first configure IPX routing on the router with the `ipx routing` command, then define an internal network number for the router, enable NLSP routing, and configure NLSP on each interface. The internal network number must be unique on an internetwork. Be careful not to use a number that identifies an actual network or that is used as an internal network number on NetWare servers, which also require an internal network number.

On a router that runs both NLSP and RIP, redistribution of networks learned via RIP is automatic. Also, there is no need to make sure RIP packets aren't sent on an interface that is enabled for NLSP, as there is with EIGRP. On a router that runs both NLSP and EIGRP, redistribution is not automatic, but it can be configured with the `redistribute` command.

When analyzing a stable NLSP network, you should see very little routing protocol traffic other than NLSP Hello packets. Designated Routers send Hellos every 10 seconds; Non-Designated Routers send Hellos every 20 seconds. In addition, the Designated Router periodically multicasts a packet called a Complete Sequence Number Packet (CSNP) that contains all the LSP identifiers and sequence numbers that it has in its database for the entire area. This ensures that other routers can detect whether they are out of synchronization with the Designated Router. The following output shows an NLSP Hello packet.

```
802.3 Header
   Destination:        FF:FF:FF:FF:FF:FF   Ethernet Broadcast
   Source:             00:00:0C:05:3E:80
   Length:             82
IPX - NetWare Protocol
```

```
    Checksum:                  0xFFFF
    Length:                    81
    Transport Control:
    Reserved:                  %0000
    Hop Count:                 %0000
    Packet Type:               0  Novell
    Destination Network:       0x00000000
    Destination Node:          FF:FF:FF:FF:FF:FF  Ethernet Broadcast
    Destination Socket:        0x9001  NetWare NLSP
    Source Network:            0x00000100
    Source Node:               00:00:0C:05:3E:80
    Source Socket:             0x9001  NetWare NLSP
NLSP - NetWare Link Services Protocol
    Protocol ID:               0x83
    Length:                    27
    Minor Version:             1
    Reserved:                  0x00
    Packet Type:               15  NLSP LAN Hello
    Major Version:             1
    Reserved:                  0x0000
    Circuit Type:              %00010001
                                       No Multicast
                                       Level-1 routing only
    Source ID:                 0x00000C053E80
    Holding Time:              30
    Packet Length:             51
    Priority:                  64
    LAN ID:                    0x00000C053E8004
    Option Code:               0xC0     Area Addresses
    Option Length:             8
    Area Address # 1
                               Address:0x00000100
                               Mask:0xFFFFFFFF
    Option Code:               0xC5     Local MTU
    Option Length:             4
    Maximum MTU:               1500
    Option Code:               0x06     Neighbors
    Option Length:             6
    Neighbor # 1
    NIC Address:               0x00000C002E75
```

Notice from the output that the station sending the Hello has learned the data link layer address of its partner. (See NIC Address: 0x00000C002E75.) You should also notice a strange thing about the output, which is that the source sends to FF:FF:FF:FF:FF:FF, the Ethernet broadcast address. NLSP should send to a multicast address. Cisco didn't support sending to a multicast address in early versions of the NLSP software, however. The router in the example is running Cisco IOS version 11.0. If you have routers running older versions of the Cisco IOS software that need to communicate with routers running newer versions or with Novell routers, you could have a problem. The routers won't understand each other's NLSP packets unless they are all configured to use broadcast or all configured to use multicast.

IPX Networks in Transition

Many NetWare networks are migrating to IP. The first step is usually to disable IPX routing in the core of the internetwork. With this approach, clients and servers can still use NCP and NCP-based applications if their IPX packets are tunneled across the IP networks. Tunneling provides network administrators the opportunity to rid the core of the network from extra traffic caused by RIP and SAP without having to implement NLSP, which is complex, or EIGRP, which only runs on Cisco routers.

With NetWare 5.0, Novell provided a *migration agent* to help you migrate from IPX to IP. If a server running the migration agent has only one NIC, then enabling the migration agent causes IPX packets destined for other networks to be tunneled in IP packets. If the server has two NICs, enabling the migration agent causes the server to function as a gateway. For example, a server acting as a migration agent might have one NIC communicating with an IP network segment and another NIC communicating with an IPX network segment. IPX requests destined to travel across the IP network are tunneled in an IP packet. IP packets destined to travel across the IPX network segment are tunneled in an IPX packet. The migration agent also handles service discovery and location by converting SAP packets to SLP packets. See Chapter 9 for more information about SLP.

NOTE In October 2001, Novell started shipping NetWare 6.0 which has additional tools to help you migrate from IPX to IP and to integrate service offerings on networks of all sorts, including the Internet. Please see www.novell.com for more information on NetWare 6.0.

Tunneling isn't the only method for migrating from IPX to IP. Novell supports numerous other methods, including using NCP with the native services of the TCP/IP protocol stack. This method is the best approach for environments that have completed the removal of IPX routing from their internetworks. On a TCP/IP network, a Novell workstation uses NCP calls to retrieve file server information, authenticate to NDS, and log in to the server. These calls can run above UDP or TCP. Most network administrators prefer TCP for its superior reliability. In a TCP/IP network, clients and servers discover and advertise services using SLP.

When a Novell client that is using the native TCP/IP protocols boots, it behaves somewhat like any IP station. First, it uses the Dynamic Host Configuration Protocol (DHCP) to determine its IP address. A Novell server can act as a DHCP server and return an address and additional information such as the address of a Domain Name System (DNS) server. The client also sends an Internet Group Management Protocol (IGMP) message to report its membership in the multicast group that receives SLP packets. It also sends SLP packets to find an SLP directory agent, and, if one exists, it sends SLP packets to find the IP address of an NCP server.

When NCP runs above TCP, you can troubleshoot it in a similar fashion as you would any TCP-based application. You should expect to see a normal TCP three-way handshake initiated by the client from an ephemeral port to the well-known TCP port for NCP, which is 524. The client then sends typical NCP calls, such as the following call to get system information about the server:

```
Ethernet Header
  Destination:          00:03:6D:16:35:4C
  Source:               00:50:8B:C9:65:A8
  Protocol Type:        0x0800  IP
IP Header - Internet Protocol Datagram
  Version:              4
  Header Length:        5  (20  bytes)
  Type of Service:      %00000000
                        000. .... Precedence: Routine,
                        ...0 .... Normal Delay,
                        .... 0... Normal Throughput,
                        .... .0.. Normal Reliability
                        .... ..0. ECT bit - transport protocol will
ignore the CE bit
                        .... ...0 CE bit - no congestion
  Total Length:         66
  Identifier:           26534
  Fragmentation Flags:  %010
                        0.. Reserved
                        .1. Do Not Fragment
                        ..0 Last Fragment
  Fragment Offset:      0  (0  bytes)
  Time To Live:         128
  Protocol:             6  TCP - Transmission Control Protocol
  Header Checksum:      0x1159
  Source IP Address:    192.168.0.101 NCP Client
  Dest. IP Address:     192.168.0.1 NCP Server
  No IP Options
TCP - Transport Control Protocol
  Source Port:          1685
  Destination Port:     524  ncp
  Sequence Number:      680922425
  Ack Number:           2567577381
  Offset:               5  (20  bytes)
  Reserved:             %000000
  Flags:                %011000
                        0. .... (No Urgent pointer)
                        .1 .... Ack
                        .. 1... Push
                        .. .0.. (No Reset)
                        .. ..0. (No SYN)
                        .. ...0 (No FIN)
  Window:               23323
  Checksum:             0xF5A8
  Urgent Pointer:       0
  No TCP Options
NCP - NetWare 5 IP
  Signature:            DmdT
  Length:               26
  Version:              0x00000001
  Reply Size:           0x00000080
```

```
        Request Type:           0x2222
        Sequence number:        2
        Low number:             8
        Task number:            1
        High number:            0
        Function Code:          23  Get System Info
        Subfunction Length:     1
        Subfunction Code:       17  Check Server Version
    Check Server Version Request
        Remaining Request Data:
        tf..              74 66 CA 01
```

Notice that the NCP header is essentially just like the NCP header we discussed earlier. The Request Type is 0x2222, which means a request. In the response from the server, this field is set to 0x3333, as seen in the following output.

```
    Ethernet Header
        Destination:            00:50:8B:C9:65:A8
        Source:                 00:03:6D:16:35:4C
        Protocol Type:          0x0800  IP
    IP Header - Internet Protocol Datagram
        Version:                4
        Header Length:          5  (20  bytes)
        Type of Service:        %00000000
                                000. .... Precedence: Routine,
                                ...0 .... Normal Delay,
                                .... 0... Normal Throughput,
                                .... .0.. Normal Reliability
                                .... ..0. ECT bit - transport protocol will
                                ignore the CE bit
                                .... ...0 CE bit - no congestion
        Total Length:           184
        Identifier:             38708
        Fragmentation Flags:    %010
                                0.. Reserved
                                .1. Do Not Fragment
                                ..0 Last Fragment
        Fragment Offset:        0  (0  bytes)
        Time To Live:           128
        Protocol:               6  TCP - Transmission Control Protocol
        Header Checksum:        0xE154
        Source IP Address:      192.168.0.1 NCP Server
        Dest. IP Address:       192.168.0.101 NCP Client
        No IP Options
    TCP - Transport Control Protocol
        Source Port:            524  ncp
        Destination Port:       1685
        Sequence Number:        2567577381
        Ack Number:             680922451
        Offset:                 5  (20  bytes)
        Reserved:               %000000
```

```
            Flags:                %011000
                                  0. .... (No Urgent pointer)
                                  .1 .... Ack
                                  .. 1... Push
                                  .. .0.. (No Reset)
                                  .. ..0. (No SYN)
                                  .. ...0 (No FIN)
            Window:               6051
            Checksum:             0x67F8
            Urgent Pointer:       0
            No TCP Options
        NCP - NetWare 5 IP
            Signature:            tNcP
            Length:               144
            Request Type:         0x3333
            Sequence number:      2
            Low number:           8
            Task number:          1
            High number:          0
            Completion Code:      0x00   Successful
            Status flags:         0x00   OK
        Check Server Version Reply
            Server Name:          BIGSRV-NW-01....................................
            File Service Version: 5
            File Service Sub-version:0
            Max Service Connections:19
            Connections In Use:   0
            Max Number of Volumes:255
            Revision:             9
            SFT Level:            2
            TTS Level:            1
            Max Connects Ever Used:5
            Account Version:      1
            VAP Version:          1
            Queue Version:        1
            Print Version:        0
            Virtual Console Version:1
            Restriction Level:    1
            Internet Bridge:      1
```

Troubleshooting IPX

This section discusses techniques for troubleshooting Novell NetWare networks that are connected via Cisco routers. On most networks, you will use a combination of router commands, protocol analyzer trace files, and client and server commands. Troubleshooting clients and servers is outside the scope of this book, although some of the commands (such as IPX ping) can be used on servers as well as routers.

Applying Your Protocol Analyzer

Perhaps the most significant observation that protocol analysts often make in a Novell environment is that multiple frame formats are in use, and that wasn't what the network designer intended. Identifying the frame formats being used by NetWare communicators is the first thing to do whenever you analyze a Novell trace file. As mentioned in the *IPX Service Advertising Protocol* section, you may be surprised to learn that network bandwidth is being consumed by packets being sent in multiple formats when only one format is sufficient.

Also, remember from the *Ethernet Frames in IPX Environments* section that one of the main things that can go wrong with client and server configurations is a mismatch of the Ethernet frame type. To communicate directly with servers or router interfaces on its LAN, a client must use the same frame type as the servers and router interfaces. A server also must use the same frame type as any clients, other servers, or router interfaces on its LAN if it wishes to directly communicate with them. If a client communicates with a server on the other side of a router, then the client and server do not need to use the same frame type. Use your protocol analyzer to troubleshoot connectivity problems that may be related to frame types.

When analyzing upper layers, it's often helpful to set up a pattern-match filter in your analyzer, which requires you to specify a byte offset for the beginning of the pattern. For example, you might wish to find all packets with a particular file handle in the NCP header. Remember that when multiple frame formats are being used, the offset will be different in the different frame formats, because header lengths differ for the four frame types (Ethernet II, 802.3/802.2, SNAP, and Novell raw).

Another thing to watch out for is the presence of a NetWare protocol that doesn't belong on the network. For example, if your network no longer implements RIP, then you should not see routers sending RIP frames. More fundamentally, if your network no longer implements any Novell NetWare, then you should not see devices such as JetDirect printers or routers sending any IPX or other NetWare frames!

IPX Ping and Trace

It may surprise you to learn that IPX has a ping utility. Usually *ping* refers to an IP Internet Control Message Protocol (ICMP) echo packet, but it can also refer to the test packets you can send on IPX networks. Cisco defined an IPX ping before Novell did, which causes an issue. Novell devices do not respond to the Cisco ping. To change to the new Novell ping on a Cisco router, use the `ipx ping-default novell` command. Cisco routers respond to either type of ping regardless of their configuration, but you need to configure the router to send the Novell ping for communication with NetWare servers.

> **NOTE** The Cisco IPX ping uses an IPX packet type of 0x01 (RIP) and an IPX socket type of 0x0002. The Novell IPX ping uses an IPX packet type of 0x04 (SAP) and an IPX socket type of 0x9086.

To use the IPX ping on a Cisco router, enter the `ping` command and press enter. One of the annoying aspects of Cisco's IPX ping is that it makes you enter the node ID in blocks of four digits, as shown in the following output.

```
Albany#ping
Protocol [ip]: ipx
Target IPX address: 100.00000c002e75
% Bad IPX address
Albany#ping
Protocol [ip]: ipx
Target IPX address: 100.0000.0c00.2e75
Repeat count [5]:
Datagram size [100]:
Timeout in seconds [2]:
Verbose [n]:
Novell Standard Echo [n]:
Type escape sequence to abort.
Sending 5, 100-byte IPX cisco Echoes to 100.0000.0c00.2e75, timeout is 2
seconds
:
!!!!!
Success rate is 100 percent (5/5), round-trip min/avg/max = 1/2/4 ms
```

It may come as a surprise that Cisco IOS routers also support an IPX trace-route utility, which is usually considered an IP command that sends UDP or ICMP packets and listens for ICMP Time-to-Live Exceeded messages. If you are running Cisco IOS 12.0 or later, then you can use trace-route on an IPX network also. To trace an IPX destination and measure round-trip delays to routers en route to the destination, use the `trace ipx [destination]` command in either user or privileged mode. In privileged mode, you can change the trace-route timeout interval, the packet count, and minimum and maximum hop count values, and go into verbose mode, which has additional parameters such as the size of the packet.

Show IPX Route

The most useful Cisco command for troubleshooting IPX networks is `show ipx route`. An example of the output from this command follows.

```
Albany#show ipx route
Codes: C - Connected primary network, c - Connected secondary network,
S - Static, F - Floating static, L - Local (internal), W - IPXWAN,
R - RIP, E - EIGRP, N - NLSP, X - External, s - seconds, u - uses
5 Total IPX routes. Up to 1 parallel paths and 16 hops allowed.
No default route known.
C         100 (NOVELL-ETHER),   Et0
C         200 (NOVELL-ETHER),   Et1
C         300 (SAP),            To0
R         400 [01/01] via       100.0000.0c00.2e75,   37s, Et0
R         500 [07/02] via       100.0000.0c00.2e75,   38s, Et0
```

The `show ipx route` command displays the IPX routing table, including network numbers, the frame type used on directly connected networks, ticks and hop counts (see [01/01] or [07/01] in the example), and the address of a router that is the next hop to the remote network (see via 100.0000.0c00.2e75). In the example, both the networks that are directly connected to Ethernet interfaces are using the Novell-Ether frame type. Network 300 is connected to a Token Ring interface and is using an 802.2 frame format, with Service Access Points, which is the default for Token Ring networks.

The output also shows the amount of time (in hours, minutes, and seconds) that has elapsed since information about a network was last received (see 37s) and the interface on which packets to the remote network will be sent (see Et0).

The text preceding the list of network numbers that says Up to 1 parallel paths lists the number of parallel paths for which the Cisco IOS software has been configured with the ipx maximum-paths command. As discussed in the *IPX Routing* section, by default, a Cisco router learns only one IPX path to a network and does not do any load sharing. Using the ipx maximum-paths command, you can tell the router to keep track of multiple parallel paths to a network, which cause the router to do load sharing. Load sharing was not enabled in this case.

Show IPX Servers

The show ipx servers command displays the IPX services discovered through SAP. For each service, the command displays the following information:

- *Type*. The type of service—for example, 4 means File Server. See Table 10.6 for a list of service types.

- *Name*. The name of the service.

- *Net*. The network on which the service is located.

- *Address*. The node ID of the service.

- *Port*. The socket number for the service.

- *Route*. The number of ticks and hops to reach the network on which the service is located. This is from the routing table.

- *Hops*. The number of hops to reach the service as specified by SAP.

- *Itf*. The interface through which to reach the service.

Show IPX Interface

The show ipx interface command displays the configured parameters and status of IPX interfaces. Following is an example:

```
Albany#show ipx interface ethernet 0
Ethernet0 is up, line protocol is up
  IPX address is 100.0000.0c05.3e80, NOVELL-ETHER [up] line-up, RIPPQ:
0, SAPPQ:0
  Delay of this IPX network, in ticks is 1 throughput 0 link delay 0
  IPXWAN processing not enabled on this interface.
  IPX SAP update interval is 1 minute(s)
  IPX type 20 propagation packet forwarding is disabled
  Outgoing access list is not set
  IPX Helper access list is not set
```

```
SAP GNS processing enabled, delay 0 ms, output filter list is not set
SAP Input filter list is not set
SAP Output filter list is not set
SAP Router filter list is not set
Input filter list is not set
Output filter list is not set
Router filter list is not set
Netbios Input host access list is not set
Netbios Input bytes access list is not set
Netbios Output host access list is not set
Netbios Output bytes access list is not set
Updates each 60 seconds, aging multiples RIP: 3 SAP: 3
SAP interpacket delay is 5 ms, maximum size is 480 bytes
RIP interpacket delay is 5 ms, maximum size is 432 bytes
IPX accounting is disabled
IPX fast switching is configured (enabled)
IPX SSE switching is disabled
RIP packets received 50, RIP packets sent 53
SAP packets received 0, SAP packets sent 53
```

Show IPX Traffic

The show ipx traffic command displays information about the number and type of IPX packets transmitted and received by the router. Following is partial output. The EIGRP and NLSP statistics are not displayed because they were all zero. The router wasn't configured to use EIGRP or NLSP. (The router displays statistics for protocols that aren't configured.)

```
Albany#show ipx traffic
System Traffic for 0.0000.0000.0001 System-Name: Albany
Rcvd:   61 total, 0 format errors, 0 checksum errors, 0 bad hop count, 0
packets pitched, 61 local destination, 0 multicast
Bcast:  56 received, 295 sent
Sent:   300 generated, 0 forwarded
        0 encapsulation failed, 1 no route
SAP:    0 SAP requests, 0 SAP replies, 1 servers
        0 SAP advertisements received, 113 sent
        0 SAP flash updates sent, 0 SAP poison sent
        0 SAP format errors
RIP:    0 RIP requests, 0 RIP replies, 5 routes
        56 RIP advertisements received, 165 sent
        7 RIP flash updates sent, 0 RIP poison sent
        0 RIP format errors
RIP:    0 RIP format errors
Echo:   Rcvd 0 requests, 5 replies
        Sent 5 requests, 0 replies
        0 unknown: 0 no socket, 0 filtered, 0 no helper
        0 SAPs throttled, freed NDB len 0
Watchdog:
        0 packets received, 0 replies spoofed
```

Most of the output from `show ipx traffic` is self-explanatory or not relevant. A few items require some explanation:

- *Format errors.* The number of bad packets discarded. If a Cisco router receives an IPX packet encapsulated with a frame type that the router has not been configured to support, it increments the format errors count and drops the packet. Format errors can also occur when the length of the received packet is smaller than 30 bytes or larger than the interface MTU, and when a packet arrives with a corrupted header.

- *Checksum errors.* The number of packets containing an IPX checksum error. This number should be 0 because IPX rarely uses a checksum.

- *Bad hop count.* The number of packets discarded because their hop count exceeded 16.

- *Packets pitched.* The number of times the router received its own broadcast packet and dropped (pitched) it.

- *Local destination.* The number of packets sent by other devices to the local broadcast address or specifically to the router.

- *Generated.* The number of packets that the router generated itself.

- *Forwarded.* The number of packets that the router forwarded from other sources.

- *Encapsulation failed.* The number of packets the forwarding software was unable to encapsulate.

- *No route.* The number of times the software could not locate a route to the destination in the routing table.

- *SAPs throttled.* The number of SAP packets discarded because they exceeded buffer capacity.

- *SAP throttling length.* The maximum number of SAP packets allowed in the buffer. Any packets received beyond this number are discarded.

Show IPX EIGRP

Three commands are helpful if you are running EIGRP as one of your IPX routing protocols:

- `show ipx eigrp interfaces`. Shows whether EIGRP is enabled on an interface and, if it is, displays detailed information about the interface, including the autonomous system number of the EIGRP process, the number of neighbors on the interface, and a count of unreliable and reliable packets queued for transmission.

- `show ipx eigrp neighbors`. Displays information about neighbor routers discovered by IPX EIGRP, including the network-layer address, the interface used to reach the neighbor, the autonomous system number, the amount of time the router has known about the neighbor (uptime), and the server list advertised by the neighbor.

- `show ipx eigrp topology`. Displays the IPX EIGRP topology table. See Chapter 8 for more information about this command, because the output is similar to that of IP EIGRP.

Show IPX NLSP

Two commands are helpful if you are running NLSP as one of your routing protocols:

- `show ipx nlsp database`. Displays the link-state database.
- `show ipx nlsp neighbors`. Shows NLSP neighbors and their states.

Debug IPX Packet

The `debug ipx packet` command displays information about IPX packets received, sent, and forwarded. The command has no arguments or keywords. It is useful for learning whether IPX packets are traveling through a router; however, it generates a lot of output on a busy network and can tax the router's CPU significantly. As you should know by now from reading this book, we recommend against the use of commands such as this. Instead, use a protocol analyzer to look at packets.

If the router is configured for IPX fast switching—which it should be—only non-fast-switched packets produce output. To generate IPX debug information for all traffic traveling through the router, you must first disable fast switching. Use the `no ipx route-cache` command on all interfaces on which you want to observe traffic. Disabling fast switching should be a temporary change, as it has a negative influence on the speed with which the router forwards packets.

Debug IPX Routing

The `debug ipx routing activity` command displays information about IPX routing packets that the router sends and receives. Approximately every 60 seconds (for RIP) the router generates a lot of information for every RIP packet sent and received. If your router receives or transmits large routing tables in and out of many IPX interfaces, use of this command is not recommended.

The `debug ipx routing events` command displays summary information about IPX routing packets the router sends and receives. This command also generates a lot of output, although not as much as the `debug ipx routing activity` command.

Debug IPX SAP

The `debug ipx sap activity` command displays information about SAP packets the router sends and receives. Approximately every 60 seconds, by default, the router generates a lot of information for every SAP packet sent and received. If your router receives or transmits large SAP tables in and out of many IPX interfaces, this command is not recommended. On smaller networks with routers that have a low CPU usage, it may be safe to use this command for a short period of time. In addition to helping you troubleshoot SAP broadcasts, it also displays output when clients send Get Nearest Server broadcasts and when the router responds to them. So it's a useful, but risky, command.

The debug ipx sap events command displays summary information about SAP packets that the router sends and receives. This command also generates a lot of output, although not as much as the debug ipx sap activity command.

Summary

This chapter has provided an analysis of Novell NetWare protocols to help you understand and troubleshoot your IPX networks. We started with an analysis of IPX addressing, explaining that devices on an IPX network have an address with three parts—a network address, a node ID, and a socket number. Novell networks support multiple routing protocols. For ease of configuration and troubleshooting, the simple distance-vector IPX RIP protocol is a good choice. RIP can cause problems on large internetworks, however, because of the amount of traffic required to advertise numerous routes. In those cases, if you have Cisco routers, you can use EIGRP on backbone networks. Another option for reducing routing protocol bandwidth usage is NLSP, which sends only updates, Hellos, and CSNP packets.

Above the network layer, the two most important IPX protocols are SAP and NCP. SAP provides a means of informing network clients, via routers and servers, of available network services. (SAP is being replaced by SLP in many Novell networks.) NCP is a client/server protocol for accessing and sharing files, printers, and other resources. NCP is still quite popular and is used in both legacy IPX networks and networks that are migrating to pure IP. IPX can be tunneled in IP to support clients and servers still using NCP on an internetwork where IPX routing has been disabled in the core. NCP can also run directly above UDP or TCP in a network that is entirely IP-based. As will be seen in Chapter 11, this is similar to the methods used in AppleTalk networks that are migrating to IP. With AppleTalk, AFP can be encapsulated in TCP for traversal across an IP internetwork. Chapter 11 delves more deeply into AppleTalk, which is similar in many ways to IPX.

CHAPTER

11

Troubleshooting and Analyzing Campus AppleTalk Networks

Over the years, AppleTalk has become the disrespected stepchild of networking protocols. It doesn't deserve this reputation. When Apple Computer designed AppleTalk in the early 1980s, the goal was to connect Macintosh computers with printers and file servers in a user-friendly manner, without the need for complex configurations. The developers of AppleTalk designed the protocols with scalability features, however, and many enterprises evolved their AppleTalk LANs into large, complicated internetworks. In some cases, AppleTalk got stretched beyond its capabilities and network engineers had difficulty managing and troubleshooting it. When AppleTalk internetworks are designed carefully, however, problems can be avoided. Also, many of the myths about how AppleTalk misbehaves are simply not true or are based on problems that Apple fixed in the late 1980s. One of the objectives of this chapter is to help you distinguish the myths from reality. The other objectives are to teach you how to avoid problems with AppleTalk and how to troubleshoot any problems that may arise in spite of how carefully you design your networks.

AppleTalk Concepts

The AppleTalk developers sought to create simple and elegant networking technologies to allow users to access remote resources and interact with other users, without adding a lot of cost or inconvenience. The goal was to seamlessly extend the capabilities and design philosophies of the Macintosh, while maintaining a "plug-and-play" experience for the user. Another goal was link independence, which means that AppleTalk can work on many data link layers, including LocalTalk, Ethernet, Token Ring, and so on. The developers also chose to make the architecture open so that both Apple and third-party developers could design applications based on AppleTalk.

AppleTalk has had a positive influence on computer networking. The AppleTalk viewpoint, which says that protocols and user configurations should be simple, is spreading to the Internet Protocol (IP) world. Consider all the protocols that start with the term *Light-Weight* or *Simple*. Also consider the move to dynamic network-layer address assignment, which Apple pioneered in the early 1980s. Although the typical method used for dynamic addressing in the IP environment (Dynamic Host Configuration Protocol [DHCP]) does not resemble AppleTalk's dynamic addressing method, which does not require a server, the philosophy is the same. The user should not have to understand arcane terms such as *dotted-decimal notation* and *subnet masks*. (The stateless autoconfiguration mechanism in IPv6 does resemble AppleTalk, by the way.)

Finding resources and services, such as servers and printers, is an important network function that AppleTalk got right from the start. Using the Chooser, a user can easily find resources, whether the user is a grade-school child or an absent-minded scientist. Also, despite what the myths say, the Chooser and the background processes that make the Chooser possible do not use a lot of network bandwidth. In an IP-based campus network, on the other hand, it's still difficult to find services. The IP protocol developers recognize that work is required in this area, however. One method for service discovery that is gaining momentum is the Service Location Protocol (SLP). Some of the creators of SLP came from Apple and the philosophy behind AppleTalk service location influenced SLP development. See Chapter 9 for more information about SLP.

While most campus networks are migrating away from AppleTalk, it remains in use, especially in schools, scientific institutions, universities, and graphics and multimedia companies. It's important to know how AppleTalk works, both because it is still in use and because it continues to have an influence on newer protocols.

AppleTalk Architectures

An AppleTalk network architecture consists of the following components:

Node.   An AppleTalk node is a device that runs the AppleTalk protocols and is connected to an AppleTalk network. The device might be a Macintosh, a PC, a printer, a router, a gateway, or some other device.

Socket.   An AppleTalk socket is a unique, addressable software location inside an AppleTalk node. It is the logical point at which upper-layer software processes interact with AppleTalk's network-layer protocol, the Datagram Delivery Protocol (DDP).

Network.   An AppleTalk network is a collection of nodes connected via cables (or wireless technologies), hubs, bridges, or switches. Routers form the boundary of an AppleTalk network, much like a router forms the boundary of an IP subnet. A nonextended AppleTalk network is identified by a single network number. An extended AppleTalk network, which is supported in AppleTalk Phase 2, is identified by a cable range, as discussed in the *AppleTalk Addressing* section later.

Zone.   A zone is a logical grouping of nodes. Nodes do not need to share a physical medium to belong to the same AppleTalk zone. A zone can span more than one network. In addition, multiple zones can exist on a single network.

Internetwork.   An internetwork is a set of networks and zones connected via routers.

AppleTalk Layering

As is the case with most protocol suites, AppleTalk protocols fit into a layered architecture. Each protocol uses the services of one or more protocols in a lower layer, and each provides a service to one or more protocols in the layer above. This layering allowed the AppleTalk developers to use a modular approach when designing and building the protocol architecture. The layering also means that other protocols can be substituted within a layer, as long as they provide the expected service. For example, the Apple Filing Protocol (AFP) can run above TCP/IP instead of above native AppleTalk protocols in campus networks that are no longer routing AppleTalk.

Figure 11.1 shows the AppleTalk protocol architecture. The lines between the boxes in the figure show the interaction between protocols, including which protocols provide services to others and which protocols use the services of other protocols. Table 11.1 describes each protocol shown in the figure.

APPLETALK'S REPUTATION FOR CHATTINESS

People often make the derogatory comment that AppleTalk is such a chatty protocol. There is no question that AppleTalk nodes frequently send many packets that are essentially background traffic. Clients and servers that use the AppleTalk Session Protocol (ASP), for example, check the session every 30 seconds by sending Tickle packets. AppleTalk's default routing protocol, the Routing Table Maintenance Protocol (RTMP), sends update packets every 10 seconds. The frequency for sending the Tickle and RTMP packets was purposely selected to provide quick recovery from problems.

As another example, when the user displays the Macintosh Chooser, the software sends multiple Name Binding Protocol (NBP) unicast packets to a router asking for help finding services in a zone. The router propagates these unicast packets to a router on each network in the zone. The recipient router sends a multicast to local nodes in the zone. This process was carefully designed to be user friendly and require minimum network configuration.

AppleTalk is not the only protocol that sends a lot of background traffic. As discussed throughout this book, many Cisco protocols send frequent keepalive and Hello packets and could be considered chatty. In Windows networking environments, discussed in Chapter 12, the automatic resource management features of the Browse function and the Windows Internet Name Service (WINS) are also chatty. Novell NetWare, using the Service Advertising Protocol (SAP), broadcasts SAP packets at regular intervals. It, too, can be considered chatty. The newer SLP techniques used in Novell, IP, and Macintosh networks also send a lot of background traffic.

The bottom line is that AppleTalk was the first of the chatty protocols because it was the first networking environment to focus on the automation of resource management. Today, it could be said that all of the popular network protocol environments are chatty.

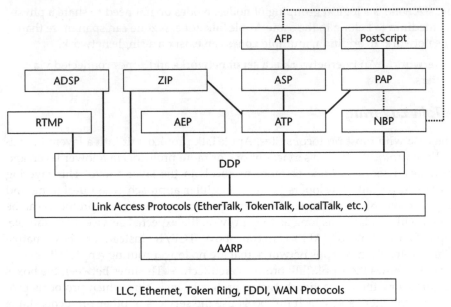

Figure 11.1 AppleTalk protocol architecture.

Table 11.1 AppleTalk Protocols

PROTOCOL	FUNCTION
Apple Filing Protocol (AFP)	Allows clients to open, close, and manipulate files and directories stored on a shared file server.
PostScript	Specifies the representation of documents that can be printed on a network printer.
AppleTalk Session Protocol (ASP)	Handles establishing, maintaining, and terminating general-purpose sessions.
Printer Access Protocol (PAP)	Manages sessions between clients and print servers.
AppleTalk Data Stream Protocol (ADSP)	Provides reliable, full-duplex bytestream services between sockets on network nodes.
AppleTalk Transaction Protocol (ATP)	Provides guaranteed transaction services between sockets on network nodes.

Table 11.1 *(Continued)*

PROTOCOL	FUNCTION
Zone Information Protocol (ZIP)	Used by routers to determine the network numbers for networks in a zone, and by end nodes to discover services.
Name Binding Protocol (NBP)	Used by servers to register named services and by end nodes to find named services.
Routing Table Maintenance Protocol (RTMP)	Simple distance-vector routing protocol used by routers to exchange routing tables.
AppleTalk Echo Protocol (AEP)	Allows a node to send a packet to another node and receive an echoed copy of the packet (similar to IP ping).
Datagram Delivery Protocol (DDP)	Connectionless network-layer protocol that forwards datagrams from socket to socket on an internetwork.
Link Access Protocols (LAPs)	Set of protocols that handle the communication between DDP and standard data link protocols, as well as Apple's proprietary data link protocol, LocalTalk.
AppleTalk Address Resolution Protocol (AARP)	Maps network-layer addresses to data link layer addresses, and verifies the uniqueness of dynamically chosen network-layer addresses.

Figure 11.1 can help you understand how the AppleTalk protocols rely on each other and how data is encapsulated at each layer. For example, when a user places a file on an AFP file server, the AppleTalk software on the client's machine creates an AFP command and encapsulates it in an ASP header, which is encapsulated in an ATP header, which is encapsulated in a DDP header. DDP uses one of the LAPs to further encapsulate the packet in the appropriate data link header, such as an Ethernet or Token Ring header.

Notice that Figure 11.1 shows that AFP also uses NBP. (See the dotted line between AFP and NBP.) Although AFP packets are not encapsulated in NBP, an AFP server uses NBP to register its name and socket number on a node, which makes the server visible to clients. (This doesn't cause network traffic.) Clients use NBP to find the server by sending *NBPBroadcastRequest* unicast packets to a local router.

Looking at Figure 11.1, you might wonder why ZIP is shown to use both DDP and ATP. ZIP packets can reside inside an ATP header or they can be carried directly by DDP. The decision to use ATP versus DDP depends on how much reliability is required and whether an application is sending a large amount of data. When a Macintosh downloads a complete list of zones, for example, ZIP uses ATP.

AppleTalk and the OSI Reference Model

Although it might be tempting to put some Open System Interconnection (OSI) labels in Figure 11.1, the figure does not show OSI layers; it shows AppleTalk layers. In other books, you will see essentially the same drawing with OSI labels incorrectly applied. Many documentation writers have fallen for the temptation that AppleTalk's protocol architecture happens to look a lot like the OSI seven-layer model and have forced the AppleTalk protocols into OSI layers. This leads to incorrect thinking about the AppleTalk protocols.

DDP, ZIP, and RTMP are all network-layer protocols. (Many documents place ZIP and RTMP at the transport layer simply because they are at the fourth level in the AppleTalk architecture.) DDP, ZIP, and RTMP handle forwarding traffic across an internetwork, dividing devices into logical and physical groups, and learning how to reach the groups. They clearly have network-layer, not transport-layer, functionality. When troubleshooting these protocols, you will focus on network-layer concerns, such as network numbers and router configurations. You won't focus on sequence numbers, acknowledgments, or flow control, as you would if they were transport-layer protocols. ADSP, which is similar to TCP, belongs at the transport layer, on the other hand. ATP, which is transaction oriented, also belongs at the transport layer. Figure 11.2 shows another representation of the AppleTalk protocols that indicates the OSI layer for each protocol.

AppleTalk Addressing

AppleTalk addresses are expressed in decimal in a *network.node* format. The network number is a 16-bit field and the node number is an 8-bit field. The node number is usually dynamically determined, whereas the network number is configured on a router. An 8-bit node number means that there can be no more than 256 nodes per network. To work around this limitation, Apple Computer introduced AppleTalk Phase 2 in 1989. AppleTalk Phase 2 provides support for an extended network, which is a network that has more than one network number assigned to it.

The assignment of more than one network number to a single physical network segment allows network administrators to have more than 256 nodes per network segment. This was something administrators said they wanted back in 1989, although most soon learned that more than 256 nodes per network was generally not a good idea anyway. (All nodes in a network are in the same broadcast domain, which can result in problems if numerous applications send broadcasts and devices on the network can't process broadcasts quickly.)

AppleTalk Phase 2 reserves three node addresses:

- 0 means a router on the network.
- 254 is reserved for future use.
- 255 means all nodes (broadcast).

OSI Term	AppleTalk Protocols
Application	AEP, NBP, AFP, Post Script
Presentation	
Session	ASP, PAP
Transport	ADSP, ATP
Network	DDP, ZIP, RTMP
	AARP
Data Link and Physical	LLC, Ethernet, Token Ring, FDDI, WAN Protocols

Figure 11.2   AppleTalk and the OSI Reference Model.

AppleTalk Addresses on a Cisco Router

When you assign network numbers to a network, the numbers must be contiguous. For example, if you have numerous nodes on a single segment, you could assign network numbers 10 to 13 to the segment. This would allow you to have 1012 nodes (4 × 253 nodes) on the segment. Cisco calls the list of contiguous network numbers the *cable range*. To configure AppleTalk Phase 2 on a Cisco router, you simply follow three easy steps:

1. In global configuration mode, type `appletalk routing`, which enables the default routing protocol, which is RTMP. (We'll cover enabling other protocols in later sections.)

2. In interface configuration mode, assign one or more network numbers to each connected network that will run AppleTalk, using the `appletalk cable-range cable-range [network.node]` command. To assign a single network number, use a unary cable range, such as 10-10.

3. In interface configuration mode, associate the network with one or more zones, using the `appletalk zone zone-name` command. Type the command once for each zone. The first zone in the list is the default zone.

AppleTalk Address Resolution Protocol (AARP)

AARP has the task of mapping AppleTalk addresses to data link-layer addresses. For example, if a node wishes to send an AppleTalk packet to another node on its Ethernet segment, AARP can map the destination AppleTalk address to an Institute of Electrical and Electronics Engineers (IEEE) 802.3 address. In this sense, AARP is just like the IP Address Resolution Protocol (ARP). As we will see in the next section, AARP has an additional job that does not correspond to IP ARP, which is to ensure the uniqueness of dynamically assigned AppleTalk addresses.

Within an AppleTalk node, AARP maintains an ARP table for each data link supported on the node. On a Macintosh, the ARP table is called the Address Mapping Table (AMT) and is hidden from the user. On a Cisco router, it is called an ARP cache. To see the ARP cache on a Cisco router, use the `show appletalk arp` command.

As with IP ARP, when a node wishes to send a packet to a destination that is not in its ARP table, the node sends a request to all other nodes on the network segment to find the data link layer address of the destination. Unlike IP, AppleTalk uses a multicast frame rather than a broadcast frame for this purpose. AppleTalk AARP frames are sent to the 09:00:07:FF:FF:FF multicast address for all devices running AppleTalk. When a station replies, the mapping of network layer to data link layer address is added to the ARP table. If there is no reply, the node retransmits.

With Cisco Internetwork Operating System (IOS) software, you can configure how quickly a router retransmits AARP requests with the `appletalk arp request interval` command. You can also configure how many times the router retransmits before giving up with the `appletalk arp request retransmit-count` number command. These commands are helpful if there are stations that respond slowly or if you are concerned about the amount of broadcast traffic caused by AARP frames.

The Cisco IOS software also automatically derives ARP table entries from incoming packets. This process, called *gleaning,* speeds up the process of populating the ARP table. During network upgrades and reconfigurations, it is sometimes helpful to disable gleaning with the `no appletalk glean-packets` command. Disabling gleaning is also a good idea to reduce a router's workload if a router has high CPU utilization.

Dynamic Addressing

One of the primary features of AppleTalk is that a node can dynamically assign its own network-layer address. This minimizes the amount of configuration required on AppleTalk internetworks. On a Cisco router, if you do not supply the `network.node` parameter with the `appletalk cable-range` command, the router dynamically selects a network and node combination using a network number from the cable range and a node ID between 1 and 253. On end nodes, no configuration is necessary. An end node automatically selects a network and node combination, and then verifies with a router that the network number is valid. The end node also uses AARP to ensure that the network-layer address is unique.

AppleTalk dynamic address assignment isn't quite as dynamic as it sounds. An AppleTalk node tries to use the same address that it used the last time it was on a network. Once a node has a unique address, it stores the address in battery-backed-up Random Access Memory (RAM), which is called *Parameter RAM* (PRAM) on a Macintosh and *Non-Volatile RAM* (NVRAM) on a Cisco router. The node uses this saved address the next time it boots. A Macintosh automatically saves its address. To save a Cisco router's address, use the `copy run start` command.

When an AppleTalk node boots, it looks in its battery-backed-up RAM for an address to use. If there is no address, the node randomly selects a node number between 1 and 253. If the node is a router, it then selects a network number from the configured cable range. If the node is an end node, and it has no saved network number, it randomly selects a network number from a special range, called the *startup range*. The startup range is 0xFF00 to 0xFFFE in hexadecimal or 65,280 to 65,534 in decimal.

Figure 11.3 shows the initial steps a Macintosh takes to determine if its address is unique. A Macintosh uses its address in PRAM, if one is available, and sends AARP packets to verify that the address if unique. Notice that these packets are sent as multicast packets, which theoretically should not require processing on non-AppleTalk nodes. (We say "theoretically" because some network interface cards are not smart about ignoring irrelevant multicast frames.)

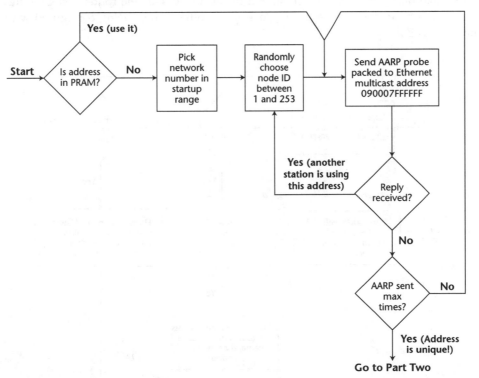

Figure 11.3 Dynamic address assignment, Part One.

Figure 11.4 shows the final steps a Macintosh takes to ensure that its address is unique. After selecting a node number, a Macintosh uses ZIP to make sure its network number is in the cable range assigned to that network, as shown in the figure.

When a Cisco router ensures that its network.node address is unique, it uses essentially the same process as that shown in Figures 11.3 and 11.4, although the time interval between AARP frames, and the number of times to send AARP frames, can be controlled on a Cisco router with the `appletalk arp probe interval` and `appletalk arp probe retransmit-count number` commands. These commands are rarely used, but they can be helpful in some situations. Cisco added the commands because of problems reported with routers using an address that wasn't unique. This can occur when a network has slow printers or low-end gateways that process AARP frames slowly.

Discovery Mode

When you assign a cable range to a network, you must configure the range exactly the same on each router on the network. If an existing router thinks the cable range is 22 through 25, for example, a new Cisco router that is configured with 22 through 26 will fail to enable AppleTalk. Zone names must also agree exactly, although they are case insensitive (*Engineering_Zone* is the same as *engineering_zone*, for example). But many AppleTalk engineers have been frustrated by such errors as one router being configured with a zone name of *Engineers_Zone* and another router being configured with *Engineering_Zone*.

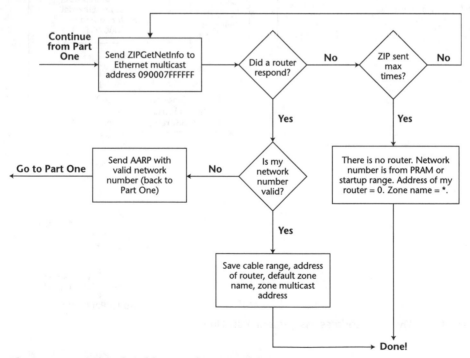

Figure 11.4 Dynamic address assignment, Part Two.

To simplify network configuration requirements, Apple developed the concept of a *seed router*. A seed router is a router where the administrator explicitly configures a cable range and zone name(s). A *non-seed router* learns the cable range and zones from other routers on the network. Cisco refers to the method of letting a router learn the cable range and zone names from another router as *discovery mode*. Discovery mode can help you avoid problems with mistyped cable ranges and zone names. Typing is required on just one router on a network—the seed router.

To configure a router as a non-seed router, assign a null cable range using the `appletalk cable-range 0-0` command. This puts the router in discovery mode. The router then learns the cable range and zone names from another router on the network.

NOTE Cisco does not support configuring a null cable range on a serial interface because it's not necessary. A serial interface on a point-to-point link automatically adjusts its cable range to match its partner. Even if you have not entered the `appletalk discovery` command, the router automatically avoids configuration mismatch problems on serial ports by changing the new router to match the existing router.

Cisco also has an `appletalk discovery` command, which sounds like it would put a router in discovery mode but actually has a slightly different purpose. You should use the `appletalk discovery` command on LAN segments when you know the cable range and zone names (and have configured them), but you want the router to change its configuration to match any new routers that advertise a different configuration. A router configured this way is sometimes called a *soft-seed router*.

Once a non-seed or soft-seed router has learned the cable range, this information is automatically entered into the router's configuration. If the configuration looks right, you can issue a `copy run start` command to save the configuration to NVRAM, so that next time the router boots, it has the right information already configured. (It becomes a seed router.) With some versions of Cisco IOS software, the router does not automatically place the zone name(s) into the configuration, however. Although the router correctly learns the zone name(s) for the network, and they can be seen with a `show appletalk zone` command, the zone name(s) are not automatically entered into the interface configuration. You must do this manually.

Configuring non-seed and soft-seed routers can be helpful when first setting up an internetwork and when troubleshooting problems with misconfigured routers that do not agree on cable ranges or zone names. The use of non-seed and soft-seed routers is not recommended on operational networks, however. Once you have worked out any problems with routers not agreeing on cable ranges or zone names, you should ensure that each router has the correct configuration saved in NVRAM. This way, every router boots with the correct information. (Every router becomes a seed router.)

When troubleshooting cable range and zone name problems, you can watch a router verify the cable range and zone names with the `debug appletalk events` command. Once the router is operational, this command should stop showing any significant output (assuming the router and the internetwork are stable), and you should issue the `no debug appletalk events` command.

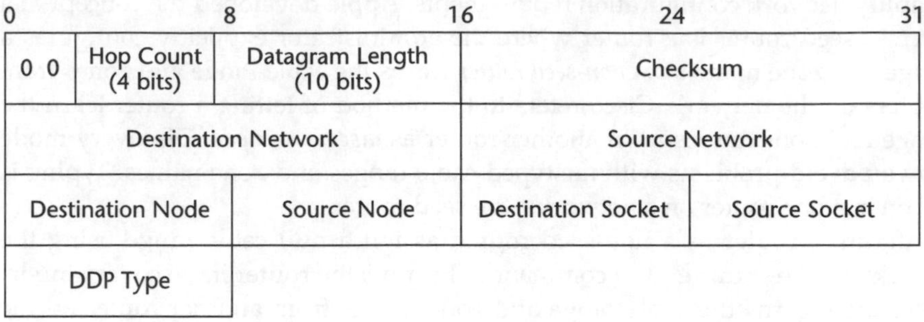

Figure 11.5 DDP header format.

Datagram Delivery Protocol (DDP)

DDP is a typical connectionless network-layer protocol that provides a best-effort delivery service for messages on an AppleTalk internetwork. A DDP datagram consists of a DDP header followed by data. Figure 11.5 shows the format of the DDP header.

The first 2 bytes of the DDP header include a 10-bit Datagram Length field, which is the length in bytes of the datagram, including the header and data. The DDP header is 13 bytes. The maximum amount of data allowed in a DDP datagram, not counting the DDP header, is 586 bytes. This is not configurable and has not changed since Apple first made this requirement in the early 1980s to accommodate LocalTalk. Unlike IP, DDP does not support fragmentation and reassembly. On data links that support larger frame sizes, such as Ethernet, AppleTalk still supports only 586 bytes of data.

In AppleTalk parlance, DDP delivers messages between sockets. A socket is an addressable software process within a network node. Each socket within a node is identified by an 8-bit socket number. Socket numbers within the DDP header identify the sending and receiving processes, as can be seen in Figure 11.5. AppleTalk uses the term *socket* essentially the same way that Novell's Internetwork Packet Exchange (IPX) uses the term. See Chapter 10 for more information about IPX sockets.

At the sending node, an application gives data to DDP, which causes DDP to form a DDP header based on the data supplied to it. DDP passes the datagram down to the appropriate data link for transmission. Similarly, when packets are received from a data link, DDP examines the datagram's destination address in the DDP header and delivers the datagram appropriately. A receiving end node delivers the packet to the appropriate upper-layer protocol based on the DDP Type field in the header. The upper-layer protocol examines the destination socket number in the DDP header to determine how to process the packet. Table 11.2 shows some common values for the DDP Type field.

Sockets are classified into two groups: statically assigned and dynamically assigned. Statically assigned sockets have numbers in the 1 to 127 range. Socket numbers 1 through 63 are reserved for use by Apple; numbers 64 through 127 arc available for unrestricted experimental use. Use of these experimental numbers is not recommended for actual (nonexperimental) networking products, however, because there is no mechanism for making sure two products don't use the same number. Instead, product developers should use the dynamically assigned socket numbers in the 128 to 254 range. DDP dynamically assigns these socket numbers on behalf of clients in a node and ensures that they are unique within the node. Table 11.3 lists the socket numbers reserved by Apple to identify basic AppleTalk processes.

A router forwards a DDP datagram based on the destination network number and node number in the DDP header. In addition to examining its routing table to decide how to forward the datagram, a router also checks the Hop Count field in the DDP header. The source node sets the hop count to zero. Each router increases the hop count by 1. A router that receives a datagram with a hop count value of 15 should not forward the datagram to another router. If the destination node is on a directly connected network, however, then the router should send the datagram to the destination node.

Table 11.2 DDP Types

TYPE	PROTOCOL
0x01	RTMP response or data packet
0x02	NBP
0x03	ATP
0x04	AEP
0x05	RTMP request
0x06	ZIP
0x07	ADSP

Table 11.3 DDP Socket Numbers and Processes

SOCKET	PROCESS
0x01	RTMP
0x02	Names information
0x04	Echo
0x06	Zone information

The DDP header also includes a checksum field. According to Apple, calculating the checksum is optional, so most end-user applications do not calculate it. If a router or end node receives a datagram with a checksum equal to zero, it can assume that the checksum was not performed by the sending station and ignore the field. On the other hand, when a Cisco router generates a packet—for example an RTMP or AEP packet—it does calculate the checksum by default. (To configure a router not to calculate the checksum, to reduce CPU processing, use the `no appletalk checksum` command.)

Name Binding Protocol (NBP)

NBP maps names to addresses. An NBP name is formatted as object:type@zone. For example, a file server's NBP name might be Galadriel:AFPServer@WildPacketsTraining. A Macintosh user finds the Galadriel AFP server in the WildPacketsTraining zone by opening the Chooser. In the Chooser, the user selects the WildPacketsTraining zone and clicks on an icon for AFP servers. NBP finds all servers of this type in the zone, and displays an icon for the Galadriel server so the user can double-click on the server icon and log in.

There are many myths about the amount and type of traffic caused by the Chooser. Despite what you may hear, Chooser traffic is not excessive and most of it is not broadcast. The packets are mostly unicast packets; some are multicast packets. Here is what really happens when a Macintosh user displays the Chooser and searches for services:

1. The Macintosh sends a ZIPGetZoneList unicast packet to its local router.

2. The router responds with a unicast ZIPGetZoneListReply that includes the zone names for the internetwork. (If there are many zones, more than one packet might be required.)

3. The user selects a zone and service type.

4. The Macintosh sends an NBPBroadcastRequest unicast packet to the router requesting the router to find all servers of the selected type in the selected zone. Notice that this is a unicast packet.

5. The router refers to its Zone Information Table and then sends an NBPForwardRequest unicast packet to a router on each network in the zone. These packets are sent to DDP node number 0 to avoid the router having to know an actual node address for other routers. Notice that this is a unicast packet.

6. Each router in the zone sends an NBPLookup multicast packet onto its local network. The multicast data link layer address is predetermined by an algorithm that hashes the zone name into a (usually) unique multicast address.

7. Any servers of the requested type respond directly to the requesting Macintosh with an NBPReply unicast packet.

If the Macintosh user leaves the Chooser window open, with a zone name and service type selected, the process repeats. In Mac OS 7.0, which Apple Computer shipped in 1989, a feature was added to reduce the number of packets that result when the Chooser window is left open. After 45 seconds, the time between the NBPBroadcastRequest unicast packets increases exponentially with each packet. The myths about the amount of traffic caused by the Chooser are greatly exaggerated. Usually the Macintosh user does not have both a zone name and a service type selected, in which case no traffic is sent. In addition, essentially all networked Macintoshes have been running Mac OS 7.0 or later for many years, so the amount of traffic is curtailed after 45 seconds.

Apple Filing Protocol (AFP)

AFP is a client/server protocol that allows users to share files across a network. A Macintosh can be both an AFP client and a server with *personal file sharing*. Third-party products also allow PCs to act as AFP clients and servers. In addition to using personal file sharing, most campus AppleTalk networks also have dedicated *AppleShare* AFP servers that run on Macintoshes or other platforms, using the Mac OS, Windows, Novell, or UNIX operating systems.

AFP is similar to the Server Message Block (SMB) protocol that is used on Windows networks for file sharing and is described in Chapter 12. In both cases, the protocols allow users to manipulate remote files using native file system commands. A data structure in local memory indicates whether the files that a user accesses are managed by a native file system or by some external file system. If the data structure indicates an external file system, the native file system redirects file manipulation commands to AFP (or SMB in the case of Windows).

Before users can access an AFP file server, the server must open a *session-listening socket*. When a server first becomes active on a network, it uses ASP to open a session-listening socket. The server also uses NBP to register the file server's name and type on the socket. (Opening a socket and registering the name are done internally and don't cause network traffic.) To find the file server, a client submits a request to NBP, as described in the previous section. NBP returns the addresses of servers that match the request. After the user picks a server, the user's machine sends an AFP *GetSrvrInfo* message to request information about the server. The server returns information that includes which AFP versions and User Authentication Methods (UAMs) it supports. From the list of versions and UAMs, the client chooses one and initiates the login process by submitting an AFP *Login* message to the server. Depending on the UAM method used, the Login message may include user login information (such as a username and password), or subsequent messages may be required to complete authentication of the user.

AFP supports a variety of methods to authenticate users. Most AFP servers use a secure method which does not send the user's password in clear text. Deriving the password from information sent over the network is essentially impossible in this case. With the most common authentication method, when a client logs in, the server generates a random number and sends the random number to the client. The client uses the password as an encryption key, encrypts the random number, and sends the encrypted random number back to the server. The server can verify that the correct password was used by encrypting the random number itself, using the known password for the user. If the two encrypted values match, then the server knows that the user typed the correct password. AFP also authenticates the server to the client. This two-way authentication prevents a hacker on the network from setting up a machine that masquerades as the server.

AFP servers running the Mac OS X operating system implement an alternative password exchange process that uses an advanced and extremely secure encryption technique called the *Diffie-Hellman algorithm*. Most AFP clients support the Diffie-Hellman method, although older Macintoshes and third-party (non-Apple) products may not support it and may send the password as clear text instead. To troubleshoot problems with UAMs, check the login screen that users see when they log in. With most implementations of AFP, the client login screen shows the UAM that the client selected from the options supported on the server.

NOTE The Diffie-Hellman algorithm is a standard asymmetric cryptographic key system that was developed in the 1970s by Whitfield Diffie and Martin Hellman. In addition to AFP on Mac OS X servers, the IPSec standard and many other technologies use the algorithm.

Although AFP has supported the random number authentication method since its invention in the mid-1980s, and Mac OS X has supported the Diffie-Hellman method since the late 1990s, some third-party products that allow a PC to act as an AFP client do not use a secure method to send the user's password. Notice in the following Ether-Peek protocol analyzer output that the client sends the password as clear text. The client in this case was a PC using AFP client software. At the bottom of the output, you will see that the user (Priscilla) typed a very nonsecure password (passwd).

```
802.3 Header
   Destination:          00:05:02:A0:43:8C
   Source:               00:00:0E:D5:C7:E7
   LLC Length:           81
802.2 Logical Link Control (LLC) Header
   Dest. SAP:            0xAA   SNAP
   Source SAP:           0xAA   SNAP
   Command:              0x03   Unnumbered Information
   Protocol:             0x080007809B  AppleTalk
Long DDP Header - Datagram Delivery Protocol
   Unused:               %00
   Hop Count:            %0000
   Datagram Length:      73
   DDP Checksum:         0x0000
   Dest. Network:        200
   Source Network:       200
   Dest Node:            199
   Source Node:          74
   Dest. Socket:         233
   Source Socket:        131
   DDP Type:             3   ATP
ATP Header - AppleTalk Transaction Protocol
   Function Code:        1   TReq
   Control Information:  %100   XO
   TRel Timeout Indicator:  %000   30 seconds
   Bitmap:               %00000001   Need Packet(s) 0
```

```
        Transaction ID:             9
(Assuming To Be ASP)
ASP - AppleTalk Session Protocol
    SPFunction:             2  Command
    Session ID:             22
    Sequence Number:        0
(Guessing To Be AFP)
AFP - AppleTalk Filing Protocol
    AFP Function:           18 Login
    AFP version:            AFPVersion 2.1
    User Authen. Method:    Cleartxt passwrd
    User Authen. Info:
    .Priscilla.passw  09 50 72 69 73 63 69 6C 6C 61 00 70 61 73 73 77
    d..               64 00 00
```

The analyzer output is interesting because of the nonsecure authentication method, but it is also interesting to see that AFP runs above ASP, ATP, and DDP. The output also shows that AppleTalk uses an IEEE 802.3 with 802.2 and Subnetwork Access Protocol (SNAP) header. Notice also that EtherPeek had to guess that this packet contains ASP and AFP data. Neither ATP nor ASP has a protocol type field that can be used to identify the next layer. EtherPeek had to remember that these packets were associated with an NBP request to find an AFP server.

In response to the login request from the user, the server performs authentication, and, assuming this works, returns a *session reference number* (SRefNum) that the client uses in all subsequent requests on this session. The next request the client makes is to obtain a list of the server's volumes using a *GetSrvrParms* message. The server returns information about the volumes on the server, including their names and an indication of whether they are password protected. The client can then open a volume, get parameters for the volume, open directories within a volume, read files, write to files, and so on.

> **NOTE** Some AFP file commands have interesting names because of the fact that a Macintosh file has two parts: a resource fork that stores information about the file and a data fork that has the actual data. So, when analyzing an AFP session with a protocol analyzer, don't be surprised to see such strange-sounding messages as *GetForkParms* and *FlushFork*.

AFP over TCP

Until around 1997, AFP worked only over AppleTalk. Now AFP also works over TCP/IP, which means it can be used for file sharing on IP campus networks and the Internet. An AppleShare client that supports AFP over TCP/IP has been built into the Macintosh since Mac OS 7.5, and AFP over TCP server software has been built in since Mac OS 9.0. Third-party products also allow PCs to use AFP over TCP/IP. AFP over TCP is usually a reasonably secure way to share files over the Internet because of the random number or Diffie-Hellman authentication methods. Because of its support for secure passwords, AFP may be preferable to the native file transfer protocol used more frequently on TCP/IP networks, which is the File Transfer Protocol (FTP). However, both the clients and servers must support AFP, and in many cases Internet servers do not support it. Also, be careful with some third-party AFP over TCP products for PCs, because they may send the user's password over the intranet or Internet in clear text.

When AFP runs above TCP/IP, you can troubleshoot it in a similar fashion as you would any TCP-based application. You should expect to see a normal TCP three-way handshake initiated by the client from an ephemeral port to the well-known TCP port for AFP, which is 548. Following the three-way handshake, you will see evidence of a new protocol, called the *Data Stream Interface* (DSI), which provides an interface between AFP and TCP. DSI uses a request/response model that supports multiple outstanding requests on a connection. After connecting via TCP, a client sends a DSI Open Session command to which the server should reply. After establishing a TCP and DSI session, the client finally sends an AFP Login command as shown in the following output:

```
Ethernet Header
   Destination:            00:05:02:A0:43:8C
   Source:                 00:00:0E:D5:C7:E7
   Protocol Type:          0x0800  IP
IP Header - Internet Protocol Datagram
   Version:                4
   Header Length:          5  (20  bytes)
   Type of Service:        %00000000
                           000. .... Precedence: Routine,
                           ...0 .... Normal Delay,
                           .... 0... Normal Throughput,
                           .... .0.. Normal Reliability
                           .... ..0. ECT bit - transport protocol will
                           ignore the CE bit
                           .... ...0 CE bit - no congestion
   Total Length:           106
   Identifier:             5120
   Fragmentation Flags:    %010
                           0.. Reserved
                           .1. Do Not Fragment
                           ..0 Last Fragment
   Fragment Offset:        0  (0  bytes)
   Time To Live:           128
   Protocol:               6  TCP - Transmission Control Protocol
   Header Checksum:        0xA4DE
   Source IP Address:      10.0.0.9
   Dest. IP Address:       10.0.0.19
   No IP Options
TCP - Transport Control Protocol
   Source Port:            1026
   Destination Port:       548  afpovertcp
   Sequence Number:        217936
   Ack Number:             563481921
```

```
        Offset:                5  (20 bytes)
        Reserved:              %000000
        Flags:                 %011000
                               0. .... (No Urgent pointer)
                               .1 .... Ack
                               .. 1... Push
                               .. .0.. (No Reset)
                               .. ..0. (No SYN)
                               .. ...0 (No FIN)
        Window:                8738
        Checksum:              0x6EA5
        Urgent Pointer:        0
        No TCP Options
  DSI - Data Stream Interface Header
        Flags:                 0  Request
        Command:               2  User Command
        Request ID:            1
        Offset:                0
        Data Length:           50
        Len Follow Data:       0
  AFP - AppleTalk Filing Protocol
        AFP Function:          18  Login
        AFP version:           AFPVersion 2.1
        User Authen. Method:   Cleartxt passwrd
        User Authen. Info:
        .Priscilla.passw  09 50 72 69 73 63 69 6C 6C 61 00 70 61 73 73 77
        d..               64 00 00
```

Notice that the AFP login looks exactly like it did in the previous example, but now it runs above DSI and TCP/IP instead of ASP, ATP, and DDP. As in the previous example, the client in this case was a PC running AFP client software that doesn't support the random number or Diffie-Hellman authentication methods, even though the server supports them, whether using AppleTalk or TCP/IP.

AppleTalk Routing

AppleTalk internetworks have three options for routing—RTMP, the AppleTalk Update-Based Routing Protocol (AURP), and Cisco's Enhanced Interior Gateway Routing Protocol (EIGRP). All of these protocols are distance-vector routing protocols. There is no link-state routing protocol for AppleTalk. Many campus networks use RTMP because it is easy to configure and has been supported for many years by Apple, Cisco, and other vendors of routers and servers that have routing capabilities. To reduce the amount of traffic caused by RTMP, some large enterprises use AURP or EIGRP on backbone networks and Wide Area Networks (WANs). RTMP must still run on LANs that support clients, however, because AppleTalk end nodes must see RTMP packets, as will be discussed in the *End-Node Routing* section. The AppleTalk routing protocols work closely with ZIP, which allows nodes to be divided into logical groups, called *zones*. This section covers ZIP as well as the three routing protocols.

Routing Table Maintenance Protocol (RTMP)

RTMP, the default routing protocol for AppleTalk, is a simple distance-vector routing protocol that is similar to the IP Routing Information Protocol (RIP). RTMP uses hop count as its routing metric with a maximum hop count of 15, as mentioned in the section on DDP. RTMP sends its entire routing table (after applying the split horizon rule) out each interface every 10 seconds. Apple chose such a short timer to promote quick convergence.

With Cisco IOS software, you can change how often a router sends RTMP packets with the `appletalk timers update-interval valid-interval invalid-interval` command, although this is not recommended. The `update-interval` parameter specifies how often RTMP packets are sent. The default is every 10 seconds. The `valid-interval` parameter specifies the time, in seconds, that the software considers a route valid without having heard a routing update for the route. The default is 20 seconds (two times the update interval). The `invalid-interval` parameter is the amount of time, in seconds, that the route is retained after the last update. The default is 60 seconds (three times the valid interval).

> **CAUTION** Be careful with the `appletalk timers` command. All routers in an internetwork should agree on timers. If they don't agree, a router might mark a route as invalid and remove it prematurely from the routing table.

Routes that have been refreshed within the last update interval (10 seconds by default) are considered *good* and are displayed in a Cisco routing table with a G. Routes older than the time specified by the update interval are considered *suspect* and are displayed in the Cisco routing table with an S. Routes may also be considered *bad* if another router advertises the route with a hop count of 31 or if the valid interval expires. Bad routes are displayed in the routing table with a B. When a route becomes bad, it is eligible for replacement by a path with a higher (less favorable) metric. During the invalid interval period, routers continue to include a bad route with a hop count of 31. If this timer expires, the route is finally deleted from the routing table.

The following Cisco IOS router output shows an AppleTalk routing table where Network 500-500 is labeled as B (bad) and the hop count is 31.

```
Albany#show appletalk route
Codes: R - RTMP derived, E - EIGRP derived, C - connected, A - AURP,
S - static,  P - proxy
5 routes in internet
The first zone listed for each entry is its default (primary) zone.
C Net 100-100 directly connected, Ethernet0, zone EthernetBackbone
C Net 200-200 directly connected, Ethernet1, zone albanyE
C Net 300-300 directly connected, TokenRing0, zone albanyT
R Net 400-400 [1/G] via 100.204, 0 sec, Ethernet0, zone bostonS
R Net 500-500 [31/B] via 100.204, 20 sec, Ethernet0, zone bostonE
```

An RTMP packet includes a tuple (set of fields) for each reachable network. The tuple lists the cable range for the network and a distance in hops to that network. The following EtherPeek protocol analyzer output shows an RTMP update for a small network:

```
802.3 Header
  Destination:            09:00:07:FF:FF:FF   ATalk Ph2 Broadcast
  Source:                 00:00:0C:05:3E:80
  LLC Length:             43
802.2 Logical Link Control (LLC) Header
  Dest. SAP:              0xAA   SNAP
  Source SAP:             0xAA   SNAP
  Command:                0x03   Unnumbered Information
  Protocol:               0x080007809B  AppleTalk
Long DDP Header - Datagram Delivery Protocol
  Unused:                 %00
  Hop Count:              %0000
  Datagram Length:        35
  DDP Checksum:           0xCE56
  Dest. Network:          0
  Source Network:         100
  Dest Node:              255
  Source Node:            122
  Dest. Socket:           1   RTMP
  Source Socket:          1   RTMP
  DDP Type:               1   RTMP Response or Data
RTMP - Routing Table Maintenance Protocol
  Router's Net:           100
  ID Length:              8
  Router's Node ID:       122
RTMP Tuple # 1
  Range Start:            100
  Range Flag:             %100   Extended
  Distance:               0
  Range End:              100
  Version:                0x82
RTMP Tuple # 2
  Range Start:            200
  Range Flag:             %100   Extended
  Distance:               0
  Range End:              200
  Version:                0x82
RTMP Tuple # 3
  Range Start:            300
  Range Flag:             %100   Extended
  Distance:               0
  Range End:              300
  Version:                0x82
```

On a large internetwork, in order to advertise all routes, RTMP can consume a lot of bandwidth. If an internetwork includes low-capacity links, it's a good idea to calculate the percentage of available bandwidth on those links that RTMP will use. When making the calculation, you can use the following values:

- Default update timer = 10 seconds
- Tuple size for each route = 6 bytes

- Size of the DDP header = 13 bytes
- Size of the RTMP header = 4 bytes
- Maximum size of a DDP datagram (not including the DDP header) = 586 bytes

On large internetworks, numerous DDP packets are required to send enough tuples to advertise every route. Because DDP datagrams cannot hold more than 586 bytes, no more than 97 extended networks can be advertised in one RTMP packet. The result is numerous back-to-back datagrams that can consume a significant portion of the bandwidth on low-capacity serial links. The workaround is not to use RTMP on the serial links. Instead, you can use static routes, AURP, or EIGRP.

When sending its routing table, an AppleTalk router uses split horizon. Neither Cisco nor Apple officially support disabling split horizon with RTMP (although disabling it with EIGRP is supported). The fact that you cannot disable split horizon can be a problem in Nonbroadcast Multiaccess (NBMA) networks, such as Frame Relay networks. In particular, there can be problems with routers learning about all routes if the network is designed in a hub-and-spoke topology, which is a typical topology for Frame Relay networks.

Looking at Figure 11.6, consider the effect split horizon has on connectivity. The headquarters router advertises only Network 100-100 when it sends its routing table out the serial (s0) WAN interface. This means that devices on Network 300-300 do not learn about devices on Network 400-400, and vice versa.

A solution to this problem is to use subinterfaces on the headquarters router. A subinterface is a logical interface that is associated with a physical interface. For the network in Figure 11.6, you should configure the headquarters router with five subinterfaces, each communicating with one of the remote routers. With this configuration,

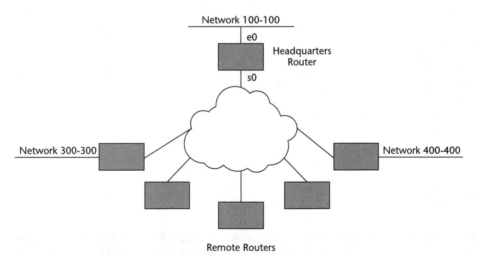

Figure 11.6 An AppleTalk hub-and-spoke network.

the headquarters router applies the split horizon rule based on logical subinterfaces, instead of the physical interface, and includes remote sites in the routing updates it sends out the s0 interface.

One other caveat with RTMP routing is that, by default, RTMP remembers only one path to a network—the path with the lowest hop count. In a network designed with redundant links, if there are multiple paths to a destination network, each with the same hop count, the router does not automatically store more than one path. You can configure a router to remember more than one path with the `appletalk maximum-paths paths` command. The software then distributes output on a packet-by-packet basis in a round-robin fashion.

End-Node Routing

Although an end node doesn't need to develop an entire routing table like a router does, it does need to know how to send packets to nonlocal destinations. In an IP environment, this is usually handled through the configuration of a default gateway on the end node. Redundancy is accomplished through use of a protocol such as Cisco's Hot Standby Router Protocol (HSRP). In AppleTalk environments, no configuration is required and HSRP is not required.

An AppleTalk end node remembers the address of the router that sent the most recent RTMP packet. Although the end node doesn't participate in the routing protocol, it does listen to RTMP update packets and copy into memory the address of the router that sent the update. If there is at least one router on an end node's network, the end node can learn about zones and can reach remote devices. If there are multiple routers on an end node's network, the end node very quickly learns a new way to reach remote networks when a router fails, because AppleTalk routers send RTMP packets every 10 seconds. There's no need for HSRP.

As you can see, Macintoshes and other AppleTalk end nodes require RTMP. Although it is a good idea to start eliminating RTMP on WAN and backbone networks, you must keep RTMP running on networks where AppleTalk end nodes reside if the end nodes need to communicate with end nodes on other AppleTalk networks. To avoid running a complete implementation of RTMP, on a Cisco router, you can configure the `appletalk rtmp-stub` command in interface configuration mode. This tells the router to send only the first tuple of an RTMP packet. The first tuple indicates the cable range assigned to the network onto which the router is sending the update, as you can see in the EtherPeek example in the previous section. End nodes can use these stub packets to learn the address of a router on the local network.

Because AppleTalk was designed in the early 1980s to run on Macintoshes with only 128 kbytes of RAM, the original AppleTalk specification stated that an end node remembers the address of only one router—the router that most recently sent an RTMP packet. The result was that an end node did not always use the best method to reach a remote station. The end node might select a path that included an extra hop. Figure 11.7 shows the workstation-to-router extra hop problem.

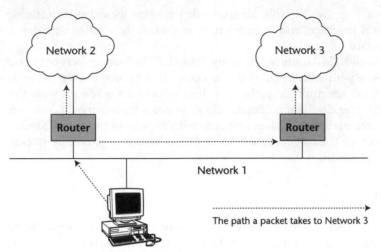

Figure 11.7   The extra hop problem.

AppleTalk Phase 2 fixed this problem by introducing the *best router forwarding algorithm*. With the best router forwarding algorithm, an end node maintains a cache of the best routers to use to reach remote networks. If a destination network is in the cache, the end node can use the router in the cache and avoid using a router that would result in an extra hop. This is similar to the behavior of an end node on a TCP/IP network, although IP nodes rely on the Internet Control Message Protocol (ICMP) sending Redirect messages, as discussed in the *Host Routing* section in Chapter 8. AppleTalk nodes, on the other hand, rely on DDP learning the data link address of routers on the node's LAN. When a packet arrives with a source network number that is not in a node's own network range, DDP looks at the sender's data link address. This is the address of the last router on the route from the network where the sender resides. DDP caches this information because this is the router that should have the best route, in terms of hops, to the network.

Zone Information Protocol

Routers use ZIP to maintain a mapping of network numbers to zone names for the internetwork. End nodes use a subset of ZIP to determine the zone(s) and cable range for the local network, and to get a list of zones for the entire internetwork.

As discussed in the NBP section, Macintosh users see the list of zones in the Chooser window. From that list, a user can request a lookup for all services of a certain type within a zone—for example, all file servers in the MistyMountains zone. By allowing an administrator to structure an internetwork into zones, Apple reduced the potential for lookup packets going to all networks and nodes. Administrators can use zones to contain broadcast traffic and subdivide an internetwork into logical groups. In this sense, zones are similar to Virtual LANs (VLANs).

A router maintains a network-to-zone mapping for the internetwork in its Zone Information Table, which sometimes goes by the uncouth name of *the ZIT*. The table consists of one entry for each network in the internetwork, and a list of zones for each network. An example of a Zone Information Table for a small internetwork follows:

```
Boston#show apple zone
Name                            Network(s)
EthernetBackbone                100-100
bostonE                         500-500
bostonS                         400-400
albanyE                         200-200
albanyT                         300-300
Total of 5 zones
```

ZIP works hand-in-hand with routing protocols. When a router receives a routing update from another router, it checks the update for any networks that it didn't know about already. If there is a new network, the router sends a *ZIP Query* to the router that sent the update, asking for the zone name(s) for that network. The router that sent the route update looks up the network in its Zone Information Table and replies to the ZIP Query. Contrary to popular myths about AppleTalk, both the query and the reply are unicast packets, not broadcast packets. (Also, it is not true that AppleTalk routers broadcast their Zone Information Tables on a regular basis, using lots of bandwidth, despite what some documentation claims. ZIP does not behave like Novell's SAP.)

The ZIP process can cause a flurry of ZIP Queries to propagate across an internetwork when routers learn about new networks. This is not a major problem if there are just one or two new networks in an update, but it can cause substantial network traffic when there are many new networks, such as during an upgrade or during recovery from a network outage. To slow the ZIP flurry and avoid ZIP storms, Cisco implemented the rule that a router does not advertise a network in its RTMP routing update until the ZIP Query/Reply sequence has completed and the zone name(s) for the network have been determined.

One disadvantage to Cisco's rule is that routing table convergence is not as fast as it could be. On large internetworks, it may take many minutes for all routers to learn about a new network because each router has to reach back and ask for the zone names before it can include a network number in its update. You can speed up the routing table convergence by telling a router to advertise routes that have no zone association by using the `no appletalk require-route-zones` command, but this is not recommended.

AppleTalk Update-Based Routing Protocol

Apple Computer designed AURP to address the problems associated with the amount of bandwidth consumed by RTMP, particularly on low-capacity WAN links. AURP reduces the network traffic associated with routing because it sends only updates after it initially sends the routing table. AURP also includes features to help a large campus internetwork migrate from AppleTalk to IP routing. AURP lets a network engineer connect two or more noncontiguous AppleTalk internetworks that are separated by a non-AppleTalk network, such as an IP network. In these types of configurations, AppleTalk still runs on the campus LANs, but it is eliminated inside the core of the internetwork to minimize bandwidth usage. IP routing replaces AppleTalk routing in the core of the internetwork.

A router running AURP can reset the Hop Count field in the DDP header to zero for traversal across a non-AppleTalk network. This permits the creation of very large AppleTalk internetworks where the hop count limit of 15 would be a problem. For example, a large university could connect many campus networks, each that already had a span of 15 hops, via an AURP backbone. Although it's unlikely that an AppleTalk campus network would span 15 hops, it's not inconceivable, especially on older educational networks where AppleTalk was once ubiquitous.

On a Cisco router, AURP is configured on a tunnel interface. Tunneling encapsulates an AppleTalk packet inside a User Datagram Protocol (UDP)/IP packet and sends the packet across the core IP internetwork to a destination router. The destination router extracts the AppleTalk packet and routes it to an AppleTalk network. You should use the following commands to configure an AURP tunnel:

`interface tunnel number`. Creates the tunnel interface.

`appletalk protocol aurp`. Creates an AURP routing process.

`tunnel source {ip-address | interface type number}`.
   Specifies the interface out which the encapsulated packets will be sent.

`tunnel destination {hostname | ip-address}`. Specifies the IP
   address or hostname of the router at the far end of the tunnel.

`tunnel mode aurp`. Enables AURP tunneling.

> **NOTE** A common mistake with AURP configuration is to give the tunnel an AppleTalk cable range and zone name. You don't need to do this, and, in fact, it brings the tunnel down.

In addition to these commands, to support route redistribution between AURP and RTMP, use the `appletalk route-redistribution` command in global configuration mode. Route redistribution is not enabled by default for AURP. Also, if your goal for using AURP is to reduce RTMP traffic, be sure to configure `no apple send-rtmps` on the interfaces that connect the tunnel, or else the router will continue to send RTMP packets out those interfaces.

When an AURP router starts an AURP process, it sends an *Open Request* message to the other end of the tunnel. AURP packets are encapsulated in IP and UDP and use 387 as the UDP port number. The other side of the tunnel should respond with an *Open Response* message. The routers then send *Routing Information Requests* to each other. The *Routing Information Responses* and *Zone Responses* that are sent in reply may be helpful when troubleshooting an AURP problem related to missing routes or zones. An example of a Zone Response follows. Notice the IP and UDP headers.

```
IP Header - Internet Protocol Datagram
  Version:                4
  Header Length:          5  (20  bytes)
  Type of Service:        %00000000
                          000. .... Precedence: Routine,
                          ...0 .... Normal Delay,
                          .... 0... Normal Throughput,
                          .... .0.. Normal Reliability
                          .... ..0. ECT bit - transport protocol will
                          ignore the CE bit
                          .... ...0 CE bit - no congestion
  Total Length:           82
  Identifier:             29
  Fragmentation Flags:    %000
                          0.. Reserved
                          .0. May Fragment
                          ..0 Last Fragment
  Fragment Offset:        0  (0  bytes)
  Time To Live:           255
  Protocol:               17  UDP - User Datagram Protocol
  Header Checksum:        0xA767
  Source IP Address:      10.10.0.2
  Dest. IP Address:       10.10.0.1
  No IP Options
UDP - User Datagram Protocol
  Source Port:            387  aurp
  Destination Port:       387  aurp
  Length:                 62
  Checksum:               0x0C41
AppleTalk Tunnelling Through IP
  Destination Domain Indicator:
                          Length:7
                          Authority:0x01  IP Address
                          Distinguisher:0x0000
                          Address:10.10.0.1
  Source Domain Indicator:
                          Length:7
                          Authority:0x01  IP Address
                          Distinguisher:0x0000
                          Address:10.10.0.2
  Version:                0x0001
  Reserved:               0x0000
  Packet Type:            0x0003  AURP
AURP - AppleTalk Update-based Routing Protocol
  Connection ID:          0x0347
  Sequence Number:        0x0000
  Command:                7  Zone Response
  Flags:                  0x0000
  Subcode:                1  Zone Information Response
```

```
  Number of Tuples:       2
Zone Tuple #1
  Network Number:         400
  Zone Name:              bostonS
Zone Tuple #2
  Network Number:         500
  Zone Name:              bostonE
```

After AURP routers have exchanged routing and zone information, they should be somewhat quiet. The only traffic should be an occasional AURP *Tickle* packet which is acknowledged. Each end of the tunnel sends a Tickle unicast packet to the other end of the tunnel every 90 seconds. Tickles are analogous to keepalives or Hello packets used in other routing protocols. (The term *Tickle* appears in other aspects of AppleTalk also. ASP and PAP also send Tickles.)

EIGRP for AppleTalk

Cisco developed an AppleTalk routing process for EIGRP to address many of the same concerns that AURP addresses. EIGRP minimizes routing traffic by sending changes rather than broadcasting the entire routing table at regular intervals. In addition, EIGRP is optimized for fast convergence. In an internetwork composed of just Cisco routers, EIGRP is more common than AURP on backbone networks. (AURP is not used much.)

EIGRP reduces resource requirements on a router. Because EIGRP supports AppleTalk, IPX, and IP, you can use a single routing protocol for multiprotocol networks, minimizing the processing and memory requirements for a router. EIGRP provides a common protocol engine that includes the Diffusing-Update Algorithm (DUAL) and reliable transport protocol for sending route updates. See Chapter 8 for more details about DUAL and the reliability of EIGRP. To create an AppleTalk EIGRP routing process, you should use the following commands:

appletalk routing eigrp router-number. Enables an AppleTalk EIGRP routing process in global configuration mode.

appletalk protocol eigrp. Enables EIGRP on an interface in interface configuration mode.

The *router-number* parameter for the `appletalk routing eigrp` command is a Router ID. The Router ID can be any decimal integer from 1 to 65,535. (Note that IP and IPX EIGRP use an autonomous system number to enable EIGRP, whereas AppleTalk EIGRP uses a Router ID.) The Router ID must be unique on the internetwork, so be sure to document which numbers are in use. If you configure a router with a Router ID that is already in use on a neighbor router, the Cisco IOS software will refuse to start AppleTalk.

By default, RTMP routes are automatically redistributed into EIGRP and vice versa. EIGRP tracks the AppleTalk hop count from end to end. (It does not have a hop count reduction feature like AURP does.) It tracks the hop count as an external metric. Redistributed RTMP routes are advertised in EIGRP as external routes. Internal EIGRP routes are preferred over external EIGRP routes. If there are multiple EIGRP paths to a destination, a path that originates from within the EIGRP routing domain is preferred over one that originates from outside the EIGRP routing domain.

You can turn off redistribution if it does not meet your needs. To disable route redistribution, use the `no appletalk route-redistribution` command in global configuration mode. EIGRP also permits disabling split horizon. To disable split horizon, use the `no appletalk eigrp-splithorizon` command in interface configuration mode. Also, if your goal for using EIGRP is to reduce RTMP traffic, be sure to configure `no apple send-rtmps` on the interfaces that use EIGRP, or else the router will continue to send RTMP packets.

Because previous chapters talked about EIGRP for IP and IPX, the format of an AppleTalk EIGRP message should come as no surprise. To help you learn EIGRP, compare the following EIGRP Update packet with the EIGRP Update packets displayed in Chapters 8 and 10. Remember, a router sends an Update packet when it boots or when changes occur.

```
DLC:  ----- DLC Header -----
      DLC:
      DLC:  Destination = Multicast 090007FFFFFF, Atalk_Broadcast
      DLC:  Source      = Station Cisco1002E75
      DLC:  802.3 length = 129
      DLC:
LLC:  ----- LLC Header -----
      LLC:
      LLC:  DSAP Address = AA, DSAP IG Bit = 00 (Individual Address)
      LLC:  SSAP Address = AA, SSAP CR Bit = 00 (Command)
      LLC:  Unnumbered frame: UI
      LLC:
SNAP: ----- SNAP Header -----
      SNAP:
      SNAP: Vendor ID = Apple1
      SNAP: Type = 809B (AppleTalk)
      SNAP:
DDP:  ----- DDP header -----
      DDP:
      DDP:  Hop count        = 0
      DDP:  Length           = 121
      DDP:  Checksum         = 7CCB (Correct)
      DDP:  Destination Network Number = 0
      DDP:  Destination Node         = 255
      DDP:  Destination Socket       = 88 (Cisco EIGRP)
      DDP:  Source Network Number    = 100
      DDP:  Source Node              = 26
      DDP:  Source Socket            = 88 (Cisco EIGRP)
      DDP:  DDP protocol type = 88 (EIGRP)
      DDP:
EIGRP: ----- Enhanced IGRP Header -----
      EIGRP:
      EIGRP: Version       = 2
      EIGRP: Opcode        = 1 (Update)
      EIGRP: EIGRP Checksum = 2B23 (correct)
      EIGRP: Flags (unused) = 0000
      EIGRP: Flags         = 0000
      EIGRP:                    Conditionally receive mode is not required
```

```
EIGRP:                       Is not an initial update packet
EIGRP: Sequence number          = 4
EIGRP: Acknowledgment number    = 0
EIGRP: Autonomous System number = 1
EIGRP:
EIGRP: Protocol ID          = 0x02 (AppleTalk)
EIGRP: Type Code            = 0x0203 (AppleTalk External Routes)
EIGRP: Field length         = 44
EIGRP: Next hop address        =
EIGRP: Originating Router ID (AT address) =
EIGRP: Originating AS number    = 1
EIGRP: Arbitrary tag            = 100
EIGRP: External protocol        = 2 (Connected)
EIGRP: Exterior flags = 01
EIGRP: .... ...1 = Destination is in the same autonomous system
EIGRP: External protocol metric    = 0
EIGRP: Time delay            = 0xFFFFFFFF (route unreachable)
EIGRP: Path bandwidth (2,560,000,000/kbps) = 256000
EIGRP: Min/max transmission unit (MTU)    = 1500
EIGRP: Hop count                = 1
EIGRP: Reliability (error percentage)    = 255
EIGRP: Load utilization percentage      = 1
EIGRP: Reserved
EIGRP: Starting cable range = 300
EIGRP: Ending cable range   = 300
EIGRP:
EIGRP: Protocol ID          = 0x02 (AppleTalk)
EIGRP: Type Code            = 0x0203 (AppleTalk External Routes)
EIGRP: Field length         = 44
EIGRP: Next hop address        =
EIGRP: Originating Router ID (AT address) =
EIGRP: Originating AS number    = 1
EIGRP: Arbitrary tag            = 2
EIGRP: External protocol        = 6 (RTMP)
EIGRP: Exterior flags = 01
EIGRP: .... ...1 = Destination is in the same autonomous system
EIGRP: External protocol metric    = 1
EIGRP: Time delay (10 msec/256)        = 512000
EIGRP: Path bandwidth (2,560,000,000/kbps) = 256524800
EIGRP: Min/max transmission unit (MTU)    = 1500
EIGRP: Hop count                = 1
EIGRP: Reliability (error percentage)    = 255
EIGRP: Load utilization percentage      = 1
EIGRP: Reserved
EIGRP: Starting cable range = 500
EIGRP: Ending cable range   = 500
```

In the example, the Cisco1002E75 router sends an AppleTalk multicast to let other routers know that Network 300-300 is not reachable via the router (see the maximum delay) and that Network 500-500 is reachable with a delay of a 512,000. Network

500-500 is an external network that another router is advertising via RTMP. It's a bit strange that AppleTalk EIGRP sends the Update message as a multicast. In the other examples in previous chapters, we saw EIGRP sending Updates directly to other routers.

In this case, there was just one other router on the Ethernet segment, and its response to the information from Cisco1002E75 about Network 500-500 was to send a ZIP Query to get the zone name(s) for the network. The following output shows the ZIP Query. It looks like any ZIP Query. (It's not different just because EIGRP is being used instead of RTMP.) Notice that it is a unicast packet. (As mentioned in the ZIP section, it's a myth that ZIP sends broadcasts.)

```
DLC:  ----- DLC Header -----
      DLC:
      DLC:  Destination = Station Cisco1002E75
      DLC:  Source      = Station Cisco1053E80
      DLC:  802.3 length = 25
      DLC:
LLC:  ----- LLC Header -----
      LLC:
      LLC:  DSAP Address = AA, DSAP IG Bit = 00 (Individual Address)
      LLC:  SSAP Address = AA, SSAP CR Bit = 00 (Command)
      LLC:  Unnumbered frame: UI
      LLC:
SNAP: ----- SNAP Header -----
      SNAP:
      SNAP: Vendor ID = Apple1
      SNAP: Type = 809B (AppleTalk)
      SNAP:
DDP:  ----- DDP header -----
      DDP:
      DDP:  Hop count      = 0
      DDP:  Length         = 17
      DDP:  Checksum       = 794C (Correct)
      DDP:  Destination Network Number = 100
      DDP:  Destination Node        = 26
      DDP:  Destination Socket      = 6 (Zone)
      DDP:  Source Network Number   = 100
      DDP:  Source Node             = 110
      DDP:  Source Socket           = 6 (Zone)
      DDP:  DDP protocol type = 6 (Zone)
      DDP:
ZIP:  ----- ZIP header -----
      ZIP:
      ZIP:  ZIP command   = 1 (Query)
      ZIP:  Network count = 1
      ZIP:
      ZIP:  --- Networks being queried: ---
      ZIP:  #1: Net = 500
      ZIP: [Normal end of "ZIP header".]
```

The Cisco1002E75 router returned the following ZIP Reply as a unicast packet to the Cisco1053E80 router.

```
DLC:  ----- DLC Header -----
     DLC:
     DLC:  Destination = Station Cisco1053E80
     DLC:  Source      = Station Cisco1002E75
     DLC:  802.3 length = 33
     DLC:
LLC:  ----- LLC Header -----
     LLC:
     LLC:  DSAP Address = AA, DSAP IG Bit = 00 (Individual Address)
     LLC:  SSAP Address = AA, SSAP CR Bit = 00 (Command)
     LLC:  Unnumbered frame: UI
     LLC:
SNAP: ----- SNAP Header -----
     SNAP:
     SNAP: Vendor ID = Apple1
     SNAP: Type = 809B (AppleTalk)
     SNAP:
DDP:  ----- DDP header -----
     DDP:
     DDP:  Hop count          = 0
     DDP:  Length             = 25
     DDP:  Checksum           = CBE7 (Correct)
     DDP:  Destination Network Number = 100
     DDP:  Destination Node   = 110
     DDP:  Destination Socket = 6 (Zone)
     DDP:  Source Network Number = 100
     DDP:  Source Node        = 26
     DDP:  Source Socket      = 6 (Zone)
     DDP:  DDP protocol type = 6 (Zone)
     DDP:
ZIP:  ----- ZIP header -----
     ZIP:
     ZIP:  ZIP command  = 2 (Reply)
     ZIP:  Network count = 1
     ZIP:
     ZIP:  --- Network-zone list ---
     ZIP:  #1: Net = 500, Zone = bostonE
     ZIP: [Normal end of "ZIP header".]
```

After each of the routers sent EIGRP Update packets and acknowledged each other's Update packets (remember EIGRP is a reliable protocol), the Cisco1053E80 router had the following AppleTalk routing table and Zone Information Table.

```
Albany#show appletalk route
Codes: R - RTMP derived, E - EIGRP derived, C - connected, A - AURP,
S - static,  P - proxy
5 routes in internet
The first zone listed for each entry is its default (primary) zone.
```

```
C Net 100-100 directly connected, Ethernet0, zone EthernetBackbone
C Net 200-200 directly connected, Ethernet1, zone albanyE
C Net 300-300 directly connected, TokenRing0, zone albanyT
E Net 400-400 [1/G] via 100.26, 1796 sec, Ethernet0, zone bostonS
E Net 500-500 [2/G] via 100.26, 1786 sec, Ethernet0, zone bostonE
Albany#
Albany#show appletalk zone
Name                            Network(s)
EthernetBackbone                100-100
bostonE                         500-500
bostonS                         400-400
albanyE                         200-200
albanyT                         300-300
Total of 5 zones
```

Controlling AppleTalk Traffic

Although AppleTalk's reputation for sending excessive network traffic is generally based on myths, it is true that RTMP's 10-second update timer is extremely short, NBP can spread like wildfire on a poorly designed network, and ZIP Queries and replies on a temperamental network make matters worse, not better. This section describes some configuration commands that can help you control AppleTalk traffic as well as implement security and access policies.

Static Routes

When using AppleTalk on low-capacity WAN links or with Dial-on-Demand Routing (DDR), to minimize bandwidth utilization, you can use static routes instead of a routing protocol. In addition, you can use floating static routes to back up routes learned by a routing protocol. A static route has precedence over dynamically learned routes, whereas a floating static route is superseded by dynamically learned routes and is intended as a last resort when the dynamic routes fail.

On a Cisco router, configuring an AppleTalk static route is similar to configuring an IP static route. To add a static route, you specify the cable range for the remote network and the address of a next hop router on the path to the network. If your goal is to reduce the amount of traffic caused by RTMP, be sure to also configure the no appletalk send-rtmps command on the appropriate interfaces.

With AppleTalk static routes, you need to know the address of the next hop router to reach the remote network. Unlike IP static routes, Cisco does not let you specify an AppleTalk static route with an interface number instead of the address of a router. This is a strange requirement considering that AppleTalk uses dynamic addressing. In fact, to use static routing, it is a good idea to not rely on dynamic addressing for your router interfaces that will be referenced in static route configurations. When you configure the interface, include the network.node parameter with the appletalk cable-range cable-range [network.node] command. That way you will know which network.node value to use in static route configurations.

When specifying a static route, you must also specify the zone(s) for the destination network. Specifying the zone(s) ensures that the router has an accurate zone list, which is important if the router is also running a dynamic routing protocol on some interfaces. In this case, the router advertises the cable range configured in the static route and must be able to correctly respond to ZIP Queries sent by other routers to retrieve the zone name(s) for the cable range.

In summary, to add a static route for an extended AppleTalk network, use the `appletalk static cable-range <cable-range> to network.node zone <zone-name>` command in global configuration mode. If the destination network is in more than one zone, then you must enter this command for each zone name. A common mistake is to enter the command only once and to enter multiple zones on one line, as shown in the following example:

```
appletalk static cable-range 500-500 to 20.14 zone Sales Marketing
```

The Cisco router will think there is one zone name in this case: "Sales Marketing." If there are two distinct zone names, Sales and Marketing, then you must enter:

```
appletalk static cable-range 500-500 to 20.14 zone Sales
appletalk static cable-range 500-500 to 20.14 zone Marketing
```

To add a floating static route for an extended AppleTalk network, use the `appletalk static cable-range <cable-range> to network.node floating zone <zone-name>` command in global configuration mode. If the destination network is in more than one zone, then you must enter this command for each zone name.

AppleTalk Access Lists

Cisco IOS software supports AppleTalk access lists for controlling access to or from specific networks, zones, and NBP named entities. Before configuring AppleTalk access lists, it's important to think about the ramifications, with a consideration for AppleTalk's unique features and Cisco's implementation of them. For example, suppose you wish to configure a list to deny access to Network 10-10 which is in the Rivendell zone. If Network 20-20 is also in the Rivendell zone, the default Cisco behavior is to also filter Network 20-20 from any route updates. To remedy this situation, you must use the `appletalk permit-partial-zones` command.

Filtering Cable Ranges

Basic AppleTalk filtering uses a list number between 600 and 699 and is configured with the following command in global configuration mode:

```
access-list access-list-number {deny | permit} cable-range <cable-range>
```

In addition to specifying the cable ranges to be filtered, be sure to define the default action to take for other network numbers, using the following global configuration command:

```
access-list access-list number {deny | permit} other-access
```

To tell the router to filter incoming or outgoing packets for the cable range, use an access group command in interface configuration mode:

```
appletalk access-group access-list-number {in | out}
```

To tell the router to filter the cable range from incoming or outgoing routing updates, use a distribute list in interface configuration mode:

```
appletalk distribute-list access-list-number {in | out}
```

Filtering Zones

To understand zone filters, remember that zone names are used by both end nodes and routers. When a Macintosh user displays the Chooser, the Macintosh sends a ZIPGet-ZoneList command to a local router. You can configure the router so that it filters zone names from the list as follows.

In global configuration mode, use the following commands:

```
access-list access-list-number {deny | permit} zone zone-name
access-list access-list-number {deny | permit} additional-zones
```

On an interface, configure the following command:

```
appletalk getzonelist-filter access-list-number
```

For ZIPGetZoneList filters to work correctly, all routers on the local segment must be configured with the same access list. You can't predict which router might respond first to the Macintosh's request for zones. For this reason, you must be careful to apply the ZIPGetZoneList filter on each router.

It is also possible to filter zones from the point of view of routers communicating with other routers. When a router advertises a route to a new network, other routers respond by sending a ZIP Query to get the zone names for the cable range, as discussed in previous sections. With a ZIP reply filter, you can control which zone names are returned. You should define the zones to be filtered with an access list in global configuration mode, as shown in the ZIPGetZoneList example. In addition, you should use the following command in interface configuration mode:

```
appletalk zipreply-filter access-list-number
```

Macintosh Networks in Transition

Macintosh networking is in the middle of a major transition due to two factors. First, the Mac OS is shifting to UNIX with the release of Mac OS X. Second, AppleTalk is starting to disappear. With the popularity of the Internet and Internet protocols, Apple is concentrating on the development of IP protocols for Mac OS instead of AppleTalk protocols. Although Mac OS X still supports the AppleTalk protocols, both Apple and Apple's customers are expected to put less focus on maintaining and troubleshooting AppleTalk protocols and more focus on Internet protocols.

From a troubleshooting viewpoint, there are many positive aspects of the transition to UNIX and Internet protocols, but there are also numerous challenges. Although Apple has done a good job of hiding the underpinnings of UNIX from the average user, experienced users (and users who think they are experienced) will be much more likely to get themselves in trouble with UNIX than they were with the older Macintosh operating systems. On the other hand, UNIX has many features that make it more robust than the older Macintosh operating systems.

Mac OS X

The UNIX operating system, which forms the basis of Mac OS X, provides a new level of reliability and performance for Macintoshes. Before Mac OS X, as many users know, a malfunctioning Macintosh application could crash or hang the entire system. With UNIX, each process runs in its own separate memory space and can't interfere with other processes or with the OS. If a process crashes, it can't impair other processes or disable the entire machine. UNIX also provides preemptive multitasking, which ensures that each process gets a fair share of CPU time and no single process can hog all CPU cycles.

NOTE The robustness of UNIX is especially beneficial for Web servers running Mac OS X. In the past, a rogue Common Gate Interface (CGI) script could crash a Web server. With UNIX, because applications run in a separate memory space where they don't have access to other applications or the OS, a buggy CGI can't crash the entire server.

UNIX was designed as a multiple-user operating system. It supports numerous ways for remote users to access a computer, which has many benefits, but also should cause concern for those of us who troubleshoot network services. An end user or server machine can provide a wide range of Internet and intranet services. A Mac OS X user can enable many services through the Sharing option in the System Preferences window. Most of the services are turned off by default to minimize security vulnerabilities and troubleshooting issues, but users may enable them and then require help from network administrators to get them to work correctly.

As in older versions of the operating system, a Macintosh can act as an AFP server. Be careful with the early versions of Mac OS X, which only supported AFP over TCP/IP, and not AFP over AppleTalk. In this case, if you have file sharing and AppleTalk enabled, your machine shows up in the Chooser of other machines. However, when those machines try to communicate with yours, they must switch over to TCP, which may not work if the machine isn't configured to support TCP/IP. (This is fixed in Mac OS 10.1 which supports AFP over TCP and over AppleTalk.)

As a network administrator, it's important to know that Mac OS X users can enable many other network services besides AFP. Mac OS X's Web sharing is similar to older versions, except that it is now based on the popular UNIX Apache server software, which is powerful but difficult to configure and monitor. What's different with Mac OS X is that users can now enable remote login and FTP server software on their machines. With early versions of Mac OS X, the remote login was Telnet, which caused security concerns because Telnet sends the user's password in clear text. With Mac OS 10.0.1, the remote login is Secure Shell (SSH), which is more secure. Nonetheless, remote login represents a troubleshooting risk because it allows authorized remote users to access a Macintosh using the UNIX command line. (In other words, it allows Macintosh users who may not be very knowledgeable to tinker with other users' machines. Permission to do this is required—the remote user must have a username and password—but nonetheless, there are some troubleshooting risks.)

FTP is another UNIX-based service with some security and troubleshooting risks. Mac OS X does not support anonymous FTP, so users must have a username and password to access the FTP service, but concerns remain because even an authorized user could cause problems. Also, as discussed in Chapter 9, FTP sends the user's password in clear text and has a tendency to misbehave with firewalls. In addition to AFP, Web sharing, remote login, and FTP, which are easy to enable, a knowledgeable user can also enable a large variety of UNIX services from the UNIX command line, including the UNIX standard for file sharing, Network File System (NFS).

When a user enables a Mac OS X service, it can be difficult to determine whether that service is being accessed and by whom. Mac OS X has no equivalent of the Mac OS 9 File Sharing Activity Monitor. Most services can output log files, but the files are written in inconsistent formats and in different places on the machine's hard drive. Mac OS X users should be encouraged to install a personal firewall that has good logging and notification features and to use a firewall log analysis application, such as Open Door's Who's There? Firewall Advisor. Mac OS X includes a standard UNIX firewall, called *ipfirewall*, which is accessible only from the command line. Ipfirewall is hard to configure and monitor and requires root privileges that are disabled on Mac OS X by default. A better solution for most Macintosh users is an end-user software firewall, such as the Norton Personal Firewall application from Symantec.

When migrating a network that is based on Mac OS 9 and AppleTalk to Mac OS X and IP, security should be a big concern. The AppleTalk protocols were designed with security in mind. The IP protocols were not, which explains the lack of encrypted passwords in Telnet and FTP. Another reason that security should be considered is that AppleTalk networks are generally isolated. The AppleTalk protocols are not routed over the Internet, so outside hackers can't easily access a node on an AppleTalk network. When migrating AppleTalk networks to IP, the use of firewalls and access lists on routers becomes increasingly necessary.

Another area for concern is that the older Mac OS versions were not a major target for virus creators and hacker attacks. Virus creators like to maximize the effect of their evil deeds by developing for the most popular operating systems, including Windows and UNIX. Mac OS X, because it is UNIX-based, is susceptible to numerous viruses and other hacker attacks that did not affect Mac OS 9 and earlier versions. Also, UNIX is *open source*, which means the source code for the OS is available for anyone who is interested, including hackers and virus developers.

> **NOTE** The UNIX root account, which is an all-powerful user account, is disabled on Mac OS X. This decreases the likelihood that some of the common UNIX attacks will succeed on Mac OS X, as many of them rely on root access. A user can use NetInfo to enable root access, but many Macintosh users don't know how to do this.

WebDAV

Mac OS X supports a new protocol called Web-based Distributed Authoring and Versioning (WebDAV), which can replace FTP or AFP for uploading files and graphics to Web servers. Apple customers also use WebDAV to access Apple's iDisk service. WebDAV is a set of extensions to the Hypertext Transfer Protocol (HTTP) to allow users to collaboratively edit and manage files on remote Web servers. One advantage that WebDAV has over FTP is that the specification (RFC 2518) states that WebDAV applications must support Digest authentication (RFC 2069) for user passwords. The Digest authentication method verifies that both communicators know a shared secret that is not sent over the network as clear text.

Service Location Protocol (SLP)

Mac OS X supports a new protocol for finding services on an IP network: SLP. SLP emulates AppleTalk by providing dynamic resource discovery and point-and-click access to services. Many organizations that have an AppleTalk heritage—in particular, universities—are starting to implement SLP.

SLP uses the concept of a *scope*, which is similar to an AppleTalk zone, and allows clients to search for services in a hierarchical manner. Services are grouped into scopes. Like AppleTalk, SLP supports dynamic naming services without the need for a centralized name server. SLP also has an option for scaling service location through the use of name servers, also called *directory agents*. Servers send *Register* messages to directory agents containing the services they wish to advertise. Clients send unicast packets to directory agents to find services.

Users and servers discover directory agents in two ways. First, they send a *Service Request* multicast packet looking for the directory agent service when they initialize. Second, the directory agent sends unsolicited advertisements infrequently, for which the client and server listen. See Chapter 9 for more information about SLP.

Mac OS X Initialization Traffic

Although the amount of bandwidth used when Mac OS X boots is not significant, the number of packets is outstanding. The authors studied a Macintosh running Mac OS X version 10.1 that was using mostly default parameters, with a few items (such as the IP address and Domain Name System [DNS] server address) manually configured. The Macintosh also had file sharing enabled. Before we had connected to any servers, accessed any resources, or even moved the mouse, the Macintosh transmitted 175 packets! This was not a scientific study because it included only one computer with a specific configuration and version of Mac OS X, but the behavior we noticed is probably similar to the behavior of many Macintoshes running Mac OS X.

The Macintosh started the boot process by sending 80 AARP probe packets to verify its own address. As expected, it sent these packets to the AppleTalk multicast address 09:00:07:FF:FF:FF. Unexpectedly, the Macintosh sent 40 AARP packets without getting a reply, and then, after 2 seconds, chose a different address and sent 40 more AARP packets. The Macintosh didn't get a response for these probes, which meant its chosen address was unique. The Macintosh used the address in the second set of AARP probe packets from there on. Earlier versions of Mac OS sent only 10 to 20 AARP probe packets. It's not clear why Apple thinks 40 packets per address are necessary or why the Macintosh wasn't satisfied with the first address it chose. Perhaps when the file sharing software started, it reinitialized the AppleTalk stack and restarted the AARP process.

The Macintosh also sent 12 IP ARP packets to verify that no other station was using its IP address. It sent these to the Ethernet broadcast address, FF: FF: FF: FF: FF: FF. It also sent numerous NBP multicast packets to verify that its NBP names were unique. (Because of file sharing, it had an AFP server name and an end-user name of type *Darwin*. (Darwin is the name of the Mac OS X open source project and appears to also be the NBP object name for Macintoshes running Mac OS X.)

The Macintosh was on a LAN with no AppleTalk router, so it didn't get any replies to its ZIPGetNetInfo requests, which it sent 12 times to the AppleTalk multicast address. The Macintosh also did a few reverse DNS lookups to get the DNS server's host name, which seems superfluous. It also sent numerous packets to the network time server at Apple. (Macintoshes can keep their system clocks current by communicating with a network time server.)

The most surprising aspect of the boot process was the SLP traffic. The Macintosh sent 15 SLP Service Requests to find an SLP directory agent. (The network didn't have any directory agents, so there were no replies.) The Macintosh also sent approximately 20 Service Requests for each type of service it wished to discover. It tried to find NFS, SMB, and Common Internet File System (CIFS) servers. (Chapter 12 talks about SMB, which is a file-sharing protocol used on Windows networks. CIFS is a variant of SMB for SMB file sharing over the Internet.) Surprisingly, the Macintosh also sent NBP lookups for NFS, SMB, and CIFS servers (four NBP packets for each service). This was before we had even moved the mouse, so this traffic wasn't caused by user action. Later we connected to some AFP servers and the traffic appeared to be typical AFP over TCP packets.

The moral of this story is that when you study your own network traffic, which you definitely should do, don't be surprised to see a lot of packets when Macintoshes running Mac OS X boot. On the other hand, don't get the wrong impression that the packets use an inordinate amount of bandwidth. In our example, 175 packets occurred in 2 minutes, but they were short packets, with a cumulative byte count of just 13,000 bytes. On a 10-Mbps Ethernet network (and especially on a 100-Mbps Ethernet network), this amount of traffic represents a minute percentage of available bandwidth. Also, when considering the amount of traffic, keep in mind Apple's philosophy regarding ease of use and minimal configuration. Mac OS X sends so much traffic in an attempt to automate service location and minimize the amount of work required for the user to find services.

Mac OS X Server Network Management Tools

Mac OS X Server software is an industrial-strength version of Mac OS X for servers. It actually shipped before the generic Mac OS X software. Like Mac OS X, Mac OS X Server runs on UNIX and supports both AppleTalk and TCP/IP. A Macintosh running Mac OS X Server software can act as an AFP, SMB, CIFS, NFS, and FTP file server. Mac OS X Server software also supports the Apache Web server software and WebDAV for uploading Web page files. A Mac OS X Server can also act as a DNS, SLP, DHCP, and e-mail (Simple Mail Transfer Protocol [SMTP], Post Office Protocol [POP], or Internet Message Access Protocol [IMAP]) server. In other words, it can act like a typical corporate intranet or Internet server, offering the services that a TCP/IP or AppleTalk campus network needs.

Mac OS X Server supports many services to help administrators manage Macintosh networks, including three that are briefly covered here: network booting (NetBoot), NetInfo, and the Macintosh Manager.

NetBoot simplifies system administration by allowing disk image files on a NetBoot server machine to act as startup disks for Mac OS clients. The server holds two standard Mac OS disk image files—one with system software and one with applications available to NetBoot clients. Holding down the N key while booting forces a client machine's firmware to look on the local Ethernet network for a NetBoot server, using the BOOTP protocol. The server returns an IP address that the administrator has assigned to the requesting computer's Ethernet address. The client then uses Trivial File Transfer Protocol (TFTP) to download the necessary files to boot. Macintosh G3 computers manufactured after January 1999 can be NetBoot clients. Macintosh G4 computers, iMacs, and iBooks can also be NetBoot clients. The machines should run on Ethernet. Apple does not recommend using NetBoot on wireless networks.

Macintosh Manager is a tool for administering Macintosh workstations, especially on educational networks. Network administrators at schools use the Macintosh Manager to implement security and control student access to software, servers, and printers. User preferences are stored on a server, so students, teachers, or administrators can access a personalized desktop from anywhere on the network. Macintosh Manager supports both AppleTalk and TCP/IP. The details of how Macintosh Manager works are outside the scope of this book, but from a troubleshooting and protocol analysis viewpoint, it's important to know that this tool exists. The tool may be adding traffic to your network and may require troubleshooting at some point.

Apple inherited NetInfo when it bought NeXT Computer. NetInfo is a distributed, hierarchical database for maintaining administrative data such as user and group accounts, e-mail configurations, NFS server configurations, and printer information. NetInfo facilitates the sharing of administrative data in a network environment. For more information on NetInfo see this article on Apple's Web site: docs.info.apple .com/article.html?artnum=60038.

Troubleshooting AppleTalk

If your Macintosh networks are migrating to IP, then a lot of your troubleshooting efforts will focus on IP protocols and you can use the techniques covered in Chapters 7 through 9. This section provides information on troubleshooting the areas of your campus LANs that are still purely AppleTalk. To troubleshoot AppleTalk, you will use a combination of router commands and protocol analyzer techniques. A few guidelines to keep in mind when configuring, monitoring, and troubleshooting AppleTalk networks are as follows:

- Every router connected to a network segment must agree on the configuration for that segment. Cable ranges, zone names, and timer values should be the same for every router on the segment. (Ensuring that zone names are exactly the same can be difficult because spaces and other non-printable characters are allowed in zone names.) If you have problems enabling a Cisco router interface due to configuration mismatch problems, use the `debug appletalk events` command to display information about initialization progress.

- Every network number in an internetwork must be unique. Document the network numbers you use in cable range assignments to avoid problems. Remember that the cable ranges cannot overlap.

- When troubleshooting routing problems, two useful commands are the `debug apple routing` command for RTMP and the `debug apple eigrp-all` command for EIGRP. These commands display output when routes are learned, advertised, and aged from the routing table. (As always, be careful with debug commands on operational networks with routers that have a high CPU usage.)

- When troubleshooting problems with zones, use the `debug appletalk zip` command. This command reports significant events such as the discovery of new zones and the sending of ZIP Queries. It can help you detect the occurrence of a ZIP storm, which is a pathological problem where ZIP packets start consuming a huge amount of bandwidth.

- Before changing a configuration, use the `show appletalk neighbors` command to determine a router's neighbors. Temporarily disable AppleTalk on routers that are on the same network segment. Make the required change, then wait several minutes before enabling the other routers. This will give the internetwork a chance to purge old information before it learns new information. Apple and Cisco recommend disabling AppleTalk for 10 minutes before making a change. This amount of time may be necessary on large internetworks, but a few minutes should be sufficient on small internetworks.

- Keep in mind that AppleTalk makes no provisions for informing neighbors in an internetwork about a changed zone list. Routers make ZIP Queries only when a new (or previously aged-out) network appears in the internetwork. For this reason, it is important to disable AppleTalk on appropriate interfaces before adding new zone data.

- When changing or adding a new interface configuration, be patient. On Cisco routers, AppleTalk interfaces take a long time (minutes) to verify that any neighbors have the same cable range and zone names configured. In general, the need to be systematic and methodical is even more important with AppleTalk configurations on Cisco routers than it is with other protocols.

- When troubleshooting either new or existing configurations, three helpful clear commands are the `clear appletalk interface`, `clear appletalk arp`, and `clear appletalk route` commands.

AppleTalk Ping (Echo)

When used with AppleTalk, the Cisco ping command sends AppleTalk Echo Protocol (AEP) datagrams to other AppleTalk nodes to verify connectivity and measure round-trip response times. The following EtherPeek output shows an AEP datagram:

```
802.3 Header
  Destination:          00:00:0C:00:2E:75
  Source:               00:00:0C:05:3E:80
  LLC Length:           108
802.2 Logical Link Control (LLC) Header
  Dest. SAP:            0xAA  SNAP
  Source SAP:           0xAA  SNAP
  Command:              0x03  Unnumbered Information
  Protocol:             0x080007809B  AppleTalk
Long DDP Header - Datagram Delivery Protocol
  Unused:               %00
  Hop Count:            %0000
  Datagram Length:      100
  DDP Checksum:         0xA1E8
  Dest. Network:        100
  Source Network:       100
  Dest Node:            26
  Source Node:          110
  Dest. Socket:         4   Echoer
  Source Socket:        253
  DDP Type:             4   AEP
AEP - AppleTalk Echo Protocol
  Echo Function:        1   Echo Request
  AEP Data:             (86 bytes)
```

To use the AppleTalk ping facility on a Cisco router, enter `ping` and press enter. When the ping command prompts for a protocol, specify `appletalk`. (You can also simply enter ping with a correctly formed AppleTalk network.node address and the router will figure out that you want to do an AppleTalk rather than an IP ping.) An example of using ping with the AppleTalk protocol follows:

```
Albany#ping 100.26
Type escape sequence to abort.
Sending 5, 100-byte AppleTalk Echos to 100.26, timeout is 2 seconds:
!!!!!
Success rate is 100 percent (5/5), round-trip min/avg/max = 1/2/4 ms
```

```
Albany#
Albany#ping
Protocol [ip]: AppleTalk
Target AppleTalk address: 100.26
Repeat count [5]:
Datagram size [100]:
Timeout in seconds [2]:
Verbose [n]:
Sweep range of sizes [n]:
Type escape sequence to abort.
Sending 5, 100-byte AppleTalk Echos to 100.26, timeout is 2 seconds:
!!!!!
Success rate is 100 percent (5/5), round-trip min/avg/max = 1/2/4 ms
```

Just to confuse network engineers, Cisco uses characters to represent the results of an AppleTalk ping that differ slightly from the characters used by IP and IPX pings. Table 11.4 lists the characters that indicate the success or failure of each packet in the AppleTalk ping sequence.

Cisco AppleTalk NBP Testing

Since Cisco IOS version 11.1, Cisco has supported a command for testing the reachability of named network entities on AppleTalk networks. The command, called test appletalk, replaces the older nbptest command that was part of the NBP option for the ping command. When you use these commands, you are prompted to select from a menu of options that includes the following:

- *Confirm.* Sends an NBP confirm packet to the specified entity.
- *Lookup.* Prompts for name, type, and zone, and then looks up a network entity.
- *Parameters.* Sets the parameters used in subsequent lookup and poll tests.
- *Poll.* Searches for all devices in all zones.
- *?.* Displays the list of tests.
- *End.* Exits the test facility.

The test appletalk command is helpful when users see zones in the Chooser but some servers are missing. You can confirm that a server has registered its NBP name by using the confirm option and specifying the server name, object type, and zone name. For example, testing 500.173 Lothlorien:AFPServer@elves confirms that the name Lothlorien is registered on the 500.173 device in the elves zone. The object type is AFPServer.

You can use the lookup and poll options to search for numerous objects. For example, =:CiscoRouter@engineering looks for all objects of type CiscoRouter in the engineering zone. As another example, =:Macintosh:c5@engineering looks for all objects in the engineering zone whose type identifier starts with Macintosh. The :c5 signifies the hexadecimal value for a wildcard character.

Table 11.4 AppleTalk Ping Results

CHARACTER	MEANING
!	The packet was echoed successfully from the target address.
.	The timeout period expired before an echo was received from the target address.
B	A bad or malformed echo was received from the target address.
C	An echo was received from the target address with an invalid DDP checksum.
E	Transmission of the echo packet to the target address failed. (The sending router was unable to send the AEP datagram due to a misconfiguration or because an AARP frame to find the data link address of the target failed.)
R	The transmission of the echo packet to the target address failed for lack of a route to the target address.

Cisco IOS Show Commands for AppleTalk

There are many Cisco show commands you can use when troubleshooting AppleTalk internetworks. One show command that is not well known, but provides a wealth of information, is the show appletalk globals command. The following is sample output so you can see the type of information that is returned from this command:

```
Router# show appletalk globals
AppleTalk global information:
          The router is a domain router.
          Internet is compatible with older, AT Phase1, routers.
          There are 76 routes in the internet.
          There are 23 zones defined.
          All significant events will be logged.
          ZIP resends queries every 10 seconds.
          RTMP updates are sent every 10 seconds with a jitter.
          RTMP entries are considered BAD after 20 seconds.
          RTMP entries are discarded after 60 seconds.
          AARP probe retransmit count: 10, interval: 200.
          AARP request retransmit count: 5, interval: 1000.
          DDP datagrams will be checksummed.
          RTMP datagrams will be strictly checked.
          RTMP routes may not be propagated without zones.
          Alternate node address format will not be displayed.
```

Table 11.5 lists some additional AppleTalk show commands in alphabetical order.

Table 11.5 AppleTalk Show Commands

COMMAND	DESCRIPTION
show appletalk access-lists	Displays the contents of current AppleTalk access lists.
show appletalk adjacent-routes	Displays routes to networks that are directly connected or that are one hop away.
show appletalk arp	Displays the contents of the AppleTalk ARP cache.
show appletalk aurp events	Displays the pending events in the AURP update-events queue.
show appletalk aurp topology	Displays entries in the AURP private path database, which consists of all paths learned from exterior routers.
show appletalk cache	Displays the current fast-switching cache.
show appletalk eigrp interfaces	Displays information about interfaces configured for EIGRP.
show appletalk eigrp neighbors	Displays the neighbors discovered by EIGRP.
show appletalk eigrp topology	Displays the AppleTalk EIGRP topology table.
show appletalk interfaces	Displays the status of the AppleTalk interfaces configured in the router and the parameters configured for each interface.
show appletalk neighbors	Displays information about the AppleTalk routers that are directly connected to any of the networks to which this router is directly connected.
show appletalk route	Displays all entries or specified entries in the AppleTalk routing table.
show appletalk static	Displays information about statically defined routes, including floating static routes.
show appletalk traffic	Displays statistics about AppleTalk traffic.
show appletalk zone	Displays all entries or specified entries in the Zone Information Table.

Cisco IOS Debug Commands for AppleTalk

There are quite a few AppleTalk debug commands. As always, be careful with debug commands. Because some of the debug commands can generate many messages, use them only when the router's CPU utilization is low. Also, be sure to disable the debugging as soon as possible. If your goal is to view packets, it's a better idea to use a protocol analyzer than some of the AppleTalk debug commands. Table 11.6 lists the most useful AppleTalk debug commands in alphabetical order.

Table 11.6 AppleTalk Debug Commands

COMMAND	DESCRIPTION
debug apple arp	Displays AARP requests and replies. This command is helpful when you experience problems communicating with a node on a local network. If the output indicates that the router is receiving AARP replies, you can assume that the problem is not at the physical or data link layers. You can also verify AppleTalk dynamic address acquisition with this command.
debug apple eigrp-all	Displays output from EIGRP processes. This command can be used to monitor the acquisition of routes, the aging of routing table entries, and the advertisement of known routes.
debug apple errors	Displays errors such as configuration mismatch problems, wrong encapsulations, invalid echo packets, unsolicited echo replies, and ZIP errors.
debug apple events	Displays information about significant AppleTalk events, such as neighbors becoming reachable or unreachable, and interfaces going up or down.
debug apple nbp	Displays debugging output from NBP processes.
debug apple packet	Displays at least one line of debugging output per AppleTalk packet processed. When used with the `debug apple routing`, `debug apple zip`, and `debug apple nbp` commands, the `debug apple packet` command adds protocol processing information in addition to generic packet details. When used with the `debug apple errors` command, the `debug apple packet` command reports packet-level problems, such as those concerning encapsulation.
debug apple routing	Displays output from RTMP processes. This command can be used to monitor the acquisition of routes, the aging of routing table entries, and the advertisement of known routes. It also reports conflicting network numbers on the same network if the network is misconfigured.
debug apple zip	Reports significant ZIP events such as the discovery of new zones and zone list queries.

Summary

This chapter has provided tips and techniques for learning and troubleshooting AppleTalk, as well as information to help you control traffic on AppleTalk networks and to migrate those networks to IP. One challenge with learning AppleTalk is that there are many myths about how it behaves and misbehaves. Hopefully this chapter has dispelled some of those myths and given you the foundation you need to configure, manage, and troubleshoot campus AppleTalk networks.

Many of the protocol techniques used in AppleTalk networks are similar to those used in IP networks. Even concepts that seem unique to AppleTalk, such as zones, are not really unusual. VLANs and SLP scopes are both similar to zones. AppleTalk concepts, such as dynamic addressing and simplified resource discovery, are becoming popular in the IP world. Learning AppleTalk will help you understand network philosophies that formed the foundation for AppleTalk and are still influential in non-AppleTalk environments.

AppleTalk was the first of the chatty protocols. AppleTalk nodes send many packets that are essentially overhead. This background traffic makes automated resource management possible. When we examine Windows networking in Chapter 12, you will find that the automatic resource management features in the Browse and WINS functions are also chatty. Many popular networking protocols are chatty. Chatty protocols are easier to use and configure, and more adaptable to changes and problems, than their nonchatty predecessors.

CHAPTER

12

Troubleshooting and Analyzing Windows Networking

This chapter describes the protocol behaviors that are observable in a Microsoft Windows–based network. Windows-based networking covers a broad range of detailed, technical, administrative, and historical topics that are beyond the scope of this book. This chapter focuses on the core protocol behavior that is quantifiable and comprehensible when a protocol analyst studies a Windows network environment. This discussion assumes that the reader has hands-on experience working with and configuring Windows networks.

Windows Networking Concepts

Windows networking refers to the networking capabilities developed by IBM and Microsoft in the 1980s to allow clients and servers running a Windows operating system to share files, printers, and other resources. Windows networking still permeates modern versions of Windows, whether it's Windows ME, Windows XP, or Windows 2000. Third-party products allow Linux and Macintosh operating systems to use Windows networking also.

You have probably used one of the key elements of Windows networking, which is the *Browse process*. The Browse process allows a client to get a list of services available on the network by clicking on the *Network Neighborhood* icon. The Browse process includes a procedure to elect a *Master Browser* that keeps track of network services.

Devices that provide services tell the Master Browser about the availability of their services.

Windows networking is usually implemented using one of three models: the workgroup model, the domain model, or the Windows 2000 model. A workgroup is simply a logical collection of computers. A domain is a more formal entity that has administrative and security properties that workgroups don't have. The term *domain*, as used here, should not be confused with the Internet domain structure implemented by the Domain Name System (DNS). Windows networks can use DNS, but they also have their own concept of a domain, as will be seen.

Many versions of Windows networking use a session-layer protocol called Network Basic Input/Output System (NetBIOS). NetBIOS handles naming, session setup, and data transfer. NetBIOS can run directly above the data link layer Logical Link Control (LLC) protocol, in which case it is called the NetBIOS Extended User Interface (NetBEUI). NetBIOS can also run on top of Novell's Internetwork Packet Exchange (IPX), and on top of the User Datagram Protocol (UDP) and Transmission Control Protocol (TCP) in Internet Protocol (IP) campus networks. In an IP environment, Windows clients can use the Windows Internet Name Service (WINS) protocol and DNS to map names to IP addresses. Windows 2000 uses the Dynamic Domain Name System (DDNS) protocol to map names to addresses.

At the application layer, clients communicate with servers using the Server Message Block (SMB) protocol. SMB provides services for the manipulation of files, such as searching, opening, reading, writing, and closing files. Figure 12.1 will help you understand how the Windows networking protocols fit together and how they map to the Open System Interconnection (OSI) Reference Model.

OSI Term	Windows Networking Protocols				
Application	SMB			WINS	DNS, DDNS
Presentation					
Session	Novell's NetBIOS	NetBEUI	NetBIOS	NetBIOS	
Transport	SPX		TCP	UDP	
Network	IPX		IP		
Data Link and Physical	LLC, Ethernet, Token Ring, FDDI, WAN Protocols				

Figure 12.1   Windows networking protocols.

The NetBIOS Basis for Windows Networking

Whether you are using the workgroup model, the domain model, or the Windows 2000 model, you'll find varying degrees of influence from NetBIOS. A simple peer-to-peer Windows workgroup could be based entirely on the NetBIOS protocol for device naming and connection-oriented communication. A sophisticated Windows 2000 environment may have none of the original NetBIOS-related protocols present, but may still carry the concepts of device naming into the realm of DDNS operation. To understand Windows networking, you must first understand NetBIOS and NetBEUI, as these form the historical—and in some cases the practical—foundation for the entire protocol environment.

The History of NetBIOS

When the IBM PC was introduced in 1981, it had a core instruction set that allowed keyboard, monitor, and disk control to be built into a permanent memory chip. This Read Only Memory chip, containing the Basic Input Output System was, of course, the ROM BIOS. The BIOS provided a set of interrupt handlers (program code routines) that handled various hardware components. To access one of these code routines, a programmer wrote assembly language code that loaded the CPU's internal registers with appropriate byte values to cause the instruction pointer to begin executing a particular routine. There were (and still are today) special microprocessor instructions, called *interrupts,* that caused the CPU to automatically save whatever it was doing and branch off to execute an interrupt handler routine. The ROM BIOS contained interrupt handlers for the common hardware functions. MS-DOS assigned interrupt number 21 (INT 21) to standard BIOS functions. The programmer loaded the command code into the microprocessor AX register and issued an INT 21 instruction, whereupon the command was carried out.

INT 21 was used for hardware control. Other interrupts were used for different special purposes. INT 5C was used for establishing communication and exchanging data with other computers across a network. The interrupt handler code for INT 5C was the Network Basic Input/Output System, and this is where the term NetBIOS originated. NetBIOS is a set of programming calls that perform specific communication functions.

NetBIOS Function Calls

NetBIOS functions can be divided into four categories: name support, datagram support, session support, and general commands. Each category includes several specific commands, as shown in Table 12.1.

Table 12.1   NetBIOS Function Calls

CATEGORY	CALL
Name support	Add Name
	Add Group Name
	Delete Name
Datagram support	Receive Datagram
	Receive Broadcast Datagram
	Send Datagram
	Send Broadcast Datagram
Session support	Call
	Listen
	Send
	Send No-ACK
	Chain Send
	Chain Send No-ACK
	Receive
	Receive Any
	Hang Up
	Session Status
General commands	Reset Cancel
	Adapter Status
	Unlink

The Importance of NetBIOS

You may wonder why it is important to know about some old DOS programming interface to troubleshoot today's networks. The answer is that the core functionality of NetBIOS has provided the essential programming interface for Windows networking through, and including, the Windows NT domain model. Even in Windows 2000 networking (where mysterious terms like *Active Directory*, *Dynamic DNS*, and *Kerberos* enter the lexicon), the vestigial remains of NetBIOS from the 1980s continue to make their presence known. Understanding Windows networking begins with understanding NetBIOS.

While the original NetBIOS implemented its command set through DOS interrupts, Windows NetBIOS implements the same commands through an Application Programming Interface (API) provided in a programming language library and compiled into a programmer's work. It's important to realize that the commands listed in Table 12.1 are not what you will see when you capture and decode a NetBIOS conversation with a protocol analyzer. The profound depth of this realization on the part of the protocol analysis engineer can not be overstated.

Consider the `Add Name` command. A communicating device on a network can be referred to by many different names. The President of the United States is called *Mr. President* when he's being addressed in his official capacity. When his personal friends play golf with him, they may call him *George*. If his wife is talking to him at home, she may call him *Honey*. In a similar way, communicating devices in a NetBIOS environment use a special identifier (called a *Qualifier Byte*) to differentiate between functions. Further, a NetBIOS communicator may be a member of one or more groups of stations. Each NetBIOS communicator maintains a table of names, any of which are recognized by the communicator as being identities for itself. Each name alludes to a different function of the communicator. Before a communicator can insert a new name into its internal table, it must confirm that no other station is currently using that name. Hence, there is external behavior associated with the issuance of the `Add Name` command. By some mechanism, the `Add Name` command must validate the name and only then place the name into the station's table.

Consider the `Call` command. In order to establish a session for the reliable exchange of data, an originating station must issue a `Call` to the destination station. The destination must then accept the `Call`. After these things are accomplished, data can be exchanged. The `Call` command is fundamentally an external command. That is, the behaviors associated with a `Call` command involve locating and connecting to a target machine.

THE MORE THINGS CHANGE, THE MORE THEY STAY THE SAME

NetBIOS was an early mechanism to validate unique device identities and then resolve those identities into specific addresses on the network. In a general way, this is similar to the contemporary behavior observed with Address Resolution Protocol (ARP) in the TCP/IP environment. A station may broadcast an ARP packet to confirm that no other station is using the same IP address. ARP is also used to resolve an IP address into a unique Ethernet address. The validation of uniqueness and the identification of a specific network address are basic communication functions that can be implemented in various ways.

When you're analyzing a trace file and you observe new or unexplained behavior, remember that what you're seeing may be simply a different method for performing a very comprehensible network operation. Always consider the end result of a protocol interaction when you're trying to explain its purpose.

NetBIOS Consistency across Different Implementations

There is a wondrous aspect of NetBIOS that has given it a long and prosperous life in the technology market: A program that uses the NetBIOS interface (whether through the original DOS interrupt mechanism or via the current API structure) is consistently using the same core set of NetBIOS commands. The way the commands are issued may differ, and the external behavior that is necessary to execute the command differs with various implementations, but the functions remain the same.

Consider the following commands that might be issued by code running in a particular NetBIOS-based machine:

```
Add Name "JOECLIENT"
Call "BIGSERVER"
Listen
Send
Send
Send
Hang Up
```

Any machine using any operating system can execute this sequence of behaviors, as long as the operating system supports a NetBIOS interface. NetBIOS is a programming interface and does not define the mechanism by which the various commands are carried out. It's that aspect of NetBIOS that gives it portability and widespread use. A program written to the NetBIOS communication standard can (hopefully) run on any machine that supports a NetBIOS API.

In the Windows networking environment, there are three families of protocols that can be used to actually carry out the various NetBIOS commands: TCP/IP; Novell NetWare's IPX; or NetBEUI, which is the original protocol that provided an interface for NetBIOS.

NetBEUI originally extended beyond the early (circa 1985) capabilities offered by simple peer-to-peer networking. NetBEUI is a protocol. It is carried directly on top of 802.2 LLC and has no Layer 3 component, making it nonroutable. When implemented with TCP, NetBIOS can use the services of TCP to establish a session when executing a NetBIOS Call. When implemented with NetBEUI, it's the NetBEUI protocol itself that is endowed with the capability of carrying out all of the NetBIOS commands.

NetBIOS Naming Conventions

Every NetBIOS-based machine is given a unique name during the Add Name process. The behaviors that implement the Add Name command differ from TCP to IPX to NetBEUI, but the end result is identical. In every case, the name must conform to a specific structure. A NetBIOS name is 16 characters. The last character is called the Qualifier Byte and is a numeric value (expressed in hexadecimal) that identifies the function associated with the name. Some examples will help clarify how the Qualifier Byte is used.

Qualifier Byte = 0x00

The 0x00 qualifier refers to the name of a machine and also the name of the domain in which a machine is a member. A machine identifies itself with its own unique name and also indicates that it is a member of a particular domain. This way the Browse process can properly identify a machine's domain membership.

Sometimes the term *Redirector Name* is applied to the 0x00 qualifier. This refers to the fact that the NetBIOS stack resident in the machine (that is, the redirector component of the operating system stack) can be the target of a request and can construct a reply. The only reason a request would be issued to the redirector itself would be for the purposes of management. The NetBIOS component of the stack can be designed to gather and report statistics regarding the number of packets sent and received, the number of active connections, and the number of available connections (sessions). It's uncommon to see any direct requests being made to the redirector.

In a Windows NT domain environment, each machine must be granted specific rights to join the domain at boot time. When a machine boots, before it has authenticated to the domain, it is not providing services to the network. Its right to be a server has not been validated yet. The machine is also not presenting a user entity to the network. Nobody has logged in because the machine is only just booting. The machine has a name, however. When a NetBIOS name has a 0x00 Qualifier Byte, it's a reference to the machine itself. This is the Qualifier Byte that is used when a machine first boots into a domain configuration.

Qualifier Byte = 0x03

The 0x03 qualifier is most commonly associated with a username after a user has logged in to a machine. It's called the *Messenger Service Name*, or *Main Name*. Messenger Service refers to the fact that this name is used to send NetBIOS messages (commands, replies, or data) up or down the stack to and from the user operating system and application software. It's also possible to see the 0x03 qualifier used for a machine that does not have a human user logged into it. A remote printer must communicate with the print server to which it's assigned. The remote printer may present itself as a user when it connects to the print queue residing in the print server. In this case, the printer name is qualified with 0x03.

Qualifier Byte = 0x05

The 0x05 qualifier is not a common qualifier in today's networks. The 0x05 qualifier identifies a name as a *Forwarding Name*. A machine could be configured to receive messages on behalf of another machine. Through some software process constructed by an application developer, the machine could forward those messages to the intended target. For example, if the CLIENT_ONE<00> machine were acting as a forwarding agent on behalf of the CLIENT_TWO<03> entity, then CLIENT_ONE<00> would announce itself as CLIENT_TWO<05>, thereby letting everyone else know that it was willing to accept messages for CLIENT_TWO<03>. Again, this behavior was more common in the late 1980s and early 1990s. Today, applications such as Outlook or Eudora manage the receipt and forwarding of messages at the application level.

Qualifier Byte = 0x06

The 0x06 qualifier is used to identify a Microsoft Remote Access Service (RAS). RAS allows users to dial in to an NT server.

Qualifier Byte = 0x1B

When the name of an NT domain is qualified with 0x1B, the machine announcing itself is the Primary Domain Controller (PDC) for the named domain. The PDC always serves as the central Master Browser for the domain and is called the *Domain Master Browser*. Hence, 0x1B identifies a PDC and identifies the sending machine as the Domain Master Browser. The PDC also contains a read-write copy of the Security Accounts Management (SAM) database, which is used to authenticate both machines and users in the domain.

Qualifier Byte = 0x1C

When NT administrators need to create read-only copies of the SAM database, they configure a server to be a *Backup Domain Controller* (BDC). The BDC announces itself with the domain name qualified with 0x1C. Authentication is always done though a conversation with a BDC. The PDC sends a copy of the SAM database to each BDC at regular intervals. If a network has only a single PDC and no other servers (hence, no other machines eligible to be BDCs), then the PDC also announces itself as a BDC. The PDC serves as both the manager of the SAM and the entity to which users and machines authenticate (as both PDC and BDC).

Qualifier Byte = 0x1D

A station that offers services uses the 0x1D qualifier to announce itself to the Subnet Master Browser during the Browse process. The Browse process is quite intricate. A station that is sharing files or printers (or offering other shared services, such as a fax gateway) must inform the Subnet Master Browser that services are available. The Subnet Master Browser then queries the station to get a list of the shared services. The station then enumerates the list of shared services. When a station informs the Subnet Master Browser about its existence, it does so by broadcasting its name using the 0x1D qualifier. In effect, 0x1D says, "I have shared resources, please ask me to enumerate them for you, Mr. Subnet Master Browser." When a station joins the network, these broadcasts occur at 1-minute intervals. Later, the interval decreases to every 12 minutes.

Qualifier Byte = 0x1E

There are many situations in which packets must be sent to select a new Subnet Master Browser. This process is quite intricate. When a station participates in this Browser

Election process, it uses the 0x1E qualifier with its name. Stations that are eligible (by configuration) to participate in the Browser Election process are called *Potential Browsers*.

Qualifier Byte = 0x1F

Microsoft defines a programming interface for the exchange of messages between Windows applications using a specified set of commands and replies. This mechanism is called the *Network Dynamic Data Exchange* (Net DDE). A machine that implements Net DDE announces itself with a 0x1F qualifier. Alternative programming interfaces compete with Net DDE, and 0x1F is not a common qualifier. The Windows NT CHAT program uses DDE and a machine running CHAT announces itself with the 0x1F qualifier.

Qualifier Byte = 0x20

The 0x20 qualifier is the most significant qualifier to see in a protocol analyzer trace file. The 0x20 qualifier is used for a *Server Service*. When a machine (either a peer-to-peer client or a file server) shares files, it announces itself with the 0x20 qualifier. Any machine acting as any kind of server (print, fax, modem, and so on) announces the service with a name qualified by 0x20. It's significant to notice that 0x20 is the ASCII code for a space character. If you examine a NetBIOS Server Service name in the hexadecimal/ASCII view provided by a protocol analyzer, you will notice that the character corresponding to the Qualifier Byte is a space.

As an example, assume that a user named Bob has logged into his Windows desktop and is sharing files on the network. Bob's machine has been assigned the name NOTEBOOKPC in the Network Control panel. The NetBIOS name for the machine is NOTEBOOKPC 0x00. (The 0x00 Qualifier Byte is used for machine names.) However, it's not the "machine" that is sharing or accessing files. You may observe the same computer using the name BOB 0x20 (where 0x20 is the 16-byte Qualifier Byte), indicating that this is Bob's computer acting as a file server. On the other hand, if Bob accesses files on Sally's machine, then BOB 0x03 accesses SALLY 0x20. (Bob, as a user, accesses Sally's machine, which is acting as a file server.)

Qualifier Byte = 0x21

A RAS client uses the 0x21 Qualifier Byte to identify itself.

The 0x0102_MSBROWSE_0x0201 Name

The NetBIOS name *0x0102_MSBROWSE_0x0201* is a special, reserved name. The name starts with the two hexadecimal bytes 0x0102, ends with the bytes 0x0201, and includes the underscore characters and uppercase MSBROWSE string, exactly as shown. The station in a broadcast domain that wins the Browser Election process and becomes the Master Browser for the broadcast domain uses this name. In the TCP/IP realm, this station is called the Subnet Master Browser. It's possible for more than one NT domain to be present in a single broadcast domain. In this case, each domain has its own Subnet Master Browser. The Subnet Master Browsers in different domains learn about the presence of other domains by hearing the broadcast with the NetBIOS 0x0102 _MSBROWSE_0x0201 name being used.

The Significance of NetBIOS Naming

From a protocol analysis perspective, a networking professional should learn to recognize the significance of the NetBIOS Qualifier Byte when examining NetBIOS traffic. Any reasonably sophisticated analyzer should decode the meaning of the Qualifier Byte along with the NetBIOS name, so memorizing the codes isn't necessary, but understanding their meaning is important. This section summarizes some important concepts regarding the Qualifier Byte.

All implementations of NetBIOS base communication on the identification of devices by name. From a machine's perspective, all 16 characters of the name are significant. That is, a unique identification is made on the basis of a 16-byte string. We, as humans, recognize the significance of the Qualifier Byte, as does the protocol stack that's processing a session's data. From a purely identification standpoint, however, the name is simply a 16-byte string. The human portion of the name (BOB, for example) is space-padded to the 15th character and then the Qualifier Byte is added. As mentioned earlier, for historical reasons, the ASCII code for a space (0x20) was chosen as the Qualifier Byte to represent a server function. Hence, if the hexadecimal/ASCII data underlying a NetBIOS name is examined, it appears as if the name itself is simply space-padded all the way to the 16th character. The 16th character, although it is the ASCII code for a space, remains the separate Qualifier Byte.

The workgroup model for Windows networking is based on each machine being assigned the name of a workgroup to which the machine belongs. A member of a workgroup can send a NetBIOS broadcast frame to find other members of the same workgroup. A Windows-based machine can share files or printers on a network in a peer-to-peer relationship with other Windows-based machines. A user—Bob, for example—can access files shared by Sally and, at the same time, Sally can access files shared by Bob. Bob is a client to Sally but he is also Sally's server. This is the essence of the peer nature of the relationship between the machines. It could be said that Bob and Sally are "back-to-back client-to-server partners." As can be seen, a particular machine has more than one function. When Bob initiates a NetBIOS session to Sally, he uses 0x03 (a username) as a Qualifier Byte. Sally responds with 0x20 (a server name). When Sally initiates her client session to Bob, she uses 0x03 and Bob responds with a 0x20 Qualifier Byte in his name.

This switching of roles and names may seem confusing, but NetBIOS handles it without problems. The NetBEUI implementation of NetBIOS refers to sessions on the basis of a *Local Session Number* and a *Remote Session Number*. Hence, when Bob is acting in the role of a client, his Local Session Number is associated with his 0x03 name and Sally, as the Remote Session Number, is referenced with her 0x20 name. When examining a protocol decode, you should consider the role played by a communicator and base your expectations of the capabilities of the communicator on the role. The Qualifier Byte will help you understand the role.

REVERSIBLE HALF-ASCII

Microsoft implements a special text encoding scheme in WINS called *reversible half-ASCII*. It was created to allow NetBIOS Qualifier Bytes (which are outside the range of printable characters) to be represented as printable characters for use internally in a WINS database. In your analyzer's hexadecimal display window, reversible half-ASCII character strings look like this: FHEJEMEE... They have lots of Es and typically end with CACACA...

The ASCII code for a character is split into two nibbles and then hexadecimal 0x41 is added to each nibble, creating a new ASCII character. Hence, two ASCII characters are used to represent a single ASCII character. This is reversible half-ASCII. It's reversible because subtracting 0x41 from each character in a pair, and reassembling the two nibbles, recreates the original ASCII character.

To encode the string WILDJOE, for example, you start by representing the string in ASCII:

```
W = 0x57, I = 0x49, L = 0x4C, D = 0x44, and so forth.
```

Next, you add 0x41 to each nibble, creating a new set of characters:

```
5 + 0x41 = 0x46 = F
7 + 0x41 = 0x48 = H
4 + 0x41 = 0x45 = E
9 + 0x41 = 0x4A = J
4 + 0x41 = 0x45 = E
C + 0x41 = 0x4D = M
4 + 0x41 = 0x45 = E
4 + 0x41 = 0x45 = E, and so on...
```

The characters WILD, represented in reversible half-ASCII and seen in your analyzer's ASCII decode in the hexadecimal window, are FHEJEMEE.

The CACACA that you see at the end of strings is the space padding at the end of a NetBIOS name, as follows:

```
C = ASCII code 0x43 and A = ASCII code 0x41.
```

Subtract 0x41 from each, yielding the following:

```
0x43 - 0x41 = 2
0x41 - 0x41 = 0
```

Reassemble these two nibbles to get 0x20, which is the ASCII code for a space character!

NetBIOS Implementation Differences

The three common implementations of NetBIOS produce packets on the network that are different. The implementations do not interoperate directly. Although each implementation uses the NetBIOS programming interface, the protocol that carries the command, reply, or data across the network is based on a different set of packets. NetBIOS is carried in TCP, NetBEUI, or IPX packets. A NetBIOS/TCP communicator cannot interact directly with a NetBIOS/NetBEUI communicator or with a NetBIOS/IPX communicator.

The terminology of NetBIOS communication can be confusing. This is because the NetBIOS acronym has been used to describe more than one thing. NetBIOS refers to the programming interface in all implementations. In the NetBIOS/TCP environment, it also refers to the portion of the packet that carries NetBIOS commands, replies, and data. In the NetBIOS/NetBEUI environment, NetBIOS refers only to the API, and NetBEUI refers to the protocol. In the NetBIOS/IPX environment, NetBIOS refers to both the API and to the protocol. To understand the details of terminology use, it's worthwhile to examine the three different frame structures for TCP, NetBEUI, and IPX.

A Windows Internet Name Service Query Carried on UDP

The NetBIOS/TCP implementation includes NetBIOS commands, replies, and data carried on both TCP and UDP. When a station wants to determine the IP address associated with a particular NetBIOS name, it sends a Windows Internet Name Service (WINS) query, which is carried on top of UDP. In this case, there is no specific NetBIOS header in the packet, as seen in the following analyzer output. The packet simply carries a NetBIOS Name Service command directly above UDP.

```
Ethernet Header
  Destination:   FF:FF:FF:FF:FF:FF  Ethernet Broadcast
  Source:        00:60:08:15:A6:9B
  Protocol Type:0x0800  IP
IP Header - Internet Protocol Datagram
  Version:            4
  Header Length:      5  (20  bytes)
  Type of Service:    %00000000
  Precedence: Routine, Normal Delay, Throughput, Reliability
  Total Length:       78
  Identifier:         43062
  Fragmentation Flags:  %000  May Fragment    Last Fragment
  Fragment Offset:    0  (0  bytes)
  Time To Live:       128
  Protocol:           17  UDP
  Header Checksum:    0x1781
  Source IP Address:  192.216.124.55
  Dest. IP Address:   192.216.124.255
  No IP Options
UDP - User Datagram Protocol
  Source Port:        137  NETBIOS Name Service
  Destination Port:   137
  Length:             58
  Checksum:           0x8FD2
NetBIOS Name Service - Network Basic Input/Output System
  Identification:     0x883A
  Parameter:          0x0110
```

```
                 Request
                 Standard Query
                 Recursion Desired
                 Packet Was Broadcast
      Number of Questions:  1
      Number of Answers:    0
      Number of Authority:  0
      Number of Additional: 0
      Query Domain Name:    MIKE-PC <20>  Server Service
      Query Type:           32  NetBIOS General Name Service
      Query Class:          1  Internet
Frame Check Sequence:  0x59DF750B
```

A TCP NetBIOS Session Setup Request

After determining the IP address of a target node, a NetBIOS/TCP station resolves the IP address to a data link layer address by sending an Address Resolution Protocol (ARP) frame. (The station uses the data link layer address of the Default Gateway for remote targets.) Next, the station establishes a TCP session with the target in the normal manner with a TCP three-way handshake. Using the established TCP session, the originator must now create a NetBIOS session. The following packet is an example of a NetBIOS Session Setup request.

```
  Flags:        0x00
    Status:       0x01
    Packet Length:130
  Ethernet Header
    Destination:  00:40:95:96:30:07
    Source:       00:60:08:15:A6:9B
    Protocol Type:0x0800  IP
  IP Header - Internet Protocol Datagram
    Version:          4
    Header Length:    5  (20 bytes)
    Type of Service:  %00000000
    Precedence: Routine, Normal Delay, Throughput, Reliability
    Total Length:     112
    Identifier:       43830
    Fragmentation Flags: %010  Do Not Fragment   Last Fragment
    Fragment Offset:  0  (0 bytes)
    Time To Live:     128
    Protocol:         6  TCP
    Header Checksum:  0xD53B
    Source IP Address:    192.216.124.55
    Dest. IP Address:     192.216.124.45
    No IP Options
  TCP - Transport Control Protocol
    Source Port:      2882  ndtp
    Destination Port: 139  netbios-ssn
    Sequence Number:  324647931
```

```
        Ack Number:         350227873
        Offset:             5
        Reserved:           %000000
        Code:               %011000
                    Ack is valid
                    Push Request
        Window:             8760
        Checksum:           0xBBCD
        Urgent Pointer:    0
        No TCP Options
    NetBIOS Session Service - Network Basic Input/Output System
        Packet Type:            0x81   Session Request
        Flags:                  0x00   Length Extension Off
        Length:                 68
        Called Name:            MIKE-PC <20>   Server Service
        Calling Name:           MOUNIR <00>  Workstation
    Frame Check Sequence:   0x0AA945E1
```

If the WINS query and the NetBIOS Session Setup packets are compared, it can be seen that the behavior desired by the NetBIOS programming interface in the sending machine is manifested as information in the WINS or NetBIOS Session Service header. In these cases, the NetBIOS portion of the stack actually has a job to perform outside the specific needs of the host application program. The application program may simply want to download a file, but the underlying mechanism of the NetBIOS interface has needs of its own, and protocol operations to fulfill those needs. After NetBIOS has done its setup work, then the NetBIOS aspect of the packets ceases to manifest any behavior. NetBIOS simply forms a thin layer inside the packet, as illustrated by the protocol analyzer output in the next section.

TCP NetBIOS Data

Notice in the next packet that the NetBIOS header does not contain any verb. It isn't a command or a reply; it simply conveys a length and some basic control information. The management of the data exchange is handled by TCP. TCP sequences the bytes, sends acknowledgments, recovers corrupted or lost frames with retransmissions, and manages memory with flow control. All of the behavior is relegated to TCP and is not handled by NetBIOS.

```
    Flags:          0x00
      Status:          0x01
      Packet Length:180
    Ethernet Header
      Destination:  00:40:95:96:30:07
      Source:       00:60:08:15:A6:9B
      Protocol Type:0x0800   IP
    IP Header - Internet Protocol Datagram
      Version:              4
      Header Length:        5  (20  bytes)
```

```
        Type of Service:        %00000000
        Precedence: Routine, Normal Delay, Throughput, Reliability
        Total Length:           162
        Identifier:             44598
        Fragmentation Flags:    %010  Do Not Fragment    Last Fragment
        Fragment Offset:        0  (0  bytes)
        Time To Live:           128
        Protocol:               6  TCP
        Header Checksum:        0xD209
        Source IP Address:      192.216.124.55
        Dest. IP Address:       192.216.124.45
        No IP Options
TCP - Transport Control Protocol
        Source Port:        2882  ndtp
        Destination Port: 139  netbios-ssn
        Sequence Number:    324648359
        Ack Number:         350228140
        Offset:             5
        Reserved:           %000000
        Code:               %011000
                Ack is valid
                Push Request
        Window:             8493
        Checksum:           0xFEFB
        Urgent Pointer:     0
        No TCP Options
NetBIOS Session Service - Network Basic Input/Output System
        Packet Type:            0x00  Session Message
        Flags:                  0x00  Length Extension Off
        Length:                 118
SMB - Server Message Block
        Protocol ID:            SMB
        Command Code:           37  Transaction - Name, Bytes In/Out
        Error Code Class:       0x00  Success
        Reserved:               0x00
        Error Code:             0  Success
        Flags:                  0x18
                Request
                Pathnames Are Without Case
                Pathnames Are Already In Canonicalized Format
        Flags2:                 0x8003
                Application Understands Long File Names
                Application Understands Extended Attributes
                Application Understands Unicode Strings
        Reserved:
        ...........   8D 80 00 00 00 00 00 00 00 00 00 00
        Tree ID (TID):          0x0800
        Process ID (PID):       0xDCA0
        User ID (UID):          0x0800
        Multiplex ID (MID):     0x0040
```

```
SMB Transaction - Name, Bytes In/OutRequest
     Word Count:            14
     Total Param Bytes:     26
     Total Data Bytes:      0
     Param Bytes To Recv:   8
     Data Bytes To Recv:    4200
     Setup Bytes To Recv:   0
     Reserved:              0x00
     Flags:                 0x0000
     Timeout (millisec.):   5000
     Reserved:              0x0000
     Params This Buffer:    26
     Params Bytes Offset:   92
     Data This Buffer:      0
     Data Bytes Offset:     0
     Setup Word Count:      0
     Reserved:              0x00
     Byte Count:            55
     File Pathname:
     Parameter And Data Bytes:
     ..h.WrLehDO.B16B   00 00 68 00 57 72 4C 65 68 44 4F 00 42 31 36 42
     BDz...h.....z      42 44 7A 00 01 00 68 10 FF FF FF FF 7A
```

According to NetBIOS, the preceding packet contains 118 bytes of NetBIOS data, as seen by the value of the Length field in the NetBIOS header. IP is carrying a total length of 162 bytes, which can be broken down as follows:

```
 20 bytes for the IP header
 20 bytes for the TCP header
  4 bytes for the NetBIOS header
118 bytes of NetBIOS data
162 Total Bytes carried by IP
```

When the 14-byte Ethernet header is added in, along with the 4-byte checksum, the value reported by the EtherPeek protocol analyzer (Packet Length: 180) is obtained. The 118 bytes of NetBIOS data are actually the bytes making up the SMB session data.

NetBEUI Data Exchange (A Browse Packet)

The next packet is a NetBEUI packet that contains 44 bytes of NetBIOS data. In this case, the data is also SMB data, as it was with the TCP example, but it happens to be a Browse frame. Nonetheless, the commonality with NetBIOS/TCP remains; both implementations are carrying some amount of NetBIOS data. It's important to note that the NetBEUI portion of the packet is carried directly on top of the Layer 2 LLC header. There is no Layer 3 identifier (such as an IP address) in a NetBEUI packet. This is why NetBEUI is nonroutable. Notice, also, that the NetBEUI/NetBIOS header is not simply a thin, behaviorless layer as was seen with NetBIOS/TCP. There is a command code in the header, and also a sequence and acknowledgment mechanism (the

Xmit/Resp Correlator number). The NetBEUI implementation doesn't use any lower-layer protocols to perform part of the work. The NetBEUI protocol stack handles all of the communication work relative to NetBIOS.

```
Flags:          0x80   802.3
  Status:         0x01
  Packet Length:184
802.3 Header
  Destination:  03:00:00:00:00:01
  Source:       00:40:95:11:56:DE
  LLC Length:   166
802.2 Logical Link Control (LLC) Header
  Dest. SAP:     0xF0  NetBEUI/NetBIOS
  Source SAP:    0xF0  NetBEUI/NetBIOS
  Command:       0x03  Unnumbered Information
NetBEUI/NetBIOS - Network Basic Input/Output System
  Length:                44
  NetBIOS Delimiter:     0xEFFF
  Command:               0x08  Datagram(Wait)
  Option Data 1:         0x00  Reserved
  Option Data 2:         0x0000  Reserved
  Xmit/Resp Correlator: 0x00000000
  Destination Name:      AG-TRAIN         <0x1E>
  Source Name:           SOCRATES         <0x20>
SMB - Server Message Block
  Protocol ID:           SMB
  Command Code:          37  Transaction - Name, Bytes In/Out
  Error Code Class:      0x00  Success
  Reserved:              0x00
  Error Code:            0  Success
  Flags:                 0x00
      Request
      Pathnames Are Case Sensitive
  Flags2:                0x0000
  Reserved:
  ............   00 00 00 00 00 00 00 00 00 00 00 00
  Tree ID (TID):         0x0000
  Process ID (PID):      0x0000
  User ID (UID):         0x0000
  Multiplex ID (MID):    0x0000
SMB Transaction - Name, Bytes In/OutRequest
  Word Count:            17
  Total Param Bytes:     0
  Total Data Bytes:      33
  Param Bytes To Recv:   0
  Data Bytes To Recv:    0
  Setup Bytes To Recv:   0
  Reserved:              0x00
  Flags:                 0x0000
  Timeout (millisec.):   1000
```

```
Reserved:               0x0000
Params This Buffer:     0
Params Bytes Offset:    0
Data This Buffer:       33
Data Bytes Offset:      86
Setup Word Count:       3
Reserved:               0x00
Additional Setup Bytes:
......          01 00 00 00 02 00
Byte Count:             50
Transaction Name:       \MAILSLOT\BROWSE
Parameter And Data Bytes:
......SOCRATES.. 0F 00 80 FC 0A 00 53 4F 43 52 41 54 45 53 00 00
........K.....U. 00 00 00 00 00 00 04 00 4B 10 04 00 0F 01 55 AA
..              00 04
```

IPX Name Query

In the NetBEUI and IPX implementations, there is nothing corresponding to the centralized name server concept embodied in WINS. All name queries must be broadcast. Following is an example of a NetWare NetBIOS packet. The NetBIOS header is carried directly on top of IPX and includes a number of reserved (padding) bytes. This packet structure is different from that for the NetBEUI and TCP implementations of NetBIOS.

An optional (and not present in this packet) field at the beginning of the NetBIOS header can list up to seven different networks that have been crossed by a broadcast NetBIOS packet. An IPX router knows how to update this field and to limit the scope of the Novell NetBIOS broadcast range.

```
Flags:        0x80   802.3
  Status:        0x01
  Packet Length:98
802.3 Header
  Destination:  FF:FF:FF:FF:FF:FF   Ethernet Broadcast
  Source:       00:40:95:11:56:DE
  Length:       80
IPX - NetWare Protocol
  Checksum:              0xFFFF
  Length:                80
  Transport Control:
    Reserved:            %0000
    Hop Count:           %0000
  Packet Type:           20   NetBIOS
  Destination Network:   0x00000000
  Destination Node:      FF:FF:FF:FF:FF:FF   Ethernet Broadcast
  Destination Socket:    0x0455   NetBIOS
  Source Network:        0x00050000
  Source Node:           00:40:95:11:56:DE
  Source Socket:         0x0455
```

```
NetWare NetBIOS
Reserved:
................ 00 01 00 00 00 00 00 00 00 00 00 00 00 00 00 00
................ 00 00 00 00 00 00 00 00 00 00 00 00 00 00 00 00
Name Type Flag:      0x00
Datastream Type:     1  Name Query
Name String:         AG-TRAIN        <0x1E>
```

IPX NetBIOS Data

Like NetBEUI, Novell NetBIOS is responsible for carrying out all of the NetBIOS work. For this reason, there's a Connection ID and Sequence Number in the NetBIOS header. Novell chose to carry its NetBIOS on top of the IPX network layer.

```
Flags:          0x80   802.3
  Status:         0x01
  Packet Length:66
802.3 Header
  Destination:  00:60:08:15:A6:9B
  Source:       00:40:95:96:30:07
  Length:       48
IPX - NetWare Protocol
  Checksum:             0xFFFF
  Length:               48
  Transport Control:
    Reserved:           %0000
    Hop Count:          %0000
  Packet Type:          4  SAP
  Destination Network:  0x00000000
  Destination Node:     00:60:08:15:A6:9B
  Destination Socket:   0x0455  NetBIOS
  Source Network:       0x00050000
  Source Node:          00:40:95:96:30:07
  Source Socket:        0x0455
NetWare NetBIOS
    Control Flag:         0xC0
              Send ACK
              System Packet
  Datastream Type:      6  Session Data
  Source Connection ID: 8669
  Dest Connection ID:   8629
  Send Sequence:        4
  Send Total Length:    0
  Fragment Offset:      0
  Fragment Length:      0
  ACK Sequence:         5
  ACK Fragment Offset:  10
  Remaining NetBIOS Data:
  ..V.            9D B1 56 C8
```

Concluding Thoughts on NetBIOS Terminology

In the NetBIOS/TCP environment, the term NetBIOS refers to the API and to the portion of the packet that carries the NetBIOS API commands, replies, and data. In the NetBIOS/NetBEUI environment, NetBIOS refers only to the API, and NetBEUI refers to the protocol and associated header information. In the NetBIOS/IPX environment, NetBIOS refers to both the API and to the protocol. Of course, when the term NetBIOS is used relative to TCP, it's referring to the thin, behaviorless header, but in the Novell world it refers to a protocol that has many different behaviors. Perhaps if these three implementations had been given dramatically different names, there would be less confusion. In fact, in the 1980s, a Novell expert would have referred to NetWare's implementation as a *NetBIOS Emulator*, alluding to the fact that NetBEUI was the actual protocol that implemented NetBIOS and Novell was emulating the functions in NetBEUI, but using Novell-proprietary protocols.

NetBIOS Name Management Mechanisms

For each of the three common implementations of NetBIOS (NetBEUI, TCP, and IPX), there are different mechanisms for managing names in a network. The name management functions, however, remain consistent for all implementations. These functions include registration, resolution, refresh, and release.

Name Registration

A station sends frames related to the Add Name command in an effort to confirm that no other station is using the desired name. If no other station is using the name, the Add Name command inserts the name into the machine's internal name table. The machine is then willing to accept data intended for that name. Remember that the name may be a unique name or a group name. The next three sections describe the terminology and packet-level decode associated with each implementation for name registration.

NetBEUI

A client broadcasts a Find Name frame several times and, if no one answers, then the originator assumes that the name is not in use. If some other station is using the name, then that station responds with a Name-In-Use frame.

TCP

Windows 95/98/ME and XP peer-to-peer networking uses WINS. Windows 2000 networking uses DDNS. A client sends a Name Query frame to a WINS or DDNS central server, if one is configured. Otherwise, the client broadcasts a Name Query. A name server responds with an Active Error if the name is in use or with no data if the name is not found. A station sends the broadcast Name Query several times. As with the NetBEUI Find Name frame, the lack of any response indicates that the name is not being used. If a station is using the name, it responds with an Active Error sent as a unicast packet.

IPX

A client broadcasts a Find Name frame. The behavior associated with the IPX Find Name frame is identical to that of the NetBEUI Find Name, although the IPX implementation of the NetBIOS protocol is different from that of NetBEUI. The lack of response indicates that the name is not being used.

Name Resolution

To send a directed frame to a specific named station, the NetBIOS name must ultimately be resolved into a particular data link (Ethernet) address to serve as the Destination Address in the directed packet. The next three sections describe the terminology and packet-level decode associated with each implementation for Name Resolution.

NetBEUI

A client broadcasts a Find Name frame exactly as when name registration was performed, but this time an answer is expected. The answer is called a *Name Recognized* frame. The client places the data link (Ethernet) Source Address in the reply in an internal table and uses it as the target for reaching the desired named station.

TCP

A client uses WINS or DDNS exactly as when name registration was performed, but this time an answer is expected. When no central WINS server is implemented, the packets are sent as IP broadcast packets with an accompanying Ethernet broadcast address. A router does not forward these packets. As a result, without a WINS (or DDNS) server, it is not possible for a NetBIOS/TCP client to contact a target that is outside its immediate broadcast domain. In fact, this is one of the problems that was initially solved through the creation of WINS and later adjusted and improved through DDNS and Active Directory in Windows 2000.

IPX

A client broadcasts a Find Name frame as when name registration was performed, but this time an answer is expected. Bear in mind that a NetWare NetBIOS/IPX packet contains a special section in the NetBIOS header that allows the packet to traverse up to seven routers. The effective broadcast domain associated with a NetBIOS/IPX packet is not bounded by the first router as it would be for an IP (or other) broadcast packet.

> **NOTE** On Cisco routers, you need to configure the `ipx type-20 propagation` command to cause the router to forward NetBIOS/IPX broadcast packets. The IPX Packet Type for NetBIOS is 20, as you can see in the *IPX Name Query* section earlier. (Chapter 10 showed the IPX Packet Type for NetBIOS in hexadecimal as 0x14.) You should configure the command on the input interface that receives the broadcast packets. To control which broadcasts are forwarded based on the NetBIOS name being queried, you can use the `ipx netbios input-access filter` command.

Name Refresh

The refresh function is implemented only with WINS or DDNS and is manifested by a Refresh Name packet being sent on the network. The effect is to reset the timeout timer that would otherwise age the name entry in the WINS or DDNS server and cause the name to be removed.

Name Release

Release occurs at the point when a NetBIOS station ceases using a particular name. You won't observe a name release in all implementations. With WINS, a client sends a Release Name packet to the WINS Server. NetBEUI and NetBIOS/IPX can use a Deregister Name packet, which is broadcast on the network. The term *deregister* refers to the fact that even though a device is not going to use a particular name anymore, it does not terminate sessions previously established with that name that are currently active. No new sessions will be accepted, and the deregistering station tells the rest of the network to no longer use the name, but sessions in progress can terminate normally.

Management of NetBIOS Names with NetBIOS/TCP

The previous sections explained that all implementations of NetBIOS must register and resolve names. NetBEUI and NetBIOS/IPX use a broadcast mechanism for both registration and resolution. NetBIOS/TCP uses WINS. This section explains the WINS process in more detail because it is the most common implementation present today and, until Windows 2000 with Active Directory and Dynamic DNS replaces the NT implementation, it will remain common in most Windows networks.

The job of both DNS and WINS is to provide a mechanism whereby a name can be resolved to an IP address. DNS and WINS differ in that WINS resolves only NetBIOS names, whereas DNS resolves fully qualified domain names, such as *bighost.wildpackets .com*. DNS can also resolve a NetBIOS server name (with a 0x20 qualifier), but cannot resolve names with other Qualifier Bytes, such as 0x03 for a username or 0x00 for a machine name. A Windows client configured with both WINS and DNS first attempts to resolve NetBIOS names through WINS. The client always resolves fully qualified domain names through DNS. A Windows NT server or workstation includes a configuration option whereby the machine can be told to attempt NetBIOS server name resolution through DNS.

WINS uses the same packet format as DNS. Every field in the DNS header is present in the WINS header. It's the same packet exactly. The difference in function between WINS and DNS is determined by the port to which the packet is sent (and, of course, by the originator of the packet, either a WINS or DNS client). Packets sent to UDP Port 53 are DNS packets. Packets sent to UDP Port 137 are WINS packets. A DNS server listens on Port 53. A WINS server listens on Port 137.

DNS provides several functions that are not available in WINS. Nonetheless, the fields that DNS uses to provide these functions are present in a WINS packet. WINS clients and servers ignore these fields, however. This is important because the value

observed in these unused fields may change. (There is no requirement that an originator of a WINS frame set the unused fields to any particular value.) The protocol analyst
must be aware that even though the value of the unused fields may appear to be significant, the fields are totally ignored and have no meaning to WINS.

DNS provides recursion, as discussed in Chapter 9. When a client makes a DNS
query, the client can specify that recursion is desired by setting the Recursion Desired
bit. That is, the client can request that the DNS server attempt to contact other DNS
servers if the desired information is not available locally. A DNS server indicates
whether it has been configured to support recursion with the Recursion Available bit.
The Recursion Desired and Recursion Available bit fields are present in WINS packets,
but they are ignored. The DNS server that maintains the names for a particular domain
(wildpackets.com, for example) is said to be the *authoritative server* for that domain. The
Authoritative Answer bit indicates that the responding server was the authoritative
server for the domain for which it answered. This bit is present in WINS packets, but it
is ignored.

Node Type Behavior

Windows clients use four different types of behavior relative to WINS. These are as
follows:

   The B-Node (A broadcast node).   The client sends WINS queries as IP and Ethernet broadcasts. This is effective if no WINS server is present. All stations in the
   broadcast domain, which is bounded by routers, hear the WINS broadcast. If the
   target machine is present, it replies with a directed WINS reply back to the
   querying station.

   The P-Node (A point-to-point node).   The client sends WINS queries as directed
   unicast packets to the IP address of the WINS server. This means that a WINS
   server can be on a remote subnet and the query will reach it through the IP routing path. The address of the WINS server is either manually configured or
   obtained through Dynamic Host Configuration Protocol (DHCP).

   The M-Node (A mixed node).   The classic description of this node type doesn't
   actually describe its observed behavior in most implementations. The common
   description of an M-Node is that it first broadcasts a WINS query and then
   sends directed packets to a WINS server. The implication is that there is some
   kind of intelligence in the M-Node that waits to see if anyone answers the
   broadcast before sending directly to the WINS server IP address. In practice, an
   M-Node broadcasts a WINS query and immediately, in the very next packet,
   sends the directed WINS query. Both packets are the result of a single WINS
   lookup request from the operating system. The M-Node behavior is reminiscent
   of the early days of Windows networking when WINS was being introduced. It
   was more probable that a target server was present in the client's broadcast
   domain than in some remote location. This is because the original Windows networking environment was based on NetBEUI, which was not routable. Therefore it made sense to broadcast in an attempt to find a target; chances were that
   the target server would be located in the local subnet.

The H-Node (A hybrid node).   A term had to be created to describe this node type, but the practical result of an H-Node's behavior is identical to that of an M-Node. The common description of the behavior of an H-Node is that it sends directed packets to the WINS server first and then it broadcasts the WINS query. Practical observation, however, shows that the H-Node sends both a directed query and the broadcast query, just in the opposite order from the M-Node. An H-Node sends the directed query first. This is probably the most common node type in use in NT networks.

Windows operating systems maintain numerous control parameters in a database called *the Registry*. While it's true that there is a Registry entry that determines a station's node type (and, hence, its behavior relative to WINS), the actual operation is a by-product of the setting of other configuration options in a node. If a WINS server address is available, then the node becomes an H-Node. If no WINS server address is configured or available through DHCP, then the node becomes a B-Node. P-Node and M-Node must be manually configured in the Registry. Remember, though, that the H-Node will probably send both the directed WINS query and the broadcast query at the same time. Whichever one is answered first becomes the answer that is recorded by the querying machine.

Troubleshooting NetBIOS Naming Problems

Troubleshooting NetBIOS naming problems should be straightforward in most cases. Capture the WINS traffic with a protocol analyzer and see who is making queries. Determine if the queries are broadcast or directed queries, and then determine who is answering these queries.

When WINS works properly, a requesting client obtains the IP address associated with a particular NetBIOS name and, in all probability, proceeds to set up a TCP connection with the target, followed by a NetBIOS session, followed by SMB communication. Also, when a client first joins the network, it confirms that no other station is using its name by making a WINS query for its name. In this case, of course, it's hoped that nobody responds to the WINS broadcast or that the WINS server reply comes back with zero answers.

Successful name registration is always the first NetBIOS process that you should observe when analyzing a NetBIOS conversation. An answer, indicating that someone else is already using the specified name, shows that there is a problem. The answer contains either the Ethernet or IP address (with WINS) of the duplicate, so the troubleshooting process simply involves determining who is the rightful owner of the name and making the appropriate configuration changes to make the names unique.

When assessing the name resolution process, keep in mind that a station is attempting to locate a particular named target probably because the station has data to send to the target. If a user can't send a print job to a printer, for example, you might observe that the user's station is unsuccessful in resolving the printer's NetBIOS name. Perhaps the user typed the name incorrectly or perhaps the target machine is not online. It may be that the target is not in the broadcast domain (for broadcast-based resolution) or that a routing configuration or connection problem exists (for directed WINS or Novell's seven-router broadcast domain).

POTENTIAL ANOMALIES WITH H-NODE AND M-NODE BEHAVIOR

Due to the fact that H-Nodes and M-Nodes ask for information twice, it is possible—though not likely—for a client machine to exhibit anomalous behavior. Suppose that a server named BIGSERVER resides in the local broadcast domain along with a client. By mistake, another server, in a remote location, is also called BIGSERVER. If the local server is not WINS-enabled (hence, a B-Node), it will not communicate with the WINS server to record its name. The WINS server will only know about the remote BIGSERVER (which, for the purposes of this example, *is* WINS-enabled).

An M-Node client sending a query may get a response from the local BIGSERVER (through the WINS broadcast), accept the answer, and ignore the different answer coming back from the WINS server a moment later. Depending on various network factors, however, it's also possible for the WINS server to deliver its directed answer before the local server has time to respond. Users might complain that sometimes they have no problem accessing BIGSERVER, but, at other times, their passwords don't work. The permutations of possible misconfigurations are endless, but it's important to recognize the types of issues that you may face when troubleshooting a WINS problem.

If the target machine definitely exists and the user typed the name correctly, troubleshooting is a matter of moving the protocol analyzer further and further away from the originating machine to see how far (physically) the name resolution packet traverses through the network infrastructure. If the packet and the target are in the same broadcast domain, then the target machine has a problem (as it can be assumed that all stations in the broadcast domain can acquire all broadcast packets). In a switched environment, the port to which the target machine is attached can be mirrored for positive confirmation that the resolution packet is, in fact, being delivered properly. With directed WINS queries, the process involves moving the protocol analyzer to the far side of the router and confirming that the router is properly forwarding the resolution packet. For directed WINS and DDNS, the query and reply packets can be examined to confirm that the WINS or DDNS server is responding with valid information.

NetBIOS Data Movement

As with any typical protocol stack, there is a reliable connection-oriented mechanism and a connectionless datagram mechanism for transporting data through a NetBIOS interface. The connection-oriented mechanism provides for session setup and teardown and for the sequencing, acknowledging, and retransmission of data. Also, flow control prevents a transmitter from overrunning a receiver's capability to accept data. The connectionless mechanism, like any connectionless protocol mechanism, provides no such capabilities and delivers data in a best-effort mode.

The functions of session setup, teardown, and reliable data transfer are provided by different components of the protocol stack in the three different NetBIOS implementations. Analysis of NetBIOS communication implies an analysis of the overall mechanism of moving data, and this may include layers other than the one labeled as NetBIOS in a protocol decode.

Session Behavior with NetBIOS/TCP

TCP/NetBIOS relies on TCP for reliability. Data is sequenced, acknowledged, and retransmitted in accordance with the normal rules for TCP transmission. This implies that, prior to a NetBIOS session being set up, a TCP session must be set up with a three-way handshake. A typical flow of behavior appears in a protocol analyzer decode with the following steps:

1. The client sends a WINS query to resolve the NetBIOS name of the server to an IP address.
2. The server (or WINS server) responds with the IP address of the server.
3. The client sends an ARP broadcast to resolve the IP address to an Ethernet address.
4. The server responds with an ARP reply that contains its Ethernet address.
5. The client sends a TCP SYN packet.
6. The server responds with an ACK for the previous SYN and its own SYN.
7. The client sends an ACK for the server's SYN.
8. The client sends a NetBIOS Session Setup packet across the newly established TCP connection.
9. The server responds with a TCP ACK.
10. The server responds with a NetBIOS Session Acknowledgment packet.
11. The client sends a TCP ACK.

Typically, the next step is that the file I/O mechanism used in Windows networking (that is, SMB) sets up its own session. SMB behavior will be discussed later in this chapter. NetBIOS simply sees the SMB packets as blocks of data that have a particular length but don't convey any particular meaning. TCP carries these blocks of data across the network with accompanying TCP acknowledgments. Moreover, NetBIOS interjects its own acknowledgment packets periodically. Each protocol layer interacts with its peer in the partner machine. That is, TCP interacts with TCP and NetBIOS interacts with NetBIOS, and both of them send data and acknowledgments autonomously.

The challenge in the protocol analysis process is to see this collage of packets as separate behavioral interactions and to assess each layer independently. The Ethernet network must be working, first and foremost. IP must be routing packets correctly. If all of this is working, then TCP can be analyzed to see if it's doing its job properly. If it is, then NetBIOS must be periodically sending an acknowledgment packet. Ultimately, SMB must be performing a logical operation, such as opening and reading files. SMB has its own set of commands and acknowledgments.

Only by careful examination of the packets involved in a NetBIOS/TCP session will these interleaved behaviors become clearly visible. There is no substitute for experience in performing this type of analysis. The way to truly learn about these behaviors is to explore them with a protocol analyzer. Capture a working conversation and identify each step of the communication mechanism as described. Remember to first track the TCP layer to verify that the sequenced bytes are properly acknowledged. Then track the NetBIOS behavior. Finally, observe the behavior of SMB riding on top of the stack. SMB behavior is reasonably intuitive to understand because its main job is the manipulation of files: searching, opening, reading, writing, and closing files.

Reliable Data Transport with NetBIOS

When NetBIOS is implemented over TCP, there is no reliability inherent in the Net-BIOS protocol manifestation. Reliable data exchange is managed by TCP in its normal manner. With NetBEUI and NetBIOS/IPX, there are sequence numbers carried in the NetBIOS header and it's the NetBIOS component of the protocol that provides reliability (sequencing, acknowledgment, retransmissions, and flow control).

In a NetBEUI implementation, there is a field called the *Transmit/Response Correlator*. This is a 4-byte hexadecimal field that is used to associate a NetBIOS data block and its acknowledgment. It is shown in the following protocol analyzer output:

```
NetBEUI/NetBIOS - Network Basic Input/Output System
   Length:                 44
   NetBIOS Delimiter:      0xEFFF
   Command:                0x08  Datagram(Wait)
   Option Data 1:          0x00  Reserved
   Option Data 2:          0x0000  Reserved
   Xmit/Resp Correlator:   0x00000000
   Destination Name:       AG-TRAIN        <0x1E>
   Source Name:            SOCRATES        <0x20>
```

The use of the terms *Transmit Correlator* and *Response Correlator* is not intuitive. When a station sends a block of NetBIOS data, the block is given a Response Correlator value. The recipient acknowledges receipt of the block by sending back the same value in the NetBIOS acknowledgment packet. In the acknowledgment packet, the acknowledgment field is technically called the Transmit Correlator, which is backward from what you might expect. That is, a station transmits the Response Correlator and the response contains the Transmit Correlator. The EtherPeek protocol analyzer simply uses the term *Xmit/Resp Correlator* for the field, whether it's the initial packet or an acknowledgment. Some analyzers change the field name. When decoding the initial packet, they call the field the Response Correlator. When decoding an acknowledgment, they call the field the Transmit Correlator.

Analyzing reliability in a NetBIOS/NetBEUI conversation is a matter of confirming that each block of NetBIOS data (identified by a Response Correlator) is met with a matching acknowledgment. The acknowledgment should carry a Transmit Correlator that is equal to the previously sent Response Correlator.

Novell's NetBIOS also uses a hexadecimal value as a sequence number. There is a Send Sequence and an ACK Sequence value in the NetBIOS/IPX header, as shown in the following analyzer output:

```
NetWare NetBIOS
   Control Flag:          0xC0
                  Send ACK
                  System Packet
   Datastream Type:       6  Session Data
   Source Connection ID: 8669
   Dest Connection ID:   8629
   Send Sequence:         4
   Send Total Length:     0
   Fragment Offset:       0
   Fragment Length:       0
   ACK Sequence:          5
   ACK Fragment Offset:  10
```

The ACK Sequence is not intuitive in its operation. When a connection is idle, the NetBIOS packets that are sent to keep the connection alive have no data, but they do have a significant sequence number. To understand this behavior, it's necessary to examine a normal exchange of packets and then see what happens when the conversation goes idle. Normally, data is exchanged on the basis of the ACK Sequence being the sequence number that is next expected.

If a station sends Send Sequence 1, for example, then the acknowledgment from the recipient specifies that the recipient expects to receive Send Sequence 2 next. The recipient conveys this by sending back ACK Sequence 2. The ACK Sequence is the number that the station expects to receive next. The two sides of a conversation aren't necessarily synchronized. A session may start with a Ping-Pong series of packets, but that probably won't continue. For example, consider the following exchange of commands:

```
Client Sends:     Search a directory for a particular file
Server Responds:  Here is the file
Client Sends:     Open the file
Server Responds:  OK, the file is open
Client Sends:     Read a block of data from the file
Server Responds:  Here is the block of data
Client Sends:     Close the file
Server Responds:  OK, the file is closed.
```

In this exchange there is a synchronized conversation between the client and server. It is a Ping-Pong conversation. Each client packet is met with a single server packet. In this type of conversation, the Send Sequence number and ACK Sequence number remain in step as follows:

```
Client Sends:     Search a directory for a particular file
                     Send Sequence 1,   ACK Sequence 1
Server Responds:  Here is the file
                     Send Sequence 1,   ACK Sequence 2
Client Sends:     Open the file
                     Send Sequence 2,   ACK Sequence 2
Server Responds:  OK, the file is open
                     Send Sequence 2,   ACK Sequence 3
```

```
Client Sends:       Read a block of data from the file
                       Send Sequence 3,  ACK Sequence 3
Server Responds: Here is the block of data
                       Send Sequence 3,  ACK Sequence 4
Client Sends:       Close the file
                       Send Sequence 4,  ACK Sequence 4
Server Responds: OK, the file is closed.
                       Send Sequence 4,  ACK Sequence 5
Client Sends:       ACK Sequence 5 (to ACK the OK from the Server)
```

Notice how the Send Sequence and ACK Sequence increment in step. This is purely an accident and is not required. It's an accident because the application-level conversation just happened to be Ping-Pong in nature. Remaining in step is not necessary. Consider this exchange of packets:

```
Client Sends:       Search a directory for a particular file
                       Send Sequence 1,  ACK Sequence 1
Server Responds: Here is the file
                       Send Sequence 1,  ACK Sequence 2
Client Sends:       Open the file
                       Send Sequence 2,  ACK Sequence 2
Server Responds: OK, the file is open
                       Send Sequence 2,  ACK Sequence 3
Client Sends:       Read a VERY LARGE block of data from the file
                       Send Sequence 3,  ACK Sequence 3
Server Responds: Here is Fragment 1 of the large block
                       Send Sequence 3,  ACK Sequence 4
Server Responds: Here is Fragment 2 of the large block
                       Send Sequence 4,  ACK Sequence 4
Server Responds: Here is Fragment 3 of the large block
                       Send Sequence 5, ACK Sequence 4
Server Responds: Here is Fragment 4 of the large block
                       Send Sequence 6, ACK Sequence 4
Client Sends:       Close the file
                       Send Sequence 4,  ACK Sequence 7
Server Responds: OK, the file is closed.
                       Send Sequence 7,  ACK Sequence 5
Client Sends:       ACK Sequence 8 (to ACK the OK from the Server)
```

Notice that the request to transfer a large file was met with several packets from the server. The server returned Send Sequence 3, 4, 5, and 6, one after the other. The server essentially dumped the data back on the client. That's an efficient thing for the server to do and it is normal behavior to observe. The effect, however, is to put the client's and server's Sequence and ACK numbers at different values. This conversation is not a Ping-Pong exchange. It's more like a Ping-Pong-Pong-Pong-Pong exchange.

When analyzing Novell NetBIOS conversations, the challenge is to keep each side of the conversation isolated. That is, it's necessary to move forward, packet by packet, and confirm that the appropriate acknowledgments are being sent. Sometimes one side will send a series of packets. The ACK number at the end of the series can acknowledge all of the previously sent data.

The behavior of the NetBIOS/IPX sequence numbers during data exchange is reasonable and reasonably intuitive. It's not dramatically different from that of many other packet-numbering sequence schemes (such as LLC Type 2, for example). When there is no data to send (when the user goes for a cup of coffee, for example), the conversation remains intact, but it becomes idle. To confirm that the other side is still alive, NetBIOS/IPX enters a keepalive state after approximately 6 seconds of inactivity. The target of the original connection resends its last acknowledgment packet. In response to this, the originator resends its last acknowledgment packet. Unlike any other protocol, however, the transmission of this keepalive resend results in the sequence number increasing. It's as if the resend of the last acknowledgment contained actual data. This is unexpected behavior in the big scheme of things, but now it should be expected behavior because it has been exposed and explained.

The Workgroup Model and the Domain Model

A Windows machine can, of course, share its file systems and printers. Permissions (and accompanying protocol-level authentication operations) must be established before someone is allowed to access a shared resource. With Windows networking, there are two general models for authentication. In the workgroup model, each machine maintains its own list of permissions and they are based on password access to resources. Anyone who knows the password can access the resource (which, for a file system, can be restricted to full or read-only access). In the domain model, permissions are stored in the *Security Accounts Management* (SAM) database. The permissions are based on a user ID and password pair, and resources can be made available with different levels of access for different users (or groups of users).

In both models, there is a mechanism by which an authentication operation takes place at the protocol level. In both cases, this consists of a series of packets in which authentication information is exchanged. The peer-to-peer workgroup authentication process is much simpler than the domain process, but the end result of successful authentication in either case is the same: The user is allowed to access the resources.

Troubleshooting the authentication process should be straightforward. Using your protocol analyzer, you must be able to identify the packets that are performing authentication. If the continuation of the protocol behavior following the authentication process consists of normal file or printer access, then evidently the authentication succeeded. If the conversation indicates that file or printer access failed, then the authentication must have failed. Of course, armed with the Windows development documentation, or having attended an in-depth course in Windows network protocol analysis, you might be able to decipher the meaning and purpose for each packet in the authentication process. Because you (probably) don't work as an operating system developer at Microsoft, you probably aren't interested in the internal workings of the authentication process; you're probably just concerned about whether it succeeded or failed. The following example will help you learn to distinguish successful and failed authentications.

Analysis of a Workgroup Authentication Operation

This section describes the protocol exchange that occurred during an authentication operation in a workgroup environment. The user at the *VIAO_Danville IP.100* client machine is accessing the *Cyrix IP.248* machine. The Cyrix IP.248 machine is sharing files on the network. Prior to the protocol exchange, the user had performed the following actions:

1. Clicked on Network Neighborhood.

2. Clicked on Entire Network, which caused a list of workgroups and domains to appear.

3. Clicked on a particular workgroup, which caused a list of machines sharing files to appear.

4. Clicked on the Cyrix server.

At this point, the trace file example begins. The software displayed a password dialog box on the user's screen, and the user typed in the wrong password (see Packet 116). When the software presented the password dialog box a second time, the user typed in the correct password (see Packet 131). To display the files in the Network Neighborhood window, the client acquired the disk attributes and a file list from the server (Packets 132 through 144), with the operation continuing beyond Packet 144.

```
Packet          SOURCE              DESTINATION   DELTA TIME
115   VIAO_Danville IP.100    Cyrix IP.248    08.719000
      SMB Tree Conn & X         C Path=\\CYRIX233\PRIVATE Service=?????
116   Cyrix IP.248    VIAO_Danville IP.100    00.003000
      SMB Tree Conn & X       R Status=Bad password
117   VIAO_Danville IP.100    Cyrix IP.248    00.000000
SMB Tree Conn & X    C Path=\\CYRIX233\PRIVATE Service=?????
118   Cyrix IP.248    VIAO_Danville IP.100    00.003000
      SMB Tree Conn & X       R Status=Bad password
119   VIAO_Danville IP.100    Cyrix IP.248    00.179000
TCP NB SessMsg       .A....,S= 237041128,L=    0,A= 690464690,W=16461
130   VIAO_Danville IP.100    Cyrix IP.248    25.052000
SMB Tree Conn & X    C Path=\\CYRIX233\PRIVATE Service=?????
131   Cyrix IP.248    VIAO_Danville IP.100    00.001000
      SMB Tree Conn & X       R Status=OK
132   VIAO_Danville IP.100    Cyrix IP.248    00.000000
      SMB Get Server Attr    C Get disk attributes
133   Cyrix IP.248    VIAO_Danville IP.100    00.001000
SMB Get Server Attr R Status=OK 1996MB total, 1550MB free
134   VIAO_Danville IP.100    Cyrix IP.248    00.001000
      SMB X2IO        C Find First File=\*.*
135   Cyrix IP.248    VIAO_Danville IP.100    00.002000
      SMB X2IO        R Status=OK
136   VIAO_Danville IP.100    Cyrix IP.248    00.144000
TCP NB SessMsg       .A....,S= 237041350,L=    0,A= 690465503,W=17520
137   VIAO_Danville IP.100    Cyrix IP.248    00.003000
      SMB X2IO        C Find Next SID=0xa329
138   Cyrix IP.248    VIAO_Danville IP.100    00.002000
      SMB X2IO        R Status=OK
139   VIAO_Danville IP.100    Cyrix IP.248    00.000000
      SMB X2IO        C Find Next SID=0xa329
140   Cyrix IP.248    VIAO_Danville IP.100    00.001000
      SMB X2IO        R Status=OK
```

```
141   VIAO_Danville IP.100   Cyrix IP.248   00.004000
      SMB Find Close C Handle=0xa329
142   Cyrix IP.248   VIAO_Danville IP.100   00.000000
      SMB Find Close R Status=OK
143   VIAO_Danville IP.100   Cyrix IP.248   00.132000
      SMB Tree Conn & X        C Path=\\CYRIX233\IPC$ Service=IPC
144   Cyrix IP.248   VIAO_Danville IP.100   00.001000
      SMB Tree Conn & X      R Status=OK
```

Notice that the client software sent the bad password to the server twice (see Packets 116 and 118). This is a normal behavior (albeit somewhat confusing, at first look). When the user entered the password properly, the behavior continued with the acquisition of the file list (Find First File=*.* in Packet 134).

Notice that Packet 143 contains a reference to *IPC$*. IPC$ is the Interprocess Communication Service in Windows networking. The dollar sign is read as *share,* so the name of the service is *IPC share.* IPC$ is the internal service (a hidden share), which is responsible for authentication and share management for a user connection. In fact, the authentication process itself is actually using IPC$ behind the scenes. The use of IPC$ is more evident when authentication is made to an NT domain, as opposed to a workgroup authentication.

The essence of the workgroup authentication process is quite simple. A client does not preauthenticate; it simply attempts to access resources. There is no initial login to a domain where a user identity is established with associated permissions. The individual servers that are offering services maintain all permissions. At the moment of access, the server checks to see if the user supplied the correct password. Note that there is no association between a particular user and a password. There's only a password. The only possible permissions are no-access, read-only, and full-access. This is quite different from the domain model, where a network administrator may assign a wide range of permissions to individual users.

By default, the user's password is the same password used to log in to the Windows desktop when the client workstation boots. Windows encrypts the user's password and sends it in a packet such as the packet shown in the following analyzer output:

```
SMB Session Set Up & X (Including User Logon)   Request
   Word count:            13
   Secondary command:     0x75   Tree Connect And X
   AndX reserved (MBZ):   0x00
   AndX offset:           228
   Max buffer size:       4356
   Max multiplex count:   50
   VC number:             1
   Session key:           0x00000000
   Case insensitive password length:24
   Case sensitive password length:24
   Reserved (MBZ):        0x00000000
   Capabilities (LSW):    %1101010000000000
                               Does not support Large Read&X requests
                               Does not support Server DFS
```

```
   Capabilities (MSW):    %0000000000000000
   Byte Count:            167
   Case insensitive
password:0xC8B6CADB2442980066E7A129A1BF77C7274D2E6B39247D38
   Case sensitive
password:0x9908CDB86FE5AB9E77F04D79BA37996094841A1850096567
   Native OS:             .............
   Native Lan Man:        ...........
```

Authentication in the Windows NT Domain Model

As discussed in the previous section, in the workgroup model, each server maintains a password for each shared resource. Authentication is handled locally. A server that is sharing a resource prompts a user for a password at the moment of access. In the domain model, authentication is accomplished through a series of centralized databases that contain user ID and password information. Authentication information in a Windows NT network is maintained in the SAM database, which is a set of disk files that can be replicated to more than one server. Only one server maintains a read-write copy of the SAM database; all other copies are read-only. The read-write copy of the SAM database is maintained in the PDC; the read-only copies are maintained in BDCs.

The user interacts with the SAM database just once (at initial login time). From then on, whenever the user wants to access a service, the server goes to the SAM database to determine whether the user has permissions. If the user does not have permissions in the SAM database, the server denies access.

The protocol behavior in an NT network using the domain model is quite complicated. It's beyond the scope of this book to explain each nuance in detail. In general, however, you'll see the following fundamental types of behavior:

Initial user login.   During initial login, the operating system acquires a list of trusted domains from the PDC and presents the list in the initial login dialog box. After the user enters a user ID and password, the login process asks the PDC to locate a BDC in the domain. The login process authenticates with the BDC. (If there's only a single PDC, the PDC plays the role of both PDC and BDC.)

Domain authentication.   When a user attempts to access a shared resource on a server, the server asks the PDC to locate a BDC. The server then authenticates the user by querying the SAM database in the BDC.

Pass-through authentication.   When a user accesses a resource in a trusted domain, the authentication process must be passed through from the user's PDC to the PDC in the trusted domain. When a user from a trusted domain attempts to log in at a machine in the trusting domain, the initial authentication must also be passed through. The concepts, configurations, and details of trusted domains and trusting domains are outside the scope of this book.

SAM replication between the PDC and BDC.   At periodic intervals (every 5 minutes by default), or when a change is made, the PDC sends a copy of the SAM database (or the changes) to each BDC.

NT Registry Parameters Controlling Replication

Windows NT maintains control parameters in the Registry database, including parameters that control the PDC/BDC replication process. The `regedit` command (from the Start/Run dialog box) allows access to the Registry. Indiscriminate or invalid changes to the Registry can make it impossible for a machine to boot properly. Horror stories abound about someone having to completely reinstall Windows after destroying the Registry. So, be careful if you plan to edit the Registry! If you are familiar with the NT Registry, you can explore the setting of the following parameters:

Pulse.   Controls how often the PDC replicates to the BDC. The value is a number of seconds between 60 and 3600.

PulseMaximum.   Controls the maximum amount of time the PDC waits to replicate if there have been no changes to the SAM database. The value is a number of seconds between 60 and 86,400 (one day).

Update.   If set to *Yes*, forces the PDC to replicate the entire SAM database instead of just the changes every time the PDC replicates to the BDC.

ReplicationGovernor.   Controls the block size and frequency of transmissions that the PDC uses to replicate the SAM database. The value is a percentage of a 128-kbyte block (for example, a value of 50 means 64-kbyte blocks are used, and they are transmitted twice as often). This value is set in the BDC, not the PDC.

The Browse Protocol

The Browse protocol makes it possible for users to see a list of shared resources when they click through the Network Neighborhood windows. The list is called a *browse list*. Windows clients and servers use a form of SMB called *MAILSLOT/BROWSE* to exchange the information that appears in the Network Neighborhood window.

There is often confusion regarding the fact that the Browse protocol uses a protocol category called Mailslot. Other functions also use the Mailslot category, including the Mailslot/NetLogon authentication process. The use of the term *Mailslot* has nothing to do with sending or receiving mail. The use of the term has nothing to do with SMTP, POP3, or IMAP. The word *mail* in the term Mailslot does not refer to e-mail. (This point has been reiterated here for emphasis!)

The term Mailslot originates with the concept of connectionless and connection-oriented protocols. In the realm of SMB, there are three mechanisms by which clients and servers exchange SMB data: native SMB, Mailslot, and Named Pipes.

With native SMB, clients and servers exchange file I/O commands (open, close, read, write, negotiate protocol, and so on) along with file data. This is essentially a connection-oriented, reliable mode of communication.

When data is sent without establishing a connection (as with the Browse and NetLogon functions), the mode is called Mailslot. The term refers to the process used in a mailroom or post office, where a clerk behind the counter places letters into people's mail boxes (their mail slots). Some time later, people come by and pick up their mail. The Mailslot protocol sends data without knowing or caring when, or if, some remote process receives it. Mailslot is simply the connectionless form of SMB. It has nothing to do with e-mail, letters, or human communication. The mail is a data message sent from one process to another, without any expectation of immediate delivery or acknowledgment.

A programmer can use the third form of SMB, called *Named Pipes,* to establish a connection-oriented, bidirectional pipe for the exchange of data. Some database systems use Named Pipes for application connectivity. The term arises from the fact that a text string identifies the connection (hence, a named pipe), as opposed to source and destination ports, which identify a TCP connection.

Maintaining the Browse List

There is potentially a nontrivial amount of traffic associated with the process of maintaining the browse list. A Subnet Master Browser is responsible for maintaining the list in each subnet. The Subnet Master Browser is elected based on a set of election criteria. Essentially, the "best" machine is the one with the most sophisticated operating system. Hence, a Windows ME machine wins over a Windows 98 machine, and an NT PDC wins over all machines.

A Windows client can be configured in three ways relative to the browse function: automatic, enabled, or disabled. This configuration is performed in the Network Control Panel by selecting `File and Printer Sharing for Microsoft Networks` from the list of installed networking components. The Properties button brings up the dialog box where Browse Master can be configured.

Automatic means that the machine participates in the Browser Election process. The machine is called a *potential browser. Enabled* means that the machine always forces a Browser Election when it enters a network. The machine is called a *preferred browser.* Preferred browsers compete with each other for the role of Subnet Master Browser. A preferred browser always wins an election over a potential browser, with the exception that a PDC is always favored over other stations. *Disabled* means that the station does not participate in the Browse process. It is not a potential browser.

When a station becomes the Subnet Master Browser, it builds a list of all shared resources. Every machine sharing a resource makes a browse announcement at periodic intervals, announcing the names of the services it offers. The Subnet Master Browser creates the browse list on the basis of these browse announcements.

When the first potential browser appears on the network, the Subnet Master Browser issues a *Become Backup Browser* packet to the new station, promoting it to the role of backup browser. The new backup browser then asks the Subnet Master Browser for a copy of the browse list. As more stations enter the network, and more shared resources are announced, the Subnet Master Browser updates the browse list and sends periodic updates to the backup browser. When the Subnet Master Browser sees 32 additional shares present on the network, it promotes a second potential browser to the role of backup browser. Additional backup browsers are created for each additional 32 machines sharing resources. Here is a review of this process:

1. The first machine joins a network. It is the only machine online. It broadcasts a request to find the Subnet Master Browser and gets no reply. As a result, the machine broadcasts a request to start an election and, because it's the only machine on the network, it wins the election.

2. The second machine joins the network. When it broadcasts a request to find the Subnet Master Browser, the first machine answers the request. If this second machine is not a preferred browser, it simply accepts that the Subnet Master Browser exists, even if the second machine would win a Browser Election over the first one. It's like politics. The best candidates for a political position may not currently be in office. They have to wait until the next Election Day before their status as being better becomes active.

3. The Subnet Master Browser promotes the second machine to the role of backup browser (if the second machine is a potential browser), and the browse list is exchanged.

4. When 32 more machines register with the Subnet Master Browser, it promotes an additional potential browser to the role of backup browser.

5. If a preferred browser enters the network, it automatically forces an election.

It should be noted that backup browsers take precedence over nonbackup browsers in an election. Because all preferred browsers can be promoted to the role of backup browsers, you could imagine a situation in which a group of preferred browsers, each of which is a backup browser, compete for the role of Subnet Master Browser. Those preferred browsers that were backup browsers would win over those that were not backup browsers. The intent is to guarantee that a browse list is available for all clients in the subnet.

The Master Browser that is resident in the PDC in a domain plays a special role. It becomes the Domain Master Browser and communicates with each Subnet Master Browser at periodic intervals (every 12 minutes) to maintain a master list of all resources in the domain. (It does this in addition to playing the normal role of Subnet Master Browser in the PDC's subnet.) This means that each Subnet Master Browser both sends its own browse list to the Domain Master Browser and also receives a copy of the consolidated browse list created by the Domain Master Browser. Moreover, because the PDC is aware of any other domains in the network, the Domain Master Browser can make these other domains part of the world known to the Network Neighborhood.

There are three Browse functions that occur at periodic intervals:

1. Each station that is sharing resources broadcasts a Host Announcement frame to the entire subnet every minute for the first several minutes after boot time, and then every 12 minutes thereafter.

2. The Subnet Master Browser uses the Microsoft Remote Access Protocol (MSRAP) to send a copy of the browse list Subnet Master Browser to each backup browser every 15 minutes. This is called a *share enumeration*.

3. Each Subnet Master Browser exchanges browse lists with the Domain Master Browser every 12 minutes.

Browsing with Multiple Protocols

Thus far we have discussed the Browse process from the perspective of a single protocol. We have discussed how a host broadcasts a Host Announcement to inform the Subnet Master Browser and all backup browsers of its presence. When a host first joins the network, it attempts to locate a Subnet Master Browser by broadcasting a Request Announcement frame. These broadcasts are protocol specific. If a station is configured to use NetBIOS/TCP, these broadcasts are IP broadcasts. If a station is using NetBIOS/IPX, it sends Novell-specific broadcasts. A NetBIOS/NetBEUI station sends NetBIOS broadcasts at the data link layer.

The entire Browse process takes place separately but completely for each of the three protocol configurations. Because a station that only uses IP doesn't recognize IPX or NetBEUI (and the same for any other combination of the three protocols), the establishment of a Subnet Master Browser takes place within each protocol community. An IP-based station becomes the Subnet Master Browser for all other IP stations. An IPX-based station becomes the Subnet Master Browser for all other IPX stations. A NetBEUI-based station becomes the Subnet Master Browser for all other NetBEUI-based stations. The entire process of broadcasting, updating the Domain Master Browser, exchanging browse lists using MSRAP, electing Master Browsers, and sending notifications occurs separately for each protocol that's in use.

In the Novell environment, a machine can be configured to use four different Ethernet frame types. The choice of Ethernet version II, IEEE 802.3, Subnetwork Access Protocol (SNAP), or Novell's own proprietary Ethernet frame format (802.3 raw) is up to the network administrator. Because a communicator using a particular frame type ignores the other three frame types, the possibility exists that a Subnet Master Browser (and the entire Browse process) could occur four times within the IPX environment itself! As you can imagine, there is a lot of traffic associated with the Browse process!

The Windows 2000 Model

When analyzing a Windows 2000 network, you will discover that quite a lot is different. You will probably have a mixture of classic NT and Windows networking protocols intermixed with the newer behaviors associated with Windows 2000.

The fundamental change in the Windows 2000 model lies in the implementation of DDNS and Active Directory. Active Directory is a dynamic database that holds the information that the PDC in an NT environment maintains in the SAM database. Active Directory also holds the IP-to-name relationships from the WINS database. Clients and servers use a protocol called *Lightweight Directory Access Protocol* (LDAP) to interrogate the Active Directory database.

Secure resource access is implemented through use of the *Kerberos* authentication mechanism. To understand Kerberos protocol messages, you must first consider a variety of administrative configurations that don't cause network traffic. To see how a user accesses a particular resource shared by a server, we'll examine the events that take place. Before you can see any packets involved with Kerberos authentication, the following actions must take place:

1. The network administrator configures a secret into the file server. The secret is a phrase that is used as part of an encryption algorithm.

2. The network administrator configures the Kerberos server with the name of the file server and the file server's secret.

3. The network administrator configures the Kerberos server with valid usernames, passwords, and access lists.

> ### WINDOWS AND MAC OS X INTEGRATION
>
> **Integrating Macintoshes that run Mac OS X into a Windows network should be straightforward because the necessary protocols are built in to the operating system. Mac OS X uses a NetBIOS Name Service broadcast (a WINS broadcast) to locate a specified service. Mac OS X does not participate in the Windows Browse process, but otherwise operates in a manner consistent with a Windows B-Node. When you connect from Mac OS X to a Windows file service, you are prompted to enter the name of the Windows service, your user ID, and a password. Entering the name of a Windows domain is optional.**
>
> **When using a protocol analyzer to investigate Mac OS X behavior on a Windows network, you will see that during SMB negotiation the Mac OS X client offers Samba as one of its supported SMB dialects. Samba is an open source version of SMB for UNIX platforms. During file transfer operations, the SMB exchange between a Mac OS X client and a Windows server is identical to what you would see between two Windows machines. If you are analyzing networks where Mac OS X and Windows machines are communicating, then you should be familiar with the Windows protocol environment, as discussed in this chapter.**

When a user wants to access a resource on a server, the user's machine makes a request to the Kerberos server, asking for a ticket. The user's request packet is called a *Get Ticket Request*. Hopefully, the server replies with a *Get Ticket Reply* packet, which includes a ticket. The user's machine will then append the ticket to a packet that it sends to the server.

A ticket is specific to the requested resource, just like a ticket for the 7:30 P.M. presentation of a Broadway show only lets the ticket holder into that specific performance. In fact, a ticket even includes a timestamp so that if it were somehow captured (perhaps with your protocol analyzer), it could not be reused at a future time. Because the Kerberos server knows the secret associated with the requested resource, it can create a uniquely encrypted ticket that can be properly decrypted by the resource. The Kerberos server and the resource share the secret key value through initial configuration.

The ticket data is appended to an otherwise normal IP packet. You might recognize the presence of a Kerberos ticket if you see a TCP SYN packet with a length of 200 or 300 bytes. Your protocol analyzer would simply show the ticket data as something like frame padding. TCP would end after 20 bytes, and whatever followed would be unintelligible to the analyzer—and rightly so!

Users are validated at the beginning of their network sessions. If the Kerberos server evaluated a user's rights each time the user's machine requested a ticket, there would be unnecessary overhead in the process. To get around this overhead, users are validated only once. The process of initially validating a user's ID and password takes some time. Based on configuration, the Kerberos server confirms that a user is authorized to ask for and receive tickets. The server gives a special ticket to the user that allows the user to then ask for specific tickets for specific resources. This special ticket is called a *Ticket Granting Ticket*. At the beginning of a user's session, you will see the Kerberos *Get Ticket Granting Ticket Request* and *Get Ticket Granting Ticket Reply* messages.

NOTE To understand the Kerberos Ticket Granting Ticket, imagine that you are a member of a very exclusive New York City club that gives its members high-quality tickets to Broadway plays. You can make the analogy that you have to show your club membership card (the Ticket Granting Ticket) to the concierge at the club before the concierge will give you tickets to a particular play.

Summary

Understanding protocol behavior in the Windows networking world implies an understanding of a number of separate but interoperable protocols. This collage of protocols becomes broader when Windows versions are intermixed on the same network, which is a common situation.

Making sense of the Windows protocol environment involves examining each protocol and each behavior independently to confirm reasonable and correct operation. It's only when practical protocol analysis experience is coupled with textbook descriptions of Windows protocols that the conversations on the cable come to light. Always remember that in a TCP/IP Windows environment you can make an assessment of TCP/IP behavior by verifying proper routing and data segment exchange, even when the specifics of the Windows protocol behavior are questionable.

This chapter has provided tips and techniques for understanding and troubleshooting Windows-based networks. This completes our exploration into campus LAN protocols. In the next and final chapter of the book, we will cover information that LAN engineers need to know about WANs.

CHAPTER

13

WAN Troubleshooting for LAN Engineers

Campus networks are usually interconnected with Wide Area Network (WAN) communication links to form large, complex organizational internetworks. As a campus network engineer, you can't focus solely on your Ethernet environment without bumping up against the WAN infrastructure that provides the communication glue between campus sites. The goal of this chapter, and of this book in general, is to teach you troubleshooting techniques to determine whether problems reside with your applications, your Local Area Network (LAN) equipment, your WAN equipment, or your service provider's WAN equipment. This chapter doesn't attempt to provide a complete dissertation on WAN engineering, but, rather, provides information to get you started learning WAN protocols and Cisco WAN troubleshooting commands. We will also explain how to troubleshoot WANs from a LAN perspective. After you finish this chapter, you should learn more about WANs by studying the excellent WAN books listed in the references section at the end of this book.

WAN Concepts

Most basic networking documents explain the differences between a LAN and a WAN by pointing out that a WAN spans larger geographic areas than a LAN. While this is usually the case, it's not always true. Some metropolitan networks are based on LAN technologies, such as Ethernet with single-mode fiber optic cabling. With high-power laser transmitters and fiber optic repeaters, single links can extend 200 miles or more and create giant, flat broadcast domains. Conversely, a WAN link, such as a leased line or Integrated Services Digital Network (ISDN) circuit, can connect two buildings that are less than a mile apart. Physical distance does not provide a clear distinction between LANs and WANs.

A better method for distinguishing LANs and WANs is to point out the differences in how they are administered. A LAN is typically owned by the organization that manages it. A WAN, on the other hand, is usually owned and operated by a service provider or common carrier, such as a telephone company. As a campus network engineer, you are a customer of the service provider and must rely on the provider to transmit your data across the provider's network. From a troubleshooting viewpoint, this complicates matters.

With LANs, you have control over configurations and can make changes as needed. Of even bigger importance, perhaps, is the fact that you can diagnose and troubleshoot problems autonomously with only the help of your co-workers and cooperative users (when they are cooperative). You don't have that luxury with WANs. With WANs, you are often required to involve your service provider when troubleshooting problems. A whole new realm of politics and human interaction issues is introduced as you walk the fine line between needing the service provider's help and pointing out that errors may be the provider's fault.

There is also a technical distinction between WAN and LAN environments. Conversations across a WAN link are based on a circuit, whereas LAN conversations are based on connection-oriented sessions or connectionless datagram message transmission. A circuit is a point-to-point connection between two communicators that is established prior to the transmission of data. Unlike a Transmission Control Protocol (TCP) session, a WAN circuit is created without any relation to the specific protocol that will be carried across it. The fundamental characteristic of a circuit is that it acts like a single piece of wire. When a bit is pushed into one end of the circuit, it comes out the other end, in bit-serial fashion, with no implied reliability or retransmission mechanism.

WAN Standards

Technical standards for WANs are developed by international standards bodies such as the International Telecommunication Union, Telecommunication Standardization Sector (ITU-T). These standards bodies tend to work rather slowly, which has resulted in industry groups forming to develop interim standards and enhancements. For example, vendors, carriers, users, and consultants formed the Asynchronous Transfer Mode (ATM) Forum and the Frame Relay Forum to promote and enhance those technologies. The Internet Engineering Task Force (IETF) also develops Request for Comments (RFCs) that address issues related to implementing TCP/ Internet Protocol (IP) protocols on WANs.

Although the Open System Interconnection (OSI) Reference Model comes from the international standards arena, and was initially focused on connection-oriented WAN services, many of the WAN services discussed in this chapter were not designed with strict adherence to that model. While the services were designed using the principles of layering, the layers of a particular WAN protocol may not fit neatly into the OSI model.

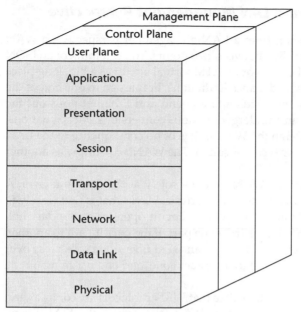

Figure 13.1   The three-dimensional OSI model.

When considering WAN protocols, it's important to recognize that many WAN protocols have control and management planes that carry signaling and overhead information. These planes are separate from the user plane that carries user data. When analyzing WAN protocols, you should think of the OSI model as being three-dimensional, with a user, control, and management plane, as illustrated in Figure 13.1.

The control plane handles call setup. Think of what happens when you make a telephone call. (Because WAN protocols have a telephone network legacy, it makes sense to use a telephone example.) When you lift the handset off the cradle of your telephone, the switch at the telephone company's local office senses that your telephone has gone off hook, provides dial tone, and accepts the numbers that you dial. This happens in the control plane. The interconnected switches that permit national and international calls also communicate with each other in the management plane, using complicated routing and administrative protocols such as Signaling System 7 (SS7). The user plane sends the actual telephone conversation. This division of tasks also occurs in both LAN and WAN networks, although one difference is that the control plane protocols for WANs are often quite complex. (In LAN environments, people don't pay much attention to the control plane, although both Address Resolution Protocol [ARP] and Internet Group Management Protocol [IGMP] could be considered control plane functions.)

NOTE See the first chapter of Howard Berkowitz's *WAN Survival Guide* for an elegant explanation of the different OSI planes and their functions.

Understanding WANs from a LAN Management Perspective

From the viewpoint of user data and from a LAN management perspective, a WAN circuit simply acts like a single data link between two points. You can think of an ISDN connection, a Frame Relay virtual circuit, or an ATM virtual circuit as a big, long piece of magical Ethernet cable that has no distance limitations. Frames go in one end of the cable and pop out the other. Ethernet feeds into one end and Ethernet pops out the other. The fact that the Ethernet frame undergoes various conversions, encapsulations, and machinations as it passes through the WAN link is of no consequence to the LAN assessment of the Ethernet-to-Ethernet conversation. The WAN acts simply as another data link in the conversation path.

From a LAN perspective, therefore, WANs operate solely at the data link layer. A dedicated WAN service (such as ISDN) includes a physical layer that is tied closely to the data link layer. An ATM or Frame Relay virtual circuit operates at the data link layer with physical layers that may change from one part of the circuit path to another. For example, an ATM virtual circuit may begin on an OC-3 fiber optic link, cross over to a copper T3 link, pass across a Gigabit Ethernet backbone, and end up going out an OC-12 link.

From a WAN perspective, it's critical to realize that WAN protocols are complex and diverse. WAN protocols such as ISDN, Point-to-Point Protocol (PPP), ATM, Frame Relay, and X.25 have user, control, and management planes. Each of these planes may have multiple layers. As far as interconnected LANs are concerned, however, the entire WAN link is simply a single data link.

WAN Components

At the most basic level, WAN protocols describe the interface between Data Terminal Equipment (DTE) and Data Circuit-Terminating Equipment (DCE). DTE devices are typically owned by an organization. The most common DTE is a router. A DCE is typically a switch inside a service provider's network. A modem is also a DCE.

A WAN implementation may use a Channel Service Unit/Digital Service Unit (CSU/DSU) to interface between the DTE and DCE. A CSU/DSU adapts the physical interface on a DTE to the interface on a DCE. The CSU/DSU also provides signal timing. A WAN circuit from a carrier enters a customer's building at a Point of Presence (POP), which is also known as a *demarcation point*. The circuit may then traverse building wiring to interface with the CSU/DSU. A DTE router typically connects to the CSU/DSU via a V.35 serial cable.

When troubleshooting WAN problems, you should start by checking the cabling between the router and the CSU/DSU and then the cabling to the demarcation point. Next isolate any problems with the CSU/DSU and make sure it can communicate with the DCE at the service provider. Most CSU/DSUs have extensive error reporting and loopback testing facilities. The error reporting may simply be a set of Light-Emitting Diodes (LEDs), which can be hard to decipher, so be sure to read the CSU/DSU documentation. Some routers have a built-in CSU/DSU, which eases troubleshooting in some ways (because there is less cabling and fewer devices that can fail) but can also make troubleshooting more difficult if you are accustomed to the LEDs and alarms provided by a typical CSU/DSU.

End-to-End WAN Considerations

In the previous section we characterized a WAN by describing the link between the DTE and DCE. A WAN also provides an end-to-end circuit that connects two LANs, as described in the *Understanding WANs from a LAN Management Perspective* section. In a Cisco environment, WANs typically represent a separate Layer 3 network. When two LANs are connected via a WAN, the two end points of the WAN circuit are routers. The WAN is assigned to a network or subnet and the WAN interfaces on the routers are configured with network-layer addresses. Figure 13.2 shows an example of a WAN that connects LANs and the IP addressing that is used.

Assigning network-layer addresses to WAN interfaces is not required, however. Cisco supports the `ip unnumbered` command, for example, which allows you to conserve IP addresses and not assign them to WAN interfaces. (The downside of this is that you can't ping the WAN interface.) IPXWAN, a protocol specified by Novell in RFC 1362 for transporting Internetwork Packet Exchange (IPX) over WANs, is another example of a WAN implementation that does not require network-layer addressing. Also, with some WAN implementations, bridges and switches are used instead of routers, in which case network-layer addressing is not needed. In addition, some WANs are implemented with an access server that allows remote nodes to join a network and appear as if locally connected. In this case, the remote nodes, local nodes, and the access server are all in the same network or subnet.

When troubleshooting a WAN, your first step should be to learn about the devices that connect the WAN network. Are they routers? Do the routers have network-layer addresses? Can you ping these addresses? Are the routers acting as access servers? Perhaps the WAN is actually a set of old-fashioned modems connected to an access server with remote modems accessing the server from end-user PCs. As part of your proactive network troubleshooting, you need to first characterize the physical and logical topology of the WAN.

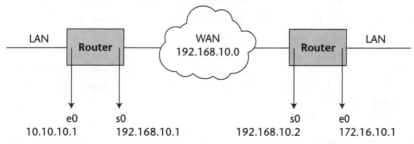

Figure 13.2 A WAN connecting two LANs.

Troubleshooting WANs from a LAN Perspective

As a campus network engineer, a lot of your troubleshooting will focus on traffic flow between LANs across WANs. Because WAN protocol analyzers are expensive and possibly beyond the budget of a campus network administration department, you will probably do a lot of troubleshooting using a LAN analyzer such as the WildPackets EtherPeek program. Your goal should be to determine if performance problems are due to packets getting lost or delayed traveling across the LAN/WAN internetwork or if the problems reside with clients or servers.

Chapter 9 discussed performance issues in the *Identifying TCP Performance Problems* section. The methods used in a TCP network can be generalized to any network that has a reliable protocol at some layer. By analyzing packet flow, retransmissions, and the response time for acknowledgments and replies, the source of degradation can be isolated. Even if your only tool is a LAN analyzer, you can often pinpoint the problem.

A client or server should send packets as rapidly as the network and application allow. When data is received, a recipient should send acknowledgments. For example, in a TCP/IP environment, the TCP layer sends acknowledgments. The application program probably has its own requests and replies. If a client sends a Read Request to a file server, for example, the server should send a Read Reply with the data the client requested. Application requests and replies may require that data be accessed from a server disk and processed in some manner by the client, which can slow down performance. When assessing performance, you should compare application response times to lower-layer response times to distinguish network problems from application client/server problems.

Consider a situation where a client issued a Read Request. A reliable protocol such as TCP, NetWare Core Protocol (NCP), AppleTalk Transaction Protocol (ATP), or Network Basic Input/Output System (NetBIOS), must acknowledge the packet. The application must also process the request and send a reply. One of three situations can occur:

1. The acknowledgment is carried with the application reply. This means that the protocol stack and application are operating at optimum performance, as is the network, including all WAN links.

2. The acknowledgment is sent immediately, but the application reply is delayed. This indicates that the network, including WAN links, is not the cause of the problem. Because the acknowledgment is able to come back immediately, the network must be working properly. The application must be the cause of the delay.

3. The acknowledgment is delayed a long time or is never seen with the analyzer. In this situation, the network is suspect. At this point, troubleshooting involves moving the analyzer from LAN to LAN, always getting closer to the WAN circuit. Examine the analyzer capture files and determine at what point packets get lost or delayed.

WANs and Retransmissions

Candidates for the Cisco Certified Internetwork Expert (CCIE) test often get confused by study questions that ask about retransmissions across WANs. The questions ask which device and which protocol retransmits if there is a problem on a WAN link that causes a bit to get dropped or changed. The study questions are an attempt to make the certification candidate think about which protocols offer reliability for end-user traffic.

Most WAN (and LAN) protocols have a Frame Check Sequence (FCS) field in the frame, which is used for error checking. The sender calculates the FCS based on the bits in the frame and places the result in the FCS field in the frame. The recipient executes the same calculation on the received bits. If the calculation doesn't yield the same FCS that is in the frame, most WAN and LAN protocols in use today simply drop the frame silently, with no notification to the sender that there was a problem. A router connected to a WAN leased line or Frame Relay circuit, for example, checks incoming frames for a bad FCS and drops a frame if the FCS is bad. The router at the other end of the circuit (that sent the frame) does not know that the frame was dropped. An end-system device must recognize that the frame never got acknowledged and retransmit if necessary. Reliability is an end-to-end service offered by protocols such as TCP.

The question about reliability of WANs has some history, however. In the past, many WAN protocols provided reliability. As is the case with LANs, old WAN protocols never completely go away. You may still encounter WAN protocols that offer reliability with retransmissions. A router running one of these protocols expects an acknowledgment and retransmits if one is not received. These protocols may be used in conjunction with TCP or other protocols that also offer reliability. Table 13.1 lists some WAN protocols and whether they provide a reliable service for end-user traffic. (Note that the table refers to end-user traffic. In some cases, signaling traffic, used for such purposes as call setup and sending telephone numbers or other identifications, is sent in a reliable fashion, even though end-user traffic is not.)

Table 13.1 WAN Technologies and Reliability for End-User Traffic

TECHNOLOGY	PROVIDES RELIABILITY? (ACKS AND RETRANSMISSIONS)
Asynchronous Transfer Mode (ATM)	No
Binary Synchronous Communication Protocol (BISYNC)	Yes
Cisco's High-Level Data Link Control (HDLC)	No
ISDN	No
Frame Relay	No
Link Access Procedure, Balanced (LAPB)	Yes
Point-to-Point Protocol (PPP)	No
Synchronous Data Link Control (SDLC)	Yes
X.25	Yes (uses LAPB)

Troubleshooting WANs from a Router Interface Perspective

Just because most WANs in use today do not have acknowledgments and retransmissions doesn't mean that WANs may not be the cause of an end system needing to retransmit. An end system retransmits when packets get dropped. Packets get dropped when they encounter errors or when a router or switch can't keep up with the flow. With a Cisco router, you should use the show interface command to determine the extent of dropped packets and errored frames. With leased lines, Frame Relay WANs, and ISDN Primary Rate Interfaces (PRIs), use the show interface serial command. If the interface is an ISDN Basic Rate Interface (BRI), use the show interface bri command. On ATM networks, use the show interface atm command.

The show interface command can tell you which type of encapsulation is in use on the interface, how many interface resets have occurred, the reliability and load of the interface, and other useful information, as shown in the following example:

```
Boston#show interface s0
Serial0 is up, line protocol is up
  Hardware is MCI Serial
  Internet address is 192.168.40.1 255.255.255.0
  MTU 1500 bytes, BW 1544 Kbit, DLY 20000 usec, rely 255/255, load 1/255
  Encapsulation HDLC, loopback not set, keepalive set (10 sec)
  Last input 0:00:01, output 0:00:01, output hang never
  Last clearing of "show interface" counters never
  Output queue 0/40, 0 drops; input queue 0/75, 0 drops
  5 minute input rate 0 bits/sec, 0 packets/sec
  5 minute output rate 0 bits/sec, 1 packets/sec
     51 packets input, 3658 bytes, 0 no buffer
     Received 18 broadcasts, 0 runts, 0 giants
     3 input errors, 0 CRC, 0 frame, 0 overrun, 0 ignored, 3 abort
     51 packets output, 3439 bytes, 0 underruns
     0 output errors, 0 collisions, 4 interface resets, 0 restarts
     0 output buffer failures, 0 output buffers swapped out
     7 carrier transitions
```

THERE ARE NO COLLISIONS ON A SERIAL INTERFACE

The output of the show interface serial command varies slightly depending on the type of encapsulation, which could be HDLC, Frame Relay, PPP, or others. One constant is that the router shows packet counts and error statistics near the bottom. The collision count should be ignored. Many networking novices think that there is a logical reason for there being a collision count on serial interfaces. There is no good reason for this other than that the Cisco programmers used a template for this bottom part of the output that is based on the output from the show interface ethernet command. There are no collisions on a serial interface, regardless of the encapsulation or technology. Collisions occur only on Carrier Sense Multiple Access networks, including Ethernet, 802.3, LocalTalk, Aloha, and 802.11 networks.

Inspecting the first line of output from the show interface serial command is vital to your troubleshooting effort. When a serial interface is enabled (not administratively shut down), but is still not working, there are two possible messages you may see in the first line of output:

1. Serial X is down, line protocol is down (down/down).

2. Serial X is up, line protocol is down (up/down).

When a serial interface is down/down, there is probably a physical layer problem. The meaning of this message is that the interface can't detect a carrier signal. In other words, Carrier Detect (CD) has not been asserted. The most likely cause is a disconnected, faulty, or improperly constructed cable. It is also possible that the DCE is having a problem and is not providing CD. Also, you should make sure that there are no faulty hardware components, including components on the router and on the CSU/DSU, if you are using a CSU/DSU.

When the interface is up/down, the router is reporting that the line protocol is down and that the router is not able to send and receive keepalive frames. Possible causes for the interface being up/down are a misconfiguration on one of the routers, a failed local or remote CSU/DSU, or a problem with the carrier's network. A router could be misconfigured with the wrong encapsulation that doesn't match the router at the other end. In the case of Frame Relay, the router could be using the wrong Local Management Interface (LMI) to send keepalives to the provider's switch, as will be discussed in the *Frame Relay* section.

Provisioning WAN Capacity

When you contract with a service provider for WAN services, you specify how much bandwidth you will need. Determining how much bandwidth you will need is the realm of network design. Many good books exist to help you with that task. (See the references section.) From a troubleshooting viewpoint, it's important to realize that WAN bandwidth is provisioned by the service provider at discrete intervals. Sometimes the designer incorrectly predicts how much bandwidth will be needed, causing packets to get dropped.

WAN bandwidth for copper cabling is provisioned in North America and many other parts of the world using the North American Digital Hierarchy, which is shown in Table 13.2. A channel in the hierarchy is called a *digital stream* (DS). Digital streams are multiplexed together to form high-speed WAN circuits. DS1 and DS3 are the most common capacities.

In Europe, the Committee of European Postal and Telephone (CEPT) defined a hierarchy called the E system, which is shown in Table 13.3.

The Synchronous Digital Hierarchy (SDH) is an international standard for data transmission over fiber optic cables. SDH defines a standard rate of transmission of 51.84 Mbps, which is also called *Synchronous Transport Signal level 1*, or *STS-1*. Higher rates of transmission are a multiple of the basic STS-1 rate. The STS rates are the same as the SONET Optical Carrier (OC) levels, which are shown in Table 13.4.

Table 13.2 The North American Digital Hierarchy

SIGNAL	CAPACITY	NUMBER OF DS0S	COLLOQUIAL NAME
DS0	64 kbps	1	Channel
DS1	1.544 Mbps	24	T1
DS1C	3.152 Mbps	48	T1C
DS2	6.312 Mbps	96	T2
DS3	44.736 Mbps	672	T3
DS4	274.176 Mbps	4032	T4

Table 13.3 The Committee of European Postal and Telephone (CEPT) Hierarchy

SIGNAL	CAPACITY	NUMBER OF E1S
E0	64 kbps	N/A
E1	2.048 Mbps	1
E2	8.448 Mbps	4
E3	34.368 Mbps	16
E4	139.264 Mbps	64

Table 13.4 The Synchronous Digital Hierarchy (SDH)

STS RATE	OC LEVEL	SPEED
STS-1	OC1	51.84 Mbps
STS-3	OC3	155.52 Mbps
STS-12	OC12	622.08 Mbps
STS-24	OC24	1.244 Gbps
STS-48	OC48	2.488 Gbps
STS-96	OC96	4.976 Gbps
STS-192	OC192	9.952 Gbps

WAN Technologies

This section introduces the various protocols and technologies used in WAN environments and provides some techniques for troubleshooting these technologies. Topics summarized here include leased lines, HDLC, PPP, Frame Relay, ISDN, and ATM. The technologies covered in this section are just a few of the many WAN options that service providers offer. The options we chose to cover are the ones that network engineers most commonly deploy to provide network services to remote offices and users. These fundamental technologies are a good starting point for broadening your horizons as a campus network engineer to include an understanding of WANs as well as LANs.

Leased Lines

A leased line is a single circuit that a customer rents from a telecommunications provider for a prearranged amount of time, usually months or years. The line is dedicated to the customer's traffic and connects two sites in the customer's network in a point-to-point topology. Typical speeds range from 64 kbps (DS0) to 45 Mbps (DS3). Enterprises use leased lines for both voice and data traffic. Data traffic is typically encapsulated in a standard protocol such as PPP or HDLC, which are covered later in this chapter.

An advantage of leased lines is that they are a mature and proven technology. Leased lines also have the advantage that the customer does not share the capacity with anyone. Most newer systems, such as Frame Relay, are shared. Historically, a disadvantage with leased lines was that they were expensive, especially in some parts of Asia and Europe. As providers upgrade their internal networks with more capacity, costs for the services that they offer to customers are dropping, however. Leased lines tend to be overlooked as a potential WAN solution because they are not a new technology. In some situations, however, they are the best option for simple point-to-point links.

High-Level Data Link Control (HDLC)

HDLC is an architecture for data link protocols for use in point-to-point and multipoint networks. It's important to realize that HDLC is more of an architecture than a protocol, and multivendor compatibility should not be expected. LAPB, Link Access Procedure on the D Channel (LAPD), and PPP are all subsets of HDLC that should interoperate between vendor implementations. On the other hand, Cisco, Codex, Motorola, and other vendors have HDLC-style framing methods that are not compatible with each other.

Cisco's HDLC framing is very simple, with no sequence numbers or acknowledgments. It provides a best-effort service and does not retransmit if a packet is dropped. Cisco's HDLC is the default encapsulation on Cisco serial interfaces, and hence is quite popular on Cisco networks. It doesn't offer many advantages over more standard encapsulations, such as PPP, but it does have some benefits. For example, it includes a function called *Serial Line Address Resolution Protocol* (SLARP), which provides dynamic IP address determination. SLARP also provides a keepalive function. Keepalives are used to monitor the status of a point-to-point link.

If a serial interface uses Cisco's HDLC, then no configuration is required. Cisco's SLARP can automatically configure a router based on a partner router's configuration. When using Cisco's AutoInstall service, a router using the default HDLC encapsulation automatically uses SLARP to learn the IP address of the router on the other end of the circuit. The router then assigns its own address based on the address of the router at the other end.

SLARP assumes that each serial line is a separate IP subnet, and that one end of the line is Host 1, while the other end is Host 2. SLARP allows Router A, for example, to request that Router B return its IP address and subnet mask. Router A then determines its own IP address based on the address of Router B. If the host portion of Router B's address is 1, Router A uses 2 for the host portion of its own IP address. Conversely, if Router B's host number is 2, then Router A uses host number 1. If Router B replies with any IP host number other than 1 or 2, Router A assumes that Router B is unable to provide it with an address via SLARP. If a router successfully obtains its IP address using SLARP, the router then tries to locate a Trivial File Transfer Protocol (TFTP) server to download the rest of its configuration.

CAUTION SLARP can be annoying when its automatic behavior is not desired. A router can take a long time to automatically select its IP address and then look for a TFTP server, which may not exist on many networks. To make matters worse, if SLARP succeeds in determining an IP address, the router automatically adds the `service config` line into the router's saved configuration file, which causes the router to look for a TFTP server every time it boots. If a router has determined its IP address using SLARP, you may need to manually configure the `no service config` command to stop the router from using SLARP and TFTP every time it boots.

Cisco's HDLC encapsulation starts with a 1-byte address field, which is set to 0x0F for unicast packets and 0x8F for broadcast packets. (Broadcast just means that the higher-layer protocol thought this was a broadcast packet. Cisco doesn't support multipoint HDLC.) The second byte is a control byte that is always set to 0x00. The next 2 bytes are a protocol type field that usually matches Ethernet EtherTypes, with some additions for packet types that don't appear on Ethernet networks. Packets with type 0x8035 carry SLARP data.

Troubleshooting Cisco's HDLC Implementation

As with any troubleshooting, you should start with the physical layer when troubleshooting circuits that use Cisco's HDLC. Check for faulty or disconnected cables, cables that are too long or too short, and other hardware problems. Serial interface cards on Cisco routers fail at times, as do other hardware components on routers and on CSU/DSUs. Also check for a timing problem. Verify that the correct device is generating the clock and that the appropriate clocking method is configured. Problems may also be related to congestion or overuse of the serial link. Use the `show interface serial` command to check the load and number of dropped packets.

A Cisco HDLC serial interface sends a keepalive frame every 10 seconds (by default) to verify that the connection is working. Unlike the Ethernet keepalive packet, which has essentially nothing in it (see Chapter 2), a Cisco HDLC SLARP keepalive packet has a sequence number that increases every time the router sends a keepalive. The sequence number starts with 0 and is independent of the sequence numbers used by the other side. In addition to including its own sequence number in a keepalive frame, a router includes the sequence number of the last keepalive received from the other router. This number is similar to a TCP ACK number and is called the *returned sequence number* or the *yourseen number*.

Each router keeps track of the last returned sequence number it received. Before sending a keepalive packet, the router compares the sequence number of the packet it is about to send with the returned sequence number in the last keepalive packet it received. If the two differ by three or more, the router considers the line to have failed and stops routing higher-level data until an acceptable keepalive is received.

On a router that is not heavily loaded, you can watch the keepalive process by using the debug serial interface command. By studying the output, you can often determine on which side of the serial link a problem is occurring. Some sample output from the command follows:

```
Boston#debug serial interface
Serial network interface debugging is on
Serial0: HDLC myseq 2, mineseen 2, yourseen 132, line up
Serial0: HDLC myseq 3, mineseen 3, yourseen 133, line up
Serial0: HDLC myseq 4, mineseen 4, yourseen 134, line up
Serial0: HDLC myseq 5, mineseen 5, yourseen 135, line up
Serial0: HDLC myseq 6, mineseen 6, yourseen 136, line up
Serial0: HDLC myseq 7, mineseen 7, yourseen 137, line up
Serial0: HDLC myseq 8, mineseen 8, yourseen 138, line up
Serial0: HDLC myseq 9, mineseen 9, yourseen 139, line up
Serial0: HDLC myseq 10, mineseen 10, yourseen 140, line up
Serial0: HDLC myseq 11, mineseen 11, yourseen 141, line up
Serial0: HDLC myseq 12, mineseen 12, yourseen 142, line up
```

In the output from the debug serial interface command, the Boston router reports that its own sequence number is proceeding normally. Notice that the *myseq* value increments with each frame. The *mineseen* value reports the acknowledgment number from the other side. In the first line, the Boston router reports that the other side has seen the Boston router's keepalive number 1 and is expecting keepalive number 2 next. In the *yourseen* field, the Boston router also reports its own acknowledgment numbers for the keepalives from the other router.

Point-to-Point Protocol (PPP)

PPP is a standard protocol for transporting various network-layer protocols across serial, point-to-point links. According to the RFC that defines PPP (RFC 1661), PPP is designed for simple links that transport packets between two peers. These links provide full-duplex, simultaneous bidirectional operation and are assumed to deliver packets in order. PPP is used with ISDN, analog lines, digital leased lines, and other WAN technologies.

WARNING: ACRONYM COLLISION

In Chapter 10, we referred to NCP as the NetWare Core Protocol. In this chapter, NCP refers to a set of protocols that form the glue between PPP and various network-layer protocols, including IP, IPX, AppleTalk, and DECnet. For DECnet gurus, however, NCP means the Network Control Program, which provides a user interface to the DEC network architecture. In an IBM Systems Network Architecture (SNA) environment, NCP refers to the Network Control Program, which controls the flow of data between a communications controller and other network resources. If you think about it, you may remember even more meanings for NCP in the networking industry!

In the output of the `show interface serial` command, Cisco calls a PPP NCP simply a *cp*. For example, the router might say that it has opened *ipcp*, *ipxcp*, and *atalkcp*, meaning that the IP, IPX, and AppleTalk PPP NCPs have been established. Try saying that three times quickly!

NOTE Per RFC 2516, "A Method for Transmitting PPP Over Ethernet (PPPoE)," PPP can also be used in an Ethernet environment. This RFC defines methods for multiple hosts on a shared Ethernet network to open PPP sessions to multiple destinations via one or more bridging modems, such as a cable modem.

PPP provides physical and data link layer services and also multiplexes and demultiplexes network-layer protocols. PPP has the following four layers:

1. The physical layer is based on various international standards for serial communication, including EIA/TIA-232-C (formerly RS-232-C), EIA/TIA-422 (formerly RS-422), V.24, and V.35.

2. The encapsulation of network-layer datagrams is based on HDLC.

3. The Link Control Protocol (LCP) is used for establishing, configuring, authenticating, and testing a data link connection.

4. Network Control Protocols (NCPs) are used for establishing and configuring various network-layer protocols such as IP, IPX, AppleTalk, and DECnet.

PPP supports two types of authentication: the Password Authentication Protocol (PAP) and the Challenge Handshake Authentication Protocol (CHAP). CHAP is more secure than PAP because PAP sends a user's password as clear text. An intruder could use a protocol analyzer to capture the password and later use the password to break into the network. CHAP provides protection against attacks by verifying a remote node with a variable challenge value that is unpredictable and used only once. Verification happens upon link establishment and can be repeated any time during a session.

Figure 13.3 shows a CHAP sequence of events when a user is authenticated. When a remote node connects to a PPP access server (or a router acting as a PPP access server), the server sends back a challenge message with a challenge value that is based on an unpredictable random number. The remote station feeds the challenge value and the remote node's password through an algorithm, resulting in a one-way hashed challenge response. The remote node sends the hashed challenge response to the server, along with a username that identifies the remote node. The server unhashes the challenge response and checks the response against a database of usernames and passwords and sends back an accept or deny message.

Troubleshooting PPP

After verifying the physical layer, the next step in troubleshooting PPP is to check the router or access server's configuration. One common mistake that Cisco administrators make is to configure the router's hostname as the PPP username. This is backward. The username should be the hostname of the router on the other end of the circuit. A useful command for watching PPP authentication as it happens is the `debug ppp chap` command. To use this command, you should shut down the serial interface, enable the command, and then enable the interface. As the interface initializes, you can analyze the PPP CHAP authentication and verify that the correct username is being transmitted across the link.

The debug ppp command displays information about PPP traffic and can be used with one of many options, including `packet`, `negotiation`, `error`, `authentication`, `chap`, `compression`, and `cbcp`. (`cbcp` refers to the Callback Control Protocol used by Microsoft clients.)

When troubleshooting a WAN serial interface problem on a Cisco router, you should use the `show interface serial` command, as discussed earlier in this chapter. Notice from the following output that when PPP is used, you can see information about whether LCP is open and which NCPs are open.

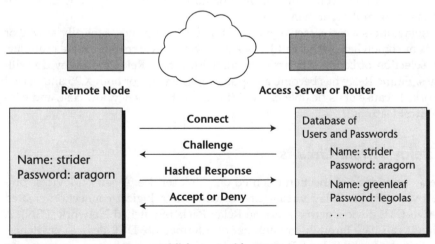

Figure 13.3 Connection establishment with CHAP.

```
charlotte#show interface s0
Serial0 is up, line protocol is up
  Hardware is MCI Serial
  Internet address is 192.168.40.2 255.255.255.0
  MTU 1500 bytes, BW 1544 Kbit, DLY 20000 usec, rely 255/255, load 1/255
  Encapsulation PPP, loopback not set, keepalive set (10 sec)
  LCP Open
  Open: ipcp, ipxcp, atalkcp, cdp
  Last input 0:00:04, output 0:00:00, output hang never
  Last clearing of "show interface" counters never
  Output queue 0/40, 0 drops; input queue 0/75, 0 drops
  5 minute input rate 0 bits/sec, 1 packets/sec
  5 minute output rate 0 bits/sec, 1 packets/sec
     978 packets input, 20781 bytes, 0 no buffer
     Received 8 broadcasts, 0 runts, 0 giants
     155 input errors, 0 CRC, 0 frame, 0 overrun, 0 ignored, 155 abort
     1017 packets output, 25277 bytes, 0 underruns
     0 output errors, 0 collisions, 178 interface resets, 0 restarts
     0 output buffer failures, 0 output buffers swapped out
     339 carrier transitions
```

Frame Relay

Frame Relay is a high-speed WAN protocol and service that is standardized by the ITU-T and the American National Standards Institute (ANSI). Frame Relay emerged in the early 1990s as an enhancement to more complex WAN technologies, such as X.25. Whereas X.25 is optimized for superior reliability on physical circuits with a high error rate, Frame Relay was developed with the assumption that circuits are no longer as error prone as they once were. This assumption allows Frame Relay to be more efficient and easier to implement than X.25.

Frame Relay offers a cost-effective method for connecting sites, typically at DS0 or DS1 speeds or somewhere in the middle. Many service providers offer more granularity in the selection of bandwidth assignments with Frame Relay than they do with leased lines. Frame Relay has become a popular replacement for both X.25 and leased line networks because of its flexible bandwidth support, efficiency, low cost, and congestion control features.

Frame Relay Virtual Circuits

Frame Relay provides a connection-oriented data link service. A pair of devices communicate over a Frame Relay virtual circuit, which is a logical connection created between two DTE devices across a Frame Relay Packet-Switched Network (PSN). A virtual circuit can pass through any number of intermediate DCE devices (switches) located within the Frame Relay PSN.

Frame Relay virtual circuits fall into two categories: Switched Virtual Circuits (SVCs) and Permanent Virtual Circuits (PVCs). SVCs are temporary connections for supporting occasional data transfer. PVCs are permanently configured circuits that are established in advance of any data transfer. An SVC requires call setup and termination whenever there is data to send. With PVCs, the call setup happens just once, which means that troubleshooting is simplified. Most networks use PVCs rather than SVCs.

A Frame Relay virtual circuit is identified by a 10-bit Data Link Connection Identifier (DLCI). DLCIs are assigned by a Frame Relay service provider (for example, a telephone company). Frame Relay DLCIs have local significance. Two DTE devices connected by a virtual circuit may use a different DLCI value to refer to the same circuit. Although you can think of the DLCI as an identifier for the entire virtual circuit, practically speaking, the DLCI refers to the connection from a DTE router to the DCE Frame Relay switch at the provider's site. The DLCI may be different for the DTE-DCE connection at each end of the virtual circuit.

Frame Relay Congestion Control

A Frame Relay network is a shared network. Although the link from your DTE router to the DCE switch at the provider's site is dedicated to your traffic, your traffic passes through the provider's network, which is shared by many customers of the provider. To make the sharing of bandwidth more fair, congestion control and feedback mechanisms are built into the Frame Relay protocol. A customer device can set a *Discard Eligibility* (DE) bit to identify less important traffic that the provider can drop when congestion occurs. In addition, Frame Relay includes congestion notification schemes that the provider can use to inform the customer of potential problems. The *Forward-Explicit Congestion Notification* (FECN) bit informs the receiver of a frame that the frame traversed a path that is experiencing congestion. The *Backward-Explicit Congestion Notification* (BECN) bit informs a sender that congestion exists in the path that the sender is using.

CONNECTION-ORIENTED PROTOCOLS MAY NOT BE RELIABLE

In the LAN world, the term *connection-oriented* is often used synonymously with the term *reliable* when referring to protocols. When we say that TCP is a connection-oriented protocol, the assumption is that TCP is also a reliable protocol. LAN engineers don't tend to differentiate the two terms.

A Frame Relay or ATM circuit is established in advance of its use through the use of a signaling protocol. The reliability, or lack thereof, associated with data being passed through the circuit is dependent on the characteristics of the upper-layer protocol being used by the communicators. Reliability is not a feature or function associated with the WAN circuit itself. A Frame Relay or ATM circuit is connection oriented, but it is not reliable. There are no sequence numbers, acknowledgments, or retransmissions associated with the WAN data link layer.

Service providers are able to keep prices for their Frame Relay service reasonably low because of the bursty nature of their customers' traffic. The service provider generally oversubscribes its internal network, making the assumption that customers won't use all of their available bandwidth all of the time. Switches within the service provider's network can use the FECN and BECN mechanisms to notify customer devices of any congestion problems. The resulting behavior at the customer devices depends on which protocols and equipment are in use.

NOTE Many protocols don't have any method for dealing with the FECN and BECN congestion notification schemes. Congestion control with TCP-based applications, for example, is usually independent of the FECN and BECN mechanisms. Upon packet loss, TCP decreases its transmit window size, effectively slowing its transmission rate. It then gradually increases the window size until congestion occurs again.

Most Frame Relay providers offer some guarantee of bandwidth availability. The guarantee is expressed as the *Committed Information Rate* (CIR). The CIR guarantee specifies that if the data transfer rate to the Frame Relay network is below or equal to the CIR, then the network will forward data for that virtual circuit. If the data rate exceeds the CIR, there is no longer any guarantee. The network might discard traffic beyond the CIR limit, although if there is sufficient bandwidth, it might continue to forward traffic. CIR is measured over a time interval T.

In addition to specifying a CIR, many Frame Relay providers also let a customer specify a *Committed Burst Size* (Bc) that specifies a maximum amount of data that the provider will transmit over the time interval T even after the CIR has been exceeded. The provider's Frame Relay switch is allowed to set the DE bit for frames at the Bc level.

Beyond the Bc, the provider can also offer an *Excess Burst Size* (Be) that specifies the maximum amount in excess of Bc that the network will attempt to transfer under normal circumstances during the time interval T. The switch sets the DE bit on these frames and also has the right to discard the frames immediately if the switch or network is congested.

To keep things simple, some service providers base their Frame Relay offerings on a physical access speed. These providers often offer a zero CIR, which means that they make only a best effort to send traffic. The advantage of a zero CIR is that it is inexpensive. The obvious disadvantage is that there is no guarantee. In actuality, there aren't any solid guarantees anyway. Even when a provider lets you specify a CIR, Bc, and Be, these parameters are based on probability. Although providers may market the CIR as a true guarantee, in fact, providers oversubscribe their networks, and cannot guarantee that their customers will correctly react to the FECN and BECN congestion feedback mechanisms, which means that no customer's CIR or Bc is truly a guarantee.

Frame Relay Inverse ARP

Inverse ARP for Frame Relay, defined in RFC 2390, allows a router to discover the network-layer address of the router on the other end of a virtual circuit and map that address to a DLCI. Inverse ARP is a method for building dynamic address mappings in networks running AppleTalk, Banyan Virtual Integrated Network Service (VINES), DECnet, IP, IPX, and XNS. Inverse ARP creates dynamic mappings, as contrasted with the frame-relay map command, which defines static mappings. With recent versions of the Cisco IOS software, Inverse ARP is enabled by default, but can be disabled explicitly for a given protocol and DLCI with the `no frame relay inverse-arp` command.

CAUTION When you configure a `frame-relay map` statement, Inverse ARP is disabled for the protocol and DLCI specified in the statement. This means that you can't use a combination of dynamic (Inverse ARP) and static mappings when configuring a router to reach multiple destinations via a particular protocol and DLCI. Use one or the other, but don't try to use both.

Frame Relay Local Management Interface

Local Management Interface (LMI) is a set of enhancements to the basic Frame Relay specification for managing Frame Relay networks. LMI provides synchronization between Frame Relay DTE and DCE devices and periodically checks on the status of a circuit with keepalive messages. LMI status messages prevent a router from sending data on a circuit that is failing or no longer exists. LMI messages are carried in a Frame Relay frame with a DLCI of 1023.

The original LMI was developed in 1990 by Cisco, StrataCom, Northern Telecom, and Digital Equipment Corporation (DEC). Later, both ANSI and ITU-T developed varieties of the LMI protocol. The fact that there are three versions of LMI is a troubleshooting issue. The LMI configured on the DCE Frame Relay switch must match the LMI configured on the DTE router. A Cisco router autosenses which LMI is in use (for Cisco IOS 11.2 and later versions). Use the `frame-relay lmi-type {cisco | ansi | q933a}` command to change the LMI type, if necessary.

NOTE The LMI type must match between a router and the local Frame Relay switch in the provider's network. Don't confuse this with the Frame Relay encapsulation type, which must match between the two DTE routers on either end of a virtual circuit. There are two options for the `encapsulation frame-relay` command, `cisco` and `ietf`. Cisco is the default.

Troubleshooting Frame Relay

Although Frame Relay is a data link layer protocol, when Frame Relay problems occur, you should check the physical layer first. For example, check to see if cables and CSU/DSUs are connected and working properly. Next, check the LMI type and encapsulation type. Also, make sure you are using the DLCI that the provider assigned to you. Don't confuse the DLCI for the local site with the one used for the remote site. When in doubt, ask the provider to verify the DLCI numbers. Then ask again. Providers are notorious for providing the wrong number.

To ensure that LMI updates are being sent and received, you can use the show frame-relay lmi command. The show interface serial command is also helpful. Notice in the following output that the show interface serial command displays different information at the top of the output when you are using Frame Relay versus HDLC or PPP. With this command you can make sure you are using the correct encapsulation and LMI type, and list the number of LMI packets of different types that have been sent and received. On a healthy network the value for LMI enq sent and LMI stat recvd should be approximately equal.

```
charlotte#show interface s0
Serial0 is up, line protocol is up
  Hardware is MCI Serial
  Internet address is 192.168.40.2 255.255.255.0
  MTU 1500 bytes, BW 1544 Kbit, DLY 20000 usec, rely 255/255, load 1/255
  Encapsulation FRAME-RELAY, loopback not set, keepalive set (10 sec)
  LMI enq sent  48, LMI stat recvd 47, LMI upd recvd 0, DTE LMI up
  LMI enq recvd 0, LMI stat sent  0, LMI upd sent  0
  LMI DLCI 1023  LMI type is CISCO  frame relay DTE
  Broadcast queue 0/64, broadcasts sent/dropped 0/0, interface
broadcasts 64
  Last input 0:00:00, output 0:00:00, output hang never
  Last clearing of "show interface" counters never
  Output queue 0/40, 0 drops; input queue 0/75, 0 drops
  5 minute input rate 0 bits/sec, 0 packets/sec
  5 minute output rate 0 bits/sec, 0 packets/sec
    135 packets input, 5122 bytes, 0 no buffer
    Received 2 broadcasts, 0 runts, 0 giants
    4 input errors, 0 CRC, 0 frame, 0 overrun, 0 ignored, 4 abort
    144 packets output, 6497 bytes, 0 underruns
    0 output errors, 0 collisions, 5 interface resets, 0 restarts
    0 output buffer failures, 0 output buffers swapped out
    7 carrier transitions
```

When analyzing LMI problems, another helpful command is debug frame-relay lmi. With this command you can verify that LMI packets are being transmitted and received. Notice in the following output from a healthy network that the myseq and yourseen values are incrementing correctly.

```
charlotte#debug frame-relay lmi
frame-relay LMI debugging is on
Displaying all frame-relay LMI data
charlotte#
Serial0(out): StEnq, myseq 219, yourseen 218, DTE up
datagramstart = 0x403F544, datagramsize = 13
FR encap = 0xFCF10309
00 75 01 01 01 03 02 DB DA
Serial0(in): Status, myseq 219
RT IE 1, length 1, type 1
KA IE 3, length 2, yourseq 219, myseq 219
```

```
Serial0(out): StEnq, myseq 220, yourseen 219, DTE up
datagramstart = 0x403F544, datagramsize = 13
FR encap = 0xFCF10309
00 75 01 01 00 03 02 DC DB
Serial0(in): Status, myseq 220
RT IE 1, length 1, type 0
KA IE 3, length 2, yourseq 220, myseq 220
PVC IE 0x7 , length 0x6 , dlci 101, status 0x2 , bw 0
PVC IE 0x7 , length 0x6 , dlci 201, status 0x2 , bw 0
Serial0(out): StEnq, myseq 221, yourseen 220, DTE up
datagramstart = 0x403F544, datagramsize = 13
FR encap = 0xFCF10309
00 75 01 01 01 03 02 DD DC
```

Another helpful command is the `show frame-relay pvc` command, which provides the status of each DLCI. Use the output from this command to verify that the DLCI usage is Local and that the PVC status is Active. Other common PVC status values are Deleted and Inactive. Deleted means that the PVC has not been configured on the provider's Frame Relay switch or that the configuration has been deleted. Inactive means that the Frame Relay switch configuration is correct on your end, but not on the remote end. An example from a healthy network follows:

```
charlotte#show frame-relay pvc
PVC Statistics for interface Serial0 (frame-relay DTE)
DLCI = 110, DLCI USAGE = LOCAL, PVC STATUS = ACTIVE,
INTERFACE = Serial0
input pkts 3779      output pkts 3771   in bytes 335733
out bytes 335117     dropped pkts 0     in FECN pkts 0
in BECN pkts 0       out FECN pkts 0    out BECN pkts 0
in DE pkts 0         out DE pkts 0
out bcast pkts 3751  out bcast bytes 333177
pvc create time 1d21h, last time pvc status changed 1d21h
```

When troubleshooting a problem reaching a Layer 3 destination address via a Frame Relay PVC, you should examine the output from the `show frame-relay map` command. The output from this command will help you notice any problems with the dynamic (Inverse ARP) or static mapping of network-layer addresses to DLCIs. In the following output from a hub-and-spoke Frame Relay network, the Charlotte router is a hub router using Inverse ARP, whereas the Boston and Albany routers are spoke routers using static map commands.

```
charlotte#show frame-relay map
Serial0 (up): ip 10.6.1.1 dlci 101(0x65,0x1850), dynamic,
              broadcast, status defined, active
Serial0 (up): ip 10.6.1.4 dlci 201(0xC9,0x3090), dynamic,
              broadcast, status defined, active
boston#show frame-relay map
Serial0 (up): ip 10.6.1.3 dlci 110(0x6E,0x18E0), static,
              broadcast, CISCO, status defined, active
```

```
Serial0 (up): ip 10.6.1.4 dlci 110(0x6E,0x18E0), static,
               broadcast, CISCO, status defined, active
albany#show frame-relay map
Serial0 (up): ip 10.6.1.3 dlci 102(0x66,0x1860), static,
               broadcast, CISCO, status defined, active
Serial0 (up): ip 10.6.1.1 dlci 102(0x66,0x1860), static,
               broadcast,CISCO, status defined, active
```

Of course, when troubleshooting a problem reaching an IP destination address via a Frame Relay PVC, you can use the ping and debug ip packet commands. Notice in the following output from the debug ip packet command that the router reports that the encapsulation failed. The router was unable to map the IP address to a DLCI due to a failure to configure Inverse ARP or static mapping correctly.

```
albany#ping 10.6.1.1
Type escape sequence to abort.
Sending 5, 100-byte ICMP Echos to 10.6.1.1,
timeout is 2 seconds:
IP: s=10.6.1.4 (local), d=10.6.1.1 (Serial0),
     len 100, sending
IP: s=10.6.1.4 (local), d=10.6.1.1 (Serial0),
     len 100, encapsulation failed.
```

Frame Relay Debug Commands

Cisco supports the following Frame Relay debug commands for looking at packets and events:

debug frame-relay verbose. This command is misnamed, as it actually displays cryptic, nonverbose, and not very useful messages about packets received on a Frame Relay interface. We mention it solely because Cisco expects you to know about it to pass certification exams.

debug frame-relay events. This command displays information about Frame Relay Inverse ARP replies that the router receives. It's somewhat useful, especially if you read RFC 2390 so that you can decode the bytes shown.

debug frame-relay lmi. This command displays information about LMI packets of different types exchanged between the router and the Frame Relay service provider. The previous section shows an example.

debug frame-relay packet. According to Cisco documentation, this command displays information about packets sent out a Frame Relay interface. However, real-world testing indicates that the command displays information about packets sent and received. This command results in the most useful output, but it is also the most dangerous of the commands because it displays a lot of data on a busy network. (Displaying data on the router console consumes CPU resources, so be careful with this command.)

NOTE To learn more about Frame Relay troubleshooting, see the excellent paper on Frame Relay by David Wolsefer at the CertificationZone Web site here: www.certificationzone.com.

Integrated Services Digital Network

ISDN is a service and protocol for transmitting voice, video, and data across a telephone provider's digital network. In many parts of the world, ISDN is a cost-effective alternative to the low-speed, analog dial-up links that were once so popular for remote access. ISDN provides a faster data rate and connection establishment time than analog modem lines, with no dialing required. ISDN is also a good choice as a backup link for another type of circuit, such as a Frame Relay circuit.

ISDN typically relies on PPP for end-user data encapsulation, although it can also use HDLC, LAPB, or other protocols. ISDN also has a set of control and management layers for handling connection establishment and signaling. ISDN has three layers (Layer 1, Layer 2, and Layer 3), which are described in the following sections.

An ISDN circuit consists of 64-kbps *B channels* that carry end-user transmissions, and a signaling channel that carries control information, such as call setup and teardown signals. The signaling channel is called the *D channel*. An ISDN BRI provides two B channels and one 16-kbps D channel. An ISDN PRI is 23 B channels and one 64-kbps D channel in the United States, and 30 B channels and one 64-kbps D channel in Europe and other parts of the world.

An ISDN network consists of terminals, Terminal Adapters (TAs), Network-Termination Devices (NTs), line-termination equipment, and exchange-termination equipment. There are two types of ISDN terminals. An ISDN-compliant terminal is called *Terminal Equipment Type 1* (TE1). A non-ISDN terminal that predates the ISDN standards is called *Terminal Equipment Type 2* (TE2).

There are also two types of NT devices. *NT1* devices implement ISDN physical-layer functions and connect user devices to the ISDN facility. Routers usually provide NT1 functionality. *NT2* devices perform concentration services and advanced ISDN functions. NT2 functions are implemented within controllers or Private Branch Exchanges (PBXs).

In the United States and Canada, ISDN enters a building or home office on a two-wire circuit at the *U reference point*, as shown in Figure 13.4. (A reference point is simply a logical interface between components in a typical ISDN architecture.) An NT1 converts the two-wire circuit into a four-wire circuit required by ISDN devices, such as ISDN phones, TAs, and routers. Many routers have a built-in NT1 interface, which is sometimes called a *U option*. In Asia and Europe, the NT1 interface is considered part of the digital network and belongs to the telecommunications provider. Thus in Europe or Asia you would typically order a router with an S/T option and no built-in NT1.

Figure 13.4 shows the following ISDN reference points:

- The R reference point defines the interface between a TE2 device and a TA.

- The S reference point defines the interface between a TE1 device or TA and an NT2.

- The T reference point defines the interface between an NT2 and an NT1. In configurations with no NT2, an S/T interface connects an NT1 to a TE1 or TA.

- The U reference point defines the interface between an NT1 and the ISDN service.

The U interface for BRI is implemented on a router or other ISDN device with an RJ-45 modular connector. Bits are transmitted across the middle (4 and 5) pins. The connected cable must be a straight-through cable.

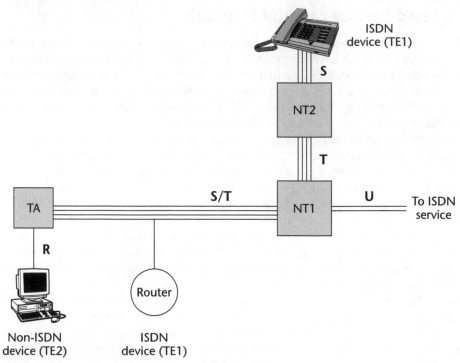

Figure 13.4   ISDN components and reference points.

NOTE To check whether a cable is straight-through, hold the cable ends side by side and verify that the colored wires are in the same order.

The S/T interface is a four-wire bus interface that typically uses the existing wiring plan in a building. Like the U interface, the S/T interface also uses an RJ-45 connector. Pins 3, 4, 5, and 6 provide transmit and receive functions and are the key pins to examine when troubleshooting an S/T problem. S/T interfaces are either point-to-point or point-to-multipoint, and may use subaddressing for the individual user devices on a shared bus. Layer 1 S/T framing provides contention resolution when several terminals contend for access on the bus.

ISDN Layer 1

ISDN Layer 1 is defined by the ITU-T in the I.430 standard. ISDN Layer 1 provides basic framing, link activation, and synchronization services. With ISDN BRI, Layer 1 framing adds 16 kbps of overhead when the U interface is used. Layer 1 framing adds

48 kbps of overhead when the S/T interface is used. (Although most documents specify the data rate for BRI as 144 kbps, you may also see the rate specified as 160 kbps or 192 kbps. These rates include two 64-kbps B channels, one 16-kbps D channel, and either 16 kbps or 48 kbps of overhead.) Data encoding schemes are defined to permit this relatively high data rate over the ordinary two-wire circuit that connects a telephone company's central office with a customer's office. Echo cancellation is used to reduce noise on the circuit.

The show controller bri command is useful for verifying that Layer 1 has been activated properly on a Cisco router. Notice in the following output that Layer 1 has been activated:

```
Boston#show controller bri
BRI unit 0
D Chan Info:
Layer 1 is ACTIVATED
idb 0x9F6E8, ds 0xA56F8, reset_mask 0x8
buffer size 1524
RX ring with 2 entries at 0x2101600 : Rxhead 0
00 pak=0x0AB0A4 ds=0x40CE70 status=D000 pak_size=0
(...)
```

ISDN Layer 2

ISDN Layer 2 uses LAPD to allow an end device to communicate with a provider's ISDN switch across the ISDN D channel. The LAPD protocol is formally specified in ITU-T Q.921, which is based on the standard HDLC architecture and resembles the LAPB used on X.25 networks and the Logical Link Control Type 2 (LLC2) used on LANs. Like these protocols, Q.921 uses supervisory, information, and unnumbered frames. Q.921 also has advanced features for handling tasks such as assigning identifiers to devices sharing an S/T bus. Figure 13.5 shows the Layer 2 ISDN frame format.

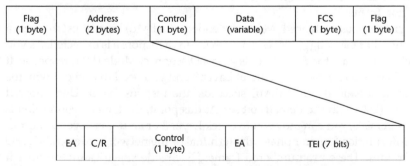

Figure 13.5 The ISDN Layer 2 Q.921 (LAPD) frame format.

In a Q.921 (LAPD) frame, the value of the Flag fields is always 0x7E. The Q.921 Address field can be either 1 or 2 bytes. If the Extended Address (EA) bit of the first byte is set, the address is 1 byte; if it is not set, the address is 2 bytes. The Command/Response (C/R) bit is used to distinguish commands from replies. The user side sends commands with the C/R bit set to 0 and responds with the C/R bit set to 1. The network does the opposite; it sends commands with the C/R bit set to 1 and responds with the C/R bit set to 0. The Address field also contains a Terminal End-Point Identifier (TEI) and a Service Access Point Identifier (SAPI). The SAPI defines the message type. Key SAPIs to look for while troubleshooting include the following:

- *SAPI 63*. Used for Layer 2 management processes, including TEI assignment
- *SAPI 64*. Used for call control
- *SAPI 0*. Used for Layer 3 signaling

A useful command for troubleshooting ISDN Layer 2 is the `debug isdn q921` command. The following output illustrates what you might see when using this command. (The exact messages depend on the ISDN switch type.)

```
Boston#debug isdn q921
2656.612 TX ->   IDREQ  ri = 14613   ai = 127
2656.648 RX <-   IDASSN ri = 14613   ai = 64
2656.652 TX ->   SABMEp  sapi = 0   tei = 64
2656.676 RX <-   UAf  sapi = 0   tei = 64
2658.360 RX <-   INFOc  sapi = 0   tei = 64   ns = 0   nr = 0
2658.368 TX ->   RRr  sapi = 0   tei = 64   nr = 1
2658.372 TX ->   INFOc  sapi = 0   tei = 64   ns = 0   nr = 1
```

Notice that Q.921 messages are similar to LLC2 messages (which Chapter 3 discussed in detail). The two Q.921 messages that may not be familiar, if you are used to LLC2, are the IDREQ and IDASSN messages. IDREQ is sent by the terminal to request an *assignment ID* (ai). The IDASSN message is the reply from the switch. The meaning of AI = 127 in the output is that the terminal is asking for any TEI. The AI = 64 in the next line of output means the switch assigned TEI 64. Each command/reply pair during this phase has a *reference indicator* (ri). These messages are sent in Q.921 unnumbered information frames.

The Set Asynchronous Balanced Mode Extended (SABME) frame establishes a connection. Notice that the Poll (p) bit is set, which means a response is expected. As you troubleshoot, check whether the SABME fails with a Disconnect Mode (DM) response. If this is the case, there is no further call setup at Layer 3 and you need to find out why the SABME was unsuccessful. If the SABME succeeds, the response is an Unnumbered Acknowledgment (UA) with the Final (f) bit set. At this point, the Layer 2 connection is up. If a problem persists, you can move on to check Layer 3 or an upper-layer protocol.

During the information transfer phase, the terminal or the network side sends INFO command (c) frames. These are numbered frames. Each side specifies the number it expects to receive next (NR) and the number it is now sending (NS). Either side can also specify that its receiver is ready (RR). The RR is used to verify the status of the data link when there are no INFO frames to transmit. Either side can end the session by issuing a Disconnect (DISC) message. When troubleshooting, if you see an unexpected DISC, you should analyze the frames that came before to determine what went wrong.

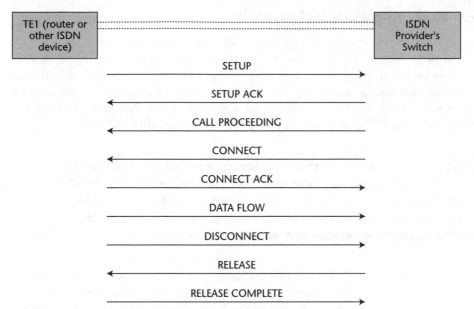

Figure 13.6 ISDN Layer 3 messages during a typical ISDN call.

ISDN Layer 3

ISDN Layer 3 is defined by the ITU-T Q.931 specification. Like Q.921, Q.931 also runs on the D channel. Q.931 includes call establishment, call termination, information, and miscellaneous messages. Figure 13.6 illustrates a sample sequence of Layer 3 messages involved during the establishment, data transfer, and release phases of an ISDN call.

A useful command when troubleshooting ISDN Layer 3 is the debug isdn q931 command. In the following output from the command, notice the SETUP, CALL PRO-CEEDING, and CONNECT messages. Also, notice that the output shows Layer 2 (Q.921) information as well as Layer 3 information. The Q.931 messages are carried in Q.921 INFO command messages (INFOc).

```
Boston#debug isdn q931
248236 TX ->  INFOc  sapi = 0  tei = 80  ns = 6  nr = 6
    SETUP pd = 8  callref = 0x02
        Bearer Capability i = 0x8890
        Channel ID i = 0x83
        Called Party Number i = 0x80, '372756'
248392 RX <-  INFOc  sapi = 0  tei = 80  ns = 6  nr = 7
    CALL_PROC pd = 8  callref = 0x82
        Channel ID i = 0x89
249460 RX <-  INFOc  sapi = 0  tei = 80  ns = 7  nr = 7
    CONNECT pd = 8  callref = 0x82
```

Troubleshooting ISDN BRI Problems

Configuring ISDN on Cisco routers is tricky and nonintuitive. When the router fails to make an ISDN call or the call doesn't go through, check your router configuration statements and then check them again. Verify the Dial-On-Demand Routing (DDR) statements, such as `dialer group`, `dialer interface`, `dialer map`, and `dialer string` statements. Also, verify with your service provider that you are using the correct phone number, switch type, and Service Profile Identifier (SPID).

> **NOTE** A SPID is a number that some service providers use to define the services to which an ISDN device subscribes. An ISDN device uses the SPID when accessing the provider's ISDN switch. Not all providers require SPIDs, and the format varies from provider to provider. Be sure to find out the specific requirements of your ISDN provider.

When troubleshooting an ISDN BRI problem, you should verify that each of the three ISDN layers is working correctly. The `show isdn status` command displays a useful summary of the status of each of the layers. It also shows the ISDN switch type, as illustrated in the following output. (On a Cisco router, you must configure the router with the type of switch to which the router will connect. This is a common area for mistakes.)

```
Boston#show isdn status
The current ISDN Switchtype = basic-net3
ISDN BRI0 interface
    Layer 1 Status:
            DEACTIVATED
    Layer 2 Status:
            Layer 2 NOT Activated
    Layer 3 Status:
            No Active Layer 3 Call(s)
```

If any layers aren't active, consider the functions of each layer and troubleshoot accordingly. For example, if Layer 1 is not active, troubleshoot cabling and physical-layer components and analyze basic framing and activation functions. In the case of an S/T bus, make sure that the bus is terminated correctly. If Layer 2 isn't working, use router commands that help you analyze Q.921 behavior. If Layer 3 isn't working, use router commands that help you analyze Q.931 behavior. The following list summarizes the most useful commands for isolating an ISDN problem:

`clear interface bri number.`   Resets the hardware logic on a BRI interface. The number parameter is the interface number (or slot/port number). Use this command to reset the statistics counters to zero so you can restart any counters you are checking.

`show interface bri number.`   Displays information about the BRI D channel for the interface selected by the number parameter.

show interface bri number 1 2. For the interface selected by the number parameter, displays information about both BRI B channels. You can also display information about only one B channel by typing just 1 or 2.

show controllers bri. Displays information about the BRI controller, including activation status for Layer 1.

show isdn status. Displays information about which ISDN switch is used and the status of Layers 1, 2, and 3.

show dialer interface bri number. Displays information about the DDR dial string, call status, and timer settings.

debug bri. Displays information about whether the ISDN software on the router is enabling and disabling the B channels when you attempt an outgoing call. This command may output extensive Layer 1 information, so use it with care.

debug isdn q921. Displays Layer 2 processes that are taking place at the router on the D channel.

debug isdn q931. Displays Layer 3 information about call setup and teardown of ISDN network connections between the local router and the ISDN network.

When using DDR, the show interface bri command may show that the line protocol is spoofing. Spoofing does not necessarily mean that the D channel is up; it tricks DDR into thinking that the interface is up/up, so that routing entries are maintained. This enables DDR to wake up and trigger a call to the ISDN network when user traffic requires the connection. The following example shows an interface that is spoofing.

```
Boston#show interface bri 0
BRI0 is up, line protocol is up (spoofing)
Hardware is BRI
Internet address is 172.16.2.1, subnet mask is 255.255.255.0
MTU 1500 bytes, BW 56179 Kbit, DLY 20000 usec, rely 255/255,  load 1/255
Encapsulation PPP, loopback not set
Last input never, output 0:00:09, output hang never
Last clearing of "show interface" counters never
Output queue 0/40, 0 drops; input queue 0/75, 0 drops
Five minute input rate 0 bits/sec, 0 packets/sec
Five minute output rate 0 bits/sec, 0 packets/sec
1948 packets input, 11442 bytes, 0 no buffer
 Received 392 broadcasts, 0 runts, 0 giants
 0 input errors, 0 CRC, 0 frame, 0 overrun, 0 ignored, 0 abort
1961 packets output, 12249 bytes, 0 underruns
0 output errors, 0 collisions, 33 interface resets, 0 restarts
24 carrier transitions
```

Asynchronous Transfer Mode (ATM)

ATM is an ITU-T standard for sending voice, video, and data in fixed-size 53-byte cells. ATM offers a high-speed, connection-oriented service that combines the benefits of circuit switching (guaranteed bandwidth and nonvariable transmission delay) with those of packet switching (flexibility and efficiency for intermittent traffic).

In the last few years, ATM has become increasingly popular in both public and private networks. Many service providers use ATM within their internal networks to take advantage of ATM's high bandwidth, low latency, and Quality of Service (QoS) features. ATM is also gaining popularity within corporate networks as both a WAN and campus LAN technology. It can be used to connect users who have very high bandwidth requirements and who use applications with advanced QoS requirements. ATM can run at T3 or higher speeds when used on copper cabling. ATM supports speeds up to OC-192 (9.952 Gbps) and beyond when used on fiber optic cabling.

One of the benefits of ATM is that applications can share bandwidth more fairly in a cell-based system compared to a frame-based system. In a frame-based system, large frames can monopolize bandwidth. Consider the case where short digitized-voice frames are waiting to be output by a serial interface on a router while the interface is busy sending a train of 1518-byte File Transfer Protocol (FTP) TCP/IP frames. The FTP user doesn't expect low delay, but voice requires it. Voice packets that are delayed result in the listener hearing distortion. Delay also causes the listener to hear silence when actually another person in the voice conversation has already started talking. This results in false starts and interruptions. Video is also sensitive to delay and appears choppy and distorted if it doesn't receive a network service that guarantees low and nonvariable delay. Because ATM divides data for all applications into 53-byte cells, serialization and queuing delay at a router or switch interface can be avoided. Small voice packets can be interleaved with chopped-up data packets.

With a connection-oriented technology such as ATM, an application can specify upon connection establishment the QoS it requires, including transmission rates, delay requirements, and the maximum acceptable level of cell loss caused by errors or congestion. In addition, an ATM application may be able to use extra bandwidth that is not used by other applications that send in a bursty fashion. Compared to older WAN technologies, ATM bandwidth usage is more efficient and flexible. Some older, non-ATM WAN technologies use synchronous Time-Division Multiplexing (TDM), which assigns a timeslot to each application. An application can only transmit when its timeslot comes up, even if all other timeslots are empty. If an application has nothing to send during its timeslot, bandwidth during that timeslot is wasted. ATM, on the other hand, is asynchronous, which means that bandwidth can be allocated on demand. High-bandwidth applications, such as digital video applications, can theoretically make use of bandwidth that less demanding applications, such as Telnet, are not currently using.

ATM Virtual Circuits and Adaptation Layers

ATM provides a connection-oriented service on a virtual circuit. Each ATM node is required to establish a separate connection to every other node in the ATM network with which it needs to communicate. Connections support bidirectional traffic and are established by means of an ATM signaling mechanism. ATM supports both PVCs and SVCs. All traffic to or from an ATM network is prefaced with a Virtual Path Identifier (VPI) and Virtual Channel Identifier (VCI). A VPI/VCI pair identifies a single virtual circuit.

Applications can encapsulate data as needed for traversal across an ATM virtual circuit. The ATM network disregards the contents of the data. The only requirement is that data be sent in a manner that follows a specific ATM Adaptation Layer (AAL) format. An AAL defines the conversion of user information into cells. An AAL segments upper-layer information into cells at the transmitter and reassembles the cells at the receiver. Five AALs are defined, although typical networks use only AAL1 and AAL5.

AAL1 and AAL2 handle traffic that requires timing synchronization between the source and destination, such as voice and video. AAL1 and AAL2 are relevant to Cisco routers only when the router is equipped with either a Circuit Emulation Service (CES) ATM interface card, or when it has voice-over-AAL2 capabilities. AAL3/4 was designed for network service providers and is closely aligned with the Switched Multimegabit Data Service (SMDS). AAL3/4 is used to transmit SMDS packets over an ATM network.

AAL5 supports typical data communications, such as classical IP over ATM and LAN Emulation (LANE). To configure a router to use AAL5, use the `encapsulation aal5` command. By default, the router sends upper-layer data encapsulated in an LLC and Subnetwork Access Protocol (SNAP) header, which is then segmented into 53-byte ATM cells. Numerous other options besides SNAP are available, however. On a router with an ATM interface, type a question mark after the `encapsulation aal5` command to determine the options for AAL5 encapsulation.

AAL5 is the simplest and most efficient of the AALs. The Segmentation and Reassembly (SAR) sublayer simply accepts packets, carves them into 53-byte cells, and sends the cells to the destination router or host for reassembly. In AAL5 format, 48 bytes of each cell are used for upper-layer data; the remaining 5 bytes are used for cell routing. The 5-byte cell header contains the following fields:

Virtual Path Identifier (VPI). In conjunction with the VCI, identifies the next destination of a cell as it passes through a series of ATM switches on the way to its destination.

Virtual Channel Identifier (VCI). In conjunction with the VPI, identifies the next destination of a cell as it passes through a series of ATM switches on the way to its destination.

Payload Type (PT). Indicates in the first bit whether the cell contains user data or control data. If the cell contains user data, the second bit indicates congestion, and the third bit indicates whether the cell is the last in a series of cells that represent a single AAL5 frame.

Congestion Loss Priority (CLP). Indicates whether the cell should be discarded if it encounters extreme congestion as it moves through the network. If the CLP bit equals 1, the cell should be discarded in preference to cells with the CLP bit equal to 0.

Header Error Control (HEC). Provides a checksum for the cell header.

Mapping a Protocol Address to an ATM PVC

An ATM interface supports static or dynamic mapping to identify the network-layer addresses of remote hosts or routers. On a Cisco router, to statically map a PVC to an address, use the `protocol` command in interface-ATM-VC configuration mode. Be sure to add the `broadcast` parameter to the `protocol` command if you expect the interface to send broadcast packets. ATM also supports Inverse ARP. Inverse ARP is enabled by default when you create a PVC using the `pvc` command. With Inverse ARP, a protocol mapping between an ATM PVC and a network-layer address is learned dynamically as a result of the exchange of ATM Inverse ARP packets. Inverse ARP is supported on PVCs running IP or IPX when no static map is configured. If a static map is configured, Inverse ARP is disabled.

ATM Quality of Service Specifications

An ATM network can provide different types of service to support different sorts of applications. The network can implement mechanisms such as connection admission control and resource allocation differently for each service category. ATM defines five service categories, each of which is described in more detail later in this section:

1. Constant bit rate (CBR)
2. Realtime variable bit rate (rt-VBR)
3. Non-realtime variable bit rate (nrt-VBR)
4. Unspecified bit rate (UBR)
5. Available bit rate (ABR)

For each service category, there is a set of parameters to describe both the traffic presented to the network and the QoS required of the network. It can be difficult to learn the many parameters associated with the different ATM services, but the effort is worthwhile because studying the parameters helps you understand the different services and select the right service for your applications.

Service categories are distinguished as being either realtime or non-realtime. CBR and rt-VBR are realtime service categories. Realtime applications, such as voice and video applications, require tightly constrained delay and delay variation. Non-realtime applications, such as client/server and terminal/host data applications, do not require tightly constrained delay and delay variation. Nrt-VBR, UBR, and ABR are non-realtime service categories.

Constant Bit Rate (CBR)

The CBR service supports realtime applications that require minimal delay variation and a static amount of bandwidth to be continuously available during a connection's lifetime. The amount of bandwidth that a connection requires is specified by the Peak Cell Rate (PCR) parameter. Digital voice and video typically use CBR, although CBR is not restricted to those applications. When CBR is used, a source end system reserves network resources in advance. The source also asks for a guarantee that the negotiated QoS will apply to all cells as long as the cells conform to the CBR parameters that the source specifies. The source can send cells at the specified PCR at any time and for any duration and the QoS commitments should pertain.

Realtime Variable Bit Rate (rt-VBR)

rt-VBR connections are characterized in terms of a PCR, Sustainable Cell Rate (SCR), and Maximum Burst Size (MBS). Sources are expected to transmit in a bursty fashion, at a rate that varies with time. The rt-VBR service may implement statistical multi-plexing of realtime data sources.

Non-Realtime (nrt-VBR)

The nrt-VBR service category is intended for non-realtime applications that have bursty traffic characteristics. No delay bounds are associated with this service category. The service is characterized in terms of a PCR, SCR, and MBS. For cells that are trans-ferred within the traffic contract, the application expects a low Cell Loss Ratio (CLR). The nrt-VBR service may implement statistical multiplexing of connections.

Unspecified Bit Rate (UBR)

The UBR service category is intended for non-realtime applications including tradi-tional networking applications such as file transfer and e-mail. With UBR, congestion control can be performed at a higher layer on an end-to-end basis. For example, TCP may handle congestion control.

UBR service does not specify any traffic-related service guarantees. No numerical commitments are made regarding the CLR or Cell Transfer Delay (CTD). A network may or may not apply a PCR restriction to the connection admission control and Usage Parameter Control (UPC) functions. (UPC is defined as the set of actions taken by the network to monitor and control traffic at the end-system access point.) In the case where the network does not enforce a PCR, the value of PCR is informational only. (It is still useful to negotiate PCR to allow the source to discover the smallest bandwidth limitation along the path of the connection.)

Available Bit Rate (ABR)

With ABR, the transfer characteristics provided by the network can change after con-nection establishment. A flow control mechanism offers several types of feedback to control the source rate in response to changing network conditions. This feedback is conveyed to the source through control cells called *resource management cells* (RM cells). An end system that adapts its traffic in accordance with the feedback should experience a low CLR and obtain a fair share of the available bandwidth according to a network-specific allocation policy. The ABR service does not require bounding the delay or the delay variation experienced by a given connection. The ABR service is not intended to support realtime applications.

On the establishment of an ABR connection, an end system specifies to the network both a maximum required bandwidth and a minimum usable bandwidth. These are designated as a PCR and a Minimum Cell Rate (MCR). The MCR can be specified as zero. The bandwidth available from the network can vary, but cannot become less than the MCR.

Troubleshooting ATM

When isolating ATM problems on a Cisco router, your first step after verifying the physical layer should be to use the show interface atm command. This command displays information that is similar to the output for any of the show interface commands. It also displays ATM-specific data, such as the encapsulation type, and whether the interface is configured as an SVC or PVC.

Cisco routers with ATM interfaces also support a `show atm interface atm` command. This command displays the type of AAL in use, the maximum number of virtual circuits supported, and the number of virtual circuits currently in use. To display information about all active ATM virtual circuits and traffic information for the circuits, use the `show atm vc` command. To be more specific, you can also use the `show atm pvc` and `show atm svc` commands.

The `show atm map` command is useful when troubleshooting a problem related to reaching another host via its network-layer address when using static mapping. This command displays the list of all configured ATM static maps to remote hosts on an ATM network.

The `show atm traffic` command displays information about traffic to and from ATM networks connected to a router, including statistics about Operation, Administration, and Maintenance (OAM) cells. You can optionally configure an ATM SVC or PVC to generate end-to-end OAM loopback cells to verify connectivity on a virtual circuit. The remote end must respond by echoing back such cells. If OAM response cells are missed (indicating a connectivity problem), the PVC state goes down. The `show atm traffic` command can help you monitor OAM cells as well as other types of packets, as shown in the following example:

```
Charlotte#show atm traffic
10 Input packets
1044 Output packets
1021 Broadcast packets
0 Packets received on non-existent VC
0 Packets attempted to send on non-existent VC
50 OAM cells received
50 OAM cells sent
```

Chapter and Book Summary

This chapter has covered WAN technologies that are typical options for interconnecting campus networks. Now that you have finished this chapter, you should learn more about WANs by studying the WAN books listed in the references section at the end of this book.

This chapter has discussed established WAN technologies, but we recommend that you also research new technologies as they gain industry acceptance. Wireless WAN technologies, for example, are not covered in this book, but are expected to expand the options available for WAN and remote-access networks in the future. Low-orbit satellite, cellular, laser, and radio frequency wireless WAN technologies are some of the numerous wireless WAN technologies that are gaining popularity.

When troubleshooting WANs, as is the case with LANs, it's important to use a systematic and logical process. Start with the physical layer first and examine cables, connectors, any LEDs that may indicate a hardware failure, and so on. Then move up the layers, considering the functions of each layer. With a good understanding of how protocols work, which this chapter and book have provided, you can start to recognize which areas in a protocol implementation might be fragile and cause problems, and which areas offer rich troubleshooting data. Keep in mind that most WAN protocols (as well as LAN protocols) have many sublayers. Consider the expected behavior of each sublayer and troubleshoot by noticing symptoms that point to unexpected behavior.

A solid understanding of protocol behavior is the fundamental basis for effective troubleshooting. This book has given you the technical groundwork to allow you to read and understand the standards that document how protocols should behave. Please take some time to peruse the references section, which will point you to the next set of documents you should read in your search to understand how your campus networks really work.

Reading documents is not enough, however! Networks don't always behave the way the documents say they will. We can't stress enough how important it is to study actual behavior with a protocol analyzer, such as the WildPackets analyzers. We have shared the knowledge we have gained over the years by studying protocol behavior with an analyzer, but there is no substitute for real-world practice. Get out your analyzer and start some captures. Access some services, both on local LANs and remote LANs across one or more WANs, and verify the communication processes. Set up a Cisco lab and practice Cisco configuration and diagnostic commands. Keep that analyzer running as you configure your routers and see what happens on the wire as different protocols initialize.

With the aid of this book and by using a combination of Cisco diagnostic commands and protocol analyzer packet captures, you can keep your campus networks relatively trouble free. Using the tools, techniques, and commands discussed in this book, you can achieve the high reliability expected by network users today. As a side benefit, you can also achieve your career goals, including Cisco and industry-wide network certifications. This book has provided the foundation you need to pass some of the most advanced Cisco and WildPackets tests in your pursuit of the CCIE and Network Analysis Expert (NAX) certifications. We wish you the best of luck with your goals and hope that your troubleshooting efforts will be eased by the protocol documentation and troubleshooting methods provided in this book.

References

This section lists documents, white papers, Web sites, and books that are recommended for further reading.

Standards Documents

Local Area Network (LAN) data link layer protocols are standardized by the Institute of Electrical and Electronics Engineers (IEEE) in the IEEE 802 series. IEEE 802 standards are available at no charge in PDF format through the "Get IEEE" program. For more information about downloading IEEE documents, see this Web site:

standards.ieee.org/getieee802

The following documents standardize LAN protocols that were discussed in this book:

IEEE 802.1D: Media Access Control (MAC) Bridges
IEEE 802.1Q: Virtual Bridged Local Area Networks
IEEE 802.2: Logical Link Control
IEEE 802.3: Carrier Sense Multiple Access with Collision Detection (CSMA/CD) Access Method and Physical Layer Specifications
IEEE 802.11: Wireless LAN Medium Access Control (MAC) and Physical Layer (PHY) Specifications

TCP/IP protocols are defined by the Internet Engineering Task Force (IETF) in Requests for Comments (RFCs). For information about the RFC series, including the processes for publishing and downloading RFCs, see this Web site:

www.rfc-editor.org

The following are classic RFCs that every TCP/IP protocol analyst should know about:

RFC 760: DoD Standard Internet Protocol (IP) [made obsolete by RFC 791, but still worth reading]

RFC 768: User Datagram Protocol (UDP)

RFC 791: Internet Protocol (IP)

RFC 792: Internet Control Message Protocol (ICMP)

RFC 793: Transmission Control Protocol (TCP)

RFC 826: Ethernet Address Resolution Protocol (ARP)

RFC 854: Telnet Protocol Specification

RFC 950: Internet Standard Subnetting Procedure

RFC 959: File Transfer Protocol (FTP)

RFC 1001: Protocol Standard for a NetBIOS Service on TCP/UDP Transport: Concepts and Facilities

RFC 1002: Protocol Standard for a NetBIOS Service on a TCP/UDP Transport: Detailed Specifications

RFC 1034: Domain Names—Concepts and Facilities

RFC 1058. Routing Information Protocol (RIP)

RFC 1122: Requirements for Internet Hosts—Communication Layers

RFC 1661: The Point-to-Point Protocol (PPP)

RFC 1700: Assigned Numbers

RFC 1752: The Recommendation for the IP Next Generation Protocol

RFC 1757: Remote Network Monitoring (RMON) Management Information Base (MIB)

RFC 1771: A Border Gateway Protocol 4 (BGP4)

RFC 1812: Requirements for IP Version 4 Routers

RFC 1905: Protocol Operations for Version 2 of the Simple Network Management Protocol (SNMPv2)

RFC 1918: Address Allocation for Private Internets

RFC 1939: Post Office Protocol (POP), Version 3

RFC 2021: Remote Network Monitoring Management Information Base Version 2 using SMIv2 (RMONv2)

RFC 2060: Internet Message Access Protocol (IMAP), Version 4rev1

RFC 2236: Internet Group Management Protocol (IGMP), Version 2

RFC 2328: Open Shortest Path First (OSPF), Version 2

RFC 2390: Inverse Address Resolution Protocol (Inverse ARP)

RFC 2453: Routing Information Protocol (RIP), Version 2

RFC 2460: Internet Protocol, Version 6 (IPv6) Specification

RFC 2462: IPv6 Stateless Address Autoconfiguration

RFC 2474: Definition of the Differentiated Services Field (DS Field) in the IPv4 and IPv6 Headers

RFC 2475: An Architecture for Differentiated Service

RFC 2516: A Method for Transmitting PPP over Ethernet (PPPoE)

RFC 2608: Service Location Protocol (SLP), Version 2

RFC 2616: Hypertext Transfer Protocol (HTTP), Version 1.1

RFC 2821: Simple Mail Transfer Protocol (SMTP)

RFC 3022: Traditional IP Network Address Translator (Traditional NAT)

Web Sites and White Papers

The following Web sites and papers were mentioned in this book as helpful for troubleshooting particular technologies or issues:

Apple Computer, Inc. "Mac OS X Server 1.x: What Is NetInfo?" <docs.info.apple.com/article.html?artnum=60038>

CAIDA. "Internet Tools Taxonomy." <www.caida.org/tools/taxonomy/>

Cisco Systems. "Enhanced Interior Gateway Routing Protocol." <www.cisco.com/warp/public/103/eigrp12.html>

Cisco Systems. "Multicast in a Campus Network: CGMP and IGMP Snooping." <www.cisco.com/warp/public/473/22.html>

Cisco Systems. "Training and Certifications." <www.cisco.com/warp/public/10/wwtraining/>

Cisco Systems. "Cisco Aironet Wireless LAN Adapters Installation and Configuration Guide for Windows," Chapter 7, "Performing Diagnostics." <www.cisco.com/univercd/cc/td/doc/product/wireless/airo_350/350cards/windows/incfg/win_ch8.htm>

Compaq Western Research Lab. "Measured Capacity of an Ethernet: Myths and Reality." <www.research.digital.com/wrl/publications/abstracts/88.4.html>

DiffServ Working Group. "Differentiated Services." <www.ietf.org/html.charters/diffserv-charter.html>

Federal Communications Commission Office of Engineering and Technology. "Questions and Answers about Biological Effects and Potential Hazards of Radio Frequency Electromagnetic Fields." <www.fcc.gov/Bureaus/Engineering_Technology/Documents/bulletins/oet56/oet56e4.pdf>

Internet Assigned Numbers Authority, "Port Numbers." <www.iana.org/assignments/port-numbers>

Internet2. "About Internet2." <www.internet2.edu/html/about.html>

Intersil. "Brief Tutorial on IEEE 802.11 Wireless LANs." <www.intersil.com/data/an/an9/an9829/an9829.pdf>

Intersil. "Complementary Code Keying Made Simple." <www.intersil.com/data/an/an9/an9850/an9850.pdf>

Intersil. "Technical Info." (on 802.11 Wireless Networking) <www.intersil.com/design/prism/wirelessb.asp>

Intersil. "Tutorial on Basic Link Budget Analysis." <www.intersil.com/data/an/an9/an9804/an9804.pdf>

Spurgeon, Charles. "Ethernet Analyzers." <www.ethermanage.com/ethernet/enet-analyzers.html >

WildPackets, Inc. "Network Analysis Expert Certification." <www.nax2000.com>

WildPackets, Inc. "The Technical Compendium." <www.wildpackets.com/compendium/main/index.html>

Wolsefer, David. "Frame Relay." <www.certificationzone.com> (CertificationZone has many other excellent papers also.)

Books

The following books are all excellent places to go to learn more about computer networking. The list is divided into four categories: books about LANs; books about WANs; books about TCP/IP; and books about other protocols, network design, and troubleshooting.

Books on LANs

Clark, K. and K. Hamilton. *Cisco LAN Switching*. Indianapolis, Indiana: Cisco Press, 1999.

Riley, S. and R. Breyer. *Switched, Fast, and Gigabit Ethernet*, 3rd ed. Indianapolis, Indiana: New Riders Publishing, 1999.

Seifert, R. *Gigabit Ethernet: Technology and Applications for High-Speed LANs*. Reading, Massachusetts: Addison-Wesley Publishing Company, Inc., 1998.

Spurgeon, C.E. *Ethernet: The Definitive Guide*. Sebastopol, California: O'Reilly & Associates, Inc., 2000.

Wheat, J., R. Hiser, J. Tucker, A. Neely, and A. McCullough. *Designing a Wireless Network*. Berkeley, California: Publishers Group West, 2001.

Books on WANs

Berkowitz, H. *WAN Survival Guide*. New York, New York: John Wiley & Sons, Inc., 2001.

Buckwalter, J.T. *Frame Relay: Technology and Practice*. Reading, Massachusetts: Addison-Wesley Publishing Company, Inc., 1999.

Freeman, R.L. *Telecommunication System Engineering*, 3rd ed. New York, New York: John Wiley & Sons, Inc., 1996.

McDysan, D.E. and D.L. Spohn. *ATM: Theory and Application*. New York, New York: McGraw-Hill, Inc., 1998.

Pildush, G.D. *Cisco ATM Solutions: Master ATM Implementation of Cisco Networks*. Indianapolis, Indiana: Cisco Press, 2000.

Books on TCP/IP

Albitz, P. and C. Liu. *DNS and BIND*, 4th ed. Sebastopol, California: O'Reilly & Associates, Inc., 2001.

Comer, D.E. *Internetworking with TCP/IP: Principles, Protocols, and Architecture*, Vol. I, 4th. Englewood Cliffs, New Jersey: Prentice Hall, Inc., 2000.

Doyle, J. *Routing TCP/IP*, Volume 1. Indianapolis, Indiana: Cisco Press, 1998.

Hafner, K. and M. Lyon. *Where Wizards Stay Up Late: The Origins of the Internet*. New York, New York: Simon & Schuster, 1996.

Halabi, B. *Internet Routing Architectures*, 2nd ed. Indianapolis, Indiana: Cisco Press, 2000.

Huitema, C. *Routing in the Internet*, 2nd ed. Englewood Cliffs, New Jersey: Prentice Hall, Inc., 2000.

Miller, M. *Implementing IPv6: Supporting the Next Generation Internet Protocols*. New York, New York: Hungry Minds, 2000.

Lemon, T. and R.E. Droms. *The DHCP Handbook: Understanding, Deploying, and Managing Automated Configuration Services*. Indianapolis, Indiana: Macmillan Technical Publishing, 1999.

Stevens, W.R. *TCP/IP Illustrated*, Vol. 1. Reading, Massachusetts: Addison-Wesley Publishing Company, Inc., 1994.

Thomas, S. *HTTP Essentials: Protocols for Secure, Scaleable Web Sites*. New York, New York: John Wiley & Sons, Inc., 2001.

Books on Network Technology, Design, and Troubleshooting

Berkowitz, H. *Designing Addressing Architectures for Routing and Switching*. Indianapolis, Indiana: Macmillan Technical Publishing, 1998.

Berkowitz, H. *Designing Routing and Switching Architectures for Enterprise Networks*. Indianapolis, Indiana: Macmillan Technical Publishing, 1990.

Buchanan, R. *The Art of Testing Network Systems*. New York, New York: John Wiley & Sons, Inc., 1996.

Chappell, L. *Novell's Guide to LAN/WAN Analysis: IPX/SPX*. New York, New York: Hungry Minds, 1998.

Chappell, L. and D. Farkas, editors. *Cisco Internetwork Troubleshooting*. Indianapolis, Indiana: Cisco Press, 1999.

Cisco Systems, *Internetworking Technologies Handbook*, 3rd ed. Indianapolis, Indiana: Cisco Press, 2000.

Comer, D.E. and R.E. Droms, *Computer Networks and Internets*, 2nd ed. Englewood Cliffs, New Jersey: Prentice Hall, Inc., 1999.

Haugdahl, J.S. *Network Analysis and Troubleshooting*. Reading, Massachusetts: Addison-Wesley Publishing Company, Inc., 2000.

Jain, R. *The Art of Computer Systems Performance Analysis: Techniques for Experimental Design, Measurement, Simulation, and Modeling*. New York, New York: John Wiley & Sons, Inc., 1991.

McCabe, J.D. *Practical Computer Network Analysis and Design*. San Francisco, California: Morgan Kaufmann Publishers, Inc., 1998.

Oppenheimer, A. and C. Whitaker, *Internet Security for Your Macintosh: A Guide for the Rest of Us*. Berkeley, California: Peachpit Press, 2001.

Oppenheimer, P. *Top-Down Network Design*. Indianapolis, Indiana: Cisco Press, 1999.

Perlman, R. *Interconnections: Bridges, Routers, Switches, and Internetworking Protocols*, 2nd ed. Reading, Massachusetts: Addison-Wesley Publishing Company, Inc., 1999.

Sidhu, G.S., R.F. Andrews, and A. Oppenheimer. *Inside AppleTalk*, 2nd ed. Reading, Massachusetts: Addison-Wesley Publishing Company, Inc., 1990.

Stallings, W. *Data & Computer Communications*, 6th ed. Englewood Cliffs, New Jersey: Prentice Hall, Inc., 1999.

Tanenbaum, A.S. *Computer Networks*, 3rd ed. Englewood Cliffs, New Jersey: Prentice Hall, Inc., 1996.

Index

Numbers & Symbols

4B/5B translation, 61–62
5-4-3 rule, 65
8B/10B encoding, 62
10Base2, 57
100BaseT2, 62
100BaseT4, 68
100BaseTX, 62
100-Mbps Ethernet
  collision domains, 66–67
  MLT-3 (Multiple-Level Transition-3) encoding, 61
  standards, 58
404 HTTP status code, 381
802.1 Bridge Spanning Tree frames, 166
802.1Q, 212–213, 222–224
802.1W features, 192
802.2 SAP (Service Access Point), 78–79
802.3 frames, 75
802.3 standard, 58
802.3x standard, 68
802.11 standard
  AP definition, 115
  distribution services mechanism, 111
802.11 WLAN
  2.4-GHz band, 122
  conflicts with Bluetooth, 108
  environmental factors affecting transmission, 133–134
  fragmentation threshold, 248
  free space propagation, 130–131
  interframe spacing, 117–118
  IP fragmentation, 248
  packet decode, 152–154
  power output, 130
1000BaseX, 62

A

AAL (ATM Adaptation Layer), 559
AARP (AppleTalk Address Resolution Protocol), 214, 448
ABR (Area Border Router), 330

ABR (Available Bit Rate), 561
access layer, 181
access-layer switches, 192–193
access links, 210
access point. *See* AP
Access to your AppleTalk network has been interrupted. error message, 189
accuracy, 33
active FTP (File Transfer Protocol), 383
Active Scanning Mode, 113
ACU (Aironet Client Utility), 142
Add Name command, 493, 494
ad hoc network, 112
adjacency, 301, 332
administrative distance, 302
AEP (AppleTalk Echo Protocol) datagrams, 38, 482
AFP (Apple Filing Protocol), 30, 459
  authentication, 455–457, 458
  file servers, 399, 455–459
  over TCP/IP, 457–459
  versions, 455
AiroPeek, 4, 18, 24, 31, 35, 99, 121
alignment error, 94
AMP (Address Mapping Table), 448
anonymous FTP, 382
antennas
  gain, 101
  isotropic, 135
  omnidirectional, 139
AP (access point), 31, 102, 110
  default IP address, 151
  ESSID (Extended Service Set ID), 151
  estimating effective range, 146–147
  functioning as portal, 110
  placement considerations, 147–148
APNIC (Asia-Pacific Network Information Center), 277
APPC (Advanced Program to Program) session, 38
AppleTalk, 3, 8, 37, 237
  AARP (AppleTalk Address Resolution Protocol), 214
  access lists, 474–475
  AFP (Apple Filing Protocol), 455–459

AppleTalk *(continued)*
architectures, 442–446
AURP (AppleTalk Update-Based Routing Protocol), 465–468
concepts, 441–459
controlling traffic, 473–475
DDP (Datagram Delivery Protocol), 452–454
debug commands, 486
dynamic addressing, 448–452
EIGRP, 468–473
end-node routing, 463–464
filtering
cable ranges, 474–475
zones, 475
finding resources and services, 442
gleaning, 448
layered architecture, 443–446
migrating to IP routing, 465–468
NBP (Name Binding Protocol), 454–455, 483
OSI (Open System Interconnection) reference model, 446
ping, 38, 482–483
protocols, 443–446
routers and split horizon, 462
routing, 459
RTMP (Routing Table Maintenance Protocol), 460–464
seed router, 451
SLP (Service Location Protocol), 375
sockets, 442, 452
static routes, 473–474
switch port startup delay, 189
troubleshooting, 480–486
ZIP (Zone Information Protocol), 464–465
zones, 443
AppleTalk addresses, 446–451
AARP (AppleTalk Address Resolution Protocol), 448
Cisco routers, 447
mapping
to data-link layer addresses, 448
names to, 454–455
network.node format, 446
appletalk arp probe interval command, 450
appletalk arp probe retransmit-count number command, 450
appletalk arp request interval command, 448
appletalk arp request retransmit-count number command, 448
appletalk cable-range 0-0 command, 451
appletalk cable-range cable-range command, 447, 473
appletalk cable-range command, 448
appletalk discovery command, 451
AppleTalk networks, 442
migrating to IP, 480–486
reducing traffic, 465–468
security, 477
troubleshooting, 484–485
appletalk permit-partial-zones command, 474
appletalk protocol aurp command, 466
appletalk protocol eigrp command, 468
appletalk require-route-zones command, 465
appletalk route-redistribution command, 466, 469
appletalk routing command, 447
appletalk routing eigrp router-number command, 468
appletalk rtmp-stub command, 463
appletalk static cable-range to network.node floating zone command, 474
appletalk static cable-range to network.node zone command, 474

appletalk timers update-interval valid-interval invalid-interval command, 460
appletalk zone zone-name command, 447
application layer, 11, 368
application-layer protocols, 368
client-server architecture, 369
DNS (Domain Name System), 369–375
FTP (File Transfer Protocol), 381–392
HTTP (Hypertext Transfer Protocol), 377–381
SLP (Service Location Protocol), 375–377
ARIN (American Registry for Internet Numbers), 277
ARP (Address Resolution Protocol), 240, 256, 268–270, 401
broadcast, 31, 159, 213–214
cache, 268, 269, 448
frames, 79, 201, 268, 269
ARPA (Advanced Research Projects Agency), 237
arp -a command, 268
ARPANET, 237–238
ASBRs (Autonomous System Boundary Routers), 331
ASCII (American Standard Code for Information Interchange), 368
ASP (AppleTalk Session Protocol), 443
association, 105
asymmetrical flow control, 73
Asynchronous Balanced Mode Extended, 82
ATM (Asynchronous Transfer Mode), 557–558
AAL (ATM Adaptation Layer), 559
ABR (Available Bit Rate), 561
CBR (Constant Bit Rate), 560
CLP (Congestion Loss Priority), 559
HEC (Header Error Control), 559
mapping protocol address to PVC, 559–560
nrt-VBR (Non-Realtime Variable Bit Rate), 561
PT (Payload Type), 559
quality of service specifications, 560–561
rt-VBR (Realtime Variable Bit Rate), 560–561
troubleshooting, 561–562
UBR (Unspecified Bit Rate), 561
VCI (Virtual Channel Identifier), 558, 559
virtual circuits and adaptation layers, 558–559
VPI (Virtual Path Identifier), 559
attenuation, 36, 130
AUI (Attachment Unit Interface), 58
AURP (AppleTalk Update-Based Routing Protocol), 465–468
authentication, 105
AFP, 455
domain model, 521
IPv6, 284
RIPv2, 310
wireless networks, 115
workgroups, 518–521
Authentication or Association Request management frame, 153
Authentication Reply, 115
Authentication Request, 115
autonegotiation, 70–72
autonomous system, 296
autoselect, 58

B
baby giants, 88, 93, 222
Backbone Fast, 192–193
back-to-back client/server traffic, 29–30
bandwidth, 33
broadcast frames, 96
EIGRP (Enhanced Interior Gateway Routing Protocol), 312, 319

Ethernet networks, 90–91
IGRP (Interior Gateway Routing Protocol), 312
interfaces, 90–91
RTMP, 461
utilization, 92–93
bandwidth command, 91
Banyan VINES, 189
baseline, 17, 33
BBN (Bolt, Beranek, and Newman, Inc.), 237
BDC (Backup Domain Controller), 496
BDR (Backup Designated Router), 332
Beacon frames, 105, 112, 114, 121, 140
BECN (Backward-Explicit Congestion Notification),
    545–546
Become Backup Browser packet, 523
bel, 124–125
Bell, Alexander Graham, 124
BER (Bit Error Rate), 136
BERT (Bit Error Rate Test), 37
BGP (Border Gateway Protocol), 245, 298
    analysis, 340–343
    connection status, 343
    Keepalive messages, 341
    monitoring, 343
    neighbor information, 343
    Open messages, 341
    processing packets, 343
    route flapping statistics, 343
    routing table, 341, 343
    Update messages, 340
Big-Endian transmission, 77
binary exponential backoff algorithm, 64
bit length, 65–66
bleedover, 114
BLERT (Block Error Rate Test), 37
blocking ports, 175
Bluetooth, 106, 107–108
Boolean AND operation, 264
Boolean logic, 262, 264–265
Boolean OR operation, 265
BPDUs (Bridge Protocol Data Units), 22
    analysis, 166–168
    BPDU Type field, 168
    Bridge IDs, 169–170
    configuration, 166
    Cost of Path to Root, 170
    Ethernet frame format, 167
    flags, 168–169
    Forward Delay, 171–172
    frames, 86, 159, 166–172, 185
    Hello Time, 171
    inconsistent reception, 187
    LLC SAP (Logical Link Control Service
        Access Point), 168
    Maximum Age, 171
    Message Age, 171
    Port ID, 171
    Protocol Identifier, 168
    Protocol Version number, 168
    refreshing, 171
    topology change notification, 166
BPSK (Binary Phase Shift Keying), 140–141
breakout box, 36–37
Brewster's angle, 133
Bridge ID, 194
bridge ports, 166
    selecting for spanning tree, 175
    states, 177

Bridge Priority, 170
bridges, 157–158
    BPDU (Bridge Protocol Data Unit) messages, 166–172
    collision domain, 66
    configuration BPDU (Bridge Protocol Data Unit), 166
    configuring priority, 197
    duplicate frames, 164
    Ethernet networks, 55–56
    filtering, 162, 164–165
    flooding, 162
    forwarding
        frames, 162, 164
        path, 56
        process for unknown destinations, 163
    identifying, 21
    MAC addresses, 159–160
    multicast address, 166
    port wait time, 171–172
    redundancy, 162–165
    tasks, 162
    VLANs (Virtual LANs), 177
bridging table, 162, 179–180
broadcast domain, 103, 109
broadcast frames, 76–77, 96–98, 165
broadcast networks, 331
broadcast storm, 97
broadcast suppression, 97–98
Browse protocol, 489–490, 522–525
BSS (Basic Service Set), 109
    cells, 110
    scanning, 113
    station association to, 115
BSSID (Basic Service Set Identification), 109
burstLength time, 74
Burst Mode protocol, 409
bus topology, 54

C

cable range, 447
cable testers, 36
CAIDA (Cooperative Association for Internet Data
    Analysis), 21
Call command, 493
CAM (Content Addressable Memory), 159
captured packets, 23, 83
CBR (Constant Bit Rate), 560
CCA (Clear Channel Assessment), 140
CCIE (Cisco Certified Internetwork Expert)
    certification, 3–4, 17
CCK (Complementary Code Keying), 140–141
CCNP (Cisco Certified Network Professional)
    certification, 3
CDP (Cisco Discovery Protocol), 21, 22–23, 77, 159
cdp holdtime command, 22
cdp run command, 22
cdp timer command, 22
CEPT (Committee of European Postal and Telephone),
    537–538
CertificationZone Web site, 550
CFN (Configuration Revision Number), 229–230
CGMP (Cisco Group Management Protocol), 165, 281
channels, 113–114, 135–136
CHAP (Challenge Handshake Authentication Protocol),
    542–543
chipping code, 107
Chooser, traffic caused by, 454
CIR (Committed Information Rate), 546
Cisco Certification Programs Web site, 4

Cisco IOS Debug Command Reference manual, 48
Cisco Support Test, 14
Cisco switches
    broadcast suppression, 97–98
    reducing startup delay on ports, 188–191
Cisco troubleshooting method, 14
Cisco Web site, 100, 142, 165
Cisco Works, 18
CIT (Cisco Internetwork Troubleshooting) class, 14
Citrix Metaframe, 31
Class I repeaters, 67
Class II repeaters, 67
Class A, B, C, D, and E addresses, 260
classful routing protocols, 297
classless addressing, 2, 262, 283
classless routing protocols, 297
clear appletalk arp command, 482
clear appletalk interface command, 482
clear appletalk route command, 482
clear cdp counters command, 22
clear cdp table command, 22
clear interface bri number command, 556
clear ip nat translation command, 279
clear trunk mod_num/port_num vlan_range
    command, 212
client/server protocols, 30, 370
CLNS (Connectionless Network Service), 37
clock synchronization, 62–63
CLP (Congestion Loss Priority), 559
coaxial cables, 36, 56
Code Red worms, 341
collision domains
    100-Mbps Ethernet, 66–67
    bit length, 65–66
    bridges, 66
    end of, 66
    extending, 66
    measurement, 65–66
    routers, 66
    segmenting, 162
    switches, 66
collisions
    802.11 network, 117, 145
    CSMA/CD network, 65
    cut-through switches, 68
    Ethernet, 63, 64–65
    hubs, 67–68
    increase in, 86
    interface rate, 94–95
    large packets, 149
    late, 65
    numerous simultaneous users, 149–150
    serial interfaces, 536
    stations detecting, 116
    switches, 67–68
    wireless networks, 145
collisions error, 94
common logarithms, 124
computing appliances, 31
conditionally-triggered debugging, 50
configuration BPDUs, 166, 175
    minimum time between transmissions, 184
    time between generation, 171
    topology change acknowledgment flag, 180
configuration settings for wireless networks, 151–152
connectionless protocols, 28, 241
connection-oriented protocols, 28, 545
contention-free mode, 119

convergence, 296
Conversation Statistics window, 35
copy run start command, 451
core layer, 180–181
count-to-infinity problem, 300
CRB (Concurrent Routing and Bridging), 303
CRC (Cyclic Redundancy Check) errors, 94, 95–96,
    108, 143, 146
CSMA/CA (Carrier Sense Multiple Access with
    Collision Avoidance), 102, 117
CSMA/CA algorithm, 149
CSMA/CD (Carrier Sense Multiple Access with
    Collision Detection), 116, 117
    collisions, 65
    Ethernet, 63
    MAC layer, 63
    switches, 68
CSU/DSU (Channel Service Unit/
    Digital Service Unit), 532–533
CTS (Clear to Send) response, 119
CTS/RTS (Clear to Send/Request to Send), 151
custom queuing, 74
cut-through switches and collisions, 68

D

Dartmouth Problem-Solving and Design Method, 13
data link layer, 11
Data Only frame, 153
dB (decibel), 122
    application of measurements, 130–133
    gain or loss, 126–130
    measurements, 123–124
    relationships between metrics, 127–128
dBm (decibel-milliwatt), 122, 123
    application of measurements, 130–133
    relationships between metrics, 127–128
DBPSK (Differential Binary Phase Shift Keying),
    140–141
DCE (Data Circuit-Terminating Equipment), 532
DCF (Distributed Coordination Function) Interframe
    Space or DIFS, 117
DDP (Datagram Delivery Protocol), 452–454
DDR (Dial-on-Demand Routing), 412, 556
dead interval, 332
debug all command, 49
debug apple eigrp-all routing command, 481
debug apple routing command, 481
debug appletalk events command, 451, 481
debug appletalk neighbors command, 481
debug appletalk zip command, 481
debug arp command, 269, 304
debug bri command, 557
debug ? command, 49
debug commands, 48–50
debug condition interface command, 50
debug eigrp fsm command, 329
debug eigrp neighbor command, 49, 329
debug eigrp packets command, 329
debug frame-relay events command, 550
debug frame-relay lmi command, 548, 550
debug frame-relay packet command, 550
debug frame-relay verbose command, 550
debug ip bgp command, 343
debug ip eigrp neighbor command, 329
debug ip icmp command, 87, 304
debug ip igrp events command, 318
debug ip igrp transactions command, 318
debug ip ospf adjacency command, 340

debug ip ospf events command, 340
debug ip packet command, 304, 550
debug ip rip command, 311
debug ip rip events command, 311
debug ip routing command, 304
debug ipx packet command, 439
debug ipx routing activity command, 439
debug ipx routing events command, 439
debug ipx sap activity command, 439–440
debug ipx sap events command, 440
debug isdn q921 command, 557
debug isdn q931 command, 557
debug messages, timestamping, 50
debug ppp command, 543
debug protocol command, 49
debug span command, 185
debug span events command, 185
debug span tree command, 185
debug vlan packet command, 216–217
DEC (Digital Equipment Corporation), 54, 158
DEC LAVC (Local Area VAX Cluster) architecture, 29
DECnet, 29, 37, 421
default
    gateways, 31, 290
    routes, 294–295
    VLAN, 224
delay
    EIGRP (Enhanced Interior Gateway Routing
        Protocol), 312
    IGRP (Interior Gateway Routing Protocol), 312
    interfaces, 91
    variation, 33
delayed ACKs, 358
demultiplexing, 347
dense-mode PIM, 281–282
Designated Bridges, 166, 175
Designated Ports, 166, 175
    electing, 174
    states, 177
designated router, 282
DHCP (Dynamic Host Configuration Protocol),
    8, 87, 200, 270–273, 430
    messages, 271–272
    monitoring, 276–277
    routers, 273–276
    server, 290
    troubleshooting, 276–277
DHCP relay agent, 273–276
Diffie, Whitfield, 456
Diffie-Hellman algorithm, 456
diffraction, 134
DiffServ Working Group Web site, 246
digital multimeters, 36
Dijkstra, Edsger, 300, 428
Dijkstra algorithm, 298, 300–301
disabled port state, 176
discontiguous subnet, 297
Discover Message, 271
DISL (Dynamic Inter-Switch Link), 22, 190, 218–222
distance-vector routing protocols, 298–300
distributed denial of service attacks, 32
distribution layer, 181
divide-and-conquer approach, 16
DIX standard, 54, 58
DLCI (Data Link Connection Identifier), 545
DNS (Domain Name System), 240, 345
    analysis, 371–375
    client/server model, 370

delegation of authority, 370
distributed database, 369
hierarchical names, 369–370
packets, 371
recursion, 370, 372
resolver software, 370
top-level domains, 369–370
zone of authority, 369
documentation tools, 20–21
documenting
    CDP (Cisco Discovery Protocol), 22–23
    logical and physical topology, 18
    network names and addresses, 19–20
    networks, 18–23
    switched networks, 21–22, 182
Domain Master Browser, 496
domains
    authentication, 521
    Windows networking, 491
dotted-decimal notation, 260
double-tagging, 88, 217
DR (Designated Router), 332
DS (Distribution System), 110
DSAP (Destination SAP), 80
DSCP (Differentiated Services Codepoint), 245–246
DSI (Data Stream Interface), 458
DSM (Distribution System Medium), 110, 111
DSPs (Digital Signal Processors), 62
DSSS (Direct Sequence Spread Spectrum), 101, 102,
    106–107, 113–114, 141
DTE (Data Terminal Equipment), 532
DTP (Dynamic Trunk Protocol), 190
DUAL (Diffusing-Update Algorithm), 319, 468
duplex negotiation problems, 71
duplicate frames, 164
Duplicate IP Address messages, 293
dwell time, 106
dynamic addressing and AppleTalk, 448–452
dynamically assigned sockets, 453
dynamic routing, 294
    convergence, 296
    differences between, 295–296
    distance-vector routing protocols, 298–300
    link-state routing, 298, 300–301
    metrics, 296
dynamic VLANs, 205

E

efficiency, 33
EIA/TIA-232 breakout box, 36–37
EIFS (Extended Interframe Space), 117
EIGRP (Enhanced Interior Gateway Routing Protocol),
    49, 91, 201, 281, 296, 298, 301, 401
    analysis, 320–327
    AppleTalk, 468–473
    automatic redistribution mechanism, 319
    bandwidth, 312, 319
    bounded updates, 319
    commands, 438–439
    delay, 312
    distance-vector algorithm, 423
    DUAL (Diffusing-Update Algorithm), 468
    enabling on interface, 438
    FSM (Finite-State Machine), 329
    guaranteed delivery, 320
    Hello packets, 320, 423
    hop count, 313
    information about neighbors, 327

EIGRP *(continued)*
  IPX routing, 423–427
  load, 313
  metrics, 423
  MTU (Maximum Transmission Unit), 313
  multicast traffic, 320
  neighbor discovery and recovery processes, 329
  neighbors information, 438
  nonperiodic updates, 319
  packet types, 320
  partial updates, 319
  queries, 325–327
  reliability, 313, 323
  route redistribution, 468–469
  routes SIA (Stuck in Active), 326–327
  routing for multiple protocols, 423
  RTMP routes, 468
  topology database, 327, 439
  traffic statistics, 327
  troubleshooting, 327–329
  Update packet, 321
e-mail protocols
  POP, 392–393, 395–396
  SMTP, 392, 393–395
empty ACKs, 358
encapsulation isl command, 215
end-node routing, 463–464
energy detect threshold, 140
environmental noise, 143–146
ephemeral (client-side) ports, 349, 350, 368
ERC (European Radio-Communications
    Committee), 122
ESS (Extended Service Set), 109, 110–111
ESSID (Extended Service Set Identification), 110, 151
established keyword, 392
Ethernet
  administratively down, 90
  architecture, 53–56
  clock synchronization, 62–63
  collisions, 64–68
  CSMA/CD (Carrier Sense Multiple Access with
      Collision Detection), 63
  flow control, 72–73
  frame corruption, 95
  frames, 75–88
  full-duplex, 68–73
  history, 53–56
  MAC layer, 63–74
  overall robustness, 56
  performance data, 88–98
  Physical layer, 56–63
  PPP (Point-to-Point Protocol), 542
  preamble, 62–63
  remote monitoring, 88–89
  retransmissions, 65
  round-trip propagation delay, 65
  signal encoding, 59–62
  topologies, 54–56
  Version I, 8
  Version II, 8
Ethernet: The Definitive Guide (Spurgeon), 24
Ethernet II, 54, 63
  EtherType, 78–79
  frames, 54, 75–76
Ethernet_II frame type, 406
Ethernet_802.2 frame format, 407
Ethernet_802.3 frame format, 407–408
Ethernet adapter promiscuous mode, 95

Ethernet frames
  average size, 85
  buffers, 84
  configuring
    multiple types on Cisco routers, 408–409
    sizes, 85–87
  delay, 93
  efficiency, 84
  fairness, 84
  footer, 83
  IPX, 406–408
  low overhead, 84
  sizes, 84–88
Ethernet networks
  bandwidth, 90–91
  bridges, 55–56
  bus topology, 54
  coaxial cable, 54
  collisions, 63
  electrical noise, 96
  excessive propagation delay, 95–96
  faulty hardware, 96
  hubs, 55
  protocol analyzers, 59
  signal reflection, 96
  star topology, 55
  twisted-pair cabling, 55
  utilization, 2
Ethernet Web site, 24
EtherPeek, 4, 18, 24, 35, 202, 354
EtherTypes, 78–79
  AppleTalk Phase 1, 83
  IPv6, 80
expert systems, 362
exponentiation, 131–133
extended AppleTalk networks, 442
exterior routing protocols, 296–297
External LSAs, 333

F

fade margin, 134, 137
Fast-Start feature, 190
fault tolerance, 193
FCC (Federal Communications Commission), 121–122
FCS (Frame Check Sequence), 83, 223, 241
FDDI standards, 61
feasible successor, 319
feedback, 302
FHSS (Frequency Hopping Spread Spectrum), 101, 102,
    106, 113–114, 141
files
  manipulating, 409
  sharing, 455–459
  transferring, 381–392
filters and protocol analyzers, 23
finger, 24, 45
firewalls and IP fragments, 248
Flags field, 247
floating static route, 294
flooding unknown destinations and unicasts, 162
flow control, 27, 72–73, 354–356
FLP (Fast Link Pulse) burst, 70
flush timer, 309
Forwarding Name, 495–496
forwarding port state, 176
fragmentation threshold, 149, 151, 248
Fragmentation was needed and the DF bit was set
    (ICMP Code 4), 247

frame error, 94
frame-forwarding path, 256
Frame Relay, 28
    BECN (Backward-Explicit Congestion Notification),
        545–546
    CIR (Committed Information Rate), 546
    congestion control, 545–546
    debug commands, 550
    DLCI (Data Link Connection Identifier), 545
    FECN (Forward-Explicit Congestion Notification),
        545–546
    Inverse ARP, 546–547
    LMI (Local Management Interface), 547
    PSN (Packet-Switched Network), 544–545
    PVCs (Permanent Virtual Circuits), 545
    reliability, 545
    SVCs (Switched Virtual Circuits), 545
    troubleshooting, 547–550
    virtual circuits, 544–545
frames
    broadcast, 76–77
    capturing corrupted, 83
    corruption, 95
    Ethernet, 75–88
    Ethernet II, 54
    format names, 75–76
    length or EtherType, 78
    looping, 165, 186–187
    multicast, 76–77
    preamble, 62–63
    tunneling and lengths, 87–88
frame size distribution graph, 86
free space path loss, 101
frequencies, 120–121
    ISM (Industrial, Scientific, and Medical) band, 122
Fresnel-Kirchoff diffraction parameter, 133
FRMR (Frame Reject) error command, 82
FSM (Finite-State Machine), 329
FTP (File Transfer Protocol), 12, 30, 240, 345
    active mode, 387, 388–390
    analysis, 383–384
    client/server architecture, 382
    commands, 384–386
    control connection, 383–384
    file types and structures, 382–383
    GUI (graphical user interface), 386
    Mac OS X, 477
    passive mode, 387, 388, 390–392
    password, 382
    PASV command, 391
    PORT command, 389–390
    replies, 386–387
    TCP connections, 383
    username, 382
full-duplex Ethernet
    100BaseT4, 68
    analysis, 69
    autonegotiation, 70–72
full-duplex links and flow control, 72–73

G
gain, 124
Garcia-Luna-Aceves, J. J., 319
gateways, default, 31
Gaussian distribution, 137
Gaussian noise, 137, 143
Gaussian variables, 133
generic problem-solving models, 12–14

Get-Bulk Request packets, 34
GET command, 379–380
Get Nearest Server request, 419–420
Get-Next Request packets, 34
Get Request packets, 34
Get Ticket Reply packet, 526
Get Ticket Request packet, 526
giant frames, 86
giants error, 93
Gigabit Ethernet, 73–74
gleaning, 448
GMII (Gigabit MII), 58
GRE (Generic Route Encapsulation) feature, 87
Gulliver's Travels, 77

H
hardware addresses, 76
HDLC (High-Level Data Link Control), 81, 539–541
HEC (Header Error Control), 559
Hellman, Martin, 456
hello interval, 331
Hello Time timer, 180
helper addresses, 201
hierarchical addressing, 266
The Hitchhiker's Guide to the Galaxy (Adams), 168
holddown timer, 299–300, 310
holdtime, 22, 184
HomeRF standard, 108–109
hop count, 296, 298
host routing, 289–291
    HSRP (Hot Standby Router Protocol), 292
    monitoring, 292–293
    troubleshooting, 292–293
host-specific route, 267
HSRP (Hot Standby Router Protocol), 291–293
HTTP (Hypertext Transfer Protocol), 30, 240, 345
    advanced commands, 380–381
    analysis, 379–381
    CONNECT command, 380
    DELETE command, 380
    GET command, 379–380
    HEAD command, 381
    OPTIONS command, 380–381
    persistent connections, 377–378
    pipelining, 378
    POST command, 380
    proxy servers, 378–379
    PUT command, 380
    replies, 381
    status code categories, 382
    TRACE command, 381
hubs, 56
    collisions, 67–68
    Ethernet networks, 55

I
IANA (Internet Assigned Numbers Authority)
    Web site, 254
IBSS (Independent Basic Service Set), 112
ICANN (Internet Corporation for Assigned Names and
    Numbers), 370
ICMP (Internet Control Message Protocol), 240
    echo packet, 38
    Redirect messages, 290
    packets, 38, 41, 87, 241, 249, 259
    types and codes, 39–40
ICMP destination unreachable (ICMP Type 3)
    messages, 41, 247

ICMP source route failed message, 257
IDF (Intermediate Distribution Frame) switches, 162
IDP (Internet Datagram Protocol), 401
IEEE (Institute of Electrical and Electronics
    Engineers), 2, 54, 406
  802.1D standard, 158
  802.1Q standard, 202
  802.2 SAP (Service Access Point), 78–79
  802.3 frames, 83, 76
  802.3 Working Group, 54
  802.11 standard, 100, 105, 152
  media standards, 56–58
IEEE 802.3 2000 Edition, 70
IEEE home page, 100
IETF (Internet Engineering Task Force), 2, 238, 292
IFG (Interframe Gap) time, 64
IGMP (Internet Group Management Protocol), 240,
    280–281, 430
IGMP Snooping, 165, 281
IGMPv2, 280
ignored error, 94
IGRP (Interior Gateway Routing Protocol), 91, 296, 298
  analysis, 312–315
  bandwidth, 312
  composite metric, 315
  delay, 312
  exterior routes, 314
  hop count, 312
  interior routes, 312
  load, 312
  load sharing, 312
  MTU (Maximum Transmission Unit), 312
  poison reverse, 315–318
  reliability, 312
  Request messages, 312
  sleeptime, 312
  summary routing information, 318
  system routes, 313–314
  timers, 312
  triggered updates, 315–318
  troubleshooting, 318
  update information, 318
  Update messages, 312
  variance feature, 312
IMAP (Internet Message Access Protocol), 346
IMAP4rev1 (Internet Message Access Protocol,
    Version 4rev1), 393
iNetTools suite, 24
information appliances, 31
Inform packets, 34
infrastructure network, 102
input error, 93
input packets with dribble condition error, 94
Intel Web site, 101
*Interconnections: Bridges, Routers, Switches, and
    Internetworking Protocols* (Perlman), 168, 188
interface fastethernet 1/0.1 command, 215
interface identifier, 286
interfaces
  administratively down, 90
  applying SAP filters, 418
  bandwidth, 90–91
  collision rate, 94–95
  delay, 91
  opening, 90
  reliability, 93–94

interface tunnel number command, 466
interframe spacing, 117–118
interior routing protocols, 296
InterMapper, 21
Internet, 238
  advertising network numbers, 278
  instability and worms, 341
Internet2, 282
interrupts, 491
Intersil Corporation Web site, 101, 141
intranets, 238
invalid timer, 309
Inverse ARP for Frame Relay, 546–547
inverse-square law, 131, 132, 138
IP (Internet Protocol), 37, 78, 240, 241
  analysis, 241–260
  best-effort delivery service, 241
  connectionless nature, 241
  datagrams, 241, 242
  fragmentation and reassembly, 246–252
  options, 255–256
  precedence, 243
  record-route, 258–259
  source routing, 256–258
  switch port startup delay, 189
  type of service, 243
IP addresses, 2, 256, 260
  ARP (Address Resolution Protocol), 268–270
  binary, 260
  Class A, B, C, D, and E addresses, 260
  Class D address, 260, 280
  converting from inside network to outside network,
      278–279
  DHCP (Dynamic Host Configuration Protocol),
      270–273
  dotted-decimal notation, 260
  duplicate, 365
  hierarchical addressing, 266
  host field, 260
  pool of, 271
  prefix field, 260
  prefix length, 260
  private, 277–278
  public, 277
  reallocation of reusable, 270
  subnetting, 261–264
  supernetting, 265–268
  wireless networks, 151
ip bandwidth-percent eigrp command, 319
IPC$ (Interprocess Communication Service), 520
ipfirewall, 477
ip forward-protocol command, 274
ip forward-protocol udp 67 command, 274
IP fragmentation, 87
IP header, 242
  DS field, 245–246
  Flags field, 247
  Fragmentation Flags field, 250
  Fragment Offset field, 247, 250
  Identification field, 247
  Options field, 254–259
  Precedence subfield, 244
  Protocol field, 254
  record route option, 42
  TTL (Time to Live) field, 252–253
  Type of Service or DS field, 243–246
  Type of Service subfield, 244–245

ip hello-interval eigrp command, 320
IP helper address, 273, 274
ip helper-address address command, 273
ip hold-time eigrp command, 320
ip icmp rate-limit unreachable command, 41
ip mtu configuration command, 87
IP multicasting, 279–282
IPng (IP the next generation), 282
ip ospf dead-interval command, 332
ip ospf hello-interval command, 331
IP ping, 38
ip rip receive version command, 310
ip rip send version command, 310
ip route network mask address | interface
    command, 294
IP routing, 289
    analysis, 304–312
    troubleshooting, 303–304
ip subnet-zero command, 262
ip telnet source-interface global configuration
    command, 46
IPv6, 241, 282
    analysis, 284–286
    authentication, 284
    Authentication Header, 286
    autoconfiguration, 284, 286–287
    Destination Options Header 1, 285
    Destination Options Header 2, 286
    Encapsulating Security Payload Header, 286
    EtherTypes, 80
    expanded addressing capabilities, 283
    extension headers and options, 283, 285–286
    flow labeling, 283
    Fragment Header, 286
    header fields, 284–285
    Hop-by-Hop Options Header, 285
    larger address space, 283
    Neighbor Solicitation message, 286–287
    privacy, 284
    Routing Header, 286
    simplified header format, 283
    source routing, 284
    stateless autoconfiguration, 286
    transition from IPv4, 284
IPX (Internetwork Packet Exchange), 399, 401
    addressing, 401–403
    anonymous switching, 422
    displaying routing table, 435–436
    Ethernet frames, 406–408, 434
    fast switching, 439
    interfaces, 436–437
    LLC (Logical Link Control) header, 406
    mismatch of Ethernet frame type, 434
    name query, 506–507
    NetBIOS data, 507
    NetBIOS name registration, 509
    NetBIOS name resolution, 509
    network number, 402
    packet forwarding, 402
    packet header, 403–404
    packet types, 404–405
    ping, 434–435
    process switching, 422
    protocol analyzer, 434
    route of last resort, 421
    SAP (Service Advertising Protocol), 414–420
    services, 436
    socket numbers, 402, 405
    trace-route, 434–435
    troubleshooting, 433–440
ipx access-list sap name command, 418
ipx-default-output-rip-delay command, 422
ipx delay ticks command, 422
ipx gns-reply-disable command, 420
ipx gns-response-delay global configuration
    command, 420
ipx gns-round-robin global configuration
    command, 420
ipx input-sap-filter command, 418
ipx maximum-paths command, 421, 436
ipx max-packetsize command, 417
ipx netbios input-access filter command, 509
ipx network {network} encapsulation arpa
    command, 406
ipx network {network} encapsulation sap
    command, 407
ipx network {network} encapsulation snap
    command, 407
IPX networks
    migration to IP, 430–433
    NCP with native services of TCP/IP, 430
    reducing routing traffic, 427–429
    tunneling, 430
ipx output-gns-filter command, 420
ipx output-sap-filter command, 418
IPX packets, 403–409, 437–438, 439
IPX ping, 38
ipx ping-default novell command, 434
IPX RIP (Routing Information Protocol), 422–423
ipx route-cache same-interface command, 408
ipx route command, 421
ipx router-sap-filter command, 418
IPX routing, 421–422
    EIGRP (Enhanced Interior Gateway Routing
        Protocol), 423–427
    IPX RIP (Routing Information Protocol), 422–423
    load sharing on equal-cost paths, 421
    NLSP (NetWare Link Services Protocol), 427–429
    node ID, 421
    one path to IPX network, 421
ipx routing command, 421
IPX routing packets, 439
ipx spx-spoof command, 413
ipx type-20 propagation command, 509
ipx update interval command, 422
ipx watchdog-spoof command, 412
IR (infrared), 107
IRB (Integrated Routing and Bridging), 302–303
ISDN (Integrated Services Digital Network)
    B channels, 551
    BRI, 551
    D channel, 551
    Layer 1, 552–553
    Layer 2, 553–554
    Layer 3, 555
    Q.921, 553–554
    Q.931, 555
    reference points, 551
    SABME (Set Asynchronous Balanced Mode
        Extended) frame, 554
    SAPI (Service Access Point Identifier), 554
    S/T interface, 552
    terminals, 551
    troubleshooting BRI problems, 556–557
IS-IS (Intermediate System-to-Intermediate
    System) protocol, 301

ISL (Inter-Switch Link), 88, 202, 212, 217–222
  mode mismatch, 219
  STP (Spanning Tree Protocol), 213
ISM (Industrial, Scientific, and Medical) band, 122
ISO (International Organization for
    Standardization), 10, 238
isotropic antennas, 135
ISPs (Internet Service Providers)
  frame sizes, 85
  static routes, 294
ITU-T (International Telecommunication Union,
    Telecommunication Standardization Sector), 530
ITU-T Q.921, 81

J

jabbering station, 96
jam signal, 64
JetDirect print server, 411

K

Kalpana Corporation, 56
keepalive frame, 90
keepalive mode, 86
Kerberos authentication, 525–527

L

LANs (Local Area Networks), 100
  administration, 530
  devices belonging to administrative group, 200
  HSRP routers, 292
  standards, 54
  switches, 56
LANSurveyor, 21
LAPD (LAP on the D Channel) protocol, 81
large packets and collisions, 149
late collisions, 65
latency, 33
LCP (Link Control Protocol), 542
LCW (Link Code Word), 70
LDAP (Lightweight Directory Access Protocol), 525
LEAP (Lightweight Extensible Authentication
    Protocol), 105
learning state, 176, 185
leased lines, 539
Leave Group message, 280
line-of-sight microwave, 102
link-local address, 286
link partner, 70
link segments, 65
link-state routing protocols, 298, 300–301
Link Test Tool, 142
listening state, 176, 185
Little-Endian transmission, 77
LLC (Logical Link Control), 4, 12, 63, 110
  connectionless mode, 80
  frame formats, 80–83
LMI (Local Management Interface), 547
load balancing, 193, 224
load sharing, 193, 224–225
logarithmic calculations, 128–129
logarithms, 123, 124
  multiplying, 131–133
  subtracting, 129–130
logging global configuration command, 49
Longley-Rice model, 133
loopback frame, 90
looping frames, 186–187
loops in bridged networks, 162–165

loose source routing, 257
LSAs (Link State Advertisements), 301, 332
LSPs (Link State Packets), 428

M

MAC (Media Access Control) address table, 159
Macintosh
  as AFP server, 476
  AMP (Address Mapping Table), 448
  integrating in Windows networks, 526
  PRAM (Parameter RAM), 449
  unique addresses, 449–450
Macintosh Manager, 480
Macintosh networks
  Mac OS X, 476–479
  Mac OS X network management tools, 480
  transitions, 475–480
MAC (Media Access Control) layer, 21–22, 36,
    55, 76, 110
  assigning to VLANs, 205
  bridges, 159–160
  Cisco switches, 170
  CSMA/CD (Carrier Sense Multiple Access with
      Collision Detection), 63
  Ethernet, 63–74
  Gigabit Ethernet standard, 73–74
  Root Bridge, 196
  routers, 161
  wireless networks, 117–120
Mac OS X
  FTP server software, 477
  initialization traffic, 478–479
  ipfirewall, 477
  network management tools, 480
  personal firewall, 477
  remote login, 477
  SLP (Service Location Protocol), 478
  SSH (Secure Shell), 477
  UNIX, 476
  viruses, 477
  WebDAV (Web-based Distributed Authoring and
      Versioning), 478
  Web sharing, 476–477
Mac OS X Server, 480
MAILSLOT/BROWSE SMB, 522
Mailslot protocol, 522–523
Main Name, 495
management VLAN, 205
Manchester encoding, 59–60, 64
master base station, 102, 109
Master Browser, 489–490, 497–498
MAUs (Medium Attachment Units), 54
Maximum Age timer, 178
Maxwell's basic laws of electromagnetism, 101
MDF (Main Distribution Frame) switches, 162
media-type interface command, 58
Membership Query message, 280
Membership Report message, 280
Messenger Service Name, 495
Metcalfe, Robert M., 53–54
metric weights command, 92, 93, 320
MIB (Management Information Base), 34
Microsoft operating systems and trace-route
    facility, 41–42
Microsoft SQL Server, 349
MII (Medium-Independent Interface), 58
mirroring traffic, 24
mixing segments, 65

MLT-3 (Multiple-Level Transition-3) encoding, 60–63
mobile networking, 87
MoM (Managers of Managers) architectures, 34
monitor-port command, 25, 26
MST (Mono Spanning Tree), 213
MTU (Maximum Transmission Unit), 87, 246
MTU Discovery, 247
mtu interface configuration command, 87
multicast frames, 76–77, 96–98, 165
multicast routing protocols, 281–282
multihomed, 340
multipath transmission, 137–138
multiple routing protocols, 301–303
multiple VLAN port, 207
multiplexing, 347

N

Named Pipes SMB, 523
named SAP filters, 418
name lookup tool, 45
name scan tool, 45
narrowband radio transmission (radio LAN), 106
NAT (Network Address Translation), 12, 278–279, 366
native VLAN, 224
natural logarithms, 124
NAV (Network Allocation Vector), 118–119
NAX 2000 Web site, 5
NAX certification program, 4–5
NBMA (nonbroadcast Multiaccess) networks, 331
NBP (Name Binding Protocol), 443, 454–455
NBPBroadcastRequest unicast packets, 445
NCP (NetWare Core Protocol), 30, 399, 409–413
    packets, 409
    print services, 409, 411
    watchdog spoofing, 412–413
NCP (Network Control Protocol), 542
NDS (NetWare Directory Services), 401
negative gain, 124
Neighbor Solicitation message, 286–287
NetBEUI (NetBIOS Extended User Interface),
        237, 491, 508
    data exchange, 504–506
    LLC Type 2 frame format, 81–82
    NetBIOS name resolution, 509
    Response Correlator, 515
    Transmit Correlator, 515
NetBIOS (Network Basic Input/Output
        System), 401, 491, 508
    API (Application Programming Interface), 493
    as basis of Windows networking, 491–518
    BDC (Backup Domain Controller), 496
    consistency across implementations, 494
    data movement, 513–518
    Domain Master Browser, 496
    Forwarding Name, 495–496
    function calls, 491–492
    history of, 491
    implementation differences, 499–507
    IPX NetBIOS, 506–507, 509
    Local Session Number, 498
    Main Name, 495
    Master Browser for broadcast domain, 497–498
    Messenger Service Name, 495
    name management mechanisms, 508–513
    naming conventions, 494–498
    Net DDE (Network Dynamic Data Exchange), 497
    PDC (Primary Domain Controller), 496
    Potential Browsers, 496–497
    Qualifier Byte, 494–498
    RAS (Remote Access Service), 496
    Redirector Name, 495
    reliable data transport, 515–518
    Remote Session Number, 498
    Server Service, 497
    Session Setup request, 501–502
    Subnet Master Browser, 496
    successful name registration, 512
    TCP, 500–501, 502–504, 510–512, 514–515
    troubleshooting naming problems, 512–513
    UDP, 500–501
    unique device identities, 493
NetBIOS emulator, 508
NetBoot, 480
Net DDE (Network Dynamic Data Exchange), 497
NetInfo, 480
NetPort print server, 411
NetPredictor, 35
NetSense, 4, 24
netstat command, 45
netViz, 20
NetWare print server, 411
NetWare protocol stack, 400
NetWare servers, 402
Network layer, 11
network maps, 18–19
    statistical monitoring, 33
    storing, 20
Network Neighborhood icon, 489
Network Statistics window, 35
network utilization, 92–93, 145, 146
NEXT (Near-End Crosstalk), 36
NFS (Network File System), 30, 240
NIC (Network Interface Card), 58, 401
    data link layer address, 268
    managing, 142
    promiscuous mode, 23
Nimbda worms, 341
NLPs (Normal Link Pulses), 70
NLSP (NetWare Link Services Protocol), 301, 401
    adjacency database, 428
    commands, 439
    default route, 421
    Hello packet, 428–429
    link-state database, 428, 439
    LSPs (Link-State Packets), 428
    neighbors and states, 439
    pseudonodes, 428
    routing areas, 428
No DHCP Servers Available error message, 189
No Domain Controllers Available error message, 189
noise, 36
non-Cisco routers and trace-route, 42
nonextended AppleTalk networks, 442
nonoverlapping channels, 114
non-seed routers, 451
North American Digital Hierarchy, 537–538
Notification timer, 180
novell-ether, 408
Novell IPX (Internetwork Packet Exchange), 37,
Novell NetWare, 3, 8, 54, 237
    concepts, 400–414
    GetNearestServer broadcast, 214
    IPX, 401
    IPX addressing, 401–403
    IPX packets, 403–409
    migration agent, 430

Novell NetWare *(continued)*
NLSP (NetWare Link Services Protocol), 401
NPC (NetWare Core Protocol), 409–412
RIP (Routing Information Protocol), 298, 401
SLP (Service Location Protocol), 375
SPX, 401
switch port startup delay, 189
watchdog spoofing, 412–413
Novell NetWare networks
IPX routing, 421–429
troubleshooting, 433–440
Novell raw frame format, 75, 406, 407, 408
nrt-VBR (Non-Realtime Variable Bit Rate), 561
NRZI (Non Return to Zero, Invert on One), 61
NSB70519—Failed to connect to a server. error message,
189
NSB83589—Failed to boot after 1 attempt. error
message, 189
NSB83619—Address resolution failed. error
message, 189
nslookup utility, 45
NSP (Network Services Protocol), 29
NSSAs (not-so-stubby areas), 331
null authentication, 115
NVRAM (Non-Volatile RAM), 449

O

Offer Message, 271
Okumura model, 133
omnidirectional antennas, 139
one-armed router, 215–216
one-level tagging, 88
one-way connectivity, 188
OpenAir, 109
Open System authentication, 115
Option Code byte, 254–259
Oracle TNS (Transparent Network Substrate)
protocol, 346
OSI (Open System Interconnection) model, 5, 10–12
AppleTalk, 446
associating network devices with layers, 11
layers, 10–11
modular protocol design, 12
protocols, 11
services offered by layers, 11
OSPF (Open Shortest Path First), 28, 91, 201,
245, 281, 296, 298, 301, 329–330
adjacencies, 332
analysis, 331–338
Area 0, 330
areas, 330
ASBRs (Autonomous System Boundary Routers), 331
BDR (Backup Designated Router), 332
broadcast networks, 331
building adjacency, 333–338
cost metric, 329–330
current router configuration, 338
DD Sequence Number, 335
dead interval, 332
distance-vector like behavior, 333
DR (Designated Router), 332
external routes, 338
general routing processes information, 339
information about adjacency, 340
information about neighbors, 339
IP precedence bits, 333
link-state database, 339
LSAs (Link State Acknowledgments), 338

LSAs (Link State Advertisements), 332
master/slave negotiation, 335
NBMA (nonbroadcast Multiaccess) networks, 331
neighbors, 331–332
network architectures, 330–331
NSSAs (not-so-stubby areas), 331
point-to-multipoint networks, 331
point-to-point networks, 331
Router ID, 334
stub networks, 331
totally stubby area, 331
troubleshooting, 338–340
virtual links, 331
ospf log-adjacency-changes command, 333
OTDRs (optical TDRs), 36
OUI (Organizationally Unique Identifier), 76
output-delay command, 306
output errors, 94
output power, 142
overrun error, 94

P

packets, 28
capturing, 23, 89
prioritizing, 244
timestamps, 23
packet-switching delay, 91
PAC (Proxy Auto Configuration) scripts, 379
PAgP (Port Aggregation Protocol), 185
PAN (Personal Area Network), 107–108
PAP (Password Authentication Protocol), 542
PAR (Positive Acknowledgment with
Retransmission), 27
passive FTP (File Transfer Protocol), 383
Passive Scanning Mode, 113
passphrase, 152
pass-through authentication, 521
pause frames, 72, 73
PCF (Point Coordination Function) Interframe
Space or PIFS, 117
PCS (Physical Coding Sublayer), 61
PDC (Primary Domain Controller), 496
PDUs (Protocol Data Units), 193
peer-to-peer traffic, 29–30
persistent connections, 377–378
personal file sharing, 455–459
phantom router, 292
PHBs (Per-Hop Behaviors), 246
PHY, 56–57
physical layer, 11
Ethernet, 56–63
PPP (Point-to-Point Protocol), 542
problems, 304
troubleshooting, 36–37
physical topologies, documenting, 19
piggyback ACK, 358
PIM (Protocol-Independent Multicast) protocol, 281
ping, 24, 37–41, 91, 304
AppleTalk, 482–483
IPX, 434–435
result codes, 40
ping command, 38, 434, 550
Ping-Pong protocol, 409
ping scan, 24, 37
pipelining, 378
PMAs (Physical-Medium Attachments), 54
PMD (Physical Medium Dependent) sublayer, 110
pods, 69

point-to-multipoint networks, 331
point-to-point networks, 331
poison reverse, 300, 315–318
POP (Post Office Protocol), 345, 393
POP3, 393, 395–396
port address translation, 279
portals, 102, 110
port block multicast command, 26
port block unicast command, 26
Portfast feature, 189–191
port monitor command, 25
port monitoring, 26–27
port numbers, 350
ports
    assigning to VLANs, 207–208
    belonging to VLANs, 209
    learning state, 185
    listening state, 185
    querying hosts, 45
    STP states, 176–177
    TCP (Transmission Control Protocol), 349
port scan, 24, 45, 46
port unreachable ICMP message, 41
Potential Browsers, 496–497, 523
PPP (Point-to-Point Protocol)
    CHAP (Challenge Handshake Authentication
        Protocol), 542–543
    Ethernet, 542
    PAP (Password Authentication Protocol), 542
    physical layer, 542
    troubleshooting, 543–544
PRAM (Parameter RAM), 449
preamble to frames, 62–63
preferred browser, 523
Presentation layer, 11
Pre-Test Study Guide and Test-Taking Instructions
    document, 5
principle of logarithmic subtraction, 129–130
print services, 409
priority queuing, 74
private IP addresses, 277–278
private port numbers, 349
proactive troubleshooting, 17
    documenting networks, 18–23
    protocol analysis, 23–26
    simulation and modeling, 35
    statistical monitoring, 32–35
    STP, 180–186
    understanding network traffic, 27–32
Probe Frames, 112, 113, 114
Probe Responses, 112, 113
problem-solving methods, 12
process layer, 368
process-switching, 49
promiscuous mode, 23, 95
propagation delay, 91, 95–96
protocol analyzers, 10, 23-26, 59
    channel scanning, 114
    corrupted frames, 95
    decoding IP header bits, 249
    detail view, 23
    Ethernet networks, 59
    Ethernet padding, 84
    examining frame sizes, 85
    FCS field, 84
    filters, 23
    full-duplex operations, 69
    hexadecimal (hex) view, 23

pause frame, 73
pods, 69
reporting of signal strength, 140–141
summary view, 23
switched networks, 24–26
taps, 69
timestamps, 23
trace file, 23
understanding network traffic, 27–32
VLANs (Virtual Local Area Networks), 202–203
WildPackets, 24
wireless networks, 105
protocol identifiers, 78–79, 83, 254
protocols
    client/server traffic, 30–31
    connectionless, 28
    connection-oriented, 28
    creative layering, 12
    distributed computing traffic, 32
    error correction, 27
    flow control, 27
    modular design, 12
    operation of, 10
    OSI (Open System Interconnection) model, 11
    PAR (Positive Acknowledgment with
        Retransmission), 27
    peer-to-peer traffic, 29–30
    reliable, 27, 28
    server-to-server traffic, 32
    terminal/host traffic, 28–29
    unreliable, 28
protocol-specific debug command, 49
Protocol Statistics window, 35
proxy ARP, 269–270, 290
proxy cache servers, 378–379
Prune messages, 281
pruning-eligible list, 229
PSN (Packet-Switched Network), 544–545
PT (Payload Type), 559
public IP addresses, 277
PVCs (Permanent Virtual Circuits), 545
PVST (per-VLAN Spanning Tree), 204, 213, 224–227

Q
queuing delay, 91

R
RARP (Reverse Address Resolution Protocol), 270
RAS (Remote Access Service), 496
RCONSOLE program, 400
reactive troubleshooting, 36–50, 186–191
real-world path loss, 138–139
receiver sensitivity, 143
receive window size, 27
record-route, 258–259
redirecting debug output, 49–50
Redirector Name, 495
redistribute command, 428
redistribute nlsp command, 423
redistribution, 301–302
redundant links, 193
reflection, 134
reflectometer, 36
refraction, 134
registered port numbers, 349, 350
REJ (Reject) error command, 82
reliable protocols, 27, 28, 545
remote devices, testing reachability, 37–41

remote loopback of request message, 381
remote monitoring
  Ethernet, 88–89
  SNMP (Simple Network Management Protocol), 34
rendezvous point, 282
Renesys Corporation Web site, 341
repeaters, 67
Request Message, 271, 272
request-response protocol, 409
resources advertising services, 414–420
Response packets, 34
response time, 33
retry packet count, 143–144
returned sequence number, 541
return paths, 42
reverse DNS (Domain Name System), 371
reverse hop count, 252–253
reversible half-ASCII, 499
RFCs (Request for Comments), 238
RF (radio frequency) signal, 31
  chipping code, 107
  engineering mathematics, 122–126
  logarithmic calculations, 128–129
  transmission, 100, 101, 103, 120–133
  transmission limitations, 136
RIP (Routing Information Protocol), 201, 281, 296, 401
  analysis, 306–309
  bandwidth utilization, 305
  default route, 421
  flush timer, 309
  holddown timer, 308, 310
  hop count, 296, 307
  interpacket gap, 306
  invalid timer, 309
  load sharing, 312
  poison reverse, 308
  request messages, 306
  response messages, 306
  RIPv1 (Version 1), 305
  RIPv2 (Version 2), 305
  routes learned through, 307
  routing table, 305
  timers, 309–310
  triggered updates, 308
  troubleshooting, 311–312
  update timer, 309
  Versions 1 and 2, 298
RIPE (Reseaux IP Europeens), 277
RIPv2, 310
RLQ (Root Link Query), 193
RLQ Response, 193
RMON (Remote Monitoring), 35, 85, 88–89
  probes, 18
RMON MIB, 34
rms (root mean square), 141
ROM BIOS, 491
Root Bridge, 169
  changing timers, 172
  cost of path to, 170
  deterministically selecting, 194–197
  electing, 172–174
  identity and location, 182
  MAC addresses, 196
  Message Age, 171
  priority, 197
  slow bridges, 197
Root Guard, 197

Root Ports, 166, 175
  electing, 174
  states, 177
Root Priority/ID field, 170
Routeing Architecture document, 239
route of last resort, 294, 421
route print command, 290
Router Advertisement messages, 286
router on a stick, 215
routers
  collision domain, 66
  debug commands supported by, 49
  DHCP, 273–276
  dropping packets, 363
  enabling bridging, 195
  helper addresses, 201
  hierarchy, 296
  ICMP destination unreachable messages, 41
  MAC address, 161
  multiple Ethernet interfaces, 214
  SAP tables, 414
  throughput, 252
Router Solicitation message, 287
route summarization, 20
Routing and Switching Qualification Exam, 4
routing loop, 300
routing protocols, 240, 289–344
routing table, 290–291
  displaying, 304
  distance-vector routing protocol, 298–299
  host-specific route, 291
  two default gateways, 291
RPC (Remote Procedure Call) with NFS
    (Network File System), 346
RPF (Reverse-Path Forwarding) mechanism, 281
RSSI (Receive Signal Strength Indicator), 140
RSSI_Max value, 141
RTMP (Routing Table Maintenance Protocol), 443
  bandwidth, 461
  hop count, 460
  path with lowest hop count, 463
  route redistribution, 466
RTMP packets, 460–461, 463
RTP (Reliable Transport Protocol), 320
RTS (Request to Send) packet, 119, 153
rt-VBR (Realtime Variable Bit Rate), 560–561
RUIP (Remote User Information Protocol) servers, 45
runt frames, 84, 86
runts error, 93

S
SABME (Set Asynchronous Balanced Mode
    Extended), 81–82, 554
SAM replication, 521
SAP (Service Advertising Protocol), 401, 443
  flash update, 414
  Get Nearest Server request, 419–420
  operations, 415
  service types, 416
SAP filters, 417–418
SAPI (Service Access Point Identifier), 554
SAP packets, 414–415
  information about, 439–440
  services, 417
SAP tables, 414
scanners, 36
scanning, 113
SDH (Synchronous Digital Hierarchy), 537–538

SDLC (Synchronous Data Link Control) protocol, 81
secondary addresses, 408
security
    AppleTalk networks, 477
    HSRP (Hot Standby Router Protocol), 293
    private network numbers, 277
    SAP filters, 417–418
    wireless networks, 105
seed router, 451
semipermanent ports, 349
serial interfaces, 90, 536
serialization delay, 91
server-based computing, 31
server ports, 349
servers, 8, 30
    locating by name, 375
    overloaded, 68
    SAP tables, 414
    transmissions between and from, 32
    wireless networks, 102
Server Service, 497
server-to-server traffic, 32
services
    advertising, 414–420
    distance to, 416
    IPX, 436
    SAP packets, 417
service timestamps debug command, 50
Session layer, 11
session-listening socket, 455
set logging level spantree 7 command, 184
set port channel mod_num/port_num off
    command, 190
set port host command, 190
Set Request packets, 34
set span command, 25
set spantree fwddelay command, 172
set spantree hello command, 171
set spantree maxage command, 171
set spantree portfast mod_num/port_num enable
    command, 190
set spantree priority command, 197
set spantree root macro, 197
set spantree root secondary macro, 197
set trunk command, 218
set trunk mod_num/port_num off command, 190
set udld enable command, 188
set vlan command, 206, 207, 208
set vtp domain command, 228
set vtp passwd command, 228
Shannon, Claude, 264–265
Shannon's Channel Capacity Theorem, 101, 136, 143, 145
Shared Key authentication, 115
show access-lists command, 292, 304
show appletalk arp command, 448
show appletalk commands, 46
show appletalk globals command, 484
show appletalk zone command, 451
show arp command, 268
show atm map command, 561–562
show atm traffic command, 561–562
show biga command, 187
show buffers command, 47
show cdp command, 23, 46
show cdp neighbors detail command, 22
show cgmp statistics command, 281
show commands, 45–48
show controllers bri command, 557

show debug command, 48
show dialer interface bri number command, 557
show environment command, 48
show frame-relay lmi command, 548
show frame-relay map command, 549
show frame-relay pvc command, 549
show igmp statistics switch command, 281
show inband command, 187
show interface atm command, 536, 561–562
show interface bri number 1 2 command, 557
show interface bri number command, 556
show interface command, 48, 72, 187, 210,
    220, 292, 304, 363
show interface ethernet command, 46, 89–95
show interface serial command, 536, 537
show ip bgp command, 343
show ip bgp flap-statistics command, 343
show ip bgp neighbors command, 343
show ip bgp summary command, 343
show ip eigrp neighbor command, 319
show ip eigrp neighbors command, 327
show ip eigrp topology, 327–328
show ip eigrp topology all-links command, 320, 327
show ip eigrp traffic command, 327
show ip igmp group command, 281
show ip igmp interface command, 281
show ip interface brief command, 215
show ip interface command, 292, 304
show ip nat statistics command, 279
show ip nat translations command, 279
show ip ospf command, 339
show ip ospf database command, 332, 339
show ip ospf interface command, 340
show ip ospf neighbor command, 331, 339
show ip pim neighbor command, 282
show ip protocols command, 304
show ip rip database command, 311
show ip route command, 215, 294, 304, 305, 307,
    309, 311, 315, 318, 320, 327, 332, 339
show ip route connected command, 311
show ip route igrp command, 318
show ip route rip command, 311
show ip route summary command, 304, 311, 318
show ip traffic command, 304
show ipx commands, 46
show ipx eigrp interfaces command, 438
show ipx eigrp neighbors command, 438
show ipx eigrp topology command, 439
show ipx interface command, 436–437
show ipx nlsp database command, 439
show ipx nlsp neighbors command, 439
show ipx route command, 435–436
show ipx servers command, 436
show ipx traffic command, 409, 437–438
show isdn status command, 556, 557
show logging command, 50
show mac aging-time command, 184
show mac command, 187
show port capabilities command, 212
show port channel command, 190
show port command, 72, 89, 220
show port monitor command, 26
show port spantree command, 190
show processes command, 47, 326
show processes cpu command, 87, 187, 248
show protocols command, 48
show running-conf command, 304
show running-config command, 47, 191, 318, 338
show span command, 182

show spantree active command, 182
show spantree command, 182–183
show spantree summary command, 182
show stand by command, 292
show startup-config command, 47
show tech-support command, 48
show time command, 184
show trunk command, 191
show udld command, 188
show version command, 47
show vlan command, 208
show vlan-membership command, 209
show vtp command, 232
show vtp counters command, 232–234
show vtp status command, 234–235
SIFS (Short Interframe Space), 117
signal encoding
    Ethernet, 59–62
    Manchester encoding, 59–60
    MLT-3 (Multiple-Level Transition-3) encoding, 60–63
signal loss, 124, 131–133
signals, 56
    absorption, 134
    attenuation, 130
    diffraction, 134
    environmental noise, 143–146
    inverse-square law of signal propagation, 131
    real-world path loss, 138–139
    reflection, 134
    refraction, 134
    reporting strength, 140–141
    strength, 140–141, 145–146
signal-to-noise ratio, 136
simulation and modeling software, 35
single-tagging, 88
site survey, 130
    antenna positioning for maximum coverage, 139
    channel power assessment, 135–136
    Gaussian noise, 137
    multipath transmission, 137–138
    real-world path loss, 138–139
    RF signal transmission limitations, 136
    Shannon's Channel Capacity Theorem, 136
    signal strength, 140–141
    techniques for WLAN troubleshooting, 146–148
    troubleshooting, 134–141
    validation phase, 148–152
Site Survey Tool, 142
size distribution, 33
Size Statistics window, 35
SLARP (Serial Line Address Resolution Protocol), 539–540
sleeptime, 312
slot time, 64, 65
slow start algorithm, 359
SLP (Service Location Protocol), 345, 375–376, 417, 442, 478
SMB (Server Message Block), 30
SMTP (Simple Mail Transfer Protocol), 240, 345, 392–393
    analysis, 393–395
    replies, 394–395
SNA (Systems Network Architecture), 12, 37, 296
    gateways, 399
    LLC Type 2 frame format, 81–82
    TCP ports, 349
SNAP (Subnetwork Access Protocol) frame format, 54, 75, 82–83, 407

sna ping command, 38
Snell's Law, 133
SNMP (Simple Network Management Protocol), 18, 34–35, 240, 346, 366
sockets, 442, 452
soft-seed routers, 451
software firewall, 45
solicited-node multicast group, 287
source-route bridging, 256, 284
source routing, 256, 284
source station, 256
SPAN (Switched Port Analyzer), 182
spanning tree, 165–166, 224
    bridge ports, 166
    enforcing topology, 197
    information, 182
    logical topology, 182
    optimizing implementations, 192–197
    reconverging, 181
    redirecting traffic flow, 179–180
    selecting bridge ports for, 175
Spanning Tree Algorithm, 21, 276. *See also* STP (Spanning Tree Protocol)
spanning-tree portfast command, 191
SPAN (Switched Port Analyzer) port, 24
spantree-option 1 priority 10 command, 226
spantree-option 2 priority vlan 40 command, 226–227
spantree-option 2 priority vlan 50 command, 226
spantree start-forwarding command, 191
spantree-template 1 priority command, 197
spantree-template (forwarding-time) command, 172
spantree-template (hello-time) command, 171
spantree-template (max-age) command, 171
sparse-mode PIM, 282
SPF (Shortest-Path-First) algorithm, 332, 428
SPID (Service Profile Identifier), 556
split horizon rule, 414
SPX (Sequenced Packet Exchange), 400, 401
SPX keepalives, 413
SPX watchdog, 413
SQL (Structured Query Language), 346
SSAP (Source SAP), 80
star topology, 55
start-of-authority record, 45
stateless protocol, 378
statically assigned sockets, 452–453
static routing, 293–295, 302, 473–474
station cache, 159
statistical monitoring, 32–35
STP (Spanning Tree Protocol), 157, 158
    802.1Q, 213
    Backbone Fast, 192–193
    behaviors, 165–180, 186
    BPDU (Bridge Protocol Data Unit) messages, 166–172
    Bridge ID, 169
    bridging table timeout, 179–180
    changing timers, 172
    convergence, 172–180
    DEC version, 167
    designated ports election, 174–175
    IEEE version, 167
    improving convergence time, 192
    ISL, 213
    load sharing, 193
    logging events
        on Cisco routers, 185
        on Cisco switches, 184–185
    monitoring, 182–186

one-way connectivity, 188
optimizing implementations, 192–197
port states, 176–177
proactive troubleshooting, 180–186
reactive troubleshooting, 186–191
reducing startup delay on Cisco switch ports, 188–191
redundant trunks, 224
root bridge election, 172–174
root ports election, 174
selecting
    bridge ports for spanning tree, 175
    Root Bridge deterministically, 194–197
spanning trees, 165–166, 224
topology change process, 177–180
Uplink Fast, 192–193
STP (Shielded Twisted-Pair) cables, 36, 56
strict source routing, 257
stub networks, 331
stuck window, 362
subinterfaces, 214, 215, 408–409
subnet mask, 260, 261–264
Subnet Master Browser, 496, 523
subnetting, 261–264
subnetwork number, 200
subnetworks, delimiting, 204
subtracting logarithms, 129–130
summarization, 266
summary advertisement frame, 229
Summary LSAs, 333
supernetting, 265–268
Support Test, 3
SVCs (Switched Virtual Circuits), 545
swap till you drop, 9
switched networks
  blocked ports, 182
  dedicated access links, 210
  documenting, 21–22, 182
  physical topology, 182
  protocol analyzers, 24–26
switches, 8, 22, 56, 66, 157–158, 199
  802.1Q, 212
  backdoors between, 181
  CatOS command line interface, 25
  Cisco IOS command line interface, 25
  collisions, 66, 67–68
  DISL modes, 219
  displaying trunking technologies, 212
  FCS (Frame Check Sequence), 223
  flow control, 73
  identifying, 21
  interconnected in VLANs (Virtual Local
     Area Networks), 202
  ISL, 212
  MAC (Media Access Control) addresses, 21–22
  mapping Ethernet address to port, 115
  mirroring traffic, 24
  parallel forwarding, 56
  performance data, 89–95
  pinging, 38
  redundancy, 162–165
  running low on resources, 187
  sending configuration information, 22–23
  switching fabric, 56
  transparent mode, 228
  trunk links, 211
  uplink group, 192
  VLAN configuration, 229
  VLAN ID, 217
  VLAN tags, 88

switching fabric, 56
switchport mode access command, 191
symmetrical flow control, 73
syslog server, 50
systematic troubleshooting method, 9–17

T

TAC (Technical Assistance Center), 328
tag domain, 202
taps, 69
TCP (Transmission Control Protocol), 72, 78, 238, 240,
    346–347
  ACK comes back immediately and application reply
     delayed, 363
  ACK delayed long time, 363
  ACK is carried with application reply, 362
  analysis, 347–366
  checksum, 365–366
  Congestion window, 359
  connection establishment, 350–354
  connection termination, 364–365
  delayed acknowledgments (ACKs), 358
  demultiplexing, 347
  empty ACKs, 358
  FIN bit, 364
  flow control, 352–353, 354–356
  header, 347–348
  header-length field, 352–353
  identifying performance problems, 362–363
  initial sequence number, 352, 353
  listening on particular port, 349
  maximum segment size, 353, 354
  multiplexing, 347
  NetBIOS, 500–501, 502–504, 508, 509
  packets in conversation between PC and
    Web server, 358
  piggyback ACK, 358
  port numbers, 348–350, 351
  ports, 349
  private port numbers, 349
  pseudo header, 366
  registered port numbers, 349
  reliable delivery, 354–356
  segments, 347
  sender begins to approach receiver's capacity, 360
  sender does not approach receiver's capacity, 360
  sender overloads receiver's capacity, 360–361
  sequence numbers and lengths, 356
  sliding window, 360
  slow start algorithm, 359
  stuck window, 362
  three-way handshake, 341, 350–351, 354, 355
  well-known port numbers, 349
  window frozen, 362
  window size analysis, 359–362
  zero window, 361
  zero window at conversation start, 361
TCP/IP (Transmission Control Protocol/
    Internet Protocol), 3, 8
  history, 237–238
  upper-layer protocols, 345
TCP/IP protocol stack, 238–240
TCP port, testing access, 46
TDR (Time-Domain Reflectometer) function, 36
Technical Compendium, 101
Telnet, 29, 240, 346
Telnet TCP port probing, 46
terminal/host traffic, 28–29
test appletalk command, 483

testing-outward approach, 16
TFTP (Trivial File Transfer Protocol), 240, 480
Thayer School of Engineering at Dartmouth College, 13
thermal effect, 122
thin clients, 31
three-way handshake, 350–351, 355
throughput, 33
Ticket Granting Ticket, 526–527
timers active-time command, 326
timers basic update invalid holddown flush
    command, 310, 312
timestamps, 23, 50
token passing, 92
Token Ring networks, 12
    frames delay, 93
    interfaces, 90
    source-route bridging, 256
tools for physical layer troubleshooting, 36–37
topology, 165
topology change acknowledgment flag, 169, 180
topology change flag, 168, 169
topology change notification BPDU (Bridge Protocol
    Data Unit), 166, 169
totally stubby area, 331
TPID (Tag Protocol Identifier), 88
trace command, 42
trace file, 23
trace ipx [destination] command, 435
trace result codes, 42
trace-route, 24, 41–44, 91, 253, 259, 304
    hiding internal hops, 42
    IPX, 434–435
    non-Cisco routers, 42
    round-trip time to destination, 41
    round-trip time to routers, 41
    unreliable results, 42, 44
traffic
    back-to-back client/server, 29–30
    client/server, 30–31
    distributed computing, 32
    peer-to-peer, 29–30
    server-to-server, 32
    terminal/host, 28–29
    trace file, 27
    understanding, 27–32
traffic-monitoring capabilities, 36
transceivers, 54
transferring files, 381–392
transparent bridges, 158–165
Transport layer, 11, 345, 346
Trap packets, 34
tree topology, 165
triggered updates, 300, 315–318
Trojan horse, 32
troubleshooting, 9, 17–36
    above Physical layer, 37–44
    active and reactive, 36–50
    AppleTalk, 480–486
    ATM (Asynchronous Transfer Mode), 561–562
    Cisco method, 14–17
    commands, 45–50
    default routes, 294–295
    DHCP, 276–277
    divide-and-conquer approach, 16
    EIGRP (Enhanced Interior Gateway Routing
        Protocol), 327–329
    Ethernet frame sizes, 85
    Frame Relay, 547–550

fundamental network considerations, 13–14
generic problem-solving models, 12–14
HDLC (High-Level Data Link Control), 540–541
host routing, 292–293
IGRP (Interior Gateway Routing Protocol), 318
IP routing, 303–304
IP source routing, 258
IPX, 433–440
ISDN BRI problems, 556–557
matching host or domain name to IP address, 45
NAT (Network Address Translation), 279
NetBIOS naming problems, 512–513
OSI (Open System Interconnection) Reference
    Model, 10–12
OSPF (Open Shortest Path First), 338–340
Physical layer, 36–37
PPP (Point-to-Point Protocol), 543–544
reliable, connection-oriented protocols, 28
RIP (Routing Information Protocol), 311–312
site survey, 134–141, 146–148
static routing, 294–295
systematic method of, 9–17
VTP, 227–235
WANS, 534, 536–537
wireless network design problems, 148–152
Troubleshooting Networks Web site, 6
trunk, 202
trunk command, 218
trunk links, 202, 211
Truth Table, 262
TSF (Timing Synchronization Function), 112
TTL exceeded message, 253
TTL (Time-to-Live) function, 186
tunnel destination command, 466
tunneling, 87–88
tunnel mode aurp command, 466
tunnel source command, 466
twinax cables, 36
twisted pair cabling, 8, 55
two-level tagging, 88, 217

U

UAMs (User Authentication Methods), 455
UBR (Unspecified Bit Rate), 561
UDLD (Unidirectional Link Detection) protocol, 188
UDP (User Datagram Protocol), 78, 240, 366
    analysis, 367–368
    checksum, 367
    header, 367
    NetBIOS, 500–501
    port numbers, 368
    SNMP, 366
    WINS (Windows Internet Name Service)
        query, 500–501
undebug all command, 49
underruns error, 94
unicast frames, 76, 163
UNIX
    IP trace-route packet, 41
    Mac OS X, 476
    nslookup utility, 45
unreliable protocols, 28, 366
update timer, 309
Uplink Fast, 192–193
URI (Uniform Resource Identifier), 379
URL (Uniform Resource Locator), 377, 379
utilization, 33, 92–93
UTP (Unshielded Twisted-Pair) cables, 36, 56

V

VCI (Virtual Channel Identifier), 558, 559
vector dot, 101
vectors, 298
vendor specifications for wireless networks, 141–143
VINES (Virtual Integrated Network Service), 37
virtual carrier sense, 119
virtual links, 331
virtual router, 292
viruses, 32, 477
Visio Enterprise Network Tools, 20
Visionael products, 20–21
VLAN ID (identifier), 202, 204, 217, 222–223
vlan-membership command, 207, 208
vlan-membership server ip-address command, 205
vlan router command, 217
VLANs (Virtual Local Area Networks), 3, 177, 199
 access links, 210
 assigning
   ports, 207–208
   VTP domain, 205–206
 assigning MAC addresses, 205
 broadcast behavior, 204
 communications, 200
 complications from, 200
 configuring, 204–210
 creation of, 206–207
 delimiting subnetworks, 213
 design of, 201–202
 device limits, 204
 frameworks, 199–204
 implementing, 205
 ISL (Inter-Switch Link), 217–222
 memberships, 204
 names, 204, 206
 network documentation, 21
 one-armed router, 215–216
 packet counts, 217
 ports belonging to, 209
 protocol analysis, 202–203
 pruning-eligible list, 229
 removing from trunks, 212
 stability, 204
 switch port configuration, 205
 tagging, 88
 verifying configuration, 208–210
VLAN tag, 202, 216, 222
VLAN trunks, 190, 191, 210–212
 802.1Q, 212–213, 222–224
 ISL, 212–213
 removing VLANs, 212
 routers, 213–217
VLSM (Variable-Length Subnet Masking), 266, 297
VMPS (VLAN Membership Policy Server), 205
VoIP (Voice over Internet Protocol) application, 74
volt-ohm meters, 36
VPI (Virtual Path Identifier), 559
VRRP (Virtual Router Redundancy Protocol), 292
VTP (Virtual Trunk Protocol), 22
 analyzing, 228–235
 assigning domain, 205–206
 monitoring, 229–235
 server mode, 206, 227
 transparent mode, 206, 227
 troubleshooting, 227–235
VTP clients, 206
VTP domain name, 206, 221
VTP frames, 159, 230

vtp mode command, 206, 228
vtp name command, 206, 228
vtp password command, 228
VTP pruning, 228–229
VTP servers, 206, 221

W

WAN protocols, 531
WANs (Wide Area Networks), 3, 8
 administration, 530
 ATM (Asynchronous Transfer Mode), 557–562
 CEPT (Committee of European Postal and
   Telephone), 537–538
 components, 532–533
 concepts, 529–538
 CSU/DSU (Channel Service Unit/
   Digital Service Unit), 532–533
 DCE (Data Circuit-Terminating Equipment), 532
 DTE (Data Terminal Equipment), 532
 end-to-end considerations, 533–535
 FCS (Frame Check Sequence) field, 535
 Frame Relay, 544–550
 HDLC (High-Level Data Link Control), 539–541
 ISDN (Integrated Services Digital Network), 551–557
 leased lines, 539
 North American Digital Hierarchy, 537–538
 OSI reference model, 530
 PPP (Point-to-Point Protocol), 541–544
 provisioning capacity, 537–538
 reliability questions, 535
 retransmissions, 534–535
 SDH (Synchronous Digital Hierarchy), 537–538
 standards, 530–531
 technologies, 539–562
 troubleshooting, 534, 536–537
WAN Survival Guide (Berkowitz), 531
watchdog spoofing, 412–413
wavelength, 120–121
Web browsers, 379
WebDAV (Web-based Distributed Authoring and
   Versioning), 478
Web servers sending forms, 380
WebStats Analysis Module, 35
well-known port numbers, 349, 368
WEP (Wired Equivalent Privacy), 105, 152
whois, 24, 45
whois.internic.net server, 45
Who's There? Firewall Advisor, 477
WildPackets
 protocol analyzers, 24
 statistical tools, 35
WildPackets, Inc. Web site, 101
WildPackets Academy, 4–5
Windows 2000 model, 525–527
Windows 2000 with Terminal Services, 31
Windows networking, 3
 Browse process, 489–490
 Browse protocol, 522–525
 browsing with multiple protocols, 524–525
 concepts, 489–490
 domains, 491
 integrating Macintoshes, 526
 IPC$ (Interprocess Communication Service), 520
 listing shared resources, 522–525
 MAILSLOT/BROWSE SMB, 522
 maintaining Browse list, 523–524
 Master Browser, 489–490
 NetBEUI (NetBIOS Extended User Interface), 491

Windows networking *(continued)*
  NetBIOS (Network Basic Input/Output System), 491
  SAM replication, 521
  switch port startup delay, 189
  Windows 2000 model, 525–527
  Workgroup model, 518–521
  workgroups, 491
Windows NT, registry parameters controlling
    replication, 522
Windows NT Terminal Server Edition, 31
WINS (Windows Internet Name Service), 443, 500–501,
    510–512
wireless clients, 31, 105
wireless networking, 100
  fundamentals, 102–103
  physical properties of electromagnetic wave
      propagation, 101
  technologies, 105–109
wireless networks, 99–101
  association, 105
  authentication, 105, 115, 152
  bad packets, 145–146
  Bluetooth, 106, 107–108
  clients, 102
  collisions, 145
  configuration settings, 151–152
  CTS/RTS (Clear to Send/Request to Send), 151
  data transfer capabilities, 142
  definition of, 103
  design challenges, 103–105
  DSSS (Direct Sequence Spread Spectrum), 106–107
  environmental noise, 143–146
  ESSID (Extended Service Set ID), 151
  FHSS (Frequency Hopping Spread Spectrum), 106
  HomeRF standard, 108–109
  interframe spacing, 117–118
  IP addresses, 151
  IR (infrared), 107
  large packets and collisions, 149
  MAC (Media Access Control), 117–120
  narrowband radio transmission (radio LAN), 106
  NAV (Network Allocation Vector), 118–119
  network utilization, 145, 146
  numerous simultaneous users and collisions, 149–150
  OpenAir, 109

  output power, 142
  PAN (Personal Area Network), 107–108
  passphrase, 152
  protocol analysis, 105
  receiver sensitivity, 143
  RF signal transmission, 103
  security, 105
  servers, 102
  signal strength, 145–146
  site survey, 121
  station initialization behavior, 112–117
  troubleshooting design problems, 148–152
  vendor specifications for, 141–143
  WEP (Wired Equivalent Privacy) key, 152
wire-mapping features, 36
WLANs (Wireless Local Area Networks), 99–101,
    109–112, 117
  RF (radio frequency) transmission, 120–133
  technical and engineering assumptions, 130
  troubleshooting site survey, 134–141, 146–148
  TSF (Timing Synchronization Function), 112
WLI (Wireless LAN Interoperability) Forum, 109
WM (Wireless Medium), 110
workgroups
  authentication, 518–521
  Windows networking, 491
worms, 341
WPAD (Web Proxy Auto-Discovery Protocol), 379

X
Xerox Corporation, 53–54
XNS (Xerox Network System), 37, 78, 305, 401
X Windows, 30

Y
Y2K problem, 8
yourseen number, 541

Z
ZIP (Zone Information Protocol), 464–465
Zone Information Table, 465
zone of authority, 369
zones, 443

CRIME

An Encyclopedia

Exercise yard at Newgate Prison, by Gustave Doré

OLIVER CYRIAX

CRIME

An Encyclopedia

ANDRE DEUTSCH

First published in 1993 by
André Deutsch Ltd
106 Great Russell Street
London WC1B 3LJ

ISBN 0 233 98821 1

CIP Data available from the British Library

Typeset by Jenny England, Woking, Surrey

Printed in Great Britain by
St Edmundsbury Press, Bury St Edmunds, Suffolk

For Holly and Jake
when they are a bit older

Contents

Introduction   ix
Acknowledgments   xi
Alphabetical entries A–Z   1
Select Bibliography   455
Index   459

Photographs

Hanratty, Alphon
Butch Cassidy and the Sundance Kid, George Joseph Smith, Donald Hume
Brink's, Bundy, Craig and Bentley
Dillinger, the electric chair, the gas chamber
Madame Fahmy, Elizabeth Short ('The Black Dahlia'), Ethel Le Neve
Dick Turpin, the Great Train Robbery, Bruce Reynolds
The Krays
Jim Garrison, Richard Bruno Hauptmann, Henry Lee Lucas

Susan Atkins, Joyce McKinney, Marilyn Monroe
Charles Manson, Kenneth Bianchi, Sirhan Sirhan
10 Rillington Place, Christie, Bywaters and Thompson
A.H. Fish, Al Capone, the St Valentine's Day Massacre
Brady, Hindley, the Moors
Michael Milken
Dutch Schultz, Dion O'Bannion, Eliot Ness
John Gotti, Joe Valachi, Alcatraz

All photographs courtesy of Hulton Deutsch

Introduction

On the walls of a shell-holed operating theatre in Mogadishu are scrawled the words 'It is better to light a single candle than rail against the dark', and it is in this spirit that the Encyclopedia of Crime was conceived. The historical sweep of criminal activity extends from the first syllable of recorded time, and its ramifications are without limit. We learn from the Book of Genesis that Cain murdered Abel and, with a liberal interpretation, almost anything can be classified as criminal: social injustice, religious bigotry, colonialism and war. Each day brings new reports of juvenile thuggery, car thefts, miscarriages of justice and husband-kills-wife.

But True Crime has an inverted hierarchy of its own, with the villains ranked in order of dishonour. For Britons, these household names include Crippen, Brady, Hindley, Nilsen and Christie; for Americans, Manson, Bundy, Dahmer, Gein, DeSalvo, Ramirez and Ng are numbered in the premier league. Russia's great contemporary contributor is Chikatilo; Germany's past master, Peter Kürten. Ranged behind them are a few hundred others, the select band of murderers or murder cases containing their nugget of forensic or historical significance.

Scores of these benchmark cases are covered, but not in isolation. The black heart of murder, that primadonna of crimes, beats within a tangled morass in part composed of forensic science, legal technicalities, the art of detection and the social mores of the time. Historically, motive was rarely ambiguous: in rough chronological order, men killed for food, shelter, territory, greed and emotional security. But the more recent phenomenon of sex and serial slayings represents a new compulsion, the practice of killing for fun, and from this dismal notion are suspended the related topics of cannibalism, sadism and torture.

In former times, men burned witches, animated at least in part by the fear that their spells sapped sexual potency. Today, sex murders are often triggered by accusations of impotence or actual impotence. Thus witchcraft, on the surface a subject more fit for the nursery bookshelf, harks back to ancient concepts of justice, the modern ones of sex discrimination, looks sideways to sex crimes, embraces the Salem trials, heralds the recent satanic ritual abuse cases, links up with the modern serial killers and sadists, and must be viewed in the light of false confessions and the claims of recalled memory.

The signposts point in every direction, and, in mapping out this book, I awarded entries to as many destinations as space permitted. Many roads led in unexpected directions through surprising landscapes, often twisted into unusual contours by the machinations of the criminal cartels. As Americans progressively discovered during the 1950s, iniquity is not the exclusive preserve of rugged individualists. It can be organised, whether by the Mafia, the Triads, the Colombian drug cartels or Britain's home-grown Kray twins. Here, too, the cornucopia of evil disgorges a rich, if fetid, harvest: the Mafia alone conjures up tales of Capone, Prohibition Chicago, the glory days of Murder Inc., the Apalachin summit, the Cosa Nostra's Sicilian roots, vendettas, J. Edgar Hoover and his G-men. All are featured, as are the great robberies and the more engaging antics of art forgers and conmen. In passing I have attempted to shed light on some of Crime's more pungent enigmas. How did America come to pass the legislation banning alcohol? What is the best way to crack a safe? How do lethal injections work? Does a head survive decapitation? What exactly is the law of rape? The story of opium?

And who invented hijacking? A gentleman named Yu, it turns out. He too has his place, under

Y, at someone else's expense. But True Crime is a broad church. There is more than enough to go round, and in this brief, digression-led volume, where every inclusion entailed a corresponding exclusion, a procession of cursory and unilluminating entries on well-thumbed criminal celebrities never seemed the way to proceed. Here, the famous rub shoulders with forgotten hoods from the third division. Sometimes familiar territory is skated over, making room for lesser-known landmarks or for a glimpse of some hackneyed underworld king in an off-guard moment; sometimes, major stories are divided into more manageable satellite entries and treated in detail; sometimes straightforward biographical narratives alternate with 'can-they-be-related?' batches marshalled under a single heading. My guiding intent was somehow to weave a representative patchwork, a tapestry of interconnected criminal endeavour, complete at least in parts.

For a subject so intimately bound up with death, True Crime is far from dead. Disclosures and new evidence continue to emerge on files which might reasonably be regarded as closed years ago. Quite apart from the hosts of current cases, like Mike Tyson, Anita Hill, Aileen Wuornos and Ivan the Terrible, still grinding their way through the mills of justice, the stories of Marilyn Monroe, Jack the Ripper, Craig and Bentley, Sir Jock 'Delves' Broughton, the Krays, Henry Lee Lucas, Kennedy and Browne, J. Edgar Hoover, and even Crippen, have benefited from the attentions of scholarship, with their original verdicts confirmed, trimmed or reversed by new research. These fables, where citizens are thrown into the limelight to become public property, are as much part of our collective memory as the wedding of Prince Charles or the assassination of President Kennedy, himself an entrant,

and are equally subject to reappraisal. Exhumations continue apace, diaries are discovered, memoirs published, letters and documentation released. Other mysteries await their first resolution, but here too I did not feel duty-bound to sit undecided on the fence.

The study of True Crime would yield few dividends were the precedence of villains graven in stone, or the investigative and judicial process disfigured by one besetting source of error. But every component in a case is open to question. Those of liberal disposition may assume that fabricated police evidence is a likely cause of injustice. This is so, but equally often, only devoted detective work beyond the call of duty ferreted out the killer. Confessions are beaten out of suspects, but even when freely given, may constitute no more than the vapourings of an attention-seeker – whereas, in other contexts, a full and open admission can carry overwhelming weight. Expert witnesses can make astonishing blunders or distort the facts, but they also blow cases wide open. In sum, famous villains may not deserve their reputations, and triumphant acquittals are perfectly consistent with guilt blacker than sin. In the intellectual backwater of crime, no particular qualification ensures immunity from error, and in these democratic circumstances, even at the risk of adding my own misapprehensions to the general heap of falsity, I have endeavoured wherever possible to point the way to a verdict.

But on one issue I have nothing to add: the Perfect Crime. The reader will search these pages in vain for a dedicated entry under P or C. Yet the Encyclopedia consists of nothing but examples of this genre laid end-to-end, and they all happened to someone else, preferably in another country, a long time ago.

Acknowledgments

Among the countless friends who provided support during the two years this volume was under compilation, David Nicholls should be singled out, first among equals, for his pithy reminder of the merits of keeping back-up diskettes; David Wilson, for repeatedly pointing out that, when something had been said once, there was little need to say it again; Simon Rae, for his unflagging support and encouragement; Patricia McClintock, for her profusion of apt and delicate artwork; Jenny England, for her flair in the face of adversity; Lizzie Owen, for persevering with the author photograph until one turned out presentable; Giles and Amanda de Margery, for one thing after another; and, for their various contributions, Anthony Berry, Julian and Charity Birch, Georgina Blomefield, George and James Brenan, Nicholas and Sarah Dent, Gian Douglas-Home, John Farmer, Anna, Jane and Pamela Foreman, Edward Littleton Fox, Jonathan Furber, Andrew Gatling, Joss Graham, Tahar Haddadi, Rupert and Helen Hardy, Richard Harvey, Rica Jones, David Keeling, Michael Merton, Francis Morris, Graham Morgan, Sophie Macpherson, Penny Moore, Sarah Nuttall, Shiela Parker and Penelope Rippon.

My grasp on the entrails of crime would never have been as firm without the kindness of Camille Wolff and Loretta Lay of Grey House Books, who took me under their wing, for months giving me the run of their library, their hospitality and their encyclopedic knowledge. Nor would the Encyclopedia have been either started or ended without the dual interventions of my editor, Laura Morris, who, having thought of the idea, told me when to start and, when she realised enough was enough, told me when to stop. I stand amazed at her forbearance, trust and culinary ability throughout, and, perhaps more important, at her finely tuned sense of revulsion which time and again helped weed out gratuitously unpalatable material.

And lastly, my very present help in time of trouble, Holly Nuttall, for her clear guidance, like a shining light.

A

A6 murder

On 4 April 1962 James Hanratty was executed for the murder of Michael Gregsten. On similar facts today, he would not be convicted. Thirty years ago, it seemed inconceivable that a Briton might hang for a crime he was tied to by almost no evidence; reviewing the case in 1964, the writer Charles Franklin observed that the English legal system was 'always thought by most people to be little short of perfect'.

Those days have gone forever, as have the traffic conditions which gave the murder its extended, dreamlike quality. For two hours on the night of 22 August 1961 Michael Gregsten and his lover Valerie Storie drove at gunpoint from Taplow, near Maidenhead, puttering almost alone through Slough and across the ghostly suburbs of northwest London before halting at the killing ground of Dead Man's Hill.

James Hanratty was convicted primarily on the identification evidence of Gregsten's companion and lover, Valerie Storie, who survived the ordeal. But only just. First Miss Storie was raped in the back seat of the Morris Minor while her lover lay dead in the front; she heard the blood falling out of his head. Then the killer shot her repeatedly at close range, paralysing her from the waist down for the rest of her life.

The incident started at dusk with a sharp tap on the car window. Gregsten wound it down to be confronted by a revolver. 'This is a hold-up,' announced an immaculately dressed stranger. 'I am a desperate man.' Then he climbed into the car. During the next six hours Miss Storie only saw her assailant once with any clarity, for a few seconds, caught in the headlights of a passing vehicle while they were face to face. At the first **identification** parade Miss Storie pulled the wrong man. At the second, she made each suspect say one sentence spoken by the killer: 'Be quiet, will you, I am thinking.' Like the murderer, James Hanratty said, 'Be quiet, will you, I am finking.'

This was not Hanratty's only connection with the killing, but there was little else. As a semi-retarded petty burglar from London, he had no motive for barging into Gregsten's car in a country cornfield at Dorney Reach thirty miles from home. Every contact leaves a trace, but despite spending six hours in the car, there was not a shred of forensic evidence: no fibres from Hanratty's clothes, no mud, no hair, no fingerprints – nothing. Hanratty volunteered to supply samples of everything and, as he expected, received the all clear. Moreover, Hanratty was a competent driver, unlike the murderer. Gregsten and Storie were obliged to show the intruder where the car lights were and how the gears worked.

More recently, it has emerged that Hanratty had a good alibi. This defence was a late entrant at the trial, where it collapsed, but only on a technicality. At first Hanratty could only remember spending the night in question 250 miles away in a bed-and-breakfast in Rhyl overlooking a railway line. This took time to find, and his landlady's credibility was damaged when, in contravention of procedural rules, she spoke to another witness. By then it was too late to dig up further corroboration. But between 1966 and 1971, after Hanratty had gone to the gallows, fourteen witnesses came forward to support, in various ways, the story of his two nights in Rhyl.

Hanratty became enmeshed in the police investigation because on 11 September two .38 cartridge cases from the fatal gun were found in Room 24 of the Vienna Hotel, where he stayed the night before the murder under a false name, as James Ryan. The highly suspicious guest there *after* the murder (when the bullets were discharged, leaving the casings) was probably the actual killer. Peter Louis Alphon, who pronounces 'th' as 'f' when excited, went missing on the night of the murder, gave the police a false alibi and spent the five days after the killing locked in a room at the Alexandra Court Hotel in a highly disturbed state, refusing to come out, talking to himself, pacing the room and rummaging noisily through his wardrobe. Alphon led a nomadic life selling almanacs door to door and was something of a misfit – a mystic and a fascist who has ever since maintained his guilt to whoever will listen, not only claiming that he was paid £5,000 to put the fear of God into Valerie Storie, who was breaking up Gregsten's marriage, but also proving the money's receipt. He was seen in the Old Taplow Inn, where Gregsten and Miss Storie shared their last drink, on the night of the murder.

Alphon is still alive, an unemployed drifter at a cheap King's Cross hotel. He claims he obtained the gun, later found under the back seat of a 36A bus, through a criminal named Charles 'Dixie' France. But Alphon was the man Valerie Storie failed to recognise at the first identity parade on 24 September, conducted in hospital when scarcely off the danger list. After Alphon's release, the police settled on Hanratty.

Recently published documents show that Miss Storie harboured misgivings before the next parade. 'My memory of this man's face is fading,' she told detectives. 'I am so afraid that when confronted with the man, I may not be able to pick him out.' Second time round, she deliberated twenty minutes before picking Hanratty. 'Oh Mr Acott,' exclaimed Hanratty, without guile, 'I've never killed a man in my life.'

Additional circumstantial evidence against

Hanratty came from Charles France. But after helping secure the conviction, France committed suicide as the day of Hanratty's execution approached. France had befriended Hanratty, who took mild liberties with his wife, and it was probably France who told the police that 'Ryan' and Hanratty were the same man.

The cartridge cases from the Vienna Hotel came from the murder weapon, but it is difficult to believe that they were not planted. First noticed on 11 September, they reposed openly on a chair, which needed moving each time the bed was made, in a room regularly cleaned for nearly three weeks. Today, sixteen boxes of papers remain secret in Scotland Yard. The Crown wants to keep them locked up for a further seventy-five years, and the Yard continues to withhold exhibits which might resolve the issue by **genetic fingerprinting**.

From the condemned cell, Hanratty wrote to his parents: 'Dear Mum and Dad, Though I will never see you again, I will know in my own mind that as my love for you is very strong, your love for me will be just as strong. I promise you that I will face it like a man just the way you and Dad would want it, and I hope this will open the eyes of many people. And what I have said before, will one day be proved to the world. So Mum and Dad until we meet again, you will always be in my thoughts. From your ever loving son, Jim.'

After watching him hang, David Lines the Under Sheriff noticed how very distressing it was to return to the vacant cell and see Hanratty's pyjamas and half-empty cup of tea, still there.

See also **Concentration**

Accidents

Loosely speaking, murder means killing the victim deliberately. Legal problems can arise when you intend to despatch A, but do away with B by mistake.

In 1907, an English case came to court involving a landlord, Richard Beck, who drank himself to death along with his wife Hilda. The couple took a swig from a bottle of stout spiked with prussic acid, left invitingly open in their rooming house by a crook named Richard Brinkley.

Brinkley, a cabinet-maker, had actually wanted to poison their lodger, Reginald Parker, whom he

THE CROYDON SENSATION.—MRS. BLUME'S BODY EXHUMED.

was meeting for a drink under the pretext of buying his bulldog. But Parker was more concerned to do business. Five pounds were at stake, and they slipped out to examine the animal without starting on the bottle. Meanwhile the Becks returned, feeling thirsty.

In court, the defence pleaded not guilty to murdering the Becks, arguing that Brinkley had no intention of killing them. But he had meant to kill someone, albeit someone else, and the prosecution triumphed through the principle of 'transference of malice aforethought'. Brinkley went to the gallows.

Today, Brinkley would be guilty of Parker's attempted murder; he tried, but failed. Nor was the death of the Becks (where he succeeded but did not try) mere manslaughter. To prove murder simply entails matching the outcome (death) to an intent to take life, and the fact that Brinkley wanted to silence someone else ranked as no more than a personal misfortune. No one else would do since Parker's testimony (if he lived) threatened Brinkley's exposure as a fraud.

Brinkley had recently persuaded Parker to witness the will of a 77-year-old widow, Johanna Blume from Fulham, with whom he was on friendly terms. Thinking to put her name down for a holiday excursion to the seaside, Blume signed away her property, and when she died two days later on 19 December 1906 Brinkley claimed her entire estate. The relatives contested the will, and disaster loomed – unless Parker could be silenced.

On learning of the Becks' deaths, Brinkley's first words to the police were, 'Well, I'll be buggered.' His next sentence was no better considered: 'If any-

one says I bought beer they have got to prove it.' But no one, so far, had. Brinkley's past career suggested that Johanna Blume's timely demise – diagnosed as cerebral haemorrhage – was no coincidence. Fourteen years previously Brinkley's wife, Laura Jane, had apparently committed suicide by poisoning herself. Thereafter Brinkley stored a chest of chemicals in his room and, on one occasion, amused himself by poisoning chickens. He made two other attempts on Parker's life, poisoning his whisky and tea. Parker, already a worried man, threw the first onto the fire and refused to touch the second.

Amidst mounting excitement the police had Johanna Blume exhumed, but the autopsy's results were unexpectedly negative. Apart from its distinctive odour, prussic acid leaves no marked signs on the organs visible to the naked eye, and theorists have posited a doctor with a defective sense of smell.

See also **Dummy**

Acid Bath Haigh (1909–49)

The confession and trial of John George Haigh in 1949 brightened the austerity of post-war Britain. It was probably the most publicised case of the century, with the *Daily Mirror* going a step too far with headlines like 'Vampire Killer'. The *Mirror*'s editor, Silvester Bolam, wound up in Brixton Prison serving three months for contempt of court.

The murderer, dapper John Haigh, made two serious mistakes. First, he was convinced that under English law the police needed a body in order to obtain a conviction. This is wrong (although it is true that the murderer must be charged with killing a particular individual). This first misconception of Haigh's encouraged his blithe confession: he believed that he had utterly destroyed the body by immersing it in a bath of sulphuric acid. This second notion was equally mistaken. His final victim – 69-year old Olive Durand-Deacon – had indeed turned into a puddle of nasty grey sludge, but enough solid evidence remained to piece together her identity.

Haigh felt so confident that on 20 February he dropped round to Chelsea police station with a friend of Mrs Durand-Deacon's to report his victim's disappearance. An astute woman desk sergeant distrusted his demeanour, and Haigh's record was checked, turning up three prison sentences, one for fraud and two for theft. On 26 February the police forced their way into Haigh's 'factory', a bare brick shed in Crawley with naked lightbulbs, a wooden workbench and a sign outside reading 'Hurstlea Products'. There the officers unearthed three carboys of concentrated sulphuric acid, rubber clothing, a revolver, and a dry cleaning receipt for Mrs Durand-Deacon's Persian lamb coat.

Under questioning Haigh came clean: 'If I told you the truth you wouldn't believe me... Mrs Durand-Deacon no longer exists! She has disappeared completely, and no trace of her can ever be found again... I have destroyed her with acid. You will find the sludge which remains in Leopold Road. Every trace has gone. How can you prove murder if there is no body?'

Given Haigh's detailed confession, the answer was 'without much difficulty' and he was hanged on 6 August 1949 after a one-day trial. His original two-and-a-half hour statement related how he enticed the crucially plump Mrs Durand-Deacon to his workshop to discuss plans for the manufacture of plastic fingernails. Then he shot her with his .38 Webley, squeezed her body into a forty-gallon drum and went out for tea at Ye Olde Ancient Priors Restaurant. After a poached egg on toast, he pumped sulphuric acid into the tank and, four days later, when he judged the decomposition complete, tipped Mrs Durand-Deacon away as fat into the workshop yard.

'Aha, gallstones!' pronounced an observant Professor Keith Simpson, the Home Office pathologist, standing in Mrs Deacon's residual sludge. The portly victim's gallstones were coated with an indigenous fatty substance that resisted the action of the acid, and the stones now lay amidst a liquescent smear some six feet by four permeating the earth to a depth of four inches. Professor Simpson had 475 pounds of the grease and muck dug up and, back at the lab, produced twenty-eight pounds of yellow animal fat, a total of three gallstones, eighteen bones and a set of dentures. The hip bone revealed that the victim was a woman, the fat suggested someone plump, the osteoarthritis indicated late adult age, and the teeth tied the remains unequivocally to Mrs Durand-Deacon.

Despite attempts to sham insanity by imbibing his urine whenever under observation, Haigh was convicted of murder after fifteen minutes consideration by the jury. Had he held his tongue for a few more weeks, it is unlikely that any evidence would have survived with the exception of the gallstones. But without finding the body from which they were missing, no one could have proved the stones belonged to Mrs Durand-Deacon.

Haigh had previously done away with the entire family McSwann as well as Archie and Rosalie Henderson, appropriating the property of these five victims for the then substantial total of £12,000 in five years. He drove the fifteen-stone Mrs Durand-Deacon to her rendezvous with death in his smart Alvis, but her killing – likewise for profit – netted a mere £100 in jewellery, with a possible £50 due from her coat. The inspiration for his method of body disposal came upon Haigh in a prison workshop, where he rehearsed on mice.

Before execution, Haigh basked in his new-found celebrity, confessing to three more fictitious murders, and professed to have relished drinking his victims' blood. As a child, he was nurtured on Bible stories, mostly those concerned with sacrifice. 'It isn't everybody who can create more sensation than a film star,' he reassured his parents in a letter from prison. 'Only Princess Margaret or Mr Churchill could command such interest.'

Much of the difficulty in putting London's **Kray** twins behind bars in the 1960s turned on the similar dearth of cadavers, which makes it harder to prove that anyone has died. Kray victim Frank 'the Mad **Axeman**' Mitchell just disappeared, and the twins got off. But **Jack the Hat**'s body vanished, and that charge stuck; there were sufficient witnesses. In Haigh's case, the body *was* found, but in a different shape and form as grease.

Acid doctor

Murders with acid are rare. The so-called 'acid doctor' was a solitary exception, a Californian who tortured his bride of five weeks to death to warn her against the perils of infidelity. As Dr Geza de Kaplany elucidated on his arrest: 'I wanted to take her beauty away. I wanted to put fear into her as a warning against adultery.' He did this on 28 August 1962 in the privacy of a San Jose honeymoon cottage at 1125 Ranchero Way, scorching out her eyes, breasts and genitals with acid, disfiguring 60 per cent of her body with third-degree burns.

His bride was a 25-year-old beauty queen, an ex-show girl and daughter of an Olympic fencing champion; he was a 36-year-old anaesthetist of noble Hungarian blood. Neighbours contacted the police because of the noise, and de Kaplany departed under escort, looking for all the world as though he were going to a dinner party. Inside the apartment was a note: 'If you want to live, 1. Do not shout. 2. Do what I tell you. 3. Or else you will die.'

The wife expired after thirty-three days, though nine specialists worked free of charge to save her; towards the end, her mother stayed at the bedside praying for death.

At the first day of the trial on 14 January 1963, the prosecutor showed de Kaplany a photograph of his dead wife, with the flesh rotting away from her bones. Her face, brownish-black, had a hard appearance, like overtanned leather. 'No, no, no,' de Kaplany screamed. 'What did you do to her?'

What did *who* do, the court wondered. That same day de Kaplany pleaded guilty; expert witnesses pronounced him a 'paranoid schizophrenic with catatonic features'. Then a Dr Russell Lee disclosed that de Kaplany himself was not the killer; the true culprit was his murderous alter ego, 'Pierre la Roche'. The accused suffered from a split personality, at that time the last word in psychiatry.

In the witness box, de Kaplany confirmed that he had attended the scene of the crime while 'Pierre' poured acid on his wife. Thereafter the trial became hard to follow. No longer clear who was under cross-examination, the defendant – split into two components – offered the court alternative versions of events. 'That evening,' de Kaplany testified, 'Pierre beat her, beat her, beat her. From that point I was vanishing and *I* was dragged and *I* was nowhere, except that I was still aware...'

After thirty-five days the jury found de Kaplany legally sane but medically insane. Sentenced to life, he served thirteen years, and was released in 1975 to follow his new **vocation** as a medical missionary in Taiwan. The parole board (the head of which subsequently resigned) had found him work as a fledgling heart specialist.

In 1991 Briton Cecil Jackson killed his wife in an acid bath. But this was by mistake. Jackson supposed that he had strangled her to death before dumping the body in a tank brimming with hydrochloric acid.

But Dassa Jackson was still alive. Two hours later, pensioners passing the garage thought they heard someone whimpering in pain. They prised open the lockup door to reveal Dassa sitting in a pool of fuming liquid, her clothes in tatters, with a vat-like container steaming in the background. She died in hospital.

See also **MPD**

Acquittals

Easy to obtain in Chicago during the Prohibition era. Most cases never reached court. In 1920 Al Capone first made news immediately after shaking hands with Joe Howard. 'Hi, Al,' said Joe, stretching out his hand in a crowded bar. Then Capone shot him dead; the next day the papers carried the mobster's photograph over the caption 'Tony (Scarface) Capone, also known as Al Brown, who killed Joe Howard by firing six shots into his body in the saloon of Heinie Jacobs at 2300 South Wabash Avenue, in a renewal of the beer war.' But with no further clues, the inquest jury affirmed that Howard was murdered with 'bullets fired from a revolver' by 'unknown white male persons'.

As the Twenties progressed, the gulf between Chicago law and enforcement assumed extraordinary proportions. On 5 May 1926 the authorities made front-page news with a formal statement: 'It has been established to the satisfaction of the State's Attorney's office and the detective bureau that Capone in person led the slayers of McSwiggin... It has also been found that Capone handled the machine-gun.' No further action was taken. After a few months Capone was officially exonerated and the charge (quite possibly ill-founded) withdrawn.

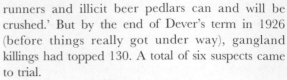

Securing a conviction proved even more fraught than bringing a case. The future leader of the Irish bootlegging contingent, smiling Dion **O'Bannion**, was apprehended by the police in 1921 on his knees with his tools embedded in the office safe of the Postal Telegraph Building. After distribution of an estimated $30,000 in bribes, the jury dismissed the evidence as inconclusive.

But at least there was a quorum; four years later, when the fearsome duo **Anselmi and Scalise** were arraigned, 234 out of the first 238 potential jurors declined to serve for urgent personal reasons.

Chicago witnesses were habitually intimidated, bribed, or just wilted from the face of the earth. The rare judge not on the take became extremely irritated. On 9 November 1926, a gloomy Judge Harry B. Miller commented on the acquittal of Saltis and Koncil in the teeth of the facts: 'I expected a different verdict on the evidence. I think the evidence warranted a verdict of guilty.'

Chicago's entrammeled reformist mayor, William E. Dever, inaugurated his career with ringing declarations: 'This guerrilla war between hijackers, rum

runners and illicit beer pedlars can and will be crushed.' But by the end of Dever's term in 1926 (before things really got under way), gangland killings had topped 130. A total of six suspects came to trial.

Five were discharged. The odd man out was unlucky Sam Vinci, but his fall from grace owed more to loss of self-control than poor planning. At the inquest into his brother's death, Vinci became uneasy that the killer, John Minnati, might avoid his just desserts. So he shot Minatti with his .45 in open court, earning a 25-year sentence. The evidence against him was simply too strong; but no stronger, one might think, than the amateur videotape of white policemen subjecting black motorist Rodney **King** to fifty-six truncheon blows in downtown Los Angles on 3 March 1991. Fear is not the only reason for a verdict of 'not guilty', and when the jury acquitted the lawmen at the first trial, Los Angeles was put to the torch.

Adipocere

A rough guide to the date of death for bodies left outside in the damp. Adipocere is a repellent yellowy-white substance engendered by the stiffening and swelling of a corpse's body fats; mostly, the limbs, chest wall and sometimes the face are affected. Once in place, adipocere maintains the outline body shape in recognisable condition and, three years after burial in 1949, the bodies of Beryl and Geraldine Evans, victims of the **Rillington Place** murders, were clearly identifiable.

In temperate conditions the conversion – also known as saponification – does not happen until some five or six weeks after death. But heat generated from, for instance, maggot infestation, can accelerate the transformation by a week or two.

Maggots adhere to a reasonably precise timetable. Flies cannot lay their eggs until the host body has cooled to about 30°C, a temperature only attained some six hours after death. Sensors in their feet direct them towards moist areas, like orifices, and the first batch of eggs hatches within eight to twenty-four hours, depending on meteorological conditions. The maggots glut on the body, favouring muscular tissues and eschewing fat, and, as they grow, evolve through three distinct stages, known as instars, in the course of ten to twelve days. Then the maggots, gorged on flesh, start to pupate, and the new generation of flies emerges from the pupa after a further twelve days.

These are minimum times, and hence the minimum period elapsed since the corpse's exposure can be computed, as can the maximum time since death: flies are attracted to smells and gases emanating from a fresh body, but after a couple of weeks they lose interest. The particular species infesting the body will show where it has lain.

Advertisements

In fiction, the cracksman John Clay advertised for a fallguy in Conan **Doyle**'s *The Red Headed League*. In real life Charles Henry Schwartz, a bogus Californian inventor, advertised for a murder victim. Schwartz had insured his own life for $185,000, and planned to fake his death. Needing a corpse of comparable physique, he specified that the preferred applicant for the post of chemist's assistant would possess small hands and feet. In the end Schwartz made do with an itinerant missionary, G. W. Barbe, three inches too tall, but death by burning causes appreciable shrinkage.

Schwartz killed Barbe with a blow to the head, extracted an upper right molar for a rough dental match, gouged out the eyes (which were the wrong colour) and burned off his victim's fingerprints with acid (see **Removal**).

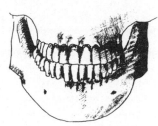

Then, on 25 July 1925, he blew up his laboratory, the Pacific Cellulose Plant in Walnut Creek, with the dead Barbe inside. A few days later, for good measure, Schwartz broke into his wife's house and stole all their photographs to further complicate identification.

The dead Barbe was horribly charred. But one of his **ears** survived in presentable condition and, perusing a studio negative of Schwartz obtained from nearby Oakland, the investigators realised that the cadaver's ear did not resemble the one in the picture. Thus Barbe's ear, with its distinct Darwinian tubercle, proved his murderer's undoing. The real Schwartz, by then hiding under an assumed name, gave himself away by categorically insisting to his new landlord, out of the blue, that the body in the local laboratory definitely belonged to Schwartz. The police were called, and surrounded the house; Schwartz committed suicide.

His invention consisted of an industrial process for the manufacture of artificial silk. But on investigation, not only were Schwartz's samples indistinguishable from the real thing; they *were* the real thing. Misgivings about his standing as an inventor initially took root because his laboratory was not connected to gas or water.

Other killers have touted for victims, including Belle **Gunness** of Indiana and Carl J. Folk, the American travelling carnival proprietor. But in these cases there was nothing ominous in the wording; Belle Gunness wanted rich suitors, and Folk, a domestic. German insurance fraudster Kurt Tetzner's quest for a corpse led him to advertise for a 'travelling companion', but in the event he killed a hitch-hiker picked up at random.

Aeroplanes

Used on 5 October 1949 by the murderer and racketeer Donald Hume to scatter the remains of his victim, a second-hand car dealer, over the Essex marshes. The corpse was first dismembered and the portions wrapped in three parcels, one of which was unwrapped a fortnight later by a farm labourer out wildfowling in his punt. He came across a sodden bundle on the mud flats.

The segments were reassembled in London by the pathologist Dr Francis Camps. Relying on his wartime experience of pilots whose parachutes had failed to open, Camps suggested that the body had been tipped out of an aircraft, and a police check on the United Services Flying Club at Elstree disclosed that a petty thief, Brian Donald Hume, had recently hired an Auster sports plane, arriving for the day encumbered by two large parcels.

Hume's first explanation was that three desperadoes – Mac, Greenie and The Boy – took him flying, compelling him to jettison what they swore were the wrapped components of an illicit printing press from a petrol coupon scheme. But the carpet in Hume's flat betrayed extensive bloodstaining.

Halfway through the Old Bailey trial the judge died. At the end of the second court case, the jury could not agree, and during the third, the murder charges were dropped when Hume pleaded guilty to the lesser charge of accessory to murder.

Released in 1958, Hume published his confession in the *Sunday Pictorial* on 1 June, changed his name to Brown, left for Switzerland, shot a man in a Zurich bank robbery on 30 January 1959, received a life sentence, went mad and was repatriated in manacles in April 1988 for hospitalisation. It is not generally known that at the newspaper party celebrating his conviction an effigy of his head was produced, stuffed with baked beans which spilled out onto its mount.

Other miscreants, intent on accomplishing limited objectives regardless of cost, have resorted to aircraft. In 1955 Jack Gilbert Graham, an American insurance fraudster, determined to murder his mother, Mrs Daisie King, for her $150,000 estate. After secreting twenty-six sticks of dynamite in her suitcase together with an activated timer, he managed to take out a last-minute $37,500 policy on her life before the scheduled flight took off from Denver airport on 1 November. All forty-four passengers lost their lives in the explosion.

Graham later admitted to being deeply resentful of his mother's decision to go away over Thanksgiving, and he was gassed at the Colorado State Penitentiary on 11 January 1957. The Canadian Marguerite Pitre was executed for a similar lack of restraint after a Quebec Airways DC3 exploded mid-air during a flight from Montreal to Seven Islands in September 1949. Twenty-three passengers and air-crew died as a result of a bomb in the forward luggage compartment. Pitre was arrested, widely remembered as the 'fat middle-aged woman' who arrived by taxi and demanded to have a parcel put on board just before take-off. Her aim, in which she succeeded, was to dispose of her lover's wife.

Aiello Brothers

Sicilian gangsters in Chicago who assumed the mantle of the Genna mob, exploiting illiterate immigrant peasants as scab labour and **poisoning** them with rotgut liquor. In 1926 the Aiellos

resolved to assassinate Al Capone, and formed a North Side coalition with Moran, Skidmore, Zuta and Bertsche.

The Aiellos broadcast an appeal for volunteers: 'Fifty thousand dollars to anyone who shows us a Capone notch.' Four men tried and four men died, their bodies each found with an unfired gun and a contemptuous nickel placed in their cold right hands. Capone knew someone was gunning for him, but not who, until the Aiellos's next ploy. The chef of the Little Italy Café, a favourite Capone haunt, was offered $10,000 to dose the great man's soup with prussic acid. But he took fright and blabbed.

The next attempt on Capone was inadvertently interrupted by Chief Detective O'Connor's armoured-car squad, which landed Joseph Aiello in jail for questioning about the machine-gun nest installed opposite Hinky Dink Kenna's tobacco shop (where Capone bought his cigars). That night, twenty-five men from the Capone mob besieged the police station angling for a go at Aiello.

'Gunmen defy police: invade law's stronghold' read the headlines the next morning. 'Chicago gun-fighters almost achieved the ultimate in assassination yesterday when they silently encircled the Detective Bureau and waited patiently for the opportunity to kill Joseph Aiello.' Three of Capone's henchmen had themselves arrested and penned in a cell next to Aiello. 'You're dead, friend, you're dead,' Louis Campagna hissed in Sicilian dialect across the bars.

But Joseph survived the night, and was released into hiding. Biding his time, in October 1930 he decided to make a run for it, bought a rail ticket for Texas and telephoned for a taxi to the station. Hurrying from his doorway, Joseph was caught in a crossfire by two machine-gunners who between them scored fifty-nine hits. The bullets in his body weighed a pound.

See also **Smokescreen**, **West Midlands Crime Squad**

Airgun

The intended weapon for the abortive 1917 assassination attempt on the British Prime Minister, Lloyd George. A group of Derby malcontents coallesced around a Mrs Wheeldon, her two daughters and her son-in-law, a chemist. Their watchword was 'Lloyd George must die' and to this end they resolved to shoot the premier with poisoned darts while he played golf at Walton Heath. For poison they chose curare, in regular tribal use in South America for coating arrowheads. It causes death by asphyxia after first paralysing the motor nerve endings of the spinal column.

There was nothing intrinsically wrong with the plan, but its execution was marred by the choice of the marksman, Herbert Booth, an anti-subversion agent from military intelligence. Mrs Wheeldon was sentenced to ten years hard labour, but Lloyd George regarded the affair as a joke and had her released early.

The case is notable for a unique prosecution collaboration between ballistics and poison experts.

Alcatraz, Birdman of

Robert Franklin Stroud (1887-1963) bears little resemblance to the saintly figure portrayed by Burt Lancaster in the 1961 film. Stroud started out as a pimp in Alaska, and when a bartender refused to pay the $10 due to his girl Kitty O'Brien, Stroud shot him dead.

Sentenced to twelve years in Leavenworth Penitentiary, Stroud was consistently unpopular as a tight-lipped, self-obsessed, predatory homosexual with fellow convicts, one of whom characterised him 'as attractive as a barracuda'. Towards the end of his term, for no known reason Stroud knifed a warder in the mess hall, saying afterwards, 'The guard took sick and died all of a sudden. He died of heart trouble. I guess you would call it a puncture of the heart.' After her laconic boy was sentenced to death, Stroud's mother secured a reprieve from President Woodrow Wilson on condition that he remained in solitary confinement. There he learned about birds, and died the best canary doctor in America.

Britain now has its Fishman of Saughton. The murderer Alex Torbet won an international repu-

tation for his expertise in breeding African tilapia. Stirling University's Institute of Aquaculture established a fish-room inside Saughton Prison, and Torbet demonstrated that the tilapia, with its rapid growth and high protein content, may have a role to play in the alleviation of Third World hunger.

Aliases

Also known as 'monikers'. A few mobster derivations include: Jacob 'Gurrah' Shapiro (for shouting 'Gurrah here'); Sam 'Teets' Battaglia ('I'll bust ya in da teets'); Vincent 'Mad Dog' Coll (shot down children in error during a gunfight); Jack 'Legs' Diamond (outpaced police); and Charles 'Lucky' Luciano (survived being hung by his thumbs and then left for dead with his throat cut). Abe 'Kid Twist' Reles's nickname came from his addiction to munching boxfuls of chocolate candy twists; Vito Gurino was known as 'Chicken Head' because he practised his aim by shooting their living heads off, and Frank Abbanando was always referred to as 'the Dasher' after being chased round the block by an intended victim when his gun misfired. Frank lapped his pursuer, reloaded, and nailed the man in the back of the head.

A false name often has some obvious connection with the criminal. Mme Bosch (executed 1910) gave her married name while making enquiries at the scene of the crime, and the American murderer William A. Dorr (executed 1914) sought to avoid detection under the alias Willis A. Dow.

Allorto and Sellier (d. 1889)

French criminals guillotined in front of an audience of sightseers in 1889, the year of the Paris Exhibition. Travel agents Thomas Cook included the double event in their list of scheduled attractions, laying on a special excursion of seven horse-drawn buses, each packed to its full capacity of forty seats.

The tourists were doubtless enjoined to listen attentively. The **guillotine** whipped off a condemned man's head with such despatch that, post-decapitation, his lungs still contained the air from his last breath. Thus the corpse was obliged to exhale and, lacking a windpipe, could be heard whistling through the neck.

This sound was noted by F. Tennyson Jesse, who attended the last public execution at Versailles in 1939, when buskers diverted the drunken crowds and spectators perched in trees. Jesse wrote: 'There came a last exclamation from Weidmann – and that was involuntary – the whistling that always sounds when a head is cut off. For the neck gives out a gasp as the last breath of air leaves the lungs, though the head be already in the basket.' For

many years previously it had been general practice to guillotine at dawn, well behind a police cordon.

The guillotine was finally abolished in 1981, when four prisoners awaited its embrace.

Amnesia

It is worth mastering the intricacies of amnesia before running it as a defence. In particular, a blow severe enough for a knock-out causes retrograde amnesia; the disturbance of the brain prevents the event from imprinting on the memory. There is a tiny time-lag between an event and its being stored, and if the system is down at the moment of the command 'save', the mind remains blank. Boxers

have no recollection of the blow that stuns them.

In South Africa, successful businessman Ronald Cohen did not know this. Thus his deposition of the struggle on the evening of 5 April 1970, when he tried to ward off the attacker of his beautiful young wife found dead, *Cluedo*-style, in the library, was marked by total recall of the impact on the back of his head from a hefty wedding present, a ram's head ornament weighing seven pounds. According to Cohen, the killer used it to knock him out.

This untoward 'island of memory' turned Cohen into the murder suspect. There had been no intruder and no fight. In prison serving a twelve-year sentence, the 41-year-old Cohen admitted to killing his wife, half his age, during a quarrel when he accused her of enjoying sexual relations with their children.

Genuine amnesia is a typical response of the perpetrator in domestic murders, often followed by a dissociative telephone call along the lines of 'There's a knife in my hand. I think my wife is dead. You'd better come quick and bring the police.' On interview the killer is likely to say, 'I don't know what happened', and this sincere memory block can persist for some time, occasionally indefinitely. In 1974 the Philadelphia psychologist in the **MacDonald** case cited an English study estimating that 60 per cent of the murderers in their survey were amnesic for the event. Likewise, the best efforts of John Reginald Christie, the British strangler, to furnish a detailed account of his killings leave the reader with the mysterious impression of women dropping dead for no apparent reason. 'She started struggling like anything and some of her clothing got torn. She then fell sort of limp as I had hold of her. She sank to the ground and I think some of her clothing must have got caught round her neck in the struggle. She was just out of the kitchen in the passageway. I tried to lift her up but couldn't. I then pulled her onto the kitchen on to a chair. I felt her pulse, but it wasn't beating.'

A form of 'false amnesia' is on the loose in America. This is the phenomenon of 'recovered memory' manifested in satanic **ritual abuse** cases, where those accused of murdering or raping children may shoulder guilt for repeated but forgotten transgressions committed over an extended period. Their accusers believe that their own recollections of the horrible incidents were similarly cloaked for years by a quirk of the unconscious mind, and these are thus unusual crimes, in that neither the victim nor the offender remembers their having happened, until seeing a therapist.

The most celebrated confessor, a puzzled Paul R. **Ingram** from Olympia, Washington, began his admissions to his daughters' accusations in 1988 with comments like, 'I can't see myself doing this', or 'There may be a dark side of me I don't know about', and peppered his ensuing statement with vague suggestions that he 'probably' did this, or 'would have' done that. After spending six months peering beyond his memory block into a visualisation of past misdemeanours, Ingram was induced to plead guilty to third-degree rape. Before sentencing, he realised that his amnesia was a false interpolation. He had never molested anyone. But it was too late to recant.

Prosecution witnesses, too, can undergo sudden attacks of forgetfulness. In 1973 Dr Keith Simpson, the Home Office pathologist, overheard an extreme regional variant while in Port of Spain for the trial of Michael X. In the neighbouring court Simpson listened to counsel for the prosecution asking the sole witness to a stabbing for her version of events. After a pause she replied: 'Ah done remember nutt'n. Coconut done fall on my head since, an ah' done know nutt'n.' The case collapsed.

See also **Memory**, **Rillington Place**

Ampere, one

Tests have shown that an electrical current of one ampere passing through the brain of the average human being will soon make him dead. This is the sort of throughput per second of a 100-watt bulb, but the high resistance of human body-tissue requires voltages in the order of 2,000. This figure must be revised upwards if the victim suffers from tuberculosis, as the lowered level of chlorine in his blood impairs his capacity to conduct. Similar allowances are called for in cold, dry weather, which makes for poor electrical contact.

A sustained electrical jolt raises the blood temperature to about 138 degrees, making restoration of life impossible, the more so as the nervous system is mangled beyond repair. If the scalp is sliced off after death, the dome of the skull underneath is revealed as completely desicated. Sawing off the top

section of the head confirms that the dura encasing the brain has lost its coloration, and when this covering is peeled away the grey matter readily discloses capillary haemorrhaging. In other words, the blood vessels at micro-levels have burst. Lifting out the brain shows that internal bleeding continues far down into its base at the level of the third and fourth ventricle, and beyond into the spinal cord.

It is said that the victim feels nothing. The theory runs that the electric current coursing into the head arrives at the brain faster than the nerves can relay the information that this sensation hurts. So the brain is paralysed before registering discomfort, and all the twitching and thrashing around in the chair is the muscle spasms of an already unconscious man.

See also **Electric chair**, **Kemmler**, **String**

Ananda VII, King of Siam (1921–45)

The death of the 21-year-old King of Siam in the Year of the Dog 2489 (i.e. 1946) precipitated one of the world's longest and more confusing criminal trials.

On the morning of 9 June the young king was discovered dead in his private suite in the Barompiman Palace by his page Nai Chit. The corpse lay bleeding from a head wound with a pistol close to its outstretched left hand. 'The King's shot himself,' Nai Chit cried, and thereafter wave upon wave of relatives and court functionaries, nannies, pages and politicians poured into the bedchamber, progressively obliterating the evidence. The weapon, an American .45 Colt automatic, was repeatedly handled and the body (which was divine) withheld from police examination.

The trial became a jamboree for conflicting theories. After the dust from a 1947 *coup d'état* had settled, proceedings started in August 1948. The prosecution called 124 witnesses, including fifteen doctors and scores of experts, none of whom thought to prove either that the bullet embedded in the mattress or the cartridge case on the floor originated from the gun by the King's side. The case unfolded on the basis of interminable woolly conjecture and disputed recollections; during the second year, two defence counsel were arrested for treason and another resigned. The surviving lawyer was called Fat Nasingkhla.

The court sat every other week for three days and not until the summer of 1950 did the defence have their say. In spring the following year the verdict was announced, whereupon the one convicted man – Nai Chit – appealed. This hearing occupied a further fifteen months and the judgment alone (which confirmed Chit's guilt and also condemned two accomplices previously acquitted) took fourteen hours to read.

Appeals to the Supreme Court were despatched in a rapid ten months, leading to the accuseds' execution after nearly six years in custody. Following the death of Dr Niyomsen, the pathologist on the first team of inquiry, his pupils had their lecturer displayed in a beautiful glass case, mounted as a skeleton at the Bangkok Medico-Legal Institute in token of their esteem. The fees of the one English participant, a very frustrated Professor Keith Simpson, were paid in cash, at night, counted out under a lamppost in London's Cromwell Road.

Apart from the king being right-handed, an early indication pointing to murder was that his body was found lying down on a bed. Suicides do not shoot themselves in this relaxed posture; they stand up or sit up.

The longest criminal trial in Britain ended on 6 February 1992 after eighteen months. The £9 million fraud case racked up £3 million in legal fees and involved 375 witnesses; computers helped the jury keep track. The principal defendant, Peter Kellard, was jailed for four years.

Animals

On the European Continent, animals featured regularly as criminals. Between 1120 and 1541 France held eighty trials conducted in the normal way with full legal formalities. The accused appeared in the dock, the Public Prosecutor brought the case, the Judge passed sentence, and the executioner killed it.

Sometimes the animals were dressed as people, and in 1386 a sow (condemned for murder) went to the gallows in human clothing. The Saint-Martin de Laon pig, convicted of infanticide in 1494, was sentenced to be 'hanged and strangled on a fork of wood', and the *Petite Chronique de Bâle* records a cross-dressing cockerel which gave birth to an egg. The deviant was burned alive in the market place, along with the egg. Buggered sheep, donkeys and pigs were frequently consigned to the same fate, and as late as 1581 the Nuremberg executioner, Franz Schmidt, recorded in his diary for 6 August, 'George Schörpff, a lecher, guilty of beastliness with four cows, two calves and a sheep, was beheaded for unnatural vice, and afterwards burnt, together with a cow.' Perhaps its three confederates could not be identified, for the concept of individual responsibility was strictly applied.

This principle was established by the brilliant young lawyer, Bartholomé Chassenée, who forged his reputation in 1510 with the case of the Autun rats, arguing that his clients could not be tried unless they were summoned individually. A transcript of a 1520 hearing shows Chassenée in fine fettle trying to save some woodworm threatened with excommunication after they devoured the Bishop of Besançon's throne in the church of Saint-Michel, a mischance which came to light when the seat collapsed under Bishop Hugo's weight on 21 April of that year. Hugo banged his head and went mad.

The woodworm were summoned on 12 August,

and on their behalf Chassenée proposed, first, that the court had no jurisdiction (since the defendants were *bestioles* and not people); second, that woodworm could not be tried *in absentia* and, say what the prosecution might about due legal process, no evidence was forthcoming that his clients had either acknowledged the summons or were in a position to travel to court; third, it could not be proved that the woodworm now in the church were the woodworm responsible for demolishing the throne; fourth, that – being woodworm and so framed by God – they were entitled to eat wood, even when inconveniently situated; and fifth, the remedy sought was inappropriate. *Bestioles* could not be excommunicated because, lacking immortal souls, they had never communicated.

In short, Chassenée behaved in the irritating way that pettifogging lawyers always have, splitting hairs. But the central plank of his submissions – that the defendants were not 'endowed with reason or volition' – shows the issue of personal responsibility already on the legal agenda: and *mutando mutandis* the same consideration was argued back and forth during Jeffrey **Dahmer**'s trial of 1992.

See also **Budgerigar, Pets**

Anselmi and Scalise (d. 1929)

A Chicago hit-man team known as the Homicide Squad. Of a noticeably gorilla-like appearance, John Scalise and Albert Anselmi had barrel-shaped torsos with short legs, dangling arms and scowling, rubbery faces. In 1925 the couple became the unlikely focus of a legal defence fund.

On 13 June 1925, accompanied by Mike Genna, the pair went looking for trouble with the Weiss gang, driving around Chicago's North Side hunting for their rivals. After a brief running gun battle, they committed a traffic offence on Western Avenue. 'Hoodlums,' cried Detective Michael J. Conway, 'let's get after them.'

The patrol car set off in hot pursuit, topping seventy miles an hour. At 59th Street a lorry crossed the gangsters' path; they skidded, mounted the pavement, felled a lamppost and juddered to a halt.

The police car came to rest a few feet distant. 'What's the idea?' demanded Detective Conway, getting out with his gun still in its holster. 'Why all the speed when we were giving you the gong?'

Hundreds of shoppers watched the mobsters respond with a fusillade from repeating shotguns, blowing away Conway's jaw and killing two of his colleagues. The gunmen fled, pursued on foot by the surviving detective, William Sweeney. In a basement shoot-out he fatally wounded Mike Genna, whose dying act was to kick a stretcher bearer in the face. Anselmi and Scalise were arrested soon after on a street-car.

'These men will go straight to the gallows,' announced State Attorney Crowe on the radio. But good Sicilians soon chipped in to the mobsters' $100,000 legal expense fund, and if not, they were shot. Four obstinate local tradesmen were murdered after jibbing when asked for their second or third contributions; one had already donated $10,000, two of the others $2,000 apiece. In retaliation, four 'collectors' were gunned down. Meanwhile the front of Detective Sweeney's house was removed by a bomb and, when the trial began on 5 October, 234 of the first 238 potential jurors declined to serve.

The defence opened with a succinct exposition of the law: 'If a police officer detains you, even for a moment, against your will, and you kill him, you are not guilty of murder... You may kill him in self-defence and the law cannot harm you.' Nonetheless Anselmi and Scalise were

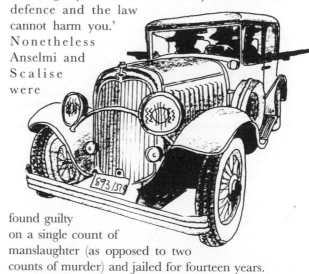

found guilty on a single count of manslaughter (as opposed to two counts of murder) and jailed for fourteen years.

This outrageous judgment was immediately appealed, and on 9 June 1927 the Illinois Supreme Court at last gave due weight to the case's previously neglected element of unwarranted aggression by the *police*. Anselmi and Scalise were released; in those days, virtually the entire apparatus of the state fell under Mob control.

Two years later, on 7 May 1929, the pair were invited as guests of honour to a Sicilian stag-party at Hammond across the state line. During the haze of goodwill and brotherhood over coffee and brandy, Anselmi and Scalise had their skulls beaten to a pulp with a sawn-off baseball bat. Then they were formally shot in the back. 'Scalise threw up his hand to cover his face,' concluded the coroner Dr Eli S. Jones, 'and a bullet cut off his little finger, crashing into his eye.' Their bodies were later dumped by Wolf Lake, Indiana. It had been rumoured that they were plotting against Capone himself.

Scalise and Anselmi were the hitmen who put an end to Dion **O'Bannion**, the troublesome Irish bootlegger. Paid $10,000 apiece in cash, they both received a $3,000 diamond ring, and Scalise sent his back to his Sicilian fiancée. In 1929 their bodies too were shipped home.

See also **Corruption, Pax Capone**

Anthropometry

An early method of identification system based on body measurements. Devised by the Frenchman Alphonse Bertillion in the 1880s, the technique was superseded by fingerprinting, not least because the French system was only of retrospective application. That is, villains hardly ever leave a detailed record of their measurements at the crime scene, so anthropometry's primary role lay in identifying habitual offenders, after arrest, when they re-presented under a new alias hoping to avoid their past records.

Bertillion, a bright but difficult child, was expelled from his Versailles boarding school for setting fire to his desk while trying to cook inside it. His father eventually landed him a clerical job in the Préfecture de Police in Paris, and there Bertillion noticed that the criminals' records portrayed them as little more than large, medium or small.

Bertillion recollected that the statistician Quetelet

– author of a tome called *Anthropométrie* – had observed that the chances against any two comparable people being exactly the same height were four to one. Bertillion reasoned that the odds could be lenthened to sixteen to one by taking two body measurements. By extension, the chance against two individuals having fourteen identical measurements, according to the generally quoted figure, worked out at 268,435,454 to one.

Thus was born anthropometry, the science of man-measurement. Bertillion set out to callibrate criminals by size. Using callipers, he perfected the art of measuring his subjects' bones, which, in adults, do not change. The five most important dimensions were the length and width of the skull, the length of the left forearm, the left foot (with the subject standing on one leg) and the left middle finger.

Bertillion's superiors at the Sureté distrusted his scheme; when Bertillion submitted his paper for the second time, the Préfect enquired if it was a joke. But in November 1882 he was granted a three month experimental run. With time running short, on 20 February 1883 Bertillion at last identified an apparent first offender, M. Dupont, as none other than the M. Martin he had tabulated some weeks previously after an arrest for stealing empty bottles, and by the year's close Bertillion recognised a further fifty recidivists.

Bertillion's system was adopted as standard by all French prison governors. Convicts were routinely measured and their particulars entered into an elaborate cross-referenced filing cabinet with eighty-one drawers. The French press greeted Bertillion's appointment as Director of the Police Identification Service with their customary restraint: 'Bertillionage is the greatest and most brilliant invention the nineteenth century has produced in the field of criminology. Thanks to a French genius, errors of identification will soon cease to exist, not only in France but also the entire world.'

Bertillion went on to categorise the standard face-shapes that would later form the basis of Identikit

ANTHROPOMETRIC LABORATORY

For the measurement in various ways of Human Form and Faculty.

Entered from the Science Collection of the S. Kensington Museum.

This laboratory is established by Mr. Francis Galton for the following purposes:—

1. For the use of those who desire to be accurately measured in many ways, either to obtain timely warning of remediable faults in development, or to learn their powers.

2. For keeping a methodical register of the principal measurements of each person, of which he may at any future time obtain a copy under reasonable restrictions. His initials and date of birth will be entered in the register, but not his name. The names are indexed in a separate book.

3. For supplying information on the methods, practice, and uses of human measurement.

4. For anthropometric experiment and research, and for obtaining data for statistical discussion.

Charges for making the principal measurements:
THREEPENCE each, to those who are already on the Register.
FOURPENCE each, to those who are not:— one page of the Register will thenceforward be assigned to them, and a few extra measurements will be made, chiefly for future identification.

The Superintendent is charged with the control of the laboratory and with determining in each case, which, if any, of the extra measurements may be made, and under what conditions.

H & W. Brown, Printers, 20 Fulham Road, S.W.

and, in 1892, triumphantly exposed the anarchist hero Ravachol as none other than the petty thief Koenigstein, wanted for grave-robbery as well as murdering a miser and killing two women shop-keepers by hammering them to death.

In Britain, the Troup Committee of 1893 recommended the establishment of the Anthropometric Registry, and Bertillionage spread throughout the world. But by the turn of the century only 18,000 British criminals had been sized, yielding a meagre 1,300 identifications.

Then in 1901 Albert Ebenezer Fox and his doppelgänger twin Ebenezer Albert Fox (who could not be told apart by Bertillionage) were differentiated by the rival **fingerprinting** system, which produced 1,722 identifications the following year. A year after, in Kansas, two blacks of identical dimensions provided further ammunition for Bertillion's detractors.

His later reputation was severely tarnished by his helping to send the innocent Dreyfus to Devil's Island. Worse, in 1913 he let the thief of the **Mona Lisa** slip through his fingers. By this stage Bertillion kept fingerprints on record but, with no classification system, his immense collection of 100,000 prints served to conceal those of the robber. Bertillion died in 1914. Although buried with national honours, his system survived him by only a few weeks. It was an idea whose time had passed.

Anti-tank mine

The murder weapon in the Eric Brown case, which anticipated the invention of the car bomb. On 23 July 1943 the teenage Eric Brown resolved to rid his family of their bullying father Archibald, an invalid. So he concealed the device – a Hawkins No. 75 Grenade Mine – under the seat of his father's wheelchair, which exploded while Nurse was taking her patient on their daily outing. She had just lit his last cigarette.

After the court heard how Eric wanted to bring some happiness into his mother's life, they found him guilty but mad.

Eric became a criminal because he exploded the mine; more recently, the Burmese army used mines to explode those already convicted. It was a new way of minesweeping: prisoners advanced ahead of the troops to see if they blew up. According to one survivor from the spring campaign of 1992, Maung Mhi Aung, some 6,000 convicts were drafted into hard labour as army porters. More than 800 were seized from Insein Prison alone, and over 300 human minesweepers died in the battle for Sleeping Dog Hill. Those merely wounded were left to bleed to death or shot out of hand.

See also **Payne**

Apalachin

Location of the Mob convention which led to America's accidental discovery of the **Mafia**. On 13 November 1957, Detective Sergeant Edgar Croswell was summoned to the Parkway Motel in rural Albany to investigate a bad cheque. Meanwhile a local kid, Joseph Barbara Jnr, swaggered into reception to block-book three double rooms for a soft drinks convention.

Croswell's curiosity was fired; he harboured suspicions about Joe's father, Joseph Barbara Snr, who ran the local bottling plant. A big spender living on a palatial estate with a small declared income, Jo Snr had pulled strings up to Governor level over a minor traffic violation the previous year.

Croswell decided to investigate, and walked over to the bottling factory. Everything was quiet, but four big limos were drawn up outside the nearby Barbara homestead. Later that night, the Motel rang Croswell. Their delegation of guests had arrived, looking very, very unsavoury: should they refuse admission? Book them in, Croswell advised, and by next morning a dozen burnished limos – Cadillacs, Chrysler Imperials and Lincolns – filled Barbara's drive, with a further twenty-five ranked in the field. Clearly, the well-heeled participants of this convention were no salesmen.

Croswell sneaked into the grounds and jotted down their registration numbers. Rounding the garage corner he ran into a group of delegates. They scattered; he too beat a retreat. On Joe's land he had no authority, but it was a different matter on the highway. Only three roads led from the

Barbara property, and two were impassable, the bridges down, flooded.

Croswell ran to his patrol car and set up a road-block before radioing for police support. Meanwhile, the local fish pedlar, Bartolo Guccia, drove up to warn about the police cars straddling the way out. By now the place was like a kicked-over ants' nest. About a dozen senior Mafiosi, in their silk tailored suits, lumbered across the fields to the woods where they were later rounded up, covered in burrs and brambles. The remainder crowded into their limousines and were duly stopped at the road block.

Croswell hauled off the nation's top hoods to the small Vestal police station and beckoned them one by one to his office for the mild questioning allowed by law – name, occupation and purpose of visit. Most said they were paying their respects to the ailing Joe Barbara Snr; many listed their professions as 'unemployed'; some were prospecting for real estate, others taking the country air. Between them, they carried $300,000 in cash.

But only one was wanted by the law, and this for a parole violation. None were packing guns. All gave their correct names. With no reason to hold them, they were freed in batches: nineteen mob leaders from upstate New York, twenty-three from New York City, eight from the Midwest, three from over the Rockies, two from the South, two from Cuba and one representative from Italy.

The law had done its utmost; now the press muscled in. If organised crime was a myth, how come sixty underworld figures gathered for an amicable convention? What were they planning? Importing narcotics? What was the FBI doing? What did J. Edgar **Hoover** have to say? An uneasy recollection surfaced about a shadowy organisation called the 'Mafia' – a fearsome secret brotherhood of criminals with its roots in Sicily (see **Inquisition**).

Thirty-four of the Apalachin gangsters within the New York jurisdiction were subpoenaed. The Watchdog Committee's sessions started on 12 December 1957; eleven hoods appeared. Most took the Fifth, with disdain. Jo Riccobono scarcely bothered to get the words right. He said: 'I refuse to answer on the grounds of not to testify against myself. Whether it means the same thing or whether it doesn't, I am not in a position to know.' Tony Maggadino pretended he could not under-

stand English and looked blank. John Montana explained that he gave hundreds of turkeys to the needy every Thanksgiving.

Highlights from the Committee's report were items 1 and 3: '1. The Apalachin meeting is strong evidence that there exists in this country an active association or organisation of criminals... 3. The incident reveals a serious defect in the state's law enforcement apparatus.' At last the secret was out.

See also **Head, Costello's**

Apologies, ritual

Many of the first wave of English **highwaymen** were former gentlemen ruined by the Civil War who failed to hit on any other socially acceptable way of earning a living.

Apologies for robbing their clients were *de rigueur*. In the words of a contemporary, 'They assure you they are very sorry that poverty has driven them to that shameful recourse, and end by demanding your purse in the most courteous manner', a trait accentuated when the victims were women. On 14 January 1797, the *Morning Chronicle* accorded favourable reviews to a 'very gallant highway robbery lately committed on Wimbledon Common on the person of a young lady'.

Behind the facade of chivalry, highwaymen were as given to brutal violence as any other rogue. But they had learned the part better. In his *Recantation*, Francis Jackson, a seventeenth-century practitioner, advised novices to hone up pretty speeches. He suggested: 'There must be a plausible account given, how you fell into this course of life, fetching a deep sigh, saying "That you were well born, but by reason of your Family falling to decay you were exposed to deep Want, and rather than shamefully beg (for you knew not how to labour), you were constrained to take this course as a Subsistence; that it is your first fault, which you are heartily sorry for, and will never attempt the like again."'

This dual-purpose speech went down almost equally well with victims and – subsequently – the judge. In the absence of fatalities, a highwayman might escape the gallows. Excessive technicalities of procedure served to attenuate the law's severity, and a successful defence, reminiscent of present-day Irish extradition proceedings, could be mounted round the misspelling of the defendant's name.

Juries too might take a lenient line, and for richer villains there was always the immunity granted by bribery. In Jackson's words: 'He can't be hanged who hath Five Hundred Pounds at his Command.' But not many had.

Arabin, William St Julian (c. 1775–1841)

British judge at the Old Bailey. According to his contemporaries, Arabin was short-sighted, deaf, eccentric and much given to 'enunciating absurdities with the most perfect innocence'.

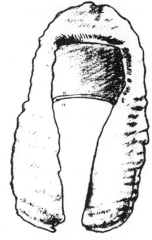

Not uncommonly, these attributes lost the accused their liberty or their lives. To a child, on sentencing him to transportation, Arabin said: 'When I first saw you, I knew you well. When you began to cry, I knew you still better. I'm tired of the sight of you. You must go out of the country.' On another occasion – *R* v. *Jarvis* 1832 – Arabin muddled the papers of two cases, one for stealing a watch, the other for stealing a handkerchief, provoking the following exchange:

Arabin Well, witness, your name is John Tomkins.
Witness My Lord, my name is Job Taylor.
Arabin Ah! I see you are a sailor, and you live in the New Cut.
Witness No, my Lord, I live at Wapping.
Arabin Never mind your being out shopping. Had you your watch in your pocket on the 10th of November?
Witness I never had but one ticker, my lord, and that has been at the pawn shop for the last six months.
Arabin Who asked you how long you had the watch? Why can't you say yes or no? Well, did you see the prisoner at the Bar?
Witness (a little confused) Yes, of course I did.
Arabin That's right, my man, speak up and answer shortly. Did the prisoner take your watch?
Witness (loudly) I don't know what you're driving at.

Arabin (after a pause, to an elderly barrister at counsel's table who had dined well) Mr Ryland, I wish you would take this witness in hand and see whether you can make anything of him, for I can't.
Ryland (after staring ferociously at the witness) My Lord, it is my profound belief that the man is drunk.
Arabin It's a remarkable coincidence, Mr Ryland. That is precisely the idea that has been in my mind for the last ten minutes.

Perhaps Arabin's most famous pronouncement came during the case of *R* v. *Chilston and Chandler* in 1832, when he concluded that, 'If ever there was a case of clearer evidence than this of persons acting together, this case is...that case.' After his stint at the Old Bailey, Arabin was elevated to Judge Advocate-General of the Army. His words were transcribed verbatim between 1830 and 1839 by an unofficial rota of ten barristers who believed his *dicta* should be commemorated for posterity.

See also **Trousers**

Arm, James Smith's

A rare example of a celebrity limb. On 25 April 1935 James Smith's arm was safely ensconced in a fourteen-foot tiger shark, itself recently confined to a public aquarium at Coogee Beach, Australia.

At five o'clock that afternoon, the shark regurgitated the contents of its stomach in front of a crowd who thus witnessed the emergence of the tattooed arm, entangled in a length of rope. Dr Coppleson, the local 'sharkologist', advised that the fish had been depressed since its capture and consequently off its food, thereby deferring its normal thirty-six-hour digestive cycle. The arm could have been consumed some days previously while the shark was at sea.

The limb's fingerprints were still intact, and it was soon identified as the property of a forger and petty thief, James Smith, last seen embarking on a fishing trip on 8 April. Basing his decision on an English precedent set in 1276 and ignored ever since, the coroner declined to hold an inquest in the absence of a body. But foul play was obvious since Smith's arm had been detached from the torso with a knife.

The case remains unsolved, although a petty criminal named Patrick Brady was charged. The principal evidence against him was a sworn statement signed by one Reg Holmes. But the court excluded his testimony, ruling it inadmissible because Holmes himself could not be called in cross-examination; he was murdered on 13 June, the day before the inquest. Brady spent over twenty years in prison for various other offences, and died in August 1965 still protesting his innocence. Sydney's then pivotal role in **opium** and heroin smuggling formed the background to the killing. Smith worked as a crewman on the motor launch *Pathfinder*, itself destroyed in an underworld spate of tit-for-tat hijackings, sinkings, tortures and murders. His boat disappeared under water, and so did he, very nearly.

Arsenic

A chemical in widespread use in the dyeing and paper industries and inexplicably popular with the modern poisoner.

Arsenic is hard to administer, almost indissoluble in cold water, which only holds about a half of a grain per ounce in suspension A hot beverage can mop up perhaps a hundred times as much, but on cooling nearly 80 per cent precipitates as a visible sediment, curdling any milk in the process; the poisoned cups of tea, coffee and cocoa beloved of fiction are unlikely instruments of doom. Moreover, the effect is unreliable. Although the smallest recorded fatal dose is two grains, Glaister's *Medical Jurisprudence* cites the abortive suicide attempt of a woman who, after ingesting 230 grains, felt no more than quite uncomfortable for three days.

Once suspected, arsenic is particularly easy to identify positively and its traces linger indefinitely in the fingernails, bones and so on. As **Napoleon**'s case exemplifies, a strand of hair – which grows at a uniform rate and likewise absorbs the poison uniformly – can provide a daily calendar of the intake.

On the upside, arsenic is all but tasteless, and readily available to the resourceful; in Victorian times, a fatal dose could be obtained by soaking a single fly-paper in water. The toxin has a cumulative effect, meaning that the victim need not be force-fed in one massive dose, and its incremental

results can be mistaken for the symptoms of many ordinary illnesses.

The long heyday of arsenic is attributable to the Arab alchemist Gber who, in the eighth century, distilled a tasteless and odourless white powder called arsenous oxide. For many centuries this afforded poisoners a clear run. The first test for the deadly substance was not developed until 1787 when Johann Metzger of Königsberg produced a deposit on copper plates suspended over the heated poison; and it was only in 1830 that James Marsh, an impoverished English chemist, devised a simple and reliable experiment on which a jury could base a conviction. His device converted arsenous residues in body tissues into arsine gas, which registered as a metallic sheen on a porcelain receptor. With refinement, a 300,000th of an ounce could be detected.

This exactitude led to the confusing finding of minute traces of this common element almost everywhere, including people. A normal, healthy person is about one ten millionth arsenic by weight; winegrowers and lovers of seafood may house three times that amount. Famous cases include Lafarge (1840), Smethurst (1859), Maybrick (1889), Armstrong (1922) and Frederick Radford (1949) who sent his wife an arsenic fruit-pie (via her father Mr Kite) as she lay dying from pulmonary tuberculosis in the Milford Sanatorium at Godalming.

On her deathbed Mrs Radford's misgivings about her husband's gifts of food, which so often preceded her severe stomach cramps, impelled her to hand the partly eaten pie to her friend Mrs Formby, telling her to send it to Scotland Yard for analysis. Instead, Mrs Formby posted it to the Sanatorium's Superintendent, mailing him an explanatory letter under separate cover. The letter went into his secretary's in-tray, arriving on a Saturday, and lay there unread; the handsome fruit pie was placed on the Superintendent's desk. He worked weekends, and bore it home for tea, ate about one sixth and fell seriously ill, vomiting so violently that the blood vessels in his eyes burst. He just survived.

Margery Radford died on 14 April, and on post-mortem her body, wasted to sixty-seven pounds, disclosed a lethal dosage of six-and-a-half grains administered over some 120 days. To the police, her husband said: 'I admit I bought the pies and gave them to Mr Kite to take to my wife. Why should I want to kill my wife? I knew she was going to die anyway.' Radford, an intelligent laboratory assistant, continued: 'I would not be such a fool as to use arsenic with my experience, as I know the police could find it easily enough. If you think I did it, charge me, and let a judge and jury decide.'

A fair challenge – but it was never put to issue. That night, released from questioning, Radford took his life with prussic acid.

See also **Poisoning, Orfila**

Arson

Arson is a recession-led crime, reflecting the endeavours of those with insurance (see **Marine fraud**) to find some way of turning their unsaleable goods or premises into money. The estimated total of British fire claims for businesses in 1991 was £800 million, up 30 per cent on the previous year. The crime is notoriously hard to prove, with probably fewer than one in ten instances leading to conviction.

In the economic boom of 1987 the FBI took a different view, ascribing only one per cent of cases to insurance frauds while attributing 49 per cent to 'vandalism', a further 25 per cent to 'excitement' and 14 per cent to 'revenge'.

In a more sombre context, arson is one leg of the 'homicidal triangle' evinced by budding serial killers. David Berkowitz, New York's 'Son of **Sam**', set the prodigious tally of 2,000 fires before raising his sights to shooting courting couples.

Less obvious is the sexual connection. The clearest, almost lyrical evocation of the obscure linkage between watching things burn and making love comes from Peter **Kürten**, the Düsseldorf sadist. 'During the firing of the haystacks,' Kürten wrote, 'the thought that human beings might be burned added to the sensations that I experienced. The shouting of the people and the glare of the fire pleased me. During big fires, I always had an orgasm.'

On the occasions where Kürten did not succeed at first, he tried again: 'If you see in my confession sometimes several arsons in one night, then I had no success with the first or second. I also had an orgasm when I fired the woods. It was a lovely sight when one pine after the other was consumed in the flames fanned by the sharp east wind... That was wonderful.'

The orthodox explanation goes to the root of the inadequacy and resentment that are the abiding features of the sex and serial killer. Needing someone, or something, to take it out on, they start by maiming animals as a prelude to torturing humans, and similarly find preliminary satisfaction in trashing property. There are many ways of doing this, but apparently it is only fire that induces the sexual criminal to urinate or defecate, a standard reaction with pyromaniacs.

See also **Pets**, **Sex crimes, Torture**

Assassins

The word derives from 'hasishim', since it was believed that the followers of the Muslim prophet Hasan bin Sabah (*c.* 1030-1124) doped themselves to the eyeballs before their solitary missions of murder. Word of the Assassins first reached the West through Marco Polo's description of a canny Old Man of the Mountains, whose followers would kill for just one more taste of paradise; these trainee assassins were surreptitiously drugged and then tended for days in a pretty garden by beautiful handmaidens.

In reality, Hasan was a competent leader short of followers. From 1092 onwards he corrected the imbalance in numbers by murdering his opponents one by one, starting with Nizam al-Mulk, and his fanatical disciples were the forebears of the modern terrorist.

The sect fell into its final decline under Rukn al-Din, a pacifist, who surrendered his fortress, the Eagle's Lair, at Alamut in about 1256 and was murdered, kicked to a pulp.

In America today, whatever the democratic theory, not everyone has the opportunity to grow up to be a president. But at least anyone can *kill* a president. In the words of the Stephen Sondheim song, composed for the character of John Wilkes Booth: 'All you have to do is to move your little finger and change the world.' Japanese assassins favour the bomb, and Middle Easterners the knife, but Americans working the dark side of their national dream prefer guns.

According to the stereotype devised by the National Commission on Violence in the 1960s, the typical presidential assassin is a failure at his job or, ideally, does not have one. Likewise his marriage (if any) is unsuccessful, his relationship with his parents strained or non-existent and his demographic profile generally that of a social misfit. Infatuation with a media star, like Jodie Foster, is par for the course.

Mark David Chapman, John Lennon's killer, left an exact account of his impulse to kill. He started his confession by denigrating his hero, the target, but within a few sentences lapsed into self-denigration. 'I came across a book about John Lennon,' he told psychologist Dr Goldstein the day after the shooting on 9 December 1980. 'I didn't hate him but I thought he was a phony. The author made the phony stuff that Lennon did sound good. I admire him in a way. I wished someone would write a book about me. It sounded like Lennon was an idiot, and he wasn't. It made me think that my life is special and I felt that no one cared about it.'

The underlying self-pity, mimicking the motivation of those who deface works of art, suggests that the destruction of property is a practicable and more considerate alternative to killing people. In a previous attempt to remind the world of his existence, Chapman had a T-shirt printed with the slogan, 'I'm unique. I think for myself.' His obsession focused on Lennon because 'I believed the Beatles. I believed John Lennon. But they were just saying all that stuff. It was all a big hoax. It's ruined my life. It's made me a nobody.'

Recently **Quantico**'s Dr Murray S. Miron opened up the field of 'psycholinguistics' with a computer programme categorising the content of threatening letters, assessing their seriousness and the writer's psychological profile. The technique identified California's 'Masked Marvel' by whittling down the initial suspect list from 7,000 to five.

The cost of Secret Service protection for the US President soared from a 1968 budget of $17.6 million in 1968 to a present-day $475 million, largely because the list of designated 'protectees' has, like the Brazilian civil service, expanded exponentially to take on board an ever-lengthening list of relatives and remote associates.

See also **Dumdums**, **Stalking**

Attaché case, poisoned

The murder weapon for an attempted 1968 killing at London's Old Bailey. As the net closed round East End gangster Ronald **Kray**, he decided to test the loyalty of his inner-circle associate Alan Cooper by insisting, in the style of the Mafia, that he carry out a murder. The target, a small-time villain, had broken the gangland peace by wounding his wife's lover in the groin with a shotgun. The man went to ground, but he was scheduled to take the stand as a witness on another case within a couple of weeks.

The killing posed obvious technical problems. But, accepting the assignment with enthusiasm, Cooper contrived

a poisoned pigskin briefcase produced to his design by ex-speedway star 'Split' Waterman. A firm tug on a small brass ring by the handle caused a long hypodermic needle to slide forwards, projecting its full length through a hole in the leading corner. Any impact on the needle triggered a spring inside the briefcase, activating the syringe's plunger which squirted out deadly poison.

The plan was to fill the syringe with cyanide; then, in the courtroom jostle, fall in behind the victim, and jab him with the case in the leg. The man would feel little more than a tiny pinprick, and die within seconds of an apparent heart attack. The post-mortem would discern no trace of poison in the stomach.

Ronnie Kray was enthusiastic, but the hitman Paul Elvey bungled the kill, complaining that his mark never showed in the Old Bailey's central lobby. Next the imaginative Cooper suggested a high-powered crossbow with steel-tipped bolts; again, the plan ran into a last-minute snag. In a final scheme – by now hoping to prove the Firm's credentials to the Mafia – Cooper and Ronnie Kray decided to liquidate George Caruana, a West

End club-owner of Maltese extraction by wiring up his bright red Mini to a bomb.

This attempt resulted in Elvey's arrest at Glasgow airport carrying thirty-six sticks of dynamite. It emerged that Alan Cooper, an ex-gold smuggler, was an informer working for the US Treasury Department in cahoots with Scotland Yard (or at least part of it). His evidence on these exotic assassinations was highly questionable, but enough to arrest the Kray twins and hold them on remand in the hope of encouraging frightened witnesses to speak. It was a chance, and on 9 May 1968 the Yard took it, pulling in the twins, their brother Charles and fourteen others.

Attorneys

A world away from the glossy television series *LA Law*, South Carolina pays attorneys staving off the death penalty $10 an hour (£5.70) to a maximum of $1,500.

Critics feel this leads to low-grade legal representation. Only serious shortcomings can have inspired the 1987 decision by a District Court in Texas that James Russell (executed in September 1991) 'was not entitled to relief solely because his lawyer may have been intoxicated during the trial'.

At the 1991 pre-execution wake of another capital offender, Andrew Lee Jones, his lawyer reportedly conceded that 'he had failed to give Andrew a proper defence at his trial', belatedly admitting that there was no evidence linking Jones to the offence. Such cases are not uncommon: the unfortunate **Rummel** of Texas, sentenced to life for stealing $120.75, relied on an attorney whose fixed fee was a miserly $250; and on Death Row in Virginia, the murderer Joseph O'Dell launched a similar appeal. 'I represented myself,' O'Dell said, 'and I wasn't competent to represent myself.'

Inadequate defences at initial trials engendered the backlog of appeals now clogging the American system, precipitating the current attack on the 'great writ' of Habeas Corpus. Under a Civil War statute, a defendant could apply for Habeas Corpus Review, often on the grounds of being denied effective legal advice, a tactic avidly adopted by those about to die. In the last sixteen years only 155 of the 3,834 sent to **Death Row** have been executed.

In its more heroic guise, Habeas Corpus freed the American black Jim Montgomery after twenty years inside. Regarded by the Illinois Ku Klux Klan as a trouble-maker, in 1923 Montgomery was jailed on a trumped-up charge of raping a 62-year-old semi-imbecile, Mamie Snow. In 1944 lawyer Louis Kurtner took up the case; he tracked down Mamie's hospital records which disclosed that the examining doctor had detected no signs of **rape**. The hospital nurse confirmed that Mamie was a virgin, and police documents recorded her failure to identify Montgomery in jail. Pardoned on 10 August 1947, he collected the standard 'going-out' fee of $10.

Today, American judges feel that the Habeas Corpus procedure is abused by lawyers trying to save undeserving mass murderers. Rather than reducing their rights of appeal, the courts could streamline the appeal process. About half the time is devoted to typing court transcripts, and a move to videotape may not be premature.

See also **Insane**

Automatism

A defence to murder or, come to that, almost anything. Crimes against the person carry a mental element, known to lawyers as 'Mens Rea', and clearly the suspension of control by the conscious mind interdicts the formation of any intent to wound or kill.

Instances of automatism are rare, featuring in law students' casebooks more than in the courts. The standard British case (*R* v. *Clarke 1972*) concerns shoplifting by a woman who argued that extreme depression made her completely absent-minded, the equivalent of saying 'I did it, but I'm not guilty.' This has clear attractions as a defence. Accordingly the burden is on the accused to prove he was, in laymen's parlance, briefly off his head.

A more plausible way of losing mental control is an epileptic seizure. In 1919 a Mrs Perry suffered an attack whilst filling a kettle and, inverting her intention, laid the kettle down on top of the oven while placing her baby on the fire. Her lawyers were reduced to pleading **insanity**, albeit temporary, with the unfortunate result that Mrs Perry was permanently confined to Broadmoor, the prison for the criminally deranged. This was better than being hanged, but today she would be acquitted on automatism.

Courts take a less sympathetic view of offences committed under the influence of drugs. In 1970 a man called Lipman had a bad trip and hallucinated that he was penned in the centre of the earth. There he assailed a giant snake which, after a fierce tussle, he slew. Coming down, Lipman found he had killed his bedmate. The LSD element reduced his conviction to manslaughter, but he was jailed for six years. Legal commentators regarded this as rather stiff.

Axeman, 'Mad' Frank Mitchell

The **Kray** twins were acquitted of Mad Frank's murder in 1966. Ronnie Kray now says (*Our Story*, 1988) that Mitchell 'is alive and well and living in... I won't reveal where.'

Mad Frank combined an impressive physique with a worryingly small brain. By 1966 he had spent eighteen of his thirty-two years in detention, and his sentence at Dartmoor was indefinite. The prison governor seemed well-disposed, promising help in extracting an early release date from the Home Office. But the day never came. Meanwhile the Kray twins decided to cut through the red tape, freeing Frank, as one of their protégés, on their own initiative. Their philosophy remains unclear, but they were probably led towards this expansive, benevolent gesture by an associate, 'Mad' Teddy Smith, who was interested in making television 'docudramas'.

Despite Dartmoor's reputation, it proved one of the easiest jailbreaks on record. First Reg Kray reconnoitred the joint. Using a false name, the notorious gangster wrote offering to bring the aged ex-boxer Ted 'King' Lewis down to hold an afternoon talk for the lags. The bait was taken. On arrival Reggie was treated to a tour of inspection before taking luncheon with the governor and padre. He coped with East End gangsters by the dozen waving in acknowledgement as he strolled round the balconies. With creditable aplomb, Reggie explained that the convicts had mistaken one of his companions (also a dyed-in-the-wool villain) for the comedian Norman Wisdom.

Reggie reported with the all-clear, so the twins sent down a car to pick up Mitchell. It was that easy. As a prisoner, Mad Frank was something of a favourite – a 'trusty' on a very loose rein. He could do more or less what he wanted, and what he wanted was to leave the prison on working parties, which were guarded by a single warder. Dressed in his shirt and denim trousers, he would wander off onto the moors for the day, feed the moorland ponies, go for a ride and perhaps meet his girlfriend, a local schoolmistress, for sex in the heather or a deserted barn. Or he might drop into a pub to fetch the liquor order for his mates. Mitchell once took a cab into nearby Okehampton to go shopping, buying a **budgerigar** for another prisoner.

While out on his rambles, Mitchell telephoned the Krays to complain about prison conditions, and under Teddy Smith's prompting they decided to court underworld popularity with a breakout. Once free, Mitchell could bargain with the Home Secretary on level terms, agreeing to surrender if his case was reviewed.

Hence the car to fetch him on 12 December. The only hitch was that the two members of the Firm assigned to Frank did not have a valid driving licence. Reggie borrowed one so that they could hire a car, a green Vauxhall. Frank's contribution consisted of a conspicuous face-mask made out of his girlfriend's nylon nightdress, and in this he toiled through the mist to the pick-up point.

Six hours passed before the prison authorities realised that anything was amiss. On arrival in London, Frank lay low at a 'safe house', a basement flat in Barking where Lennie Dunn and 'Scotch' Jack Dickson minded him night and day.

Over the ensuing days Frank's status regressed. The *Daily Mirror* and *The Times* published his letters, which included the line 'Sir, I ask you, where is the fairness of this?', but the Home Secretary paid them no regard. The Krays wondered What To Do About Frank, and after the first week they devised the stopgap expedient of an expensive callgirl. Frank bedded this attractive woman for two days; he fell for her, and penned a Christmas card that survived as almost the sole physical memorial to his existence. It said: 'To Lisa, the only one I've ever loved.' Afterwards he became increasingly obstreperous, railing against his confinement. The Krays grew fretful, and on 24 December sent round a van, ostensibly to take him to 'a farm in Kent'.

Frank was never seen again, alive or dead. The Krays were tried for his murder, but the uncorroborated evidence of their henchman Albert Donaghue failed to secure a conviction in the absence of a body.

According to Donaghue, two gunmen lay in wait for Frank inside the van, one with a silenced automatic and the other with a revolver. The van lurched forwards as he grabbed for their weapons. They shot him several times in the body and three more times in the heart. Frank lay still. Then he lifted his head and they shot him twice more in the brain. Afterwards, Donaghue telephoned Reggie Kray.

'The geezer's gone,' he said. Reggie broke down and wept.

B

Bamber, Jeremy (1960–)

A famous British police bungle. In the early hours of 7 August 1985 Jeremy Bamber stole into White House Farm and shot his adopted father and mother, his sister by adoption (a model known as 'Bambi') and her two children.

Bamber left his fingerprints on the rifle, an Anschutz .22 automatic, concealed the silencer (still with blood and hair on it) in the gun cupboard, bolted the farmhouse doors and climbed out through the lavatory window. He bicycled to his cottage and, two hours later, telephoned the police, alleging that his father had just managed to put through a call – before the line went dead – saying that Bambi was on the rampage with a rifle.

While Bamber sat down to a fried breakfast, the police surrounded his parents' farmhouse and, after a four-hour wait, broke in and discovered the five bodies. Soon the search started for the culprit. The helpful Bamber was clearly out of the running, as he had no particular motive other than a £436,000 inheritance; anyway, he was on the telephone to the police at the time he said the killings occurred.

But in practice, Bamber would still have been connected to the phone found off the hook at the farmhouse. Lacking this information, the culprit's identity remained wide open until the first major police breakthrough when they missed the open window through which Bamber made his getaway.

This mistake narrowed the suspects to one of the deceased *inside* the building. Then, against all the odds, detectives overlooked the silencer smeared with Bambi's blood. So the rifle found in her hands could have been a suicide weapon, if only the barrel, when pressed against her neck, was not too long for her to reach the trigger.

But the case did not close around Bambi without further corroboration. Her father fought for his life ferociously, sustaining two black eyes and cuts to his face before the rifle stock was broken over his head. So after careful deliberation a clear picture emerged. According to the police, first the frail and diminutive Bambi, on heavy tranquillisers, beat up her six feet four father, a former fighter pilot, without bruising herself, even on the knuckles. Then she shot him and, placing the rifle barrel against her head, unreeled her arms beyond their natural extent and killed herself with a shot to the brain. But the powder marks to her wounds showed that one bullet was fired with the silencer and the other without. So as soon as Bambi was dead, she unscrewed the silencer and shot herself again in the neck – an open-and-shut case.

It seems that the detectives' misgivings, aroused five weeks later, may have been attributable to Bamber's girlfriend, Julie Mugford, who informed them that he admitted responsibility. 'Tonight's the night,' he announced just before the event, and afterwards had told her of his clever planning. At first, she thought it a joke.

Bamber was convicted on 28 August 1986 and sent down for a minimum of twenty-five years. Colin Wilson, the crime writer, makes the point that 'detection only comes into its own when the investigator is aware he has something to detect'.

In this case Bamber 'packaged' a ready-made solution. He insists on his innocence from prison, not by disputing the facts but by proffering alternative 'scenarios'. From his late teens he **fantasised** about eliminating his family, and in the months preceding the killings he talked of 'rubbing them out' to get his hands on their money, either by burning down White House Farm while they slept or by engaging a London **hitman**. Julie Mugford said he devised 'plot after plot', dismissing the fire scheme because it would destroy too many valuables. Consumed by resentment at his sister's – his *adopted* sister's – £20,000 allowance, Bamber was going nowhere under his own steam; he worked casually as a waiter or barman, while Bambi produced children who constituted further obstructions to his inheritance, and his parents continued their pointless existence as pillars of the local community.

Bath, drowning in the

The correct technique is to seize the victim by the knees and raise the legs in the air. This immerses the head. Tests have shown that no other method is comparably effective.

In 1914 the case against George Joseph Smith (1872–1915) was considered vulnerable when Sir Charles Mathews, the Director of Public Prosecutions, pointed out the difficulty of drowning anyone in the bath who put up the slightest resistance; potential victims could easily keep their heads above water by propping themselves up on their elbows.

The circumstantial evidence against Smith was strong. He had married three times, losing his first wife Bessie Mundy in 1912 (found dead in the bath), his second – Alice Burnham – passing away

George Joseph Smith

the following year (found dead in the bath) and the third, Margaret Lofty, expiring shortly afterwards in December 1914 (found dead in the bath). While Margaret lay dead or dying, Smith played 'Nearer my God to Thee' on the sitting room organ.

Smith's matrimonial career came to light when the father of Number Two read a *News of the World* item on Number Three: 'A Bride's Tragic Fate'. The evidential hurdle was finding a plausible way of satisfactorily drowning bathers.

Sir Bernard **Spilsbury**, expert witness for the prosecution, set out to solve the riddle. Together with Detective Inspector Arthur Neill he practised on young ladies, attired in bathing suits, who obliged by sitting in a narrow bath while he attempted to drown them. But, just as Sir Charles feared, even the slenderest specimen could not be submerged. Nothing worked until an inspired Neill grabbed his prospect by the knees. She went under immediately and lost consciousness.

At Smith's trial, the public gallery was packed with women, to whom he proved most attractive. He 'married' scores of them, once under the name George Oliver Love; in a typical case, after a brief courtship, Smith would lay his hands on any cash and then, the day after the ceremony, nip out for a stroll from which he never returned. His trial ran for an unprecedented eight days, and it took 112 witnesses and 264 court exhibits to unravel his numerous aliases and deceptions. Smith's motive was money, pure and simple; he netted £2,500 from his first killing.

In those days, baths were not so common. Smith had to insist on lodgings with baths, or buy one himself. He purchased Alice Burnham's on 9 July 1913, beating the price down from £2 to £1 17s 6d, and, after the murder four days later, returned it to the shop scarcely used. 'I did not like the way he asked about the bath,' recalled Mrs Heiss, an astute landlady who refused accommodation to Smith and his third victim.

'Brides in the Bath' Smith was hanged on 13 August 1915, still claiming that the deaths were a tragic coincidence. His last days were spent in almost constant tears, but probably his most trying moments came after each killing, as he stood by the bath, encouraging the local doctor in his endeavours to revive the murder victim.

See also **Exhibits**

Benefit of Clergy

An early English legal defence. The gradual extension of this principle, according to Sir James Stephen, the great (if stern) Victorian judge, 'reduced the administration of justice to a sort of farce'.

Originally, Benefit of Clergy exempted those in Holy Orders from the jurisdiction of the ordinary courts, a benign manoeuvre when the death penalty was mandatory for every felony. Its progressive extension to other groups of the population marked an early effort by the legal profession to mitigate the full rigour of the law.

A statute of 1350 extended Benefit of Clergy to minor religious functionaries such as church door-keepers, exorcists and so on. To avoid limitless immunity for successive murders, from 1487 criminals were branded on the thumb, and second time round the exemption was withheld, unless the supplicant was ordained. In due course, virtually anyone able to read and write was entitled to the concession, except women, and this legal stratagem staggered on down the centuries, saving the life of the playwright Ben Jonson in 1598. As late as 1765, Lord Byron (the poet's great-uncle) avoided his just desserts for the manslaughter of a Mr Chaworth by pointing out that he could read. Particularly heinous crimes – for instance, **petty treason**, piracy and murder in church – stayed beyond forgiveness, and by 1769 some 160 offences were classified as 'non-clergyable', that is, worthy of instant execution. For the remainder, the death sentence was optional.

The procedure involved the defendant falling to his knees and reading out the first verse of the 51st Psalm (the 'neck-verse'), which begins, 'Have mercy upon me, O God, according to thy loving kindness'. The more wily illiterates learned the passage by rote. Rather than attempting to discriminate against those who seemed able to read in favour of those who really could, in 1705 the law formally conceded that Benefit of Clergy covered anyone

able to memorise the lines. Women only qualified if bona-fide nuns, and not until 1692 did they achieve parity with men.

For many years a replica of a medieval cage discovered in the moat of the Sicilian castle of Hilazzoa was exhibited in Madame Tussaud's Chamber of Horrors. In Sicily, prisoners in holy orders could not be executed; but it was permissible to cage them up until death resulted from hunger, thirst and exposure.

Berry, James (1852–1913)

British hangman. In his disastrous year of 1885 Berry tangled with the redoubtable John **Lee**, whom he failed to despatch despite three attempts. Then on 30 November, Berry decapitated the murderer Robert Goodale despite reducing the drop to a minimal 5 feet 9 inches; after separation, Goodale's headless trunk descended into the pit underneath the scaffold. The episode reduced the prison governor to tears.

The ensuing Committee of Inquiry recommended a drop to produce a blow of 1,260 foot pounds to the neck, with a diligent mathematician observing that the weight of the head should be discounted in any calculations since it was situated above the noose.

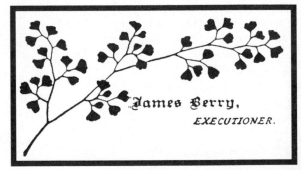

Berry's business card, printed in black, green and gold

Berry survived these early disappointments and, by his retirement, had officiated at more than 200 executions, averaging a comfortable £200 a year. Of stout moral fibre, at his interview Berry told the Sheriffs of London he had no qualms about **hanging** an innocent man 'because the crime committed would be that of the law and not mine'. Selected from 1,400 applicants for the post, his business card featured an attractive ivy-leaf motif together with his trade: 'Executioner'. Before killing his clients, he sent them a set of fortifying verses entitled 'For one under sentence of death'.

It was Berry's experience that a good rope improved with service, using one sixteen times and another twelve before presenting both to Madame Tussaud's. Berry also donated a large knife used to behead seven Chinese pirates, an item he obtained in a swap for another rope. On retirement, shorn of glory, Berry was unable to find another profession. Ostracised and threatened by those who recognised him, he depended on anonymity for survival. But his autobiographical *Life Story and Strange Experiences* proved popular enough.

See also **Initiation, Recruitment**

Biggs, Ronald (1929–)

A decorator and hopeless small-time thief sentenced to thirty years for his part in the **Great Train Robbery** of 8 August 1963. A last-minute addition to the gang, his role was to supply the substitute train driver (who lost his nerve and flunked the job).

On 8 July 1965 Biggs escaped from London's Wandsworth Prison, scaling the walls with a rope ladder and leaping down onto the roof of a waiting furniture van. The jailbreak came free, but honour among thieves is at a premium, and by the time Biggs was reunited with his wife Charmian and their three children in Australia in January 1966 he was £55,000 out of pocket for extensive plastic surgery in France and the forged passport issued in the name of 'Terence Furminger'. The family lived peaceably for several years in the Melbourne suburbs while Biggs traded incognito as a carpenter, shedding another £30,000 when a surefire investment went wrong. Then, recognised from a newspaper picture, he fled to Brazil just ahead of a police raid.

There he established a new life. But in 1974 an English journalist unearthed his whereabouts and started on a biography; the newspaper executives

A relaxed-looking Biggs in his Copacabana days

tipped off the British police, and on 1 February 1974 'Slipper of the Yard' arrived in Rio for the arrest in a blaze of publicity.

But Brazil has no extradition treaty with Britain and, before this obstacle could be **straightened**, Biggs was again beyond the reach of the law. His new girlfriend, Raimunda, announced her pregnancy, and the father of a Brazilian child cannot be deported. A crestfallen Slipper returned to England; a triumphant Biggs blossomed, making a record with the Sex Pistols and taking drinks on a Royal Navy destroyer. Seven years passed before the next attempt on his person.

This time the mastermind was a 36-year-old British ex-serviceman, John Miller, who concocted the idea of remaindering Biggs at auction. Heading a four-man team, Miller knocked Biggs out with Mace gas outside a Copacabana bar, zipped him into a sack and smuggled him out of the country through the northern port of Belem on a chartered yacht. The kidnappers sailed to Barbados, and while the boat stood offshore beyond territorial limits, Miller informed the world's press from his hotel base that Biggs was now 'available' to the highest bidder.

Meanwhile, the yacht's engine broke down. The boat drifted into Barbadian waters to be seized by coastguards; Biggs was thrown into Bridgetown jail to await repatriation and the rest of his thirty-year sentence.

But his best friend from Rio, cockney John Pickston, hired a high-calibre lawyer and, after three weeks' deliberation, Chief Justice Sir William Justice ruled that the longstanding extradition treaty with Britain was invalid. Freed to a welcoming crowd, Biggs paraded through the streets in triumph. He flew back to Rio for an emotional reunion with his little son, to be greeted with a newly issued Brazilian passport and work permit.

Biggs was last heard of in 1992, starring in a celebrity product-endorsement advertisement on Brazilian TV. The final sequence shows him roaring off into the sunset in a vehicle stacked with mailbags. To the camera, Biggs says: 'When you have a tough job to do and need reliable transport, you can always rely on Land Rover.'

Perhaps this exemplifies Brazil's ambivalent attitude towards law and order. The country is about the size of Europe and, in its further reaches, gun law prevails. It holds the record for the world's highest murder rate, with 104 homicides per 100,000 of the population, as against 1.3 for Britain and nearly 10 for the United States. In 1983 Brazilian killings totalled 370 per day; a productive week in New York during the peak season yields about 60 fatalities.

Birch

The size of the 'birch' – a bundle of birch twigs – was precisely regulated by law and varied according to the age of the recipient. Boys over ten were beaten with a cane measuring no more than forty inches long and no heavier than nine ounces, but adults could be chastised by a more expansive instrument, four feet long with a circumference of nine inches and a weight of twelve ounces. Before application, the birch was soaked in water for added pliability. The victim, tied to an easel-like apparatus known as the triangle, was bent over a pad placed on the crossbar and bound by the hands and ankles. In this posture he received anything up to thirty-six blows from a prison officer paid two shillings and sixpence for his pains.

In the 1920s, some 30 per cent of those convicted of robbery with violence received corporal punishment, but by the 1940s this figure dropped to 14 per cent. Birching was finally abolished by the Criminal Justice Act of 1947, whereupon the then Lord Chief Justice, Rayner Goddard, instituted a campaign for its restitution. Sentencing two brothers for robbing two other boys, he observed: 'What they want is a thundering good larruping.'

Thrashings have recently been re-introduced in Singapore, where courts can impose a particularly violent form of caning on prisoners guilty of offences like attempted murder, robbery and rape. 'Prisoners feel like the blood is exploding out of their bodies,' said Tony Poh of the Ministry of Home Affairs. Supposedly, the beatings constitute an effective deterrent. According to Poh: 'Only five per cent of prisoners who have been caned are ever charged with another crime. The memory of their suffering lasts all their lives.'

In Japan, teachers face severe disciplinary action for beating pupils to death. Between 1979 and 1981, four students died after their thrashings at a single establishment, the Totsuka Yacht School. One – Makoto Ogawa – was found on post-mortem to have 144 external wounds; his wire teeth-brace was smashed back into his throat. Ten years later the school's headmaster was convicted of manslaughter, but Judge Hiroshi Kojima set him free on a suspended sentence, depicting the pupil's punishment as 'largely legitimate'.

See also **Trousers**

Blackmail

Put on the legal map by Alexander Chaffers in 1872. Historically, blackmail took a long time to emerge because it preys off respectability, and it took some time for civilisation to become respectable. Not until the Victorian era could men be ruined by imputations of fornication and the like.

When the Chaffers case came to court in 1872, the blackmailer was branded as 'an object of contempt to all honest and well-thinking men', but otherwise escaped scot-free. As the law stood, Chaffers had done nothing illegal. His victims' recourse was not to report him to the police but to sue for libel, and since Chaffers's allegations were true, the trial ended not in his but in their contumely. So in 1873 the new offence of 'demanding money with menaces' was created.

Chaffers was a London solicitor who, while taking the air in Kew Gardens, came across the promenading Sir Travers Twiss and his wife. Sir Travers was an eminent barrister and professor; his spouse, the former prostitute Marie Gelas. Sir Travers did not know this. He thought Marie, his wife of some years, was a Van Lynseele, daughter to a Polish Major-General. He had married Marie on this basis, presenting her at court to the Prince of Wales and Queen Victoria.

Chaffers recognised Lady Twiss from their shared afternoons in a Belgian brothel, and sent her a bill 'for services rendered', first for £46 and then, when she failed to respond, for £150. Lady Twiss spun Sir Travers a story and he paid Chaffers off with £50, but demands continued to arrive. Finally the blackmailer told his tale to the Lord Chamberlain and deposited a sworn affidavit with the Chief Magistrate at Bow Street. Sir Travers could no longer dismiss Chaffers as a madman with a grudge. He had to sue for libel.

On the trial's eighth day, Lady Twiss withdrew her case and entrained for the Continent. She never saw Sir Travers again. He was disgraced in turn, resigning from all his posts. Sadly, the court hearing had gone well for Lady Twiss, with the respectable witnesses testifying she was Van Lynseele and the less respectable witnesses testifying she wasn't Marie Gelas. But the testimony was probably bribed; presumably Marie found her witnesses under increasing pressure from the threat of perjury.

The word 'blackmail' originally derived from the Highlands of Scotland in Elizabethan times, where it meant unlawful rent ('mail') or 'black-rent'. Chieftains extorted this protection money from local farmers. In the East End of **Jack the Ripper**, blackmail acquired a technical meaning for a blunter form of extortion practised on prostitutes. One exponent was the suspect known as 'Leather Apron'. He carried a sharp knife and demanded money with menaces, threatening: 'I'll rip you up.'

See also **Pedigree Chum**

Blackmail, computer

Probably the most notorious blackmail attempt in the history of computer crime was the brainchild of the American anthropologist Dr Joseph Lewis Popp. Found unfit to face trial in November 1991 after a few days on remand in Brixton jail, Dr Popp took to wearing a cardboard box and threading curlers in his beard 'so that he could detect the radioactivity'. The authorities packed him back to the United States.

In December 1989, Dr Popp mailed out 20,000 floppy disks to World Health Organisation medical researchers and other professional users. The software, entitled *Aids Information – Introductory Diskette*, came with an invoice priced at $189 or $378 (depending on the anticipated usage) from a Panamanian company, and the accompanying leaflet specified that unauthorised use would result in computer malfunction. The disks carried a virus that hid all the pre-existing memory on the user's hard disk.

The operation cost about £10,000 to mount, including postage, with a maximum take in excess of £3 million. But Dr Popp lacked the nerve to see it through; on 21 December he cracked up during a Nairobi–Amsterdam flight after reading the first press reports on the resulting havoc. First Popp thought he had been contaminated in mid-air. Then he accused a colleague in the next seat of being an Interpol agent. Finally, on arrival, he attracted attention by scrawling 'DR POPP HAS BEEN POISONED' on another passenger's briefcase. A Dutch police officer informed the head of Scotland Yard's Computer Crime Unit.

No one knows why Dr Popp did it. After gaining a Harvard doctorate in 1979, he spent a decade with commendable African development agencies like the Flying Doctor Service.

Apart from motivation, the case raises interesting legal considerations. Blackmail entails an 'unwarranted demand'. But Dr Popp hoped to exact his licence fee, neither an unwarranted nor an unreasonable ambition. The alternative charge of criminal damage might cover destroying data. But Dr Popp's virus was designed not to obliterate information but to conceal it. In the event, his mental breakdown meant the issues never came to trial.

In 1991 Chile reported an unusual case of a crime committed not with but by a computer. A few days after the installation of a new system in a Valpariso bank, a security guard noticed one of the terminals running a horned demon graphic on its own initiative. The machine did for two employees and put a third into a coma. In the words of Police Detective Raul Lopez: 'An evil spirit inhabits that machine and the death of two innocent people proves it. Computer experts tried to examine the terminal, but they had no success. One of them started babbling like a madman when he came within ten feet, and a dozen more were flung to the floor like rag dolls by some unseen force. We can't turn the system off because everyone who tries to blacks out and falls to the floor.'

The ordinarily reliable British magazine, *Computing,* carried this story on 5 December 1991, reporting that the bank faced closure unless the efforts of Father Hector Diaz, an exorcist, bore fruit.

Bloodstains, a short history of

The science of serology was a late-comer. Until the twentieth century, dried human bloodstains could not be 'typed' or even distinguished from animal blood. This afforded a first line of defence obvious to the most dim-witted of killers, with the victim's blood routinely ascribed to the results of skinning a rabbit, spilling woodstain or tearing frogs to pieces.

It was the series of animal blood transfusions by a Dr James Blundell in 1814 that instigated serious scientific inquiry. Some of Blundell's charges prospered, others perished in agony, a pattern repeated when he progressed to humans four years later and, by the turn of the century, the survival rate stood at around one in two. The 1871 tally was 146 fatalities out of 263 transfusions.

The talk was of two antipathetic types of blood, a theory put to the test in 1900 by an Austrian, Dr Karl Landsteiner. Watching for visible signs of coagulation ('clumping'), he mixed the blood of five colleagues into six specimens of a single master sample. Repeating the procedure five more times with different masters, he produced a cross-referenced table suggesting the existence of three types of blood: A, B, and C (subsequently better known as O). To these was soon added a fourth group, AB, and the approximate percentages for the overall population were later established as A, 42 per cent; B, 10 per cent; O, 45 per cent and AB, 3 per cent. The figures vary from one part of a continent to another. Thus 'A' group frequency is high among Europeans, western Asians and Australian aboriginals.

At about that time, following in the footsteps of Pasteur and von Behring, another Viennese doctor discovered the precipitin test, based on the defensive reaction of blood serum (blood minus the cells) to invasion by foreign blood cells. Paul Uhlenhuth established that animal blood (except for apes, which are too closely related) reacts to human blood by throwing a visible white precipitate, and

	GROUPING SERA		
	Anti – A	Anti – B	Anti – A,B
Group O Cells	●	●	●
Group A Cells			
Group B Cells			
Group AB Cells			

Testing for the four main blood groups

a suspect's bloodstained clothes, soaked in salt water, yielded a sufficient concentration to produce the reaction.

At last the forensic pathologist could tell whether bloodstains originated from the same species as the victim, and today police laboratories carry stocks of anti-sera of the common animals, enabling an immediate check on the truth of a suspect's story.

Over the years, the four blood groups were split into subdivisions, and protein analysis separated out distinguishing factors, or combinations of factors, in ever smaller population categories. In 1925 Landsteiner realised that all body fluids – sweat, saliva, urine, semen and so on – could be similarly 'typed'; about 86 per cent of the population are 'secretors' whose fluids carry tell-tale blood cells. In the post-war era Stuart Kind, a Home Office scientist, devised a simple and reliable way of testing old bloodstains, and today the modern radioimmunoassay technique enables samples, in many cases, to be sexed; female white corpuscles display microscopic drumstick-like shapes.

But although blood-grouping theoretically provided ever narrower differential bands, in practice it failed to deliver results. Not until 1934 was the first major trial settled by forensic serology. Flecks of blood proved too small – or their investigation too complex – for the jury's taste, a depressing contrast with companion disciplines securing convictions from microscopic shreds of cloth, fluff or hair.

And rightly so. Australia's '**dingo**' trial showed that, as late as 1982, experts could mistake paint for blood. Even in the British Backhouse case of 1984, suspicions of foul play revolved around more Holmesian deductions about the *shape* of the blood **drops**, not their composition; common sense suggested that a wounded man fighting for his life (the Backhouse version) would spatter blood around, producing drops with flying tails, rather than the neat, round markings actually found, more characteristic of blood dripping from a stationary casualty.

That same year everything changed when Alec Jeffreys from the University of Leicester unveiled the Holy Grail of Serology: **Genetic fingerprinting**

Bobettes

American journalese for the swarms of female admirers flocking to the trial of Robert Chambers, the upper-crust 'Preppie Murderer'. With one more turn of the screw, the killer evolves into a love object while behind bars, with **romances** blossoming during prison visits from strangers.

Ordinary women may wonder exactly what it is about multiple murderers and wife-slayers that proves so attractive, for – in the words of Sheila Isenberg, author of *Women who Love Men who Kill* – 'There is no serial killer who has not been pursued by dozens of women', and the more presentable one-off cases, like the family murderer Jeff **MacDonald**, are also treated to marriage proposals while awaiting trial. Psychiatrist David Abrahamsen, of the Berkowitz case, puts forward an explantion: 'Most of these women are unhappy, frustrated and dissatisfied. They have low self-image and want to attach themselves to figures they think are powerful.'

There is a curious correspondence between a serial killer – an outcast in pursuit of an identity – and his suitor, an outcast seeking a relationship. Their affairs have much to recommend them. An incarcerated love-object is easy to idealise since there is little prospect of the bond being put to the test or consummated. This combination of celibacy and suffering-through-separation makes an ideal fit for strict Catholics, disproportionately represented amongst murderers' suitors. The romances occasionally lead to marriage; Ronald **Kray** (with his 'old-world manners and gentlemanly behaviour') wed former kissagram girl Kate Howard in 1989, and when handsome Richard **Ramirez** (the 'Night Stalker') proposed to mother-of-two Christine Lee, she could not say no.

Florida boasts a handful of prisons with matrimonial apartments that start the marriages off on the right foot with regulation 42-hour honeymoons. It is when the inmate is freed that trouble begins. The prisoner's gratitude fades, and the relationship is exposed as a fiction; according to prison counsellor Kathryn Parris, 'Most of the women involved with prisoners describe a level of emotional intimacy and passion only found in books.'

Body language

Sometimes a dead give-away. Perhaps the most extreme example was the American serial murderer Gerald Stano, who found it hard to lie without backing away, pushing back his chair and crossing his legs, left ankle on right knee. For the truth, he earnestly leaned towards his questioner.

This made police interrogation easy. Had Stano ever met Mary Carol Maher, whose body was found in Florida on 17 February 1980? Yes, he had given her a lift (leaning forwards). By herself? No, she was with another girl (back, legs crossed). Where had they gone? To a nightclub called 'Fannie Farkel's' (back, legs crossed). Did he have sex with her? Yes (leaning forwards).

The questioning turned to whether Mary Carol resisted his advances. When Stano was asked, 'She could hit pretty hard, couldn't she?', he leaned forwards and replied, 'You're damned right she could.' But the next question, 'So you hit her?', propelled him backwards as he crossed his legs and demurred, 'No, I let her out.' And so it continued until, angled forwards, Stano confessed and then, inclined backwards, recanted.

The inquiry took a macabre twist when Stano was asked about a missing black prostitute, Toni Van Haddocks. Did Stano know anything about her? No (back, legs crossed). How often did he pick up black girls? He didn't (back, legs crossed). So what about Toni? Stano adopted his posture for deceit and said, 'That's the only one I ever picked up.' At this stage the investigating officer, Detective Crowe, experienced a sinking feeling that he was dealing with a serial killer.

Eventually Stano admitted to murdering thirty-four women between 1969 and 1980, generally leaving his 'signature' at the site by the careful, ritualistic display of branches arranged round the corpse. On 2 September 1981 Stano was jailed for seventy-five years for six murders, but a subsequent trial awarded the death sentence. Quoted in the *New York Times* as saying, 'I just can't stand a bitchy chick', according to the Florida police he thought only of three things: 'stereo systems, cars, and killing women'.

Bodysnatchers

A grisly British occupation. In 1540 Henry VIII granted a charter to the Company of Barber Surgeons entitling them to the bodies of four felons a year for dissection. As long as surgeons were content to develop anatomical theories without reference to their patients' actual physique, this allotment – bolstered to twelve by the Murder Act of 1752 – proved sufficient, and until the end of the eighteenth century, bodysnatching remained a tiny trade supplying the demand of a dozen or so anatomical pioneers. The rest of the profession practised, if at all, on model skeletons made of papier-mâché.

For centuries there was no legal sanction against bodysnatching; since a corpse did not constitute 'property', nothing was actually stolen. But the legal framework changed with the 1788 case of *R* v. *Lynn*. Lord Kenyon, the presiding judge, suddenly and erroneously recollected a 1744 precedent involving St Andrew's churchyard, and ruled that, in truth, to disturb a grave was a misdemeanour. He fined Mr Lynn, a surgeon, £10.

In fact the 1744 case dealt with the theft of lead coffins, but as a result Lynn's conviction avoided classification as a felony since it lacked the element of theft: the victim's clothes and coffin were left in the tomb. This nice legal distinction had practical ramifications, since felonies entailed a mandatory death sentence, making convictions an unlikely outcome on even the clearest evidence. But misdemeanours carried a real threat of enforcement, and after 1788 doctors preferred to pay others to do their dirty work.

This untoward change in the law combined with a vast expansion in the medical profession to foster the novel industry of bodysnatching. The number of medical students quintupled to 500, and their new professors wanted them each to try their hands on at least two bodies before qualifying. This put the quota for London alone at 300 corpses a year, at the very period when the rate of criminal executions was declining. One contemporary commentator on this problematic statistical area stated that 'in all Great Britain, from 1805 to 1820, there were executed eleven hundred and fifty criminals, or about seventy-seven annually'.

Resurrectionists, resurrection men or sack-em-up men came into being to supply the shortfall.

Doctors might pay two to three guineas for a full-sized body ('large', three feet or more), with children ('large small') or babies ('foetuses') at a guinea or less. Prices inflated steadily, by 1812 attaining four guineas for a 'large' and doubling again by 1828.

The trade, despite its illegality and the endemic bouts of gang warfare, was efficiently administered and controlled by racketeers, notably the ex-boxer Ben Crouch. Like any other wholesaler, at the start of each academic term Crouch negotiated directly with the medical schools' professors, agreeing prices and quantities for the forthcoming term. Crouch ran a tight ship, beating up rivals, turning them into the law or, if all else failed, spoiling a rival's graveyard (his source of supply) by digging up the graves and heaving the rotting corpses onto the ground. As a last resort he would break into hospitals and shred cadavers purchased from other purveyors.

After his retirement in 1817, Crouch was summoned by the 1827 Select Committee when an alarming legal development resulted in a fine for a medical student, rather than the uncouth bodysnatcher. The Committee estimated that ten full-time resurrectionists were working in London, together with about 200 freelances. Asked if bodies could be imported from the Continent, Crouch attested that the trade was already international, with bodies crossing the borders between England, Ireland and Scotland. Customs sometimes impounded putrefying corpses too long in transit.

The construction of operating theatres in four major London hospitals at the end of the 1820s bolstered demand, forcing the bereaved to mount watch over their relatives' gravesides until the cadaver had sufficiently decayed to be worthless. Spring-guns and mantraps proliferated in the churchyards; a castellated watchtower from this era can still be seen in Edinburgh's New Calton Burial Ground. Outlandishly deep graves became popular, particularly among boxers, who believed that their exceptional musculature was favoured by the anatomists; pugilist Tom 'the gas man' Hickman was buried eighteen feet down. The rich too remained relatively immune in their deeper graves.

An experienced team, working hard in relays, could spirit away a corpse in a quarter of an hour. To prevent outsiders jumping on the bandwagon, the resurrectionist cartel circulated disinformation, suggesting that the body was best extracted through a shaft excavated to a point adjacent to the head of the coffin. They recommended that the coffin's wooden top next to the deceased's cranium should be banged out, the corpse's arms folded down, and the body eased out like toothpaste from a tube. In fact, the real bodysnatchers dug straight down, attached hooks and cords to the coffin itself, which they raised by the head to ground level, and then broke open the lid.

Earnings were good; one gang of six or seven confederates grossed over £1,000 in a single year from the sale of 312 bodies. **Burke and Hare** took bodysnatching a step further, murdering people rather than digging them up. In the aftermath of their 1829 trial, a Member of Parliament, Henry Warburton, framed 'A Bill for Preventing the Unlawful Disinterment of Human Bodies', which became law in 1832. It enabled the legal custodians of a corpse – notably unwanted cadav-

The rear of Burke's lodgings, his window marked A

ers in the workhouses – to release it for dissection. Bodysnatching ceased forthwith, although Warburton's name was reviled long after by doctors. With its emphasis on a proper inspectorate and by putting an end to the illegal trade, his Bill decreased supply.

In modern Thailand, the days of bodysnatchers may be numbered. In April 1991 the Thai cabinet was poised to suspend the two charities responsible for collecting the corpses of Bangkok's murder and accident victims. The charities were paid by the number of bodies delivered to the morgue. It seems that the system, which in principle entailed handing in those *found* dead, was subject to abuse.

Bolero, Ravel's

A **fingerprint** case from the twilight zone. Ravel's Bolero was the music played by a 1961 **ghost** in northern England. The nocturnal spirit displayed such mastery of the violin that a Manchester widow realised that the other occupant of her home – her sleeping son – could not be responsible.

David Cohen of the Society of Psychical Research was summoned. The seances that followed in the small terraced house featured the standard levitating table, together with the more unusual manifestation of a luminous tambourine zooming round the darkened room, supported by sporadic appearances from a disembodied pair of spirit hands. The tambourine was real, and the ghostly hands might have belonged to one of the sitters round the table. To eliminate fraud, Cohen resolved to check the tambourine for fingerprints, and called in Sergeant Rowland Mason of the Manchester Fingerprint Bureau.

Mason was said by colleagues to possess second sight, and on his second visit he touched the spirit's hands. They felt real, if dry and scaly, but subsequent examination revealed no fingerprints on the tambourine, and findings were similarly negative when he prepared it with mercury dust.

Mason recognised that subterfuge had failed, so he asked the spirit's permission to take its fingerprints on a chemically sensitised pad. The ghost agreed, giving Mason a firm impression at the next session. By now the local police were in a frenzy of excitement, and Mason's ghostly imprints were developed amid intense anticipation. But they amounted to no more than three parallel scratch marks suggestive of fingernails or perhaps a bird's claw.

Forsaking fingerprinting, Mason brought in a Constable John Cheetham to try infra-red photography. The spirit posed for a snap, producing an excellent likeness of an empty armchair with an indentation in its back cushion made by the otherwise invisible head, a photograph revered by the Manchester police for its strange, suggestive powers. Sadly the investigation went no further. The *Daily Mail* got wind of the story, and the Chief Superintendent called a halt to avoid public ridicule.

This odd tale is told by Detective Chief Inspector Tony Fletcher of the Manchester Fingerprint Bureau in his *Memories of Murder* (Weidenfeld, 1986).

Bones, ground

Dr Joseph Mengele, Auschwitz's 'Angel of Death', is definitely dead. He drowned in a Brazilian swimming accident on 7 February 1979.

In February 1992, a master sample of genetic material derived from his son, Rolf Mengele, a German lawyer, was matched with the graveyard skeleton of his supposed father. A new technique enabled the extraction of the tiny amounts of DNA left in Mengele's bones after years of decomposition and provided a positive match with a probability in excess of 1:500. Similar investigations were recently conducted on the supposed bones of Tsar Nicholas and his family found in a pit at Ekaterinburg; the master blood sample came from a distant relative, the Duke of Edinburgh.

The pioneering work for this type of case identified the remains of Karen Price, a Welsh schoolgirl whose murderers were convicted ten years after the killing. Her body lay buried in the rear garden of Cardiff's 29 Fitzhamon Embankment for eight years before building workers deepening a trench sliced into a roll of carpet in 1989. Inside was a skeleton dressed in socks, bra and panties.

Traditional forensic techniques led to identification of the body and thus to the arrest of the killer. But to prove the case in court required firmer evidence. Analysis of the corpse's rotting clothing showed that the victim wore a Levi-Strauss sweatshirt first marketed in December 1980. Other garments, like her 'Karman Ghia' slacks, were on sale in the Cardiff area during the early 1980s. The fact that her teeth were still developing put her age at about 15, and 'Dr Zak' (Zakaria Erzinclioglu) of Cambridge University pronounced that the presence of a well-established colony of woodlice to eat the fungus gathering round the skeleton's exposed bones indicated that its soft tissues had first been consumed by Phorid flies (the so-called 'coffin flies'),

and that the combined processes must have taken a good five years. This placed the murder between early 1981 (the sweatshirt) and 1984 (the Phorid flies), enabling the police to question the inhabitants of 29 Fitzhamon Embankment.

No. 29 had been knocked together with No. 27, and the two houses partitioned into bedsits and small flats for a floating population of lodgers. Some 700 people lived there during the 1980s. But one of the sergeants assigned to the case had seen a television programme about an archaeological technique, **facial reconstruction**, and in December 1989 a sculptured head of 'Little Miss Nobody' was commisioned from Richard Neave of Manchester University. Photographs of her clay bust were distributed to the press and television, and within two days a social worker put a name to the face: 15-year old Karen Price, who absconded from a children's home some eight years previously.

The BBC's *Crimewatch UK* broadcast an appeal for help. Among the viewers was one of Karen's murderers, Idris Ali. In the company of friends, Ali rashly exclaimed, 'I knew her... I used to go around with her', and was persuaded to go to the police.

The sorry tale soon unravelled. Karen Price, the disturbed child of a broken marriage, had been in care since the age of ten. During 1981, aged fifteen, she repeatedly absconded from her Pontypridd assessment centre and drifted into a life of prostitution in a run-down area of Cardiff. Sixteen-year-old Idris Ali acted as her pimp, and one client was doorman Alan Charlton. Sometime in July 1981 the two men took Karen back to Charlton's basement flat in Fitzhamon Gardens and ordered her to pose for pornographic photographs. When she refused, Charlton went berserk and strangled her. Idris Ali helped him dig the garden grave.

This was fine for the police, but insufficient for the courts. The first forensic hurdle involved extracting the DNA from the skeleton. Erika Hagelberg, an Oxford biochemist, began with a clean-up, sandblasting Karen's bones. Then she ground the residue into a fine powder at low temperatures. This revealed plenty of DNA, 99 per cent from contaminating fungus and bacteria. So the human component was amplified by the polymerase chain-reaction test.

But standard genetic identification is based on DNA sections between 1,000 and 10,000 units long, and nothing this large had survived intact. So in concert with Professor Alec Jeffreys, Hagelberg devised a miniaturised process that read sections of a mere 100 units

In addition to the novelty of the minute samples and the polymerase chain-reaction test, the trial was the first to present an analysis from decayed bone as court evidence. On 26 February 1991 Alan Charlton (who played 'the greater part' in the killing) was sentenced to life imprisonment, and Idris Ali detained 'during Her Majesty's Pleasure'.

Bonnie and Clyde (1910–34; 1909–34)

A couple of small-time hoods (then known as Clyde and Bonnie). Their largest haul came to no more than $2,500, and one month their takings totalled $76. Clyde was driving shoeless on 23 May 1934 when the 187 bullets smacked into their old jalopy; Bonnie, clutching a half-eaten sandwich, wore no pants under her dress. But as word of their death spread, the roads for miles around were jammed with cars. An estimated 9,000 sightseers flooded into Arcadia, Louisiana, and when the truck towing their car broke down, schoolchildren thrust their hands into the vehicle to smear their fingers in blood, pulled tufts from Bonnie's hair and tore shreds from her dress. Thousands shuffled past their bullet-torn corpses displayed in a local furniture store. Their car was still being exhibited forty years later at $2.50 a time. It was sold in 1973 for $175,000, and is said to be at the Haçienda Nàpoles in the possession of Pablo **Escobar**, Colombia's cocaine billionaire.

Bonnie was tiny, no more than four feet ten. She came from a background of narrow respectability in the small Texas town of Rowena. Although no particular rebel, she threatened to razor her best friend when aged ten, tattooed her boyfriend's name, Roy Thornton, on her thigh at fifteen and married him a year later. But she never achieved independence from her mother, and Thornton made himself scarce. In 1929 he was sentenced to five years for robbery, and in January 1930, bored and lonely, Bonnie met young Clyde Barrow in West Dallas.

Clyde, the sixth of eight children, grew up in wretched poverty on a Telico farmstead. As a child he was unsupervised, unpunished and neglected,

nearly suffocating once and nearly drowning on another occasion. His family scraped and saved even to buy a ukulele costing $1.98, and his parents frequently billetted him with relatives to save money. He landed in trouble several times for torturing animals, and by 1926 was a member of the juvenile Root Square Gang, who cut their teeth on stealing tyres and matured to robberies in Waco and Sherman.

Cartoon from the Dallas Journal of 9 April 1934

Clyde had already escaped three times from police gunfire and that, to a romantic young girl, meant glamour. So she took him home to meet her mother, and there, next morning, he was arrested. But Bonnie had hopes for the future, writing as he awaited trial, 'I want you to be a man, honey, and not a **thug**. I know you are good and I know you can make good... We are young and should be happy like other boys and girls.'

Her love for Clyde dragged her down. On 11 March 1930, at his request, she broke into a fellow-prisoner's house, searching for a hidden Colt .32, and smuggled it into his Waco jail. Clyde escaped, but was recaptured and sentenced to fourteen years. He was unexpectedly paroled on 2 February

1932, and within a month Bonnie languished in jail in Kaufman after a joint attempt at robbery misfired. They were caught in the act, fled by car down small dirt roads and got stuck in the mud. So they ran over the fields and, spotting some mules, leapt onto their backs. But the animals refused to budge. So Bonnie and Clyde crawled away down a ditch while bullets flew overhead. Clyde made off looking for a car to steal and, that evening, Bonnie was picked up trudging alone down a country road.

While she was awaiting trial, Clyde killed for the first time, on 27 April shooting 61-year-old John Bucher for no good reason; he had already opened the **safe** to his general store. On 17 June Bonnie was released by a grand jury. Clyde's next killing came on 5 August, during a pointless gun-battle after he attracted a sheriff's attention at a Stringtown country dance. Instead of telling the lawman to drop his weapon, Clyde shot him, and continued to blaze away in the dark, killing a deputy and wounding a dancer before driving off in such disarray that he crashed

the first car and wrote off its hijacked replacement. The next morning he had Bonnie collected and driven to his hideout, an abandoned farmhouse near Grand Prairie. That night he described their future with the words, 'Driving, just driving from now till they get us. Kansas, Missouri, Oklahoma, Mexico – Texas, always Texas, where we were born.' Scarcely out of their teens, Bonnie and Clyde spent the rest of their days in stolen cars, on the run, robbing grocery stores and making furtive visits to Bonnie's mother.

It is no easy thing to be an armed robber if your first and invariable reaction is panic. Nor is it an enviable life. The only place Bonnie and Clyde felt safe was in a car. They lived in them, sometimes sleeping inside, sometimes camping rough, robbing gas-stations for pocket money. On 11 October 1932 they killed a man, Howard Hall, during a $28 raid which also netted a few vegetables. On 25 December 1932, after Christmas dinner, they shot salesman Doyle Johnson while stealing his car, abandoning it a few minutes later. From then on, at constant risk of ambush and betrayal, they took care to shoot first. In all, the 'Barrow Gang' claimed a dozen lives. Of a killing of 6 January 1933, Clyde said he felt 'like I always felt, sick inside, sick and cold and weak – and a sort of dull wishing I had never been born'. A year later, on 31 March 1934, just outside Grapevine, Texas, an elderly farmer, William Schieffer, watched as two lawmen dismounted from their motorcycles, casually approached a couple sitting by the roadside, and were blasted by shotguns. Schieffer saw Bonnie walk over to a wounded man, fire twice into his face, and reportedly heard her say, 'Look-a-there, his head bounced just like a rubber ball.'

Bonnie and Clyde drove endlessly, leading a nomadic life as motorised versions of their direct predecessors, the Western outlaws. Driving was almost the only thing for which Clyde showed aptitude. He knew the back roads, and they were immune from pursuit if they could cross a state boundary. The police, hampered by low morale and low pay, often had to buy their own weapons and transportation. Their cars were no match for Clyde's stolen Ford V-8s. **Hoover**'s Department of Investigation, with less than 300 **G-men**, had still to make its mark.

There was the ambush at the Wharton bridge, the stakeout at West Dallas, the attack on their apartment in Joplin; the capture of a motorcycle policeman who tried to book them for speeding; the drive with their partner W.D. Jones wounded in the head; the kidnapping of a young undertaker and his fiancée during a car theft; the Red Crown Tavern ambush spearheaded by an armoured car, at which Buck was shot in the temple, and Clyde alone unwounded of the four in their car; the crash at Salt Fork River when Bonnie was horribly burned and they dared not contact a doctor – she hovered, in agony, between life and death for a week; the Dexfield Park ambush, where Buck was killed; the abortive Dallas Highway ambush; the Eastham Farm breakout, when Clyde 'sprang' five convicts from Huntsville penitentiary; the bickerings between the gang members; the fast-and-loose Mary O'Dare who advised Bonnie to dope her lover and then, 'While he's out, take his roll and beat it'; Sheriff Smoot Schmid's plan to trap and perhaps squash the gang with a large four-wheel drive gravel mover; the gunfight outside Commerce, when a 63-year-old constable perished; and the final ambush, led by Ted Hinton, half a mile outside Irvin Methvin's farm in Lousiana.

Bonnie penned the 'Story of Bonnie and Clyde', possibly the best literary composition by a major criminal, and Clyde sent a famous 'since then I have used no other' letter to Henry Ford. 'While I have still got breath in my lungs,' Clyde wrote, 'I will tell you what a dandy car you make. I have drove Fords exclusively when I could get away with one. For sustained speed and freedom from trouble the Ford has got every other car skinned.' Otherwise, the pair were hardly more attractive than **Brady** and **Hindley**, the Moors murderers, and many of John **Dillinger**'s exploits were appropriated by the 1967 film to make Bonnie and Clyde more palatable.

'Johnny and Clyde' was Truman Capote's working title for a proposed exposé of Hoover and his aide, Clyde Tolson.

Bonny, Anne (b. 1700)

Female pirate captain who disappeared from history at the age of twenty after a spectacular early career.

Born in Ireland in 1700 from the illegitimate union of a lawyer and a serving girl, Anne was raised by her father, who emigrated to South Carolina. As a tomboy, Anne was trained in the rapier; and her father's tracker, an Indian named Charlie Fourfeathers, taught her to handle guns, knives and hatchets. At thirteen, Anne stabbed her mother's maid. At fifteen, her breasts assumed 'the size and strength of melons'. At sixteen, she married a destitute wretch, James Bonny.

Distraught at this dreadful news, Anne's mother died of shock; her father barred her from the house. Anne laid siege to, and then stormed, the parental home, breaking every window; Pa called out the militia. In high dudgeon, the new Mrs Bonny sailed away to New Providence in the Bahamas, on arrival shooting off the **ear** of a huge desperado blocking her way on the pier.

She dispensed with her husband in favour of the local receiver, Chidley Baynard, temporarily single after killing his mistress. By now a friend of Teach and Blackbeard, Anne put to sea as a pirate in a special outfit of velvet trousers and a scarlet silk blouse. A lawful privateering voyage turned to piracy when the drunken Jack 'Calico' Rackham mutinied and took over the ship. Anne became his lover and, after landing to raze her former husband's house and shipyard to the ground, she cruised for two years in *The Queen Royal*, falling for a handsome young sailor to whom, by way of preliminaries, she disclosed that she was a woman, only to learn that he was no man but the disguised pirate Mary Read.

Anne was captured in October 1720 off the Jamaican coast near Negril Point; she was carousing with a crew of turtle fishermen when her ship surrendered to Captain Jack Barnet's sloop. Legend has it that Anne and Mary were the last to lay down their arms and, along with their shipmates, the two women went on trial at St Jago de la Vega, where they were sentenced to death.

Asked as a formality if there was any reason why they should not be executed, the women responded, 'My Lord, we plead our bellies', and were reprieved on account of their pregnancies. Rackham was hanged at Gallows Point. As Anne remarked, 'I am sorry to see you there, Jack, but if you had fought like a man you need not have been hanged like a dog.' Freed within the year, she married a man called Michael Radcliffe, forsook piracy and left for America. She was last heard of moving West with a train of settlers.

Academics at the cutting edge of piratical scholarship are increasingly dubious about accounts of female buccaneers. It seems that these women, in their gorgeous attire, were often men, and that the Caribbean provided an early refuge for the gay community.

Borden, Lizzie (1860–1927)

To murder enthusiasts, 'Lizzie' will always mean Lizzie Borden, the middle-aged spinster absolved of one of history's great 'locked house' murders. On 4 August 1892 Lizzie's elderly father and step-mother were viciously axed to death at their home, 92 Second Street, in prosperous Falls River. The front door was locked, the house surrounded by a high barbed-wire topped fence, and the only serious suspects were the four people staying in the house. Of these, two were out, one of them fifteen miles away, so only Bridget Sullivan, the maid, and Lizzie Borden, the disaffected 40-year-old daughter of the house, remained as possible killers.

The double murder caused an immediate sensation in the highly stratified town; Falls River was one of those prosperous Massachusetts communities where the Durfees and the Braytons spoke only to the Bordens, and the Bordens spoke only to God. By the next day, business had ground to a virtual standstill; jostling crowds gathered on the sidewalk.

On 11 August Lizzie was arrested; it was she who had discovered her father's body, his skull crushed by eleven blows from an axe while he slept on the ground-floor couch, one eye cut in half and his nose severed.

At the time, Lizzie had summoned the maid Bridget with the famous words: 'Come down quick! Father is dead! Somebody came in and killed him!' Checking upstairs, they found Abby Borden – Lizzie's dull, overweight stepmother – killed by twenty-one axe blows to the head. Unlike her husband, who was still dripping gore, Abby's blood had congealed. So she had already been dead for a good hour.

VIEW OF THE VICINITY OF THE MURDERS.

I. Borden house.
II. Borden barn.
III. The well.
IV. Fence with barbed wire on top.
V. Side entrance.
VI. Churchill residence.
VII. Dr. Bowen's house.
VIII. Dr. Chagnon's house.
IX. Kelley house.
X. Yard from which officers watched the Borden house.
XI. Kelley's barn.
XII. Pear orchard.

'It must have been done while I was outside in the barn,' said Lizzie. After her arrest she was portrayed in the press as a heroine and martyr, a frail woman hounded by police and prosecutors, and, at her trial in June 1893, the verdict of 'innocent' was greeted with acclaim. Overnight, Lizzie became an idol, inundated with congratulatory messages, courted by clergymen, and headlined in the papers: 'Church and Charity will Claim Lizzie'.

But two days later, the public mood abruptly changed. With Lizzie off the hook, the conundrum remained. Who had killed her parents? On all the evidence, Lizzie was the only person with the opportunity. Barring an intruder committing a very leisurely double murder, it must have been her.

Amid snide comments about 'self-made heiresses', Lizzie moved upmarket on the proceeds of her father's $250,000 estate, buying a mansion called 'Maplecroft' where she lingered on for another thirty-four years, at first ostracised and then a curiosity, in her later years motoring through the streets in a gleaming limousine with a liveried chauffeur at the wheel.

A century after the killings, the corpses of Lizzie's parents are on the shortlist of proposed exhumations by America's amateur sleuth Professor Starrs. It is now appreciated that a head blow here may produce damage there, so the true number of axe blows may be elucidated. The blade of the fatal axe, on display in the Falls River Museum, is to be microscopically matched against the broken skulls.

The real mystery is how Lizzie escaped the murder charge. She had the motive – money, and an intense dislike of her stepmother, conventionally depicted as a grasping hypochondriac. Before the killings, the atmosphere in the house was terrible. Inner doors were blocked off, and the family ate separately, forcing Bridget to serve each meal twice. Nor was her father a lovable man. A miser and a strict patriarch, he regarded Lizzie as his 'special girl', barring her from contact with outsiders, and commentators have surmised a background of incest. Evidence barred from the trial included two attempts by Lizzie to buy prussic acid to 'mothproof a fur cape' only hours before the murders, and she evidenced her guilt by making inconsistent statements about her whereabouts during the killings.

In court, Lizzie did not testify; her defence hinged on the absence of blood on her clothing. But stepmother Abby died at least an hour before Lizzie's father – ample time to change and freshen up. And the head of her sleeping father lay flush by the door leading from the dining room. Lizzie could have killed Father in one room while standing in another, above and behind.

In any case, Father's blood would not have squirted anywhere in the absence of the *double* circumstance of his heart continuing to beat after an artery had been severed. Even then, Lizzie still had

fifteen minutes to make herself presentable before 'finding' the body, and the Sunday after the murders she burned a soiled dress only ten weeks old 'to tidy up her wardrobe'.

Lizzie was not – as she claimed – rummaging in the barn for fishing tackle at the time of the murders. It was suffocatingly hot up in the roof of the outbuilding, almost unendurable after only a few seconds, and the dusty floorboards showed no footprints from her alleged half-hour visit.

Why was Lizzie discharged? The local prejudice ran against executing women. The last one to hang in Massachusetts, Bathsheba Spooner, claimed to be with child, despite expert evidence to the contrary. But on autopsy she was found five months pregnant. Further, on 1 June 1893, a few days before Lizzie's trial, the papers reported another axe murder in Falls River. The *Boston Globe* ran the headline: 'Many Points of Resemblance'.

With Lizzie already locked up, her attorney took full advantage: 'Are they going to claim Lizzie did this too?' In fact, an arrest was made on 4 June, but this was not published until the following day. The news came too late for the jury; the trial had already started.

Brady, Ian (1938–)

The dominant half of the Brady–**Hindley** team, perpetrators of Britain's Moors Murders. Brady swamped Hindley with his personality, and his personality was, in turn, a product of his upbringing. Today's psychological profilers would recognise many constituents of an '**organised**' serial killer's background.

Brady came from the tough Gorbals slums of Glasgow, the illegitimate son of a waitress. His real name was Ian Duncan Stewart. Raised by foster parents, he won a scholarship to an expensive school for children from more prosperous backgrounds. Resentment led to a spate of housebreaking and a disturbing reputation for bullying his juniors; at thirteen he was sentenced to two years probation in the course of which he re-offended ten times, earning a further two years. A teenage drunk, he landed a job in a brewery which culminated in his dismissal for stealing. A spell in a tougher borstal in Hull followed.

At twenty-one Brady found work as a clerk in a Midlands' chemical firm. In his youth, he had amused himself with cruelty to animals, lobbing cats out of the tenement windows. Now he devoted himself to a study of the Nazis, True Crime (particulary *Compulsion*, the story of the Leopold and Loeb murder) and the Marquis **de Sade**. He could quote from *Mein Kampf* at length, and amassed a collection of books on leather fetishism, sexual sadism and bondage in an era when these things were hard to come by.

In early 1961 this hardened, vengeful individual dictated a letter at work to an innocent young typist from Gorton: Myra Hindley. The events which followed are described elsewhere, and in 1966 Brady was sentenced to three life terms for murder. Nineteen years later he confessed to two more killings on Saddleworth Moor and, in 1987, provided vague stories about five other murders from his youth, including a woman thrown to her death from a Manchester canal bridge, a man stabbed in Glasgow, and a hitchhiker shot near Loch Lomond. By then Brady had wasted to eight stone, just skin and bone with shrunken cheeks and his hands devoid of flesh, suffering from delusions, hallucinations and paranoia. Transferred to mental hospital as a shambling wreck, in a lucid interval he drew parallels with Dostoevsky's *Crime and Punishment*: 'I led the life that other people only think about... In other words, Raskolnikov's situation was a synopsis of precisely how I was. That's what I believed at the time.'

See also **Fantasising, Pets, Privilege, Tapes**

Brank, brake or Scold's head

These days, we hear little of the brank. It was a relatively modern English device, not mentioned until 1623 in Macclesfield.

It consisted of a skeletal metal helmet with a protrusion, sometimes spiked, inserted into the

wearer's mouth to immobilise the tongue. The Walton-on-Thames brank bears the inscription 'Chester presents Walton with a bridle/To curb women's tongues that talk too idle.'

An excellent contemporary account survives in Dr Brushfield's recollections from an 1856 lecture. In the village of Congleton, 'There was generally fixed on one side of the large open fireplaces a hook so that when a man's wife indulged her scolding propensities, the husband sent for the town jailor to bring the bridle and had her chained to the hook... I have often heard husbands say to their wives "If you don't rest up with your tongue I'll send for the bridle and hook you up."' The last record of the Congleton brake's use is in 1824, and for the Shrewsbury brake, 1846.

There is no record of a brank for men, but the punishment seems mild compared with the fate of disorderly American women who, in the 1860s and 70s, were routinely handed over to gynaecologists for ovariotomy (female castration).

See also **Hopkins, Sexism, Witchcraze**

Brink's

The FBI called it the 'crime of the century'. The *Boston Globe* billed the heist as 'the biggest all-**cash** stick-up in the US'. But the only person to make

usable money out of the 1950 robbery at the North Terminal Garage was Joseph F. Dineen, a journalist with the *Boston Globe*. He wrote the book of the crime, filmed as *Six Bridges to Cross*, earning a fee of $150,000.

Brink's was the security firm handling $10 million a day in local payrolls. On 17 January 1950 the thieves made off with $2,775,395, $1,218,211.29 of it in cash. The seven-man team were in and out in seventeen minutes, carting their 1,200 pounds deadweight of loot back home to Adolph 'Jazz' Maffey's. Next morning they went to work as normal, only collecting their share a month later. Then they frittered it away, leaving the police without a lead.

But one of the gang, 'Specs' O'Keefe, entrusted some $90,000 to another member of the team, who later declined to give it back. 'Specs' threatened to blow the gaffe; the gang put out a contract on him with Elmer 'Trigger' Burke, who failed; and Specs did blow the gaffe, on 12 January 1956, only five days before the expiration of the six-year Statute of Limitations. All ten raiders went to jail. The aftermath of Britain's **Great Train Robbery** is depressingly similar: an unprecedented criminal venture followed by years of filching and misery.

The Brink's break-in was well rehearsed over eighteen months while the gang made a total of twenty-seven night-time sorties, wandering round the premises more or less at will. Five locked doors barred their way to the main counting room; over the months, their locksmith Henry J. Baker removed each lock, cast a duplicate key overnight and then replaced the cylinder. So on the day the raiders walked through to the final wire-mesh grille, donned their rubber masks and chauffeurs' caps, showed their guns and said: 'This is a stick-up.' The FBI investigation into the robbery cost an estimated $29 million.

The co-planner of the robbery was smiling Anthony 'Fats' Pino, an inspirational crook and monumental liar born in 1907. As a child Pino showed unusual promise at pilfering coal for his parents' stove. He sold off the surplus at three cents a pound, earning his first arrest for stealing a streetcar ride. When shot in the buttock by the police at the age of fifteen after purloining some cake and milk, he already had eight arrests under his belt, as well as three spells on probation and seven months in a reformatory for filching $20. While sitting out World War II in Charlestown prison, he was beaten up by other inmates for stealing the buttons from their uniforms. Released on parole in September 1944, he faced deportation and, to raise the $5,000 bribe to reverse the decision, worked nights as a cart pusher at a Stop and Shop warehouse. In the eight weeks before being sacked, Pino stole $6,000. One morning after his shift, inspired by the sight of the Brink's trucks rumbling up Congress Street towards the Chamber of Commerce building, he thought of doing something worthwhile.

Pino studied the comings and goings at Brink's, wearing a variety of disguises from his collection of stolen costumes, dressing up as a milkman, busboy, chef or doorman. His favourite outfit, stolen from a circus, was the lion tamer's, which he only wore in private. In January 1946 he tailed Truck 48 to a garage and stole a set of keys from the office hook. That February he opened the van door, while the guards were on delivery, and removed a bag containing $3,500; ten days later, he helped himself to $5,000, and thereafter, together with the gang, he embarked on a regular schedule of robberies of the premises to which Brink's made deliveries. In February 1946 the first safe yielded $7,300, and the gang did the rounds of Brink's customers twice, some even three times, netting $600,000 in addition to the $400,000 from the trucks.

Smiling Anthony 'Fats' Pino

In June 1948 Pino married, and while honeymooning in Baltimore he devoted himself to stealing hideous rubber masks from an arcade. Later that year he earned a twelve-month term for stealing a dozen golf balls. Meanwhile the gang agreed to terminate their professional relationship with Brink's by robbing Truck 48 as it loaded on the premises. The raid was set for 7 January 1949, but

Brink's moved offices to the North Terminal Garage Building in Prince Street, and a new plan evolved to divest the entire building of cash, dressed as chauffeurs, wearing Pino's masks.

Pino was released from prison in July 1971 and died two years later, still vowing to kill Specs O'Keefe. Brink's remains a favourite target. On 30 March 1976 one of their delivery trucks was stopped on a Montreal street. The gang, who threatened the van with an anti-aircraft gun, made off with $2.8 million.

Budgerigar *et al*

A long-term prisoner may get permission to keep a budgerigar in his cell. Paid for out of his own pocket, this expensive acquisition indicates a prisoner's acceptance of his sentence. Thereafter he is regarded as quietly settled, *doing his bird*.

A budgerigar may represent the prisoner's most significant relationship and, in the vindictive atmosphere of prison, this constitutes an Achilles heel. Budgies can be assassinated to satisfy a grudge or even be kidnapped: an ounce of tobacco or your bird comes back – dead. In a December 1992 modification, a convict's pet rabbit, 'Lucky', was abducted in a Scottish maximum security jail and ransomed for two cans of ginger beer.

Rabbits are rarities in mainstream crime. Colleeen Stan, the sex-**slave**, was confined to a hutch-like box, and the eighteenth-century British conwoman Mary Toft conjured rabbits up, but not by pulling them out of a hat.

Delivery was effected with the aid of an accomplice who helped Toft load the struggling creatures into her womb, where they caused such discomfort that their miraculous ejaculation was provoked by painful spasms simulating labour. She hoped for a royal pension, and succeeded in convincing Mr Howard, the local doctor; he confirmed that in one month he had assisted at the birth of twenty live rabbits, provoking widespread awe.

Toft's credibility was much enhanced by her poor education. It was supposed that she lacked the intelligence to mislead sophisticated medical opinion, and rumours of her proclivity reached the household of her sovereign, King George I. He had Toft appraised by no less a luminary than the Royal Surgeon, St André, who dissected one of Toft's offspring in the royal presence to prove that they were real rabbits.

Confidence in Toft became a political issue at court, where a cynical Queen's faction took issue with the King and his supporters, and when the Queen despatched her physician, Sir Richard Mannington, to examine the girl, his misgivings were aroused by the pig's bladder she secreted vaginally in error. Toft confessed, and was consigned to Bridewell in 1726; she had briefly made a good living from her exploits.

The murder of Eddie Evans by Ian **Brady** on 6 October 1965 is the only killing known to the author observed by a budgerigar. It was called Joey, and it played no part in the proceedings. Indeed, birds are seldom called in evidence (but see **Carrier Pigeons**), except perhaps in Argentina where the eye-witness testimony of a parrot can be decisive. In 1990 Rosella DeGambo brought an action against her husband Carlos, whom she suspected of two-timing, her apprehensions inflamed when the family cockatoo, Bozo, started giggling in an unfamiliar, high-pitched, female voice.

Summoned to the stand, Bozo reacted strongly to photographs of a young beautician who allegedly visited Carlos on the sly. 'Honeybun, I love you!' exclaimed Bozo in apparent recognition of the woman's picture. Bozo added: 'Ruby loves Carlos. Ruby loves her baby.' The husband's secretary was called Ruby.

Despite the protests of Carlos's lawyer, Bozo's evidence was adjudged admissible. But this is a third-hand report of a civil case from another country, noted in the Canadian journal *The Lawyers Weekly*, summarised in the *Toronto Sun* on 9 March 1990, and digested in the *Fortean Times*.

In America, a 1942 murder case was solved by an eponymous parrot. On 12 July the proprietor of the East Harlem Green Parrot Bar was gunned down in front of twenty customers, none of whom had the good fortune to witness the incident. But the police soon knew the motive. 'Robber, robber,' chanted the parrot. With no further leads, the investigation foundered, but an intrigued detective John J. Morrisey persisted in a study of the bird's linguistic abilities, finding its elocution flawed by a tendency to drop the final consonant, and, further, that its vocabulary was confined to the names of the bar's regular clientele. Checking his files for a likely-sounding Robert, Morrisey came upon a Robert Butler, by then living in Maryland, and on 10 February 1944 Butler was sentenced to seven years after making a full confession.

In Brazil, a 'parrot's perch' denotes a form of **torture** where the victim is suspended in mid-air with his knees bent double over a metal rod and his ankles bound to his wrists.

Bundy, Theodore Robert (1946–89)

This pernicious American serial killer not only depersonalised his victims, he depersonalised himself, preferring to speak of his encounters in the third person. Asked if there was much conversation with his victims, Bundy told the police: 'There'd be some. Since this girl in front of him represented not a person, but again the image, or something desirable, the last thing we would expect him to want to do would be to personalise this person.' So he called them things like 'cargo' or '**throwaways**'. Bundy could not acknowledge his crimes directly, but only 'speculated' about what had happened, hiding behind a fiction of innocence while helping investigators build up a 'picture' of what the killer was like.

It took Bundy years to work up from his first faltering steps as a voyeur, via stalking his quarry home, to overt sexual assaults and thence to rape and finally murder. His first homicide was Lynda Ann Healey on 31 January 1974; his youngest, 12-year-old Kimberley Leach. In July 1974, Bundy killed two in one day, abducting his victims from the crowded beach at Lake Sammamish Park, bringing back the second girl to the house where he had already raped the first, and then raping the second in front of the first before killing both. Returning to his fiancée Cas Richter that evening, Bundy said he felt 'real bad', but later recovered sufficiently to go out to dinner.

Bundy escaped from prison twice, the second time by dieting and then, on New Year's Eve 1977, squeezing through a loose ceiling panel around a light socket and crawling through the overhead space to the jailers' lounge. He might have remained at large indefinitely, but under his alias Chris Hagen he continued killing. On the night of 15 January 1978 he ravaged four women in a Florida Chi Omega student residential block, moving from room to room in some thirty minutes. Two lived to tell the tale, two were clubbed to death and strangled during vicious sexual assaults. A few minutes later, Bundy broke into a student house a few blocks away. There he attacked ballet student Cheryl Thomas. Her flatmates heard the struggle, and she survived despite massive head injuries.

Next month, during a failed abduction in Jacksonville, the registration number of his stolen white Dodge van was noted. The following day, on 9 February, he kidnapped and murdered schoolgirl Kimberley Leach. The van was found abandoned on 13 February, replete with forensic evidence, and two days later Bundy himself was approached by Patrolman David Lee, his attention caught by an awkwardly parked VW Beetle in a Pensacola side-street at 1.30 a.m. Bundy drove off, was overtaken and arrested at gunpoint. He was sentenced to death the following year and executed nearly ten years later.

Bundy, a good-looking charmer with an easy manner, found work with the Seattle Crime Prevention Advisory Commission before (and while) plunging off the rails. In the words of Barbara

43

Grossman, a TV reporter: 'The first time I saw him I said to myself, "Wow, all he had to do is ask me to go with him and I'd go"' – exactly what many of his victims did, falling for his pick-up **lines**. Grossman was not alone in her assessment; Cathy Swindler, who met Bundy when he was twenty-one, depicted him as 'a figure that people met and loved'. His contemporaries believed him destined for high office, 'a man who might well have been Governor of Washington'.

Too much has been made of Bundy's brilliant future and social talents. His killings formed the counterpoint to his emotional life. The illegitimate son of a respectable secretary, he was left almost alone for the first weeks of life, when the ability to give and receive affection is imprinted. His father's identity remained a secret; his maternal grandfather (with whom he lived until the age of four) was a violent despot. Bundy grew into a keen **masturbator**, formidable liar, a fantasist and a compulsive thief, as an adult once stealing an eight-foot tree from a greenhouse and driving away with his booty sticking out through the car roof. When his lost love, the beautiful, sophisticated and wealthy Stephanie Brooks, dropped him in 1966, the distress caused a surge in his thieving.

Bundy wanted to impress her by studying Chinese at Stanford University, but his grades were poor and he could not compete with his own standards of success. Reduced to working as a salesman in a department store, he stole for kicks, nurturing an interest in violent pornography. An accidental glimpse of a woman undressing in a lighted room led to a career as a campus Peeping Tom, and by degrees, in between interludes of self-disgust, he sought 'more active kinds of gratification', first following the girls, then tinkering with their cars to disable them, then stalking, weapon in hand, then lying in wait, and finally making his first attack with a piece of wood as his victim fumbled with her keys by her front door. The next stage, in 1973, was forced entry, hiding inside a student's room against her return.

At this stage Bundy's star was temporarily in the ascendant. His acceptance as a law student, coupled with his job at the Crime Commission, imparted a spurious aura of self-confidence and maturity. He won Stephanie Brooks back with a high-power courtship. Dazzled by his new sophistication, she

agreed to marry him during Christmas 1973, which they spent in a borrowed condominium at Alpental. But she flew back to California on 2 January, hurt and confused by a change in his manner. She later concluded he had made her fall in love with him for the pleasure of rejecting her.

Maybe this made Bundy feel good: three days later he committed his first rape. It was symbolic; he violated student Sharon Clarke with a metal bed-rod. She was found in a coma the following day, scarcely alive. Then he refused to take Stephanie's bewildered telephone calls. Maybe that made him feel better, and during this phase of satisfying demonstration of power he killed for the first time.

The victims were all attractive Stephanie-clones, sporting the same long hair parted in the middle and the same good, even features. Often penile dominance was not enough; Bundy stuffed his victims' vaginas with twigs and dirt and, on one occasion, sodomised a corpse with an aerosol can. Such activities cannot claim to be primarily sexual. His regular girlfriend during this period, Magan Roberts, reported that she and Bundy progressed through anal sex to bondage and thence to mock **strangulation** with distressing rapidity. Sex became an arena for anger, and Bundy was angry with everyone – his girlfriends, his family and his associates.

After his arrest, Bundy always kept at least one woman under his spell, living for her brief jail visits, running his errands and proclaiming his innocence. When one drifted away, another took her place. But his fragile self-image must have taken a knock after sentence as he walked down the prison corridor towards Death Row. Jeers, threats and howls of execration echoed from the other cells. 'He was scared to death,' said one of the guards. Prisoners regarded him as the lowest of the low, a child molester and sex killer.

Bundy confessed to twenty-three murders. Hours before his electrocution at 7.16 a.m. on 24 January 1989 he gave a radio interview, discoursing on the evils of pornography which, he claimed, caused his crimes – hence the nicknaming of the current Pornography Victims' Compensation Act as 'Bundy Bill'. His was a popular execution. More than a thousand applicants wrote in asking to witness his death, and outside the Florida State Penitentiary a huge crowd wearing 'Burn, Bundy, Burn' T-shirts let off fireworks in celebration, while the local radio station enjoined listeners to switch off domestic appliances 'to give them more juice down there at the jail'.

See also **Preview, References, Throwaways, de Sade, Trolling**

Burke and Hare

A Scottish **bodysnatching** partnership who together despatched sixteen or perhaps seventeen victims, nearly all drunk old wives or drunk old men. The couple made their living by selling the victims' corpses, shocking the Edinburgh citizens so deeply that until the passage of Warburton's 1832 Anatomy Act children were kept off the streets; families huddled indoors long before dark and working men travelled home in groups for safety.

Burke (1792–1829) was of a tolerably amiable disposition, a flautist who never attracted the vilification heaped on his accomplice. Born in County Tyrone, Burke emigrated to Scotland where he worked as a navvy. He took up with Helen McDougal, and ran into Hare (1790–c.1860) at Log's Lodgings in Edinburgh's West Port, a doss-house where the latter was ensconced with the widowed owner, Margaret Laird.

Not long after Burke's arrival, one of the lodgers – a decrepit pensioner called Desmond – died of dropsy. He owed £4 in back rent, a loss the pair

more than recouped by marketing his body. The eminent surgeon Robert Knox paid the going rate of £7 10s, representing about six months' wages for a labourer. 'We would be pleased to see you again,' Burke and Hare were told by the hospital.

Thereafter the pair obtained their corpses by murder. The first victim was Joseph the Miller, suffocated with a pillow after being rendered insensible during a companionable drinking session. Their method was for one to lie on top of their 'prospect', keeping him down while the other covered the mouth and nose. This left little trace of violent death, and Knox accepted the murdered bodies in good faith. Joseph the Miller netted a handsome £10. Next came a match-seller; then Abigail Simpson, the salt pedlar; then a young whore Mary Paterson; then more 'drunk auld wives': one-toothed Peggy Haldane and Effy the cinder gatherer. The victims – referred to as 'shots' – were picked up in the Edinburgh streets and, if it seemed their absence would not be missed, befriended and asked back for a drink.

After snapping the spine of a deaf-mute and packing him into a pickled herring barrel along with his grandmother, Burke suffered from sleeplessness, keeping a lighted candle and a bottle of whisky at his bedside. But his partnership with Hare continued, their tally soon including a misguided relative, Mary Haldane, who came to stay for a holiday.

Burke (left) and Hare (right)

Margaret Laird took a pound from every body-sale as 'rent' for the murder premises which, according to the contemporary Professor Wilson, looked pleasantly 'like a minister's manse'. Similarly, Burke's room 'was one of the neatest and snuggest little places' that Wilson ever saw.

To supplement his income, Burke took in paying lodgers, a tactical error compounded by disposing of popular 'Daft Jamie' Wilson, a mild-mannered but well-known local idiot whose unexplained disappearance had the neighbourhood seething with rumours of a new gang of cannibals like Sawney Beane (see **Cannibalism**).

Burke and Hare sealed their fate with their next murder of 'Madgy or Margaret Campbell or Duffy or M'Gonegal or Doherty'. Whatever her true name, this tiny woman in a conspicuous red gown was unambiguously seen at Burke's lodgings on the evening of her death. Next morning Burke concealed her body in straw under his bed and invited friends in for breakfast, spraying whisky around as a disinfectant. Eventually his guests went about their daily business, leaving Mrs Gray the lodger to wash and sand the floor. There she came across an arm poking out from under the straw.

Her husband dragged out Madgy's body and the couple fled in terror, instantly running into Helen McDougal, who offered them the extravagant hush-money of £1 a week for life. But she could only manage six shillings down. The three discussed it over a drink and the Grays decided to inform the police, but by the time Constable Fisher arrived, the body had vanished. Burke had already flogged it to Knox, and very nearly succeeded in shrugging off Madgy's bloodstains on the straw as a visitor's menstrual bleeding.

A post-mortem on Madgy's recovered body furnished no proof of foul play and Burke realised he had to explain away a corpse, not a murder. After a couple of imaginative false starts (including a tale of a stranger 'in a greatcoat' who arrived with a tea chest out of which, like a conjurer, he produced a body before disappearing) Burke shrewdly admitted everything about Madgy except the manner of her death. He insisted that she had died peacefully overnight. True, he had sold his windfall to Knox, but why not? With no firm evidence of foul play, no fair jury could convict: there was a reasonable doubt.

So the police offered Hare exemption from prosecution if he turned King's evidence. He duly confessed, and the legal proceedings began on Christmas Eve 1828 in the tiny Edinburgh courtroom.

Burke stood accused of three murders, Helen McDougal was indicted as 'art and part' to the killings, and Hare appeared as principal prosecution witness, earning particular disgust for his congenital simper.

The defence opened with a novel gambit, arguing that if the case proceeded then evidence of a nature prejudicial to the defendant's reputation would be aired in public. This was true, but the trial started anyway and continued all night, the judges sipping coffee on the bench as the grim story unfolded; the following morning Burke was sentenced to death. Helen was acquitted. But for police intervention, she would have been torn to pieces, recognised by the crowd at her release on Boxing Day.

Before his execution on 28 January Burke made a full confession, but his regret, though real, was limited to Knox having only made part-payment for the last body. He was hanged on a very short drop in front of a huge gathering, including such luminaries as Sir Walter Scott; to the crowd's gratification, he struggled in protracted agony. The body was exhibited the following day in the medical school, and then dissected. His tanned skin sold at a shilling a square inch for presentation **tobacco** pouches.

Although cleared by a Committee of Inquiry, Knox was suspected by the mob, who strung up his effigy and broke his windows. Attendance at his lectures tapered off and he moved south to the London borough of Hackney as a general practitioner, dispensing free obstetric care to the poor. H. R. F. Keating, the writer of crime fiction, affirms that Knox was last heard of in America as a travelling showman with a band of Redskins.

Hare, smuggled out of Scotland, took a factory job. But he was recognised by his workmates, who hurled him into a **lime** pit. His sight was destroyed, and it seems he made his way to London, where late Victorians recalled seeing him in their youth as a blind beggar around Oxford Street and the British Museum.

See also **Coffins, Memorabilia**

Butch Cassidy and the Sundance Kid, the fate of

The recent work of American anthropologist Clyde Snow may have unearthed the bodies of the two men immortalised by Robert Redford and Paul Newman. In the 1969 film the outlaws perished in a doomed act of bravado, charging ranks of massed troops. In reality, a suicide pact is probable.

They died in 1909 in San Vincente, Mexico, where their fate was investigated by the US Bolivian Consul. He learned from the soldiers in at the kill, that the bandits holed up in a shack and, after an inconclusive gun-battle, shot themselves rather than surrender. Today, the closest account comes from a manager of the Chocaya Tin-Silver Mine called Roberts, who told his story to the mining engineer Victor J. Hampton in the 1920s.

During their last day, the gangsters held up a mule train led by a mozo or native guard, making off with both the money from Roberts's mine and one of the pack-animals. Soldiers tracked them down. Hampton recalled: 'The soldiers arrived as darkness was closing in. The mozo, who had been the payroll's guard, went inside and found the mule. He came out and told the officer in charge of the detachment that the two Americans cooking inside the hut were surely the robbers. Cassidy and the Kid were in the adobe hut, their rifles outside. They were using a small beehive-type baking oven and could be seen eating in the glow of the candle. The officer led his men into the gate and shouted an order to surrender. That's when the shooting started. Roberts said they found the pair dead the next morning.'

To reduce their risk, the soldiers sent an Indian woman on ahead, carrying a baby. Cassidy lay dead on the floor, and the Kid squatted on his haunches, shot through the eyes. Roberts said that one was wounded going for the rifles, the other committed suicide.

The bodies were buried in the local cemetery, and in January 1992 a local, who had the story from his father, pointed out their supposed grave to Clyde Snow. On excavation, it disgorged the bones of two bodies of Caucasian origin, both with a bullet hole to the skull.

C

Cadaveric spasm

An important pathological finding. Cadaveric spasm is a form of rigor mortis associated with violent death including drowning, when the victim clutches at straws. The fingers grip whatever they held at the time of death with such force that they cannot be prised open.

Since it is impossible to simulate, the condition carries great evidential weight; investigators can be certain that whatever the cadaver's hand holds was there at the moment of expiry. One of G. J. Smith's murdered wives clasped a piece of soap in *prima facie* corroboration of his unlikely tale that she drowned in the **bath**.

This fierce grip must be distinguished from standard rigor mortis, a point underlined in 1885 when an apparent suicide's body was discovered in a locked bedroom clutching a revolver. Lacassagne, the great French pathologist, established experimentally that the fingers of a newly-dead corpse *could* be made to encircle objects like a pistol, albeit loosely, and the onset of ordinary rigor would temporarily mimic cadaveric spasm as the hand tightened around the butt.

This observation confirmed his suspicions, originally aroused by the corpse's arms which lay under the bedclothes pulled up to its chin, a point missed by the local Savoy doctors, who diagnosed suicide. But Lacassagne thought it unlikely that the man would blow his brains out *before* tidying up his bedding.

Lacassagne's persistence led to the conviction of the deceased's son, who had shot his father before escaping through a window.

See also **Mortal combat**

Camargo, Daniel (1931–)

The so-called 'Beast of the Andes', currently serving sixteen years – the maximum penalty under Ecuadorian law – for murdering seventy-one or perhaps 150 young girls.

Camargo's story bears suspicious parallels with the life of Henry Lee **Lucas**, the discredited American serial killer. Both were arrested by luck as pathetic hoboes in middle age; both claimed wretched childhoods from broken, violent families; both maintained that they attended school forcibly dressed as a girl; both staked claims to an extraordinary number of murders committed in a very short time, and both were greeted by the police as the answer to a backlog of unsolved killings.

Lucas's **success** in hoodwinking sophisticated American law enforcement agencies suggests that such feats would be easy for well-briefed serial confessors in the Third World. Camargo is intelligent and well-read, fluent in three languages, and one of the things he may have read before his 1986 arrest is the dizzying climb to celebrity that followed Lucas's capture in 1983.

Camargo, born in the Colombian Andes on 22 January 1931, says that his mother died when he was one, his stepmother beat him, his uncle drank, his sister was a bully and his father stole his piggy bank. He left Bogota's Leon XIII College at the age of twelve, married Alcira Castillo when he was twenty-nine and walked out seven years later on the day he discovered her in bed with another man. Then the slide started.

Obsessed with virginity, Camargo forced his next lover to drug young girls with sleeping pills so that he could rape them, and in 1965 he was sentenced to six years after being identified by a victim. On release, by his account he went to Brazil, but according to journalist Alberto Uribe Gomez he stayed in Colombia for a rampage that ended the lives of at least eighty adolescent girls. Not in dispute is his arrest in May 1974 and a twenty-five year sentence for a single rape and murder.

Ten years into his term on the penal island of Gorgona, Camargo stumbled across an abandoned canoe. After three days at sea, on 26 November 1984 he made shore on the mainland where he evaded capture for fifteen months until his chance arrest, when two inquisitive officers opened his battered suitcase to discover a bundle of bloodstained clothing.

Camargo confessed to seventy-one killings. In his words, 'I took my revenge for several years of humiliation. I took revenge on women's unfaithfulness... After I spent five years in jail for rape, the only thing I feared was to return there. So I had to kill without leaving traces... I had an extra shirt with me and when I had blood on my hands I pissed on them.'

His apparent motivation dovetails with the psychological orthodoxy of today: 'Some of my victims fought so violently that they set off my impulse to violence and I couldn't control it. It was a natural prolongation of the sexual impulse which had not always been satisfied through **rape**.' Nor is Camargo a stranger to the concept of the cooling-off period (see **Terminology**). After a murder, he said, 'I swore never to start again. And then it came back. A desire inside me, like a drug. I had to kill another one.'

Asked why he removed one victim's heart, lungs and kidneys, Camargo replied, 'That's an entirely invented story... At best I might have taken out the heart, the organ of love.'

See also **False confessions, Success**

Cambo, Judge

An eighteenth-century Maltese judge famed for his prowess at distinguishing between **justice** and the law. One day in 1720 Cambo witnessed a murder outside his house and took a good look at the culprit as he ran off, dropping a knife sheath in the process. A passing baker picked up this incriminating clue (matching the dagger left embedded in the victim), and was duly arrested.

As luck would have it, the innocent baker came up for trial before Cambo, who quite properly found the circumstantial evidence insufficient for a conviction. Eschewing personal favouritism, the judge followed standard procedure and subjected the accused – who he knew was not the murderer – to **torture**. When he confessed, the wretch was executed.

This miscarriage of justice came to light when the true culprit admitted the killing on his deathbed. The Grand Master of the Knights of Malta took Cambo to task for condemning a blameless man, but he pointed out it was his duty to uphold the law rather than to act on knowledge he happened to have acquired in his private capacity. Even so, Cambo lost his job.

Camels, homing

Normal drug couriers are known as '**mules**', except in the border area of Rajasthan where the job is done by camels. These ships of the desert, laden with satchels of heroin strapped to their bellies, are turned loose to plod unescorted through the sands to the border collection point, and their rare interception represents no coup for the police, producing neither arrests nor intelligence. On safe arrival, the **narcotics** are removed and buried to await shipment through India.

In the nineteenth century the daily price for **opium** throughout the subcontinent was formally 'fixed' each morning by the Rajasthan cartel from their desert mansions in Shekhwati. The going rate was broadcast to India after reaching the railway line at Bhowani Junction, where it arrived by bush telegraph, that is, drumming.

Campden Wonder, The

A famous **false confession**. On 16 August 1660 William Harrison, a 70-year-old steward from the village of Chipping Campden, vanished while on his rounds. A bloodstained hat was found, and under interrogation Harrison's servant – John Perry – implicated his brother and mother in the killing. He said they had strangled Harrison with a hair-net and pitched the body into the lake by Wallington's Mill. The three accomplices were tried and executed the following year.

Two years later, in 1663, Harrison turned up alive and well, claiming that a band of highwaymen had beaten him about the head, clapped on handcuffs and escorted him to the coast to be shipped abroad in a convoy and sold as a slave to a Turkish doctor in Smyrna. 'It was my chance to be chosen by a grave physician of eighty-seven years of age,' he said. Harrison's wife – 'a snotty covetous Presbyterian' – hanged herself after his return.

This mysterious train of events, related by Sir Thomas Overbury in his *True and Perfect Account*, highlights the dangers of bringing a murder charge without producing the body. Harrison's story has long excited disbelief; highwaymen were not equipped with handcuffs, and no marauding Turkish traders supplied Smyrna with septuagenarian English slaves. More recently, suspicions grew that the entire story was a fiction: the return of the wanderer is a stock literary theme.

But records surfaced showing that a steward called Harrison stopped signing the local grammar school accounts between April 1660 and October 1663. Other documentation chronicles the delivery on 3 March 1661 of John, Richard and Joan Parry to Gloucester Jail for execution. So Harrison did disappear and the Parrys were hanged.

Today, the phenomenon of Parry's **false confession** is better understood. As for Harrison, he went missing in the year of the King's restoration after the Civil War, when many people found it expedient to make themselves scarce while old scores were settled. If Harrison was not forcibly abducted, then he must have bloodied his own hat, leaving it as a misleading clue.

Cannibalism

Eating people is not against the law provided they are dead. The element of cannibalism adds a macabre dimension to a killing, but the defendant does not face the additional charge that he consumed his victim. Thus men like Chase, Fish and Haarmann were tried for murder, whereas those who – after plane crashes or similar interruptions to their journeys – devour their deceased companions rather than perish from hunger have simply broken a taboo.

It is vital to wait until the prospective meal has expired. On 25 July 1884 Captain John Dudley, starving to death on a drifting lifeboat 1,600 miles off the Cape of Good Hope, resolved to kill the cabin boy Richard Parker for food. The lad was barely alive, but Dudley pipped the Grim Reaper to the post. A replenished Dudley survived his ordeal to make land, only to face a charge of murder. He pleaded 'necessity' by way of defence, but was convicted and sentenced to death. Eventually the Crown relented and let him off with six months.

Cannibalism was practised until recently in parts of Africa. On 11 May 1888 the explorer James Jameson was chatting to the slave trader Tippu-Tib in deepest Congo. Cannibalism was all travellers' tales, said Jameson. By way of reply one of Tippu-Tib's men fetched a young girl and knifed her. 'Three men then ran forward, and began to cut up the body of the girl,' wrote Jameson in his diary. 'Finally her head was cut off, and not a particle remained, each man taking his piece away down to the river to wash it. The most extraordinary thing was that the girl never uttered a sound, nor struggled, until she fell.' Tippu-Tib resumed the conversation. A CBS correspondent in the Congo during the 1960s recalls tribal feasts where he dined off the flesh of infants (roasted on the spit) who had died of natural causes.

Many other societies continued to eat people into the modern era. Thus the Basuto tribesmen excised the hearts of their enemies and ate them, as did the Sioux Indians. Head hunters sucked out the brains of their prey, and the Zulus consumed the forehead and eyebrows of their foes. The underlying rationale was to imbue the victor with the power of the fallen, and the best documented inheritor of this tradition is Jeffrey **Dahmer**, the Milwaukee serial killer. His love of corpses, in the final phase, extended to eating them. He prepared a total of five meals from their body parts.

Dahmer's words, 'I suppose in an odd way it made me feel as if they were more part of me', grope towards some truth, most notably the tenet at the heart of Christian ritual, the transubstantiation of communion where the faithful partake of Christ's blood and body.

Christianity derives from paganism and the florid rites of pre-history. But the primmer, more pedestrian Protestant doctrines dispense with the elements of primitive mysticism and superstition subsumed in Catholic ritual and iconography, leaving a religion bowdlerised of its pagan roots. On this analysis, throwbacks like Dahmer uncover lineaments of paganism in their unconscious, falling prey to the unacknowledged bogey of cannibalism and erecting primitive shrines in its honour.

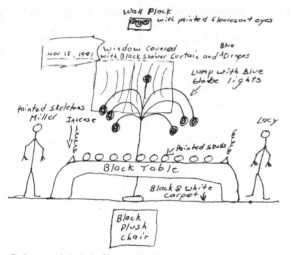

Dahmer's 'shrine', in his own hand

Almost the only project ever undertaken by Dahmer was the construction of a home-made shrine in **Oxford Apartments**. There his black table, supposedly corresponding to an altar, was to be flanked by skeletons and adorned by skulls. Numerous Christian places of worship incorporate similar reliquaries. 'What was it a shrine to?' Dahmer was asked. 'Myself,' he replied. It represented a place where he could feel 'at home'. Occasionally members of North American tribes are similarly possessed by the so called 'windigo' spirit, which takes over hunters who spend their harsh lives in the wilderness, bereft of human companionship and lacking a place to call their own. Indians absorbed by the windigo devoured all who crossed their path. Saskatchewan furnishes a well-attested case from 1879 involving a Cree Indian called Swift Runner. At his trial in Edmonton it was obvious that nothing would shake Swift Runner from his course.

'You might as well hang me,' he said after eating his family, 'because I'm going to kill lots more.'

The Russian serial killer **Chikatilo** laboured under a similar affliction, telling the Rostov Chief of Police: 'I cannot help myself. When the call comes, I must kill.' Both Dahmer and Chikatilo evinced a sexual fascination with their victims' innards. Dahmer made love to the intestines prior to cooking their more digestible parts, but the act of consumption was a leisurely, post-coital confirmation of a relationship during a phase distinct from **dismemberment**. The processing of his victims, elaborated into a ritual extending over hours or days, culminated in a formal meal they shared to the extent that both were present, although one of the participants was merely on the menu. Even then, the bones were destined for incorporation into his shrine.

Dahmer is the thinking man's cannibal; with Chikatilo, eating formed part of the sexual frenzy, an extreme extension of the love-bite which, in the clearest parallel, involved biting off his victims' nipples but progressed to slicing off the tips of tongues, severing the sexual organs or biting off the boys' testicles. In grosser violation of his female victims, Chikatilo excised the uterus. 'I did not so much chew them as bite them, they were so beautiful and elastic,' he said. This is consumption for sexual rather than liturgical purposes, and the love and the biting are no longer conjoined.

British cases lack conviction. In Scotland the sixteenth-century Sawney Beane supposedly sired an entire incestuous clan of eight sons, six daughters and thirty-two grandchildren, cannibals every one of them. The Beanes inhabited a cave on the Galloway coast, eating 1,500 people in twenty-five years, the bodies 'hung up in rows, like dried beef'. King James I led an expedition of 400 soldiers against them, fought a pitched battle and dragged the clan's surviving members to Leith where they were burned at the stake without trial. There is, however, no historical documentation of these events, and 'Sawney Beane' is almost certainly a legend.

See also **Fish, Sagawa, Sex crimes**

Canonisation

The latest manifestation of the American crime craze is a new saintly figure: the Victim. Celebrity status awaits 'survivors' who testify on chat shows.

The Central Park Jogger, left for dead after a vicious assault, was honoured by the tribute of flowers from Frank Sinatra. In mid-1992 Rodney **King**, the Los Angeles victim, stood a chance of becoming a movie and merchandising property; he attracted favourable comparison with Martin Luther King's 'I have a dream' speech by saying 'Can't we work together?' in the aftermath of the 1992 riots.

Truman Capote's 1964 *In Cold Blood* made respectable the chronicling of mundane gore. Norman Mailer, with his 1980s dalliance with the convicted murderer Jack Abbott, made it risible. Today, *Vanity Fair* carries regular crime features with glamour photos of leading *mafiosi* like John Gotti by star snapper Annie Leibowitz, and the recent reversal of the 'Son of **Sam**' law by the Supreme Court has left criminals free to profit from their rush into print and celluloid.

On American television a spate of 'reality shows' and televised trials blurred the distinction between real life and entertainment. The FBI retained Robert Stack (of *Untouchables* fame) to host *Unsolved Mysteries*. *The New FBI: the Untold Stories* uses Pernell Roberts (from *Bonanza*). *The American Detective* shows real cops on the job. Celebrities like Mickey Rourke and Anthony Quinn flocked to John Gotti's **trial**; the televised Kennedy rape trial was selected for video release. *Top Cops* too is just like real life: true stories and voice-overs from the actual policemen involved. The only difference is that the actors are better looking.

David Simon, a police reporter from the *Baltimore Sun*, has remarked how local jurors, depressed by the quality of real courtroom casting and screenplay, encumber proceedings with interjections of lega-babble culled from *Hawaii Five-O* reruns.

Hinckley's shooting of Ronald Reagan was no less confusing (see **Stalking**). He tried to kill the President because actress Jodie Foster (whom he admired in the film *Taxi Driver*) failed to respond to his letters. The attempt landed him on television, thereby adding to Miss Foster's resonance in her subsequent role in *The Silence of the Lambs*.

Instant television 'docudramas' are big business. On the day of the 1993 World Trade Tower bombing, the FBI logged nineteen calls claiming responsibility while CBS received fifteen from movie producers wanting to cut a deal. An audience of 80 million tuned in to watch the story of Amy Fisher, the 18-year-old 'Long Island Lolita' who shot her lover's wife dead, but the six-month schedule between the murder and its screening as entertainment proved too tight for a quality production. In the words of Professor Robert Kubey from Rutgers University, 'The main issue for Hollywood is, "Can this person sue us?"; not "are we distorting or offending?"'

The extent to which Britain lags behind the United States in the rush to dramatise personal tragedies can be precisely computed. It is two weeks. Hardly a year after Oxford student Rachel McLean was strangled by her boyfriend and concealed under the floorboards, a reconstruction was filmed for the 1992 television series *Michael Winner's True Crimes*. After Rachel's parents objected that its broadcast might be upsetting, the showing was postponed by a fortnight. A year later, the murder of the Liverpool toddler Jamie Bulger by two ten-year-old children prompted immediate American interest in a two-hour television show. The British researcher charged with obtaining the 'buy-ins' (exclusive rights) to the 'story' from relatives and acquaintances encountered only occasional resistance. He noted, 'The public weren't the problem. Most were only too pleased at the thought of appearing on American television.'

The British True Crime boom owes much to the economic recession. Distressed or anxious readers can comfort themselves with case-histories of warped perpetrators, whose lives are worse than their own, and stories of the victims, brought low more or less at random.

See also **Wuornos**

Cards, collector's

The latest craze in collector's cards for American schoolkids is the set of 'Mass Murderers/Serial Killers'. This replaces their former predilection for baseball card series immortalising non-toxic sporting heroes like Babe Ruth. Instead, children can gaze on the visage of Edmund **Kemper** and turn over to find that: 'Edmund as a child showed severe psychological disturbance. At age 13 he cut the family cat into pieces...' Or they can learn about Pogo the Clown, the popular entertainer at Chicago children's parties during the 1970s. The man behind the mask was a local building contractor with a civic streak and an active interest in Democratic politics, John Wayne Gacy, and in the crawl-space under his house he disposed of the bodies of twenty-eight young victims. Their smell finally alerted a policeman on the premises, who had called round to ask about the disappearance of a youth last seen on his way to Gacy's for a job interview.

The card on Jeffrey **Dahmer** is particularly prized.

Carrier pigeons

Trained by an ingenious and unidentified Taiwanese robber in the collection of ransom money, traditionally the most dangerous stage of such operations. Flying off with the victim's money in a pouch hung round its neck, a pigeon can soon shake off police pursuit. 'It is not easy to follow them,' admitted Superintendent Chen Jaioqin, head of the Changwa criminal affairs department in November 1991.

The ruse involved a car thief who telephoned to offer return of the owners' vehicles on receipt of 3,000 Taiwanese dollars. This is only £70 but constitutes the maximum payload for successful take-off.

Victims were directed to a bamboo birdcage in a public park. There they found a homing pigeon sporting a miniature wallet round its neck, together with instructions to fill its pouch with money and turn the bird free.

Disgruntled owners complained to the police that their cars were never returned, probably because they were not stolen by the Birdman of Changwa in the first place. In Taiwan, robbery victims customarily advertise in the classifieds asking for help, making them an easy touch for conmen posing as 'fixers'.

In the 1950s, the New York Mafia employed carrier pigeons to transmit bets for an extensive illegal gambling network, posing the police with serious problems in bringing charges, since the *mafiosi* could simply trip the cages, allowing the only two bits of hard evidence (the pigeons and the rice-paper betting slips) to fly away. Eventually a young plain-clothes detective, Michael Falcione – later a scourge of the Mafia – devised a solution. He bought a falcon. But it was too hungry. It ate the evidence. A better-fed successor eventually brought a pigeon to earth in a state fit for production in court, thereby earning Falcione his nickname: the Falcon.

Cash

For Joe Public, cash is what you buy things with. For a middle-ranking mobster it is what he is forced to spend. There is little else to do with the Niagaras of folding stuff. He cannot buy stocks and shares or real estate (for fear of the IRS); safe-deposit boxes and banks are out (for fear of the IRS and the FBI), and not every hit-man fancies the post-impressionists. But pockets are fine for the five or ten thousand dollars of day-to-day pin-money.

So the money is blown. A typical medium-term financial strategy for a *mafioso* involves eating out continually; longer-term investments amount to little more than snappy clothes, like $500 shoes or $2,000 suits, with cars as a good retirement bet. Surplus cash is mopped up by betting, say, $5,000 a card on baccarat, maybe totting up seven-figure losses over the years; the infamous John Gotti ran through $200,000 in the first half of the 1982 football season. But there was plenty more where that came from. Even in the late 1970s, captains with another New York clan, the Bonanno family, pulled in up to $30,000 dollars a week.

The prudent mobster keeps a cache of 'lawyer money' against a rainy day, of necessity entrusted to a partner who – after the eventual arrest – will probably steal it.

Further up the scale, the inflow of drugs money creates problems by its physical size. On Good Friday, 1982, Turkish businessman-turned-informer Paul Waridel was struck by the length of the table in a Lugano bank that supported the two-feet-high stacks of twenty and fifty dollar notes. The money was eventually crammed into six voluminous suitcases which, between them, only accounted for $5 million, or 400 kilos of morphine base at wholesale prices.

A few months later, in July, the Merrill Lynch headquarters in Lower Manhattan refused to countenance further deposits of luggage containing low-denomination notes. So the Mafia front-man rang to ask if they would reconsider their position if he lobbed in $50 million cash.

Inevitably, serious drug dealers have recourse to the banking system for transmission of funds, and this leaves a trail. Traffickers increasingly resort to offshore **tax havens**; they buy a company off the shelf, appoint themselves a signatory, fly the money in, and then draw it out, untraceable and freshly laundered.

Cash dispensers

It is easier to extract the cash machine than the cash from the machine.

On 22 April 1992 the London police arrested a London gang red-handed as they levered out a cash dispenser from a Romford building society. They used a fork-lift truck, with a van at the ready to transport the machine away. For the previous raids, netting an estimated total of £200,000, JCBs were employed. All the robberies concentrated on branches of the Abbey National, suggesting either an inside source to notify the outside robbers when the machines were full, or a clear preference for the soft-target setting of the Abbey's hole-in-the-wall machines, installed in glass windows as opposed to brick walls.

This type of bank raid may yet raise complex legal arguments about whether the offence constitutes theft or robbery. The latter is more serious but requires 'breaking-and-entering'. The gang broke, but did not enter.

Cash dispensers are tempting propositions containing up to £60,000 each. Mounted on substantial concrete plinths, they are only secured by a few bolts, which yield easily to the onslaught of heavy machinery. Subsequent manoeuvring of the dispenser is facilitated by its handy rollers. At this stage the problems multiply, one venture coming to grief when – in the course of cutting their dispenser open – the thieves incinerated its contents.

A historical precedent for the take-away robbery dates to 1922 when Matt and George Kimes hit the bank in Pampa, Texas, with a pick-up truck. With their accomplice Ray Terrill, the gang reversed through the front window, tethered the safe to their vehicle and drove away, dragging their 'box' behind them. They netted $35,000.

Cathedral, The

'The Cathedral' was one nickname for Pablo **Escobar**'s lavish hillside prison in Colombia, also known as 'Club Medellin', or 'Club Med' for short. He left on 22 July 1992.

Escobar planned his stockade on the lines of a retirement home, designing a luxury complex of ranches on his own land. Barbed wire fences and minefields suggested that the prison's function was to keep Escobar in, rather than others out, and the man in charge was no prison governor but Colonel Homero Rodriguez, a specialist in protection, well aware that Escobar's death in captivity could precipitate a civil war. Rodriguez got wind of a plan by the rival Carli cartel for an airstrike on Escobar from an A-37 armed with four 250-pound bombs, and authorised the construction of a concrete bunker. But the attack never came.

Escobar surrendered on 19 June 1991 after negotiating a nine-year-sentence for a minor trafficking charge. Effectively, Escobar and fifteen henchmen received military protection to run his cocaine empire from the Club Med's offices with eleven telephone lines, cellular telephones, three radio telephone systems, nine bleepers, fax machines and a flock of microchip-carrying homing pigeons. His primary prison duties thus consisted of murdering rivals and arranging drug distribution, while living at the government's expense, and in July 1992 he summoned two powerful underlings, Galeano and Moncada, for interrogation after growing suspicious that they were welching on the deal to pay a monthly tithe of $100 million. The pair were killed, along with twenty associates.

Inside Club Med, Escobar lived well. His private suite incorporated a bedroom with a king-size bed; the fitted wardrobes held thirty-seven tailor-made shirts and nine pairs of identical Nike sneakers. His reception area had a padded bar and a balcony with a fixed telescope for the panoramic views. The interiors, dotted with cane sofas covered with scatter cushions, were liberally decorated with potted plants and photographs of Escobar dressed up as a Chicago gangster. Over his bed hung a portrait of the Virgin Mary, and his library included five Bibles. The tiled bathroom, complete with huge jacuzzi and gold-plated taps, bulged with expensive oils and essences from Paris. Other attractions included a fully-illuminated football pitch, motorcycles, a gymnasium (with a natural waterfall for showers), a discotheque lined with solar system murals, and a playroom with billiard tables and toys.

In July 1992, as news of Escobar's lifestyle leaked out, embarrassed authorities threatened to send him to a proper prison. It is perhaps an over-dramatisation to say he escaped. Rather, he checked out. His position had become precarious.

President Bush was trailing in the election polls; Escobar might be seized to boost his ratings. Overhead surveillance by DEA planes made Escobar jumpy, as did the price of $1.5 million on his head and the discovery of an AR-15 rifle fitted with a nightscope in the surrounding forest. Then a survivor from the Galeano-Moncada purges went to the police, and on the night of 21 July the Cathedral was surrounded by the military. In Escobar's words, 'We left in the middle of the shooting that started about seven in the morning. I was wearing blue jeans and sneakers... We went out the back on foot up the mountain.' He is still at large, probably hoping to engineer another surrender. One future envisaged for 'Club Med' is a tourist attraction.

Cat's eyes, dead

Crucial evidence in the 1893 trial of New York's Dr Robert W. Buchanan. In November 1890 he divorced his first wife for adultery. Her replacement, a fat brothel keeper twice his age called Anna Sutherland, had little to recommend her and indeed became a personal and professional liability. But she was rich, and Dr Buchanan stood to inherit. In 1892, when he booked a passage to Scotland, she threatened to cut him out of her will.

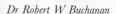

Dr Robert W Buchanan

Four days before he was due to sail on 25 April, Anna fell seriously ill and died. The death certificate, issued by a Dr McIntyre, specified 'cerebral haemorrhage', and Buchanan benefited to the tune of $50,000.

A tip-off from a suspicious partner of Anna's alerted the *New York World*. A reporter interviewed Dr McIntyre, who vouchsafed that the prime symptom of morphine poisoning was lacking; the pupils of Anna's eyes, which would have contracted to pin-points with an overdose, were normal. Further enquiries unearthed two highly suggestive facts, first that Dr Buchanan cancelled his ticket ten days before his wife fell ill, not four as claimed, and second that he remarried his former wife three weeks after Anna's death.

Exhumation revealed 1/10th of a grain of morphine in her body, the residue of a fatal dose of some five grains. But the pin-point pupils were absent. Then a *New York World* staff writer subjecting Dr Buchanan to a hostile grilling noted that the apparent size of his quarry's eyes was greatly magnified by his thick-lensed spectacles. This reminded the journalist of his childhood when belladonna – administered to a schoolfriend's eyes – achieved the same result.

Anna's nurse confirmed that Dr Buchanan had given her patient belladonna drops for no apparent reason, and he came to trial on 20 March 1893. Witnesses testified that he bragged about his method for disguising morphine poisoning, which was put to the test in court. A cat was injected with morphine and then soused in belladonna. It gave its life that another might die, and on 2 July 1895 Dr Buchanan was electrocuted in Sing Sing.

See also **Exhibits**

Champagne

The murder weapon in a 1953 case from New York. When Dr and Mrs Fraden were discovered dead in their apartment after drinking champagne dosed with potassium cyanide, the case was initially viewed as a suicide pact. But it soon emerged that the couple had been poisoned by their son Harlow Fraden, who described his escapade as 'a delightful game'.

Harlow got away with a verdict of serious mental disorder. In his twenties he had struck up a close but platonic relationship with Dennis Wepman; and the two young men egged each other on in fanciful self-indulgence culminating in murder. Wepman too admitted to being 'enthralled'; he felt that by paying close attention to the process of killing he could further his literary ambitions. Perhaps he was right. The long-standing drug addict William Burroughs is highly regarded as a writer at the age of seventy-seven, but his wife is no longer with us after Burroughs (under the influence at the time) accidentally drilled her through the forehead while demonstrating how he thought he could shoot fruit off the top of her head. He has said that this experience helped turn him into an author.

See also **Poisoning, Privilege**

Chaplin, Charles (1889–1977)

Chaplin was buried in a small cemetery at Corsier-sur-Vevey overlooking Lake Geneva; on 2 March 1978 his body disappeared.

A local Bulgarian car mechanic in Switzerland on political asylum, Galtscho Ganev, had been going though a difficult patch. In his own words: 'As a result I decided to hide Charles Chaplin's body and solve my problems.' Ganev failed to grasp the basic point about **kidnapping**: he demanded a ransom of £330,000 from the family if they wanted to see their loved one again, dead. The asking price was soon down by half and the situational dynamics needed bolstering by more traditional threats to kill living members of the family: Geraldine Chaplin's younger brother and sister. But since they had not been kidnapped, this proved beyond Ganev's powers.

Ganev's accomplice was caught after keeping a promise to ring through further demands at exactly 9.30 in the morning; the police captured their man by mounting a watch on 200 local telephone boxes. The main problem with recovering Chaplin's body was that the kidnappers forgot where the coffin was hidden; police officers had to use mine detectors. Ganev was sentenced to four-and-a-half years hard labour, and the film star's tomb is now protected by a concrete lining; in life, his person formed the target of one of **Hoover**'s many maliciously-motivated investigations, the Joan Barry Mann Act case of the 1940s.

Cheerleaders

Wanda Holloway's travails in smalltown Texas began in 1989 when she removed her 14-year-old daughter Shanna from elementary school and sent her to the Alice Johnson High. This move ensured her eligibility for the 1990 seventh-grade cheerleading tests.

But Wanda learned that her friend and neighbour, Verna Heath, had gone one better. Despite keeping her daughter Amber at the elementary school, Verna persuaded Johnson High to accept her girl for the 1989 Pom-Pom trials.

Wanda protested that this was hardly fair; Amber was not even enrolled at Johnson High. The girls themselves remained friends, even after a playoff for the last two places on the cheerleading squad when the school picked Amber rather than Shanna. But Wanda felt devastated, and Amber's mother noted her altered disposition: 'I felt tension. Wanda was very upset because my daughter got to be cheerleader.'

Wanda would not admit defeat. She campaigned on her daughter's behalf, running off a special set of rulers with printed slogans and handing them out in school. But the Parents' Association said this contravened the rules. Forced to find a way of helping her daughter secretly, in January 1990 she met John Harper – her ex-husband's brother – in the local shopping centre and asked him to have Amber and her mother killed. 'I'm serious about it,' she said. 'I've just got to come up with the money.'

Harper demurred, saying that he did not know anyone who would murder a 13-year-old girl. Wanda replied: 'There's car wrecks. Houses burn down.'

'Yeah, but not on purpose,' objected Harper. But Wanda persisted, and the pair met regularly over the following months. Eventually Harper put forward an offer of $20,000 for the two. Wanda expressed dismay at the expense. 'Lady,' Harper reminded her, 'this ain't no five-and-dime burglary.' So they set about whittling down the cost, and soon he reported that another contact would do the mother for $2,500 and the daughter for an additional $5,000.

But why bother about the girl? With her mother eliminated, Shanna would be too upset to manage the cheerleaders' complicated gymnastic routines. So, on 28 January 1991, the conspirators settled on $2,500 for just the mother. As Wanda said: 'I can't afford to do both. The mother's the one who's screwed me around.' She gave Harper a pair of diamond earrings in part payment and agreed to make up the final $500 within a month of the hit.

Two days later Wanda was arrested. The full story came out at her August 1991 trial. After Wanda's first approach, Harper had gone to the police. 'If anything happened to this woman or little girl,' he said, 'I wanted the cops to hear it from me first.' After initial scepticism a Sergeant Blackwell wired Harper up with a microphone for his last six meetings, and the police had monitored contract negotiations throughout. Harper's packaged bargain, priced at $7,500 for two, was their idea.

At the trial, the defence contended that Harper had proved an enthusiastic salesman. On tape Wanda was heard saying: 'Blow it off. I don't want to go through with this' while Harper cajoled: 'Have I got a deal for you!' The defence argued that Harper was the true instigator from his opening remark to Wanda: 'I can take care of that for you.' In their version, Wanda tried to back off when she realised Harper meant business. She said he turned threatening in an unrecorded telephone conversation, insisting it was too late.

Wanda allegedly realised it was a put-up job when Harper offered to take her earrings in lieu of cash; she handed them over just to be rid of him. In support, the defence produced Harper's estranged wife. She testified against her husband, saying he hoped to worm his way back into his family's favour and back into the family will. Harper's brother was Wanda's ex-husband Tony, the family executor, and – according to Harper's wife – the two had plotted against Wanda in order to regain custody of Tony's children by Wanda. This seems plausible on paper, but the jury did not believe it. Neither did Wanda. After the verdict she sobbed in the dock, saying: 'I lost sight of a wrong from a right.'

Wanda Holloway is currently serving fifteen years. In the late 1960s, her life as a teenager was blighted by the refusal of her God-fearing father to let her join the cheerleaders. He thought their costumes too skimpy.

Chikatilo, Andrei Romanovich (1936–)

Russian serial killer echoing the personality traits of his Western counterparts. Born in a small Ukrainian village during the era of purges and famines, when millions died, their corpses often littering the streets and fields, Chikatilo heard on his mother's lap that his cousin had been killed and eaten. At primary school he was introverted, unable to admit to short-sightedness; he obtained his first glasses at the age of thirty, and wet his bed until he was twelve. His father, captured by the Nazis in the war, was branded an enemy of the people, and Chikatilo lapped up stories of partisan heroes roaming the woods in search of prey.

Humilated at school, Chikatilo took refuge in Communism, reading *Pravda* to his classmates; his fixation with political dogma verged on a mental disorder. Shy with girls, he vowed to remain pure until marriage. His first attempt at sex failed and, during army service, he was rumoured impotent. Once, while cuddling a girl, she tried to withdraw from his arms, and he climaxed during the few seconds he held on tight. Thereafter he preferred unrequited love, once praising a girl in a newspaper instead of approaching her directly.

Chikatilo was twenty-seven when his sister dragooned him into marriage with a miner's daughter, Fayina. A week later he had his first marital erection. Sex was for making babies – they had two – but otherwise a chore, and fantasies of sexual prowess began to interpose. In 1971 a university degree qualified him as a teacher, but he could not control his class and turned ever more sullen. Girls under twelve exercised increasing allure, and he barged into their dormitories, **masturbating** in his pocket while eyeing pupils in their underwear. In May 1973 he sexually assaulted a girl in the swimming pool. At his next school he molested boys as they slept. To pursue his interests in private, he bought a run-down shack on the edge of town, to which he lured drunks and prostitutes with offers of food and drink. But adults succumbed willingly to his advances, and Chikatilo could not respond.

On 22 December 1978, he befriended Lena Zakotnova, aged nine, in the street. She needed to go to the toilet. Chikatilo took her to his shed and stripped her violently, accidentally drawing blood. This conferred an immediate erection, making the fatal connective spark between blood and sex. So he pulled a knife and stabbed her in the stomach. Each blow brought him closer to orgasm. So he stabbed her again and again.

That night he threw Lena's body into the nearby river; it was found downstream two days later, as was a smudge of blood in the snow by his shack. Chikatilo was questioned, but the police soon arrested another sex offender, Aleksandr Kravchenko, shot in 1984.

Over the next twelve years Chikatilo disposed of fifty-three women and children. In 1981 he became a supply clerk for Rostnovnerud, and his job of travelling the region provided the perfect cover. Rostov, his base, attracted the poor of the surrounding area, and an underclass of teenagers from broken homes slept rough in the railway station, trading their bodies for a drink or a crust of bread. They were outsiders like him but, in his estimation, worse: 'They followed me like dogs.'

On 3 September 1981 Chikatilo met his second victim, Larisa Tkachenko, and offered to take her to a nearby complex of concrete cafés. Probably she had sex in mind, but for Chikatilo one thing now entailed another. On a short cut through a wood, Chikatilo lost his self-control. He strangled her and ejaculated over her body. Then he performed a war dance, whooping round the corpse. 'I felt like a partisan,' he said later.

Chikatilo knew he would kill again. Thereafter he made no attempt at intercourse, but he often inflicted as many as thirty carefully sited stab wounds, slicing up his victims, extracting their organs, and chewing them. Nearly all had their eyes stabbed out, perhaps to avert their shaming gaze.

Chikatilo drew his victims from different ages, sexes and backgrounds. To the police there seemed no link between ageing alcoholic prostitutes and little boys – except that he killed them. But that *was* the link. Chikatilo liked killing people. In November 1984 his twenty-three, highly distinctive murders were united under Operation Forest Path. Moscow's Serbsky Institute produced a profile of an ostensibly normal man, probably married, with a regular job, and sperm found on the shirt of his twentieth victim showed the killer had AB blood.

Killing became a periodic endeavour undertaken for pleasure to satisfy a physiological need and, by the end of 1982, Chikatilo had claimed six more lives. Not until Sasha Chepel's killing (number thirty) in August 1984 were the murders admitted in the local Party daily, *Molot*. The police initially assumed that the culprit was mentally handicapped, and Chikatilo kept his secret from his wife, maintaining that his scratched face and the flecks of blood on his shirt came from handling sheet metal. Given his apathy about sex with her, she never considered him a likely sex killer.

On 14 September 1984 Chikatilo was arrested in Rostov's market after a series of pick-up attempts. In his briefcase was a jar of vaseline, a rope and a long-bladed knife. Chikatilo fitted the killer's rough description, but the files did not show his previous record. He seemed a respectable married man, and was conclusively exculpated when his blood tested group A. Chastened by his escape, in the next two years he only killed twice. By then 26,500 suspects were on file; card number nine was Chikatilo's.

The widely dispersed killings suggested a murderer with access to a car, and in Russia this constituted an eliminating factor. Or maybe the killer had police ID to lure away the tramps who comprised the bulk of his victims. Maybe the skilled incisions indicated a butcher. Investigators checked 5,845 men with previous convictions, particularly sex offences, 10,000 of the mentally ill, 419 homosexuals, 163,000 drivers – 500,000 in all. Among the paperwork languished a 1988 circular, quoting Japanese research that in one case in 10,000, a man's sperm did not match his blood group.

In March 1989 Chikatilo cut off Tanya Ryzhova's head and legs, wrapped her in a bundle and towed her through the snowy streets on a sledge with the help of a passing stranger. Tanya's body was stuffed into pipes by the tracks, and many other victims had

been found near the line or last seen at a station. So the police mounted a watch over the platforms, put men picking mushrooms in the nearby woods, and installed officers in holes covered in branches by the side of the track. Decoy policewomen acted as bait, sprawling drunk in the carriages.

On 17 October 1990 Chikatilo killed Vadim Gromov in the forest by Donleskhoz station. Sixty specialists established their headquarters in nearby Shakhti, drafting in the local police and a crack riot squad a hundred strong. Two weeks later Chikatilo struck again, and 600 detectives were deployed along the line through the forests, with three or four officers covering even the most isolated halts.

On 6 November 1990 Sergeant Igor Rybakov at Donleskhoz saw a man in a suit and tie emerge from the nearby woods. When the stranger washed his hands at the water hydrant, Rybakov noticed his bandaged finger and his stained cheek. He asked for his papers and filed a routine report. Five days later a detective at the Gromov site spotted a new piece of ripped pocket dangling from a tree, and a search revealed Sveta Korostik's body, dead for about a week. The killer must have passed through the station, and Rybakov's report named the suspicious stranger as Chikatilo.

Arrested on 20 November, his sperm (but not his blood) tested group AB and he claimed not to have been at Donleskhoz. The following day he conceded a weakness for 'perverted sexual displays in films', admitting he was not 'a complete man'. Of the tramps, he said, 'the question arose of whether these degenerate elements had the right to exist.' On 27 November he said, 'I am ready to

give evidence of my crimes, but please do not torment me with details. My psyche could not cope.' Two days later he cracked when a psychologist was sent to discuss his 'problems'. Chikatilo eventually admitted to fifty-three killings and guided investigators to the murder scenes, vaguely hoping that the number of dead would make him a valuable scientific specimen. Indeed, the *Moscow News* reported that the Japanese were interested in acquiring his brain.

Chikatilo appeared at his trial penned in a metal cage with his head shaven. On the first day he delighted photographers by brandishing a porno magazine. Later he became dejected, stripped off and waved his penis in court, shouting 'Look at this useless thing, what do you think I could do with this?' On 15 October 1992 he was sentenced to death. He concluded a rare interview in June 1993 with the words, 'Remember me to my friends, to my colleagues, to everyone I knew. Tell them I am sorry, so sorry...'

China travellers

Early escapees from the first years of the Australian convict settlements. The conditions of brutality and near-starvation encouraged bands of desperate prisoners to vanish into the dunes or make a run for the bush. They headed for China, the fount of milk, honey, opium, silk and yellow girls.

The Irish proved peculiarly susceptible to this fantasy, placing China about a hundred miles north of Sydney on the far side of a wide but navigable river. The first band of twenty men and one woman slipped out of Rose Hill in November 1791. Three believed they came so close to the promised land that on their recapture they ran away again. This time they lost their lives. Others set off, heading for China inland from the beaches of Tasmania, and the phenomenon is reported as late as 1798 with batches of Irishmen sixty-strong setting off for the Orient.

Lacking proper compasses, the China Travellers made their own makeshift version, consisting of a crude circle, drawn on paper or bark, showing the positions of north, south, east and west. And yes, they omitted the needle. Mostly the men died, the victims of thirst, hunger or Aboriginal spears. Recaptured survivors faced 500 lashes.

Christmas

A criminal offence in England for sixteen years. The celebration of Christmas was banned on account of its 'carnal and sensual delight' by the Long Parliament of 1644. Cromwell's Puritans abhorred the Christian elements of the Christmas ritual because they were Catholic, the pagan parts because they were pagan, and the festive bits because they were festive. Instead, Christians were directed to fast, and the army sent out yuletide snatch-squads on house-to-house searches for illicit Christmas dinners which they doubtless consumed themselves. In 1647 the ban was extended to Easter and other festivals.

Christmas was reinstated along with Charles II in 1660.

Cicero

In the early 1920s, Cicero was a pleasant Chicago suburb with 50,000 inhabitants, 68 per cent home ownership and its own Rotary and Kiwani clubs.

In 1924 a small-time fixer, Ed Konvalinka, realised there was a danger of the Democrats unseating the Republicans in the coming elections, ending six years of Republican control over the area's politics and saloons. To ensure election of Klenha's Republican ticket, Konvalinka hit on the scheme of importing an outside electioneering specialist. Local politician Big Ed Vogel approved the plan; together they agreed to approach a young 'mover-and-shaker', Al Capone, offering him free run of the district provided the right candidates were returned.

Capone did a thorough job. According to the Illinois Crime Survey, 'Automobiles filled with gunmen paraded the streets slugging and kidnapping election workers. Polling places were raided by armed thugs and ballots were taken at the point of the gun from the hands of voters waiting to drop them in the box. Voters and workers were kidnapped, taken to Chicago and held prisoner until the polls closed.' Capone's brother Frank was killed in a firefight, and Al shot his way out of trouble with a gun blazing in either hand.

Mayor Klenha and his cronies came sailing through their democratic ordeal with immense majorities. But the day of their election marked their last day in power. Overnight, placid Cicero changed into Mob City, with government by, for and of the bums, sprouting a profusion of dance halls, night-clubs, gambling dens, betting shops, dog tracks and 160 night-and-day bars. There were no whore-houses because of an inter-gang agreement.

Capone ruled the roost. He took $100,000 a week out of Cicero, beat up the editor of one paper, kidnapped the editor of the other and got rough with the Mayor for showing insufficient respect. Once, Capone had to go down to City Hall personally, drag Klenha out of his mayoral office, knock him down the outside steps and then kick him repeatedly. A policeman watched, twirling his nightstick before strolling off. It was said you could tell when you crossed the parish boundary from Chicago to Cicero by sniffing. 'If you smell gunpowder, you're there.'

See also **Hawthorne Castle, Pax Capone**

Coffins

A good Chicago mobster deserved a great coffin. When Antonio Lombardo was shot in the head with **dumdums** in 1928 he became the third president of the feudal Unione Sicilione to die by gunfire. He rated a heavy bronze container, crested with a brass eagle, and his funeral train needed twelve pall-bearers. Another prime example received the body of Frank Capone, Al's brother who lost his life in the line of duty rigging the 1924 **Cicero** elections. Frank went to his grave in a silk-lined silver-plated casket.

Vincent 'the Schemer' Drucci lay in state in a $10,000 silver-and-aluminium affair. **O'Bannion**, the Irish gang leader, went one better. His coffin was rushed to Chicago in a private freight car all the way from Philadelphia. Its design is reminiscent of the showpiece version in Walt Disney's *Sleeping Beauty*, with solid silver-and-bronze airtight walls, and the thick plate-glass on the top made for clear viewing of the smiling killer, who lay in repose on a bed of white satin with tufted cushions. The heavily carved corner posts were of solid silver.

In the nineteenth century the British favoured a baser metal. Iron coffins were constructed to Edward Lillie Bridgman's patented design. His impregnable subterranean containers countered the epidemic of graverobbers, and by 1822 Bridgman was advertising in *Wooler's British Gazette*. 'Many hundreds of bodies will be dragged from their wooden coffins this winter, for the anatomical lectures... The question of the right to inter in iron is now decided... The only safe coffin is Bridgman's Patent wrought-iron one.'

Not unreasonably, the advertisement invited those 'about to inter a mother, husband, child or friend' to consider if they really wanted their loved ones to be dug up by rabble and sliced into bits by medical students. Subsequent advertisements reported a brisk trade. Bridgman charged a hefty £31 10s for his product, which featured interior locking bolts.

The iron slabs and protective railings commonly seen round early Victorian graves served a similar defensive function.

Kidnap victims are often confined under peculiarly grim conditions. Colleen Stan, the sex **slave**, spent years immured in a double-lined wooden crate, and in 1993 Stephanie Slater from Birmingham told the court how, after her abduction in January 1992, she was led into a large darkened garage. 'I hope you are not claustrophobic, because you are going into a box within a box,' her kidnapper said, shovelling Miss Slater into a coffin, itself contained in a large wheelie bin. He cautioned her against any attempt at escape since boulders were balanced overhead and she was ringed by electrodes. In addition, he handcuffed, gagged and blindfolded her.

On her first night, Miss Slater all but froze and, in due course, concluded that she had perished. 'I was so cold, I thought I had died,' she recalled. 'I thought I had gone, completely gone. Then I saw a very, very vivid picture of Christ in front of me in the total blackness.' In court, Miss Slater reduced both the jury and her captor to tears.

See also **Bodysnatchers, Flowers, Neilson**

Colombia, Little

Name given to an area of New York centred round 83rd Street off Roosevelt Avenue. The district is awash with cocaine money, although the local drug of choice is *bazuko*, a cocaine by-product. The incoming consignments of 500 kilos of 'Snow White' are broken up among, say, five Colombians who handle the sub-distribution through a network of Dominicans for the actual street-work. Apparently no one wants to work with Cubans.

Defenestrations in Little Colombia are a regular occurrence. In the words of a detective interviewed in 1992 for *Vanity Fair*, 'You raid Dominicans, you always need a man covering the windows. You've got them all lined up with a gun on them and they start shuffling sideways. You say, "Hey, what the hell are you doing?" And suddenly he's out of the window, three, four, five stories up... You either find a pile of broken bones down there or he staggers away.'

At the Cali cartel in Colombia they assume two fatalities per 500 kilo consignment by the time it reaches the streets. New York police regard Colombian homicides as the hardest to solve; those who break the Wall of **Silence** are 'hit', and if they are not, their families are. The price for murder is $200.

The cocaine comes in to feed the voracious appetite of Wall Street, with Learjet pilots landing it at Westchester for $1,000 per kilo unit. A single successful run earns the intrepid aviator upwards of half a million dollars; New York's total cocaine imports for 1990 were estimated at 400,000 kilos.

Comparatively speaking, New York police relish arresting Colombians; it is high-profile stuff perfect for the evening news bulletins – red Ferraris, stacks of cocaine, guns and cash. Putting a middle-aged, besuited Chinese accountant behind bars for five kilos of heroin does not attract the same kudos. But the Chinese are patient, careful criminals, likely to run in five kilos a week, year in, year out, while the Colombians go for broke, shipping hundreds of kilos until they are busted, often second time round.

See also **Escobar**

Concentration

It is said that the prospect of execution concentrates the mind wonderfully. In the case of William **Palmer**, the poisoner, this operated to the exclusion of the general in favour of the particular. His last words on the morning of 14 June 1855, delivered standing on the trap door of the gallows, were 'Are you sure this is safe?'

One can understand Palmer's point; a sentient being facing imminent extinction has the responses of a living person, even though he is, for all practical purposes, dead. On his way to the scaffold Palmer minced along like a dainty schoolgirl, taking great care to avoid getting wet in the puddles from a heavy overnight downpour. George Orwell was struck by precisely the same conduct in his 1931 essay 'A hanging'.

Orwell watched as a condemned native walked towards the gallows and execution; the man stepped aside to avoid splashing through rainwater. In Orwell's words: 'All the organs of his body were working – bowels digesting food, skin renewing itself, nails growing, tissues forming – all toiling away in solemn foolery. His nails would still be growing when he stood on the drop, when he was falling through the air with a tenth of a second to live... He and we were a party of men walking together ... and in two minutes, with a sudden snap, one of us would be gone – one mind less, one world less.' These reflections made Orwell appreciate 'the mystery, the unspeakable wrongness, of cutting a life short when it is in full tide'.

In Russia, the apprehension of imminent extinction is infinitely extended. The condemned never learn their date of execution, and the prisoner fears the worst each time footsteps approach his cell. To be ushered into a room is to anticipate a Ministry of the Interior executioner stationed above the door with a specially adapted Makarov service pistol, waiting to fire a nine gramme bullet down through the top of the skull. Such a fate awaits **Chikatilo**, currently in cell thirty three of penal establishment UH 398 ST3.

Condemned sermon

Traditionally delivered to prisoners awaiting execution in **Newgate** Chapel. Lest they forgot, the men were seated in a black-painted pew grouped around a coffin.

Edward Wakefield left a contemporary account of a condemned sermon where one listener was clearly off his head. 'At length the Vicar pauses,' Wakefield wrote, 'and then in a deep tone which, though hardly above a whisper is audible to all, says, "Now to you, my poor fellow mortals, who are about to suffer the last penalty of the law"... The dying men are dreadfully agitated... The poor sheep-stealer is in a frenzy. He throws his hands far

from him and shouts aloud: "**Mercy**, good Lord! mercy is all I ask; There! There! I see the Lamb of God! Oh, how happy! Oh! This is happy!"'

The service was a popular spectacle with the general public.

See also **Treadwheel**

Condoms

A useful device for drug runners (known as '**swallowers**') who shepherd rubber-clad contraband through Customs in their stomachs. Contrary to the normal pattern, a burst sac means instant death.

Irina Ratushinskaya reports a more unusual application in her account of the Russian gulag: *Grey is the Colour of Hope.* Prisoners keen to smuggle alcohol into labour camps would slip a condom down their throats and attach it with an airtight seal to a long piece of plastic tubing which, poking up into their mouth, was firmly wedged between any surviving set of adjacent molars.

Outside the workcamp, the *zek* was topped up with a syringe by squirting alcohol into his condom via the tube until it expanded to line the duodenum and stomach, his maximum load of three litres sufficient to make seven litres of vodka. Safely through the guards and back in the camp, the *zek*'s jubilant colleagues would drain their hero by suspending him head downwards from the barrack rafters with his tube held over a dish.

According to Detective Dick Woodman of the West London Drug Squad, a similar trick is used today by crack dealers on the capital's streets. But the technique is more akin to fishing than ballooning. First the dealer's crack 'rocks' are wrapped in tin foil. Then the sachet is attached to one end of a length of twine; the other is secured to a tooth, and the **narcotics** are lowered into the throat for retrieval on each sale.

Contempt

A Mafia expression of this extreme emotion is to cut off the penis and testicles with a stiletto, leaving them beside the victim's body after first blowing out his brains.

One intended recipient of this treatment was Eliott Ness of the Chicago **Untouchables**, who received a telephone call promising he would shortly be found in a ditch with his 'wang slashed off'. He wasn't.

The regular Mafia punishment for messing with a *capo's* woman was severing the man's penis and then stuffing it into his mouth. One unnamed hood guilty of this breach of etiquette suffered the ultimate in contempt. According to the 1989 book *Mobster*, Carlo Gambino had the man fed, still alive and limbs first, into a large meatgrinder.

See also **Faithful**

Contempt of Court

An offence entitling a judge to mysterious and far-reaching powers. In 1631 an English thief, Noy, was convicted of a felony at the Salisbury Assizes; in a fit of pique he threw a 'brickbat' at Judge Richardson who, dodging the missile, had the prisoner indicted for contempt. Noy was strung up in the presence of the court, with the exception of his offending hand, hacked off for separate display on a gibbet.

These draconian powers were re-examined in 1975. In that year Lord Balogh's son, Stephen, was devilling as an articled clerk in St Albans. He made £5 a day helping out a firm of solicitors involved in an interminable pornography case  The days passed, the boredom rose. Eventually Balogh decided to enliven the proceedings. The court building was state-of-the-art; it had air-conditioning. Balogh pinched a small gas cylinder containing N_2O from a nearby hospital car-park and, that night, sneaked onto the court roof. There he located the ventilation ducts which had their outlets in the court below, near the bench where the barristers who had tormented him for days with their tedious speeches would take up their stations the following morning. All that remained was to judge his moment, slip out of court, position the cylinder and open the valve to flood the chamber with nitrous oxide.

Next morning he arrived with his briefcase at the ready. But court officials spotted him skulking on the roof the previous night; they searched his case

and discovered the gas canister. That afternoon Balogh was arraigned before Judge Melford Stevenson in the neighbouring courtroom on a charge of contempt. With commendable presence of mind, he argued: 'I am actually in the wrong court at the moment; the proceedings which I intended to subvert are next door. Therefore, it is not contempt against your court for which I should be tried.' Unimpressed, the judge sent him down for the inordinate period of six months. Balogh greeted his sentence with the words: 'You are a humourless automaton. Why don't you self-destruct?'

After a fortnight cooling his heels, Balogh thought his debt to society must surely be paid and appealed via the Official Solicitor. The court's powers came under scrutiny, and it was held that their exercise should be restricted (since the judge was acting as prosecutor, judge and jury) to emergencies where it was 'urgent and imperative to act at once'.

In Balogh's case there was no emergency. No trial had been upset and no proceedings disturbed. So his offence rated not so much as contempt as attempted contempt. Nor was his plan actually workable, since the laughing gas would have been too diluted by the air-conditioning to reduce the court to its proposed state of giggling hysteria. Hence the crime represented an attempt at attempted contempt, and Balogh was released.

Cornhill Burglary, The

A turning point in the story of safes. Until this 1865 burglary, manufacturers were happy to emblazon their steel 'boxes' with impressive seals, the public were happy to buy them, and thieves happy to prise them open. Afterwards, the industry buttressed its damaged reputation by making genuinely secure safes; thirty-six patents were registered in the following year and a host of new entrepreneurs entered the trade.

The **safe** that started the furore was a Milner's List 3 ('Quadruple Patent, Fraud-resisting, recommended for Cash and Valuables, Doors half-inch, Bodies quarter-inch, lined throughout, unequalled Fire-resisting Chambers') installed in John Walker's jewellers at 63 Cornhill, London, where it held some £6,000 worth of gold watches, diamond rings, chronometers, bracelets and so on.

The strongroom, illuminated by gas all night, had walls lined with iron. The interior was visible from the street through holes in the metal window grilles, and mirrors placed round the safe itself ensured that anyone in its vicinity was highly visible. Yet at start of business on Monday 6 February 1865, the Milner was found with its door burst and the contents vanished. The raiders had entered the building on Saturday and were accidentally locked in by Walker as he left for the weekend. The strongroom's iron walls defeated the gang's first assault, but they attacked from another direction, from the basement, emerged through the floor, and then forced the safe open with wedges.

The press revelled in the story ('The enemy applies the principles of war to the acquisition of gold and jewels') linking it to recent raids in Threadneedle Steet, Lombard Street and the Strand, and the gang were soon behind bars after one of their women, animated by spite, shopped her man to the police.

Walker decided to sue Milner's, claiming that their product did not match its 'thief-proof' advertisements. It proved an easy matter to produce the safe in open court and demonstrate its flimsy construction, but Walker's case needed the additional support that only a convincing expert witness could provide. Who better than the cracksman himself? Recently convicted Thomas Caseley was released from Millbank Penitentiary to give evidence, and on 14 February 1866 he testified before the Lord Chief Justice and eight counsel (four for the defendant, four for the plaintiff).

Casely was charm itself, good-looking, self-assured, and gifted with 'the most amusing coolness'. He explained how the gang had ducked their heads once every nine minutes to avoid being observed by the regular police patrol.

Their success was assured from the moment the first small metal wedge banged into the crack round the safe's door stayed there. For where a small wedge will go, a bigger will follow.

'You have had some experience in opening safes?' counsel enquired. 'Yes, unhappily I have,' Caseley conceded, and then related how 'two of us purchased two of Milner's safes to experimentalise upon, and we succeeded upon one after seven hours... the other safe was opened in six hours.' It was all done with wedges and bars of ever-increas-

ing size, until finally the 'alderman' or head-bar could be inserted to rip the door off its hinges. As Caseley left the witness box, the Lord Chief Justice remarked, 'It is a pity you did not turn your talents to better account.'

'It is a pity the police did not let me,' Caseley replied. But for all his sang-froid he had a fourteen-year sentence to serve, which perhaps inspired the *Daily Telegraph*'s favourable report of his courtroom performance. It helped launch yet another criminal legend, the insouciant cracksman with 'a keen wit... a fine dramatic instinct, infinite readiness, surprising fluency; the instinct of an actor for effect.'

Walker lost his case despite Caseley's evidence. Nonetheless, public awareness grew that existing safes were not, in fact, safe. And so the modern security industry was born.

See also **Gutshot**

Corruption

There have been corrupt police as long as there have been police, and few more corrupt than Charles Becker. Given control of New York's Special Squad Number One, charged with cleaning up prostitution, graft and gambling, Becker cleaned up, charging 25 cents on every criminal dollar. He was arrested for the murder of Herman 'Beansie' Rosenthal when his henchman, 'Billiard Ball' Jack Rose, landed in jail for the job and Becker failed to secure his release. Billiard Ball sang, and Becker was electrocuted on 7 July 1915.

Chicago was always something special. In the words of Alderman Robert Merriam: 'Chicago is unique. It is the only completely corrupt city in America.' By the mid-1920s the Capone-Torrio gang were doling out $30,000 dollars a week in bribes, mostly paid over the counter on Fridays to an orderly queue of minor government officials, **Prohibition agents** and policemen. Further up the scale the emoluments were higher. Capone is believed to have contributed $250,000 to the election campaign of *laissez-faire* Mayor Big Bill Thompson; and Morgan Collins, police chief from 1923 to 1927, refused $1,000 a day for looking the other way. Despite such setbacks, during Thompson's three terms as Mayor it was Capone and Torrio who controlled Chicago and Cook County's machinery of government.

Another Chicago gang, the Terrible Gennas, ran a Prohibition warehouse at 1022 Taylor Street conveniently situated just four blocks from the Maxwell Street police station. Their business made $150,000 clear a week. Eventually the government extracted a twenty-five page affidavit from the warehouse manager describing how the premises had run unmolested for years, operating heavy trucks round the clock except during the occasional raid. Police visits were notified in advance, generally in writing, and 'the entire... enterprise was done with the full knowledge, consent and approval of the law'. Liquor shipments through hostile gang territory merited a pre-arranged police escort.

By April 1925 the Gennas' bill for police protection money reached $6,500 a month; as a supplementary inducement, alcohol was available to the force at bargain rates. Some 400 uniformed police attended the warehouse each month together with numerous representatives from the State Attorney's office. To prevent fraudulent claims for protection by unallocated personnel, each week the Maxwell Street station submitted a written list of the accredited officers together with a note of their individual star numbers and the amount due; policemen collecting their wages presented their numbered star as identification.

The Gennas' pay-outs were logged in a ledger (subsequently captured) naming the guilty men, but this evidence disappeared after falling into police hands following one of the Anselmi and Scalise trials. No fewer than 187 police were transferred from the Maxwell Street station, but otherwise no action was taken.

Corruption extended to the judiciary. An undated story has a reporter mid-interview with Capone when the gangster learned that one of his men had been arraigned in court. Capone telephoned the offending judge and shouted: 'I thought I told you to release that fellow.'

More recently, a striking example of corruption comes from Mae Sai in Thailand's '**Golden Triangle**'. The town boasts one main street and a single dirt road. The official salary of the Chief of Police is $100 a month; the job can be bought from the local council for $40,000 down together with monthly 'refreshers' pitched at around $12,000. This is significantly less than the backhanders from the heroin traffickers for turning a blind eye; the

dusty border town consists mostly of an unbroken line of banks.

See also **Oaths, West Midlands Serious Crime Squad**

Court of Appeal

Not established in Britain until 1907. Until then a condemned man's only hope was to ask the King for a pardon; some monarchs, George III among them, took the Royal Prerogative of **Mercy** very seriously. The 1901 case of Adolph Beck highlighted the need for change.

Beck suffered the misfortune of a criminal lookalike; but since the other man preyed on women, the fact that Beck's double had been circumcised was well established. Beck was uncircumcised, but this conclusive distinction did not suffice to end his seven-year sentence. Public disquiet after Beck's second arrest in 1901 for the misdeeds of his near-twin culminated in the establishment of a court of last resort.

Sadly the first judgment to be overturned by the Court of Appeal protected not the innocent but the guilty. On 21 August 1911 Charles Ellsome, a real low-lifer, stabbed his girl Rose Pender to death. She worked as a whore; he was her pimp, and she left him for an Italian.

Ellsome gave a detailed account of the killing to a friend, the thief Jack Fletcher, and was later arrested. Tried during an afternoon session at the Old Bailey, Ellsome was quite properly found guilty and sentenced to death. But the condemned man appealed on a point of law. Since Fletcher was a thief, he was a questionable witness; his statements needed corroboration. In the summing-up, the judge pointed out that Fletcher's story had never varied: there were no inconsistencies between his initial statements to the police and his evidence in the dock. This constituted internal corroboration.

But Fletcher's initial statements had never been put in evidence at the Old Bailey. True, Fletcher had not wavered from his story but this had not been *proved in court*. A surprised Ellsome had his conviction quashed. Traumatised by the experience, the Court of Appeal allowed a further twenty years to pass before overturning another murder conviction. On 9 January 1923 even the wretched Edith **Thompson** had to swing, condemned for little more than her immoral role in what the Court's President characterised – irrelevantly – as a 'squalid and rather indecent case of lust and adultery'.

This resilient tradition has been maintained more or less intact, and the recent British flood of overturned convictions – the Birmingham Six, the Guildford Four, the Darvell Brothers, Judith Ward, Stefan Kiszkow, the Cardiff Three, the Broadwater Three, the Maguire Seven and Jacqueline Fletcher – may well prove shortlived.

The Court of Appeal's primary function is to uphold British justice. This could explain the February 1993 decision of the Home Secretary, himself a member of the Bar, to uphold the Bar's reputation by refusing leave to appeal in the Carl Bridgewater case. As with other miscarriages of justice, it has been patently obvious for years to anyone who studied the facts that the accused are innocent of Carl's murder, with the additional twist that this particular crime was committed by someone else who is identifiable.

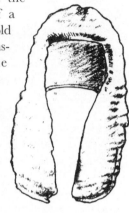

Carl Bridgewater was a newspaper boy who died from a shotgun blast to the head at Yew Tree Farm on 19 September 1978. Supposedly he interrupted a burglary. A petty thief, Pat Molloy, admitted to being upstairs in the house at the time of the shooting, and three other men – James Robertson and the two Hickeys, Michael and Vincent – also earned lengthy sentences almost entirely on the strength of Molloy's brief confession, beaten out of him by a corrupt police officer, now deceased, Detective Constable John Perkins of the West Midlands Serious Crime Squad. Molloy withdrew the confession as soon as he was allowed to see a lawyer, and the absurd document is now believed by no one, including the Home Office's own expert, Eric Sheppard. Nonetheless it is far and away the prosecution's strongest evidence, and at the trial Molloy was advised to stick to his confession, in the hope of receiving a sentence for manslaughter, rather than recant and risk the stiffer penalty for murder.

James Robinson became involved because Vincent Hickey, following his arrest for another robbery, traded the 'information' in the hope of obtaining bail. A prison officer named Gibson has come forward with convincing evidence (obtained in conversation with a prisoner) that the only eyewitness against Robinson was lying.

According to the then Home Secretary, 'Other prison officers do not support Gibson's version of events.' But as Gibson makes clear, no one else was within earshot. Similarly, Michael Hickey was convicted because his cousin Vincent Hickey was found guilty. Why? Because of Molloy's bogus confession, which meant that Vincent's alibi – that he spent the afternoon with his cousin Michael – must be false, and since, however, Vincent *had* spent the afternoon with Michael, then Michael must have spent the afternoon with Vincent. So he must be guilty too.

The Bridgewater case was rejected on appeal after a nine-week hearing in 1988, but this happened before the Guildford Four case first showed that the unjustly condemned could be released. To air the prosecution case (now unsustainable and virtually non-existent) again would be too humiliating; hence the 1993 decision not to review it.

See also **Trousers, Virtual Reality**

Courtesy

The hallmark of the crack English **highwayman**. He did not rob; he collected.

A typical report, from the *Birmingham Gazette* of 6 May 1751, describes a highwayman who behaved 'very civilly to the passengers, told them that he was a stranger in distress, and hoped that they would contribute to his assistance. Each passenger gave him something, to the amount of about £4, with which he was mighty well satisfied, but he returned some half-pence, saying that he never took copper. He warned them that there were two other collectors on the road, but he would see them out of danger, which he did, and begged that they would not at their next inn mention the robbery nor appear against him if he should be taken up hereafter.'

Similar acts of gentility are so widely reported that they must have had a basis in reality. But courtesy ran only skin-deep and amounted to little

Crack

So called after the snap, popple and crack that cocaine 'rocks' make as they burn. It takes six seconds for the body to respond, as chemicals swoosh into the brain's reward centre where pleasure is registered. Thanks to the influx of dopamine and noradrenaline it registers a great deal.

But each hit only lasts a few minutes, and at four hits a rock the whole trip is over in a quarter of an hour, with the user just £20 short (or $5 in the US, or 25 cents in the West Indies) of paradise by doing it all over again. Addicts become unusually venomous in pursuit of their next hit, and when they have had that one, feel like another. Heroin can dampen the pangs of the aftermath.

In Britain, the users' craving spawns petty crime; the inter-dealer violence leads to murder. In the 1992 words of Detective Inspector Francis Sole of Britain's Crack Intelligence Unit: 'In most Metropolitan Police murder and serious crime investigations in the past year, crack has been involved.'

Ordinary dealers can make £2,000 a week, and this sort of money needs guns for protection. The distribution networks, generally controlled by Jamaican **gangs** – 'Yardies' – teeter on the edge of small wars as the epidemic takes root in the inner cities. London's Notting Hill is the home of an estimated 800 crack addicts.

In America, the writer Thulani Davis, discussing black urban violence after the 1992 Los Angeles riots, underscored the drug's corrosive nature. 'The crucially destructive factor was introduced in the Eighties,' she said, 'when crack appeared in black communities. It's one of the worst things that ever happened, because women take it. Mothers ceased to be nurturers and carers, which led to a generation of children receiving no socialisation. Enormous numbers of homeless children are now growing up in our cities exactly as though they were orphans, completely disenfranchised people.' In Britain too, recent studies show that the great majority for whom crack is the primary drug of dependence are black.

Here is a representative selection of what the habit means at street level, taken from 1992 verbatim reportage by American journalists Tim Wells and William Triplett. From a pusher: 'When I first started dealing heroin back in 1978 there wasn't so

An idealised version of Old Mob (Thomas Sympson) robbing the Duchess of Portsmouth

more than not shooting those who put up no resistance. Outside this convention, and even within it, all was brutality.

The pick of present-day *mafiosi* observe similarly stringent double standards. Sicily's Salvatore 'the beast' Riina, finally arrested in January 1993 after twenty-three years on the run, seemed the embodiment of soft-spoken Old World courtesy. Prosecutors were impressed by the deferential way he rose to his feet whenever they entered the courtroom, and associates recall him weeping as he mused on his **mother**'s early hardships. A good family man, at funerals he reduced hardened mourners to tears with his eulogies of those whose assassinations he had blessed, and, as an informer from the Catania Mafia told the police, 'His philosophy is "If someone's finger is hurt, it's better to be safe and cut off his arm."'

much unnecessary violence. But these days the young kids out hustling don't understand that. They don't understand the importance of fear. The only things they care about are gold chains and fancy cars. If some dude smokes up some dealer's money, the dealer don't go back with a baseball bat and put fear in the dude. He thinks he's got to save face, so he goes straight back with his gun and kills the dude straight off the top.'

And an addict: 'After four or five months of heavy crack use, I didn't even look like a human being. I lost a lot of weight and my eyes looked all bloodshot and wired out. I looked like a person off the streets. My boyfriend would let me have all the crack I wanted, but he wasn't nice to me anymore. Him and his friends would beat me and rape me... They'd tear off my clothes and screw me, with a bunch of people in the room.'

One of the problems with cocaine is its plethora of production areas and distribution points. Unlike the heroin trade, largely in the hands of organised crime, crack-dealing is open to all-comers, giving rise to the phenomenon of *dis*organised crime, a free-for-all with a commensurate incidence of random violence.

In the panic which followed the 1989 visit of San Francisco detective Robert Stutman, who issued dire warnings about the new drug wave at a police conference, the British set up a National Crack Squad. But it had little success. Crack can be made from cocaine in an ordinary kitchen with a bit of baking soda; it was as if the authorities were trying to stamp out tea-drinking, but not tea.

See also **Kids, crack**

Craig and Bentley

To the layman, the case of Craig and Bentley has always represented the apotheosis of unreason. The fatal words 'Let him have it, Chris' have passed into British popular history.

On the night of 2 November 1952, Christopher Craig and Derek Bentley broke into the premises of Barlow and Parker in London's Tamworth Road and climbed onto the warehouse roof. Then the police arrived. Detective-Constable Fairfax shinned up a vent pipe and succeeded in nabbing Bentley on the roof. Meanwhile Craig pulled out a revolver and opened fire. In Fairfax's statement: 'Craig was

then on the westerly side of the stack. Bentley broke away from me and as he did so, he shouted "Let him have it, Chris." There was a loud report and something hit my shoulder.'

So one policeman was down. Moments later, PC Sydney Miles burst onto the roof. Craig continued firing and Miles collapsed forwards, dead, hit in the forehead. Then the cornered Craig jumped from the roof, waking up three days later in hospital. A policeman at his bedside noted down his first words: 'If I hadn't cut a bit off the barrel of my gun I would probably have killed a lot more policemen. That night I was out to kill.'

Murder then ranked as a capital offence. Craig was only sixteen – too young to hang. But Bentley was old enough. And under the legal principle of 'joint ventures' he was as guilty as Craig. In the words of the indictment: 'Bentley incited Craig to begin the shooting and, although technically under arrest... was party to that murder and equally responsible in law.' So Craig, who had committed the murder, received a prison sentence; and Bentley, who had not, swung on 28 January 1953, while a hostile crowd battled at the prison gates, tearing down the Notice of Death as it was posted.

By then it was apparent that Bentley was a subnormal with an IQ of 66. Born in 1933, he had fallen off a lorry at the age of four and suffered periodic epileptic fits thereafter. He remained illiterate until the end of his days, thinking his first name was spelt 'Derk', and his deputy head teacher at Norbury Manor uncharitably described him as 'an utterly worthless piece of humanity'.

Craig and Bentley's trial was steamrollered through by Lord Chief Justice Goddard, who in effect acted for the prosecution. Puzzling discrepancies in the evidence were dismissed as irrelevant, and, in 1991, the publication of John Parris's *Scapegoat* put forward a troubling new scenario.

According to Parris, Craig did not shoot PC Sydney Miles. He was shot by the police. Of the three officers said to have witnessed the incident – Fairfax, MacDonald and Harrison – two could hardly have seen what transpired, one because it was dark and he was too far away, if he was there at all, and the other because it is extremely unlikely that he ever reached the top of the roof. A fourth police officer, Claud Pain, actually on the roof, was never officially admitted as present.

Officer Fairfax did climb to the top where – as he testified – he collared Bentley. They sheltered together behind the skylights as Craig loosed off sporadic shots from his revolver. Then the officer persuaded Bentley to help make Craig surrender. Bentley warily left his shelter and came within six feet of Craig. 'For Christ's sake, Chris,' he pleaded, 'what's got into you?' He repeated this a number of times, and started edging forwards. 'Fuck off, otherwise I'll shoot you too,' said Craig. Bentley scampered back to Fairfax and safety.

Meanwhile the local police station summoned two Scotland Yard marksmen with rifles. They took up position opposite on the roof of 26 Tamworth Road while Craig went on firing haphazardly. But it was pitch-dark, with no one in clear view for him to fire at, even if he wanted to. Fairfax was only hit by a ricochet, very possibly aimed wide, the bullet stopped by his braces. After a total of six rounds Craig's gun ran out of ammunition. He pulled the trigger four more times, the hammer falling on an empty chamber. 'See, it's empty,' he shouted.

At that moment the police reinforcements appeared, bursting onto the roof through an internal staircase. First up was PC Miles, immediately drilled clean through the forehead by the marksmen on the far side of the street. More shots rang out, and Craig threw himself over the parapet in a bid to escape.

That night the shocked and angry police cobbled together Bentley's confession, forging his signature a total of six times. Over the ensuing days the officers concocted a complete scenario for the gunfight, agreeing who had been where and seen and heard what. In particular, they invented the shout 'Let him have it, Chris' to put a noose round Bentley's neck in revenge for their colleague's death.

These damning words, designed to be legally watertight, had already been tested in court – in the case of *R* v. *Appelby* which featured in the force's standard bible *Moriarty's Police Law. Appelby* set an exact precedent, where a burglar captured by the police urged his mate, still at liberty, to shoot the arresting officer. He did, and the first burglar swung for his pains. The words that hanged him were 'Let him have it', and there was no reason why they should not hang Bentley too.

At the trial, Bentley elected to run a truly fatuous defence, claiming that he had simply popped out that evening for a bus-ride and had no intention of breaking or entering anything. He was rightly regarded as a stupid liar. Out of loyalty he kept quiet about his attempt to disarm Craig.

More important, Craig never disputed that he killed PC Miles. Why should he? He had been firing away, and there was the dead body. True, Craig felt puzzled by this turn of events, later saying, 'What I've never been able to understand is how I shot him between the eyes when he was facing away from me and was going the other way.'

Lord Chief Justice Goddard made great play of the boys' possession of a knuckleduster

The truth is that Craig could only have fired six rounds. According to Parris's computations, the fatal shot was the seventh one heard, after which there were three or four more shots. Craig's gun was wildly inaccurate, almost incapable of hitting anyone intentionally. When he sawed off the barrel to a stub, he also removed the sights. His ammunition did not fit: he used .45 calibre bullets for a .455 gun. On test, the deflection worked out at six feet either way over a range of thirteen yards.

PC Miles was hit in the head, the bullet entering one side and exiting the other. If fired by Craig this should have shattered the glass panel in the door behind Miles as he emerged onto the roof. But it remained intact. Further, Miles could only have been shot in the forehead if he was looking left as he was turning right. More likely, he looked right and turned right. In this case he could have been shot in the front of the head from the opposite direction, from Tamworth Road, with the expended rounds lodging in the woodwork round the door frame.

Marks were later found, but any bullets had been removed. Further, the best evidence now available is that Miles's head-wound came from .32 to .38 calibre ammunition. Police sharpshooters were issued with .32s.

At the time, the Lord Chief Justice advised against clemency for Bentley. Forty years later the Home Secretary, Kenneth Clarke, rejected a posthumous pardon on the grounds that the jury's verdict was correct on the evidence *then* available.

Crank, The

The crank was introduced to British prisons along with the **Separate System** during the mid-nineteenth century. This pernicious device ranks as an early feat of miniaturisation, enabling prisoners to be stationed outside a small **treadwheel** instead of inside a large one.

The Victorians implemented the principle that convicts needed the moral uplift of work by making them turn a heavy handle attached to a drum-shaped container installed in their cells. The bottom of this inspiring machine – known as a 'crank' – was filled with sand, and the handle rotated an internal system of scoops. These raised the sand to the top of the drum. When the sand reached the top, it fell down to the bottom.

The crank's pressure was adjustable, with a normal setting of around twelve pounds, and a dial in front of the drum registered the number of rotations. A convict failing to meet his target was liable to further punishment, a system open to sadistic abuse. At a rough guess, the standard quota of 10,000 rotations a day took nine hours based on a notional three seconds a turn. Keener staff insisted on prisoners 'earning' their food by demanding, say, 2,000 turns before breakfast, and a Royal Commission in the 1870s discovered an inmate who had qualified for only nine meals in twenty-one days.

The crank featured an adjustable screw to make the job easier or, more likely, harder. By this means the prisoner could be 'wound up' by the 'screws'.

Unlike the treadwheel, the crank had no end-product. Its use was banned in 1898.

See also **Prison**

Crime passionel

In France, disposing of one's lover or spouse in a fit of passion can constitute a defence to the charge of murder. The court may reduce the offence to manslaughter or, in especially sentimental circumstances, direct an acquittal.

On 12 August 1952 Yvonne Chevalier, the country wife of a rising political star, shot her unfaithful husband Pierre four times with a 7.65mm Mab automatic. It was his first day as a Minister.

Pierre represented something of a paragon, a real French war hero. A doctor by day, by night he ran the local Resistance, leading the attack on the Germans which expelled them from his native Orleans. And now he had been gunned down by his cloddish peasant wife! Feeling ran so high that she had to be tried in distant Rheims. But the public mood changed on hearing Yvonne's side of the story.

Yvonne recounted how her husband had long refused to share the marriage bed; how he flaunted his relationship with his mistress, the glamorous Jeanne Perreau; how he rebuffed her time and again at public receptions, refused to see her when she visited him at work, suggested that she take a lover, reacted indifferently to her attempted suicide and finally announced that he was leaving to marry his mistress. 'And you can remain in your own filth,' he shouted, 'I'm a Minister.' On this last occasion, the distraught Yvonne produced the Mab automatic and waved it in his face, threatening to end her life there and then. 'Go ahead,' Pierre replied. 'It will be the first sensible thing you've done in your life.'

'I'm serious,' cried Yvonne. 'Well,' said Pierre, 'for God's sake kill yourself, but wait until I've gone.' Then she shot him four times. Meanwhile her young son, Mathieu, started crying downstairs. Yvonne went down to soothe the child, handed him over to the maid and then returned upstairs where, in a fit of passion, she shot her husband again.

With a defence like this, the prosecution did not dare ask for a penalty of longer than two years. But the French jury found Yvonne innocent of everything, and she left the court to cheers.

British courts are beginning to invoke the 'slow burn' concept of provocation in an effort to mitigate the sentences of women driven to kill their husbands. For a historical yardstick, the Chevalier case comes from the era when the British could find no alternative to condemning Ruth **Ellis**, who shot her lover, to be hanged by the neck until dead.

See also **Sex discrimination**

Criminals

The British judiciary still draws a fairly clear distinction between crime and criminals. A member of the middle classes can commit a crime, but this does not make him a criminal *per se*. Belonging to the right class can diminish the gravity of an offence, and hence the social system now performs the same function as the old **Benefit of Clergy**, of which it is a vestigial relic.

Thus in January 1992, David Vaughan, a former merchant banker with Kleinwort Benson, was convicted on eighteen charges of embezzling a total of £455,280 from his employers. The most he took at one time was £230,000; normally it went in dribs and drabs, a thousand here and a thousand there, and the theft came to light soon after he left for early retirement.

Passing sentence at Knightsbridge Crown Court, Judge Christopher Compton pointed out that the money had not been squandered on loose living; rather, it was *invested* in a bigger and better home so that his family could maintain a standard of living for which Vaughan had insufficient income. It was true that none of the funds had been recovered, but on the plus side the defendant was a devout Christian. In the circumstances, a suspended sentence seemed appropriate, and a relieved Mrs Vaughan said, 'Things are going to be very difficult for us now', as her husband left the court a free man, thereby irritating hundreds of prisoners serving lengthy sentences for robbing parking meters or stealing bicycles.

This does not imply one law for the rich and another for the poor. Although the distinction between a course of fraud undertaken to support one's family in a style to which they are not accustomed, as against a systematic career in theft aimed at unjust enrichment, might be a tricky one, the fact is that some men prey on society whereas others deserve to be rescued by it.

From the defendant's point of view, the crux is a successful presentation of the offence as an extraordinary aberration. From this perspective, Vaughan's case is a creditable exercise in damage-limitation. Probably the Methodist minister came closest to the mark: 'I have never at any time doubted Vaughan's honesty and this is completely out of character.'

In other words, Vaughan may have committed a crime, but he was very far from being a criminal. Full-blown *mafiosi* feel the same, regarding hoodlums working outside the family as crooks and bums.

Crippen, Hawley Harvey (1862–1910)

Sometimes a murder attains the status of a coat peg on which a generation hangs its sense of dread and love of morbidity. For the British, it was Sutcliffe in 1970s, Brady and Hindley in the 1960s, Christie in the 1950s, Jack the Ripper in the preceding century and Hawley Harvey Crippen (1862–1910) in between.

Crippen poisoned his wife with hyoscine on 1 February 1910, buried her in the basement, told their friends that she had left him, took up with his mistress, successfully fobbed off the police, lost his nerve, fled to America, was caught, tried and executed.

The case exemplifies the difference between crime and violence. A 'good' murder – of the old-fashioned kind – towers above the run of juvenile muggings, 'drive-bys', or drunken brawls that end in death. Crippen's full story displays the compact drama of a play, unfolding from early suspicions, via the sensational discovery of the body, to the attempted escape ended by the technological marvel of wireless telegraphy. There were unusual names, an unfamiliar poison, a background of domestic duplicity supported by a large cast of secondary characters, a horrible act of dismemberment, an extended charade of concealment, a disguise, and the clash of experts in court, culminating in Crippen's extinction by the hangman's noose. If the entertainment ever seemed base, Crippen's unfailing love for his mistress redeemed it. He was buried holding her photograph and surrounded by her love letters.

Many killings afford only the ephemeral interest of a grisly death or a novel weapon, but Crippen ran the full five acts, absorbing the nation for half a year. The transatlantic pursuit in July 1910 generated such excitement that newspapers carried diagrams each day showing Inspector Dew's *SS Laurentic* gaining on the fugitives' *SS Montrose* at three-and-a-half knots an hour. The chase elevated readers to the status of gods, granting them crucial information denied to the human participants. Cut off at sea and disguised as 'the Robinsons', the Crippens calmly dined at the Captain's table on board the *Montrose*, unaware of their status as objects of international fascination over whom hung the sword of retribution.

No one would remember Crippen had he been arrested at his home, or had he fled and disappeared, or had he lacked the complication of a lover. By his hanging on 23 November 1910, the impedimenta of Edwardian society was laid out for public dissection: love and marriage, home, hypocrisy, ambition, the mistress, the stage, music halls and medicine, the loyal friends, the murderer's fatal mistake, Scotland Yard, detectives, ocean liners, disguises, telegrams, courtroom drama and Justice.

Crippen's was thus a murder of quality, and the better the story is told the more intriguing it becomes, hinging on the finer social niceties. It can be argued, for instance, that his wife Cora was vain on the compelling grounds that she had the house redecorated in shades of pink to better set off her hair, dyed blonde from its natural raven black. But perhaps this was no act of premeditated

colour-coordination. Perhaps she just liked pink. But this might suggest poor taste. The reader is willy-nilly caught up in arcane considerations of snobbery. Did Cora ask their lodgers to leave because they disturbed her gentleman-callers? Or because she had aspirations to improve her social standing? And is such a desire compatible with modesty and good sense?

With Crippen, the major actors were fully rounded characters. There are many ways to play their parts. The line adopted by the press was to cast Crippen as the brutal 'cellar murderer', an inhuman monster who disposed of his wife, a flamboyant actress, for the love of his mistress, the beautiful Ethel Le Neve. Closer scrutiny suggests that Crippen was an insignificant little man encumbered by a brassy wife who pretended to have been a music-hall favourite. Behind this version is the kindly, mild-mannered doctor, a model of generosity yoked to an hysterical bully who squandered his money on broken dreams and taunted him with a succession of lovers. This Crippen set the table for their lodgers' breakfasts before going to work while his wife lay in bed, planning her day's flirtations. Here, Ethel is a quiet, modest girl, first Crippen's confidante and then, after seven demure years, his lover.

Then there is Crippen the Quack, salesman for the Munyon Homeopathic Home Remedy Co., whose remedies included a nostrum for piles. He was fired when it emerged that he managed a music hall singer – his wife – and he drifted into work as a bogus ear specialist notable for his filthy equipment and vulgar way of dressing. His firm went into liquidation after a conviction for medical negligence for the death of a locksmith. Crippen acquired the bankrupt stock, and set up in business on his own account with Ethel as his secretary.

The real name of this Ethel was Ethel Neave, who considered Ethel Le Neve more romantic. Her hypochondria earned her the nickname of 'Not very well thank you'. She hated her father, and grew up as a whining child almost continuously afflicted by delusional bouts of neuralgia, anaemia, headaches and fibrositis. Her biographer brands her as a pathological liar, telling fibs 'from sheer perversity – in fact she seemed incapable of telling the truth'.

Her rival, Cora Crippen, born Kunigunde Mackamotzki, trod the boards under the stage name of Belle Ellmore, by her mid-thirties best described as a monument to corsetry. In her twenties Crippen was content to pay theatres to allow Cora to appear, writers to compose her songs and costumiers to dress her. His support extended to dispensing real £5 notes when Cora's role required her to hold stage money.

As a performer Cora may not have been such a disaster. Producer Clarkson Rose adjudged her perfectly competent: 'She was not a top-rank artist, but, in her way, not bad – a blowsy, florid type of serio', and to the end Crippen funded expensive *toilettes* to fit her for the role of Honorary Treasurer to the Music Hall Ladies' Guild. But Cora drank to excess, adorned the parlour walls with photographs of her lover and was caught in bed with a lodger.

The trial was clear cut, since the quixotic Crippen elected to protect Ethel by denying that his wife had died. He claimed that the body in the basement belonged to someone else, deposited there by a former tenant who somehow included Crippen's pyjama tops in the consignment. This defence introduced a new player into the drama – forensic science – and with it a new public figure, the young pathologist Bernard **Spilsbury**, whose calm, authoritative manner speedily demonstrated that a fragment of skin under the coal cellar floor was derived from a stomach, not a thigh, and that its crease was not a fold but a scar, identical to one that disfigured Cora's stomach. Spilsbury thus put a name to a body that lacked a head, fingers and sexual organs. He became a household name and remained so for decades.

Ethel Le Neve proved no less **durable**. She survived until 1967, but in a different guise. After the trial, briefly the most famous woman in the world, she slipped away to Toronto and changed her name to Harvey before slinking back into Britain, where she took work at Hampton's furniture store near Trafalgar Square. She married a bookkeeper, Stanley Smith, settled down in east Croydon and produced two children, Bob and Nina.

Her offspring had no inkling of their mother's tumultuous past until the seventy-fifth anniversary of the trial in 1985. Six years later they were interviewed for BBC radio; Ethel was described by her daughter as 'straightlaced' and 'perfectly ordinary', and by her son as an 'ordinary housewife sewing on buttons'. He dimly realised that at some stage his mother had 'been' to Canada, but Ethel was too cagey to acknowledge even her assumed name and told her daughter, who once found a book inscribed 'E. Harvey', that it belonged to a friend.

One striking casualty of the case was Cora's body. Spilsbury's notes only record discovering the 'medical organs of the chest and abdomen removed in one mass. Four large pieces of skin and muscle, one from the lower abdomen with old operation scar, four inches long – broader at lower end.' Of the rest – the head, the limbs and bones – from which these components had been excised, there was no trace.

Crown jewels

The Crown Jewels of England were stolen by the Irishman Colonel Thomas Blood. Born in 1618, the son of a blacksmith, Blood fought with the Parliamentarians in the English civil war, gaining forfeited estates to the tune of £500 a year. These were reappropriated under the Restoration, confirming his views on the monarchy.

After a series of abortive plots, in 1671 the Colonel disguised himself as a parson and befriended the elderly Mr Edwards, keeper of the Crown jewels in the Tower of London. Mr Edwards had a lovely daughter, and Blood offered his 'nephew's' hand in marriage. But on 9 May, instead of effecting the promised introduction, Blood gagged the keeper, hit him on the head with a mallet and then ran him through with a sword. Edwards nearly died.

Meanwhile Blood crushed the crown of England flat so that it fitted under his cloak. When the alarm was raised, his accomplices decided to leave the sceptre behind – it took too long to file in half. But the golden orb, symbol of sovereignty, was thrust down a robber's trousers, where it made running difficult. So the orb too was relinquished, the thief melting into the crowd. Next, the squashed crown fell out of Blood's cloak as he rode off.

Apprehended in a Hampshire pub, the 'Crown and Cushion', Blood was sent back to the Tower in chains. There he refused to bandy words with anyone except his sovereign. Charles II responded, visiting the prisoner, and subsequently exercised clemency to restore his Irish estates. After release, Colonel Blood remained influential at court, where he continued plotting and scheming until his death in 1680.

Across St George's Channel, the Irish Crown jewels faded away in July 1907. It soon emerged that the thief had taken an impression of the key to the Dublin Castle safe held by Sir Arthur Vicars, Ulster King of Arms. The most likely culprit was a member of Sir Arthur's staff, Frank Shackleton, Herald of Dublin, a homosexual and a close friend of the Duke of Argyll, King Edward VII's brother-in-law.

The royal connection threatened the throne with scandal and the investigation was cut short, but not before it emerged that Shackleton's lover, Captain Richard Gorges, had been present when a joke was played on Sir Arthur a few weeks before. Sir Arthur drank himself unconscious at a party in the castle, and a friend took his key ring and removed the Crown Jewels as a prank, replacing them on his desk the following morning. Omitting this final stage, Gorges gained access with a key furnished by Shackleton on or about the night of 5 July.

Despite a £1,000 reward, the Insignia of the Order of St Patrick were never recovered. Shackleton was later imprisoned for fraud and died in disgrace, Gorges shot a policeman and outlived his sentence in Dartmoor to die in the 1950s, and Sir Arthur was relieved of his post and killed by the IRA in 1921.

Cuthbert, Cyril (d. 1984)

Police constable from Devon, in charge of the station pay ledger, who became the reluctant founder of Scotland Yard's forensic science laboratory.

For a constable, Cuthbert had an unusual background: an uncompleted medical training and the rudiments of dentistry, rounded off by evening classes in chemistry. On joining the police he developed an interest in criminal medicine, eventually spending half his weekly wages on a thirty-five shilling microscope, keeping it at home to avoid official reprimands about time-wasting. But his superiors, mindful of his hobby, relegated Cuthbert to the backwater of the Criminal Records Office. Nothing daunted, Cuthbert persisted in helping out his colleagues with their more difficult cases.

Matters came to a head in the 1930s when the Assistant Commissioner, Sir Norman Kendall, received a request for Cuthbert to give evidence in court, referring to him as Cuthbert 'of the Metropolitan Police Laboratory'. Kendall felt outraged by the presumption; there was no police laboratory. He refused permission, but in the end Cuthbert was subpoenaed. By this stage Cuthbert would have left the force had he been able to find another job. But at the trial his well-presented evidence secured a conviction, and his work – reprimanded by Kendall – was commended to the attention of the Police Commissioner, Lord Trenchard.

Trenchard, intrigued to hear of his force's exciting new facility, insisted on a personal tour of inspection. In a panic Cuthbert collected up all his odds and ends, spreading them out in one of the photographic department's cupboards. For added authenticity he borrowed a white coat from a hospital, and Trenchard was so alarmed by this pitiful display that he forced through the establishment of a proper, well-funded facility with lecture halls, dark-rooms and laboratories. A promoted Cuthbert supervised the installation of the apparatus, including microscopes, epidiascope, centrifugal separator, X-ray apparatus, one of the latest reversion spectroscopes and so on.

The new building was opened on 10 April 1935 to highly favourable press comment. But the police themselves were less enthusiastic. 'For the first ten years the lab never really prospered. The 'Old Guard' at Scotland Yard were suspicious,' the laboratory's fourth director, Dr Hamish Walls, recollected in 1976. This complaint was repeated in 1987 by the retiring director, Dr Raymond Williams, who considered that the value of forensic science had never been fully acknowledged by the Home Office.

Cutpurse, Moll (c. 1584–1659)

Also known as Mary Frith and Mary Markham, a startling underworld figure so far ahead of her time it is surprising that her life has not been filmed. She was the first bisexual, cross-dressing, pipesmoking, entrepreneurial highwaywoman, and she may also have been England's first professional actress. Her voice alone resonated so powerfully that it was capable of 'drowning all the city'.

By the age of 26, Moll had sufficiently progressed from her humble beginnings as a pickpocket for the Jacobean dramatists Middleton and Decker to pen a play in her honour, *The Roaring Girle*. Rather than lose the profits of thieving to the fences, Moll set up as her own receiver, spending

The Roaring Girle.
OR
Moll Cut-Purse.

As it hath lately beene Acted on the Fortune-stage by the Prince his Players.

Written by *T. Middleton* and *T. Dekkar.*

her earnings on a large house staffed by three maids and a footman. Moll's critics maintained that she was so big, strong and ugly that there was no real need for her to disguise herself as a man, and she enjoyed a string of lovers both male and female, becoming the first English woman known to have smoked. Still game at the age of sixty, Moll overstepped the mark by robbing General Fairfax on Hounslow Heath, shooting him in the arm, and she had to buy her way out of trouble with a massive £2,000 bribe after being captured at Turnham Green, now an underground station on the District Line.

Otherwise Moll kept her nose clean, with a solitary exception in 1612 when she was compelled to do penance at St Paul's Cross, first bracing herself by drinking six pints of sack and then disturbing divine service in the cathedral with her caterwauling.

She died at the age of 75, doling out handsome bequests to her friends along with the unusual injunction that she be buried upside down ('with her breach pointing upwards'). In the words of the contemporary ditty, 'Here's no attraction your fancy greets. But if her features please not, read her feats.'

D

Dahmer, Jeffrey L. (1960–)

American serial killer and psychological test-bed showing Man stripped bare of everything that makes existence tolerable. Dahmer's negative posture provided no lover, no friends, no contacts, no job, no interests, no conversation, no hobbies, no sports, no occupation, no money, no prospects and nowhere to live. He thus remained utterly unsocialised, and his cavernous emotional interior progressively degraded, the void filling with phantasmagoria.

Dahmer was born on 21 May 1960 to a troubled marriage between a respectable research chemist and an emotional, self-pitying neurotic. A shy child, he seemed forlorn at school. Animals provided an early interest – snakes, toads, rabbits and fish. He kept a heap of bones (which he called 'fiddlesticks') under his house, and was intrigued to feel the same fiddlesticks inside the live animals he handled. His family moved six times before settling into 4480 West Bath Road, Ohio, in 1968, and at the age of ten he first tried bleaching chicken bones. He spent much of his childhood tucked away in a wooden shed up on the hill, collecting insects in pickle jars and preserving them in formaldehyde. He worked his way up through the animal kingdom, via squirrels and raccoons, to large road-kills, carrying their bodies to the woods where they were left to rot. Then he soused the remains in bleach to clean the bones.

His mother, on tranquillisers, set a family precedent by blotting herself out with drugs, and after a spell of hospitalisation she spent her days at home in bed. Dahmer withdrew into unbreakable isolation. At eleven, he talked in a monotone. He turned into a solitary 'class clown', bleating like a sheep during lessons or acting retarded in shops,

and he took to drink and **masturbation**. His grades plummeted. By sixteen he was regularly drunk in class, his only friend Jeff Six, the local marijuana supplier. The two were continuously stoned. At seventeen Dahmer masturbated three times daily; for stimulation he used male magazines, focusing on the models' muscular torsos, daydreaming of strangers who lay passively by his side. Like any consumer of pornography, he related not to the models' personalities but to the beautiful shiny pictures. His other preoccupation was with the insides of animals, and later these interests fused when he used the insides of people as pornography.

When Dahmer reached seventeen, a jogger – an attractive, healthy youth – regularly ran past his house. Dahmer wanted to meet him. Lacking any social skills to detain him, he took a baseball bat and lay in wait, planning to attack as he passed. But the runner never came. The following year his father left home, and on 18 June Dahmer picked up a young hitchhiker, Stephen Hicks, asked him home and then murdered him rather than allow him to leave. After slitting the body to inspect the innards, Dahmer placed it in some trashbags which he dumped in a nearby ravine.

Thereafter Dahmer renounced life in a brooding descent into self-disgust and withdrawal. His father sent him to Ohio university, where he downed a couple of bottles of whisky a day, never made classes and antagonised his roommates by stacking their furniture in a corner and spreading pizzas over the walls. In December 1978 his despairing father made him enlist as a soldier. But military liquor is half-price and Dahmer drank himself into oblivion, off and on duty. After his discharge in March 1981 he was packed off to his grandmother in West Allis, Wisconsin. Dahmer went to church, read the bible, and limited his self-abuse to once a week, keeping his cravings at bay, and found work at Milwaukee's Ambrosia Chocolate Factory. But one day in the public library he was handed a note reading 'Meet me in the second level bathroom. I'll give you a blow-job.'

Dahmer's veneer of self-control collapsed. His masturbation climbed to four times a day, and he stole a shop mannequin and took it home as a sexual partner. Then he discovered Milwaukee's 'bathhouses' where homosexuals met for anonymous and impersonal sex. But he had difficulty obtaining erections while his partners were awake and, after obtaining sleeping pills on prescription, gave his contacts a heavily doped drink. They passed out for the night; between bouts of masturbation Dahmer put his head to their chest and listened to their heartbeats. But he was banned when an oriental took two days to revive.

So Dahmer searched the obituary columns for a corpse of his own. He attended the funeral of a suitable 18-year-old, and visited the cemetery at night to dig him up. But the ground was frozen. Meanwhile he lived like an automaton, working in order to live in order to work, and an arrest for indecent exposure in September 1986 led to his first psychological assessment. The professionals were unanimous: Dahmer was in a dangerous state, and on 20 November 1987 he killed for the second time. The victim was Steven Tuomi, a black youth he met outside the 219 Club. Dahmer took him to the Ambassador Hotel, offered him a doped drink and woke up the next morning on top of a bloodied body with no recollection of what had happened. He put the corpse in the cupboard, rebooked the room, bought a large suitcase and ferried it by taxi to his grandmother's.

There he stored Tumoi in the basement cellar and dismembered him, keeping the head for two weeks in a blanket on his top shelf. Then he boiled the skull and bleached it. Thereafter Dahmer killed whenever an opportunity presented. His technique hardly varied: first the pick-up – he offered money

for sex – then the Irish cream, mixed with coffee and crushed sleeping pills, then the **strangulation**. After the kill he embraced the corpse. In life, contact was harder; as he put it, 'I did my drinking alone, and bar-hopping alone... no one... no one.' Dahmer's next victim was Jamie Doxator. He explained, 'I knew grandma would be waking up and I still wanted him to stay so I strangled him.' He had anal sex with the corpse, put it in the cellar and went to church. By now he only related to the dead.

Dahmer wanted to keep the heads, and gradually devised the concept of a shrine adorned with bones. Richard Guerrero was killed next, but on 26 September another victim managed to leave before the drugs took effect. The police pressed charges, but their house search missed Guerrero's skull, and Dahmer was found guilty of Second Degree Sexual Assault on 30 January 1989. Before starting his one-year sentence he killed Anthony Sears, storing the body in the upstairs bathroom, mutilating it as a sexual aid and spray-painting the skull.

Dahmer moved into the run-down Oxford Apartments in March 1990. He purchased a long black table and two plastic griffins, laying out the next body on this makeshift altar to take Polaroid snaps. He froze the organs and other preferred items, boiling up the rest in a huge eighty-gallon kettle filled with water and wallpaper stripper, before putting the resulting morass into a large trash container primed with acid. Two weeks later he tipped the slush down the lavatory. This seemed a waste, so the body of Eddie Smith – his next victim – went into the freezer. But it would not dry out properly, and when he tried baking the skull, it exploded. Again, nothing remained.

So Dahmer kept his next victim's head in the fridge, cut up the body, ate some of the flesh, bleached the bones, and tried to reassemble the skeleton. The skull he painted; by now he had three. Of the successors, some he ate in part and one he flayed, hoping to keep the whole skin. But it disintegrated. Normally he slit the bodies from neck to groin, slipped his hands into the chest cavity, and caressed the viscera before having sex with them, either by lowering himself onto the body, or by rubbing himself with the intestines. His Polaroid photospreads became increasingly elaborate; he might lay out the hands, head, and severed genitals in a still life on the kitchen draining board. But the pleasure to be derived from corpses was transitory, and he determined to manufacture '**zombies**' he could keep. He bored through his subsequent captives' skulls and injected fluid into the brain so they would stagger round his apartment in a stupor.

On 19 July Dahmer was sacked from work for absenteeism. By then he showered with two corpses in the tub; there were hearts in the fridge, heads in the freezer, skulls in the filing cabinet, and a body on the bed, crawling with maggots. He was arrested on 23 July after the escape of an intended victim, Tracy **Edwards**.

Dahmer's trial began on 27 January 1992. It seemed clear from the start that he was driven by mental disease and equally clear that he would not be 'let off' as insane. After the verdict Dahmer spoke to the court for the first time. 'Your honour, it is over now,' he said. 'I feel so bad for what I did to those poor families, and I understand their rightful hate... I take all the blame for what I did... I have hurt my mother and father and stepmother. I love them all so very much.' Sentenced to a minimum of 900 years, on his first day the prison authorities were inundated by 200 requests for interviews and good wishes from strangers all over the world.

There is a theory that Dahmer's problems originated from a double hernia operation at the age of four, when his abdomen was opened and the doctor rummaged around his insides; the black table on which he laid the bodies of his victims' supposedly mimics the operating table.

Database

The FBI's Behavioral Science Unit compiled its initial database between 1979 and 1983 from interviews conducted with thirty-six incarcerated sex and serial murderers. No one had thought of talking to these people before. They had been tracked, arrested, tried in court, convicted and sentenced – but never interviewed to find out exactly what they did to their victims.

The unofficial survey was a risky process based on a 57-page questionnaire which initially involved lengthy one-to-one cell sessions with convicted killers, one of whom (Edmund **Kemper**, a habitual decapitator) told his interrogator, 'I could screw your head off and place it on the table to greet the guard.'

The emphasis in the questioning was more on a murderer's 'how' than his 'why', thus bypassing the notoriously self-serving accounts of motivation which, in any case, do not procure arrests. 'We don't get hung up on why the killer does the things he does,' FBI Special Agent Roy Hazelwood wrote in *Psychology Today*. 'What we're interested in is that he *does* it in a way that leads us to him.' The behaviour at the scene of the crime, manifested by the way the victim (and subsequently the body) was treated, provided clues about the type of assailant.

Of the thirty-six interviewees, twenty-five were serial killers. As to their 'rearing environment', fifteen had been sexually abused in childhood, twelve in adolescence and thirteen as adults. Typically they came from broken homes with a non-caring mother and an absent father. Seventy per cent felt 'sexually incompetent' and relied heavily on pornography, preferring the type featured on the covers of detective magazines, showing a terrified woman, bound and gagged, looking up at her violator. Such images have more to do with sadism and dominance than sex.

To put it another way, these people had terrible childhoods, with a characteristic upbringing of illness, accidents, interference, beatings, abuse, bullying, ridicule, neglect, desertion, resentment, isolation, ostracism, poverty and often head injuries. As yet, there is no serial murderer from a good background.

It transpired that the child, who set fire to buildings or tortured animals, was father to the man, whose emotional focus was random killing. A gradual split emerged between two distinct personality types of killer, the '**organised**' – who plans – and the 'disorganised', who does not: in the initial database sample, the organised/disorganised ratio stood at twenty-four to twelve. The two categories treated their victims in different ways and themselves exemplified different personality traits. Thus *how* the victims were killed indicated *who* they had been killed by.

The hundreds of indicators from the database survey went onto computer in the form of 'rules' to form the basis of the computer programme now known as '**Profiler**'. One of the technique's early success cases was the murder of Francine **Elveson** which ensured that as from 1982 the interviewing of convicted killers became official policy.

See also **Sex crimes, Zombie**

Date rape

Date rape has been in the news since 1989, when Dr Koss at the University of Arizona discovered in a nationwide survey of 6,000 students that 15 per cent had been penetrated without their consent. Four out of five of Koss's victims knew their assailant and these findings were mirrored by British studies, the most recent conducted by Cambridge University on 1,600 students nationally, showing that one in five had been raped: a figure exceeding conventional rape figures by a factor of hundreds. Clearly this was helpful in moving the concept of rape out of big city ghettos and into the realms of everyday life. But why the discrepancy?

Indubitably, **rape** – like any other crime – is under-reported: the British Home Office figures for 1988 estimate that only 21 per cent of serious sexual offences against adults ever reach the police.

It is likely, if not certain, that date rape has always been with us, but only recently discovered. In the words of Helen Peggs, of Victim Support, women 'are realising that what happened to them was unacceptable and that they were not to blame'. Rape itself still carries the same definition – of unauthorised penile penetration – and thus it is the perception of rape that has broadened.

On the hard feminist line, the concept is extended almost beyond recognition. Germaine Greer has argued that the commonest form is 'rape by fraud – by phoney tenderness or false promises of an enduring relationship'. But Greer acknowledges this as non-criminal and it is, of course, practised by both sexes. A leading QC, Helena Kennedy, dismisses the idea of a half-way house, a 'rapette' as it were, saying that there is no need to differentiate the crime: 'The varying seriousness is reflected in the sentencing.'

On a more practical level, juries tend to take a fairly robust view. According to the barrister John Parris, women jurors frequently argue that the victim 'got what she asked for'.

In four out of five British rape cases the defendant is found not guilty, and with date rape the fact of a previous relationship is often treated as indicative of a consensual element – a tendency only increased by joint ventures such as going out together, having a drink or a meal, returning home, kissing, petting and issuing an invitation to spend the night on the sofa or in the bed – 'but no funny business'.

Juries presumably consider it unduly harsh to brand a man for life when the woman changes her mind only just before, during, or after the act; or where she feels ambivalent but tending more to the negative about actual intercourse. The prosecution's problems are exacerbated by the absence of corroborative evidence such as scratches or torn clothing. Moira Lasch, the prosecutor in the 1992 Kennedy Smith rape trial (see **Modus Operandi**), was reduced to making unsubstantiated allegations to such an extent that the judge threatened her with legal action.

In a sexual relationship of which the cultural essence, for centuries, was that the woman surrendered, there will always be scope for misunderstanding about exactly what constitutes 'consent'. This difficulty is compounded by the predilection of some women to say 'no' when they mean 'yes', a tradition reconfirmed by Charlotte Muehlenhard's recent survey at Texas University where nearly half the female psychology students interviewed admitted to feigning reluctance in the run-up to intercourse to make the man 'more sexually aggressive'.

During the televised hearings of the 1991 Anita Hill Judge Thomas sexual harassment case that kept Americans glued to their sets, Laura Berman of the *Detroit News* noted a progressive fragmentation of opinion: 'There was this huge gap between what I was reading in the *New York Times* – the standard elitist-feminist line about Anita Hill being this great heroine, and how she reflected the experience of all women – and what I was hearing among women in my own office, out there in middle America, which was a lot of scepticism and speculation about her motives.'

Two years on, these doubts seem well-founded. Despite Hill's canonisation as a feminist icon, study of her sworn testimony – as dissected in *The Real*

Anita Hill by David Brock – shows it either to conflict with the facts or omit them. Nor was Thomas her first harasser. Diane Holt, who worked for her in Washington, commented: 'She always bragged that all the men in the office were coming on to her.' Another lawyer, a former colleague from Oklahoma, says: 'Everything was sexism or sexual harassment. She was obsessed with it... Every time she walked through a crowd someone was grabbing at her breasts. When she really got going, every guy she ever worked with sexually harassed her. The sheer numerosity of it struck me.'

But like so much of the most damning material in *The Real Anita Hill*, this last source remains anonymous. Its author, David Brock, is not an unbiased journalist but a right-wing polemicist and fellow of the Reaganite Heritage Foundation. Many of his verifiable assertions are misleading; for instance, the **lie-detector** test passed by Miss Hill was not administered by an inexperienced novice but by the chief of the FBI's polygraph division, and the witnesses cited by Brock as failing to corroborate her evidence were not interviewed by him and, when they are, support her story. So although truth may out, in this case it has not yet, and the sledgehammer of court procedure may be too blunt an instrument to unravel the finer points of interpersonal relationships. Meanwhile, Judge Thomas's career is on hold, while Hill makes after-dinner speeches on gender politics for fees of up to $12,000.

More than in the assault-by-a-stranger cases, date rape turns on whether the sexual interaction is seen from the man's or the woman's perspective. When a victim clearly and repeatedly expresses her opposition to sex, but her protestations are not believed by the accused, one of two consequences arises. In America, the man goes to prison as a rapist. In Britain, he is acquitted, since from his viewpoint she acquiesced.

US official figures put the annual total of rapes at 85,000. The standard extrapolation from Dr Koss's report, which found that only one date rape case in twenty reached the police, turns that into 1,700,000 rapes per annum or one every 18.55 seconds.

In Britain, the 1991 total of reported rape cases stood at 3,900; if confined to women aged between sixteen and thirty, this puts the chances of being raped at one in 1,600.

Death, Certification of

In Britain all deaths must be certified by a doctor, but it is not necessary to see the body *after* death. Before will do just as well. The law prescribes only that – provided a colleague has seen the actual corpse – the certifying doctor 'should have been in professional attendance during the patient's last illness and within fourteen days of his death'. In 1993, an analysis of 500 British deaths showed that 29 per cent of certificates contained one or more inaccuracies.

In 1978, the American 'Friedgood Bill' banned doctors from signing the death certificates of their own relatives. This was because Dr Friedgood, who murdered his wife with a course of fatal injections, certified her as expiring from a stroke. In an earlier case a Dr Clements got away with signing the certificates of his first three wives, each richer than the last. But when Number Four passed away on 26 May 1947 the cause of death was queried by other doctors, their suspicions aroused by the deceased's pin-point eye pupils, and a second post-mortem confirmed that she had been poisoned with morphine. Clements committed suicide before he could be questioned.

There is of course no law against doctors conducting autopsies on their own murder victims. The crime is the antecedent killing. Thus in 1847 Dr Valorus P. Coolidge proved delighted to sign off his deceased creditor Edward Matthews, whom he had only just finished murdering. In 1855 a similar train of circumstances led to the attempted theft of a very unusual object, the stomach belonging to man called Cook. This had been poisoned by the famous Dr William **Palmer**, called in to assist at the autopsy. Subsequently Dr Palmer tried to bribe the laboratory assistant charged with transporting the stomach to London, begging him to destroy the goods in transit. But to no avail; he went to the gallows on 14 June 1856.

Death, Life after

During his late twenties, Britain's Dennis **Nilsen** had plenty of homosexual contacts with strangers. But he found the experience of London's gay scene demoralising; his partners never stayed.

In late 1975 Nilsen had a shot at living with

someone, practically kidnapping a young derelict, David Gallichan, who was having trouble in a street brawl. They set up home together, buying a cat, a dog and a budgerigar. Their flat was cosy enough and they cleared the rear garden, where today apple and plum trees still blossom.

But the pair had little in common; both started bedding strangers. When Gallichan – nicknamed 'Twinkle' – left in the summer of 1977, Nilsen had few social outlets. Sometimes he secured casual sex from one of London's gay pubs but normally he went to work, came home, and waited for tomorrow. On Fridays, he waited till Monday. As he put it, 'Loneliness is a long unbearable pain.'

Come the dread hurdle of Christmas 1978, Nilsen spent six days by himself. On the evening of the 30th he could bear it no longer, and walked over to the 'Cricklewood Arms' hoping for company. There he met the man of his dreams – someone who would stay. They returned to Nilsen's flat and drank themselves to sleep. 'I remember thinking,' Nilsen wrote later, 'that I wanted him to stay with me over the New Year whether he wanted to or not.' Sometime in the early morning Nilsen killed the sleeping youth, strangling him in bed with a necktie.

Nilsen gave the boy – his name never emerged – a bath, and washed his hair. Then he pulled him out of the tub, deposited him on the lavatory seat and towelled him dry. Later, when it was time for bed, Nilsen snuggled the body down, pulling the bedclothes up to the chin.

Next day Nilsen dressed up his dead guest in Y-fronts, a vest and a brand new pair of socks. He looked so nice that they went to bed together. 'I held him close to me with my arms around him,' Nilsen wrote, 'and I began to remove his pants and explore his body under the blankets (I had an erection all this time).'

But the sex did not work. The boy's body was too cold. Nilsen fell into a deep sleep and that evening he decided to snug the body away under the floorboards. But the corpse would not co-operate; it had rigor mortis. This allowed Nilsen to prop him up for the night against the wall. By the following day, the rigor had passed off and Nilsen eased him under the floor.

A week later Nilsen pulled his lover out again. In his words: 'I stripped myself naked and carried him into the bathroom and washed the body... I carried the still wet youth into the room and laid him on the carpet.' There was a kind of loving: 'Under the orange side-lights his body aroused me sexually. I knelt over him and **masturbated** onto his bare stomach.'

Then the couple spent one last night together. 'Before I went to bed I suspended him by the ankles from the high wooden platform,' Nilsen recorded. 'He hung there all night, his fingers just touching the carpet. The next day while he was still hanging there upside down I stood beside him and masturbated again.'

At last they parted. The youth's body went under the floorboards for seven months. Nilsen took it out to burn on 11 August 1979 and a few months later he felt ready for his next lover, Kenneth Ockendon, who stayed for two weeks after his demise. They spent hours together sitting in the tiny kitchen, relaxing in the armchairs, or lying side by side on the bed watching television while Nilsen chatted, relating the events of the day, telling the corpse how good it looked. Whenever he wanted, Nilsen could give the body a stroke; but there was nothing sexual, just affectionate caresses.

For the first night Ockendon shared his bed, and next morning Nilsen bought a Polaroid to take some snaps. Soon they settled into a domestic routine. 'Good night, Ken,' Nilsen would say at the end of another companiable evening. Sometimes the body sat docilely on Nilsen's knee and let itself be undressed. Sometimes they shared non-penetrative sex. At night, Nilsen put the corpse to bed in the cupboard, covering it with a curtain for a blanket.

With time, Ockendon decomposed slightly and leaked bodily fluids, but Nilsen wiped the muck away and touched up the face with make-up. It was his standard practice to bathe new visitors in a ritual of purification. Nilsen wrote of another dead victim, Stephen Sinclair: 'He looked really beautiful, like one of those Michelangelo sculptures. It seemed that he was really feeling and looking the best he ever did in his whole life.' Nilsen scrutinised his victims' corpses minutely for hours on end. He wrote: 'Even if I knew the body to be dead, I felt that the personality was still within, aware and listening to me.'

To Nilsen, the murders almost seemed acts of mercy. 'I entertained no thoughts of harming him, only concern and affection for his future and the pain and plight of his life,' he said of Sinclair. 'I remember wishing he could stay in peace like that for ever. I had a feeling of easing his burden.'

The actual killing was not important or particularly gratifying; it constituted a preliminary process enabling Nilsen to transmute base human flesh into something far, far finer. In fact, if he got lucky, as accidentally happened in April 1982 with Carl Stottor, he would not *quite* kill his man. The aftermath of near-strangulation compelled the intended victim to stay all day while Nilsen nursed him back to health.

Nilsen never knew who he was going to kill; many visitors came to his flat and left unscathed. Many did not; on 27 January 1983 he woke up to note with surprise a dead man seated in his armchair.

When the bodies ceased to be fit for social role-play, Nilsen was in no hurry to be rid of them: he stored them. Even the task of **dismemberment** – revolting enough to make him repeatedly sick – never really destroyed Nilsen's relationship with his victims. A drawing entitled 'The last time I saw Stephen Sinclair (final image)' shows Nilsen's farewell glimpse of his friend lying in the kitchen on a plastic sheet. In the picture, Sinclair's upper body is missing, severed at the waist.

THE LAST TIME
L SAW STEVEN
SINCLAIR
(FINAL IMAGE)
SUNDAY/MONDAY
6AM 7am
FEB

In December 1980 Nilsen gave the bodies a great send-off, incinerating his hoard of cadavers on a huge garden bonfire. He noted 'the sparks, heat, hot air, smoke and energy of life arrowing skywards in a great visual display of living natural forces, like some Viking ship glowing westwards to Valhalla.' Nilsen turned his hi-fi speakers face out through the French windows and watched the blaze to the accompaniment of *Tubular Bells*. The neighbourhood children gathered round the flames, and at the day's end Nilsen wrote, 'The sun is setting on the glowing embers and I, weeping, drink the bottle dry.'

By his arrest on 9 Febrary 1983 – 'the day help arrived', as he put it – Nilsen claimed fifteen or sixteen murders; he was desperate for the nightmare to end, no matter how. In prison, he remained a stickler for formality, waiting exactly three months before writing to tender his resignation from the Civil Service.

See also **Mirror**

Death Row

At time of writing, 2,547 men and 41 women are backed up on America's Death Row. Eight have been there since 1974.

Fifteen states have no capital punishment and, until the death of Robert Harris in April 1992, executions were largely confined to conservative 'renegade' states, like Nevada and Utah. Texas produced a quarter of the total.

Since the reintroduction of the death sentence in 1976, 169 prisoners have been executed. Blacks – who comprise 12.1 per cent of the population at large – account for almost half. Of these, four out of five died for killing white men; in September 1991 'Pee-Wee' Gaskins became the first white for half a century executed for killing a black. But statistical evidence of racial discrimination does not constitute grounds for appeal.

The process that allowed killers such as Robert Harris to lodge fourteen separate appeals, delaying their execution for years or even decades, was rejected by the Senate in a June 1991 vote which barred further legal manoeuvres once a federal judge has ruled that the accused received 'a full and fair hearing' in the original state court. This abolished the traditional ground of appeal that gassing was unconstitutional as a 'cruel and unusual' punishment. In any case, twenty-three states have switched to execution by lethal **injection**.

In 1989 the prisoner's stupidity became another line of defence excluded by a Supreme Court ruling that the mere fact that the condemned man was mentally retarded did not preclude execution, even with a mental age of less than twelve. The 1992 gassing of Robert Harris, the first in the comparatively liberal state of California for twenty-five years, was expected to inaugurate an era of increased throughput.

Some prisoners might welcome a more speedy determination of their fate. The correspondence of Andrew Lee Jones (executed in July 1991) provided a glimpse of his life before death: 'I been here on Death Row since November 15 1984,' he wrote. 'I have had seven execution dates. I don't have any children and I don't have any friends here on Death Row. It don't pay to have one, because it's no telling when he might get executed... Like we are lock down for twenty-three hours a day. We get to go outside three days a week for one hour. Every time I'm out of my cell, I'm handcuff... The cell that I'm in is right in front of the light and it stay on twenty-four hours a day. Like, since I've been here, I have seen men lose their mind... It gets worse in the last few days because they start checking to see if the chair work, and sometimes the lights go dim.'

San Quentin has a holding room for those about to die. Known as the 'death watch cell', it is thirteen paces from the gas chamber. Judging by the level of 'on-off' appeals, this proximity is an important convenience. In 1992 Robert Harris was repeatedly bundled back and forth during the four stays of execution that filled the last day of his life.

The southern states are known as the 'death belt'. Some penitentiaries have truly weird names, like the 'Diagnostic and Classification Centre' in Jackson, Georgia, which houses more than a hundred Death Row prisoners.

See also **Attorneys**, **Lifelines**.

Death, time of

The main method of establishing time of death is still body temperature. The interior of a well-fed, clothed, dead adult will not cool down to the ambient temperature for about a day. At first the corpse loses 1° F an hour, but this increases slightly with the passage of time to average out at 1.5°.

In his *Medical Jurisprudence* Glaister presents this formula: (98.4 − rectal/vaginal temperature) divided by 1.5 = approx hours since death.

The skin and the extremities cool first. Warmth in the armpit continues for about six hours. As a rule, the body loses all its natural heat in eighteen to twenty-four hours, but appropriate allowances must be made; nudes, for instance, cool down twice as quickly as the clothed, and fat people retain body heat better than thin ones.

In sexual cases, readings are often taken from the interior of the abdomen to avoid disturbing evidence in the vagina, and, quite soon, decay radiates out from the corpse's abdomen. According to Glaister: 'A body decomposes in the air twice as quickly as in water, and eight times as rapidly as in earth.' A year outside is generally sufficient to reduce a cadaver to bare bones.

The abdomen turns greenish a couple of days after death as bacteria break down the blood. Then 'marbling' sets in: the veins under the skin gain unusual prominence, imparting a pattern to the body. Next comes gross disfiguration, followed by bloating, with partial disintegration after a month or so. Some poisons, arsenic and alcohol included, act as preservatives.

See also **Adipocere**

Debt, imprisonment for

Often fatal. Initially this draconian sanction was a right reserved to the sole use of the Crown, deployed against those who could but would not pay. By the eighteenth century it was in widespread use and abuse. In 1716 Baston recorded in *Thoughts on Trade and a Public Spirit*: 'tis reckoned there are about 60,000 miserable debtors perishing in prisons in England and Wales', a figure in excess of today's entire British prison population.

Imprisonment for debt made little sense since the prisoner had to pay for his board and lodging. He thus became even poorer or, quite often, dead. In 1792 the Oglethorpe Committee detailed a common Marshalsea sequence whereby an imprisoned wretch soon wore out the kindness of his friends, sold his clothes, ate his last allowance, grew ill, went into the sick ward, lingered for a month or two on charitable rations and then perished. Unquestionably a significant proportion of cases were maliciously inspired for fictitious sums.

Marshalsea and Whitechapel were the principal prisons for defaulters, the former the setting for much of Dickens's *Little Dorrit* and his own father's temporary home. In Elizabethan times, the most desirable jail was the Rules – ordinary London dwellings clustered round the Old Bailey. In effect, the lucky 300 inmates were sent to houses, where they came and went at will. But they remained on the prison register and hence beyond further arrest, since they were already prisoners. Debtors paid to get in. In **Newgate**, the debtor's section went under the name 'Tangiers' since the conditions were reminiscent of the barbarities inflicted by Arab pirates trading on the Barbary Coast. Inmates were called 'tangerines'.

Decline and fall

The **Mafia**'s grip on America is loosening. After the **Pizza Connection** bust of 1984, the FBI estimated the number of 'made' Mafia members had dwindled to 1,700 nationwide together with about a 1,000 associates – about half the strength of the twenty-four Mafia families two decades before. Symbolic of their decline was the wholesale arrest, on 26 February 1985, of the New York Mafia Commission. Its leading lights, mostly respected men with an average age of seventy, were not so much frightened as infuriated, raising their bails, set in Castellano's case at $4 million, in a matter of minutes.

But the defendants were sentenced to 100 years each on 13 January 1987. The dawn raids of 31 March 1988 netted another sixty-four suspected drug traffickers, and on 2 April 1992 the only remaining head of a big American crime family not in jail, John Gotti, was convicted. On the day the Gotti jury retired, 'Little Vic' Orena, the alleged head of the Columbo family, was arrested. In New York two of the five Mafia families are essentially bust and a third is on its knees. The Genovese clan remains largely inviolate, but the mob are on the run or defeated in Kansas City, Philadelphia, Cleveland, Chicago, New Orleans and Boston, with twenty bosses put behind bars in the last ten years.

Legal stratagems have played their part. The conspiracy charges in the Pizza Connection case showed that any one individual could be sentenced for the overall acts of the team; previously, the boss (whose hands, if little else, were clean) remained above the law and only his underlings took the rap.

Today the FBI eliminates whole families with a stick-and-carrot approach, on the one hand penetrating the homes of *mafiosi* with electronic surveillance to garner evidence, on the other proffering a workable witness protection scheme to 'turn' mobsters into informers.

Sometimes the hoods can hardly wait. Modern mobsters, even at the highest levels, do not just talk; they wear wires, write books and hire agents to dispense revelations of their lifestyles that today seem increasingly outdated, even quaint.

At the same time, civil RICO (Racketeer Influenced and Corrupt Organizations Act) charges chipped away at the Mob's economic base, in New York breaking its stranglehold on the staples of the Fulton Fish Market, the International Longshoreman's Association and the Teamsters. But this did not happen overnight. RICO's mob-busting potential went largely unappreciated until June 1980 when Professor Robert Blakey held a seminar at Cornell University, explaining to FBI agents how the law could be turned against the Mafia's entire organisational structure. Until then the FBI had concentrated on specific crimes; within a year the Agency was redeployed into nine elite squads, five individually targeted on the Mafia's five New York families.

The onslaught does not bode well for Mafia recruitment. Formerly, the mob's attractions were twofold: there was not much else for poor immigrants to do, and the inner ring possessed legal immunity. In the late 1950s mobster Frank Scalice marketed 'membership' to would-be 'soldiers' for $50,000 a head. Today, these old certainties have faded. In America this represents a golden opportunity for someone else, perhaps the conspicuous Colombian cartels, the violent Jamaican posses or the street-level Dominicans, but more probably the **Triads**.

Elsewhere the Mafia continues to thrive, proliferating from Italy into Germany. During the two years to July 1992, Germany launched sixty-eight investigations into Mafia-related crimes, with twenty-eight Mafia suspects arrested in the most recent three months, mostly on Italian tip-offs. The break-up of the Soviet bloc channelled substantial underworld investments into eastern Germany, where the Mafia crowded in on the ground floor as a substitute form of oppression.

See also **Inquisition, Techies, Trial, Whacks**

de Crespigny, Sir Claude

Latter-day amateur British hangman who in 1886 volunteered to assist **Berry** at the triple execution of three thieves named Rudge, Martin and Baker. The well-heeled Sir Claude paid Berry £10 for the privilege, selecting the alias 'Charles Maddon' for his cameo role.

After the formalities, the prison governor, spotting a man of quality, invited Sir Claude and his boss to tea, and the executioners lingered on for dinner. The incident created quite a *frisson* in Victorian society, and Sir Claude felt constrained to explain his motivation through the columns of *The Times*. Apparently he thought that one day he might attain the post of Sheriff of Essex, and felt it his duty not to ask anyone to do something he would not do himself.

In 1626, another nobleman suffered an adverse experience, this time not as, but at the hands of, a novice. It took twenty-nine blows to slash off the Comte de Chalais' head; the wretched man remained alive after the twentieth stroke. This epic decapitation was conducted by an amateur to save his own neck.

Dementia Americana

Ingenious medical condition said – in court – to afflict rich Americans, making it excusable for them to kill their wives' ex-lovers. The case in question involved one very pretty woman, Evelyn Nesbit, and two very unattractive men, Harry Thaw and Stanford White, America's most distinguished architect.

White designed New York's landmark building, the Madison Square Gardens, on the top of which he was shot on 28 June 1906 while watching a roof-terrace performance of a dreary new musical, *Mam'zelle Champagne*. On the Garden's pinnacle loomed a statue of the naked goddess Diana, rumoured to be a likeness of Evelyn Nesbit sculpted while she was one of White's mistresses. White kept several, throwing dinner parties at which young ladies popped out of immense pies, and by the time of the trial he stood blackened as an unscrupulous roué, a portrayal he was no longer in a position to dispute.

White's first encounter with the 16-year-old Evelyn, then a chorus girl, concluded with her romping Fragonard-style on a velvet-upholstered swing while the architect pushed her higher and higher. Soon White had his quarry half-naked, posing for photographs in a kimono. The final seduction took place while Evelyn, although technically present, lay asleep and quite possibly drugged in a room whose walls and ceilings were lined with mirrors. 'A pounding began in my ears,' she recalled, 'and the room began to spin.'

Evelyn Nesbit

White's eventual murderer and rival for Evelyn's affections was Harry Thaw, a playboy heir to railroad millions with an $80,000 a year allowance. Thaw's youthful escapades included stunts like driving a car through a display window, throwing a $50,000 party for the leading whores of Paris and losing $40,000 in a poker game. He ran across Evelyn while she was in tow as White's mistress, and for her it seems a case of money at first sight. The pair absconded to Europe, renting the Schloss Katzenstein where Thaw treated her to a good hiding, ensuring that she was confined to bed for a further three weeks. 'Without any provocation,' she recalled, 'he grasped me by the throat and tore the bathrobe from my body, leaving me entirely nude except for my slippers. His eyes were glaring and he had in his right hand a cowhide whip.' It emerged that Thaw was seriously unbalanced and would beat her savagely at the least provocation. Nonetheless, and despite the additional disincentive of Thaw's cocaine habit, the couple married on 25 April 1905.

According to one account, White arranged the marriage himself at the instigation of Evelyn's parents, persuading Thaw to propose and threatening to expose him on charges of corrupting a minor – Evelyn – if he refused. Whatever Thaw's motivation, they moved into a Pittsburgh mansion where he fostered a penchant for pistols.

A year or so later the Thaws came up to town for the premiere of *Mam'zelle Champagne* which was, by chance, also attended by Stanford White. The performance was too dull to sit through; the Thaws made for the elevator, Harry pausing on the way to pump three bullets into the architect while the unsuspecting Evelyn waited at the lift.

Thaw rejoined her with the smoking pistol still in his hand. 'Good God, Harry, what have you done?' she asked, and, as guests stampeded for the exits, the stage manager jumped on a table and shouted, 'Go on playing. Bring on the chorus.' The dead man too would have left early, had he not been hoping for an introduction to another chorus girl after the show.

Moments later Thaw was arrested. To the sergeant in charge, who asked 'Why did you do this?', Thaw replied 'I can't say' with no great show of interest. He proved more forthcoming to the District Attorney, commenting, 'I saw him sitting there, big, fat and healthy, and there Evelyn was, poor delicate little thing, all trembling and nervous.'

The rooftop slaying

The aftermath turned into a legal farce. Thaw's novel medical condition of *dementia Americana* was diagnosed by expensive defence doctors and at the first trial the jury could not agree. At the second, in 1908, he was found not guilty by reason of his affliction.

This verdict reflected the successful efforts of the Thaws' press agent to promote a popular morality fable of a wronged waif (Evelyn) seduced by an ageing roué (White) and rescued by a chivalrous knight (Thaw) undergoing a brainstorm. One component of the orchestrated campaign was a Thaw-backed play based on the shooting, culminating with the killer's last-scene declaration from his cell in the Tombs: 'No jury on earth will send me to the chair, no matter what I have done or what I have been, for killing a man who defamed my wife. That is the unwritten law made by men themselves, and upon its virtue I will stake my life.'

Seven years later, with the aid of a waiting limousine, Thaw escaped from his asylum. He was recaptured, but on 16 July 1915 his wealthy family contrived to have him released by reason of his newly certified sanity: he had never been found guilty of murder, now he was no longer mad, so out he came. Thaw lost little time in kidnapping a Kansas City youth, Frederick Gump, and set about him with a horsewhip. This time, the millionaire was not re-adjudged sane until 1924.

Thaw appointed Delmonico's restaurant as

caterers for his spell on remand in New York's Tombs prison; all his meals were shipped in. He died in 1947.

Dempster

A verb, as in 'to be dempstered'. In the 1770s this entailed being hanged, an expression commemorating the name of a contemporary London lackey, fond of giving himself airs, who made his living from other people's misfortunes. He hanged them. A common epithet for his trade was the 'crap merchant'.

Another eponymous hangman, from the sixteenth century, went under the name of Derrick. He was saved from execution by his patron the Earl of Essex, whom he subsequently beheaded. The initial arrangement was that Derrick's life would be spared provided he hanged the twenty or so other felons with whom he had been convicted for rape, and the modern derrick is named after his design for the gallows, suggesting that the condemned were winched to their deaths.

Detection, risk of

Contrary to the tortuous mysteries of fiction, murder remains about the easiest crime to solve. With the exception of the random doodlings of serial killers, only the most extreme personal antagonism will serve as a trigger. Thus the motive, connecting victim to murderer, runs through the fabric of their lives like a scarlet thread, with the culprit's identity flowing naturally from identification of the victim.

Of Britain's 1991 crop of 708 homicides, as at 8 January the following year only sixty-seven (9.46%) had not resulted in charges. Most were cleared up within a few days of the crime. In a July 1992 case, a man loaded the corpse of his common-law wife into the car and drove it as evidence to the local police station at Kingstanding. Experienced homicide detectives will, where possible, first ask of the gaggle of spectators that tends to gather round a body, 'Do you know who did it?' and then, 'Where does he live?'

The crowd may include the murderer. Sex killers, particularly the '**organised**' ones, often haunt the scene of their crime, returning to gloat, and may try to insert themselves peripherally into the investig-

ation. Peter **Sutcliffe**, the Yorkshire Ripper, returned to one of his victims a few days after the attack and tried to remove her head with a hacksaw. Peter **Kürten**, the Dusseldorf sadist, relished the excited throng jostling round his victims' bodies, and in 1931 this trait was turned to advantage by the Rumanian detective Franculescu, baffled by a corpse found behind locked gates in a Bucharest courtyard. The only clue, furnished by the dead man's fingernails, was that his assailant had red hair. After running every other line of enquiry into the ground, Franculescu re-examined the police photograph of the body which showed, in the background, the usual knot of onlookers.

Did any of them have red hair? Yes. And who was it? The murderer, Bardica. As this happened before the invention of colour photography it took some time to work out by patient enquiries, but Bardica eked out the rest of his life in the Kimpolung convict mines.

One of the most obvious reasons for killing someone who is a wife is being her husband. Typical of the domestic cases that parade through the newspapers is that of 47-year-old Hazel Wood, shot fourteen times with her husband's hunting rifle as she lay asleep at home. No great deductive powers were needed to pin the crime on her spouse who, inflamed by jealousy, told friends and relatives that he intended to kill her. Defence lawyers are apt to listen to their clients' protestations of innocence with jaundiced ears. As Bernie Segal, the defence lawyer in the American **MacDonald** case, remarked, 'The police only arrest the obviously guilty. They don't know how to catch the others.'

Over 300 of British cases in 1991 involved domestic disputes and, for 1989, 81 per cent of female and 58 per cent of male victims were killed by someone known to them personally. In America the corresponding figure hovers around 55 per cent overall, well down from the 80 per cent of two decades ago. Thirty-one of the 1991 British killers had committed suicide within a year.

In 1992 the mere fact that a backlog of unsolved murders had accumulated in London led senior Scotland Yard detectives to speculate on the existence of a hitman syndicate, although national newspapers reported that the police were reluctant to state that professional assassins existed for fear of causing public anxiety. Somewhere between five and twenty murders were involved, all sharing an absence of motive, a dearth of clues, and a wall of **silence**.

History provides almost no precedent for the eminent 'consulting detectives' who saunter so brilliantly through the pages of fiction.

The word 'murder' is derived from the Anglo-Saxon 'murdrum', originally a fine imposed on the natives for killing Normans. If the person responsible was not caught, the whole community paid, literally.

Diatoms

Primitive but tough microscopic algae found in unpolluted fresh water and the sea. A corpse dumped in the sea or river fills its air passages with diatoms as the water swamps the lungs. But the diatoms do not penetrate further. In contrast, the continued breathing of a drowning man will, as he struggles, draw the air, water and diatoms into his bloodstream. Once in the system, the acid-resistant silica shells are pumped round to the heart and then distributed throughout the kidneys, stomach, brain and bone marrow.

On post-mortem examination, sample body tissue can be broken down to reveal the diatoms' presence, thereby proving death by drowning. More than 25,000 diatomic varieties of local origin are known to science; hence their identification may indicate the place of death, in one case allowing scientists to show that a corpse washed up on the Belgian coast had fallen off a yacht by the Isle of Wight.

There is 'wet drowning' and 'dry drowning', when death occurs within seconds and little or no liquid is found in the lungs. This happened to Robert Maxwell, the financial fraudster, but traces of diatoms in his bloodstream proved that he was alive when he hit the water, establishing that he had not killed himself *before* falling off the *Lady Ghislaine* near the Canary Islands in November 1991. In dry drowning, a sudden influx of unexpected water through the nose can produce a spasm of the larynx, which in turn squeezes the vagus, the long nerve monitoring blood pressure via a bulb in the neck. In these circumstances the vagus erroneously deduces that blood pressure has reached dangerously high levels, countered by stopping the heart, an instruction issued by the brain forthwith.

Even in wet drowning cases, death may result from heart failure rather than oxygen deprivation. Fresh water sluices into the bloodstream via the lungs, increasing its volume by perhaps 50 per cent in a minute, and the heart cannot take the strain. Sea water, with its higher osmotic pressure, reaches no further than the blood vessels of the lungs. They swell, but this is not fatal of itself, and hence it often proves easier to drown a man in fresh water. There are no reported cases of drowning faked by an *in vivo* infusion of diatoms.

Dickens, Charles (1812–70)

An influential opponent of public hangings. Dickens wrote to *The Times* in 1849 after witnessing the hanging of Frederick and Maria Manning. The spectacle attracted almost unprecedented excitement and 500 constables were drafted in to keep the peace outside Horsemonger Lane jail.

The thrill centred on the novel execution of a husband-and-wife team, with much speculation about who would 'go' first. In the event, they 'went' together. A skeleton summary of Dickens' letter describing the crowd reads: 'levity... shrillness... howls... screeching... laughing... prostitutes... ruffians... fightings... faintings... whistlings... callousness... as if the name of Christ had never been heard in the world.'

Dickens's liberal record is hard to fault; when the avant-garde were firmly wedded to the supposedly benevolent prison regime, the **Separate System**, he wrote: 'I hold this slow and daily tampering with the mysteries of the brain to be immeasurably worse than any torture of the body; and because its ghastly signs and tokens are not so palpable to the eye and sense of touch as scars upon the flesh, therefore the more I denounce it.'

Dickens also coined the word 'detective', using it in 1850 for a journalistic series in *Household Words*. The first fictional detective was Inspector Bucket of *Bleak House*, inspired by Inspector Charles F. Field, who accompanied the writer round London's docklands. In the same work, Maria Manning was reshaped as the villainess Hortense.

Maria Manning's execution had a dramatic impact on women's fashion. She dressed in the

Sunday staple of black satin for her hanging and, thereafter, black satin was very definitely out. The conviction of Franz Müller fifteen years later for the first British railway murder had the reverse effect. After killing a Mr Thomas Briggs for his gold watch on the 9.50 p.m. from Fenchurch Street Station, Müller swapped his victim's respectable top hat for his own 'beaver'. Müller's headwear was a distinctive

Müller's cut-down topper

truncated version of the topper with a low crown, and after his execution the 'Müller cut-down' enjoyed a brief vogue.

See also **Handkerchiefs**, **Fagin**, **Yuppies**

Dillinger, John Herbert (1902–34?)

A formidable bank robber with good looks and a pleasant manner, who employed his gun sparingly and, when caught by the camera, often appeared relaxed and well turned-out. Dillinger's mother died when he was four and he was raised by his father, a strict Quaker disciplinarian who believed in sound thrashings. They moved to Indiana in 1920, and three years later Dillinger joined the navy. He deserted from the USS *Utah* a few months later, and left his new wife, Beryl Hovis, shortly after that, imprisoned for trying to rob the local Mooresville grocer. An ex-con managing his baseball team had cut him in on the deal, and when it misfired Dillinger accepted an offer of a lenient sentence in return for pleading guilty.

Released on parole nearly a decade later, he set about robbing banks, starting in Daleville on 17 July 1933 and eventually extracting a million dollars from at least ten banks dotted through the Midwest. The raids were meticulously planned and rehearsed against the clock; Dillinger's trademark was an athletic spring over the railings protecting the tellers' cages, and his public image benefited from a refusal to take money from customers caught up in the raid, on the grounds that he robbed banks not people. Afterwards he would hightail it over the nearest state boundary and, in the wake of his first five successes, the Chicago police set up a forty-man 'Dillinger Squad'. When caught in September robbing the Bluffton bank and thrown into prison in Lima, Ohio, three of his men turned up posing as prison officials, shot the sheriff, and let him out.

The robberies resumed, clocking up their first fatality during a $20,000 raid on the First National Bank in Chicago when a policeman died. Dillinger was arrested again, this time with three confederates, in Tucson on 27 January 1934 after a tip-off from a detective story fan. Flown to East Chicago, he was locked up in the Crown Point prison, from which he escaped on 3 March, brandishing his famous wooden pistol (blackened with shoe polish) to force the guards to release him before driving off in the sheriff's car; embarrassed officials started the rumour that he wielded a smuggled .38 Colt.

A bent lawyer, Louis Piquett, helped restock the gang with arms and bullet-proof vests; Dillinger submitted to crude facial surgery (to conceal a scar) and tried to burn off his fingerprints with sulphuric acid (see **Removal**). By now almost a national hero, on 13 March 1934, in the company of 'Baby Face' Nelson, he hit the First National Bank of Mason City for $52,000. To cover their escape, Dillinger ordered twenty hostages out at gunpoint and festooned his car with them, standing some on the running boards and putting others on the hood or draping them over fenders and bumpers. A frustrated Police Chief E. J. Patton watched the large tourer lumber out of town.

Acting on a telephoned tip-off, in late April a posse of FBI agents encircled Dillinger in a lodge at the lakeside resort of Little Bohemia, Wisconsin. Closing in after dark under the leadership of Melvin 'Nervous' Purvis, they opened fire on customers leaving the restaurant, killing one diner and wounding two more. 'The fever for action,' Purvis reported, 'dissipated all other emotions.' Dillinger escaped, receiving the accolade of 'Public Enemy Number One' in a poster proclamation of 25 July which pegged a price of $10,000 to his head. The FBI looked increasingly ridiculous. Attorney General

Cummings said agents should 'shoot to kill', although Dillinger was not known to have killed anyone himself. But he had irritated **Hoover** with a series of taunting postcards, and his death became a personal priority.

Anna Sage, the 'Lady in Red', was an immigrant brothel madam in trouble with the law. Needing a permit to stay in the United States, she told the police of her date with Dillinger to see *Manhattan Melodrama* at Chicago's Biograph cinema on 22 July. As he emerged from the performance at 10.30 p.m. he found himself ringed by agents. In Purvis's words: 'I was very nervous. It must have been a squeaky voice that called out, "Stick 'em up, Johnny! We have you surrounded." Dillinger drew his .380 automatic pistol, but he never fired it. He dropped to the ground; he had been shot.'

Other reports say Dillinger never went for his gun. As he lay on the pavement, the awestruck crowds dipped their dresses, handkerchiefs and even scraps of paper in his blood.

The ambush represented a great public relations coup for Hoover, helping to establish the FBI as a major investigative force. Hoover kept Dillinger's straw hat, his smashed spectacles and damaged .38 on display in his reception room for decades to come. But the pistol on show – serial number 119702 – never belonged to Dillinger. It did not leave the Colt production line until December 1934, and Dillinger's gang were soon claiming that the FBI shot the wrong man.

When the autopsy records finally materialised after thirty years, they were riddled with discrepancies. The dead man had blue eyes, whereas Dillinger's were grey, and they may have stayed that way for decades afterwards.

Dillinger's associate 'Baby Face' Nelson came to a bloody end in a shootout on a country road near Barrington, Illinois. He killed both the FBI agents who lay in ambush for him, but took seventeen slugs himself. The next day his body was found naked by the roadside, dumped out of the car by his wife.

These smalltime hoods were typical FBI targets. Alvin 'Creepy' Karpis, the thief, was another propaganda victim. For years his comments on his own arrest in New Orleans on 1 May 1936 were regarded as sour grapes. Hoover was lionised in the press for personally disarming the gangster, but Karpis grumbled, 'It's an old practice of the FBI to dress up the truth with lies that make them look more clever and powerful than they are. The most obvious flaw in the FBI story of my capture lies in Hoover's own character. He didn't lead the attack on me. He hid until the coast was clear. Then he came out to reap the glory.' It was, however, always conceded that Karpis shambled through the streets bound up with his necktie because the FBI had forgotten the handcuffs.

Years later, Karpis whiled away his term in McNeil Island penitentiary by teaching the steel guitar to a young prisoner named Charles **Manson**, and it was his pupil's musical ability that helped seduce the **Family**'s first members.

Dingo

The disappearance of Lynne Chamberlain's daughter at Ayers Rock on 17 August 1980 at Ayers Rock launched Australia's sensational 'dingo' case.

During the summer of that year, the encampments and tourist areas round Ayers Rock saw a steady rise in dingo attacks; in early June, several were shot after going for children. On 23 June, little Amanda Cranwell was dragged from her car and just rescued from the animal's jaws by her father. The dingoes became ever bolder, scavenging through tents for food; on 4 August the Chief Ranger posted up warning signs. Then on 15 August a Mr Backhaus-Smith woke to find an unfazed dingo in his tent, and another traveller, Erica Letsch, had the pillow tugged from under her head as she slept. The next day two young tourists were bitten. The day after, the Chamberlain family arrived from Mount Isa. There was Lynne, her husband Michael, and three young children including baby Azaria.

That evening Lynne settled Azaria in her carrying basket and stayed chatting to Bill and Sally Lowe in the tent alongside. Suddenly Bill was alerted by a menacing growl. Then Sally heard the wail of a baby, abruptly cut short.

'I think that is bubby crying,' said Aidan, the Chamberlains' eldest. Lynne covered the few yards to her tent just in time to see a dingo emerging. The animal's lower body was hidden behind a low fence, but Lynne thought it held something in its jaws. It shook its head from side to side before running off. Lynne threw herself into her tent, fearing that Azaria had been savaged. Inside, the central pole was knocked askew, blood was spattered around, and Azaria had vanished. 'A dingo has got my baby,' Lynne screamed.

Within thirty minutes three hundred searchers were combing the bush. With every moment the chances of finding Azaria alive dwindled: she had been snatched by a predator, to be killed and eaten. That night the Chief Ranger and his Aboriginal tracker discovered the animal's tracks. Starting seventeen yards from the tent in a sand-dune, the trail consisted of a shallow drag-mark some eight inches wide from Azaria's clothing, with depressions in the sand where she had been rested on the ground. Paw marks circled the tent, bunching outside where Azaria lay as the dingo caught her scent. On 22 August, her mangled and blood-stained jumpsuit was found on the far side of Ayers Rock. Azaria herself was never seen again.

Dingoes may sound fierce in suburban Britain, but in Australia, with its man-eating crocs, they are considered small beer, normally running scared at the word 'shoo'. Baby Cranwell's lucky escape never reached the papers, so the tourist-hardened dingoes of Ayers Rock remained unknown. Azaria became the first reported snatch.

Public reaction played a crucial role; in its initial stages, the case was a trial by media and rumour, and the parents proved fertile targets for gossip. People react in different ways to grief, and Michael was a pastor for the Seventh Day Adventists, his wife a devout follower. When they tried to reconcile their loss with their faith, regarding Azaria's death as part of God's plan, the average Australian thought it a weird parental stance.

The professionals too turned sceptical; the Mount Isa police reported that Lynne 'appeared not to care for baby... did not feed it... dressed it in black... and did not react like a normal mother.' They disclosed that Azaria meant 'sacrifice in the wilderness'. This was all untrue, but as the rumours grew so the wooden coffin in the family's garage, used by Michael as a prop for anti-smoking classes, evolved into a small white coffin in Azaria's bedroom; soon her clothes on Ayers Rock had been found neatly folded. At school, the Chamberlain children endured taunts of 'Dingoes don't come into our house and steal babies.'

At the inquest on 16 December 1980, expert evidence suggested – on the basis of fairly impromptu tests – that a person, not a dingo, had shredded Azaria's clothing and extracted her body from the jumpsuit. These were inexact sciences; by comparison, the eye-witness testimony proved overwhelming, and the coroner ruled that Azaria 'met her death when attacked by a wild dingo'. The alternative of murder seemed a near-impossibility, since Lynne was in view of Bill and Sally Lowe throughout. She could hardly have reached the tent unseen, spirited her child away to the car, slit its throat, concealed the body in something like a camera bag, and returned a few seconds later to continue the conversation.

The coroner's emphatic judgement was televised; the police felt publicly humiliated. But six months later they were vindicated when one of their expert witnesses took Azaria's clothing to London for a second opinion from Professor James Cameron, a renowned forensic pathologist.

His conclusions were dynamite. Azaria's neck had been slit not by a dingo but by a sharp instrument. The bloodstains came from an injury inflicted before her clothing was unbuttoned. And on the back of the babysuit Professor Cameron found the blood-stained imprint of a female hand. On 19 September 1981, during a series of raids on witnesses and suspects, four hundred items were seized from the Chamberlain's house and their car flown by Hercules to Darwin for minute examination.

At the second inquest on 14 December 1981 the Chamberlains heard that bloodstains had been discovered in their vehicle – beneath the seat and, more importantly, in a fine spray under the dashboard, as though caused by a severed artery. Tests showed that this blood could only originate from a child younger than three months. Similarly, minute traces of blood and hairs were detected in the Chamberlains' camera bag, where it now seemed the body had been secreted.

A textile expert confirmed that the ripped jumpsuit was cut rather than torn, and a London odontologist, Bernard Sims, showed that the rips were not what one would expect from a dingo. He also proved that Azaria's head was not clamped in the dingo's jaws (as the defence alleged) because dingoes cannot open their mouths wider than ten centimetres. Further, twenty-five tufts from the jumpsuit were found in the car. But a tuft is a single fibre severed twice and, when a strand has parted at one end, it is no longer taut; accordingly, it cannot be *torn* again. A sharp instrument is needed to cut it twice.

The trial opened on 13 September 1982 and ran for nearly two months. It followed a familiar pattern: all the eyewitness evidence (heard first) went the Chamberlains' way. But this was a fading memory after weeks of forensic argument. The prosecution wisely conceded they knew neither why nor exactly how Lynne killed Azaria: they simply knew that she had. The judge summed up broadly in her favour, but juries are entitled to their views, and on 28 October 1982 Lynne was found guilty.

Her initial appeal was turned down in the absence of new evidence, and the second could not hear the new evidence which had then emerged, since its remit was simply to review the legitimacy of the verdict based on the old evidence – largely discredited when, on 24 November 1983, a Seventh Day Adventist, Les Smith, finally found the explanation for the bloodstains under the dashboard.

The stains were not blood but paint. During manufacture, the wheel arches of the car, a Holden Torana, were coated with a sound-deadening material, Dulux Dufin 1081. In 10 per cent of the models, a burst of spray carried through a drain-hole to the underside of the dashboard. The other microscopic bloodstains under the seat and in the camera bag were only dirt. Serology is an extremely complex science (occupying 108 pages in the final Inquiry) but at base the prosecution's orthotolidine test was simply a *prima facie* indicator, showing that the traces *might* have been blood. Another thing they might have been was copper dust. The Chamberlains lived in the copper-producing area of Mount Isa, and dirt taken from their street produced an identical reaction.

Similarly, it turned out that dingo teeth *were* a sharp instrument. True, Azaria's clothes had been cut rather than torn, but no one checked whether dingoes cut or tore clothes. Les Smith conducted the first experiments, holding out chunks of meat wrapped in cloth, and found that dingo teeth possessed a clean scissor-like action – sharp enough to slice through seat belts in a straight line or sever wire cable. And although dingoes cannot open their mouths wider than a baby's head in theory, they can in practice, as witness a medium-sized dingo videoed grasping a frozen chicken, diameter 13.5cms. Again, experts were baffled by how the dingo managed to undo Azaria's bootees, leaving them in the feet of the jumpsuit, before extracting her body by the head. This was because they had never watched dingoes in action fixing jumpsuits by the feet and shaking out their prey.

The bloodstained female handprint of Professor Cameron's evidence proved invisible. No one else could see it. Likewise the overall pattern of bloodstaining on the jumpsuit was not what Cameron *expected* from a dingo-inflicted wound, but his expectations lacked evidential weight. The 'tuft theory' too had not been submitted to dingoes; given a test-garment to shred, they ripped it into tufts and snippets.

In June 1987, after seven years, two inquests, one trial, two appeals, a £6 million inquiry, and paperwork weighing five tonnes, Lynne Chamberlain won a pardon. Her conviction was quashed on 15 September 1988, and in May 1992 she received A$900,000 compensation.

Dismemberment, reasons for

There are four good reasons for dismembering a corpse. First, to complicate identification. Second, to facilitate transportation of the resulting components. Third, as an act of vengeance where mere killing has constituted insufficient punishment. And finally, for sexual gratification (see **Cannibalism**).

Readers contemplating cutting a body up should set aside a good day for the project. Dennis **Nilsen**, the British serial killer, was an army-trained butcher from the Catering Corps, and he devoted an entire (if leisurely) weekend in February 1983 to carving up Stephen Sinclair into his main chunks.

A great British virtuoso was the British multiple murderer Henry Jeremiah McKenny, a London hard man six feet five inches tall. By the late 1970s McKenny became browned off with life as an armed robber. Whenever an eyewitness described a gangster attending a raid as more than six feet high, the police pulled in 'Big H' for questioning. So one day he observed to his associate John Childs, 'It would be a lot easier to do people in for money.'

They already possessed the know-how. Childs rented a council flat at 13 Dolphin House, Poplar, which had a brick fireplace with a tiny grate, and in October 1974 its living room carpet was covered with polythene to receive the first body: 'Teddy Bear' Eve, killed to facilitate the takeover of his soft-toy business. The corpse was ferried through the estate at night and then underwent preliminary dissection prior to insertion into a £25 electric meat mincer. But the machine jammed. So they burned Eve bit by bit, and three months later an unlucky witness followed him up the chimney.

In 1978, 'Big H' moved into murder on commission, and when at last the police came by they gazed at the eighteen-inch fireplace of Number 13 in disbelief. It seemed to lack both the capacity and the high-temperature potential for the throughput of the eventual total of six bodies.

Could it be done? Pathologist James Cameron purchased a dead eleven-stone pig. He cut it up and, to his surprise, over the course of thirteen hours, reduced most of it to a heap of ashes, in the process recording a core-heat of 1,000° F. Cameron's only problem came when the intestines released such quantities of fluid that the blaze faltered, but John Childs explained that the secret of Big H's technique was to dry the intestines separately in front of the fire before immolation.

Dismemberment of the living is an exceedingly rare criminal enterprise. John Gotti allegedly divided his neighbour in two with a chainsaw, and on 8 November 1980 Londoner John Bowden devised a plan to divest Donald Ryan, a 47-year-old boxer, of £20. After spending the evening drinking cider together, Bowden battered his friend over the head with a bottle, placed him in a bath and then, while he was still alive, cut off his arms and legs with a saw, a machete and an electric carving knife before disposing of the body in a plastic bag on a waste tip. Neighbours called round by chance to find the door opened by an accomplice, Michael Ward, stripped to the waist and covered in blood. Arrest followed. At the Old Bailey trial, four members of the jury were so affected by the photographic evidence that they fell ill.

See also **Contempt**, **Durability**

Dolphins, sex with

In 1991 Alan Cooper, a British animal rights campaigner, was acquitted of the unusual charge of committing an act of a 'lewd, obscene or disgusting nature' with a wild dolphin. Spectators on a boating trip thought he masturbated it.

The case took five days and amused every-

one apart from the defendant. Crucial to Cooper's case was an understanding of what dolphins use their penises for. With humans the penis is of restricted utility. As defence counsel pointed out: 'Men do not employ their penis to push the supermarket trolley. They do not use it to greet each other.' But things are otherwise in the world of dolphins. A penis is an extra – or only – limb. Mr Cooper explained: 'It's like a flick knife. He flicks it in and out at will.' Expert testimony supported this view. In the words of Dr Dobbs, who had watched the dolphin at play: 'I have seen him catch fish with his mouth, throw it in the air and catch it on his penis.'

The crux was that the dolphin's permanently rigid member had non-sexual applications. The prosecution accepted that when the dolphin hooked divers in the crook of the arm or leg with its penis and towed them round the bay this meant – in the words of Dr Dobbs – no more than 'extending the finger of friendship'. Cooper received two death threats in the run-up to the trial; he was cleared in December 1991.

But experts are not always right. In the correspondence aroused by the case a Mr R. J. Henry from Pearce, Australia, cited anecdotal evidence from his 1974 friendship with a woman dolphin-handler from the Hong Kong Sea World. She told him that male dolphins were, like so many people, 'in a perpetual state of rut and only became tractable if they were regularly masturbated'. Mr Henry asserted that **masturbation** was the standard reward in training, maintaining that the Asian sex industry boasts a number of establishments with specialised dolphinaria catering for Western divers wishing to fraternise with fish.

See also **Animals**

Dougal, Samuel Herbert (1846–1903)

Samuel Dougal was a pivotal Victorian murderer. His case revolves around a degree of rural isolation and an absence of communications that are today inconceivable. But his story has elements that go back further, to a style of imposture and sexual shenanigans of an almost feudal resonance.

In 1899 Dougal killed his common-law wife, 55-year-old Camille Holland, in a moated house in bleakest Essex hours from the nearest railway station, so remote that the local tradesmen never called; Dougal ensured that the postman – the last

link with civilisation – did not come too close by meeting him in the lane. There was no one to notice that Camille had disappeared, so after a while Dougal realised that, for financial purposes, he might as well treat her as alive. He learned to forge Camille's signature and for the next four years

Miss Holland's undoubted signatures (above) and Dougal's forgeries (below)

lived handsomely off her income, toffing it up as a local squire, buying one of the first cars in the district; he referred to it as a 'locomobile'. Meanwhile Dougal recalled his real wife from Ireland, who 'hollandised' herself, assuming Camille's identity and making progressive inroads into her predecessor's wardrobe.

Dougal's victim was that vanished breed – the wealthy spinster, living in semi-retirement. Serving wenches, another historical relic, figure large in the case; Dougal loved them, making them pregnant in droves. In an outlandish twist, Dougal specialised in teaching Essex girls how to cycle in the nude. 'What a picture,' wrote the chronicler of Dougal's 1903 trial, 'in that clayey, lumpy field, the clayey, lumpy girls naked, astride that unromantic object, a bicycle.'

Dougal had a way with women. His first wife bore him four children; she died suddenly in 1885 after eating oysters. His second wife perished of stomach cramps and vomiting the same year. Both may well have been poisoned. In the intervening years Dougal lived with many different women, siring many more children before his third marriage in 1892 to an Irishwoman. But disaster struck with his imprisonment for forging a £35 cheque in the name of 'Lord Frankfort'. The pension from his eleven years service with the Royal Engineers, previously a steady payer at 2s 9d a day, was forfeit.

Strapped for cash, in early 1899 Dougal attended the Earl's Court Exhibition on the lookout. There he met the well-off, unaccompanied Camille Holland, a resident of a lodging house in fashionable Bayswater. Dougal paid court, and although she knew he had a wife in Dublin, Camille agreed to set up home together.

With Camille's money the couple bought the isolated Moat Farm. They moved in during April 1899 but it at once came forcibly to Camille's attention that her 'husband' had made advances to their 19-year-old servant Florence. The girl took fright when Dougal tried to break down her door and she sheltered overnight in Camille's bed.

Camille Holland

Camille apologised for Dougal's conduct, but the girl left the following morning. Camille too could have fled, embarrassed and shamed but alive. She stayed on, and sometime during the next three weeks Dougal shot her in the head, burying the body in a drainage ditch which he then had filled and planted. Learning to forge Camille's handwriting, he released some of her capital and transferred Moat Farm into his own name.

By 1902 Dougal was still at his philandering; he took advantage of dozens of servant girls, including a mother and her three daughters. The real Mrs Dougal departed, and his shady back-

ground emerged when he attracted public notice by contesting an affiliation order. Camille's nephews came forward; they confirmed that nothing had been heard of their aunt for years. But the bank and solicitors maintained they were in constant correspondence with the vanished woman, and produced her last cheque, dated 28 August 1902. At last Dougal's game was up.

He was arrested on suspicion of murder after his return from a weekend in Bournemouth with yet another woman he had impregnated. The house was searched for Camille's body; the moat dragged and then drained, the grounds probed with long iron rods – all without result. In the absence of the corpse, Dougal regained his bluster and threatened to sue the Chief Constable for £1,000 compensation for disfiguring his land. Then a labourer remembered the old infill of the 1899 ditch. Up came a woman's boot, size 2, with some bones in it, then a skull with a bullet-hole and a round of Union Metallic Ammunition still inside. At the trial the prosecution replicated the hole in the skull by firing bullets into a sheep's head.

It seems that Dougal was remembered by his many *amours* without rancour. He wrote from prison to one old flame suggesting that they hire communal transport for their massed appearance as witnesses at his trial. 'It is a delightful drive through undulating country,' he wrote, 'and at this time of year would be a veritable treat for them all.'

Dougal was hanged on 14 July 1903. As the executioner started to pull the lever the prison chaplain enquired: 'Guilty or not guilty?'

'Guilty,' the hooded Dougal replied. From his photographs he looks a fine, bluff fellow with an Edward VII beard-and-moustache.

Doyle, Sir Arthur Conan (1859–1930)

Conan Doyle, the creator of Sherlock Holmes, meshed with the world of real crime during the case of Oscar Slater, a German Jew wrongfully convicted of the murder of an old lady, Miss Marion Gilchrist, bludgeoned to death for her jewellery. The only evidence linking Slater with the December 1908 killing was eye-witness **identification**.

But of the three crucial witnesses against Slater, one stated, 'It's not the face I went for, it's the walk... I could not tell his face, I never saw his face.' Another succeeded in pointing out Slater as the man wanted by Justice when he appeared before her handcuffed between two court officers. The third was near-sighted. None had caught more than the most fleeting glimpse of the culprit as he fled from the murder.

All the twelve witnesses who identified Slater, an obvious foreigner, had previously seen newspaper photographs which showed him to be obviously foreign. In the identity parades, they selected the man most like the accused from an assortment consisting of Slater, an obvious foreigner, standing out like a sore thumb alongside nine plainclothes Scottish policemen and two railway officials. When one witness suggested mixing

Marion Gilchrist

Slater with men of similar appearance, the officer in charge replied: 'It might be the fairest way, but it is not the practice in Glasgow.'

There was nothing to connect Slater with the deceased, nothing to suggest he was acquainted with her or had heard of her jewellery. His supposed murder weapon – a light tin-tack hammer from Woolworths – was too flimsy for the fearful damage suffered by the victim and, like Slater's clothes, disclosed no bloodstains. He produced a perfectly reasonable alibi and was extradited from America (to which he had travelled openly) only because a bicycle-dealer saw him trying to sell a pawn ticket, allegedly for one of the missing diamond brooches. It was not, but by the time the police ascertained that Slater's brooch had been in pawn since 18 November, well before the killing, they had him fingered as the culprit.

Slater went down on a majority verdict after the judge, Lord Guthrie, explained that 'a man of his kind has not the presumption of innocence in his favour'. The sentence was reduced to life imprisonment two days before the scheduled execution of 27 May 1909.

On release of the trial transcripts, which marched from puzzle to puzzle, Conan Doyle took issue, writing an impassioned booklet entitled *The Case of Oscar Slater*. He showered the newspapers with letters of protest, and approached successive Secretaries of State for Scotland demanding to have the case reopened. The Scottish Office stonewalled and the campaign fizzled out.

Fifteen years later, the publication of *The Truth about Oscar Slater* resurrected the controversy. Conan Doyle took the opportunity to circularise Members of Parliament, finally forcing a retrial before the Court of Appeal. The conviction was grudgingly set aside on 20 July 1928, leaving Conan Doyle to bear Slater's legal fees of some £1,500, which he guaranteed to get the case off the ground. During the hearing Conan Doyle described Slater's face as 'terrible for the brooding sadness that is in it'.

Conan Doyle's creation of a skilful, if fictional, detective was largely attributable to his lacklustre medical career. His Southsea practice attracted not a single patient and he whiled away his empty hours by composing fiction. In part his inspiration derived from Edgar Allan Poe's detective, Auguste Dupin, who made his debut in *The Murders in the Rue Morgue* in the 1840s. But Conan Doyle had his own plans; as he told a fellow student in 1880, he wanted a detective based on 'the system of Poe, but greatly simplified and brought down to the level of ordinary people'.

Real police work furnished no precedent; Sherlock Holmes's magnifying glass, his tape measure, his minute study of the crime scene, his mono-graphs on the different types of cigarette ash and the composition of various clays and muds, were all Conan Doyle's invention. When *A Study in Scarlet* came out in 1887 **fingerprinting** and even **anthropometry** still lay in the future, and detec-tion, such as it was, consisted not of assessing the physical evidence, even in blatant cases, but on trapping the culprit red-handed, or accepting hearsay and rumour, or checking suspects one by one in an endless round of elimination (see **Lacenaire**). Juries remained extremely sceptical of any intellectual bias.

Conan Doyle's solitary emphasis on the pre-emi-nence of logic made him a **court** of last resort for those adjudged guilty who could prove their inno-cence; he also played a part in the Edalji and Beck cases.

His contribution to **Ripperology** was the theory of Jill the Ripper: since a female midwife could wander bloodstained through the East End streets without attracting attention, the author considered the occupation an ideal disguise for a male killer.

His brother-in-law, the journalist Edward William Hornung, created the gentleman burglar Raffles, who first appeared in the 1899 bestseller *The Amateur Cracksman*.

Drawing and quartering

Until the introduction of the long drop, hanging achieved slow and agonising death through strangu-lation. It was thus possible to interrupt the process before death supervened and disembowel the vic-tim, compelling him – for instance – to eat his own entrails before chopping the body into quarters. The punishment, reserved for treason, was also known as 'Godly Butchery' since its proponents claimed to find scattered authority for the practice in the Bible. Forgery was considered a direct assault on the apparatus of the state, and many coiners suffered dismemberment.

The victim was sentenced to be 'hanged by the neck until half dead, and then cut down and his entrails to be cut out of his body while living and burned by the executioners. Then his head to be cut off, his body to be divided into quarters and afterwards his head and quarters to be set up in some open places directed.' Clearly the perfor-mance had a strong theatrical element, standing as a paradigm for the might of the state and the piecemeal destruction of its enemies.

Efficient workers – butchers were preferred – often removed the innards with such despatch that they could still attract the victim's attention by wav-ing his guts in front of his face. More showy execu-tioners sliced open the chest to excise the heart, which they held out to the populace with the words: 'Behold the heart of a traitor.'

Possibly the first victim was William Marise, pirate, in 1241. The last provincial display hap-pened in Derby in 1813, and seven years later in London the Cato Street Conspirators were decapi-tated after being hanged; when the executioner dropped the last head, someone from the crowd shouted 'Butterfingers!' As late as 1839, two years into Queen Victoria's reign, the Chartist John Frost was sentenced to the full penalty, later commuted to transportation for life to Australia.

See also **Exactitude**, **Pressing**, **Quartering**

Drops, of blood

Drops of blood behave as one would expect, in a Newtonian fashion, and a great deal can be deduced just from their shape. Blood falling verti-cally makes a circular mark with neat, spiky edges, and the distance fallen can be estimated by the number of pointed 'spines' round the circumfer-ence. From a height of about five feet, the blood tends to splodge out towards one side.

Circular **bloodstains** come from a stationary source (since otherwise they would not have fallen vertically). Drops of blood from a moving person (or object) land in the form of exclamation marks, their outline varying according to the speed of impact and direction of travel. Smears on the floor emanating from a bleeding corpse as it is dragged away show which way it went. Lines of blood on the ceiling are flung off when an assailant flourishes an axe overhead. Level trails of blood deposited along the walls suggest a weapon brandished hori-zontally.

These mundane considerations played a crucial role in the 1984 case of Graham Backhouse. As a hairdresser, Backhouse prospered. But soon after inheriting Widden Hill Farm outside Bristol in mid-dle-age and turning his hand to agriculture, he found himself nursing a £70,000 bank overdraft. Meanwhile the traditional hairdresser's perk of extra-marital philandering brought him into bad odour with his neighbours. After a string of abusive telephone calls and poison-pen letters, a worried Backhouse notified the police that on 30 March 1984 his herdsman had found a severed sheep's head impaled on his fence with a note reading 'You next'.

It was no idle threat. On 9 April Backhouse asked his wife to drive into town to collect some antibiotics, and she got into her husband's Volvo and turned on the ignition. This triggered the detonator in a steel pipe packed with the powder from twelve shotgun cartridges, firing 4,000 lead pellets upwards through the driver's seat and removing half her thigh. She was lucky to survive.

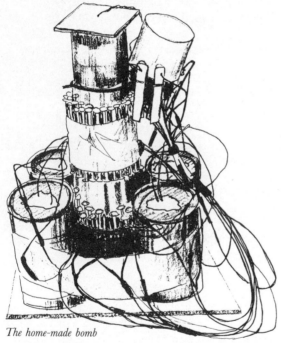

The home-made bomb

This apparent attempt on her husband's life inspired an intensive police investigation, and it transpired that Backhouse was locked in dispute with many of the locals over soured business deals or seductions. One among several suspects was a troubled near-neighbour, Colyn Bedale-Taylor, with whom Backhouse had quarrelled about a right of way. The police provided round-the-clock protection, but after nine days the impatient Backhouse ordered the men off his land.

By the evening of 30 April the police had a corpse on their hands. A bleeding Backhouse related how Bedale-Taylor had called round to Widden Hill Farm on some pretext and, after an amicable cup of coffee in the kitchen, gone beserk. First he accused Backhouse of causing his son's death in a car crash two years before. Then he admitted to planting the bomb. Then he pulled a Stanley knife and tried to finish the job, slashing Backhouse across the face and chest as the two men grappled for their lives.

Backhouse struggled free and fled into the hall, where he seized a shotgun. He warned off the advancing Bedale-Taylor, then shot him twice in the chest. A police search of the dead man's land revealed the remainder of the steel pipe used in the car bomb.

But the drops of blood in Backhouse's kitchen were the wrong shape and in the wrong disposition. They should have been spattered around the walls and furniture by the violent fight, producing distinctive 'flying tails'. Instead they lay sedately on the flagstones, forming neat circles with indented edges, as though Backhouse deliberately stood still and allowed his blood to spill evenly to the floor.

On further examination, one of the envelopes containing a threatening letter disclosed a few fibres of wool stuck to the gum under the flap, and the microscope matched them perfectly to fibres from one of Backhouse's own sweaters. In a desk drawer a detective found a notepad, and on one page was a doodle corresponding with indentations carried through to the 'You next' note.

Backhouse had been sending himself threatening letters. The reason? So he could murder his wife and collect her life insurance, recently doubled to £100,000. He could have pulled back from the brink after the failure of the bomb plot, but he may have felt that both the police and his wife needed further proof of innocence. He was sentenced to life imprisonment on 19 February 1985.

Duelling

The German Chancellor Bismarck was quick to take offence in his youth, fighting – some say – twenty-five duels as a student at the University of Göttingen during the 1830s. An unusual affair of honour involved a professor who, given the choice of weapons, selected a matched pair of **sausages**, one of them poisoned. Bismarck declined to participate, but he was game for nearly everything else. Back on his Pomeranian estates after his student excesses, he remained a tearaway, drinking recklessly, womanising and letting loose with a pistol through the bedroom windows of his occasional guests, and all this before he started to cause serious trouble. Bismarck provides a perfect example of the high-dominance, high-ability personality. He became a statesman. His high-dominance, low-ability counterparts grow up as criminals.

Jeffrey Hudson, dwarf by appointment to Queen Henrietta Maria (the first bride of Charles I), killed a man in one duel and defeated a turkey in another. Cyrano de Bergerac, the seventeenth-century French wit, is reputed to have fought and won over 1,000 duels, during one three-month period running through his opponents at the rate of four a week. Between 1601 and 1609 some 2,000 French nobles died in duels.

Affairs of honour were less frequent in England, where the victor stood a reasonable prospect of a murder charge. When Ben Jonson, the Elizabethan playwright, killed an actor with his rapier in a duel in September 1598, he was brought to trial and duly condemned to death. But he pleaded **Benefit of Clergy** on the grounds that he could read as well as write, demonstrating his knack by declaiming from a book handed to him in court. The sentence was commuted to branding, with the letter T (for Tyburn) scorched into his thumb.

In 1654 Oliver Cromwell reaffirmed the illegality of duels, but the practice continued unabated, not least since Army regulations obliged officers 'to redeem their honour in a duel' until 1844. The last duel on British soil occurred at Egham in Surrey in 1852, fought by two Frenchmen.

Duffy, John Francis (1954–)

The 'Railway Murderer' was the computer-caught British sex-killer who committed his first known **rape** on 10 June 1982. The police had little more to go on than a distinct *modus operandi* coupled with a vague physical description of a small, slightly built man with staring eyes. This fitted hundreds of suspects on their list of 1,999 sex offenders, already whittled down from 4,874 by eliminating improbables and those in prison or dead.

The distinct style of the rapes afforded few clues. Most of the attacks happened on or close to London railway stations, generally in the footpaths and alleys nearby. First the rapist chatted to his victim, then he produced a knife. The woman's hands were bound behind her back, and after the assault he wiped down her privates with a paper tissue and brushed through her pubic hairs with a plastic comb to remove forensic evidence. Apart from the obvious inference of their suspect's familiarity with the railway network, the police had no real pointers.

For the first sixteen attacks the rapist operated in tandem with a taller partner. Both men wore balaclavas. After a void period in late 1983, the shorter of the two went solo. He had committed a total of twenty-five rapes by 29 December 1985, the day that a London secretary, Alison Day, set off to Hackney Wick station to meet her boyfriend. She never arrived. Two weeks later her body, weighted down with stones, was recovered from a canal a short distance from the station.

Alison had been raped and beaten about the head with a brick. Her hands were tied behind her back, and her assailant tore a strip from her tartan shirt, tied it round her neck, inserted a stick through a turn in her 'collar' and then twisted it round until she died. She was nineteen.

Other rapes led to murder. On 17 April 1986 a 15-year-old schoolgirl, Maartje Tamboezer, rode her bicycle to the village sweetshop half a mile away. She took a shortcut down a narrow lane beside East Horsley station, to be knocked off her bike by a nylon rope across the path. She too had her hands bound; she too was bludgeoned about the head. She too was raped and strangled. This time the killer stuffed her vagina with paper tissues which he set alight to eliminate traces of his spermatozoa. Witnesses saw a small wiry man in a blue parka running for the 6.07 train back to London. Two million railway tickets were collected and examined for the suspect's fingerprints without result.

A month later a third woman died, this time a bride just back from honeymoon. The police correctly considered the Railway Murderer as a latter-day manifestation of the Railway Rapist, and he, in turn, should be among their 2,000 'possibles'. But where?

The year before, in July 1985, a diminutive young man from Kilburn, John Duffy, had broken into the bedroom of his estranged wife and subjected her to a violent rape; later he attacked her new boyfriend. Duffy was released on bail, but the arrest added him to the list as suspect 1594, and a detective took a traumatised 20-year-old rape victim to his court hearing to see if she recognised him. She did not, but it is likely that Duffy saw her and understood the threat posed by survivors.

Artist's impression of Duffy

On 17 May 1986, three weeks after Maartje Tamboezer's murder and the day before the final death, two police officers driving through North Weald in Essex came upon Duffy twenty-five miles from his home, loitering by a tube station. A search revealed a sharp knife and a wad of paper tissues in his pocket. Duffy explained he was a Zen Budo enthusiast and needed the weapon for martial arts classes. He could not be charged, but by now the investigation had established the rapist's blood group and his phosphoglucomutase reading, enabling the elimination of four suspects out of five. In addition the police had clothes fibres, and knew that the string used to tie up victims was a distinctive type of 'Somyarn' dating from 1982. They could convict the right man, if they could find him.

On 17 July Duffy was called in for routine questioning. He arrived with a solicitor, itself unusual, and, curiouser and curiouser, refused to supply a blood sample. The following day he staggered into West Hampstead police station after being violently attacked in a street mugging, his face bruised and his chest bleeding profusely from a razor slash. A side-effect was partial memory loss, and Duffy committed himself to the psychiatric unit at Friern Barnet Hospital.

The police ploughed on through their other suspects. Meanwhile they contacted David Canter, a psychology professor from Surrey University, to see if an American-style '**profile**' might help. Canter had no previous police experience, but he asked for the witness statements and forensic reports, and two weeks later produced seventeen 'personality indicators' of which thirteen proved well-founded. Many were computer-friendly, allowing instantaneous elimination of whole categories of suspects.

Thus the 'centre of gravity' of the attacks suggested a resident of Kilburn or Cricklewood. Statistical probability put his age between twenty and thirty. The recurring feature of bondage suggested an interest in bondage. Witnesses described their assailant as physically small, and small men given to rape may feel themselves unattractive, particularly if they have acne, and small acned men given to violent rape may be interested in martial arts, and small martial arts hobbyists fascinated by bondage who are given to violent rape are unlikely to have a stable marriage. But they may well keep a collection of hard-core porn and knives and swords. And so on. Detectives keyed the information in, and the computer identified suspect number 1594.

The police now discovered that Duffy was not safely hospitalised, but an outpatient, and while out on 21 October he raped again. Still without hard evidence, Superintendent McFadden ordered his arrest. A search of Duffy's home yielded a collection of knives and 'Kung fu' weapons. In a cupboard at his parent's house the police found a ball of Somyarn. Forensic analysis of thirteen 'foreign' fibres on Alison Day's body proved a perfect match for one of Duffy's sweaters, and a fellow martial arts devotee, Ross Mockeridge, described how he had been persuaded to subject Duffy to a simulated mugging.

Duffy's wife filled in the picture. She married the former altar boy in June 1980. Amidst increasing recriminations they tried hard for a child; he took their failure to procreate as a personal insult and their love life went awry. Before having sex he insisted on tying her hands to replicate rape; the more she struggled the more he liked it. His obsession with bondage and violence bred endless rows, and an attempted reconciliation in the autumn of

1983 corresponded with the temporary cessation of the rapes. Their marriage broke down in June 1985. 'The nice man I had married had become a madman with scary, scary eyes,' said his wife. In 1988 at the Old Bailey, Duffy was sentenced to a minimum of thirty years.

Dumdums

Bullets designed to fragment inside the target on impact. Dumdums were first employed in India in 1897, to such terrible effect that their military application was banned by the Hague Convention of 1899. But the Feds in Prohibition Chicago used them, and more recently they constituted the favourite ammunition of both Ronald **Kray** and **van Schoor**, the South African security guard.

The Armalite rifle now achieves the same objective legally. Instead of entering the body cleanly, its high-velocity bullets tumble through. Alternatively, Americans can purchase a type of ammunition known as 'Devastators'. These bullets, developed for sky marshals in hijacking cases, contain a small aluminium canister filled with explosive. John Hinckley Jnr fired them into President Reagan, but they failed to go off.

John Lennon was not so lucky, and it is interesting to see that his assassin, Mark Chapman, thought his plans through to envisioning the dilation of the ammunition – hollow-point Smith & Wesson Plus Ps – within the target body. 'I chose the right type of bullet so that it expanded inside him rather than going in and just laying there,' Chapman told psychiatrists. 'This way, the expansion of the bullet, it instantly damaged more of Lennon's internal organs and death was more quickly there for him.' Chapman's subtext is of caring for his victim, and evidently **assassins** who care use dumdums.

See also **Stalking**

Dummy

One legal constituent of murder is killing with 'malice aforethought'. This requires the formation of intent and there is thus a long line of 'mistake' cases where death was caused without the requisite intention.

Among the more unusual scenarios is the Waterloo Dummy case. It started on the morning of 8 December 1950 when William Donoghue, a 42-year-old bus conductor, stood outside his south London flat staring in horror at a corpse on the landing, muttering: 'Is it a dummy or a body? Take it away.' Later, when the police arrived, Donoghue said: 'If that is a real man, I done it.'

It emerged that Donoghue had been out for a drink the night before. First he downed six or seven bottles of Guinness in the 'Prince Albert'. Still thirsty, he set off for the 'Brunswick Arms', Southwark, where he met an old friend, Thomas Meaney. Together they drank beer laced with gin and then returned unsteadily to Donoghue's flat, rounding off the evening with a bottle of spirits. Donoghue fell asleep in a chair while Meaney dozed off on the bed.

Later that night Donoghue climbed into his bed which – much to his irritation – he found encumbered with some sort of dummy, a person-shaped object presumably put there by his mates as a practical joke. Donoghue threw the 'guy' on the floor and then savaged out its stuffing with his old Army bayonet, stabbing it sixteen times. Realistic-looking red gunge oozed out. Then he kicked it onto the landing and went back to his drunken stupor.

Was this murder? Manslaughter? Or an **accident**? Donoghue's urine sample showed 450mg alcohol per cent, sufficient to threaten his own life and enough to bar the formation of any intent to kill. At his trial the prosecution accepted a plea of manslaughter and Donoghue went down for three years.

This case is in sharp contrast to one where a killer drinks for 'Dutch courage' to stiffen his resolve, an aggravating factor indicative of premeditation.

See also **Accidents**, **Ghost**

Durability

Never underestimate the durability of the human body; no matter what, parts keep on turning up. Killers should clearly visualise the scale of the problem.

A corpse is a large object to conceal and soon broadcasts its presence by the stench. Burial is hard in cities, and in the country the grave is readily distinguishable by traces of disturbed soil. Shallow graves give up their dead. Deep ones take hours to dig, and neighbours think it odd. Transportation to the disposal site is fraught.

Dumping the body in a trunk at Left Luggage is asking for exposure. Hiding a corpse around the house destroys the ambience. **Dismemberment** is a vast task which produces blood and bits everywhere, and even then the chunks have to be concealed. **Acid** does not work. Nor do bombs (see **Payne**). Incineration leaves the **teeth** and often even the **hair**. Identification evidence survives the rivers and the sea. Hence the attractions of faked accidents and **poisoning**. Once the first hurdle of packaging the death as 'natural causes' is surmounted, the problems are over. For a killer with a corpse on his hands, they are just beginning.

John Perry's 1992 experience in Clwyd, Wales, typifies the difficulties caused by an unwanted body. After killing his wife, a Filipina half his age, 52-year-old Perry carried her body to the bathroom to cut her up. The Home Office pathologist Dr Wayte estimated that this task alone would have taken a good twelve hours of intensive effort, but the results were impressive – uniformly diced chunks. The bones Perry sawed and snapped.

Then he started on the cooking. To make it easier to open, the head was baked separately in the double oven. Then Perry drilled and chiselled the skull in two, depositing the contents, together with some twenty gallons of blood and body fluid, in the countryside on repeated night trips. This left a bin full of human organs, two plastic bags stuffed with ancillary material and a container filled with congealed human grease. The house smelled of roasted and decaying flesh, the carpet was covered with blood, and Perry still had fresh gore on his forehead when detectives called to investigate. They had been summoned by neighbours, who noticed an excess of soap suds round the drains.

The police asked Perry where his wife was. He replied, 'I have fed some to the cat.' The family pet thus became the macabre object of photographers' attentions and an excellent portrait appeared in the *Independent*, a paper not normally renowned for its humour. The creature's present whereabouts are not known, but Perry was sent down for life in November 1991.

Durable

Nickname given to the irrepressible Mike Molloy, an Irish inebriate from New York. A syndicate from his Third Avenue speakeasy in the Bronx reckoned that no one would miss Mike much. He was already aged sixty and, at that, a wreck. So, insuring his life for $1,788 as a healthy forty-six-year-old, they set about doing him in. It looked like easy money to the five-man team of Kreisberg, Green, Pasqua, Murphy the bartender and Tony Marino, the bar's proprietor; the gang was fresh from their triumph of killing Tony's mistress for her insurance. All they did was get the girl drunk, fix the window open, add water and collect when she died of pneumonia.

For the repeat performance on New Year's Eve 1932, the boys made Mike paralytically drunk on liquor spiked with anti-freeze and left him for dead. But next day Mike staggered back into their lives, desperate for a drink. Over the following days they dosed him with turpentine, and with wood alcohol bumped up with rat poison, and with sardine sandwiches filled with tin tacks. Mike blossomed.

Luckily one of the team – Green – worked as a taxi driver; he ran Mike over, but to no effect. So Green ran him over again. Results were better, a broken shoulder, but still not good enough. So they made Mike very drunk yet again, stripped him, doused him in water, waited until the ice formed and then left his body on the streets to freeze.

When that failed, Mike Molloy must have thought he was having one helluva start to the year. But on 22 February the boys took the Great Survivor out carousing one more time and gassed him with carbon monoxide, stuffing a rubber tube down his throat. Word got out because one of the gang *boasted* of the killing.

On exhumation the conspicuous red blotches on Molloy's skin testified to the cause of death, and all five of his friends went to the **electric chair**.

Dutch, The

Very naive. Dutch liberal policies towards soft drugs in the 1970s attracted the major Chinese heroin traffickers seeking a hospitable European base. Legally speaking, the odds were heavily stacked in the dealers' favour: no *agents provocateurs*, no convictions in the absence of possession, no effective conspiracy laws, no plea-bargaining with informers, no wiretap evidence admissible in court and, until 1977, a maximum sentence of four years for drug trafficking, with remission for good conduct. The prisons were so pleasant they resembled hotels, housing one inmate per cell, with televisions, radios, magazines, books, gymnasia, conjugal visits, full access to telephones, and limited inspection of packages in and out.

In the early 1970s no one in the Dutch police force had seen any heroin, so it was reasonably safe to leave it lying around in buckets. The first haul came in 1971, consisting of a mere two ounces found on a Chinese sailor in a Chinatown gambling den; two years later, when Amsterdam was one of the main conduits for 'China White', total seizures edged towards a pound.

Richard Weijenburg, chief of the intelligence division on Chinese crime, tells a story from the early 1970s when two officers inspected a Chinese restaurant. They ran across millions of dollars' worth of a strange white substance. 'In the kitchen,' recounts Weijenburg, 'they saw a large wicker basket with plastic bags stamped with a tiger on the front.' This was the logo of the Double U-O Globe brand, the world's most famous branded heroin. 'The bags were filled with a white powder and there must have been a hundred large bags in there. The police asked the chef what the bags contained and were told it was a common spice used in the restaurant's cooking. When one of the police asked if he could have some for his wife, an avid

cooker, he was politely refused because it was very expensive and hard to get.'

The officers left to go about their business. In 1973 America's exasperated DEA lent a hand in mounting the first big arrest – for fourteen kilos of heroin – which very nearly miscarried when at the critical moment, rather than making the bust, the Dutch police nodded off.

Worried by the growing American intervention, the head of the local 14K **Triad**, nicknamed the Unicorn, was recalled to Hong Kong. He had single-handedly developed the European **narcotics** trade following the American withdrawal from Vietnam; now he needed polishing with an intensive course in socialisation. Back in Amsterdam, a refurbished Unicorn made a big play to the Dutch authorities, stressing his benevolent role as Chairman of the Chinese Overseas Association. Decorated for his contribution to public service, he inveigled his way into the confidence of Amsterdam's Police Commissioner, Gerard Toorenaar, for whom he acted as a personal informer as well as the unofficial peacekeeper of the Chinese community. In return for the Unicorn betraying his rivals, Toorenaar allegedly issued letters of immunity clearing him of involvement in the heroin trade.

The Unicorn was assassinated on 3 March 1975; by then, the Dutch police were becoming suspicious. But in 1988 they had no more than three full time officers on the Triad connection – reminiscent of **Hoover**'s taskforce, several strong, devoted to rooting out organised crime in America.

E

Ears, severed

Perhaps the best-known ears are J. Paul Getty III's and Lord Erroll's. The former hit the headlines after being sent through the mail to a newspaper in Rome.

Getty had been kidnapped. His captors cut off his ear and consigned it to the mercies of the notorious Italian postal service on 21 October 1973; it was lucky to be received by the press in early November. After further threats that other parts of the kidnapped youth would follow, his grandfather, Paul Getty himself, agreed to a record $2.9 million ransom. Since this was paid as three billion lire, the money was delivered to Calabria by truck.

Lord Erroll's detached ear made a brief appearance in the courtroom scene of the film *White Mischief*. This was no dramatic licence. On the night of 23 January 1941, Josslyn Victor Hay, twenty-second Earl of Erroll, was shot twice in the head from point-blank range with ammunition charged by a black powder propellant, a point demonstrated in court by Erroll's stained ear, handed round in a jar of spirits. 'This really is *too* much. Poor Joss,' said Diana, his ex-lover (see **White Mischief**).

The ear of Donald Merrett's mother became a similar forensic curiosity in 1924 after she was shot in the head while sitting at the desk in a recess of her living room. The police, suspecting suicide, confined her to a secure ward under conditions of near-arrest for her sin, and when she died four days later, her ear (attached to a six inch slab of flesh) was scrutinised for clues. No scorch marks or traces of 'tattooing' from unburned flecks of powder were found, suggesting that the gun had been at least nine inches from her head at the moment of discharge – unusual for suicides, and it seemed more than a coincidence that her son, who stood to inherit, had been in the room at the time. Donald Merrett purchased the pistol a few days previously, and his mother's last recollection before hearing a bang was of saying: 'Go away, Donald, and don't annoy me.' But the verdict was 'not proven', and Merrett killed twice more before committing suicide in 1954.

In a more mundane incident from October 1991, Scotsman Kenneth Docherty was jailed not for theft but assault. After biting off his opponent's ear in a fight, he ran away with it clenched between his teeth.

The forensic possibilities of earprints are under appraisal by Professor Starrs of George Washington University. Professional criminals wear gloves on a job as a matter of course, but do not appreciate the dangers of listening, with one ear pressed to the door, before effecting entry.

See also **Kidney**

Eastern bloc

With the collapse of the Communist empire, parts of the Soviet Union regressed to the state of brigandage prevalent throughout Europe centuries ago. At the most basic level, customs officials started freelancing, forming themselves into mafia cartels. In late 1991 on the Ukraine/Polish border, vehicles leaving Russia faced a single-line tailback of six miles and a wait of two weeks or more for their turn to be fleeced. Customs officers simply peered into the car and fixed a price – whatever the travellers could pay.

In the words of the Polish writer Ryszard Kapuscinsky: 'The Moscow authorities said they no longer controlled the Ukraine; and the Kiev authorities said that the customs officials were still under the control of Moscow. The truth is they're both right and they're both wrong, because in fact neither has any control. The customs officials operate as free agents, exacting arbitrary tolls without appeal and for themselves alone.'

With these tempting yields, borders became increasingly popular propositions. The Kiev–Minsk–Warsaw train developed a previously non-existent Ukrainian–Byelorussian frontier for the extraction of levies. Heading the other way into Russia, drivers travelled in convoys. Cars on the Byelorussia highway were liable to be shot up, and arrived – if at all – with shattered windscreens.

When the film-maker Piotr Bikont caught the Moscow–Warsaw train, he witnessed the nightly robbery routine. Come the small hours, 'several of the more beefy Russians took to gazing expectantly out of the windows at the endlessly flat, snow-covered terrain, and suddenly, as if on cue, they all heaved themselves up from behind their tables and stalked off to the Russian cars. There they barged into one sleeping compartment after another... yanked open the windows and proceeded to toss every suitcase, package, purse or unattached bundle out of the train. Five seconds, ten seconds – bam! And then on to the next compartment, same thing. Their confederates were positioned out there along this particular stretch of railway.'

In Vladivostok, law and order all but disappeared. Conditions were so bad that robbers stole potatoes, digging up whole fields. Students supplemented their monthly grants of £0.50 by turning to prostitution; tourists were openly mugged in city restaurants for their cash, and the import of second-hand cars shipped across the Sea of Japan created Mafia-style gang warfare responsible for about eight bullet-riddled corpses a week.

With the progressive decay of central authority, the infection spread to Moscow by the summer of 1992, with eleven gang-warfare fatalities in one 24-hour period, three gunned down in restaurants. Some were casualties of the Icon Wars; six thousand of these 'wooden roubles' are seized at Moscow's Sheremetyevo Airport each year, on their illegal way out of the country, many for thefts commissioned by Western dealers. Smugglers kill for stock. The month of August saw the recovery of a cement-filled box from the river near Tula. Inside was a dead body, but it had been alive when the concrete poured in.

More fortunate gangsters, who reached the top of the heap, settled in London; the brothers Ruslan and Nasabeck Utsyev paid cash for a luxurious £1 million penthouse with fully fitted cupboards, from one of which their bodies, shot in the head, were retrieved in early 1993. British police suspected that big-time Russian gangsters, with access to limitless supplies of Eastern bloc arms and drugs (some irradiated by Chernobyl), were forging links with both the Mafia and the Colombian cartels.

The Russians act with peculiar savagery. Western gangs generally steer clear of killing journalists, but the Russian investigative reporter Vladimir Glotov turned up dead in his Moscow apartment with his face cut off. Abroad, Russian *mafiosi* appreciate that the worst they face at the hands of the authorities is imprisonment in relatively comfortable conditions.

As an antidote to increasing violence, in 1992 Russia was poised to legitimise the sale of firearms for home use.

See also **Whacks, Zlotys**

Edwards, Tracy (1959–)

A lucky man. On the afternoon of 22 July 1991, 32-year-old Edwards stood chatting to two friends in Milwaukee's Grand Avenue Mall when he was approached by an acquaintance, Jeffrey **Dahmer**.

Dahmer, by that stage virtually destitute, said he felt 'real bored' and offered them $100 each to come back to his house and keep him company. Pressed for details, he added that he wanted to manacle somebody. Edwards accepted, and they took a cab back to Dahmer's home at 213 Oxford Apartments.

Inside the apartment, Edwards commented on the overpowering stench: 'It smells like someone died in here.' They shared a couple of beers but, disturbed by the smell, Edwards became restless. So Dahmer handed him a spiked rum and coke, snapped a pair of handcuffs round his wrist and pulled a knife.

Dahmer easily dragged the groggy Edwards into the bedroom, where they sat on a sheet that appeared to be covered in dried blood and watched *Exorcist II* on video. On the walls Edwards noticed photographs of naked mutilated men, one almost destroyed by acid. Halfway through the tape, Dahmer said, 'I want to show you something', pulled a man's **head** out of a filing cabinet and gave it a good rub. 'This is how I get people to stay with me,' he told Edwards. Then Dahmer pointed to a shelf in the closet, drawing his attention to a pair of severed human hands.

Edwards now observed that Dahmer was trying to force the handcuffs onto his other wrist. It's all right, Dahmer reassured him, it's just to take a few photographs. Then Dahmer man-

handled him to the floor and sat on top with the butcher's knife at his captive's chest. Dahmer said that he intended to cut out Edwards's heart and eat it. Edwards played for time, characterising himself as a friend, and they drifted back into the living room where Dahmer slipped in and out of a reverie.

'It's time, it's time,' Dahmer chanted, brandishing the knife. With his last strength Edwards slugged him in the jaw and then knocked him clear with a karate kick. Edwards reached the door and struggled with the locks while Dahmer scrabbled from behind. He broke free and staggered into the street, running screaming through the night until he flagged down a passing patrol car.

'He's going to kill me, he's going to kill me,' Edwards babbled to the police, but the dangling handcuffs made Officers Rauth and Mueller mistake this strange apparition for a fugitive from justice. Edwards persisted until they checked out his story and found that, indeed, 213 **Oxford Apartments** was a charnel-house.

Within hours Dahmer's grisly secret splashed over the world's press and airwaves. Edwards became a familiar face as he told and retold the story of his escape to the cameras, so much so that police watching the transmissions in Tuepolo recognised him as the alleged rapist of a 14-year-old girl. Edwards faces thirty years if convicted.

But at least Edwards survived. Not everyone was so lucky. Only a few days before, on 27 May, 14-year-old Konerak Sinthasomphone ran into

Dahmer in the shopping mall. Dahmer offered him a few dollars to pose for some photographs.

Back home Dahmer gave the boy some sleeping pills in a drink. On this occasion, Dahmer's programme included an attempt, with the aid of an electric drill and an injection of muriatic acid, to perform a prefrontal lobotomy. Halfway through, Dahmer realised he had overlooked something important: canned beer. So he left Konerak groaning in semi-consciousness and jogged over to a bar on 27th Street. Meanwhile, Konerak came to and found himself in an apartment reeking of death. Despite the incomplete surgery and his drugged stupor the boy meandered out onto the street, nearly naked, walked into a tree and crumpled to the sidewalk.

Among the crowd that gathered as he lay on the pavement was the returning Dahmer and a concerned neighbour, Nicole Childress. She flagged down a passing patrol car. 'There's this young man,' Childress told the police. 'He's buck naked and he has been beaten up. He can't stand.' The officers summoned an ambulance from the Fire Department. In minutes Engine 32 arrived, but by then the police had decided to send the paramedics back. Konerak did not seem seriously hurt. 'You know this guy?' asked one of the officers, turning to Dahmer.

'I do,' said Dahmer, and explained that Konerak was his 19-year-old lover who had overdone things with a bottle of Jack Daniels. So the police escorted the couple back to their love-nest, with one of the officers carrying Konerak in his arms because the boy still could not stand. Inside No. 213 the officers put Konerak down in a chair, and left as soon as they could – it smelt like death in there – saying 'Well, you just take care of him.' Dahmer did.

This lamentable chain of events inspired Edwards to file a $5 million lawsuit against the Milwaukee police on 12 September 1991. Edwards claimed for the mental anguish he suffered as a result of the police's failure to apprehend Dahmer sooner.

This was the Sinthasomphone family's second brush with Dahmer; on 30 September 1989 he went down for a second-degree sexual assault on one of Konerak's brothers. Nine years before, the family had risked their lives to reach America from their native Laos, building a boat and making a nighttime run across the Mekong.

Eiffel Tower

Sold not once but twice by the Czechoslovakian-born conman 'Count' Victor Lustig (1890–1947). Part of the scheme's beauty lay in the reluctance of his dupes to complain about their losses. In theory, Lustig could have lived off the trick for life.

In March 1925 Lustig was staying at the luxury Crillon Hotel in Paris when he read a newspaper item on the government's growing concern about the expense of the Tower's upkeep. Forging Ministerial stationery, he approached five scrap merchants, inviting them in strict confidence to the hotel's conference rooms. There he disclosed that they had been selected to pitch for the Tower's demolition and its potential yield of 7,000 tons of scrap. Lustig gave the dealers a personal guided tour of the Tower, arriving incognito so that the staff would not get wind of this sensitive project.

Lustig settled on an ambitious Monsieur Poisson as his dupe and put the deal above suspicion by the authentic Continental touch of demanding a bribe to clinch the contract. Lustig fled the hotel by the back entrance as his victim left by the front. The 'con' went unreported, so next year Lustig did it again.

In the course of his career Lustig – the son of the Mayor of Hostinne – accumulated a total of twenty-five aliases and forty-seven arrests. Before the First World War he spent several years working the transatlantic liners as a cardsharp, and in the post-war era netted $25,000 by selling the millionaire Herbert Loller a patent device for duplicating banknotes.

Imprisoned in the Tombs, New York, on 1 September 1935 Lustig escaped by climbing out of a window and down a sheet. After his final conviction in December 1945 for distributing $134 million in forged banknotes, he passed his declining years in the company of Al Capone in the laundry at Alcatraz. They had met before, when Lustig relieved the great man of $50,000 in a 'double-your-money' Wall Street scheme. Thinking things over, Lustig realised that this was rash and went back – money and cap in hand – to Capone, who rewarded him with $5,000 for his honesty.

Scotsman Arthur Ferguson was another talented salesman of larger items. In a six-week period during 1925 he sold Buckingham Palace for £2,000, Big Ben for £1,000 and Nelson's Column for £6,000. The buyers were American tourists, whose homeland must have seemed a source of almost limitless wealth. So he emigrated in late 1925, on arrival attempting to rent out the White House for $100,000 a year to a Texas cattleman.

Before his eventual arrest Ferguson got some way towards disposing of the Statue of Liberty for a six-figure sum to an Australian visitor. But he was identified from a snapshot taken by his client, which clearly showed the con-man posing in front of his monumental sculpture of a woman with a tiara holding a torch.

Sent down for five years, Ferguson served his time and died in 1938 in prosperity in California.

During his younger days he had worked as a repertory actor, once taking the role of a gullible American conned by a trickster.

Eighteenth Amendment

'A noble experiment', according to J. Edgar **Hoover**, but one to which no great thought was given. Prohibition came about almost absent-mindedly.

It followed a long, slow run-up. The revulsion against the wild drinking of the frontier days melded with America's deep-rooted puritanism to produce an anti-drink crusade which, by 1907, turned Georgia teetotal. Other large rural states succumbed: Tennessee, North Carolina, Mississippi, West Virginia and Oklahoma. A Yale professor, Dr Charles Foster Kent, contributed his mite to the cause of abstinence by producing an alcohol-free Bible; he deleted all references to drink, for instance changing the 'flagon of wine' of II Samuel vi, v. 19 to 'a cake of raisins'.

In 1914, the Eighteenth Amendment gained 197 votes in the House of Representatives, with 190 opposed. But the requirement for a two-thirds majority meant that the issue was not recontested until 1917. By then America was undergoing the sobering experience of war with Germany, which owned many of the breweries, thereby bringing drink into further disrepute, and the eventual victory in the contest of arms would, it was known, usher in a utopian era with little need for artificial stimulants. When the Eighteenth Amendment came up for the second time it passed after a mere thirteen hours. A few months later the House of Representatives nodded the proposal through after a day's debate, and by January 1919 the necessary thirty-six states appended their approval. Apart from President Wilson, no one objected much except the American Federation of Labor, belatedly concerned about the working man's glass of beer.

Despite predictions, there was no last night binge, even in the notoriously wet cities of New York, Chicago, Detroit, New Orleans and San Francisco. At one minute past midnight, on the morning of 17 January 1920, the Eighteenth Amendment became law with very little thought for the morrow. All breweries would close, all imports cease, all bars stop serving, and everyone would stop drinking for ever.

The story rated only a single column halfway down the page in the Chicago *Tribune*: 'Liquor's knell to toll in US at midnight', above an even shorter item, 'US to be dry as Sahara'. The paper carried no editorial on the subject. As the newly appointed Prohibition Commissioner, John F. Kramer, commented: 'This law will be obeyed in cities, large and small, and in villages, and where it is not obeyed it will be enforced.'

Apart from appointing 1,500 **Prohibition Agents** (an average of about thirty a state), almost the only other practical measures were the partial closures of the Chicago City House of Correction and of the *delirium tremens* ward of Cook County Hospital, now surplus to requirements, since lawlessness and alcoholism would soon cease. In this manner, America was delivered to the Mob.

Electric chair

Early electrocution was not a pretty spectacle. 'The man's lips peel back, the throat strains for a last desperate cry, the body arches against the restraining straps,' wrote reporter Don Reid of a Texas execution. 'The features purple, steam and smoke arise from the bald spots on head and leg while the sick-sweet smell of burned flesh permeates the little room.' The smell of burning comes from the electrodes at a temperature high enough to melt copper – 1,940°F.

In Britain the executioner James **Berry** attended a series of experiments conducted in Manchester in 1888 to see if electrocution represented an improvement on hanging. Together with a 'small committee of gentlemen', Berry assisted at the extermination of a dog and a calf. The process was not impressive.

Nowadays the electric chair is made of stout wood and equipped with leather restraining straps. It stands on a thick rubber mat. As a preliminary the prisoner's skull is shaved; then a Tin Man 'death cap' is strapped on his head over a sponge soaked in salt water to maximise electrical contact. The other electrode is clamped to the inside of the victim's left calf, similarly shaved. The exact dosage varies from one account to the next. But Dr Amos Squire of Sing Sing Prison, who presided at 138 executions, writes of '2,000 volts for ten seconds, reduced to 250 volts for from 40 to 50 seconds, then raised to a higher voltage for five seconds'. Then 'a second contact is almost always given, lasting for three to five seconds'.

The chair at Starke penitentiary is known as 'Old Sparky'. It executed Ted **Bundy**. The leather face mask at Louisiana State Penitentiary – and presumably elsewhere – is a little charred round the edges by its former victims. Martha Beck of the 'Lonely Hearts' murders was so fat that she could hardly squeeze into her seat on 7 March 1951.

To avoid the guilt of lawful killing tainting any one individual, at Cook County Gaol four identical death switches were installed, only one of them connected.

See also **Kemmler**

Ellis, Ruth (1926–1955)

Few cases have the open-and-shut simplicity of the murder of David Blakely by Ruth Ellis who, shortly after 9 p.m. on Easter Sunday 1955, walked down a Hampstead street towards her lover outside the Magdala pub.

As they stood side-by-side, she produced a Smith and Wesson .38 from her handbag. When Blakely tried to run she pulled the trigger twice, and the first bullet struck him from a range of three inches. He stumbled on, and Ruth walked after him. 'Get out of the way, Clive,' she said to a friend, and shot Blakely again. This time he fell to the pavement and she continued pulling the trigger until the six-chamber magazine was empty.

Drinkers rushed out of the pub to see Ruth standing stock-still with a smoking revolver in her hand. 'Phone the police,' she said, and in the second sentence of her statement to Detective Superintendent Crawford later that night she admitted, 'I am guilty.' By 20 June, Ruth was on trial at the Old Bailey for her life. But she did not want it.

Mr Christmas Humphreys, QC, for the prosecution, only asked one question in cross-examination: 'Mrs Ellis, when you fired that revolver at close range into the body of David Blakely, what did you intend to do?' She replied without hesitation: 'It is obvious that when I shot him I intended to kill him.' This excluded any possibility of manslaughter, and thus necessitated a finding of murder. That took the jury fourteen minutes, and the judge was compelled to pass the death sentence, whereupon Ruth smiled faintly. From her cell she wrote to Blakely's mother: 'I shall die loving your son, and you should feel content that his death has been repaid.'

To a friend Ruth confided that the prospect of execution seemed no more alarming 'than having a tooth out'. At 7 a.m. on the morning of 13 July she penned her last note: 'Everyone (staff) is simply wonderful in Holloway. This is just to console my family with the thought that I did not change my way of thinking at the last moment. Or break my promise to David's mother.' At 8 a.m. she prayed in front of a crucifix. At 9 a.m. she downed her tot of brandy, thanked the officers for their kindness, and steadily walked the few feet to the Execution Shed.

By then Ruth Ellis was one of the few who did not object to the procedure. As the mother of two children, the youngest aged three, it was hard to see the exact way her death contributed to the greater good of society. 'Should hanging be stopped?' demanded the headlines of the *Daily Mirror*. Her supporters included the crime author Raymond Chandler, who wrote to the *Evening Standard*, 'This was a crime of passion under considerable provocation. No other country in the world would hang this woman... This thing haunts me and, so far as I may say it, disgusts me as something obscene. I am not referring to the trial, of course, but to the medieval savagery of the law.' Lawyers, MPs, friends and relatives campaigned for a reprieve – one petition collected 50,000 signatures – but there were no grounds on which to apply.

Ruth Ellis was perhaps an unlikely target for sympathy. First a waitress, then a nude model, then a club hostess, then a call girl, then an occasional prostitute and manageress of a seedy Knightsbridge drinking club, with one illegitimate child, a broken marriage and several abortions behind her, Ruth ran two lovers, sported a full peroxide rinse typical of a brassy tart, was strung out on tranquillisers and drunk on Pernod.

She killed her feckless lover, ex-public schoolboy David Blakely, after a couple of on-off years together. At the time of his death they were sharing a one-roomed flat in Chelsea with her son. But the rent was 'lent' to Ruth by her back-up lover, company director Desmond Cussen. Blakely had no job and squandered his £7,000 inheritance on motor racing; his last car, The Emperor, fell to pieces on its first track outing.

Sometimes Blakely beat her. Sometimes they made up. Sometimes he proposed. Nothing went anywhere, they drank to excess and eventually Blakely took fright. On Good Friday 1955 he made the momentous decision to stand Ruth up.

Blakely ran into some friends, Carole and Anthony Findlater, who found him sitting sadly in the Magdala public house. Why not, they suggested, make the break with Ruth and forget their date for 7.30 that night? Why not spend the weekend with them in Tanza Road?

Ruth already suspected Blakely of an affair with Carole, and when he failed to materialise she telephoned the Findlaters' flat repeatedly; they replaced the receiver. She made Cussen drive her to Tanza Road, but they would not answer the door. When she stove in the windows of Blakely's car, they called the police and Cussen drove her home.

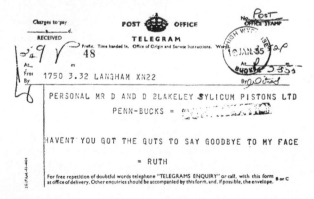

Ruth did not sleep that night, and by ten the following morning, again on station in Tanza Road by the front door, she saw Blakely emerge and get in a car with Anthony Findlater. Leaving her son at London Zoo with enough money for the afternoon, she spent the day driving round town with Cussen,

trying to track down her errant boyfriend. That evening she was back at Tanza Road listening from the street as the Findlaters held a small party. Inside she thought she made out David talking to a woman – who laughed. Then some bedroom curtains were drawn. Ruth, overwrought, concluded that the Findlaters were dangling an *au pair* as bait to lure her man away.

That night Ruth again did not sleep. Her thoughts unspooled: 'I had a peculiar feeling I wanted to kill him.' The following evening, blurry-headed but determined, she hit the Pernod. According to a statement made on the last day of her life, 'We had been drinking for some time. I had been telling Cussen about Blakely's treatment of me. I was in a terribly depressed state. All I can remember is that Cussen gave me a loaded gun... I was in such a dazed state that I cannot remember what was said. I rushed out as soon as he gave me the gun.' Then, by her account, she caught a taxi to the Magdala, where she shot her lover dead.

Elveson, Francine (d. 1979)

A New York schoolteacher and murder victim. Her case marked an early success for the FBI's Behavioral Science Unit, who all but identified the murderer from a desk in **Quantico**, 300 miles from the crime scene.

The state of a victim's body can be a good general guide to the killer's age. The teenager tends to kill with the haste and tempestuousness of youth; a murderer of more mature years may take his time. So when Francine Elveson died in a sex attack, it proved possible to estimate her assailant's age.

FBI Agent John Douglas considered that the murderer was unlikely to be far into his thirties since any sex killer (a repetitive occupation) would by then be in prison. On the other hand, the ritualistic posture of Elveson's body on the rooftop of Pelham Parkway House, the severed nipples placed on her chest, and the deliberation with which he forced the umbrella into her vagina suggested a leisurely slaying. This put her attacker between twenty-five and his early thirties, and the knifework had been such a protracted business that the murderer must have known he would be undisturbed. 'He spent hours up there mutilating the body,' recalled Douglas. 'What's strange is that he spent so much time there that he had to defecate on the steps, and he covered it over! Somehow, *that* was repulsive to him... He felt too comfortable there.'

Francine Elveson was accosted while leaving the building for work, and then forced up the stairs. She had not screamed, and all this implied a killer who knew both the building and his victim, the more so since the attack had the personal element of face mutilation. Psychologically, no murderer wants anyone resembling someone he knew left to tell tales, and it is when the killer's identity can be traced through the victim's that the face must be obliterated.

The murderer would be white; sex killings are nearly all intra-racial. The style of the murder did not suggest a good family man. The killer was probably a loner, indubitably a sadist, most likely living by himself and with a predilection for bondage-type hard porn; the body was laid out like a magazine spread. In FBI jargon, the killing was primarily 'dis**organised**' and thus the murderer would be an under-achiever.

New York police had already questioned and cleared some 2,000 suspects. One, Carmine Calabro, had given an alibi which withstood the perfunctory scrutiny of the initial screening, but he matched the '**profile**' prepared by Agent Douglas. An unemployed, unmarried 32-year-old actor and high school drop-out, Calabro shared a pornography collection with his father, a Parkway House resident, and his alibi fulfilled two major requirements. First, it supplied the element of emotional instability: Calabro had been – in theory at least – sequestered in a mental hospital at the time of the murder. And second, the alibi proved easy to break. On closer examination it transpired that the hospital's institutional patients were at liberty to come and go as they pleased. Calabro's **teethmarks**, corresponding to the bites on the victim's legs, clinched the case and he is currently serving twenty-five years.

In traditional detection the clues lead to a specific individual, with the motive often pointing straight to the killer. Detective work is primarily a physical process – collecting, tagging, logging, examining and so on. But in random murders, nothing connects a particular killer with a particular victim. Instead, the scene-of-the-crime is analysed to find the specific *type* of murderer, creating a theoretical framework against which suspects, in their thousands if necessary, can be compared for exactness of fit. This is both a matter of applied behaviourial science and of convenience. Crime scenes do not often contain forensic clues, but murderers inevitably leave behind behaviourial clues in the form of the victim's body and exactly how it was treated.

See also **de Sade**

Escape from Alcatraz

Conscientious 1979 Don Siegel movie starring Clint Eastwood and based very closely on the facts. There *were* three escapees, they did scrape away their cell walls with mess-hall cutlery, and the resulting holes were covered with grey-painted bits of cardboard. Just as in the film, the gang left dummy heads in their beds to fool the guards. There was an ascent to a ventilation shaft on the roof, a slide down a drainpipe and – almost certainly – an escape by raft. After that, no more is known. So the film stops.

The three convicts were Frank Lee Morris (who had an IQ of 133) and the two Anglin brothers; their absence was not noticed until the roll call on the following morning. At dawn, on 13 June 1962, a woman saw three men rowing across the San Francisco bay, and a crude paddle was found in the water near Angel Island. The three are regarded as still at large.

Their escape led to the prison's closure and the relocation of its inmates to the maximum security penitentiary at Marion, Illinois. Alcatraz witnessed twenty-six attempted breakouts; the previous standard was set on 16 December 1937 by Ralph Roe and 'Sunny Boy' Cole, who certainly made it into the water, but probably not out of it.

Today, the prison is part of the entertainment industry. Parts of *Point Blank* were filmed there, as was *Escape from Alcatraz* itself. In 1992 three quarters of a million visitors made the trip across the bay for a guided tour. Only two of the thirteen buildings are safe to enter, and the top of the crumbling warden's house is likely to blow off with the next big wind.

Many trippers are struck by the contrast between the harshness of the prison itself and its stunning setting; the tantalising vision of San Francisco shimmers across the bay. On New Year's Eve the inmates could watch the shore fireworks from their five-by-seven cells and even hear snatches of the honking traffic drifting over the waters.

Alcatraz opened in 1934 for the incorrigibles of the American prison system, and for the first five years the regime operated under the 'silent system' discarded elsewhere in the nineteenth century. For the duration of their sentence, prisoners were not allowed to talk.

Escobar, Pablo Emilio (1949–)

Colombia's equivalent of Al Capone, a gangster who made his fortune by meeting the public's needs. Born on a small farm outside **Medellin**, Escobar started in petty crime by stealing gravestones and selling hot cars, and worked briefly as a triggerman for a small Mafia cocaine operation. By the mid-1970s he ran drugs on his own account, and the explosion in demand created the major drug 'cartels' – distribution and insurance services for third-party producers. In Escobar's words, 'You bribe someone here, you bribe someone there, and you pay a friendly banker to bring the money back.'

You also kill people. Alongside the pages of lawyers, accountants, and rural security divisons in Escobar's organisational chart are listed some forty urban extermination squads like *Los Nazis* and *Los Escorpiones*. Escobar opened recruiting offices in the slums so youths could work their way up, if they lived, from minor dirty work to prestigious assassinations at two million pesos each.

Escobar became the undisputed boss of his local trade association. Like the Mafia's governing Syndicate, Escobar's Medellin cocaine cartel regulated the various sub-groups of traders, each retaining their own business networks, their own objectives and their own army, and by the early 1980s Escobar and his friends were making their first millions. As a former girlfriend put it, 'They were peasant boys, adventurers, they were fun. They had lots of airplanes and helicopters and zoos.' The centre of Escobar's empire was the 7,000 acre Haçienda Nàpoles, and guests recall the contant racket of computer games, and the visiting Saudi

prince so proficient on jet-skis.

Escobar nurtured political ambitions, in 1982 gaining a Liberal seat in Congress. He believed that his backgound of poverty tailored him for the Presidency, and he channelled money into public works, building over 200 houses for the homeless and funding the unrivalled social welfare system of Envigado, his home town (see **Zoo**). But he lacked the finesse for non-violent negotiations and, after the patrician power-elite – the 'Men of Always' – forced him out of politics in 1983, he returned to running the cartel with a gun stuck in his belt, playing fast and loose, occasionally telling independent traders that their consignment was 'lost in transit', and deciding who should, and who should not, be killed. By the late 1980s, *Forbes* magazine put his wealth at $3 billion.

Escobar's downfall started in 1989, when a former ally, Luis Carlos Galán, ran for the presidency on a platform including the extradition of cocaine traffickers to the United States. Escobar's name headed the list, and Galan was assassinated. Galan's successor, Virgilio Barca, declared war on the *narcotraficantes*.

Escobar rallied the Medellin city-state behind the banner of non-extradition. Engaged on two fronts, he did battle with his rivals from the Cali cocaine cartel and the government, itself a fairly labyrinthine concept. Car bombings, assassinations, kidnappings, airliners destroyed mid-flight, bounties for dead policemen and helicopter gunship attacks followed in a round of shifting alliances as money changed hands. Army soldiers, on a monthly pittance of $20, were easily bribed, and Escobar's widespread intelligence network infiltrated men and radios into operations supposedly mounted against him. Throughout 1989 the Medellin cartel funded Escobar's campaign, and in 1990 he made the government a tempting offer. He would surrender – provided they shelved plans to deport drug dealers to Miami.

The idea of Escobar behind bars increased Colombia's standing with Washington. But his surrender package involved the construction of a lavish ranch (see **Cathedral**) for a prison. In a back-to-back deal, other cartel members paid him $100 million monthly as compensation for his loss of liberty, and in the autumn of 1990 the Colombian constitution was reworded to make extradition illegal, a deviation accepted by Washington in return for support in the UN for the Gulf War.

Escobar moved into his newly-completed retreat overlooking Medellin in June 1990, and left a year later when political realignments threatened real imprisonment. He remains a fugitive, and his hunters include 500 American troops and advisers. The Medellin cartel is divided, the Cali cartel are in the ascendant and a reward of $5 million dangles over his head. But, according to a friend, Escobar 'is still on top. He still thinks he will be president of Columbia.'

Escobar is a good family man with two children and a longstanding wife, Tata. The best clues to his personality, apart from the gravestones in Medellin's Campos de Paz, and Colombia's 1991 total of 28,284 homicides, come from the Cathedral's interior where bibles, shrines with candles, tiled portraits of the Virgin Mary and Barbie Barbecue Playsets jostle for space among videos of The **Godfather**, *Bullitt*, indifferent oil paintings, gold taps, books by Graham Greene and García Márquez and a photograph of Escobar dressed as a Chicago gangster. On the Colombian adage of 'Don't sleep on your own poison', he never indulged in cocaine or **crack**. But he savoured his press, often asking 'What are they saying about Reagan and me?' His real thrill was to fight, taking the war into the enemy's camp, and his primary motivation power. It was certainly not sex, although the two became confused. Asked to whom he would most like to make love, Escobar replied, 'Mrs Thatcher.'

Evidence

Cowed witnesses occasionally testify against all the odds to bring down a criminal empire. This takes courage. By 1935 'Lucky' Luciano was raking in $10 million a year from prostitution. Not surprisingly, the vice squad detectives found none of his 1,200 women prepared to take the stand, and Luciano bragged to newsmen that the investigation would never get anywhere; his girls were just 'gutless whores'.

Mildred Harris, 'Cokey Flo' Brown and the aptly named Nancy Presser took umbrage at this professional slur. They had the guts to testify in court and it took the Second World War to get Luciano out of jail. His sixty-two counts of prostitution earned

him a thirty-to-fifty year sentence, only curtailed by his much-disputed contribution to the cause when he arranged for partisan cover to the Allied landings on Sicily.

In Britain, the **Kray** twins were similarly laid low by a humble barmaid. Their trial's turning point came when she was asked to identify the man who had entered a London pub, The Blind Beggar, on the night of 8 March 1966 and put a bullet in George Cornell's head; while the killer remained at large, a whole area of east London stayed under gang law.

In the words of a detective, 'We knew that thirty or so people had seen what had happened, yet there was no one prepared to talk. The bar staff's version was that Cornell had been the only customer. The staff themselves had all been "out the back" when the shooting happened and hadn't seen a thing.'

For months the barmaid (known only as 'Miss X') held her tongue, terrified for her two children and frightened that she herself would be killed if she spoke.

When the trial started on 8 January 1969, she entered the witness box pale and drawn from a legacy of sleeplessness and nightmares; one observer, Professor Keith Simpson, feared she would pass out under the pressure.

Kenneth Jones, QC, took her through the evidence, finally asking: 'Did you see the man who shot Cornell?' There was a pause of several seconds. Then the barmaid raised her arm and pointed: 'It was No. 1 over there. Ronald Kray.'

'Have you any doubt?'

'No – oh no. That was him.'

Witnesses do not always stay the course. In Sicily, an early attempt to break the Wall of **Silence** put thirty *mafiosi* in the dock charged with a total of nine murders when a courageous widow, Rosa Messina, told all she knew to the local magistrates. She had lost her husband and two sons to a **vendetta**, and in 1963 this brave woman was hailed by the international press. On 19 September, amidst massive publicity, the court usher at the Assize Court in Palermo called her to the witness box.

But Rosa's nerve failed in the final hours; she was tracked down later that day, quaking with fear in her home village, adamant that even if the police dragged her to court she would utter not a word.

See also **Omerta**

Exactitude

When it came to hanging, **drawing** and quartering, getting the judicial words right mattered. In 1694 an execution was declared void because the sentence failed to specify that the victim's entrails were to be burned while he was still 'living'.

The case (*R* v. *Walcott*) did not lack interest. On appeal, the Crown contended unsuccessfully that the omitted words were not substantive, being merely 'in terrorem' (as a warning), and in any case constituted an impossibility since it was 'inconsistent in nature for a man to be living after his entrails were taken out', an objection overruled on the basis that the court had no discretion to vary the proscribed form of punishment. It was additionally noted that the celebrated Colonel Harrison (one of the regicides who signed the death warrant of King Charles I) had, after his disembowelment, 'strength enough left to strike the executioner'. The sentence was remitted, albeit posthumously, with the action brought by the deceased's son.

Execution Dock

The place at Wapping on the Thames where British pirates were hanged, led to their deaths by an official carrying a silver oar. A special set of gallows, erected for the occasion on the foreshore, stood at the exact point of the low-water mark. This was not just for the convenience of viewers in the boats moored midstream or for the huge crowds watching from the opposite bank. The siting underlined the Admiralty's jurisdiction over all crimes committed on the high seas and waterways up to the low-water mark.

Unlike those executed by the civil authorities on land, the bodies were not immediately cut down but were left to hang until three tides washed over them. One of many sentenced to this fate, Scotsman James Buchanon, was a well-regarded sailmaker who stabbed to death the fourth mate of the *Royal Guardian* on 16 October 1737 while his ship was berthed in the Canton River, China. Returned to England, Buchanon faced his hanging at Execution Dock with courage, leading the singing of the 23rd Psalm before confessing to the crowd that he was a Sabbath-breaker, swearer and drinker who deserved to die for the killing. Then the platform was kicked away from under his feet, whereupon some sixty seamen and friends stormed the scaffold, overthrew the officials, cut Buchanon down and jubilantly carried him away to Deptford. Despite a reward of £200, he was never seen again.

Executive action

What the CIA takes against trouble-makers. It kills them. One failed executive action, an attempt on Castro's life, used Marita Lorenz – a jealous lover – as the assassin. She was issued with poison capsules, which she stored in a jar of cold cream. But they melted.

Castro was long a recipient of American hate mail. One item was the guerrilla leader Che Guevara's severed hands and, with the cessation of the Cold War, a string of more mischievous CIA harassing schemes came to light. In May 1993 Agent Walt Elder described a plot to induce a drug into Castro's cigar to make his beard fall off, whereupon he would be swept from power on a wave of ridicule.

The CIA's other weird plans included 'Project Artichoke', a post-war experiment in brainwashing which continued into the 1960s, its objective to hypno-programme individuals into performing involuntary acts (like assassinations) of which they subsequently had no recollection. According to the project's Dr William Bryan Jnr, 'You can brainwash a person to do just about anything.' By the late 1960s hypno-programmed killers were ready to go.

But the only operation imputed to the Project was an 'own goal', the 1968 murder of Senator Robert F. **Kennedy** in a Los Angeles hotel, for which Dr Bryan (now deceased) allegedly claimed responsibility with his successful indoctrination of Sirhan Sirhan. Robert Kennedy's assassination is fertile ground for the conspiracy theorists: Sirhan's trial was blatantly stage managed by the Los Angeles Police Department. The ballistic evidence was inconsistent; inconvenient witnesses were intimidated, testimony suppressed, Officer Sharaga's report falsified, photographic evidence (2,410 pictures) destroyed and the coroner smeared.

Perhaps the LAPD wanted to force the case through before a miasma of conjecture clouded the issues. Alternatively, they may have covered up the fact that Sirhan was not a lone assassin but acted in concert with another couple, one of them probably the so-called 'polka-dot dress girl' seen in the Ambassador Hotel's lobby. The conspiracy scenario has Sirhan shooting at Kennedy and missing, hitting five bystanders instead. The accomplices shot at Kennedy and hit, killing him. This explains numerous discrepancies, like Sirhan's apparent feat of producing ten or perhaps twelve bullets out of an eight-bullet clip. It tallies with the autopsy finding that Kennedy died from shots fired from behind at a range of few inches; Sirhan opened fire from in front at a range of a couple of feet.

Sirhan was immediately apprehended, but an unknown couple escaped, observed by numerous witnesses, including a bystander, Sandy Serrano, who to this day goes in fear of her life. As for Sirhan, he cannot remember a thing about the attack, and CIA involvement looms large in subsequent police stonewalling.

See also **Hamilton**

Exhibits

Unusual exhibits materialised at the Old Bailey in 1915, when the three baths of George Joseph Smith appeared in evidence. The exact size, shape and angulation of these domestic novelties were described in great detail in the contemporary reports, supplemented by technical illustrations. During the trial Mr Justice Scrutton suggested to the jury that they try the baths out. 'When you examine these baths in your private room,' he said, 'you should put one of yourselves in. Get some one of you who is about the height of five feet nine.'

It was perhaps because of the general scarcity of baths that Smith – who drowned his wives – thought he could get away with murder. He remarked to a Miss Pegler, who unwisely expressed a desire in his hearing to take a dip: 'I should advise you to be careful of those things, as it is known that women often lose their lives through weak hearts and fainting in a **bath**.' Nowadays, no one would believe him.

Apparently Smith's persuasive powers were abetted by his eyes, said by his first bigamous wife to have a strange, hypnotic quality. 'He had an extraordinary power over women,' she recalled. 'This power lay in his eyes. When he looked at you for a minute or two you had the feeling you were being magnetised. They were little eyes that seemed to rob you of your will.' At the time of his trial, rumours abounded that Smith had employed hypnotic suggestion to make his wives remove their clothes and drown themselves.

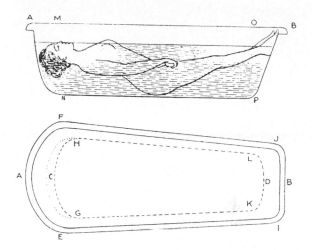

The occasional severed **ear** makes its way into court, and in 1893 a dead cat was put in evidence. During the **Crippen** case of 1910, the defence argued that the identifying scar supposedly found by the pathologist Bernard **Spilsbury** on a piece of the corpse's stomach was no more than a crease in some skin taken from a thigh. For the prosecution, Spilsbury enlivened proceedings by placing the disputed segment of flesh in a soup bowl, and handed it round to the judge and jury, pointing out the vestiges of the rectus muscle attached to the abdominal wall.

Eyes

In criminal folklore, a dead man's eyes retained an imprint of the last thing they saw. The superstition survived into the 1920s when – according to the traditional account – Englishman Frederick Browne shot Constable William **Gutteridge**. As the policeman lay groaning on the ground, Browne was disturbed by his continuing gaze. 'What are you looking at me like that for?' Browne asked, blowing out Gutteridge's eyes with two more shots. This grizzly detail made the killing front-page news throughout Europe.

For the forensic scientist the eyes can provide valuable information, including the rough time of death, and asphyxia produces hundreds of tiny haemorrhages in the eyes in response to the increase in blood pressure. In America, the diameter of the pupils is often recorded during the postmortem; **insulin** causes the pupils to dilate and morphine will make them contract.

Other famous eyes include 'Bugsy' Siegel's, which bounced across the room after being shot out. The man who made legal history by insisting on his own execution, Gary Gilmore, got his eyes on television to the background of a song called 'Gary Gilmore's Eyes', in reference to his expressed wish to donate his eyeballs to the community. The Russian serial killer **Chikatilo** inflicted vicious eye-wounds that almost became his hallmark. Investigators theorised that these mutilations signified a residual sense of shame as the killer tried to avoid his victims' gaze.

In 1937, eyes formed the highlight of a case from provincial France when the badly mutilated bodies of Madame Lancelin and her daughter were discovered lying on the first floor landing of their home in Le Mans. Blood was splashed round the walls to a height of seven feet; upstairs, two maids lay huddled naked in a single bed. The elder, Christiane Papin, made a meticulous confession: 'When Madame came back to the house, I informed her that the iron was broken again,' she said. 'When I saw Madame Lancelin

was going to jump on me, I leaped at her face and scratched out her eyes with my fingers.'

Then Christiane corrected herself: 'No, I made a mistake when I said that I leaped on Madame Lancelin. It was on Madamemoiselle Lancelin that I leaped and it was her eyes that I scratched out.'

She continued: 'Meanwhile, my sister Lea had jumped on Madame Lancelin and scratched her eyes out in the same way. After we had done this, they lay and crouched down on the floor. I then rushed down to the kitchen to fetch a hammer and a knife. With these two instruments, my sister and I

fell upon our two mistresses; we struck at the head with the knife, hacked at the bodies and legs and also struck with a pewter pot which was standing on a little table on the landing. We exchanged one instrument for another several times. By that I mean that I would pass the hammer over to my sister, so she could hit with it, while she handed me the knife, and we did the same with the pewter pot...'

At the trial, Christiane demonstrated how she had torn out the eyes with her fingers, tossing the first one down the stairs. During cross-examination, the magistrate asked: 'You knocked Madame Lancelin down with a blow from a pewter pot. As she cried out, your sister came running. What did you say to her?'

'Tear her eyes out,' Christiane replied promptly. Doctors, psychologists and lawyers were baffled. The girls – stolid peasant types – were not mad; they harboured no particular grudge against their employers, with whom they stayed for eleven years; there was no prior plan to kill them; conditions of service and pay were normal; their characters excellent. Nor had they espoused communism.

But they were servants, and this point was overlooked by contemporary commentators. Born and bred as menial skivvies, the Papin sisters spent their lives under the watchful eye of a mistress who checked the polished furniture for dust with a white glove and counted the sugar lumps to guard against theft.

The domestic iron that precipitated the killings had already broken down a few days previously, when Madame docked five francs from the girls' wages for its repair. On the afternoon of 2 February the iron shorted again, provoking the fatal outburst. At the trial, asked whether she 'loved' her employers, Lea appeared not to understand. 'We served them, and that's all,' she said. 'We never spoke to them.'

F

Facial reconstruction

Sometimes the only way of establishing a murder victim's identity is to reconstruct the face from the skull and then see if anyone recognises it.

At the turn of the century, Swiss research culminated in the publication of tables listing the average depth of the overlying soft tissues at twenty-six points on the human face. Today the world leader in this lumbering technology (described in the best-seller *Gorky Park*) is Russia, inspired by the work of anthropologist Professor Mikhail Gerasimov.

Following his acclaimed remodelling of the face of a Cro-Magnon woman unearthed before the Second World War in a Late Upper Palaeolithic grave, Gerasimov was approached by the Moscow head of Forensic Medicine. As a test, they collected a dozen heads, numbered and photographed them, stripped away their flesh and then sent them off to Gerasimov, who correctly and recognisably reconstructed the samples as four Russian men, one Russian woman, three Ukrainians, a Pole, a Chinaman, a Caucasian and a man of Baltic origin. Gerasimov went on to make some 140 models for criminal investigation.

Great excitement heralded the technique's first use in Britain during the early 1980s. The body of an unknown woman, dead for some sixteen years, came to light in a house in Bolton, and Detective Chief Inspector Fletcher resolved to attempt a reconstruction, coupled with extensive publicity, to put a name to her face. The make-up by Ruth Quinn of Granada Television aimed for historical veracity by simulating the mid-60s style with an unobtrusive blusher and a choice of six different wigs, and the bust was unveiled at a crowded press conference.

Only seven couples came forward; all had lived in the house where the body was found and, with nothing further to add, were eliminated from the enquiry. Two other leads surfaced, one from an elderly woman who could not identify the photographs for certain because she was blind, and the other from a confident old lady unable to share her information, as she had expired by the time detectives arrived.

In 1990 the police enjoyed greater success with another body. A skull unearthed after eight years in a Cardiff garden was rebuilt into a recognisable face by a medical artist from Manchester University, and police posters prompted two social workers to identify the face as that of Karen Price, a Welsh schoolgirl missing since the summer of 1981. From there, the police work proved easy; they soon had their man, Alan Charlton, but to satisfy the court that they had the right body was another matter. At the trial the prosecution relied on DNA fingerprinting, basing their analysis on a novel technique using samples of decayed **bone**.

Fagin

The model for **Dickens**'s Fagin is reputed to be the Jewish pickpocket and fence known as 'Ikey' (Isaac) Solomon, who operated in London during the 1820s.

In 1827 Ikey was finally convicted of theft. But our exits here are often entries elsewhere; Ikey soon materialised on the far side of the globe. Since the Black Maria that conveyed Ikey from the court to Newgate was driven by his father-in-law, he never reached the prison gates. His wife had just been transported to Australia with their four children, so Ikey set off to rejoin them on an elliptical journey via Denmark, the United States and Rio. On arrival in Tasmania as a free man and something of a criminal celebrity, Ikey invested his loot in a house and some land.

For the time being, he remained immune from prosecution. A warrant for his arrest could only be issued by the Colonial Office, which was in London and hence unaware of his presence in Australia. So he stayed at liberty until the papers could cross the sea and back again. Ikey used his months of grace to buy back his wife, putting up a bond of £1,000 to have her assigned to him as a servant.

In November 1829 Ikey's warrant arrived; he was returned to London for trial, but not before petitioning the Governor for work as an informer. Back in England, Ikey was sentenced to fourteen years transportation, so by Christmas 1831 he found himself in Hobart again. Reunited with his family under the ticket-of-leave system in 1835, he bickered with his wife incessantly. The pair separated in 1840 and he died ten years later, not a pauper, but poor, with an estate worth £70.

Fahmy, Madame (1891–1971)

British lawyers are rather patronising about the Gallic exemption of the '**crime passionel**'. Like the vanished concept of **Benefit of Clergy**, it makes laws pointless. But in 1923 the beautiful Madame Fahmy escaped scot-free after shooting her brute of a husband, 22-year-old Prince Ali, in their suite at London's Savoy Hotel. Her defence consisted of little more than the considerable eloquence of her counsel, Sir Edward Marshall Hall, in denouncing the millionaire Prince as a cad and a toad.

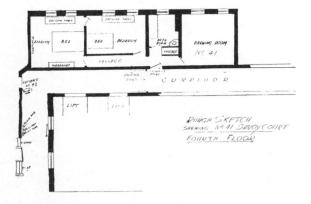

Hall denigrated Ali as 'a psychopath of revolting depravity, a homosexual and a sadist', and harped on about his 'filthy and perverted taste ... vile tempers ... and demands for unnatural sexual intercourse.' In those days, such epithets were easily earned by foreigners.

Not in dispute was Ali's great wealth. His annual income never fell below £40,000 and at the end of the war exceeded £100,000. Ali loved speed. In 1923 his stable of cars included one Mercedes, two Rolls Royces, a Buick, a Berlier, a Renault and a Peugeot, as well as a couple of run-abouts, several motorbikes and a fleet of speedboats. He drove through Cairo like Mr Toad. Then there were the jewels, the villas, palaces, footmen, tapestries, rugs, hashish, and of course his retinue of hangers-on.

Cartoon depicting Ali Fahmy (right), his secretary and his secretary's secretary: 'the Light, the Shadow of the Light, and the Shadow of the Shadow of the Light.'

Prince Ali first set eyes on Marguerite, ten years his senior, in July 1922. She had an extremely expensive lifestyle and a daughter to support; she needed someone with money. They married the following year, and within a week things started to go adrift. Marguerite's conversion to Islam was no more than skin-deep. She continued to entertain and dress décolleté like an emancipated Parisienne; he carried on like an Egyptian prince, insisting she drape a shawl over her shoulders. During the six months of their stormy marriage Marguerite endured scenes in the Hotel Majestic in Paris and, it seems, the most terrible privation on a Nile cruise ship. She wrote to her lawyer, very likely laying the groundwork for a lucrative divorce, with exaggerated reports of confinement: 'I have to bring you notice of very grave incidents. For the last three days, I have been a prisoner on board. I am absolutely unable to get out. Threats were made.'

By June 1923 there was a record of running around brandishing expensive pistols and late-night matrimonial fisticuffs. Then on 9 July, Ali put Marguerite on drip-feed for shopping, cabling Cartier and Vuitton to prevent delivery of two handbags valued at £4,027 the pair in a period when Britain's finest battleship, the *Queen Elizabeth*, cost about four million.

Marguerite had done well for herself financially. Starting her working life as a provincial prostitute, she evolved into a modish Parisian courtesan with the help of the kindly Madame Denart, a brothel keeper who shaped her protégé with instruction in dress sense, conversation, elocution and the piano. Marguerite married well at the age of 27, taking the young and wealthy Charles Laurent for a husband in 1919. After her divorce a year later she was well-off in her own right, and her marriage to Ali made her rich.

According to Marguerite, on the night of 10 July 1923 she fired a warning shot in her husband's general direction during a row. Then, thinking the gun empty, she put the .32 pistol to his face and squeezed the trigger twice more. He fell down dead.

She was taken to Holloway Prison in a taxi. But at the trial she was discharged, her defence contending (with tremendous theatrical panache) that she did not realise that the gun was an automatic. In the words of Marshall Hall: 'An inexperienced person might easily reload the weapon thinking that, in fact, he was emptying it.' That is, loosing off a single bullet to clear the chamber simply resulted in the weapon reloading itself. This was the line taken by Marguerite in the witness box. 'The cartridge having been fired,' she said tortuously, 'I thought the pistol was not dangerous.' In fact Marguerite knew enough about the weapon to cock it by pulling back the sliding breech cover. To fire off each round required the heavy finger-pressure of eight-and-a-half pounds – hardly the sort of gun that goes off by accident or feminine indecision.

After the verdict Marguerite left London for the Continent, hoping to assume control of Ali's estate, valued at £2.5 million. Unfortunately there was no will, although under the Muslim law of intestacy a male descendant's entitlement stood at somewhere between a quarter and a half of the inheritance. So Marguerite would be in the money – if she could produce a posthumous heir.

And she could, at least on paper. She paid a Dr Kamel £2,500 to sign a birth certificate for a phantom child. When the scheme was exposed, she became the laughing stock of Europe, and wisely departed for the watering hole of Carlsbad. There she earned a name as the 'Queen of the Bohemian Watering Places' and broke into films, in a minor way, playing an Egyptian wife. She died in Paris in 1971, at the age of eighty, without remarrying.

Her lawyer, Sir Edward Marshall Hall, possessed innate theatrical sense, in his closing speeches often addressing the hushed courtroom with his arms outstretched to symbolise the scales of justice, finally dropping into one hand the invisible presumption of innocence, like a golden nugget, to tip the scales in favour of the accused. His courtroom tactics included the use of a noisy throat spray during key points of his opponent's speeches, and in Marguerite's case he achieved marked results by entering into learned confabulations with his own expert witness during the prosecution's testimony, apparently in rebuttal but actually in discussion of the prospects for the shooting season.

Faithful, the

When a Mafia boss got 'hit' in the 1930s, his lieutenants had to burn too. In the words of Joe Valachi, *mafioso* turned informer: 'I asked Vito how come there had to be these killings, and he said that whenever a boss dies, all his faithful have to go with him, but he explained that it was all over now and we didn't have a thing to worry about.'

The elimination of influential opponents is a reasonable tactic, but it does not explain why, in the wake of Salvatore Maranzano's gangland murder in 1931, it was necessary to hammer an iron pipe up Sam Monaco's bottom before throwing him into the Passaic River, nor why Louis Russo's head had to be crushed after his throat was cut. The Mafia have always believed in brutality; when they drag a man across the floor, they do it by the testicles. The body of one unfortunate who crossed the *mafioso* Carmine Fatico (founder of New York's Bergin Hunt and Fish Club) was believed decapitated until, on autopsy, the police discovered his missing head smashed into the chest cavity.

The aftermath of a gangland coup was always tense while the victors decided who the faithful were; after the first few days, survivors on the losing side put out feelers from their hiding places to establish (without getting themselves shot) whether the new management would take them on the payroll.

See also **Contempt**

Fakes

Two of the most impressive written forgeries of modern times are the 'Hitler Diaries' and Clifford Irving's 'auto'-biography of Howard Hughes. Both share something in common with another famous impostor, the **Tichborne Claimant**, namely massive bulk.

In the Hitler case, the forgery was so amateurish it would scarcely deceive a child. Conrad Kujau was a German conman who earned his first prison sentence in 1963 for counterfeiting twenty-seven Marks worth of luncheon vouchers, and by the 70s he started dabbling in paintings of battle scenes and war **memorabilia**; he found their value rocketed if fake documentation was attached. For instance, he would certify that an old jacket had once been worn by the **Führer**.

Certificates were easy to run up with Letraset on modern paper aged with spilt tea, inscribed with a few words from 'Bormann' or 'Hess'; the public display of Nazi material was illegal and collectors did not check too carefully. Then one afternoon in 1978 Kujau sat down and copied out bits from *Hitler's Speeches and Proclamations* into a school notebook. When his pen ran out, he switched to pencil. On the cover he stuck some plastic initials, made in Hong Kong, which read AH. And there it was, a genuine fake Hitler diary. Actually, Kujau slipped up; the letters were 'FH'. But no matter, when he showed his work, an aged collector reverentially accepted it as the real thing.

Eventually word of the notebook's existence reached a gullible reporter, Gerd Heidemann, obsessed with the Nazis, and in January 1981 he dragooned *Stern* magazine into investing two million Marks in twenty-seven Hitler diaries. These did not exist, even as fakes, so Kujau churned out the first batch of three more notebooks in ten days, still sprinkling the pages with tea. At 85,000 Marks per volume, this represented good money, so Kujau kept on discovering more diaries. In the end, *Stern* parted with 9.3 million Marks for their scoop.

The scale of Kujau's work demanded belief. When the historian Hugh Trevor-Roper verified the diaries, he was so distracted by the quantity of bogus material that he neglected to assess its quality. Well versed in the period, Trevor-Roper knew little German and could not read the manuscripts' pages of archaic script. Had he understood the entries, he would have been appalled by their banality, little more than schoolboy material along the lines of 'Got up. Had breakfast.' But Trevor-Roper relied on appearances.

These were overwhelming. After much cloak-and-dagger business, including an oath of secrecy, in April 1983 Trevor-Roper was ushered into the presence of an entire Hitler archive in a private chamber of the Zurich Handelsbank: a stack of fifty-eight diaries, a boxful of paintings and drawings, letters, notes, memorabilia, and Hitler's First World War helmet, authenticated by Hess. All were fakes, but as the historian leafed through the material, which he could not understand, his doubts 'gradually dissolved'. Trevor-Roper reported in the *Sunday Times*: 'It is these other documents ... which convinced me of the authenticity of the diaries', later explaining that he was 'impressed by the sheer bulk of the diaries. Who, I asked myself, would forge sixty volumes when six would have served his purpose?'

The answer was anyone paid on piece-rate. Given the knack, documents can be forged endlessly. After his exposure for the Howard Hughes fiasco, Clifford Irving commented: 'Once you have the mood, you can go on for ever... I could write sixty volumes of Howard Hughes autobiography and they would pass. Once you can do one page, you can do twenty. Once you can do twenty, you can do a book.' Irving's forgery – described as 'beyond human ability' – sailed through layers of verification.

Apart from Trevor-Roper's historical vetting, the Hitler diaries were subjected to two other batteries of tests. One, the scientific examination of the physical constituents of the notebooks, speedily exposed the fraud, since the paper and bindings contained a chemical whitener discovered in 1955, the red threads on the seals were of polyester and viscose, and the ink of a type unavailable during the war. The chloride evaporation test showed that the diaries had been written within the last few years.

But this was established *after* the diaries started serialisation. Until then *Stern* relied only on journalistic hunches and the flawed reports of three hand-writing gurus, their task complicated by several factors. First, they were not informed that by approving a couple of letters, some of them photocopied, they would authenticate an entire set of the world's most important diaries. Second, one of the experts could not speak German, and the other was really an authority on the investigation of biological micro-traces.

But the fatal source of confusion arose when two of the three experts compared the new 'Hitler' extracts against old 'Hitler' material which included samples produced by the same forger: Conrad Kujau. So the writing matched.

It would be vexing if large-scale hoaxes became extinct. But this is unlikely. As the serialisation of the Hitler diaries loomed ever nearer, journalist Philip Knightley begged his employers at the *Sunday Times* to learn from past experience. Setting out in detail the lessons of the famous Mussolini forgery of 1968, which cost the paper £100,000, he warned: 'You cannot rely on expert authentication. Thomson engaged five experts, including the author of the standard work on Mussolini, the world's greatest authority on paper, a famous hand-writing expert, an internationally known palaeographer and an academic who authenticated the Casement Diaries. Not one expert said they were fake.'

His words were ignored. Not only can thorough investigation come up with the wrong answers; in a well-conducted fraud it is psychologically and practically impossible to make the checks at all. Throughout the Hitler scam, the buyers were convinced that the scoop would be ruined if anyone discovered their amazing secret. This is the heart of a good con – a deal so dazzling and so profitable that if one word ever leaks out the contract would be snapped up by a million outsiders.

Obsessive secrecy and obsessive urgency became the order of the day at *Stern*. When Kujau received a four-year sentence on 8 July 1985, the judge remarked that *Stern* had acted so recklessly that it was a virtual accomplice. The *Sunday Times* weathered a storm of derision, perhaps taking heart from the example of the *Boston Globe* nearly a century before.

Four months after the sensational **Borden** murders of August 1892, the *Globe*'s ace crime reporter

Henry Trickey managed to subvert the private detective – Edwin D. McHenry – who worked with the police on the case when it first broke. On 9 October 1892, for a mere $500, Trickey secured the prosecution's testimony in its entirety, including verbatim copies of their affidavits.

The following day the entire issue of the *Globe* was devoted to the scoop. 'Lizzie had a secret, Mrs Borden discovered it, then a Quarrel, Startling testimony of 25 new witnesses' ran the headlines. The edition sold out.

But the *Globe* had been duped. The witnesses were fictitious, their addresses did not exist, and the story devoid of any factual basis. The fraudulent McHenry disappeared, and on 2 December 1892 the journalist Trickey earned an indictment for interfering with the course of justice. A lesser paper might have gone under.

See also **Morals**, **Provenance**, **Ripperology**

Fallout, alcoholic

The effects of America's 'Prohibition' were shattering. By 1930, 550,000 citizens had been arrested for drink offences. Two hundred and thirty thousand served a total of 33,000 years in prison. Thirty-five thousand died of liquor poisoning, and countless more were crippled or blinded. Deaths from alcoholism increased sixfold. Two thousand gangsters and beer runners perished in the fighting, together with 500 **Prohibition agents**. In Chicago alone, the 'Feds' killed twenty-three innocent bystanders by mistake, sometimes with **dumdum** bullets.

Worse, the administration of justice degenerated into a farce, its erratic ferocity typified by such cases as the 1928 jailing for life of Fred Palm from Lansing, Michigan, for possession of a pint of gin. Police and local government became an extension of the underworld. By the time Franklin Roosevelt swept to power on one of history's simplest and most appealing slogans, 'A New Deal and a Pot of Beer for Everyone', the ghetto gangs of Italian and Sicilian immigrants had burgeoned into a criminal empire of confederate mafia families, based on booze, controlled by their governing Syndicate and intricately interwoven into the nation's social and commercial fabric.

It was only in the mid-1930s, after the FBI's headline successes as the nemesis of the Midwestern bank-robber gangs (see **Dillinger**), that **Hoover** turned his attention to organised crime. He established the Hoodlum Watch, declared Dutch Schultz 'Public Enemy Number One' and in 1936 roundly denounced racketeering as 'a problem which, if not solved, will eventually destroy the security of American industrial life and the faith of our people in American institutions'.

By 1937 Hoover was taking his men into the Mob's financial heartlands, personally leading raids in four states against brothels operated by Italian gangsters. In August he linked one of the arrested pimps to crime boss Lucky Luciano, and correctly identified 'the tide of dirty money that flowed from the houses to the racketeers and through them filtered out to local protectors, policemen, small-time politicians and even ultimately into the coffers of state political machines'. This was fighting talk. Luciano was the architect of the first 1929 **Mafia** convention, and Hoover's onslaught suggested the FBI meant business.

But he abruptly changed tack. In 1938 Hoover announced that the American criminal was 'not of a foreign country, but of American stock with a highly patriotic American name'. He retained and elaborated this fiction, with brief lapses, until the day he died. The mob flourished; the FBI stood idle. Thus in the 1940s FBI agent Pete Pitchess was contacted by Bugsy Seigel (see **Las Vegas**) who offered to rat on his criminal enemies as a 'deep-throat' informant, but Pitchess neither dared tell the Bureau about the contact nor, after it had taken place, dared file the information under 'Mafia', since it did not exist.

In the 1950s, Agent Neil Welch was driven to despair by wasted investigations confined to the theft of single truck-loads of chickens when it was obvious that the Teamsters Union were in cahoots with the Mafia, subjecting the entire national distribution network to illicit taxation. Two years after the 1951 Kefauver Commission (which detected 'a nationwide crime syndicate known as the Mafia'), the FBI's Assistant Director wrote, 'the Maffia [*sic*] is an alleged organisation... The organisation's existence in the U.S. is doubtful.' Organised crime, which took root during Prohibition and proliferated unchecked for half a century, was Hoover's most abiding legacy to America.

See also **Eighteenth Amendment**

False confessions

Not just concocted by the police. Often innocent outsiders can hardly wait to get in on the act; false confessions are one of the commonest causes of wrongful imprisonment.

Historically, the classic example is the **Campden Wonder**. Judith Ward provides a contemporary British case; and in July 1992 David McKenzie was dubbed a 'serial confessor' by his defence counsel after admitting to a dozen murders he could not have committed, including one that never happened.

A 1992 work, *The Psychology of Interrogation, Confessions and Testimony*, by the forensic scientist Dr Gisli Gudjonsson, identified three distinct psychological types prone to fabricate confessions. There are the depressives, animated by a sense of guilt and a general desire to be punished for something; the publicity seekers, and the fantasists, who cannot distinguish between illusion and reality. An impressive new subdivision of this category is furnished by the American phenomenon of 'recalled **memory**', where perhaps hundreds of thousands of citizens have, with the aid of their therapists, recalled a similar number of murders at satanic **ritual abuse** ceremonies, without producing a single body.

Covert admiration for **sex** criminals is reflected in the unusually high numbers of false confessions they attract. In America, the horrific 'Black Dahlia' killing of 15 January 1947 elicited twenty-eight confessors in the first few months; what with the victim, 22-year-old Elizabeth Short, being mutilated round the breasts, covered in cigarette burns, beaten about the head, slit along the torso, cut in half, exsanguinated and washed clean, mostly while alive, it was a very macho claim to make.

'Well, I'm *capable* of doing it,' John Andry told detectives after bragging for weeks in a Long Beach bar about carving up cadavers. One step further down the line, on 24 January the police received a pre-emptive false confession from a man walking off the street to surrender, saying 'I'm afraid I *might* kill a woman.' The eventual total of Black Dahlia confessors topped forty, embracing those unborn at the date of the murder and several women, Emily E. Carter among them, who entered the San Diego precinct yelling, 'Elizabeth Short stole my man, so I killed her and cut her up!'

Another telling indicator of the deep desire to confess is revealed in pathologist Professor Keith Simpson's autobiography. Simpson describes an unpublicised 1956 murder in Hertfordshire to which he was summoned post-haste by telephone. Three false confessions were logged before he had time to reach the police station.

In a separate category are the involuntary false confessors, those whose psychological weaknesses make them vulnerable to pressure. These are the suggestible: often compliant or anxious inadequates with low self-esteem, low intelligence and poor memory.

One of Britain's 'Birmingham Six', Hugh Callaghan, was a classic 'involuntary' case in a highly susceptible phase. At the time of his arrest, Callaghan was in the midst of a heavy drinking bout. Unemployed for three years, he was undergoing hospital treatment for depression and suffered from a duodenal ulcer. A night in the police cells without food or sleep, followed by abusive accusations from the heavies, proved sufficient to crack his resistance. Callaghan recalls: 'I was totally disorientated. I was physically weak. My hands were shaking. There were four or six guys coming at me, shouting at me. The pressure is so bad you'll do just anything to run away from it. I didn't read the statement when I signed it but I knew I had involved myself in the bombings.'

Judith Ward, convicted for the M62 bombing, broke in much the same way. First the police kept her awake for four nights. Then, she said, 'You get all these people screaming at you. So in the end you think: "Oh God! say what they want, get them off your back."' Another confessor, Pat Molloy, wrote to the **Court of Appeal** on 8 October 1980, detailing the similar circumstances surrounding his 1978 admissions: 'Detective Constable Perkins rushed back in again and struck me a severe blow in the stomach... I was disturbed by the uniformed staff every half hour banging on the hatch to wake me up. The meals I received were liberally doused with salt and I was not given anything to drink... In the morning I signed the confession out of revenge on the others and out of fear of more beatings and ill treatment.' Molloy is dead, but his statement secured life sentences for three associates in the Carl Bridgewater case.

See also **Ingram**, **West Midlands Serious Crime Squad**

Family, The

The genesis of Charles **Manson**'s 'Family' was described by the biker and gun-freak Danny DeCarlo. The story began in March 1967, with Manson just out of prison. He hung out on the steps of the Santher Gate entrance to the University of California, playing his guitar. Mary Brummer, 23, with a BA in history, was then an assistant librarian at the University. Unattractive, with a high-buttoned blouse and her nose in the air, she would pass Manson while exercising her poodle.

DeCarlo describes what happened next. 'So one thing led to another. He moved in with her. Then he comes across this other girl. "No, there will be no other girls moving in with me!" Mary says. She flatly refused to consider the idea. After the girl *had* moved in, two more came along. And Mary says, "I'll accept one other girl, but never three!" Four, five, all the way up to eighteen. This was in Frisco. Mary was the first.'

Susan Atkins, a Family stalwart, recorded her first impressions of Manson: 'I was sitting in the living-room, and a man walked in and he had a guitar, and all of a sudden he was surrounded by a group of girls.' Manson started to sing. 'I knew at the time that he was something I'd been looking for... and I went down and kissed his feet.' During their first sexual encounter a few days later, Manson suggested that she regard him as her father. 'I did so,' she noted, 'and it was a very pleasant experience.'

In 1968, the Year of Love, Manson decided to quit the increasingly bad vibes that spilled out as the Haight-Ashbury dream turned sour. He acquired a bus and loaded up his followers for a Magical Mystery Tour – just like the Beatles' album – and set off on the journey that ended in Death Valley at Spahn's movie ranch in the desert. Mary accompanied them, and bore Manson's child, a boy called Michael.

At Spahn's, the Family first took over the Jailhouse Barn, then colonised the outbuildings of the Long Branch Saloon and Rock City Cafe. At its maximum the Family numbered perhaps a hundred members, but the inner core was only twenty-five to thirty strong. Mostly teenage runaways, they were cut off from friends, parents and the framework of their previous life. No books sullied the commune's intellectual freedom and, since time was just a bourgeois convention, clocks were not allowed either. The word 'why' was banned. As Manson pointed out, in conformity with the prevailing orthodoxy of the period, 'Never ask why. Everything is good. Whatever you do is what you're supposed to do. You are following your own karma.'

At first the kids indulged in endless rounds of love-making and drugs and role-play in their desert commune. A rape victim later described her impressions: '20–25 people sitting, standing, lounging around in a living room; men, women, girls, boys and even little children; strobe lights going off and on; things hanging from the walls, everything psychedelic; some on the floor plunking on some types of musical instruments; and they were all drinking out of a dirty jug and smoking something.'

Manson made the Family dress up as pirates and had them slash away at boarders; next day, they would be cowboys fighting Indians, or Mexican knife-fighters, or devils. It was always them-against-us, even to the extent of outstaring snakes in the desert. Later the Family staged the world's first outdoor LSD crucifixion ceremony.

But the real gambit was sex. Manson had it seven times a day. Love-vans and mattresses were scattered round the site and, in the hidden gullies and remote woody areas, nudity was the order of dress. Sex 'deconstructed' the girls; they arrived with their middle-class morality intact and finished up in group orgies. Brooks Poston, a Family member, put it this way: 'One of Charlie's basic creeds is that all that girls are for is to fuck.' If a girl was plain, Manson convinced her she looked beautiful; if she wanted a father figure, he turned paternal; and if she needed a leader, he revealed he was Christ. Manson could sniff out an individual's weaknesses.

Manson sent out his sidekick Paul Watkins to collect more girls whenever he ran short, sometimes teenyboppers from Sunset Strip, sometimes hitch-hikers. Family orgies happened about once a week, starting with drugs. Manson would distribute supplies of 'grass', peyote and LSD. He orchestrated the whole event, beginning the dancing himself; then he stripped and led the naked Family behind him in a long snake while he beat out a rhythm on his drum. Next, they lay naked on the ground, rubbing themselves against each other, until...

Manson, the master of ceremonies, treated the intertwined couplings like plastic art, arranging the combinations into pleasing compositions. In Paul Watkins's words: 'He'd set it all up in a beautiful way like he was creating a masterpiece in sculpture.'

Manson made his disciples 'confront their fears'. Any disinclination or inhibition – whether against homosexuality, lesbianism, buggery or cunnilingus – became the task for the day. Manson initiated one 13-year-old who did not want to be sodomised while everyone watched by doing just that. The normal ratio stood at five girls to every man; Manson needed the women to lure in the men.

The last orgy happened on 22 July 1969, but by then the sex had tapered off. At the end of 1968 the Family's preoccupation shifted to bloodletting. Manson would intone 'You can't kill kill' and drone on about carnage. 'If you're willing to be killed, you should be willing to kill.' According to a neighbour from nearby Steele Ranch, 'They talked about killing all the time.'

In this deranged atmosphere Manson seized on the release of the Beatles' 'White Album' as a prophecy that he would conquer the world. The Family knew that the end of Western civilisation was nigh – after a fearful bloodbath. By the autumn of 1969 the final Armageddon of the Book of **Revelations** was expected daily. Teams scoured the desert for the 'bottomless pit', their hiding place for the duration. Other squads worked on building look-out posts and fortifications. Stolen beach buggies came pouring in with new recruits, some heavily armed.

By then Sharon Tate and the others were dead (see **White Album**). The final number of Manson's killings remains in doubt; he himself claimed thirty-three.

The gradual evolution of Manson's supposedly loving and peaceful commune into an armed camp follows a traditional and largely American pattern typified by the fate of the Bhagwhan's city of love built in Oregon in 1981, where distrust of the local population rapidly turned the encampment into an armed stockade. The Bhagwhan went everywhere escorted by guards, and the bitter factional jockeying for position spawned an electronic surveillance system to tap every telephone and every room. The network of spies needed control by an inner clique, one of whom tried to poison 900 of the inhabitants of a nearby town with salmonella in order to induce a fitting degree of respect. The Bhagwan's misadventure ended without loss of life after the FBI were called in amid allegations of financial fraud.

Few quests are more perilous than the pursuit of perfect love, particularly when sought through self-sacrifice and martyrdom. The cult of Jim Jones claimed the lives of 913 disciples in the jungle of Guyana in 1978, and David Koresh, the leader of the Branch Davidians and 'reincarnation' of Christ whose followers were immolated in Waco, Texas, during early 1993, is merely the most recent example.

Fantasising

Serial murderers fantasise on a scale way beyond ordinary daydreaming. The subject matter, too, is different. For the killer, protracted indulgence in sadistic fantasies plays a central emotional role as compensation for his imagined grievances. Mostly his visions are of blood. In the words of crime writer Colin Wilson, 'the basic psychological pattern of the sex criminal is a slow development through fantasy.'

Peter **Kürten** dreamed of weakening railway bridges and watching whole trainloads plunge to their deaths (see **Viaducts**). Or he brooded on individual acts of vileness: 'The long sentence I served when still quite young had a very bad effect on me. I did not masturbate. I got my climax of enjoyment when I imagined something horrible in my cell in the evenings. For instance, slitting up someone's stomach and how the public would be horrified. The thought of wounding was my particular lust.' Two other quotations from the FBI's database interviews echo the same mood: 'I was dreaming about wiping out the whole school' and 'I knew long before I started killing that I was going to be killing. The fantasies were too strong. They were going on far too long and were far too elaborate.'

At these potent levels, the fantasy is poised to erupt into real life. No take-over could be more damaging. The proper place for fantasies is in the head, and their attempted re-creation within the confines of ordinary life, warts and all, brings only contamination in its wake. Nor, for that matter, are fantasies greatly improved by the deadening hand of reality. The two realms are irreconcilably distinct and, during the public debate over the nuclear deterrent, it was argued that it was necessary to descend into a prophylactic hell of the imagination in order to *forestall* a descent in reality.

Ian **Brady**, the sex killer, staged in real life the type of motiveless murder depicted with such fluency in Dostoyevsky's *Crime and Punishment*. But once a fantasy has happened, it is reality, and its original fabulous aura, sullied by enactment, can only be reinstated by variation on repetition. Thus begins an uneasy commerce between the two realms, with the elaborated fantasies bringing only disappointment in their wake.

The serial killer Jeffrey **Dahmer** may have been beyond salvation by the time his sexual daydreams first focused on lying beside the body of another man, calm and still, perhaps even dead, whom he could explore at will. Had these visions remained fantasies, then *his* life alone would have been poisoned. But Dahmer was, as it were, already heavy with dreams, and no amount of **masturbation** could rub the images away. Bit by bit the ideas developed. Whose body would the stranger be? How could they meet?

Dahmer constructed a scenario in which he picked up a handsome, bare-chested man while cruising the highway – a self-evident fiction, since Dahmer had no car and rural Ohio had no hitch-hikers. But one day in June 1978 the dream happened in real life. As Dahmer drove home in his father's Ford, he saw young Steven Hicks from Illinois thumbing for a lift, standing by the roadside without a shirt. Dahmer picked him up, asked him back for a beer and, when he said he had to leave, killed him. Then, just as in his dreams, Dahmer masturbated over the dead body. So there was a waking dream, death in life.

At his trial, Dahmer's defence counsel laboured manfully to conjure up his dread of receiving disconcerting messages from the Other Side. 'How would you like at age fifteen to wake up and have fantasies about making love to dead bodies?' he asked the jury. 'What kind of person would wish that on another human being? Who do you tell it to? Do you tell it to your mother? To your best friend? None of us can possibly have gotten anywhere near to the fantasy level that this kid was at, at fourteen or fifteen years of age. I would not be Dahmer for one day.'

See also **Ng**, **Sex crimes, Zebra**

Fantasies

On 16 July 1973 a crazed teenager, Mary Ellen Jones, burst into a police station in Fort Lauderdale, Florida with a cock-and-bull story about her dead boyfriend. She spun a tale about accepting a lift from a man called 'Eric', who had driven them to his Miami home, forced the pair to strip at gunpoint and then taken photographs while they engaged in 'unnatural' sex acts.

Mary Ellen detailed how Eric had shot her boyfriend Mark Matson dead and then shackled her to a wall in a soundproofed torture-room festooned with whips, padlocks and chains. Eric then embarked on a twenty-four hour stint of rape. Finally he wearied, saying: 'I've taken a life, but now I'm going to give you your life.' So he had just taken Mary Ellen back to Fort Lauderdale, and here she was.

She was not believed. The police telephoned home, and discovered Mary Ellen's record as a runaway and a compulsive liar. Her mother wired them her fare, and they packed the young attention-seeker back to Kentucky.

The following Saturday, a young Fort Lauderdale boy had better luck when he pointed out to his mother that their neighbour had sat stock-still in his back yard for two days. She telephoned the police: 'I think there's a dead man in the garden next door.' On arrival the officers found the body of Albert Rust; he had poisoned himself with a glass of chocolate cyanide. In his bathroom, a freshly rendered wall behind the shower curtain wept blood.

There, embedded in concrete, the police found the dismembered body of Mark Matson. For the final entry in his diary, the 41-year-old Rust (probably a virgin until his bout with Mary Ellen) wrote in a mood of anti-climax: 'I see no good reason for going on. What would come next? The whole business is not worth it; life is not worth the trouble after all.'

One of John Wayne Gacy's surviving victims encountered a similar credibility gap. The youth related how he had been stopped by a policeman, handcuffed, taken to a house, sodomised, half-drowned in a bath, urinated on and then made to play Russian roulette with his abductor – who predicted, correctly, that the police would never believe his story.

It is often said that 50 per cent of all advertising works, but no one knows which 50 per cent, and it is a pity that truth is no easier to discern. Among current allegations receiving widespread credence are reports of satanic **ritual abuse**. During the late 1980s, America's Erika **Ingram** recalled an extended pattern of rape and extreme sexual violation, convincing the Thurston County Sheriff's Office to press charges against her father. She recounted, 'One time, my mom open my private area and put a piece of died baby inside me. I did remove it after she left, it was an arm [*sic*].' Erika's father made her 'perform sexual acts with animals including goats and dogs'. On another occasion, 'he urinated all over my body. He didn't defecate on me this time.'

Such recollections landed Erica on television on 2 December 1992, where she recalled satanic ceremonies attended by policemen, judges, doctors and lawyers. 'First, they would start with just, like, chanting,' Erika said. 'Sometimes they would kill a baby.' She mentioned having sex on an altar-like table, and described the ritual abortion performed on her child: 'The baby was still alive when they took it out. And they put it on top of me and then they cut it up. And then, when it was dead, the people in the group ate parts of it.'

Sadly, Erika's impressionable father believed her and in May 1989 pleaded guilty to six counts of rape. He is now serving twenty years.

See also **False confessions**

'Female Offender, The'

Title of an influential 1895 work by the criminologist Cesare Lombroso, who pioneered Social Darwinism by applying the doctrine of 'survival of the fittest' to people. Lombroso suspected that women destined to be murderers developed unusual strength, whereas whores followed their calling because they were particularly attractive.

Such views are difficult to reconcile with direct observation and, after years of studying pictures of female offenders, measuring their crania and quantifying their moles and tattoos, Lombroso seemed no nearer to proving his case. The unequivocal signs of degeneration, like misshapen skulls or thick black primate-like hair, were only apparent in a tiny minority of cases.

Eventually Lombroso realised that women offenders revealed fewer signs of degeneration because they were less highly evolved than men. Hence the female primitives were less conspicuous among their backward sisters. He contended that as women were naturally more law-abiding than men,

the rare female criminal was thus genetically male. This meant that women convicts suffered both through application of the law and social ostracism. In his words: 'As a double exception, the criminal woman is consequently a monster.'

The idea passed into the cultural mainstream of received wisdom. The FBI's director, Edgar **Hoover**, claimed: 'When a woman does turn profesional criminal she is a hundred times more dangerous than a man... acts with a cold brutality seldom found in a man.' To a New York Round Table audience Hoover went further, assuring them that a female criminal 'always has red hair... She either adopts a red wig or has her hair died red.' A case in point was flame-haired Katherine Kelly, wife of George 'Machine-Gun' Kelly, who served twenty-six years in prison for masterminding the 1933 Urschel kidnapping. But this was to put the cart before the horse. It emerged in 1970 that the FBI had suppressed the exonerating report of their own handwriting expert.

See also **G-Men, Sex discrimination**

Ferrers, Lord Laurence (1720–60)

The star of England's smartest execution. All the Earl's efforts to have his death sentence commuted to the socially acceptable fate of beheading failed; he had to settle for a fashionable **hanging**.

On 5 May 1760, Ferrers was duly taken to Tyburn, but not in the common cart. He was conveyed in his own carriage, drawn by six horses bedecked with black ribbons, and followed by mourning coaches packed with friends. His coachmen wept all the way to the gallows, a set custombuilt in the Earl's honour with a central flight of steps leading up to a silken noose beneath which, on a platform covered in black baize, reposed some plump cushions. These allowed the Earl to say his last prayers in comfort. Dressed for the occasion in his wedding suit of white satin, he processed to Tyburn accompanied by a splendid turnout from the Grenadier Guards, with the Life Guards bringing up the rear.

The scaffold incorporated a collapsible platform, precursor of the trap-door. But this innovation only represented a more dignified way of stepping off the gallows; the drop itself was still too short. The

Earl's dangling feet touched the ground, and it took him some four minutes to choke to death. The only other hitch came when the Earl handed a tip of £5 to the man he believed to be the hangman. He was not. A fight immediately broke out on the gallows, only broken up by intervention of the Sheriff.

Contemporary engravings show the scaffold ringed by a huge circle of mounted cavalry, with a mobile coffin, drawn by its six horses, waiting in the wings. The day's box-office receipts in the packed grandstand (Madame Proctor's Pews) totalled £500.

Ferrers was overdue for execution. A high-handed, hot-tempered aristocrat, he had a long record of violent assaults on family and domestics. He kicked his wife unconscious, stabbed a servant for impertinence and finally, on 18 January 1760, shot his steward Johnson for suspected embezzlement. It was for this crime that he met his end, condemned by his peers in the House of Lords, where a descendant still sits making speeches about the European Economic Community.

Fielding, Henry (1707–1754)

The English novelist and playwright who, after the introduction of official censorship, was reduced in 1748 to taking up work as a magistrate; he landed the job through a friend from Eton.

During his six-year tenure and with the aid of a £600 grant (only half of which he used), Fielding brought the first semblance of law and order to the streets of London. He urged victims of recent robberies to repair forthwith to his offices in Bow Street, whereupon a specially formed group of constables would set off, at a run, in pursuit of the culprit. Hence the 'Bow Street Runners', originally consisting of the only six of the eighty constables in Westminster not on the take.

Fielding himself was scrupulously honest, and strove to introduce the concept of justice into the administration of law (see **Cambo**). The *Covent Garden Journal* contains a report of 'another defendant, who appeared guilty of no crime but poverty, and had money given to her to enable her to follow her trade in the market'.

Fielding's Bow Street snatch-squads proved surprisingly effective, mostly because criminals, unused to the idea of pursuit, were apprehended in scores relaxing in their customary haunts. These arrests came as a shock, since previous attempts at deterrence consisted of the largely academic enactment of a savage penal code, with scant attention paid to its implementation by catching anyone. Fielding reinforced success by advertising, for instance proclaiming on 5 February 1750: 'Near forty highwaymen, street robbers, burglars, rogues, vagabonds and cheats have been committed within a week.'

Fielding's campaign marked the first 'criminalisation' of the criminal. Before, the thief was more of an accepted feature of society, endured if not necessarily admired; thereafter, a felon was expected to use guile and deceit to avoid detection. This new, furtive attitude stood in stark contrast to the traditional values typified by one eighteenth-century highwayman who, at his trial, explained why he had failed to avoid detection: 'Gentlemen do not resort to trickery.'

See also **Horse patrol**

Fifth Amendment

According to the FBI, 'taking the Fifth' was invented by the hoodlum Llewellyn Morris 'Murray' Humphreys (1899–1965), the heir to Capone who eventually rose to become America's Public Enemy Number One.

By 1930 Humphreys controlled some 70 per cent of the Chicago rackets, which produced a gross income of $80 million a year. Nearly thirty years later, Humphreys weighed in as the elder statesman of the Chicago Mob to negotiate the so-called 'Family Pact' with Agent Bill Roemer of the FBI.

The problem started with J. Edgar Hoover's belated 1957 recognition that organised crime existed. This led to the 'Top Hoodlum' programme, and the Mob reacted to the unfamiliar strain of police surveillance by harassing the wives of FBI agents. Roemer only took action when the *mafiosi* stepped up the pressure by shadowing his children on their way to school. He went direct to Humphreys and outlined a deal: you stay away from our families and we will stay away from yours.

The Family Pact remains in force, one aspect of a code which makes the police relatively comfortable when the Mafia are around. Everyone knows where he stands. Disorganised crime, typified by the **crack** trade, is a different ballgame.

Fingerprints, discovery of

Fingerprints are patterns formed by papillary ridges which facilitate the discharge of sweat through tiny raised ducts. As early as the 1820s Johann Purkinje, an anatomy professor, observed that every individual's fingerprints were unique. But this unprecedented opportunity for identification held an apparently insoluble problem. If each print was different, how could it be classified? Without categorisation, it would be impossible to find the single matching set in a filing system perhaps millions strong.

As early as 1858 the British magistrate William Herschel used fingerprints successfully in India to prevent illiterate government pensioners from claiming that the money they received last week had in fact been collected by someone else of similar appearance but fraudulent intentions the week before. The idea was not pursued; Herschel's enthusiastic letter to the Inspector-General of Bengal Prisons was politely ascribed to the wanderings of a fevered man weakened by dysentery. But two decades later, in 1880, an acerbic Scottish doctor, Henry Faulds (who afterwards cast himself as the only begetter of fingerprint identification), secured the discharge of a suspect in Tokyo whose prints did not match those found at the crime scene.

The quest was next taken up by Sir Francis Galton. Scheduled to lecture on *Bertillionage* in 1888, he became interested in fingerprints instead. Galton, a highly methodical type who once attempted to tabulate statistically the United Kingdom's distribution of female beauty, contacted Herschel and within three years confirmed that each individual's fingerprints really were unique, or – to be precise – the chances against two identical sets were 64 billion to one.

Ever up-to-the-minute, on 19 February 1939 the *News of the World* tried to boost circulation, venturing a prize of £1,000 for 'the reader who can reproduce a finger-print identical with any one reproduced at the top of this page'. There were no successful claimants. Forty years previously, Galton too was stymied on the problem of classification. Nonetheless he wrote a book called *Fingerprints* which passed into the hands of Edward Richard Henry, the Inspector-General of the Nepal Police. Henry had grappled with the intricacies of introducing bemused hill-tribes to **anthropometry** with all its paraphernalia of callipers and filing cabinets, and while on leave in England obtained access to Galton's material.

Henry made the conventional observation that each finger displayed the pattern of an arch, a loop or a whorl. Beyond that, and like many before him, he stared at his fingertips in vain. Then, on a railway journey in 1896, he made the breakthrough. Each fingerprint (with the exception of the simple arch) has a 'delta', a roughly triangular space around the central whorl formed by the lines running off to either side. Henry realised that the size of this area has an exact numerical quantity – its width in terms of the number of papillary lines.

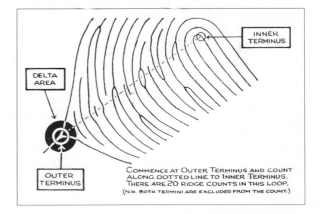

INNER TERMINUS

DELTA AREA

OUTER TERMINUS

COMMENCE AT OUTER TERMINUS AND COUNT ALONG DOTTED LINE TO INNER TERMINUS. THERE ARE 20 RIDGE COUNTS IN THIS LOOP. (N.B. BOTH TERMINI ARE EXCLUDED FROM THE COUNT.)

With the aid of a needle, these were easily counted and the prints then sub-classified according to whether they were whorls or one of the four basic types of arches and loops.

The following year, *Bertillionage* was scrapped throughout India and replaced by the fingerprint system, which soon gave Henry his first arrest. But the culprit, a servant named Charan who had cut the throat of a tea-plantation manager, was cleared of murder because the jury regarded the new-fangled evidence as inconclusive. Nonetheless, in May 1901 Henry was appointed Assistant Commissioner at Scotland Yard and founded the Central Fingerprint Branch in July 1902. That year, a total of 1,722 suspects were identified, more than achieved by *Bertillionage* since its inception.

America got off to a slower start. Its first centralised bureau was not established until 1923 when it took over the 800,000 prints from the Leavenworth files, and even this undertaking was crippled by lack of funds for a further year.

Throughout the 1920s American juries remained suspicious of the novel evidence, which was, like so much else, vaguely unconstitutional. The routine fingerprinting of American offenders did not become legal until 1928 and, as the implications sank home, this led to a spate of largely abortive fingerprint **removal**. Today the FBI's library of over 200 million prints handles 30,000 enquiries each day.

Firefights

Careful ballistic work based on pure deductive logic can reconstruct the precise pattern of firefights.

On 4 December 1969 the Cook County Attorney, Edward V. Hanrahan, announced that the Chicago police had been involved in a fierce gun battle with diehard elements of the Black Panthers. Hanrahan described how, following a tip-off, the police arrived at a house in West Monroe Street to search for arms only to be met by a hail of bullets. The gang refused to surrender despite repeated entreaties, and by the time the shooting stopped the building was riddled with some eighty bullet holes. Two Black Panthers lay dead and four were wounded, but providentially the police suffered no casualties. The seven surviving gang members were charged with attempted murder.

At the Panthers' trial, Herbert Leon McDonnell – the defence ballistics expert – reconstructed the precise course of the gun battle. The direction (ingoing/outgoing) of each shot, its flight path and the main firing sequences of the battle were plotted on a scale-drawing of the apartment. McDonnell showed that the first shot had been fired through the apartment door by the police when it was partially open, and the second in response by the Black Panthers when the door was wide open. Thereafter, every single bullet came from the police. The police had decided to kill some Black Panthers, burst into the house unannounced and started firing. Not surprisingly, the Panthers felt their civil rights had been violated and thirteen years later, in 1982, won $1.85 million in damages from Cook County.

The seminal British ballistics case was the 1927 murder of William Walker, a gamekeeper. Towards midnight on 27 October, Walker (together with his underkeeper George Rawlings) caught the local poacher red-handed in a wood near Bath, Whistling Copse. Shots were exchanged in the moonlight. When the smoke cleared Walker lay dead and Enoch Dix, the poacher, was arrested with a peppering of buckshot down his back.

Dix protested his innocence. With one of the three protagonists dead it was simply his word against the under-keeper's. Or so he thought. He said he had only opened fire by accident as he reeled away under the impact of hits from both barrels of Rawlings's shotgun. But examination of the crime scene showed that most of the pellets fired at Dix were still embedded in the tree trunk by which he had been standing. From the spread of shot in the tree and Dix, it was clear that Rawlings had fired from a range of fifteen yards; to prove the point, firearms expert Robert Churchill banged away with Rawlings's gun at a series of white-washed metal plates, providing the court with a precise computation showing the spread of shot at different ranges.

By contrast, Walker's corpse showed that his fatal wound was inflicted from a range of five yards or less. He had died of a single, closely defined gash to the throat five inches in diameter; the pellets had no time to spread. In other words, the poacher had fired from a range of five yards and been fired at from a range of fifteen. Of course, the gamekeeper could have pulled the trigger first while Dix ran towards him, but since Dix's wounds were to his rear, this entailed charging forward, backwards. The poacher was sentenced to fifteen years.

See also **Hamilton**

Fish, A. H. (1870–1936)

A nauseating American serial murderer still hard at it in his sixties. A father of six, Fish was brought to justice in 1934 by the almost single-handed efforts of Detective Will King of the New York Police.

The murder that brought him down was the June 1928 killing of 10-year-old Grace Budd. Fish got away with the crime itself, but six years later he wrote to Grace's mother describing how he had cut her child's little body into pieces and then eaten it. From a parent's point of view, the missive must mark an all-time nadir. It reads in part, 'Grace sat in my lap and kissed me. I made up my mind to eat her... How she did kick, bite and scratch! I choked her to death, then cut her in small pieces so

I could take my meat to my rooms, cook it and eat it... How sweet and tender her little ass was, roasted in the oven. It took me nine days to eat her entire body. I did not fuck her tho I could of [*sic*] had I wished. She died a virgin.' Fish cut Grace's flesh into strips which he cooked with 'carrots and onions and strips of bacon'; this excited him sexually.

With the aid of a spectroscope, an otherwise invisible mark on Fish's envelope led Detective Will King – who had kept the case alive all these years – to the New York Chauffeurs' Benevolent Association, where a driver, Lee Siscoski, admitted to stealing office stationery, some of which he had left in a doss-house at 200 East 52nd Street. There the detective found a signature in the register corresponding to the handwriting on Mrs Budd's letter. King rented a room at the top of the stairs and waited for three weeks before he got his man, who surrendered submissively and then tried to razor his captor.

According to the psychiatrist Frederick Wertham, Fish looked every inch 'a meek and innocuous little old man, gentle and benevolent, friendly and polite. If you wanted someone to entrust your child to, he would be the one you would choose.'

This was exactly how he snared Grace. Her father, a doorman in straightened circumstances, advertised for work in the *New York World Telegram*, and on 28 May 1928 a well-dressed elderly gentleman arrived at the family's basement flat in the Chelsea district of Manhattan with an offer of employment at $15 a week. He gave his name as 'Frank Howard' and returned a week later to firm up the details. This time Howard and the Budds had lunch together; he produced a sizeable bankroll, peeled off some bills to send the elder children to the cinema and then volunteered to escort Grace to a children's party given by his sister. Instead, he took her to Wisteria Lodge, an unoccupied house in Greenburgh, choked her, removed her head and then sawed the body in half before carrying the portions home to eat. Wertham related how Fish's account of the culinary process was 'like a housewife describing her favourite methods of cooking. You had to remind yourself that this was a little girl he was talking about.'

A good half of Fish's psyche was resolutely genial. He delighted in his 12-year-old grandson, said, 'I love children and was always soft-hearted',

and often read the Bible. But God told him to kill, and his lodgings contained a suitcase packed with press cuttings on another source of inspiration, Fritz Haarmann, the cannibalistic murderer of Hamburg who turned boys into **sausages**. Dr Wertham adjudged Fish mad, but his subject dissented: 'I am not insane, I am just queer.'

Fish confessed to many child murders, sometimes fifteen, sometimes 400, between 1910 and 1934; the true total is anyone's guess since his idea of a good time was highly individual. X-rays revealed a plethora of rusted needles in his testicles. He would thrust them in through his scrotum just for kicks,

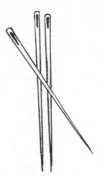

and he revelled in eating human excrement and setting light to alcohol-soaked cotton wool stuffed into his victims' – or even his own – anus.

Fish also experimented with poking needles into the soft flesh under his fingernails. But it hurt too much. 'If only pain were not so painful,' he complained. To the press he said, 'Going to the electric chair will be the supreme thrill of my life', and this was no mere bravado. Dr Wertham, appealing for clemency, noted, 'This man is not only incurable and unreformable, but unpunishable. In his own distorted mind he is looking forward to the electric chair as the final experience of supreme pain.' He received double value; on 16 January 1936 the first electrical charge failed, supposedly shorting on his intra-testicular stock of twenty-nine needles.

Fish's last words were, 'I don't know why I'm here.' The jury were similarly confused. A majority had concluded that he was legally insane, but they still thought he should die.

See also **Cannibalism, Sacher-Masoch**

Flowers

Chicago mobsters said it with flowers. As early as 1924 the passage of Capone's brother Frank to the Great Beyond was soothed by $20,000 worth of flowers. The tradition grew: in 1927 Vincent 'the Schemer' Drucci went to his last resting place preceded by twelve cars piled high with flowers, wreaths, bouquets, flower Bibles and set-piece tributes including a vacant chair of white and purple blossoms bearing the inscription: 'Our pal'.

But it was the Irish gangleader Dion **O'Bannion** who put floral tributes squarely on the map. A keen killer and lover of flowers, in 1922 O'Bannion bought a half-share in William E. Schofield's florists opposite Chicago's cathedral and there the gangleader whiled away shop-opening hours amidst the lilies and terracotta vases.

O'Bannion supplied many of the flowers for Mike Merlo, who died on 3 November 1924 from natural causes – almost unprecedented for a President of the Unione Siciliana. A $100,000 cascade of wreaths and orchids descended on Merlo's home, overflowing into the garden to carpet the winter lawn with blooms. Capone sent an $8,000 order; even Merlo's wax effigy, exhibited in the open tourer leading the cortege, was bedecked with flowers.

After he had been shot six times on 10 November while making up one of Merlo's wreaths, it was O'Bannion's turn for a fine send-off. He all but received a state funeral, lying on display in his silver and bronze glass-topped coffin for three days while 40,000 shuffled past to pay their respects in Sbarbaro's Funeral Parlour. According to the *Chicago Tribune's* funeral correspondent: 'Silver angels stood at the feet with their heads bowed in the light of ten candles that burned in solid golden candlesticks they held in their hands. Beneath the casket, on the marble slab that supports its glory, is the inscription "Suffer the little children to come unto me." And over it all, the perfume of flowers. Vying with the perfume was that of beautifully dressed women of gangland, wrapped in costly furs.'

Twenty-six lorry-loads of flowers followed O'Bannion to his grave at the Mount Carmel Cemetery. Showpieces included a seven-feet-high arrangement in the shape of a heart woven from American Beauty roses, a massive wreath from the Teamster's Union, a duvet of orchids to cover the grave, and a basket of roses labelled 'From Al', sus-

Digitalis purpurea. *In 1775 Dr Withering discovered that two grammes of its dried leaf extract will kill.*

pected of masterminding the hit. Mounted law officers cleared a path through the crowd of 20,000 lining the streets, and the mile-long procession was led by three bands and a police escort. Five municipal judges were among the mourners; the warring gangster chiefs – Torrio, Capone, Moran, Weiss and Drucci – faced each other over the grave. The only flaw came from the Archdiocese's refusal to allow burial on consecrated ground, but even in death O'Bannion coasted round these moral strictures. Within five months he was re-interred next to Archbishops Feehan and Quigley.

The first of the great gangster funerals was accorded to Big Jim Colosimo, underworld boss of Chicago from 1910 to 1920. In his youth, Big Jim laboured as a terrorist, pickpocket and pimp; in maturer years he became Diamond Jim, the Czar of Prostitution with a 'stable' of thirty-five $1 and $2 houses and two rather plusher establishments. When Johnny Torrio had him shot through the head, Colosimo's obsequies were graced by 5,000 mourners. His honorary pallbearers numbered eight Chicago aldermen, three judges, two Congressmen and a State Representative. Hymns were sung by the Apollo Quartet.

In Sicily, the *capo-mafia* Cesare Manzella received an unusual send-off after being blown up in April 1963. All that remained was his hat and one shoe, placed in the coffin alongside a dummy wearing his suit.

Footprints

True footprint evidence is rare in British criminal cases, since most people wear shoes; for the opposite reason, it is fairly common in places like Africa and India.

As with the fingers, the ridges on the soles of the feet are unique to each individual. So when Stephen Tomkinson of Bristol removed all his clothes apart from a pair of goalkeeping gloves prior to a rape, he provided investigators with two clues. They were not just looking for a goalkeeper; they wanted a goalkeeper with corresponding footprints. On 13 April 1992 Tomkinson was sent down for fourteen years on the evidence of a **fingerprint** expert seconded for the occasion.

Until now, the fact that no comparison between the culprit and his footwear was practicable until he and it are caught, vitiated the prospects for foot- and shoeprint evidence. But the April 1992 edition of the *Journal of the Forensic Science Society* outlined a device called a pedobarograph which, by encoding images into a computer, showed the pressure patterns on a shoe during a complete step. This allowed assessment of an individual's gait and build from his tread pattern.

In 1946, the body of Dorothy Eggars, recovered from California's San Bernardino Mountains without a head or hands, was identified by the chiropodist who treated her bunions.

Franz Ferdinand, Archduke (d. 1914)

Interspersed in the crowd lining the streets of the Bosnian town of Sarajevo on 28 June 1914 were seven conspirators lying in wait for Archduke Franz Ferdinand, heir to Franz Joseph, ruler of the Habsburg monarchy. Resplendent in full-dress uniform topped by plumed headgear, the Archduke motored slowly through the town in an open tourer.

Five of the assassins jibbed at the last moment. One failed to recognise the Archduke, the next felt sorry for his wife, the third was unprepared for the complexities of a moving target, and a fourth fell prey to the delusion that he was standing next to a policeman. Meanwhile their target progressed unharmed through a regular avenue of assassins.

The least reliable of the group, Cabrinovic, proved the most enterprising. He asked a constable: 'Which is His Majesty's car?' and then whipped off the detonator and lobbed the bomb into the designated vehicle. The detonator cap struck the Archduke's wife, bruising her neck. The bomb itself rolled off the folded hood into the street where it exploded under the car behind and made a hole in the paving, injuring a dozen bystanders. Dismayed, the conspirators scattered; a testy Archduke drove on to the Town Hall where he complained: 'I come

here on a friendly visit and someone throws a bomb at me.'

The Archduke's humour was quickly restored; he agreed to go to the local hospital to visit the morning's wounded. But since his driver was not informed of the change in plan, the Archduke's car took a wrong turning and then backed slowly past a corner delicatessen where, as it happened, the sixth assassin, Gavrilo Princip, sat despondently, contemplating suicide.

Two years earlier, Princip's attempt to join the Serbian guerrillas had been thwarted by his puny physique. Now, hardly able to believe his good fortune, Princip drew his pistol and shot both the Archduke and his wife. She died instantly. Mortally wounded, the Archduke turned and said: 'Sophie, live for the children.' Then he whispered, 'It is nothing.' Then he died.

Princip and twenty-three other youthful conspirators were rewarded with lengthy jail sentences. Princip himself survived in prison until dying of tuberculosis in 1918. He fared better than millions of others, indirectly killed by the choreography of Ruritanian alliances that led from the Sarajevo assassination to the First World War, the bloodiest conflict the world had ever seen.

After the war, King Zog of Albania proved altogether more fortunate. While Zog was opening Parliament in Tirana, a young assassin rose to his feet from a few benches back and levelled a pistol. The youth had his monarch cold and, in accordance with the blood-feud formalities of the Balkan tradition, embarked on the ritual formula of denunciation before pulling the trigger. But the killer suffered from a very bad stutter and was disarmed.

French Connection, The

Not just a film. The French Connection peaked in 1971 when it delivered about ten tons of heroin to the USA – a strong recovery from the parlous state of the American drugs trade immediately after the Second World War, when the interdiction on shipping, coupled with the prevalence of serious border problems, whittled down the number of heroin addicts to an estimated 20,000.

In the post-war era the Corsicans in France and the Mafia in Sicily retained strong connections with Indochina through the French colonial presence.

Opium collected from the hill tribes of Southeast Asia was transported to Saigon for processing into morphine before shipment to Marseilles. There, refined into heroin, it was smuggled to the United States in an enterprise undertaken with the connivance of De Gaulle, by way of retaliation for the American failure to rally to the relief of Diem Bien Phu in 1954. Or so the gossip runs. In the words of Agent Thomas C. Tripodi of the Drug Enforcement Agency: 'De Gaulle had to know about it. And he obviously permitted it because he could have stopped it if he wanted to.'

The American crackdown of 1972 ended the French Connection. Among the principals, Sarti was dead, and Ricord, Nocoli, David, Pastou, Catania and Buscetta languished in jail. But nature abhors a vacuum. In one way, the successor to the French Connection was the Sicilian – or '**Pizza**' – Connection; in the other direction, far more important, the Chinese Connection through the **Triads**.

See also **X, Operation**

Führer, The (1889–1945)

Adolf Hitler was one of history's greatest war criminals. In addition he may have murdered a young girl in 1931.

At the least, the circumstances invite suspicion. On 19 September 1931 Hitler's half-niece, the attractive 23-year-old Geli Raubal, was found dead in her bedroom in the Munich apartment she shared with Hitler, shot through the chest by a bullet from Hitler's 6.35mm Walther pistol. On her desk lay a letter, broken off midway through a word, with the final 'd' of the *und* omitted. 'When I come to Vienna,' Geli was writing, 'hopefully very soon – we'll drive together to Semmering an...' There the letter ends.

Earlier that day, at lunch, Hitler and Geli had quarrelled violently over whether she could leave for Vienna. Only the previous week, she tried to escape from her claustrophobic life in Hitler's flat, reaching his cottage in Berchtesgaden before receiving orders to return.

Now Geli was dead and, whether it was murder or suicide, a corpse in Hitler's apartment constituted an embarrassment to his meteoric political career. Despite the damage limitation by Hitler's advisors, the periodical *Die Fanfare* ran the headline: 'Hitler's lover commits suicide: bachelors and homosexuals as leaders of the party.'

Long before then, over the weekend, Geli's corpse was spirited down the block's back stairs for a cursory medical examination. Then the sympathetic police hastily announced that Geli had taken her own life. The Bavarian Minister of Justice (already in Hitler's pocket and subsequently well promoted) put an end to any further investigation and the body was shipped to Vienna. There Geli was unaccountably buried on hallowed ground, a right normally denied to suicides.

Meanwhile a distraught Hitler went to earth at an isolated lakeside cottage on the Tegernesse where, in one version, Rudolf Hess snatched a gun out of his hand to prevent suicide. Scandal sheets printed rumours that Hitler had killed Geli; the *Münchner Post* said that 'the nose bone of the deceased was shattered and the corpse evidenced other serious injuries'.

But with the body buried, no police inquiries, and no coroner's report, the story lacked staying power. The only man to pursue it was journalist Fritz Gerlich who, eighteen months later, was ready to reveal the truth in his paper, *Der Gerade Weg*. In March 1933, before he could publish, a squad of fifty stormtroopers burst into his newspaper office, smashed his face, burned his files and bundled him off to Dachau. A month later one of Gerlich's main sources, George Bell, was murdered. Gerlich himself perished during the Night of the Long Knives. But he reportedly smuggled out documentary proof that Hitler had ordered Geli's death; the recipient, Karl von Guttenberg, lodged this dangerous material in a numbered Swiss bank account and then took his secret to the grave as a participant in the July 1944 coup against Hitler.

Who killed Geli? At the heart of her fate is her relationship with 'Uncle Alfie'. It started shortly after his nine-month prison sentence in 1923 when Hitler summoned the 17-year-old Geli and her mother to Munich to act as live-in housekeepers. By 1925 Geli had blossomed: tall, vibrant, a golden girl who turned heads in the street. Hitler squired Geli around town, went riding with her, paid for her music lessons, mooned over her at the opera and, according to Fest (a party leader from Württemberg), turned in 'a very plausible imitation of adolescent infatuation'.

Of the seven women with whom Hitler had intimate relations, six committed suicide or seriously attempted it. Before her death in the Bunker in 1945, Eva Braun tried to take her own life in 1932 and 1935. Actress Renaté Mueller, later found dead beneath her Berlin hotel window, confided in her director that on her date with Hitler he 'fell on the floor and begged her to kick him... condemned himself as unworthy... and just grovelled in an agonising manner... She finally acceded to his wishes. As she continued to kick him he became more and more excited.'

Heiden, a respected writer on Hitler, calls the future Führer 'a man with masochistic–coprophil inclinations, bordering on what Havelock-Ellis calls undinism'. Geli confided in Otto Strasser, a one-time Nazi insider, on the way back from a Mardi Gras ball in 1931. Strasser recalls: 'Hitler made her undress while he would lie down on the floor. Then she would have to squat down over his face where he could examine her at close range, and this made him very excited. When the excitement reached its peak, he demanded that she urinate on him and

that gave him his sexual pleasure.'

It is possible that Geli, trapped in a gilded cage with only Hitler for social and sexual recreation, took her own life. But her last, interrupted letter is the opposite of a suicide note; the girl is looking forward to life. But Geli constituted a serious threat to the future Führer. Two years before, in 1929, Hitler wrote her an explicit and degrading love letter which fell into the hands of his landlady's son. Hitler's fixers managed to buy the missive back. But it was clear that any future revelations by Geli could unleash deeply damaging press smears.

Perhaps Geli was carrying Hitler's child, and killed herself out of grief; for Hitler was just beginning to show an interest in Eva Braun. But if Geli was with child, it is most likely she had spurned Hitler's advances in favour of another admirer, either her suitor in Vienna or an art teacher from Linz, both Jews. Such an alliance would not have gone down well with the leader of the Master Race.

Perhaps Geli Raubal shot herself. Perhaps she was made to shoot herself. Perhaps she was shot on Hitler's orders. Perhaps Hitler shot her. No one knows, and unless her body is exhumed from its zinc coffin in the featureless pauper's burial ground outside Vienna, it is unlikely that they ever will.

G

Galvanic research

The scientific hocus-pocus of the *Frankenstein* films once comprised mainstream medical research. On 13 January 1803 the corpse of George Forster, an English murderer, was subjected to an electrical experiment in order to restore him to life. Professor Alkini wired up the cadaver, made a connection and induced the dead Forster to grind his jaw and open one eye. Under further electronic encouragement, the body clenched its right hand and waved its legs around, with the *Criminal Recorder* remarking that this 'showed the eminent and superior powers of Galvanism to be far beyond any stimulant in nature', although Mr Pass, the beadle of the Surgeons' Company who observed the process, died of fright.

More recently, Charles Manson believed in the existence of the Bottomless Pit, and, in the hope of locating the source of evil, today's galvanic researchers evince a fetish for the brains of serial killers. Leonard Lake's (see **Ng**) has been preserved for posthumous study, and the Russian authorities say that **Chikatilo** will be shot with particular care to avoid damaging his cerebella, for which several psychiatric institutes are in open competition. As Chikatilo says, 'There are two parts to my brain. Part of it says kill and the other part says do not', so it should be relatively straightforward to see which is which.

Gangs

A non-word among the Los Angeles street gangs. 'We'd rather be considered a community inside a community, you know?' said Bone, an Athens Park Blood aged a miraculous twenty-seven. 'But the word "gang" puts a stigma on our love. And it's all about love.' This is partly true; the gangs confer a sense of belonging, a family and – perversely – vestigial security.

The main warring factions are the Bloods and the Crips, distinguished by their respective house colours of red and blue. In addition to shooting each other, they shoot themselves; perhaps the biggest of the Crips's internecine feuds was the War of the Stolen Leather Coat, claiming some thirty lives – a toll that stands comparison with major Mafia bloodlettings over multi-million dollar rackets. In the chilling words of a probation officer, 'By the time they're seventeen, they've done their drive-bys.' Many houses round the South Central district have ramps going up the steps, not because of the high percentage of aged occupants but because so many are paraplegics disabled by the fighting.

An escalation in the bloodletting accompanied the introduction of **crack** in the late 1980s, when disputes abruptly ceased to concern territory and centred on money, corroding traditional restraints on violence. The new wars were fought with assault weapons like the high-velocity Kalashnikov AK-47s, which blasted through not just the target house but the ten houses behind. The gangs themselves never made significant money out of dealing; profits stayed higher up, with the Cubans and Colombians.

After twenty years of fighting, in 1992 the Bloods and the Crips declared a truce. The gangs bonded during the Los Angeles riots against a common enemy, the police.

The expression 'plug uglies' is derived from plug hats, or top hats, and the Plug Uglies were an early New York street gang. Their rivals included the Dead Rabbits and the Shirt Tails, and in Britain of the late eighteenth-century it was worth giving a wide berth to 'Macaronis'. A vicious gang of criminal yobs, fond of gambling, drinking, duelling, their direct antecedents were the founders of the Macaroni Club, reserved for young men of fashion who travelled in Italy, on their return daringly introducing pasta to Almack's assembly rooms off St James's. Their criminal namesakes regarded themselves as above the law. Historian Christopher Hibbert cites the case of young Plunket who, exasperated by his wig-maker's refusal to knock more than a guinea off his bill, razored the tradesman's throat from ear to ear.

The word 'hoodlum' is an American creation, coined in San Francisco during the 1870s. Cutthroat gangs formed a scrummage round their intended victim, shouting 'Huddle 'em, huddle 'em', and more recently, the thuggish John Gotti earned a reputation as the 'Hoodlums' hoodlum'.

The term 'racketeering' probably derives from American politics. In the late nineteenth century New York City political clubs held boisterous gettogethers called rackets, an idea adopted by local gangs who held rackets of their own, and the racket was that you bought tickets, or else.

Gas chamber

The problem with gassing murderers is that they must collaborate in their own demise. Sympathisers enjoin the condemned man to make things easy by taking a few deep breaths to draw the gas down into his lungs. But even the most obliging type may find this runs contrary to inclination and instinct, and the gas chamber is survivable for as long as the man can hold his breath. At least with hanging, shooting and electrocution the state does the job for you.

Death by gas is not pleasant to watch. As Clinton Duffy, Warden of San Quentin, put it: 'In a matter of seconds the prisoner is unconscious. At first there is extreme evidence of horror, pain, strangling. The eyes pop, they turn purple, they drool. It is a horrible sight; witnesses faint.' Observers of Caryl Chessman's execution on 2 May 1960 saw him 'gasping, drooling, rolling his head – surviving the engulfing gas for several seconds'. On 6 April 1992 an Arizona convict took 10 minutes 31 seconds to die.

On 21 April 1992 the final throes of the murderer Robert Harris were viewed by forty-nine specta-

tors. Some were official witnesses, some well-wishers, others quite the reverse. Representing Harris's murder victims were two bereaved mothers, one father and two sisters. All peered into the death chamber through the glass panels. Inside, a videocamera whirred to aid post-mortem legal evaluations of whether gassing could be construed as cruel and unusual.

In the words of reporter Dan Morain: 'Harris inhaled four or five times. His head snapped back and then dropped as he strained against the straps. After a minute, his hands appeared relaxed. His mouth was wide open and his face flushed and then almost purple. Whether he was unconscious, in pain or numb, he seemed oblivious two minutes into his execution. But then, as his body seemed to have relaxed, his head rose eerily.'

Gas chamber technology is simple enough. Under the death chair is a tank, linked by a pipe to a reservoir of sulphuric acid. Above the tank, a pound of cyanide in a gauze bag is suspended on a hook. The condemned man is strapped into the chair, the door locked, and the acid released; presumably the convict hears the trickle. Then the executioner operates a lever, dunking the cyanide in the acid to produce the lethal hydrocyanic gas. Afterwards, a liquid ammonia spray neutralises any gases lingering on the corpse. The procedure was summarised by a placard waved outside San Quentin on the day of Harris's execution: 'Plop, Plop, Fizz, Fizz, Oh, what a relief it is.'

The gas chamber was invented as a humane alternative to the electric chair by a Major D. A. Turner. The first gas execution took place in Nevada in 1924, whereupon the process was adopted by ten states, including California where San Francisco's city authorities tested the apparatus on live pigs; some of the journalists attending the experiment described the procedure as more savage than **hanging**, **drawing**, and **quartering**.

In a recent adaptation, a Welsh magistrate constructed a portable gas chamber for personal use out of a plywood hood shaped like a large sewing machine case. He connected it by a pipe

to his car exhaust. With the engine running, the device proved capable of despatching the family cat when placed inside and, thinking to replicate the feat with his wife's head, Cranog Jones extended the piping from the garage, over the conservatory and into the marital bedroom.

On the night of 7 December 1991, Margaret Jones awoke to the sound of her Ford Fiesta, eerily loud, as though she had parked upstairs. Crouched at the bedside was her husband, clutching a box about two feet square from which carbon monoxide fumes emanated. 'What are you doing?' she asked, and then tried to ring the police. But the line was dead.

Cranog Jones was sentenced to nine years for attempted murder on 23 April 1993. The couple, married for twenty years, were embroiled in a divorce likely to cost Jones his house. He planned to gas his wife, place her body in the car, and pass off the death as suicide.

Gein, Edward (1906–1984)

A very strange American. One of the garments that Ed Gein crafted from human skin was a waistcoat. He also made a nipple belt, that is, a belt of nipples.

Gein's ideas on interior decor were equally bizarre. In his room, a wastepaper basket and lampshades fashioned of human skin jostled for space alongside bowls made from skullcaps. 'You wanted to use them as containers?' asked the incredulous investigator, Joe Wilimovsky, after Gein's 1957 arrest. 'I think you got the right idea,' responded Gein cheerfully, 'I think that's taken from an old Norwegian style.'

Gein came from the rural mid-western town of Plainsfield. He decorated the interior of his timber house with scatter masks – the skin stripped from faces – and finished off the bedroom with a display of skulls perched on his bedposts. Upholstered chairs, backed with human skin, had strips of fat still visible on the underside.

Another feature not widely copied was the woman's flayed torso slit up either side. Tanned and freestanding, it could be worn in the style of a breast- and back-plate; Gein kept it for those

moonlit nights when he pranced round the yard in a state of sexual excitement, draped with the face, hair, breasts and vaginas of his human trophies. In the kitchen he put Mrs Worden's heart fair and square on the stove in the saucepan. On his arrest, her fermenting head was found stashed in a burlap bag, with steam coming out. But basically Gein was a muddled man, storing his stock of nine vulvas in a shoebox. He found that a little sprinkled salt dried them out nicely.

In his capacity as a butcher Gein worked in the woodshed, hauling up Mrs Worden with a block and tackle by the ankle before eviscerating and decapitating her. It was tidy work; he had dressed the corpse like a carcass in a slaughterhouse when the police found it swinging. In the words of the medical report: 'The body had been opened by a median incision from the manubrium sterni and extending in the mid-line to the area just above the mons veneris... the empty body cavities were glistening and free from blood and appeared as if they had been washed.'

In real life, Gein was a precursor of Jeffrey **Dahmer**, the Milwaukee serial killer and kindred spirit. Both were **cannibals**, both inhabited shadowy inner worlds redolent with primitive superstition, and Gein's home was the 1950s hick equivalent of Dahmer's urban Oxford Apartments. In cinema and fiction, Gein's influence is discernible in more literal characters like Buffalo Bill, the skin-transvestite of *Silence of the Lambs*, and he rates a mention in Bret Easton Ellis's *American Psycho*. Gein also inspired the smalltown 'Leatherface' whose handiwork with bodies featured in *The Texas Chainsaw Massacre*. And fifty miles from Plainsfield lived a young writer, Robert Bloch, who worked Gein's story into a novel, *Psycho*, transferring the action to a motel in order to ensure an adequate influx of victims.

Bloch homed in on his anti-hero's Oedipal motivation: there had to be a *reason* for Gein's way of life (see **Lucas**), and his mother's bedroom was the only normal place in the house. It contained a bed, a cedar chest and other furniture, all coated in a thick layer of dust. The room had been nailed shut as a shrine ever since the death of Gein's mother in 1945, twelve years previously. Since then Gein felt that things were unreal. A loner with few social outlets, he never enjoyed sexual relations with anyone and, before she died, Ma Gein drummed into him that sex before marriage was bad and that **masturbation** was worse. During his intensive police debriefing in 1957, Gein devoted hours to discussing his relationship with his mother, dead for more than a decade. She was, he said, 'good in every way'.

Ma kept in touch after she passed on, chatting away for the next year or so while her boy drifted off to sleep; Gein told the police that during this period he developed a fascination with anatomy. He was impressed by contemporary reports of Christine Jorgensen's sex-change operation and toyed with the idea of becoming a woman. Then, in tandem with another weird local, Gus, Gein opened his first grave to provide material for his medical experiments.

Many of the household knick-knacks and furnishings discovered on Gein's arrest came from grave-robbing. For years he ferreted around in local graveyards, sometimes lugging complete cadavers home, sometimes cutting off the interesting bits as mementoes. But his yearnings were not restricted to predeceased bodies. Although tried for only one murder – Mrs Worden, shot in the head in 1957 – Gein also admitted to killing Mary Hogan. Psychologists were quick to point out that both these women bore a strong resemblance to his mother, but in addition his brother died of a mysterious accident, leaving Gein as sole heir to his mother's estate, and a man called Travis disappeared after Gein offered to take him hunting. Two local girls also vanished without trace. But it was only after the Worden murder that outsiders, in the form of the police, entered Gein's home, finding it bedecked with human remains. At his trial on 6 January 1958, Judge Bunde stated 'I can't see how my opinion can be anything other than to find this defendant insane', a view judicially confirmed ten years later.

Gein's home was razed to the ground on 30 March 1958 after rumours that it was destined to become a House of Horror tourist attraction. But his 1949 Ford pickup survived, sold at auction for $760 after brisk bidding. The vehicle went straight into harness at local fairs. A placard announced, 'It's here! See the car that hauled the dead from the graves.'

Gein died on 26 July 1984 after decades as an ideal patient at a psychiatric unit. Today, fans can buy latex Gein masks, collect Gein ephemera, or join the Ed Gein Fan Club. Cultists swap Gein jokes: he couldn't operate his farm – all he had left was a skeleton crew. What did he keep in his sewing box? 'Belly buttons.' And how were Gein's folks? 'Delicious.'

Genetic fingerprinting

In 1985 Alec Jeffreys from the University of Leicester discovered DNA fingerprints: the Holy Grail of serology, hailed as the 'forensic breakthrough of the century'.

Jeffreys was studying myoglobin protein when he isolated a block of repeated DNA sequences within the so-called hypervariable region. This is the DNA section responsible not for universal information common to all humans (how to grow arms and legs) but their personal characteristics. These blocks are particular to each individual (with the exception of identical twins) and are derived from bands present in either the mother or the father.

Jeffreys highlighted the hypervariable sections with radioactive probes so they registered on film, producing darkened bands not dissimilar in appearance from supermarket barcodes. At last blood specimens (or any type of genetic material) could be attributed with certainty not to a type of person but to a specific individual. Equally important, they could be unambiguously related to his antecedents and successors.

In its civilian guise, the procedure set to work resolving paternity and immigration disputes. Then in 1987 genetic fingerprinting secured the conviction of the British murderer and rapist Colin Pitchfork, a cake decorator, matching his blood to semen found in his victim. It was a copybook case, with the new wonder-evidence simultaneously exculpating a 17-year-old false confessor. The American author Joseph Wambaugh felt inspired to write: 'The scourge of rape and other violent crimes could largely become a thing of the past.'

In 1988, DNA evidence secured its first conviction in the US when Tommie Lee Andrews went down for two rapes. And in 1989 a British publican, Ian Simms, was convicted of murdering 22-year-old Helen McCourt on the strength of the bloodstains on his discarded clothes. The stumbling block had been to obtain a match with his victim's blood, since her body was never found; the prosecution was only the third British case without a corpse. Ingeniously, a sample taken from her parents tallied at one remove with those found on the murderer.

The most recent figures show that about 15 per cent of the 4,500 DNA tests conducted annually in Britain are for criminal cases. The DNA specimen may be degraded by a body's exposure to poor storage conditions, the process is often complicated by the tiny size of the specimen (see **Bones**), and in closely linked population groups the DNA similarities may exceed the patterns achieved by random mating.

Thus both 'false positives' and 'false negatives' remain a possibility, and the reliability of the DNA test began to be challenged in the courts. In two Australian cases, DNA evidence was ruled non-admissible. In one, it was disputed that the apparent barcode 'match' constituted a true match – they looked the same, but were they identical? In the other, the statistical evidence of probability (once put as high as 1:738,000,000,000,000) was dismissed because it did not include samples from the suspect's ethnic group.

In December 1991, the American journal *Science* suggested that realistic odds could not be calculated without greater knowledge of DNA patterns in ethnic communities. The authors, respected academics, were warned off by a US Department of Justice official and the magazine asked the writers to 'tone down' their findings. These included a Missouri case where the accused was initially found guilty on odds of one in 150 million, a figure the authors revised to one in 256. Six American courts have now excluded DNA evidence, ruling that 'the scientific uncertainty over the role of population substructure in calculating the chance of DNA matches is too great to pass the so-called Frye test' by which the admissibility of forensic evidence is judged. Thus the status of genetic fingerprinting is unclear in the United States, but less so in Britain, which has no equivalent of the 'Frye test' to satisfy.

In Britain, where techniques are accepted on an *ad hoc* basis, order prevails. Ethnicity is regarded as a statistical red herring since the odds are so high that the exact number of noughts is irrelevant. Ian Evett, from the Home Office Forensic Science Service, took the most extreme example (a single

'probe' as opposed to the usual four, confined to an Afro-Caribbean sample) and still derived a probability of one in 50,000. The most recent investigations suggest that genetic differences are greater *within* races than *between* them, and in Britain the mere mention of DNA evidence often secures guilty pleas when legal aid committees refuse funds to fight the case.

Nonetheless it is now apparent that 'genetic fingerprinting' is a misnomer. The evidence is subject to technical errors both in carrying out the test and in the inferences drawn from it.

Ghosts

The supernatural provided the key to Allan Pinkerton's most far-fetched case. In 1885 a county clerk and pillar of rectitude, Alexander P. Drysdale, murdered a bank-teller out West and robbed the safe of $130,000. Pinkerton had his suspicions but not the proof, and called in three operatives to help with the case. It transpired that his youngest sleuth, Green, bore a remarkable resemblance to the murder victim.

Pinkerton turned this to fantastical advantage. He disguised Green as a ghost, caking his hair with blood. Then another assistant, Andrews, inveigled the suspect Drysdale out for a stroll at the witching hour; they made their way at dusk to the local haunted spot of Rocky Creek. There Green put in an appearance as the ghost of the deceased. Drysdale uttered a great shriek but his companion, unperturbed, asserted that there was nothing to be seen.

Soon Pinkerton's third spy, by now a friend of Drysdale's wife, reported that the suspect was prey to nightmares and sleep-walking. Meanwhile, in his capacity as a spirit, Green embarked on a series of nocturnal rambles round Drysdale's house. Finally Pinkerton arrested the murderer and took him to the bank where the disguised Green popped up again, still shamming dead. Drysdale fainted and, with modest encouragement, confessed.

Eighty-one years before the Pinkerton case, Francis Smith was sentenced to death for opening fire on a ghost at point blank range. His target was the notorious sprite of Hammersmith, then a village outside London, and on 3 January 1804 Smith loaded his fowling-piece and went on the prowl with the night-watchman. A few minutes after eleven he cornered a pale spectre in flowing garb lurking near the ghost's usual haunt at the end of Black Cross Lane. Smith brought his gun to his shoulder and challenged the apparition. It did not reply. 'Damn you, who are you?' Smith called. 'Stand, else I'll shoot you.' It advanced towards him. Smith fired.

The phantom had frequented the district for weeks, flitting across the fields as the church-bell tolled one in the morning. At the sight, according to a local newspaper, 'Women and children have nearly lost their senses.' A pregnant woman was confined to her bed with shock, and a waggoner driving a team of eight horses fled in terror, deserting his fifteen passengers. One ghost, accosted in Church Lane, was unveiled as an impostor, a girl dressed in white out courting. Another was seen unrobing in Harrow Lane, removing a white sheet. But reliable reports persisted, with many sightings detailing the spirit's eyes flickering like glow-worms, and its nostrils, exhaling fire and smoke. Few would venture out after dark.

Sadly, Francis White's target proved to be Thomas Milward, a young plasterer in his whitened work-clothes which reached to his shoes. Milward's sister told journalists that she had never thought of warning him that he might be mistaken for the ghost, since it had glass eyes and long horns. But even though Smith held his fire to the last moment – as evidenced by the blackened powder on Milward's face – he faced a charge of murder. Three days later he went on trial for his life at the Old Bailey.

Smith was a pleasant, mild-mannered young man, but the Judge, the Lord Chief Baron, made no allowance for the obvious element of mistake (see **Accident**), expounding the law in peculiarly drastic terms. To prove 'malice aforethought' did not entail demonstrating active hatred by the accused; a mere intention to kill sufficed. To their credit, the **jury** paid no attention and returned a verdict of manslaughter. The judge objected that this was wrong, and instructed them to reconsider. This they did, and the Recorder passed the sentence of death. 'Francis Smith,' he reassured the prisoner, 'you have been tried by a most attentive and intelligent jury.' In the normal course of events a grateful Smith would have been hanged the following Monday.

But he was reprieved that evening, and on 20 January George III reduced his sentence to one year's imprisonment.

The ghost, caught a week after Milward's shooting, proved to be James Graham, a bootmaker. He had begun his series of nocturnal appearances clad in a sheet with the intention of scaring his apprentices and his lodger, a one-armed postman who had terrorised his children with ghost stories. So Graham waylaid them going home, and enjoyed the impression he created so much that it became a hobby.

The 1970s haunting of 112 Ocean Avenue, Amityville, discloses no firmer basis in the supernatural. In 1974 the house was home to Ronald DeFreo, a well-liked car service manager, his wife and their five children. But their eldest son, Ronnie Jnr, was a spoiled brat with a vicious streak, and on 12 November 1974, aged twenty-three, he slipped barbiturates into the family supper and then shot them dead with a .35 Marlin rifle. His feeble cover story deceived no one, and in December 1975 he was found guilty on six counts of murder. Two weeks later, a Mr and Mrs George Lutz bought 112 Ocean Avenue as a home for their three children and dog.

Twenty-eight days after moving in the Lutzs fled Ocean Avenue in terror, and their experiences formed the basis for Jay Anson's book, *The Amityville Horror*. Anson, a TV documentary scriptwriter, described how a family friend, Father Frank Mancuso, arrived to bless the house the day they moved in. But the ceremony was suspended when a voice called 'Get out!', and while driving back home Mancuso nearly crashed, and a colleague who shared his car for part of the journey became involved in a serious accident soon afterwards. The Lutz family fell to arguing, and were disturbed by mysterious noises at night; George Lutz stopped washing, and saw a ghostly pig his daughter claimed to keep as a pet. Green slime oozed from the walls, the basements stank of excreta, the lavatory bowls filled with black gunk, and his wife assumed the guise of a toothless hag and levitated.

Lutz became suspicious of the house and researched its history. He learned of the grisly DeFreo murders, and discovered that his home was built on an enclosure for sick and demented Indians. It was their burial ground. Under the front steps he found the entrance to an open cistern, through which, he surmised, evil spirits made their way to infect Ronnie DeFreo Jnr.

Ghost stories are all in the telling, and the slightest distortion turns fact into fiction. No medium is better suited to this transmutation than film, and the smell of excreta, betokening the presence of Satan, may have been indicative only of plumbing problems. We, or our children, have all heard things that go bump in the night, and clever depiction of atmospherics can capture terrors which are nonetheless baseless.

The Shinnecock Indians never established a compound for their mad or dead anywhere, least of all at 112 Ocean Avenue, and it is surely unlikely that George Lutz, a house broker, was unaware of the DeFreo murders. The killings attracted a blaze of publicity. Lutz, a resident of Suffolk County, purchased 112 Ocean Avenue, presumably at an advantageous price, two weeks after Ronnie Jnr was sentenced at the end of the county's longest trial.

Gibbets

As a rule, gibbeting in irons was reserved for corpses. But occasional reports describe a condemned man as lingering alive in his ironwork after a bungled execution. The gibbeted highwayman John Whitworth was saved from this fate in 1777 by the guard of a passing stagecoach, who shot him.

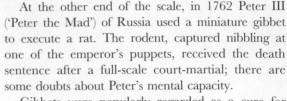

The display of the criminal's body was intended as a deterrent, and, after the invention of 'tarring' to act as a preservative, Newgate prison installed a 'kitchen' where the bodies could be processed. Gibbeting remained within the discretion of individual judges until 1752, when hanging in chains became part of the legal sentence, and soon gibbets lined the Thames and the six approach roads to London. The practice was banned in 1834 after reaching new heights the year before, when James Cook, a murderer, was gibbeted from a set of gallows thirty-five feet high in Saffron Lane, Leicester.

At the other end of the scale, in 1762 Peter III ('Peter the Mad') of Russia used a miniature gibbet to execute a rat. The rodent, captured nibbling at one of the emperor's puppets, received the death sentence after a full-scale court-martial; there are some doubts about Peter's mental capacity.

Gibbets were popularly regarded as a cure for toothache; the Spennymore gibbet eventually disappeared completely, removed sliver by sliver for medicinal purposes.

Girl from Botany Bay, The

There was nothing special about Mary Broad's crime or her punishment. A sailor's daughter from Fowey in Cornwall, she stole a cloak, rendering herself eligible for seven years transportation. She reached Australia alive and there married another convict, William Bryant, in April 1790 giving birth to her second child.

Bryant was a fisherman, and in October 1790 he wangled a chart, a compass, a quadrant and a set of muskets out of a passing Dutch ship. Judging his moment, Bryant stole the governor's six-oar cutter and put out to sea from Port Jackson on the night of 28 March 1791, taking six convicts with him as well as his wife and their two infant children.

In ten weeks they sailed their open boat 3,250 miles north. Hugging the coast, they found themselves blown out to sea, where for three weeks they were lashed by gales and thrown onto the Barrier Reef; they survived on turtles, caulked their boat with soap, fought off hostile natives and headed away from the northernmost tip of Australia into 500 miles of open water, pursued by cannibals in canoes. But on 5 June they made harbour at Koepang, Timor.

There the band of escapees presented themselves to the Dutch governor as shipwrecked mariners and waited for a boat back to England. But Bryant rowed with his wife and, perhaps while drunk, confessed to the governor. They were thrown into prison, and then shipped back to England clapped in irons.

During the harsh voyage both Mary's children died and, on arrival in London, she was bundled off to Newgate to await transportation back to Australia as an escaped felon.

Word of Mary's epic journey leaked out; the

press dubbed her 'the Girl from Botany Bay'. Her cause was espoused by James Boswell, Dr **Johnson**'s biographer, who approached both the Home Secretary and the Under Secretary of State on her behalf, and in May 1793 the Girl from Botany Bay received an unconditional pardon. Boswell settled an annuity of £10 on her; she returned to Cornwall and faded from history, but not before giving Boswell a little packet of dried Australian 'sweet tea' that had shared the vicissitudes of her heroic voyage. These few leaves are now in the archives of Yale University.

Glatman, Harvey Murray (d. 1959)

Possibly the ugliest of the sex killers. Glatman possessed an IQ of 130, but the lower half of his face betrayed a slightly inflated, ape-like look which, when coupled with his jug ears, made him unappealing to women. Solo sex was his only recourse, and it took the form of self-strangulation in mock hangings. At the age of seventeen his lunges at the opposite sex consisted of snatching their purses in the streets of his hometown in Boulder, Colorado, and then tossing them back. This progressed to making a young girl undress at gunpoint, albeit with a toy gun. Finally a string of robberies – by now with real firearms – on New York women led to a five-year spell in Sing Sing. Released in 1951, he set up a television repair shop in Los Angeles.

The lonely, frustrated Glatman joined a photographic club for the titillation afforded by nude models in studio sessions. Then, on 30 July 1957, he made a service call to the apartment of an attractive young woman, Judy Ann Dull, a model recently arrived from Florida. By chance, he was a photographer for a New York True Crime magazine. Could he see her portfolio? Would she like a job? How about $50 for a series of bondage pictures in his studio?

Judy Ann agreed, and two days later Glatman drove her to his apartment. He explained that his plans had changed. They would do the shoot there. Would she put her hands behind her back while he bound them? Then he could put on the gag and tie up her legs. She acquiesced, and soon sat helpless in his armchair while he pulled down her sweater,

raised her skirt and started to click away. For the first time in his life he had a semi-clad pretty girl in his home.

Whatever his original intentions, Glatman lost his self-control. He tore off her clothes, put a gun to her head, and raped her, twice. Then the pair sat naked on his sofa watching television. She begged him to let her go. She promised not to talk.

But could she be trusted? Glatman's record meant that if she was lying he would be put away for a long time. The logic was inescapable. He loaded her into his car and drove 125 miles into the desert near Idaho. There he took another series of photographs as Judy Ann begged for her life in her underwear. Then he strangled her. Alone with her body, he begged for forgiveness and drove back to Los Angeles in a mood of self-revulsion to await arrest.

But nothing happened. No police came knocking on his door. With time, Glatman's panic and remorse began to mutate. He developed his photographs and sneaked another look. Then he pinned enlargements to his walls.

By the following spring Glatman was ready to kill again. He joined a 'lonely hearts' club under the name of 'George Williams' and on 8 March 1958 he drove 24-year-old Shirley Ann Bridgeford into the desert of Anza State Park, east of San Diego. There he followed the established routine: first the gun, then the rape, then the bondage photo-session, and then the kill. He left Shirley Ann to rot behind a cactus, and four months later, on 23 July 1958, a striptease dancer and nude model, Ruth Rita Mercado, met the same fate. Glatman contacted her through the personal columns of the *Los Angeles Times*. He wanted to let her go, but by now it was even riskier than before. 'Ruth was the only one I liked,' he recalled. 'I didn't want to kill her. I used the rope, the same way.'

By September it was the turn of another model, Joanne Arena. When Glatman offered her a photographic job, she thought his manner 'creepy'. But a friend, Lorraine Vigil, needed the money. Lorraine and Glatman drove off together down the Santa Anna Freeway and, just outside the town of Tustin, he pulled over onto the hard shoulder and produced his gun. Strip, he said.

'I knew he was going to kill me,' Lorraine said later. 'I tried to plead, but I knew pleading wouldn't do any good.' She grabbed for the gun. Glatman shot her in the thigh but she twisted the barrel round until it pointed at him, and the struggling pair tumbled out onto the road.

At that moment a police patrol car came to the rescue. Glatman gave himself up. Sentenced to death after a three-day trial, he refused to lodge an appeal. 'It's better this way,' he said. 'I knew this was the way it would be.'

He was executed on 18 August 1959.

See also **Hansen**

G-men

Abbreviation allegedly coined by Machine Gun Kelly, who was extremely pressed for time. His words were: 'Don't shoot, G-men!' uttered as the FBI agents burst into his bedroom with guns drawn early on the morning of 26 September 1933. The 'G' stood for government.

Kelly died twenty-one years later, still in Leavenworth Penitentiary for the July 1933 **kidnapping** of the Oklahoma oil millionaire Charles F. Urschel, 'snatched' from his porch during an after-dinner hand of bridge.

Urschel had been released on payment of the $200,000 ransom, and he provided the FBI with their crucial clue. Every day during his week of blindfold captivity he listened as two planes droned overhead, one at 9.45 in the morning and the other at 5.45 in the evening. The only intersection where airline timetables showed this to happen in Texas was the town of Paradise.

Urschel proved a meticulous observer. From his room he heard the barnyard sounds of cows and hens, and his drinking water – which had a strong mineral taste – was drawn from a creaking well to the north-west of the house. The FBI flooded Paradise with undercover agents, touring the homesteads kitted out as as bankers offering agricultural loans and found a farm fitting the description, owned by a man called R. G. Shannon, and his stepdaughter Kathryn was married to a George Kelly, Machine Gun Kelly.

Thirteen men stood trial for Urschel's kidnapping, but Kelly and his wife were still at large when proceedings began. They were caught in a dawn raid in Memphis, Tennessee, after a little girl named Geraldine Arnold confided in a schoolfriend that she had been 'borrowed' by a couple needing a child for the sake of appearances. The playmate told a friend, and the friend told her father, a policeman.

What Kelly actually said when he saw the shotgun pointing at his heart was, 'I've been waiting for you all night.' The phrase 'G-men' was already in popular usage, and **Hoover** concocted the story for publicity.

Despite his ferocious soubriquet, George Kelly was a relatively amiable man who never fired at any one; it was Kathryn who bought him his gun, Kathryn who landed him a job with a two-bit gang and then – after two feeble bank raids in the towns of Tupelo and Wilmer – Kathryn who talked him into the Big Time with the Urschel kidnapping. But she could not persuade him to kill their captive after the ransom was paid.

Kathryn served twenty-six years. It emerged in 1970 that the FBI had suppressed the handwriting evidence by their own expert, which would have destroyed their case, clearing her of writing the ransom demand notes.

See also **Female Offender**

Godfather, The

The movie's fictional Don Vito Corleone was derived from the Mafia boss Carlo Gambino, on the outside the very model of an Old World benevolent patrician.

Prior to *The Godfather*'s release, pressure from the newly founded 'Italian-American Civil Rights League' compelled the deletion of all the film's references to the Mafia. The League, which campaigned against the stereotyping of American Italians as gangsters, was the creation of mobster Joseph Colombo, who embezzled the League's funds for distribution to himself and other Mafia bosses. Colombo rose to prominence through Gambino's influence and was murdered in 1971 for his bungling; he died at an open-air League rally in a Mafia hit.

Godmothers

A recent phenomenon in the 'dead-man's-shoes' world of the Italian Mafia. After a family Godfather is rubbed out or jailed, his spouse or sister takes his place as Godmother.

Among these *grande dames* are old 'Ice Eyes', Rosetta Cutolo, who stepped in when her brother Raffaele was sentenced to life for murder and extortion; Elvira Palumbo, taped nagging her husband during a prison visit: 'Enzo, wouldn't it be better to give that job to someone else? The guy you're talking about can't shoot to save his life'; Pupetta Maresco, who inherited her husband's criminal empire after liquidating his killer; and Anna 'the Black Widow' Mazza, living off the fat of the land in a million-dollar villa surrounded by bodyguards in bulletproof vests.

'Ice Eyes' was captured during Italy's anti-Mafia spasm of 1993. She had been sought ever since escaping from a police raid in September 1981, and was sentenced *in absentia* to nine years in 1990. On 8 February 1993, acting on a tip-off, the police knocked on the door of a fortified villa outside Naples. She came quietly to the entrance saying, 'I am tired of being a fugitive', thus becoming another casualty of the recent confessional spate by former *mafiosi*.

In the summer of 1992 Italy at last established a workable witness protection package (the basic tool of organised crime investigations) offering informers a new name, a new home and a new nose. Special telephone hot-lines enabled those with guilty consciences to confess from the comfort of their own homes; page 166 of domestic Teletext asked repentant viewers to dial Rome 33170804, and in the first nine months some 280 'penititi' took the opportunity to shop former associates, a figure standing favourable comparison with the dozen or so who came forward in the previous four decades.

As with the black race riots (see **King**), it is the highly-publicised physical outrages that bring retaliation from an incensed populace. The 1963 Italian Mafia crackdown was inspired by the dynamiting of seven policemen with a car bomb, the 1982 campaign by the assassination of General Dalla Chiesa, and the current paroxysm by the devastating 1992 murders of prosecutors Giovanni Falcone and Paolo Borsellino.

They did not die in vain. Despite official reprimands for 'ruining the Sicilian economy', Falcone persevered to become the architect of Palermo's maxi-trial which culminated in 1987 with 350 convictions, reducing the Mafia's wall of **silence** to rubble while maintaining sufficient judicial equilibrium to hand down 114 **acquittals** for lack of evidence. As with the **Pizza Connection** trial, culpability extended into the higher echelons, with nineteen of the most powerful bosses sentenced to life.

Optimistic commentators, many of them astute, consider that the Mob overreached itself with the 1992 Falcone-Borsellino assassinations, and the killings may may yet prove the Italian Mafia's worst mistake. In Palermo, between the nineteenth and the twenty-third of every month – the dates of their deaths – the streets are hung with sheets bearing anti-Mafia slogans, and women fast in the Piazza Castelnuovo. The pavement outside Falcone's apartment has become a public shrine.

Golden Triangle, The

Source of about 70 per cent of the world's opium and heroin; the Middle East produces less than half that amount, and nearly all their crop is consumed locally.

The Golden Triangle is an area of rugged terrain occupying parts of Thailand, Laos and Burma. The region, about the size of Greece, is dominated by sharp mountain ranges, deep valleys and thick jungle, populated by fierce hill tribes who harvest some 1,500 tons of **opium** annually under **Triad** control. The crop, refined down to 100 tons of heroin, is then distributed worldwide through the Chinese Connection. Each year, a few tons are intercepted, but most law enforcement agencies prefer to concentrate on traditional targets like the Italian Mafia, leaving the Triad distribution network all but untouched.

From the hill farmers' perspective, opium is a perfect crop. With an average yield of two kilos an acre, the harvest is non-perishable and easy to sell. The growers do not go to market: the drug traffickers and opium warlords send their agents to buy at source. Many farmers are addicts – a further incentive to replant – and are bound into economic servitude by accepting loans. Sometimes their payment is in kind, with goods like salt and matches. For cash, the crop fetches about $40 a kilo.

In the Burmese section, the Shan States of the Golden Triangle are a legacy of the British Empire. The area was never colonised and, on gaining independence after the Second World War, Burma inherited a country within a country of thirty-four independent 'Sawbwas' (feudal warlords) indulging in low-scale opium cultivation. American know-how founded the modern industry; the CIA, along with French Intelligence, regarded the creation of independent criminal empires as an excellent buffer against communist expansion.

At harvest time the opium trails with their mule caravans sometimes a mile long are all but invisible, screened by an impenetrable jungle canopy. Nonetheless the opium is brought out at night and, with 40,000 armed insurgents controlling the area, subjugation or control of the Triangle remains a hopeless task. Every jungle laboratory is fiercely defended; in 1987 the US Drugs Enforcement Agency busted a run-of-the-mill lab defended by thirty guards ensconced behind landmines and armed with machine guns, M-16s, Russian AK-47s, M-79 rocket launchers and grenade launchers.

About 80 per cent of the Golden Triangle's narcotics ultimately emerge along the Chiang Mai paved road and its corresponding route to the north, the contraband concealed in ordinary commercial vehicles. In 1987 perhaps seventy tons passed this way. But a big lorry may carry 400 bags of rice, or two tons of fish packed in ice, and a single search takes hours, backing up traffic for miles. American DEA officials depend on the approval of the Thai police, who generally wave the vehicles through after a few minutes. Apparently the local officers meet every one of the FBI's criteria defining organised crime, except that they are not organised.

Some efforts at drug containment are little more than propaganda exercises. For the purposes of cosmetic aerial photography a few hill farmers have taken to planting coffee, but they still harvest opium on the next square of land.

Gordon, Lord George (d. 1793)

A prisoner who brought style to **Newgate**. In 1781, Gordon was tried for high treason following of the Gordon Riots. Not only was he innocent of

fomenting the disturbances; he got off. But from then on he was a marked man, finally brought to injustice in 1787, sentenced to five years for libel; he had sponsored a petition criticising the British legal system.

Gordon took up private rooms in Newgate, passing his mornings in correspondence and reading before the arrival of his midday guests. Luncheon was served for around half a dozen friends at about 2 p.m., and once a fortnight he threw a formal dinner party, sometimes with music and dancing. Gordon had the benefit of two personal maids, one of them the beautiful Polly Levi, possibly his mistress.

This Newgate story does not end well. After serving his full term Gordon was unable to find the sureties that would have assured his release. In the end he became deranged, adopting the Jewish faith and devoting himself to the bagpipes. He died of jail fever in 1793, intoning the French Revolutionary ditty 'Çà ira'.

It would be a mistake to regard a spell in Newgate as festive, but on 28 August 1790 the prison formed the venue for the so-called 'Monster's Ball', a party thrown by Renwick Williams, of necessity in advance, to celebrate his hanging. Forty guests attended his *thé dansant*, pirouetting until eight in the evening to the accompaniment of violins and flutes. Then the gathering, comprised largely of those who had attempted to provide their host with alibis, sat down to a cold supper with meat and a selection of wines. The following morning Williams – popularly known as the 'Monster of London' – was hanged.

The Gordon Riots form the background to Charles Dickens's *Barnaby Rudge*.

Graphologists

Experts contend that by examining a specimen of handwriting they can discern the characteristics of a thief, rapist or murderer, and spot tell-tale symptoms of impotence, frigidity, deceit, father influence, aggression, homosexuality and the like.

These ideas seem simplistic rather than simple. For instance, handwriting analysis is based on three zones, the upper, the middle and the lower. The 'upper' area is the penstrokes which stick up at the top, the 'lower' those that stick down below and the 'middle' the bits in the middle. These supposedly correspond to the subjects' higher instincts (spiritual and intellectual), lower instincts (sex and the subconscious) and the bits in between (day-to-day attitude). Ideally all three zones should be in proportion, and a lack of balance suggests ... a lack of balance.

There are many rules. Small a's and o's which are not closed at the baseline indicate deceit, as do capital letters which stray leftwards and squiggly 'enrolled' capitals. Inflated capitals suggest an inflated ego. A variable slope denotes an unreliable character; messy writing speaks of a messy mind. Broad m's show the extravagant approach of the bluffer, while a cross-bar to a t which starts low down at the base reveals that the writer is capable of zipping off in extraordinary directions – in other words, a liar. Narrow loops clambering up the stem a little way without crossing it are a sure sign of sexual anxiety, whereas short spiky underlengths tending towards the right are typical of a stifled sex drive.

To the layman, Jack the Ripper's writing looks a mess, Myra Hindley's is childish, and Himmler's spiky in a robotic way. The same applies to the handwriting of millions of ordinary individuals.

'Revealing' signatures. Crippen's (above) and Himmler's (below), which 'shouts of aggression and a complete lack of warmth or emotion'.

But to the professional graphologist even the smallest detail may assume overwhelming significance, especially after the event. Thus the unexceptional signature of the famous British murderer **Crippen** discloses his inferiority complex (by the small capitals), his desire to manipulate others (by the threadlike strokes), his sociability and ardent nature (by the rightwards slant), his craving for prestige (by the heavy pen-pressure) and his domestic discontent (by the small g's with their pointed downstrokes).

Except on the Continent, graphology is not thought to have a scientific basis. This is quite distinct from the study of handwriting to detect forgeries, which remains more or less a science.

Great Gatsby *et al*

The figure of Gatsby was inspired by F. Scott Fitzgerald's New York neighbour in Great Neck, Long Island, a high-profile bootlegger called Larry Fay. The millionaire gambler Arnold Rothstein, responsible for fixing baseball's 1919 World Series (by paying a reputed $70,000 to eight members of the Chicago White Sox), provided the starting point for the character of Wolfsheim, and in real life Rothstein seldom left home with less than $200,000 pocket money in new $1,000 bills.

Dashiell Hammett was another author who stuck to what – and who – he knew. Hammett was a one-time Pinkerton detective, and Nora Charles, the wisecracking wife in his *Thin Man* series, derives from his lover Lillian Hellman. The husband – a suave, sophisticated metropolitan – is a pen-portrait of Hammett.

The film director D. W. Griffith was a similar stickler for accuracy in his early days. He made the first gangster movie in 1912, *The Musketeers of Pig Alley*, based on the New York murder of gambler Herman 'Beansie' Rosenthal on 21 July of that year. For added verisimilitude, Griffith hired the actual gangsters, 'Kid' Brook and 'Harlem' Tom Evans, to play themselves. But his background research was not always so careful. In *Birth of a Nation* he cast the Ku Klux Klan as social liberators.

Arnold Rothstein's estimated fortune of $50 million just melted away in his bad year of 1928, entering the final tail-spin on 8 September with a three-day poker marathon, when he lost $320,000 to two West Coast gamblers, 'Nigger Nate' Raymond and 'Titanic' Thompson in a game hosted by bookie George 'Hump' McManus. Rothstein welched on his debts, and it was McManus's duty to collect. On 4 November, Rothstein set off to meet him at New York's Central Park Hotel and was found there with a bullet in his stomach. The police asked Rothstein what had happened. 'I won't talk about it. I'll take care of it myself,' he said, and died. Charges against McManus were dismissed after a chambermaid, on better consideration, withdrew her identification evidence.

In the 1934 film version of the Rothstein story, *Manhattan Melodrama*, the hero was 'blown away' by Clark Gable, and, after watching a screening of this movie on 22 July 1934 in the Chicago Biograph, John **Dillinger** (or someone very like him) died at the hands of the FBI. Crime boss Albert Anastasia was another gangster who met his end in the Central Park Hotel, gunned down in the barber's shop on 25 October 1957 by the infamous Gallo brothers, 'Crazy' Joe, 'Kid Twist' Larry and 'Kid Blast' Albert. The site is now on the tour organised by Sidewalks of New York, an outfit specialising in visits to the Big Apple's crime spots.

'Not a dry eye in the group,' says founder Sam Stafford of his trip to the Dakota apartment building where John Lennon was assassinated. 'There are only two sure things in life – death and taxes, and nobody wants to see where the rich and famous pay their taxes.'

Great Train Robbery

So mesmerised were the British public and authorities by the audacity of the Great Train Robbers that in February 1966 the police announced that they needed the Army's help to guard Durham prison, then holding three of the gang. 'I am satisfied,' declared the Chief Constable of Durham, 'that Goody's friends would be prepared to launch a full-scale military attack, even to the extent of using tanks, bombs, and what the Army calls "limited" atomic weapons.'

Information played the crucial role in the theft: the gang were 'tipped off' that the mail train from Glasgow to London the weekend after the Bank Holiday would be laden with anywhere up to £5 million in used notes. Thus the robbery involved stopping the train and breaking into the second coach behind the engine, the so-called High Value Packages Coach. Compared with busting a bank vault (see **Nice**), the second stage was easy, entailing a few blows from a crowbar, but the first necessitated tampering with two signals, switching one to amber and another, at Sears crossing, to red. Lightbulbs wired up to rogue batteries placed behind the coloured filters did the trick, and the green 'go' signal was masked by a pair of cricket gloves that nearly toppled the government.

For these were worrying times. The Profumo scandal had reached its height with osteopath Stephen Ward committing suicide on 3 August. Scarcely a month before, Kim Philby defected to Russia, turning MI5 into a laughing stock, and England had been humbled at the Fourth Test match at Headingley, with demands for the removal of cricketer E.R.Dexter vying for space with calls for the Prime Minister's resignation. Britain was already on its metaphorical knees by the time the commando-style Great Train Robbery brought the patrician 1950s to a close, at exactly 3.03 a.m. on 8 August 1963.

In obeisance to the signals, the Royal Mail train ground to a halt a few hundred yards short of Bridego Bridge, Buckinghamshire. Fireman David Whitby dismounted to investigate and set off through the dark to the emergency telephone behind the signal gantry. Buster Edwards, a villain, bundled him down the embankment, and moments later the train driver, Jack Mills, was coshed on the head. With the rear coaches uncoupled, the engine and the two front coaches trundled on to Bridego Bridge where the gang smashed through the doors and windows of the High Value Packages Coach, and five Post Office guards were forced to lie on the floor while a human chain passed 120 sacks

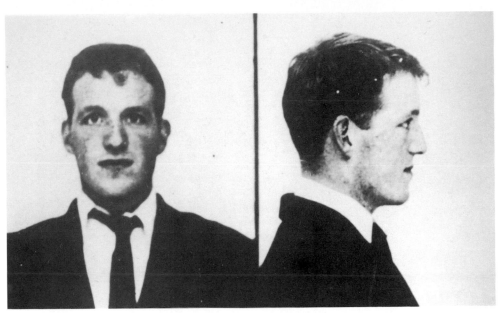

A rare photograph of James Hanratty, the petty criminal
hanged for the A6 murder.

Hanratty's father outside the House of Commons
leafleting passers-by, seven years after his son went to the
gallows.

Dapper Peter Alphon, discharged
on 4 October 1961.

Butch Cassidy (front right), the Sundance Kid (front left) in the ill-judged New York photograph of 1900 that put their faces on 'Wanted' posters across the country.

That special day. George Joseph Smith in a studio photograph with his first murder victim, Beatrice Mundy.

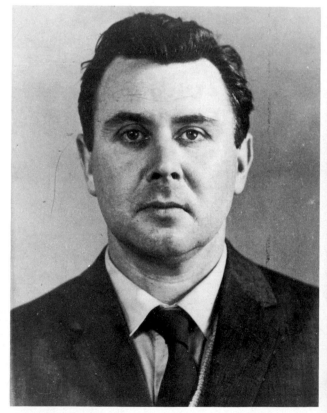

Donald Hume, whose inventive method of body disposal landed him in prison, where he was privy to Timothy Evans's partial confession to the Rillington Place murders.

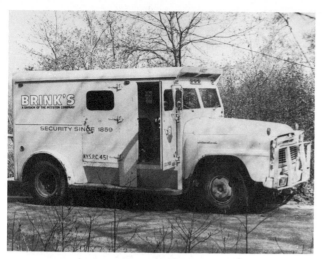

A Brink's van, taken over by bandits with sub-machine guns, yielded $700,000 in Brockton, Massachusetts on 23 May 1967.

(Right) Ted Bundy in a disassociative stance as the County Sheriff indicts him for the Chi Omega slayings.

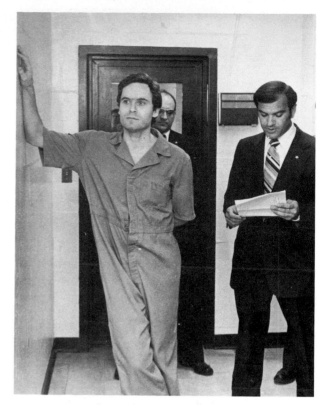

Christopher Craig at sixteen – too young to swing.

His accomplice, Derek Bentley, a few days before arrest.

WANTED

JOHN HERBERT DILLINGER

On June 23, 1934, HOMER S. CUMMINGS, Attorney General of the United States, under the authority vested in him by an Act of Congress approved June 6, 1934, offered a reward of

$10,000.00

for the capture of John Herbert Dillinger or a reward of

$5,000.00

for information leading to the arrest of John Herbert Dillinger.

DESCRIPTION

Age, 32 years; Height, 5 feet 7-1/8 inches; Weight, 153 pounds; Build, medium; Hair, medium chestnut; Eyes, grey; Complexion, medium; Occupation, machinist; Marks and scars, 1/2 inch scar back left hand, scar middle upper lip, brown mole between eyebrows.

All claims to any of the aforesaid rewards and all questions and disputes that may arise as among claimants to the foregoing rewards shall be passed upon by the Attorney General and his decisions shall be final and conclusive. The right is reserved to divide and allocate portions of any of said rewards as between several claimants. No part of the aforesaid rewards shall be paid to any official or employee of the Department of Justice.

If you are in possession of any information concerning the whereabouts of John Herbert Dillinger, communicate immediately by telephone or telegraph collect to the nearest office of the Division of Investigation, United States Department of Justice, the local addresses of which are set forth on the reverse side of this notice.

JOHN EDGAR HOOVER, DIRECTOR, DIVISION OF INVESTIGATION, UNITED STATES DEPARTMENT OF JUSTICE, WASHINGTON, D. C.

June 23, 1934

Hoover's bête noir, John Dillinger, in a 1934 poster.

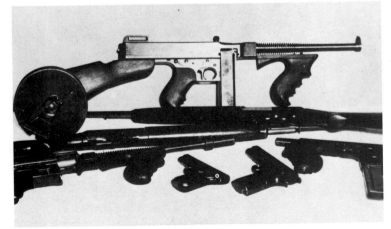

A collection of guns allegedly used by Dillinger.

The Ohio electric chair in a bland setting, 1973. Note the telephone for last-minute instructions and the framed Rogues' Galleries.

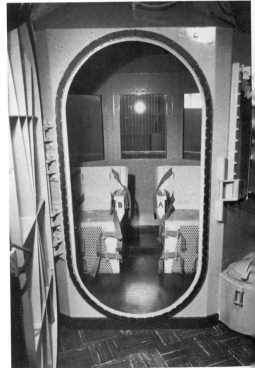

The San Quentin gas chamber, which claimed 194 lives up to 1967. The last moments of Robert Harris in 1992 were recorded on video.

(Right) The former prostitute Madame Fahmy, begowned in all her glory.

(Above) Elizabeth Short, the Black Dahlia (see **False Confessions**). True Crime writers traditionally characterise female victims as beautiful. Miss Short was.

(Right) Young Ethel Le Neve (see Crippen), briefly the most romanticised woman in the world, wearing a fine hat.

A famous but imaginary incident in Turpin's legend-encrusted life.

Bridego Bridge after the Great Train Robbery, the so-called 'last decent crime'. To the left is the embankment down which the human chain ferried 120 mailbags.

Great Train Robber Bruce Reynolds after his high life in Mexico palled.

The young Krays, known locally as the Terrible Twins, with 'Our Queen', their mother Violet.

Reg (left) and Ronnie (right), released after thirty-six hours of questioning about George Cornell's murder.

Jim Garrison (see **Kennedy**) announcing that the trial of Clay Shaw will start on 21 January 1969, nearly two years after indictment.

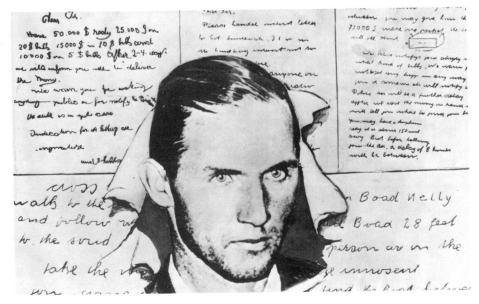

Richard Bruno Hauptmann, electrocuted for the kidnapping and murder of Charles Lindbergh Jnr (see **Ladders**). To the left, the scrawled ransom note, to the right, the handover instructions.

Henry Lee Lucas on 4 April 1984, eleven months after his first arrest and well into his confessing spree.

bulging with banknotes down to a waiting lorry and two Land Rovers.

In twenty-four minutes the Great Train Robbers made off with £2,631,648, about £25 million in today's terms. Their haul weighed two and a half tons and, split seventeen ways, amounted to a minimum of £150,000 each. When a local policeman, alerted by the blacked-out windows, discovered the gang's abandoned hideout at Leatherslade Farm, among the wealth of fingerprints and forensic clues was a Monopoly game played with real money. Only £50,000 of the loot was recovered, turning up in a telephone box on

11 December, but most of the gang were under lock and key by the end of the year. The following April they received swingeing terms ranging up to twenty-five years – commensurate with the penalty for armed robbery, suggesting that future robbers might as well go equipped with guns to reduce the number of partners, thereby increasing each individual's take. Villains today do not conduct their business in bands of twenty.

Hence the depiction of the Great Train Robbery as 'the last decent crime'. But wealth beyond the dreams of avarice did not bring happiness. On the lam, Buster Edwards was no longer a poor criminal. He was a rich one, and after three years of frittering his money away on high living in Mexico, he preferred to return to England to face his sentence.

Where are the Train Robbers now? After serving their time, Wisbey, Hussey and Goody went back inside for further offences. Charlie Wilson got himself shot in Spain in 1990. Jimmy White works as a house painter; Buster Edwards runs a flower stall at Waterloo station. That leaves Ronnie **Biggs**, a ray of hope in a grey world, sunning himself on the Copacabana in Rio, making celebrity-product endorsements. In the shadows behind him

lurk a handful of unnamed associates. During an August 1993 telephone interview, Biggs confirmed that four gang members escaped, three because they never removed their gloves at Leatherslade Farm and one because his prints were not on file.

Guillotine

A humanitarian device, which most people know was invented by Dr Guillotin. Less widely appreciated is that the guillotine swiftly became such an object of French veneration that, in Robespierre's 1794 Festival of the Supreme Being, it starred as a quasi-religious totem, appearing draped in blue velvet embroidered with roses. Lord Byron was another great admirer, finding the device 'altogether more impressive than the vulgar and ungentlemanly 'new drop''.

Dr Guillotin (1738–1814) was described by his contemporary Bonneville as 'devoid of either talent or repute', and his mental capacity to give birth to his mechanical marvel is traditionally ascribed to the impulse that expelled him from the womb when his mother suffered a nasty shock, coming unexpectedly upon a criminal undergoing torture on the wheel.

In fact, little inventing was needed; there were precedents aplenty, not least the **Halifax Gibbet**. But the first well-documented claim to mechanical decapitation belongs to the Irish. Holinshed's 1577 *Chronicles* contain a detailed woodcut of a working guillotine, unequivocally affirming its use in the execution of one Murcod Ballagh on 1 April 1307, near Merton.

In France, on 10 October 1789, Dr Guillotin suggested to the Revolutionary Assembly that death without **torture** and by decapitation (hitherto a privilege reserved for nobles) should be the sole means of execution. On 1 December he added a single sentence specifying that this objective 'should be achieved by means of a simple mechanism'. The intention was that loss of life, rather than the pain inflicted while losing it, should constitute sufficient punishment, and even before its invention Dr Guillotin's device became known as the guillotine. But his contribution consisted of proposing that someone should invent it.

The project went forward to various committees, and on 17 March 1792 a droll personage called Dr Louis submitted a detailed review of beheading round the world, *Avis motive sur la Mode de la Décolation*. Apart from its imaginative description of the 'standard' English practice of guillotining, the document is packed with interesting *aperçus*. The aged Dr Louis pointed out that botched executions were often conducted with the condemned man kneeling but otherwise unsupported. All too often the first axe-blow simply knocked him sprawling. This observation inspired the corrective invention of the bottom half of the guillotine with its solid restraining platform. Dr Louis continued: 'Everyone knows that cutting instruments have little or no effect when they strike perpendicularly... You must saw the object to be cut... You cannot decapitate with a single stroke of an axe or blade of which the cutting edge is horizontal.' This observation entailed the corrective invention of the oblique blade of the top half of the guillotine.

The Legislation Committee were impressed by Dr Louis' report, according him 'the merit of having benefited humanity when the law's blade strikes the head of the guilty'. Over the next few weeks Dr Louis discussed refinements of his gadget at his Sunday evening salons attended by literati, medical men and politicians, finally submitting a detailed specification to M. Guidon, the state scaffold-builder.

Guidon put in an inflated estimate of 5,600 livres to cover extra payments to his artisans for the unpleasant nature of the work. So on 10 April 1792 the contract went elsewhere, to a German harpsichord-maker, Tobias Schmidt, who threw in a free leather bag for a total price of 960 livres. This little sack was to put the heads in; Schmidt's later inventions included a patent chimney.

According to the unreliable M. Begin (Dr Louis's great-nephew) the new gadget was first tested on 11 April when it removed the heads of two or three sheep. But when the official trials opened three days later using human cadavers, two of the necks were only partially severed, their heads left dangling forwards, the blade embedded in the last few shreds of cartilage. The disapointed party of official observers withdrew to a lunch of capon and excellent wines, specifying an increase in the height of the two uprights and modifying the shape of the blade.

On 21 April a revised model was tried out on 'three corpses of Herculean dimensions' and passed with flying colours. The machine's design never became fixed. According to the executioner Henri **Sanson** in 1811, in one variant 'the body is allowed to fall through a hole in the scaffold into a sort of tomb'. It was alleged (by Guyot de Fère) that Danton asked the retired Dr Guillotin to devise a three-bladed machine. A four-bladed version was actually built and installed in Bordeaux with trap doors through which the bodies tumbled into waiting carts. In 1793, a M. Guillot (of truncated nomenclature) carried out experiments on a massive nine-bladed installation (which failed). The executioner Heindrecht resisted the proposal to construct an all-metal mobile variant mounted on wheels.

The guillotine's first victim was the highwayman Nicolas-Jacques Pelletier, beheaded on 25 April 1792 to ambivalent reviews; *La Chronique de Paris* noted that 'the speed with which it struck' left little by way of improving spectacle. At the height of the Revolution's guillotine fad, its fodder included the corpses of those who had escaped justice by suicide (for instance, Valazé), children (Nantes, 17 December 1793), dummies of notorious émigrés, birds for the dinner table, effigies of reigning monarchs and, allegedly, a dog taught to howl whenever it heard the word 'Republican'.

Guilt

According to FBI agent Howard Teten, the best approach for a policeman interviewing a young suspect in the grip of guilt is to gaze fixedly into his face and enunciate: 'You know why I'm here.' Sadly, Teten's formula was never put to the test. An instinctive 'profiler', Teten devised this approach in response to a frenzied killing of the early 1970s in California. Over the telephone he suggested to the Californian police that the murderer was a lonely teenager living locally – very probably skinny, acned and bursting to confess. Teten advised: 'If you walk round the neighbourhood and knock on doors, you'll probably run into him.'

Teten erred on the side of caution. It was merely necessary to stand close to the killer and say nothing. 'You got me,' conceded a young, acned interviewee on opening his door, before the cop could get a word in edgeways.

Teten joined the FBI National Academy at

Quantico in 1972 and was a long-time admirer of Dr Brussel of '**Mad Bomber**' fame. He formed part of the 1973 team that caught sex killer David Meirhofer, an early profiling breakthrough that led to the implementation of VICAP (see Quantico) some ten years later.

Britain's Dennis **Nilsen** proved similarly resilient under interrogation. Returning home on the evening of 8 February 1983, Nilsen found himself confronted by three detectives making enquiries about the human flesh in the drains.

'Good grief, how awful,' said Nilsen. Chief Inspector Peter Jay replied, on a hunch: 'Don't mess around, where's the rest of the body?'

'In two plastic bags in the wardrobe,' Nilsen replied. 'I'll show you.'

Guldensuppe, William (d. 1897)

William Randolph Hearst was a newspaper magnate and gutter press pioneer not always associated with investigative reporting. But in 1897 he played a part in solving the Willie Guldensuppe murder.

Hearst's interest was fired by the discovery on 26 June 1897 of a headless torso wrapped in oilcloth in Brooklyn's East River, and he assigned a team of the *Journal*'s reporters to the case. Journalist George Arnold recognised the calluses on the cadaver's hands as a common characteristic of Turkish bath masseurs and, taken in conjunction with a tattoo, this led to the first breakthrough, the identification of the corpse.

The newspaper tracked down the purchaser of the body's distinctive oilcloth wrapping, and delivered her as a suspect to police headquarters. An unlicensed midwife of majestic proportions called Augusta Knack, she denied any intimate connection with the deceased, saying in the morgue: 'I don't believe those are Willie's **legs**.'

But Hearst knew better. The *Journal* established that Guldensuppe and Knack were lovers and, further, that Augusta had taken up with a barber called Martin Thorn who lost his job after a beating from the masseur. Shortly afterwards, Thorn bought a pistol and swore revenge.

'Murder Mystery Solved By *Journal*,' trumpeted the paper on Thorn's arrest. Then the journalists

found the murder cottage. It was quietly situated; the bathroom drained into a pond, and on the day of the murder the local farmer had been perplexed by the way his ducks turned pink.

The lovers had wrapped up Willie's body in a number of parcels, dropping them off from the Greenpoint ferry. Thorn went to the electric chair on 1 August 1898, but Augusta Knack escaped with twenty years. Paroled after ten, she set up a neighbourhood delicatessen, performing much the same function in New York as the Patty Hearst ransom money was later to play on the West Coast.

The full demand for the return of Miss Hearst after her February 1974 kidnapping consisted of a $400 million Food Aid programme for hungry Californians. Eventually this was parleyed down into the mass distribution of $25 lunch boxes, containing emergency rations of chicken, steak, turkey and frozen fish.

Gun control

In America, it is said that 'Guns don't kill people, people kill people.' This view receives typical expression in the 1983 book *Under the Gun*: 'Unless we solve the problem of interpersonal hatred, it may not matter very much what we do about guns... It definitely does not follow that, in the complete absence of handguns, crimes now committed with handguns would not be committed. The more plausible explanation is that they would be committed with other weaponry.' In fact, from the gun lobby's standpoint it seems that 'few homicides due to shooting could be avoided if a firearm were not immediately present' (*Patterns in Criminal Homicide*, 1958).

So entrenched are these opinions that rational American assessments – for instance *Gun Control* (1987) – of the resulting mayhem proceed with tentative pedantry bordering on the surreal. Thus: 'In addition to providing greater range for the attacker, it is argued, firearms are more deadly than other weapons.' The second of these two contentions is supported by statistical tables.

About 200 million firearms are in circulation in the USA, with about 10 per cent of households owning four or more. Some 60 to 70 per cent of householders with handguns keep them for 'self-protection'. But this is not a good idea. Figures from the Violence Policy Centre show that a handgun is 118 times more likely to be involved in a suicide, a fatal accident or a murder than in eliminating a criminal. Seventy-one per cent of homicides involve friends and acquaintances, and are presumably bitterly regretted; eighty per cent are over domestic disputes like love, money and other transient irritants.

Resistance to armed robbery increases the risk during a commercial attack by a factor of fifty, and during a personal robbery by some fourteen times (*Journal of Legal Studies*, 1986). Accidental killings in the home account for about a thousand lives annually, in addition to the hundreds of thousands of firearms-related injuries and the overall total of a million 'gun incidents' in any given year.

In 1991 these figures included the case of Vicki Childress, an asthma sufferer, who reached under her pillow on the night of 21 October, pulled out what she hoped was her inhaler, and shot herself in the face. She survived, as did Joe Petrowski of Manitobi, shot by his dog. Deputy Sheriff Todd Rollins from Oregon was another survivor; he discovered that he had wounded himself in the right thigh with his 9mm semi-automatic when he awoke drenched in blood the following

morning. Rollins got off lightly; in 1989 one in every four of the police officers killed in the line of duty with handguns were victims of their own handguns.

Shortly after the assassination of John Lennon (see **Stalking**), the President's wife Nancy Reagan went on television to oppose gun control, saying that legal restrictions encouraged 'the wrong persons' to obtain guns. She disclosed that she kept a weapon herself, saying it was 'just a tiny little gun. I don't know anything about it', provoking a columnist to enquire whether a tiny little gun fired itsy-bitsy bullets that left the victim just a little bit dead.

Laurette Brunson of Tampa, Florida, encapsulated the arguments in favour of gun control in two sentences. After being wounded by her husband during her wedding reception in April 1992, she said: 'I don't think he meant to shoot me. He just got mad and had a gun in his hand.' Surprisingly,

a 1990 Gallup poll found wide support for restrictive measures, with 81 per cent of Americans behind handgun registration and 95 per cent backing a seven-day waiting period before purchase. Virginia's Governor Wilder has sponsored legislation limiting purchasers to one gun per month, but there is little chance of more useful legislation. Congress is terrorised by the National Rifle Association with its an annual operating budget of $100 million, and senators who step out of line put their careers at risk.

American schoolroom slang for a gun is a biscuit, burner or cronze. A 'streetsweeper' means a sub-machine-gun.

Gunness, Belle Brynhilde Paulsetter Sorenson (1859–1908?)

Accident-prone professional widow. Belle's father was an itinerant conjurer and in her youth she graced his shows as a tightrope walker. But life on their small Norwegian farm palled and in 1883 she emigrated to America.

The following year she married a Swede, Mads Sorenson. Their union was childless, but she adopted three children: Jenny, Myrtle and Lucy. Then one day in 1900, when two insurance policies overlapped, her husband died of 'an enlarged heart'. Belle collected $8,500 in insurance and left Chicago (where Sorenson's relatives demanded an exhumation) for Austin, Illinois. But her new home, a rooming-house, caught fire, and after collecting the insurance she returned to Chicago to buy a confectionery store.

This too burst into flames. Belle collected the insurance and bought a farm in La Porte, Indiana, with the proceeds. There she met a jovial Norwegian, Peter Gunness. They married, but in 1903 he was involved in a fatal accident which broke his skull when a heavy sausage grinder toppled onto his head. Belle collected the insurance of $4,000. Then, to the general admiration of her neighbours, she settled down to a hardworking routine as a widow, homesteader and mother. Her unhappy personal life attracted some sympathy. Relationships with a succession of farm workers and prospective husbands never prospered; the rejected men disappeared after a few days. Meanwhile she gave birth to Gunness's posthumous son. But as one child arrived, so another left; young Jennie departed in her early teens, sent to Los Angeles to complete her education.

By now Belle had lost her teeth. She weighed about 280 pounds and was reduced to advertising in the matrimonial journals for suitors where, as devotees of Lonely Hearts columns would expect, she depicted herself as rich, goodlooking and young. One advertisement ran: 'Comely widow who owns a large farm in one of the finest districts in La Porte County, Indiana, desires to make acquaintance of gentleman equally well provided, with a view of joining fortunes. No replies by letter considered unless sender is willing to follow answer with a personal visit.' Sometimes she added the tagline 'Triflers need not apply', and responded in this vein: 'I feel sure you are the one man for me... I am worth at least $20,000, and if you would bring just $5,000 to show you are in earnest we could talk things over.' No one stayed long, but in 1906 a hired hand, Ray Lamphere, added a stable element to her life.

This timid man became Belle's on-off lover. She continued to entertain other suitors; when they arrived, he moved out. In January 1908 the bachelor Andrew Helgelien rode up from Aberdeen in South Dakota. Helgelien stayed for weeks, inflaming Lamphere with jealousy, but shortly after drawing $2,900 in cash from a local bank he too vanished. When Lamphere was overheard remarking to a drinking partner, 'Helgelien won't bother me no more', the locals became suspicious. Meanwhile Helgelien's brother pestered Belle by letter about Andrew's whereabouts. He had not been seen since Belle's note arrived saying, 'My heart beats in wild raptures for you. Come prepared to stay for ever.'

By now Lamphere was quarrelling openly with Belle. She fired him and took on a replacement, Maxon, to run the farm. Lamphere left to live with a woman known as 'Nigger Liz' Smith, but he continued to stalk Belle's land. She had him fined for trespass, and on 27 April she confided in her attorney about her fears for her family's safety. Lamphere had threatened to torch her home.

Early the following morning the farm went up in flames, and in the ashes the searchers found the charred remains of three children aged eleven, nine

and five, together with a headless female body with Belle's rings on its fingers. In the smouldering debris were watches and human teeth, and three weeks later a jawbone, with Belle's dentures attached, was discovered in the cellar. Traces of **strychnine** in the woman's body encouraged the coroner towards a finding of 'death by felonious homicide, perpetrator unknown', and Lamphere was charged with the murder of Belle and her family.

Asle Helgelien arrived to look for his brother. Nosing around the fields, his attention was caught by a rubbish pit in the corner of a bog pen, and Sheriff Smitzer set his men digging. They unearthed four bodies with several limbs missing. Andrew Helgelien was one victim, furled in an oil-cloth, and young Jennie another. Further excavations brought the total of dismembered corpses to fourteen, including two more children and a human skull dredged from the cesspool. Among the dead were Thomas Lindboe, a labourer from 1905; Henry Gurholdt, a Scandinavian suitor who had brought $1,500 in earnest of his intentions; Olaf Svenherud, a Norwegian admirer; and two others called Budsberg and John Moo. The rest remained nameless.

Meanwhile Belle was seen everywhere and frequently arrested: 'Mrs Gunness Very Numerous' ran the newspaper headline. Lamphere came to trial on 9 November 1908, and after nineteen ballots a divided jury pronounced him guilty of arson. He died in prison of tuberculosis in December 1909, but not before leaving a confession with the prison minister, describing his role as Belle's accomplice in a total of forty-two joint murders. He admitted to chloroforming the Gunness children on the night of the fire and related how Belle had substituted another – presumably spare – female corpse for her own. Then he drove her away, disguised as a man, before doubling back to set fire to the house.

But this story bears a striking resemblance to the theory already advanced in a shocker called *The Mrs Gunness Mystery*. Belle was the possessor of what the crime writer Colin Wilson terms a 'High Dominance' personality (like Brady in the **Brady–Hindley** combination). Lamphere was under her thumb, and one possibility is that they set the scene months before, hoping to be reunited after the fire. Perhaps Belle died in the blaze. Or perhaps she escaped and lived to a ripe old age. The one certainty is that her suitors perished in droves, killed with strychnine and axe or hammer.

Gutteridge, George William (d. 1927)

On the morning of 27 September 1927 the body of Police Constable George William Gutteridge was discovered sprawled in the road outside the Essex village of Howe. He had been shot four times. His right hand clutched a pencil, and his notebook lay nearby. Cartridge cases were scattered on the ground.

The time of death was estimated at four in the morning, when it was still dark. But Gutteridge's torch remained in his pocket, and he needed to see in order to write. His colleagues surmised that he met his death in the glare of car headlights. It soon emerged that a Morris Cowley had been stolen from Dr Edward Lovell's home fourteen miles away, and the vehicle turned up that same evening, abandoned in London, with splashes of blood on the running board.

Seven months later two small-time villains, Frederick Browne and William Kennedy, were convicted at the Old Bailey. The murder weapon had a distinctive damaged breech, and the professional testimony of Robert Churchill represented a major step towards the acceptance of forensic ballistics as a valid discipline.

After the verdict, Browne told the court, 'It will come out later that I had nothing to do with it', and sixty-five years later it has. Frederick Browne was undoubtedly a hardened villain, a violent crook with Essex connections and a car thief to boot, and during the early stages of the investigation, Chief Inspector James Berrett became 'convinced that Browne was mixed up with the murder even if he had not actually committed it'.

Browne was arrested in a dawn raid on 20 January 1928 for an unrelated theft of a Vauxhall car the previous November. At his garage the police found a loaded Webley revolver. Browne casually admitted ownership without being shown the gun in question (later to become Exhibit 31);

he had a small arsenal of unlicensed weapons. At this stage there was no hint of a murder charge, but the following day the police uncovered *another* Webley in the garage, which Robert Churchill correctly identified as the fatal weapon (Exhibit 17). Browne had swapped an automatic for this revolver, taking possession on 7 October; on the day of the shooting Exhibit 17 belonged to an associate, William Kennedy.

Berrett later used Browne's 'sight-unseen' admission to tie him to Exhibit 17, and by the time Browne appreciated his error it was too late for a convincing retraction. But when Browne accepted responsibility for Exhibit 31, the existence of Exhibit 17 was unknown. So Chief Inspector Berrett knew the admission, which hanged Browne, arose from a misunderstanding.

After Kennedy's arrest on 25 January, Berrett extracted the famous confession in which Kennedy, the true murderer, detailed how Browne had shot Gutteridge. Kennedy claimed they had travelled to Essex together to steal a car. On the way back, PC Gutteridge flagged them down and asked for a driving licence.

When Browne prevaricated, Gutteridge demanded, 'Do you know the number of this car?' 'Yes,' said Browne, 'I know the number, but do you?' Kennedy chipped in, 'It's TW6120', and Gutteridge took out his notebook. Then, said Kennedy, 'I heard a report, quickly followed by another one. I saw the policeman stagger and fall over by the bank at the hedge. I said to Browne, "What have you done?", and then saw he had a large Webley revolver in his hand.' *Kennedy's* account went on to describe how *Browne* had shot out Gutteridge's **eyes** as he lay dying.

Where one man's defence is to incriminate another, the two are normally tried separately. On these particular facts, the jury were merely enjoined to disregard Kennedy's statement. But his vivid tale dominated the hearing, and it comprised the only evidence against Browne. He was not seen stealing the Morris Cowley, nor seen travelling in it or to it, nor were his fingerprints detected in it. He was not proved present at the murder and, even if he had been, there was nothing to show he knew his companion was armed. It is almost certain that Browne spent the night of 26 September at home with his wife, as he maintained. But in the course of the trial the two revolvers became inextricably muddled, and Kennedy's allegations stuck to Browne like glue. Both were hanged on 31 May 1928.

Gutshot

Safecrackers' technical term. A gutshot was the basic way of opening a **safe** with explosives. After knocking off the **lock** dial with a hammer, the box was tipped on its back, and the nitroglycerine squeezed into the exposed workings from a pipette; a dropper and a half was more than enough. A detonator laid across the top blew the charge, destroying the lock's innards, and the whole operation took about five minutes.

A variant, the 'ragshot', prevented the explosive from dribbling harmlessly away and, by removing the reliance on gravity, allowed safes to be tackled upright. It entailed inserting a bit of cloth saturated in nitro but, like the gutshot, sometimes fused the lock mechanism solid.

The radical solution of the 'jamshot' blew the safe's door right off. Apart from nitroglycerine, the technique required steady nerves, a bar of well-kneaded soap and a strip of cellophane, pressed in along the top of the door to keep the hairline crack free from the soap. This was worked into a semicircular 'cup' or dish straddling the gap and, after withdawal of the cellophane, the nitroglycerine was poured carefully into the cup on the face of the door. The liquid seeped into the crack, trickling round the edge of the doorframe.

In the old days, the safeman lit a fuse dangling into the cup. Timing was all. Needing five seconds to get clear, he had to forecast whether, as he struck his match, the explosive would complete its run round the door by the moment of ignition. Too soon, and some of the nitroglycerine remained in the cup, with not enough in the crack; too late, and it drained away.

This was the golden age of safecracking. Practitioners were underworld kings, revered by their colleagues and the press, like the **highwaymen** of yore. In 1894 the *New York Times* described cracksmen as 'the gentlemen Joes of their trade, who scorn small affairs... They keep step with science, and they have every new invention at their command.' Down the decades their robberies were celebrated as 'bold', 'daring' and 'expert', and as late as 1965 Britain's *Star* newspaper characterised safecrackers as 'Master Technicians, or even graduates in Crime Technology'.

The advent of electric detonators banished the days of spluttering fuses and turned a craft into a dull, if predictable, science. The final indignity came in the 1960s, when cash payrolls were diluted by increasing reliance on cheques. Safes no longer held enough money to be worth robbing.

Apart from finding the key, the easiest way to open a safe today is with a core drill, a standard building trade item consisting of a water-cooled tube with a diameter anywhere between one and nine inches, tipped with diamond or carbide chips.

H

Hair

The year 1857 saw the publication of the first monograph on hair. Magnified some 2,000 times under the microscope, hair became easy to categorise. Emile Villebrun, one of Lacassagne's students, pointed out that animal hair possesses a continuous central core – the medulla, which contains air. With humans the core is only intermittently visible, enabling the two to be differentiated.

Under the microscope, the outer casing – the cuticle – of animal hair displays tiny overlapping scales which vary from species to species, and forensic laboratories now keep quick-recognition charts for animal identification.

Hair thickness can be measured to the nearest hundredth of a millimetre. Its rate of growth is constant, about .44 mm a day and, since hair absorbs poisons such as arsenic, it provides a precise calendar of the dosage inflicted (see **Napoleons**). Its provenance – from pubic area, head or armpit – can be readily established. Head hairs are circular in cross-section, facial hairs triangular, eyebrows taper towards one end, and pubic hairs are triangular or oval (and curly) and tend to drop out during sexual assaults. By the early twentieth century, hair was a forensic discipline in its own right.

Until the advent of **genetic fingerprinting**, hair evidence remained inconclusive, indicating not that the hair did come from a particular person but that it might. 'Consistent with a common source' is the scientist's cautious phrase. Sometimes the common source could be very broad indeed. The pubic hair attributed to Beryl Evans, killed at 10 **Rillington Place**, was identical to that of some 15 to 20 per cent of the population. But the 'co-ed' killer, Edmund **Kemper**, was implicated by old-fashioned hair evidence, as was Ted **Bundy** after

being stopped in his Volkswagen in Granger, Colorado, for a traffic violation in August 1975.

Bundy's vehicle was vacuumed from top to bottom, yielding two pounds of dust and debris, and this was shipped to the Quantico laboratories where, spread out on a back-lit glass-topped table, it was minutely scrutinised with an illuminated magnifying glass. Strands were extracted with tweezers, and a comparison microscope produced perfect matches for tresses taken from Melissa Smith (murdered on 18 October 1974) and Caryn Campbell (murdered on 12 January 1975). Bundy was charged with Caryn's murder, but only convicted of the abduction of Carol DaRonch on the strength of her resolute eyewitness testimony.

Things are different today. DNA technology recently secured the conviction of the murderer Patrick Hasset when a hair sample was genetically matched against his semen, which had been removed from his strangled and raped victim fourteen years previously and stored in a freezer (see **Sperm**).

Half-hanged Smith (b. 1662)

John Smith, a Yorkshireman, enlisted in the Second Regiment of Foot Guards and, like many of his fellows, regularly engaged in housebreaking. On 5 December 1705 he was charged at the Old Bailey for the theft of fifty pairs of shoes, 900 yards of cloth, 400 pounds of silk and 148 pairs of gloves. Caught red-handed, he was sentenced to death, and executed at Tyburn on Christmas Eve by a charitable hangman who swung on Smith's feet to expedite his demise.

Somewhere between five and fifteen minutes later – depending on the version – a horseman galloped up to announce that Smith had been reprieved. So he was cut down and taken to a nearby public house where, by a fortunate coincidence, he turned out to be alive. Smith remained under a suspended sentence of death, but on 20 February he received an unconditional pardon after informing on some '350 pickpockets, house breakers, etc, who got to be soldiers in the guards'.

Half-hanged Smith's narrow escape

For many years 'Half-hanged' Smith continued a lucky if not a prudent man. On two occasions he came up on a capital offence; he extricated himself from the first on a legal technicality, and from the second because the prosecutor expired the day before testifying. But in September 1721 he was arrested burgling a warehouse and, despite a plea based on his advanced years, was transported to Virginia where in all probability he died.

Of his near-death experience, Smith said he beheld 'a great blaze or glaring light which seemed to go out at his eyes with a flash, and then lost all sense of pain'. Seeing a radiant haze is a common experience of many survivors of hangings. A

Captain Montagnac, from the Religious Wars, spoke of 'a light of which the charm defied description' (although an 1849 contributor to the *Quarterly Review* was probably gilding the lily in his reference to the 'pleasurable feeling' of execution).

Evidence of the incandescent colour is fragmentary, but an Irish youth who recovered from an 1825 hanging for sheep-stealing commented on its scarlet tint. He reported that 'though he felt the jerk of the rope when the ladder was turned, he did not become unconscious. He seemed to have the power of seeing all round, above and below him. Then everything turned a bright red colour, and a sort of half sleepy sensation crept through his frame, till he became insensible.' An unfortunate actor who nearly perished in the course of a stage execution during the 1890s provides partial corroboration: 'Mr H said he felt a burning sensation in the head for a second or two, then everything seemed to become a brilliant red, changing suddenly to a bright green... Of actual pain, he experienced very little, save for the fact that his head seemed to feel too small.'

This green hue was noted by the British serial killer Ian **Brady**, who knows what Death looks like. In 1985 he told the journalist Fred Harrison: 'I have seen death, a green face, warm, not unattractive... green, not black – people always associate death with black. The face is not really formed, it's a radiation, a warmth. Warm green.'

Halifax Gibbet

The Halifax Gibbet was an English guillotine, already ancient by the publication of Holinshed's *Chronicle* in 1587.

A local law prescribed that anyone found guilty of a theft valued at more than 1s 1½d should be 'forthwith beheaded on the next market day', and the miscreants perished at the hands of the Halifax Gibbet. The blade of this tremendous engine weighed 7 pounds 12 ounces, and decapitated heads were said to bound a huge distance, anecdotally coming to rest in washerwomen's panniers.

The gibbet incorporated a highly idiosyncratic communal release mechanism, triggered by removal of a pin attached to a rope pulled by 'every man there present' – except in cases involving the theft of animals, when the creatures themselves were roped up and herded away from the gibbet to pull out the pin.

Some twenty-five unfortunates were executed during the rein of Elizabeth I; the last recorded use came in 1640. The gibbet's stone base was rediscovered in 1840 by the Halifax Town Trustees in the course of levelling Gibbet Hall.

A weird echo of the Halifax Gibbet, crossed with the solution to Agatha Christie's *Murder on the Orient Express*, cropped up in the 1740s when a gang of Hampshire smugglers cornered a Customs Officer called Galley and his travelling companion Chater at the inn of Rowland's Castle. After crushing Galley's testicles, the smugglers whipped him to death. It was then proposed that Chater be killed with a pistol, its trigger attached to a length of string. All fourteen gang members would give the fatal tug together. In the event, a simpler expedient was adopted. They threw Chater into a well and dropped rocks on top of him. Seven of the smugglers swung for the killings.

Hamilton, Dr Albert

Early twentieth-century American charlatan with a bogus doctorate who posed as a ballistics expert when the science was still in its infancy. During the Stielow case of 1915, Hamilton helped obtain a conviction by spotting imaginary but otherwise distinctive scratches on the test bullets, twinning them with the murder ammunition.

The jury accepted the existence of the markings – missing from the pictures produced in court – believing Hamilton's explanation that he had unluckily photographed the wrong side, and Stielow was found guilty of murdering his employer, Charles Phelps.

Phelps was shot dead by a .22 on the morning of 22 March 1915 at his Orleans County farm. Stielow, a farmhand, denied owning a gun, but he was lying. He had a .22, and Hamilton's evidence secured the death sentence.

But the slow-witted Stielow seemed too amiable for a plausible murderer, and after the case was reopened it transpired that his gun was clogged with grease and dirt of some antiquity. The weapon had not been fired for years, and when it was, the test bullets looked quite different from the murder ammunition even to the naked eye. Stielow

was released in 1918, and an assistant on the case, Charles E. Waite, then in middle age, embarked on his life's work, cataloguing the specifications of every type of gun made in America since the first Colt. By 1922 Waite had amassed a collection of some 1,500 weapons, and he established New York's Bureau of Forensic Ballistics, making reliable assessments with the newly invented comparison microscope.

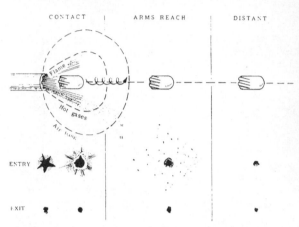

Effects of discharge of fire-arm with body surface in contact, up to arm's reach, and beyond

One of Waite's notable collaborators, Calvin Goddard, later became the author of the definitive *History of Firearms Identification* (1936), and Goddard too was impelled towards the serious study of ballistics after a spell with Hamilton, who recaptured the limelight during the 1923 **Sacco and Vanzetti** case with an attempt to doctor the evidence. He planned to substitute new guns for old, and set the scene by bringing a pair of Colt revolvers into the courtroom to compare with Sacco's original revolver. Running through some patter, Hamilton dismantled the batch in front of the judge. Then he reassembled them with Sacco's fatal barrel on his own gun, and tried to leave the court with the original exhibit. His ruse failed and the motion for a new trial was rejected.

When falsification is required, scientific findings can still be tailored to fit. Thus the 1968 report on the assassination of Robert Kennedy produced a tidy official account of Sirhan Sirhan's eight bullets which killed the Senator and wounded five others (see **Executive Action**). Meticulous diagrams plotted the reconstructed path of each shot. But it is now apparent (as it was then) that ten or possibly twelve bullets had been fired; Sirhan's magazine only contained eight rounds. Witnesses were unanimous in affirming that Sirhan shot at Kennedy from in front at a distance of two to three feet; he certainly never came closer than eighteen inches. But the autopsy showed that the Senator died from gunshot wounds fired from a range of three inches, from the side or behind. Three years later, in 1971, three independent experts affirmed that the fatal bullets (said at the trial to be a perfect match for ammunition fired from Sirhan's gun) could not have come from his weapon.

See also **Firefights**

Hand

Martha Sheward's hand was sniffed out in 1851 by a dog and taken to its master, on an English country walk. But no one knew to whom it belonged, and Sheward's other portions, which turned up all round the Norwich ditches, similarly defied identification when presented to the police. So the entire assortment was pickled, and the jar put into long-term storage in the Norwich Guildhall.

Eighteen years later Martha Sheward's husband, overcome by remorse, felt moved to stand outside the house in Walworth, London, where he first met his wife, and confess her murder to the nearest policeman. The disassembled body in Norwich was produced and, despite subsequent retractions, William Sheward went to the gallows.

The pair had been grindingly poor and quarrelled bitterly over money. Sheward found it galling that shortly after her demise his wife came into a substantial inheritance which she could not claim, being dead. This quirk of fate lay heavy on his mind, and led to his fatal confession.

Half-a-century later, burglar George Mitchell was arrested after breaking into a crockery warehouse in Clerkenwell. The constable on the beat identified the fixture surmounting one of the spikes on the wooden gate outside the premises as a human finger. It had separated from Mitchell's right hand as he scrambled over the gate and a gold ring snagged on the tip of a spike. The digit, forwarded to the Fingerprint Bureau, acquired a certain measure of renown in the *Police Gazette*, which printed the gate's photograph with a helpful arrow indicating the railing on which it was found. The alert went out for a four-fingered criminal, and Mitchell was arrested a month later on suspicion of pilfering in a crowd at a tramstop. Producing his bandaged hand in proof of innocence, Mitchell not unreasonably objected, 'How could I pick pockets with a hand like this?' The detective replied, 'I don't know about that, but I reckon you've lost a finger. The blokes at the yard are looking after it for you.' Mitchell was sentenced to twelve months' hard labour.

Handkerchiefs

Charles Dickens's **Fagin** constituted a viable financial proposition; it was feasible for a London receiver of stolen goods to prosper by specialising in handkerchiefs. By the early 1800s, a Mrs Diner of Field Lane, Holborn, was reckoned a woman of property, and she dealt exclusively in handkerchiefs for many years, 'buying them from pickpockets of every description. Men, women, boys and girls, but chiefly boys, whose practice it is.' The loft above her shop was crammed to bursting. Mrs Diner remained beyond the short reach of nineteenth-century law by removing the identifying marks and initials from her stock.

In those pre-conglomerate days, London receivers were many and various. Robert Charles was the specialist for stolen ducks. His near neighbour, Edward Memmery from Old Pye Street, preferred pilfered foodstuffs: butter, cheese and bacon. Joshua Roberts of Pump Lane handled hot game. In Tottenham Court Road, Mr Brand concentrated on lead. And a fence called Reed, who had a Rag and Glass shop off Fitzroy Place, ran what amounted to a school for young thieves, starting his pupils off by lending them housebreaking implements.

The young went to prison in droves. Many were transported, some were hanged, 'dying game' in stolen finery, cheered at the gallows by their friends. In 1816, a conservative estimate of 6,000 London boys and girls supported themselves solely by thieving. Known as 'boys on the cross' or 'cross boys', from a middle-class perspective they must have seemed irretrievably lost, perhaps the 'lost boys' of J. M. Barrie's *Peter Pan*.

Hands Up

A succinct formula devised by the remarkable Bill Miner (1847?–1913), who ran away to California 'to become a cowboy' at the age of thirteen. 'Old Bill's' first stagecoach robbery in 1869 earned him a few hundred dollars and ten years in San Quentin.

After his release, Old Bill travelled, doing a spell in Turkey as the partner of a trader who abducted desert women for resale to harems. Then he worked as a gun runner in Rio before returning to his interrupted career as a stagecoach robber. But in 1881 he was caught again. Sent down for twenty-five years, he gained his freedom in 1901 only to find that the era of the stagecoach had passed.

So at the age of fifty-four, Old Bill took to robbing trains, concentrating on the Canadian Pacific. Jailed for life in 1906, he escaped and held up a bank in Oregon before reverting to railways. Pinkerton's W. H. Minster captured the sexagenarian Miner after a swamp shoot-out and, during his next life sentence, Old Bill escaped three times from the Georgia State Penitentiary.

He spent the final years of his life, like the last Emperor of China, tending a flower garden; in breaks between horticulture, he dictated his life story to a friendly prison detective, and died in his sleep in 1913.

The last person and first woman to rob a stagecoach was Pearl Hart. Obsessed by derring-do dime novels in her twenties, Pearl persuaded the local town drunk to collaborate in a hold-up; and in 1899 the pair stopped a stage somewhere outside Globe, Arizona. They never found out exactly where; inextricably lost, the pair were rounded up by an unarmed posse still with their $450 of loot. She served five years in the Yuma Penitentiary.

Hanging, a short history of

Hanging is thought to be a Persian invention which reached England in the twelfth century. It soon achieved a momentous throughput. In the single year of 1279, Jews alone accounted for 280 executions for clipping coin. According to the historian Stow, some 72,000 criminals were hanged in the reign of Henry VIII when the total population stood at not much more than a couple of million; the 2,000 executions a year represented an annual mortality rate of one in a thousand across the population, some ten times the current British road accident rate.

While Edward VI was on the throne (1547–53), hangings reached an annual average of 560 at Tyburn alone. Every law day twenty or thirty were executed in a batch. London was referred to as the City of Gallows and it is commonplace to find road directions in Ogilby's *Itinirarium Angliae* with gallows as the nearest reference point. Three sets disfigured the highway between London and East Grinstead, some forty miles distant.

Excessive zeal on 23 March 1738

The habit of doling out the death sentence continued without respite down the centuries. Between 1825 and 1831 a total of 9,136 were condemned to death, but by then only a minority of the sentences were carried out. Of the 410 convicted of horse, sheep and cattle stealing only seventy actually swung, and the proportion of reprieves steadily increased from the mid-eighteenth century, inspiring old lags to reminisce fondly of times past. One, reported by John Townsend – the most famous of the Bow Street officers – remarked: 'Why, Sir, where there is one hung now, there were five when I was young.' But horrors still abounded. In 1833 a boy of nine was killed for poking a stick through a window and stealing tuppence worth of paint.

Thereafter the number of executions fell very rapidly, thanks largely to the work of Sir Robert Peel who wiped capital offences off the statute books by the score. In 1837, 438 prisoners were capitally convicted, but two years later the figure had dropped to fifty-six. Public executions were only banned in 1868.

For many years it was the custom to dump the bodies of the deceased on the doorsteps of those who had been instrumental in their demise. Thus the Annual Register of 1763 records that the body of Cornelius Sanders was taken to the house of Mrs White in Lamb Street, Spitalfields, from whom he stole the £50 for which he went to the gallows. The mob sacked her house, burning her furniture in the street. In the provinces, civic feasts were often held at public expense to mark executions, a practice which continued in Scotland until the nineteenth century.

The gallows provided work for the lowest of the low, and those who lived by the rope often died by it, with executioners ending up on the scaffold as a matter of routine. Other functionaries were also at risk. On 23 March 1738 a drunken executioner at Hereford was only just restrained from hanging the parson reading from the Book of Prayer.

Family firms – notably the **Pierrepoints** – often dominated the hanging business. Payment was per capita, fixed at ten guineas from the mid-nineteenth century, and last-minute reprieves generated a certain amount of ill-will. Payment came in two instalments, half in advance at the time and the remainder two weeks later for good post-execution conduct. This included not holding court in the local pub afterwards as a freak attraction. During the nineteenth century executioners still received the clothes and personal effects of their victims as a perk, hawking them as souvenirs for a tidy sum. The training course took about a week.

The art of hanging developed very gradually. In the old days at **Tyburn**, the cart holding the accused stopped beneath the gallows; after the noose was fitted, the horse ambled on, leaving the victim to dangle, perishing slowly of asphyxia. Death might not come for many minutes and there are several cases of effective reprieves arriving some time after the victim was hanged. Nor were 'resurrections' unusual. When the murderer William Duell was hanged with four others at Tyburn on 24 November 1740, he revived in time to find himself in one piece (but only just) in the macabre surroundings of a dissection room. He was returned to **Newgate** and transported for life.

Sometimes the executioner pulled on the victim's legs to hasten his demise, and often relatives fought for the corpse to prevent its delivery to the Worshipful Company of Barber-Surgeons for anatomisation.

The most significant technological development, the long drop introduced by William Marwood, produced, in theory at any rate, instantaneous extinction. Almost equally important was the placement of the knot in its optimum location, empirically established, under the angle of the left jaw. This tilted back the chin, thereby assisting in the rupture of the spinal cord. The body was left on the end of the rope for an hour to avoid any chance of premature burial.

Reading the memoirs of the nineteenth-century hangmen it is hard to avoid a dispiriting sense of their professional jealousy about who ranked as the 'best' hangman or 'chief' executioner. Nor do the minor refinements or stylistic variants of each practitioner seem matters for great pride. But in a strange transference of celebrity, the victim's fame rubbed off onto the executioner, who in later periods serialised his memoirs in the newspapers. Public status of the craft was reflected in the hangmen's calling cards. James **Berry** had an attractive card with an ivy-leaf design giving his name and trade of 'Executioner'. William Calcraft's (1800–79) painted shop sign stated 'Boot and Shoe Mender' and, in much larger letters, 'Executioner to Her Majesty'.

Fond of animals, Calcraft hanged people off a three feet drop, and indulged in one of the more peculiar ruses to segregate his personal from his professional life. On arrival at a prison for a hanging garbed in a black suit, he would change his clothes, donning another black suit of identical design. It is supposed that he purchased these duplicate outfits in multiples, two or three at a time, and perhaps no criminological issue is quite so fraught with insignificance as the speculation over whether he preserved his suits particular to their usage, unless it be the question of erections.

It is widely believed that the victim of a hanging achieves instantaneous erection, which may account for the last words of Dr Thomas Neill Cream, executed on 15 November 1892. 'I am Jack...' he said as the hangman pulled the lever, suggesting that a confession to his true identity as the Ripper was imminent. But Cream was a well-spoken man, and it is equally likely that he was commenting on the phenomenon of involuntary emission ('I am ejaculating.').

See also **Initiation**, **Recruitment**

Hansen, Robert (1939–)

Alaskan baker from Anchorage who gave his victims a sporting chance. If they agreed to oral sex he spared them. Only when a woman refused did he strip her at gunpoint. Then Hansen gave his quarry a head start, waiting as she ran off screaming into the frozen woods.

Hansen relished the stalking, sometimes allowing his victim to think she had escaped before flushing her out for the excitement of another chase across the icebound wastes. When his prey became too exhausted to move, he killed her with his .223 Ruger Mini-14 high-velocity hunting rifle.

He tracked naked Paula Golding along a sandy river-bank, following the footprints until he spotted her lying bleeding and exhausted under a stand of brush. Rather than kill outright, he shouted until she staggered to her feet, and then took her on the run with a bullet between the shoulder-blades.

Cats do much the same, growing petulant with mice which won't 'work' any more, hoping to paw them into revived spasms. For Hansen too, nationally recognised for bagging specimen Dall mountain-sheep with a bow and arrow, the thrill was in the hunt. It felt 'like going after a trophy Dall or a grizzly bear'.

In psychological terms, Hansen's move to bigger quarry was motivated by feelings of resentment, in turn provoked by a well-founded perception that he was unattractive. At school, as a pimply, skinny stutterer, Hansen enjoyed little success with girls, and as an adult he preyed on the floating population of busty topless dancers working the red-light district in Anchorage.

Episodes normally began with a bout of torture in the basement of Hansen's pleasant suburban house. Lured to his home by an offer of two or three hundred dollars for oral sex, the unwary soon found themselves handcuffed to a post. Women who demanded money (as though they needed *paying* to have sex) were generally killed, whereas those who admitted servicing Hansen out of carnal desire went free. Maybe thirty or forty victims were released alive after hours, or even days, of sex and torture but, as bar girls on the wrong side of the law, they did not pester the police with complaints.

In 1982 one of the women escaped, declining to get into Hansen's Piper Super Cub at nearby Merrill Field for the flight to the killing ground. She struggled free and ran for her life towards the streetlights where Officer Gregg Baker spotted her on Fifth Avenue. But her detailed report was disbelieved, no more than the word of a frightened teenage hooker against a married local businessman with a teenage daughter. Hansen ran a popular bakery, and two respectable cronies provided an alibi.

A few months later hunters working the Knik River twenty-eight miles from Anchorage noticed a curious mound of earth. Digging a few inches down, they exposed the stiffened body of a naked young  woman. Two brass shell casings lay beside her in the shallow grave, and she was easily identified as a 23-year-old topless dancer, Sherry Morrow, missing since November 1981. About this time another body – Paula Golding's – broke through the soil in a half-dug grave on the banks of the River Knik. Paula's clothing showed no bullet holes; she too had been shot while naked in an Alaskan winter. Investigators checking missing-persons reports for other disappearances came across Officer Baker's report, and District Attorney Krumm broke Hansen's alibi by threatening to make his friends repeat their story under oath. A home search located Hansen's .233 Ruger, and tests produced firing-pin marks identical to the shell casings found in the Golding and Morrow graves.

Hansen offered to talk if, by pleading guilty to four murders, he could spare his family the ordeal of a trial. His twelve hour confession was recorded over two days, and it is possible that he only included 'prostitutes' in his seventeen admitted killings. Krumm commented, 'He liked and respected women who he felt, in his mind, were good', and Hansen may have drawn a veil over the fate of respondents to his advertisements seeking 'a woman to join me in finding what's around the next bend, over the next hill'.

Many of Hansen's victims had simply fallen on hard times. Paula Golding was a secretary until a botulism scare closed the local canneries, and she worked just eight days in a topless bar to make ends meet before Hansen approached her.

On 28 February 1984 he was sentenced to 461 years. Hansen kept a tally of his victims on a little map, marking their graves on the rugged Kenai Peninsular with asterisks.

Harding, John Wesley (1853–1895)

A stone-cold killer. Harding was the second son of a Texan Methodist minister, and (in his own words) 'distracted his parents' with his first killing at the age of fifteen. The victim, a black called Mage, seized Harding's bridle. So Harding 'shot him loose'. As he put it, Mage 'kept coming back and every time we would start, I would shoot him again and again until I shot him down'. Harding spent the following ten years on the run, killing three more times before his next birthday, reaching a total of twelve victims before he started to shave, eventually clocking up forty-four notches.

Harding was captured early on and locked up in the log jail at Marshall with an armed prisoner, whose Colt .45 he purchased, enabling him to avoid trial by shooting his guard dead. Then he killed the three soldiers who recaptured him. He sawed his way out of another jail and, in a fight with Mexican cattlemen, claimed five more victims. He lent a hand in the Sutton-Taylor feud, and fell out with Wild Bill Hickok (then the Marshal in Abilene), who took umbrage when Harding killed a fellow hotel guest through the wall for snoring.

On the night of his twenty-first birthday, on 26 May 1874, Harding killed the Brown County Deputy Sheriff Charles Webb (his thirty-ninth victim), who was prudently trying to shoot him in the back. A posse hung Harding's cousins Tom and Bud, his brother Joe was strung from a telegraph pole, and two friends were executed by gunfire. Despite the price of $4,000 on his head, Harding himself remained at large for another three years, finally trapped in the smoking car of a Florida train by Texas Rangers when his pistol got caught in his suspenders.

In prison Harding studied algebra, theology and law. On his release in 1894 he set up as an attorney-at-law, portraying himself in the *El Paso Times* as a 'peaceable, dignified man...that never yields except to reason and law'. But he was overheard threatening local lawman Young John Selman for jailing his mistress McRose overnight, and on 19 August 1895 Old John Selman found Harding playing dice in the local bar and blew the back of his head off. Selman successfully pleaded self-defence at his trial.

In the eponymous album, Bob Dylan characterised Harding as a friend to the poor, 'never known to hurt an honest man'. Dylan's music also featured in a 1987 Australian killing, precipitated when Gladys Dickinson asked her son to turn down the volume of the LP *Desire*, which he was playing at four in the morning.

Mistaking his mother for the record's evil character Isis, Richard Dickinson trampled her to death to the accompaniment of the track 'One More Cup of Coffee for the Road'. Then he sprinkled her body with instant coffee grains. Five years later the schizophrenic Richard was let out of prison for the evening to attend a Dylan concert, but not until a medical team evaluated and dismissed the risks of Dylan singing the offending song live.

Hawthorne Restaurant

Site of one of Chicago's most impressive set-piece onslaughts. After the notorious **Cicero** election of 1924, the Hawthorne Inn became known as 'Capone Castle' and, on 20 September 1926, at 1.15 in the afternoon, Capone was finishing lunch in the street-level restaurant, sipping coffee by the window on West Twenty-second Street.

Hymie Weiss planned to take Capone head-on. First he sent in a black tourer, mocked up like a detective bureau car. With its gong clanging, the decoy roared down the road at fifty miles an hour in apparent hot pursuit of escaping mobsters while a heavy on the running board blazed away with blanks from a Thomson sub-machine gun.

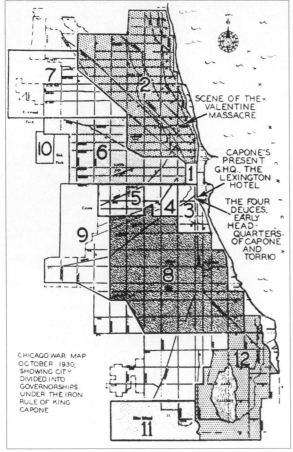

Chicago fiefdoms ruled by Capone in 1930, showing his henchmen's spheres of influence, including: (1) Jake Gusick, (4) Jack McGurn, (8) Spike O'Donnell, (9) Ralph Capone and (10) Joe Montana.

Capone fell for it. The moment the wagon passed, all sixty customers of the packed restaurant – Capone included – dashed to the window to see the fun. They were caught by Weiss's back-up. Ten cars, spaced at three-yard intervals and loaded with machine-gunners, drew up in a slow procession outside the Hawthorne.

Inside, Capone's bodyguard flung his boss to the floor under a table. Weiss's cars opened fire, pouring concentrated streams of bullets through the plate glass, stitching rows of neat horizontal holes in the rear-wall plaster. From the penultimate vehicle stepped a man in brown overalls nursing a Tommy gun. He strolled over to the restaurant, and the final car disgorged his guards, who took up station, with sawn-off shotguns, to either side on the sidewalk. The machine-gunner peered into the entrance, knelt, set the gun to rapid-fire and administered the *coup de grâce*, emptying an entire drum into the premises from point-blank range, methodically spraying from side to side.

The gunfire ceased, the killers quietly returned to their cars and on a triple blast of the horn the majestic caravan drew away, heading back east towards Chicago. A thousand rounds had been fired. The restaurant was shot to pieces, thirty-five cars were holed and no one died. But a Mrs Freeman, sitting in a nearby parked car, was wounded in the elbow. Her right eye was struck by flying glass; a stray bullet perforated the hat on her husband's head, and their son's overcoat was likewise punctured. In addition, a Capone gunman suffered a shoulder wound.

Two weeks later, on 5 October, Weiss pulled up outside his gang's headquarters above **O'Bannion's** old **flower** shop on North State Street. Accompanied by his bodyguard, his lawyer, their driver and a local politician, Weiss walked across the pavement into a hail of machine-gun crossfire.

Capone's men had rented two overlooking rooms and, to judge by the hundreds of cigarette butts ringing their seats, waited a week for their chance. The gunmen scored twelve hits on Weiss and fifteen on his bodyguard; the two others were badly wounded but survived.

Capone was not questioned. 'It's waste of time to arrest him,' said Morgan A. Collins, Chief of Police. 'He's been in before on murder charges. He has his alibi.' Capone reimbursed the Hawthorne shopkeepers and shelled out $5,000 dollars to save Mrs Freeman's sight. He could afford it.

See also **Pax Capone**

Head, Billy Moseley's

Said to have been shot in 1974, cut off and driven down to Brighton for exhibition as a trophy to a local publican before its burial at sea.

This was the prosecution's version of events and, at the end of the longest murder trial in English history (November 1976 until June 1977), Bob Maynard and Reg Dudley were sentenced to life imprisonment for murder. The evidence consisted of their own confessions coupled with the testimony of Tony Wild, a violent criminal, who contributed the Gory Head story.

The killing came to light on 5 October 1974 when a birdwatcher observed a torso, minus the hands, wallowing in the Thames near Cold Harbour Point. Detectives suspected that the body belonged to William Henry Moseley, a 37-year-old small-time crook, but it was hard to be sure without the head or fingerprints. The discovery of Moseley's friend and associate Michael Cornwall buried in Chalkdell Wood increased the chance that the two had fallen victim to a gangland feud and, at a second post-mortem on 24 October 1975, Professor James Cameron noted a rare 'metabolic' or pure cholesterol gallstone. Moseley was undergoing treatment for such a condition, and his chest X-ray from a health campaign showed eight points of similarity with a radiograph of the torso.

This painstaking forensic work was not matched by Commander Alan Wickstead's investigation, which earmarked Dudley and Maynard as the culprits. Their life sentences supposedly marked the break-up of one of the big gangs (dubbed '**Murder Inc.**' by the press) inheriting the **Kray**'s mantle of terror. Their outfit was credited with four killings and, even in the courtroom, the jury demanded special protection.

In London's East End, Dudley and Maynard went under the sinister epithet of 'Legal and General'. But the nickname was coined in their local pub one day when they arrived wearing mackintoshes and carrying umbrellas, like a couple of gents from an insurance company. Certainly both were criminals, Maynard a petty crook and Dudley a bent jeweller, but there was no weapon, no fingerprints, no forensic evidence, no witnesses to tie them to the killings and, come to that, no gang. Dudley's daughter had married Michael Cornwall, and the two families remain friends, bound together by a joint misfortune rather than sundered by a blood feud. Pundits commented that at the conclusion of the seven-month trial the jury felt that it would be disloyal or even rude to hand down acquittals.

The prosecution witness Wild later admitted that he fabricated his testimony to police specifica-

tions in return for a shorter sentence for armed robbery. Maynard's and Dudley's confessions consisted not of detailed admissions but, at best, of a failure to rebut the accusations in detail, and the accuracy of the police interview transcripts has always been disputed.

Perhaps more to the point, Billy Moseley's head turned up on 28 July 1977. But since it was found in a bundle of newspaper in an Islington public lavatory, it could hardly have been washed ashore after a sojourn at sea. On the contrary, judging by its partially defrosted state, it spent the last few years in a deep freeze. Nor had it been shot.

Head, Exxie Wilson's

Discovered beautifully presented, frozen, in an ornate wooden box in a Burbank driveway on 24 June 1980. Its hair had been posthumously washed, the features freshly made up with lipstick, eye shadow and blusher in the style of a Barbie Doll. The sperm in the mouth resulted from a post-decapitation sex session in a shower.

Wilson, a pretty 21-year-old from Little Rock, Arkansas, drifted into life as a Hollywood prostitute with her friend Karen Jones. Douglas Clark, the 'Sunset Slayer', enticed her into the front seat of his car and shot her in the head before cutting it off and driving it away, running over Karen and shooting her to death on the way home. According to Carol Bundy, Clark's accomplice, 'We had a lot of fun with Exxie' once she was safely in their apartment. They kept her head in the refrigerator.

Carol Bundy was a fat nurse, and she too caught the decapitation habit, severing the head of former lover John Robert Murray and tossing it into a ravine to prevent his sneaking to the police. 'I did it for Doug,' she told investigators. 'I loved him.'

A lonely 37-year-old diabetic on the rebound, Carol allowed Clark to move in the night of their first meeting and thereafter did his shopping, cooking and washing. She lent him her car. She paid an attentive ear to his lurid stories of teenage streetwalkers on Sunset Boulevard, and voiced no objection when he brought them to her apartment. She photographed the girls giving him oral sex, and rose to the occasion when Clark produced the bodies of two young runaways he picked up hitchhiking. She enthused over his making love to their bodies. She applied the make-up to Exxie Wilson's head. She went cruising with Clark and passed him the gun to kill a teenager near Tuna Canyon. She sat with him while he stabbed a girl twenty-seven times in his car in a parking lot and, after telling John Murray too much over a late-night drink, killed him herself.

Carol broke down during a coffee break at her job at a Burbank convalescent hospital. 'I can't take it any more,' she sobbed. 'I'm supposed to save lives, not take them.'

On 28 January 1983 Clark was sentenced to the gas chamber for these and five other murders. Carol received two consecutive life sentences. According to crime writer Colin Wilson, Clark only killed women out of resentment at their failure to bring him to orgasm, the so-called 'right man' phenomenon.

See also **Jekyll and Hyde**, **Romances**

Head, Frank Costello's

Shot on 2 May 1957 by Vincent 'the Chin' Gigante in a hotel lobby. Frank Costello was Manhattan's **Mafia** chief, and hence the natural target for a Mafia conspiracy, in this case fomented by the hot-bloods Anastasia and Genovese. They disliked Costello's diplomatic style, which in their view risked turning the Cosa Nostra into a bunch of sissies.

It proved an easy contract. Costello had no retinue of bodyguards, and Gigante's bullet hit him smack in the temple, where it was deflected and veered off round the skull, travelling beneath the skin. After completing the circumnavigation of his cranium, the bullet came upon the original entry hole, through which it exited, leaving Costello with no more than an unusual flesh wound.

Nonetheless, Costello judged it time to retire. In the aftermath, Anastasia indulged in such a rampage of violent killings that he had to be put down, meeting his end riddled with holes in a New York barber's chair on 25 October 1957. The removal of two such senior personnel in rapid order left the Mafia in a turmoil – hence the ill-fated Mob summit at **Apalachin**.

Costello took to the grave the secret of his long-standing, friendly relationship with J. Edgar **Hoover**. The pair first met in the 1930s, when the Director of the FBI was out window-shopping on Fifth Avenue, and they maintained regular contact through the decades, often meeting in the Waldorf Hotel where both made use of apartments. It was through this conduit that Hoover stage-managed his apparent coup of Louis 'Lepke' Buchalter's arrest on 24 August 1939, in a spirit of continuing peaceful co-existence between the Mafia and the FBI.

Head, John Hayes's

In pre-photographic times, identification was achieved in a relatively direct and robust manner. On 2 March 1726 a severed head, noted on the muddy Thames foreshore near Horse Ferry Wharf in London, was washed, brushed, and impaled on a stake outside St Margaret's, Westminster, with a twofold objective: first, to find out to whom it belonged and second, to arrest anyone 'who might discover signs of guilt on the sight of it'.

But no one recognised it. On becoming excessively decayed for continued public display, the head was immersed in a jar of spirits (most likely gin) and exhibited, on request, to those who thought they might be able to help. In due course someone said it might be John Hayes, a carpenter who had gone missing. His wife Catherine attracted suspicion to herself, lying about her husband's whereabouts, saying variously that he had left for Hertfordshire, gone out for a walk, and fled to Portugal after killing a man in a quarrel. She confirmed the identification, exclaiming in tears, 'Oh, it is my dear husband's head', before embracing the glass container.

Catherine subsequently confessed to murdering her husband after making him very drunk indeed: on six pints of wine. Clearly a high-dominance woman, she compromised two men, Thomas Billings and Thomas Wood, in her plot by depicting her husband as a heartless atheist and the killer of his two children. As a further inducement she offered to share an inheritance of £1,500. The men hatcheted Hayes to death, but it was Catherine's cunning plan to remove the head, complicating identification, and she who held the bucket underneath the neck to catch the sluice of blood. The dismembered trunk turned up in Marylebone pond and, in an early feat of forensic detection, was crudely fitted to the head. The case is well-documented, but makes no mention of the sexual bond that today's reader suspects bound the conspirators together.

On 9 May 1726 Catherine Hayes was burned alive and kicking when the executioner was unable to strangle her at the stake before the flames took hold. Her story passed into fiction in Thackeray's 1839 novel *Catherine*.

Head, Lord Lovat's

Re-attached for cosmetic reasons. George Selwyn, man of fashion and smart friend of Horace **Walpole**, was addicted to viewing executions; his wide circle of upper-class acquaintances thought the habit in questionable taste.

In Lovat's case, Selwyn stayed the distance. Reproached for sneaking off to watch the removal of the noble lord's head on 8 April 1747, he replied, 'Why, I made amends by going to the undertaker's to see it sewn back again.' The same thing happened to the head of King Charles I.

Lord Lovat, a venerable eighty, was the last man to be executed by the axe in England, and twenty others perished with him when a grandstand by Tower Hill collapsed, crushing both the carpenter who erected it and his wife, selling liquor underneath.

Head, Max Rubin's

An American survivor. Rubin, an ace operative at labour racketeering, had a difference of opinion with Louis 'Lepke' Buchalter, the celebrated boss of **Murder Inc**.

'By the way Max, how old are you?' Lepke enquired in the autumn of 1937. Rubin replied that he was forty-eight.

'That's a ripe age,' said Lepke. A few weeks later, on 1 October 1937, Rubin turned into Gun Hill Road in the Bronx with his head still on his shoulders. A hitman fell in behind, put the muzzle of his revolver on the base of Rubin's neck, adjusted the angulation upwards and pulled the trigger. Rubin heard something go bang. The bullet traversed his neck, emerging via the bridge of his nose between the eyes, and the gunman did not consider a *coup de grâce* worthwhile.

For thirty-eight days Rubin lay in hospital between life and death. Then he staged a full recovery, but his head stayed crooked until the end of its days.

Most survivors of head wounds are shot in the front; many parts of the brain have little to do and, in the absence of infection, it is perfectly feasible to recover from a bullet that enters the head on one side and exits on the other. The business end is at the rear.

Head money

Trouble with Chinese buccaneers prompted the enactment in 1825 of the statute for 'Encouraging the Capture or Destruction of Piratical Ships and Vessels'. Under this act, the Royal Navy's Treasurer paid £20 for every dead Chinese pirate, a reward known as 'head money' although the heads were not lodged in evidence. The Admiralty accepted any 'sufficient' proof as to quantity. Qualitatively, the issue of whether the foreign seafarers – eliminated on a lawless coast on the far side of the globe – actually were pirates was taken at face value.

Certainly Chinese corsairs were not always able to mount effective resistance; during a couple of days in October 1849, a force under Commander J.C.D. Hay killed 1,700 in the waters near Chokeum without suffering a single fatality.

The cost of the 1825 Act had reached £93,005 by its repeal in 1850, with the more acerbic Members of Parliament asking how claimants *knew* their victims were pirates and wondering aloud about the temptations of the money-for-corpses policy.

See also **Wuornos**

Head, William Gallo's

Gullible but lucky. William Gallo was a small-time hood who, with his associate Ernest 'The Hawk' Rupolo, was assigned to take out Ferdinand 'The Shadow' Boccia in 1934.

The killers' boss, the devious Vito Genovese, awarded Rupolo the task of murdering his partner to tie up the loose ends for $175 all-in. Later, Genovese changed his mind and placed the original Boccia contract with Mafia professionals, and when they killed the 'Shadow', Rupolo believed it was still incumbent on him to murder Gallo.

So one night Rupolo and Gallo went to the movies and, as they strolled home, Rupolo decided to earn his keep. He drew his gun, put it against his partner's head and squeezed the trigger. The weapon misfired, so Rupolo tried again, but it failed again. Meanwhile, Gallo, surprised at the way his friend was holding a pistol to his head and repeatedly pulling the trigger, grew suspicious, and demanded some clarification of his intentions.

Rupolo shrugged off the episode as horseplay with an unloaded weapon, and the pair continued amicably on their visit to a friend. There Rupolo examined his revolver and found that the firing pin had rusted. So he oiled it, and later that night, as they walked another couple of blocks, tried again. This time the gun worked. But since Gallo was only wounded, he experienced no difficulties in identifying his assailant, and Rupolo spent the next ten years in prison.

This was one of the favourite anecdotes of Joe Valachi, the Mafia informer. There is a sequel. In 1937, Vito Genovese staged a tactical withdrawal to Italy, accompanied by $750,000. Seven years later Rupolo was released on parole; shortly afterwards he came up on charges for another shooting. By now it seemed certain that Genovese had left the country for good, so Rupolo had few qualms about incriminating him in the original Boccia.

But in 1945 Genovese was repatriated to face trial, where he promptly had the only material witness poisoned. At liberty, Genovese started trading again, creating endless mayhem until his imprisonment in 1958 for a narcotics conspiracy. Meanwhile, Rupolo made himself scarce, eking out a fearful existence for nearly twenty years as an informer on the run. His tightly bound corpse was found in New York's Jamaica Bay on 17 August 1964, mutilated, with a bullet in the back of his head.

Like many underworld bosses, Vito Genovese was a stickler for appearances. He told one of his enforcers, the toothless Johnny D, 'The next time I see you, I want to see you with some teeth.'

Heads, Jeffrey Dahmer's

No section on heads would be complete without mentioning Jeffrey **Dahmer**.

When the police entered his apartment shortly after midnight on 23 July 1991, they noticed the first one on the bottom shelf of the fridge alongside some pickles and mustard. In the freezer were three more, frozen solid. Another three were packed in a cardboard box marked 'computer equipment', but these, like the two kept in the top drawer of the filing cabinet, were only skulls, with their flesh and skin scraped clean. That was all, apart from the two on the kitchen shelf above the stove where Dahmer was boiling up some hands and a genital organ. He told the police he had eaten Oliver Lacy's heart and biceps after frying them in vegetable oil.

In the words of Dahmer's former schoolmate Dave Borsvold: 'I kept my distance from him. He was generally one weird dude.'

See also **Torso**

Heads, living

Something funny happened to the head of Charlotte Corday. Charlotte, it will be remembered, assassinated the journalist Marat on 13 July 1793 during the French Revolution.

Immediately after being guillotined, her head was shown to the crowd by an assistant executioner, François le Gros. He slapped her on the cheek in a gesture of **contempt**. It was noted that in her blush of indignation '*both* Charlotte's cheeks reddened perceptibly... It cannot be claimed that this flush resulted from the blow itself, for the cheeks of corpses may be struck in this way in vain.' In other words, Charlotte was still 'alive'.

A learned correspondence ensued in the Paris daily *Le Moniteur*, with the German anatomist S.T. Soemmering professing that the biological technicality of death did not necessarily supervene just because the head was cut off. 'Feeling, the personality, the ego,' Soemmering argued, 'remain alive for some time in the head which has been detached from the victim's body, and there remains the *arrierè-douleur* from which the neck suffers... If the air still circulated through the vocal organs, these heads would speak.'

Most medical men remained sceptical, but the seeds of doubt were planted, and nearly a century later the debate revived after an experiment by three French doctors, the Decaisne brothers and Dr Everard.

After the execution of the murderer Théotime Prunier on the morning of 13 November 1879, the trio started work on his head in the cemetery, trying to get in touch. Putting his mouth very close to the deceased's ear, one doctor tried to rouse Prunier, repeatedly shouting his name. Then they pinched Prunier's cheek; stuffed a brush dipped in ammonia up his nostrils; drew a pencil of silver nitrate over the conjunctiva; and held a lighted candle so close to their subject's eyes that his eyeballs were singed. But nothing worked. Prunier's head was definitely dead.

The following year, Dr Dassy de Lignière experienced better luck with the murderer Menesclou, executed on 7 September 1880. Three hours after his decapitation, Menesclou perked up. With his head receiving the life-support of a blood transfusion from a dog, Menesclou's skin reddened, his features firmed, his eyelids twitched and his lips stammered. De Lignière concluded: 'This head, separated from its body, hears the voices of the crowd. The decapitated victim feels himself dying in the basket. He sees the guillotine and the light of day.'

Twenty-five years later a Dr Beaurieux provided disturbing support for this proposition. At half past five on the morning of 28 June 1905 the freshly guillotined head of the murderer Languille tumbled upright onto its base, semi-sealing the neck and keeping the haemorrhage to a minimum. After Languille's eyelids and lips worked in irregular rhythmic contractions for some five or six seconds, the head seemed to die with the lids half-closing on the eyeballs.

'Languille!' barked Dr Beaurieux. Slowly Languille's head opened its eyes, looked round, saw the doctor, focused on him and returned his gaze. 'I was dealing,' wrote the doctor, 'with undeniably living eyes which were looking at me.'

After a few seconds Languille again shut his eyes. The doctor shouted for the second time; again Languille was roused, and stared 'with perhaps even more penetration than the first time' before a final half-closing of the eyelids. Then his eyes glazed over. Dr Beaurieux's meticulous and convincing report is contained in *Archives d'Anthropologie criminelle, t. XX, 1905*.

As late as 1956 the researchers Dr Piedlièvre and Dr Fournier affirmed that death from decapitation 'is not instantaneous... Every vital element survives decapitation... It is a savage vivisection followed by a premature burial.' Since then, countries with advanced medical facilities have ceased research, but in March 1993 a Dr Steven Seddon from Staffordshire volunteered to the *Guardian* newspaper that a beheaded man's suspension of consciousness results from the interruption of oxygen supply to the cortex.

Thus decapitation simply initiates the process by isolating the head from newly oxygenated blood and, Seddon reported, the cortex only 'shuts down' after some twenty seconds; the process of irreversible brain death takes a further three-and-a-half minutes. The severing of the spinal cord hardly matters; it causes total paraplegia of both the voluntary and involuntary muscles, but in the nether regions to which, by a happy chance, the head is no longer connected. Clearly the accidental 'sealing' of Languille's neck prolonged the presence of arterial blood in his skull, allowing it to drain away rather than gush out, and the sparks of life would persist for longer than normal until the complete 'suffocation' of his brain.

High finance

Fraud at the highest levels is sometimes depicted as a matter of childish simplicity. In his bitterness at losing the Harrods takeover battle, businessman 'Tiny' Rowland circulated a booklet, *Hero from Zero*, which made nine- or even ten-figure gains seem the work of a moment. At the peripheries of the Harrods-Al Fayed saga, Rowland's confabulations included a story about the son of Carl Hirschmann Snr (an adviser to the world's richest man, the Sultan of Brunei) who he alleged appropriated $100 million. The money, Rowland maintained, was originally intended to put his father in funds to buy the Sultan of Brunei a long-distance 747-SP so that he could fly around with polo ponies and racing cars in an aeroplane. Rowland alleged that Hirschmann's son added the word 'Jnr' after the payee name on the banking forms, and then paid $100 million into his own account.

Another of Rowland's baseless contentions is that the respected financier Al Fayed duped the Sultan of Brunei out of $1.5 billion by the simple expedient of telling him he would, following receipt, place the funds in a joint account.

Money does not grow on trees, but in the nineteenth century the mighty department-store oak of the Sears, Roebuck empire did spring from an acorn of dubious origins. Starting his working life as a railroad telegraph operator, Richard W. Sears dealt in watches on the side, buying them in at $2 and mailing them out at $20 to imaginary customers at non-existent addresses. Sears took care to open the packages 'returned to sender' in his workmates' presence, allowing them to snap up his stock at a bargain $10 each.

It is wrong to underestimate the limitless tenacity and guile exercised by fantasists and conmen in achieving their positions of trust. Nonetheless, at the highest levels the 'sting' itself may bear no clear relationship to complicated financial machinations. When a House of Commons committee reported on Robert Maxwell, who filched £500 million from company pension funds, it described his methodology as 'startlingly simple'. Maxwell was fully entitled to sell the pension fund shares. So he did. But there was nothing to ensure that he gave the sale proceeds back. So he did not.

The latest scam on the international financial markets involves the large-scale sale of 'prime bank notes' at a discount. The scheme has the special allure of free money; buy a dollar for, say, 85 per cent of its face value and see how much more it can be sold for. Translated into inter-bank finance, institutional punters took up millions of dollars worth of secure debt ('standby letters of credit') at 15 per cent below par. The notes, supposedly issued by major international banks to the privileged few, were traded at a surefire profit in conditions of intense secrecy (somehow connected with furtive 'ethical' investments) under the supervision of the federal authorities in Washington.

If you believe that, you will believe anything. Buying the notes was effortless, but their sale proved impossible. By late 1992 the South Pacific island of Nauru and the Bank of Croatia had squandered $20 million before calling in the police, and in February 1993 the Salvation Army joined their ranks with an $8.8 million loss.

Highwaymen

A curiously schizophrenic English entity, straddling the realms of fantasy and real life.

Highwaymen comprised the elite – the cavalry, as it were – of eighteenth-century criminals, if only because the ability to acquire a horse was restricted to those of relatively high competence or standing; in their pedestrianised version, robbers were merely footpads. Even Lord Macaulay, the distinguished historian, type-cast highwaymen as holding 'an aristocratical position in the community of thieves'.

By the time of the Romantics, highwaymen were elevated to the status of paragons. The writer De Quincey praised their 'strength, health, agility and excellent horsemanship, intrepidity of the first order, presence of mind, courtesy' and concluded: 'The finest men in England, physically speaking, throughout the last century, the very noblest specimens of man, considered as an animal, were the mounted robbers who cultivated their professions on the great roads.'

Highway robberies might go smoothly when the victims handed over their valuables without protest; in general, the prudent highwayman was loath to kill 'for fear of provoking the law to an implacability'. But resistance (or even sometimes compliance) could produce barbarity verging on the psychopathic.

The highwayman Thomas Wilmot thought a passenger slow in handing over a ring and cut off her finger. William Cady was so provoked by a woman who swallowed her wedding ring that he shot her dead and retrieved it via the stomach. Bob Congden murdered his first victim and did away with his landlady together with her baby and maid. Patrick O'Bryan sliced off the nose, lips and ears of a traveller who refused to part with his money, and on another occasion raped, and murdered, and then burned a woman together with her servants.

Notwithstanding, the myth of the cultivated highwayman had some basis in reality. Many were from the upper classes. Smith's contemporary *Complete History of the Lives and Robberies of the Most Notorious Highwaymen* contains two distinct skeins: apocryphal anecdotes lifted from Boccaccio, and fact. Of the fifty-nine practitioners mentioned, thirty-two came from good homes and of these eighteen were the sons of the wealthy, including three Oxbridge men (Brasenose, King's, Trinity) and three law students. The sons of clergymen figure disproportionately.

Highwaymen who were not former students or gentlemen of leisure had almost without exception followed a decent line of work: as goldsmiths, farmers, shoemakers, glovemakers, tailors or servants to the well-off. Footmen – exposed to riches from which they were excluded – often progressed to a career as highwaymen, like many a man of spirit who had exhausted his inheritance on gambling and whores. A wife of mettle might share her spouse's distaste for the world of work. '*Do? Do!*' exclaimed a shocked Mrs Picken in response to her impecunious husband's vacillations about his job prospects, 'Why, what should any man do that wants money and has courage, but go upon the highway!'

Leaping Hornsey toll gate.

" Shout for your lives," cried Patterson, " the turnpike man will hear us—the gate is shut." Dick coolly calculated its height, spoke a few words to Bess, gently patted her neck—stuck spurs into her sides, and cleared the spikes by an inch.   No 2.

The takings might be good, but expenses were high. Mounted robbers were expected to pursue a course of prodigal debauchery, surrounded by conniving innkeepers, whores, dressmakers, tailors, astrologers, hangers-on and wine merchants who made them pay through the nose in return for service and – more important – silence. Few highwaymen ever put by the £500 that was the going rate to bribe their way out trouble.

But prospects were sufficiently attractive to plague the capital with an early form of protectionism when, 'in order to maintain their rights' – according to the Abbé le Blanc writing in the 1720s – highwaymen 'fixed up papers at the doors of the rich people about London, expressly forbidding all persons, of what condition or quality whatsoever, to go out of town without ten guineas and a watch upon them, upon pain of death'.

No police existed to check their activities and not until the reign of William and Mary was the casual system of informers confirmed by Parliament, when a payment of £40 (and the horse) was authorised for information leading to a conviction – a system subject to abuse, culminating in thieftakers like Jonathan **Wild**, who presented gullible young men with the horse, pistol, tuition and even the opportunity with which to commit highway robbery so that he could shop them for the reward. Between 1749 and 1761 some 250 highwaymen were executed at Tyburn, and by 1786 the prize money ran at over £10,000 a year.

Often the corpses were gibbeted, suspended in an iron cage, swinging in the breeze near the scene of their crime. For added longevity the body was coated in tar, making it an attractive proposition for pyromaniacs as well as a local landmark under which, not infrequently, further robberies were committed.

Progressive gentrification of open spaces and heaths eroded the highwaymen's freedom of operation, as did a growing tendency to withhold licences from inns that harboured them. But the highwayman's grip on the English roads was broken by blind John **Fielding** and his introduction of a civilian **Horse Patrol**.

Hindley, Myra (1942–)

Myra Hindley was a pleasant working-class Manchester girl, a Catholic convert. She delighted in animals and children, babysat locally and, at eighteen, was still shocked by bad language.

Myra suffered an early romantic disappointment, breaking off her engagement with Ronnie Sinclair, a low-paid tea blender, dismissing him as too 'immature'. On 16 January 1961, aged nineteen, she started as a typist at Millwards Merchandising, where her very first letter was dictated by a lanky, good-looking young man in a three-piece suit. He was the Stock Clerk, Scotsman Ian **Brady**, and Myra fell head over heels in love. 'Ian looked at me today' became the first entry in her diary. She wrote later: 'I hope he loves me and will marry me some day.'

Brady seemed quite a catch. Mean and sullen, he looked like Presley, and cut a dashing figure on his motorbike in a long trenchcoat, leather headgear and goggles. Outside work, Brady favoured black shirts; at the office, his suits were a fashionable grey, with just the correct proportion of terylene.

Myra stayed in ignorance of Brady's true character, largely because he proved so unresponsive. Throughout 1961, her diary charts his indifference. On 25 July she noted, 'Haven't spoken to him yet', on 18 October, 'Ian still ignores me', and on December 2nd, 'I hate Ian, he has killed all the love I had for him.' But on 22 December Myra wrote triumphantly: 'Out with Ian!', and at the end of the year he walked her home from the office party. Even so, she would not let him through the front door. On New Year's Eve, when Brady presented her father with a bottle of whisky, Myra confided to her diary: 'Dad and Ian spoke as if they'd known each other for years. Ian is so gentle he makes me want to cry.'

Later, as their relationship deepened, Myra noticed that Brady disliked Jews. He preferred things German. On dates, he insisted on German wine. Brady was well-versed in the philosophy of the Marquis **de Sade** and the Nazis. He had tape-recordings of Hitler's Nuremberg Speeches. Soon Brady was encouraging Myra to read *Mein Kampf, Six Million Dead* and *Eichmann*. As the local librarian Barbara Hughes noted: 'He always walked straight to the true crime shelves.'

The couple's sex life started to go adrift. After making love a few times Brady wearied of vaginal intercourse. Anal penetration was different. It hurt Myra – but Brady enjoyed it. In the next sexual development she was all but omitted, her participation limited to inserting a candle in his rectum while he masturbated. On at least one occasion – we know, because they took time-lapse photographs – the pair had sex wearing hoods. There are whip marks on her buttocks. On another occasion Ian photographed himself urinating against a curtain.

Brady put Myra wise to a lot of things, like the fact that everyone was corrupt. He explained that God had died; in fact, God was no more than a superstition, a cancer injected into society. Come to that, de Sade believed that rape was no crime, but only a state of mind. According to de Sade, there was little wrong with killing: 'Indeed, such destruction does good, what does it matter to Nature whether a certain mass of flesh which is today a living two-legged animal should, by the action of another two-legged animal, be destroyed?'

For Manchester in the early 1960s, this was exotic stuff; and Hindley too went to Brady's head. Whatever he said, she lapped up. They fed off each other. Soon Myra hated babies, renounced her religion, rejected marriage and scorned social occasions like dances. She bleached her hair and allowed herself to be photographed in jackboots posing as Irma Grese, the 'Beast of Belsen'. Isolated from her own background (see **Family**), she merged her character into Brady's.

Brady basked in the admiration, and by 1963 their *folie à deux* threatened to expand from fantasy into reality. Brady devised a plan for a payroll robbery; Myra would play the driver's part, but she repeatedly failed her test. Nonetheless she bought a van, and on 16 April Brady wrote to her about his plans to case the joint prior to their raid: 'I shall grasp this opportunity to view the investment establishment situated in Stockport Road, next Friday, to go over details.'

Brady moved in to share Myra's grandmother's house in Bannock Street, and persuaded her to join a pistol club where she bought an unlicensed Webley .45 and a Smith & Wesson .38. But in July 1963 they relegated the robbery to the back burner after Brady outlined an even bolder scheme – to commit the perfect murder.

Killing children was Brady's ambition. They would tour the residential side-streets of Manchester and find someone to abduct. Doing it as a couple in the form of ritualised slaughter would provide a fillip for their relationship. Myra would drive ahead in the van, and when Brady, on his motorbike, spotted a likely-looking prospect he would flash his lights. Myra was to stop and lure the child into the van, offering a reward for help in finding a valuable glove lost on the moors during a picnic.

The victim Brady selected was 16-year-old Pauline Reade. Hindley was on speaking terms with the girl's mother, making the pick-up all the easier. She drove Pauline to the beauty spot of Hollin Brow Hill, introduced her to Brady and left the two together to 'look for the glove' while she found a better parking space. By the time Hindley returned, Pauline lay on the ground with her skirt pulled up, bleeding to death. On 23 November it was the turn of John Kilbride ('lifted' while buying six-penny-worth of broken biscuits) and, seven months later, Keith Bennett and, six months later, Lesley Ann Downey and, ten months later, on 6 October 1965, Edward Evans.

On this occasion they staged a show, inviting Myra's 17-year-old brother-in-law David Smith to witness the killing in the hope of inculcating him as a new disciple. Smith owed £14 8s in rent arrears, and Myra and Brady scoured the town for a 'queer to roll'. Instead, they brought back a young homosexual, Eddie Evans, for a drink. Late that night Myra went to fetch Smith, who lived round the corner, and inveigled him back: 'See me home through the houses, it's dark and I'm scared.'

In principle, Smith agreed with Brady and de Sade that 'people are like maggots, small, blind and worthless'. In practice, stunned by the spectacle of Brady axing Evans to pieces amid pools of blood in the living room, he helped lug the body upstairs to Myra's bedroom, and then lingered, mesmerised, while Brady and Hindley chatted over wine and tea. Brady said, 'That was the messiest yet.' Myra remarked, 'Did you notice how when you hit him, his eyes registered astonishment?', propped her blood-covered feet on the mantelpiece and reminisced: 'Ian, do you remember the time we went on the moors with a body in the back...'

Smith left at three in the morning but, far from converted, he sprinted home in a blind panic, threw up and, at 6.10 a.m., rang the police from a phone box, cowering there armed with a screwdriver and carving knife in case Brady was on the prowl.

Brady was arrested after the discovery of Evans's body in a locked room, but no one thought to take Myra into custody for another five days. Neither confessed, and at their trial one of the victims' fathers, Patrick Downey, bought a .32 Webley pistol to kill Brady in court; the pair were tried with shatterproof glass screens behind their backs.

Joint killers normally blame each other, but Brady tried to exonerate Hindley. During nine hours of cross-examination, he never acknowledged either his culpability or hers. They both blamed David Smith, no more than an unwilling spectator, and in 1985 Brady confirmed, 'All my evidence was to get her off.' His act of self-sacrifice stored up trouble for the future. After sentence, the pair were separated, and away from Brady's spell Hindley saw herself as others did, not a social pioneer but a monster. She had to hand the raw material of her rehabilitation, Brady's fictionalised testimony.

Thus began a strange double act: the more Hindley proclaimed her innocence as Brady's innocent dupe – always 'out of the room' or 'in the car' at the moment of the killings – the more he recanted, affirming her guilt. In 1979 she submitted a virtual thesis to the Home Secretary, a 30,000-word document requesting parole on the grounds that she was an impressionable young girl serving a sentence for crimes she had little to do with. In January 1985 Brady countered that if he ever 'expanded' on events, Myra 'would never get out in a hundred years'. That year he confessed, for the first time admitting the killings of Pauline Reade and Keith Bennett. The police searched Saddleworth Moors and, under this renewed pressure, in February 1987 Hindley finally confessed. It took seventeen hours, and she remains one of Britain's most hated women.

In July 1987 Pauline Reade's body was found in a shallow grave 150 yards from the road over the moors. The remains of Keith Bennett were never discovered.

See also **Remorse**, **Tapes**

Hirasawa, Sadamichi (1893–1987)

Japanese poisoner who spent a record thirty-nine years on Death Row after his robbery of the Teikoku Bank, Tokyo. It is doubtful whether his technique would work in other countries.

On 26 January 1948 Hirasawa donned an armband of the Welfare Department, walked into the bank and asked the manager to muster the staff for immunisation against amoebic dysentery. Hirasawa presented a doctor's card, and issued each of the sixteen employees with a teacup into which he squirted some cyanide from a syringe.

On the command 'please' they all drank it. Hirasawa waited until everyone was immobilised in agony or dead, and then left with 164,400 yen (about £350). There were twelve fatalities.

Hirasawa died in prison in 1987, aged 95. He avoided the death penalty because his lawyers contended, for decades, that hanging was illegal since the Japanese constitution protected its citizenry from self-destruction (including, by extension, the commission of acts attracting the death penalty). Fundamental doubts persist about his guilt, and in February 1992 his posthumous lawyers filed their nineteenth request for a retrial, alleging a cover-up. According to documents still to be assessed, the poison used was not sodium cyanide (corresponding to samples found in Hirasawa's house) but acetone cyanohydrin (available only to military personnel).

The 1991 efforts of Seichi Kawaguchi relied on similar fanatical subservience to authority. Kawaguchi, a gifted mass blackmailer, embarked on a programme of standard threats distributed in indiscriminate direct mail shots to some 4,000 candidates. He extracted five million yen (£20,000) from 130 respondents before being reported, and is now awaiting trial. His victims were mostly professional men, their addresses culled at random from trade directories. At his peak, Kawaguchi took on extra staff to help lick the stamps; plagued by heart trouble, he wanted a nice sedentary business.

Hitmen

It is said that hitmen work more for prestige than for cash. The classic statement comes in *Joey*, a 1973 autobiography of an anonymous American killer. The author writes that after his first contract, 'the realization came to me that I was a made individual. I was a force to be reckoned with. A lot of people who had looked down at me as a snot-nosed wise-ass kid would now be speaking of me in different tones. The job paid $5,000.' This is first about kudos, last about cash.

But for a man reduced to 'rubbing out' strangers for money, almost *any* job offer would increase his self-esteem. In 1972 Martin Benitez, a Mexican, told police, 'If I hadn't done it, someone else would. And it was better paid than work as a labourer.' Benitez cut off his victims' heads to show to his clients as proof of completion.

Investigations into the **Murder Inc.** killers found that each was motivated by a personal blend of ambition, fear and sadism. One operative observed of his bosses: 'One of those guys tells me to do something, I do it. If I don't, I'll get myself killed.' Hitman Harry Strauss put himself forward for jobs even when it was not his turn, just to curry favour with the big guys. But Luigi Ronsisvalle, a mob enforcer from Sicily in the 1970s, cast his role in more chivalric terms: 'A man of honour no go around stealing and killing for money. A man of honour, he kill for some reason, to help people.' He drew the line at drug trafficking: 'You give to me $30,000, and I am sent to kill a person. You kill him, not me. But to move pounds of heroin, you destroy thousands of young American generations.' Of Ronsisvalle's thirteen commissions, the most sordid came in 1977 when he was approached by a policeman with $2,000 collected in a whip-round to finance the hit, and it did indeed concern honour. The officer's sister was married to a compulsive gambler who, unable to cover his last wager in a poker game, had staked his wife. Then he lost the next hand.

The day after the husband brought the two winners back for sex with his mate, she complained to her brother, and in due course Ronsisvalle shot the gambler dead as he left home to go fishing. The following year, Ronsisvalle declined to help the Italian swindler Michele Sindona, who was offering $100,000 contracts on the liquidator and the attorney rummaging through his financial affairs.

The cost of murder varies widely. The Mexican Zosimo Montesino, credited with 150 slayings, charged anywhere between £3 and £150 per job.

Prices are higher in the developed world, but first-time buyers should be wary of five-figure asking prices. One of many British cautionary tales befell businessman Malcolm Stanley, who in 1992 negotiated a £30,000 purse for his wife's killing. 'I want a complete termination job, I do not want a hospital job. I want it completely zappo,' said Stanley to the prospective killer, who was, it transpired, an undercover detective.

That same year, Susan Gill, an English businesswoman, went higher, allegedly agreeing a £90,000 fee to have her unfaithful husband eliminated. Again the 'hitman' was a plain-clothes police officer. Similarly, the *agent provocateur* in America's **Cheerleaders** case began bargaining at $20,000.

All these buyers were middle-class, acclimatised to substantial bills from professionals like lawyers and accountants. However one rates their services, there is little of the professional about 'contracts', which in real life are fulfilled by the dregs of society for a pittance. In Britain, it is hardly worthwhile retaining someone; beyond the very limited confines of south London gang warfare, where crooks kill each other with metronomic regularity, mostly over soured drug deals, there is no indigenous hit-man tradition. 'Applicants' are posers chancing their arm.

Linda Calvey hired one in November 1990, and it was a waste of time. Known as the 'Black Widow', Calvey agreed on £10,000 with Daniel Reece. After pumping a shot into her lover's elbow, Reece 'froze', and his client snatched the gun back and finished the victim herself.

In 1993, journalist Simon Bell made a determined effort to find a British hitman available to the public. A fortnight passed before he tracked down a contact, 'Ralph', who said, 'If it's an End Job you want... you give me a phone number. You don't get any phone number from me. It may be five or six people down the line.' Ralph mentioned a 'starting price' of between £10,000 and £15,000, largely destined for the intermediaries.

In London's traffic conditions a 'get-away car' is a contradiction in terms. The British hitman of the gang wars goes to work on a motorbike, relying on a pre-planned escape route down a set of stairs or a narrow alley where a back-up bike awaits. The helmet conceals his face.

Killing comes cheap in America. It always has (see **Westies**). Walter Stevens, a Prohibition gunman from Chicago, charged $25 for roughing up a man and twice that for killing him. A quiet, decorous individual, Stevens nursed his invalid wife for twenty years, inveighed against lax morals and the contemporary theatre, adopted three daughters and refused to let them wear lipstick.

In 1993, the going rate in New York's 'Little Colombia' was $200, but there is clear evidence of a two-tier pricing structure: a few dollars for a punk killing and tens of thousands for a prestige Mafia job. Frank Bavosa reportedly netted $40,000 for his February 1987 attempt on Pietro Alfano in Greenwich Village. Nonetheless, Alfano survived his three bullets in the back, albeit paralysed from the waist down.

See also **Dismemberment**, **Head, William Gallo's**

Hoover, J. Edgar (1895–1972)

Until recently, Hoover's life provided a shining example of how an individual of almost unbelievable wrong-headedness and limitations could achieve great power. Synonymous with the core values of American society and the safety of the nation, Hoover was eulogised at his death by the Vice-President for his 'dedication to principle and complete incorruptibility'.

Perhaps more than anyone else, Hoover devoted his life to combatting the organised crime syndicate whose corrupt tentacles corroded the American Way. In his view, this was the Communist Party, which he pursued tirelessly, from his paper on a 1919 bombing through to the era of Senator McCarthy and beyond.

A decade after McCarthy's demise, Hoover still had most of the FBI on Red Alert, to the extent of putting three harmless septuagenarian Greeks under surveillance for months while they played dominoes. When President **Kennedy** swept to power, Hoover still emphasised that 'The Communist Party USA presents a greater menace to the internal security of this nation than it ever has.' Robert Kennedy, the new Attorney General, riposted, 'It couldn't be more feeble and less of a threat, and besides its membership consists largely of FBI agents.'

FBI anti-Mob staffing levels were risible; in 1992 agent Bill Roemer recalled that just before Kennedy's 1960 election the ten agents assigned to organised crime in Chicago were cut to five. In New York, in 1959, four full-time operatives kept tabs on organised crime; and a hundred times as many toiled on the communist threat.

For Hoover, the 1957 syndicate conference of seventy leading *mafiosi* in **Apalachin** never took place and, when it had, all twenty-five of the FBI reports describing it were shredded. The barrage of press questioning extracted the concession that *something* was going on, leading to his memo of 27 November 1957, quaintly entitled 'The Top Hoodlum Program'. Two more years passed before Hoover finally seemed convinced. In 1959 the FBI bugged the Chicago mob, producing conclusive evidence of the 'Commission', the five leading **Mafia** families who met to arbitrate inter-gang disputes. But Hoover's campaign mysteriously lost impetus, and by 1962 he was again assuring Robert Kennedy that 'No single individual or coalition of racketeers dominated organised crime across the nation.'

Was Hoover really that boneheaded? Not necessarily. It was easier to grab headlines by bagging a few mid-western bank robbers like John **Dillinger**, Machine-Gun Kelly and Alvin 'Creepy' Karpis, than to tackle the Mob. It was also more expedient. Strong evidence has emerged that the Director's personal life required very careful handling. Apart from the long-rumoured homosexual affair with his aide, Clyde Tolson, with whom he discretely held hands in public, it now seems that Hoover may have been exposed to continous Mafia blackmail.

Hoover's homosexuality was common knowledge among the Mob. The clinching detail was the photographs. William Donovan, director of the Office of Strategic Services and himself a target of Hoover's intrigues, allegedly obtained compromising pictures of Hoover and Tolson *in flagrante*, which fell into the Mafia's hands – specifically, Meyer Lansky's hands – and from then on organised crime ceased to exist. It had hardly existed before; Hoover was a long-standing associate of the mobster Frank Costello, whom he met on a regular basis, and it is likely that Costello had known his secret for years (see **Runyon**).

When the 'Top Hoodlum' programme went into reverse, Hoover was seeing a lot of the liquor baron Lewis Rosenstiel, who maintained well-established links with both Costello and Meyer Lansky. Rosenstiel shared Hoover's interest in young boys, and Rosenstiel's wife Susan has claimed that in 1958 she twice met the head of the FBI attending orgies in a private suite at New York's Plaza Hotel. On the first occasion, Hoover was 'wearing a fluffy black dress – very fluffy with flounces, and lace stockings, and high heels, and a black curly wig. He had make-up on, and false eyelashes.' At the next, he sported a red dress with a feather boa draped round  his neck, and at about this period Hoover's brief campaign against the Mafia faltered. But prudent commentators have observed that the only person to see Hoover in drag was a gangster's widow, later charged with perjury, and that no photographs have survived.

There is no disputing that Hoover was a vicious blackmailer who corrupted every administration he served, and little doubt that he became increasingly deranged throughout his tenure as Director. After assuming control of the agency in 1924, he welded a corrupt and incompetent force into fearless crime fighters. But by his death, the FBI had returned to its original low morale (see **Prospects**). Neutralised by the Mob, Hoover's principal mission was to cling on to power, and to this end he accumulated enough dirt on President Kennedy's indiscretions to make his dismissal unthinkable.

First came the 1941 'Inga-Binga' tape, recording the future President making love to Inga Arvad (who may have nurtured Nazi sympathies). 1959 produced the Pamela Turnure recordings, succeeded by surveillance of Kennedy's relationship with Judith Exner, his use of mob-controlled whores in Los Angeles, his contacts with Giancana, and Operation Mongoose – the Mafia plot against Castro. Then there was the Angie Dickinson recording from the flight to Palm Springs. Finally Hoover bugged the Lawford house, wiring the living room, bathroom and bedrooms (where **Monroe** and Kennedy met). All this compromising material festered in his files.

Hoover's prurient attentions ran riot over Washington in a series of reports and recordings that reduced national security to a matter of who was sleeping with whom. He degraded the FBI into thought-police, infiltrating more than fifty colleges and universities to oust teachers with left-wing leanings. By his death the Bureau held 883 files on senators and 772 on congressmen, packed with derogatory information that ensured solid support on Capitol Hill, and he broke the lives and careers of those who crossed him. Hoover lived virtually free, milking the FBI as his personal fiefdom, despatching agents to hand-deliver orchids round Washington; having the Exhibits Section do his home building work, painting and maintenance; the Radio Engineering Section to see to his home appliances; and the Recreation Fund to pay for his public relations, personal gifts, accommodation and holiday transport. He lunched gratis daily in Harvey's, one of Washington's best restaurants; at home he went to the lavatory on a special FBI invention, the heated toilet seat; and his particular brand of ice-cream, stockpiled in a basement freezer in the Justice Department, was freighted in by air. Hoover degenerated into what he had set out to destroy, Public Enemy Number 1, the most dangerous man in America.

His recruitment policies were particularly unhelpful. He preferred his agents as white, conformist and Protestant – or preferably Mormon – six-footers, and denigrated Dr Martin Luther King, the black civil rights leader, as 'the most notorious liar in the country'. By 1974, after years of racial equality campaigning, one hundred of the FBI's 8,000 agents were black. Fifty were added in the following decade – in agencyspeak, mostly 'house niggers'. Hoover himself directly employed several per cent of the total, one as his chauffeur, another as receptionist and a third, Jim Amos, for old times' sake.

Such racism reflected the FBI's head-in-the-sand approach to organised crime; it seemed almost a matter of indifference that one bunch of Italian immigrants should exploit another bunch of Italian immigrants, and by the end of Hoover's stewardship the Mafia was deeply entrenched in legitimate business. Today an older and wiser agency cracks down far more quickly on ethnic groups.

Hopkins, Matthew

Mid-seventeenth century 'witchfinder general' and a rare English manifestation of a predominantly Continental form of hysteria. Hopkins was an Essex lawyer and, after finding an old crone in Manningtree with three teats, he arrested another thirty-one women, successfully descrying nineteen as witches. They were hanged.

Word of Hopkins's special skill spread rapidly. Soon he was paid by the head at £6 a time. He went the whole hog, resorting to 'witchpryking' and the indiscriminate throwing of suspects into ponds to see if they should be executed for floating. Hopkins hanged sixty-eight victims in Bury St Edmunds, raking in £1,000 of blood money in a single year.

In those superstitious times, witches were easy to come by. Conventional wisdom depicted them operating in tandem with a 'familiar' lent by the devil to do their dirty work. The sorcerers' apprentice might be the toad, weasel, rabbit, cat or dog that a seemingly innocuous old woman, living by herself on the edge of poverty, kept as a pet. But

Hopkins interpreted the concept of 'familiars' broadly. The mere settling of a fly on a suspect's shoulder was strong evidence of guilt. For Hopkins, a 'third teat' under the arm, or elsewhere, or some other physical irregularity attendant on birth or old age furnished corroboration. He discovered that most communities had their lucrative share of witches.

Unusually, Hopkins was discredited by a courageous man of the cloth, Gaule, who denounced him from the pulpit. Gaule pointed out that torturing witches was a criminal act (or, as one judge said, reviewing the law: 'It is not a legal offence to fly through the air.'). Thrown into a pond by an angry crowd, Hopkins died a year later of tuberculosis.

In Europe, men of his ilk were legion, between them responsible for perhaps hundreds of thousands of **Witchcraze** deaths. But in Britain, wrote Reginald Scot in 1584, 'It is indifferent to say in the English tongue "she is a witch" or "she is a wise woman".'

Hopkins aside, black witches were executed, but not on a lavish scale. In 1563 it was made a capital offence to kill by witchcraft. But murder has always been against the law no matter what the method, and although James I cracked down harder on witches than his predecessor, between 1558 and 1736 (when witchcraft ceased to be a legal offence) no more than 513 cases came before the Courts of the Home Circuit and only 109 persons were hanged.

British witches had to be accused of something specific; it was not enough to just *be* a witch, and thus many English cases lacked the vague Continental razzmatazz of covens and devil worship. Margaret Harker, hanged at Tyburn in 1585, was more mundanely accused of stopping a neighbour's peas from growing by cursing a field. More dramatic cases, like John Palmer (who in 1649 *confessed* to turning himself into a toad) were rarities. In all the trials, a broomstick is only mentioned once, and Britain only fell into line with Continental practice in the late 1980s with a series of baseless satanic **ritual abuse** cases.

Horse, Nails Morton's

Samuel J. 'Nails' Morton was a citizen of style. In the trenches of the First World War he won the *Croix de Guerre* as a first lieutenant, leading his men over the top despite being wounded twice. In Chicago he found a niche as one of the **O'Bannion** gang, killing two policemen in a café, and for recreation he rode daily on the Lincoln Park bridle-paths, mingling with society equestrians.

One morning his stirrup leather parted; he fell and was kicked to death by his cantering steed. Perhaps he was not all bad: on 15 May 1923 the *Daily News* ran the headline, 'Tribute to Nails Morton: Five Thousand Jewish People attended the funeral acclaiming him protector'.

Morton's friends resolved to track down his killer and take their revenge. Two-gun Louis Alterie presented himself at the stable and rented Morton's horse. Then he trotted to the fatal spot, where the O'Bannion mob were assembled, and the horse was ceremonially executed, each gangster firing a shot into its head. Honour satisfied, Alterie telephoned the stables: 'We taught that goddamn horse of yours a lesson.'

Killing horses can be lucrative work. In the words of Tommy Burns, the leading equine hitman arrested on 2 February 1991 after nine years in the trade, 'I got paid a lot more for killing racehorses than many people get for killing people.' Burns received up to $35,000 a time from financially distressed owners anxious to claim windfall profits on their insurance. A typical victim was *McBlush*, a 3-year-old Colt from Conneticut, valued at $100,000 but worth only fifty cents a pound as horsemeat.

Burns's attached one end of an electric wire to the animal's ear with an alligator clip, the other to its rectum, and then plugged it in. 'They go immediately,' he reported.

Horse Patrol

The final solution of the English **highwayman** problem, devised by the blind John Fielding who succeeded his brother, the writer Henry **Fielding**, as Justice of the Peace at London's Bow Street in 1753. It is a story of exemplary official blundering.

After soliciting Fielding's proposals for controling the chronic infestation of highwaymen, and then rejecting them, the government contributed £600 towards an experimental civilian Horse Patrol. Instead of the occasional mounted foray, this was full-time, and by 1763 Fielding had five two-man teams out each night patrolling London's approaches.

No one had tried to *catch* highwaymen before; the only previous recourse involved self-defence or retrospective complaint to the Bow Street Runners, who were, as their name implies, based at Bow Street in central London and in any case on foot. Fielding's men achieved dramatic results, limiting robberies to two in the first fortnight. Both villains were caught, and by the spring of 1764, for the first time in living memory, he had secured the six roads out of London.

Government reaction was swift. They pointed out that as the highways were now crime-free, little would be gained by continuing the patrol, and it was abolished despite Fielding's vociferous protests. Whereupon the relieved highwaymen returned in swarms, and by June 1764 things were as bad as ever with eight incidents in six days.

Grudgingly, the government allowed Fielding another chance. Once again, he miscarried: that is, no one was waylaid while the patrols continued, but when they withdrew his funding for the second time, the highwaymen flooded back. Clearly, the idea was a flop.

Distinguished victims of the ensuing spate of robberies included the Prime Minister, the Prince of Wales, the Duke of York, the Lord Mayor, Admiral Holborn and the Neapolitan Ambassador. Not until 1805 was the patrol reinstated, this time on a permanent footing with the addition of uniformed officers guarding the roads for ten miles round London until midnight. The scheme achieved the usual purgative results.

Hulks

Cheaper than prisons; an unseaworthy vessel could be converted into an intolerable **prison** at a fraction of the cost of a new building. With their patched sides and outcrops of platforms and lean-to's, the vessels resembled bloated slum tenements.

After 1775, the American War of Independence made the transportation of British prisoners to foreign parts problematic. As a temporary expedient, convicts awaiting shipment were packed into the hulks of a couple of motley three-deckers on the Thames.

This stop-gap expedient became standard procedure. Over the years more and more criminals were sent to the hulks, until by 1816 a convict establishment of 2,500 festered in five decaying vessels; twelve years later, the total had risen to 4,446. Captain Cook's *Discovery* degraded ungracefully as a prison ship.

After arrival on board, the new prisoners were sodomised as a matter of routine and then had a fourteen-pound iron riveted to the right ankle, extinguishing any hope of escape by swimming. The following day the men were put to work on chain gangs in the Royal Dockyards. Sightseers came to gawp. Of the buggery (see **Tobacco**), Jeremy Bentham wrote: 'An initiation of this sort stands in place of garnish [tips] and is exacted with equal rigour... As the Mayor of Portsmouth, Sir John Carter, very sensibly observes, such things must ever be.'

Conditions on board were terrible. Men and boys, murderers and pickpockets were jumbled together, with the newcomer confined to the lowest of the three decks. There was no air or light, just claustrophobic, guttering candles. At night the hatches were screwed down. Gambling and disease were rife, death rampant, with fellow-prisoners encircling the dying like vultures, eyeing 'anything about the bed, so that they might take it, flannels or money'.

Captain Cook's Discovery *at Deptford, where it spent its final ten years as a convict hulk*

According to George Lee, sentenced to transportation for possession of a forged banknote, 'Nine at a time out of four hundred have lain dead on the shore, the pictures of raggedness, filth and starvation.' Typically, all the officials on board – the captain, the victuallers, the quartermaster and the jailers – were on the take. Even the surgeons were corrupt. Doctors retailed the corpses from the hospital hulk at five or six pounds apiece, and did not always strive officiously to keep their patients alive.

After 1823 the boys were held separately at Chatham on the frigate *Eurylis*, which offered a diet of gruel and potato parings, bullying, scurvy, ophthalmia and the saddest sight of all: child convicts taking silent exercise on deck, trudging round and round, like wizened monkeys.

Hurkos, Peter (b. 1911)

A Dutch psychic detective born with a caul over his head, in Britain superstitiously regarded as evidence that the child is proof against drowning and in Holland a touchstone for the sixth sense. Hurkos showed no exceptional abilities until 1941, when he fell thirty feet off a ladder while painting a house and banged his head.

Coming round, Hurkos found that he had lost his memory but gained X-ray vision. By handling a person's belongings (or making a 'pass' over them with his sensitive hands) he could receive an accurate impression of the owner's personality and background, a process called 'psychometry'.

His local reputation for the recovery of missing objects and people spread, and in 1958 the Miami police called for his assistance in the case of a murdered cab driver. Hurkos flew to Miami and installed himself in the deceased's taxi to soak up a psychic portrait of the killer; he intuited that the culprit was a mariner known as Smitty. Strange to tell, a sailor called Smith was later convicted.

On 29 January 1964, Hurkos came to the aid of the police hunting the Boston Strangler (see **Insatiable**). Presented with 300 case-photographs to study, he placed them face down on a table and scrutinised them carefully by passing his hands over their blank backs. Then he described their contents to the detectives. They knew Hurkos was right because they could look at the photographs face up, and he convinced his remaining detractors when an officer arrived late, claiming that his car had broken down. Not so, said Hurkos, and correctly detailed how the latecomer had stopped to make love to his girlfriend, a divorcee in her late twenties, on her kitchen table.

Six days of gruelling telepathic immersion followed. Hurkos shed fifteen pounds as he seeped into the killer's psyche. Then he 'saw' the murderer. 'I lived through the killings,' he recalled later, 'I lived through the mind of that man.' He presented a detailed description to the police; the suspect weighed 130 to 140 pounds and was slightly built with a pointed nose and a scar on his left arm. 'And he loves shoes.'

So the police picked up a door-to-door shoe salesman, 'Thomas P. O'Brien' (real name withheld). After a face-to-face confrontation with Hurkos, he opted for voluntary psychiatric confinement in the Massachusetts State Mental Centre, and has stayed there ever since. As Hurkos predicted, the killings stopped – until October when Albert DeSalvo was arrested after the final 'Strangler' murder.

Since then Hurkos concentrated on his work as a clairvoyant in the entertainment industry, although he contributed briefly to the 1968 **Manson** case on behalf of the friends of victim Jay Sebring, the hair stylist. A week after the slayings, Hurkos visited the house at 10050 Cielo Drive to cadge some Polaroids of the murder scene from a *Life* photographer. He told the press: 'Three men killed Sharon Tate and the other four and I know who they are. I have identified the killers to the police.' The officers never logged his information, whatever it was, and in due course one man and three women were identified as the murderers. To the papers, Hurkos enlarged that the slayings erupted during a black magic ritual of 'goona goona'.

The author is unaware of any murder case irrefutably solved by psychic intervention.

I

Identification evidence

The **Tichborne** Case suggests that, given flair, the similarity required for successful imposture need not be close, an historical deduction confirmed in 1990 by journalist John Louvet on his release by Austrian border command. For months, Louvet travelled round Europe with a picture of his cocker spaniel 'Chummy' as his passport photograph, said by the police to be a 'very good likeness'.

The converse ability to recognise a person from a photograph does not always come naturally. In November 1942 an unknown woman's body, the victim of a vicious strangling, was found near Luton, naked in the shallows of the River Lea, loosely covered in sacking, ankles trussed together and knees strapped to her chest. The left-hand side of her face was crushed by a single blow, but she had probably survived the attack for another half hour; her legs bore traces of bruising from the tight ropes (showing that she was still alive when her lower limbs were bound) but there were no corresponding marks by the time her assailant secured her arms. The woman wore no clothes, no jewellery, no ring and no teeth – even her dentures had been removed. Her blood group was the common O, she lacked any distinguishing characteristics or deformities, and carried no trace of foreign fibres or hairs.

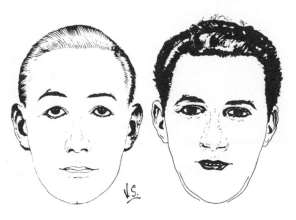

Alternative identikits issued after the A6 murder. Valerie Storie's version (left) and other witnesses' (right). Although better than nothing, they unleashed hundreds of false sightings.

As an identification aid, the victim's good side was photographed in profile but, despite post-mortem refurbishment, her features were coarsened by the facial bruising, and the pictures must have been as unintelligible as train announcements.

The photographs were shown by the police house-to-house, and the dead woman's sons, aged fourteen and fifteen, failed to recognise their mother, although they had inklings quashed by their father, the murderer. But the 17-year-old daughter saw the likeness advertised on a cinema screen without evincing so much as a flicker of recognition. Neighbours shook their heads blankly after studying the photographs. Nine times the corpse was wrongly identified, as four different people.

Eventually a name was put to the body by a dry cleaner's tag. The methodical Detective Chief Inspector Chapman had ordered the collection of all the bits of clothing and rags dumped in local garbage tips and dustbins around the date of the killing. Three months into the investigation, the whole collection was minutely re-examined, producing a distinctive section of black coat with a dyer's tag still attached. The trail led to the local branch of Sketchley's, and their books provided the customer's name: Rene Manton. Conclusive evidence was furnished by her dental records.

It took only two days to pin the murder on the husband, Bertie Manton. During an argument on

18 November, she had flung a scalding cup of hot tea in his face, shouting, 'I hope it blinds you.' Manton lost his temper and smashed her head with a heavy wooden stool, but had the presence of mind to tidy up before the children returned from school. He told them Rene had gone to visit their grandmother, and that evening disposed of the body by wheeling it through town, wrapped in sacks on his bicycle's handlebars. The next morning, thinking her departure in mid-winter without a coat might look odd, he cut it into pieces and discarded it in a dustbin.

Sentenced to death, Manton was pardoned by the King after presentation of a 26,000-signature petition for clemency. He attempted to preserve the fiction of his wife as still alive by mailing himself letters 'from' her. The messages made mention of Hampstead, misspelled without the 'p' and, in classic style, Chief Inspector Chapman asked Manton to write a sentence in which 'Hamstead' duly appeared.

Even under favourable conditions, eyewitness identifications have long been a source of disquiet. The most troubling recent British case involved a balaclava, the headgear surmounting all four men who burst into the home of 74-year-old Robert Forrest on 17 June 1989. Only the burglars' eyes and mouths were visible through the slits.

Under normal circumstances this might make the robbers hard to recognise. But the tallest intruder wore a black leather jacket, and when Forrest was asked by the police whether anyone in the identification parade 'resembled' his assailants, he saw one who did: the only man in a black leather jacket, unlucky Robert Campbell, now serving five years for armed robbery. The only other evidence against Campbell was an ambiguous confession, later retracted.

In 1992 Professor Graham Davies of Leicester University conducted a scientific study to resolve the thorny issue of whether it is easier to recognise people when their faces are visible. Apparently it is. Professor Davies explains his theory thus: 'The face is the primary source of identification for identification purposes. If you are deprived of that information, you are forced back on other clues, such as voice and body movements, and your chances of making a mistake go up.' The professor convinced doubters by staging a dummy burglary, showing that the ability to recognise hooded raiders rated no higher than chance.

See also **Bloodstains**, **Doyle**, **Fingerprints**, **Genetic fingerprinting**, **Teethmarks** and individual cases.

Inflatable dolls

Beware of imitation women; they are not the same. The Canadian Robert Poulin tried to wriggle off the horns of his dilemma in 1975 by purchasing a blow-up doll. In high hopes he wrote in his diary: 'I no longer think that I will have to rape a girl.'

But he was wrong: the inflatable proved a disappointment. So in October 1975 the 18-year-old Poulin raped and killed schoolgirl Kim Rabat. Then he shot seven classmates before committing suicide, turning the gun on himself.

Canadians have carved out a niche in schoolroom slayings. On 6 December 1989, Marc Lepine entered Room 230 in Montreal University armed with a Sturm Ruger semi-automatic rifle. He separated the women students at gunpoint, ordered the men to leave, and then told the nine female engineering majors that he was there 'to fight against feminists'.

'But we're not feminists,' one student demurred. Then Lepine pulled the trigger, spraying out a thirty-shot clip. Six died. Lepine shot another one in the corridor, three more in the cafeteria, and four in Room 311. Then he removed his anorak, wrapped it round the gun barrel and shot himself upwards through the head. His baseball cap flew off.

Lepine was a 25-year-old at the end of his road. As a child, he was thrashed by his father; as an adult, he was rejected by Montreal University, by the Army and by his girlfriend. His suicide note jumbled up a pathetic desire to appear intelligent with a vendetta against women.

Lepine wrote: 'I continued my studies in a haphazard way for they never really interested me, knowing in advance my fate. Which did not prevent me from obtaining very good marks despite not handing in my theory works and the lack of studying before exams... The other day, I heard they were honouring the Canadian men and women who fought at the frontline during world wars. How can you explain then that women were not authorised to go to the front line? Will we hear

Caesar's female legions and female galley slaves who of course took up fifty per cent of the ranks of history, though they never existed.'

His points are no less misconceived than many notions aired in the newspaper correspondence columns, and in fact Lepine sent his suicide note to Francine Pelletier, a columnist for *La Presse*. But Lepine did not kill to get in the papers. Like most mass murderers, he exacted revenge on his supposed oppressors; and he had no desire for them to be any better off than he was shortly to become. As Charles Starkweather said after his 1958 murder rampage across Nebraska and Wyoming: 'Dead people are all on the same level.'

See also **Luby's Cafeteria**, **Terminology**

Informality

American procedure permits judges greater latitude for homilies than their British counterparts. After condemning serial killer Ted **Bundy** to death, the judge continued: 'Take care of yourself, young man. I say that to you sincerely. It's a tragedy to this court to see such a total waste of humanity. You're a bright young man. You'd have made a good lawyer. I'd have loved to have you practise in front of me. I bear you no animosity, believe me. You went the wrong way, partner. Take care of yourself.'

British courts occasionally dispense career advice, notably in 1977 when the Recorder of York Crown Court awarded Mr Philip McCutcheon a conditional discharge, saying: 'I think you should give burglary up. You have a withered hand, an artificial leg and only one eye. You have been caught in Otley, Leeds, Harrogate, Norwich, Beverley, Hull and York. How can you hope to succeed?'

But this is mere badinage compared to the conduct of Judge Fleet of Miami, as reported in the *Daily Post* of 3 July 1992. He opened fire in court, loosing two bullets from his .45 across the accused's head before sentencing him to five years, goaded beyond endurance by the defendant's cry of defiance from the dock after hearing the verdict of 'guilty'.

'Judge Fleet is a bastard, and if I had a gun I would kill him,' Mynette shouted, whereupon the judge produced his weapon, drew a bead on the prisoner and said: 'Get down on your knees – or I will condemn you to death and execute you here and now.' Then he fired his warning shots.

In England, this sort of lapse would never do; nor would the tear-jerking that intermittently vitiated the **Dahmer** trial of 1992, when the prosecution handed round photographic portraits of each of the fifteen victims. Since there was no dispute about whether Dahmer had killed them or who they were, the exercise was scarcely germane. Nor could the ritual of allowing relatives of the deceased to hurl abuse at the convicted man prior to sentencing be said to contribute greatly to judicial objectivity.

Ingram, Paul R. (1945–)

America's showcase satanic **ritual abuse** (SRA) offender. For the seventeen years before his 1989 conviction, Ingram led a blameless life in the sheriff's office of Olympia, Washington.

In the late 1970s, the Ingram family found itself drawn to Pentecostalism. Paul was a stern father, and his two daughters, Erika and Julie (born in 1966 and 1970 respectively), were shy with boys. During three years in her late teens, Erika only dated twice, and in August 1988 the sisters attended a two-day retreat sponsored by the Church of Living Water. A charismatic facilitator, Karla Franko, enlightened the teenage audience about sexual abuse, and after the session a number of tremulous girls, Erika among them, declared themselves victims.

Erika left home, telling her mother that she had endured years of forced sex from her father and her two brothers. 'You're the only one who didn't know,' she said. But neither she nor Julie could tell if their ordeal had ceased ten years ago or last month. Apparently traumatised, they only responded to questions after lengthy pauses, and on 28 November 1988 their bemused father was charged. Anxious to co-operate, Ingram said, 'If this did happen, we need to take care of it', and, at his first interrogation, he produced halting snippets like 'I would have removed her clothing'. The police psychologist assured him that, once he confessed, his misdeeds would come flooding back.

Meanwhile Julie wrote to her teacher: 'A lot of men would come over and play poker with my dad, and they would all get drunk and one or two at a time would come into my room to have sex with me.' So a sex ring of paedophiles was at large and, in a gruelling interview, Ingram tried to 'visualise' the rapes. 'I just don't see anything,' he said, enjoined to remember his friends having sex with Julie tied to a bed. 'Let me see if I can get in there. Assuming it happened, she would have had a bed, bedroom, by herself I would think...Uh...' Ten-minute silences came and went while he cudgelled his brains. The interrogators exhorted him to 'choose life over living death', crying, 'God has given you the tools to do this.'

At full stretch, Ingram saw the past, envisioning Julie with her hands tied to her feet. He noticed 'a penis sticking up in the air'. Asked if anyone was taking pictures, he replied, 'Uh, it's possible, let me look. I see, I see a camera... I don't see a person behind that camera... Well, the person that I see is Ray Risch.' So his friend Risch was arrested, and Jim Rabie too, the man behind the waving organ. Ingram said, 'Boy, it's almost like I'm making it up. But I'm not.'

When Rabie was charged, the police pointed out that he remained in the 'denial stage'. 'I must be,' replied Rabie, 'because I honestly do not have any recollection of it happening.' Meanwhile, Ingram reflected, 'If I can't remember this, then I am so dangerous I do not deserve to be let loose.' Soon his **memory** was on the mend, aided by Pastor Bratun who, on 2 December, exorcised his demons. First Ingram remembered that he was the Green River killer. Then he 'saw' Rabie raping his son, Chad. Under questioning, Chad spoke of his childhood dreams: 'People outside my window looking in... short people walking on me.' They reminded him of the Seven Dwarfs.

'You want to believe it's dreams,' urged Detective Schoening. 'You don't want to believe it's real. It was real, Chad.' Well-versed in the ways of SRA, the officers realised that Chad suffered from 'destruction of his sense of reality... total, absolute subservience to the group', and in due course Chad agreed. Conditioned to obliterate the years of abuse, he had not dreamed of having a cloth stuffed in his mouth. It was a real penis. Paul's wife, Sandy, wondered if she too had blanked the past. 'Has my life been a lie? Have I been brainwashed, oppressed – controlled – without knowing it?' she asked her diary in December 1988.

Under further prompting, Erika and Julie hinted at their mother's involvement. 'She'd just watch,' said Erika at first. Afraid of being branded 'in denial', Sandy sought solace from Pastor Bratun. He told her that she was '80 per cent evil', recommending confession, and on 18 December the police located the eldest of the Ingram children, Paul Ross, living in Reno. Paul hated his father, saying 'I'd like to shoot my dad', and depicted a horrific scene glimpsed through a door. His mother was tied to her bed. 'Jim Rabie was screwing her and his dad had his 'dick' in her mouth,' the detectives recorded. Ray Risch and another man were there too, 'jacking each other off'.

But Paul did not think that he, or Erika and Julie, had been molested. Indeed, the Ingrams all remembered different things and, in frustration, Detective Schoening backed Paul against the wall, shouting 'We know you're a victim'. But if Paul was stuck in denial, Erika continued in full flow. Too damaged to answer verbally, she took to writing notes: 'Then he urinated all over my body in bed. He didn't defecate on me this time.'

Meanwhile, Ingram wavered, taking sexual deviation tests in triplicate, basing answers on (i) how he would have replied before his arrest, (ii) before being exorcised by Pastor Bratun, and (iii) afterwards. His results ranged from normal to a monster, but he was keener than ever to be punished after Erika submitted an essay on the full-blown satanic ceremonies he conducted in regalia. Skeletal excerpts read, 'middle of the night... high priestess... dad wore a gown and a hat resembling a viking hat with horns... blood everywhere... sacrifice... chant... baby... dead... They would say, "You will not remember this."'

On 23 January 1989, in disclosures transcribed by a friend, Erika divulged: 'My father made me perform sexual acts with animals including goats and dogs.' But as the case entered its pre-trial phase, the prosecution's testimony was muddled. Julie hid under a table when questioned by attorneys, Erika described the sacrifice of twenty-five babies, and the Thurston County Sheriff's office compiled a wall-chart of Satan's underground, with 225 inter-connected headings like 'phibinite cult', 'heavy metal', 'eating faeces', 'urban hysteria', 'buried alive with insects and snakes', 'killing babies', 'eating pets', and 'you will die if you remember'. The sheriff was overawed by the conspiracy's sheer scale, musing 'It isn't just a matter of people running around and killing babies... When you look at the chart, don't you more or less go, like 'Wow'?'

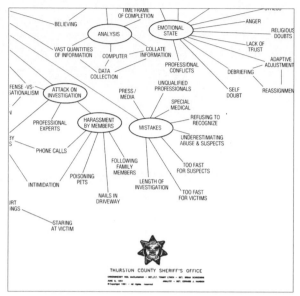

Satan's underground. A corner of the official chart showing how it all fits together.

Asked to explain the mind-control devices 'scrambling' the suspects' memories, a Dr Richard Ofshe demonstrated that Ingram was highly suggestible, with an ability to float into trance states and a desire to please authority. He 'remembered' to order. Ofshe suspected a mass folly initiated by the sisters, who unleashed avalanches of new allegations to cover old inconsistencies, outraging one detective so much that, at a court hearing, a private detective had to mount guard in case he tried to shoot the defendants. But Ofshe could not persuade Ingram to recant and, on 13 April 1989, after a convulsive effort, he retrieved the names of ten cultists in the Sheriff's office acting in collusion with the canine unit. Their dogs had raped his wife.

The sheriff, by now famous on the SRA workshop circuit, lauded the investigation as the first case 'confirmed by an adult offender in the nation's history', and Ingram happily pleaded guilty to six counts of third-degree rape. Then, awaiting sentence, he started a log dividing his recollections into three categories: 'Definitely happened', 'Not so definitely happened', and 'Not sure'. On 19 July, while at prayer, a voice said, 'Let go the rope', and he realised that he had made everything up.

In April 1990, before sentencing, Ingram told the court: 'I stand before you, I stand before God. I have never sexually abused my daughters. I am not guilty of these crimes.' To the judges, he sounded like any other rapist, and they gave him twenty years. 'Satanic abuse is real,' commented the Sheriff, 'this case proves it.'

Initiation rites

The day he gets 'made' is a big one for a *mafioso*. In the typical ritual of the Philadelphia mob (now virtually destroyed), the ceremony was marked by a summons to a luxurious gang house where forty confederates awaited his arrival, seated round a long table sumptuously laden with meatballs, olives and spaghetti.

The *capo* at the head of the table formally demanded of the newcomer: 'Do you know why you're here?', expecting and receiving a 'no'. Next the recruit was advised to disclose any 'bad feelings' about anyone present; again, the prudent response was in the negative. A recitation followed of his working contribution to the family, after which the invitation to join – 'to be one of us' – was extended, together with a token assurance that he could decline and leave as a 'friend'.

Some ceremonial business with the gun and knife lying on the table ensued: would he use these for his colleagues? Yes. Clutching a lighted tissue paper, the new member intoned: 'May I burn like the saints in hell if I ever betray my friends.' For the closing formalities his trigger finger was ritually pricked; then, after kissing his associates, the assembled hoods fell to feasting. Thereafter, the rules were elucidated: no kidnapping, no counterfeiting, no drug dealing on your own behalf. Striking another member meant death. And never so much as look at another member's wife (see **Contempt**).

According to Nick 'The Crow' Caramandi, now under the witness protection scheme: 'It's a strong, deep and very meaningful ceremony. Here are forty guys, we're all killers and we're all one. The ceremony's gorgeous. It's just beautiful. It's a sacred thing. You pray together. We all hold hands.' Salvatore Contorno, inducted in Sicily in 1975, outlined a similar ritual, except that he held a burning picture of a saint; the blood from his finger trickled over the image as it crumbled into ashes.

From that day on, the respect shown by non-members to the new *mafioso* is palpable. His life alters fundamentally. Instead of subjecting the general public to beatings, murder and extortion to gain peer approval, his focus shifts to in-fighting, eliminating rivals in a scramble to expedite promotion: a sort of do-it-yourself dead man's shoes.

Hangmen, too, observe rites of passage, and a British ceremony, now defunct, commemorated the initiation of a public executioner. Probably the last inductee was William Calcraft in 1829, when, after his successful candidacy, he was greeted by the traditional conclave of berobed dignitaries bearing their insignia of office. The Lord Mayor, the Sheriffs and City Marshal, the Governor of Newgate, a Crown Judge and the Town Crier, together with a host of minor functionaries, waited in fearsome solemnity while the bell tolled the funeral knell. Then the Sheriff commanded, 'Bring in a well-sharpened axe', whereupon it was borne in by the Keeper of the Axe. 'Bring in the usual leg-irons, handcuffs and other fetters,' he continued, and these articles were proffered by the Keeper of the Irons. 'Now,' directed the Sheriff, 'bring in the halter and a pair of white caps and the beheading knife.' These too were produced by the relevant Keeper, and at this stage the 'candidate' entered, taking his oath of office kneeling, with his left hand on the axe and his right hand on the Bible, while the Judge kept the great sword of justice poised over him.

After Calcraft had completed the oath, which began with the words, 'I do most solemnly swear to hang or behead, or otherwise destroy, all felons of our Lord the King', a veil bestowing theoretical anonymity was draped over his head and he was hounded out of the assemblage to general groans, with the Judge's final injunction ringing in his ears: 'Get thee hence, wretch!'

Injection, lethal

The lethal injection of today is machine-administered, its operation regulated by a computerised control console fronted with a burnished steel fascia peppered with flashing lights. The contraption is the invention of Fred A. Leuchter, a professional 'execution technologist' who supplies equipment complete with a 'Manual of Operation'.

The business end of the machine embodies a firing sequence of three syringes delivering chemicals into the bloodstream through a single manifold. The first injection of sodium pentothal puts the victim to sleep, the second paralyses his respiratory system, and a final shot of potassium chloride stops the heart. Within nine minutes the prisoner is dead.

Does this hurt? No, but it must be the only part of the sanitised process that is painless. Missouri ordered the first machine in 1988. It came with a full maintenance contract, and fifteen prison officials attended a training course on the theory and practice of execution, compiling a step-by-step guidebook known as the 'Missouri Protocol', now in its thirteenth edition. The manual governs everything that happens to the prisoner from his first isolation in the 'Death Watch' cell to the order for two warders simultaneously to depress the buttons – one of them redundant – to initiate the injection process.

This final act generates huge antecedent requirements in terms of press witnesses, staff witnesses, duty rotas, extra staffing, machine preparation, dress rehearsals, paperwork, medicals, legal appeals and additional security, and the Missouri Protocol covers the countdown in such detail that it is now standard throughout America. A refinement under consideration for the fourteenth edition is the installation of an intercom so that witnesses divided from the death chamber by glass panels can hear the reading of the death warrant. This is followed by the last exchange, 'Do you have anything to say?' and then, 'God bless you.'

Despite the attention to procedural niceties, it is hard for the condemned man to overlook the fact that he is being killed, particularly during his last half-hour as he lies strapped to a trolley with a plug in his anus and a needle in his arm, watching the clock tick the seconds away, waiting for the stay of execution that may still come while his friends and relatives gaze from the far side of the windows.

The first to die from a lethal injection was Missouri's 'Tiny' Mercer in January 1989. When Billy White, a 34-year-old rubbish van driver, was 'turned off' in Huntsville prison on 23 April 1992, medical attendants ferreted around for some forty minutes to find a vein for the needle. White, even then, must have had hopes.

See also **Lunette**

In-laws

A perennial source of detestation. In 1955 Lincoln Sayre of West Virginia decided that he had tolerated his for too long. He resolved to kill his four brothers- and sisters-in-law in one clean sweep.

Sayre was a violent alcoholic who felt that the twenty-four years his relatives spent persuading his wife Hazel to leave him were more than enough. After she walked out for good on 25 August 1955, Sayre moped for five weeks and then, on 30 September, stole a friend's high-powered Japanese hunting rifle fitted with telescopic sights.

For an alibi he faked a hunting trip for wild boar; he would 'return' after his weekend in the woods to be greeted by the news that Phloe Johnson, Alice Martin, Vance Grimes and Elmer Grimes (all of whom he was known to hate) had been slain in four isolated attacks by a mysterious gunman. Sayre supposed that he could talk his way out of any suspicion; after all, he harboured no designs on his mother-in-law and the rifle did not belong to him.

On the morning of 30 September, Sayre was duly seen driving out of town. He doubled back through the woods in his pick-up, and at 9.18 that evening he was crouching outside the window of prim Phloe Johnson. While he waited, Phloe entered the living room for her evening tipple of soda and, as she lowered herself into her favourite rocking chair, Sayre shot her through the mouth. A woman came running to the door of the next house. It was Alice Martin. Down went number two, hit in the throat, and Sayre loped away to the home of Vance Grimes, a block away.

Here he encountered his first hitch. Vance had unexpectedly gone out for the evening. So Sayre hurried to nearby Robertsburg to kill Elmer, loosing off a fusillade of shots as his target traversed a window. Then he hightailed it for the woods.

But Sayre had missed Elmer, albeit by inches, so his tally stayed at two. As so often in murder, **detection** took several seconds: the sobbing mother-in-law told the police, 'It was Lincoln Sayre. Nobody else would have done such a thing.' Ballistic evidence tied the bullet to a gun reported missing from his friend's back porch, and on investigation Old Mammy Cole, who worked locally, said she saw Sayre running off with the weapon that morning.

Coming in from the wilds the following evening, Sayre overheard the townsfolk discussing his imminent arrest. He fled, and early the next morning committed suicide.

See also **Oral Hygiene**

Inquisition, The

In Sicily, the Inquisition assumed a particularly invidious form. In the absence of any real religious dissent, its heretical net widened to snare bigamists, philosophers, usurers, carnal priests, parvenus and eventually anyone with more money than they needed.

Membership of the Inquisition was restricted to the aristocracy and, on conviction, all the defendant's property was forfeit. So the cult represented oppression of the poor by the rich: arrests on suspicion, an accused presumed guilty, a prosecutor doubling as judge, and a defendant precluded from calling women, children or servants as witnesses in his support – although they could testify against him. Nor was legal representation permissible, since it constituted a seditious challenge to the Inquisition's authority.

For three centuries Sicily groaned under the yoke of religious predators, never less than 2,000 of them, whose dominion helped maintain feudalism. The only shield against their random depredations was a subversive brotherhood based on respect for natural justice and true honour, an honoured society or, in other words, the **Mafia** – a term possibly derived from the Arabic word meaning 'place of refuge'.

In later years, the Sicilian Mafia did quite nicely itself. In October 1992, Palermo police confiscated the property of one local family, the Madonias, seizing sixty-two legitimate businesses, 160 apartments, six boats, 202 cars and forty-three plots of land with an aggregate value of $400 million. Since the Madonias are one of two dozen local clans battening on the region, it is not surprising that parts of downtown Palermo, bled dry, look as though they have just been bombed. Indeed, many buildings destroyed by the hostilities of 1943 remain untouched.

Insane

Under English law, a defendant is presumed innocent until proven guilty or insane. This is quite distinct from the technical defence of madness under the McNaghten rules, where the accused avoids *criminal* punishment, a risky defence since it often prefixes an indefinite stay in a secure hospital.

But actual insanity can carry even more drastic repercussions. Here, the accused may be found guilty whether or not he committed the offence. A deranged defendant is adjudged 'unfit to plead': he cannot say whether he wishes to contest the charge, so there can be no trial (see **Pressing**). Detention in psychiatric prison follows. In other words, the mere bringing of the accusation results in a custodial sentence without the customary preliminary of a hearing.

There are only some fifteen English cases a year, which can produce the exciting result of prolonged incarceration for trivial offences the accused may not have committed or, worse, which have not been committed at all. In 1986 Glenn Pearson was sent down indefinitely on a charge of stealing £5 and three light bulbs, and in 1987 Valerie Hodgson acquired a certain notoriety following release from Wakefield's Newton Lodge secure unit. Two years previously she had confessed to stabbing her father to death and, being mentally handicapped and thus unfit to plead, the court never considered whether she actually had killed anyone. She had not, but this took two years to find out.

In the ten years following 1976, some 300 Britons were detained as 'unfit to plead'. About a quarter are still hospitalised, and fifteen (who are now fit) await their first trial. Perhaps these injustices will be ended by the 1992 Criminal Procedure (Insanity and Unfitness to Plead) Act.

In 1992 a sharp-eyed social worker, John Wasson, stumbled on a similar American case. He realised that 94-year-old Junius Wilson, who is black, was not mad but deaf. Wilson was confined to a mental home for sixty-seven years after being branded 'unfit to plead' to a charge of attempted rape in North Carolina. Judging by Jim Montgomery's story (see **Attorneys**), Wilson's 1925 crime may have been a fiction, but despite the absence of a trial he suffered the standard penalty for the period, castration. Prudent British psychiatric cases should likewise take pains never to indulge in mindless acts of petty arson. If the court considers the accused 'of unstable character', it may imprison him for life.

In principle, such a sentence allows the Home Secretary to order the prisoner's early release on recovery – a power he lacks with fixed-term sentences. In practice, petitions are rejected since they entail proving a negative: the appellant must show that he is no longer dangerous. But this proposition is only demonstrable retrospectively, after death.

So he disappears into the bowels of the prison service. Among the missing are a Mr Thornton (Christian name unknown), jailed for life in 1974 after igniting the curtains in a hospital interview room. Also sunk without trace is one Ellis Blogg, last seen in 1980 at his sentencing for burning down a cardboard box.

Insatiable

One of the few **sex** killers motivated largely by sex was the Boston Strangler. The normal sex murder represents the fulfilment of other needs by sexual means, with impotence looming large as a precipitating factor. But Albert Henry DeSalvo (1931–73), the Boston Strangler, suffered from *penile dementia*. He wanted sex all the time. He could make love once and then, right away, do it again. Compulsive recourse to sex, intermingled with casual brutality, permeated his upbringing. His father would bring back prostitutes and take his pleasure in front of the children. He beat his wife senseless, and once broke her fingers one by one. DeSalvo had intercourse with his sisters and, as he matured, wanted sex with any woman he met. His prowess was unusual in matching his desires and, rather than becoming assimilated into a civilising framework, it made a stable relationship unsustainable.

Word of DeSalvo's mesmeric abilities first began to circulate in 1948 when he was a 17-year-old vacationer at Cape Cod. College girls 'would even come up to the motel sometimes looking for me and some nights we would spend the whole night doing it down on the beach, stopping for a while, then doing it again'. During Army service in Germany, DeSalvo married a Frankfurt girl, but his demands for intercourse six times a day soon exhausted her libido, and his hypersexuality burgeoned into a hideous affliction.

In 1956, a year after he was charged with molesting a 9-year-old girl, DeSalvo settled in Boston. He did the rounds of apartment blocks, persuading women to open their doors to him as a talent scout for a model agency. He took their vital statistics, sometimes with mild molestation and sometimes procuring consensual sex by offering photographic assignments. The police dubbed him the 'Measuring Man'. He was caught on 17 March 1960, sentenced to two years for 'lewd and lascivious behaviour', and released a year later. But his offence was classified as 'breaking and entering'.

Between 14 June 1962 and 4 January 1964, thirteen Boston women were strangled, often after being raped repeatedly – an attribute which might have directed attention towards DeSalvo. The attacker posed as a workman and left his victims ritually displayed with a crude bow tied around the neck with a housecoat, stocking or pillow case. Several victims were sexually assaulted with bottles, and the first five were elderly, aged between fifty-five and eighty-five. Sometimes investigators found the intruder had ejaculated almost everywhere apart from the vagina, on breasts, thighs and the carpet. But after the killing of Mary Sullivan, the murders ceased.

A rapist continued in operation, an altogether gentler man who occasionally relented and often apologised, and on 27 October he abandoned an assault on a Massachusetts housewife with the words, 'You be quiet for ten minutes... I'm sorry.' His polite demeanour reminded detectives of the 'Measuring Man', and the artist's impression was, for once, clearly recognisable. On arrest, DeSalvo was identified by one of his victims, and routine dis-

Albert Henry DeSalvo

tribution of his photograph to neighbouring forces precipitated hundreds of complaints about similar incidents by a 'Green Man', named after the colour of his trousers. Police put the number of assaults at 300; DeSalvo estimated his total at 2,000, and both agree that on 6 May 1964 he attacked four women in four different Connecticut towns.

But the Boston Strangler was still believed at large. The city remained in the grip of hysteria, and a Brockton housewife died of fright when a stranger knocked on her door selling encyclopedias. The *Boston Advertiser* offered counselling in an 'Appeal to the Strangler', advising, 'Don't kill again. Come to us for help. You are a sick man.' By then a psychological team had drawn up a complicated **profile** of two or more killers, discernible by their different methodology. Only Dr Brussel, of **Mad Bomber** fame, united their exploits under the umbrella of a single individual with shifting behaviour patterns. 'Over the two-year period during which he has been committing these murders,' Brussel reported, 'he has gone through a series of upheavals – or, to put it another way, a single progressive upheaval. What has happened to him, in two words, is instant maturity. In this two year period, he has grown, psychosexually, from infancy to puberty.'

Brussel detected a classic victim of the Oedipus Complex. DeSalvo's early concentration on the elderly represented a 'search for potency'. Theoretically, the rapist's unconscious desire for his mother had left him impotent, an inference reinforced by his assaults with broom handles and bottles. The Boston Strangler sought to expunge his mother's image by murdering older women, and the switch to younger women, initiated by his killing of 20-year-old Sophie Clark on 5 December 1962, showed that he had 'found his potency'. So the Boston Strangler was cured: 'This came about, of course, in the most horrible way possible. He had to commit these murders to achieve his growth. It was his only way to solve his problems, find himself sexually, and become a grown man among men.' He stopped killing, Dr Brussel opined, because he was better.

But the Oedipus Complex was by then an intellectual placebo, and although Brussel proved correct in diagnosing the hand of one assailant, it was for the wrong reasons. DeSalvo was not a well man. He continued raping, but stopped killing because, out of some fundamental decency, he could no longer endure the act of murder and preferred to risk capture by letting his victims live. DeSalvo felt particularly disgusted by his defilement of Mary Sullivan. She was only nineteen, and he left her in a grotesque state with a 'Happy New Year!' card propped against her foot. His penchant for talking to his victims like people – a posture studiously avoided by the likes of Ted **Bundy** – eroded his resolve, the objectives of which fluctuated. DeSalvo would hurry home from a murder to be sure not to miss playing with his children before bedtime.

Sent to the Bridgewater Mental Institute in Massachusetts, De Salvo was adjudged mentally ill. Meanwhile the vast manhunt for the Boston Strangler dragged on until he bragged to a fellow inmate, and his detailed confessions to thirteen murders, recorded on fifty hours of tape, convinced investigators of his guilt. But an insane DeSalvo was unfit to stand trial, and if sane, there was no case to answer since he would be advised not to repeat his confession, the only convincing evidence. In a legal compromise, DeSalvo stood trial as the 'Green Man'. Sentenced to life in 1966, he was stabbed to death by an unidentified fellow inmate in Walpole State Prison on 26 November 1973.

Peter Kürten was similarly oversexed, like Charles Manson, described by Sandy Good as 'perma-rigid'. Of these three, DeSalvo is alone in concentrating his sexual fantasies on sex.

Insulin

A good way of killing people; so good that it seemed perfect until the fine forensic detection of the 1957 Barlow case.

On the evening of 3 May a doctor was summoned to Kenneth Barlow's Bradford home, where his wife's dead body lay in the bath. Barlow said she had been ill and must have passed out and drowned while he dozed in their bedroom. The doctor noticed that her pupils were widely dilated and called the police; when Barlow described his frantic attempts at in-bath artificial resuscitation, the officer noted that his pyjamas were dry.

A preliminary post-mortem investigation excluded drowning. So Elizabeth Barlow had died of something else. But what? Her vital organs were untainted by disease. Poison was suspected, yet exhaustive analysis detected no traces of toxin in the stomach or elsewhere, nor any method of administration. Detectives found syringes in Barlow's house, but this was nothing remarkable; he worked as a male nurse.

As a last resort, the police had the body illuminated by powerful lamps and then minutely inspected, head to toe, with a magnifying glass. And there, in the folded, freckled skin under the right buttock, were two tiny puncture marks.

Barlow had told detectives that on the evening of her death his wife complained of vomiting, sweating and weakness. Specialist advice confirmed that these were common symptoms of hypoglycaemia, a deficiency of blood sugar – the opposite of diabetes, conventionally treated with insulin to drive the blood-sugar level down. Administering insulin to a normal person could induce hypoglycaemia and, in extreme cases, cause death by shock.

There were serious problems with this idea, the first being that it was only a theory and one contraindicated by the *high* readings of blood sugar in Elizabeth Barlow's heart. Proof positive entailed discovering insulin in her body. But there was no test; insulin disappears very quickly once in the bloodstream.

Combing through medical literature, the forensic scientists learned that in cases of violent death, the liver releases a massive boost of sugar to help the fight for life. If the victim dies quickly, the residue remains in the stopped heart, exactly the finding with Mrs Barlow. Eventually a Professor Thomson devised a test-by-proxy. Some of her tissue was injected into mice, producing various repercussions (one of which was death) including an identical response of the blood-sugar level to a control group injected with insulin. So although the pathologists could not prove that she had been dosed with insulin, they knew that an insulin injection would produce the same effect. Further research revealed that insulin is preserved by acid. A dead body forms lactic acid in the muscles, and tests on Elizabeth Barlow's buttock yielded eighty-four units of insulin.

The trial hinged on the scientific evidence. Barlow's defence contended that the body manufactures insulin naturally, along with adrenaline, during moments of stress. But the concentration of eighty-four units in his wife's buttock near the point of injection suggested a body-wide count of 15,000 units. According to the prosecution's expert testimony, the maximum natural output is twenty units.

Barlow had strengthened the police's initial suspicions by telling several colleagues that insulin was *the* way to commit a perfect murder. 'If anybody gets a real dose of it, he's on his way to the next world,' he said. Sentenced to life, Barlow was dragged from the dock protesting his innocence; no motive for the killing emerged, but his previous wife expired the year before at the age of thirty-three with no clear cause of death.

By a strange coincidence, working in the trial judge's chambers at the time of the case was a young Danish lawyer, Claus **von Bülow**

Iowa

The 1989 explosion in Number Two turret of the battleship *Iowa* exposed the FBI's Behavioural Science Unit to ridicule and contempt. Recommissioned in 1984, the *Iowa* retained her main battery; and shipboard guns – like any other – are subject to periodic explosion whether from enemy action, premature detonation, unstable cordite or machine malfunction. At 9.53 a.m. on 19 April 1989 the *Iowa* was four rounds into a practice shoot when the hoist officer of Number Two turret shouted, 'Hold up just a minute, we've got a problem here.' At 9.55 the gun turret blew up, killing forty-seven crew.

At first the inquiry drew a blank. Then on 8 May a letter from the sister of a dead crewman, Clayton Hartwig, asked about his parents entitle-

ment to their son's life insurance policy even though he had assigned it to a shipmate, Kendall Truitt.

So Truitt stood to gain $100,000 from his friend's death, and Hartwig was gun captain on the fatal day. The ordnance inquiry had established that the explosion started between the first and second powder bags in the barrel. Could – or would – Hartwig have put a detonator there?

A 'psychological autopsy' was requested from the FBI's Behavioral Science Unit, widely venerated for its work in profiling serial killers. To crime buffs and the media, pioneering FBI agents like Brooks, Douglas, Hazelwood and Ressler had acquired supersleuth status. But the case was off their patch. It was one thing to analyse fragmentary evidence on a serial killer, but the suspects in this case were professional sailors with reputations and families. For the first time the FBI findings were destined for high-profile critical scrutiny.

On 2 June the FBI took delivery of some 300 dossiers on Truitt, Hartwig, Hartwig's parents, his siblings, schoolmates, and shipmates. They dismissed the idea of murder by Truitt. But Clayton Hartwig had a more suggestive personality. His sister thought him a loner; only in eleventh grade did he develop a close friend, Brian Hoover. Their bond was curiously intense; Hartwig sent Hoover over a thousand letters, gave him $200 a month from his Navy pay, and wrote a will in Hoover's favour in gratitude for his preventing a suicide attempt. The association ended abruptly when Hoover had sex with a mutual friend, and Hartwig's affections switched to Truitt; again, the pair became very close, but they stopped speaking after Truitt married. Then one day Hartwig said, 'Hey Ken, if ever I die you are going to be a rich man.' It was his first mention of the insurance policy.

Hartwig seemed largely asexual, and his letters hinted at rejection, alienation and stress. Like many emotional defectives familiar to the Behavioral Science Unit, he contemplated joining the police (see **Vocations**), and spoke of important – but imaginary – assignments. He discussed suicide with a crew member, who recalled: 'We came to the conclusion that the quickest way we had ever seen anyone die was by explosion.' Hartwig told shipmates that the powder bags could be detonated with a blow from a hammer. He owned a copy of *Improvised Munitions*, talked of bomb-making, and a sailor saw something like a timing device in his locker. On visits home, Hartwig's conversation dwelt on gun-turret explosions.

The profilers decided that Hartwig was 'a very troubled young man who had low self-esteem'. They concluded: 'In our opinion, it was a suicide. He did so in a place and manner designed to give him recognition and respect that he felt was denied', and on 15 July 1989 Admiral Milligan reported that the explosion was 'a wrongful intentional act'. Hartwig had blown himself up.

BODY DISPOSITION

136. There Is Reason to Believe the Offender Moved the Body from the Area of the Death Site to the Area of the Body Recovery Site:
   1 ☐ Yes   2 ☐ No   3 ☐ Unable to Determine

137. Evidence Suggests the Offender Disposed of the Body in the Following Manner:
   1 ☐ Openly Displayed or Otherwise   3 ☐ With an Apparent Lack of
       Placed to Insure Discovery   Concern as to Whether or Not the
   2 ☐ Concealed, Hidden, or Otherwise   Body Was Discovered
       Placed in Order to Prevent Discovery   99 ☐ Unable to Determine

138. It Appears the Body of the Victim Was Intentionally Placed in an Unnatural or Unusual Position *after Death Had Occurred* (e.g., staged or posed):
   1 ☐ Yes   2 ☐ No   3 ☐ Unable to Determine

139. Body Was Discovered...
   1 ☐ Buried   5 ☐ In a Container (e.g., dumpster, box
   2 ☐ Covered   refrigerator)
   3 ☐ In a Body of Water (stream, lake, river,   6 ☐ In a Vehicle
       etc.)   7 ☐ Scattered (body parts)
   4 ☐ In a Building   8 ☐ None of the Above

140. If the Body Was Discovered in Water, Was It Weighted?
   1 ☐ Yes –– With What? _____   2 ☐ No

Part of the FBI's profiling questionnaire

The resulting furore could only be assuaged by a full Capitol Hill inquiry. Was not the evidence circumstantial? Were not most young men 'very troubled'? Was not Hartwig in good spirits at the time of his death? How had he ignited the charges? And had the Navy found a clever way of salvaging its billion-dollar battleship programme, jeopardised if defective design was responsible for the blast? When the hearings opened on 12 December 1989, the FBI were castigated for being too categorical, for unquestioning acceptance of everything in the Navy's files, for selectivity in reviewing evidence, and for failing to consider whether the explosion was accidental.

Fourteen psychologists testified in summary that suicide by Hartwig was of 'a relatively low probability'. The final report was damning: 'The FBI's psychological analysis procedures are of doubtful professionalism. Their false air of certainty was probably the biggest single factor inducing the Navy to single out Clayton Hartwig.' The *Times* commented: 'Deep within the FBI there exists a unit of people who – without ever talking to you or anyone who knows you – are prepared to go into

court and testify that you are a homicidal maniac.'

The outcry prompted renewed investigation into the explosion. The Sandia National Laboratory discovered that a charge could be ignited prematurely by excess ramming speeds, and on 24 May the Navy replicated their results. On 16 October 1991 the Navy conceded it had no proof that the explosion was not an accident and apologised to Clayton Hartwig's family.

So whither the science of profiling? The FBI were not asked to investigate the explosion or query the Navy's findings. Their remit was to give an opinion, based on information received, on whether Hartwig had committed suicide. They thought he had. Their conclusion was not invalidated by an accidental explosion, although it would have been helpful to know it was a possibility. A man with suicidal tendencies can still die in an accident; Hartwig could still have been troubled and depressed.

The FBI's opinions were firmly expressed. But they remained opinions, largely endorsed by the other psychologists. Thus one said: 'The psychological profile drafted by the FBI is very plausible', another, 'Hartwig would appear to be at a high risk for self destruction', a third, 'Yes, he may have done it. No, the investigation does not present clear, cogent, and compelling evidence that he did do it.' The ridicule directed at the FBI stemmed from a misunderstanding of their role, journalistic over-simplifications, and the Navy's ineptitude. In criminal cases, too, **profilers** rely on evidence from outside experts, and if garbage is put in, it is garbage that comes out.

Ivan the Terrible

The ghoulish war criminal of Treblinka. Ivan the Terrible ran the engine which pumped carbon monoxide into the gas chambers, despatching 850,000 victims in a single year. He derived gratuitous pleasure from his work, smashing the prisoners' skulls with an iron pipe and slashing them with his sword as they passed, slicing off ears, noses, women's breasts. The ears he picked up and gave back, like dropped litter, as the Jews filed to their deaths.

Thirty years after the war, an American journalist returned from the Ukraine bearing a list of some sixty Nazi collaborators resident in the United

States. Among them was an 'Ivan Demjanjuk' of the Sobibor death camp, and more than a decade later, after a massively publicised Israeli trial, Cleveland car worker John Demjanjuk was identified as Ivan the Terrible and sentenced to death.

The trial had several bizarre features. Rather like the **Tichborne Claimant** case, which ran for so long that the issues were obscured rather than illuminated, the central issue of identification fell by the wayside. The court deliberated not on whether John Demjanjuk and Ivan the Terrible were one and the same, but on the crimes committed by, and the fitting punishment for, Ivan the Terrible. In the event, John Demjanjuk was convicted for the acts of someone else, Ivan Marchenko.

Two strands of evidence linked Demjanjuk to Treblinka. The first, which occupied fifty days of court time, was equivocal. The prosecution produced an SS identification card showing that Demjanjuk (like thousands of others) had indeed been a concentration camp guard. But at Sobibor, not Treblinka. If the card was genuine, it proved only that Demjanjuk worked in the same country as Ivan the Terrible. The second strand of evidence consisted of direct identification by survivors. Again, this fell into two types, the first of which was fraudulent.

At the June 1981 hearing which stripped him of American citizenship, Judge Frank Battisti held that Demjanjuk was at Treblinka in 1942 and 1943, a finding based on the testimony of Otto Horn, an ex-Nazi. Horn worked with Ivan the Terrible on a daily basis, and the court heard that Horn positively identified Demjanjuk as Ivan.

Had this been true, it would have been powerful evidence. But in the 1980s, the janitor at the U.S. Office of Special Investigations fell into the habit of dumping surplus paperwork in bin-bags outside a McDonald's on Washington's K Street. The documents, removed from the skip by a sympathiser, reached Demjanjuk's son, who unearthed two papers describing in consistent detail what happened at Horn's photo-parade.

Horn identified John Demjanjuk not as Ivan the Terrible but as John Demjanjuk. First Horn was shown a series of photographs and 'studied each of them at length, but was unable to positively identify any of the pictures... The first series of photographs was then placed in a stack, off to the side of the

table – with that of Demjanjuk lying face up on top of the pile, facing Horn.'

Next, Horn studied a second set of pictures, including another photograph of Demjanjuk, and he correctly observed that this was the 'same person' as the man at the top of the first stack. In other words, Horn said that Demjanjuk looked like Demjanjuk – no more, no less. By the 1981 hearing this became:

Attorney: Did you in fact identify or recognise someone in those photographs?

Horn: Yes, this Ivan.

So the only valid testimony at the Jerusalem trial came from concentration camp inmates. As the Ivan investigation gathered impetus in the 1970s, several survivors picked out Demjanjuk from photospreads, saying (in the words of Eliyahu Rosenberg) 'That man looks very similar to the Ukrainian Ivan' and (Pinchas Epstein), 'This photo reminds me very strongly of Ivan.'

These witnesses were asked not whether they recognised anyone, but whether they recognised anyone as Ivan. In the courtroom's emotional atmosphere, ten years later, Rosenberg confronted Demjanjuk in the dock: 'Ivan. I say so unhesitatingly and without the slightest doubt. This is Ivan from the gas chambers. The man I am now looking at. I saw his eyes. I saw those murderous eyes. I saw that face of his.'

Thus the eleven-month case boiled down to this: Demjanjuk might have followed the right line of work, at the right time, in the right country; and four aged witnesses, separated from Ivan for more than forty years, believed they recognised him. Even with Horn's misleading testimony, the guilty verdict was hardly sustainable.

A contributory factor in Demjanjuk's downfall was his fragmented defence team. *The American Lawyer* stated that Demjanjuk's first attorney had 'little if any experience as a trial lawyer'. His second, the highly respected Dov Eitan, received many death threats and died on 29 November 1989 after unexpectedly plummeting from a fifteenth-storey window. The third, Yoram Sheftel, nearly lost his eyesight in an acid attack two days later. Across the benches, the prosecution case, endlessly padded out by the inclusion of appalling but largely extraneous background material on the Holocaust, fulfilled an important educational function for the coming generation; the hearings were televised, with 250,000 spectators passing through the courts.

After the 'guilty' verdict of April 1988, Demjanjuk's son John took up his father's case. In September 1990 John visited Russia with Sheftel and, through a sympathetic judge, secured the Simferol KGB's file on war criminals, including depositions from Soviet survivors of Treblinka. All sixty-one of these statements identified Ivan the Terrible not as the John Demjanjuk of the SS photo-card but as Ivan Marchenko, last sighted during a June 1943 posting at a prison camp in Trieste.

His long-time colleague Nikolai Shelayev (a gas-chamber motorman who accompanied him to Italy) stated that in the spring of 1944 Ivan defected to the Yugoslav Communist partisans. Most of this information had been known to the American Department of Justice since 1978 and in August 1993 Demjanjuk's appeal was allowed but, at time of going to press, the possibility remained that his conviction might be salvaged by finding him guilty for crimes committed as Ivan the Less Terrible, an unknown concentration camp guard from Sobibor. Israel has never before prosecuted this level of minor functionary.

The name 'Ivan the Terrible' was adopted by one of the most feared drug traffickers of Colombia's Cali cartel. He specialised in cutting off his victims' **hands**.

J

Jack the Hat

A very English murder. Jack 'the Hat' McVitie was an old-style East End villain in the London of the 1960s.

At the time, the **Kray** Twins were campaigning for recognition as 'proper' criminals. Ronnie Kray had already staked his claim, on 8 March 1966, by striding into the bar of the 'Blind Beggar', a large Victorian pub in London's Mile End Road, and shooting George Cornell of the Richardson gang with a 9mm Mauser automatic in front of several dozen witnesses. As Ronnie was fond of recounting, George's head 'burst open'. The way Ronnie saw it, that was how gangsters should deport themselves, killing publicly.

This bravado put his brother Reggie on the spot; Ronnie demanded to know when his twin would 'do his one'. By the autumn of 1966, Ronnie's mania was in full flower. More and more people who 'needed killing' were 'on the **list**'. If the Krays were ever to rank as a serious brotherhood alongside the Mafia, its high-ups should all be killers. The pressure mounted on Reggie to follow his leader.

In the end Jack the Hat drew the short straw. Well past his prime, Jack was prematurely bald (hence the hat), a drunk zonked on pep pills, and definitely not the man to kill Leslie Payne, a former Kray associate and now a suspected informer. But in September 1966 Ronnie issued Jack the Hat with a pistol and a £100 deposit for the hit. Jack bungled the job but hung onto the money, infuriating Ronnie, but Reggie felt so sorry for the old-timer that he advanced another £50.

'You should've paid George Cornell as well,' stormed Ronnie. He wanted his £100 back, and this triggered Jack the Hat's final spiral. Jack went on a blinder and staggered into the Krays' Regency Club – 'North London's Smartest Rendezvous' – brandishing a sawn-off shotgun and threatening to blast the twins. They were not there, but someone blabbed. Ronnie decided Jack the Hat had to go, even if it meant doing it himself.

This was too shaming for Reggie. So on the last Saturday in October, well and truly drunk, he set off for the Regency to shoot McVitie. When his intended victim failed to show, Reggie let the club manager to talk him out of his gun and then returned disarmed, mission unaccomplished. Not surprisingly, Ronnie felt let down. He despatched one minion to reclaim the pistol, ordering his henchmen the Lambrianous brothers to scour late-night London, find Jack the Hat, ply him with drink and then bring him for a party to Blond Carol's house in Evering Road, Stoke Newington.

Just before midnight Jack the Hat burst into the house. He was drunk. 'Where's all the birds, all the booze?' he roared. Reggie stepped out from behind the door, wedged the gun against McVitie's head and pulled the trigger. It jammed. Outside, one of the Lambrianous brothers realised what was happening and start to weep. Meanwhile, Reggie pinioned Jack from behind. He broke free and dived through the window into the garden, shattering the glass and frame.

He was pulled back by his legs. 'Be a man, Jack,' shouted Ronnie. 'I'll be a man,' returned Jack, 'but I don't want to die like one.' Now Ronnie held McVitie tight. Clutching a carving knife, Reggie faced the bald, wretched crook. 'Kill him, Reg. Do him,' urged Ronnie. 'Why are you doing this to me, Reg?' said Jack. In reply, Reg shoved the knife into his face below the eye. Then he stabbed him in the guts, then the chest and finished by skewering his throat to the floor.

Within a day or so, Ronnie felt sufficiently composed to talk about how it had all gone, about how Jack looked and the gurgles he made and the amount of blood. Reggie anaesthetised himself with drink, but he had earned his brother's approval.

Jack's body was never found, but after the Krays' arrest on 9 May 1968 one of those present at the killing, Ronnie Hart, turned Queen's evidence, and in March 1969 the twins were sentenced to a minimum of thirty years for the McVitie and Cornell killings.

Both murders were pointless. The Richardson gang had already disintegrated: Cornell was the last survivor. And Jack the Hat was just a drunken nobody. The Krays were enmeshed in make-believe, aiming for the smooth prestige of American gangland killings. They finished up with an East End rough-house while an accomplice, Chrissie Lambrianou, sat blubbing at the horror on the stairs, the venture a prelude to a spiral of self-destructive drinking, remorse, self-pity and prison.

Across the Atlantic, as Ronnie surmised, they did things differently. Of the Dutch Schultz killing in October 1935, the jaunty Joe Valachi recorded: 'Right after this Vito Genovese tells me the Dutchman has got to go... He says not to go out looking for him, but to shoot him if we happen to bump into him', a distinctive stance within the frame of reference of a small-time London gangster interviewed in 1992: 'There's a lot of instability in drug dealing – the exchange of money, credit. So you need guns. Killing is part of the scene. It's not like the Krays. They didn't need to kill. The only reason they killed is because that's what gangsters did in America. Now blokes have revolvers, semi-automatics... It's about presenting yourself as someone who will use a gun.'

Jack the Ripper

The benchmark by which all sex killers are judged. Jack the Ripper stands at the gateway to the modern age. Before, men killed for a reason, or so it was assumed. Afterwards, it gradually became apparent that the sexual impulse could entwine round and fuse with violence, engendering the amalgam familiar today as 'sex-and-violence'. In its most extreme form, the mutation becomes the sexual satisfaction that an individual derives from killing, his blood-lust sharpened by social alienation.

Often the point of these assaults is to leave the female body subjugated and humiliated, spreadeagled and disembowelled in a position of ritual supplication. This demonstrates male supremacy more forcibly than intercourse.

The fact that the Ripper was never caught has contributed powerfully to his status as a cultural icon. At large, Jack is imagined as guileful, cunning, and still very much alive, with each new sex-killer billed as his successor. As a legend, Jack is enshrined with the immortals, and he materialised – still at it – on another planet, in an episode of *Star Trek*, 'Wolf in the Fold'.

During the 1888 killings, London's Whitechapel resembled an area under siege. Eight newspapers followed the story daily, magazines picked it up, and the penny dreadfuls amplified its reverberations. But despite the contemporary fracas, the Ripper's real populariser was Marie Belloc Lownes's 1913 best-seller *The Lodger*, which ploughed through thirty-one editions, eighteen languages and five films, the first by Hitchcock.

Today, serial killers still take their cue from their Victorian hero. **Kürten** averred that the Ripper exercised a profound influence over him and, like his master, exchanged letters with the newspapers; one of the **Son of Sam**'s few possessions was a book on the Ripper; DeSalvo promised the police he was about to break something really big, 'like Jack the Ripper', and **Bundy** was designated by the *Reader's Digest* as 'America's Jack the Ripper'. Perhaps this tradition, abetted by the media, inspires emulation rather than aversion.

The facts on Jack are threadbare. There were five accredited killings: Polly Nichols (31 August), Annie Chapman (8 September), Elizabeth Stride and Catharine Eddowes (both 30 September) and Mary Kelly (9 November). All were prostitutes, all had their throats slit, all were mutilated (time permitting), all were killed within a quarter of

Elizabeth Stride

a square mile in Whitechapel, and all died in the early morning, in the first or the last weekend of the month. None was sexually assaulted.

Any talk of royal suspects, or the Freemasons, barristers or medical men, and any image of plush brothels, should be set beside the district's grinding, unremitting poverty. At maybe tuppence a trick, prostitution was the last bulwark against starvation, with many using their clothes like a house, to keep their possessions in. Catharine Eddowes, the Mitre Square victim, was found on post-mortem with all her belongings in her garments: a blunt table knife, a scrap of red flannel for her pins and needles, and two tin boxes, one for sugar and the other for tea. Annie Chapman, discovered in Hanbury Street, was all but dead on her feet before her fatal encounter: undernourished and raddled with chronic diseases of the lungs and brain membranes. Local doss-houses crammed up to eighty into a single dormitory, and many rents were collected daily. The

The sketch issued by the press.

public houses of the area did not close until three in the morning, and opened at six to serve a liquid breakfast. The police ventured into Whitechapel only in groups and, a mile to the east, in the **Ratcliffe Highway**, dared not venture at all.

Jack the Ripper astonished the world by his florid displays. Rather than covering up his transgressions, he broadcast them. The bodies, with their scattered entrails, were left out on exhibition, surrounded by ritually placed objects, often taken from the victim – rings, coins, pills wrapped in paper, and the famous leather apron. He maintained a taunting correspondence with the police, press and citizen groups.

The Ripper's crimes were without historical precedent, leaving commentators bewildered. What was the *point* of the killings? The coroner's suggestion after the inquest on 10 September that 'both Nichols and Chapman had been murdered...to secure some pathological specimen from the abdomen' was eagerly embraced for its comforting

sense of purpose. The London *Times* exhibited typical incomprehension, reporting that the police were 'confronted with a murder of no ordinary character, committed not from jealousy, revenge or robbery, but from motives less adequate than many which still disgraced our society'. The double murder of 30 September demonstrated that the malice was not directed against any particular individual, and represented an exponential leap in horror.

The epicentre of the social tremors was the state of the victims' bodies. The autopsy report on Mary Jane Kelly, by Dr Thomas Bond, reads in part: 'The viscera were found in various parts viz the uterus & Kidneys with one breast under the head, the other breast by the Rt foot, the Liver between the feet, the intestines by the right side & the spleen by the left side of the body. The flaps removed from the abdomen and thighs were on a table... The whole of the surface of the abdomen and thighs was removed and the abdominal cavity emptied of its viscera. The breasts were cut off, the arms mutilated by several jagged wounds and the face hacked beyond recognition of the features. The tissues of the neck were severed all round down to the bone... The pericardium was open below and the heart was absent.'

Such savagery was new, in wild excess of any requirement to extinguish life, beyond the previous high water mark of pointless violence recorded in the Ratcliffe Highway murders seventy years previously. The concept of 'Rippers', together with its alternative, 'stabber', had been popularised by the nineteenth-century press before 1888, but they were faltering antecedents of the modern sex criminal, content merely to stab their victims in the breasts, genitals and buttocks as they walked through the streets. Although commonplace by the 1880s, with exponents in London, Paris, Texas, Moscow and Nicaragua, it was Jack the Ripper who catapulted his exaggerated version into mass cultural consciousness.

For the killings, it is likely that the Ripper stood in front of his victims in the normal position for standing intercourse and then seized them round the neck. This would simultaneously ensure silence and induce unconsciousness. Next he thrust his victim to the ground with the head to his left, and then slit the throat, starting at the far end to direct the blood away.

As to the killer's identity there is little to go on, but enough to found an industry: **Ripperology**. The police had their suspects, but 1888 was too early for forensic science to play a significant part. *The Times* asserted that a good fingerprint might be 'almost as useful' a clue as a **footprint**, and a proposal to equip constables with rubber-soled shoes to deaden their approach was seriously entertained. The victims' eyes were photographed in case they retained an imprint of the killer (see **Optographs**).

More usefully, rewards were offered and, less usefully, a pair of champion bloodhounds from Scarborough, called Burgho and Barnaby, were assigned to the case. But they got lost on Tooting Common and had to be tracked down by police. Queen Victoria joined the general public condemnation of the force, sending a lengthy missive beginning 'The Queen fears that the detective department is not so efficient as it might be'. But for all the flood of well-intentioned advice, short of catching their man red-handed, there was little the authorities could do.

See also **Ripperology, Sex crimes, Solution**

Jails, best

With America's prisons filling up with the likes of Ivan Boesky, Leona Helmsley, Michael **Milken** and Mike **Tyson**, a need arose for a guide to the country's best jails. *Playboy* plugged the gap in July 1992 with a listing of the nation's top ten.

Most of the rated prisons are small, some housing only a few dozen inmates, like Olmsted County Jail with its 'tradition of great cooking established by the sheriff's wife'. Over at Evans County Jail in Georgia, the twenty-five prisoners 'dress in robes and slippers, lounge on down pillows and watch movies. The jail is relatively new; it smells like a new car.' But be warned; Kentucky's Crittendon may have a TV satellite hook-up, but *there is no remote control*.

The place to be seen in Britain is Ford Open Prison in Sussex, as a Category D prisoner. The institution looks like a collective farm for cricketers; huts huddle round the pitch, and inmates trundle their wheelbarrows across the country road intersecting the grounds.

The three city financiers jailed at Ford for the Guinness share-ramping scam founded its reputation as a club for upper-crust lags honing their share portfolios. But the social tone declined after a number of petty offenders and car thieves wormed their way in.

Jake

Prohibition drink. Brewed from Jamaican ginger, jake was some 90 per cent alcohol and allegedly possessed medicinal properties for stomach disorders; hence its availability on prescription in prodigal quantities. A small Texas druggist took delivery of 200 barrels in 1928, and by 1930 jake was in widespread demand throughout Kansas. Indiscriminately sold at thirty cents a shot to previously healthy citizens, it produced the interesting side effect of selective paralysis.

The condition was manifested by loss of control of the muscles which traditionally ensure that the heel lands before the toes when walking; victims were known as 'jake-trotters'. Frequently the muscles of their thumbs and index fingers wasted away, and initial amusement palled after the Prohibition Bureau estimated the number afflicted nationwide to total 15,000, many of whom in due course recovered partial control of their hands and feet.

See also **Fallout**

Jaws

Despite his nickname of 'Metal Fang', Nikolai Dzhumagaliev from Kazakhstan did not use his white-metal gnashers for the kill.

Nikolai dates back to the pre-*glasnost* era of 1980, so reports are fragmentary. But after his day's work on an Alma-Ata building site, the neatly dressed Nikolai would take a woman for a stroll by the river, rape her, hack her to bits with an axe, light a fire, cook her and then invite friends back for supper with real meat. Such meals were a welcome rarity in Russia. But Nikolai became careless; it was a mistake to leave a woman's head and intestines exposed on the kitchen table, where they were noticed by two guests.

Charged with seven murders, Nikolai was adjudged insane and sent to a mental institution in Tashkent, from which he escaped in 1989. He was rearrested in Uzbekistan in August 1991.

Jekyll and Hyde

A 60,000-word novella. Robert Louis Stevenson finished the first draft in one three-day stint, as though he were on speed. In fact he was on cocaine, which thus constituted his inspiration, means of production and, in part, the subject. His model for a double life probably came from the career of William Brodie, which Stevenson had already adapted as a stage play, first produced at the Prince's Theatre in London on 2 July 1884.

Brodie was born wealthy and died poor after dissipating his fortune on gambling. From his large house in the Lawnmarket, he played a prominent role in Edinburgh social life as Deacon on the Town Council and a luminary of the exclusive Cape Club. But by 1785, with his money gone, he turned to crime, robbing the houses of his wealthy clients and acquaintances. The following year he formed a gang with three professional thieves and, after a burglary on the Excise Office on 5 March 1788, two confederates were arrested and turned King's evidence. Brodie was hanged on 1 October 1788 before a huge crowd exulting in his fall from grace, and Stevenson's *Jekyll and Hyde* charts his hero's progressive degeneration from high intentions and respectability to a hideous reality from which, one day, there is no return.

In recognition of this tendency, many sadistic killers collaborate in their own capture, using their residual good side (Dr Jekyll) to ensure annihilation of their bad side (Mr Hyde). The youthful serial killer William Heirens expressed this vividly on 10 December 1945, scrawling his message with lipstick on a wall by the dead body of Chicago woman Frances Brown: 'For heavens sake catch me before I kill more I cannot control myself'. He was captured six months later, on 26 June 1946, but not before distributing 6-year-old Suzanne Degnan in five different sewers. Her head was found beneath one manhole cover, with her left leg, right leg, arms and torso occupying four more.

According to graphologists, Heiren's childlike script, with its downward slope and poorly formed letters, shows emotional stress, nervousness and maladjustment

Heirens's sexual drive went haywire during adolescence, when it was his custom to don women's underwear and stare at pictures of Nazi leaders. Arrested for carrying a loaded pistol at the age of thirteen, he had already accumulated a sizeable home arsenal. His upbringing on matters sexual had been deeply repressive, but sex, like truth, will out. His longings focused on the forbidden, and hence the unlawful, leading to an incremental confusion between sex and crime. Originally this evidenced itself through burglary, when he achieved orgasm as he 'entered' a building through the symbolic vagina of its window.

But one thing leads to another, and on 3 June 1945, while housebreaking, Heirens slashed the throat of Josephine Ross, and from then on murder, in its more strident forms, represented his ultimate pleasure. But he took no pains to avoid capture and was arrested prowling round an empty apartment; routine checks revealed that his **fingerprints** matched those at the murder scenes. His attempt to shift Suzanne's killing on George Murman (his alter ego) was indicative more of self-disgust and denial than legal manoeuvring (see **MPD**), and he was sentenced to three terms of life imprisonment.

Other sex killers, like Britain's Neville Heath, telephone the police and offer to assist in their enquiries or, like Dennis **Nilsen**, regard their capture as 'the day help arrived', a longed for curtain-call ending their course of self-destruction. Serial killers often display a kamikaze tendency, with their murders constituting a suicide note, the outcome of acute depression, an inability to relate and an unlived life. 'Low self-esteem' and 'under-achievement' are recurring features of psychological **profiles**.

Apart from sensual gratification, the murders may be motivated by resentment against the world and its failure to take proper cognisance of the killer, whose clever handiwork puts him on the map. But only at the very bottom. It gradually dawns that he is only important for bludgeoning innocent bystanders to death, and even then nobody knows he did it; his lot is worse than when he started (see **Ng**, **Zodiac**).

The killer can only achieve celebrity in his own right after being caught. 'I wanted to be famous... I thought you were never going to catch me,' complained Kenneth Erskine, London's Stockwell Strangler, who throttled seven pensioners in 1986, sodomising five. By this terminal stage, many serial killers welcome or even ask for the death sentence. On 28 January 1983, Douglas Daniel Clark, America's 'Sunset Slayer', presented his own case during the penalty phase of the court proceedings. He appointed himself the thirteenth member of the jury and recommended his execution. 'We have to vote for the death penalty in the case,' he declared. 'The evidence cries out for it.' Numerous other killers have echoed these sentiments.

But Clark felt reasonably safe, since at the time California's last execution was in 1967. Similarly, although the killings may be a suicide note, serial killers rarely take their own lives. To pursue the analogy *à l'outrance*, the **sadism** – a distorted mirror-version of ordinary sexuality – produces the murders which, in a grotesque parody of ordinary existence, represent a displaced plea for help.

Johns, Tommy (1922–88)

Leading but dead Australian sot. Johns celebrated his 2,000th arrest for drunkenness on 9 September 1982 and, shortly before his death, estimated his total at 'nearly 3,000' since 1957, a rate of nearly two arrests a week over a career spanning three decades. Despite these selfless endeavours Johns failed to drink himself into an early grave.

A famous nineteenth-century English drunk was Annie Parker, who served over 400 sentences. She devoted her time inside the Clerkenwell House of Correction to sewing tiny needlework 'samplers' of ivory-coloured lace, delicately emblazoned with religious motifs such as: 'I will instruct thee and teach thee in the way which thou shalt go. I will guide thee with mine eye. Thine home is in heaven.' The words 'Prudence' and 'Temperance' figured in two corners of each cushion. Annie used her hair as thread, giving the embroideries to the prison vicar, who donated them to Scotland Yard's Black Museum.

Johnson, Dr Samuel (1709–84)

A hard-liner. Johnson characterised the proposed relocation of the gallows to **Newgate** in these terms: '**Tyburn** itself is not safe from the fury of innovation. Executions are intended to draw spectators; if they do not, they do not answer to their purpose. The old method was most satisfactory to all parties; the public was gratified by a procession, the criminal supported by it. Why is all this to be swept away?'

The views of the diarist Samuel Pepys (1633–1703) on **hanging** are perhaps more illuminating. He advocated the use of silken rope, 'it being soft and sleek it do slip close and kills, that is strangles presently, whereas a stiff one do not come so close together and so the party may live longer before being killed'. Pepys was right, but this was not appreciated for nearly two centuries.

Jury

Initially comprised exclusively of the accused's personal acquaintances, who were well placed to know if he was guilty. The word derives from the French *juré*, meaning sworn.

In America, the Fully Informed Jury Association's exertions are directed towards publicising the widely unknown power of 'jury veto'. This neglected provision, enshrined in the Constitution as a final check on government powers, entitles jurors to acquit regardless of the evidence, on the basis that they disagree with the law itself.

Jury selection was already big business in America by 1975 when a Duke University psychology professor received $15,000 in the Jeffrey **MacDonald** case to 'profile' potential jurors predisposed to an acquittal. Nine hundred randomly selected citizens were subjected to telephone interviews including demographic questions about their age, race, marital status, educational background and churchgoing habits, and each factor given statistical weight. The ideal juror, it turned out, was exactly the type which conventional wisdom decreed would be most sympathetic to the prosecution, namely white, conservative and over thirty-five: solid, upstanding citizens like accountants, chemists and ex-policemen.

In the event, MacDonald was convicted after six and a half hours of consideration. A younger, more liberal jury would probably have reached the same conclusion more quickly.

Justice

Easy to achieve in former times, the task simplified by the inviolability of the person of a 'freeman', by definition almost incapable of guilt.

Until the twelfth century, criminal procedure remained a matter of self-assessment. The victim reported an offence to the officers of justice and then made his accusation in court. There the defendant swore on oath that he was innocent, whereupon proceedings terminated in his acquittal. The equivalent commercial process today is known as 'self-regulation'.

The accused's sworn oath was virtually irrefutable as the truth in front of God, thought to intervene continuously in earthly affairs to ensure that wrongs received fitting retribution. Only in the most outrageous cases would the accused's oath require reinforcement from other oath-helpers, called 'compurgators'. But unlike modern witnesses, compurgators did not give testimony as to events; instead, they rendered evidential support by consenting to the swearing of the accused's original oath.

Tricky cases might go one step further, to **mortal combat** where the litigants fought to determine the innocent party. This was the survivor, since it was observed *ex post facto* that God, who moved in mysterious ways, accorded victory to the pure in heart. Nonetheless, prudent litigants often nudged the scales of justice by designating someone bigger and stronger to trade blows on their behalf.

This system was prevalent throughout Christendom until the twelfth century, when the recovery and adaptation of the written body of Roman law introduced a new element: proof. The judgement of man supplanted the judgement of God, inaugurating the familiar process of examining the written record and interrogating witnesses.

The most powerful of all evidence in this uncertain undertaking was a confession, soaring above the vagaries of judges, juries and evasive witnesses, as the *regina probatiorum*, the queen of proofs. It put matters beyond argument; moreover, confessions could be made at any time, in sharp distinction to the fleeting availability of criminals caught red-handed. In cases of inconclusive evidence, the court could rely on the testimony of the one man who *knew first-hand* whether the suspect was guilty, and for some crimes – chiefly capital ones – it was unsafe to convict in the absence of a full admission.

Fortunately, the technology for extracting confessions had long since been mastered, and by the start of the thirteenth century – in the interests of fair play and justice – **torture** was integral to the legal system. It remained in ordinary usage throughout Europe until the 1800s, except in England where it played no official part after 1166. King Henry III instituted the petty jury whose members, confronted by perplexing circumstantial evidence, proved capable of making up their own minds; in other countries, guilt was determined not by the jury but by the judge who, as a state prosecutor, followed the state's rigid hierarchical procedure, of which torture was an established element.

Under English law today, the accused is assumed innocent until proved Irish.

Justification

Murderers often feel obliged to justify their killings to themselves or the police. A common rationalisation is 'obeying voices', often God's but in the case of Son of **Sam**, God spelt backwards. He obeyed a barking dog. Peter **Sutcliffe**, the Yorkshire Ripper, explained that he was animated by the best civic motives (see **Sex crimes**): 'The women I killed were filth... I was just cleaning the place up a bit.'

The Son of Sam still revelled in his mission during the courtroom proceedings; seeing the parents of his last victim, Stacy Moscowitz, in the spectators' section, he chanted: 'Stacy is a whore, Stacy is a whore. I'll shoot them all.'

In October 1964 John William Stoneley, a 21-year-old cable-maker from Southampton, battered taxi driver George Newbury into unconsciousness with a metal pipe and then, while his victim lay slumped over the wheel, stove in his head with five more blows. The police learned from Stoneley that his victim's demise 'was caused by him not getting help'. At his trial this statement told against him, and he was sentenced to death, later commuted to life imprisonment. Five months into his sentence, Stoneley married a 19-year-old in a brief ceremony with a prison guard for best man.

Sometimes murderers worry that the jury and public do not understand. In 1979 Californian Lawrence Singleton, accused of raping a 15-year-old and chopping off her arms with an axe, explained his ordeal with perfect clarity: 'My night of terror had begun. Everything I did was for survival...' A stubborn jury took the reverse view and found him guilty as charged.

Singleton's last letter to the author Amanda Spake contained a word-for-word rewriting of his indictment, save that his own name was substituted throughout by the true perpetrator of the crime, his victim. In Japan, during 1972 the leader of the Red Army Faction, Hiroko Nagata, worked herself into a similar 'logic grave', killing one of her followers for wearing earrings.

Given the right frame of mind, something can be the motive for anything. On 20 September 1991 Alec Bell was jailed for three-and-a-half years after demolishing a woman's house with a mechanical digger when she refused to heat up his dinner, and in February 1992 Sylvester Simon was convicted of the manslaughter of his 70-year-old friend Cephus John, who denounced him for cheating at dominoes. Similar instances are without number.

Cases where the crime is out of all proportion to its engendering circumstances have always been with us. The leap for mankind was the so-called motiveless murders, where the impulse to kill sprang from the criminal's internal dictates without input from the victim, a trait which came to the attention of criminologists like **Locard** in the 1940s.

K

Kangaroo

A singular disguise. The only land bridge from the penal colony on the Tasman Peninsular was Eaglehawk Neck, a 100-yard isthmus leading to mainland Australia, and in 1831 the Lieutenant-Governor, Sir George Arthur, established a guard station on the narrow strip of land after the first flurry of escapes when desperate convicts walked, crept or waded across to an uncertain future on the mainland.

A former actor as well as a convict, William Hunt decided to dress as a kangaroo for his escape. He had nearly bounded to the safety of Forestier's Peninsular on the far side when he was spotted by two picket guards, who could scarcely believe their luck. At last there would be something decent for dinner. The guards gave chase and levelled their muskets at the animal, which capitulated with the words, 'Don't shoot, I am only Billy Hunt.'

Thereafter Captain Charles O'Hara Booth, the Port Arthur commandant, put a stop to such indignities. To the complement of the nine guard dogs tethered at intervals across the Neck, in 1832 he added a row of oil lamps which illuminated a white background of crushed cockle shells. Behind, Booth constructed a line of sentry boxes together with guard-houses for an increased squad of twenty-five men. When the convicts took to the waters, so did Booth, building seaborne rafts as dog outposts. And according to rumour, when the prisoners tried to bypass the platforms by swimming further out, his guards dumped blood and offal into the sea as a beacon for sharks.

Kelly, Ned (1855–80)

Australian national hero, the inspiration for three movies, a rock opera, several paintings and a jazz suite.

Kelly's father, an Irishman transported for stealing two pigs, was imprisoned in 1865 for rustling, and he died shortly after release, leaving his widow to raise their seven children in squalor. Ned, the eldest, was jailed at sixteen after sundry robberies for 'rooting both his spurs' in a constable. Of his chain gang years, Kelly said, 'I'd rather face the gallows than go to jail again.' A fine figure of a man, six feet tall, a good horseman and a skilled boxer endowed with a luxuriant beard, he stayed out of trouble despite stealing some 200 horses. But in September 1877 he was arrested by a Constable Lonigan and dragged across the road by his privates. Kelly bawled, 'If ever I shoot a man, Lonigan, you will be the first.' He was.

The following April Constable Fitzpatrick called at Kelly's slab-and-bark hut to arrest his 17-year-old brother, Dan. According to Fitzpatrick, Ned burst in, took aim from the range of a yard and missed. Meanwhile, the boys' mother banged Fitzpatrick's helmet down over his eyes with a spade; Ned fired again, winging him in the wrist. According to Ned, and this is more likely, he was 400 miles away at the time; Dan duped Fitzpatrick with the oldest trick in the book, crying 'Here comes Ned now', seizing his pistol as he wheeled round. Whichever, Fitzpatrick retired hurt, but his report turned both the Kelly boys into outlaws and landed their mother with a three-year prison sentence.

On 25 October 1878, two noisy search parties set out hunting the Kellys. Informers directed one group to a small clearing by Mount Wombat on Stringybark Creek where Ned ambushed their camp. Constable McIntyre surrendered, but his companion – Lonigan – took to his heels, reaching for his weapon. Kelly blasted him with a shotgun: 'It was him or me. What a pity the bastard had to run.' When the two others, Kennedy and Scanlon, returned they too died in a gunfight, and Kennedy's **ears** were missing when his body was discovered five days later. All Victoria was agog at the news; the confrontation was rehashed as a play, the *Vultures of the Wombat Ranges*, and Kelly's character was cheered to the echo. With £1,000 on his head, an army of police scoured the bush, but rather than lying low, on 9 December 1898 Kelly took over Euroa, a settlement of 300, first investing the station at Faithful's Creek in genial mood, confining twenty-two passengers

In all his glory

and staff to the storehouse before riding into town clad in pilfered finery to relieve the bank of £2,060.

Kelly placed the loot in a sugar bag and, after sharing a bottle of whisky with Mr Scott, the manager, insisted on taking him, his wife, seven children and two servants on an outing to Faithful's Creek where he ordered dinner for thirty, delivered a firebrand speech, showed off his riding skills and then, to general acclaim, rode off into the Strathbone Ranges.

Such exploits are the stuff of legend, and the reward was raised to £4,000. On 8 February 1879 Kelly took the town of Jerilderie hostage, locking the local police in their cells, donning their uniforms and forcing the unfortunate Constable Richards to introduce his gang round town as a new contingent hunting the Kellys. Next day, they robbed the Bank of

New South Wales of £2,140. Kelly briefly considered burning the mortgages, adding another twist to the legend, but was distracted by the complication that the bank's deedbox also contained pension policies. He hosted another party where, lionised by the townsfolk, he stood drinks all round, alternately threatening to execute Constable Richards on the spot and then magnanimously pardoning him. In sentimental mode, Kelly ordered the return of a gold watch and a favourite horse to their former owners, and he left behind a spirited, unpunctuated note, characterising his detractors as 'a parcel of big ugly fat-necked wombat-legged narrow-lipped splay-footed sons of Irish bailiffs and English landlords'.

The reward was raised to £8,000. The Kellys had friends everywhere, but eighteen months in the bush took their toll and by June the following year Kelly devised a masterplan to lure a trainload of lawmen into his clutches, derail it and then, invincible in ploughshare armour, gun down the survivors. With all the district's police dead, he would plunder every bank from Benalla to Beechworth. His plan worked like clockwork, but its intended victims did not, and the mistimed scheme backfired.

On 26 June 1880 Kelly baited the trap with the shooting of Aaron Sherritt, an informer, at a hut guarded by four live-in police. Kelly rightly reasoned that this would prompt Melbourne's Captain Standish to despatch reinforcements to Beechworth. But the officers cowered in the hut overnight, and when the news did reach Melbourne, Standish could not be found, and when he was, the engine took hours to work up steam. The train did not leave until 10.15 p.m. on the 27th, twelve hours later than Kelly calculated, and he made his dispositions too soon.

Late on the 26th, Kelly commandeered the Glenrowan Inn by a small railroad halt and ripped up the track a mile down the line on a precipitous embankment. His sixty-two prisoners needed entertaining all morning under mounting tension; games and dancing to a concertina whiled away the hours, but one man of spirit, Thomas Curnow, the local schoolteacher, resolved to avert the impending massacre. He begged Kelly to release him and his family: 'You've got no cause to fear me, I'm with you heart and soul.' Kelly acceded, and at 3 a.m. on the morning of the 27th Curnow ran down the track clutching a candle while the Kellys faced their second night without sleep.

Curnow flagged down the pilot engine short of the break in the line. The police debouched, as did numerous reporters, artists and several ladies, who were treated to a grandstand view of the shootout. Thirty officers fanned out towards the hotel; the gang donned their armour and lined the verandah, blazing away in the dark for fifteen minutes as the police returned fire from the field's perimeter. 'Come on, I'm Ned Kelly and I'm made of iron,' Kelly taunted his assailants, but he was soon hit in the foot, elbow and hand. Volleys poured through the wooden walls as the hostages lay on the floor.

At 97 pounds, Kelly's armour proved an encumbrance. Hardly able to move, or sight a weapon, or raise a rifle to his shoulder, he shambled out into the fields unobserved, hoping to outflank his tormentors. But at first light he determined to regain the hotel and lumbered from the treeline through the mist like a mythic figure, his coat flapping over the iron plating. Railwayman Jesse Dowsett takes up the story: 'I emptied my revolver at him, but he came on steadily, saying, "Fire away, you bloody dogs, you can't hurt me"... I fired again, hitting him full in the head, but not having the slightest effect... He seemed to fall backward. I ran up, and jumping over the log, saw Steele and he on the ground. I grasped the revolver from him.' Kelly, bleeding from twenty-five minor and five serious wounds, was asked why he had not deserted his gang to save himself. 'A man would have been a nice sort of **dingo** to walk out on his mates.'

Later that morning the hostages were released, and in the afternoon the hotel was torched. Inside, the other three gang members were already dead. After recuperating in the Melbourne jail infirmary,

Artists were on hand to sketch the battle almost as it unfolded. An accurate depitction of Kelly's capture by Dowsett and Steele.

Kelly was tried on 28 October, charged only with the murder of Lonigan, to which he could have pleaded self-defence. On receiving the death sentence, Kelly steadily addressed Judge Barry from the dock: 'It is quite possible for me to clear myself from this charge if I liked to do so... I dare say the day will come when we shall go to a bigger court than this. Then we shall see who is right and who is wrong.' A petition 60,000 strong failed to secure a reprieve, and he was hanged on 11 November 1880. 'Such is life,' Kelly said, as they tightened the noose around his neck. Two days later, Judge Barry collapsed and died.

Kemmler, William (d. 1869)

William Kemmler (who hatcheted his girl, Tillie Zeigler, to death on 29 March 1889) was selected as the first victim of the **electric chair**.

A host of curious, besuited physicians attended the experiment at New York's Auburn Prison on 6 August 1890. They awaited Kemmler's arrival expectantly, seated in a circle round his empty chair. He had dressed to the nines in a new suit for his big day, looking 'better than he had ever been before', and the Warden ushered him into the killing room with the announcement, 'Gentlemen, this is William Kemmler.' He walked over to his chair, bowed to the assembled company, and took up his seat.

'Now we'll get ready, William,' said the kindly Warden. As he was strapped in, Kemmler reassured the nervous Deputy Sheriff: 'Don't get excited, Joe. I want you to make a good job of this.' Kemmler wanted everything just so, calling for an adjustment to his skull cap. When all was shipshape, the Warden took his leave: 'Goodbye, William.'

'Goodbye,' replied Kemmler calmly. Then they killed him. But not very well. A thousand volts banged through Kemmler for seventeen seconds; the fascinated doctors gathered round his body. When Kemmler took a deep breath, everyone scattered in panic. Then they gave him the treatment again.

With the exception of the *New York Times*, condemnation of this barbaric implement was universal, and fifteen states adopted electrocution as their official method of execution.

The murderer William G. Taylor survived for longer than Kemmler. On 27 August 1893, after the first electric jolt extended his legs and broke the front part of the chair, a guard fetched a box to prop up the sagging seat. Then the warder threw the switch again, but nothing happened. The generator had burnt out. The groaning Taylor, comatose but still alive, was unstrapped and settled in a cot while the electricians frantically restrung power lines over the prison walls to bleed off the city's current.

But Taylor died before he could be executed; in other words, the sentence had not been carried out. So they executed him dead, installing his corpse in the chair for one last, thirty-second blast.

The first woman to be electrocuted in Pennsylvania was Irene Schroeder who, in tandem with her lover Glenn Dagus, murdered a policeman in 1931. As they tightened her straps, Schroeder was asked if she wanted anything. 'Yes,' she said, 'there is something. Tell them in the kitchen to fry Glenn's eggs on both sides. He likes them that way.'

George Appel, a Chicago gangster, managed a joke while they buckled him in. 'Well folks,' he told the watching press men, 'you'll soon see a baked Appel.'

Kemper, Edmund Emil III (1949–)

The 'co-ed killer', a cornucopia of deviant psychiatric tendencies marked by the usual childhood symptoms including cruelty to animals, especially cats (see **Pets**).

Kemper killed his grandparents in 1964 at the age of fifteen. Afterwards he said, 'I just wondered how it would feel to shoot grandma', and when grandpa ran into the room he wondered how that would feel too. Released in 1969 by the California Youth Authority against psychiatric advice, Kemper progressed to sadism, murder, necrophilia and cannibalism, finishing with matricide.

For a while the 6ft 9in, 21-stone Kemper confined himself to female university students, picking up hitch-hiking co-eds and cutting off their heads. 'Alive, they were distant, not sharing with me,' he recounted. 'I was trying to establish a relationship. When they were being killed, there wasn't anything in my mind except that they were going to be mine.' To make the girls more truly his, Kemper ate parts of their bodies.

Interiors exerted a strange fascination. Kemper said of his February 1973 victim Rosalind Thorpe: 'She had a rather large forehead, and I was imagining what her brain looked like inside and I just wanted to put a bullet in it.' So he did, delivering her to his mother's house at Santa Cruz where he removed her head and gouged the slug out. In life, death was always with him; asked how he would react if he saw a pretty girl on the street, Kemper said: 'One side of me says, "Wow, what an attractive chick, I'd like to talk to her, to date her." The other side of me says, "I wonder how her head would look on a stick."'

Kemper's **mother** was at the root of his problems. She never stopped nagging, so on Easter Saturday 1973 he cut off her head. Then, to make doubly sure, he excised the larynx and stuffed it down the garbage disposal unit. But when Kemper switched the machine on, it clogged and spewed her throat back at him. 'Even when she was dead,' Kemper recalled, 'she was still bitching at me. I couldn't get her to shut up.' Next, Kemper invited his mother's friend, Sarah Hallett, for tea. After crushing her head with a brick, he cut it off and made love to the torso. Then, leaving a note for the police (which concluded 'I got things to do!'), he drove to Colorado to await arrest.

But this proved beyond the capacity of American law enforcement; even though Kemper was stopped for a traffic violation, he had crossed a state boundary and did not feature on the local wanted list. With growing frustration, he made repeated, pleading telephone calls to the Santa Cruz police, eventually persuading them to send the Colorado cops to collect him outside a phone booth.

Convicted of eight murders, Kemper asked for 'death by torture'. But he was running out of steam, like many a serial killer. 'The original purpose was gone,' he later told the police, explaining his decision to surrender. 'It was starting to weigh kind of heavy. The need I had for continuing death was needless and continuous. It wasn't serving any physical or emotional purpose. It was just a pure waste of time. I wore out of it.'

But the homicidal embers still flickered. Sentenced to life, Kemper was interviewed in jail by the FBI for inclusion in their serial killer **database**. He told his questioner, waiting nervously for the long-overdue arrival of a guard to let him out of the cell: 'The rooms are soundproofed here, nobody can hear your screams. By the time you push that button I'll tear you apart... I could screw your head off and place it on the table to greet the guard.' Heads were Kemper's speciality. As he told the FBI: 'You know, the head is where everything is at, the brain, the eyes, the mouth. That's the person. I remember being told as a kid that if you cut off the head, the body dies. The body is nothing after the head is cut off. The personality is gone.'

With hindsight, it is clear that Kemper was a necrophiliac precursor of Jeffrey **Dahmer**.

Kennedy, John F. (1917–63)

President Kennedy was enmeshed – before, during and after his tenure of office – by intelligence agencies operating to a secret agenda who covertly manipulated governmental policy to their own ends. These included war; and in this warped political context it is not unreasonable to query the official account of his assassination. The original Warren report, far from being exhaustive, was required by Johnson before the 1964 election, and after only three months the investigators learned that they were supposed to be 'closing doors, not opening them'. The continuing revelations about **Hoover**'s predilection for blackmail and his links with the Mafia, together with the Kennedy–Exner–Giancana–Operation Mongoose–Mafia nexus, hardly inspire confidence.

The leading theories are that Oswald killed the President at his own prompting ('the lone nut' con-

cept), or that Oswald was 'sponsored' by Khrushchev, or Castro, or big business, or the Mafia. Or Oswald was set up as a fall-guy by a disaffected clique within the CIA.

The problem with the 'lone nut' theory is that it involves two lone nuts, the second being Jack Ruby,

The shooting of Oswald

who had ties with the Mafia and died in custody with (to judge from his words to Chief Justice Warren) his tale still untold. Ruby gained access for a clear shot at Oswald with perfect timing hard to replicate without inside assistance. Nor is Oswald's assassination weapon satisfactory. The 1940s 6.5mm Mannlicher Carcano had a stiff bolt action, a misaligned sight and was notoriously inaccurate. According to the FBI, it took 2.25 seconds to aim and fire. The famous Zapruder film shows Kennedy and Governor Connally taking hits less than two seconds apart, and material from the President's brain splattered backwards onto the car trunk, some impacting on a motorcycle policeman riding behind and to the left.

But firing tests on melons and stuffed skulls show that detritus is not expelled towards the rifle. An alternative point of origin for at least some of the gunfire is the 'grassy knoll'. The evidence is no more than verbal, but it seems persuasive. Thus William Newman, a Korean War veteran, was standing on the pavement between the knoll and the motorcade. He heard the first two shots as no louder than distant firecrackers, and thought they registered a hit. But then he flung himself and his family to the ground as a loud boom rang out from close behind, simultaneous with the disintegration of the President's head.

Doubts remain about Oswald's motivation and the capacity in which he acted, if he acted at all. His palmprints were not found on the rifle until 24 November, and this was after FBI agents – allegedly – visited the funeral parlour to obtain a set of transferable prints. In the seconds following the shooting Oswald was seen unconcernedly strolling around the second-floor lunchroom in the Depository with a bottle of Coca-Cola.

Oswald appears to have trained as an American intelligence agent, and his purported communist sympathies may have been a front. In the days before the assassination, he was seen cloistered with the eccentric David W. Ferrie, an impassioned anti-communist who glued pieces of orange fur to his head to hide his alopecia, and Clay Shaw, a wealthy ex-army officer. Jim Garrison's conspiracy case against Shaw was defeated on 1 March 1969, but not before three of his main informants died, and his investigation formed the mainspring of the recent film *JFK*, which in turn inspired the movie's distributors to issue study guides, further permeating the national consciousness as agreed fact.

In April 1967, Garrison informed the media: 'My staff and I solved the assassination weeks ago. I wouldn't say this if we didn't have evidence beyond a shadow of a doubt.' But for Garrison, almost anything constituted evidence. A few hours after complaining to the Washington *Post* on 22 February 1967 that Garrison was persecuting him, Ferrie died. The coroner attributed his death to natural causes – a cerebral haemorrhage resulting from a ruptured blood vessel – but, rather than challenging the autopsy, Garrison arrested Clay Shaw, and within days he announced he had firm evidence linking Shaw to Oswald.

Both their address books contained an identical five-number digit: 19106, Shaw's prefixed by the words 'PO Box' and listed under 'Lee Odom'. When deciphered, Garrison said, the numeral produced Jack Ruby's unlisted telephone number (WH 1-5601) and 'no other number on earth'. This transformation entailed reassembling 19106 by taking digits alternately from each end (making 16901) and then subtracting 1,300. The fact that a man called Odom did have PO Box 19106 (a number only allocated after Oswald's death) failed to shake Garrison's ardour, and, after watching a television programme on 23 February, he devised a scenario where Ferrie, Oswald, and Shaw met a man named Perry Raymond Russo in September 1963 to plot the assassination.

Since Ferrie and Oswald (both of whom Shaw denied meeting) were dead, Russo was Garrison's only possible witness. On television Russo affirmed that his partner, Ferrie, had once mentioned that it

would be easy to kill a President. But on questioning by a Garrison attorney, Russo maintained that he never heard *Kennedy*'s assassination discussed. Nor had he ever met Shaw.

So on 27 February, on Garrison's instructions, Russo was drugged with sodium pentothal and hypnotised, told to imagine a screen in his mind: 'There will be Shaw, Ferrie and Oswald... They are talking about assassinating somebody.' Under direction, Russo remembered (see **memory**) witnessing the plot, but Garrison knew perfectly well that this contradictory testimony would not withstand cross-examination in court. So he devoted the next twenty-two months to delaying tactics by arresting a broadcaster, Edgar Eugene Bradley, and issuing arrest warrants against three journalists. By the time Shaw's trial began in January 1969, the powers behind Garrison's conspiracy theory had expanded to include homosexuals, anti-Castro Cubans, oil millionaires, the Dallas police, arms manufacturers, White Russians, CIA agents and the invisible Nazi substructure.

Garrison's case against Shaw collapsed, since it was based on a witness, Russo, who had given evidence in support of the defence. Garrison only attended the hearing intermittently, and the sole support for his hypotheses came from a smartly dressed New Yorker, Charles I. Spiesel, who suffered from paranoid delusions. Spiesel went to a party in May 1963, overhearing a plot to kill Kennedy, and was the target of a conspiracy involving fifty hypnotists. He testified that he regularly fingerprinted his daughter to ensure that she was not an impostor. After this fiasco, Garrison continued to home in on 'missing' evidence, asserting what it would reveal when found. There were four frames missing from the Zapruder film, a missing brain, missing bullets, missing gunmen, missing witnesses and unexamined autopsy photographs and X-rays.

Garrison declared that the missing film would show a street sign (now missing) scarred by the marks of a stray bullet, proving the existence of more than one gunman. But on publication they disclosed nothing of the kind. So Garrison said the marks had been airbrushed out. Then he produced newspaper photographs taken ten minutes after the assassination which showed a man. He was wearing a suit. So he was a federal agent. In the first picture the man gazed at the pavement. So he had noticed a bullet, and, in the second, his fist was closed. So he had picked it up. Garrison informed the press that the bullet 'which fell into the grass with pieces of the President's head was in the hands of federal government ten minutes after the President was dead'.

In his 1970 book *A Heritage of Stone* Garrison went further. America was run by 'an invisible government that began and ended with deception', a power elite engaged in thought control operating in another dimension above and beyond mundane reality. This may be true, but not in the way Garrison intended.

Unravelling the truth behind the assassination would be aided by declassification of material locked away until 2029; by unveiling the Lopez Report (detailing the inquiry into Oswald's supposed Mexico trip shortly before the shooting); and by release of the files on Operation Mongoose and the CIA-Mafia plots. Thirty years after the event, investigation of the killing spirals away into trails where unreliable sources provide glimpses of underworld figures and double agents who may, or may not, have had ulterior motives which governmental agencies perhaps wished to conceal. It is unlikely that the truth will ever be known.

Ketch, John (d. 1686)

Also known as Jack Catch, although his real name was probably Richard Jacquet. He was a seventeenth-century executioner held in execration throughout England for his butchery and incompetence, and his name became generic to his trade, still used to terrorise children in Victorian times. For centuries he survived as a stock character in Punch and Judy performances where he met his just desserts (as in real life) by being hanged. 'While Jeffreys on the bench, Ketch on the gibbet sits' ran the saying.

Specifics of Ketch's early misdeeds have not survived. Dwarfish and pockmarked, he embarked on his career as an executioner in 1663. Like others in the trade, he would have done a bit of whipping, branding and nose-slitting on the side. But he caused widespread revulsion by his habit of clowning on the scaffold, rifling through his victims' pockets and stripping them naked while their bodies

still twitched. In 1679 Ketch landed the plum job for the execution of thirty men betrayed by Titus Oates, and traipsed round London hawking a 'Plotters Ballad, being Jack Ketch's incomparable receipt for the cure of traytorous disease'.

Four years later Ketch bungled the decapitation of Lord Russell, condemned for his plan to kidnap Charles II. On the scaffold, Russell offered Ketch (as was customary) a bonus or 'tip' for a clean job. The first blow merely wounded Russell who observed, 'You dog, did I give you ten guineas to use me so inhumanely?', and it took three more swipes to finish the job. In 1785 the Duke of Monmouth fared worse. Although finally dead after five swings of the axe, his head still needed severing from its trunk with a knife. Monmouth's servant, the stakeholder, walked off without paying Ketch his six guineas.

Ketch was imprisoned twice, once for insulting a sheriff and once for a debt of £22. He celebrated his second release by going on a binge in the course of which he beat a gingerbread woman to death. To general satisfaction, he was hanged in November 1686 by one John Price who, in the manner of the times, later swung from the same gallows.

The Law Journal of 28 August 1926 reports an old case in which a Norwich Court held that to say to a man 'You are Jack Ketch' was *per se* 'undoubtedly actionable as defamation'. And rightly; the innocent lookalike was hurled into a duck pond by an angry mob.

See also **de Crespigny**

Kidd, Captain William (1645–1701)

Hanged twice for a pirate on 23 May 1701 at **Execution Dock**. On the first occasion the halter snapped, but – despite the crowd's exhortations – Kidd proved unable to make a run for it. He was blind drunk. The second time the rope held, and his body was tarred and gibbeted, swinging from Tilbury Point as a landmark for years to come. The chaplain turned Kidd's temporary respite to good use, remarking that it presented a golden chance to make further supplications to the Almighty.

Despite his fearsome reputation as the 'Archpirate and common enemy of mankind', Kidd was more of a scapegoat than a corsair. Born in

Scotland, he preyed on the French as a licensed privateer from 1689 to 1691. But after his marriage to a wealthy widow, he moved into a Wall Street mansion and traded as an easy-going merchant skipper, the master of the brigantine *Antiqua*. Then in 1695 this fussy middle-aged man was enticed into accepting a commission as a privateer in an expedition against the pirate Thomas Tew. The backers, a Whig syndicate, comprised most of the British cabinet including the First Lord of the Admiralty and the Lord Chancellor – but not King William IV, who was unable to raise the money. Kidd struck a poor bargain: the backers were to receive 60 per cent of any profits, the King 10 per cent, the crew a standard 25 per cent and Kidd himself (who had to stump up a fifth of the costs) the remaining 15 per cent.

The swashbuckling Kidd of legend.

Mathematicians will have noticed that this comes to more than 100, and Kidd was meant to persuade his men to take a reduced share, making it almost impossible to assemble a decent crew and, as Kidd sailed down the Nore in his thirty-gunned frigate, the *Adventure Galley*, he was stopped by HMS *Duchess*, who commandeered his best men in a press gang. On arrival in New York he made up his complement of 155 by signing the scourings of the waterfront, pirates themselves, and set sail on 6 September 1696 amid grim forebodings: 'Twill not be in Kidd's power to govern such a hoarde of men under no pay.'

It was not. Basically, his voyage was a disaster, a three-year 'lost cruise'. The first prize, the Dutch *Rouparelle*, did not come his way for eighteen months. The crew had mutinied long before, in October 1697. Kidd killed one of the mutineers, gunner William Moore, with a blow on the head from a wooden bucket bound with iron hoops. Then he barricaded himself into his cabin and burned the ship's log. Kidd breasted this challenge to his authority, and in January 1698 captured a valuable ten-gunner, the *Quedah Merchant*. She seemed a legitimate quarry, carrying French documentation, and her cargo fetched a handsome £10,000. In November 1698 he set sail for New England.

But unknown to Kidd, the Nine Years War against France had ended, and in any case the *Merchant*'s French passes were papers of convenience. The ship was Armenian, and when Kidd limped into Anguilla he found himself branded as the piratical 'Scourge of the Indies'. But the Governor of New York, the Earl of Bellomont (one of the original syndicate), advised him, 'You may safely come hither...and I make no manner of doubt but to obtain the King's pardon.' Kidd landed at Boston on 4 July 1700 and was told to prepare a report.

Two days later he was arrested and shipped to Britain, where he languished in an underground dungeon at **Newgate** for six months, a pawn in a political power-play. The government was at risk if Kidd revealed the role played by Privy Councillors and three Whig ministers in financing a piratical expedition. They wanted him dead, and in May 1701 a blatantly political hearing indicted him on five counts of piracy and Moore's murder.

The Admiralty impounded his papers, precluding Kidd from producing his two commissions, his original sailing orders from Bellomont and the French passes from the *Quetta Merchant* in his defence. The judge commented, 'For ought I can see, none saw them but himself, if there were any', and he was condemned to death.

Early this century, after two centuries of vilification as a blood-drenched rogue, Kidd's papers were unearthed in a bundle of papers in London's Public Record Office.

Kidnapping, invention of

In the first reported case, dating from 1 July 1874, 4-year-old Charlie Ross from Philadelphia was not returned and the ransom of $20,000 not collected; clearly the ploy required fine-tuning to become a paying proposition. To complicate matters, the boy's parents had just gone bankrupt, although they succeeded in raising the money.

Charlie was 'snatched' along with his brother, 6-year-old Walter, from the sidewalk outside their home on Washington Lane by two men in a buggy. The kidnappers released Walter the same day, but Charlie was never seen again, and an ex-policeman, William Westervelt, was later convicted on circumstantial evidence. It seems that money formed an ancillary motive; Westervelt preferred to drown Charlie for kicks.

Until the ransom demand for Charlie arrived, no one understood the reason behind the theft; why steal a *baby*? Nearly fifty years passed before the next kidnapping, when the practice aroused so much undesirable publicity that in the 1920s the focus shifted to wealthy businessmen. Although just as valuable to their families, as wage-earners, the public did not miss millionaires as much as their children, and the gangsters suffered less at the

hands of the press.

The poverty of the Depression era fuelled the craze, with the *New York Times* reporting in March 1932 that 'abduction for ransom has become a big money crime, taking its place beside the liquor, vice and drug traffic among the prominent rackets of this country'. The practice peaked the year before, with 279 recorded American instances, including the national catastrophe of the Lindbergh kidnapping; the parents were deluged with 38,000 letters in the first week. In New York, a hysterical committee of 600 mothers convened to demand plainclothes police protection for their children playing in Central Park, and Pinkerton's detective agency quadrupled their operatives in a single week.

Before the Charlie Ross snatch, kidnapping was not a specific legal offence – since no one had committed it, no one had legislated against it. But in its wake, Pennsylvania enacted the first laws which carried the ferocious penalty of twenty-five years in solitary together with a $100,000 fine.

The word 'kidnap' derives from the seventeenth-century English practice of siezing children and transporting them as slaves to the **tobacco** plantations in the American colonies. The American innovation was to make money not by sending children away but by sending them back. Australia did not record its first case until 1960, nine years before Britain.

See also **Ladders**, **Nilsen**, **Public Relations**

Kidney, human

On 16 October 1888, George Lusk, the head of the Whitechapel Vigilance Committee, received an unsigned letter. It read [*sic*]:
'From Hell
Mr Lusk sir I send you half the Kidne I took from one woman prasarved it for you tother peice I fried and ate it was very nise I may send you the bloody knif that took it out if you only wate a whil longer. Signed. Catch me if you can Mishter Lusk.'

The organ, initially dismissed as of canine origin, arrived in a three-inch square cardboard box preserved in spirits of wine.

The accompanying missive was one of thousands received by Scotland Yard during the Ripper crisis; in one month, 14,000 poured into the Yard and the newspapers. In all, 128 pieces of correspondence

Charlie Ross, projected forwards in time. The painting, based on a photograph of the boy at two and a half, was done with suggestions from the Ross family to show him aged four.

purported to be from the killer, suggesting that an appreciable portion of the population considered him a model worth emulating. The consensus is that three missives are from the genuine **Jack** – the one above, and two more, those of 28 and 30 September in which the killer expressed an affinity for **ears**. All three letters evince the same chirpy tone.

In the first, the writer promised: 'The next job I do I shall clip the lady's ears off and send them to the police, just for jolly, wouldn't you.' In the second, he apologised for his failure: 'Double event this time. Number one squealed a bit. Couldn't finish straight off. Had not time to get ears for police. Thanks for keeping last letter back till I got to work again.'

Recent research has cast serious doubt about whether Lusk's kidney came from Catharine Eddowes' body.

See also **False Confessions**

Kids, Crack

'Crack' is often the first word assimilated by children in America's inner cities. 'It is when mom gets more and more angry,' according to one 5-year-old. The term 'crack kids' denotes children who suffer brain damage while in the womb from their mother's habit.

It was thought that the neurological damage occurred when the drug intake reduced the womb's oxygen supply; as she inhales, the mother feels her unborn child kick madly as though being strangled. But evidence is accruing that the crack chemicals, which invade a woman's bloodstream, wait in the uterus to latch onto the spermatozoa as they turn up. Thus the egg is poisoned *ab initio*.

Some crack kids are violent, others autistic; some are prone to fits, some to rages. A few are born physically impaired with very small heads or deformed hearts and lungs. All experience learning difficulties which first emerge as problems with basic locomotive skills like walking. Collectively, crack kids constitute a 'biological underclass' which, in the Third World conurbations of New York, Washington and Los Angeles, accounts for some 20 per cent of all deliveries. The current estimate for California's 1992 intake, or output, is 72,000. As the first wave hits the schools, it remains unclear whether, given care, they will ever lead normal lives.

Half a dozen crack babies were reported in Liverpool in the six months to May 1992 but, given the phenomenon's novelty in Britain, others have probably gone undiagnosed.

Killer Bimbos *et al*

They do not actually kill anyone; Killer Bimbos flock to the ski resort of Aspen, Colorado, in the hope of bedding some celebrity or billionaire. The competition is fierce – and savage internecine Killer Bimbo violence the result. They slash, scratch, bite, and attack each other with champagne glasses; over Christmas 1991 at the Aspen Club Lounge, Dewi Sukarno put 'Mini' Osmena in hospital by nearly gouging out her eye. She needed thirty-seven stitches.

'There is no other place with such a concentration of fat wallets and mansions within one square mile,' said Miss Texas USA of Aspen in 1991. Sean Connery took refuge in a wine cellar when charged by a swarm of Killer Bimbos; Michael Caine was mobbed and three bodyguards bitten when they tried to stem an Invasion of the Killer Bimbos at an exclusive party. 'There is no doubt' says David Koch (worth $1.7 billion and suffering from Bimbo Fatigue), 'Aspen is more ferocious and frantic than ever before.' Even the pavements are heated in this socialites' version of **Medellin**, Colombia, and the prison is so comfortable that it reputedly needs walls to keep people out.

First blood went to singer Andy Williams's ex-wife in 1976, when she accidentally shot her lover dead saying: 'Bang! Bang!' Her sentence totalled thirty days inside, served segmentally to dovetail with the school holidays. The following year the Aspen courthouse was the scene of Ted **Bundy**'s celebrated escape. After an interlocutory hearing on 6 June 1977 about the status of the death penalty, Bundy suddenly found himself alone. He sauntered into the law library on the second floor, crossed to a large window, opened it, jumped and ran, thinking 'They don't shoot you in Aspen.' Inside, his absence passed unremarked until a relaxed young woman walked into the Sheriff's office and asked, 'Hey, is it kind of unusual for someone to be leaping out of the courthouse window?'

Despite a sprained ankle, Bundy remained at large for five days, swimming the Roaring Fork River and holing up for one night in a hunter's cabin. But he could not break out of the area with its mountains on all sides. It was on these snowy slopes, years later, that the Ivana Trump/Marla Maples War first blossomed. In 1989 real shots were fired at a paparazzi helicopter hovering over the wedding of Don Johnson (star of TV's *Miami Vice*). Then in 1990 Hunter S. Thompson, the bad man of alternative journalism, landed himself in hot water for allegedly assaulting a girl in a steam tub. And in 1991 Lord White, a sugar grand-daddy and Aspen regular, was charged with assaulting his beautiful companion, Victoria Tucker.

Killer Bimbos are blonde, leggy, and immaculately groomed. Snooty about first-class travel, they are freighted in by private jet, their arrival only marginally preceded by their silicone-enhanced breasts. As short-term sexual assets these accessories are extremely expensive, retailing (according to one exponent at a Christmas 1991 dinner party) at $3,000 a week and a New York condo.

See also **Queen Poison**

King, Rodney (1965–)

Briefly the world's most famous victim, victimised anew by his exploitation as a major financial asset.

King is the ex-convict videotaped during his drubbing from the Los Angeles police on the night of 2 March 1991. From then on he was a made man, the centre of a swirling vortex of agents, lawyers and film-makers who fought tooth-and-nail for a slice of the action. On his first release from jail after the televising of his fifty-six blows, King was so hot a property that he was lucky to hack his way through the crowds of ambulance-chasers. The deal-making mania eventually engulfed Stacey Koon, one of the officers involved in the beating, who signed with a television network, as did Los Angeles police chief Darryl Gates.

As soon as he was safely under contract, King spent his days confined in a secure house in Ventura County, guarded round the clock and dosed with pharmaceuticals under the supervision of his personal psychiatrist. It made King lonely and miserable, but with their client locked away from exploitation and alternative offers, his business advisers could map their commercial strategy. They had King's image to protect; his marketability was

seriously dented by an arrest in May 1991 after he engaged the services of a transvestite hooker.

The stakes were high. At one stage the personal injury specialist Stephen Lerman wanted $56 million for the Rodney King 'supersuit', but he later trimmed his demands to a $10 million lump sum plus an annuity. Lerman's fees might have absorbed a third of any receipts; then there were disbursements, like King's advance, his security and living expenses, and the bills due to the medical team of psychiatrist, plastic surgeon and neurologist. Eventually the Los Angeles Council offered $1.5 million in settlement, but Lerman held out for $5 million, and was sacked after negotiations broke down.

Meanwhile the film rights to the Rodney King story were sold to some unknown producers, Triple 7, for a rumoured (and measly) $20,000; they planned a feature film and a domestic mini-series, together with a book of the film and the book of the making of the film. That left the merchandising and endorsement rights; King's Aunt Angela – a Lerhman supporter – was warned off producing T-shirts of her nephew's copyrighted face, and his relatives split into warring elements divided between his wife's faction and his own family, with King, a one-man victim corporation, caught in the middle, pulled this way and that by his kith and kin while the media claimed him as a celebrity, spokesperson or cautionary tale. Whether as icon, demon, potential gold-mine, poor businessman or modest retiring citizen, King remains a shy and pleasant man unsuited to the demands of fame; his new lawyer is called Milton Grimes.

The exceptional facet of the King case is that it was captured on tape; otherwise his brutal treatment followed the familiar Los Angeles code for blacks that if you run from the police you are beaten up. But such thrashings play with fire. Although blacks will apparently tolerate economic injustice almost indefinitely, five of America's massive race riots stemmed directly from physical oppression by law enforcement officers: Watts (1965), Newark and Detroit (1967) Liberty City and Brownsville (1980) and South Central itself (1992). That is, race riots are provoked by white policemen, and an examination of the record shows a compelling reason for their addiction to thuggery.

They can get away with it. Police are almost never prosecuted for 'excessive force'. In Los

Angeles county, well over a thousand citizens have perished from police gunfire since 1945. But of the fifty-four cases referred to the District Attorney between 1986 and 1990, fifty-three were dismissed and the single exception concerned an officer-on-officer assault.

Thus not one of the 387 shootings by Los Angeles Police Department officers between 1985 and 1991 (which included 153 fatalities) resulted in charges, although numerous survivors received substantial civil damages, with a culmulative total in excess of $20 million.

Similarly, fifty-six of the 202 shootings by the sheriff's department during the corresponding period were seriously questionable (involving, for instance, unarmed victims hit in the back) but again no cases resulted, even for the 1988 execution by a sheriff which the city settled for $1 million out of court. Cynics with long memories can take heart from the 1973 incident when an officer killed a 12-year-old boy while 'playing' Russian roulette, perhaps to secure a confession. He was charged, and two more indictments were laid only last year.

Following the Los Angeles riots, the Christopher Commission reviewing the LAPD monitored dozens of patrol car messages, such as 'I would love to drive down Slauson with a flamethrower. We could have a barbecue' and 'I almost got me a Mexican last night but he dropped the gun too quick.' The hard-core LAPD racist element is thought to constitute no more than 10 per cent of the force, but it is beyond the rule of law.

Kray, Ronald and Reginald (1933–)

East End twins, with a strangely cinematic penchant for violence, who controlled the London underworld in the late 1950s and the 60s. They thought Cagney, but filmed Ealing: stock East Enders who drank tea, worshipped their **mother** ('Our Queen'), wore spiv suits from Saville Row, drove flash cars and were on nodding terms with the celebrities of the day.

Not that the twins provided much to laugh at. As children they were boxers and street fighters; as young men they routed Army discipline in head-on conflict (see **Officer Material**). By their late teens

they were already, in the words of one old villain, 'a thoroughly evil pair of bastards', with a reputation for unrestrained savagery. They loved fighting. As an associate said, 'If I was cutting somebody or putting the boot in, I'd usually hold back a bit – never the twins though. If you watched their faces while they did it, you'd see real hate. They always went the limit.'

Their first foothold in their early twenties was a rowdy East End snooker hall, the Regal; after a month of brawls the owner installed the Krays as the legal tenants at a weekly rent of £5. The hall became their headquarters; a gang formed round the twins, who led raiding parties for fun, to smash up a dance hall or pub, rather like a club outing. They ruled with fear, holding court martials for breaches of discipline, and Ronnie earned the nickname of 'the Colonel' for his military acumen and network of spies. He accumulated a formidable arsenal, kept at his mother's house – an old Mauser, sawn-off shotguns, revolvers, and a Beretta .32. His **swordstick**, Gurkha knives, bayonets, cutlasses and sabres were sharpened on a grindstone in the rear yard. A barber called daily to administer his morning shave while he lounged in a purple dressing gown, and for a while he retained a personal masseur. His yoga fad proved shortlived.

The twins rapidly moved into protection, 'putting the arm on' dozens of local pubs, restaurants, illicit betting shops and unlicensed gambling dens. By 1956 their outfit acquired a name as 'The Firm', and that autumn Ronnie gained tremendous prestige by shooting a docker in the leg after an argument about a car. On 5 November 1956 he received a three-year sentence for causing grievous bodily harm (to another victim), and in prison keeled over into certified madness. On release, in an unstable mental state, he was appalled to find that Reggie had almost gone straight.

Reggie – more diplomatic, more intelligent, less of an out-and-out psychopath – founded a flourishing West-End-style club in the East End, 'The Double R', which he fronted in a smoking jacket. He was halfway to quitting the rough-and-tumble of dirty work and Ronnie's bar wars; he '**straightened**' the law and made peace with their old enemies, the Italian gangs of Clerkenwell.

But Ronnie had no time for such trifling; his craving to intimidate and exploit impelled him to demand protection from a club they already owned. He stormed out of inter-gang councils and suddenly all Reggie's administration and self-imposed restraint counted for nothing. It was us-and-them, the twins together against the world, and the Krays' reversion to strong-arm tactics secured a potent victory when they muscled in on Peter Rachman's Notting Hill rent collectors. Rachman tried to buy them off with an ill-considered bouncing cheque and then realised he had to come up with something better fast. It was 'Esmerelda's Barn', a prime Knightsbridge casino, and Rachman agented its takeover from Stephan de Faye in the autumn of 1960. The twins paid £1,000 for an asset producing some £80,000 a year. Their fortunes were made.

Reggie Kray

But only in theory. Ronnie pined for a plusher version of the Regal billiard hall and ran the *Barn* into the ground, personally mismanaging credit limits and encouraging admission of riff-raff. He was offered £1,000 a week by the manager (who had been kept on) to stay away. But Ronnie needed a showcase for his violent theatrics, and within a few years the casino went bust. Elsewhere business boomed. The Krays pulled off some fifty 'long-firm frauds' in the early 60s, netting an estimated £100,000 from this source alone in 1962. Their arrest on 10 January 1965 for demanding money with menaces was followed by a bungled prosecution (or perhaps a tampered jury) that made them seem untouchable. By now the Mafia had put out feelers for a reliable outfit to guarantee the well-being of the planeloads of punters they proposed to fly into London on gamblers' junkets. Serious money, in the form of casino and hotel investments, was at stake. Could the twins guarantee protection?

The Krays' only rivals were the Richardson gang (see **Torture**) and, spoiling for a firefight, Ronnie bought two Browning sub-machine guns. But luck went the Krays' way. After a couple of skirmishes, an unrelated shoot-out on 8 March 1966 – the 'Battle of Mr Smith's Club' – put most

of the Richardsons into hospital, behind bars or under the ground, leaving the Krays as the undisputed criminal kings of London.

But Ronnie wanted to kill someone. He picked on the one worthwhile survivor from the Richardson debacle, George **Cornell**, who had in any case called him a 'fat poof'. His killing meant that Reggie had to murder **Jack the Hat** to keep up. Then they had Mad Frank the **Axeman** – one of their own – put away, and two more members of the firm – a man called Frost and 'Mad' Teddy Smith – vanished without trace. By now Ronnie was drowning in paranoia verging on madness and the Firm awash with suspicion.

A new police commissioner, Sir Joseph Simpson, felt compelled to target the Krays. The full-scale investigation was led by Inspector Leonard 'Nipper' Read (after whom the Krays named their pet boa constrictor, purchased at Harrods) heading a team of fourteen men, and he insisted on legal immunity for informers. When the twins' ex-accountant Leslie Payne panicked, Read interrogated him for

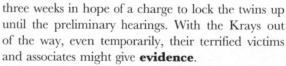

three weeks in hope of a charge to lock the twins up until the preliminary hearings. With the Krays out of the way, even temporarily, their terrified victims and associates might give **evidence**.

On 7 May 1968, in the wake of the '**attaché case**' revelations, Read arrested the Krays in an early morning raid together with a dozen cohorts, charging Ronnie and Reggie with the Cornell and McVitie murders.

One by one members of the Firm talked – first Lennie Dunn, then Billy Exley, then Liza, then the Blind Beggar barmaid, then Albert Donaghue, then Blonde Carol, then Ronnie Hart. The Krays were jailed for a minimum of thirty years in March 1969.

Kürten, Peter (1883–1931)

One of the most sinister photographs in all the demonology of crime shows Peter Kürten, the Vampire of Düsseldorf, just standing still, doing nothing, wearing a suit and somehow radiating evil. Proud of his appearance, he used a dab of make-up here and there, staring at himself for ages in the mirror, a compulsion shared with Britain's Peter **Sutcliffe**, the Yorkshire Ripper.

Kürten was adept at obtaining orgasms from unusual stimuli. 'It was not my intention to get satisfaction by sexual intercourse,' he later explained, 'but by killing.' In fact almost anything destructive would do; Kürten set fire to haystacks or woods to bring himself to a climax. What really excited him was blood; if he witnessed a road accident he would ejaculate involuntarily. In adolescence he discovered that the experience of sodomising sheep could be enhanced by stabbing the animal in a frenzy.

In maturer years Kürten regularly experienced emission when seizing a human victim's throat or sticking in the knife (see **Stabs**). If possible, he gulped the blood down as it pumped from the wound; he once gave himself an orgasm in a park by cutting off a swan's head and sticking its spurting neck into his mouth. The gurgling sound was music to Kürten's ears, and just before his execution he told psychiatrist Karl Berg that he looked forward to momentarily hearing his own blood cascading from his trunk into the basket and onto his head.

Kürten spent twenty-four of his forty-eight years in prison. The more he was sentenced, the more he seethed with rage at the inhuman penal conditions. He broke minor prison regulations just to be confined in solitary so that he could better indulge in

detailed sadistic daydreams of immense catastrophes when he weakened railway bridges (see **Viaducts**), or introduced bacilli into drinking water, or gave arsenic-laden sweets to schoolchildren. He recalled, 'I would derive the sort of pleasure from these visions that other people got from thinking about a naked woman.'

Kürten's first victim was 13-year-old Khristine Klein, killed on 25 May 1913. The murder is a textbook example of a fascination with blood coupled with the get-even mentality that underpins a serial killer's motivation. 'I heard the blood spurt and drip on the mat beside the bed,' Kürten later recounted. 'It spurted in an arch, right over my hand... Next day I went back to Mulheim. There is a café opposite the Kleins' place and I sat there and drank a glass of beer and read all about the murder in the papers. People were talking about it all round me. All this indignation and horror did me good.'

To his Düsseldorf neighbours, Kürten seemed a model citizen – decent, modest, kindly and married. He parted his hair meticulously, buffed his gleaming shoes, and scented himself with eau de Cologne. Children liked him instinctively, and he was finally arrested after befriending a woman stray, Maria Budlick, whom he brought back to his flat for a glass of milk and a sandwich before taking her through the woods, where he assaulted her. But he stopped short of the kill, and within days Maria led the police to his home.

Kürten knew his time was up, but when he notified his wife that he was the 'Beast of Düsseldorf' she thought it a joke. Then, realising he was in earnest, she proposed a suicide pact. But Kürten had a better idea. There was a substantial reward out for his arrest; she might at least earn some money by turning him in. So she did, on 24 May

1931, arranging to meet her husband and the police outside the St Rochus Church.

Kürten was executed on 2 July 1931 for nine murders and seven attempted murders, with the court unable to detect any trace of insanity in his brisk, composed and lucid manner.

His background furnishes all the constituents of a serial killer, and more besides. There is the drunken, brutal father; marital rape; whippings from his mother, the incest and attempted incest, the cruelty to animals, the masturbation of dogs, the buggery of goats and pigs, the **arson**, the rapes, and quite possibly the murder of two children drowned while playing round a raft on the Rhine when he was aged nine.

After his inaugural killing of young Khristine Klein in 1913, Kürten only got into his stride in 1929. He started the year with Rosa Ohliger, a child stabbed thirteen times with a pair of scissors, his favourite weapon. One wound was to the vagina. On 23 August, Kürten killed two children, slitting their throats, and tried to rape and kill a woman, Gertrude Schulte, leaving her for dead.

With such a clear motive for killing – orgasmic gratification – premature ejaculation could be a lifesaver; when Kürten climaxed *before* completing a murder, there was no point in continuing the assault. He would shamble off apologetically, mumbling 'That's what love's about.'

It may be that this trait led to Kürten's arrest, which flowed from Maria Budlick's survival. Just as she was about to lose consciousness, Maria felt her assailant's grip round her throat relax.

'Do you remember where I live?' Kürten asked. 'In case you're ever in need and want my help?'

'No,' gasped Maria, and Kürten quietly showed her out of the woods.

See also **Detection, Fantasising, Organised**

L

Lacenaire, Pierre-François (1800–35)

Poet and murderer who achieved a very brief stay of execution when the guillotine's blade jammed inches above his neck. Lacenaire managed to twist his head round to view the second and final approach of the engine of his destruction.

Lacenaire represented a new kind of criminal, the alienated middle-class intellectual. After a string of convictions for petty theft, he axed an old Parisian woman and her son to death, hoping to steal a hoard of 10,000 francs. All he found was some *bric à brac*. Betrayed by his accomplices, Lacenaire was thrown into prison where, being well-educated and articulate, he attracted fashionable attention, not least for his callow but undeniable sense of style. 'It would have been very disagreeable to be executed by a *provincial* executioner,' he sighed on learning that he would tried in Paris.

As a free man, Lacenaire composed songs and verses; as a prisoner, he corresponded with the papers, attaining the renown that previously eluded him. In his cell in La Force he conducted Socratic dialogues with an entranced audience of doctors, barristers and journalists. 'There was a day in my life when I had to choose between suicide and crime. I chose crime,' he expounded. In less flam-

boyant mood, Lacenaire described the time in March 1829 when, as a deserter, he exhausted the last of the 500 francs mailed by his mother. 'Within a matter of days, I was reduced to a point at which I almost died of hunger,' he recalled. 'From that moment I became a thief, and in spirit at least a murderer.' This obvious piece of cause-and-effect constituted a novel inversion for an era which assumed that crime caused poverty.

Lacenaire's *Memoirs* – unfinished at his execution – promoted the notion of a neglected man of destiny waging his struggle against a corrupt society, and included a number of modern concepts. **Prisons**, for instance, he dismissed as 'Universities of Crime'. He blamed his misshapen life on the inadequate rearing of his uncaring parents, and lectured visitors on social justice, earning the opposition's favour by his censure of Louis-Philippe's regime.

His fame spread to Russia, where the *Memoirs* were released in magazine form by a young editor, Dostoevsky, who was intrigued by his views on crime and punishment.

Lacenaire's capture resulted from one of the great pieces of foot-slogging detection. On 16 December 1834, a neighbour noticed blood seeping under the door of widow Chardon's lodgings at 271 rue St Martin. Inside lay the widow and her son, both dead, and two weeks later a bank messenger was called to the rooms of a man named Mahossier at 66 Rue Montorgueil. On entry, the door slammed shut and the boy was pinioned from behind. He broke free and reported the assault to the Sureté, who assigned both cases to Chief Inspector Louis Canler.

The messenger had noticed that one of his assailants, a distinguished man with a silky moustache and a high forehead, had a copy of Rousseau's *Social Contract* protruding from his pocket. Canler visited every cheap hotel in the area, combing their registers for a 'Mahossier', lighting upon the name in a rooming house on the Rue du Faubourg. The hotelier remembered little, but on the next line of the ledger the name 'Fizellier' was printed. The two had shared a room, and the proprietor's wife volunteered that Fizellier was a large red-haired man – like someone already under arrest. The imprisoned Fizellier admitted to the bank job, and the hotelier's wife let drop that Mahossier had an alias, Bâton.

The real Bâton, a known homosexual thief, did not resemble Mahossier. Nor was he a great reader. But Canler reasoned that Mahossier must know him – why else appropriate his name? He interrogated all Bâton's associates, finally hearing rumours of an upper-class gentleman with a silky moustache known as 'Gaillard'. But Paris boasted many Gaillards, so Canler toured the hostels to find one whose handwriting matched 'Mahossier's' signature and, after two days, tracked down Gaillard's rooms. The landlady remembered a courteous poet with well-trimmed whiskers.

So Canler returned to Fizellier, who related how an inebriated 'Gaillard' claimed to have axed a widow to death while an accomplice kept watch. Canler now realised that 'Gaillard' figured in both the murder and the bank job. Fizellier was the accomplice for one, and Canler followed his hunch that a stool pigeon, Avril, had played a part in the other. Avril squealed, revealing that Gaillard had a well-to-do aunt in the rue Bar-du-Bec. There Canler located a Madame Gaillard and she, it transpired, had a shady nephew called Pierre-François Lacenaire who, as it happened, was arrested in Beaune on 2 February 1835 for passing a forged bill of exchange.

Brought to Paris, eight months later Lacenaire died with courage and composure.

Ladders

The conclusive evidence in the trial of Richard Bruno Hauptmann, a German carpenter executed for the kidnapping and subsequent murder of nineteen-month-old Charles Lindbergh Jnr.

The kidnapping on 1 March 1931 inaugurated an extended ordeal for the parents which only ended with the grisly discovery of their child's decomposing remains on 12 May 1932. By then the Lindberghs had lived through thirteen ransom demands, one paid in full through their intermediary Dr John F. Condon at St Raymond's cemetery. It was a hoax.

The investigation centred round the wooden scaling ladder, abandoned in the garden after the kidnappers climbed to the second floor windows of the Lindberghs' New Jersey home. Two years later, 'the greatest feat of scientific detection of all time' (according to *The Trial of Richard Hauptmann*) traced the ladder to Hauptmann. But it now seems the evidence was both inconclusive and fraudulent.

The ladder, crudely made in sections, had three upright runners were of North Carolina yellow pine which showed, under the microscope, tiny grooves indicating that the wood was machined in a sawmill with a defective planer. Arthur Koehler, a wood technologist, circularised the 1,598 lumber mills handling yellow pine and pinned the source to the Dorn Lumber Company in South Carolina. They had despatched forty-seven loads of yellow pine to thirty timber merchants, each of which Koehler and Detective Bornmann visited in turn.

One of the wood yards was in the Bronx, and on 19 September 1934 the police arrested a local German carpenter, Richard Bruno Hauptmann, for handling the marked ransom notes, $10 gold certificates. Hauptmann was a regular customer of the Bronx National Lumber and Millwork Company.

This meant that, like other Americans living round the thirty designated timber yards, he could have bought wood from the Lindbergh consignment. The ransom money, laundered on the New York underworld at around forty cents in the dollar, was similarly disseminated into many hands. Hauptmann's $13,000 allegedly came his way through a crooked business partner, Isidor Fisch. This was all very suspicious, but far from conclusive.

The evidence that clinched Hauptmann's fate was Rail Sixteen. The Lindbergh ladder incorporated a section of a different kind of wood – a wide chunk planed down from something like a floorboard. And when Detective Bornmann searched Hauptmann's attic, he came upon a torn-up floorboard with a matching sawn-out section. The interpolated wood from the ladder fitted the plank perfectly, with the four nail holes in Rail Sixteen coinciding with the nail holes in the exposed attic joist. Hauptmann, evidentially tied to the ladder, was buckled into the electric chair on 3 April 1936.

In 1985 Ludovic Kennedy's *The Carpenter and the Airman* established that Hauptmann was framed. At the original hearing the court learned that Hauptmann habitually made the cod Teutonic misspellings exemplified on the ransom note – 'gut' for 'good' and 'singature' for 'signature'. But in the first police test, Hauptmann spelled the text correctly; the detectives insisted that he wrote it again spelled wrongly, producing this second version as evidence. The entire prosecution case was similarly vitiated. One witness altered his story after money changed hands. The telephone number of Lindbergh's intermediary, Dr John Condon, was scrawled on Hauptmann's lavatory door by a journalist, Tom Cassidy, as a joke. Hauptmann's partner Fisch did have strong underworld connections.

As for Rail Sixteen, the cannibalisation of the attic floor only came to light after Hauptmann's wife left the family home, giving the police a free run of the premises. Was it likely that the meticulous, prosperous Hauptmann went up into the roof, prised up the floor and carved out one piece of wrong-sized timber? Or was he framed? Hauptmann's descendants are petitioning for a posthumous pardon.

Another famous ladder, now based in Scotland Yard's Black Museum**,** is the collapsible burgling ladder of Charlie Peace, the nineteenth-century murderer.

Peace's collapsible burgling ladder

When folded, it measures fifteen inches by nine by two, fitting comfortably in a briefcase. As a burglar, Peace made his approach from above, roping the top of the ladder to a rooftop chimney and then climbing *down* to effect entry. His crucible for melting the stolen valuables is also housed in the Museum, as is his violin, which he played professionally at private gatherings, thereby casing the joints of the houses he later robbed.

Laing

Long established British construction company. Laing's motto is 'We Build for People', and in 1987 they accepted an order for two termite-proof gallows for the Abu Dhabi regime. As the Foreign Office pointed out: 'The manufacture of execution equipment in the UK is legal and its export is not subject to any form of control.'

In January 1992 Amnesty International, the human rights organisation, claimed that other British firms were exporting artefacts such as leg-irons and an electronic torture chamber nicknamed (although not by its occupants) 'The House of Fun'. Amnesty opposes the continued trade in lethal **injection** equipment. Indeed, it seems hard to endorse traditional commercial arguments that manufacturers have no idea what, for instance, gallows will be used for. The likely ultimate end-use of small arms may be no more obscure, and the ageing Mikhail Kalashnikov's 1993 recommendation that the armaments industry set up a charitable fund for those wounded in conflicts is the thin end of a very large wedge indeed: product liability for weapons manufacturers.

The 1954 edition of a popular book on hanging, *Shadow of the Gallows*, includes a pleasant photograph of elderly craftsmen toiling in a workshop. The caption reads: 'Modern hanging ropes being made at the South London factory which supplies them for Britain and the Empire. The operator is burnishing the metal 'eye' which now replaces the slip-knot.'

Landru, Henri Desiré (1869–1922)

French murderer of unusual appearance. On 21 July 1904, in his mid-thirties, Landru collected his first prison sentence. An ostensibly respectable married man, he made a modest living dealing in second-hand furniture and cars, but he could not keep his hands off other people's property. Days before the outbreak of the First World War he was sentenced *in absentia* to four years for fraud, his sixth conviction, and only avoided prison by going into hiding under various aliases.

Landru's speciality was inept attempts to swindle elderly widows: fraud by seduction. His three-year sentence in 1910 stemmed from his advertisement for a wife in a Lille newspaper. A Madame Izoret responded, handing over her cashbox (containing 20,000 francs). He reciprocated with his deeds (worthless paper). Landru disappeared, she went to the police, and in prison he must have reflected how much better it would have been if she had disappeared rather than he.

In 1914, posing as the widower Raymond Diard, he charmed an attractive widow, Jeanne Cuchet, in a lingerie store, and they set up home with her 17-year-old son in the Paris suburb of Chantilly, where he appropriated her 5,000 francs savings. Jeanne persisted in the affair, despite the misgivings of her relatives, the discovery that 'Diard' had a track record of fraud, that his real name was Landru, and the revelation that this Landru was, in fact, already married. The Cuchets were last seen on 15 January 1915. Landru almost certainly incinerated their bodies; neighbours saw thick black smoke streaming from his chimney.

Landru hired another villa, where he disposed of a Mme Laborde-Line. Then he rented a pretty stone house, the *Villa Ermitage*, thirty miles south of Paris in Gambais. He never furnished it properly, but he did install a large stove in the basement. Landru was no figurative ladykiller – short, bald, middle-aged and handicapped by a bizarre spade-shaped beard – but each day the hostilities on the Western front created swathes of new widows. In May, Landru advertised in the Parisian *Le Journal* under the name of Freymet: 'Widower with two children, aged 43, with comfortable income, affectionate, serious, and moving into good society,

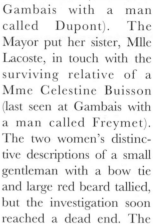

desires to meet widow with a view to matrimony.' During the war years some 300 women succumbed to his blandishments. He escorted his murder victims to Gambais by train, buying himself a return ticket and them a single, thus saving a franc. Every one counted; on average, the murders netted 3,000 francs from the victim's savings or the sale of her trinkets, bonds and furniture. Landru, who killed for money, was permanently broke.

And so it went without mishap until the 1918 disappearance of Mme Anna Colombe (last seen at Gambais with a man called Dupont). The Mayor put her sister, Mlle Lacoste, in touch with the surviving relative of a Mme Celestine Buisson (last seen at Gambais with a man called Freymet). The two women's distinctive descriptions of a small gentleman with a bow tie and large red beard tallied, but the investigation soon reached a dead end. The tenant of the *Villa Ermitage* had given a false name and address.

But on 12 April 1919, while promenading on the rue de Rivoli, Mlle Lacoste recognised Landru entering a porcelain shop, and the police extracted the customer details from his invoice. Landru had adopted the name of Monsieur Guillet, and taken up lodgings at 76 rue de Rochechouart with a delightful 19-year-old actress, Fernande Segret. She met Landru on a tramcar, thinking him a 'funny old man' until becoming his mistress. As the police dragged him away, Landru bade farewell by bursting into an aria from the Massenet opera *Manon*, 'Adieu, notre petit table'; like '**Acid** Bath' Haigh, who followed in his footsteps, Landru trained as a chorister in his youth.

At the Préfecture, an envelope in Landru's pocket disclosed his true identity. The police examined his little black notebook with growing dismay. On one page, eleven names were listed, four of people known to be missing or presumed dead: the two Cuchets, and Madames Buisson and Collomb. The remaining seven had disappeared. Other pages detailed Landru's dealings with 283 women; the mere mention of this figure passed as a joke in France for some time afterwards, and investigators established that Landru had enjoyed 'relationships' with at least 179 respondents. On 29 April the *Villa Ermitage* was searched and the gardens excavated, but the only remains in the grounds came from two dogs which, Landru said, he had kindly agreed to **strangle** on behalf of their owner, Mlle Merchardier (one of the vanished eleven). 'It is the gentlest and easiest of deaths,' he reassured the court, speaking like one who knew.

Apart from 295 unidentified bones in the cinders near the basement furnace, some clothes, buttons, and forty-seven teeth, no bodies were ever found, and this evidential hiatus allowed Landru to taunt the prosecution. His frequent appearances before the magistrates became a popular diversion. The music-halls nicknamed him Old Bluebeard, The Ladykiller and The Red Man of Gambais, and Fernande Segret's stage career briefly blossomed. Landru played to the gallery, crammed with women, offering his seat in the dock to a latecomer who could not find a space. But it was gallows humour, and it upset the jury.

Landru was convicted on 30 November 1921 of eleven murders. His victims' relatives and the members of the jury signed a petition for mercy, but he went to the guillotine on 25 February 1922, protesting his innocence. Forty-one years later the daughter of one of his trial lawyers removed a picture frame from a presentation drawing by Landru to find a confession, translated in the *Daily Express* as 'I did it. I burned their bodies in my kitchen oven', and in the *News of the World* as 'The trial witnesses are fools. I killed the women inside the house.'

In 1965, Landru's life was filmed. A surprise member of the first-night audience was the aged Fernande Segret, long presumed dead. After the trial she had withdrawn to the Lebanon, working as a governess. Returning forty years later to sue the film's producers for 200,000 francs, she won 10,000, but her renewed notoriety prompted a fatal plunge into the castle moat at Flers-de-l'One. Her suicide note read: 'I still love him, but I am suffering too greatly. I am going to kill myself.'

Of all the attempts to make murder pay, Briton Frederick Henry Seddon made history's most avaricious attempt to squeeze out the last penny. After duping Eliza Barrow out of £1,500 in 1911, he poisoned her with arsenic, augmenting his take with a final twelve shillings levied from the undertaker as commission for introducing the business.

Las Vegas

The invention of Benjamin 'Bugsy' Siegel (1906–47), a mobster from Williamsburg, Brooklyn, who first made his name as a New York bootlegger. He was among the four who on 15 April 1931 executed one of the last old-time bosses, Joe Masseria, in a Coney Island restaurant during a meal with Lucky Luciano.

Siegel moved to Hollywood and apparent respectability in 1936, spattering his underwear with monograms and parking a Cadillac, a Buick and a Dusenberg in the drive of his $250,000 mansion. He lined his bathroom with red marble, the principal bed was mounted on a two-foot dais, and the house concealed three secret refuges behind sliding partitions operated by hidden buttons.

Siegel's children enroled in the best schools. They took riding lessons; he joined the Hillcrest Country Club and tussled nightly with the *Reader's Digest* feature 'It pays to increase your wordpower'. As mobsters go, Bugsy had a real sense of refinement and courtliness; his charisma won friends like Cary Grant, George Raft, Jimmy Durante and Jack Warner, and Grant took Bugsy as his role model for the 1940s movie *Mr Lucky*.

After bedding numerous starlets in his love nest at the Garden of Allah, Bugsy romanced the Countess di Frasso (née Dorothy Taylor, an American heiress) who, sadly, was married. The Countess whirled Bugsy away on a European tour, passing her mobster off as a baronet from an old English family.

It was a business trip. Bugsy had acquired – or rather, had been duped into buying – the rights to an awesome new explosive, 'Atomite', which he felt sure would interest Mussolini. He was right: the dictator produced a $40,000 advance payment for an exclusive licence. But at the formal demonstration in front of the Italian War Office, the detonator was pressed only to produce a tiny detumescent wisp of smoke. Mussolini demanded his money back and demoted Bugsy and his Countess socially, summarily ejecting them from their guest accommodation in Rome's Villa Madam into the mansion's converted stables. Into their vacated quarters went another pair of visitors, Goebbels and Goering.

This prompted Bugsy's next idea. 'I'm gonna kill him, and that dirty Goebbels too,' he told Dorothy. But she talked him down, pointing out that her Italian husband would be blamed as a scapegoat for the murders. The course of world history might have been very different if Bugsy had stuck to unmarried women, and this crime of omission remained one of his great regrets.

Bugsy's first stab at finding treasure in the sand started in September 1938, when he set sail in a three-masted rented schooner, the *Metha Nelson*, on an expedition to Cocos Island 300 miles off Costa Rica, where $90 million of pirate gold was surely buried. They had a treasure map, property of an individual called Bill Bowbeer.

In eighty-five degree temperatures, through tropical cloudbursts, in the choking jungle, the crew set to work with spades, explosives and heavy drills. 'We drilled through rocks and shale,' recalled one crew member. 'The climate was murderous but we couldn't stop. We dynamited whole cliffs.' But the island extended over eight square miles. After ten days Bugsy called a halt and cruised back to reality and the limelight of the press. The glare of amused newspaper interest led to exposure of his murky past, and the public's worst suspicions were confirmed by rumours about his November 1939 killing of Big Greenie Greenburg for his efforts to chisel $5,000 out of the boys from **Murder Inc**. Siegel had to resign from his clubs. Later, he admitted to a career total of twelve homicides: 'But don't worry, we only kill each other.'

With the advent of war, Siegel's eyes strayed over the state line to the small township of Las Vegas with its population of 6,000, mostly Hoover dam construction workers and descendants of the early Mormons. As well as a street of brothels unromantically entitled 'Block 16', Vegas had a group of sawdust joints where gambling was legal. Siegel looked at the dross but saw glittering lights. He envisaged a future of hydro-electric power driving the air conditioning in glittering hotels accessed by Highway 91 and – maybe – mass air travel.

Together with the new woman in his life, the archetypal moll Virginia Hill, Siegel developed his fantasy. He sold his Trans America wire service to the Vegas joints; then he bought into them. Next

he acquired thirty acres of desert for a few dollars, set up the Nevada Projects Corporation, and secured Mob finance. In December 1945, work started on his casino-hotel, 'The Flamingo'.

It is easier to shoot people for not running a tight construction site than to run one yourself. Siegel's penthouse suite needed rebuilding at a cost of $22,500 when he noticed that the planned ceiling height was only five feet eight. The air conditioning throughout proved too noisy; it was ripped out and replaced, and the kitchen reconfigured at a cost of $30,000. The boiler room was too small, building materials just walked off site, it rained in the desert for nine days nonstop and the construction budget mushroomed from $1.5 million to $6 million. Mob pressure intensified and in December 1946 Siegel opened before the hotel was finished.

The first night was catastrophic. Nobody who was anybody came, apart from George Raft whose career had already faded. Nobody stayed; the rooms were not ready. Many guests could not even secure admission; Siegel imposed arbitrary dress restrictions, and he refused to allow the fountains to be turned on for fear of disturbing a cat and her six kittens trapped in a water sump. Over the next two weeks the casino was taken to the cleaners by professional gamblers, losing $300,000 across the tables. Siegel closed 'The Flamingo'; the Mob closed Siegel.

In a December 1946 meeting at the Hotel Nacional in Havana, Siegel's backers heard that their man had syphoned off $600,000 cash from the casino. In the words of Lucky Luciano: 'There was no doubt in Meyer's mind that Bugsy had skimmed this dough from his building budget... Lansky said, "There's only one thing to do with a thief who steals from his friends. Benny's got to be hit."'

He was. At 10.30 p.m. on 20 June 1947, a .30/30 carbine fired nine rounds through the open window of Virginia Hill's house. Six hit Siegel, the first one bouncing his eye fifteen feet across the room and plastering it to the tiled floor. The eyelashes separated from the eyelids, and were later found glued to the door jamb. Thus did Siegel become only the third person to be killed in exclusive Beverly Hills in thirty-five years.

Within minutes, Siegel's backers were at 'The Flamingo' announcing a change of ownership. It was territory the Mob never relinquished; in 1965

Caesar's Palace was built with $20 million from the Teamster pension funds which were, in the New York and New Jersey branches, under the control of Mafia stooges for the Genovese family.

Only five mourners attended Siegel's funeral. A few days later, on 2 July, Virginia Hill attempted suicide in Paris, and she went on trying until she finally succeeded in March 1966 in a small village outside Salzburg, where she swallowed pills beside a little mountain stream.

The recent film of Siegel's life, *Bugsy*, correctly stresses that only the unwary used his nickname to his face. It does not mention that most of his Hollywood income was creamed from the Film Extras' Union. The 1993 disclosures of J. Edgar **Hoover**'s troubled sexuality affirm that additional support for Siegel came from the Director of the FBI who 'helped get the OK' for the Flamingo. Returning a favour to Meyer Lansky would be a plausible motive; Lansky was one of many *mafiosi* reputedly blackmailing Hoover, and Lansky remained at liberty until he died in 1983. His immunity from federal prosecution continued until 1970, two years before Hoover's death. Even then, the IRS and not the FBI spearheaded the attack – which failed.

In May 1992 Siegel's car, a 1933 V-12 Packard, went to auction with an estimate of $25,000.

Lawnmower

The intended murder weapon in the Whybrow and Saunders case of 1991. This English couple, who were lovers, planned to rid Susan Whybrow of her wealthy husband in a faked accident. He planted the seed of his undoing by reading his wife an excerpt from the *Daily Telegraph*, describing an unusual fatal mishap in which a gardener fell off a tractor-type lawnmower into a ditch.

Whybrow and Saunders concocted a plan, primarily over the car telephone, to drown their victim in the duckpond and then claim he had plummeted into the depths on his lawnmower with the throttle open. Hoping to lull her husband into unsuspecting satiety, she baited the trap by expressing an interest in making love on the floor. But this prompted Mr Whybrow to undress. Realising that nude lawnmowing would look suspicious, she told him to put his clothes on again and, while thus engaged, Saunders

attacked from behind. But their prey broke free and escaped, swimming across the lake to arrive at a neighbour's house bedraggled with weeds.

In March 1991 the conspirators were convicted of attempted murder. Elizabeth Saunders was previously better known for her support of the local church.

Lee, John (1865–1933?)

The man they could not hang. John Lee was one of three servants looking after an elderly widow, Emma Keyse, in her two-storey thatched cottage near Torquay. Early on the morning of 16 November 1885 a fire broke out, and upstairs they discovered their employer's brutally murdered body soaked in paraffin, her throat cut so violently that the knife notched the anterior aspect of her vertebrae.

Lee was arrested on strong but circumstantial evidence. Miss Keyse had accepted Lee back into her employ despite his conviction for stealing silver, but she gave him a boy's rate for a man's job, and shortly before her death denigrated his work, cutting his wages by sixpence to two shillings a week.

His two colleagues were women, and the killing bore the stamp an 'inside job': no signs of forcible entry, nothing stolen, and weapons – a hatchet and knife – which came from the pantry.

Lee told the police that, like the other retainers, he slept through the blaze. But his bloodstained clothes reeked of paraffin, and a human hair, similar to Miss Keyse's, adhered to one of his bloodied socks. Lee lied in the witness box, invoking his excellent relationship with the deceased and maintaining that he had cut himself on a broken window, and it took the jury only forty minutes to find him guilty. Unruffled by the verdict, he said to the judge, 'The reason, my Lord, why I am so calm and collected is because I trust in my Lord and he knows that I am innocent.'

The night before his execution, Lee dreamed that he would not die. It is unlikely that this is unusual, but Lee envisioned standing on the trap door while it failed to open three times, and told his warders so before the noose was placed round his neck in Exeter jail on 23 February 1886.

Berry the hangman pulled the lever, but the floor beneath Lee's feet did not open, and the

Chaplain, Reverend John Pitkin, read stolidly from the Book of Common Prayer as the lever was jerked to and fro. Then Berry asked Lee to stand to one side while he sent for an axe, saw and plane and, when the mechanism was functioning perfectly, the pinioned and hooded Lee was put back on the spot.

PRICE SIXPENCE

THE MAN THEY COULD NOT HANG

THE LIFE STORY OF JOHN LEE

PUBLISHED AT 17 AND 18, HENRIETTA STREET, LONDON, W.C.

Lee's apologia, putting forward an unconvincing account of his innocence

Berry gave the handle such a mighty yank that it bent. Again the trap doors stayed shut, even when the warders stamped on them, and Lee was directed to wait in the basement until the trap door was eased again. On the third attempt, still nothing happened. 'The noise of the bolts sliding could be plainly heard, but the doors did not fall,' wrote Berry in his memoirs.

As the Chaplain observed, 'For the third time I had concluded the service; for the third time the prisoner had felt the agonies of death; for the third time the responsible officers had failed to put him to death.' He announced that he would tarry no longer, thus terminating the proceedings. Lee, somewhat disgruntled, was escorted to his cell where he assured the Chaplain that he wanted to die, and the following day wrote to his sister saying he remained in hopes of being hanged.

But it was not to be. Against some opposition, the Home Secretary Sir William Harcourt commuted the sentence to life imprisonment. Lee's later history is vague, but he was released in December 1907 and married a nurse, Jessie Augusta Bulleid. Their union failed in 1912, and he died in obscurity in Milwaukee in 1933.

Of his brush with death, Lee concluded, 'It was the Lord's hand which would not let the Law take away my life.' Berry took a different view, believing that the centre of the trap fitted too tightly: 'The woodwork of the doors should have been three or four times as heavy with ironwork to correspond.' Another temporal explanation is foul play. The author Ernest Bowen-Rowlands, in his *In the Light of the Law*, quotes a 'well-known person' who heard from someone, who had it from the old lag in question, 'that in those days it was the practice to have the scaffold erected by some joiner or carpenter among the prisoners. The man inserted a wedge which prevented the drop from working, and when called in as an expert he removed the wedge and demonstrated the smooth working of the drop, only to reinsert it before Lee was placed on the trap.' This sounds plausible, but the information is fourth-hand.

Leg, stabbed

Perhaps the most unusual of the many clues that could have solved the **Manson** case sooner. As a rule, legs do not get stabbed much.

On 31 July 1969, nine days before the Tate murders, two homicide detectives were summoned to investigate the murder of Gary Hinman, a 34-year-old music teacher stabbed in his Los Angeles house. A coded message was scrawled on his wall, in his blood, 'Political piggy', and there was thus a chance that his death might be linked to the Tate murders, when the victims were stabbed in their Los Angeles house, with a coded message scrawled on the wall, in their blood: 'Pigs'.

Hinman was murdered for his unreasonable attitude. He had rebuffed Manson, saying: 'I'm sorry Charlie. I'm not going to sell all my things and come and follow you.' After the killing, Manson's hit squad, including Susan Atkins, felt so hungry that they sat down to cherry cake and coffee in the nearby Topanga Kitchen.

On 6 August, Officers Guenther and Whitely pulled in a youth, Bobby Beausoleil, still with blood on his shirt, still driving Hinman's 1965 Volkswagen bus. He was charged with murder. Two days later the officers read the details of the Tate massacre and were struck by the uncanny similarities. But Guenther and Whitely worked for the Los Angeles County Sheriff's Office, and the Manson killings were handled by the highbrows in the Los Angeles Police Department, who were unimpressed by Whitely's hunches. Sergeant Jess Buckles responded: 'We know what's behind these murders. They're part of a big dope transaction.'

Before his arrest, Hinman's killer Beausoleil had shacked up in Death Valley on an old movie set at Spahn's ranch, where a hippy commune centred round a man called Charlie who believed he was Jesus Christ. And as it happened, on 9 August the encampment was raided on suspicion of car theft, and thus Manson was in custody at the time he should have been arrested on suspicion of murder. But everyone was released.

The Tate killings remained unsolved nearly two months later when the local Inyo County police paid another visit to Spahn's ranch about some stolen dune buggies. This time they corralled twenty-six **Family** members, one of them a young woman called Susan Atkins. As the police cars bumped over the desert, two frightened girls emerged from the bushes begging for police protection. They were fleeing the wrath of the Family, they said, and feared for their lives. One of the women was Kitty Lutesinger, Bobby's Beausoleil's 17-year-old ex-girlfriend, long wanted for questioning about the Hinman killing.

At the County Sheriff's Office, Kitty Lutesinger admitted being present at Hinman's during the

murder, but in another room. She said she accompanied Bobby and a girl, Susan Atkins, who later mentioned knifing a man three or four times in the legs.

But Hinman's legs were unmarked. So the police reasoned that the legs stabbed by Susan Atkins belonged to someone else.

The officers recollected a recent case: Voytek Frykowski, one of the Tate Massacre victims, knifed fifty-one times. It was hardly a surprise that some of the wounds strayed onto his limbs, but when Officer Whitely pestered the LAPD once again, they were no more interested than before.

Lie detector

The first generation of this device was the 'hydrosphygmograph', and the second the 'cardio-pneumo-psychogram'; the third wave was known as the 'polygraph'.

The cardio-pneumo-psychogram became the 'lie-detector' for short. In 1921 William Marston of Fordham University published an article reiterating his belief that lies affected the blood pressure; a progressive Californian Chief of Police, August Vollmer, prevailed upon his sergeant to run up a version based round the traditional blood-pressure armband. The machine was responsive to small fluctuations, and during a mock interrogation instantly penetrated Vollmer's fibs: 'It registered every time I lied – about not liking roast beef and about going to bed before midnight.'

Rumours of the machine's omniscience reached such a pitch that local criminals broke down and confessed at the mere sight of the device. Nationwide publicity followed the Hightower case of 1921.

William A. Hightower was a nut. On 2 August 1921 he kidnapped a priest, Father Patrick E. Heslin, from his home just outside San Francisco; later he crushed his victim's skull with a blow to the head, burying him near Salada beach close to a billboard of a man frying pancakes.

Despairing of the ransom, Hightower resolved to collect the advertised reward by selling information about Heslin's whereabouts. Who could have been better placed? On 10 August Hightower presented himself at Archbishop Hanna's house and recounted how he had stumbled across Heslin's scarf while digging for bootleg liquor in the sand. Heslin's body, Hightower said, had to be nearby; he did not know *exactly* where, but somewhere close.

Hightower led the police to the scarf on the beach, discoursing the while on his invention of the machine-gun and his patent substitute for candied fruit. Then, predicting the very spot where Heslin lay, Hightower seized a spade and set to. 'Be careful,' cautioned Police Chief O'Brien, 'you might damage his face.'

'That's all right,' Hightower reassured the policeman, 'I'm digging at his feet.'

Hightower insisted on his innocence despite this inadvertent confession. So Vollmer's lie-detector was brought to the San Mateo jail, where it hardened a very strong suspicion into certainty. Hightower was sentenced to life imprisonment, convicted on overwhelming evidence.

In 1926 a refinement of Vollmer's machine expanded its repertoire to take simultaneous readings of blood pressure, pulse, breathing rate and sweat. But by 1930 it emerged that suspects have a limited inventory of adrenalin. Prolonged exposure to questioning exhausts the stock, allowing placid body-responses during the most monstrous falsehoods. This led to the introduction of three-minute interrogation sessions. But J. Edgar **Hoover** did not hold with the new device and in 1935 the machine-wonder took a further knock when the Illinois rapist Gerald Thompson passed its scrutiny with flying colours. Asked whether he had killed 'Mildred', Thompson said 'no' and the lie detector stayed steady.

Later Thompson explained that he had outwitted the machine by thinking of a different Mildred, whom he had not killed. Those with advanced powers of self-deception posed additional problems. A madman, when asked if he was **Napoleon**, lied. He said 'No', and the machine spotted the attempted deception. In 1960 multiple killer Chester Weger took a risk which paid off when he washed down aspirin with Coca-Cola before taking the test. More disturbingly, the innocent can register as guilty through worries about the machine's accuracy.

According to Chris Gugas, founder of the National Board of Polygraph Examiners, the modern polygraph is all but infallible in the hands of a properly trained operative. A 1950s study of 4,280 criminals showed a success rate of 95 per cent, exculpating the innocent as well as incriminating the guilty. But the equipment is expensive, at over $10,000 including training, and is inadmissible in a court of law unless both sides agree or the judge so demands.

The complicating factor is that the machine's results need interpretation. What the operator looks for is a sequence where the subject's nervous tension mounts as he approaches the leading question and then tails off. This requires a properly structured sequence of questions, a properly trained user, and a proper interpretation: factors which reintroduce by the back door the subjective element the machine removed by the front. The subject's state of mind can be critical. Psychological pressure, or his own inadequacies, can induce the misapprehension that he is guilty, particularly when allegations are of 'denial' and 'suppressed **memory**'. In the **Ingram** satanic ritual abuse case of 1989, the lie detector indicated that suspect Jim Rabie's assertions of innocence were false; and by then, for all he knew, perhaps they were.

See also **False Confessions, Lombroso**

Lime

It is worth ordering the right type. Lime strips away the flesh of a body, rendering identification harder or even impossible. But slaked lime only disposes of the beetles and maggots which would otherwise eat the corpse. It thus acts as a preservative. The error is occasionally made by murderers, who unintentionally present the police with a body in first-class condition. One who made this mistake was Harry Dobkin.

Dobkin's brief matrimonial career began and ended in September 1920, when his arranged marriage to Rachel Dubinski culminated in a separation after three troubled days. During this interlude he fathered a child, and for the next two decades Dobkin was dogged by their misalliance as his luckless wife waylaid him in the London streets pleading for maintenance. On at least four occasions he reacted with violence, and on the afternoon of 11 April 1941 he strangled her after a meeting in a Dalston café.

After carving up her body, he buried it the cellar of a Baptist Church off Vauxhall Road, and for good measure sprinkled the remains with slaked lime. This preserved part of her voice box, and not long afterwards the Luftwaffe set fire to the church during the Blitz. On 17 July 1942 a workman completing the demolition unearthed the corpse, and the following day in the Southwark mortuary it was still possible to discern the distinctive fracture to the upper horn of the thyroid cartilage: the hallmark of strangulation. An adjacent blood clot indicated that the damage had occurred in life, and Rachel Dubinski's body was conclusively identified from dental records.

Across the Channel, the French killer Dr Marcel Petiot needed lime in bulk for his victims, and during the early stages of the police investigation his brother (the supplier) claimed that Marcel wanted the quicklime to exterminate cockroaches. Since he delivered 400 kilos (over a third of a ton), the brother was initially charged with conspiracy to murder.

Petiot created a lime pit to treat the bodies with which he fuelled the stove of his home in Paris's smart XVIth *arrondissement*. An outhouse contained one heap of bodies marinating in quicklime; another lime pit suppurated in the stable, and when Petiot was accused in 1945 of twenty-seven murders, he angrily dismissed the charges, claiming sixty-three victims.

Petiot nearly came to grief the year before, on 11 March 1944 when his chimney went up in flames. Summoned to his home by telephone, Petiot arrived to find the police and fire brigade ensconced in his basement, gazing in consternation at corpses in every stage of decay. Asked if he knew anything about them, Petiot said yes, they were his bodies, adding that it was imperative that he leave at once to alert the Resistance network that their headquarters had been overrun. Off he scurried, and, by the time the police realised that the deaths had no connection with the summary execution of pro-Nazi collaborators, Petiot was nowhere to be found. But this is no place for a prominent serial killer. Eschewing anonymity, Petiot initiated a correspondence with the magazine, *Résistance*, claiming under a new name, but with the same handwriting, that the corpses had been dumped in his home by the Gestapo. On 2 November 1945 he was arrested at his return address.

Petiot inveigled wealthy Jews to his house under the pretext of securing their safe passage out of France. They brought their valuables, perhaps a

million pounds in total, and he took their lives, administering fatal **injections** under the guise of complying with foreign inoculation requirements. Petiot slept through some of his trial, and scored telling points when awake. The President of the Court opened by reading the accusation and then observed: 'As a child you were noted for a your violent temper.' 'Oh come now,' interrupted Dr Petiot, 'if we start like this we shan't get on very well.'

For much of the time the case went his way. Of the twenty-seven murders, Petiot asserted that nineteen were German collaborators and the other eight were still alive. His defence, part bluster, part abuse, was based round his membership of the Resistance, the details of which he refused to disclose, and his acquittal as a patriotic hero remained a real possibility to the end. He was executed on 26 May 1946.

Lincoln, President Abraham (1809–65)

The Lincoln conspiracy-theory suggests that his assassination was too easy, the assassin's escape incredible, his death suspicious, the investigation bodged, the trials rigged and the true culprit unpunished.

On 14 April 1865, three days after the Civil War ended, Lincoln was killed by John Wilkes Booth, who discharged his derringer at the President from a range of four feet during Act III of *Our American Cousins* at Ford's Theatre, Washington.

Lincoln's bodyguard, John F. Parker, considered the play boring. So he deserted his post and went for a drink, giving Booth access. Yet Parker never received an official reprimand. Similarly, Booth's escape route included a surprisingly clear run over the heavily guarded Anancostia Bridge on his way to Maryland. His flight was further facilitated by a mysterious electrical fault which put all the telegraph wires from Washington out of commission for the two critical hours after the killing.

Booth was eventually cornered in a barn near Bowling Green, Virginia, on 26 April. Told that he could safely surrender, he was shot by a Union soldier, Boston Corbett, who later committed suicide himself. Corbett was rumoured to be in the pay of the Secretary of War, Edwin McMasters Stanton, to whom he handed the diary found on Booth's

John Wilkes Booth

body. When Stanton – the hub of the web – released the diary to the investigators, eighteen pages were missing. Among the extant pages were Booth's puzzling and perhaps overlooked lines: 'I have a greater desire and almost a mind to return to Washington, and in a measure clear my name, which I feel I can do.'

Stanton was a staunch opponent of Lincoln's plans to reconstruct the South after the bitter Civil War. Following the President's death, Stanton pushed through the conspirators' trials, even securing the death sentence for one of their wives, Mrs Surratt. But he was reluctant to have her husband arrested; Surratt only returned to America against Stanton's orders after his capture in Egypt. At the trial, Surratt was acquitted, with Stanton's legal friends handling the defence.

Stanton destroyed the master-plate of the only photograph of Lincoln in his coffin. Only one print survived, and this by accident. Later, Lincoln's son burned many of his father's documents, explaining: 'These papers contain the documentary evidence of treason of a member of my father's cabinet... It is best for all that such evidence be destroyed.'

A more humdrum explanation is that Lincoln was shot by a lone nut, operating in concert with other lone nuts, the half-dozen or so co-conspirators. It was Booth's fourth attempt on the President.

Lines, pick-up

The best way to 'slay' at leisure is to lure the victim into a car. From which flows a simple rule-of-thumb for women threatened with sexual assault or abduction: make a stand outside the assailant's vehicle. Do not get in.

The book *Sexual Homicide* (by John Douglas, Robert Ressler and Anne Rule) contains general recommendations for the early stages of a hijack, advocating a first and invariable response of attempted escape, with verbal confrontation as the next defence and offensive physical resistance as the third.

Three approaches are open to the rapist: the 'blitz' (sudden, overwhelming violence), the surprise (an ambush), and the con, a technique espoused in various guises by the Russian serial killer **Chikatilo**. With runaways, he asked if they were hungry or thirsty. To young boys he offered to show his stamp collection, to their elders, his horror videos. To girls he proposed money for sex. Or Chikatilo fell in alongside and asked, 'Where are you off to?... Oh, I'm going that way myself, let's go together', before suggesting a short cut through the woods. In the words of Rostov's Chief of Police, 'He had something for everyone. For the drunkards, there was vodka. For others he was the friendly teacher who could give them a lift.' He lured his first victim, a 9-year-old girl, to her death by purporting to escort her to his toilet. Chikatilo commented, 'They followed me like dogs.'

Ted **Bundy** was another personable fellow who had no need of violence to snare his prey. To 17-year-old Carol DaRonch, Bundy posed as Officer Roseland. 'Excuse me miss,' he said, 'we think there's been an attempted burglary of your vehicle. I'd appreciate it if you'd go with me to identify a suspect my partner is holding out.' But instead of driving Carol to a police station, he headed out of town, clapped a set of handcuffs round one of her wrists before she flung herself out onto the road, and pursued her on foot, brandishing a tyre iron, until the approach of another car frightened him off.

Bundy accosted another survivor, Raylene Shepherd, in the lobby of the Viewmount High School theatre in Bountiful, Utah, during the intermission. 'I wonder if I could get you to help me for a minute with my car in the parking lot?' he asked. But Raylene, the drama instructor, was busy. As so often after a rebuttal, Bundy tried again. He was noticed later in the auditorium 'breathing kind of heavily', and that night young Debbie Kent fell for a similar approach.

Then there was Bundy's gambit of the Bad Arm and Books, which he deployed against Janet Carstensen on Washington University's Central Campus. One evening, outside the library, she saw a young man in difficulties carrying a stack of text-books. In her words: 'He dropped the books and was making a noise (pain) as though his arm was hurting. A castlike bandage was on his arm. I went over to offer him some assistance.'

Bundy pulled this trick on a number of women, but it only got them *to* his vehicle, not *into* it. With Janet Carstensen, he arrived at the car complain-ing, 'Oh my arm hurts.' Then he opened the door and told her to start the engine. She refused. Bundy turned nasty, snarling 'Get in', and Janet ran off.

Bundy perfected his method with the Bad Arm and Boat. On a hot July afternoon in 1974 he drove to Lake Sammamish ten miles outside Seattle, mingling with the 40,000 swimmers and sun-bathers crowding the beach. Wearing a plaster cast, Bundy first approached Jennifer Rutledge on the sands and said with a deprecating smile that he could not manage his boat with just one arm. Would she help unload his dinghy from the car? As they strolled to the parking lot he introduced him-self as 'Ted', chatting about his racketball injury.

But when they reached the car park, Jennifer noticed at once that there was no boat. Bundy pointed to the hillside some miles distant and said, 'Oh, it's up at my parents' house.' At this stage Jennifer backed out, but later that day Bundy some-how glossed over this problem with both Denise Naslund and Janice Ott. The exact technique in these cases is unknown; both girls are dead.

The Dutch film *The Vanishing* shows the anti-hero trying a Bad Arm and Trailer without success; a Bad Arm and Furniture features in *Silence of the Lambs*.

See **Trolling**

Lingle, Alfred Jake (1892–1930)

An accomplished saver. Thrifty Jake Lingle, an obscure crime reporter with the Chicago *Tribune*, entered a crowded pedestrian subway heading for the Illinois Central suburban railway on 9 June 1930. As he neared the east exit, a man with blond hair dropped behind him, drew a Colt .38 (known as a 'belly-gun') and fired a single shot upwards through Lingle's neck. It traversed the brain before exiting through his forehead, and the killer escaped, his pursuit impeded at the critical moment by a mobster dressed as a priest.

Shell-shocked Chicago reacted with outrage. It was one thing for gangsters to bump off each other, and even to kill law-abiding citizens by mistake. But Lingle's murder represented a new twist in the downward spiral.

The *Tribune* launched a massive hunt for his killers. The paper clubbed together with the *Evening Post* and the *Herald and Examiner* to offer a $55,000 reward. Eight columns of the *Tribune*'s edition of 10 June were devoted to this civic crusade, and on 12 June it editorialised under a clarion heading, 'The Challenge': 'The meaning of this murder is plain... Mr Lingle was a police reporter and an exceptionally well-informed one... What made him valuable to his newspaper marked him as dangerous to the killers... It was very foolish ever to think that assassination would be confined to the gangs who have fought each other for the profits of crime in Chicago... The *Tribune* accepts this challenge. It is war.'

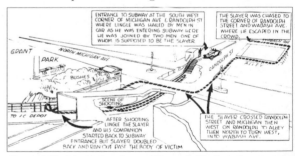

Scene of Lingle's death as he set off towards his favourite racetrack

A humble reporter with a byline-free career, Lingle pulled down $65 a week. As the investigation unfurled, it transpired that he maintained a chauf-feur-driven Lincoln, a summer house at Long Beach, a suite of rooms at the stylish Hotel Stevens, a jew-ellery collection and an expensive gambling habit. A friend of millionaire businessmen, judges and county officials, Lingle shared golfing holidays and stock market speculations with the Police Commissioner, and died with $9,000 in cash in his pockets, girded with the ultimate symbol of gangster chic, a dia-mond-studded belt presented by Capone himself.

Lingle's underworld role was as the fixer of police promotions. He mediated between mobland and the political machine as the unofficial Chief of Police. In the words of the Hotel Stevens' house detective, 'He was up there amongst the big boys and had a lot of responsibilities.' A disappointed Chicago returned to its habitual state of lawless torpor.

More than half a century later, on 11 March 1992, New York witnessed a rerun of Lingle's killing when the crusading journalist Manuel de Dios Unanue was gunned down in the restaurant Meson Asturias on 83rd Street to almost identical headlines: 'Slain newsman made criminals quake' and 'He did his job too well – maybe that was deadly'. News organisations sponsored a reward fund that rapidly climbed to $67,000, and a joint task force of the police and federal agencies worked round the clock. The city's Governor, Mayor and ex-Mayor all attended the memorial Mass.

At first it was conjectured that Unane was hit on the orders of the Colombian drug lords, whom he constantly harried in the press. But the moral certainties quickly evaporated. 'This case is a nightmare,' said a detective. 'The day after he was shot we hear he was a hero. Two weeks later, he's a dirtbag... Five hundred people hated this guy.' His former employer, the editor of *El Diario*, put in a good word for him, but only one: 'He deserves credit for being consistent. A consistent asshole.'

Lists

On 22 April 1922 a methodical youth, Ernest Walker, wrote out a list:

1 Ring up Sloane Street messenger office for boy.
2 Wait at front door.
3 Invite him in.
4 Bring him downstairs.
5 Ask him to sit down.
6 Hit him on the head.
7 Put him in the safe.
8 Keep him tied up.
9 At 10.30, torture.
10 Prepare for end.
11 Sit down, turn gas on.
12 Put gas light out.
13 Sit down, shut window.'

Steps one to twelve proved straightforward. As Walker explained in his intended suicide note: 'I brought him into the pantry and hit him on the head with a coal hammer *so simple*. Then I tied him up and killed him. *I* killed him, *not* the gas. Then I sat down and turned the gas full on. I am as sane as ever I was, only I cannot live without my dear mother. I didn't half give it to that damned boy. I made him squeak. Give my love to Dad and all my friends.'

But step thirteen – when Walker sat there and died – proved a stumbling block. He decided to leave it out, and went to Charing Cross Station instead, catching the 7.35 p.m. to Tonbridge. On arrival, still elated by his brilliant coup, Walker shared the secret of his murder with a constable on the beat. PC Sheepwash noted the dried blood on the youth's hands, and arrested him.

Meanwhile, Raymond Davis was found bleeding from a headwound in the butler's gas-filled bedroom at 30 Lowndes Square, London, with a gag in his mouth. He died the next day. Walker confessed: 'I do not know what made me do it... I hit him with a piece of iron bar. I have felt bad since last Wednesday, and I lost my mother last January, when the flu was about.'

Walker, an 18-year-old-footman, was looking forward to joining his mother on the far side of the grave. But he needed a companion to stiffen his resolve, and devised the scheme of ordering up a boy from the District Messenger Company in Sloane Street (see **Murderee**). Raymond Davis, in his new uniform of a pillbox hat and cape, drew the short straw. At the trial, Walker's list showed clear premeditation, and his letter to the butler started on an upbeat note: 'Dear Mr Pallance, I expect you will be surprised to see what I have done.' Walker was found guilty but insane.

Another famous list was compiled by John George Haigh on the eve of his 1949 encounter with Olive Henrietta Helen Olivia Robarts Durand-Deacon. It went like this:

Large oil drum
Stirrup pump
Rubber gloves
Apron
45 gallons sulphuric **acid**

He dissolved her. The 'Brides-in-the-**Bath**' murderer, George Joseph Smith, also committed his thoughts to paper after his murder of Alice Burnham in 1913. In a passage echoing T. S. Eliot's dreary précis of life as no more than 'birth, death and copulation', Smith wrote: 'certificate of birth, certificate of marriage, certificate of death, wife's will, policy, receipt for premium paid, official acceptance, receipt for burial.'

Lividity

Also known as **livor mortis**. A corpse's skin assumes the livid hue of a bruise as the blood gravitates to the body's lower portions. The areas of discoloration, restricted to the body parts not in contact with a hard surface, are established within some twelve hours after death.

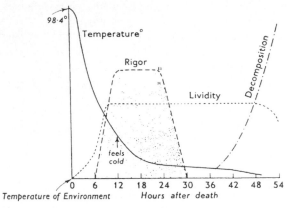

Chart showing the major changes by which the lapse of time after death might be estimated. The first hour often shows little fall in temperature

A typical supine cadaver exhibits lividity in the small of the back and the posterior aspect of the neck and thighs, the reverse of the symptoms expected from a prone corpse, and when Petrus Hauptfleisch left his mother (whom he had killed) lying face down for some hours before rearranging her the other way up in a staged accident, the local doctor was surprised to find symptoms of lividity on her frontal aspect. Hauptfleisch, a South African, was hanged in 1926.

Locard, Edmond (1877–1966)

Eminent French criminologist whose youthful reading of *The Adventures of Sherlock Holmes* kindled his interest. Against entrenched indifference, in 1910 Locard founded the first police laboratory in Lyon

and became a minor celebrity the following year for his conviction of Emile Gourbin.

Gourbin was a bank clerk whose girlfriend, Marie Latelle, lived in a villa on the outskirts of Lyon. Her flirtations gave him pangs of jealousy, making Gourbin the obvious suspect when she was strangled at her parents' home. But he proffered an unbreakable alibi. Medical evidence put Marie's death at around midnight, and Gourbin had passed the whole evening with friends some miles away; they drank deeply, dined well and played cards until one in the morning.

Summoned by the local police, Locard examined Marie's body, detecting abrasion marks on her throat where the murderer's fingers scraped away her skin. He obtained some of Gourbin's fingernail scrapings and, under the microscope, among the traces of epithelial tissue, noticed a strange granular dust. It was powdered rice, a basic cosmetic ingredient, and further analysis disclosed vestiges of other chemicals – iron oxide, zinc oxide, bismuth and magnesium stearate – common in the manufacture of pink face powder.

A police search of Marie's room revealed a box of identical make-up. Gourbin confessed; he had duped his friends by advancing their wall-clock from 11.30 p.m. to 1 a.m. and broken up the evening early. The prosecution argued that this betokened premeditation, and Gourbin was sentenced to death for murder. But he claimed that Marie's death happened accidentally; he altered the clock only because he was bored and wanted to see his girlfriend. He said that at their assignation he asked her to marry him, and when she refused, lost his temper and choked her in a rage. The jury did not believe him.

Locard's guiding tenet was that 'every contact leaves a trace' (the so-called 'Locard Principle'), a philosophy borne out by his 1922 case of the postmen's heads. As he observed, 'Nothing resembles the head of one postman more than the head of another', particularly when viewed from above, and the French postal authorities discovered this empirically during an investigation into the internal theft of registered letters. An enterprising postmaster suspected that the robberies took place in his post office, with the mail opened in the lavatories, and he stationed spies in the attic to watch for suspicious activity. They spotted the thief in action in his cubicle, but his pate was unfamiliar, and the observers banged on the ceiling, dislodging a dusting of fine plaster which drifted onto the culprit's left arm and shoulder.

But the building dust proved invisible on clothing. So the suspect uniform was sent to Locard, who easily detected traces of sulphate of **lime**. Such procedures are routine now, but were cutting-edge technology then, and to this day many laboratory procedures derive from Locard's work. He discovered the distinctive patterning of the microscopic pores in the papillary ridges and is the reputed inventor of the eight-feet long portable microscope. An account of many of his cases was published in 1922 under the title *Policiers de roman et policiers de laboratoire* and his major work, *Traité de Criminalistique*, came off the presses the following year.

When the seventh volume in the series appeared in 1940, it included a sinister new category, Crime Without a Cause. Locard approached this modern staple with caution, citing a case from 1886 where, against the evidence, a chemist's assistant from Le Havre, Pastré-Beaussier, was absolved of a string of arsenic poisonings after convincing the jury that he lacked any *motive* for murder. The deaths included his employer M. Decamps (who had accused him of petty theft), Mme Decamps, M. Delafontaine (the new owner) and the housekeeper Mme Morisse. Numerous others collapsed with vomiting but recovered, and a simple process of elimination demonstrated that Pastré-Beaussier was the culprit, propelling a reluctant Locard towards the conclusion that he 'killed for pleasure, and perhaps, after his first murders, from habit'.

See also **Success**, **Young**

Locks, combination

Not since the late nineteenth century could a crook *feel* when the right number was dialled into a combination lock. The countless film plots hinging on safecrackers with sensitive fingers, or sophisticated auditory devices, are baloney. For the last hundred years, the bar releasing the lock has made no contact with the internal dials until the number is correctly set, at which point the safe opens anyway.

A more reliable way of outwitting a combination lock is to find where its owner has written the number, typically in a nearby card index or filing cabinet, under 'S' for 'Safe'. If not, then the words of the American cracksman Harry King afford useful guidance. King 'found it to be the rule among cashiers to use numbers easily divisible. For example, a train of numbers selected would be four, sixteen and thirty-two, or twelve, twenty-four and thirty-six.'

Other safe-owners never revise the original settings dialled in by the manufacturer, likely to be testing sequences such as 10-20-30-40. Or the number corresponds to an anniversary or hobby. Golfers prefer 9-18-36-72, whereas bridge players plump for 4-13-26-52.

This principle allowed the nuclear physicist Richard Feynman to penetrate the Los Alamos safes in the 1940s. Feynman's hobby was lockpicking, and for a lark he postulated that his colleagues would employ a mathematical constant for their combination locks. He tried the base of natural logarithms (2.71828) and the doors to nine cabinets swung wide. 'I accessed the safes which contained all the secrets of the atomic bomb,' he wrote. 'All the schedules for the production of plutonium, the purification procedures, how much material is needed, how the bomb works, how the neutrons are generated, what the design is, the dimensions...'

Unaware of Feynman's success, during the last decade British nuclear weapons scientists still adopted *pi* as the numerical base for their strongboxes. The computer hackers of today, who circumvent electronic security systems by guessing the 'password', operate on a similar mix of cod psychology and intuition.

With combination locks, if all else fails, it is worth filming, photographing, listening or watching as the owner unlocks his door, an approach utilised, on a highly sophisticated level, during the famous 1975 raid on the Bank of America in London's Mayfair.

The gang's inside informant worked on building maintenance and, while checking the ventilation systems prior to an attempt with a thermic lance (which generates heat and smoke), discovered that the lobby overlooking the vault door had a false ceiling.

Above the removable panels was a void some eighteen inches high, enough for an accomplice to crawl into, suspend himself from a cradle and wait all day until the safe was opened. He viewed the operation through a tiny hole with a spyglass, wrote the numbers down and left the building after work hours.

On 24 April 1975 the gang unclicked the vault door and 'caned open' the deposit boxes, described as 'chock-a-block with pound notes and francs and dollars. There was gold this and gold that alongside piles and piles of diamond rings, bracelets and necklaces.' The eight-man team made off with as much as they could carry, valued at £8 million.

On aged domestic safes, the lock should be given a good bang with a heavy hammer. Often the spindle is driven into the case, freeing the handle. A variant, with a long, hard spike, is known as 'punching a can'; it only works with the more elementary safes, but even today is the first thing Americans try.

London Bridge

Before it fell down, the gatehouse of London Bridge was garnished with up to thirty-five rotting heads impaled on poles. Since the heads were customarily drawn larger than life, this feature is sometimes visible in contemporary engravings of general prospects of London or the Thames.

The **heads** provided snacks for scavenging birds, and for added longevity the trophies were first parboiled and then dipped in tar. The culinary preparations are described in detail in the seventeenth-century *History of the Life of Thomas Ellwood*.

Ellwood wrote of his depressing induction to Newgate: 'There lay the quartered bodies of three men who had been executed some days before... and the reason why their quarters lay so long there was, the relations were petitioning to have leave to bury them, which at length was obtained for the quarters but not for the heads... I saw the heads when they were brought up to be boiled. The hangman fetched them in a dirty dust basket, and setting them down among the felons, he and they made sport with them. They took them by the hair, flouting, jeering and laughing at them, and then giving them some ill names, boxed them on the ears and cheeks. Which done, the hangman put them into his kettle, and parboiled them with bay-salt and cummin seeds that keep them from putrefaction and this to keep off the fowls from seizing on them.'

Until 1550, London Bridge provided criminals with an easy avenue of escape. On the south bank of the Thames lay the borough of Southwark, beyond the writ of the city. It consisted mainly of brothels, and a thief had only to walk across the river to dissipate his gains in safety.

Lombroso, Cesare (1836–1909)

A former army surgeon and father of modern criminology. His findings, embodied in the science of phrenology, are now discounted.

In 1876 Lombroso rocketed to fame with his publication of *L'Uomo Delinquente*. His revelations were inspired by examination of the brain of the deceased brigand, Vilella.

Just by the spot where Vilella's spine met his cerebellum, Lombroso noted a little concavity, similar to the depression found in the brains of rodents. Lombroso realised that criminals were animals. He wrote: 'At the sight of that skull, I seemed to see, all of a sudden, lighted up a vast plain under a flaming sky, the problem of the nature of the criminal – an atavistic being who reproduces in his person the ferocious instincts of primitive humanity and the inferior animals.'

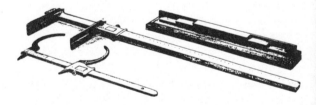

Anthropometric instruments for phrenological purposes

Lombroso distinguished two types of wrongdoers: the environmentally driven 'occasional criminals' and the 'born criminals'. The latter were doomed throwbacks, easily recognisable by their elongated, neanderthal arms. His survey of 7,000 criminal subjects confirmed that criminals had acute eyesight (like birds of prey), heavy jaws, jug ears and asymmetrical faces. They were predisposed to epilepsy and often covered in tattoos.

Lombroso is significant not for what he discovered but for what he investigated, and his mistaken thesis endowed criminology with an aura of respectability. Apart from his views on women (see **Female Offender**), his legacy included the 'hydrosphygmograph', an aqueous precursor of the **lie-detector.** In 1905 he put a mendacious robber, Bersonne Pierre, to the test, sealing his hand in a rubber membrane and inserting it into the glass vessel filled with water. The level visibly altered with each heartbeat, and these fluctuations were transferred to a column of air in another glass tube graduated like an old-fashioned barometer. A revolving drum registered the pulse rate linearly.

Lombroso's contraption correctly predicted that no, Pierre had nothing to do with a railway theft but that, yes, Pierre had relieved a man called Torelli of his passport.

At the 1992 gathering of the British psychological Society, Professor Ian Hunter pointed out that phrenology, the science of cranial bumps, furnishes a good example of researchers' tendency to dismiss evidence which does not support their assumptions ('confirmation bias'). The skull of Descartes was examined by a nineteenth-century phrenologist anxious to get to grips with his magnificent frontal lobes. But Descartes's were of the ordinary variety. So the researcher decided that he was not a great thinker.

Lottò

An otherwise insignificant hood whose 'death' displays the Sicilian Mafia on peak internationalist form in the early 1920s. Lottò, a *mafioso*, committed a murder in 1922 with such blatant disregard for the niceties of concealment that even in Sicily he courted arrest, posing a serious threat to Mafia prestige. The local chief, Don Calo Vizzini, had Lottò declared insane and confined to a lunatic asylum in Barcelona.

There he 'died', was buried (in a ventilated **coffin**), and on the third day or thereabouts rose again, was issued with false papers and smuggled into the United States. For his provenance, Lotto identified himself to the New York reception committee of *mafiosi* by tendering a yellow silk handkerchief embroidered with the initial 'C', for Calo.

Sicily retains its split personality of grinding, feudal poverty and extensive criminal enterprises, uniting these attributes until recently in the person of Salvatore Riina. A paunchy diabetic dressed in ill-fitting clothes, with a crude haircut and the stubby fingers of a peasant, Riina attempted to pass himself off as a farmhand at his arrest in downtown Palermo, apprehended driving a nondescript Citroën saloon on 15 January 1993. During the two decades he evaded capture, often by living openly in his own home, Riina clocked up convictions in absentia for some 150 murders while building a billion-dollar operation in narcotics and money-laundering.

The mere influx of six-figure sums will not loosen a *mafioso*'s stranglehold on the meagre pittance derived from local extortion. The account books of the Madonia family seized by the police a few years ago recorded eighty-five local businesses paying monthly protection of a few hundred dollars – hardly a major income stream for an outfit worth $400 million, but essential to maintain 'domination of the territory'.

See also **Inquisition, Vendetta**

Luby's Cafeteria

To date, America's worst mass killer is George Hennard, who drove his blue Ford Ranger truck through the plate-glass window of Luby's Cafeteria in Killeen, Texas, on 16 October 1991.

This dramatic entry into the crowded diner crushed one table and its occupants. Hennard jumped from the vehicle, drew his 9mm Glock semi-automatic and opened fire, calmly and deliberately, reloading as he exhausted each seventeen-round clip, walking through the tables, drilling customers through the head as they scattered to the ground. Hennard killed twenty-two and wounded another twenty-three, and there is no doubt that he would have gone on until his ammunition ran out. He carried a spare pistol with another forty-five rounds.

But it was Hennard's bad luck that two undercover policemen were on a case almost next door; they reached the cafeteria within a minute of the first shot. In a brief exchange of fire, Hennard took four hits. He staggered to a rear hallway and put a bullet in his brain.

There was little to investigate when the gunfire ceased. The police assigned two dozen detectives to the case, and all they unearthed was Hennard's background. Aged thirty-five, he had not distinguished himself at school, and did not get on with his mother. He had no known friends or girlfriend, and his seaman's licence, his last link with the world of even semi-decent work, had been suspended. At one stage Hennard played the drums, but to a different rhythm from the rest of the group, who chucked him out. Most of his victims were women.

Hennard falls into the classic type of mass murderer – an aggrieved social and sexual failure approaching middle age. His grudge's existence is easy to deduce; almost the only clues to its nature are his babbled words as he gunned down his victims: 'Look at what Belton's done to me! Tell me people, was it worth it? Wait till those women in Belton see this! I wonder if *they'll* think it's worth it!... Take that, bitch!... This is what Belton done to me! Is it worth it? Is it worth it?... Hiding from me, bitch?'

Hennard lived alone in nearby Belton, and in January 1991 he wrote to two local sisters asking them for a date: 'Please give me the satisfaction of someday laughing in the face of all those mostly white, treacherous female vipers from those two towns who tried to destroy me and my family.' The sisters declined.

See **Terminology**

Lucan, 7th Earl (1934–?)

The rich may have more money, but this does not necessarily make them interesting. As Melissa Wyndham, a girlfriend of one of Lucan's 'Clermont Set', recalls: 'Of course, I thought Lucan was the most depressing person ever. He was fantastically gloomy. He may have had a good point, but I certainly didn't spot it.' Others describe Lucan as charming and intelligent.

Good-looking enough to screen-test for the role of James Bond, Lucan was an addicted gambler who made £20,000 at *chemin de fer* during a two-day winning streak in 1960, on the strength of which he devoted himself full-time to gaming. By the early 1970s he had frittered his fortune away, declining into a bit-part as the Clermont's house player, a lure for other punters.

In 1963 Lord Lucan contracted an ill-fated marriage. He separated from his wife ten years later, and she won custody of their children in a bitter court case while he became enmired in debt and drink. On the night of 7 November 1974, wearing gloves, carrying a ten-inch length of lead pipe and a canvas US mail sack, he stole into his home at 46 Lower Belgrave Street. His wife and children were upstairs watching *The Six Million Dollar Man*. Lucan removed the lightbulb over the stairs and waited in the basement kitchen for his wife to make a cup of tea after putting the children to bed. Shortly after 9 p.m., he heard the descending footsteps and attacked, bludgeoning his victim's head. Blood spurted everywhere. When the body was still, he folded it in two and wedged it into the sack.

The rest was easy. Lucan had left time to return to his flat and clean himself up before meeting four friends for an after-theatre supper at the Clermont Club. Then he would drive the corpse to the coast, take it onto a boat and dump it overboard, weighted down, in the middle of the Channel. He had – according to writer Taki Theodoracopoulos – made two practice runs, rehearsing the transfers and timing the journey. Next morning he would learn, from the police or the nanny, that Lady Lucan had disappeared.

Few would be sorry or surprised. Lady Lucan had once fled from a psychiatric hospital, even if only for a few hours, and was widely regarded as difficult and unbalanced. A hotel manager's stepdaughter, she was variously described as tense, joyless and a manic-depressive. The custody battle had cost Lucan £40,000 he did not have. He ran four overdrafts, was borrowing heavily from his friends in the 'Eton Mafia', and received an annual remittance of £12,000 against expenditure of £17,000. With his wife dead, the outgoings on his rented flat and the matrimonial private detectives would cease, and he could reinstate himself in the family home with his children, whom he adored. Posted as a 'Missing Person', Lady Lucan would probably be dismissed, after a judicious interval, as a suicide.

Indeed, eight years later Lady Lucan did try to take her life, and on that night in November 1974, after waiting fifteen minutes for her tea, she called, 'Sandra? Sandra? What's keeping you?' In the dark, Lucan – probably drunk – realised that he had killed the nanny, Sandra Rivett, five feet two like his wife. She had changed her day off because of a boyfriend. Lucan climbed the stairs, stuck his gloved fingers down his wife's throat and battered her round the head. But she fought back, reaching for his balls and squeezing until he stopped. Then she calmed Lucan down and, apparently, they started to chat. While he was in the bathroom damping another towel to tend her wounds, she bolted through the front door and ran to the quiescent 'Plumber's Arms' covered in blood, screaming, 'Murder, murder, he's murdered my nanny.' By the time the police arrived Lucan had disappeared, and he has not been seen since. No one now knows whether he is dead or alive.

After fleeing from Lower Belgrave Street, Lucan drove forty-four miles south to call on Susan Maxwell-Scott. There he downed a few stiff drinks, telephoned his mother, and scribbled a letter to his friend Bill Shand Kydd with a cock-and-bull story about how he had 'interrupted a fight at Lower Belgrave Street and the man left'. The letter continued, 'I will also lie doggo for a bit.' Lucan left Maxwell-Scott at about 1.15 a.m., and his borrowed Ford was discovered two days later, half-an-hour's drive away at Newhaven, the Channel port.

The car's location suggested that Lucan took the ferry to France. Perhaps this is what he wanted the police to think. Gale force winds blew that night and, when the ferries resumed, they sailed almost empty. Lucan's photograph was splashed over the headlines and he would have been spotted. He had no access to a speedboat, and no boat was stolen. If he threw himself into the sea, the twenty-foot waves would have regurgitated him somewhere along the coast or, more probably, hurled him straight back. So suicide or conventional flight are both improbable.

But Lucan was part of a coterie of extremely wealthy men. It might have been diverting to give him asylum or spirit him away on a yacht or a private plane. Much is made of Lucan's friends' grand disregard for law and order, but perhaps it is not unusual to wish to keep a friend out of prison.

Detectives searched Warwick Castle, Holkham Hall, the cellar of banker Algy Cluff, Aspinall's estate, Goldsmith's house in Paris and telephoned the wealthy Claus **von Bülow** to ask if he was sheltering Lucan. The fugitive was reliably seen in Cherbourg, Belgium, Brittany, the Netherlands, Ireland, the Orkneys, South Africa and South America.

Today, Lucan's friends are reluctant to talk, and outer members of his circle occasionally let drop remarks like, 'Friends chipped in to pay for the education of his children... Oh, God, I'm not supposed to say that', or, 'There's more, but I can't tell you... We were talking about this down in Mexico at Jimmy's. They said I could only talk about the dinner the night before.'

It has also been proposed, with varying degrees of conviction, that Lucan employed a bungling hitman, that a cover-up concealed Sandra Rivett's death at the hands of a policeman, and that Lucan took his own life in Aspinall's private **zoo** and was fed to the tigers.

Lucan's children have prospered. His wife lives in reduced circumstances, and the affair's aftermath numbered two unexpected casualties. Dominic Elwes, the painter, committed suicide after talking to the press about the Clermont Set, who cut him dead; and Christabel Boyce. She replaced Sandra Rivett as the Lucans' nanny and, in February 1985, in an unrelated incident, her body was found dispersed over the East End. Boyce's husband confessed and was sentenced to six years for manslaughter.

Lucas, Henry Lee (1937–)

A self-proclaimed serial killer from Texas, a penniless drifter remarkable for his ghoulish appearance and grim family background. Lucas was so badly beaten by his mother, a Chippewa Indian prostitute born Nellie Viola Dixon, that he suffered brain damage. She raised him as a girl, and he arrived for his first day at school with permed hair, in a dress. His father froze to death, ejected from home with no legs after a railway accident. Lucas himself sported a downturned mouth and a glass eye; he tried to kill himself repeatedly, and in 1960 raped and murdered his 74-year-old mother during an argument. He spent four years in a mental hospital on electric shock therapy.

After his release from Michigan's Jackson prison in 1975, Lucas embarked on an eight-year killing spree, for the later stages teaming up with a child sex murderer and pyromaniac, Ottis Elwood Toole. His rampage ended on 9 May 1983 when Ruben Moore, a preacher from the House of Prayer in Stoneberg, tipped off the police that a member of his flock was armed.

Arrested on suspicion, an ill-kempt Lucas confessed to two murders, but hinted at others. As the implications sank in, the Texas Rangers set up a 'Henry Lee Lucas Task Force' to coordinate efforts to unravel his years on the road. Soon Lucas was alluding to sixty killings, and on the day the Rangers opened their telephone lines they fielded seventy long-distance calls from police forces anxious to clear up their unsolved murders. One by one Lucas admitted responsibility for the slayings, providing details only the killer could know.

His turn of phrase was vivid: some victims he 'filleted like fish'. Others he crucified. As he explained: 'Killing someone is just like walking outdoors. If I wanted a victim, I'd just go get one.' And again, 'I've killed by strangulation, knifing, hit and runs, shootings, robbings, stabbings, hangings, every type of crime...' He worked part-time as a contract killer for a shadowy organisation known as 'the Hand of Death', kidnapped children and smuggled them into Mexico and, for sex, would rape people or kill animals and make love to their bodies.

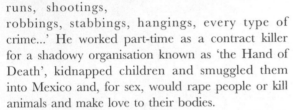

Lucas's grisly body-count multiplied to 150 and, as his prestige as a sweeper-up of unaccounted crimes grew, so the stature of the Task Force soared. In 1984 more than eighty detectives from twenty states booked into a Louisiana Holiday Inn, and for two days the convention studied a special screening of the Henry Lee Lucas videotapes. Speaking to camera, Lucas rambled through a litany of murders and mutilations, and by the time the dust settled some 210 killings were cleared. A detailed computerised ledger provided a chronological record of his wanderings over the interstate highways. In an ordinary month, say October 1979, he killed six times, on the 1st, the 2nd, the 5th, twice on the 23rd and again on the 31st.

As Lucas dredged through his memory the tally climbed to 360 killings. It reached 630, and finally hit 1,000. A media celebrity, he featured in a spate of surprisingly nebulous books. No longer a destitute drifter, he appeared in a three-piece suit with groomed hair and dark glasses. 'It was interview after interview,' he said. 'I was staying on television twenty-four hours a day... I thought I was the biggest movie star in this country, I think I even beat Elvis Presley.'

Lucas developed a close professional relationship with his 'minders'. 'I was real close to Sheriff Boutwell,' he recalled. Like father and son.' He needed careful handling. As Boutwell said, 'If at any time you indicate you disbelieve him... you'll ruin your credibility with him.' But their restraint brought a rich harvest as day after day they called the press with new reports of cases solved.

Murder is a grim business for relatives of the deceased, and to initiate the grieving process they need to know how their loved one died. The ordeal of Bob and Joyce Lemons ended nine years after the August 1975 killing of their 18-year-old daughter Debra Sue Williamson, when Lucas recounted how he broke into their white suburban bungalow through the patio door and stabbed their daughter to death in her bedroom.

But the Lemons' relief proved short-lived. As they pointed out to the Task Force, although their house was now white it had been green at the time of the killing; the patio door was sealed shut on installation, and their daughter met her death outside in the garden. The Lemons' objections went unheeded. By now Lucas was an unstoppable juggernaut, living high and wide. In his words, 'I was a king, I had everything I wanted, everything possible that a man could want, I had money, I had a colour TV, all kinds of food, stacks of cigarettes.'

Obsessed with the case, the Lemons tracked down Lucas's half-sister, who maintained that he spent the day of Debra Sue's death 2,000 miles from the murder site in Lubbock, Texas. As bereaved parents, the Lemons lacked official standing, and still Lucas piled new iniquities onto his dizzying heap of confessions. 'Every time they would bring a murder case in I would accept it, no matter what it was.'

Meanwhile Vic Feazell, District Attorney from Waco, Texas, landed the job of prosecuting Lucas for three specimen murders. Disturbed that the only evidence was Lucas's own confessions, he too started an investigation.

Feazell obtained copies of Lucas's paychecks, his work records, his applications for food stamps and his traffic tickets which yielded an indisputable day-by-day record of his whereabouts. It bore no relation to the Task Force log. For 1979 Feazell found that Lucas had cashed forty-three weekly cheques at the Buy-Rite grocery store in Jacksonville. But during that same year the Texas Rangers had him committing forty-six murders in sixteen different states. Killing after killing proved a physical impossibility. A murder of 5 March 1981 in Corpus Christie, Texas, fell on the day that Lucas was selling scrap metal in Jacksonville, Florida. Two claimed murders took place while he was in prison. And so on.

Feazell compiled a meticulous day book with Lucas's actual whereabouts set against the corresponding murder sites and, thus equipped, confronted Lucas in the Huntsville Penitentiary, Texas. Feazell spread out his day book. 'We *know* you didn't do these killings,' he stated. Lucas smiled. 'I was wondering when someone would get wise to this.'

Feazell was in head-on conflict with the Task Force. With its credibility at stake, Feazell found himself targeted by a virulent FBI corruption investigation, and he was dragged off in handcuffs to face accusations of racketeering, burglaries and homicides. Feazell conducted his own defence, vindicating himself and winning a record $58 million in libel damages.

By now Lucas appreciated the drawback of impersonating the world's greatest serial killer. He was on **Death Row** awaiting execution. He started to retract, and his downward revisions of the death toll left the figure of one: his **mother**, a murder for which he had paid the penalty. His terrible childhood remains uncorroborated.

Perhaps Lucas gleaned the names of his supposed victims (when he provided them) from newspaper clippings. But this would involve ambitious forward-planning. A simpler explanation is to hand. As Lucas said, 'I didn't go to the police about these killings, they would bring the murders to me and tell me about them.' By the Task Force's procedure, outside police agencies submitted detailed offence reports; only after receipt was Lucas interrogated, suggesting that he was 'primed' with details.

In Britain, IRA cases revealed a judiciary unable to swallow the bitter pill that the police might be corrupt; in America, the innocence of Lucas would turn the Texas Rangers and a dozen agencies beside into a laughing stock. As Lucas says, 'This is Texas, and I'm trying to fight a legend.'

On television, Lucas comes across as a likeable, bumbling man who relished his limelight years. 'It's like being a movie star,' he reminisces. 'It's just like playing a part.' But there are tears in his eyes. He may still have to die.

The otherwise admirable film by John McNaughton, *Henry: Portrait of a Serial Killer*, depicts Lucas as a man who just woke up and killed. But he didn't. He just woke up.

See also **Cormorgo, False Confessions, Success**

Luciani, Albino (1912–78)

Also known as Pope John Paul I, who died on 28 September 1978 thirty-three days after his election. Six years later the British investigative author David Yallop published *In God's Name*, a massive research piece whose contents are fairly summarised by the Cataloguing Data on the title verso: '1. Catholic Church – Finance, 2. Organised Crime.'

Yallop assembled a convincing if circumstantial case that the Pope was murdered. It seems that Luciani was bent on rooting out corruption at the Vatican bank, overturning established Catholic doctrine on birth control and ending the Church's involvement with the illegal but powerful branch of Freemasonry known as P2. Careers and reputations at the highest Vatican levels were at stake; the exposure of massive financial fraud imminent.

Yallop contended that the evening before his death the reformist Luciani discussed a dramatic reshuffle of staff with his Secretary of State, Cardinal John Villot (himself destined for the chop). Next morning, Luciani – previously in good health – was dead, but forty-five minutes *before* the official discovery of the corpse by Villot, the Signoracci brothers, embalmers, were called to the Vatican.

Items beside Luciani's body, including a medicine bottle, vanished. Without troubling to hold an autopsy, a Dr Buzzonetti vaguely passed off the death as 'myocardial infarction' (heart attack); within fourteen hours the body (and any evidence with it) was embalmed. A few days later the hard-liner Karol Wojtyla was elected, the old gang of corrupt cardinals were safe in their sinecures, and Luciani's reforms lay dead in their tracks.

Murder, said Yallop. But his book is a fine example of a conspiracy manufactured out of thin air. None of the main evidential planks bears investigation. Thus the wicked Cardinal Marcinkus was supposedly wandering round the Vatican very early on the morning of the killing: 'What the President of the Vatican Bank, not a renowned early riser, was doing so early remains a mystery,' comments Yallop. In fact, Marcinkus motored early to work every day to avoid the traffic.

Nor were the embalmers summoned to the Vatican with untoward prescience. Old men with failing memories, the Signoraccis' evidence is contradictory and unreliable, with Ernesto later saying: 'It's all confused... it could have been seven in the morning... or... it could have been at ten in the morning... or... at three in the afternoon... I don't know.' It would be easy to put words into their mouths, and there were five doddery brothers in the same line of business to put them into or take them out of.

Again, the Pope's prompt embalming was in anticipation of his imminent public display, spanning several days, quite possibly in sultry weather, and although such conservation might be illegal in Italy, it is lawful – and normal – in the Vatican, a separate country.

There are wider problems, not least that the Vatican is incapable of conspiring to do anything, let alone kill a Pope. In a hive of factional gossip, a concerted cover-up is impossible. Nor was there any point in conniving against Luciani. No clean broom, he was a befuddled old man of sixty-five out of his depth. His previous administrative experience was restricted to the decaying see of Venice with its small flock of 90,000. Suddenly – and mistakenly – elected Pope, he was plunged into the deep end as the Chief Executive of one of the world's biggest, most demanding businesses.

Luciani did not want the job; he did not understand it; as Pope, he was a provincial embarrassment at his wits' end, and seriously ill to boot. His legs were so swollen that he could not wear shoes – strongly indicative of thrombosis of the inferior vena cava. In his prayers, Luciani begged the Lord to let him die, and on the day of his death complained three times of feeling ill, and of a severe pain in the chest.

Luciani probably took anti-coagulants to improve the circulation in his legs. If he neglected to take his pills, his blood would become more coagulable, making the chest pain of his last afternoon consistent with a minor blood clot in the lungs, and his death that evening consistent with a massive pulmonary embolism. Throughout his brief tenure, Luciani went without the ordinary medical attention that could have saved him.

Luck, hard

Countless thousands of criminals come to grief each year through no more than bad luck. These stories of unhappy coincidences cumulatively suggest that a life of crime is a high-risk occupation liable to detection one way or the other.

Thus in February 1991 an 18-year-old thief, Freedom A. Hunter from Arizona, achieved simultaneous felonious possession of a chequebook (property of a Nebraska couple) and a driving licence (belonging to one Tim Holt). Using the latter as identification, he went to a drive-in bank with a forged cheque for $275 made out to himself under his new alias. As the bank clerk to whom he handed the cheque was Tim Holt, Freedom Hunter ended up in jail.

Such incidents progressively shade into stories where bad luck is attributable to **stupidity**. On 27 March 1990 the Atlanta *Constitution* reported a striking *faux pas* by William J. Collins. He walked into Atlanta police headquarters and threw a bag of crack down on the desk of Officer V. J. Williams. Shortly before being booked for possession, Collins complained that he was fed up with bad stuff and wanted his supplier arrested.

Many of the more mundane 'hard luck' stories centre on cars – getaway vehicles running out of petrol or being clamped, or fleeing villains flagging down a police car to ask for directions. But despite appearances, it is not so much that criminals are stupid as that they habitually commit crime. Anyone could get arrested doing it.

Lunette

French term for the wooden halter clamping the condemned man's neck on the **guillotine**; in the plural, *lunettes* means spectacles. At the decapitation of Maître Georges Sarret on 10 April 1934, the severed head remained affixed to the *lunette* for some ten minutes after the blade got stuck.

Prior to execution, a French convict signed his record-sheet to acknowledge that everything was in order; the prison director added, 'Handed over to M. the Executioner for carrying out of the sentence', whereupon the prisoner, received in operational condition, became the responsibility of his executioner.

America has equally stringent requirements. A man about to have his life removed by the State must be conscious, alert and 'physically able to withstand the shock of execution'. So the day before he dies he receives a medical examination. In the words of Doyle Williams, who survived to tell the tale after the postponement of his 20 March 1991 'event': 'They take your temperature and they weigh you, and the doctor hits your knee to see if you have reflexes. And if I remember right, he took his stethoscope and listened to my heart. I thought it was kind of silly. I said, "What are you going to do if I'm sick?"'

In France the assistant executioner's job was to ensure that his client did not imitate the action of a tortoise, drawing his head back into his shoulders as the blade approached. This he accomplished either by pulling the prostrate victim forwards by the hair or (if bald) the ears, thereby assuring a properly extended neck, and his obsession with settling the condemned man in position accounts for his slang title as 'the photographer'.

M

MPD

Acronym for 'Multiple Personality Disorder'. In 1962 California's '**acid doctor**' was well into his murder trial when he first intimated that, really, his *alter ego* should be held accountable for the killing. 'Let me out of here,' said an astonished policeman as he grasped the nature of the doctor's defence, 'I think I'm going to be sick.'

At the time, psychiatry was a fad tossed into movies to explain the hero's motivation. *Sybil*, based on a woman with no less than fourteen personalities, became the forerunner of several MPD films, and in 1979 similar psychological fragmentation formed the defence strategy of the Hillside Strangler, Kenneth Bianchi (see **Romances**).

Although weak-willed, Bianchi was resourceful. He set himself up as a psychiatrist on the basis of a diploma from California State University, culled by submitting a thesis stolen from someone else. Luckily, Bianchi had no patients, so he slid into life as a pimp, and from then on it was downhill all the way.

After his January 1979 arrest, Bianchi stonewalled with impressive sincerity, adamantly denying knowledge of the killings. Then he watched *Three Faces of Eve* on prison television. Soon Bianchi's defence lawyer and psychiatric social worker glimpsed hidden depths in their client, wondering if the most likely explanation for his disavowals was a multiple personality disorder; perhaps the murders were the work of unacknowledged *alter egos*. The authorities called a specialist, and when an excited Professor John G. Watkins from the University of Montana put Bianchi into hypnosis, who should turn up but 'Steve'.

Steve was the Mr Nasty who had spent years inside Kenneth's Mr Nice. Steve spoke through Bianchi with a weird, low voice ingrained with hatred. He held his cigarettes in a different way, first tearing off the filters and gripping the stub between thumb and forefinger. Steve was vengeful and aggressive, and had done those 'jobs' with pleasure. If Kenneth wasn't careful, he would fix him too.

Obviously Bianchi was insane. Another psychological authority was summoned: Ralph B. Allinson, author of *Minds in Many Pieces*, who confirmed the MPD diagnosis. Allinson discovered that 'Steve' even had his own surname: Walker.

Bianchi's insanity meant that he could not be brought to book as the Hillside Strangler, and it was only when Dr Martin T. Orme (like Bianchi, familiar with *Sybil*) subjected him to a simple test that the sham was exposed. Orme introduced a hypnotised Bianchi to an imaginary lawyer. Bianchi leaned forwards and shook hands with the invisible attorney. But a subject under hypnosis knows better than to touch his hallucinations. Then Bianchi said to Orme: 'Surely you can see him?' If Bianchi *had* been able to see the lawyer, he would not have known that no one else could.

Next, Orme insinuated that most MPDs had more than two sides to their personalties. And, sure enough, Bianchi's internal family gave birth to another cohabitant, a whining child called Billy. Later, a police sergeant pointed out that 'Steve Walker' and Bianchi were hardly bedfellows of longstanding; it was the name of the psychiatry post-graduate from whom Bianchi stole the thesis. The Hillside Strangler was hastily reappraised and sentenced to five life terms.

The more churlish British school of psychology has long regarded MPDs with warranted scepticism, treating them as hysterics or malingerers. In America, the dysfunction is linked to the rise of satanic **ritual abuse**, where many 'survivors' claim previous MPD diagnoses.

McCummings, Bernard (1961–)

First mugger to retire a millionaire. In the summer of 1984, 23-year-old Bernard McCummings grabbed an elderly subway passenger at a West Side Manhattan station. By chance, a Transit Police detective standing nearby intervened and shot McCummings twice. One bullet severed his spine, paralysing him from the chest down, but after the trial McCummings was able to serve his 37-month sentence in a wheelchair.

A police board of inquiry cleared Detective Rodriguez of 'excessive force', accepting that the mugger had lunged for the gun. This was because the departmental pro-ceedings never established that McCummings was hit in the back, a fact which the police captain in charge said he only learned during his cross-examination at the subsequent trial in April 1992. Awarded $4.3 million in damages, McCummings, confined to a wheelchair, lives in a Harlem housing project with his mother while the judgement is appealed.

McKinney, Joyce (1948–)

An all-American girl and a regular at Bible camp. Born in 1948, she was voted Miss North Carolina High School by her classmates. But one day in 1975, while driving with a friend in her new Stingray convertible, a handsome young man popped his head through her car window.

In Joyce's words: 'I found myself gazing into the deepest pair of baby-blue eyes. He put Paul Newman to shame. My heart did flip-flops. I turned to my girlfriend and said: "Hey, get out – I'm in love."'

Joyce's beau was a 6ft 2in Mormon missionary, Kirk Anderson, and for a time their affair flour-ished. A besotted Joyce was anxious to please; according to a friend, she visited porn films and live sex-acts to amass tips on sensual arousal. When Anderson tired of their Salt Lake City affair, she harassed him, with escalating violence. Anderson's windows were broken, his tyres ripped and his car smashed. He requested a transfer to California, but Joyce followed him. So Anderson took an overseas posting in Britain.

Joyce blamed the tyrannical Mormon Church for stealing her lover; she wanted him back, depro-grammed and freed of sexual inhibitions. So she advertised in an underground magazine for the comprehensive abduction services of 'a muscle man, a pilot and a preacher to help in a romantic adven-ture'. Joyce never assembled the team, but she did have a car crash, and the $15,000 insurance money funded a visit to, or perhaps a raid on, Britain. Arriving with a false passport, she hounded Anderson out of East Grinstead to Reading and thence to Epsom.

It was there she struck on 14 September 1977. Outside his church, Joyce and a male accomplice hustled Anderson into a car at imitation-gunpoint, put him to sleep with a bottle of chloroform and then motored to Devon for The Cure. At the cot-tage, Joyce explained her terms. Anderson could go free as soon as he agreed to marriage. Thereafter, what happened depends on who you believe, but only for one detail. Everyone agrees that Anderson spent three days tied to a bed with chains and a leather strap; that he had oral sex with his ex-lover; that she spreadeagled him on his stomach and gave a back-rub clad in a negligee; that she turned him over, and tied him business side up with ropes, chains and padlocks; that they had intercourse. The dispute centred on that familiar bone of con-tention, consent.

Joyce said Anderson loved it; he let himself be trussed up and lay there 'grinning like a monkey'. Anderson maintained the sex was forced. 'But he would, wouldn't he?' said Joyce. Anderson would hardly *invite* excommunication.

The element of consent was not crucial. In law, a woman cannot **rape** a man. So when Anderson ran to the police after three days on the rack, Joyce and her accomplice were charged only with abduc-tion and possession of an imitation revolver. From the prison van taking her to court, a tearful Joyce distributed messages to newspapermen, 'Please ask Christians to pray for me', scrawled on the torn-out pages of a Bible. At the preliminary hearing, she was granted bail, but on a curfew, a restriction lifted on 13 March 1978 to enable her to visit the cinema. But she went to America instead, emerging from hiding garbed as a nun to court the popular press. For six years little more was heard. Then in June 1984 the papers announced: 'Sex-in-chains Joyce is at it again.'

By now, Anderson had given up his calling as a missionary; married to a girl called Linda, he worked as an airline company executive. When Joyce stationed herself outside his office, Anderson braced himself for another snatch and called the police; they charged her with disturbing the peace. Joyce carried a notebook detailing Anderson's every move, and through her lawyer, explained that she was 'writing a screenplay about her experiences and wanted to see how the story ended'. For the time being, the story stops there.

See also **Crime Passionel**

MacDonald, Dr Jeffrey (1944–)

The front cover of *Esquire*'s March 1970 edition read, 'Lee Marvin is afraid – Evil lurks in California.' Inside were features on the **Manson** slayings and a candlelit LSD orgy presided over by a long-haired 'witch' with a retinue of four. One subscriber to the magazine was 26-year-old Dr Jeffrey MacDonald at the Green Berets' Fort Bragg, and two nights after he drew a neighbour's attention to the articles, the police responded to a late night emergency call to his home. They found a dazed MacDonald lying by his pregnant wife in the master-bedroom, her skull fractured and both her arms broken. She had thirty-seven stab wounds. 'Pigs' was daubed in blood by the headboard, and down the corridor lay their two children, both stabbed to

death. MacDonald gasped, 'Four of them... She kept saying, "Acid is groovy... Kill the pigs."'

MacDonald realted how he had dozed off on the living room couch at 2 a.m., waking to find himself under attack from intruders wielding knives, an ice-pick and club. One of the men had a moustache,

and the girl wore a floppy hat over her long hair. She held a candle. Somehow MacDonald's pyjamas were ripped over his head and became entangled with his hands. As he fainted, he heard Colette, his wife, screaming and his children crying. Coming to, he pulled a knife out of Colette's chest, covered her with his pyjamas and, at 3.42 a.m., called for help.

MacDonald was the boxing team doctor, an Ivy League School graduate and a weightlifter. Perhaps two notes jarred: he aired his suit on the clothesline if he went to a party where guests smoked tobacco. And no one groovy enough to take acid still said 'groovy'. Nor did the forensic evidence tally. Almost a hundred threads from his tattered pyjama tops were found in the three bedrooms – which he went to *after* covering his wife. Some fibres lay *under* Colette's body. But none were shed during the living room fight, which left MacDonald almost unscathed. His single stab-wound was a slit one centimetre wide, as though self-inflicted with a scalpel, and his home was virtually undisturbed. The greeting cards still stood, and the coffee table found on its side proved top heavy: when investigators knocked it over, it turned upside down.

The MacDonald family all had different blood types. Colette's was present in Kristen's bedroom, Kimberly's in the hall and in the master bedroom, MacDonald's by the hall cabinet housing the scalpels. So the forensic evidence directly contradicted his version of events. 'Step one, you lose your family, step two, you get blamed for it,' he objected on 6 April, and later that day, as he stood in the canteen queue, the radio announced his arrest. MacDonald's in-laws, the Kassabs, rallied to his defence.

The Army hearing discovered that the crime scene had been irreparably compromised. Twelve military police had trampled through MacDonald's apartment; his pyjama bottoms were lost, the lavatory flushed, a bloody footprint destroyed, and scrapings of skin under Colette's fingernails and a blue fibre from Kristen's fingers mislaid. A flower-pot (supposedly found upright) was set back on its base by a medic. A doctor shifted Colette's body and moved the pyjamas, her 'hair' came from her coat collar, and one of MacDonald's from his pony. The police saw a girl in a floppy hat loitering nearby on the night, but nothing was done; Fort Bragg had a population of 50,000 and thirty-one access points, so no roadblocks were set up.

An embarrassed Army cleared the court. Then a man named William Posey recalled that his neighbour – a teenager called Helena, a witchcraft druggy who affected floppy hats – had returned in her Mustang at 4 a.m. with two or three raucous men on the murder night. On the day of the MacDonald funerals, Helena wore black, and draped wreaths from her porch. Later she said of her boyfriend, 'Well, we can't get married until we go out and kill some more people.' Posey testified; Helena was located, but under questioning she betrayed no recollection of the murder night.

MacDonald's lawyer mocked the investigation for its listless pursuit of the Helena lead. Charges against MacDonald were dropped for insufficient evidence, and, in a *Newsday* interview, he enumerated his nineteen stab wounds. He put out feelers for a book deal with *Esquire* and the North Carolina *Observer*, and appeared on television, castigating the army for framing him. By now he spoke of twenty-three wounds.

Despite MacDonald's veto on taking a lie test, the Kassabs remained stalwart allies. Clearing his name was a prerequisite to renewing the hunt for their daughter's real killers, and Kassab lobbied 500 congressmen on MacDonald's behalf. But he needed the thirteen volumes of Army hearing transcripts to argue his case in detail, and MacDonald seemed reluctant to allow access. Instead, on 18 November, he telephoned: 'All I can say is, one down, three to go'. Next day MacDonald vaguely described how he had tracked down one of the killers and beaten him to death.

This made the Kassabs curious. Who was it? What did the culprit say? Why had MacDonald killed a man who could prove his innocence? Pushed for details, MacDonald said that the girl in the floppy hat was called 'Willie the Witch'; she had left with the moustache man. Two months later Kassab's efforts produced a new investigation, but when Helena was traced, she proved a rambling heroin addict. 'I don't know whether I did it or not,' she said. 'I really and truly don't know anything.' Much of Posey's testimony was untrue.

Background inquiries on MacDonald revealed a domestic martinet addicted to indiscriminate affairs. Re-evaluation of the forensic evidence showed that the smooth knife-holes in MacDonald's torn pyjamas, allegedly deployed in defence while tangled round his hands, were inflicted on a *stationary* garment. Slits in Colette's clothing showed that the knife MacDonald claimed to have extracted from her chest was never used against her. Its blade matched cuts to *his* pyjamas, suggesting that he stabbed himself. And some of Colette's blood sprayed onto his pyjamas in circular blobs; the cloth had later been torn in two.

In March 1971 Kassab took delivery of the Army transcripts. He pored over MacDonald's 153-page testimony with mounting disbelief. How had Colette cried, 'Help, help, Jeff why are they doing this to me?', when her throat was cut? If MacDonald was knocked out, where were his contusions? Why wasn't he killed while unconscious? Everyone else had been. Why was only one of his wounds more than 5mm deep? Why were his daughters found on their *sides* if he gave them mouth-to-mouth respiration? Why deny an ice-pick was in the house?

Kassab secured access to the MacDonald apartment. The ceiling was too low to wield the club overhead. Soundproofing was poor, yet the family above slumbered through the screams. With the lights extinguished it was too dark to see an assailant's moustache. And stamping in the corridor toppled the greeting cards in the dining room.

The new investigation was complete by June 1972, but MacDonald remained at liberty until 1979. By then he had a $350,000 West Coast condominium, drove a Citroen-Maserati, owned a ten-metre yacht, and his many supporters considered him a heroic figure. Although MacDonald's guilt was clear, the Department of Justice evaluated the evidence as circumstantial and the chances of a conviction slim. Nor did MacDonald pose a threat to others. But Kassab's tireless efforts for a prosecution finally bore fruit.

The killings probably began with a bedroom row. Weapons came to hand and Colette's blood spurted onto MacDonald. Kimberly intervened and was killed in her bedroom. Colette revived and tried to protect Kristen. Both were killed. To explain Colette's blood on his pyjamas, MacDonald used them to cover her bleeding body. Then he stabbed her repeatedly, and, when the pyjamas were refolded in replication of the crime-scene photographs, their forty-eight knife-holes could be duplicated by twenty-one ice-pick thrusts, delivered in the pattern of Colette's twenty-one chest wounds.

MacDonald always insisted on his innocence, but an early defence report depicted a selective **amnesiac** with suspect credibility, and his factual statements revealed tiny distortions which, in aggregate, constituted a big lie. In 1970 he was on amphetamines, then considered harmless and prescribed for weight loss, and in the month preceding the murders – already lean and fit – he lost a further stone. The side-effects of his probable dosage are insomnia, irritability and hallucinations. On top of his job, MacDonald worked every night of January at one hospital, did weekends at another, applied for a third moonlighting post, and worked out with the boxing team. Before the murder, he stood a twenty-four hour shift, put in a day at the office, played basketball and stayed up late. Then, something happened.

See also **Jury**

Maconochie, Alexander (1787–1860)

This son of a Scottish lawyer ranks as one of Australia's unsung heroes. As a young man, Maconochie spent two years from 1811 imprisoned by the French during the Napoleonic Wars; the experience may have been formative.

A quarter of a century later, invited by Sir John Franklin to Australia, Maconochie's colleagues at the Royal Geographic Society commisioned a report on the convict system of Van Diemen's Land. Maconochie correctly depicted its inhabitants as callous slave-owners exploiting convict labour. The system, he wrote, was 'cruel, uncertain, prodigal, ineffectual either for reform or example; can only be maintained in some degree of vigour by extreme severity'.

In Britain, the report's 1838 publication was a bombshell; six months later, when the mails arrived in Australia, it became a scandal. Maconochie was ostracised, libelled and slandered. But he assured London: 'The cause has got me complete... I will neither acquiesce in the moral destruction of so many of my fellow beings nor in the misrepresentation of myself.'

Maconochie's insight was that all the systematic policies of convict degradation served no purpose.

The prisoners had done nothing to deserve their floggings, and were not benefited by them. Other than for the perpetuation of tradition, there was no reason to whip the men within an inch of their lives.

Maconochie devised a disciplinary theory based on a system of marks, as in schools. Points for good conduct would earn convicts better conditions, enabling ascent from solitary confinement to 'social treatment both night and day'. The fiercest punishment was taking marks away, condemning the convict to solitary again. Thus each prisoner's fate lay in his own hands. Maconochie fondly imagined that his scheme would turn the convicts from objects into people, in whom jailers could take a personal interest, and he rounded off his system with proposals for a prison ombudsman.

Ticket-of-leave, issued to convicts of good behaviour, allowing them to seek employment outside government service.

Maconochie's ideas were as alien as the Coca Cola cans that occasionally drop out of aircraft to land at the feet of stone-age tribesmen. The Australian way was to work convicts to near or actual death, flog them without mercy for misdemeanours like 'looking up from work' and then flog them again for being unable to work after being flogged. But the deliberations of the 1838 British Molesworth Committee resulted in Maconochie's surprise appointment as commandant of **Norfolk Island**, the heart of darkness of the Australian penal colony a thousand miles from Sydney.

Maconochie landed in May 1840 to be greeted by the mustered ranks of 1,200 brutalised degenerates who for years had endured a daily round little better than **torture**. In his inaugural speech, Maconochie announced that the old system had ended. Then he outlined his pet plan of schoolboy marks.

After stunned incredulity the compound resounded with cheers. In the words of Thomas Cook, an old hand, 'From that instant, all crime disappeared', and in fact most of these reprobates had been transported for petty theft involving clothes or food.

To celebrate Queen Victoria's birthday on 24 May, Maconochie declared a holiday. He ran little pennants up the prison flagpole, fired off the cannon, threw open the prison gates, allowed the dazed convicts to wander over the island, gave them permission to swim, served special rations for barbecues, issued pannikins of rum and lemon, and staged a play (the comic opera *The Castle of Andalusia*) before winding up the evening with a firework display. Maconochie noted: 'Not a single irregularity, or anything even approaching an irregularity, took place.'

When trouble started, it was the backlash from the mainland. What about the regime of terror? Where was the hardship? Counter-orders poured in from Sydney. Why had he ignored the regulations about punishment-labour for the new prisoners? On the irksome question of his contravening the law, Maconochie replied: 'It can scarcely be doubted that this Act will be repealed. I never thought of these rules as a guide.'

Instead, he pressed ahead with liberalisation, requisitioning shiploads of encyclopedias, magazines, stories of exploration, history books, poetry and enough Waverley novels to found a library; sheet music, a trumpet, fife, horns, drums, reed accordions and other orchestral instruments; he distributed good conduct marks, dismantled the gallows, threw away the cat-o'-nine tails, built a church, instituted a makeshift synagogue, allocated vegetable plots, held gardening classes, let the men grow **tobacco** and allowed them decent burials with headstones.

The prisoners were transformed. In Cook's *Exile's Lamentations*, Maconochie earns a hundred pages of praise. Another set of memoirs refers to him as an 'angel', stating, 'Justice stares us in the face, the Almighty has now sent us a deliverance.' At a stroke, the Norfolk Island convicts returned to their former identities as ordinary, reasonably docile citizens. Many were former denizens of the Home Counties.

Meanwhile the colonists on the mainland were in a ferment of outrage; in London, Lord Stanley decided to drop his protégé. At the age of fifty-six Maconochie was dismissed from his post, but not before discharging 920 of his prisoners: a mere 2 per cent re-offended in the first two years. After his departure, Norfolk Island was plunged back into the dark ages.

Back in Britain, Maconochie was marginalised, briefly serving as a governor of Birmingham Prison where all his efforts were countermanded. Almost the only person to take him seriously was Charles **Dickens** and he died largely ignored in 1860. His 1846 *Crime and Punishment* remains a classic of modern penology.

See also **Negative blocking**

Mad Bomber

For more than sixteen years George Metesky terrorised New York. His campaign started on 16 November 1940, marked by a dud bomb on a windowsill at a Consolidated Edison plant on West 64th Street. An accompanying note, handprinted in neat capitals, read 'Con Edison Crooks – this is for you.'

Ten years later, on 24 April 1950, the unknown bomber raised his game to devices that exploded, and by 1957 his bomb tally had reached the high fifties. Some were duds. Injuries were few, and for the war years his harassment ceased altogether when, still out of step, he wrote a note vowing: 'I will make no more bomb units for the duration of the war – my patriotic feelings have made me decide this.'

But the underlying trend was for bombs of ever-increasing size, and on 2 December 1956 six cinemagoers were hurt in an explosion at the Paramount Theatre in Brooklyn. In January 1957 the Mad Bomber responded to an open letter from the publishers of the *Journal-American* with an explanatory note: 'I was injured on a job at Consolidated Edison plant – as a result I am adjudged totally and permanently disabled – I did not receive any aid of any kind from company – that I did not pay myself – while fighting for my life – section 28 came up.' Section 28 is New York's two-year Statute of Limitations.

Here was the first solid clue – the Mad Bomber had been on Consolidated Edison's payroll. But when a trawl through the company's records drew a blank, Inspector Howard E. Finney called in a Dr James Brussel from New York State's mental health department. Brussel perused the case-files, the photographs of the unexploded devices and the many notes and letters. And this is what he thought.

It was common ground that the bomber was waging a public **vendetta** against Con Ed, blaming the utility for his troubles. So the suspect was paranoid. Most paranoids do not get into their stride until their early thirties. So, by now a middle-aged paranoiac who, to judge by his handwriting, was meticulously, obsessively neat. A clean-shaven type who favoured a double-breasted suit. Buttoned up. And, going by the notes' stilted phraseology, an immigrant. Or, more likely, in view of his age, the first generation son of an immigrant. A son because most bombers are, statistically, male. And possibly Slavonic, since Slavs, historically, have a taste for bombs. In any case, not German, Italian or Spanish, to judge again by the phrasing. So very probably Slavonic. And hence a Catholic, like most immigrant Slavs. And, like most middle-aged paranoiacs, the Mad Bomber would live either by himself or with an elderly relative. And since he had been seriously ill (according to his letters) for a long time, but remained alive, he either suffered from TB, or chronic heart disease, or cancer.

On arrest, the Mad Bomber proved to be George Metesky, a middle-aged, neatly dressed, paranoid, church-going Catholic Pole, who lived alone with two doting elder sisters and wore his double-breasted suits buttoned. He suffered from TB.

Misleading trimmings of Freudian junk permeated Dr Brussel's analysis. Thus the shape of the bomber's handwritten 'w's and 'u's, which were tantalisingly plump and round, suggested an obsession with female breasts characteristic of an Oedipus Complex. So Con Ed symbolised *male* authority, and the Bomber's campaign, which included explosive devices left in *holes* in cinema seats, was motivated by *sexual inadequacy*. Otherwise,

Brussel was spot-on.

Brussel's profile did not lead directly to the arrest since, in the meantime, Metesky sent one note too many to the *Journal-American*, disclosing the date of his 5 September 1931 accident. His capture followed immediately, and he whiled away the rest of his life in an asylum.

Brussel was dubbed the 'Sherlock Holmes of the Couch' by the press, and the subsequent development of '**profiling**' flowed from attempts to implement his insights on a systematic basis. Brussel stayed ahead of the pack in the Boston Strangler fiasco (see **Insatiable**), when he was the first to realise that the attacks were not the handiwork of two distinct killers but of one. His final 'psychofit' of a strongly built 30-year-old, of average height and clean-shaven, dark-haired, of Spanish or Italian origin, fitted DeSalvo precisely.

Mafia, discovery of

The best kept secret in the annals of law enforcement. The Mob's existence remained unsuspected by educated Americans until 1950, when Senator Estes Kefauver's investigating committee stubbed its toes on something familiar to every cop and every street-corner punk: 'a sinister criminal organisation known as the Mafia'. Even then this was regarded as a questionable fantasy, with Robert Kennedy in a 1957 cross-examination enquiring of a gangster whether he was 'born into' or had 'married into' the Mob, as though it were the Royal Family.

The core-information went on record after the discovery of **Murder Inc.** in 1940, when the killing of a minor hoodlum, 'Red' Alpert, prompted hitman 'Kid Twist' Reles to furnish mountainous evidence that a gang of professional gunmen worked full-time on the orders of Mafia high-ups.

If this was a bombshell, no one heard it. In the words of the case's District Attorney, penned a decade later: 'Kid Twist's confession reached its climax with the incredible disclosure that there existed in America an organised underworld, and that it controlled lawlessness across the United States. For the first time in any investigation anywhere, the lid was lifted to lay bare a government within a government, in which the killings and the rackets worked hand in hand in a national combine of crime. Law enforcement had hardly any concept even of what a national combination meant. A lot of officialdom, it would appear, still remains in the dark about this danger from within.'

This was because **Hoover**, refusing to acknowledge what he knew to be true, squandered the FBI's resources on Communists. New York had four agents working on the Mob, and 400 assigned to the Reds, beavering away on vital issues like whether the head of the Communist Party travelled to work by subway or cab. Meanwhile the Mafia pursued its business undisturbed.

The shooting of the *mafioso* Joe Masseria over supper on 15 April 1930 was a turning point for the Mob, paving the way for the coming generation of hoods. Masseria was one of the last old-timers, believing that every gang should fend for itself, and after the killing, young Lucky Luciano (who shared dinner with Joe but tactfully withdrew to the men's room at the vital moment) assumed the Presidency of the Italian Society. On 11 September 1931 he launched 'Purge Day', a Spaghetti Night of the Long Knives. Thirty plus of the Mob's older leaders were liquidated. On the East Coast, the Big Six emerged: Costello, Luciano, Adonis, Lepke and Gurrah, Siegel and Lansky, Zwillman, and Schultz (who did not last long).

In 1934 Johnny Torrio of Chicago mustered the top shots at a meeting and opened with the proposal, 'Why don't all you guys work up one big outfit?' He continued: 'One guy gets hit, and his troop hits the outfit that did it.' These troublesome inter-gang feuds aroused the attentions of the law. Torrio recommended a Syndicate to end indiscriminate rivalries, with disputes referred to a Commission, which thereafter regulated the myriad rackets in industry, the ports, the rag trade, trucking, labour, strikes, strikebreaking, gambling, the ice business, loan sharking, car-theft, slot-machines, hot dog stands, prostitution, pornography, protection, extortion,

Joe Valachi testifying to the Senate

construction, narcotics, garbage and the mozzarella trade. In a word, the Mafia was in business, and the Commission's decrees were enforced by Murder Inc. operatives, who killed trouble-makers.

Hoover remained sceptical until the **Apalachin** summit of 14 November 1957, when a New York State detective blundered into a formal conclave of sixty or so mobsters at Joe Barbara's house. Even then, official recognition came slowly; the public first grasped the true extent of organised crime from Joe Valachi's testimony during the McClellan Senate hearings of 1963. Only the year before, on 8 September, FBI agent James Flynn terrorised Valachi by mouthing the dread phrase 'Cosa Nostra'. In the words of the official account: 'Valachi went pale. For almost a minute he said nothing. Then he rasped back hoarsely, "Cosa Nostra! So you know about it."' As late as the early 1970s, Attorney General John Mitchell ordered the word 'Mafia' struck from the Justice Department's vocabulary.

Times change. In 1984, an alibi witness for the drug trafficker Salvatore Catalano feigned ignorance of the term, saying: 'I don't know what that is. Is it something that one eats?' The court burst out laughing.

See also **Decline and Fall**, **Whacks**

Magic Eraser

A 1975 hi-tech gambit in the cocaine business. A Colombian stamp on a passport intensified the chances of arrest, and an Englishman known as 'Dr Richard', with a prototype pigtail and wire-rim spectacles, made his money in Colombia under the trade name Downstream Plastics, selling two aerosols at $5,000 a throw.

The first can sprayed an invisible micron-thin protective layer onto paper documentation; the sheen dried off in a few seconds. A burst from the second aerosol fragmented the coating like a smashed windscreen; the frosted shards could be shaken free, leaving no trace and the paper undamaged. A passport veneered with Magic Eraser allowed removal of the tell-tale Colombian entry and exit stamps after departure but before arrival, and the courier 'Rosalita' used the stratagem for six of her forty-three undefeated trips. The technique had one patent drawback: the whole passport needed treating each time, since it was impossible to foresee on which page an Immigration official would put the stamp. The latent pitfall was that the laminate proved susceptible to heat, as Rosalita discovered when she accidentally left her passport on the windowsill of the Hotel Tequendama in Bogota. The coating baked in the sun, crinkling up on the pages like a fried egg. She binned her passport and abandoned the aerosols.

Rosalita was last heard of in the mid-80s living in a half-finished apartment in Quinta Paredes, Bogota, with a single-bar electric fire and an expensive habit. If alive, she is now aged 43. She made a number of runs disguised as a nun, Sister Dominica, carrying her cocaine stuffed into crucifixes.

See also **Narcotics**

Male rape

Surprisingly popular among heterosexuals, underlining the point that rape concerns subjugation rather than sex. Nor is it confined to **prison**. A 1990 survey in the *British Journal of General Practice* found that 72 per cent of the victims were acquainted with their assailants socially, regarding them as heterosexual.

Male **rape** differs from the female version in two non-biological respects. First, the maximum penalty is ten years as opposed to life. Second, its exponents are all but immune from prosecution. In the words of the late Richie McMullen, author of *Male Rape: Breaking the Silence on the Last Taboo*: 'If you and I decided that we were going to go out tonight and rape a boy or a man, we could almost guarantee – 99.99 per cent certain – that we would get away with it. We know the victim is not going to report the crime.'

But the humiliation endured by the victims is no different. 'Survivors' recall the usual symptoms of defilement, outrage and depression, frequently coupled with a loss of the will to live. Some burn all their clothes, take to obsessive washing, and are scared to leave home, while their lives collapse around them. Unlike the abscess of female rape, which can be partially lanced by confiding in sympathisers, male victims, lacking a reservoir of social comprehension, have no one to tell because no one understands. One distressed victim telephoned the Rape Crisis Centre, to be told tartly: 'We are for women.'

Malory, Sir Thomas (ca 1400–1471)

English Member of Parliament as well as a brigand, robber, horse thief and rapist. After campaigning in France under the Earl of Warwick, Malory ravaged his native county as a gang leader. He extorted money 'by threats and oppression', attempted the murder of the Duke of Buckingham, rustled cattle, ransacked Coombe Abbey and raped Joan Smyth not once but (a few months later) twice. Generally, the law caught up with him and, while serving his third or fourth **Newgate** sentence, Malory amused himself by jottings of fantasies harking back to more chivalric times. Some fourteen years after his unmourned death, the manuscript came into the hands of William Caxton. He thought it had potential.

Malory's *Morte d'Arthur* became an instant best-seller, and stayed so for centuries, profoundly influencing Western culture. The book's elevated tone ensured the posthumous rehabilitation of its author, until the mid-1920s when an American scholar uncovered the truth while researching in the Public Records Office.

Manson, Charles Milles (1934–)

Manson was extremely small, a pint-sized 5ft 2in; so tiny that during the 12 October 1969 raid on the **Family** ranch he nearly avoided detection by hiding in a cupboard – partitioned by a horizontal shelf – under a small hand-basin. But his hair stuck out.

To the Family, even Manson's name was imbued with potency. As Susan Atkins said: 'I want you to dig on his name. Now listen, his name is Manson – *Man's Son!*' That was the name they booked him under: 'Manson, Charles M., aka Jesus Christ,

God'. Manson himself went further, upgrading his middle name from Milles to Willis, producing the aphorism 'Charles' will is Man's Son'. On the ride back to Independence in the police pickup, the arresting officer, Patrolman James Pursell, overheard Manson making utterances 'that caused the others to say "amen" two or three times in unison'. Interrogating the Family women, Deputy District Attorney Vincent Bugliosi was struck by the way the girls smiled almost continuously, repeatedly intoning 'Charlie is love.' Their supine, undifferentiated complaisance reminded him of Barbie Dolls, and initial investigations into the Family's enterprises made little headway. Pressed for details like dates, the girls replied: 'There is no such thing as time.'

Manson was born on or about 12 November 1934, the illegitimate son of a 16-year-old mother. As a child, he experienced 'uncle' after 'uncle' – his mother's new lovers – living in run-down hotel rooms. His first armed robbery came at the age of 13. Confined to juvenile reform school, Manson raped a number of inmates, sodomising one boy with a razor to his throat. By the time he was thirty-two, Manson had clocked up seventeen years behind bars for offences like burglary, car theft and forgery. His overall sentence would probably have totalled less than five years had he been tried for comparable crimes in state rather than federal courts, and it is as though he sought out offences that carried the most severe punishments.

Atkins, Krenwinkel and Van Houten arrive at court singing, wearing party dresses

By his Family days, Manson did not think twice about killing. His domination of the group was absolute. Often he dined alone on top of a large rock in the desert while the rest of the Family sat in a reverential circle on the ground, listening to his evocations of the imminent confrontation between blacks and whites.

To trigger this holocaust, he sent out his followers in squads to kill. On 8 August 1969, Manson despatched Susan Atkins, Patricia Krenwinkel, Leslie Van Houten and Charles 'Tex' Watson' to the house of record producer Tony Melcher. He had moved, but they killed the new occupants with the appalling brutality that Atkins afterwards characterised as loving care.

Two days later, Leno LaBianca and his wife Rosemary were done to death under equally gruesome circumstances.

Manson was tried and convicted not for killing, but for masterminding the killings. His comprehension had become inverted. At the trial, he threw his crimes back at his accusers: 'You make your children what they are... You taught them. I didn't teach them. I just tried to help them to stand up... These children – everything they have done, they have done for the love of their brothers.' In short, his hands were clean, and any dirt attached to his female disciples. Manson remarked to biker Al Springer, 'Whatever happens the girls will take the rap', and, left to their own devices, they would have shouldered responsibility for planning the slayings. Defence lawyers decided not to question Atkins, Krenwinkel and Van Houten lest they incriminated themselves on the stand.

'To Charlie, death was no more important than eating an ice-cream,' one Family member recalled, and Manson's true number of murders may be somewhere in the mid-thirties. Recollecting the high points of his 1969 career from the relative tranquillity of 1986, Manson showed some insight into his manipulative skills. At the time of the Tate murders, he was edging towards 40, a father-figure to his teenage acolytes. They may not have known what they were doing, but he certainly did.

Here is Manson in 1986, summarising his 1969 reactions – calculating, self-interested, distant – to the Family's rapturous description of the Tate killings:

'A normal person would find the details of the night's events shocking and horrifying, but I had long ago stopped measuring myself by society's standards... My only concern was whether it resembled the Hinman killing. Would the police now have reason to believe that Bobby was not the slayer of Hinman? And were the kids, loaded with drugs, clever enough to avoid leaving prints or evidence of their identities? Knowing Sadie and Tex and their flair for dramatic exaggeration, I doubted the slayings went down as they had described. More importantly, did they leave a trail that would lead to the ranch?'

The murders set a new low for the number of **false confessions**; even the most chronic publicity seekers had no desire to be tarred with Manson's brush. He is now eligible for parole.

See also **Leg, stabbed, Revelations**, **White Album**

Marine fraud

Marine fraud is a cyclical business linked to the ups and downs of world trade; its life-blood is insurance claims.

In boom years shipowners draw perfectly respectable operating profits from their vessel, even if bought on an 80 per cent mortgage. But as with houses, so with ships: come the slump and a $5 million ship tumbles to a fraction of its purchase price. Meanwhile it lies idle and, if unsold, racks up finance and maintenance charges.

In this predicament it makes sense to sink the vessel, the more so since its submersion unlocks windfall profits as well as stopping the loss. Ships are covered on 'valued' policies, with the amount payable agreed in advance, and, to boost premiums, underwriters traditionally endorse over-valuation. A vessel bought for five million, mortgaged for four, and now worth two, may be insured for eight.

The commercial downturn of the early 1980s induced a surprising amount of old Greek tonnage to burst into flames for no apparent reason, typically at lax ports like Piraeus, preferably at the anchorage's far end beyond easy reach of any fire-fighting facilities. The standard explanation was a 'carelessly dropped cigarette falling on an oily rag in the bilges', just within the outer reaches of credibility.

But fires are a risky business. Crews are – rightly – scared of starting them at sea, and in harbour, even in Greece, the blaze is sometimes extinguished, leaving a charred ship which the insurers insist on repairing and an owner no better off. Worse, the

arson may be detected, particularly if the flare-up began in several 'seats' simultaneously.

So owners turned to sinking their ships outright, developing a scenario that, among investigators, aroused scepticism bordering on derision. The wearying pattern was of a vessel making a ballast run towards Suez, passing relatively close to shore on the pretext of helping the crew conserve their drachmas by taking advantage of cheap VHF rates on calls home.

Despite light seas and clear weather, a Master would receive the astonishing intelligence that his engine room was awash with water. Luckily the discovery normally happened early in the morning, allowing all day for a leisurely sinking and rescue in pleasant conditions. Many losses occurred miraculously close to shore, and one particular tug acquired a reputation in London legal circles for the canny regularity with which it arrived in time to save the crew but just too late to save the ship. In graver cases, owners seeking a more plausible scenario ensured that at least some of the crew drowned.

Legitimate cargo claims flow directly from the Bill of Lading, a pre-printed standard form embellished with a couple of stamps, stating what was – theoretically – loaded onto the ship and hence what sank with it. But the sea-bed is no longer a Black Hole beyond verification. When the MV *Lucona* foundered with half a dozen crew in 2,000 fathoms in 1977, ROVs (Remote Operated Vehicles) photographed the wreck, establishing not only the cause of loss (a deliberate explosion in Number One hold) but also the fate of her cargo. The containers marked as Uranium Ore Processing Plant and insured for 30 million Swiss francs had spilled over the ocean floor, disgorging scrap farm machinery. The shipowner, Udo Proksch, is now serving a twenty-year sentence for fraud and six murders.

The Honduras have overtaken Panama as the Mecca of slack shipping regulations. Some 90 per cent of the vessels that disappear (with their cargo) by virtue of name-changes are now Honduran-registered. One ship, the *Jupiter 8*, managed two aliases in a single voyage (first the *Joyce* and then the *Wing-Tai*) under the acquiescent eyes of a Chief Officer who, as an unemployed Burmese labourer, had never been to sea before in his life.

Marlowe, Christopher (1564–93)

Marlowe, the Elizabethan playwright, died in a tavern brawl on 30 May 1593 when his companion Ingram Frizer stuck a twelvepenny dagger, via the eye-socket, into his brain. They were arguing over the bill.

But perhaps none of this happened. The conspiracy theory is that Marlowe did not die. The fight was a ruse, a prelude to interring somebody else in his stead. At the time of the taproom squabble, Marlowe was on bail pending his trial for the capital offence of blasphemy. Like Marx and **de Sade**, he held that 'The first beginning of Religioun was only to keep men in awe', and only three days before his death a damning report forwarded to the Privy Council recommended that 'All men in Christianity ought to endeavour that the mouth of so dangerous a member should be stopped'. Marlowe was in fear of his life.

The most extreme theory casts Marlowe's lover, Walsingham, as stage-manager for his boyfriend's vanishing, supplying a substitute corpse and spiriting the playwright away to France. There Marlowe settled down to work; *Venus and Adonis* appeared a few months later. Officially dead, he could not publish under his own name, and coaxed an undistinguished burgher of Stratford, William Shakespeare by name, into 'fronting' his work for a small fee. Later this became common practice in McCarthyite Hollywood.

Or so Calvin Hoffmann proposes in *Murder of a Man Called Shakespeare*. The exotic Shakespeare component goes too far, but Marlowe's death remains suspect. A tamer rendition has the playwright not saved but killed by Walsingham, the Queen's spymaster, to forestall embarrassing sexual disclosures at the writer's trial. Another theory has Marlowe set up and killed by Walsingham's wife.

The truth is probably simpler. All the men in the fatal room were acquaintances of Marlowe's; two – Nicholas Skeres and Robert Poley – came from the shady world of espionage and the third, Frizer, was a fixer, a young man on the make, later pardoned for the killing. Marlowe himself was not only a poet, but also a homosexual spy enmeshed in intrigues: with Walsingham's secret service, with the Earl of Northumberland, with the occultism of Giordano Bruno, counterfeiting in Holland, anti-Catholic espionage, and the Essex-Raleigh rivalry. Complicated cross-alliances made backing the wrong horse an occupational risk for spies, and it seems that Marlowe was summoned to Deptford for an ultimatum – either implicate Raleigh or take the consequences.

The England of Elizabeth I was a virtual police state where multifarious networks and shifting allegiances meant that players traded scraps of information for preferment. The truth behind Marlowe's death may never be known, but it is unlikely that he died squabbling over a bill. He certainly did not die in a tavern; the house, a private residence, belonged to Widow Bull, a well-connected woman who called Lord Burleigh 'cousin'.

Masturbation

Excessive indulgence in this harmless recreation is an early pointer to a budding serial killer.

Serial killers cannot (or will not) have relationships with people. So they derive their thrills from pictures; and masturbation over pornographic images forms a prologue to a career as a Peeping Tom and, eventually, sexual assault. The murderer Albert Hamilton **Fish** proved an avid practitioner even in his sixties on Death Row; the prison Chaplain requested him not to 'holler and howl' so loudly while on the job during divine service. One of the prime Ripper suspects – a Polish Jew, Aaron Kosminski – was billed in the Macnaghten Memorandum as a great exponent. First the habit drove him insane. Then it killed him; the Swanson marginalia cites 'self-abuse' as Kosminski's cause of death.

The modern serial killer Jeffrey **Dahmer** did it in public, earning an arrest for 'lewd and lascivious behaviour' on 8 August 1986 for his performance on the banks of the Kinnickinnic River. 'You having a good time?' asked one of the spectators. 'Yeah, I'm having a great time,' Dahmer called back. In all, Dahmer exposed himself in public six times; such exhibitionism is, perhaps, sadistic, compelling bystanders to see something they would rather not.

Masturbation and the serial murderer fit each other like fingers in a glove. Often he kills because he lacks the solace of ordinary human relationships. His sex-drive is normal, his associative powers and social skills low, producing a dearth of sexual partners. Masturbation furnishes the natural outlet, since no one else will consort with him – at least not while alive, and by the time the object of his affections can no longer decline his attentions – in other words, when his victim is dead – the killer is thrown back on the same problem which leads, again, to the same solution. Despite all the excitement and its attendant arousal, he is still by himself and still unsatisfied. Hence the frequent phenomenon of sex-killers masturbating onto corpses. The element of disjointed time, where the killer works out of sequence, is exemplified by **Chikatilo**: impotent while his victims were alive, he achieved satisfaction by killing, and then attempted retrospective intercourse, packing his sperm manually into his preys' orifices. Full-blown necrophilia is only a step away.

Murder can become a means to an end where the desire to experience sex, coupled with the inability to have it (which may take the form of impotence when confronted by normal stimuli) engenders extreme frustration. This is vented by the restorative of sadistic murder, which reinstates sexual prowess. Analogously, the absence of sexual power calls for the demonstration of power by other means, for instance, brutality.

New York's serial killer Arthur Shawcross, who claimed eleven victims, was finally caught in 1990 masturbating on a bridge in the forest near the site of his last victim's body; the police kept watch by helicopter against his return. Likewise, Jeffrey Dahmer used his trophies as sexual props. He took the severed head of his first victim, Steven Hicks, up to his bedroom, set it upright on the floor as a stimulant and then sought relief. His behaviour came under scrutiny at his 1992 trial, where the psychiatrist Dr Dietz suggested that 'it facilitated the fantasy of the entire person, the fantasy of the living person to whom the head had belonged, and cut out awareness that the rest of the body was missing'.

But like most psychiatric evidence, this is speculation. Perhaps Dahmer was titillated by the absence of the body. He may have found severed **heads** sexy *per se*. Like the British serial killer, 'Reggie-no-dick' Christie, Dahmer could not achieve erections in the face of the living, and throughout the nine years when he refrained from killing, his frequency of masturbation provided a mental health index. Once a week, under control; four times a day, and an unrequited Dahmer was teetering at the edge.

Masturbation is a starting point for most people's sexual careers; from it, they progress to shared sex. Dahmer's sexual boundaries were more closely confined, extending not to pleasuring a partner, but only to pleasuring himself, using his partner, like a pornographic picture, as a masturbatory aid. Exclusive recourse to this practice produces a dead inner world, where people are objects, and, before raising his sights to corpses, in 1984 Dahmer stole a shop mannequin from the shop window of the Boston Store in Southridge, keeping it for weeks as a sexual companion.

See also **Torture**, **Zombies**

'Mattress, to go on the'

Mafia expression dating from New York's Castellammares War of 1930 and 1931, when rival gangs shifted from one apartment to another, often at a few minutes' notice as they staked out the opposition for a 'hit' or fled an ambush. The only item the soldiers carried as luggage was their bedding, so 'going on the mattress' meant being at war.

The Castellammares War claimed some sixty lives, ending in complete victory for Salvatore Maranzano after the killing of Joe Masseria. He rashly proclaimed himself *Capo di tuti Capi* at a mass Mob rally held in the Bronx at a hall off Washington Avenue. It was standing space only. A good 500 hoods attended, and Maranzano suspended a crucifix over the platform at the far end of the assembly room and posted religious paintings to the walls, so that outsiders blundering in would mistake the gathering for a religious convention.

Maranzano only held office for a few months; he was liquidated in the nationwide Mafia purge of September 1931.

Medellin, Colombia

Figures hardly convey the slaughter in this cocaine city-state with a population of around two million. More than 300 police officers died in 1990, part of the tally of 5,300 homicides. Of these the majority

– some 3,000 fatalities – were concentrated in the age group 14 to 25, and by 1991 the toll for the city and its environs reached 7,900 fatalities, ten times the total for the whole of Britain.

Wary members of Colombia's elite anti-drug squad mount guard in Medellin after the 2 June 1993 assassination of Escobar's brother-in-law

Medellin's youth is wiping itself out. **Hitmen**, drug gangs, street gangs, death squads, militias, paramilitary squads and extortion brigades fight it out on a neighbourhood basis. Youngsters kill yesterday's friends in endless internecine feuds. The sixth of the seven Mosquera brothers met his end on 28 October 1992; the family's surviving son is temporarily safe, doing time in New York. But he is wanted for murder back home. In February 1993 a vigilante gang, Los Pepes, lined up seven men and machine-gunned them at a petrol station. A boy called Tono, dying of gunshot wounds, was said by Alonso Salazar (a professional chronicler of the epidemic violence and hence a *violentogos*) 'to almost salivate when he told the stories about all the people he'd killed'.

When Jorge Mario Mejias – another youth who is probably dead by now – was asked what he wanted to do with his life, he replied 'I'm a bum. What's the point of making plans if I'm not going to get anywhere anyway? All the **kids** round here are getting killed. We're all going to die.' His brother had already been shot dead. In the words of Victor Gaviria, a local film-maker: 'I think that in the end the kids kill just to see what it's like, they want to know how their own passage from one world into another will be.'

The violence is the outcome of the vicious contrast between local, traditional poverty and the rich pickings from cocaine. The government's war against the drug barons (see **Escobar**) has made things worse. According to one observer: 'There's tremendous unemployment amongst the drug gangs now, and they're all fighting for the available crumbs. All sorts of old scores are getting settled... Everybody's freelancing.'

The Medellin cartel, with their partiality for death squads, have a reputation for playing rough. By contrast, their rivals in Cali are better known for their fine art collections and sound business sense. When Cali's Rodriguez Orejuela was jailed in Spain in 1985 he had a 'cultural adviser' flown over to continue his education in the history of art. But the tuition had no perceptible impact on his taste; a visitor to Orejuela's home reported that the lavatory seat had gold coins plastered around its edge.

Cocaine retails locally at around $2,000 per kilo, with two more noughts added by the time it reaches Europe. The cartels have diversified into **opium** and its derivative, heroin. Growing poppies is bad for the environment; the cultivation process on the jungle hillsides drags thousands of acres into an ecological grinder of slash-and-burn agriculture aggravated by indiscriminate bombardment with fertilisers and pesticides.

Medellin's urban warfare has spawned an evocative *argot*, with new terms thrown up as rapidly as the bodies: *narcocondominico* (drug trade apartment), *punketos* (gangs devoted to punk music), *pistolocos* (crazy gunmen), *desechables* (throwaway kids) and *quietos* (corpses).

A good place to see the fun is the casualty ward at the San Vincente de Paul Public Hospital. On weekend nights the taxis ferry in about ninety gunshot victims, a quarter of whom die.

Other regional specialities include a revival of the tradition of **Burke and Hare**. In March 1992 a badly mauled garbage collector barely escaped from the Free University campus in Barranquilla, lured there by security guards who attempted to kill him. A police search of the medical school disclosed a stockpile of ten illicit bodies, together with twenty skulls, the same number of brains, fifteen lungs and twelve limbs. None of the corpses had undergone autopsy by the state pathologist; all had been shot or bludgeoned to death within the preceding two months.

Five security guards were arrested. Police said the killings were for profit, with the bodies sold to the medical students for their 'practicals' at 130,000 pesos each.

Memorabilia

Why not make money out of crime by investing in souvenirs? The revolver used by Jack Ruby to kill Lee Harvey Oswald in November 1963 originally cost $62.50, but on 28 December 1991 it was knocked down at auction to a gun collector for $220,000. The following year, Oswald's hospital body-tag fetched $6,600. The lot included a lock of bloodstained hair and his shoes.

In the late 1970s, an autograph of John Wilkes Booth, Abraham Lincoln's assassin, was worth about £500, twenty times more than that of his law-abiding brother Edwin, the most renowned actor of his day. A square inch of the skin of the graverobber Burke originally retailed at a shilling; in January 1992 a specimen went to auction with an estimated price-tag of £500. Applied pro-rata over the average individual's extent of eighteen square feet, it values Burke's hide at £1,269,000.

In Britain, auctions of hanging impedimenta were common until the turn of the century. The last recorded sale was in 1906 when a length of cord, guaranteed used by **Berry**, realised a disappointing seven shillings. Half a century before, the rope which hanged William **Palmer**, cut into two-inch sections, fetched half-a-crown a piece, and the rope which ended the life of William Corder, the Red Barn murderer, achieved a guinea an inch. According to *The Times* of 1866, Parisian ladies of fashion believed that a segment of a hangman's noose in their pockets conferred good luck at cards.

Hitler's personal guillotine, a decorative focal point, was recovered by Gerd Heidemann of the **fake** Hitler's Diaries three years after its 1989 disappearance from a Hamburg auction house. The thirteen-foot-high machine dates from the French Revolution and, together with Hitler's piano (a 50th birthday present) had an auction estimate of £175,000.

In April 1992 a job lot of Capone memorabilia made £30,000, including an initialled jug at £1,000. A stuffed fish caught by the great man in 1929 went for three times that amount. As a comparative yardstick, **Napoleon**'s penis was reportedly sold for 7,000 francs at a 1977 auction, but Christie's, the fine art dealers, have cast aspersions on its authenticity.

In 1976 an English conman, Barry Edward Gray, purchased a pair of shoes for $3.50 in a junk shop and then offloaded them to the *New York Times* for $50,000 as the former property of the missing US Teamster boss Jimmy Hoffa (whose last resting place, according to hitman Donald 'Tony the Greek' Francos, is six feet under, opposite section 107 of the New York Giants' stadium in the Meadowlands). The newspaper, although out of pocket, can comfort itself with the reflection that their investment must possess a value in excess of Gray's original cost as a memento of his coup.

Memory, recalled

A feature of satanic **ritual abuse** (SRA) cases, based on the supposition that sexual offenders bury the memories of their transgressions as too horrible to contemplate. In 1988 the first influential survey, by psychiatrists Young and Braun, surmised that the 'recovered memories' of their thirty-seven interviewees recorded the real experiences of people suffering from dissociative conditions (like the multiple personality disorder (**MPD**)), often affiliated to an unintegrated sense of identity.

A 1991 paper by a Dr George Ganaway drew different conclusions from the same data. Ganaway argued that highly hypnotisable subjects would, while in a trance, suspend critical judgment and seek to acquiesce to suggestions posed by their therapists. He depicted 'recalled memories' as a colourful 'screen memory' – a Hollywood version of real life, masking mundane forms of genuine abuse and neglect like beating, rape or straightforward deprivation. On this basis, SRA victims correctly identify themselves as damaged, but by something else.

From a sufferer's point of view, the misattribution may not matter. In August 1992, Professor Michael Nash cited a client who, under hypnosis, discovered that he had been shanghaied by aliens. The trauma exposed, the patient recovered. Nash commented, 'Here we have a stark example of a tenaciously believed-in fantasy with all the signs of a previously repressed memory. I work routinely with sexually abused adult women, and I could discern no difference between this patient's clinical presentation... Worse yet, the patient seemed to recover as he elaborated the report of his trauma (abduction by spaceship) and integrated it into his view of the world.' Nash concluded, 'In terms of clinical utility, it may not really matter whether the event happened or not.' That is, just because a victim believes something, it does not mean it is true, nor does a favourable response to treatment indicate a condition based on actual events.

Paul **Ingram**, the supposed satanic rapist, gave an account of the workings of recalled memory. First he imagined entering a warm, white fog. After a few minutes, images welled up which his interrogators assured him were real because, they said, God would bring the truth. Likewise, Ingram's wife appreciated her questioner's help. 'He kind of prods,' she said. 'When we start, initially he describes a scene to me.' Then she remembered it.

Recalled memory hinges on the theory of repression, originating from Freud. But what did he know? The notion that painful or dangerous memories are blocked from consciousness, thereby inducing irrational conduct, was posited but not proved. Therapists strive to ferry repressed material to the surface, but what is remembered may not be what has happened. Research by Professor Loftus on subjects told of invented incidents by a source regarded as reliable (for instance, an elder brother) shows that they may accept the tales as true and then add details of their own, rapidly achieving a seamless tapestry of fabrication. Thus an acorn of untruth can sprout into an oak of falsehood, a procedure formally entitled the false memory syndrome.

It is a quantum leap from masking a single brief incident (the 'traumatic amnesia' of combat or rape) to blanking protracted episodes of SRA endured time and again over years or decades. To regard their suppression as an equal likelihood produces the curious state where the mere absence of untoward memories is immaterial. On such a *carte blanche*, false accusations and **false confessions** are writ large.

Mercy

Towards the end of the eighteenth century the disparity between trivial offence and frightful punishment increasingly tormented the British liberal conscience.

Perhaps the most infamous hanging statute was the Waltham Black Act of 1723, a response to minor rural disturbances at Waltham Chase, Hampshire, when protesting labourers poached fish, burned hayricks and the like. The Act made nearly everything punishable by death, creating more than 200 new capital offences: cutting down an ornamental shrub, standing on the highway with a blackened face, setting fire to a hut or poaching a rabbit.

In part, the waning authority of the Church suffered encroachment from a new ritualised orthodoxy, the rule of law. Before the might of the legal system, even its berobed functionaries, the judges themselves, broke down and wept. At the Salisbury Assizes in 1831, during the sentencing of two agricultural protestors, Peter Withers and James Lush, a reporter from the *Dorset County Chronicle* noted, 'The judges were frequently obliged to rest their faces on their extended hands, and even then the large drops were seen falling in quick succession.'

Sometimes the victim petitioned for the offender's pardon. When agricultural worker Thomas Tate was given seven years transportation for stealing sacks of flour, the farmer William Tidman begged Viscount Sidmouth to let him off the hook in consideration of his wife and four children, 'as I freely forgive him myself'.

Transportees rarely escaped their fate, but hanging was a different matter. Juries bent over backwards to value goods at thirty-nine shillings (forty was a hanging matter), and the proportion of death sentences carried out dwindled from the mid-eighteenth century. In the decade from 1749 to 1758, 365 (69.3%) of London and Middlesex's 527 capital convictions were hanged. For the ten years from 1799, convictions were up to 804 and executions down to 126 (15.7%).

Pardons were granted in batches. Prisoners favoured with leave to appeal 'at the next general pardon' grovelled for their lives. As the Old Bailey's *Post Boy* for 31 August 1700 noted, 'The last day of the sessions 85 criminals pleaded on their knees for the King's most gracious pardon, acknowledging his Majesty's great clemency and mercy; they presented the court with gloves according to custom.' Most were successful.

Villains did not always extend the same courtesy to their monarch. According to William IV, his great-grandfather George II was accosted by a highwayman who scaled the walls of the royal gardens in Kensington. After a hollow show of deference, he deprived the king of his purse, watch and buckles.

See **Court of Appeal**

Milken, Michael

Bond trader with New York's Drexel Burnham and Co. In 1975 his employers set his remuneration at 35 per cent of the profits from his backwater activities dealing in low-grade, unquoted securities – the so-called 'junk bonds'.

Since junk bonds were low-grade, no one else much sold them; as they were unquoted, no one else knew their prices. Milken could buy cheap and sell dear. He could buy back cheaply from companies to whom he had sold dear, and sell dearer. He could buy dear and sell dearer still. By early 1977 Milken had cornered one quarter of the entire USA market in junk bonds, building a massive buy-and-sell 'spread' into their price. He awarded one-eighth of a point to his salesmen, retaining $29^7/_8$ points for himself. This made individual sales exceptionally profitable.

But Milken did not just do the occasional deal. He preached and sold the gospel of junk bonds nationwide. Junk bonds, he argued, carried no higher risk than other securities, but they paid higher interest. Soon everyone wanted them, and they all bought from Milken, fuelling the corporate mania for takeovers. By 1986 Milken was paying his top men like Jim Dahl $10 million while keeping back $550 million for himself. To boost his income from an increasingly rigged market, in 1984 Milken instigated a tranche of insider-deals with Ivan Boesky.

Or did he? The extent of Milken's guilt remains obscure. In 1983 and 1984, 72 per cent of companies involved in takeovers and mergers saw their stock price rise in the month before going public. Insider-trading was rife. But Milken played no part

in it. He was jailed primarily on the evidence of Ivan Boesky, and Boesky – widely regarded as a highly objectionable character – needed a sacrificial scapegoat to lay on the altar of the Securities and Exchange Commission.

In August 1986 Boesky was subpoenaed by the Commission. He rapidly decided to deal, negotiating a settlement in exchange for the downfall of Milken and three other Wall Street figures. Boesky had to act fast; on 14 November 1986, his SEC investigation would become public knowledge. So he telephoned Milken on 1 October, angling for a meeting at the Beverly Hills Hotel, and recorded the call, making a number of heavy references like 'Do you understand what I'm talking about?' He mentioned 'having a kind of like a *private* meeting' so that they could 'spend a little time recalling what we had talked about'.

At the 9 October conference Boesky arrived wired for sound. But the discussion focused mostly on Milken's breakdown of an invoice for $5.3 million for investment banking work. At worst, it was vaguely illustrative of a diffused pattern of manipulation; but two-and-a-half years later, in March 1989, the full indictment against Milken ran to ninety-eight felony counts for a possible total of 520 years in jail.

Milken, ground down piecemeal by a year of legal proceedings, capitulated on 24 April 1990 with guilty pleas to six charges. But the court report noted that the 'Milken Foundations are now among the largest charitable institutions in the country', that Milken himself always made time for family and friends and that his wealth was 'the result of legitimate business activities'. Asked to furnish the judge with three clear-cut examples of Milken's 'pervasive criminality', the prosecutors were unable to link him unequivocally to two crimes, and for the third, an insider-trading case, could not show that a crime had been committed.

Nonetheless on 21 November 1991 Milken was sentenced to ten years at the work camp of Pleasanton where, *sans toupee*, he shared a four-man 'dorm'. On release, he faced 5,400 hours of community service.

Why such a stiff sentence? Probably because, in the broad view, the harvest of Milken's labours proved catastrophic. Junk bonds lived up to their name, degenerating into junk. But insurance companies, pension funds, savings-and-loans all held them, and the corporate raids and the takeover battles left a billion-dollar legacy of debt, enshrining Milken as 'the Hannibal Lecter of American business' alongside Boesky who, during the peak years between 1984 and 1986, telephoned as a client thousands of times, yelling and screaming abuse. Milken would agree to anything to get Boesky off the phone; hence the imputation of a general criminal alliance, and the narrow picture – that the charges may be based on inaccuracies and factual errors – counted for little.

Milken paid off his $600 million fine in 1990, turned his hand to teaching, and in June 1992 started testifying against former colleague Alan Rosenthal in a bid to shorten his own sentence and secure early release to full-time community service. He was freed after twenty-four months.

What Milken wanted his $1.1 billion fortune for remains unclear. He favoured ready-made clothes, never touched alcohol and despised designer fizz, preferring tap water or fruit juice. The deepest fantasy envisaged by his wife, Lori, was to buy any hardback book she wanted. When she read in November 1986 that her husband was worth $15 million – a gross under-estimate – she told him to 'get rid of it': having so much money 'didn't look good'.

Mirror image

Dennis **Nilsen**, Britain's most prolific serial killer, arrived in London in 1972, aged 25 and almost without friends.

Some five years had elapsed since his first homosexual experience during his Army days, but his most abiding sexual relationship as a Non-Commissioned Officer was with his own likeness. 'By placing a large, long mirror on its side strategically beside the bed,' he noted, 'I would view my own reflection', and from the first he kept his head out of the frame, making believe that he was someone else. Nilsen moved while he watched, but that proved unsatisfactory. 'The pleasure could dwell much longer on a mirror image which was asleep.' So he stayed inert, gazing at an anonymous, headless version of himself.

Nilsen continued in this vein on settling in London. 'My most fulfilling sexual feasts were savoured with the image of myself in the mirror,' he wrote. 'To detach this image from identifying it directly with me, it evolved from an unconscious body into a dead body.' That is, Nilsen pretended his mirror-image was a stranger's corpse. Then he could **fantasise** that he was someone different, the violator of the inanimate trunk he eyed in the reflection, sometimes suspended by its wrists. This set-up was 'emotional and physical perfection', a great improvement on the unsettling reality of the one-night stands of London's gay scene.

By the summer of 1977, after the failure of his live-in affair with David Gallichan, Nilsen's approach had turned distinctly bizarre. Instead of pretending to be dead, Nilsen dressed up dead: 'I put talc on my face to erase the living colour,' he wrote. 'I smeared charcoal under my eyes to accentuate a hollow dark look. I put pale blue on my lips. I rubbed my eyes to make them bloodshot.' Then he riddled his tee-shirt with imitation bullet holes and dripped simulated gore onto his wounds. He lay there, watching himself playing a corpse with saliva dribbling from his mouth, and dreamed.

Nilsen imagined that he had been shot by the Nazi SS and left for dead in the woods. This much he could see in the reflection. But he still needed to visualise the other actor in the drama: an aged hermit. In Nilsen's words: 'The old man pulls my now naked body off the bed onto the floor. He washes me. He ties my penis and puts some wadding in my anus. He sits me on a chair then he puts me over his shoulder and carries me back into the woods and buries me. Later he returns and digs me up and takes me back to the shack. He masturbates me and my penis comes to life and I ejaculate.'

To imbue his fantasy with life, only one ingredient was lacking: the corpse. Then Nilsen could play the hermit, or whoever, with everything for real. He would have a familial unit of his own, over there, in the reflection.

Nilsen started killing in December 1978 to make his contacts stay so that he could talk to them. Four years later his description of Stephen Sinclair's murder on 27 January 1983 shows his mirror-life in full flower. By then there really were two bodies, one of them really dead.

'I lay beside him, and placed the large mirror at the end of the bed,' Nilsen wrote after the trial. 'I stripped my own tie, shirt and grey cords off and lay there staring at both our naked bodies in the mirror. He looked paler than I did... I put talcum powder on myself and lay down again. We looked similar now... He looked sexy but I had no erection. He just looked fabulous. I just stared at both of us in the mirror.'

Later, Nilsen's dog Bleep jumped up on the bed. 'Come on old girl, get your head down,' said Nilsen. 'Stephen is all right now. He's OK.' They started to doze off. Nilsen wrote: 'I turned Stephen's head towards me and kissed him on the forehead. "Goodnight," I said, switched off the bedside light and went to sleep.'

At last Dennis Nilsen was at peace, on the other side of the looking glass.

See also **Chikatilo**

Modus operandi

It is generally agreed that the date-rape case against William Kennedy Smith failed on the first day of the trial, 2 December 1991, when the prosecution was barred from calling evidence of similar assaults by Smith.

The rules against 'similar evidence' are strict. Nothing is more likely to lead a jury to a finding of guilty – on the seventeenth occasion – than to hear the suspect committed (or has been acquitted of committing) the same offence sixteen times before. But the previous instances are not in issue, and evidence of prior acts is only admissible if the crimes show a clear and unique 'signature' or *modus operandi*. If only the accused has a track record of behaving in a particular and idiosyncratic way, it is reasonable to infer that if anyone did the same thing again, he did.

At the Kennedy trial, Patty Bowman's attorney, Ellen Roberts, wanted to put in evidence the stories of three other girls who tangled with William Smith. Roberts adduced the defendant's distinctive behaviour pattern thus: 'The attacks, Judge, on all these women were violent and without provocation. They were pinned down, and they were rough

attacks... He ordered each of them not to resist.' She explained how Smith made a habit of seeking out 'attractive young brunettes' at 'a party, a picnic or a night spot'.

Although not mentioned in court, behind these three attacks glowered a stack of other cases. In the words of *Newsweek*'s Spencer Reiss: 'Lots of us know about lots more. So does Moira Lasch [Miss Bowman's other attorney]. She knows of at least sixteen others. That's the reason she's so venomous. She is convinced she has a real, live rapist on her hands, and she can't fucking pin him.'

Nor could she. As Smith's counsel observed, where else would his client meet girls other than at parties, picnics and night spots? By their nature, all rapes are violent, and many men prefer attractive young women to ugly old ones. Ms Roberts's motion foundered and her client lost the case.

For American detectives, a killer's modus operandi has attained investigative rather than legal significance. In the 1960s, Dr James Brussel constructed a psychological portrait of the Boston Strangler (see **Insatiable**) based on the behaviour (or symptomatology) exhibited at the scene of the crime, that is, by the way DeSalvo treated his victims. Britain's L.S Atcherley of the West Riding Constabulary developed a similar 'MO system' for Scotland Yard from his experience that a criminal's signature was often betrayed by 'small, irrelevant acts which had no relationship at all to the actual commission of the crime and could be accounted for only by the individual'.

See also **Mad Bomber**

Mona Lisa

Probably the most valuable object ever stolen, spirited away by Vicenzo Perruggia, a house painter on friendly terms with one of the Louvre's workmen. On 21 August 1911 he found himself alone in a gallery with the painting, which he simply lifted off the wall. Removing the frame, he slipped the wooden canvas under his smock and walked out through a service exit.

Within a day the theft had been spotted and a squad of a hundred police combed the museum in vain. A clairvoyant attributed the robbery to a 'young man with a thick neck' and suspicion fell on a painter called Picasso – a friend of the poet

Apollinaire – whose former secretary was much given to purloining the Louvre's smaller statues (the ears of one of which stood service as a model in *Les Demoiselles d'Avignon*). Apollinaire spent a week in prison, and Picasso followed in St Peter's footsteps, disentangling himself by denying that he had ever set eyes on his old friend.

For Perruggia, all went smoothly for the next two years while he kept the painting under his bed. Then he attempted to sell it for a reported $95,000 to Alfredo Geri, an Italian art dealer, who inspected the merchandise in Perruggia's *pension*. The picture, stored under a beaten-up pair of shoes, a mangled hat and some plastering tools, looked familiar. Geri went to the police.

The French police triumphant

Perruggia was an Italian immigrant with a grudge against the French, who called him a 'macaroni eater' and dosed his wine with pepper. He received a light prison sentence and the Italian *pension* changed its name to the 'Gioconda'.

See also **Anthropometry**, **Valfierno**

Monroe, Marilyn (1926–1962)

According to Chuck Giancana, Marilyn Monroe died from a doctored suppository. This was considered both safe – since it left no telltale needle marks – and certain, as there would be nothing in her stomach for any rescuers to pump out.

This new twist is reported in the 1992 book *Double Cross*, by the brother of Mafia Godfather Sam Giancana. The story goes that Marilyn was dangled as bait by the CIA to set up world leaders for blackmail. Meanwhile producer Joseph Schenck, who had Mafia connections, assiduously promoted her career, and by 1960 Marilyn was romantically involved with President John **Kennedy**. Then, in 1962, she fell for his brother Robert. Marilyn became distraught at the way the brothers passed her back and forth like 'a piece of meat', and by July she was threatening to 'blow the lid off the whole damn thing'.

Marilyn now posed a threat to both the Mob and the CIA – who contacted Giancana to have her eliminated. He scheduled the hit to coincide with Robert Kennedy's visit to California planned for the weekend of 4 August. On the night, 'Needles' Gianola and 'Mugsy' Tortorella were stationed outside Marilyn's Brentwood home on electronic surveillance. They saw Kennedy call round, accompanied by another man; they heard Marilyn become hysterical.

Kennedy instructed his friend, a doctor, to give Marilyn a shot to calm her down. When they left, the killers entered the house, taped Marilyn's mouth and inserted the suppository into her anus. Her unconscious body was replaced on the bed; then the tape was removed and her mouth wiped clean. Marilyn died, with Giancana hoping that Kennedy, a crusading Attorney General, would be implicated as the last man to see her alive.

But over their wiretaps 'Needles' and 'Mugsy' heard the cover-up get underway. Kennedy was alerted to Marilyn's death and mobilised a team of FBI agents, ordering Detective Fred Otash to sweep the place clean. And thus Marilyn's murder was passed off to the world as suicide.

Or so the story runs. Variants have the Mob killing Marilyn as a favour to the Kennedys, as part of their mutual support over Cuba. Incidental backing for the rival theory of suicide comes from FBI Agent William Roemer. He bugged Giancana's headquarters and learned that Marilyn was depressed about the events of the previous weekend at the Cal-Neva casino, where she had allegedly been bedded and humiliated by both Giancana and Frank Sinatra in an orgy. Coming on top of the

Kennedy 'meat syndrome', she must have found the experience upsetting.

The Giancana murder scenario is compatible with many of the known facts, not least the 'purplish discoloration' of Marilyn's colon noted on autopsy. The Los Angeles Chief of Police, William Parker, a friend of Robert Kennedy, had the death labelled as self-inflicted from the start, allocating the case to the suicide investigation squad. After five days, with her studio's active co-operation, Parker closed the file, and all but thirty pages of the 723-page report into Marilyn's death were destroyed.

A cover-up is beyond doubt, but what was being covered is not clear. The problem with Marilyn's death is her inconclusive autopsy. She died of a Nembutal overdose, with 4.5 per cent barbiturates in her blood. But preliminary examination showed her kidneys were clean, strongly suggesting that her stomach was likewise free of drugs – which would exclude her having taken by mouth the drugs she was supposed to have swallowed. At the time, on post-mortem, Dr Thomas Noguchi ordered microscopic analysis of tissue from her small intestine, and requested tests on her liver, kidneys and stomach. But the tests were never performed; Noguchi learned that Marilyn's organs had been accidentally destroyed.

The exact time of Marilyn's death is suspect. Rather than being found dead at 3.30 in the morning, she may have been discovered comatose at 11.30 p.m. Walter Schaefer, owner of the local ambulance service, maintains that the star was still alive when his ambulance men arrived *before* midnight; according to him, she was driven to the hospital and then returned home after death, allowing time for a 'clean-up' before her official discovery. In confirmation, rigor mortis had set in when Sergeant Jack Clemmons arrived at half past three. Marilyn's enigmatic housekeeper, Eunice Murray, now says: 'I don't know why I didn't call the police until 3.30.'

The original suicide theory is hard to sustain. To achieve her blood-level of barbiturates Marilyn needed to gulp down between seventy-five and ninety capsules, a nightmare for someone who simply hated taking pills, particularly without water. There was no glass by her bedside, and the water in the adjoining bathroom was turned off pending plumbing work. In any case Marilyn did not have

enough pills. On the best estimate, she was down to twenty-two Nembutals on the morning of 4 August and had no hidden reserves. A week before, her housekeeper drew a blank searching the house for a secret cache, and in the days preceding her death Marilyn tried to borrow from friends.

Psychologically, many observers thought Marilyn in fine fettle during her last days. Her psychoanalyst, Dr Ralph Greenson, says: 'Suicide is not an option in this case.' Fox's production chief, one of the last to talk to the star, confirms this view: 'We had hired her back at a salary of half a million dollars. And she was ecstatic.' Nor was the body found in a setting which contra-indicated foul play. Marilyn adhered to a strict bedtime routine, always sleeping in a fresh brassiere, with earplugs and eye mask, in a darkened room with the curtains closed. She was discovered naked and unencumbered, with the curtains open and the lights on.

So it looks like murder, whether by injection, suppository or enema. True, Noguchi detected no needle marks on the body, but medical records show that Marilyn had received two jabs since the preceding Thursday. So Noguchi's examination was not infallible and, in any case, punctures made by fine surgical needles can disappear within a few hours. Recently, Noguchi alluded to other findings. 'I did find evidence which indicated violence. There were bruises on her lower back area – a very fresh bruise – and bruises on her arms.'

A key factor concealed from the American public was Marilyn's association with Robert Kennedy. His presence on the day of her death is still officially denied, but the helicopter company which flew Kennedy out of the area has the flight records of the transfer. The day of her death the FBI pulled General Telephone's records of her frequent calls to Kennedy at the Justice Department in Washington; the papers were recovered only five years ago from a homicide detective's garage.

One of Marilyn's many misfortunes was to pose a serious threat to the political stability of the United States. Just like her scatty screen persona, the girl was always in a muddle. 'How can we carry on a conversation about current events if you can't remember the details?' Kennedy once snapped. So she kept track with a diary full of 'Bobby says this' and 'Bobby says that'. One of the things that Bobby said was that the CIA had hired the Mafia to kill Castro – the administration's deepest secret, of itself enough to have Marilyn killed before she started blabbing.

Then there were the tapes. It seems that the Mob were using Marilyn to provide compromising evidence on the Kennedys. The Hollywood detective Fred Otash was allegedly paid indirectly by the Mafia to install eavesdropping equipment at the star's home. Apparently he recorded exotic love scenes with the President, interspersed with discussions of state secrets, together with similar indiscretions by the Attorney General. In addition, the Lawford house was thoroughly bugged by the FBI for nearly a year during the period that the President bedded Marilyn there. The tapes formed J. Edgar **Hoover**'s favourite listening.

England's King Henry II had to demand outright 'Who will rid me of this turbulent priest?' to have Thomas à Becket assassinated. Things are simpler now. 'All the President or Attorney General has to do is *insinuate* displeasure with somebody, and then somebody else picks it up and does it,' said a later Republican Attorney General of Marilyn's death. 'That's the kind of power that really, truly exists.'

So one solution goes like this. Marilyn threatened to expose the President and his brother. On the evening of 4 August 1962, Robert Kennedy made a placatory visit. They quarrelled; she was given a sedative. Kennedy returned to his brother-in-law's house to find Marilyn ranting on the telephone, threatening to call a press conference. Kennedy knew what he'd done, knew what he'd said, and knew of the tapes and the notebooks. So later that evening someone else paid a visit to Marilyn – Hollywood's most famous beauty – and, on behalf of the Attorney General and the President of the United States, killed her.

Her death heralded a remarkable *volte-face* in Kennedy's perspective on Hoover, whose FBI agents helped in the cover-up and in whose hands the incriminating evidence now resided. For years Bobby had derided his weird stance on Communism, and on 7 August W. H. Ferry, vice president of the Fund for the Republic, lambasted Hoover's views on the Reds as 'sententious poppycock'. Now Kennedy leapt to Hoover's defence: 'I hope he will continue to serve the country for many years to come.'

See also **Executive action**

Mooney, Tom (b. 1884)

A striking American miscarriage of justice. Mooney, a San Francisco labour leader, was arrested for the July 1916 bombing of the Preparedness Day parade in which nine bystanders died.

At the trial, the evidence showed that Mooney had been both seen and heard by prosecution witness Frank C. Oxman: seen, wedging a satchel against the wall of a Steuart Street saloon, and heard, remarking to his accomplice: 'We must run away, the cops will be after us.' Moments later, the bomb exploded.

Only part of Mooney's defence was a chance photograph of the parade. Produced in court, the picture showed an unmistakable Mooney in the throng exactly 6,008 feet away from the point of detonation. By his side stood his wife, Rena. In the background was a civic clock, showing the precise time of the explosion. Nonetheless Mooney received a life sentence. When it emerged that prosecution witness Oxman was somewhere else at the time of the bombing, ninety miles away, President Wilson commented: 'The utilities sought to get Mooney... With Oxman discredited, the verdict was discredited.'

But California had archaic perjury laws preventing the review of cases based on false evidence. Although discredited, the 'guilty' verdict was immutable (see **Virtual Reality**), and Mooney spent twenty-two years in prison before his pardon on 7 January 1939.

See also **Wobblies**

Morals, art forgers'

Morally speaking, art forgery is not always clear-cut. According to the British painter Eric Hebborn, a forger is merely 'an artist working in the style of other people'. He claims to have infused the great art collections with more than a thousand fake Old Masters over the past three decades.

Hebborn, an artist, places the blame squarely on dealers. On the one hand, they commission work 'in the style of' Van Blank, and then pass it off as an original for hefty profits; on the other, they are easily fooled, unwittingly making false attributions. Thus the canvas leaves the artist as a lawful item in its own right; it only becomes a forgery when the dealer ascribes it to the wrong artist. But perhaps Hebborn is disingenuous. He would present a carefully balanced portfolio, with an accomplished fake lurking among the originals, and encourage dealers towards misattribution with vague but suggestive pointers of a **provenance**.

Experts tend to follow experts. When a work is passed by one, it joins the club, accepted by all. Perhaps more difficult than passing off a fake as genuine is exposing a fake as a fake. Owners are reluctant to concede that costly Gainsboroughs are modern facsimiles, and even when this is pointed out by the original artist the response is typically, 'Have you got a degree in Art History?'

In this vein, Hebborn's offer to tour the National Gallery 'outing' his work and other forgeries was rejected. Galleries prefer the idea of false confessions, a concept which opening the door on a world of mirrors more commonly associated with the double and triple agents of espionage. The position is complicated by pranksters like Magritte, who not only repudiated certain of his early paintings but also sanctioned 'copies' of his work. Perhaps not surprisingly, Hebborn was an intimate of Anthony Blunt, Keeper of the Queen's Pictures and Soviet spy.

In his 1991 book *Drawn to Trouble*, Hebborn claimed that only some thirty of his thousand fakes had been identified; he did not disclose what the remaining 970 were, nor where they now hang, although they included eighty Augustus Johns, thirty-seven Castigionis, and works by Walter Sickert, Degas, Picasso and Breughel.

Forgers generally specialise in less expensive items, like preparatory sketches, where expert involvement is of diminished probability. Picasso and Chagall are among the usual 'suspects', with a new frontier opening in the Russian avant-garde.

In his youth, Hebborn was expelled for setting fire to his school in retaliation for being accused of playing with matches. Resentment against the Establishment also fuelled the careers of **Van Meegeren** and of Tom Keating, the British forger who claimed a career total of 2,500 fakes. Keating first took umbrage on discovering that works he was paid £5 to copy finished up in West End galleries for £500 and, as a restorer, witnessed a steady procession of paintings returned to their owners substituted by imitations, with the originals retained for resale. Keating's friends suspect deeper grievances. In his cups, he would discourse at tedious length on his naval service as a stoker in the Second World War, when he was treated with disrespect by the officer class.

Keating's unintended move into forgery seemed a dream come true. Anxious for recognition in his own right, he was disconsolately burning paintings on a bonfire when his girlfriend suggested putting them into a local auction. Experts praised Keating's draughtsmanship to the skies, discerning the hand of Samuel Palmer, and his works changed hands for thousands of pounds each. At his 1979 Old Bailey trial Keating took particular delight in denigrating his output. Of his famous ink-wash of *Sepham Barn* – sold for £9,400 as a genuine Samuel Palmer – he said, 'I am ashamed of this piece of work', dismissing the figure of the shepherd as 'un-Palmerish' and the sheep as 'un-sheeplike'. Similarly, his drawing of *Shoreham Barn* (sold for £2,500) was a doodle. 'That must have taken me about half an hour,' he said.

But when he was good, Keating formed a neutral conduit for the talent of his master. Van Meegeren, too, felt in mystical contact with Vermeer and, at this level of empathy, surely a little artistic licence is allowed. As Keating said, 'I'd sit in my little room waiting for it to happen. I had never drawn a sheep from life but then Palmer's sheep would begin to appear on the paper. With Sam's permission I sometimes signed them with his own name, but they were his, not mine. It was his hand that guided the pen.' Quite.

Mortal combat

An infallible method of apportioning guilt. The last instance occurred in England as late as 1817 during the retrial of Abraham Thornton for the murder of Mary Ashford, a local beauty.

Mary's body was dredged up from a pond the morning after a village dance at Tyburn near the small town of Birmingham. Her bonnet, shoes and neatly folded frock reposed on the bank by her bloodstained stockings. Thornton admitted to deflowering Mary *al fresco* that very night – hence the traces of blood, also found in a nearby patch of grass that bore the impress of a human body lying full length. But Thornton was seen three miles from the pond near the time that Mary must have died, and it seemed that some third party had come upon Mary after her lover departed. Thornton may well have been guilty, perhaps throwing Mary into the water unconscious after a rape, but he was acquitted after only six minutes deliberation by the jury.

Local feeling ran high. It was still possible to be tried twice for the same offence, and Mary's brother William mounted an appeal. Arraigned in court, Thornton was asked how he pleaded. 'Not guilty,' he cried, 'and I am ready to defend the same with my body.' Then he flung down a glove in front of a surprised Lord Chief Justice, Lord Ellenborough. Thornton correctly stated that this constituted a valid challenge to single combat, and was freed when his accuser, who was smaller, declined to pick up the gauntlet.

Murder aficionados have developed ingenious theories to explain Mary Ashford's demise, sifting the clues provided by the intricacies of footsteps zigzagging across the fields.

The case exudes the attraction of an open air 'closed room' mystery, one of the most remarkable of which concerned the death of Isidor Fink in New York in March 1929.

Fink ran a laundry from a New York tenement, and inhabited a single room measuring twenty by forty foot at 52 East 133rd Street. His neighbour  Locklan Smith heard a disturbance on the evening of 9 March, and when Patrolman Albert Kattenborg broke into Fink's apartment, he found him dead from two gunshot wounds to the chest, lying in solitude on the floor ten yards from the entrance. Fink's windows were barred and unbroken, the front door of solid construction bolted from inside, as were the windows, and entry was only effected by a small child smashing through the fanlight and wriggling through to release the door.

Cleverly, the dead Isidor Fink was not holding a gun. Nor was a weapon secreted in the apartment.

This ruled out Fink either shooting himself or being shot by anyone else inside his home, and although the police made heavy weather of the conundrum, to state the puzzle in these terms is to solve it. Fink must have been shot by someone *outside* his apartment. To allow the bullets access, the door must then have been open and, as it was found locked from the inside, this necessitated locking by Fink, having been shot. And as his body lay some distance away, and there was no one else in the room, he must have gone there under his own steam, and died.

Mothers

One of the many vexations confronting a murderer is the unendurable stench emitted by the victim as decomposition proceeds. In 1954 the teenage New York killers Theresa Gresh and Billy Meyers adopted a radical solution. They encased their cadaver in a plaster-of-Paris sarcophagus and deposited it in the bath as a short-term holding measure.

In a macabre twist, the mummified body was that of Theresa's mother, whom they had bludgeoned and stabbed to death in the hope of removing her as the obstacle to their matrimonial plans. Billy was a 17-year-old schizophrenic homicidal Marine, considered by Mrs Gresh to be an unsuitable spouse for her immature daughter. He went to the chair; Theresa received a twenty-year sentence.

On the feminist analysis, mothers are such well-established scapegoats that a confession to serious sexual crime lacks weight without a token domineering matriarch.

As one astute psychiatrist pointed out to Kenneth Bianchi, the Hillside Strangler, 'If you add the letter *s* to "mother", you get "smother".' The hypothesis runs that a witch of a mother creates a monster of a son. Witch-hunts are a regular feature of serial killings, and the Boston Strangler profile (see **Insatiable**) snagged on precisely this misconception.

Feminists maintain that the figure of the wicked matriarch is largely confined to the patriarchal fantasies of film and pulp fiction. Apparently the facts can be safely ignored. When the 'Son of **Sam**' pursued his vendetta in obedience to the dictates of his father – '"Go out and kill" commands father Sam' – the psychiatrist most closely associated with the case deduced that the killings were actuated by Berkowitz's relationship with his mother. Some say that it is only a minor transition from blaming Mother to condemning the victim, particularly female victims of sex crimes who 'ask for it'.

This predisposition has not escaped shrewder killers seeking to prove that their transgressions were not their fault or staking a claim as properly accredited **criminals**. Both Bianchi (see **Romances**) and Henry Lee **Lucas**, the 'wannabe' serial killer, claimed to have suffered sexual abuse from their mothers almost as a talisman of authenticity. Similarly, the 'Co-ed killer' Edmund **Kemper** precluded further investigation into his motivation by blaming his mother: 'Six young women dead because of the way she raised her son, and the way her son is raised and the way he grows up', although no one knows her side of the story because he killed her too.

Who can forget Norman Bates in the dead hand of matriarchy in *Psycho*, or James Cagney on 'top of the world, Ma'? But these are mere films. In fact, mobsters doted on their mamas. Chicago gangster Johnny Torrio endowed his mater in Italy with a coastal estate, retaining fifteen servants to tend to her wishes. She rode around in a chauffeur-driven limo. Hymie 'the Polack', whose crucifix dangled from his neck next to an armpit holster, was another attentive son. Capone too idolised Momma. **O'Bannion** installed his in a fine house, paying weekly visits with stacks of new gramophone records. Dutch Schultz, from New York, said it all with his dying breath: 'Mother is the best bet and don't let Satan draw you too fast.'

The tradition continues, as witness the **Krays**, and, in the 1980s, the New York Bonanno still downed tools on Mother's Day.

See also **Godmothers**

Mozart, Wolfgang Amadeus (1756–1791)

Soon after Mozart's death, rumours began to circulate that he had been poisoned by his musical rival, Antonio Salieri. Mozart's widow Constanze laid the theory's cornerstone with an account of her husband's last drive in the Prater in Vienna during the autumn of 1791. 'Mozart began to speak of death and declared he was writing the Requiem for him-

self,' Constanze reported. ' "I feel definitely," he continued, "that I will not last much longer. I am sure I have been poisoned. I cannot rid myself of this idea." ' Mozart imputed his forthcoming death to ingestion of *aqua toffana*, an arsenous preparation.

Mozart's illness was diagnosed as 'military fever' by his doctors. His body was painfully swollen and he could only move with difficulty. He ran a fever, had 'the taste of death on his tongue', and in the final stages suffered spasms of nausea – symptoms consistent both with kidney disease (progressing to kidney failure, oedema and uremic poisoning) and a fatal intake of mercury, which attacks the kidneys.

Salieri, the prime candidate for murderer, makes an unlikely poisoner; as a leading composer of the period, he was an important teacher (Beethoven was a pupil), an admirer of Mozart's work and one of the few to attend his funeral. He tutored Mozart's son and engineered his first appointment. Salieri exerted a powerful influence over the distribution of court patronage through his position with the emperor, Joseph II, but merely to possess power to harm in one way is no proof of its exercise in another.

Despite the gossip, Salieri made no deathbed confession, other than inspiring a sickroom visitor to remark, 'Morally speaking Salieri had no doubt by his intrigues poisoned many an hour of Mozart's existence', and the famous discovery of 1953, billed as firm historical evidence by the Soviet musicologist Igor Boelza, consisted of the research of a dead colleague, which Boelza declined to reveal. As with **Jack the Ripper**, this evidential vacuum attracted the spectre of the Freemasons. They killed Mozart. He failed to follow the Masonic line with sufficient

rigour in *The Magic Flute* or, in the alternative, divulged too many of their secrets, and was sentenced to death, a conjecture corroborated by the unsurprising deaths of his librettists Schikaneder and Giesecke decades later.

The truth is that Mozart did succumb to poison. At his death he was undergoing treatment for a combination of depression and acute military fever, for which the contemporary remedy was mercury and antimony. Mercury precipitates kidney failure, and in the Vienna of the eighteenth century, antimony was frequently contaminated with arsenic, which kills. Meanwhile the antimony would cause military fever as well as pneumonia and death. Mozart suffered from all three.

With almost every avenue of survival covered, it was asking too much of Mozart to survive his leeches' attentions for more than the fifteen days of his terminal illness. Or so said Dr Ian James in October 1991, addressing the British Association for Performing Arts Medicine.

Münchausen syndrome by proxy

An enhanced version of the Münchausen syndrome, when patients persistently seek unnecessary medical attention for themselves. Such individuals need to feel ill. The Münchausen by proxy syndrome happens when they need someone else to feel ill, if necessary by force.

The condition is named after the fictional Baron Münchausen, addicted to fantastical storytelling. The syndrome itself was first noted in 1951, and Professor Meadows of Leeds encountered the first 'proxy' case in 1977. Habitually, the disorder involves grandmothers suffocating their grandchildren, mothers **poisoning** their offspring, or spouses devoted to nursing their partners with noxious 'medicine'.

In principle, the affliction stops short of murder, but the exact moment is hard to judge. A recent American survey of 117 young victims found ten fatalities, another ten seriously affected in the long term, and ten more unexplained deaths among siblings.

The perpetrator is typically a woman, superficially eager to please but with low self-esteem, often with a history of sexual abuse and marital difficulties. The condition languished in the footnotes of medical literature until the case of Nurse Beverley Allitt, convicted on 17 May 1993 of four child murders as Britain's worst female serial killer of the century.

Allitt's symptoms dated from childhood when, as an attention seeker, she would arrive at school covered in plasters and bandages. 'We could not tell if she was hurt or not,' recalled a fellow pupil. As a nurse, Allitt pestered staff with an endless string of minor ailments, aches and sprains of obscure origin,

some self-inflicted, attending the casualty department of Grantham and Kesteven Hospital twenty-four times. But the damage was all in her head. During 1990 Allitt took ninety-four days off work, and she progressed to increasingly anti-social behaviour, unattributed at the time, starting fires under her hostel grill and leaving excrement on display. Then, in the spring of 1991, Allitt seemed to stabilise. Her visits to Casualty ceased.

In fact, she had deteriorated. During this fifty-nine day 'proxy' phase, Allitt switched from molesting herself to attacking babies on Ward Four, accounting for twenty-one unexpected collapses and four fatalities. Afterwards, staying with a friend, Allitt receded into a hinterland where she stole money, embedded a knife in her pillow, poured bleach over the carpets and fed noxious pills to the family pet.

Just as a patient asking why he has muscular pain may be told he has rheumatism, which means no more than muscular pain of unknown origin, the words 'Münchausen Syndrome' designate neither the cause of the condition nor the way to make it better.

See also **Weber**

Murder bag

The invention of the great pathologist Sir Bernard **Spilsbury**. Arriving at the bungalow site of the Mahon murder in 1924, Sir Bernard was appalled to see Superintendent Percy Savage rummaging through the victim's remains.

As Savage later recalled, 'Spilsbury...expressed astonishment that I had handled putrid flesh with my bare hands, and he pointed out that I ran a grave risk of septic poisoning. He said that no medical man outside a lunatic asylum would dream of such a thing, and that I ought to at least wear rubber gloves. I told him we were not provided with rubber gloves... We lacked many other things essential to the efficient performance of our duties. If we wanted to preserve human hair on clothing, or soil or dust on boots, we picked it up with our fingers and put it in a piece if paper. We had no tapes to measure distances, no compass to determine direction, no apparatus to take fingerprints, no first-aid outfit, no instrument to find the depth of water, no magnifying glass. In fact we had no appliances available for immediate use on the scene of the crime.'

In conjunction with Sir Bernard, Savage drew up a list of Holmesian impedimenta for inclusion in a 'Murder Bag', which thereafter accompanied chief inspectors on their callouts.

The Mahon trial was distinguished by particularly loathsome medical evidence. In court, Spilsbury ran through a seemingly endless litany of the body parts he had pieced back into a recognisable corpse. In addition to the two-gallon saucepan half-full of a reddish fluid, with a layer of thick grease at the top and a piece of boiled flesh at the bottom, and a hat-box crammed with thirty-seven chunks of flesh, Spilsbury described a suitcase containing four large portions which, carefully assembled, formed practically the whole trunk of a woman. Questioned about the large biscuit tin, Spilsbury responded: 'I found the organs of the chest and of the abdomen in nine separate pieces. Shall I detail all the pieces separately? One long piece was a portion of the large intestine eight inches long.'

'And the second?' enquired counsel. Spilsbury reported that when he squeezed the nipple of the right breast, milky fluid escaped. The victim, Emily Beilby Kaye, had been pregnant.

Patrick Mahon was a dishonest Irishman from Liverpool with good looks and charm. He embezzled from his employers and cheated on his wife, and in 1916 earned a five-year sentence when identified by the charlady of Sunningdale's National Provincial Bank after a break-in. First Mahon knocked her out with a hammer. Then, when she revived, he took her in his arms and romanced her, and in 1924 Mahon won the heart of Miss Kaye. But she discovered his past while cleaning out a drawer lined with the newspaper reporting his trial. When Mahon made her pregnant, she demanded a 'love experiment', spending time together at a bungalow on a bleak stretch of coast near Eastbourne. In anticipation of bliss, Miss Kaye purchased an engagement ring, told her friends she was leaving the country and suggested to Mahon that they sail for South Africa.

Mahon bought a tenon saw and chef's knife before catching a train to Eastbourne on 12 April. It rained, and he shared his **umbrella** with an attractive young woman, Ethel Duncan, making a date for the following Wednesday. On the Tuesday, Mahon killed Miss Kaye, most probably with a vio-

lent blow to the head, and set about her dismemberment. Her head he placed on a blazing fire in the kitchen and, as he did so, a thunderstorm burst and the dead eyes flickered open. Mahon ran screaming onto the beach, but by the next day he had regained sufficient composure to escort Miss Duncan to dinner. The following weekend they shared the bed formerly occupied by the late Miss Kaye, next to the room where her corpse lay in a travelling trunk. When Miss Duncan expressed interest in the locked room, Mahon sent himself a telegram and decamped for London, taking his Gladstone bag so he could toss bones out of the train windows. He visited his wife in Richmond, attended the Plumpton races, and returned to Waterloo's Left Luggage to collect his portmanteau. There he was arrested.

His wife, suspicious of Mahon's erratic movements, had handed his luggage ticket to an ex-railway policeman, who found a knife wrapped in a large quantity of bloodstained cloth. The police were waiting for Mahon at Waterloo, and he was hanged on 9 September 1924 for premeditated murder. The prosecution produced receipts from a hardware store in refutation of his tale that the tenon saw and chef's knife were bought after the killing, and the jury rejected his story of an accidental fall during a scuffle, their deliberations assisted by the absence, among all the body, of the head (suggesting concealment of a vicious injury) and the womb, suggesting attempted concealment of Miss Kaye's pregnancy.

Murder Inc.

Not just a film. Established in New York by Louis 'Lepke' Buchalter in the early 1930s, Murder Inc. provided a nationwide killing service for anyone willing to meet their standard fees of around $500. The customer-base consisted of gangland figures taking out rivals, informers or obstinate businessmen behind with their protection. Thus it was strictly for 'business reasons'.

The **hitmen** often remained in ignorance of the target's identity until afterwards, when they read it in the papers. Body disposal, available for an additional fee, was not included in the basic charge.

Murder Inc.'s exposure came hard on the heels of the 1940 killing of 'Red' Alpert in New York, when informer Harry Rudolph ratted on the hit-man, 'Kid Twist' Reles, one of the permanent pay-roll. In the wake of the Kid's confessions it emerged that Murder Inc. had evolved as the enforcement arm of the Mafia Commission, the regulatory body of the leading Mob families. The Commission acted as a loose confederation minimising inter-gang dis-putes and 'unnecessary' killings. Their decisions had to be respected – hence the need for experts to conduct sanctioned eliminations.

Under Lepke's management the Brooklyn killers acquired a reputation for proficiency, becoming the Mob's semi-official execution squad on $12,000 annual retainers. Work came flowing in, often as fairly casual com-missions. According to Reles in 1940: 'Lep gave us eleven con-tracts for witnesses when he was on the lam. We knocked off seven before Dewey put him on trial last year.' 'Muddy' Kasoff's offhand instructions were: 'This bum is cutting in on my play with the stuff. You guys take him.'

Pittsburgh Phil in jail

Reles was unperturbed by his arrest for Red Alpert's murder; it was routine, his forty-fourth spell behind bars. The prosecution case looked weak, lacking corroboration, and no one suspected his string of previous killings, which included two black men shot in broad daylight on the streets; one died for failing to wipe a smudge from Reles's front fender after a car-wash, and the other was dilatory in fetching Reles's vehicle from a parking lot. So, when his wife walked into Brooklyn police headquarters on 22 March 1940 announcing, 'My husband wants an interview with the Law', it came as a surprise. But the new Assistant District Attorney, Burton Turkus, had a backlog of 200 unsolved murders on his desk and was eager for help. 'I can make you the biggest man in the coun-try,' Reles told Turkus. 'But I got to make a deal.'

By four in the morning he had his bargain, and Reles started his narrative with the words, 'I can tell you all about fifty guys that got hit; I was on the inside.' He kept talking for twelve days, filling twenty-five shorthand notebooks. The stenographers worked in relays. For the first time the astonished authorities learned of the existence and the work-ings of Organised Crime – a government within a government.

According to Reles, Murder Inc.'s total body-count ran into the hundreds; about a thousand is a fair estimate. One operative, Pittsburgh Phil, accounted for more than thirty men in more than a dozen cities. Reles preferred to work with an ice-pick; he admitted eighteen Murder Inc. killings. An eventual victim was his former client Muddy Kasoff, one of many seized in a spate of inter-mob-ster kidnappings, mostly for ransom, sometimes, like Kasoff, for information.

When Kasoff dried up, Reles blew off his head with a shotgun. As Reles explained to the court, recalling his part-ner's reaction: 'It handed Phil a laugh. We left the bum under a billboard that says "Drive Safely". Lucky was sat-isfied plenty.' Most pho-tographs of Reles show him laughing.

'Bum' was the hitmen's standard terminology and amounted to a moral dis-claimer; there was little wrong with shooting one of them. When Turkus probed deeper into Reles's attitude, he gathered that after the first few, 'you get used to it'.

Reles was given round-the-clock police protection on the seventh floor of a Coney Island hotel. But the Brooklyn District Attorney sold his whereabouts to Mafia boss Anastasia, and on 11 November 1941 Reles was levered out of a window by his police guard, primed with a $100,000 bribe, giving birth to the mobster adage that 'canaries can sing, but they cannot fly'. Lepke, his boss, survived another couple of years before perishing, albeit indirectly, at the hands of associates, when Lucky Luciano gave orders, via Costello and Meyer Lansky, for him to surrender personally to **Hoover** as a sop to public opinion. The plan was to relieve police 'heat' on Mob operations. In return, Lepke was promised lenient treatment. But he was condemned to die in the electric chair on 15 September 1943.

Murder Inc.'s finest hour came with the destruc-tion of the Dutch Schultz gang on 23 October

1935. Dutch needed killing. A natural hothead, he determined to 'take out' the unusually aggressive New York Special Prosecutor, Thomas E. Dewey. 'Dewey's gotta go,' Schultz used to say. 'He has gotta be hit in the head.' Gangland was aghast at the prospect of the resultant police crackdown, and Charles 'the Bug' Workman accepted the commission. He walked into the Palace Chophouse, Newark, with two automatics blazing, shooting dead three of Schultz's henchman after first mortally wounding Dutch himself, mistaking him for a bodyguard washing his hands in the men's room.

Workman waived his fee for this prestigious assignment and, widely recognised, served twenty-three years. Another walk-on player for Murder Inc. was Oscar 'the Evaporator', renowned for his legendary prowess at atomising hot vehicles so that no trace of evidence survived. For years the Mob paid him $50 per car, leaving Oscar to work the vehicles over with blow-torch and acid until not a scrap of fender or bolt remained. Oscar's prowess was truly legendary; what he actually did was sell the cars on, intact, at $5 each. Oscar liked poetry; the place to find him was reading in the park, lucky to be alive.

Murderee

Word invented by the writer F. Tennyson Jesse to designate those whose occupation or character makes them particularly subject to lethal force – for instance, prostitutes.

An obliging murderee tumbles into the killer's lap. Thus call-girl Kimberly Diane Martin was simply ordered up, like a pizza, from her escort agency by the Hillside Stranglers. They specified hair and underwear colour, blonde and black respectively.

A broader version of the murderee is the catch-all concept of the innate 'victim', to be contrasted with an 'unvictim'. Janice Hooker, wife of Cameron the **Slave**maker, said of their house-girl: 'I chose not to be a victim. I hope Colleen makes that choice. Not just to walk out, but to make a total change, to become an unvictim, to take charge.'

It is not only feminists who find the idea of 'choosing' not to undergo random sexual assault hard to stomach. But the concept contains a grain of truth. Serial killers, sex killers and sex offenders often select their victims, stalking them perhaps for

days. Sometimes a killer nurtures a preference for a certain type whose apparent vulnerability triggers his fantasies (see **Trolling**).

In Britain the term 'murderee' was first popularised by Martin Amis in his novel *London Fields* (see **Rillington Place**). The occupational catchment area has been extended to include **Planning Officers**.

Musicals

By most reckonings, **Jack the Ripper** constitutes an unlikely subject for a musical. The show made its debut on 17 September 1974 at London's Ambassadors Theatre in a production by comedian Brian Rix. It was not a long run, but the stage directions make good reading. Excerpts include: 'He draws a knife across her throat... At this point the cabinet door is flung open and from the cabinet slumps the dead and bloody body of Polly... The Figure cuts Annie's throat... The Ripper creeps up and cuts Lizzie's throat. She is carried off to the 'Death March'.' The entertainment featured a chorus of massed whores.

The life of Robert Maxwell, the international financial fraudster, is perhaps a more catchy subject. Evan Steadman, who sold his company to Maxwell for £16 million, is backing a stage version of his patron's life. As Steadman says, 'Not to spend two hours in the company of Robert Maxwell is to deny the fruits of one of life's unrepeatable experiences. Admittedly the fruit goes bad, squashy and then makes you sick. Maxwell was impossible, ruthless, remorseless, but always with a smile, though it wasn't funny for the buggers he didn't buy out for £16 million.'

The broad canvas of opera may be a better vehicle for *The Manson Family*. In the 1992 words of the opera's composer, John Moran from Nebraska: 'The violence of the case doesn't interest me at all. What does interest me is the nature of Manson's personality... In the way of a revivalist preacher, it's not what he says but the way he says it that's so fascinating.' Manson's rhythmical, sing-song delivery is echoed in the music, now available on CD, and his earlier musical career included an abortive joint venture with the Beach Boys, a pop group. One evening in the spring of 1968 their drummer, Dennis Wilson, returned home to find a kneeling

Manson inviting him into his own Sunset Boulevard property. Inside, the **Family** were in residence as irremovable, uninvited guests, and their visit cost Wilson about $100,000 in stolen clothes, unreturned loans and a wrecked Ferrari.

Wilson later said: 'Except for the expense, I got on very well with Charlie and the girls.' At any one time, his living room might contain twenty-five nubile 'chicks', all of them deeply into caressing. For food, the Family took Wilson's Rolls Royce on garbage runs to the San Fernando supermarkets, loading the rear seat with top-grade discarded pro-

duce. For music, Manson collaborated with Wilson, writing the song 'Cease to exist'. But the Beach Boys missed the point. First they changed the words to 'Cease to resist' and then retitled his offering as 'Never Learn not to Love'.

The New Orleans bandleader and part-time pimp, Jelly Roll Morton, was another artistic beneficiary of crime. Jelly Roll found the Chicago whore-business too tightly controlled for his freelancing, and while in town he was – for the first time in years – compelled to devote himself to music.

See also **Sweeney Todd**

N

Names

No less than anywhere else, Chicago hoodlums had splendid names. Among the more outlandish were: Sam Samoots Amatuna, Bugs Moran, Vincent the Schemer Drucci, Nails Morton, Three-gun Louis Alterie, Mike de Pike Heitler, Tony Mops Volpe, Roger the Terrible Tuohy, Dominic Cinderella, Orchell DeGrazio, Buttons Capone, Mitters Folley, Toots Mondi, Potatoes Kaufman, Slippery Frank Rio, Diamond Joe Esposito, Bummy Goldstein, Jack Greasy Thumb Guzik, Machine-gun Jack McGurn, Eddie the Eagle Baldelli, Orrazzio the Scourge Tropea, and Hop Toad Guinta, so named for his addiction to dancing. John Dingbat O'Berta was a fox-faced Italian with an assumed Irish apostrophe.

Nearly all met violent ends. Cinderella went not to the ball but as one, trussed into a sphere with rope, dropped into a sack and slung in a ditch. He died with his slippers on. Vincent the Schemer Drucci came to grief in an equally mortifying way for a gangster: outraged at being arrested, he got himself shot by a policeman.

The saddest fate was reserved for Roger The Terrible Tuohy. He was not terrible at all. An honest and intelligent young man, he invested his profits from oil leases in a trucking business, and during the early 1920s, like everyone else, moved into bootlegging. His liquor was of high quality, his kegs did not leak, and he kept the local police and politicians in Des Plaines, Illinois, happy with a Special Brew of bottled beer.

Capone decided to take Tuohy over. But the great man's emissaries returned from their visits with awesome tales about the Tuohy gang, an impression Tuohy carefully fostered by stacking his office with borrowed pistols and machine guns, some loaned by the police, while friends trooped through his rooms talking like plug-uglies. The local garage attendant was primed to ring so that Tuohy could sound fierce when he took the call.

In 1933 **Hoover** denounced Tuohy as one of 'the most vicious and dangerous criminals in the history of American crime', and his capture was hailed as 'a credit to the entire Bureau'. But the FBI were not involved: Tuohy was spotted by an unarmed policeman out on a fishing trip. Nor was Tuohy. He had been framed – perhaps by Capone – for the kidnapping of Chicago businessman John Factor, and he served twenty-six years of his ninety-nine year sentence before being cleared in 1959. Less than four weeks later he was dead, gunned down in the Chicago streets.

Machine Gun Jack McGurn and Louise Rolfe

Machine Gun Jack McGurn (real name Jack De Mora) was another near-survivor. After his father's death in 1923 at the hands of the Genna gang, he worked as a hired gun for Capone, concentrating his fire on the Gennas, and he was one of the St Valentine's Day Massacre gunmen. Police charges against McGurn were dropped, but he was indicted for perjury. When he realised that the only witness against him was a girl called Louise Rolfe, he knew what to do. He married her. Then McGurn faded from sight. But seven years to the day after the Valentine's day shooting, he was shot in Chicago's Avenue Recreation Club, still wearing his spats.

Three-gun Louis Alterie survived. A former cowboy, he found Chicago too hot and went back West.

Napoleons

Even before his death on 4 May 1821, Napoleon knew he had been murdered. After months of inexplicable physical degeneration, the Emperor wrote: 'I am dying before my time, murdered by the English oligarchy and its hired assassin.' But historians considered cancer, or any one of a dozen other infections, a more likely explanation.

Then in the 1950s the publication of the St Helena diaries of Napoleon's chief valet, Louis Marchand, gave a detailed description of the day-to-day course of the Emperor's last illness. In 1955, Swedish dentist Sten Forshufvud, who was also a toxicologist, realised that Napoleon's decline exhibited every known characteristic of **arsenic** poisoning: the loss of hair, the swollen feet, the failing legs, the icy chills, the obesity, the alternating bouts of somnolence and insomnia, the enlarged liver found on autopsy and the well-preserved state of the body exhumed in 1840.

Forshufvud's hypothesis could only be verified by analysis of Napoleon's hair. But five grams were needed – about 5,000 strands. Then in November 1959 the journal *Analytical Chemistry* reported a new technique whereby nuclear bombardment of a single hair produced accurate results. The following year, Forshufvud tracked down a lock of the Emperor's hair shaved from his head the day he died; tests conducted in Scotland revealed an arsenic content of 10.38 micrograms per gram – thirteen times the norm. Sectional studies of a 13-centimetre strand (representing about a year's growth) showed that the poison was regularly administered over an extended period, with peaks

and troughs ranging from a low of 2.8 micrograms to a high of 51.2. This finding excluded constant exposure to a background source and effectively proved that Napoleon was poisoned.

French historians did their best to disparage and obstruct Forshufvud's work. The principle of a meddlesome Swedish dentist solving major French mysteries was bad enough. The practice was worse. Forshufvud's discovery meant that history's most famous Frenchman had been assassinated by...a Frenchman. Napoleon's British captors could have contaminated his entire St Helena household, but only a member of his immediate entourage was in a position to poison the Emperor alone.

The motive seems clear. After Napoleon's defeat at Waterloo, the Bourbons were reinstated as rulers of France. Napoleon had swept the dynasty away without a single shot in 1815 and, as long as he survived on St Helena, he might do so again.

Among the exiled Emperor's attendants was the improbable figure of Charles Montholon, a playboy aristocrat recently let off the hook by the Bourbons on a serious charge of embezzlement. Oddly, Montholon rallied to the Emperor's banner *after* Waterloo, and he stayed on with the Emperor in St Helena when even the most loyal of associates departed for France. Nor did Montholon object to Napoleon using his attractive wife Albine as a mistress.

Montholon was master of Napoleon's cellar, and Napoleon always drank from his own private barrel of Vin de Constance. It would have been a minute's work to poison the cask itself before the vintage was bottled.

It looks as though Montholon acted under orders as an assassin, and careful study of the Marchand diaries shows him adhering to the classical routine of the arsenic poisoner. First he dosed his victim repeatedly. Then in 1821 he stopped the arsenic, and induced the Emperor's physicians to prescribe a combination of otherwise innocuous drugs which would finish the patient without leaving arsenic residues for the autopsy. Thus, on 21 March 1821, Montholon ensured that Napoleon received a dose of tartar emetic, corroding the mucous lining of the stomach and destroying its capacity to vomit up further toxins. On 29 March, Montholon set up the daily tonic of 'orgeat', a drink of bitter almonds. Harmless of itself, the hydrocyanic acid in the

NARCOTICS, SMUGGLING

orgeat combines with the inert mercury in calomel – another popular remedy – to produce lethal mercurous cyanide. On 3 May, Montholon persuaded the doctors to administer a huge dose of calomel. By the following evening the Emperor was dead and, in France, the cause of his death is still unknown.

Another murdered Napoleon, perhaps more familiar to True Crime enthusiasts, was Serge Rubinstein, the Napoleon of Fifth Avenue, discovered strangled in his five-storey home by his butler on the morning of 27 January 1955.

Rubinstein, a short individual, enjoyed dressing up as the Emperor for costume balls. He made his millions through stock market manipulation and insider trading, driving companies into liquidation, defrauding stockholders, engineering currency fluctuations, and operating through aliases and nominees with such panache that on the eve of his 1941 marriage he was invited to dine at the Roosevelt White House.

Rubinstein liked women, and women liked him. He attended the 1955 New Year's Eve White Russian Ball with a bevy of seven lovelies in tow, juggled perhaps half a dozen lovers – actresses, singers and models – at a time, and handed out the keys of his Fifth Avenue Mansion to his current favourites.

Rubinstein was found trussed up on his bedroom floor in a silk dressing gown, and the police soon had a list of suspects. His loose-leaf notebooks provided the names of some 2,000 associates, lovers, pimps, politicians, business partners, creditors and informers, all of whom might have wanted him dead and any of whom could have secured access. After a sporting try, the police abandoned the case.

Another great admirer of Napoleon was Henry Fauntleroy (1785–1824), probably the first modern financial fraudster. Over the course of some nine years Fauntleroy embezzled £500,000 from the London bank, Marsh Sibbald and Company, in which he was a partner. Of diminutive stature, Fauntleroy had the drawing room of his mistress's Brighton villa decorated as a reproduction of the Emperor's travelling tent and, on his eventual arrest inquired of the police officer, named Plank, 'Good God! Cannot this business be settled?'

But it could not, and Fauntleroy was sentenced to death for forgery, in part convicted on the evidence of Robert Browning's father, who worked for the Bank of England (see also **Wind in the Willows**). The tremendous public outcry on his behalf achieved nothing; even the entreaties of the language teacher Edmund Angelini to be executed in his stead fell on deaf ears. The financier met his end with dignity on 30 November 1824, but rose again – at least in legend – to start a new life abroad as a nineteenth-century Lord **Lucan**, saved not by a silver spoon in the mouth but by the silver pipe that popular myth adroitly inserted into his windpipe.

Apart from Napoleon himself, and Mussolini and Goebbels, the list of unusually short delinquents includes **Manson**, Issei **Sagawa** and **Bonnie** Parker.

Narcotics, smuggling

In January 1992, British Customs and Excise exhibited a captured false leg, former property of a smuggler hoping to walk 1.5 kilos of cocaine through Heathrow airport (see **Thiefrow**). Other containers include the stomach, spectacle frames, television cathode tubes, shoe heels, children's books, nuns' habits, fish cakes, artificial hair braids, factory-sealed liquor bottles, impregnated suitcases, antique chair-legs, hollowed-out jacket buttons, salsa records split down the centre (filled and re-bonded) and a St Bernard dog. A single dummy aerosol can hold several million dollars of heroin at street prices.

In April 1992 the *Independent* newspaper referred to a deranged woman in Holloway, imprisoned for smuggling drugs in the body of a dead baby. Surgical implants are another innovation, with one Puerto Rican arrested with slabs of cocaine introduced into his thighs. He was stopped because of his waddling gait.

A recent stratagem of almost fiendish cunning has clean merchandise shipped in contaminated packaging. When the goods are extracted from their containers for scrutiny, the drugs are laid to one side; and, the examination over, they are replaced for onwards shipment. One version has the heroin stuffed into long, specially made straws inserted between the serrated walls of cardboard boxes; a large package can carry perhaps two kilos. The first Customs 'bust' was at Rotterdam when a crate accidentally dropped during handling. A variant secretes the contraband in the hollowed-out chocks of wooden pallets.

The latest high-technology ploy is infusion of fibre glass and plastic products with cocaine. The only recorded seizure was a batch of cocaine dog kennels imported from Colombia, surely the perfect mainspring for the plot of a 'mistaken identity' thriller. The three kennels were impounded on arrival in Los Angeles in October 1992 and, when ground to powder, yielded seventeen kilos of cocaine with a street value of $1.5 million.

More antiquated ruses include strips sewn into the bra, and vaginal caches; female crack vendors now employ an updated version with the 'rocks' first popped into a little plastic egg of the type found in Kinder chocolates.

With domestic vehicles, a favourite hiding place was a petrol tank rewelded to take drugs instead of fuel. This reduced range. In the era of the long overland haul from Spain to **Sweden**, cannabis smugglers made the journey with a one-gallon petrol capacity, allowing twenty-five mile runs between fuel stops. Drug smugglers with camper vans prepared for their trip through Customs by a three-day in-vehicle stint of cooking onions.

Some 80 per cent of Europe's heroin now comes in through the Balkan route. For many years, the repressive regimes of Iran, Turkey and Eastern Europe, with their strict controls on through-traffic, kept the influx of drugs from Pakistan and Afghanistan in check. But the road to Istanbul is now clogged with tourists and lorries, and it can take a day to search a single vehicle; narcotics worth millions (or birds worth thousands) can be concealed in a compartment measured in cubic inches.

The illegal trade in rare birds, now attracting serious smugglers, has obvious financial parallels with the exponential mark-up on drugs: an African Grey plucked out of the jungle for almost nothing fetches £500 in the UK and £7,000 in Australia. The contraband

is stuffed into tiny cardboard boxes or specially designed cavities in a dashboard; fatalities in transit are high. For the traffickers the penalties are trivial, a fine of £250 or maybe £400; for the birds, seventy-seven of the world's 300 species of parrots are facing extinction.

Lucky Luciano's horticultural contribution was the invention of wax oranges, injected with 100 grams of heroin, for shipment from Sicily to the United States.

See also **Condoms, Magic Eraser, Pizza Connection, Swallowers**

Negative blocking

A concept invented by the American penologist Dan McDougald. His views owed much to Jouvet's 1950s Harvard experiments on a cat wired for sound. When confronted by a jar of appetising white mice, both the cat and the oscilloscope (connected to its ear) ignored a sharp click. The machine itself no longer detected the sound. That is, the cat was so distracted by its prey that it somehow prevented the signal from reaching the eardrum.

As with cats, reasoned McDougald, so with criminals. He argued that 'negative blocking' ensured that a villain's fixation on Looking After Number One made him blind and deaf to the claims of love, honesty and fellow-feeling. Dyed-in-the-wool criminals would not know what these words meant. They were linguistically challenged, and the way to defeat their blocking mechanism was by inculcating the definitions of these key concepts, first persuading hard-core psychopaths to expose their defective preconceptions during conversation, and then subjecting them to a course of remedial tuition. When convicts grasped the basic vocabulary of ordinary life – that is, what the words really meant – they would be reformed. McDougald named his method 'Emotional Maturity Instruction'.

In 1967, McDougald decided to pit his theory against the toughest nuts in Georgia's maximum security prison near Reidesville. Shortly afterwards a startled Dr C. D. Warren, medical director to the penitentiary, reported: 'You would not believe the results. In two weeks with the 22-man group, the constructive changes were impressive... In eight weeks, they had successfully rehabilitated 63 per cent of men under instruction.'

The important thing with prisoners is to make *some* attempt at re-education; anything is better than the standard policy of locking men up in cells and leaving them there. Today, Britain has only one jail – Grendon in Buckinghamshire – where sex-offenders are treated as opposed to being merely confined. The **prison** houses about 190 inmates from a national pool of 3,000 offenders.

Traditionally, sexual criminals are despised by everyone else, but at Grendon the men are marshalled into small groups where, during encounter sessions, their problems are brought nearer home. The men find that they despise each other, and, subsequently, themselves. Nationally, 42 per cent of prisoners re-offend. The figure for Grendon inmates after a year and a half of therapy is 18 per cent.

Neilson, Donald (1936–)

On 6 March 1975 the search for kidnap victim Lesley Whittle drew to its close as Detective Constable Phil Maskery clambered into the Glory Hole, a shoulder-high octagonal structure protecting the entrance to the Bath Pool drainage system in Britain's Midlands.

Maskery climbed down the rungs of the dark concrete shaft, and forty feet into his descent he reached the culvert, a five feet high sewer pipe. His torch picked out a Dymo lettering machine discarded among the debris and grime. The kidnapper had laid his trail of messages with trigger-gun strips, but there was no sign of his teenage captive, and Maskery returned to the surface, tramping over to the second entrance to the underground complex. This time he found nothing.

The third and deepest shaft started at the top of a nearby hill. But a gas gauge showed – incorrectly – that dangerous levels of methane were present, and the following morning Maskery made his descent with breathing apparatus. He reached the first metal inspection platform twenty-two feet down, and ducked through the grille to the next section of steel ladder. On the second platform twenty-three feet below, he peered into a narrow culvert at knee height and saw a tape recorder – presumably used to dictate the ransom demand. Then he lowered himself to the final level in the pitch dark.

It was soft underfoot. Maskery was standing on a foam mattress. His flashlight picked out a dressing gown dangling over the edge of the platform from an iron stanchion. A taut steel cable ran from the base of the ladder over the metal lip and, swinging

below, with her toes seven inches above the tunnel's floor, was Lesley Whittle, naked, hanging by the neck. She had died not of strangulation but vagal inhibition, that is, fright.

Lesley spent the last days of her life in this concrete-and-iron dungeon, and had perished after falling off the platform. Divers later found a sticking-plaster blindfold, a gag, her blue slippers and her zipped-up sleeping bag, which had perhaps slithered from her body as she swung.

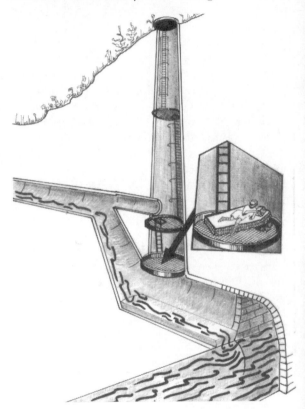

Lesley Whittle's last resting place

Lesley's death may have been an accident, as the kidnapper Donald Neilson claimed with disconcerting vagueness ('As I stood on the platform she went over the side and was suspended by the wire'), but it is unlikely the jury were in any mood to care, and he was jailed for life on 21 July 1976. To add to the family's torment, all attempts to ransom Lesley's life misfired. The first secret rendezvous, with £50,000 packed into a suitcase, was scheduled for the day of the kidnap, but the 'drop' aborted after an alert freelance journalist splashed the story over the news. The second demand miscarried when the kidnapper was interrupted while laying his trail. Gerald Smith, a British Rail overseer at the local freight depot, accosted a stranger skulking round his yard. The prowler shot him six times, and then pulled the trigger again with the pistol to Smith's head. But the magazine was empty.

The bullets extracted from Smith (who died a year later) proved a perfect ballistic match with ammunition used in a series of eighteen small-time robberies, in which three postmasters died. The raider, dubbed the 'Black Panther' for his habitual garb of a black hood with a slit for the eyes, was equated with the Whittle kidnapper a week later, on 23 April, after the discovery of his Morris saloon parked 250 yards from the scene of Smith's shooting. Inside was paraphernalia from the kidnapping – ropes, a mattress, plastic sheeting and four Dymo tape messages with ransom instructions.

By then, Ronald Whittle had tried to hand over the money for the last time. On 16 February a recorded message directed him to the Kidsgrove Post Office telephone box where it took an hour to find his next clue, a Dymo strip behind the backboard. This ordered him to Bathpool Park: 'Go to the wall and flash lights look for torch run to torch further instructions on torch then go home and await further instructions.' Ronald Whittle came so close, and yet so far. In the dark he drove through the grounds, with its football pitches, artificial ski slope and a dammed-up lake called the Bath Pool, from which the overflow was drained by an underground culvert accessed by three vertical concrete shafts. Unable to find the right wall or the torch, that night he stood alone in the park, above his entombed sister, shouting 'This is Ron Whittle. Is anybody there?'

Three weeks later, a schoolboy handed in a strip of Dymo tape found under some twigs two days after the kidnapping. It read, 'Drop suitcase into hole.' Next day some children produced the torch from which this message had worked loose. They had discovered it perched between the iron railings surrounding the first shaft of the Bath Pool drainage system. This was 'The Glory Hole' where Phil Maskery started his search on 6 March.

After his chance arrest five months later, Neilson began his interrogation in baby-talk. 'I no the shoot anybody,' he mouthed in a foreign accent. 'I would shoot dog but no policeman. I no Black Panther.

When Black Panther work, he shoot to kill.' By then he was nearing forty. Born Donald Nappey, at school he was ragged and scruffy, known as 'Dirty Nappy', and in 1965 he changed his name to avoid the same fate for his daughter. After his mother's death when he was ten, Neilson became the household drudge, and grew into a shy, introverted youth. His happiest days came during Army National Service, serving in Kenya against the Mau Mau and in Cyprus against EOKA terrorists.

Neilson married his first girlfriend, and cajoled her into indulging his obsession with guerrilla warfare. Photographs recovered from his home showed the family at play, kitted out in combat fatigues, pitching dummy grenades at one another or lying 'wounded' in wrecked jeeps, and his home was stuffed with combat gear and equipment. In prison awaiting trial, Neilson continued his routine of 200 press-ups a day, and application of these specialist survival skills in the outside world had seemed to offer his only chance of decent money, which self-employment failed to deliver. As Neilson told Dr Hugo Milne, 'So there was only one thing left for me. There was no other way than crime', and by the late 1960s he started housebreaking. Then came armed robbery, then murder, then murder and **kidnapping**.

Four decades separated the Whittle case from a commensurate act of premature burial. On 25 April 1934, 6-year-old June Robles was walking back from kindergarten school in Tucson, Arizona, when a man beckoned her into his car. The stranger explained that her father had sent him. A ransom demand for $15,000, signed 'XYZ', arrived that afternoon, but nothing more was heard of the kidnap victim for nineteen days. 'Is little June dead?' asked New York's *Daily News*.

Then a letter to Governor B.B. Moeur of Arizona advised a search of the desert some ten miles east of Tuscon. There the rescue party pulled away at a pile of cactus and deadwood to reveal a crude box, six feet long and three feet high, dug into a sand pit. Its tin lid, burning hot and punched with ventilation holes, was ripped off to reveal a blistered and bleeding June, chained to a metal bar by a padlock round her ankles. She survived, and four days later President Roosevelt signed federal legislation making kidnapping punishable by death.

See also **Coffins**

Newgate

A prison popularly known as 'hell on earth', built between 1130 and 1137 on the guardhouse site by the new gate of Roman London at a cost of £36 0s 11d. Its administration hardly changed until well into the nineteenth century.

The main entrance

Gaolers had to pay their own turnkeys, so the prison was woefully understaffed, and inmates were kept in irons, fetters or the dreaded skull cap throughout their sentence. The warders' main source of income was the money wrested from their prisoners, and the staff sold or hired beds, blankets, sheets, mattresses, coal, firewood, candles, food and drink. In 1717 visits from friends were charged at six pence, furniture at a pound a fortnight, and whores for the night at a shilling a time.

Prisoners could 'choose' one of three standards of accommodation – the Master's Side, the Knight's Side or the Hole, roughly corresponding to First Class, Second Class and Steerage.

As money ran short, conditions deteriorated, and since everything had to be paid for repeatedly, funds never lasted long. On arrival, wealthy prisoners would subscribe to the Master's Side and, on payment of a bribe or 'garnish', were ushered through the appropriate doorway. This led to a passage at the end of which stood another locked door and another warden, exacting another bribe. This second payment only secured admittance to another Kafkaesque corridor. And so it went on.

As long as a Master's Side inmate could pay, there was meat and claret at every meal and plenty of tobacco. Men of quality (see **Gordon**) dined alone or were waited on in the company of friends. For a few shillings more, the prisoner remained out of his cell after dinner, and his companions from outside might drop round for a game of cards. But every item, every service, entailed more garnish. Come the evil day, the prisoner was packed off to the Knight's Ward (again for a fee), and thence to the final indignity of the Condemned Hold, a large fetid dungeon underneath the prison gates with an open sewer oozing down the middle. Food was flung in through a hatch and, according to a Colonel John Turner, the prisoners 'lay like swine upon the ground, one upon another, howling and roaring'.

No public funds were set aside for poor convicts; if they lived, it was off citizens' bequests. Donations filtered through the warders' hands, to which they stuck and, at the end of Queen Elizabeth's reign, prisoners in the Hole submitted a petition complaining of their 'lying upon bare boards, still languishing in great need, cold and misery... almost famished and half-starved to death; others very sore sick, and diseased for want of sustenance'. Fennor, author of *The Counter's Commonwealth*, writes of 'the child weeping over his dying father, the mother over her sick child; one friend over another... they lie together like so many graves.'

Constantly swept by epidemics of 'gaol fever', Newgate threatened those outside its walls with contagion. During the famous Black Assizes of May 1750 a hundred inmates were squeezed into Bail Dock and, in the ensuing outbreak of gaol fever, the Lord Mayor, two judges and over forty officials, barristers and jurymen lost their lives. Fee-paying was not abolished until 1823, when Newgate was found to house a man serving eleven years for a debt of 1s 5d and another incarcerated for **debts** of fourpence. The keepership became a valuable office, in 1696 reportedly sold for £3,500. In a 1708 pamphlet, it was said to give £8,000 security. Celebrated convicts provided windfall profits for the Warden, who charged admission for viewing. In 1724 the exhibition of highwayman Jack Sheppard netted £200.

Newgate had just been enlarged and rebuilt in 1780, after a fire in 1762, when it was put to the torch during the Gordon Riots. Some 300 prisoners were rescued from the flames and escorted by the jubilant mob to local blacksmiths, who struck off their irons. Puzzled by their new-found freedom, many drifted back to the smouldering debris, and were rounded up the following day.

Three years later the main London gallows were shifted from **Tyburn** to Newgate to eliminate the traditional procession of the condemned across the capital.

This was more convenient for the convicts, who could be executed on their own doorstep in the shadow of the Debtor's Gate, and the new gallows got off to a cracking start on 9 December 1783 when ten men were hanged in a single session. The impact on local property values was good; houses facing the gallows acquired new rental potential, charging three guineas a spectator for popular executions, and even the roofs could be filled at two guineas a place. But the new venue proved too cramped for proper crowd control. At the 1807 hanging of Haggerty and Holloway a mob of 40,000 gathered in the narrow streets; twenty-eight were killed in the crush when someone tripped over a pieman, and a further seventy were injured.

Newgate survived into the twentieth century as a relic of medieval barbarity at the heart of the Empire opposite the new Old Bailey. Demolished in 1902, the contents went to auction. The Tussaud brothers were enthusiastic bidders, acquiring the toll bell for £100 in addition to the complete cells of Lord George Gordon and Jack **Sheppard**. These were dismantled, carted down the Marylebone Road and reassembled in the Chamber of Horrors where they remained until the 1970s. Newgate's plaster casts of hanged criminals fetched £5 each (many going to the Black Museum) and the execution shed, £5 15s 0d.

The gallows themselves went on to Pentonville, and were soon back in harness.

Ng, Charles Chiat (1961–)

One half of an American sex-killer duo. Ng met his partner, Leonard Lake, through a magazine personal advertisement. Ng was on the run from the Marines for stealing a brace of machine guns in 1981, and ten years previously Lake had been released from the military with signs of an 'impending schizophrenic reaction'. Lake's in-laws gave him the freedom of a two-acre ranch north of San Francisco in the Sierra Nevada, and in 1984 and 1985 the pair made this Wisleyville property the base for their Nordic survivalist fantasies, of the variety where **slave** girls are tortured in dungeons. Together they snatched transient women, or men and women, or men and women and their babies, exercising the women as sexual drudges before they were discarded, dead. Meanwhile they stalked their male captives through grounds rigged with trip wires and booby traps in a crazed re-creation of the Vietnam War. Investigators were to remove forty-five pounds of bones from the compound.

The real 'fun' took place in the concrete bunker, built by local workmen as 'a food storage area, to keep apples and walnuts in a cool place'. The hut measured sixteen feet by fourteen, and behind a removable partition was a tiny bedroom with a viewing panel through a one-way mirror. In this torture chamber, which doubled as their home movie studio, the manacled women were terrorised, raped, mutilated with power tools and then murdered.

The case unravelled on 2 June 1985 when Ng ran off with a $75 vice from a San Francisco lumber yard. Lake, waiting in a car, was caught, and from this prosaic start flowed horror after horror. Lake requested a drink of water and then collapsed dead from a cyanide capsule. He had given his name as Robin Scott Stapely, and investigators identified Stapely as a San Diego Guardian Angel, reported missing some months before. Another Lake alias was Charles Gunnar (also missing), and Lake's 1980 Honda Prelude was registered to a car dealer, Paul Cosner (missing). Lake carried a bankcard belonging to Randy Jacobson (missing), and when the San Francisco police contacted the Calaveras County Sheriff about the Wisleyville homestead, where Stapely had been Lake's immediate neighbour, they were dismayed to hear the fate of Stapely's three housemates: missing. The Sheriff drove to the ranch, where a pickup truck carried a sticker, 'If you love something, set it free. If it doesn't come back, hunt it down and kill it.' Ng and Lake were eventually linked to twenty-seven missing persons.

Lake was cremated with the exception of his brain, conserved for medical research. Ng escaped over the Canadian border to be captured a month later, down to his last ten dollars, shoplifting in a Calgary department store. He could not be extradited – Canada is opposed to capital punishment. But by September 1991 the Canadians were prepared to make an exception in Ng's case; his trial was scheduled to open in California in April 1992. For the time being most of the information is hearsay; the videotapes, for instance, have not been screened. These productions would command a massive premium as 'snuff movies', and rumours abound that Ng sold copies to Hong Kong contacts prior to capture. The **tape** which Sergeant Ronald L. McFall found himself watching after the Wisleyville raid was labelled 'M Ladies Kathy/Brenda', and the show started with a handcuffed woman (Kathy Allen, missing since 12 April 1985) listening to a voice invoking her boyfriend Mike as the well-worn mainspring of a porn movie plot.

'Mike owes us and unfortunately he can't pay. We're going to give you a choice... You co-operate, and in approximately thirty days we'll take you back to the city and let you go... If you don't co-operate with us, we'll probably put a round through your head and take you out and bury you someplace... While you're here you'll wash for us, you'll clean for us, you'll fuck for us.' After this prologue Leonard Lake walked into shot and took off Kathy's handcuffs, put on her leg irons, and made her undress.

The tape cut to four days later. Kathy, strapped to the bed, listened as Lake castigated her for some bent hasps on a lock. In passing, he mentioned that they had killed Mike; it would soon be time for her to join him.

They did 'slay' Kathy, but not on screen. Instead the tape switched to a terrified Brenda O'Connor, with Ng slicing off her shirt with a knife and then shearing her bra in two. 'If you don't do what we tell you,' Ng threatened, 'we will tie you to the bed, rape you, shoot you in the head, and take you out and bury you.' Later footage showed Brenda

imploring Ng for the life of her baby while he responded with taunts: 'I don't think you're a fit mother.'

A friend of Ng's, interviewed on the television show *Inside Edition*, said, 'The **torture**, the pure **terror** – Ng wanted to see terror... I don't think the sexual act was very gratifying... They had to beg for it to stop... And then, once they stopped, it was no longer fun. Then it's time to put a round in their head and move on to find another one.'

Lake, middle-aged and balding, wrote in his diary, 'There is no sexual problem with a submissive woman. There are no frustrations – only pleasure and contentment.' His idea that peace of mind was attainable through tying people up and killing them marked the intrusive triumph of long-nurtured fantasies over his nondescript everyday existence.

Although Lake maintained that his life started when he joined the Marines, he saw no active service in Vietnam. Instead, he bragged about his heroic exploits. After discharge, he degenerated into a gun freak, amassing scores of weapons, and thence into a paramilitary freak, stoking his dreams with war magazines. He wore combat fatigues round the neighbourhood, offered to instruct high school pupils in the use of explosives, liked to photograph his sex partners handcuffed, and progressed to pornographic home movies. His preoccupation with the John Fowles novel *The Collector* (in which the first kidnap victim is Miranda) cross-fertilised his survivalist obsessions. Hence Lake's 'Operation Miranda', where he would wait out the nuclear inferno in his bunker, consoled by weapons and sex slaves. In Lake's imagination, his insignificance was displaced by a sense of omnipotence, and he carried his philosophy through; the *San Jose Mercury News* quoted a neighbour who reported Lake saying, 'If somebody deserves to die they should be dead.'

Murder is no counterweight for personal inadequacy, and serial killers are typically left encumbered by gore with their troubles unresolved. Lake's later diary entries show that the growing number of bodies in the trench behind their bunker brought only misery. His problems can be traced to his childhood, when he was raised by his grandfather, a strict disciplinarian, and his sisters allowed Lake to have sex with them in return for protection from his brother.

Ng was a hard case from childhood. Of wealthy Hong Kong parents, he was expelled from two schools, the second time for stealing; he was caught shoplifting; became involved in a hit-and-run accident; intimidated his fellow Marines; boasted about killings, and stole weapons before contacting Lake. In his Canadian prison, he compiled a **list** of seventy-seven witnesses and law officers scheduled for execution.

See also **Fantasising, Preview, Reading material, Souvenirs, Zodiac**

Nice, France

Scene of the 1976 bank raid on the Société Général, masterminded by Albert Spaggiari, an unsavoury right-wing criminal.

By his own account, Spaggiari's career started in 1948 with a bid to join a band of Sicilian bandits at the age of sixteen. He applied in writing. He served as a paratrooper in Indo-China, then robbed a nightclub, and later enlisted in the OAS where he tried to assassinate De Gaulle. It is said that Spaggiari had the President in his sights from an upper window above his mother's shop in Nice; but the order to fire never came.

After a four-year prison sentence for distributing inflammatory political pamphlets and the unlawful possession of firearms, Spaggiari hatched a plot for the perfect robbery. Despite its glamorous outcome, the project resembled a large-scale civil engineering exercise.

Spaggiari's first accomplice was a lady who tackled the undercover work with relish. She rented a safe deposit box in the underground vault of Nice's Société Général and arrived for her visits with a miniature spy-camera. She installed a concealed radio-transmitter to eavesdrop on the bank guards' daily routine, and her detailed questions about locks, alarm systems and patrols seemed perfectly natural for a nervous old woman nearing eighty who was worried about her savings.

Meanwhile Spaggiari boned up on commercial security from technical journals like *Science et Vie*. A frontal assault on the bank seemed bound to fail. The only remaining approach was through the walls or floor, but the vault was set into solid rock. Spaggiari experimented by leaving an alarm clock, then a radio with a timer, and finally a siren in the

deposit box to prove that if ever the walls were breached he could work undisturbed.

Attempts to procure a thermal lance embroiled Spaggiari with a gang from Marseilles, to whom he divulged his plan. They 'wanted in' and undertook to supply seven men, leaving Spaggiari to rake up the rest from his military low-life acquaintances. Together they bought a van identical to the Public Works department's vehicles. Then they acquired official overalls, uniforms and a set of traffic signs, and mapped the sewers of Nice in broad daylight, setting up 'Roadworks' signs while they disappeared through manholes in the middle of the road. They needed an entrance large enough to admit heavy mechanical gear, giving good access to a point near the strongroom, preferably with electric power. They found it.

Spaggiari stockpiled equipment with the diligence of a quartermaster, making purchases in dispersed sorties to allay suspicion. In addition to hi-tech items like a small laser and walkie-talkie radios, and the basic requirements of electric drills and a heavy-duty hydraulic lever, he thought the plan through to the last details. After assembling their checklist of toolbags, scissors, 300 metres of cable, chisels, hammers, jemmies, bolt cutters, oxyacetylene torches, gas cylinders, buckets, cement, boots, work gloves, surgical gloves, portable stove, smoke extractor and wheelbarrow, the gang took to the sewers, setting up first base in early May 1976 a hundred yards down a twisting route in the network of conduits, lugging eighty pounds of gear at a time during repeated trips.

Then they drilled towards the vault. The rockface was unyielding. Four inches an hour constituted good progress. Drill bits snapped and tempers flared, but after two weeks their shaft was twenty feet long, extending to the bank's concrete footings. Three pneumatic jacks and more than a hundred

drill bits later, on 24 June, their seventh week in the sewers, the gang pierced the five feet-thick foundations. The wall of the vault itself was the only remaining barrier.

They breached it easily. But the way was barred; they had come out behind a fifty-ton safe. First they tried budging it with jacks. Then they torched through its back. The steel casing yielded, but they were defeated by its concrete lining. Finally the entire unit was shifted and wedged out of the way, and on Friday 16 July the gang climbed into the strongroom with a whole weekend ahead.

The 1,500 deposit boxes were themselves inside safes, and Spaggiari assumed that the most strongly defended contained the most precious spoils. By four o'clock on Saturday afternoon only twenty-eight had been ruptured, sometimes disgorging cash, sometimes mouldy biscuits, or sugar, or jewels, gold, securities and pornographic pictures. The gang worked in relays, sleeping on the floor, slurping down hot soup prepared on their butane stove, and by Sunday evening they had opened a total of 317 boxes.

The value of their haul as they pulled at midnight on Sunday, staggering under their sackloads in the rising sewers, is estimated at between a conservative $8 million and an extravagant $75 million. Behind them, the main door to the vault was welded shut from inside, and the walls bore their final message: 'No hate, no violence and no guns'.

The police were so impressed by the tunnelling, propped at the correct intervals, that they first suspected miners. Spaggiari, arrested three months later, was traced through one of the shops from which he bought his equipment, as well as by his predilection for Dom Miguel cigars; his butts littered the strongroom. But at a courtroom appearance on 10 March 1977 he broke free and leapt out of the window, breaking his fall with a paratrooper's roll on a parked car twenty feet below, and roared away on the back of an accomplice's motorcycle.

Spaggiari was never recaptured, and died on the run from natural causes. The money probably passed into the hands of sundry right-wing terrorist groups.

The best fictional account of the raid is Robert Pollock's novel *Loophole* published in 1972, four years before the event and a quarter of a century after the world's greatest robbery, when some £2,500 million of gold (at today's values) vanished from the Reichsbank following Germany's collapse in the spring of 1945.

Nicholl, Charles (1950–)

Author of one of the great passages of comedy-thriller crime reportage. In *The Fruit Palace* (1985), Nicholl recounts how an undercover story on the Colombian cocaine trade nearly came unstuck when his drug-dealing contacts discovered his true identity. The dealers considered 'checking his oil' with a knife in the guts, but veered in favour of giving him a little job: smuggling cocaine on to the *Nordic Star* in the Santa Marta docks. Nicholl had no choice but to comply.

He dressed in pristine whites as a *gringo* reporter for his big day out. A five kilo sack of cocaine was thrown over the harbour's perimeter fence for him to collect once he had negotiated security, and Nicholl slunk unobserved through the harbour's outbuildings only to find that the bag had burst. Cocaine was blowing everywhere. He crammed the leaking sack into his briefcase. But it had been manufactured in Taiwan and the hinges broke. Nicholl tried to clean himself down with his hands, which were covered in oil, and in this state, smeared in grease and cocaine, he found himself button-holed at inordinate length by the harbour's Director of Operations.

In mid-conversation in his capacity of journalist, Nicholl looked down to find the white powder still trickling from the case's loose corner, making a little narcotic pyramid on the ground. He covered the cocaine pile with his foot. Still talking, he plugged the leak by clamping the briefcase close to his chest like a teddy bear, and the chit-chat droned on while the precious seconds of his hand-over time ticked away.

It was only by feigning convulsive diarrhoea that Nicholl tore himself away. He insisted on using the *Nordic Star*'s lavatories, where his hand-over was scheduled, and scampered up the gangplank with seconds to spare. But his contact, an irate Swede, refused to take delivery; the cocaine was spoiled, spilling loose inside the case. Wiping the briefcase down, Nicholl unthinkingly put his fingers to his nose, hoovering up pure 'Snow White'. As well as paralysing his speech centres, this laid waste to most of his motor co-ordination.

Nicholl's plight was now parlous. He could not deliver the consignment: it had been rejected. He could not dump it: he would be liquidated. He could hardly move; he was zinging at the eyeballs.

Luckily, what he lost in ability he gained in confidence, and he approached the task of running the drugs back out of the ship, down the gangplank and through the guarded harbour complex with unshakeable optimism. He attributes his survival to his innovation of smuggling cocaine *into* Colombia, for which the authorities were ill-prepared.

Nicholl is alive and well and still writing. The guards manning Colombian ports are open to financial persuasion; their weekly wage is £2.

Nilsen, Dennis (1945–)

Britain's most prolific serial killer, whose exploits are described elsewhere (see **Death, Life after** and **Mirror Image**).

Why did Nilsen become a murderer? The best source is Brian Masters, author of *Killing for Company*, who makes the point that Nilsen's family were fishermen from eastern Scotland, a harsh coast savaged by wind and sea, where the inhabitants – fatalistic and suspicious – regarded good and evil not as thin religious concepts, but as reality. Inbreeding in the fishing villages was rife, stretching back for centuries, bringing in its wake mental and emotional disorders regarded locally as no more than quirks. Many of the menfolk were lost at sea. Life was poor and hard.

In 1942, Betty Whyte from Fraserburgh, a fisherman's daughter, rushed into marriage with an officer of the Free Norwegian Forces, Olav Magnus Nilsen. They lived in a single room in her mother's house, eventually with three children. In Nilsen's words, his father 'in the heat and uncertainty of war, married my mother primarily on lustful grounds and ignoring irreconcilable cultural and personality differences which doomed the match to failure'.

During his early years Nilsen was quiet and withdrawn, liable to wander off on his own. He

depicts himself as an 'unhappy, brooding child, secretive and stricken with inferiority'. He never saw his father, and remembers nothing of him save a photograph. His grandfather, Andrew Whyte, became his surrogate father and filled his head with tales of a seafarer's life, and this relationship became the core of the young Nilsen's life.

During 1951, Nilsen's grandfather weakened, and on the morning of 31 October his shipmates found him dead in his bunk. Whyte's body was despatched by train to the family home, where it lay in an open coffin amid the lamentations of his relatives and friends.

Nilsen knew something drastic had happened. Aged six, he was ushered into the parlour and lifted up to see the corpse in the coffin. His mother explained that grandfather – his 'father' – was asleep. Everyone cried, and Nilsen experienced a sense of dread and excitement. The next morning he watched a mysterious procession of besuited men troop past the window. He discovered that grandfather had disappeared without waking or saying goodbye, and from that day Andrew Whyte's name was never mentioned.

Nilsen waited patiently for his 'father' to return. He wrote later, 'It is the custom in Fraserburgh that when there is a death in a household they draw the blinds and curtains. When my grandfather died it seemed that these blinds were drawn across my life... Relatives would pretend that he had gone to 'a better place'. "Why," I thought, "should he go to a better place and not take me with him?" "So death was a nice thing," I thought. "Then why does it make me miserable?" Father and grandfather had walked out on me, probably to a better place.'

Elsewhere Nilsen wrote of the 'emotional death' that stemmed from this incident. By the age of eight he would sit for hours on the rocks by the sea, watching its shifting patterns to the screech of gulls. He described his near-death by water in an incident that seems half-imagined: 'Many years ago I was a boy drowning in the sea... The retreat of the wave carried me out further. I panicked, and waved my arms as I submerged. I could hear a loud buzzing in my head and kept gasping for air which wasn't there. I thought that Grandad was bound to arrive and pull me out. I felt at ease, drugged and dreamlike under the silent green weight of water. I felt myself suspended in a void.'

Later, as a schoolboy, Nilsen helped in the search for an old man from the village who had wandered into the river to a watery grave. He found the corpse. 'He reminded me of my grandfather,' he noted, 'and the images were fixed firmly in my mind... I could never understand the reality of death.'

In a 1993 interview, Nilsen claimed twelve victims rather than the previously accepted figure of fifteen. He says that the misconception arose during an exchange in the police car immediately after his arrest. Asked how many men he had murdered, Nilsen reached for a number, and then stuck by his story to keep the police happy. During the interview, he pinpointed the high point of the killings. It came when he raised the dead bodies up, and their arms splayed back. 'The most exciting part of the little conundrum was when I lifted the corpses,' he recalled. 'It was an affirmation of my power to lift and carry and have control, and the dangling element of the limbs an expression of their passivity.'

Nonce

British prison slang for the lowest of the low, the sex offenders. Everyone needs someone to look down on, and 'nonce' means a nothing, a nonsense, a no one, or a non-thing. Nonces live in constant fear, always insulted and whenever possible pushed, tripped, beaten, burned and stabbed. They are generally segregated in Section 43, a prison within a prison, kept apart for their own protection.

There is a pecking order even for nonces; the sex offender spits on the child molester, in his turn a cut above the child killer. The bottom of the heap is Ian **Brady**, the child killer who tortured his victims. But even Brady found someone lower than himself. In 1967 this wretched individual, Raymond Morris, was convicted of the murder of 7-year-old Christine

Darby on Cannock Chase in the West Midlands. Both Brady and Morris were confined to Durham Prison, and on 12 December 1969 Brady poured scalding tea over his inferior, earning himself twenty-eight days in solitary. Afterwards Brady went for Morris at every opportunity, on one occasion pushing him down the stairs. 'Years later,' said Brady, 'I realised that, in a way, I was attacking myself.'

Norfolk Island

A stain on British history, Norfolk Island was 'the old hell' of the Australian penal colony. After its horrific opening stint under Major Foveaux, the settlement reopened in 1825 as the ultimate in convict degradation. A first-hand account of life under the regime of the new commandant, the sadistic Lieutenant-Colonel Morisset, survives in the memoir of transportee Laurence Frayne, an indomitable Irish thief who arrived on the island in late 1830.

Frayne had already taken fifty lashes for trying to jump ship and another 150 for cursing the overseer; he landed with his untended flesh ripped open, crawling with maggots. He was immediately set to work as a porter, his festering back piled high with heavy gear. 'I really longed for instant death,' he wrote. He soon came up before Morisset on another serious charge: he had broken a flagstone in the quarry. Frayne was awarded a further hundred lashes.

'After the sentence,' the undaunted Frayne recorded, 'I plainly told the Commandant in the Court that he was a Tyrant. He replied that no man had ever said that about him before. I said they knew the consequences too well to tell him so: "But I tell you in stark naked blunt English that you are as great a tyrant as Nero ever was." The moment I expressed these words I was sentenced to an additional 100 and to be kept ironed down in a cell for life and never to see daylight again.'

To allow Frayne's wounds to heal, these 200 lashes were administered over four sessions so that his back could be opened up time and again with special heavy-duty whips. Frayne's flogger was himself threatened with a flailing at any hint of leniency.

Frayne lived, to find himself up before Morisset a few weeks later on the pretext of assault. Again Frayne spoke out: 'It is useless for me to gainsay anything... If you actually knew my innocence yourself, I well know that you would punish me... If you acquit me for the assault you will flog me for what I have now said to you.' Morisset called Frayne a 'damned scoundrel', decreeing a further 300 lashes. Frayne took his life in his hands: 'I am no Scoundrel no more than yourself.'

After his second instalment of 100 lashes they banged Frayne untended into solitary, where he was reduced to pouring his miserly water ration on the floor and urinating into this puddle so that he could lie in a little lake of liquid to ease his agony. 'I was literally alive with Maggots and Vermin,' he noted. Next they cooped him up in a soundproof isolation chamber for two months solitary and, on emerging, this remarkable man earned 100 supplementary lashes for consorting with women.

Frayne survived Norfolk Island. Others opted for suicide in semi-institutionalised rituals. William Ullathorn, Vicar-General of Australia, summarised the process in 1834: 'Lots were even cast; the man on whom it fell committed the deed, his comrades being witnesses, with the sole view of being taken to Sydney.'

For this temporary respite the men would kill. Convicts banded into co-operative units, about a dozen strong, choosing straws. The two finalists proceeded to a further draw to establish who was the murderer, and who the **murderee**. So one man died, meeting his end in a strange mixture of brutality and nobility: he gave his life that others might live. His attacker was arraigned on a capital charge, but at least he went to Sydney, accompanied by the witnesses, who provided muddling testimony at the trial and hoped for escape.

To end this practice, in September 1833 the authorities instituted kangaroo courts on Norfolk Island to hang the men there. On 15 January 1834 the convicts rose. The rebellion lasted seven hours and cost the lives of five prisoners, with about another fifty crippled. The guards resumed control, instigating months of what can only be described as systematic **torture**.

When fifty-five of the wretches came for trial they begged, in whispers, for death. One man, reprieved with his mates on a former occasion, told the court: 'We wish we had been executed then. It was no mercy to send us to this place. I do not ask for life. I do not want to be spared... Life is not worth living on such terms.'

Fourteen were condemned to be hanged. The men heard the news from Ullathorn, who recounted: 'Those who were to live wept bitterly, whilst those doomed to die, without exception, dropped on their knees, and with dry eyes, thanked God that they were to be delivered from such a place.' Ullathorn noted that the convicts' language had inverted: they transposed 'evil' with 'good', 'virtuous' with 'wicked' and so on. Prisoners habitually blinded themselves so that they would be left alone as useless human trash, and it is worth remembering that the great majority were initially transported for subsistence thefts of clothes and food.

Norfolk Island improved dramatically under the influence of the penal reformer Alexander **Maconochie**. But in 1843 the settlement plunged back into the dark ages with the appointment of the abhorrent Major Joseph Childs, a flogger who distributed over 1,500 lashes a month.

Of this period the Reverend Thomas Rogers wrote that some mornings, 'The ground on which the men stood at the triangles was saturated with human gore as if a bucket of blood had been spilled on it, covering a space three feet in diameter and running out in various directions in little streams two or three feet long.' July 1846 saw another uprising, and after a hearing where the accused were allowed no representation and called no witnesses, twelve men swung. Then came the worst of all the Australian commandants, John Giles Price, who implemented a routine of savagery beyond anything previously imagined.

Price suffered a fitting retribution. After retiring in 1853 he secured an appointment as Inspector General of the Victoria hulks. Four years later in the quarry at Williamstown, on 26 March 1857, he was surrounded by a crowd of convicts, who closed in to trample, beat, kick and bludgeon him to a dead pulp.

North Marshall Street

America's equivalent of **Rillington Place**. On 25 March 1987 the police, investigating the wild claims of a young hooker, Josefina Rivera, forced their way into 3520 North Marshall Street in a run-down residential district of Philadelphia.

Gary Michael Heidnik, the occupant, surrendered peaceably, mumbling about being late with his alimony payments, and at the station the police relieved their well-heeled captive of $2,000 in cash, numerous credit cards and the documents for four cars, including a Rolls-Royce, a Lincoln and a Cadillac Coupé de Ville.

Heidnik styled himself a Bishop, but only of his own sect, the United Church of the Ministers of God, and in his basement the officers found two semi-naked black women, brutally scarred and chained to a sewer pipe, huddling under a thin blanket. 'Hosanna – we're free,' they shouted, kissing the officer's hands. In a dark pit in the floor, covered by a board, crouched another woman, naked, manacled and handcuffed, too weak to move. A single bulb illuminated the mildewed, littered chamber. Upstairs, where Heidnik had conducted his bouts of sex and torture, was a stack of pornography. In the fridge, near the blackened stove surmounted by a sinister pan, an officer discovered a human forearm.

At his peak, Heidnik housed six women in the downstairs dungeon. He preferred mentally retarded black prostitutes, subjecting them to a routine of thrashings, rape, oral sex and three-in-a-bed sessions. Often he compelled the prisoners to beat each other. Two had perished: the troublesome Deborah Dudley, electrocuted on 18 March, and Sandra Lindsay, who expired on 7 February after swinging from the ceiling by her hands for a week. Heidnik roasted her dismembered body, ground up the remains, and mixed them with dog food in a processor to supplement the survivors' normal diet of gruel. He fed one of the arms intact to the Doberman in his yard.

Heidnik started his collection of 26 November 1986, picking up Josefina Rivera in his Lincoln. At North Marshall Street he clapped on handcuffs, threw her into the basement and outlined his plans for their future. Josefina represented the first of a projected harem of ten black women required to sire his children. 'We'll all be one big happy family,' he told her. 'Society owes me a wife and family.' But Heidnik resorted to extreme duress to keep his captives in order, and took pleasure in it, gouging out their eardrums with a scewdriver (so they could not hear any rescue attempt) and on occasions forcing the women into the pit and filling it with water. By degrees he came to rely on Josefina. She snitched on the others, reporting plans to escape and their disrespectful talk, and beat them to his command. Heidnik liked to watch, and he mistook this arrangement of convenience for a relationship, taking Josefina out for meals or rides in his Rolls. On 23 March they picked up his final captive, Agnes Adams, together. The following day he gave Josefina permission to visit her family on the strict understanding that she returned after setting their minds at rest but, unlike Colleen Stan, the sex-**slave** who endured years of such treatment, Josefina broke her word.

Opening the defence at Heidnik's trial on 20 June 1988, his attorney stated, 'My client is not innocent, he is very, very guilty', and asked for a verdict of insanity. Heidnik came from a broken home and a violent, loveless background. Born in 1943, his parents separated two years later. He last saw his father in 1967, his mother committed suicide in 1970, and in childhood he fell from a tree, injuring his head. It became slightly deformed, giving rise to a school nickname of 'football'. Discharged from the Army at the age of eighteen as a schizophrenic with an IQ of 130, Heidnik committed himself to mental hospitals twenty-one times and survived thirteen suicide attempts. He registered his church, a delusion of grandeur, as a charity in 1971. Heidnik did hold services, but also ran it as a front for loan-sharking. Female members of his flock often finished up sharing his bed, two at a time.

An inadequate drawn to inadequates, in his mid-thirties Heidnik fathered one child by a semi-retarded black woman and helped her sister escape from a mental institution, installing her as a captive in his home where he subjected her to deviant sex. This led to a four-year prison sentence. Released in 1983, he continued to limp towards the goal of a family, impregnating Sandra Lindsay. But she had an abortion. A film, *The World of Susie Wong*, suggested that a compliant Oriental might provide the answer, and he obtained one from a matrimonial agency. A week after the wedding, his wife came back from a shopping expedition to find him bedding three women. She rejected his explanation that this was a standard American custom, and in 1986 brought charges of 'spouse rape'. Still impelled by matrimonial urgings, Heidnik blundered on towards the mirage of connubial harmony through the acquisition of multiple sex-slaves, capturing his first that November.

Heidnik could not hold down a relationship or a job, but one sector of his brain – the part that makes money – remained enviably intact. Within five years of opening a Merrill Lynch account with $1,500, he amassed half a million dollars. Joesfina told the court that after making a killing, literally, Heidnik would stop off to check his stocks and shares. On 1 July 1988 he was sentenced to death.

Nuremberg, injustice at

The Americans made a botch of the Nazi executions in October 1946. A Master-Sergeant, John C. Woods, volunteered, putting on a brave face for an interview with the *Stars and Stripes*; 'I did a good job. Everything went A1... I wanted this job so terribly that I stayed here a bit longer.'

Woods had the requisite experience, with 347 hangings to his credit in America over a fifteen-year career. But the trap-door for each of the three specially-built gallows in the Nuremberg gymnasium proved too small, slicing off the noses of the descending Nazi leaders. Nor was the drop long enough. Keitel survived for twenty minutes dangling on the end of the rope, Jodl took eighteen minutes to die, and Ribbentrop ten. Goering attempted to 'cheat the hangman' by taking his own life, but in vain. They hanged his corpse.

The hanging impedimenta were burned. Woods had received an offer of $2,500 for one of the ropes from a souvenir hunter before the executions. Recently discovered documents from KGB files reveal that the corpses of the Nazi warlords were flown overnight to Munich, cremated, and then flown back to Nuremberg. During the return journey the ashes were vented over Germany.

Albert **Pierrepoint**, the famous hangman, was asked by the American United Press Association to contribute a critical review on the botched hangings. He declined, but he did agree to train the post-war Austrian executioners, who were addicted to a short drop, compensating by clinging to the condemned man's legs.

Nor did the Nuremberg trials provide a great advertisement for justice. At first Churchill wanted to shoot the Nazi leadership out of hand, and the political context of the hearings ensured that truth became the first casualty.

It remained so to the last. The authority of Air Chief Marshal Sholto Douglas, head of the Allied Control Commission, to review the sentences was taken out of his hands. The Russians blamed the Nazis for the massacres at Katyn, a fiction nodded through by the judges although Soviet responsibility must have been apparent, and, since the defendants were in the dock for waging a war of aggression, any allusion to Russia's attack on Poland or Finland was taboo, as was the British intervention in Norway.

The twenty-four defendants were selected with haste and negligence. Gustav Krupp, senile and bed-ridden, was indicted in place of his son Alfred. The duplicate charges against General Jodl served no purpose once General Keitel had been accused. Admiral Raeder and Doenitz landed in the dock, despite accurate evaluations by the British Foreign Office that the German Navy had 'behaved pretty well'. Even though Admiral Chester Nimitz let the side down, testifying that American naval practices were identical with the German, his opposite numbers were jailed.

During cross-examination, Goering was denounced for keeping the troop movements along the east bank of the Rhine secret, and the court could not restrain its mirth when he replied, 'I am not aware that the Americans ever informed us of their mobilisation plan.' Goering could only be tenuously linked to the shooting of escaping RAF officers. But he was a primary architect of the 1938 Munich conference, which temporarily averted war, and he endeavoured to dissuade Hitler from invading Poland the following year. Nonetheless he was found guilty.

Goering may have been repulsive, but it is bad law to condemn a man for crimes other than those with which he is charged; a tendency from which tribunals where the accusers sit as judges are not exempt.

O

Oakes, Sir Harry (1874–1943)

The rich may have more money, but this does not necessarily make them any nicer, and by the time Sir Harry Oakes's gold strike east of Swastika with his partners the Tough Boys made him the richest man in Canada, he lacked friends and social graces.

At smart dinner parties Sir Harry used foul language, whistled under his breath and spat grape-seeds across the table: the oblique legacy of two decades' hard graft, prospecting in Alaska, Canada, the Belgian Congo and Death Valley. But Oakes had to be invited everywhere as uncrowned king of his adopted home, where he maintained half a dozen residences, built a golf course, ran the British Colonial Hotel, and owned a third of New Providence Island, as well as an airline and an airfield. In 1937, the year Oakes settled in the Bahamas, the islands were a one-horse attraction, geared to the upper-crust few, playing host to a meagre 34,000 visitors during a three-month season. But the Bahamas had potential, particularly if gambling was legalised.

It is unlikely that Sir Harry saw it that way. He was happy with his bulldozer, and he went on buying land from the local real estate promoter, Harold Christie, so that he could knock down more trees. As the editor of the *Nassau Times* commented, 'As long as Christie could find something for Sir Harry to destroy, he knew he had a sale.' His other recreational outlet was golf, where he sparred with another unacknowledged king, the Duke of Windsor, posted to the Bahamas as Governor after the outbreak of World War II. The Duke found Bahamian society insufferably dull, and might well have considered a few casinos a welcome diversion.

As would *mafioso* Meyer Lansky, who acquired the gambling concession to Havana's Hotel Nacional in 1937 after a $250,000 bribe to Fulgencio Batista. But the war made life difficult for him. Passenger services to Cuba from the American mainland were in short supply, planes were scarce, and indigenous punters few and far between. From Lansky's perspective, the Bahamas lay nearer to America, were more stable politically, stocked with monied war-wives and Allied personnel, and made a nicer resort. A 1939 amendment to the Bahamas' Lotteries and Gaming Act of 1905 empowered the Duke to grant gaming licences as he saw fit – provided, of course, that its leading citizen, Sir Harry Oakes, assented.

Harold Christie, an astute operator, would have supported the move, like many other legitimate businessmen. For too long the Bahamas had been dependent on the whims of a few rich individuals, and the wartime boom was edging nearer to peacetime bust. Year-round mass tourism would ensure long-term prosperity, and Christie knew the man to put the package together: Meyer Lansky, to whom he ran bootleg liquor in Florida during Prohibition. Christie had access to the Duke and was a close associate of Sir Harry's.

On the night of 7 July 1943, Christie stayed at Westbourne, one of Sir Harry's homes. His host slept two bedrooms down the hall, and the following morning Christie discovered Sir Harry dead in bed, his body partially burned, and his skull fractured by four heavy blows. He had been set alight while alive and, intriguingly, the body was moved after the attack. Found face-up, it had blood from the back of the head running across the face. Mud tracks sullied the main staircase. But Christie declared that he had passed the entire evening and night at Westbourne without hearing a thing.

The killing created headlines round the world, ousting the Allied invasion of Sicily as the lead feature in American newspapers. It seemed that the Duke, who took personal charge of the investigation, delighted in another chance of snatching the limelight. It is unfair to assume that the resulting bungle was deliberate, but he started on the wrong foot by dispensing with the services of the local police and Scotland Yard, instead summoning two Miami detectives (one of whom, it later transpired, was in the Mob's pay), reputedly asking them to 'confirm the details of a suicide'.

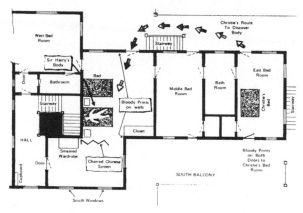

Plan of second storey at Westbourne

Soon an exotic playboy, Count Marie Alfred 'Freddie' Fouqereaux de Marigny, was under arrest, enhancing the case's newsworthiness. The Duke hated Freddie; he had not shown the deference due to an ex-monarch, and his caddish lifestyle represented an affront to the British community. Freddie bolstered his finances by marrying well, owned a speedboat called *Concubine*, was French, and had run off with Sir Harry's daughter when she was seventeen. In addition, he remarked to a detective, 'That guy, Sir Harry, the old bastard, should have been killed anyway.'

It is reasonably certain that Freddie was framed, perhaps with the Duke's collusion, and the Commissioner of Police, R. A. Erskine-Lindop, was transferred to Trinidad when he balked at pressing charges. This peremptory move prevented Erskine-Lindop from testifying. He would probably have expanded on his 1951 statement to the *Nassau Tribune* that an unnamed suspect, who 'continued to move about in high society...broke down under his cross-examination'. At the trial, the fingerprint evidence looked dubious in the extreme, and Police Captain Edward Sears gave evidence that he saw

Christie on the murder night in downtown Nassau, on a route connecting Westbourne and Prince George's Wharf, three blocks from the sea. Sears had a good view of the Christie-lookalike; the two were both at the wheel, driving in opposite directions and passed only a couple of feet apart.

Freddie was discharged, and the murder remains unresolved. Solutions abound, but they are no more than scenarios, mostly orbiting round the casino issue, whereby Sir Harry refused to have his island paradise spoiled and was 'hit' by the Mafia. A Bahamian watchman at Lyford Cay reportedly watched as an unfamiliar, powerful speedboat docked on the night, disembarking two strangers who left before dawn; his story could not be verified because shortly afterwards he was 'found drowned'. Or perhaps Sir Harry and Christie kept a late-night rendezvous with Lansky's men on a boat. Discussions broke down, and Oakes was killed at sea, landed through the mud, and then driven back to Westbourne by a terrorised Christie.

In this version, Oakes's body was burned in ritual desecration to underline the lot of those who thwarted the Mafia, leaving Christie in no doubt that a dire fate awaited him and the Duke if they stepped out of line. The more drastic imputations against the Duke – for instance, that he had Freddie framed to avoid exposure of a proffered bribe for agreeing to legalise gambling – stem from his inexplicable conduct. But that is his hallmark.

Other theories range from robbery-gone-wrong to the exotic voodoo premise expounded by Charles Higham in his biography of the Duchess of Windsor. In this version, Christie imported a Brujeira dwarf from Florida to slaughter Sir Harry (to whom he was in debt) with a pronged fish spear, thus accounting both for the bloody handprint four feet from the bedroom floor and the unusual wounds. A less exotic **weapon** would be a winch handle with a serrated spindle.

Casting Christie as the killer or witness to the killing has its attractions, and not just because newly declassified FBI documents name him as their front runner from the start. Christie is the most obvious suspect, a sound line to follow with murder. His bed was unrumpled on the morning of 8 July – not slept in, but merely lain on, and either he perjured himself by his insistence that he discovered Sir Harry on his back (and he had thus rearranged the body, or witnessed his rearrangement) or his slumbers, so light on the bedding, made him deaf to all comers.

The casinos finally arrived in 1963, four years after Castro's seizure of power in Cuba made a new locale a financial imperative. Patience is all: they were under Meyer Lansky's control.

Oaths

On 18 July 1816, the London *Times* – then known as 'The Thunderer' – called for an end to 'the horrible trade in blood demands'. This was during the last days of the old reward system. Thief-catchers and police received a capitation fee for the criminals they arrested, and the worse the crime, the greater the reward.

Thief-catchers were no fools and recognised that it made commercial sense to nurse a criminal along until he did something serious; the more avaricious would, through an intermediary, set up a dupe to commit a capital offence and then seize him, literally making a killing. Forty pounds was the price for death, 'weighing forty' the phrase as informers assessed a villain's worth.

The 1816 case which shocked the nation involved three Irish lads, Reardon, Quinn and Thomas Connell. Approached in London's Cheapside Market, they were offered work by Barry (the criminal intermediary). 'My master has plenty of employment for some smart fellows,' said Barry, 'but it is very *hard* work... there is some *hazard* in it.' One of the boys replied: 'So has every kind of work; mounting a ladder five storeys high, with a heavy hod of mortar is attended with great hazard; but an Irish labourer does not care much for danger.'

Barry exacted a vow of secrecy: 'My master would not hire anyone, but such as will take a solemn oath that if he leaves the work, he will never speak about it.' Installed in a hired room, the boys were issued with base metal, files, scissors and tools and instructed to make things looking ominously like shillings. The penalty for forgery was death; they suddenly grasped their predicament and tried to leave, saying it was lunch-time. Barry countered that food was on its way. Meanwhile, police officer Brock obtained a search-warrant and together with Barry's contact, Constable Power, made the arrest. The boys went on trial for their lives.

The stark choice between a hanging and dishonouring their oaths was hardly an issue. As good Catholics the boys kept their word, offered no defence and were duly sentenced to death in Barry's presence. But Sir Matthew Wood, Chief Magistrate, overheard a chance remark during the trial and, discovering the obstacle, thought of the remedy. He summoned a priest, who assured the youths that in the circumstances their vows were not indissoluble. Thus the conspirators were exposed and, remarkably, the boys returned to Ireland with sufficient funds (from a subscription organised by Wood) to buy a smallholding.

The reputation of the London police had never been lower. There were not many of them, and most were corrupt. Little came of the Select Committee established in 1816, but Robert Peel's first abortive attempt to set up a centralised police force was only seven years away, and his Criminal Law Act of 1826 curtailed the courts' powers to disburse blood money.

See also **Ratcliffe Highway**, **Wild**

O'Bannion, Dion (1892–1924)

Chicago gang leader portrayed by James Cagney in *Public Enemy* and eventually eliminated, possibly by Capone, after an impressive sting. Born in Chicago's Little Hell, just by Death Corner, O'Bannion was noted for his fixed smile which remained in place even while he shot you. With one leg four inches shorter than the other, he was psychologically asymmetric: a bootlegger who deplored alcohol, a racketeer who eschewed prostitution, and an expert florist credited with twenty-five killings.

On his way up, O'Bannion served a stint as a singing waiter in McGovern's Cafe. At the top, he was Chicago's most dangerous mob-leader, carrying the North Side as well as three guns in his specially tailored pockets: one in his trousers, one in his overcoat and one under his armpit. Capone considered him cocky and impulsive, instancing O'Bannion's grudge shooting of Dave Miller in the La Salle Theatre foyer on the first night of a musical comedy, but he received civic recognition at a 1924 banquet thrown in his honour by the Democrats. In addition to a shining galaxy of thugs, bodyguards, hit-men, plug-uglies, bludgeon men, bootleggers and pimps, the O'Bannion feast (the first blatant linking of politics and gangsterdom) was attended by upholders of Prohibition like the Chief of Detectives, police lieutenants, a County Clerk, a Commissioner of Public Works, a Union President and Secretary, an Assistant State Attorney and numerous other lesser police and politicians who, after downing quantities of illegal whisky, wooed O'Bannion to the Democrats' cause with a platinum watch encrusted with rubies and diamonds. It was money and effort wasted. Come the day, O'Bannion and his boys backed the Republicans.

In early 1924 he heard word that the Feds were moving to close the important Sieben Brewery, hitherto supervised by the precinct police. O'Bannion blithely told Capone and Torrio that he was contemplating retirement, and sold them his share in the brewery for $500,000. To allay suspicion, he arranged for a handover at Sieben's at the exact time of the raid. Any sooner, and the deal would abort; any later, and O'Bannion would go irritatingly scot-free.

The **Prohibition agents** hit the site on 19 May as soon as the money changed hands, grabbing Torrio and O'Bannion along with thirteen truckloads of beer. Despite a proffered $50,000 bribe, eleven defendants had to suffer the unusual inconvenience of a court hearing. But O'Bannion was not among them. Torrio smelt a rat, and exacted retribution.

At noon on 10 November 1934, O'Bannion was idling in his **flower** shop opposite the cathedral, clipping the stems from a bunch of chrysanthemums. Three customers entered. O'Bannion recognised them and turned to his young porter, saying, 'The floor's in a mess, Bill. Better brush all those leaves and petals up', and went forward, secateurs in one hand, the other arm outstretched in greeting. He shook hands with his killer, who did not let go.

Thus immobilised, O'Bannion was shot twice in the chest, twice in the throat, once through the cheek and then, sprawled among the lilies, in the head. A few days later one of his buddies, Two-gun (or sometimes Three-gun) Louis Alterie, issued a public challenge to the murderers to shoot it out fair and square on the corner of State and Madison Streets; Alterie was fresh in from the West and a life as a cowboy. Mayor Dever protested, 'Are we living by the code of the Dark Ages?'

O'Bannion's killers were almost certainly the Sicilian 'torpedoes' **Anselmi and Scalise**. As a minor refinement, they prepared for assignments by rubbing their bullets with garlic in the belief that this enhanced the likelihood of their victims' wounds turning gangrenous.

Oesterreich, Walburga (b. 1867)

A queer Californian case from 1922. The story started nineteen years before, when the redoubtable Walburga Oesterreich already felt disenchanted with her husband, Fred, a slave-driving drunk who owned a Milwaukee apron factory. In 1903 he hired a new repairman: an undersized, introverted 17-year-old, Otto Sanhuber.

Walburga, then thirty-six, took a fancy to the newcomer. First the sewing-machines in the factory broke down continually; then the one in Walburga's bedroom malfunctioned. Otto started paying home calls, and soon Wal-

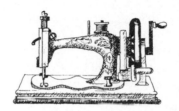

burga's Singer needed his ministrations so regularly that her husband became jealous. He suggested that Walburga buy a new sewing-machine.

'No, I like this one,' she said firmly, and set off with Otto, by now her lover, for a protracted tour of Chicago and St Louis. Fred had them tailed, infuriating Walburga, and she cracked him over the head with a silver candlestick on her return.

Walburga realised that the only way to ensure that she was not followed when visiting her lover was for him to move in. So one day in 1905, while Fred went to work, Walburga installed Otto in the loft of their large mustard-coloured Milwaukee home, and there this shy, retiring man spent his next seventeen years. Walburga scratched three times on the ceiling when she wanted him, ascending through a trapdoor in the master bedroom ceiling.

By day, Walburga lived with Otto. By night, she lived with Fred. So everything happened at different times, but in the same place, although there were occasional changes of scene when the Oesterreichs and Otto moved house. The three finished up in North St Andrews Place in Los Angeles.

Sometimes Fred heard scufflings overhead or noticed that this or that had been moved. His cigars kept disappearing and drink vanished at an alarming rate. Provisioning Otto was a major undertaking. Walburga ferried up armfuls of tinned meat, milk, bottled beer, canned fish, vegetables, bread, bolognas, whole liverwursts and entire cheeses. Otto's career provided another challenge, but convention has always allowed an outlet for solitary men of no particular aptitude confined to attics. They become writers, and after eleven years of rejection slips Otto's intensely-visualised tales of sacred and profane love in the South Seas were eagerly sought by editors of pulp fiction.

When Fred heard things go bump in the night, Walburga responded with references to an infestation of rats, and his bewilderment at the way food seemed to eat itself made her heap scorn on his drunkard's memory. Finally, out in the garden, Fred swore that he discerned a face peering through the dusty attic window. This drove Walburga into a derisive frenzy.

The years passed, the First World War came and went, the Oesterreich Garment Company flourished. Then on 22 August 1922, Fred came back early from work and fell into an argument with Walburga while Otto, caught short, was downstairs. Intervening, he shot Fred dead with four bullets from his .25, a gift from Walburga.

Walburga called the police, explaining that her adored spouse, by now a millionaire, had been gunned down by a burglar. She was not believed. The .25-calibre weapon was a 'lady's gun' avoided by professional crooks, and everyone knew that Walburga detested her husband. She was arrested on suspicion after imprudently giving her lawyer, Herman Shapiro, a distinctive diamond-studded ring that she claimed had been stolen during the robbery.

In prison, Walburga sent for her attorney and asked him to call at her house, go to the bedroom, open the cupboard door, and scratch three times on a panel above a shelf. Then, Walburga explained, her ne'er-do-well half-brother in the attic would appear. Shapiro was to assure him that all was well.

But when pale Otto emerged, the truth came tumbling out; after nearly twenty years he was probably glad to talk to someone. Otto confessed to the shooting. What should he do? The attorney advised him to leave town. Otto did, settling in Portland, Oregon, where he married a compliant stenographer who accepted his selective **amnesia** covering the years from 1903 to 1922. Meanwhile, without Otto, the circumstantial case against Walburga folded.

Another seven years passed. By now Shapiro feared for his own life. Walburga had taken to paying threatening calls to his office, and he lodged an affidavit revealing the truth about Fred Oesterreich's murder.

In 1930 Otto and Walburga were indicted. Otto was tried first, and the jury convicted him of the lesser crime of manslaughter, an offence covered by a three-year Statute of Limitations. As the trial was out of time, Otto could not be guilty since he could not be prosecuted, and Walburga was absolved on account of the previous finding that Fred had been killed by Otto. In her declining years, she lost all her money and lived above a garage in the Wilshire district of Los Angeles.

Officer material

The **Kray** twins' unusual military career merits attention. Fierce and vicious fighters, they came from London's East End, an area largely beyond the law even in the 1950s. National Service provided the novel taste of an authority larger than their own: army discipline.

On 2 March 1952, their first day with the Royal Fusiliers, the brothers cut short a corporal's exposition on the virtues of highly polished boots. 'We don't care for it here,' they announced. 'We're off home to see our Mum.' The corporal grabbed one of the boys; they knocked him down and arrived home in time for tea. After recapture the next morning, each twin blamed the other, and the pair got off lightly with a week in the guardroom. On release, they went AWOL again, only to find that their diet of bar brawls at home palled after a couple of weeks. So when a policeman spotted them in a Mile End café, the twins meekly returned to the fray at the Fusiliers.

After their next sojourn in detention, the Krays beat up a sergeant. Separating the pair produced adverse results. Reggie honed his left hook on NCOs while Ronnie refused to shave or wear his uniform. Their next cells, in Colchester's Detention Barracks, supplied the twins' first encounter with hardened criminals, making a future of armed robbery a serious option.

The twins escaped again, were recaptured, and broke out once more, on Christmas Eve. A Constable Fisher spotted them in Mile End's 'Red Caff' and, after offering to come quietly, they roughed him up and ran off. Collared a few weeks later, they served a month in the Scrubs before being locked in the Howe Barracks guardroom to await military trial. The worst they faced was a Dishonourable Discharge preceded by another spell in prison – exactly what they fancied.

So Ronnie and Reggie settled down to enjoy themselves. On their first day, after smashing the cell furniture, they ripped their bedding and uniforms into tiny shreds. When the colour sergeant arrived to restore discipline, the twins emptied the latrine bucket over his head. Caged up, they demanded water, and handcuffed the guard's outstretched wrists to the bars; it took an hour to cut him free. They burned their replacement bedding and uniforms, earning a drenching with fire hoses, and the following morning clambered onto the roof for a sing-song. But still they longed for home. Dressing up neat, they told the guards they were leaving, asked to visit the lavatory, put their escort in a necklock, stole the guardroom keys and broke out again.

Rather than lock the Krays away for five expensive years, the Army called a truce. A court martial on 11 June 1953, condemned the twins to spend their nine remaining months of military service in prison at Shepton Mallet, where they completed their criminal education.

The only soldier to overawe the Krays was a languid, upper-class cavalry captain, who interrupted the pair mid-rant: 'I know perfectly well what you're up to and it's all right by me. But for God's sake, *do* stop making such a bloody row. You'll frighten the horses.' In a seminal incident the year before their conscription, Ronnie was arrested for punching a constable on the jaw outside Pellici's café. The fight ended before Reggie could come to his aid. Rather

than let his twin down, Reggie spent the rest of the day hunting the policeman and, the moment he could, assaulted him. Thus did Reggie wangle his way *into* his brother's dungeon, a psychological pattern repeated in the years to come.

Omerta

Strictly speaking, *omerta* means the ability to be a man, a key concept of the Sicilian Mafia. It involves double moral standards: those inside the group must be treated well whereas those outside are fair game, subject to *false omerta* (feigned courtesy, masking, for instance, the intent to deceive or kill).

Similarly, the ideal Sicilian male is virile, whereas the perfect woman is a virgin; there is an inherent contradiction here. In Sicily, either quality – virility and virginity – could be easily misplaced, the former by any momentary default in responding appropriately to a threat touching personal honour, and the latter in the usual way. But sexual honour might also be forfeit by a broken engagement, with its imputation that the intended bride was unworthy to be a wife.

Within the household, the two qualities were complementary: the men's virility shielded the women's virginity, and the women's virginity proclaimed their menfolk's virility. But beyond the family, all was marauding mayhem. Between 1940 and 1950, more than 60 per cent of Mafia murders in Calabria were sexually inspired.

A man could earn respect (*uomo di rispetto*) – no matter how humble his origins – by demonstrating *omerta*. The pursuit of honour was a democratic business; hence its appeal for the poor to whom no other avenues were open.

Today, *omerta* denotes **silence**. This is because, in Sicily, it was manly to stay quiet; in a society of oppressive injustice, little was gained by complaining. For almost thirty years in America, from Luciano's establishment of the 'Commission' in 1931 right through to the 1960s, if a gangster talked, he died. Some 5,000 *mafiosi* went through their lives, and even to their deaths, adhering to this doctrine in the face of law enforcement entreaties to co-operate.

Things are different now. In 1993 Sammy the Bull Gravano, former underboss of the Gambino family, occupied Court 318 on New York's Centre Street, testifying against his former associates, and the prospect that he will be hunted down by omniscient hoods seems remote.

See also **Decline, Inquisition, Murder Inc., Vendetta**

One-way ride

Everything, no matter how mundane, has to be invented by someone and tested on someone else. In July 1921, Steve Wisiewski, picked up in Chicago's Maxwell Street ghetto, received an experimental 'one-way ride', the world's first, all the way to Libertyville twenty-five miles north of the city, where his body turned up the next day. The term was coined by the leading labour racketeer Big Tim Murphy, shot in 1928.

Wisiewski paid the price for hijacking a consignment of beer, becoming the first of Prohibition Chicago's 703 gangland killings.

Onorevole

More to do with strength than honour. Being *onorevole* was the other concept underpinning the Sicilian Mafia's code of conduct; it can be translated roughly as 'violently touchy'. Any successful act of aggression was *onorevole*, and the more aggressive the better. The traditional bandit Marlino Zappa attracted veneration because 'he wasn't violent as a rule, but when he had to be, then he amazed everyone, he stunned his enemies'.

Mafiosi always behave honourably; that is, they attain honour through violence. In Pitré's words from the turn of the century: 'The *mafioso* is simply a brave man, someone who will put up with no provocation... The Mafia is a certain consciousness of one's own being, an exaggerated notion of individual force and strength.'

In Sicily, those without honour were often physically segregated from the rest of the community. The writer Asprea describes a Calabrian village in the 1930s where the besmirched outcasts were cordoned off like lepers: 'To the south of *il Calvario* was *il Pilieri*. There, alongside the main sewer of the town was a string of huts, battered by the east wind.' These smoke-blackened hovels gave refuge to the most wretched dregs, feeble-hearted men whose defenceless womenfolk (and children) were at the mercy of anyone more powerful. Andrea described the killing of Pepinello, a prostitute's child from Oppido Mamertina, who was retained by local youths as a target for their shooting competition.

Failure to pursue a **vendetta** provided one sure means of forfeiting any claim to social standing. But it was not a bad plan. Before taking revenge on the violator of a daughter or on your wife's lover (for which you would die in turn), convention demanded you first dispose of your sullied offspring or unfaithful wife. For the squeamish, emigration provided the only way out.

See also **Contempt**

Opium

A drug with an extraordinary history. In nineteenth century Britain, opium ('laudanum') was regarded as a relaxant, good for headaches or spicing up the after-dinner port. Devotees included Wordsworth, Coleridge, peasant women and babes-in-arms. In America, opium – known as the 'Mongolian curse' – reached San Francisco in 1853 along with the coolies working the railroads; by 1870, the town boasted a good 200 opium dens. Twenty-four were lavish joints with silk-lined bunks catering exclusively for whites, notably society matrons and their rich daughters.

Fortunately, as the grim facts of addiction emerged in the second half of the century, so did the cure, in the form of the opium derivative, morphine. When it transpired that this was no less habit-forming, doctors were relieved by the 1898 discovery of a heroic antidote to contain the morphine epidemic.

The new wonder-drug, heroin, not only weaned patients from their morphine dependence; it was, according to German chemists, a panacea for bronchitis and tuberculosis. By the turn of the century Bayer distributed heroin in a dozen countries, and in 1906 the American Medical Association approved it for general use. It acquired tens of thousands of followers through patent medicines like Dover's Powders or Sydenhams's Syrup, and by the early 1920s, New York had 250,000 addicts, allegedly responsible for 95 per cent of the city's crime.

Opium has long been an instrument of national policy, political for the Americans and commercial for the British who, in the nineteenth century, became the largest organised drug traffickers in history, targeting China as their most profitable market. In 1800, 200 tons of Indian opium were shipped to China, a figure increased tenfold by 1840, and forty years later imports stood at 6,500 tons, supporting some 100 million users and 15 million addicts. Not until 1906 did the House of Commons pronounce the trade immoral, and opium was not banned in Hong Kong until 1946.

Decades before, Chinese smokers and licensed Chinese opium merchants had spread throughout South-east Asia, deriving additional stimulus from French colonial policies in Vietnam. This long-standing co-existence of the means of production and supply (an interlinked network of growers, Chinese traffickers and **Triad** distributors) ensured that opium became an ingrained part of South-east Asia's social fabric. Inevitably, any major player in the region was enmeshed in the heroin trade, and none more deeply than the CIA, who promoted the **Golden Triangle** into world's foremost centre of opium production. In 1945 the area yielded a hundred tons a year piecemeal. Within fifteen years, CIA policies had raised output by a factor of seven.

The post-war Truman administration wanted a bulwark against communist contagion, and in 1949 America backed the refugee troops fleeing from revolutionary China to northern Burma, arming and provisioning them through the CIA's Air America. But northern Burma was the Cradle of Opium and, once ensconced, the soldiers mutated into the world's largest private heroin armies.

Their leader, General Li, launched a couple of abortive strikes against China in 1951 and 1952. Meanwhile, he found himself commanding well-equipped forces in lawless territory. First Li extended his control throughout the Shan States. Then he taxed the hill tribes, then he taxed the smugglers, then he laid on protection for the smugglers, and finally he became a trafficker himself – buying direct, organising plantations, working hand-in-hand with the Triads. Still receiving CIA backing, he boosted production from its modest level of forty tons in 1949 to 350 tons within a decade. With 10,000 troops at his disposal, armed with the latest American weapons, General Li met the CIA's requirements for an anti-Communist buffer state.

It was the same pattern elsewhere. In Laos, after Kennedy cut off the country's monthly drip-feed of $3 million aid in 1961, the CIA maintained their nominee (the right-wing Phoumi Nosavan) in power with funds raised through the opium trade. Taking the backward Laotian narcotics industry by the scruff of the neck, the American military encouraged farmers to cultivate opium and oversaw the crop. Output increased tenfold, to 200 tons a year. In Thailand, the CIA's principal government contact, Chief of Police General Phao Sriyanonda, went into partnership with the Triads to run the drugs business. Phao became a massive trafficker himself, inculcating widespread corruption, and when he took refuge in Switzerland in 1957 the Triads stepped into his shoes and into the regime, monopolising the trade.

Today, America reaps the harvest. As her forces poured into Vietnam, the dealers realised that here was a whole new mass market. In 1970 the Cholon Triad sponsored a test campaign, feeding the troops with free samples of injectable heroin; even when money changed hands, it was a pittance, with 99 per cent pure vials at five dollars. By mid-1971 some 40,000 GIs were hooked, and the Hong Kong Triads (the 14K and the Wo Shing Wo) were so impressed that they sent official observers to learn the business. The war's end saw 100,000 soldier-addicts; and the Triads, already billions of dollars to the good, viewed the American withdrawal with some chagrin.

Then the Triads regrouped under the far-sighted guidance of the Ma brothers from China's Chiu Chau region. Their customers might have left, but they had not ceased to exist. Why not establish a distribution network to trail the retreating troops home and supply the American market? And why stop there? Why not feed the world?

Hence today's international heroin traffic, dominated by billionaire Triads.

Optographs

In 1881, Professor Willi Kuhne of Heidelberg University peered into the eyes of a dead frog and discerned, etched on its retina, a faint impression of his laboratory bunsen burner. The frog had gazed fixedly at the flame before it died, and thus the professor could see an image of the last thing the frog saw.

Professor Kuhne realised that the criminological implications would be immense if the same held true for human beings: a deceased's eyes might 'photograph' his assailant. Kuhne could not conduct experiments on people, but he systematically repeated his work on frogs, confirming that images of bright, high-contrast objects remain imprinted on the retina for half an hour after death. The same applied to rabbits, and it was for this reason that in 1888 the British police took an 'optograph' of **Jack the Ripper**'s last victim, just in case.

To no avail. Nonetheless the legend of optographic images passed into criminal folklore. It inspired the grisly shooting of PC George William **Gutteridge** on 27 September 1927, and as late as 1947 an investigative photographer from California begged the coroner to release the Black Dahlia's eyeballs (see **False Confessions**) so that he could obtain a likeness of her murderer.

Research from the 1980s by Professors Sandheim and Alexandridis of Heidelberg suggests that people do 'photograph' the last thing they see. But the images, very poor at best, blur after the first half hour. Successful detection requires prompt development with specialised techniques, and a frontal assailant who remains immobile at length in bright sunlight.

Oral hygiene treatment

Invented by the Austrian nurse Waltraud Wagner at Vienna's Leinz hospital. Wagner devised her 'oral hygiene treatment' as a counter-measure to the interminable misery and suffering of her elderly charges.

In Britain, a concoction known as the 'Brompton Mixture', consisting of morphia, codeine, alcohol and syrup, provided a popular but informal method of euthanasia. During the final stages of terminal disease a large bottle was placed by the patient's bedside, with a warning that on no account should he or she to drink it for fear of fatal consequences.

The medical profession at large, with its power to mete out life and death, has spawned its fair share of murderers. Pre-eminent among them is the industrious Dr Clarke Hyde of Kansas. Married to a niece of Thomas Swope, the millionaire founder of Kansas City, Hyde counted a total of seven relatives – surely a manageable total – interposed between him and inheritance, and in 1909 he set to work.

Swope perished in October, followed to the grave by his financial adviser James Hunton. Five brothers- and sisters-in-law fell ill from a familial epidemic of typhoid, and Chrisman Swope expired under Hyde's care. Suspicions against Hyde hardened when the condition of the survivors markedly improved during his absence on a trip to New York. He was followed, and observed discarding a capsule from his pocket which, on analysis, smelled of cyanide, as did the body of Thomas Swope after exhumation. Hyde was found guilty of murder, but a well-funded defence contrived his release in 1917.

Hyde's motive was clear, as is the ostensible element of perverted 'mercy-killings' for Waltraud Wagner. More obscure was the compulsion animating Britain's Nurse Beverley Allitt, who in February 1993 was charged with twenty-six counts of murder, attempted murder and causing grievous bodily harm. She worked on Ward 4 of the Grantham and Kesteven Hospital, where four children inexplicably died between February and April 1991. The body of the first victim, 5-month-old Paul Crampton, contained a huge amount of **insulin**, and the duty roster showed that none of the twenty-five suspicious collapses occurred when Nurse Allitt was not on duty.

See also **In-laws, Münchausen**

Orfila, Joseph Bonaventure (b. 1787)

Father of modern toxicology. Orfila discovered his purpose in life halfway through a chemistry lecture to his students in April 1813. After summarising the standard tests for arsenious acid, he turned to his practical demonstration. It did not work.

At his bench after class, Orfila verified that most of the orthodox chemical tests for the better known poisons were worthless. Toxic residues could not be detected in food, drink or bodies; the most reliable forensic indicator was to feed an animal with an extract of the suspect substance and see if it died. Orfila rapidly ascertained that no one knew anything. He wrote: 'The central fact that struck me had never been perceived by anyone else. My first words were these: *toxicology does not yet exist.*'

Orfila was a child prodigy. Born in a school-free Minorcan village, by the age of fourteen he had mastered five languages and written a Latin thesis on philosophy. After a brief interlude as a sailor he won a chemistry scholarship to Barcelona and then took a medical degree in Paris. There he eked out his slender resources by teaching – hence his fateful lecture on poison.

Ambitious and energetic, Orfila signed up a bookseller to take on a two-volume textbook, *Treatise on Poison, or General Toxicology*, published that same year. Like today's unfathomable *Brief History of Time*, the title became a surprise best-seller and Orfila found himself catapulted into social prominence. He married well in 1815 and three years later was appointed professor in 'mental maladies' to the Paris Medical Faculty. As well as putting toxicology on a scientific footing, Orfila became a celebrated expert witness, perhaps most notably in the 1840 case of the romantic young Marie Lafarge.

The drawback with arsenic is that it does not readily dissolve, and when Marie Lafarge gave her husband a cup of poisoned milk after he became indisposed from poisoned cake, their maid noticed white flakes floating on the surface. The girl, Anna Brun, saw Marie surreptitiously taking pinches of white powder from a malachite box, and carried the milk dregs to the local doctor. Nine days after Charles Lafarge died on 16 January 1840 from an obscure gastric ailment, Marie was under arrest.

She cut an attractive and newsworthy figure, particularly when contrasted to her uncouth husband. Marie was well-born, of royal descent through an illegitimate line, and her cousin had married the Vicomte de Léautaud. Orphaned at the age of eighteen, Marie viewed with reserve the exertions of a wealthy aunt to offload her onto a suitable husband. The first contender, a local sub-prefect, did not correspond to her aristocratic

expectations. But in 1839 a matrimonial agency proposed a candidate purportedly matching her 90,000 franc dowry. This was Charles Lafarge. He may have looked like a fat, crude rustic, but he was billed as a man of fortune, an ironmaster with 200,000 francs of property and an annual income of 30,000 francs.

The ill-matched pair were married in August that year, and a protesting Marie was dragged away to the social wastes of deepest Limousin. In her words, 'Upon arriving at Le Glandier, instead of the charming château I had been led to expect, I found a dilapidated ruin.' Her fashionable aspirations were utterly confounded. Her husband was a bankrupt, his family were peasants, and their farmhouse crawled with rats. A distraught Marie refused to consummate the marriage, and as the year progressed she discovered that her spouse, in his efforts to raise money, forged her signature, and that her mother-in-law had tampered with her will. At **Christmas** she sent Charles, on business in Paris, a large arsenic cake, and he died three weeks later .

The murder case was preceded by a preliminary trial for the theft of a diamond necklace which vanished from Léautaud's château while Marie was a guest. High-society allegations of Marie's kleptomania and compulsive lying monopolised the French headlines for months before she arrived to face capital charges in Tulle on 3 September 1840 as a convicted thief. The local chemist attested that he found arsenic traces in the fatal glass of milk and in the malachite box, as well as in her husband's stomach and vomit.

The defence consulted Orfila. He refuted the prosecution's case: the yellow precipitates discovered to be soluble in ammonia were not necessarily arsenic, and although boiling the dead man's stomach was said to have produced metallic deposits on the arsenic 'mirror' this could not be validated in court because the apparatus had exploded. Nor had the prosecution heard of the much more sensitive Marsh test, discovered ten years previously.

With their arguments in tatters, the prosecution volunteered to try the Marsh test themselves. Results were negative on the stomach contents – Marie was innocent – but positive on the malachite box and the suspect preparation of eggnog – Marie was guilty. Summoned to resolve the discrepancy, Orfila arrived by stagecoach on 13 September and worked well into the night in the presence of the local pharmacists.

The following afternoon he revealed that residues of arsenic (which did not originate from the soil) were present in Charles Lafarge's stomach, liver, heart, brain and intestines. Orfila left one tiny crack of hope; there was no trace of arsenic in the flesh, so perhaps Marie's husband had been contaminated *after* death. This was not sufficient to save her from a sentence of hard labour for life, later commuted to ten years, and she died a few months after her release in 1851.

See also **Poisoning**

Organised and disorganised

Interviews conducted by the FBI's Behavioral Science Unit in the early 1980s (see **Database**) resulted in the classification of sex killers into two major types: the 'organised nonsocial' and the 'disorganised asocial'. The first word of each designation means what it says. The murders are, to a greater or lesser extent, planned and controlled; and as so often happens, the 'organised' practitioner is a cut above his 'disorganised' counterpart – more intelligent, more employable, with his own car and perhaps a live-in lover.

Where the type of murderer can be gleaned from scene-of-the-crime evidence, investigators are provided with initial indicators on the suspect's characteristics: his type of job, whether he lives alone or with a partner, whether his home is near the scene of the crime, and so on. Sex killers leave few other clues, since the target is essentially random, making traditional detection (working back from the victim's identity) redundant.

The 'organised nonsocial' sex killer may dislike people in general. Superficially, however, he appears warm and even charming. Typically regarded as a troublemaker by acquaintances and colleagues, his prime concern is 'number one'. His latent social hostility materialises with the onset of adolescence, and the murder is generally triggered by some specific event, like losing a job.

As a rule, the organised killer does not take a local victim. He has the prudence to browse, cruising for the next hit, and the foresight to carry his weapon with him, both to and from the crime. He will not normally snatch his prey by immediate

recourse to violence; his social skills beguile the prospect into going his way. The assault is a slow process as the victim is tortured and mutilated preparatory to the kill, making for a tidy crime scene. The infliction of **terror** and pain supplies the pay-off, and the organised killer lingers over his solitary pleasures, often elaborated into a ritual of **dismemberment**.

The organised killer obtains retrospective audience reaction, transporting the disfigured corpse to a place where someone is bound to stumble over it. As a follow-up he maintains an eye on the investigative progress, waiting to see if the body has been discovered, and ideally becomes peripherally involved in the investigation (see **Vocation**). He may taunt the police with messages. On his 'free' evenings he sometimes, like the Son-of-**Sam**, returns to the site of a previous killing and dreams of the parades gone by.

By contrast, the 'disorganised asocial' does not just dislike people deep down inside. A quiet loner unable to cope with personal relationships, he keeps himself to himself and is generally tied to a menial job. In adolescence, he steals women's clothes, particularly underwear; this is less risky than approaching them openly. In maturity, he is classified as 'sexually incompetent', and any sexual acts occur after the victim is safely dead. The disorganised killer finds his victims near home, overwhelming them in a frenzied 'blitz'. Up to the fatal moment, he may have had no intention to kill; the offence is unplanned, devoid of precipitating stress. Normally the body is abandoned where it lies with only a feeble attempt at concealment. There may be mess: bloody footprints and fingerprints. The murder weapon – often a weapon of opportunity – is frequently discarded nearby. Taking parts home to eat is a disorganised trait.

Thus the initial police investigation concentrates on the probable sequence of events during the killing (*in vivo*/posthumous mutilation), the location of the body (hidden/exposed) and the presence/absence of the weapon. Sometimes the signs are clear, sometimes they are mixed, but either way they form the basis of a psychological '**profile**', quite possibly sufficiently revealing for the police to work a neighbourhood door-to-door asking questions beginning, 'Have you ever known someone who...', which lead to the culprit.

The system is by no means perfect. FBI Agent Robert Hazelwood keeps a profile on his office wall specifying that the suspect from a Georgia case was a divorced high-school drop-out from a broken home with a low-skill job who lived miles from the murder scene and hung around cheap bars. The culprit proved to be a non-drinking, married, high-flying executive from a reasonable family background with a neighbourhood home.

See also **Detection, Lines, Masturbation, Terminology, Torture**

Oxford Apartments, no. 213

Everybody likes good neighbours. Number 213 Oxford Apartments was home to Jeffrey **Dahmer**, the Milwaukee serial killer, and in the run-up to July 1991 the block's residents became acclimatised to the regular thumpings, crashings and screams from his flat.

Following Dahmer's arrest, it transpired that his neighbour Aaron Whitehead had listened to the sound of dismemberment, taking Dahmer for a hobbyist. 'I would hear a buzz saw running in the early evening,' he recalled. 'I thought he was building something.'

The noise was bad, but the stench was very nearly intolerable. Nanetta Lowery, who lived above Dahmer, commented, 'The smell got so bad, it got into my clothes and I couldn't get it out, even after washing.' According to neighbour John Batchelor, 'It was terrible. It almost made me throw up.'

The odour (see **Mothers**) was noticeable even from adjacent properties. Identifying its cause posed unfamiliar problems for civilians. After Dahmer's arrest, Ella Vickers, another neighbour, said, 'We've been smelling things for weeks, but we thought it was a dead animal, or something like that. We had no idea it was humans.' Larry Marion believed that combat experience would have helped. 'Had we been war veterans, we would have known the smell of death.'

Dahmer's neighbours constantly remonstrated with him; he attributed the stench of the dozen festering cadavers in his flat to a 'balky fish tank' or the 'spoiled meat' stored in his unreliable freezer. After the truth emerged, on the night of 22 July 1991, the building attracted such waves of antagonism that Milwaukee residents actually shot it, peppering it with random gunfire.

P

Packer, Alferd (d. 1907)

America's leading cannibal. In autumn 1873 Packer left Salt Lake City as one of twenty frontiersmen on an ill-fated expedition prospecting for gold. Close to starvation, ten men later turned back, and soon the expedition consisted of a rump of six survivors heading for the Rio Grande through the Colorado mountains under Packer's leadership.

Only Packer remained by the following spring. He dragged himself back from the wilds into the Los Pinos Indian Agency, exhausted but – all things considered – strangely plump.

The 2 April discovery of human flesh not far from the outpost prompted Packer's first confession. The famished prospectors had been reduced to eating roots over the winter; then one morning, after a fruitless five-day scavenging foray, he staggered into to their lakeside camp to find Israel Swan on the menu, his leg roasting on the camp-fire under the super-

vision of Shannon Wilson Bell. Everyone else was dead, either from hunger or from Bell's murderous hatchet.

Swan was the group's oldest, and after he ran out, fat Frank Miller was consumed. But it was clear that when James Humphrey and George Noon were exhausted, Packer and Bell would have no provisions left. Bell ran amok despite a non-aggression pact, and Packer shot him dead in self-defence, sitting out the winter on the remains. Come spring, he stripped Bell down for provisions and struggled away, discarding the last cuts of meat when he came in sight of the trading post. If Packer's story were believed, he was blameless. But it wasn't.

Packer's first bid to lead a party back to his encampment in what is now known as Deadman's Gulch proved unsuccessful. By June, the team knew why. Near a cabin on the shores of Lake Christoval they found five corpses, four with their skulls shattered. The brains of Frank Miller had been dashed out with a rifle butt.

Packer escaped from custody. Retaken in 1883, he was sentenced to death in ringing terms for the murder of Israel Swan. 'Stand up, y'voracious man-eating son of a bitch, stand up,' Judge Melville B. Gerry is said to have roared. 'There was seven democrats in Hinsdale County and you've ate five of them. God damn you. I sentence you to be hanged by the neck until you is dead, dead, dead, as a warning against reducing the Democrat population of the state.' More restrained versions of these sentiments appear in the published transcripts. On a retrial the charge was reduced to manslaughter, and a pardon trimmed Packer's forty-year term to eighteen years. He eventually made good as a posthumous local hero, and his bust now stands in the Colorado State Capitol.

What really happened at Deadman's Gulch? Today, a replica of one of the prospector's skulls squats on the desk of Professor James Starrs in Washington; massive photographic enlargements of the cannibalised bones grace the walls of his university office. In 1989 Starrs located the bodies with ground-penetrating radar and subjected them to modern forensic techniques, putting it beyond doubt that the cadavers had been filleted; Starrs detected the carving nicks on the skeletons made by a skinning knife. No evidence of any gunshot wounds emerged, but examination disclosed defence cuts on the upraised arms, indicating that the men had perished trying to ward off blows from a hatchet. Starrs confirmed the rifle butt injury to 'victim C'. Thus the prospectors were murdered and eaten, although there was nothing to show by whom, except that the manner of their deaths was inconsistent with Packer's story. Professor Starrs, clearly conversant with the intricacies of living off the land during a Colorado winter, commented, 'Packer was having his fillets morning, noon and night, even though he could have survived by killing rabbits.'

See also **Cannibalism**

Palmer, Dr William (1824–56)

A Victorian case of overpowering circumstantial evidence. Dr Palmer was a betting man accustomed to heavy losses, and on 12 November 1855 he accompanied a horse-owner called John Parsons Cook to the Shrewsbury races.

Cook's mare, Polestar, romped home and the two friends retired to the Talbot Arms in Rugely to celebrate. Cook downed a glass of brandy and then leapt to his feet, exclaiming, 'Good God, there's something in that which burns my throat.' Palmer soothed him and appeared to sip the last drops without ill-effects. But Cook was taken ill, and the local physician, a venerable 80-year-old called Bamford, prescribed a diet of 'slops' together with a 'night pill'. Palmer fed the patient with capsules from his own hand, and his condition progressively deteriorated. On 20 November, Cook went into spasm and died as his heels arched back against his head.

The High Street, Rugely, showing the Talbot Arms where Cook died (left)

Palmer fought a spirited rearguard action against growing suspicion. He attended Cook's autopsy in his medical capacity, and jostled the doctor's assistant against Charles Devonshire, the medical student who was, at that moment, slicing open Cook's stomach. Nearly all its contents spilled into the body cavity, but the organ was carefully placed in a sealed vessel, which Palmer attempted to steal. 'Where's the jar?' demanded Dr Harland. 'It's here,' called Palmer, slinking towards the door at the other end of the room. 'I thought it more convenient to take it away.' Then Palmer offered the groom £10 to stage an accident destroying the specimen jars in transit.

When Cook's remains arrived unscathed at the London laboratory of Professor Taylor, the leading authority on poisons, they contained only a small quantity of antimony (rather than the expected **strychnine**, for which there was as yet no real test) and Palmer managed to intercept the post-mortem report in the post. Meanwhile he sweetened the local coroner with a bribe of a twenty-pound turkey, a brace of pheasants, a barrel of oysters and a fine cod.

Professor Alfred Swaine Taylor

But to no avail. By now the extensive conglomeration of Palmer's dead friends and relatives was a matter of public discussion, as was the imposing accretion of the fourteen illegitimate children he sired as a medical student. Palmer's first job with a Liverpool firm of druggists ended in embezzlement; his second apprenticeship was cancelled after difficulties over women and money. As a doctor, Palmer confined his interest to racing, which fuelled a downwards spiral into debt. But he was cheerful, a church-goer, and an inveterate liar whose bare-faced deceit inspired unwarranted credence.

First among the dead was a Mr Abley, who passed away after sharing a glass of brandy with Palmer in the Staffordshire Infirmary. Palmer was mid-affair with his wife. Then came the turn of Palmer's mother-in-law, reputedly worth £12,000. 'I know I shan't live long,' she had objected in January 1849 when invited for a visit which ended a week later, as she predicted, with her demise. This loss marked Palmer's first recourse to the obliging Dr Bamford who ascribed the death to 'apoplexy'. Then a bookmaker, Leonard Bladen, came back from Chester Races, his pockets bulging with winnings of £1,000. Palmer asked him to stay. He too expired after a week, and both his money and his betting book (in which Palmer figured as a heavy loser) disappeared.

William Palmer

By now Palmer's wife, Annie, was fed up. 'When will it all end?' she asked. The answer was not with Palmer's four children, who perished in convulsions after licking honey from his fingers. Palmer next disposed of a creditor called Bly, to whom he owed £800, and an uncle, Joseph 'Beau' Bentley, who succumbed after a brandy-drinking competition. That left Annie herself. Palmer secured a policy of £13,000 on her life and paid the first premium. Then she died, goaded on her way by nine days of dosing with antimony. 'My poorest dear Annie expired at ten minutes past one,' Palmer noted in his diary before bedding their servant girl Eliza. 'She was called by God to the home of bliss she so well deserved.' Dr Bamford diagnosed 'English cholera'.

Now it was the turn of Palmer's younger brother Walter, an ailing alcoholic. Palmer insured him for £13,000, installed him in a local hotel and plied him with gin. But even on three bottles a day, it takes unremitting effort to drink a man to death, and on 15 August 1855 the landlord came upon Palmer at the bedside measuring out some accelerating medicine. He asked how the patient was. 'Very ill, very low,' conceded Palmer. 'I'm going to take him something stimulating.' Next day Walter was dead. This time the insurance company put an investigator on the case, and he learned from a boot boy, James Myatt, that Palmer was seen pouring something into Walter's glass. Palmer had a talk with this damaging witness over a drink; Myatt gradually made a full recovery.

Walter's widow unexpectedly claimed on the policy, so Palmer – harried by his creditors – cast around for another source of funds, and when Polestar came in at 7–1 at the Shrewsbury Races, Cook netted £2,050. He was ripe for the picking and, after his suspicious death, the authorities exhumed Annie's body. It too contained traces of antimony. At Palmer's trial the medical evidence was too weak to secure a conviction, but his general course of dealing proved overwhelming. The judge's summing-up was deadly, and, as Palmer told the prison governor, 'When the jury returned into Court, and I saw the cocked up nose of the perky little foreman, I knew it was a gooser with me.' His defence was assisted neither by the forged cheque for £350 he drew on Cook's account as he lay dying, nor by his endeavour to forge a document showing that Cook owed him £4,000.

Palmer was hanged on 14 June 1856 after a hearing at the Old Bailey. It was felt that he would not receive a fair trial locally, and a special statute – the so-called Palmer Act – was passed for his benefit. Judge James Stephen observed that 'Palmer's career supplied one of the proofs of a fact of which many kind-hearted people seem to doubt, namely that such a thing as an atrocious wickedness is consistent with good education, perfect sanity, and everything in a word which deprives one of all excuse for crime.'

Palmer was not unique in turning children's sweet-tooths to fatal advantage. On Hallowe'en

1974, 8-year-old Timmy O'Bryan from Houston died in convulsions shortly after admission to hospital; his post-mortem suggested death by poisoning, confirmed by stomach analysis which detected traces of cyanide. This matched the cyanide discovered crammed into the candy straws – 'Pixy Sticks' – handed round as a Hallowe'en treat to Timmy and his friends. Police impounded the rest of the confectionary before it claimed more victims, finding six more Pixy Sticks laden with a fatal dose.

Timmy's father, who murdered his son for the insurance money, went to the electric chair.

Panopticon, The

In 1791, the British philosopher Jeremy Bentham published a pamphlet, 'The Panopticon or Inspection House', setting out his thinking on the perfect **prison**.

Bentham's edifice was to be constructed to the plan of a multi-storeyed wheel, with a circular rim housing the prisoners' individual dungeons and overlooked by a central hub, the inspection tower, a layout combining solitary confinement with a sense of continuous supervision from warders, who could peer in through the cell windows.

This represented the worst of both worlds. Bentham submitted his proposal to successive governments to no avail, despite undertaking to run the concern himself at a modest profit derived from the prisoners' work.

In due course Bentham became such an enthusiastic proponent of his design that he advocated it as a substitute for Australia, arguing against the policy of transportation in his *Panopticon versus New South Wales*.

When this failed, Bentham tirelessly lobbied David Phillips, then setting off to colonise Port Phillip Bay, insisting that he build a Panopticon in Australia, a sort of a prison within a prison. Before Phillips sailed, Bentham demanded: 'Are you serious in your intention of building a prison, and moreover of building it on the central inspection principle?' Phillips was not, but he was too polite to say so. The thinking behind Bentham's scheme, intended to avoid 'contamination through association', gave rise to the catastrophes of the **separate system**.

Panty Bandit *et al*

In the summer of 1988, the Panty Bandit became California's Public Enemy Number One. He was a hybrid, a sex burglar.

First came the sex. The Panty Bandit would raid a Los Angeles beauty parlour and force a woman, at gunpoint, to remove her knickers. Then he draped the garment over his face and masturbated in front of the assembled customers. Phase two supplied the burglary. The Panty Bandit emptied the till and left. When arrested on 23 October 1988, the culprit Bruce Lyons was carrying a carton of trophy underwear in his Honda Civic.

People take their pleasures in different ways. An American, Edgar Jones, was detained in 1992 on suspicion of being the St Louis Serial Toe Sucker; he faced two charges of sexual abuse and five other related offences. His victims were all schoolgirls. Jones posed as a jogger, knocked the girls to the ground, ripped off their shoes and gave their toes a good sucking. In Britain, Jonathan Thomas of Oxford experienced a similar attack on the night of 10 April 1992 when he was bound, blindfolded, and remorselessly tickled on the soles of his feet.

Thomas informed the police, but the mute pavements, footpaths and underpass with which twenty-year-old Karl Watkins from Worcestershire enjoyed sexual relations could take no such action.

Pedestrians and passers-by protested that Watkins would remove his trousers, lie down and make love to the flagstones, and on 19 February 1993 he was convicted on five charges of outraging public decency.

In Britain, Hampshire's Meon Valley became the favourite hunting ground of a sex attacker during 1991. Five of his twenty assaults included horrific mutilations to the horses' genitals.

See also **Horse, Masturbation, Pets**

Parker, Marion (1925–27)

Los Angeles **kidnapping** victim. Marion was returned on 17 December 1927. The kidnapper pulled up at the handover location with the wide-eyed child in the front seat of his car. But after paying the $1,500 ransom, her father discovered that William Edward Hickman, the kidnapper, had already detached his child's hands, legs and intestines. Her eyes were wired open. Hickman was very definitely mad, but this proved insufficient to avert his execution on 4 February 1928.

His arrest followed a clear logical evolution. By the roadside near Marion's body, a woman noticed a suitcase stuffed with torn newspapers, some blood-drenched towels, a few scraps of wire and a paper pad identical to the one used in the ransom demand. The towels came from a nearby hotel, where traces of human flesh clogged the drains. A set of fingerprints enabled the police to broadcast Hickman's description and, a few days later, a Seattle haberdasher's suspicions were aroused by a young man trying to buy a change of clothing with a $20 bill. The note was traced to the ransom; and a local garage attendant reported that a man answering Hickman's description was driving a green Hudson. He was picked up heading back towards Los Angeles.

Parricides

In France, parricides were led in a black veil to the scaffold, where – until 1832 – their right hand was cut off prior to decapitation. Regicides suffered the same fate, since their crime was against the father of the nation.

This relatively humane treatment contrasts with the staggering and extended brutality of the *amende honorable* with which the regicide Damiens was disjointed on 2 March 1757, a spectacle described with scrupulous particularity by a Monsieur Bouton, officer of the watch, in one of the most disgusting passages ever printed. Interested readers are referred to *Discipline and Punish* (Allen Lane 1975).

Pax Capone

On 26 October 1926, Al Capone convened a mobster Summit at the Hotel Sherman to partition Chicago and Cook County into formal spheres of interest between the four main gangs. The delegates met without weapons or bodyguards, and agreed the framework of a treaty under Capone's Five Terms: 1. A general amnesty; 2. No future killings or beatings; 3. All past killings and beatings to be forgotten; 4. All malicious rumours to be ignored; 5. Gang leaders to be responsible for acts of their gang members.

'Let's give each other a break,' began Maxie Eisen in the chair to murmurs of assent. Then the hoodlums settled down to hard bargaining. This was fine-print business rather than thuggery, where (for instance) Drucci and Bugs Moran ceded their territorial gains south of Madison Street, limiting themselves to the Forty-second and Forty-third precincts; their rights for beer and spirits to be exclusive as to both retail and wholesale, with their North Side prostitution and gambling concessionaries operating henceforth as Capone licensees.

The convention concluded with warm handshakes, shoulder slapping and smiles all round. Then the colleagues fell to feasting, yarning about the old days. A newspaper man slipped in, later describing their celebratory supper as the ultimate in the macabre. 'Thugs who had taken a shot at each other with murderous intent admitted the effort to the proposed victim, laughing heartily. Thugs who had actually killed explained the details of the killing to friends of the deceased and gave their version why there was no way of getting out of it. The most frightful things in violence were discussed and chuckled over.'

Interviewed about the negotiations the next day, Capone said, 'I told them we were making a shooting gallery of a great business and that nobody profited by it. It's hard and dangerous work, aside from any hate at all, and when a fellow works hard at any line of business, he wants to go home and forget about it.'

For the next two months not a shot was fired. Capone's settlement worked tolerably well until Big Bill Thompson's re-election in April 1927 inaugurated Chicago's final free-for-all.

At the height of his powers, Capone ran his empire from a suite of six rooms on the fourth floor of the Hotel Lexington near the present-day McCormick Place. Staff patrolled the lobby, and their leader in Salon 430 was reached, via ranks of sentries and bodyguards armed with .45s, through an oval vestibule where the initials AC were enclosed by a crest on the parquet floor. The bathroom – with purple tiles, gold fittings and an immense sunken tub – was off left. Capone liked to transact his morning business in a dressing gown and blue silk pyjamas with gold piping, sporting an eleven carat blue-white diamond on his middle finger.

A New York dishwasher when Prohibition took effect, by 1925 Capone ruled a criminal empire with an annual income of $125 million. His house on Prairie Avenue was crammed with oriental rugs, antique furniture, jade and exquisite sculptures. Distended before his time by mountains of pasta, Capone was a music lover readily moved to tears and, unlike many of his colleagues, he held press conferences, attended opening nights at the opera and distributed $100 tips. People waved at the sight of him on city streets. One elderly widow knelt and kissed his hand and, on his appearances at the racetrack or Wrigley Field, hundreds rose to their feet in spontaneous applause. Today the Lexington is derelict; and on the warehouse site of the 1929 St Valentine's massacre they put up a parking lot.

Capone's machine-gunning of seven members of the North Side Gang proved a turning point, burying his affable reputation under the first real public outcry. Two prominent Chicago publishers, Knox of the *Daily News* and McCormick of the *Tribune*, travelled to Washington to complain to Hoover in person, and the upshot was a dual onslaught on Capone's kingdom. The Treasury Department,

under Special Agent Frank J. Wilson, was instructed to build an income tax evasion case, and the Justice Department, not before time, enjoined to connect Capone with bootlegging. But their **Prohibition agents** were corrupt, and District Attorney George Q. Johnson determined to establish a special Capone squad. On 29 September 1929 he summoned a promising young agent, Eliot Ness by name, to his office. Thus were born the **Untouchables**.

In the event, Capone was indicted on 5 June 1931 and brought to justice by the Treasury's case (despite a $4 million bribe) with Ness's bootlegging charges kept in reserve. Sentenced to eleven years, Capone was paroled on 19 November 1939, 'nuttier than a fruitcake' in the advanced stages of syphilis, and died eight years later.

In 1968 George Patty, a food company executive, bought the pock-marked St Valentine's Day garage wall at auction, intending to reassemble it for posterity. Capone's car became another curiosity. A real monster, his mobile fortress was based on a V8 40hp Cadillac, custom-built at a cost of £6,000, and its seven-ton mass owed much to the armour-plated bodywork, a steel-lined fuel tank and bullet-proof glass one and a half inches thick. The car featured a police siren, a secret gun-locker and a removable back window for the rear gunner.

Bought by a British speculator, in 1934 the vehicle, exhibited on a dais, toured England with Bertram Mills's Circus. A placard reading 'The Car of Scarface Al Capone, King of the Gangsters' stood alongside a photographic display of the great man together with his lieutenants, many pictured lying dead in the gutter amid pools of blood.

See also **Cicero, Eighteenth Amendment, Fallout, Hawthorne, Public relations**

Payne, A.D. (d. 1930)

A Texas lawyer. Payne was sentenced to death for exploding his wife and son on 27 June 1930; he wanted to be free to live with his secretary. Awaiting execution, he blew himself up in his prison cell by detonating a charge strapped to his chest.

Miami gangster Creighton Randall 'Randy' Bethell suffered a similar fate in February 1975. Acting on a tip-off, on 4 September 1975 police drove to the reported site of his corpse in a wood opposite utility pole 136 on Card Sound Road, only to find a four-foot crater. Bethell had been detonated with five sticks of dynamite.

But half-measures will not destroy a body. An intensive search of hundreds of square feet of woodland yielded myriads of bone shards. Enough of Bethell's shirt and wig survived to be recognised by his father. The skull was largely intact, showing the passage of a large calibre bullet, and a section of the lower jaw, containing teeth numbers 30, 31 and 32, displayed dental work that matched Bethell's army records.

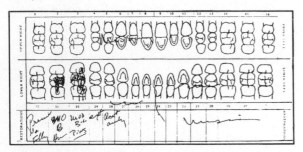

Bethel's dental chart, showing the pin work to teeth 30, 31 and 32 (lower left)

The medical examiner's report detailed the course of events. Bethell had been abducted from his home, driven to Card Sound Road and shot. Later the killers paid another visit to knock out his teeth and jaws, smashing his skull with a boulder. On ascertaining that both Bethell's knees were surgically pinned, they came back to blast his legs with a shotgun. Finally, they blew Bethell up, checked the site and gave it the all-clear.

Even so, his remains helped put Richard Douglas Cravero behind bars. Cravero headed a vicious team of drug-runners credited with thirty-five killings. Bethell, a former associate, had been executed for holding money back.

See also **Durability**

Pearce, Alexander (d. 1824)

Alexander Pearce's head was removed in 1824 by a Mr Crockett of the Hobart Colonial Hospital, Australia, who adapted it as a **souvenir**. Crockett stripped off the flesh, extracted its brains and eyes and then boiled it. In the 1850s the relic was presented to Dr Samuel Norton, the skull collector, who appended it to his one thousand other speci-

mens in 'The American Golgotha'. Today, Pearce's head may be viewed in a display cabinet at the Academy of Natural Sciences in Philadelphia.

It is a head worth having. Pearce, its first owner, was born in Ireland in 1790. Sentenced at 29 to seven years' transportation for stealing six pairs of shoes, he wound up in the penal colony of Macquarie Harbour on Van Diemen's Land. There, on 20 September 1822, he commandeered an open boat and, together with seven companions and one axe, rowed across the bay and hightailed it into the forest.

The convicts found themselves entangled in rough terrain, battling up sharp mountainous escarpments through a morass of scrub, creepers and rotted trees. After a week their stores were exhausted. In Pearce's words, taken from his deposition: 'We then consulted who should fall. Greenhill said, "Dalton; as he volunteered to be a flogger, we will kill him."'

That night, while Dalton lay asleep, Greenhill's axe 'struck Dalton on the head, and he never spoke a word after... Matthew Travers with a knife also came and cut his throat, and bled him; we then dragged him to a distance, and cut off his clothes, and tore out his inside, and cut off his head; then Matthew Travers and Greenhill put his heart and liver on the fire and ate it before it was right warm; they asked the rest would they have any, but they would not have any that night.'

Cannibalism exudes a terrible logic, immediately clear to the seven survivors. Dalton would soon run out and someone had to be next. The weakest were most in fear. Two slipped away in the forest mazes of the Engineer Ranges; the others hunted them, to kill, but the pair struggled back to Macquarie Harbour where they died from their privations. That left five convicts at large, and on 15 October, somewhere near the Loddon Plains, Greenhill rounded on Bodenham and split his skull. Then they devoured him.

Four remained. They reached the Western Tiers in a mania of sullen suspicion, vowing never to eat each other. But on the open plains, no man could hide, no man could hobble faster than his companions, no man could make a run for it, and still Greenhill had the axe. They were bound together in a stranglehold, destined to eat or be eaten, kill or be killed, and in late October, while Mather was sicking up some roots, 'Greenhill still showing his spontaneous habit of bloodshed seized the axe and crept up behind him and gave him a blow on the head'.

Mather beat off his attacker, and lived; that night the unhappy four gathered round the camp fire. Mather knew his time had come. 'They told him they would give him half an hour to pray for himself, which was agreed to; he then gave the prayer book to me, and laid down his head, and Greenhill took the axe and killed him.' And then there were three.

The next to go was Travers, Greenhill's bosom friend. So, at last, on the great Australian plains, just Pearce and Greenhill remained. Together this odd couple dragged through a pleasant landscape of undulating fields and copses, keeping a fixed distance apart, one stopping when the other did. Both knew that the first to sleep was a dead man. They eyed each other day and night, watching across the camp fire. One day passed, then another, and then another.

Finally Greenhill succumbed. He nodded off and Pearce killed him, continuing on his way alone but replenished, with his companion's arm and thigh for sustenance. A week later, after nearly two months of surviving on people, Pearce ran into a convict-shepherd, McGuire, on the edge of the River Ouse. McGuire gave him food and shelter, and Pearce avoided capture for two more months. Summoned before the acting magistrate, Reverend Robert Knopwood, he confessed everything.

But since his grotesque tale was not believed, the authorities sent Pearce back to Macquarie Harbour from which, on 16 November 1823, he escaped again. This time he headed north, making for Port Dalrymple with Thomas Cox, whom he ate on 19 November. On this occasion, Pearce's captors found a mangled body, cut through the middle and partially stripped.

Shipped down to Hobart, Pearce was tried, executed, and anatomised, with his head passing into the hands of Mr Crockett.

Pedigree Chum

Dogfood contaminated by Rodney Whitchelo, who blackmailed the manufacturers. He also spiked cans of Heinz babyfoods with caustic soda, razor blades and rat poison. At the height of the scare, Heinz and Cow & Gate – victims of a copycat threat –

recalled 100 million units from the supermarket shelves after baby Victoria Coppock cut her lip on a razor implanted in a jar of yoghurt. Although Whitchelo only netted £32,000 from his £3.75 million demand before being caught in October 1989, he secured access of a peculiarly irritating kind to almost limitless funds.

As an Essex detective, Whitchelo formed a low opinion of police intelligence. He lived alone with his mother, founded the Sado Masochistic Pen Pal Club and rented hotel rooms for sex with women contacted through magazine advertisements. With the approach of his forties, he was loosely engaged on the early drafts of a book about the 'perfect crime', and the template for his blackmail scheme was a similar but secret plot by William Frary, an unemployed microbiologist who dosed Bernard Matthews's turkeyburgers with mercury. The Detective Training School attended by Whitchelo at Ripley put the clandestine details of Frary's scheme on their 1986 syllabus; Whitchelo, impressed, put them into action. He set up a mailing address in Hammersmith and whiled away two years before making his move, so that any recollection of his voice or appearance would have faded.

The crime was nearly perfect, and its ingenuity lay in the method of ransom collection. At first Whitchelo extorted £100,000 in a brisk letter explaining that he had poisoned the dog food with biocides because they were 'colourless, odourless and highly toxic'. The funds were paid into a building society account opened under a false name, and Whitchelo drove cross-country to make withdrawals from any one of 900 cash machines to a maximum of £300 per day. He reasoned that his colleagues could not mount a nationwide watch without his knowledge.

The police countered with Operation Roach, enlisting 3,000 officers for round-the-clock surveillance on building society branches on selected days. This massive undertaking required the collaboration of the Regional Crime Squads, and Whitchelo duly learned of the plan and its timing from his workmates in the pub. On Operation Roach days, he stayed home. He handled his cashcard with gloves, and when a machine 'ate' it acting under police orders it revealed no fingerprints. Caught on videotape at a branch in Ipswich, he was wearing a hood. And when a public reward was offered, Whitchelo applied for this too, requesting payment in his usual way.

The police guessed that the blackmailer had inside knowledge. So they set up an inner plan, Operation Agincourt, to disseminate the disinformation that Operation Roach was winding down. Whitchelo became careless. With no fears about his financial prospects, he took early retirement and confined his withdrawals to London. Meanwhile, Special Branch offered to maintain a discrete guard over the fifteen 'best-guess' **cash dispensers** on the night of 20 October 1989. Whitchelo went elsewhere, only to find the machine out of action. Workmen had severed an electric cable. So he drove to another cash point at Enfield, approached it wearing a mask, and was arrested.

Sentencing him to seventeen years, Judge Nina Lowry commented: 'You knew there were millions of dog owners in this country and a threat to poison dogs would be particularly compelling.' The case inspired copycat **blackmail** schemes by the sackload – 750 in all, triggering twenty-four charges for wasting police time.

Recent blackmail cases include threats of a poison gas blitz on Cyprus (1989), releasing animals injected with rabies (1989), poisoning a blind man's guide dog (1989), stuffing cyanide into cigarettes (1986) and threatening to destroy an original collection of photographs of Charlie **Chaplin** (1986). Robert Telford, a failed businessman, was jailed for ten years on 30 May 1991 for his million-pound plot to defile Cadbury's Creme Eggs with Paraquat weedkiller. 1980 furnished a relatively endearing scheme to spoil crumpets with cigarette-ends, and a recent attempt, from a duo calling themselves Laurel and Hardy, involved toothpaste contaminated with poison, an idea perhaps gleaned from the 1987 film *Black Widow*.

The British counselling experts in food contamination, public relations consultants Burson-Marseller, handle about a hundred incidents a year; about a quarter can be attributed to disaffected present and former employees. Insurance cover must be kept secret, and policies come complete with expert security services, including rehearsal of operational scenarios. Control Risks, leaders in the field, note that, 'Collecting the money is the most dangerous part for the criminal', and Whitchelo nearly had the problem licked.

Perera, Dr Samuel (1943–)

Sri Lankan dentist who killed his adopted daughter and used sections of her body as bedding soil for houseplants.

Perera settled in the West Yorkshire village of Sandal after winning a research post as a lecturer at the Dental Department of Leeds University. He had two children by his wife Dammika, but in December 1981 he decided (for reasons which remain obscure) to acquire another and flew to Colombo where he purchased a 10-year-old village girl, Nilanthe. Renamed Philomena, she was brought back to Sitwell Close, a series of redbrick 'executive style' dwellings.

In November 1983, Nilanthe disappeared. The neighbours asked what had happened. First Dr Perera's wife explained that she was banned from playing outside because 'she made eyes at all the men'. After Christmas the story changed: 'She grew homesick and my husband decided it was kindest to send her back to her father in Sri Lanka.'

Contrary to the general run of tales about compliant neighbours who listen unmoved to thuds and screams emanating from next door, the Sitwell Close residents called a community meeting and drafted a collective letter to the police. Detectives took Dr Perera to task, but he maintained that he had taken Nilanthe to Sicily for the weekend and handed her to his brother for repatriation.

Flight records showed no trace of Dr Perera's booking. And there the matter rested for nine months. The police had no body, but they pursued the case by talking to Dr Perera's colleagues at the Dental Department. Dr Perera shared a desk there, and on 4 February 1985 his fellow-lecturer happened on some human remains – a jawbone and segments of skull – in a manilla envelope in one of his drawers. A rapid scout through his office revealed a clutch of further fragments from the foot, pelvis, forearm, shoulder and neck – variously distributed in a five-litre glass beaker, a coffee jar and a stainless steel tray.

The next day the police searched 16 Sitwell Close. In the back garden they unearthed a shallow grave, recently vacated, containing a vestigial tooth, a hank of hair and one small bone.

Inside the house, three large plastic flowerpots stood on the hallway carpet and perspex sidetable.

Susan Atkins leaving the courtroom after her arraignment for the Manson slayings. The newsmen are caged.

Marilyn Monroe.

Joyce McKinney maintains a high profile at a movie premiere with the editor of the *Daily Express* in April 1978, a few days before absconding.

Charles Manson at the preliminary hearing in Independence, California, March 1969.

Kenneth Bianchi, the Hillside Strangler, carefully groomed for his courtroom appearance.

A puzzled Sirhan Sirhan after Robert Kennedy's assassination (see **Executive Action**).

The shambling figure of Albert Howard Fish, multiple murderer and cannibal.

Capone travelling in style to Atlanta Federal Penitentiary at the start of his eleven year sentence.

The St Valentine's Day Massacre, 1929. Capone taught the Bugs Moran gang a lesson, but Bugs himself escaped, late for his appointment.

The grimy exterior of 10 Rillington Place. *Inset:* John Reginald Halliday Christie.

Frederick Bywaters (left) at the October 1922 inquest into the death of his lover's husband, Percy Thompson (right). Edith, Percy's wife (centre), shows some of the sexuality she later exuded from the dock.

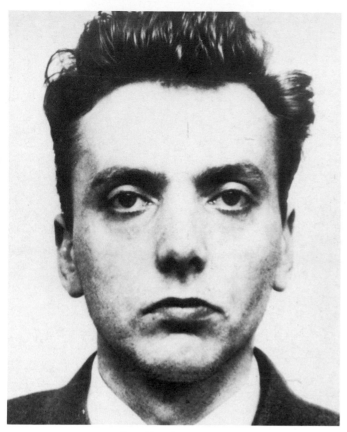

Ian Brady.

Myra Hindley. This 1965 photo shows her withered at the age of twenty-three.

Ann Downey, the picture of sorrow, as the police search the moors for her daughter's body in 1964.

The only good boy in class? Milken urges the 1989 California Forum to push for forgiveness of Latin American debt.

A shifty Dutch Schultz Flegenheimer, on charges of income tax evasion in January 1935. He died in a Murder Inc. hit nine months later.

Chicago bootlegger Dion O'Bannion was said to look just as composed as he pumped bullets into you.

Handsome Eliot Ness, God's gift to public relations. But his reputation was deserved.

Gambino family godfather John Gotti in transitional sartorial style, arriving for his 1986 trial in safari suit.

Mafioso Joe Valachi testifying at the 1963 Senate Investigation subcommittee.

Alcatraz Penitentiary – a view from the hills of San Francisco.

Two contained geraniums. In the words of forensic scientist Professor Usher, 'The plants were very small for such large pots, and did not seem to be doing very well; they were wilting somewhat.' Usher fetched a dustbin lid and placed it upside down on the carpet. On tipping out the contents of the largest pot, a complete human spine, coiled round the roots, slithered free. Decanting the geraniums disgorged semi-liquid clumps of decaying flesh. Then the police noticed a human rib in a butter dish.

In all, 105 bone fragments retrieved from Dr Perera's home were reunited with their associates from the University to form a total of 130 pieces, previously hidden in eight locations, and reassembled into a skeleton, in part to establish the age, sex and race of the deceased, but also to ensure that, say, two or more right arms were not present.

Perera was convicted on compelling evidence on 11 March 1986. As Professor Usher observed, 'I could conceive of no legitimate purpose for what was literally half a human torso being concealed in a domestic flowerpot.'

Perera's motive never emerged. Colleagues thought him a disagreeable, arrogant man, and perhaps the most revealing insight was afforded by a throwaway line to Detective Inspector Hodgson on his first visit to Sitwell Close: 'She's only a jungle girl, after all.'

'Planting a tree' is an arcane Trinidadian term meaning 'to kill'. The expression derives from Michael X, who issued orders for an execution in 1972 and then had the body buried in a trench, instructing his gardener to 'plant something in it'. In the case of Joseph Skerrit, decapitated for refusing to raid a country post office, the 'something' was lettuces. These grew tall and yellow, and his last bedding place came to light.

Pets

'Homicidal triangle' is the psychiatric term for the three character traits often found in serial killers: childhood bedwetting, acts of delinquency especially arson, and a delight in torturing animals.

Cruelty to animals is usually as much as a child can manage, but when he becomes a man he progresses to people. Ian **Brady**, the Moors Murderer, flung cats out of tenement windows as a Glasgow

child; Ed **Kemper**, from California, cut his family cat into pieces with a knife. **Kürten** mutilated dogs and, on one occasion, a swan. He sexually assaulted sheep. The underlying pattern is the pet today, the world tomorrow. The **torture** of animals is almost as satisfying as torturing people: pets can whimper, scream, struggle and bleed. But the essential difference remains. At the end of the day, they are only animals.

Jeffrey **Dahmer**, the Milwaukee serial killer, is not on the list of animal sadists, despite devoting much of his childhood to collecting insects in empty pickle jars and preserving them in formaldehyde. Dahmer started with butterflies and moths, and progressed via chipmunks, squirrels, raccoons, opossums and cats, often killed in road accidents. He carried a St Bernard's body back to the woods, left it to rot, and then doused the remains in bleach to clean the bones.

Dahmer created an animal cemetery, spiking the skulls on crosses. Neighbours recollect that skinned and gutted dogs were nailed to nearby trees; one find had its gutted intestines draped round the tree. But on the best evidence, Dahmer's morbidity was restricted to creatures already dead, although on fishing expeditions he chopped up bluegills and bass, still alive and wriggling, into tiny pieces, before tossing them back. 'I want to see what it looks like inside, I like to see how things work,' he said. But fish hardly count, and Dahmer was not preoccupied with cruelty; he yearned for a relationship and, lacking the social skills to handle the living, lavished his attention on the dead, evolving a macabre preoccupation with his companions' innards – the mere *machinery* of life. He had a two-dimensional appreciation of the normal person's desire to see what makes his friends tick; in Dahmer's literal vision, it involved physical exposure of the heart.

His first human victim was Stephen Hicks, a hitchhiker. Dahmer smashed in his head on 18 June 1978 without preliminary torture, and then processed the body up at the shed in the usual way. Thus his lack of cruelty to animals presaged his lack of cruelty to people. But, like **Nilsen**, he still had to kill them.

Bedwetting only acquires significance if it persists beyond the age of twelve. **Arson** is considered separately.

Petty Treason

A crime that embraced coining and other assaults on the body politic, murdering a husband among them. The sentence for women, whether for high or petty treason, was burning, a practice which continued until 1790.

But at least they were burned dead, not alive. The executioner tied the victim to a chair or to the stake and, after lighting the pyre, quickly strangled her with a noose round her neck. The timing could go awry, as with Catherine Hayes on 9 May 1726 (see **Head**). According to the *Newgate Calendar*, 'She rent the air with her cries and lamentations. Other firebrands were instantly thrown on her; but she survived among the flames for a considerable time.'

Condemned cell, Newgate

Using the term colloquially, the two notable transgressors of recent times were the writer P.G. Wodehouse and William Joyce, also known as Lord Haw Haw. Their treason was so petty it was not treason at all. In 1941 Wodehouse recorded a series of jocular (and even courageous) broadcasts to neutral America covering the Nazis' arrival in France, and was for ever after *persona non grata* with the British establishment. As for Joyce, his wartime broadcasts (which started 'This is Jairmany calling') may have annoyed the Allies, but his indiscretions were all abroad and, besides, he was not a British subject.

Joyce once owned a British passport, but he was not entitled to it and therefore was not British. His passport application gave his place of birth as Galway, Ireland instead of Brooklyn, New York.

In effect, the courts claimed jurisdiction over an alien for a crime committed abroad. If this were

the law, the principle would be of limitless application and could, with similar justification, condemn anyone, anywhere, for anything unlawful in Britain. It was a political trial.

It is no matter for pride that Joyce was hanged, and on 3 January 1946 a crowd of 300 gathered round the prison gates. Some parents brought their children.

Philips, Judith

A 'cunning woman' who had it in for men. By and large, con-tricks from the Elizabethan era lose something in the telling; but not this one.

Judith Philips lived in Upper Sambourne, near Winchester, where her near neighbour was an unnamed but rich 'churl'. First Philips researched his background. Then, unobserved, she buried some money on his land and introduced herself as a white witch.

Philips intimated that she could tell by certain magical signs on his forehead that he was involved in a lawsuit with a local landowner, a fact she had already ascertained. Then she pointed out that the man's wife possessed a rather 'fortunate' face. This reminded Philips of the treasure she felt sure lay in his grounds, not least since she had just put it there. 'Have you not,' she enquired, 'a hollow tree standing near unto your house, with certain weeds growing about the root?'

It so happened that the neighbour had, and, after some testing excavations, a small gold coin and a silver sixpence were duly unearthed. Philips promised to find the rest of the buried hoard. But for her final act of divination she wanted £14 in cash together with a decent room, fit for an audience with the Fairy Queen.

Philips listed her requirements: 'You must set five candlesticks in five several places in your chamber, and under every candlestick you must put a golden coin.' The apartment for the enchanted reception was to be sanctified with the finest linen and set about with the household's most precious objects. As a last detail, Philips insisted that her mark obtain a brand new saddle and two girths.

Come evening, when all the valuables were neatly arrayed, Philips ordered her man into the yard. Then she saddled him up and rode him round and round the holly bush. Dismounting, she explained to the man and his wife: 'You must lie three hours one by another grovelling on your bellies under this tree, and stir not, I charge you, until I come back again. For I must go into the chamber to meet the Queen of the Fairies and welcome her to that holy spot.' Then she stripped the house bare and fled into the night with her spoils.

Sad to tell, Philips was caught and whipped through the City of London.

See also **Hopkins**

Pierrepoints

A Yorkshire 'family firm' of executioners who dominated the English **hanging** trade from 1900 to 1956. The first in the line was Old Harry Pierrepoint (1877–1922), a former butcher who resigned in 1916 with ninety-nine victims to his credit, including the last double female hanging. He passed on the torch to his elder brother Tom (1871–1955), a phlegmatic carrier given to sucking sweets during executions.

After the retirement of his rival John Ellis, Tom Pierrepoint rose to become Britain's chief hangman. By the time he hung up his rope in 1948, he had logged forty-five years in harness to become Britain's longest serving executioner, often assisted by his nephew Albert (1905–92), selected at the age of twenty-seven from a shortlist of ten applicants. During his interview Albert declared that the job was 'something to take pride in' and later referred favourably to the opportunities for travel.

Albert, an extremely fast worker, could clock in at somewhere between seventeen and twenty seconds. This included pinioning the victim, escorting him to the scaffold, and fitting the noose as well as pulling the lever. After the Second World War his professionalism was applied to despatching some 200 war criminals; he once hanged twenty-seven in twenty-four hours.

In 1946 Pierrepoint took over a pub, unremarkably named 'Help the Poor Struggler', known locally as 'Help the Poor Strangler'; one of his underlings, Harry Allen, ran the 'Rope and Anchor'. A publican's hours suited Pierrepoint well. As he wrote, 'I found that I could take a three o'clock plane from Dublin after conducting an execution there (Eire having no home-grown hangmen) and be opening my bar without comment at half-past five'.

Pierrepoint's pub sign

It was while emerging from another pub, the Fitzroy Tavern in London's Charlotte Street, that Pierrepoint first laid eyes on the villains Jenkins and Geraghty who had just driven their stolen car through a jeweller's window in a smash and grab raid. They shot dead a passer-by who 'had a go', and five months later, on 19 September 1947, briefly met Pierrepoint again, when he hanged them. A fastidious man, he liked to be photographed in a bow-tie and, during the Royal Commission of 1953, confessed himself 'very much put out' by the impropriety of discussing his work in the proximity of a female typist. He retired in 1956.

In 1974, after profiting from the hanging of 530 men and 20 women during a career spanning three decades and nine countries, Albert Pierrepoint wrote: 'I do not believe that any of the hundreds of executions I have carried out has in any way acted as a deterrent against future murder. Capital punishment, in my view, achieves nothing except revenge.' This statement is often quoted by opponents of capital punishment, among whom Pierrepoint must rank as the most bizarre.

See also **Recruitment, Sansons**

Pillory *et al*

A wooden clamp fixing a miscreant's arms and neck. The punishment, intended to expose its victims to ridicule rather than pain or injury, was in constant demand from the Anglo-Saxon era until its wholesale abolition in 1837. Its staple fodder was scolds, bakers adulterating their bread and suchlike, but it could rise to graver occasions. In May 1613 Messrs Waller and Bostock, seditious rumour-mongers, were fined 5,000 marks apiece and sentenced to 'stand on the pillory, to lose their ears and be whipped thence through the streets'.

By the end of the seventeenth century a spell in the pillory not infrequently ended in a public stoning. In 1756, when **highwaymen** M'Daniel and Barry were exhibited in London, 'it was with the utmost difficulty that one of the sheriffs and the keeper of Newgate, who stood on the balcony just by, prevented their being utterly destroyed'. Three days later their confederates, Eagan and Salmon, fared worse. They 'were instantly assaulted with showers of oystershells, stones, &tc., and had not stood alive one half-hour before Eagan was struck dead and Salmon was so dangerously wounded in the head that it was thought impossible he could recover'. Clearly the bombardment could be vigorous in the extreme: in 1732 two men were convicted of murdering a prisoner in the pillory 'by pelting him with cauliflower stalks'.

Pillories were often combined with whipping posts and stocks to form a multiple facility, generally occupying the market square. The Manchester pillory remained in use until its removal in 1816. From then until 1837 the pillory was reserved for perjurers. Drunks and rowdies had their feet clamped in the stocks – a form of punishment that was never abolished but just faded away in the nineteenth century. The last recorded case was in Rugby in 1865, and the practice survived just long enough to be photographed, showing everyone (including the victim) smiling.

In the nineteenth century, some English local authorities would accept a public apology for a minor offence in lieu of prosecution. An otherwise obscure Mary Kelly made one such abject submission on a wall poster in Stockport on 27 July 1864 'for plucking flowers in Vernon Park'. The poster is signed with an 'X' placed in the space between the words 'Her Mark'.

Pizza Connection, The

On 24 October 1984, twenty-two members of the Sicilian and American Mafia were arraigned on conspiracy charges of smuggling heroin and cocaine into the United States by the ton. The gang's imports from 1979 to 1984 were estimated at $1.6 billion. Only $250 million in cash was recovered, but the Sicilian network – successor to the **French Connection** – was shattered by the eighteen convictions, which included a 45-year sentence for Gaetano Badalamenti, former head of the Sicilian Mafia's ruling commission.

The investigation started nearly five years before, in July 1979, after the murder of the Bonanno Family boss Carmine Galante, shot through the eye in a Brooklyn restaurant. The survival of his bodyguards suggested that they had sold his life, not theirs, dearly, in a pre-agreed hit probably engineered by the Gambino clan. Galante became a likely candidate for liquidation after his attempt to monopolise American heroin distribution, charging a 'licence fee' of $5,000 per kilo, but at the time these machinations were unknown, and surveillance agents found themselves stationed outside New York pizzerias, noting the delivery of mysterious cardboard cartons or paper shopping bags by hitherto unknown hoods.

Years passed before investigators realised that they had stumbled on the rear end of a vast heroin network. The bags contained kilos of money, and the bundles of cash were shipped out of America either as profits or as advance payment for the next consignment. Not until 7 March 1983 did the FBI accumulate sufficient evidence to run wiretaps; by the start of the court case two years later they had recorded approximately 100,000 conversations on hundreds of cassettes which, if played end to end, would last a year.

Transacting all the illegal business from payphones in code made it difficult to tell who was ringing whom about what. Officers had to put names to voices, and distinguish between genuine orders for pizzas and encoded exchanges about narcotics. The syndicate possessed no formal cypher; the glossary shifted from day to day, often depending on intonation. A typical snippet from 1983 had one conspirator saying to his wife: 'Tell them that I'm making a pizza and then I'm coming.'

What did this signify? 'And ask to bring the calzones,' someone chimed in from the background. These were real pizzas. But other innocuous commodities like lemons, shirts, tangerines, salted sardines, plants, tables, ovens, onions, suits, pants, pears, bread rolls, the 'thing that is being manufactured' or the state of the weather could allude to the shipment of merchandise. Again, 'My daughter wants a pizza with extra cheese, Sicilian not American' might mean just that. 'Is it still raining?' could refer to the level of police activity.

Perhaps the clearest sequence of dialogue was taped from 8 February 1984, recording

Badalamenti masterminding the deal: 'I met the guy with the shirts of four years ago... but there's a little problem... There's another guy here that has, there's 10 per cent acrylic... the good suits, you're talking 180 dollars... 175... 185... it depends... 190, it has also gone to. It depends on the situation.' The 'shirts' designated the cheaper heroin with 10 per cent impurity, the 'suits' the real McCoy, and the prices quoted were per kilo minus three noughts.

It was confusing for the agents and equally confusing for the slower conspirators, like Badalamenti's nephew Pietro Alfano from a pizzeria on South Fourth Street in Oregon. When he could not make up his mind if his instructions were in plain language or code, Alfano, the syndicate's Rosetta Stone, asked straight out over the wiretapped lines. Where were the 'salted sardines' kept? At Filippo's? Did 'town of the sun' mean Fort Lauderdale? What exactly was a '*little* shirt?' Were 'prickly pears' a place, a key of cocaine or ordinary fruit? Even references to a Howard Johnson threw Alfano; he thought it was a person. Understandably, he had problems calculating the syndicate's finances over the telephone by subtracting 'little things' from 'big shirts' to arrive at a dollar total.

Alfano's role was to assemble the syndicate's cash – no easy matter – for the next transaction. 'The thing is,' Alfano at last volunteered to Badalamenti on the telephone, 'I can do this thing tomorrow. Today is Tuesday.' 'Today is Thursday,' interjected Badalamenti while his nephew reckoned off the mid-week days still to come.

As the final deal started to fall apart, Alfano realised that without the cash the shippers were liable to turn nasty. He might be chopped into pizza: 'Ping, ping, ping, ping... piece by piece.' In the event the Pizza Connection was busted in a series of co-ordinated raids on 9 April 1984.

Alfano was arrested along with Badalamenti in Madrid, and in the second year of his trial he was shot in the back three times outside a delicatessen. He recovered, pleading guilty by telephone from hospital, paralysed from the waist down, and was jailed for ten to thirty years.

See also **World Wide Business Centre**

Planning Officers

The British Town and Country Planning Acts of 1947 empowered local authorities to control the right of ordinary citizens to build as they pleased. At a stroke, even the minor details of a small home extension could be indefinitely delayed or altogether banned. Planning Officers and council committees often imposed their personal taste on detailed questions of layout and appearance, deliberating for weeks, months or sometimes years on the precise type of glazing bars or railings on a residential extension, at the same time as authorising or encouraging the construction of large-scale developmental disasters.

It has long been the tradition for Planning Officers to claim that the real power is vested in their local councils. But in practice, councillors normally defer to the advice of their professionals, and thus Planning Officers can and do inflict almost limitless loss and distress on their applicants. So it is probable that most people with first-hand experience of the planning process have, at some stage, wanted to kill their Planning Officer, and thus even in law-abiding Britain it was only a matter of time before one got himself shot.

The man who did it was Albert Dryden. On 20 June 1991 he murdered Derwentside's Principal Planning Officer, Harry Collinson. As the confrontation and killing were filmed, Dryden became an instant television celebrity.

Albert Dryden was a well-liked local eccentric, a bachelor of 51 with a streak of self-taught mechanical ingenuity. In the 1970s he was known in the neighbourhood as the 'Rocket Man' for his hobby of building missiles which he launched from Stanhope Moors; the government took him to court because they flew too high. At the time of the killing, Dryden had the world's longest car under assembly.

After his redundancy from British Steel, Dryden invested his £15,000 pay-off in building a bungalow for his mother. He bought a plot of land and, in an off-the-record meeting as the planning wrangle developed, Collinson said he *could* put up a house – provided it was less than three feet high.

So Dryden built the bungalow in a hole. This meant that to all intents the structure could not be seen from the surrounding terrain. But, as many applicants for roof terraces can confirm, mere invisibility has never been an extenuating criterion for planners.

Dryden foolishly felt that he did not need permission for a building no one could see; quite properly, Collinson and the subsequent planning inquiry held otherwise. When Dryden's mother died, the *Northern Echo* ran the story that it was the row over the bungalow that killed her.

On the morning of 20 June 1991, the Council bulldozers arrived to flatten Dryden's bungalow. Harry Collinson was at their head, and Dryden shot him dead. According to eye-witness Michael Peckett: 'I saw Dryden straighten his arm and take very careful aim. When the gun went off, I jumped a foot in the air with surprise. To be honest, it was no noisier than a cap gun, not like you hear on TV.' Dryden shot Collinson four times.

In March 1992 Dryden was jailed for life despite pleading **amnesia** since, whether he could remember it or not, he had certainly committed murder. The public too felt strongly. That year Dryden received eighty-three Christmas cards.

Clearly Collinson had made many enemies. Terry Batson, an aggrieved town councillor for Tow Law outside Consett, commented: 'May you rot in hell, Harry Collinson, after what you did to my father.' Denise Bullivant, another local, was equally vehement: 'Harry Collinson was the officer who dealt with my planning application. He objected to the red tiles we wanted to use, even though they are traditional... it changed the whole course of our lives. Mother had to sell the big house and ended up in Lanchester.'

Local hostility was intensified by Dryden's conviction. The chief executive of the Council, Neil Johnson, complained that 'some of the people around Mr Dryden have threatened and actually assaulted officers of the council. There've been threats of "We'll smash your car windows" and "We know where you all live."'

Other officials considered the episode and its outcome avoidable. For instance, Dryden and his mother could have been granted a purely personal right to occupy the bungalow, such right to cease on death. In retrospect, the council escaped lightly with just the one fatality. Before the shooting, Dryden envisaged a kamikaze attack on the Town Hall. According to local newspaperman Garry Willey: 'Albert talked in the past about loading one of his American cars with explosives and ploughing it into the Civic Centre and taking eighty or ninety with him.'

Planning Officers in Turkey travel armed.

Poisoning

A source of macabre fascination but relatively few deaths, only accounting for about five per cent of murders. Generally the prosecution has little difficulty in proving malice aforethought. Extreme practitioners, like Graham **Young**, view their victims' protracted agonies as a spectator sport.

Although poisons are regarded as a 'coward's weapon' favoured by women, they are the special province of male doctors, with their unfettered access to lethal substances and their control over the legal formalities on death.

The wide latitude under which medical men can operate according to the dictates of their clinical opinion means that mere doubt about the propriety of any treatment is insufficient to establish guilt. Like everyone else, doctors disagree, and the main plank of the 1957 prosecution case against Dr Bodkin Adams (accused of giving lethal **injections** to his elderly patients) foundered when their expert witness was asked, 'Is there, in your opinion, any justification for injecting morphia and heroin immediately after a stroke?'

'No justification whatsoever,' replied Dr Douthwaite. But this was only Dr Douthwaite's opinion and it was, as it happened, incorrect.

From the other side of the fence, the allure of poison is that the resulting process often replicates the manifestations of an ordinary ailment, and few doctors query an apparently natural death. Death from arsenic evinces symptoms resembling those of severe gastroenteritis, and until quite recently a patient complaining of pain of obscure origin might have his condition diagnosed as 'neuralgia', which means no more than pain of obscure origin. In many cases a toxin degrades into the constituents conventionally found in a corpse; thus deadly succinylcholine chloride splits into the succinic acid and choline one would expect in body tissue. Other poisons have unknown active ingredients. They evidently work, because the recipient dies, but although modern laboratory techniques can discern quantities down to a single molecule, the pathologist does not know what to look for without advance knowledge of what the poison is. Despite progressive attempts at regulation, a murderer can generally get his hands on something lethal; Britain's Arsenic Act of 1851 represented an early attempt to prevent strangers or children from buying arsenic at will. Because of the relative scarcity both of black foodstuffs and beverages tasting of coal, the Act prescribed that soot, in the proportion of an ounce to a pound, be mixed with the poison prior to sale.

The diligent pathologist starts by evaluating the contents of a corpse's stomach and then samples the blood from at least six locations. Different organs favour different poisons. In the words of toxicologist Dr Alan Curry, 'The liver is a marvellous organ... That's where I'd look for inorganic material. There, and in the kidneys. The brain is where I'd look for volatile substances or solvents such as chloroform. Analysis of blood should reveal substances like strychnine.'

Perhaps the most famous delivery vehicle was the poisoned scone that the fastidious Major Herbert Armstrong handed Martin over tea in Hay-on-Wye in 1921, remarking 'Excuse fingers'. But, like the box of chocolates that Armstrong had sent to Martin's home earlier that week, the dosage proved too small to kill. The local chemist recognised Martin's symptoms, as did the Major when he passed his intended victim wobbling down the street. 'You must have eaten something which disagreed with you,' Armstrong pointed out, 'and I have a feeling you will have another illness very similar.'

It was easy to work out what the something was. On the day of Martin's stomach cramps he had eaten exactly the same as his wife, apart from the scone. A urine sample was despatched to the Home Office pathologist, together with the confectionery. Back came the reply: 'Two of the chocolates in this box had the appearance of being tampered with. A cylindrical hole nearly $\frac{1}{2}$ inch long has apparently been bored and filled with a white powder... found on analysis to be white arsenic to the extent of 2.12 grains. Two grains of white arsenic has been known to cause death in an adult.'

The social imperative attaching to boxes of chocolates – they must be *shared* – invests the victim's precise identity with an element of uncertainty. It was not Oswald Martin who ate them, but his wife's sister. Similarly, the poisoned chocolates put in the mail by Professor John Buettner-Janusch in 1987 hit the wrong target. The professor, an American anthropologist of unusual brilliance, put the seal on his long record as a war protestor and civil rights supporter with a 1980 conviction for making and possessing drugs. He was paroled, but the court case lay heavy on his mind, and for St Valentine's Day in 1987, he sent the trial judge, Charles L. Brieant, a lethal box of 'Golden Godiva' chocolates. A former colleague at Duke University was another recipient, and two more boxes were intercepted in the post after the judge's wife nearly died.

Buettner-Janusch was caught by the imprint of his little finger on the packaging; five years into the sentence, a ruling that his release would not be before the year 2,000 destroyed his will to live. He stopped eating and, despite force-feeding, died on 2 July 1992.

Poisons are either organic or inorganic (of mineral origin) and they work by latching onto enzymes, impeding their proper function. They can be classified into four main categories: those impairing the blood's ability to carry oxygen (carbon monoxide, cyanide); corrosive acids and alkalis which perforate the stomach (mustard gas, chloroform); systemic poisons causing widespread damage (**arsenic**, antimony, mercury, **strychnine**, morphine and hyoscine); and poisons which leave no trace on entry, like ricin, but wreak havoc only after their absorption.

Precociousness

Startling evidence was presented to the 1816 British Select Committee on the police. The Newgate chaplain, Reverend H. S. Cotton, a man with an advanced social conscience, was asked if the prisoner-boys in his charge kept mistresses. 'All of them,' he answered. 'Burnet, who is only nine years of age, has also a person he terms his girl.' Cotton affirmed that there was a constant procession of women at the prison gates 'calling themselves sisters and relations of the boys, who had been prevented afterwards from coming, from its being found out that they were common prostitutes and kept by the boys'.

'Prostitutes' was a term broadly used at the time, often designating an unmarried woman, other than of upper class extraction, who had a boyfriend. 'Girl' or 'woman' would be a fair contemporary equivalent.

William Crawford, of the Society of Friends, provided the Committee corroborative testimony. He maintained that it was normal for boys on the loose to cohabit with girls of their own age. He cited the case of a youth lodging in a 'flash' house who 'had slept there upwards of thirty times with girls of his own age, and he particularly named five. This boy was fourteen.'

By this age, the reputation of the American Jesse Pomeroy (1860–1932) was already well-established. A double child killer, Pomeroy was a Bostonian child with a blind white eye and a hare-lip who murdered children. At 12 he was sent to the West Borough Reform School for his uncontrollable addiction to stripping youngsters naked, tying them up and beating them into unconsciousness. Paroled in February 1874, he turned to murder, stabbing four-year-old Horace Mullen thirty-one times before trying to cut off his head. He confessed to twenty-eight other killings, and the police unearthed twelve mutilated bodies buried round his mother's house.

Pomeroy's death sentence was commuted to solitary confinement because of his age; he served fifty-eight years, and perhaps the only uplifting feature of his life was an attempted jail-break of 1890. Chiselling away at his cell, Pomeroy's exertions exposed a gas pipe, and he hit on a four-stage escape plan. First, he took a deep breath. Second, he ruptured the pipe. Third, he held his breath. Fourth, he lit a match.

The explosion blew Pomeroy clear out of his cell but knocked him unconscious when he slammed into a wall. Meanwhile, the prison caught fire; three inmates perished in the blaze.

More recently, in April 1992 a girl of six was assaulted and allegedly raped in an Indianapolis junior school lavatory. The two males charged with the offence, aged seven, were confined to 'house arrest' with their parents.

At the other end of the scale, rapes of octogenarians are commonplace. A representative offender was Keith Walker, sentenced to life on 21 July 1992 for raping and then murdering an 82-year-old widow. He spent her savings of £70 in a Nottinghamshire night-club.

Pregnancy

In the court of Henry VIII, a page's punishment was to go without beer for a month; the crime, making a chambermaid pregnant.

Until the twentieth century the social opprobrium directed at birth out of wedlock meant that the mother's fate might well be death. The centuries-long cycle consisted of poverty and pregnancy, followed by theft or prostitution to keep body and soul together. An expectant unmarried woman would be shown the door by any employer and probably turned onto the streets by her family.

Transportation or the gallows were thus frequent repercussions of sexual indiscretion, and the poor were often reduced to killing their illegitimate offspring. The better-off might foster them to the sinister 'baby farms' of the Victorian era; the most famous was run by a Mrs Amelia Dyer, whose main assets were a neat, bonneted appearance and a reassuring line in Salvation Army sentiments. With these she plied her trade for fifteen years, charging between £10 and £15 to relieve distressed mothers of their misbegotten children.

It was the dead baby she tossed into the Thames by Caversham Lock, trussed up in brown paper bearing her name and address, that brought Mrs Dyer to grief. The neat little parcel was fished out by a bargeman on 30 March 1896, and the wrapping tore to reveal a leg. In the five days it took the police to ascertain that '20 Wigott's Road, Caversham' should have read 20 Pigott's Road, and that the 'Mrs Harding' who had recently left was the same person as Amelia Dyer, now resident at 45 Kensington Road, she killed again.

Dyer drummed up custom by advertising in the *Bristol Times and Mirror*, posing as a childless woman yearning to care for a baby. She ran the operation in concert with her daughter and son-in-law, Polly and Ernest Palmer, who were forever picking up or dropping off Mrs Dyer from hand-overs at railway stations, watching a succession of babies arrive and heavily laden carpet-bags leave. The police dragged the Thames at Reading, dredging up another six bodies. 'You'll know mine by the tape around their necks,' Mrs Dyer observed, a point underlined in 1900 when four tiny skeletons were unearthed from the garden of a house she occupied in Bristol.

Polly gave evidence against her mother, and at the trial a Dr Lyttleton Stewart Forbes Winslow for the defence endeavoured to prove that his client was insane, a task to which Mrs Dyer had already applied herself with enthusiasm, inducing him to diagnose 'melancholia' and 'delusional insanity'. Forbes Winslow favoured the direct approach. 'Do you ever see any visions?' he demanded in a prison interview. 'Pray do not ask me,' Mrs Dyer replied, looking scared. 'What do you see?' Forbes Winslow continued. Mrs Dyer elaborated: 'I can't tell you; that is why I keep awake at night. The sounds I hear and the sights I see are dreadful.'

Dyer went to the gallows, as did many a mother who, in confusion or distress, slew her offspring within a year of birth. Only in 1938 did the Infanticide Act remove the onerous compulsion on judges to pass the death sentence in such cases; one beneficiary of this enlightened attitude was Australia's Barbara Wilkinson, who disposed of her six babies over a seven-year span, starting in 1961 at the age of twenty-one. She killed the first because she was unmarried, the second because she conceived before marrying, and the next four because she could not face explaining their fate to a midwife or doctor (who would inevitably notice that the new child was not her firstborn).

Barbara Wilkinson produced all six infants without her husband, mother-in-law or friends noticing. She had two techniques. One was to understate the length of her term and, after the infanticide, conceal the corpse and claim a miscarriage. But when caught short staying at her mother-in-law's house at Mangrove Mountain, while her husband was away as a long-distance lorry driver, she explained that the swelling in her stomach came from an influx of 'fluid' which needed draining every year or so.

Wilkinson's past came to light when she haemorrhaged after having (and killing) her sixth. Her husband, Les, drove her to hospital where the doctors, like him, believed they were confronted by a still-pregnant woman. But foetal movement was completely lacking. They diagnosed and treated Barbara for an intra-uterine death, only to find no baby.

She was not a woman of great emotional depth.

After telling the police about the 'binning' of her first child, she continued: 'After that, I went on to Les's place and that night I went to his twenty-first birthday party.'

See also **Münchausen, Weber**

Pressing

Not until 1827 were English courts empowered to enter a plea of 'Not Guilty' on behalf of an accused who stayed mute. His trial could not start without a plea, and thus an obdurate prisoner might defer his fate and, moreover, enrich his descendants by staying silent, since conviction as a felon entailed automatic forfeiture of all property to the Crown.

To prevent justice being cheated, taciturn suspects were sentenced to 'peine forte et dure'. They were 'pressed', that is, squashed. In about 1406 this supplanted the practice of starving them to death.

In **Newgate's** dedicated Press Yard the prisoners, spreadeagled on their backs, had weights heaped on their chests until they spoke or died. Often the wretches' backs were snapped by positioning them over a central ridge. In Elizabethan times this served as a form of execution, but by the eighteenth century it was regarded as a **torture** to induce a plea. During the first twenty years of James I's reign, in Middlesex alone forty-four prisoners, including three women, were crushed to death.

In 1721 the highwayman William Spiggot withstood a load of 350 pounds for half an hour before a further fifty pounds compelled him to utter. He was hanged. In 1658 a Major Strangeways held out to the bitter end. To safeguard his estate from confiscation, a group of friends helped flatten him in a record eight minutes.

The practice was abolished in 1772.

See also **Insane**

Preview

Murder is such an obliterating event that it is hard to see where the sex comes in. What can be sexy about a sex killing?

A few weeks before the double murder at Lake Sammamish, Ted **Bundy** staged a dry run which stopped short of death. But the other constituents were in place, in diagrammatic form, and it is perhaps easier to discern the roots of Bundy's pleasure.

In June 1974, Bundy arranged a raft trip on the River Yakima with an acquaintance from the state legislature, Larry Voshall. The young men invited two women, Becky and Susan, buying life jackets because neither girl was a proficient swimmer. Three of the group took the raft, and the fourth was towed behind on a rubber inner-tube.

As they entered the white-water rapids, Bundy's mood suddenly changed. In the Voshall's words, 'All at once, Ted who's behind Becky, unties the string of her halter top. It fell off, exposing her breasts. We were all just flabbergasted, embarrassed. You know, we didn't really know each other at all. Ted seemed to get some kick out of that. Later on we were in a pretty swift current, and Becky was behind the raft in the inner-tube. Ted reached for the rope and said, "What'll you do if I untie this rope?" Well, Becky's screaming. Just scared to death. And I looked at Ted's face and I couldn't believe it. He had a look on his face as though he was enjoying subjecting her to that terror – hearing her scream. He had untied the rope. And I got really upset.'

Lust killers are normally highly 'organised'. First comes the fantasy, replayed many times in the head, followed by the hunt, then the murder, an intensely personal act often preceded by mutilation and accompanied by extreme overkill; in a representative 1990 incident from Cardiff, shipping clerk Geraldine Palk was stabbed eighty-three times.

Bundy's dress rehearsal on the raft was aborted at a preliminary stage. He achieved sexual humiliation by ripping off Becky's clothes, and had settled into the phase of **terror** induced by domination: 'What'll you do if I untie this rope? What'll you do if I knife you just here?' There are clear parallels with an exaggerated version of sexual congress – the girl goes completely out of control, in a frenzy, she has eyes only for you, your slightest movement makes her squeal. Two thousand years ago, the amphitheatres of Rome were sexual arenas.

Normal intercourse is followed by psychic discharge, and sex killers like Bundy gradually devise the form of displaced sexual behaviour that meets their needs. In a hideously distorted form, many conventional motivational elements of the courtship ritual are embodied in a sex killing: the phase of establishing contact, the excitement, the 'inter-course' proper, and the afterglow. Although the killer adapts each stage to his own ends, the objectives remain the same.

Ordinary people may experience perfectly containable sadistic fantasies during sex. For a sex-killer the two components (sex and sadism) diverge, with the killer's perverse sphere (sadism) progressively ousting the conventional side (sex) until it assumes an independent existence outside the sexual context, as a substitute for it.

Thus the Russian serial killer **Chikatilo** bit off his victims' nipples in mimicry of the love bite. **Masturbation** over the corpse is another common thread, as is the factor of the killer's sexual disfunction, most often impotence, extending to an apparent lack of interest in sex and an awkwardness with women. The lethal combination is a desire to have sex coupled with the inability to have it, and the Russian investigator Kostoyev observed of Chikatilo that no-one capable of having normal heterosexual relations would have needed to kill as he did. Sadism of this order may confer sexual ability, but not the partner, who is dead.

See **Cannibalism, Sex Crimes, Torture**

Prison system, a brief history

Historically, Britain had little need of prisons. If guilty, the normal sentence was death, and if innocent, the accused was released. The idea of sentencing miscreants to a fixed term of confinement did not evolve until more civilised times.

Thomas More's *Utopia* (1516) contained an early proposal for imprisonment as a punishment. As an alternative to execution, More suggested that thieves should be locked up and reduced to slave status for a prescribed term of years. But there was hardly anywhere to send them. State prisons did not exist.

Until the nineteenth century, most prisoners were incarcerated not for crime but for **debt**. The remainder awaited their fate in a ragbag of local prisons, county prisons, debtors' prisons and private prisons. About half the jails were privately owned, rented out to sub-contractors by their landlords, like the Duke of Portland or the Bishops of Ely or Leeds. Thus **Newgate** was a profit-making commercial enterprise run by and for the Warden, with any surplus after expenses accruing to his pocket.

Unnecessary amelioration of the inmates' conditions was not a priority, and when the prison reformer John Howard began his visits in the 1770s, he preferred to travel by horse rather than carriage. His clothes became so heavily impregnated by their brief exposure to prison interiors that their stench in a post-chaise proved intolerable.

Transportation provided a long-standing alternative to the shortcomings of the prison system. From the seventeenth century onwards, the British shipped many of those who avoided execution to the plantations in Virginia or the last-ditch islands of Jamaica and Barbados. All went smoothly enough until 1775 and America's War of Independence. Thereafter, until the development of the Australian penal colony, convicts who were not hanged still had to be put somewhere.

Thus were born the **hulks**, clapped-out vessels where men and boys were kept ironed throughout their sentence. The ships' capacity was supplemented by the 1779 Act authorising the first state prison, Millbank, which opened thirty-two years later on the site of today's Tate Gallery in London. Remarkably, it had individual lavatories in each cell, the outcome of the standing requirement for solitary confinement (the **Separate System**), but the contamination through substandard drainage claimed a dreadful death toll.

The policy of continuous solitary represented an abrupt volte-face on the previous regime of foul (but social) slumming, where inmates were bundled together in a heaving mass. Under the new order, convicts were obliged to contemplate their navels for years on end in supposed eradication of their criminality – a cruel distortion of the thinking of John Howard, who favoured classification into small groups of appropriately graded offenders.

Millbank may have been intended as a semi-religious reformatory, but its policies were conducive only to madness. This initial failure led to the implementation of steadily harsher measures, like flogging, until thirty years after its opening the government denounced Millbank as an 'entire failure'. By then the structure was little more than a reception centre before prisoners were farmed out to the hulks or transported.

But Australia increasingly resented the influx of unreformed convicts. So the government endorsed the construction of a new model prison, Pentonville,

which espoused the Separate System with even greater ferocity. Opened in 1842, Pentonville ushered in an era of nationwide solitary confinement exacerbated by such soul-destroying devices as the **crank** and the **treadwheel**.

Discipline became stricter, and in 1877 prisons were unified into a monolithic state-run service under their first commissioner, Du Cane, architect of the great nineteenth-century prison construction programme of Wakefield, Reading, Wandsworth and the Scrubs (built entirely by convict labour). Du Cane enforced programmes of bread and water, solitary labour, religious instruction, and seclusion; more importantly, the cells were built without lavatories, and the ones in Pentonville were ripped out. Du Cane believed that the inmates had only to ring a little bell for attentive staff to come running.

Thereafter the prisons were closed to press and public alike, and the solitary rigours instigated at Pentonville extended throughout the system. Convicts had to maintain absolute silence, wear masks, and walk with their heads turned to face the wall when outside their cells to avoid eye contact. These practices continued into the present century; separate confinement was only abolished in 1922.

Today's regime represents a slightly mollified version of its nineteenth-century predecessor enacted within the same physical fabric. In 1991 an inmate commented, 'I've been on active service in Cyprus picking up dead bodies eaten by rabid dogs, but I found the conditions in Pentonville barbaric', and on 31 May 1992 the Human Rights Watch organisation characterised the British prison system as 'just coming out of the Dark Ages'. The next day the Chief Inspector of Prisons likened Dartmoor to a 'dustbin', lamenting the dual use of lavatory brushes for dish scrubbers. He pointed out that the inmates' only source of satisfaction was confrontation with the warders. Elsewhere, the twelve British mother-and-infant cells spawned a curious evolutionary mutation: babies who cannot crawl. Their mothers were afraid to let them loose on the cockroach-infested floors.

But things are worse in Thailand. In 1982 (and probably now) Bangkok's notorious Mahai Chai prison, with its design capacity of 600, housed 6,000 inmates, all without the benefit of plumbing.

The only water was dumped into a large horse trough. The then commandant, Prasan Prasert Prasert, turned a blind eye to violence and torture by the guards; killings were particularly rife in the hospital unit. Overcrowding meant that prisoners were not alone even in solitary confinement.

In America, more black men are in prison than in college. For the 15–25 age group, one quarter are in prison, or on bail, or on parole. But this is only the average. In Washington, the figure rises to 40 per cent.

Privilege

Some convicts are more equal than others. The murder-for-fun couple, Leopold and Loeb, were incarcerated in conditions of inexplicable luxury in the 1920s. The crowded Statesville penitentiary allocated them each a two-man cell, with space for a desk, a filing cabinet and a small library. The boys were allowed their own toiletries and their own meals, prepared to their personal specifications, and dined in private in the officers' mess. Special washing privileges gave them access to the officers' shower room, and the prison storeroom was available round the clock for telephone calls. Their doors were seldom locked, and the pair – lovers since the age of fourteen – saw each other when they wanted, often taking a stroll outside the prison walls to visit Leopold's garden, or wandering off to buy dope or booze.

Photographs suggest that their standard of living was roughly comparable to a second-rate English public school, and indeed Leopold and Loeb were still teenagers at the start of their sentences in 1924. Had they been upper-crust English schoolboys, they would hardly have noticed the difference. As it was, they were upper-crust American, Leopold the son of a multimillionaire shipping magnate, and Loeb the son of a vice-president of Sears, Roebuck. Both were law students.

The 1924 murder of Bobby Franks supposedly manifested their innate superiority over other mortals, who must have found the boys' immunity to the normal consequences of their actions very galling. Loeb was the leader of the two, and he accepted Leopold as his lover after insisting on a signed contract agreeing joint participation in teenage criminal ventures. The pair worked their way up through the petty thrill of stealing a typewriter from the fraternity house to their perfect version of the ultimate crime: murder 'for kicks'. According to Loeb, it was Leopold who 'suggested it as a means of having a great deal of excitement, together with getting quite a sum of money'. At the time, both ideas – kidnapping and recreational murder – were novelties.

On 21 May Leopold and Loeb hired a car and 'trolled' for a young victim, male or female, enhancing their excitement by watching through binoculars from the cover of an alley at some youths playing basketball, part of the selection process. Two hours passed before 14-year-old Bobby Franks hove into view. As a friend of Loeb's younger brother, Franks had no qualms about accepting a lift. He was killed with a chisel, stripped naked and disfigured with hydrochloric acid, and his parents received a pre-typed ransom demand for a meagre $10,000. But the next day their son's body was discovered wedged into a culvert on waste ground near Wold Lake outside Chicago.

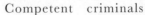

Lucky Luciano

Competent criminals might have concealed the body better. Its feet stuck out, and the boys were careless in three other respects. The Leopolds' chauffeur saw them scrubbing down blood from the back of the car; and they elected to dump Franks in a deserted marshy area which they were known to frequent as bird-watchers. Doubtless Leopold and Loeb were titillated by their inclusion in the initial investigative stages, but it was a more serious oversight to type the ransom note on their stolen portable, with its distinctive 'i', 't' and 'm'.

Bad luck took a hand in their conviction when Leopold mislaid his glasses near the culvert. They were picked up by one of the workmen summoned to shift the body, and the optical company Almer Coe recognised the spectacles as one of 54,000 pairs sold in Chicago, identical save for the refinement of the hinges machined by Bobrow Optical. Leopold's were one of only three sets made. He attempted to fob off his interrogators by describing how his glasses had slipped out of his top pocket when he tripped during a bird-watching expedition the previous week. Invited to replicate the incident, he fell forwards on his face. But the glasses stayed put.

Leopold and Loeb were saved from the death penalty by Clarence Darrow's sterling defence, and their lenient treatment meant the trial judge needed police protection for months afterwards. Family money ensured the boys a comfortable existence, but in 1935 a homosexual inmate razored Richard Loeb to death, inspiring the headline: 'Sentence ends with a proposition'. Leopold was released on parole in 1958, whereupon he sued the author of *Compulsion* (a novel and subsequently a film based on the case) for defamation. The $3 million action failed, and he died on parole in Puerto Rico in 1971.

More recently, Ivan Boesky fared well in his jail of first choice, the minimum security prison at Lompoc, Santa Barbara. Given the free run of the administrator's telephones, he habitually dined on steak and fresh fruit in the visitors' room and went into town whenever he wanted. Sometimes he was collected by a blonde in her early thirties.

Inside prison, men of importance do not lose caste. Lucky Luciano all but held court during his 1940s spell in the maximum security State Penitentiary at Dannemora (known as 'Siberia'). According to a guard: 'He practically ran the place. He used to stand in the yard like he was the warden. Men waited in line to talk to him. Charlie Lucky would listen, say something and then wave his hand. The guy would actually *back* away.'

Procession

This is not the schematic disposition of a prison football team with the Chief Warder as goalkeeper:

Chief Warder
Warder   Warder
Warder   Chaplain   Warder
Convict
Executioner
Principal Warder   Principal Warder
Warder   Warder
Governor   Sheriff
Wand bearer   Wand bearer
Surgeon and Attendant

It was the rigid Victorian order of procession as the condemned man walked across the courtyard to the gallows. The strict protocol and the sheer number of state and institutional officials emphasised that his termination was very far from haphazard retaliation.

An unfortunate incident involving the murderer Andrew Carr at Dublin's Richmond Prison on 28 July 1870. His trunk continued to quiver for three minutes.

'Profiler'

Profiling is the buzz-word for the accurate psychological portraits of serial killers constructed from seemingly trivial details; 'Profiler' is the FBI Behavioral Unit computer programme. It operates according to rules culled from investigative experience. For instance, most violent crime is intra-racial: whites prefer slaughtering whites; and Hispanics, Hispanics. Most serial murderers are white; the majority take their first life between 25 and 30. Sexual assaults on the elderly are generally the province of blacks. Similarly, in British homicide cases with a female victim under seventeen, the assailant is 62 per cent likely to be single, rising to 83 per cent if the victim is male. In 70 per cent of child homicides unaccompanied by sexual molestation, the culprit is a parent or guardian, but in sexual cases parental involvement drops to near zero. And so on.

The FBI's Profiler prototype began with 150 rules; by 1990 this had topped 270, and the list is still growing. For each case, the input to Profiler is everything known about the crime and, in particular, about the victim and the state of the body. Profiler output is the *type* of culprit: his age, sex, race, marital status, IQ, school record, present type of job (if any), outline employment history, 'rearing environment', personality traits, hobbies, appearance and grooming; whether he is **organised** or disorganised, whether he is liable to return to the crime scene and whether he lives near to or far from it, his connection with the victim and, of course, the motive. More graphically, Profiler provides an itemised reconstruction of the murder, starting with Phase One (contact) and ending with Phase Four (disposal).

For fine tuning, results of the computer-generated profile are adjusted against the human operative's assessment. Even getting only five or six of the twenty-five personality 'indicators' right may pinpoint the culprit, and today the headquarters for the Analysis of Violent Crime at **Quantico** handles about 900 cases a year.

Profiling received an inauspicious start in the 1960s when the medical-psychiatric team deployed on the Boston Strangler case suggested that his killings were the handiwork of two people: one a schoolteacher and the other a man living alone. One was a homosexual. Both were consumed by a festering hatred for their domineering **mothers** who, it seemed, were probably dead. It seemed likely that during the killers' childhoods, their mothers walked about 'half-exposed in their apartment, but punished them severely for any curiosity'. These objectionable experiences encouraged the Stranglers to play out their resentments in adulthood, murdering and mutilating older women in a manner simultaneously 'loving and sadistic'. Both killers had a weak and distant father.

Arrested in one piece, DeSalvo proved a family man motivated by an **insatiable** sex-drive and a vitriolic hatred of his brutal, domineering *father*. DeSalvo actually liked his mother, who was still alive.

It was the alteration of DeSalvo's *modus operandi* during his criminal career that misled the profilers. In the initial stages he concentrated on elderly victims; later, he picked on his own age group. A dissenting member of the investigative team, Dr James Brussel (see **Mad Bomber**) correctly reconciled the apparent differences in the killers' style as a single individual's process of maturation. 'In this two year period,' Brussel noted, 'he has suddenly grown from infancy to puberty to manhood.'

Profiling remains an inexact science, at least partly governed by psychiatrists' capacity to infer what they want to believe. Shrewder villains exploit this tendency. The Hillside Strangler, Kenneth Bianchi, nearly wriggled off the hook by feigning an exciting multiple personality disorder (**MPD**), fooling every expert apart from the police and a lone psychiatrist, Martin Orme, who happened to have read the books (*Three Faces of Eve, Sybil* etc.). Similarly, the **false** taped **confession** to the Yorkshire Ripper killings, which sidetracked the police investigation for months, may have invited belief by its conformity to the largely mythic stereotype of **Jack the Ripper**. Other critics maintain that psychiatrists are overly gratified by suggestions of a deranged mother/son relationship, regarding this as a touchstone indicative of authenticity.

In Britain, profiling was viewed with mistrust until very recently. But Professor Canter of Surrey University has now collaborated with the police on fifty-two investigations, including the case of John **Duffy**, the first conviction secured by computer.

Jack the Ripper was profiled posthumously as a male in his late twenties living locally. Since the murders were associated with weekends, he was probably in employment – but free from family accountability, as the killings occurred between midnight and six in the morning. The profile pointed to someone from the lower classes, since the murders evinced 'marked unfastidiousness'. The Ripper was not surgically or anatomically skilled, and had probably been in some form of trouble with the police before. He would be regarded by his associates as a loner. And he was a likely victim of child abuse, especially from, or with the consent of, his mother.

Much of the scepticism about profiling centres round its clusters of jargon. Put more simply, many objections melt away. For instance, few people would dispute that it takes a particular type of cretin to be a serial killer; profiling tries to establish which. Professor Cantor is admirably succinct: 'We can correlate the behaviour and the characteristics of the crime. From this we can draw indications of what sorts of criminals committed what sorts of murders. We will put a file of suspects into an order of priority.' Killings often throw up 'suspect lists' several thousand strong from their catchment area, and without a profiling system the police are left to plod endlessly through, say, reams of married businessmen when they should be concentrating on unemployed teenagers.

See also **Elveson, Mad Bomber**

Prohibition agents

A motley crew, despised by the Mob and public alike, and perhaps even more by the police as an unwarranted Federal intrusion.

Qualifications were minimal, the wages $200 dollars a month. But the prospects for extortion and kickbacks were without obvious limits, opening a vista of rich pickings which attracted the dregs of political appointees and near-criminals into the initial draft of 1,500 'Feds'. One agent was reportedly offered a bribe of $300,000 a week.

Prohibition agents became a byword for corruption, earning their first three indictments for selling confiscated liquor to bootleggers and accepting bribes within ten days of the **Eighteenth Amendment** coming into force; appropriately, the charges were issued in Chicago. Between 1920 and 1928, when the Department of Justice assumed control,

the Treasury dismissed 706 agents for larceny. Too many of the remainder acquired justified reputations as hoodlums on the take, lolling in chauffeur-driven limousines with show-girl mistresses on their arms.

Captain Dan Chaplin, chief of the New York Prohibition force, purged his squad in a few seconds. At a meeting of his agents round a large table, he rapped out, 'Put both hands on the table', then, 'Every one of you sons-o-bitches with a diamond ring is fired.' A good half left. In the Chicago of 1929, District Attorney George Emmerson Q. Johnson was perturbed by the young Eliot Ness's plan to form an elite caucus of a dozen **untouchables**. 'Can we find enough honest agents?' he asked. Ness unearthed ten, most from outside Chicago.

New York agents Izzy Einstein and Moe Smith were men of integrity and substance, tipping the scales at 240 pounds each. Dubbed 'Tweedledum' and 'Tweedledee' by the press, the pair raided speakeasies in disguise, dressed up as rabbis, fishermen, bootleggers or football players.

The best evidence to make a charge stick in court was a sample of the liquor on sale. Einstein and Smith would order a drink at the bar and pour the tipple into a concealed funnel linked by a tube to a back-pocket flask. Between them, they were instrumental in making 4,392 arrests and impounding five million bottles of rotgut.

Prospects

According to the research of criminologist William West, professional criminals in America fare considerably better than their more opportunistic colleagues, who spend an average of two-thirds to three-quarters of their working lives in prison. A professional should get away with incarceration for about a quarter of his time.

The low clear-up rate presented by government statistics gives a different impression, but official figures relate only to the percentage of crimes solved on an annual basis. Habitual criminals commit more than one offence a year for more than one year. 'If you want to play, you have to pay' runs the adage.

According to Charles E. Silberman, author of *Criminal Violence, Criminal Justice*, 'None of the criminals I interviewed knew, or had ever heard of, anyone who had been a criminal for any length of time without having been imprisoned.'

An intractable problem is that after pulling off one paying job, the criminal must devise another. But any operation earning money through repetition is tantamount to business or, in other words, very like work, requiring much the same qualities of reliability and applied intelligence. Thus a life of crime is not better than working for a living; it *is* working for a living. Mobster John Gotti put in fourteen-hour days under constant threat from law enforcement agents and his own colleagues.

In organised crime, the consequences of a hostile takeover or under-performance are often fatal. Although at first sight there is little to choose between Robert Maxwell and John Gotti as a boss, the blunt truth is that when Maxwell put his employees through the grinder it was only a figure of speech. Even the hoods assigned to mowing Gotti's garden lawn went in fear of their lives in case they tackled the task the wrong way and, under **Hoover**, the FBI achieved moblike status as a similarly terrorised organisation. John Dowd, the prosecuting attorney investigating misuse of Bureau funds in 1975, observed: 'There I was, interviewing employees just as scared as the people I'd had to deal with in pursuing Mafia chieftains. People in my office were absolutely trembling, relating twenty or thirty years of sordid conduct. They were still afraid, even though Hoover was dead.'

In America, a life of crime beckons early. It is as they enter Third Grade that pupils notice whether they form part of the cultural mainstream or its underclass. According to Dr James Comer, professor of psychiatry at Yale, the marginalised children appreciate what their background has failed to supply and what their future will fail to deliver, and slip off the edge academically as their attention fixes on two alternative scenarios: a life spent frying burgers for risible wages, or a bright-lights career for easy money dealing in drugs. The choice is theirs, to an extent, but the 1954 experiments of psychologist John B. Calhoun on the reaction of rat communities to gross overcrowding are not encouraging. Calhoun found that five per cent of the population turned into criminals, giving way to such anti-social ventures as rat rape and rat cannibalism. Contemporary statistics show parallel results with people, with the American urban homicide rate three times the norm for small towns, and the sex crime rate up by a factor of four.

According to American criminologist Bruce Jackson, underworld figures spend an inordinate amount of time asleep. Lacking a proper job and, generally, the corrective framework of a wife and family, they have little reason to get up.

This has been true down the ages. In 1808 an English seaman in Tunis recorded his impressions of the celebrated pirate John Ward: 'Speaks little, and almost always swearing. Drunk from morn till night. Most prodigal and plucky. Sleeps a great deal and often on board when in port.'

Provenance

Technical term for corroborative evidence establishing the pedigree of a work of art. Until the Second World War, the authentification process tended to rely on the word of connoisseurs. But their opinions were erratic in the extreme. The art expert Abraham Bredius was over eighty and half-blind when he accepted **Van Meegeren**'s pastiches as genuine Vermeers. Bernard Berenson too was famed for his partial, almost cantankerous attributions. Unsupported expert opinions can be just that: opinions. In 1984 a stone head dredged from a canal in Livorno, Italy, was proclaimed a priceless Modigliani by the curator of the local Museum of Modern Art before its exposure as a student prank, the fruit of four hours work on a paving stone with two chisels, two hammers, a screwdriver and a power drill.

After the Second World War, academics like Anthony Blunt pioneered the careful inspection of the documentation related to a painting as an essential tool for the art historian. The legacy is a boom in forging not the paintings themselves but their authenticating papers. Even a genuine picture is more marketable with the appropriate paperwork. So the documents are faked. Since most galleries were extremely lax with their records until the 1960s, the door is wide open for imaginative interpolations.

Provenance can be established by almost anything: a letter, a diary entry, a line in an inventory or a receipt, and to mock up such scraps of paper is relatively straightforward. This means, paradoxically, that a fake provenance does not necessarily connote a bogus picture.

Intriguingly, there are a number of 'unclaimed' provenances. Thus a contemporary diary sometimes records that a famous artist painted a certain picture on such-and-such a day. But the picture itself may never have been discovered. A current example is the 1957 memoir of the French writer Jean Genet, 'The Studio of Giacometti', which details how Giacometti produced several versions of the writer's head, finally proffering one as a gift. Genet wrote: 'I decide to take a small head... it is only seven centimetres high and three-and-a-half or four wide.' Several versions of this painting exist, but none this size.

A competent forgery to these dimensions could beguile an unsuspecting art historian into the excited 'discovery' of the missing Genet head, easing its path to acceptance, and this project (suggested here for the first time) might well pay dividends. Similarly, an assiduous trawl through period diaries and letters would uncover other sitting targets, works of art known to have been created but which have never come to light.

Even today scientific tests are of limited application. Porcelain can be separated into 'ancient' and 'modern' by the thermo-luminescence test. But statues are beyond verification: all stone is old. Dendrochronology ascertains the age of wood in a Renaissance panel painting. Lead isotope ratios reveal whether paint includes American lead, which at least puts a work as before or after the sixteenth century, and patient scholarship has clarified various pockets of information, like the number of threads per inch in Rembrandt's canvases. But counts outside these norms are not of themselves conclusive.

Crystallography can distinguish without equivocation between the regular machine-ground particles prevalent in nineteenth-century paint, and their rougher, earlier counterparts. But irrefutable evidence of counterfeit work most often comes from analysis of the pigments (and their binding medium) in the lower layers of a picture, indicating foul play if their ingredients post-date any overpainting, or the artist himself. But it is rare to expose a fake on scientific evidence alone. The great majority of artworks stand or fall on a rounded assessment of style, provenance and technical considerations conjointly, in other words, on opinion.

Save for his use of Bakelite, the physical constituents of the paintings by conscientious forgers like Hans Van Meegeren might pass muster today, but the paintings themselves are dreadful. Today's experts are astonished at how easily Van Meegeren duped yesterday's experts. Here the adage is that '**fakes** date'. The forger unwittingly absorbs stylistic nuances from his period, and a generation later it suddenly becomes clear that his compositions are distinctively of his own time. These days, with the perfect vision of hindsight, any fool can tell that Van Meegeren's *Christ and the Adulteress* was heavily influenced by Picasso's blue period.

Possibly the world's finest assemblage of forgeries was housed in Tito's Jesuistski's Museum outside Zagreb. The collection of 4,000 Old Masters, amassed by Ante Topic-Mimara and valued locally at $4 billion, contained hundreds of laughable Woolworth-style works in whose corners words like Turner, Michelangelo or Velazquez were written. Imelda Marcos is another mainline investor in expensive but obvious forgeries.

It is said that an expert cannot be fooled while drunk.

See also **Morals**

Public relations

One of the Mafia's more serious preoccupations. In Sicily a 'man of respect' fulfilled a social function, wielding his power with a word here and there to straighten out day-to-day social conflicts. A mediator, even a public benefactor, he represented threatened individual or collective interests. According to the writer H. Hess: 'The *mafioso* recoils with shocked surprise from any suggestion that he is a criminal.'

The return of stolen goods is a Mafia speciality with an honourable lineage. In 1932, in Sicily, the bombastic Prefect Cesare Mori reported a 95 per cent success rate when the Mob was called in to mediate, and the semi-formalisation of this process of recovery (with a going rate of about one third of the face value of the goods) epitomised the usurpation of the state's traditional monopoly of law and order.

When Mafia backs are against the wall, the gestures become grander. In his declining years, Capone spent time and money cultivating his role as a philanthropist. During the Depression, he set up Chicago's first soup-kitchens. 'Block restaurants for the unemployed, free food with compliments of the Organisation,' said a sociologist with first-hand knowledge, 'and you didn't have to listen to any sermons or get up and confess. You sat down and they gave you a real meal with tablecloths on the tables, and no one rescued you.'

The theft of national heirlooms provides real opportunities for gangland. After the Lindbergh kidnapping (see **Ladders**) of April 1932, Capone undertook to retrieve the child in return for temporary freedom. From Atlanta Penitentiary, he announced, 'I believe I can find the baby. I won't run away... What a lot I could do outside! I don't know a thing about the Lindbergh kidnapping, but I'm known to all the racket crowd as an honest guy, an honest guy who would keep his word if it's money they're after.' Lindbergh accepted the offer; the authorities declined.

Joseph Profaci, reputed head of the Colombo family, reinforced the tradition in 1952 by arranging for the return of the jewel-encrusted golden crowns lifted from New York's Regina Pacis Votive Shrine; these plangent relics were fashioned from the melted-down wedding rings of war widows. And when the icon from the Greek Orthodox church in Astoria, New York, was stolen at gunpoint on 23 December 1991, John Gotti put out word that he expected it returned. This was the famous 'weeping icon of peace' which shed tears at the start of the Gulf War.

At the time Gotti, in jail awaiting trial for racketeering, needed all the help he could get and, by the end of the week, amid much bell-ringing, the relic was safely back in the fold – minus its frame, a gold setting encrusted with rubies and diamonds, valued at $800,000.

It is not only *mafiosi* who crave respectability. Among the the droves of Chinese drug traffickers infesting Bangkok, serious dealers who have made their fortune expend their millions on buying power

and influential friends; for added social acceptability they distribute big money to worthy philanthropic causes. Accordingly, major traffickers make six-figure donations to anti-drug campaigns, helping to educate the public in the crusade against the addiction from which their riches sprang.

Puente, Dorothea (1928–)

Arsenic and Old Lace, the play by Joseph Kesselring, premiered at Broadway's Fulton Theatre in 1938, with the comic theme of the two aged Brewster sisters who poisoned their way through a dozen lodgers, despatching them with arsenic-laced elderberry wine. Serial killers in America were then such rare aberrations that they made safe figures of fantasy; during the 1920s, a mere thirty-nine deaths were recognised as the handiwork of multiple murderers.

Today, serial killers are no longer a joke, and it is unlikely that a revival of *Arsenic and Old Lace* would attract wide audiences either in Milwaukee, the home town of Jeffrey **Dahmer**, or in Sacramento, California, where Dorothea Puente is currently embroiled in a legal misunderstanding. Dorothea is the frail, diminutive grandmother who ran the boarding house on F Street. A keen gardener, she grew giant tomatoes, apricots and wonderful roses which sucked their nutrients from the lush soil near her back-door statuette of St Francis.

Dorothea provided work for prison parolees who sometimes laboured at digging her flower beds, and she turned her powder-blue Victorian home over to the welfare of the state's poor and muddled pensioners in their declining years, charging an affordable $350 for a month's board and lodging.

Dorothea prospered over the years. She took taxis everywhere, invested in a snappy wardrobe, favouring mauve and pink, and earned a reputation as a generous tipper at the local bar where she stood drinks all round. Always on the lookout for a new homeless senior citizen, she gave free financial advice on the welfare jungle, and many lodgers were picked up over a vodka-and-orange. When her guests fell ill, she dispensed special care upstairs in her sickroom. She replaced its carpet a number of times at her own expense; as she told friends, sometimes 'bad things' happened up there.

Two strict rules governed Dorothea's establishment. First, guests had to be punctilious in the maintenance of their pension, welfare and disability allowances. Under the second, Dorothea alone could collect the post. Otherwise, her guests – and neighbours – only needed to acclimatise themselves to the F Street smell. For scrub as Dorothea might, spray what lemon deodorant she would, dump as much fish emulsion on the garden as she could, the place still stank.

In 1988 social worker Judy Moise enquired about the fate of one of the lodgers, a 52-year-old retarded immigrant from Costa Rica named Alvaro Montoya. Dorothea maintained that he had left to visit his relatives in Mexico.

But Moise knew that Montoya's only relatives lived in New Orleans. She called the police, who spent three days excavating Dorothea's garden, unearthing the decayed remains of seven tightly-wrapped bodies, all lodgers, buried under the rosebeds and the vegetable plot. Their former land-lady was charged with a total of nine murders including another guest whose boxed corpse cropped up in the river, and yet another lodger previously regarded as a suicide.

The prosecution contend that Dorothea poisoned them for their monthly pensions which she neglected to cancel, eventually netting some $5,000 a month, and a survivor spoke of declining offers of bitter-tasting iced tea and coolaid.

The defence insists that the lodgers died of natural causes. Whatever the outcome, Dorothea is destined for a starring role, but not necessarily in a comedy.

Q

Quantico

The US base forming the headquarters of the FBI's NCAVC: the National Centre for the Analysis of Violent Crime. Set up by Reagan in June 1984, its primary mission is the apprehension of serial killers, and its first investigative step to establish whether a new killing displays the hallmark of a villain already on file.

Operatives work sixty feet underground in an old nuclear bunker. The ten senior profilers are designated 'criminal investigative analysts' (the 'A team') and, since their job is analysis not arrest, the premises house neither cells nor offenders. The business end is the computer system, known formally as VICAP – the Violent Criminal Apprehension Programme – and informally as 'Old Red-Eye' for the pulsing red light in the console's steel face.

Details of new cases come into Quantico clinically described on an exhaustive ten-part questionnaire completed by local police. Headings include everything known about the victim, the state of the body (including details of '**souvenirs**' removed, any **torture** and so on), the **modus operandi,** cause of death and forensic evidence. Thus Section VII ('Condition of Victim when Found') incorporates a sub-section, 'Restraints Used on Victim', beginning with Question 141 'Was the Victim bound?', followed by eight multiple-choice questions. Number 142 asks respondents to select between: restraint with an article of clothing; tape; cordage; chain; handcuffs; or other ('please specify').

This standardised data is sent down the line to the mainframe in Washington, which reciprocates with a print-out – the 'Template' – of the ten best matches: similar killings elsewhere, listed in order of resemblance. A junior analyst adds the human element, assessing which (if any) are the work of

the same hand. A positive identification of two or more 'events' with a matching 'signature' means that the various law enforcement agencies involved are put in contact with each other and with Quantico which, on request (indicated by a tick in the relevant box), forwards a copy of the killer's 'profile'.

This system, the brainchild of Commander Pierce Brooks, represents the fruit of twenty-five years work. The Commander's inspiration dates to 1958. Driven by a hunch that a murder victim had perished at the hands of an experienced killer, Brooks was reduced to combing through newspapers at public libraries to check for a previous mention of an unidentified killer. The search took a year of his free time, but it yielded a news clipping on an arrest for an analogous slaying in a different city. The fingerprints in that case matched those in his. As Brooks attested at the 1983 Senate Committee, 'Over the years that primitive system worked two or three times.'

Until the 1980s there was no alternative to similar feats of clerical drudgery. Local law officers remained in ignorance of the case-load of colleagues in other jurisdictions. Many forces in many states could want the same man, with no one the wiser, and police on the spot might be unaware that their murder was the work of a serial killer sought (or behind bars) elsewhere. In an era of advanced technology, American police lacked any means of pooling information, and the overwhelming consensus for reform voiced at the 1983 Senate Committee hearing prompted Reagan to implement the VICAP proposals without delay.

Today, VICAP constitutes a centralised, updated directory of homicides nationwide. Staff reckon on detecting the handiwork of about fifteen new serial killers a year. Perhaps half are caught.

One of Quantico's more unusual features is the mock town of 'Hogan's Alley' for anti-terrorist training, based on Hollywood's Universal Studios. Next to the Bank of Hogan, the most robbed financial institution in the world, stands the Biograph Theatre, perpetually playing *Manhattan Melodrama* in tribute to the death of John **Dillinger**. Agents, brought up to regard themselves as 'doing God's work', incessantly rehearse tactical manoeuvres, scaling walls, firing at pop-up targets and simulating drug raids. Their FATS device (firearms training device) stages **virtual reality** gunfights where agents hone their skills on changing scenarios; one time, the electronic suspect reaches for a gun, the next for a cigarette, and the recorded fall of shot shows who dies when. In many ways, Quantico fosters a culture of action, and critics of the Waco debacle, where more than eighty Davidians died in an inferno after the FBI rammed a tank into the compound, question whether the Agency is best equipped to handle situations of psychological stasis calling for protracted inaction.

See **Database, Organised, Profiler**

Quartering

Unpopular with French executioners. The process was complicated and time-consuming since each of the condemned man's limbs had to be stoutly harnessed to a **horse**, and the four animals might strain for an hour before the victim was torn apart. Worse, each animal needed to be goaded by an assistant, whose fees came out of the executioner's pocket.

Queen Poison

Title awarded to Lydia Sherman, a manic American poisoner who escaped the death penalty. In 1864 Lydia grew tired of her whingeing husband, Edward Struck, a New York policeman who lost his job after flunking the arrest of a mad knifeman. First Lydia mocked her spouse into drink and despair; then she poisoned him with **arsenic**. Next she did away with her six children, including her nine-month-old baby, weaned on contaminated milk.

At last she was free, and in 1868 Lydia married the elderly Dennis Hurlbrut, whom she poisoned.

Her third husband, Nelson Sherman, met the same fate on 12 May 1871, laid low by a mug of poisoned cocoa; by then she had already put his two daughters underground.

Altogether, Lydia is credited with forty-two killings. But she confessed to only eleven and another dozen or so 'possibles', and at her trial in April 1872 was convicted of second-degree murder. She died five years into her life sentence.

A strong British claimant for the epithet of Queen Poison is Mary Ann Cotton. Born in 1832 to a Durham miner, she was raised as a devout Methodist. At its maximum, Mary Ann's tally includes her own mother, two husbands, two lovers, her best friend, five of other people's children and ten of her own, but her fatal swathe is normally put at fourteen or fifteen, mostly identified by the telltale certification of death from 'gastric fever'. Mary Ann was atypical in her occasional poisonings to clear the way to a marriage rather than from one; other motives included insurance policies of a few pounds or even burial money. She often moved house, shedding spouses and children in her wake.

Mary Ann was arrested on 18 July 1872 after the unexpected demise of her stepson, Charles Edward, in the village of West Auckland. On 6 July she had implored the local public relief official, Thomas Riley, to make room for her boy in the workhouse. Riley enquired if she wanted to get married. 'It might be so,' responded Mary Ann, 'but the boy is in the way.' Six days later Charles Edward was dead. 'I was surprised,' Riley recounted. 'The boy had seemed a perfectly healthy little chap. I went straight to the police and the village doctor.' On exhumation, the child's viscera were found riddled with arsenic; £8 was due on a policy with the Prudential.

By the time Mary Ann came to court on 5 March 1873 her past was public knowledge, and the trial was a one-sided affair since the judge, Sir Thomas Archibald, admitted evidence of similarly suspicious deaths among her friends and relatives. Beyond arguing that Charles Edward had succumbed to some green floral wallpaper, heavily impregnated with arsenic, her counsel had nothing to say. Mary Ann was hanged on 24 March 1874, with the *Newcastle Journal* commenting: 'Perhaps the most astounding thought of all is that a woman could act thus without becoming horrible and repulsive. Mary Ann Cotton, on the contrary, seems to have possessed the faculty of getting a new husband whenever she wanted one. To her other children and her lodger, even when she was poisoning them, she is said to have maintained a rather kindly manner.'

R

Ramirez, Richard (1960–)

Julian and Mercedes Ramirez – poor Mexican immigrants – had seven children. Like all his family, Richard, the youngest, was brought up in the Catholic faith in El Paso, Texas. But by the age of nine he preferred glue-sniffing and video arcades to churchgoing.

Then Ramirez discovered dope, funding his habit by theft. Robbery led to burglary and school truancy. He dropped out at the age of seventeen, and on 7 December 1977 underwent his first arrest, for suspected possession of marijuana. He was carrying a ski mask and a toy gun at the time. After his fourth arrest he was sentenced to three years' parole. Thereafter Ramirez lived rough, subsisting on a diet of Coke and hamburgers. He stole cars. By 1983 he had moved to Los Angeles, where he slid into an existence in the abyss. A tall, lanky dope-head with hollow cheekbones, obsessed with satanism and heavy metal rock 'n' roll, Ramirez financed his injections of cocaine by stealing videos and microwaves.

He was caught, jailed for car theft, served his term and was released. Then in June 1984 Ramirez raped and killed Jennie Vincow. She was seventy-nine. Nine months later, on 17 March 1985, he broke into the apartment of Dayle Okazaki, a traffic-manager from Hawaii. In the kitchen he shot her dead, and when her flatmate returned, he shot her too. Then he pressed on to Monterey Park where he dragged Tsai Lian Yu from her car and killed her. On 27 March he forced his way into the home of Vincent and Maxine Zazzara; he owned a pizza restaurant, she was a lawyer. Ramirez shot him dead; she died after her eyes were cut out. On 14 May he broke into William Doi's home, shot him dead, beat his wife and raped his daughter. The next rape came on 30 May; the victim – Carol Kyle – survived, and on 27 June Ramirez slit the throat of Patty Elaine Higgins, and on 2 July Mary Louise Cannon suffered the same fate.

Five days later Ramirez bludgeoned to death Joyce Lucille Nelson, a grandmother. On 20 July Max Kneiding was shot dead in bed in his Glendale home. Ramirez stabbed Kneiding's wife, Lela, before attempting to cut off her head. That night he shot Chainarong Khovananth and raped his wife, and then on 5 August he left the Petersons for dead. Three days later he murdered Elyas Abowath in San Gabriel Valley before raping his wife. Then on 17 August he shot a man called Peter Pan and his wife Barbara through the head.

As early as June, Detective Sergeant Salerno of the LA County Sheriff's Department knew that a serial killer was on the loose. Salerno tracked Ramirez's progress through his persistent use of the same .22 calibre pistol and its matching bullets. Two hundred police were assigned to the case, but by August they had accumulated little more than an Avia shoeprint and various sightings indicating that the killer was tall, thin and dark-haired. When the detailed descriptions provided by the Petersons were converted into Identikit sketches and flooded onto the newspapers and television screens, Ramirez showed the results to a friend in San Francisco, Donna Myers, an older woman who did his laundry and was virtually his only stable relationship. 'Do you think that could be me?' he asked.

Donna said no. So after breaking into William Cairn's home on 24 August, shooting him dead and raping his fiancée Inez, Ramirez remained unconcerned. He went to Phoenix Arizona to buy cocaine and caught the Greyhound back on 31 August. At about 8.30 that evening he walked into Tito's liquor store on Towne Avenue to buy a can of Coke and some doughnuts. By the checkout he noticed a stack of newspapers with his clearly-recognisable photograph on the front page. Ramirez panicked and ran, pursued by shoppers.

He was identified because, the week before, survivor Inez Erickson told the police that her assailant had driven an orange Toyota. That same day a sharp-eyed teenager, James Romero III, spotted a suspicious orange Toyota circling his home in Mission Viejo. He noted its number, which matched the registration of an orange Toyota abandoned in the Los Angeles suburb of Rampart. A fingerprint lifted from the vehicle by laser scanning was transmitted to the state computer in Sacramento, just updated with the prints of those born after 1 January 1960. Ramirez's birthday fell on 28 February 1960, and his photographs were on file.

Ramirez sprinted two miles down the broad Los Angeles avenues, twisting into the side streets to shake off a growing crowd of pursuers. Two teenagers, Jaime and Julio Burgoin, jumped him. Then the police arrived. 'Save me, please! Thank God you came,' blurted Ramirez. A mob gathered round Hollenbeck police station, eager for a lynching.

After legal manoeuvring his trial did not open until January 1989. A refurbished Ramirez appeared in the dock. No longer a shabby loner with T-shirt and decaying teeth, his hair was groomed, his dental work shone, and he wore a pinstripe suit. But he declined to testify and was sentenced to death on 20 September 1989.

What was the *point* of the murders? Ramirez bragged to a cellmate, 'I've killed twenty people, man. I love all that blood.' To Sheriff Jim Ellis he expanded, 'I love to kill people. I love watching them die. I would shoot them in the head...or I would cut them with a bread knife and watch their faces turn real white. I love all that blood.'

After sentence Ramirez told the court, 'I have a lot to say, but now is not the time or place... I am beyond your experience. I am beyond good and evil.' To the press he said, 'Death always went with the territory.'

See also **de Sade**

Rape, Law of

In England, rape is punishable by a maximum of life imprisonment (Section 1, Offences Against the Person Act 1956) but the offence only received statutory definition in 1976 as 'unlawful sexual intercourse with a woman... who does not consent.' Thus a woman cannot rape a man, although this exploit was attributed to Joyce **McKinney** in 1977 by the tabloid press. The word 'unlawful' appears – or did appear until 1991 – to mean extra-marital intercourse.

The basic constituents of rape have long been established. The 1841 case of *Hughes* laid down that the hymen need not be broken; in the words of the 1956 Act, 'it is not necessary to prove... emission of seed, but intercourse shall be deemed to be complete upon proof of penetration.' Nor is it a defence that the victim was asleep (*R* v. *Mayers* 1872) or even unconscious (*R* v. *Camplin* 1845), since both states preclude the victim's consent. At the time of writing there remains an irrefutable legal presumption that a boy younger than fourteen is incapable of sexual intercourse.

The fraud cases follow the firm stand taken by the American wit Dorothy Parker, who remarked to a diminutive colleague: 'Never make love to me again, and if I ever find out you have I shall be extremely annoyed.' In *R* v. *Case* (1850), a doctor duped his patient into having intercourse under the pretence that this constituted treatment. The victim regarded the insertion as a surgical operation.

In fact it was rape, and nearly seventy-five years later the principle was upheld in *R* v. *Williams*, where a singing master procured sex with a 16-year-old pupil by depicting intercourse as a method of voice training. It may be that with the greater emphasis on sexual education this particular approach is defunct; there are no recent cases. But Section 2 of the 1956 Act still prohibits the misguided venture of inducing a married woman to make love by impersonating her husband.

Dense thickets of problems surround the notion of 'consent', the absence of which turns sex into rape. This area was notoriously expounded by Lord Denning: 'If a lady says "no" she means maybe, if she says "maybe" she means yes and if she says "yes" she is no lady.'

It is clear from *Olugjuba* (1982) that rape need not entail violence or even the threat of violence. Nor is acquiescence during or after the act pertinent; it is the woman's state of mind immediately prior to penetration that matters. There is no requirement for the victim to put up resistance. But the accused has a good defence if he genuinely considers – however unreasonably – that the woman agreed to intercourse. In *DPP* v. *Morgan* (1975) three friends were invited back for sex with a man's wife. The husband cautioned that her protestations were not to be regarded as lack of enthusiasm; she enjoyed it better that way. Initially, the three were convicted on the grounds that their belief in the woman's willingness had to be reasonable, but this was overturned on appeal, a decision reinforced by *R* v. *Satnam and Kewel* (1983), when the victim's lack of consent should have been 'obvious to every ordinary observer' and the participants alone deluded. Provided the belief is genuine, it need not be reasonable; being stupid is one thing, reckless quite another.

American law has followed the alternative route, as the 1992 **Tyson** case exemplifies. Convictions are based not on whether the man thought he was raping the woman but on whether the woman thought she was being raped by the man.

In England, until 1991, a bizarre but absolute presumption remained that a woman consented to intercourse with her husband, irrespective of the facts. Over the years the exemption's broad sweep was progressively eroded. In 1949 legally separated couples were excluded (*Clarke*), nor has it applied during a decree nisi since 1974 (*O'Brien*), or where the husband was under an injunction not to cohabit with his victim.

The landmark case of *R* v. *R* abolished the defence, for which no authority later than 1736 could be found. Lord Lane commented that the exemption was socially outmoded, and in October 1991 Lord Keith averred that marriage was a partnership in which the wife no longer constituted a subservient chattel.

Judges' comments made after conviction but during sentencing often attract widespread press discussion, perhaps most notably when a young woman was deemed to have asked for it because she hitchhiked home, after nightfall. A companion case from 1993 ended with the freeing of the 15-year-old assailant after Judge John Prosser ordered him pay £500 'compensation' to his schoolgirl victim so she could have a holiday 'to recover'.

But it is easy to make smoke without much fire. On 11 April 1991, Brian Huntley from Hull was convicted of raping a 19-year-old prostitute. When his intentions became clear, his victim begged him to use a contraceptive and, remarkably, he did. Judge Arthur Myerson took this act of vestigial concern into account when arriving at a sentence of three years' imprisonment. The following day, the *Daily Mirror* carried the headline 'Judge praises rapist who wore condom', printing calls from Women Against Rape for his dismissal. In America, a similar 1992 case caused even greater outcry when the request for a condom inspired a defence based on the victim's consent.

There were 4,110 reported rapes in Britain during 1992; the average sentence was six years four months. In America the total reached 160,000 – about ten times the British *per capita* rate. In Mississippi the offence carries the possibility of the death sentence, perhaps a historical legacy intended for blacks.

Probably the single greatest contributor to the global figures is Mustapha Tanet, the police commissioner of Casablanca. In three years 1990, he raped the astonishing total of 1,500 women in his *garçonnière* at 36 Boulevard Ben Yacine. Tabet was above the law. His bank account groaned under a credit balance of £1.8 million accumulated on an annual salary of £2,000, and he lived by rake-offs and bribes, the traditional perks of a local chief of police. But Tabet went further. He bought a blue Mercedes, hired a chauffeur and drove round Casablanca offering rides to young women. He video-taped his assaults, enabling identification of 516 of his victims, and is currently awaiting execution.

Ratcliffe Highway

The main thoroughfare running east out of London, through the worst districts of the capital. In 1811, Number 29 was occupied by a young linen-draper, Timothy Marr, his wife, their three-month-old baby, their maid and apprentice boy.

Late on 7 December 1811, the maid went out to buy oysters for the family supper. On her return, the Marrs could not be roused; it was as though they had all suddenly disappeared or died. She waited half an hour before waking her neighbour, who climbed over the backyard fence. In the shop he stumbled over the apprentice's body, his head smashed so badly that parts of his brains dripped from the ceiling. Nearby lay Mrs Marr, her skull likewise battered. Behind the counter was Timothy Marr's corpse, and downstairs the baby swung in its cradle, its head caved in and the throat cut to the bone. If the motive was burglary, the till was untouched, and a bedroom drawer still contained £152 in cash. Two sets of footprints led from the back of the house, and a long ripping chisel, perhaps used as a jemmy, reposed on the counter. Upstairs was a heavy iron mallet covered in blood.

A wave of horror and indignation swept the capital. *The Times* doubted the killings had any 'equal in atrocity', and sightseers clogged Ratcliffe Highway. Three separate authorities launched investigations: the parish churchwardens, the Shadwell magistrates and the River Thames Police. Their efforts were paltry, confused and disjointed. They failed to follow leads and fed on rumour, arresting dozens of suspects, most of them drunks, madmen or foreigners. The ripping chisel had last been seen in the possession of a carpenter, Cornelius Hart, who worked on Marr's shop, but his alibi went unchecked, and only on 19 December was it noticed that the iron mallet bore a set of dotted initials punched on its head: 'IP'.

Late that night, two minutes' walk from Marr's shop, a near-naked man lowered himself on a set of knotted sheets from the upper floors of the King's Arms, crying, 'They are murdering the people in the house.' Neighbours broke in and found three bodies, again with their throats slit and their heads pulped, this time with a three-foot crowbar. The intruder or intruders escaped out of the rear window, jumping onto a muddy bank.

John Turner, the lodger, had been saved by the housemaid's cry, 'Lord Jesus Christ! We shall all be murdered.' Tiptoeing down to the first floor he saw the killer, a tall man six feet high in a Flushing coat, with two brained bodies at his feet, his back turned as he rifled through the parlour cupboards. This tallied with a stranger in a brown jacket observed loitering outside the pub only minutes before. A tentative sighting of two suspects described one as lame.

According to crime writer Colin Wilson, public hysteria attained such heights because the murders were imputed to a single man rather than to run-of-the-mill gang violence. De Quincey put his literary seal on the concept of a demented individual in his fanciful 1854 essay, *Murder considered as one of the Fine Arts*, extolling the killings as 'the sublimest and most entire in their excellence that ever were committed'. Why, De Quincey demanded, cut a man's throat after beating out his brains? Why smash a baby's skull as it slept in its cot? Why razor its throat? De Quincey took hold of the cruelty and barbarity of the event, most probably an interrupted robbery, and added the thrilling element of pointless sadism. The scare had long tentacles. De Quincey mentions a friend in an isolated rural area in Grasmere, who 'never rested until she had placed eighteen doors... each secured and bolted, between her bedroom and any intruder of human build.' It only remained for **Jack the Ripper** to breathe life into the fantasies of recreational killing.

On 23 December, a young sailor of shabby elegance, John Williams, was summoned before the magistrates. A former shipmate of the dead linen-draper, he was a man of superior education and foppish disposition lodging at the Pear Tree Inn. It was said that on the murder night Williams came home late and asked a roommate to extinguish the candle, as though anxious to conceal his appearance. He had been drinking at the King's Arms, starting the evening with sixpence and ending it with a pound. In addition, he was billed as short, lame and Irish (see **Xenophobia**).

On arrival in court, it was clear that at 5 feet 9 inches Williams was tall, even-limbed and Scottish. He admitted visiting the King's Arms, where he was friendly with the landlady, and accounted for his money with a tale of pawning his clothes. And, as a sailor with a dread of fire at sea, it was natural for him to be alarmed at finding his roommate lying in bed with a pipe in his mouth and a candle in his hand. Like many another suspect, Williams was consigned to Coldbath Fields Prison, but the next day the news broke that the Pear Tree's landlord had recognised the iron mallet. It belonged to John Peterson, a German sailor, who stored his tool chest at the inn, and Williams was recalled for renewed questioning under mounting suspicion.

John Turner, the survivor from the King's Arms, failed to identify him, although a laundress testified that four or five days *before* the second murders she found lightly spattered blood round one of Williams's shirt collars. Clearly this had no bearing on the later killings, and Williams gave details of a scuffle after a drunken game of cards. But he was returned to custody. Then on Christmas Day, the Pear Tree landlord stated that the crowbar also came from Peterson's tool chest, and Boxing Day brought the revelation that the morning after the murders Williams had washed a muddy pair of stockings. 'We are not yet certain he will prove the man,' the magistrates wrote to the Home Secretary. But charges were imminent.

On 27 December, the warders found Williams dead in his cell, suspended from an iron bar by his handkerchief. This dramatic development was interpreted as an admission of guilt, and the half-hearted examination of another suspect, William Ablass, the subject of much neighbourhood gossip for his unpleasant disposition, was not pursued. Following the route of least resistance, the magistrates concluded that Williams alone was guilty, and on 31 December his body was loaded on a cart, his head resting on a wooden stake, with the crowbar, mallet and ripping chisel arrayed around him. The corpse processed through Wapping, watched by a crowd of ten thousand in stony silence, and Williams was dumped in a hole at the crossroads of Back Lane and Cannon Street, with a stake hammered through his heart.

John Williams, drawn in the prison cell soon after he was cut down

The case against him remains flimsy. Had the magistrates searched the Pear Tree thoroughly, and cross-examined everyone with access to Peterson's tools, the truth might have been established. But, over-impressed by having a suspect in custody, they looked no further.

Was his death suicide? Williams left no note, and asked for no pen and paper. He was in confident mood when last seen, remarking that 'the saddle was on the wrong horse'. If innocent, he stood a fair chance of acquittal: his alibi might yet be confirmed, and he had not even been committed for trial. If guilty, he could save his skin by turning King's Evidence. The individual most endangered by his existence was the true murderer, facing either betrayal or a renewed investigation.

The bar in Williams's cell stood 6 feet 2 inches from the floor, and he presumably jumped from his bed. But the *Morning Post* of 28 December states that 'the state of his body clearly demonstrated that he had struggled very hard'. If so, Williams could probably have saved himself in the minutes before asphyxiation, either with a toehold on his bed or by calling for help.

If Williams was not the culprit, then who? The Marrs' murderer did not act alone. Two, or possibly three, men loitered outside the shop earlier in the evening; two sets of footprints were found, and one man would hardly enter the premises encumbered by the long mallet and the long chisel as well as a razor. It would be interesting to put William Ablass back in the dock. He was tall, lame, and a dangerous man who had organised a mutiny on the *Roxburgh Castle*. He had access to Peterson's tools. The woman who vouchsafed his alibi was his wife, and he had money for which he could not account. Similarly, the armchair detective might recall Cornelius Hart and verify his alibi.

John Williams's burial

The Ratcliffe Highway murders made it very clear that London – still safeguarded by the antiquated system of decrepit **watchmen** – was unsafe for law-abiding citizens, and the idea of a 'police force' was hotly debated in the press. 'I had rather half-a-dozen people's throats be cut in the Ratcliffe Highway every three or four years,' affirmed one commentator just back from France, 'than be subject to the domiciliary visits, spies and the rest of Fouché's contrivances.' A more vigorous Home Secretary than the incumbent, Richard Ryder, might have pushed through worthwhile legislation, but his proposals were costed at £74,000 and voted down for the 'alarming powers' they conferred. It was 1829 before Robert Peel set up the Metropolitan Police.

See also **Oaths**

Reading material

J.R.R. Tolkien's *The Lord of the Rings* is often dismissed by intellectual snobs as a literary ghetto for the emotionally retarded. One great fan was Jeffrey **Dahmer**.

For many serial killers, *The Collector* is a favourite choice. This 1963 novel by John Fowles tells the story of a shy young man who 'collects' a beautiful young girl and holds her captive until she perishes for want of medical attention. Then he looks for another specimen.

The would-be presidential **assassin**, John Hinckley, took his cue from J.D. Salinger's *The Catcher in the Rye*.

During Al Capone's brief 1929 spell in prison, his preferred authors were reputed to be Bernard Shaw and Shakespeare. At the time the public would swallow anything about Capone; 'genius' was a common epithet, and a Philadelphia newspaper characterised him as a 'stern highbrow'.

The reading list of actor Sean Penn, jailed for assaulting a photographer, was equally impressive. It included Montaigne and William Burroughs (see **Champagne**). But Penn says: 'I recommend Thurber for everyone in jail.' By a strange coincidence, British prisons are crammed with Walter Mitty characters professing to be Ulster secret agents or members of the Parachute Regiment and the SAS.

George Bernard Shaw was another perceptive man. According to his secretary, Bernard Blanche, in the early 1940s they were lunching together at London's Onslow Court Hotel when a sudden fracas broke out at a nearby table. A smart looking gentleman shocked his fellow diners by savagely berating a troublesome child, snarling, 'If you do that again, I'll kill you.'

'That man will hang,' commented Shaw. Haigh did. Another writer imbued with prophetic powers was Mark Twain. In 1883, he published *Life on the Mississippi*. Chapter thirty-one described the identification of a murderer by a bloodstained **fingerprint**. This pre-dated the first such occurrence (Francisca Rojas, Argentina) by nine years and was written before any police force anywhere was aware of the possibilities of fingerprints.

According to Shaw, the artist is judged by his highest moments, and the criminal by his lowest.

Recruitment

The Chinese street gangs infesting today's New York incorporate cultural elements derived in equal measure from the **Triads** and American gangster movies. Their members, who may live several to a room, can be as young as thirteen, and an unusually forthright – and cynical – description of their high school recruitment was given by David Chong, an undercover police officer and former *dai lo* (street boss) of the 'Flying Dragons'.

'I would have my kids go to a high school in Chinatown and look for the turkey right off the boat,' said Chong. 'You want him in ninth or tenth grade, he can't speak English, he's got a stupid haircut. And when you find this kid, you go beat the shit out of him. Tease him, beat him up, knock him around. We isolate this kid; he's our *target*. What will happen is one day I'll make sure I'm around when this kid is getting beaten up, and I'll stop it with the snap of my finger. He'll look at me – he'll see that I have a fancy car, girls, I'm wearing a beeper – and I'll turn around and say, "Hey, kid, how come these people are beating on you?" I'm gonna be this kid's hero, this kid's guru – I'm gonna be his *dai lo*.'

The softening-up complete, 'I'll take the kid for a drive, take him to a restaurant, order him the biggest lobster, the biggest steak. Eventually, I'll take him to the safe house where I keep kids and guns. Then I slowly break him in.'

Forty dollars a week and a bedroom shared with five others is a fair starting rate for a recruit. Training includes instruction on killing 'cleanly': shoot the victim repeatedly, make sure there are no witnesses, and – for economy – use a cheap gun. The murder weapon must always be discarded.

In Britain, finding a new recruit for the position of public hangman required no such coercion; the death of the executioner William Marwood on 2 September 1883 provoked a flood of unsolicited applications. Selected excerpts from assorted correspondents eager to prove their mettle read as follows [*sic*]: 'Dere Sir, I am waiting outside with a coil of rope, and should be glad to give you a personal proof of my method'; 'I would hang either brothers or sisters, or anyone else referred to me, without fear or favour'; 'I have witnessed Executions among all nations; consequently there is no fear of my getting sick at the right moment'; 'In my Line of Business as a Barber I have had some Great Experience of the Formation of necks and windpipes of all people'; 'Deer Sur, I am ankshus to be yure publick exechoner, and i hereby apply for the job. i am thurty yeres old, and am willing to hang one or two men for nothink'; and, 'I have at various times made some very successful experiments in the art of hanging (by means of life-size figures) with a view to making myself thoroughly proficient in the despatch of criminals.'

Thirty applicants were invited to an interview at the Old Bailey. Seventeen turned up, and after two hours the Sheriffs settled on Bartholomew Binns, a coalminer. He bungled his first four jobs, and was sacked after arriving drunk for the fifth. Thereafter, he briefly made a living in fairground booths demonstrating his prowess on wax effigies.

References

Like everyone else, hangmen must pitch for work. James **Berry**, the meticulous Victorian executioner, customarily issued new clients with a written estimate. His pre-printed form had various blanks to fill in, notably the Quote Number and the missing bits in the following sentence: 'I am prepared to undertake the execution you name of ... at ... on the ...'

As proof of his workmanship, Berry collected references. One testimonial, dated 2 September 1884 and signed by a Dr Bar, began: 'I have never seen an execution more satisfactorily performed... This was very gratifying to me. Your rope was of excellent quality; fine, soft, pliable and strong.'

But few testimonials can have been as glowing as the one submitted by the serial killer Ted **Bundy** to bolster his 1973 application to law school. His reference, signed by Washington State Governor Dan Evans, read in part: 'It was the consensus among those of us who directed the operation that Ted's performance was outstanding. Given a key role in the issues, research, and strategy section, he demonstrated an ability to define and organise his own projects, to effectively synthesise and clearly communicate factual information and to ... tolerate strain and sometimes critical situations. In the end it was probably his composure and discretion that allowed him to successfully carry out his assignments.'

Who could resist an applicant of this calibre? After Bundy's first conviction, Dr Carlisle of Utah State Penitentiary completed another assessment scarcely less flattering, although on careful reading the doctor's crucial final qualification is perceptive;

REG KRAY, BOOK OF EXERCISES

anyone who needs to be 'clever' to appear 'close' to the 'edge' of normality must be way off beam.

'In general,' Dr Carlisle wrote, 'the scores for the objective tests portray the picture of a person who is happy, confident and very well adjusted... In conclusion, I feel that Mr Bundy is either a man who has no problems or is smart and clever enough to appear close to the edge of "normal".'

It is probable that Bundy himself penned most of Governor Evans's panegyric. In prison awaiting trial, he sent the *Seattle Times* an open letter revealing a less confident touch: 'I address this letter to my many friends and acquaintances who have offered their prayers, concern and support in my behalf. When time permits, I shall do my best to reply personally to each of you. You are truly beautiful people.'

These are the flawed perceptions of a pop star, of a man with an admiring audience of depersonalised units.

'Reg Kray Book of Exercises for People in Confined Places, The'

Said in 1983 to be Reggie **Kray**'s joke title for a short manual compiled during his interminable prison sentence, setting out his physical fitness regime. The Kray twins' actual book *Our Story* is an affectionate piece of auto-hagiography, liberally sprinkled with photographs of the famous: Diana Dors ('a true friend'), Barbra Streisand ('To Ronnie, happiness!') and Lord Boothby ('a friend and business associate of Ron's').

Fifteen years in close confinement as a 'Category A' prisoner is generally reckoned sufficient to turn a jailbird into a human vegetable. Reggie has been inside since 1969 and, to his credit, is still *mens sana in corpore sano*, painting with water colours and enjoying a good book. He is scheduled for release in 1998. His brother, Ronnie, was in a bad way when he went into prison and is now a patient in the Broadmoor psychiatric hospital. But this did not prevent him from getting married. Nor did his former penchant for young boys constitute a just impediment.

In August 1993 it finally emerged that the establishment politician Lord Boothby had indeed shared a joint enterprise with Ronald Kray: the pursuit of young men. Ronnie pandered for him.

Scotland Yard's intelligence section, C11, kept them both under observation, and Boothby had to sue for libel after the *Sunday Mirror*, campaigning against organised crime in London, ran its July 1964 headline, 'Peer and a gangster: Yard inquiry'.

Ronnie's joint sexual escapades with a peer of the realm did more than titillate his appetite for celebrities. He hoped that the relationship would confer immunity from prosecution.

It did. Boothby's cronies rallied round to defend their colleague against the imputations of homosexuality, and Sir John Simpson, Scotland Yard's commissioner, denied ordering any investigation. The police inquiry was speedily wound down. Boothby won damages of £40,000, but, with incriminating letters and photographs in the Krays' possession, he remained wide open to **blackmail**. It seems that he bankrolled the twins' successful 1965 defence against extortion charges, and in February of that year spoke out on their behalf in the House of Lords.

It became increasingly clear that an attack on the Krays would involve tackling both Boothby and his influential friends, who had lied to maintain his innocence. The police backed off, as did the press, leaving evil alone. Thus began the Krays four-year breathing-space, during which they constructed a criminal empire that was well-nigh impregnable.

See also **Attaché case**, **Bobettes**

Reis, Professor A.R.

Master detective and founder of the Lausanne Institute of Police Science, probably Europe's first forensic science laboratory. In October 1909, Reis performed a deductive feat worthy of Sherlock Holmes.

Reis received a summons from a baffled Préfet de Police in the south of France to assist in a murder investigation. After crawling round the crime scene with a magnifying glass and a pair of tweezers, Reis tendered the solution: 'The man you seek is a left-handed sailor who has recently been in Sicily. He has a cut on his left hand and a red moustache.' This narrowed down the population of Marseilles to a field of one; and the arrest of the culprit Forfarazzo on board the *Donna Maria*, fresh in from Sicily, speedily followed.

The case involved the death of Marie Pallot, a receiver of stolen goods. Forfarazzo, the sailor, gashed his hand jemmying open her door, leaving a trail of blood down the left-hand side of the corridor and a trail of wax from a guttering candle down the right side. This suggested that he carried his weapon in his left hand, an observation confirmed by the damage to the left side of Mme Pallot's skull from a blow struck from behind.

Reis's magnifying glass located two **hairs** on the carpet which, under the microscope, proved red and of a length and width consistent with a moustache. Chemical analysis of the candle-wax – one of Reis's specialities – revealed that the candle was of a type made and sold only in Sicily. Since no one carries a candle around for ever, it seemed likely that the murderer had just been in Sicily, and since he was now in Marseilles, a port, he was probably a sailor.

Reis's deductions were correct. Tracked down by the police, Forfarazzo sealed his fate by taking a proffered slip of paper with his left hand. A search revealed the telltale candle stump in his pocket. Forfarazzo was tried, convicted, and later confessed.

See also **Locard**

Religion, abuse of

Down the ages, religious bigots have been accountable for untold suffering. But in Sicily, from the middle of the last century, Christianity degenerated into a straightforward criminal enterprise promoted for profit by the Mafia. The rot started in the outlying villages when the Mob seized control of the standing committees representing individual patron saints; maladministration of the funds earmarked for their annual feast days yielded easy money.

Thereafter the Mafia expropriated the religious function, monopolising the manufacture of devotional candles, hiring out church pews and, in the twentieth century, moving into mass production of religious relics. Many lines consisted of no more than statuettes and medallions churned out by the million, with the revenues creamed off by organised crime; others were hand-crafted speciality items. In 1962 the Italian newspaper *Le Ore* researched one distributor exporting to America and discovered that the year's sales included twenty suits of armour worn by St Joan, the same number of gowns (property of the late Francis of Assisi), fifty of St Bernadette's rosaries, and Moses' wand (one only).

The 'originals' of these and other artefacts were owned by the Mafia; to ensure a copy was infused with at least part of the original's rectitude, the two had only to be brought briefly into contact, a practice which lapsed into blessing dubious relics by the truckload, such as the ashes of Abraham (in presentation urns) or piscine bones from the Miracle of the Bread and Fishes.

When sales declined, a judiciously staged 'miracle' – like the stigmatisation of Padre Pio, the San Giovanni monk – drove pilgrims into a buying frenzy, transforming a locality's infrastructure. Mafia-run guest houses, hotels and hospitals burgeoned round the holy site, to which the pious flocked in their thousands, spending expensive weeks awaiting confession. The queue for absolution could be jumped, on payment of a fee. Or the unwary were confessed by false Padre Pios in back-street rooms, again for a fee. Meanwhile, sales of guidebooks and recordings of the priest at Mass boosted the Mob's coffers, as did the merchandising of hundreds of yards of bloody bandages as authentic souvenirs of the monk's stigmata; even the 1960 newspaper revelation that they were slaked in the blood of chickens had no impact on income.

But the Franciscan fathers of Mazzarino take pride of place in the Sicilian annals of religious abuse. The monks were all gangsters, of itself nothing untoward in a country where as recently as 1923 a Benedictine mobster from Santo Stefano beheaded his Abbot on the refectory table. In Mazzarino the monks made their living from robbery and extortion, preying off the villagers. They dealt in property, traded as usurers, disposed of healthy bank accounts under their lay names, spent their nights whoring in the monastery and amassed a huge collection of pornography. One of the fathers, Guglielmo by name, blazed away at night with a heavy automatic, shooting at the stars; another, expelled by the brethren, was seen by a servant packing a sub-machine gun as he left. Often the confessional box in the village church was used to transmit blackmail threats, and the nave became the 'drop' for payments.

In the late 1950s a prominent villager, Angelo Cannada, rejected the Franciscans' demand for ten million lire; he remained adamant even when the prior himself motored over to make him see sense. A few days later the intransigent Cannada was gunned down by four masked men in his vineyard, leaving his wife to inherit the bill. The aged prior, a malevolent octogenarian called Carmelo, conducted negotiations with the widow, dropping his fee to three million after threatening to kill her only son. The mere sighting of a monk in the village streets sent the locals scurrying for cover.

A new police chief, Di Stefano, started an inquiry. In 1961, one of his men was shot dead near the monastery. The three attackers fled, but one dropped his gun; this was recognised and the murderers arrested. In prison, they admitted to Cannada's murder, absolving themselves by blaming the monks' wicked gardener, who 'made' them do it. Within hours of his imprisonment in Caltanissetta, the gardener was found hanged in his cell.

A search of the monastery unearthed the typewriter used for the blackmail notes, and in March 1962 Padre Carmelo and three other monks were charged with extortion and complicity in murder. An ecstatic crowd greeted their arrival at the Messina courtroom; Padre Carmelo responded to the effusions of applause with the sign of the cross. While awaiting trial, the fathers continued to say Mass and hear confessions and, when proceedings started, prominent ecclesiastics streamed over from the mainland to demonstrate solidarity. The prosecution agreed to stay its hand, withholding evidence about the orgies, the extortion and the secret bank accounts; and Cannada's widow refused to testify (see **Vendetta**).

The three **hitmen** accused the dead gardener; in the absence of religious orders they received thirty years apiece. The monks went free, successfully pleading duress, a defence which requires the physical impossibility of escape.

A 1963 appeal resulted in thirteen-year terms for the monks. With a parliamentary commission on the Mafia in the offing, the social climate had temporarily changed.

In medieval Britain, the Lord of the Manor was historically empowered to hang miscreants, as was every town and abbey. This gave rise to 'private' gallows, of which Edward I's Commissioners discovered ninety-four in Yorkshire alone, owned by such worthies as the Abbot, the Dean and the Archbishop of York.

See also **Inquisition**

Remorse

As they return from the sick moments of killing to more ordinary moral considerations, murderers often suffer extreme remorse. The nightmare of the event is succeeded by the nightmare of guilt from which there is no easy escape.

One third of British killers commit suicide. Here are extracts from a letter from one who did not, written thirteen years after the spilling of blood. The exact wording posed its author with complex problems, since the recipient was the bereaved mother of the victim:

'My own mother, and my family have endured terrible sufferings through me, and are still serving, like yourself, an unbearable life sentence. This is yet another burden of guilt I carry, and the weight of it is almost more than I can bear. The same is true of the sufferings and heartaches I have caused you and the other families... I do understand your hatred, of course I do, but believe me Mrs West, you couldn't hate me more than I hate myself. I have asked God for his forgiveness, but I couldn't ask you for yours, for how can I expect you to forgive me when I cannot forgive myself? I have to live with the past for the rest of my life, with self-inflicted wounds to my mind and heart which I doubt will ever heal.

'Having finally and fully acknowledged and confessed these heinous crimes, and realised the dreadful enormity of them, the guilt and remorse I feel is agonising – the wounds have re-opened and are raw-edged and festering. But I deserve it all ... please don't add to your suffering by a hatred that I'm not worthy of.'

These words were sent by way of reply to Ann

West, the mother of Lesley Anne Downey, murdered for kicks on 26 December 1964. The letter was published word for word in the *Daily Mirror* of 12 October 1987 and prompted renewed national vilification of its author, Myra **Hindley**.

Mrs West clearly remained locked in a psychological feud with her daughter's killer. 'I set a trap for Hindley,' she commented, 'and this letter proves she's fallen right into it. I've conned her... How can she lie like that? She obviously doesn't know I've heard the tapes and seen the photographs...'

Fury, bitterness and desolation are not easily reduced to words. Mrs West had written to Hindley in scrawled capitals: 'I could never forgive or forget my Lesley, I expect if you was in my position you would feel the same.' It may be that language, however used, is an inadequate vehicle to convey grief.

Murder is thus a crime for which it is difficult to apologise. There is no agreed protocol, nor is it clear what degree of personal abnegation can ever be acceptable to the bereaved. The serial killer Dennis **Nilsen** was not unreasonable in believing that mouthing the word 'Sorry' would add insult to injury. As author Anne Rule pointed out in her testimony to the 1983 Senate Committee (see **Repeat Killers**): 'I have seen the agony of parents, children, spouses and friends of murder victims. For each of these violent deaths there is a ripple effect, and scores of lives are forever blighted. It is not just the victim who is lost; it becomes a kind of death for their families, and, indeed, the death of a small part of our entire society.'

To be included among a murder's detritus are the friends and family of the killer himself.

Removal, of fingerprints

After the FBI's establishment of a permanent Division of Identification and Information in 1930, harassed American gangsters toyed with the idea of having their **fingerprints** surgically removed, and in 1934 Freddy Barker and 'Creepy' Karpis – members of the Ma Barker gang – went under the knife only to find that as the fingerpads healed, so their fingerprints reappeared. But their doctor, Joe Moran, was never seen again.

In 1934, John **Dillinger** attempted a variant, scorching off his fingerprints with acid in a troublesome operation conducted at gunpoint, during the

course of which he swallowed his tongue and nearly choked. But the telltale papillary patterns were already showing through when he was, they say, gunned down a few months later.

Daily Express fingerprint competition, 1905

In 1941 Robert Pitts, a hold-up gangster, went one better with a bid to have 'neutral' skin grafted onto his surgically pruned fingertips, spending six weeks with his arms folded, fingerpads clamped to his chest while the graft took. But on his next arrest in Austin, Texas, it transpired that being the only man in the world with no fingerprints attracted almost equally unwelcome notice. Exhaustive research by the FBI produced a positive identification. This time the doctor, a Leopold Brandenburg of Union City, survived the operation but received a prison sentence, while his patient was sent down for a robbery where he left prints of the left ring-finger below the joint, the point where his skin graft stopped.

During the late 1950s and 60s, Hong Kong deportees sought readmittance to the colony by having their fingerprints cut out and repositioned upside-down. But scar tissue round the join ensured that the inversion was easily spotted, and their true identity could thus be established by turning the records the other way up.

In 1933 a set of prints were accidentally detached by a natural process. The skin of the body's hands was 'sloughed off' by prolonged immersion in a river near Wagga Wagga, Australia. The fingerprints were later discovered intact, in the form of a detached skin 'glove' snagged on the river bank, enabling identification of the corpse, and hence of the murderer, Edward Morey.

Repeat killers

Ronald Reagan was prone to muddling up countries and calling Princess Diana 'David'. But when he announced the formation of the FBI's Behavioral Science Unit in 1984 to track 'repeat killers' this was the accepted terminology of the time. The phenomenon was so recently and dimly recognised that no one knew what to call it. The FBI had five categories of murder: felony murder (during a robbery), suspected felony murder (probably during a robbery), argument-motivated murder (domestic disputes), other motives (anything else, if known) and unknown (anything else, if unknown).

FBI special agent Robert Ressler, a **Quantico** instructor, gave birth to the media-friendly term 'serial killings'. According to a *New York Times* article of 26 October 1986: 'Mr Ressler started using the term because such an offender's behaviour is so distinctly episodic, like the movie serials he enjoyed as a boy.'

Three years earlier, the phrase made its official debut during a 1983 Senate Judiciary Committee debating the unwieldy concept of 'patterns of murders committed by one person in large numbers with no apparent rhyme, reason or motivation'. One subheading was the more succinct 'Serial killers', and the American edge extends beyond the timely conferral of nomenclature. British serial killers can be counted on the fingers; Jack the Ripper, Christie, Brady and Hindley, Sutcliffe, Nilsen, Erskine, Duffy and Nurse Allitt. But America has everything, the biggest, the best, the most horrible. The names come tumbling out: Holmes, Manson, Bundy, Gacy, Gein, Panzram, Dahmer, DeSalvo, Fish, Ng, Kemper, the Night

Stalker, the Skid Row Slasher, the Hillside Stranglers and so on.

The general American per capita murder rate is some eight times Britain's but, with 6,000 killings a year officially ascribed to 'unknown' motives, its pre-eminence in serial killings is probably by a factor of hundreds.

Puritanical zealotry gave birth to Prohibition, which sired organised crime, and it is possible that the same repressive trait, directed at sexuality, has inspired the white American wave of middle-class sex killers. Early practitioners, like Gein and Heirens, raised to regard sex as a sin, fell into a greater heresy, and a common feature of the lust murder is the victim's denigration as a whore for indulging in sex, often under coercion.

Revelations, Book of

Charles **Manson** was inspired by the Book of Revelations which – with its emphasis on death, blood, judgment, and slaying the third part of men – provided a fertile stomping ground for his inflamed imagination. The ninth chapter provided his favourite reading.

The key biblical concept was the four angels 'standing at the four corners of the earth holding the four winds of the earth'. According to Manson, their names were John, Paul, George and Ringo. For the Bible says: 'Their faces were as the faces of men', although 'they had hair as the hair of women'. The Beatles were prophets, girded with 'breastplates of fire', updated as electric guitars, and their lyrics comprised the 'fire and brimstone' issuing from the angels' mouths.

Revelations 9:11 introduced the fifth angel: 'And they had a king over them, which is the angel of the bottomless pit.' Manson knew who this was: Charles Manson, a star descended from heaven to earth. In Latin, the fifth angel's name is Exterminans.

To Manson, the Armageddon of Revelations 9 was imminent and the 'bottomless pit' a real place. It had no zip code, but 'Crazie Sadie', a Family member, believed it was reached through the Hole in Death Valley to whose exact whereabouts only Manson was privy. There, beneath the ground, inside the earth, lay another civilisation with chocolate fountains and food trees. One of the entrance portals lay submerged in a lake off Route 127, just past the town of Death Valley Junction, and Manson obtained an estimate for pumping the water out. But the $33,000 price tag proved too steep for the privilege of direct access, so the Family devoted days to scouring the desert for another way in.

Similarly, Revelations 9 told the literal truth in verse 18: 'By these three plagues was the third part of men killed, by the fire and the smoke and the brimstone.' Manson could see the bloodshed coming to California right then in 1969, for it was written, 'in those days men shall seek death'.

The carnage would be triggered by the black-white revolution. Blacks would surge into the exclusive Bel Air and Beverly Hills districts for an orgy of slaying – with stabbings, blood on the walls, and words like 'pigs' daubed in the victims' own blood. When the killing finally stopped, Manson divined that 'blackie' would be left in control of a devastated world, lumbered with his usual job of 'cleaning up the mess, like he always has'.

But the blacks needed leadership, and that was where Manson and his family came in. Out in the desert, their numbers swollen to 144,000, the Family would wait for the call, a world government under Jesus Charles Manson Christ.

To set this momentous train of events rolling, only the slightest of nudges was needed, and on the evening of 8 August 1969 Manson gave orders to one of his followers, Charles 'Tex' Watson, issuing him with a knife and .22 revolver, and selecting two girls, Susan Atkins and Patricia Krenwinkel, to accompany him. 'Go with Tex,' he told them, 'and do whatever he tells you to do.' As they started up their '59 Ford, Manson leaned through the window and added: 'Leave a sign. You girls know what to write. Something witchy.' Then they headed off to 10050 Cielo Drive.

See also **White Album**

Rillington Place, Number 10

The London house in which a total of eight bodies were secreted, at least six by John Reginald Halliday Christie. The street was named Ruston Mews to escape its sinister reputation and, after demolition and redevelopment, the site was rechristened as Wesley Square, where Housing Association starter-homes for newlyweds now cluster round a pleasant garden.

The habitual watering holes of another resident at Number 10, Timothy Evans, are just down the way: the Kensington Park Hotel and the Elgin Arms. They remain fairly startling places, comprising the backdrop to Martin Amis's murder novel *London Fields*.

Christie's 1953 arrest provided a double shock. Britons were not accustomed to regard themselves as a nation in which a respectable citizen would occupy a home where he had buried two bodies in the garden, three in the outhouse and another under the living-room floorboards. The newly-arrived Jamaican who moved into the empty flat in March 1953 and peered into the sealed-off kitchen recess may never have achieved the traditional, cosy image of the British as law-abiding sons of Empire, creators of an outstanding police force and a system of justice envied throughout the world. His surprising discovery of three stacked corpses in the cupboard brought in detectives, who unearthed another body and two skeletons, and the manhunt for the previous tenant of Rillington Place put the address back in the headlines. For it was in this same house that Timothy Evans, a mentally retarded illiterate from Wales, had strangled his wife and child in 1949.

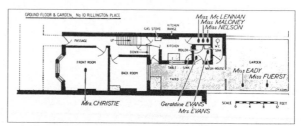

Or so the court found. At his trial, Evans settled on the line – properly regarded by lawyers as the feeblest of inventions – that the principal witness against him, John Christie, was none other than the perpetrator of his crimes. Evans was hanged on 5 March 1950, largely on the strength of a confession he subsequently withdrew, and three years later newspaper readers could not help wondering about the integrity of the original investigation and the fairness of the courts. The 1949 searches of the house had overlooked the two skeletons buried in shallow graves in the tiny back garden, where a bush grew through part of a human spine, and a femur stood upright, deployed as a fence post.

Was it likely that Evans, convicted as a strangler, lived in the same house as Christie, a strangler? And if not, how had the police obtained Evans's confession to the original murders? Why had Christie admitted to one of the same killings? Why were the case's shortcomings not exposed in court? And was execution an appropriate penalty when a man found guilty on capital charges might be innocent? The mood of public scepticism was heightened by the publication of John Scott Henderson's official report, which exonerated everyone except Timothy Evans.

The murder of Beryl and Geraldine Evans remains one of True Crime's most complex tangles. Sherlock Holmes's maxim may be of assistance: first eliminate the impossible, and whatever remains, however improbable, must contain the truth. Christie's confession to the murder of Beryl Evans included a description of how he 'turned the gas tap on and as near as I can make out, I held it clear to her face. When she became unconscious I turned the tap off.' Later he said, 'There is the possibility that as the gas tap was used for only a short time (1 to 1½ minutes) there may not have been signs in the body.'

But if Beryl was gassed into unconsciousness, however briefly, the cherry-pink signs of carbon-monoxide poisoning would have been evident on autopsy. No such traces were apparent in 1949, nor were they detected in her body tissues or **teeth** during the 1953 exhumation. So Beryl was not gassed, and thus the main component of Christie's confession is a fabrication. This reasonable starting point leads to the reasonable supposition that Christie's confession was false – he did not kill Beryl – and that Evans's confession was true.

Who killed baby Geraldine? With the mother dead, Evans's only hope of avoiding detection lay in disposing of the child. Provided the bodies were not found, he could brazen out their disappearance or flee. After his arrest, Evans talked with the murderer Donald Hume (see **Aeroplanes**) in Brixton prison. Hume reported that Evans said: 'Christie came to an arrangement with his wife and that Christie had murdered her. Then Evans told me about the child. He said: "It was because the kid was crying." I said: "So you did it?" He said: "No, but I was there while it was done." He told me that he and Christie had gone into the bedroom together, that Christie had strangled the kid with a bit of rag while he stood and watched.' There are few compelling reasons for watching a man strangle your child, and being innocent of its mother's murder is not among them. Guilt might just suffice.

It is possible that the 'arrangement' mentioned by Evans has a bearing on the four clumps of pubic **hair** found in Christie's tobacco tin. One ringlet resembled Beryl's hair, but exhumation showed no sign that a tuft had been snipped from her pubis. Thus the trophy provided no support for Christie's confession to her murder – unless he did have an 'arrangement', and it was of sufficient duration to allow Beryl's hair to regrow. An unsavoury dalliance would give *Evans* an additional reason for killing her. But this is to speculate.

Christie's motivation for his confirmed killings exemplifies the familiar paradox of sex murders by an impotent man. Desire plus inability creates frustration. After his first abortive attempt at sex as a youth, the shouted epithet of 'No-Dick Christie' in his home streets of Halifax can have done little to foster self-esteem. In maturer years Christie found that if he gassed the objects of his desire, he could manage intercourse just before, during, or after death.

Ripperology

Many – perhaps most – eminent Victorians have been fingered as the true **Jack the Ripper**; the suspects range from a future King of England downwards, with the added attraction of captivating conspiracy theories involving the Royals, the government, and the Freemasons. Many of the twenty-seven non-fiction books on the Ripper promote solutions devoid of evidential support which fly in the face of the evidence. The latest suspect is Virginia Woolf's cousin, James Kenneth Stephen, his culpability proved by a nonagenarian psychiatrist residing in New York. Apparently Stephen acted in concert with his royal pupil as an early homosexual killer couple.

In more traditional versions, the story of the royal connection derives from Joseph Sickert, an artist and picture restorer, who alleged that Prince Albert Victor married Annie Crook, his grandmother; the Ripper murders were to cover up this shameful misalliance. But the marriage never happened and, as a suspect, the Prince is a nonstarter. His movements are well documented from Court Circulars and diaries; thus for the double murder of 30 September 1888, which took place in London between one and two in the morning, the Prince was in Abergeldie, Scotland, as he had been for three days. On the 30th, he lunched with Queen Victoria.

The 'Freemason Connection' is based almost entirely on one word: 'Juwes'. This formed part of the graffiti found after one of the killings in Goulston Street: 'The Juwes are the men that will not be blamed for anything'. It is true that these words might have been scrawled by the killer, but not true that 'Juwes' is a collective noun for Jubela, Jubelo and Jubelum, the murderers of the master mason of Solomon's temple. Even if it were, 'Juwes' bears a more obvious interpretation. But Stephen Knight, champion of the Freemasons' involvement, expired shortly after publishing his views in *Jack the Ripper: The Final Solution*, thereby fuelling speculation that he was liquidated by the Brotherhood. In fact, Knight died of cancer.

Individual suspects include Dr Thomas Cream (see **Strychnine**), incarcerated in Joliet Prison, Illinois, during the relevant period at the end of 1888 for the murder of a man called Stott; Sir William Gull, who suffered a severe stroke in 1887; the writer George Gissing, because he married a prostitute; the Prime Minister William Gladstone, because he took a charitable interest in prostitutes; and Randolph Churchill, because he went funny in the head. In 1888, the speculation was no less intense; a woman writing from the Isle of Wight affirmed that Jack was really a large ape on the loose from a wild beast show.

Beyond suggesting familiarity with the work of Edgar Allen Poe, her response constituted a denial that any member of the human species could be sufficiently depraved to perpetrate the revolting Ripper murders. Another popular theory promoted a disfigured murderer: 'He probably had his privy member destroyed and he is now revenging himself on the sex by these atrocities.' The concept of internal disfigurement was still to be accepted.

For murders dating back more than a century, new evidence comes to light with impressive regularity. Modern Ripperology only started in 1959 with the rediscovery of the 1894 Macnaghten Memorandum recording the views of the detectives on the spot. Six more years passed before a name was put to two of Macnaghten's prime suspects (Druitt and Kosminski); the third (Ostrog) was only identified after the 1987 discovery of the Swanson Marginalia and the unravelling of some thirty aliases. Similarly, the posthumous photographs of the victims unearthed by Francis Camps were not printed until 1972, and Dr Thomas Bond's autopsy report on Mary Jane Kelly was only recovered by Scotland Yard in 1987.

The proliferation of 'soft' theories, which evolve all by themselves, is scarcely affected by the continued emergence of 'hard' information, which may one day establish the true identity of the killer and, as this book was going to press, preliminary details of the discovery of the 'Ripper's Diary' were

Early forensic detection from the Police News' front page. Note the corpse undergoing assemblage (left).

announced. Leaked advance information suggests that a sixty-five page notebook was found undisturbed after a hundred years in a Liverpool attic, written by cotton-broker James Maybrick, who signed himself 'Jack the Ripper'. One excerpt is said to read, 'Oh, what deeds I shall commit. For how could one suspect that I could be capable of such things? I will take the first whore I encounter and show what hell is really like.'

Maybrick died in 1889, poisoned by his wife, although it was never clear that she poisoned him to death. As a gifted hypochondriac and a glutton for **arsenic**, which he regarded as a medicine,

Maybrick may well have killed himself. At the age of forty-two he married Florence Elizabeth Chandler, twenty-three years his junior, and they led an extravagant life, which he could not afford, in a twenty-roomed Liverpool mansion staffed by five servants. He kept a mistress, and frequently travelled to London where he visited his brother.

Two evidential hurdles remain: first, to show that the diaries are genuine, and second, that any claim laid on the Ripper's deeds is true. The diary could have been forged on paper bought from an antique shop, and anyone can *say* he is Jack the Ripper; he provided a role model for an appreciable proportion of the population. During the investigation, the London police received 128 letters from persons claiming his mantle.

See also **Solutions**

Ritual abuse, satanic

From the late 1980s, Britain was plagued by a series of 'satanic ritual abuse' (SRA) cases involving children. Caped adults were supposed to prance around, first molesting infants and then sacrificing them in late-night orgies of devil worship. These stories received wide press coverage; in February 1992 the respected television programme *Dispatches* produced conclusive evidence, broadcasting a grainy videotape with scenes of sexual mutilation and the buggery of young children.

A few days later it transpired that the tape was an old promo video made by an arts group. Such anticlimaxes have typified revelations; the caped molester of the Orkney Islands turned out to be the blameless local priest in his vestments, the Reverend Morris McKenzie.

Even a case reaching the Old Bailey proved without substance. In November 1991 five adults in a 'ring' were arraigned on twenty specimen counts of rape, buggery and assault, on the evidence of two sisters aged ten and fourteen. In the opening speeches the court heard how babies and little children – at least three of each – were slaughtered at a gypsy memorial stone in Epping Forest while the cloaked and masked adults sipped blood from a chalice and chanted 'Lucifer'. The two girls were obliged to dismember the corpses and eat their flesh; then they were raped, buggered and made to perform oral sex on each of the adults round the

stone monument, which was surmounted by horns and a black cross.

On the fourth day of the trial, the basis of the case became clearer. The girls testified that they had made their stories up. The prosecution conceded that there were no bodies, no reports of missing children, and no reliable evidence of abuse. The stone memorial, which appeared in photographs to lurk deep in a creepy wood, lay a few yards from a main road; and one of the principal defendants, George Gibbard, was incapable of having sex due to horrific injuries suffered in the army. Meanwhile, the girls' parents – also among the accused – lost their homes and their jobs and were held in prison.

The credulity of the social workers, doctors, police, solicitors, barristers and the other myriads of professionals involved makes it easy to understand the former mania for burning witches (see **Witchcraze**). The parallels with the hysteria of Salem are distressingly clear. Today, a drawing of a love heart with 'Mum' in the middle has been interpreted as evidence of 'inappropriate sexual knowledge' and those sinister codewords used by children, like 'snow', 'rainbow' and 'brownie', regarded as Satanic indicators.

Transcripts of the Orkney Island interrogations by social workers anxious to procure convictions make pathetic reading. Here are fourteen consecutive answers of a child being browbeaten to admit that a party where a friend dressed up as a Teenage Ninja Turtle was in reality a Satanic Ritual. To save space, the questions have been omitted, but it is easy to get their general drift and assess the truth behind the allegations. Nothing happened.

First the child replies: 'I don't want to do that', then 'No', then 'No' again, then 'I don't want to do it. Can I play now?', then 'You are boring me', then 'That's all', then 'Morris', then 'I don't know', then 'Nobody else', then 'Who?', then 'I don't know', followed by 'I don't know' and 'I don't know', before concluding with the explanation 'Because I don't', at which stage the child bursts into tears.

These wayward stories pale into insignificance alongside American extravaganzas, which started in the early 1980s with imputations of sexual abuse in day-care centres, in part fuelled by the publication of *Michelle Remembers* cataloguing the ordeals endured by the Canadian Michelle Smith as a child. Smith recovered these buried **memories** while in therapy and, although there was no evidence to support her contentions, her story served as a blueprint for an escalating number of victims. In 1988 the first clinical study by the psychiatrist Bennett G. Braun unearthed common threads of being drugged during rituals; of witnessing the torture of others or the mutilation of animals; of attending the sacrifice of babies or adults, and the like, all features of *Michelle Remembers*.

By 1991, 30 per cent of the respondents to an American Psychological Association survey had treated patients suffering from SRA; 93 per cent of respondents believed that their patients' claims were true. In California, half the social workers interviewed accepted that SRA was a conspiracy of national proportions, extending through the generations, involving baby-killers who led otherwise exemplary lives and held respectable positions in the community.

In October 1988 the notion received a massive boost from two prime-time NBC television documentaries, 'Satanic Breeders: Babies for Sacrifice' and 'Devil Worship: Exposing Satan's Underground', which began with a voice-over intoning: 'No region in this country is beyond the reach of Devil worshippers... The children you're about to meet were born into it. They say their parents forced them to witness bloody rituals and even, they say, to participate in ritual murder.' The Satanist delusion is backed by fundamentalist Christians primed to drive the populace into the arms of God by scare stories about the Devil, their efforts aided by books like Lauren Stratford's autobiographical best-seller *Satan's Underground*, now said by her sister to be a work of fiction.

It is easy, but not necessarily facile, to draw comparisons between the Communist threat and the onslaught of SRA. As international communism collapsed, so SRA replaced it. Bennett G. Braun drew an exact parallel, referring to the devil worshippers' 'national-international type of organisation' which exhibits a 'communist cell structure, where it goes from ... small groups to local consuls, district consuls, national consuls, and they have meetings at different times.' The sophisticated use of brainwashing, drugs and hypnosis is supposed to keep members quiet for much of their lives.

The FBI's expert on SRA, a sceptical Kenneth V. Lanning, recently commented that the devil-

stories are so unsubstantiated that it is 'up to mental health professionals, not law enforcement, to explain why victims are alleging things that don't seem to be true'. By the mid-1980s, the number of SRA murders was said to be in the tens of thousands annually. A prison official from Utah revealed that sacrifices were running at 50,000 a year, a figure which became the accepted benchmark. But the FBI have investigated 2,000 cases without uncovering any concrete evidence, the absence of which does little to curtail panics in rural areas, where distraught mothers drive to school to snatch their children back from class before marauding Satanists arrive.

America was the country briefly brought to its knees in 1938 by the Orson Welles-produced radio play 'War of the Worlds'. Citizens fled the Men from Mars *en masse*, and the nearest to a solid SRA case is the trial of Paul **Ingram**, detailed elsewhere.

Rodine

A brand of rat poison containing phosphorus. In 1953 Rodine was still freely available over the counter at all good chemists. A one-shilling tin held enough to murder a large colony of humans; the phosphorous content was ten grains, and a lethal dose is one. Louisa Merrifield used it to poison Sarah Ricketts, an elderly widow who took her on as a live-in companion. Within a month of starting work Louisa was named as sole beneficiary under her employer's will and, a few days later, at 3.15 on the morning of 14 April 1953, the widow died in agony. Louisa waited until tea-time before summoning help, presumably animated by a justifiable sense of apprehension. 'It was not a nice time to go out on the streets and call a doctor,' she demurred. She was hanged on 18 September 1953, aged forty-six, and her husband, a quarter of a century her senior, was also charged with murder. But the jury could not agree and, notwithstanding his inheritance of a half-share in Rickett's bungalow, he eked out his days as a side-show on Blackpool promenade.

Four years later Mary Elizabeth Wilson, a serial husband-killer, used such quantities of phosphorus that her three exhumed spouses were found still glowing. The last two had only survived the first fortnight of their nuptials, and Wilson's total gross from these killings for profit exceeded £200. Aged sixty-six, the 'Widow of Windy Nook' was regarded as past her prime for hanging and died soon after in prison. The sale of Rodine is now banned.

Rolling pin

The murder weapon in the 1992 June Scotland case. A century ago, bashing in a husband's head with a rolling pin and burying his body in the garden was the form expected from the worst murderesses of the melodramatic Victorian era. In those days, the perpetrator could count on general opprobrium and a well-received hanging. Today, June Scotland escaped a custodial sentence and left the court under a two-year probation order. Modern judges are more inclined to take into account the guilt of the accused, and June Scotland had withstood twenty-two years of domestic torture by her husband, driving her twice to attempted suicide.

There was no dispute as to the facts of the killing; to avoid the obligatory life sentence for murder, June Scotland's lawyers pleaded 'diminished responsibility'. But in successful cases the accused (although absolved of murder) is liable to confinement in Broadmoor for indefinite psychiatric detention, an outcome the judge avoided by conceding that June Scotland had been demented *at the time*. But now, five years later, with her husband dead, she felt much better.

The discovery of her husband's skeleton highlights the risks of shallow burial in a tiny back-garden near a neighbour's fence.

See also **Sexism**

Romances

There is a kind of security in loving a man behind bars. The prisoner is a sitting target for affection, liable to respond to any advances with enthusiasm. Men who kill have a certain glamour and Kenneth Bianchi killed a lot; as one of the Hillside Stranglers, his criminal career included schoolgirl victims, rapes committed with beer bottles and murders with plastic bags over the head, injections of cleaning fluid, gassing and electric shocks. Before strangling Lauren Rae Wagner, he plugged her into the mains.

Bianchi finally settled down to marry his pen-pal Shirlee J. Book in a prison ceremony during 1989.

But Shirlee was not his first suitor. Veronica Lynn Compton stole his heart away in 1980.

Veronica was a fetching brunette aged twenty-three who loved True Crime murder and fancied her chances as a poet, playwright and actress. In June 1980 she mailed a fan letter to the imprisoned Bianchi, soliciting his expert advice on a play she was writing. Veronica's creation was a female serial killer who misled investigators by injecting semen into her victims' vaginas.

In fictional terms this is no mean ruse, and indeed Scott Turow's best-seller *Presumed Innocent* employs a similar plot-motif. Bianchi was intrigued by Veronica's request, and even more intrigued when he saw her in the flesh on a prison visit. Soon she visited twice a day, and together the couple concocted a dream future where they travelled the world on a voyage of murder, cutting off their victims' genitalia for permanent display in jars of embalming fluid.

Come to think of it, and they did, with Veronica at liberty this was perfectly feasible. Since Bianchi was locked up, she would kill for the two of them, and better still, provided she had the spunk, it could be just like her play. If she used Bianchi's, he would not just accompany her in spirit; he would be with her in spermatozoa, deposited in the corpse. Further, this might secure Bianchi's release by showing that an identical murderer remained at large.

And so it was. Before her next visit Bianchi masturbated into a rubber glove and later passed her the bulging finger concealed in the spine of a book. Veronica and her precious cargo flew to the small coastal town of Bellingham. There she checked into the Shangri-la motel, and in a local bar she identified a likely-looking cocktail waitress, Kim Breed. After a few drinks Veronica asked her new friend to drive her back to the hotel, where she lured her into the bedroom for a nightcap. Veronica slipped into the bathroom, took out her strangling rope, tiptoed behind her victim and drew the cord tight round her neck.

Kim Breed, a fitness fanatic, lofted Veronica over her head, and soon Bianchi's sweetheart was languishing unsubdued in jail for attempted murder, where she directed her love mail at a new beau, California's 'Sunset Slayer' Douglas Clark. He reciprocated, sending her snaps of a body whose **head** he had cut off.

Bianchi was hardly more of a catch than his successor in Veronica's affections. Officially credited with a sequence of ten Californian murders starting in October 1977, he was finally caught in Washington after disposing of two co-ed students in January 1979. Bianchi became a suspect when the police heard that he had offered the girls $200 to house-sit on the night they disappeared; in corroboration, police found the keys and address of the empty house in his car.

At first sight Bianchi made an improbable killer. Friendly, handsome and gentle, regarded by neighbours as a good family man, Bianchi lived amicably with his girlfriend, Kelli Boyd, and their young son. But the charm of serial murders is an overrated commodity, and Bianchi may have been psychologically fissured almost at birth. From the age of only three months, after his adoption by Nicholas and Francis Bianchi, his upbringing was a model of stability and affection. But his true mother, a teenager with a drink problem and a reputation for promiscuity, handed Bianchi to a foster mother straight after delivery, and she, in turn, farmed him out to a series of neighbours. Bianchi matured as a liar, a thief and a two-timer. After visiting his cousin Angelo Buono in Los Angeles, he degenerated into a pimp, rapist and murderer.

Another prison liaison from the early 1970s involved Myra **Hindley**, the child killer, and Patricia Cairns, a former Carmelite nun turned warder. They met for sex in the prison chapel and, when apart, masturbated at pre-arranged times. Hindley was sentenced to an additional year inside, and Cairns to six years, for plotting an escape. Veronica succeeded; she is still at large.

Hindley's initiation into the world of romance was strikingly unfortunate. Just before Christmas 1961 she confided in her diary, 'Eureka! Today we have our first date. We are going to the cinema.' The film was *Trial at Nuremberg* and her escort Ian Brady.

See also **MPD**

Rummel, William James (1942–)

American drop-out whose plight was considered by the fearless Supreme Court. Born in 1942, Rummel was reared by his grandparents and left school to take up casual work in San Antonio, Texas. In 1964 he had his first brush with the law, pleading

guilty to a minor credit fraud after running up an $80 debt on new tyres for his old Studebaker. Released in 1966, Rummel kept his nose clean until 1969 when he forged a cheque for $28.36 to cover his rent at the local Angeles Motel.

In August 1972, Rummel landed in trouble again when the owner of the local Captain Hook's Lounge, David Shaw, asked him to repair his air conditioner. Shaw produced an advance cheque of $120.75 for a new compressor; Rummel cashed it but never got round to doing the work.

At that date Texas had a 'Three Time Loser' law imposing a mandatory life sentence on anyone convicted of three felonies. It is far from clear that on the air-conditioning charge Rummel was guilty of theft, or of theft by pretext, or of anything, and in fact Shaw signed a non-prosecution agreement asking to withdraw the case. But Rummel's state-appointed lawyer, William B. Chenault III, on a fixed fee of $250, felt it would be irksome to call witnesses and advised his client not to testify. So Rummel, found guilty of wangling the $120 advance, was automatically sent to prison for life.

Several years later Rummel's cause was championed by a young lawyer, Scott Atlas, at a smart Houston firm. Against tooth-and-nail resistance from the state of Texas, by 1980 Atlas succeeded in referring the case to the Supreme Court.

There he argued that Rummel's sentence was so disproportionate that it constituted a 'cruel and unusual punishment' and hence was unconstitutional. But he was wrong. On 18 March 1980 both Rummel's sentence and the right of Texas to do what it wanted were upheld in a majority decision. Justice William Rehnquist explained that unlike mere traffic offences, for which life imprisonment would be excessive, Rummel's crimes were serious.

Later, after Rummel had served seven years, nine months and fifteen days, Atlas secured his release on the grounds of the inadequate defence by his first attorney, and in 1983 Texas deleted the mandatory life-sentence clause from the statute book.

See also **Attorneys**

Runyon, Damon (1884–1946)

Highly paid Hearst journalist and author of the *On Broadway* short stories. From his arrival in 1910 to his death from throat cancer in 1946, Runyon created the deadbeat folk-lore characters (immortalised in his *Guys and Dolls*) who encapsulated underworld New York, enriching our vocabulary with terms like 'monkey business', 'kisser' and 'croak'.

Some of his cast were based on real people. The last days of Arnold Rothstein (see **Great Gatsby**) are dramatised in the story *The Brain Goes Home*. Nightclub hostess 'Texas' Guinan became 'Miss Missouri Martin', mobster Frank Costello (see **Head**) turned into 'Dave the Dude' and Al Capone made a starring appearance as 'Black Mike Mario'. 'Waldo Winchester' was the fictional alter ego of gossip columnist Walter Winchell, a late-night buddy on Runyon's forays with the police.

Winchell's unofficial office was his table at the New York's Stork Club, and from this vantage point two guests first spotted J. Edgar **Hoover** holding hands with his male lover, Clyde Tolson, on New Year's Eve 1936. It is unlikely that this particular cat stayed in the bag for long. Not only was Winchell a compulsive gossip anxious to impress the likes of mobster Costello; in addition, the front-man for the Stork Club, former bootlegger Sherman Billingsley, reportedly had the celebrity tables wired for sound and installed two-way mirrors in the lavatories. In any case, Billingsley was in Costello's pay.

Capone was a pal of Runyon's, and before his 1932 prison sentence presented him with his prize pair of whippets for safe-keeping.

R v. Collins

An English criminal case of 1973 dearly beloved by law students. The defendant, a youth called Collins, was tried on a technical charge of burglary contrary to Section 9 of the Theft Act 1968, in that he had entered a building as a trespasser with the intention of raping a girl.

The facts were that one night Collins, feeling randy, had determined to have sex – by force if necessary – with a distant female acquaintance. So he found a step-ladder, went to her home, took off nearly all his clothes and ascended to her window. Case reports regard it as peculiarly comical that at this stage he was clad only in a pair of socks, left on to facilitate a rapid escape.

When Collins reached the top of the ladder he heaved himself onto the ledge of the bedroom's latticework window. Inside, the girl awoke and, observing a naked man with an erect penis crouching on the windowsill, mistakenly inferred that her boyfriend had arrived. She pulled Collins in. He had sex; she made love; they had sexual intercourse.

Afterwards the woman felt that 'somehow, something was different', perhaps the length of Collins's hair, or perhaps his voice as they exchanged pillow-talk, and he was exposed as an unwitting impostor. Captured despite his getaway socks, Collins presented the police with a legal dilemma. He could hardly be charged with rape; the girl had willingly submitted to his embraces.

So the police went for Section 9 burglary, citing his intention to rape at the moment of entry into the home. But on appeal Collins was exonerated. While outside the girl's window he had planned to rape her. But in the event she asked him in. The crux was that she extended her invitation to Collins while he remained *outside* the house. True, he was squatting on the windowsill, but he was not yet *in the house*. So he entered not as a trespasser but a guest.

Perhaps in a more solidly built home with a deeper window embrasure Collins would be adjudged as perching 'inside'. So burglars with charm should concentrate on houses of flimsy construction.

S

Sacco (1891–1927) and Vanzetti (1888–1927)

Electrocuted in 1927 and feted ever since as innocent victims of capitalist oppression. But there is little doubt of their guilt. The original 1921 trial took place in the infancy of forensic ballistics. The firearms evidence was unquestionably ambivalent, and although Sacco and Vanzetti were convicted, they were not executed. But when a 1927 committee re-examined the case, peering through the newly invented comparison microscope at slides of a test bullet fired from Nicola Sacco's Colt .32 into cotton wool, even defence firearms expert Augustus Gill conceded defeat, a conclusion confirmed in 1961 by another forensic team. The case against Bartolomeo Vanzetti is strong, but not conclusive.

The accused – a fish pedlar and a shoe-factory worker – were members of an anarchist cell advocating violence and, as labour agitators with Communist sympathies who sidestepped the First World War by fleeing to Mexico, they presented an unsympathetic face to middle America, an impression enhanced by charges of a brutal double murder on 15 April 1920 when the paymaster and a guard at the Slater shoe factory in South Braintree were shot dead carrying two cashboxes containing $16,000. Frederick Parmenter was gunned down as he ran, even though he had already dropped his box, and the other victim, Alessandro Berardelli, was repeatedly shot as he lay wounded on the ground. By the time Sacco and Vanzetti came to trial on 31 May 1921, Vanzetti was already serving ten years for an attempted hold-up at Bridgewater when he had again opened fire on payroll guards.

Their conviction on confusing evidence (including 158 identification witnesses) sparked an international outcry fostered by the defence attorney's insistence that this was a political trial dispensing capitalist justice. Judge Webster Thayer, presiding, did not allay these fears by calling the couple 'those anarchist bastards' in his club, and after the verdict his home was bombed. But the hearing was fairly conducted, the convictions proper and, despite the efforts of the Red Aid committee and numerous petitions (whose signatories included H. G. Wells, Albert Einstein and John Galsworthy), Sacco and Vanzetti died in the electric chair as propaganda heroes on 23 August 1927.

See also **Hamilton**

Sacher-Masoch, Leopold von (1836–95)

Austrian inventor of masochism. A novelist by trade, Sacher-Masoch's literary endeavours were spurred on by his wife, who whipped him. A proponent of **torture** and subjugation, he particularly commended being lashed 'by a successful rival before the eyes of an adored woman', remarking that this sensation could not be described.

Sacher-Masoch devoted his life to refining the sources of pleasure, spiking himself on needles or adding flesh-retentive hooks to the tip of a whip. Like the celebrated serial murderer, A.H. **Fish**, he enjoyed slashing himself with razors, a tendency noted by his contemporary Richard von Krafft-Ebing, professor of Psychiatry at the University of Vienna. Observing that some people derived gratification from inflicting pain and suffering on themselves, the professor (who pioneered the study of sexual deviation) coined the word 'masochism'.

Sadism differs only in that the discomfort is inflicted on someone else and hence is more popular. Krafft-Ebing's work led to the progressive recognition of 'lust murder', which we know today as sex killing; his *Psychopathia Sexualis* of 1886 incorporates a section on **sexual crimes** which encompasses the ritualised slaughter of women, anticipating **Jack the Ripper** by two years. 'Very likely,' Krafft-Ebing surmised, 'the murderous act and subsequent mutilation of the body were substitutes for the sexual act.'

Masochism may be fun, but is it legal? A related issue came before the British House of Lords in March 1993 after fifteen men in a homosexual ring were sentenced to prison for consensually assaulting each other. That is, they all agreed to it. The defence argued that it was not against the law to stick wires down a friend's penis, or sandpaper his testicles and nail his organ to a board through a hole in the foreskin, providing he made no objection, but their Lordships ruled that Sections 20 and 47 of the Offences Against the Person Act 1861 had been infringed. Lord Templeman commented, 'The victim was usually manacled so that the sadist could enjoy the thrill of power and the victim could enjoy the thrill of helplessness. But the victim had no control over the harm which the sadist, also stimulated by drugs and drink, might inflict. In one case a victim was branded twice on the thigh and there was some doubt as to whether he consented to or protested against the second branding.' It seems that these pleasures are best savoured in solitude.

Sade, Marquis de (1740–1814)

French inventor of sadism. The high point reached by the Marquis in real life was carving small slits in the skin of prostitute Rose Keller and pouring in hot wax. This and similar misdemeanours, like administering sweetmeats containing aphrodisiacs to Marseille prostitutes, caused him to be locked up for thirteen years so that only his imagination could run riot. In prison Sade turned to literature, describing every sort of perversity by way of making a political rather than a sexual point.

Sade's premise was that there was no God. It followed that the dominant institutions of the state, like law and religion, were fraudulent in their efforts to bamboozle citizens into moral (or at least legal) conduct. Sade argued that to be selfish was to be honest, and the best an honest man could do was embark on a life of criminal debauchery. This is the 'plot' of *The 120 Days of Sodom*, where the four principal libertines include a bishop and a Lord Chief Justice, as well as a supporting cast of corrupt monks and nuns.

There was nothing too extreme about these views in the revolutionary France of 1789. So Sade was released. But theory is one thing, practice another. Once free, with both motive and opportunity, Sade passed up the chance to get even with his mother-in-law, responsible for his original incarceration. On his travels Sade professed to be outraged by the *castrati* and transvestites of Florence, and he was soon indicted by Robespierre's regime for excessive moderation. As from 1801 he spent the rest of his life in prison, dying in the madhouse at Charenton in 1814. His other books include *Justine* (1791) and *Juliette*.

Across the Channel, Sade's tracts became popular, inspiring English mutations which progressively eliminated the intellectual content and accentuated the sexual, until there emerged fully-fledged Victorian pornography, precursor of the era of the **sex crime**.

The underlying aim of the sadist may not necessarily be the derivation of pleasure from another's agony. Ensuring compliance may be equally important. In words penned by one unusually articulate serial killer on the **Quantico** files, 'The wish to inflict pain is not the essence of sadism. One essential impulse: to have complete mastery over another person, to make him/her a helpless object of our will, to become the absolute ruler over her, to become her God. The most important radical aim is to make her suffer since there is no greater power over another person than that of inflicting pain.' For FBI Agent Robert Hazelwood, a sadist's hallmark is contempt for women as 'sluts and bitches', in part a defensive reaction to mask the perpetrator's own failure at normal interaction which simultaneously justifies brutality, forcing many a 'nice' girl to comply with deviant demands and thus justify her death as a whore.

See **Slave, Torture**

Safes, how to crack

Of the two most comprehensive guides to safe-cracking, one was published by the American 'Commission of scientific or mechanical experts to report on the best methods of safe and vault construction'. It put the makes of safe on the market at the end of the last century through their paces and found all (with one exception) could be opened, whether with drills, wedges or explosives.

Through some oversight, the Commission released details of its deliberations, setting out exactly how each model should be tackled and producing comparative studies on the relative efficacy of different techniques. Thus it noted that 'the wedging off of sheet after sheet is found a better method of attack than drilling',

The rotund Corliss, cast in a single piece of manganese steel

thereby saving the inexperienced from hours of wasted exertion, quite apart from needless investment in costly drilling equipment.

On the delicate area of explosives the Commission promulgated clear guidelines on the appropriate type, quantity and technique. Best results were obtained when 'nitroglycerine was poured into the crack (between the door and frame) until three ounces had entered and it had begun to drip from the lower side of the door'. Did this work? Apparently, yes: the outcome was 'the complete destruction of the lower part of the door'. For the faint-hearted, the Commission offered reassurance that 'the sound of the explosion was not very startling'. To assist scheduling, it advised that a well-conducted job took no longer than seven minutes. And so on, for page after page.

Corners were always a safe's most vulnerable point, and the only make to resist the Commission's attentions did without them. This was the Corliss, a strongbox shaped like a cannonball with a round door set in a round hole; circles are easier to engineer to fine tolerances than rectangles, making for a more exact fit, minimising the fatal gap between door and frame through which wedges or explosives could penetrate. A mere five-hundredth of an inch is sufficient for nitroglycerine to seep in.

One of few documented successes against the Corliss was achieved by Herbert Emmerson Wilson (with alleged career takings of $16 million), who adopted the alternative approach of an axe. First he torched a groove round the safe one inch deep, then he weakened it with his axe, tapping out the channel all the way round, and finally he split the 'egg' in two with a single mighty blow. He related: 'I took aim with the blacksmith's tool, prayed my hunch was right, hit the groove at the top of the safe only one sharp blow, just one... The haul came to $170,000.'

In the late nineteenth century, American cracksmen could learn their craft at Frederika Mandelbaum's educational establishment; she provided tuition in return for a percentage of her students' profits. In the 1920s, amateur cracksmen in Los Angeles took diplomas at the Wayne Strong School of Safework in 'safe opening, safe repairing and safe lockwork', and in the 1960s the Canadian police discovered a classroom in a Toronto garage, complete with sample oxyacetylene cutting gear, drills, nitroglycerine, detonators, and a course textbook footnoted, cross-referenced and divided into instructional modules.

REWARD
$100,000

has been offered by BRINK'S, INCORPORATED, Chicago, Illinois, "for information leading to the Arrest and Conviction of the Persons involved in the Holdup of the Office of Brink's, Incorporated, 165 Prince Street, Boston, Massachusetts, on January 17, 1950." The person or persons to whom the reward shall be paid and the amount will be determined by a specially designated reward committee.

If you have any information concerning the identity or the whereabouts of any of the perpetrators of the robbery of Brink's, Incorporated, at Boston, Massachusetts, on January 17, 1950, please communicate with the undersigned or with the nearest office of the FEDERAL BUREAU OF INVESTIGATION, U. S. Department of Justice, the local address and telephone number of which are set forth on the reverse side of this notice. The telephone number can also be obtained from page one of your telephone directory.

If such information leads to the arrest and conviction and / or recovery of money, the FEDERAL BUREAU OF INVESTIGATION will, if specifically requested to do so by the person furnishing information, advise the Reward Committee of the information so furnished.

JOHN EDGAR HOOVER, DIRECTOR
FEDERAL BUREAU OF INVESTIGATION
U. S. DEPARTMENT OF JUSTICE
WASHINGTON, D. C.
TELEPHONE NATIONAL 7117

In Britain, it was only in 1965 (when the era of safe-cracking had all but gone) that criminals received a properly printed thirteen-step guide to safeblowing, each stage illustrated with captioned photographs starting with removal of the keyhole cover. Pictures showed how to wire the detonator, drill the hole for the second charge (packed in a **condom**) and then fire the door itself. Only the amount of gelignite was omitted, but presumably the *Sunday Times*, with its several million readers, took legal advice on its liabilities.

See also **Gutshot**

Sagawa, Issei (1949–)

Japanese celebrity cannibal. On 11 June 1981, while studying at the Sorbonne in Paris, Sagawa invited a Dutch girl, Renée Hartevelt, to dinner. The pair had known each other for some time; Sagawa was a long-standing admirer, much taken by Renée's white arms, and had previously escorted her to the theatre and concerts. They had even danced together, their bodies touching. But this was the first time the diminutive Sagawa succeeded in enticing Renée back to his sixteenth *arrondissement* apartment. In Sagawa's words, she had 'nice breasts, a slender build, a long white neck, transparent white skin, and a beautiful and gorgeous face'.

After shooting her in the back of the neck, Sagawa chopped Renée up and consumed her. A student of comparative literature, he recorded his impressions meticulously. 'I touched her hip and wondered where I should eat first. After a little consideration, I ate right in the centre of the abundant, bouncing part of the right hip... but I could not bite it out, so when I opened my mouth, I could see the teeth print in her white hip... so I took a meat knife, and when I stabbed, it went right in... a little came out and I put it into my mouth... it had no smell or taste, and melted in my mouth like raw tuna in a sushi restaurant. Finally I was eating a beautiful white woman, and I thought nothing was so delicious! Then I moved to the thighs...'

Over the next few days Sagawa ate the rest, some fried in salt, pepper and mustard, and others *sushi*-style, raw. When the best parts were finished, Sagawa placed the leftovers into two cardboard suitcases and flung them into a pond in the Bois de Boulogne. But a severed arm and hand stuck out of one of the cases, so the incident attracted the attention of a watching couple. Arrested on 15 June, Sagawa confessed immediately.

Found insane by Judge Jean-Louis Brugière in 1983, Sagawa avoided a conviction for murder and was detained in Paris's Paul Guiraud asylum. But there were language difficulties. According to Dr Tsuguo Kaneko, the French mistook Sagawa's 'enteritis' (an inflammation of the intestines, like indigestion) for the more serious 'encephalitis', an inflammation of the brain (like incipient death). Regarding their patient as an incurable psychotic destined for an early grave, the French shipped him back to Tokyo after a year, on the understanding that he would be sequestered in a mental hospital. He was, but he did not enjoy it. 'My time in the mental ward was like hell,' Sagawa says. 'Everyone else in there was crazy.'

Problems arose because Sagawa had never been committed to Tokyo's Matsuzawa Hospital. His parents simply *consented* to his confinement. But their boy was not guilty of anything in Japan and, on reflection, he was not guilty of anything in France, where the charges were dropped because of his mental derangement. So after fifteen months his father, a company president, had him released. As Sagawa was not insane, he could not be detained.

By then he was moderately famous. In 1983 the Japanese playwright Kara wrote a 'factional' novel about him, *Letters from Sagawa*, which sold 320,000 copies in a month and won a literary prize. The same year Sagawa published his own memoirs, *In the Fog*, penned while in prison. His sales topped 200,000, and the book was acclaimed as 'beautifully done, outstanding amongst recent Japanese literature'. Forty pages were devoted to a detailed culinary description, starting with his first abortive attempts at eating Renée's corpse with his teeth (excerpted above).

Sagawa's *oeuvre* now comprises two more titles, *Health* and *Mirage*. In December 1991 he produced a magazine feature with the more graphic title of 'I ate her because of fetishism', and he is currently working on an anthology of **cannibalism**. In March 1992 Sagawa nearly precipitated an international diplomatic incident when he travelled to Germany for a television chat show with a regular audience of nine million.

Like many famous trouble-makers, Sagawa is short, well under five feet. His hands and feet are undersized. Interviewed in January 1992, he said: 'I still adore the sight and shape of young Western women, particularly beautiful ones. I was a premature and unhealthy baby, I am ugly and small, but I indulge in fantasies about strong healthy bodies. I'm essentially a romantic.'

Sagawa's fetish took root at the age of five with a nightmare about being boiled inside a pot. By adolescence, this had transmuted from a fear of being eaten into a desire to eat, and that is what he still craves. But sometimes this finds expression as a desire to be devoured by a beautiful Western woman.

Conscientious reporters often point out that Renée's parents must find Sagawa's high profile extremely painful.

Saltillo Prison

Site of a famous Mexican jailbreak. In November 1975 the convicts started digging the tunnel through which, on 18 April 1976, some seventy-five escapists set off for the outside world. The tunnel came up in the nearby courtroom. All were recaptured.

In January 1913 an attempted escape from San Quentin by Herbert Repsold, a burglar, came to a more macabre end. Repsold had both nouse and money, using the one to pull the fuses from the prison's power station and the other to pay for a boat waiting at the water's edge. In pitch darkness he scaled the prison wall and rowed out to sea. But his dinghy capsized and next morning he was taken back and dumped in the penitentiary's reception area where he remained on display for two days, dead, *pour décourager les autres*.

'Sam, Son of'

Pudgy David Richard Berkowitz turned violent at the age of twenty-two. On Christmas Eve 1975 he drove to New York's Co-Op city looking for a woman to kill.

His intended target escaped. As Berkowitz ran off, his eye was caught by a 15-year-old in a doorway; he attacked her instead, stabbing the girl six times with his hunting knife. Elated by his success, that night he gorged himself on junk food. For the

next venture he bought a pistol, a Charter Arms Special Bulldog, and in the year from 28 July 1976 he earned a name as 'The .44 Calibre Killer', attacking seventeen victims, killing six, blinding one and paralysing another. He concentrated on women, shooting courting couples through their car windows, sometimes gunning for the man too.

Like many 'dis**organised**' serial killers, Berkowitz was a no-hoper condemned to menial jobs, a shy recluse inhabiting a bare room with a blanket nailed over the window for a curtain and a dirty mattress on the floor. There he dreamed of women, of his enviable physique, of his superb stamina as a lover, and of the bouts of oral sex he later replicated by shooting Virginia Voskerichian through the mouth. This was the drab reality of his psychological state; but in court Berkowitz made much of the monsters, the demons, the voices in the head baying for blood and, most notably, the dog who urged him on.

Berkowitz claimed that he took his orders from a labrador belonging to his Yonkers neighbour, Sam Carr. The dog kept him awake with its barking, and at his trial Berkowitz declared that the animal had been possessed by the spirit of a 6,000-year-old demon who demanded sacrificial victims.  Berkowitz assumed the name of 'Son of Sam' after the dog's owner, and only on his interview, post-conviction, for the FBI's Quantico **database** did a more sceptical picture surface.

In his cell, Berkowitz launched into his dog routine. FBI Special Agent Robert Ressler cut him off: 'Don't hand me that bullshit about the dog, David, I'm not buying.' Taken aback, Berkowitz replied, 'You're right', and conceded that the tales about demons were inventions concocted for the press. Under thorough questioning a more equivocal image emerged, of a timid loner given to sexual fantasies and addicted to TV horror movies.

Some shootings seemed almost reluctant. At his first killing, Berkowitz hoped the couple would drive away. Of the second, he said: 'I just wanted to get it over and head home', and of the seventh set of victims, Judy Placido and Salvatore Lupo, Berkowitz commented: 'I saw them and just finally decided that I must do it and get it over with.' But the afterglow was pleasant. 'You felt very good after you did it,' Berkowitz reported. 'It just happens to be satisfying, to get to the source of the blood.'

Berkowitz entered criminal record books as the only serial killer arrested on the strength of a parking ticket. Moments after his last attack on the night of 26 June 1977, a witness saw a man running to a car which had been ticketed only a few minutes previously. Police checked the parking records and found Berkowitz listed as the owner.

The cosmetics firm Max Factor made subliminal commercial capital from his 'reign of terror' by introducing a new female face moisturiser, 'Self-Defence', promoted by a poster reading, 'Warning! A Pretty Face Isn't Safe In This City. Fight Back With Self-Defence.' Berkowitz was well known for his pride in concentrating on shooting 'pretty girls', referring to them as 'tasty meat', and the linkage between sex, violence and fashion was underlined by the pop group, the Sex Pistols, who peaked at exactly the same time with a New York tour.

Sansons

Charles-Henri was probably the most famous of the great Sanson dynasty of French executioners, which included plain Charles (the first of the line, appointed in 1688), his successor Charles-Jean-Baptiste, and – in alphabetical order – Henri, Henri-Clèmont, Jean-Louis, Louis-Charles-Martin, Louis-Cyr-Charlemagne, Louis Henri-Gabriel, and Nicholas-Charles-Gabriel.

The Sansons could not all trade as executioners in Paris, so they dispersed throughout the country, to Tours, Reims, Dijon and Provins. But it was Charles-Henri who cut off King Louis's head, and Robespierre's too; and his son who fell off the Paris scaffold and broke his neck.

In France, the selection process for executioners was analogous to the English procedure for choosing a monarch. There isn't one. French executioners, like kings, were born. Thus in 1706 Charles-Jean-Baptiste Sanson inherited his title at the age of seven, and a regent was appointed in the form of François Prud'homme until the lad came of age. So it was not just Charles-Henri's son who perished,

but his apprentice and heir, and until 1775 it was a position worth inheriting. Executioners were entitled to the proceeds of *havage*, a tax levied on food which brought in revenues estimated at 60,000 livres a year. Charles-Jean-Baptiste maintained his large mansion in Paris in considerable style.

The black sheep of the family was Henri-Clèment (1799–1889), a Regency buck of a fellow who dissipated his considerable inheritance on wine, women, gaming and the theatre. He took over the family business in 1840 and, as his fortune ran out, moved into harmless freelancing.

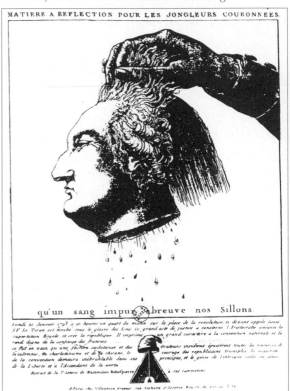

Their end-product

Henri stored his **guillotine** in a shed near home and, for a fee, would exhibit the machine in action, slicing straw-bales in half. But this additional income proved insufficient. So in 1847 Henri carted his guillotine round to the pawnbrokers. Inevitably, before it could be redeemed, he was instructed by the Procureur-général to cut off a head. In panic, Henri begged his creditor to release his equipment for just one day; then he would return it. But to no avail. Henri was obliged to make a full confession to his employers, who sacked him. By 1854 this guillotine was again in pawn when Henri, still struggling, had a windfall. A certain M. Tussaud bought the device outright for £220 (half due to the pawnbroker) for display in his waxworks; this particular model has a dubious but stimulating provenance as the specimen that Henri Sanson told Alexandre Dumas was used by his father to decapitate King Louis XVI.

Travellers may visit the Sanson family sepulchre in the Cimetière Montmartre, where the tombstone describes Charles-Henri as 'the benefactor of his whole family, who will never cease to pray for him'.

Sausages

The final format of Fritz Haarmann's victims. Haarmann (1879–1925), an epileptic homosexual butcher and police informer, frequented Hanover's railway station in Germany's depressed postwar years. The police issued him with a badge; Haarmann used it to pose as a policeman, picking up young unemployed workmen who slept rough on the platforms, part of the homeless flotsam tramping though the country in the 1920s.

Haarmann escorted the youths to his Neuestrasse lodgings in the thieves' quarter. There he violated them sexually, then killed them – supposedly with a bite through the windpipe – before selling their boned and dismembered bodies as meat. As the *News of the World* reported: 'All his victims were between twelve and eighteen years of age, and it was proved that the accused actually sold the flesh for human consumption. He once made sausages in his kitchen and, together with his accomplice, cooked and ate them.' But more often Haarmann swept the boned chunks of youth into small buckets which he hawked round Hanover's open market, retailing the boys as horsemeat, selling their pathetic clothes and trinkets.

The butchery went on in the attic, its walls crusted with blood. Haarmann kept the neighbours awake chopping his way through the night. Bones were the problem. When Haarmann's neighbours started to query his persistent gifts of the suspiciously white bones for their stock-pots, he took to ejecting the mangled skeletons – including whole skulls – from his window into the river Leine which ran by the back of his house. In partnership with his lover Hans Grans, Haarmann ploughed through any-

where between twenty-seven and forty victims. Upper estimates of their toll extend into three figures; at this period, young men disappeared in Hanover at the rate of hundreds a year.

On 22 June 1924 Haarmann fell under suspicion for indecent behaviour, and when his rooms were searched the police discovered some of the missing boys' possessions. On the foreshore a heap of bones, 500 in all, from twenty-three bodies, came to light; skulls had been found by urchins on the river banks as early as 17 May. Haarmann confessed, and the evidence for the first few days of his trial was considered so revolting that proceedings were heard behind closed doors.

Like many of his ilk, Haarmann was a pleasant enough man subject to periodic and irresistible urges. He claimed that he killed while in a trance-like state, unaware of the nature of his act. Court psychiatrists discerned a loathing of his father, who allegedly beat him. His three sisters became prostitutes while young; Haarmann himself was institutionalised at the age of seventeen for sexual attacks on young children.

Haarmann kept his pride to the bitter end. Confronted with a picture of a missing boy, Herman Wolf, shown by his worried father, Haarmann exclaimed: 'Such an ugly creature as, according to his photographs, your son must have been, I would never have taken to... You ought to be ashamed to have let him go about like that... Such a youngster was far beneath my notice.'

He embraced the prospect of extinction with open arms, pleading: 'Condemn me to death. I only ask for justice. I am not mad. It is true that I often get into a state of which I know nothing, but that is not madness. Deliver me from this life which is a torment. I will not petition for mercy, nor will I appeal.' Before going to the guillotine, he insisted: 'On my tombstone must be inscribed, "Here rests the mass murderer, Haarmann."'

Schaefer, Gerard John (1947–)

Police deputy Gerard Schaefer of Martin County, California, brought about his own arrest in a rather unusual way. On 22 July 1972 he contacted his superior, Sheriff Robert Crowder. 'I've done something very foolish,' Schaefer said. 'You'll be mad at me.'

Crowder was. The previous day, cruising in his patrol car, Schaefer had given a lift to two girls on State Highway A1A, making a date to meet again and go to the beach. On 22 July the three set off as arranged but, with the girls safely in the vehicle, Schaefer settled into a long harangue about the dangers of hitchhiking.

Then he handcuffed them, fitted gags, and dragged the women off the road into the swampland forests. There Schaefer slipped rope nooses round their necks and made them balance on the exposed tree roots to which their feet were bound. If they fell, they died.

At this stage Schaefer seemed to realise that he was late for an appointment, perhaps his call to Sheriff Crowder. Glancing at his watch, he exclaimed, 'Oh oh, I gotta go.' The girls wriggled free and, still gagged and handcuffed, struggled through the swamps to the road where they were collected by the sheriff.

Schaefer was charged with false imprisonment and aggravated assault. But as a law enforcement officer he remained at liberty until his trial some four months later and, on 27 September, local teenagers Susan Place and Georgia Jessup were last seen driving off with a new friend, 'Jerry Shepherd'. On 23 October, Mary Briscolina and Elsie Farmer, 14-year-olds from Fort Lauderdale, disappeared, and their sudden absence was linked to other neighbourhood 'missing persons', Leigh Hainline Bonadies, Carman Hallock and Belinda Hutchins.

When Schaefer's case came up in November he was sentenced to six months. Before his release date the skeletons and torsos of young girls were turning up around the county, the first on 17 January 1973 in the undergrowth near Plantation, the second 200 yards away a month later, and two more on 1 April in a pit by Blind Creek on Hutchinson Island. The two known numerals – 42 – of 'Jerry Shepherd's' numberplate were traced to Gerard Schaefer's blue Datsun, and a search of his room yielded the usual clutch of **souvenirs**, weapons and aids to masturbation.

Mementos taken from his victims included teeth, a driving licence, jewellery and a passport. Schaefer kept eleven guns, thirteen knives, pin-ups enhanced by the addition of pencilled ropes and bullet holes, 'live-action' blurred photographs of women being hanged and even a picture of Schaefer himself swinging from a tree in female underwear. A 300-page notebook meticulously detailed numerous murders including those of 'Belinda' and 'Carman'.

Schaefer had been divorced for 'extreme cruelty' five months into his 1970 marriage. Nor did he last long as a law officer. His previous job at Wilton Manors rapidly ended in dismissal for misuse of police computers to obtain the telephone numbers of girls he stopped while on traffic duty. In his student days at Broward Community College, he had avidly espoused clean-living, right-thinking values, joining a group called 'Sing Out 66' in reaction to the moral corrosion of his hippy contemporaries.

In September 1973 Schaefer was sentenced to two life terms, and today makes money by publishing 'fictional' murder stories.

See also **Vocation**

Separate System, The

The nineteenth-century term for a supposedly elevating and actually extreme form of solitary confinement, enshrined by the Prison Act of 1839 as official government policy: 'Any prisoner may be separately confined during the whole or any part of the period of his or her imprisonment.'

The objective was the prisoners' permanent moral benefit, achieved by preventing contamination from association, and the idea followed the intense interest in the even more immoderate 'Silent System', an American regime which kept prisoners mute throughout their sentences while they contemplated their transgressions. But the British Prison Inspectors rejected the American model, recognising its overriding drawback. It was unenforceable. Instead, the Home Office plumped for the Separate (or 'Philadelphia') System, and as a showcase built the Model Penitentiary, Pentonville, really more of a convict academy. It boasted 500 separate cells of a relatively good size, each with its own lavatory.

The fact that Pentonville was accurately characterised as 'the culmination of three generations of thinking' provides a telling insight into the human condition. Inmates were rigorously isolated in continuous solitary, each convict identically regulated by an inflexible daily routine of twelve hours of repetitive task-work. Prisoners were known and addressed only by their numbers and, when they left their cells, were obliged to don black hooded masks. They were thus incognito, incommunicado and deprived of all human contact.

In daily assembly at chapel, each man occupied his own box, a type of vertical coffin, preventing his gaze straying from the straight and narrow to his left or right, affording only a vision of the preacher. Prisoners left divine service one-by-one in a numerical sequence dictated by a silent, central numbering machine. The warders themselves knew neither the names nor the crimes of their

Masked prisoner from Pentonville

charges; their shoes were soled in felt so that even the sound of footprints was erased, and no mail got through. The original allowance of one fifteen-minute visit from the outside world every three months was pruned to a more ideologically pure twenty minutes twice a year.

Results were impressive. The insanity rate achieved at Pentonville was ten times higher than at any other British establishment. According to Ken Smith, author of *Inside Time*, 'After the experience most prisoners were found to be quite daft.' In 1861 the Reverend John Clay, Chaplain at Preston Gaol, said the same thing in different words: 'As a general rule, a few months in the separate cell can render a prisoner strangely impressible. The chaplain can then make the brawn navvy cry like a child; he can work his feelings in any way he pleases... and fill his mouth with his own phrases and language.'

This was considered so satisfactory that the system set the standard for forward-thinking penologists everywhere: an exact scaled-down replica was built on the far side of the globe in Australia's Port Arthur in 1848.

See also **Crank, Dickens, Treadwheel**

Sex crimes

Apart from the occasional wayward aristocrat, this staple of modern life hardly existed before the First World War. For centuries the term 'sex crime' had a different meaning imposed by the church, which can today be loosely translated by the word 'sex'. It included enterprises such as fellatio, masturbation, homosexuality and fornication.

The Ripper case of 1888 was probably the first modern sex murder, and the practice remained a rarity for several decades thereafter. The First World War, where horrors beyond imagination were played out in real life, brought a surge in the genre, as did the Second World War. It is argued that in previous centuries men had more important things to worry about, such as survival, and that the legacy of Victorian prudery was responsible not only for bizarre fetishistic fixations on anything remotely feminine (like footwear) but also for the pent-up frustration unleashed in frenzied killings. It seems likely that to earlier eras the idea of murdering for mere sex or sexual gratification would be incomprehensible.

Sex killings presented the police with a new problem. The absence of a clear connection between the killer and his particular victim left no line of enquiry to follow. But this has been counterbalanced both by tremendous strides in detection and by the tendency of many killers, once their violent spasm is over, almost to invite arrest (see **Jekyll and Hyde**) in sharp contrast to the self-protective instincts of the average criminal.

Criminologists regard the sex itself as a fairly unimportant component in a sex crime, a view shared by a multiple rapist who confided to FBI Agent Robert Hazelwood: 'Rape is the least enjoyable part of the entire crime.' Apparently, Charles **Ng** did not relish the sex; even in the absence of consent, it is a real experience between two parties, very fraught, most likely disappointing in the extreme, and one that makes reification of the victim a little bit harder. Other than **terror**, human interaction is not the sex criminal's purpose. Indeed, many victims are prostitutes, and if sex was what the attacker desired, he had only to ask. His craving for violative intimacy is typically reflected in a preference for a knife or an axe rather than an impersonal gun.

The 'sex' is furnished by the chosen method of assault and, even in the absence of ritual mutilation, the onslaught can be frenzied beyond any desire to extinguish life. The sex is often omitted. Instead, the sexual organs are attacked; tearing people to pieces is easier to do, easier to control, and more reliable. Moreover, it provides what the attacker wants: domination, so often sought by the weak.

A man capable of asserting himself in a socially acceptable fashion has no need to be vicious; it is the weak who are prone to stab in the back and, by extension, the impotent who gravitate towards sex crimes. Many serial killers are either pushed over the brink by imputations of impotence (**Sutcliffe**), are impotent (Christie), find they can only achieve erections during the frenzy of killing (**Chikatilo**) or have sex with corpses (**Dahmer**). Impotence, which does not negate sexual desire but merely prevents its release, is thus a potentially dangerous condition, and few experiences are as inimical to sexual fantasies as real life. Individuals reduced to inhabiting a world of sexual make-believe, having no other vent for their drive, often prefer their subjects dead, gaining transitory (and unsynchronised) potency in the process. In **Chikatilo**'s words: 'I could not control my actions. What I did was not for sexual pleasure, rather it brought me peace of mind and soul for a long times.' But he obtained his satisfaction during the murders, and his killings represented a displaced sexual procedure, where his frenzy conferred release and, thereafter, calm.

Impotence has psychological roots, and one cause is repression stemming from childhood abuse or social conditioning. William Heirens's mother assured him at the age of thirteen, 'All sex is dirty, if you touch anyone you get a disease.' As a teenager locked in an embrace with a girlfriend, Heirens succumbed to an attack of revulsion at his fall from grace, first bursting into tears and then retching. Thereafter, his sexuality found other channels, coagulating into an obsessive fantasy involving female underwear, cross-dressing, photographs of Nazi leaders, masturbation, weapons and prowling through the unoccupied apartments of strange women. His sex life thus centred around almost anything apart from shared consensual heterosexual sex, which remained illicit, a depraved activity associated with degradation, thus putting Heirens's outlook on all fours with many victims of sexual abuse.

If sex is vile, then only vile people have sex, a proposition which (in the sadist's eyes) speaks volumes for the great bulk of the female population. They are whores. In the words of FBI Agent Robert Ressler, 'Most if not all the organised killers have tremendous anger towards women, often expressed in the belief that a certain female is not 'woman enough' to 'turn him on'.' By this stage, the sexual criminal and his prey are trapped in a downwards spiral. Women are filth. So they are treated like filth, coercing them into filthy behaviour, thus reinforcing the original premise. The FBI's working definition of a sex murder is a killing made 'in the context of power, sexuality and brutality', and its outer manifestations are 'the attire or lack of it found on the body; sexualised position of the body; sexual injury; evidence of sexual activity on, in or near the body and evidence of substitute sexual activity or sadistic fantasy'. The murders can normally be differentiated from run-of-the-mill sadistic homicides by the special emphasis placed on mutilation or removal of the breasts, rectum or genitals. The latest thinking on rapists (most of whom have been raped, making it an inherited condition) depicts them as depositing their self-hatred in another person, literally. On a practical level, rapists may feel obliged, against their better nature, to murder their victims to escape identification.

Triumphant armies have always raped their way through the womenfolk of their foes. In the recent Balkans conflict, the rape of Muslim village women by former neighbours evolved into an instrument of diplomatic policy. One 28-year-old mother from the town of Foca was raped perhaps 150 times in all, including thirty-three times in the course of her last night during a bout which presumably inflicted the last iota of defilement without producing the least tremor of recognisable sexual pleasure in her assailants. Humiliation of the enemies' women represents a triumph over, and attack on, their menfolk, and most assaults are conducted in groups, when the individual conscience is subservient to mob rule.

It might seem that murder for sexual gratification represents the end of the emotional road. But even at this stage, choices remain. At the outer reaches of the macabre, decapitators face a final option. Which part do they fancy? Edward **Kemper** made love to the torsos, but Douglas Clark preferred the severed **head**.

See also **Fantasising, Masturbation, Male Rape, Preview, Terminology, Torture, Trolling**

Sexism

Women claim that they receive a rough deal from the courts. In 1991 the British discrepancy was encapsulated by the divergent fates of Sara Thornton (sentenced to life for murdering an alcoholic husband) and Joseph McGrail (given probation for disposing of his bullying wife). Similarly, on 29 January 1992 Bisla Rajinder Singh, aged forty-four, received a brief suspended sentence after killing his wife for nagging; she had shouted at him non-stop for (by some standards) a modest two hours.

According to the *New Law Journal*, 37.5 per cent of women who kill their spouses are found guilty of murder rather than manslaughter; the comparable level for men is 26.6 per cent. These figures conflict with official Home Office research, which shows almost the exact opposite. For the general record, of the thirty-three British women convicted of homicide in 1991, exactly one-third engaged in murder, as against a level of nearly half for the 408 male killers. Women tend to kill people they know.

Trial-by-media is no more reliable than trial by the courts. Press reports depicting Sara Thornton as a female scapegoat on the altar of male oppression do not always investigate her case thoroughly. It is true that her husband, Malcolm, was an alcoholic, but not a violent alcoholic. According to his previous wife, who tolerated him for fifteen years, after getting drunk he would go to sleep.

On all the evidence this was the pattern on the fatal night. His son last saw Malcolm dozing on the sofa. From his room upstairs, he heard no sound of the brutal altercation which Sara maintained triggered the killing. But her hunt for a knife in the kitchen was perfectly distinct, so the quarrel should have been audible. It seems as though Sara stabbed her husband while he slept; the couple had been married for ten months.

Apologists argue that the courts are perplexed by the differing gender-concepts of provocation. A man is taunted; he lashes out and kills, but he was provoked. A woman is taunted for twenty years. She does nothing, then suddenly, without apparent provocation, lashes out and kills. That looks like

pre-meditation. Others believe a patriarchal court system treats the killing of a man by a woman as a violation of the natural order deserving of fearsome retribution.

One undeniable sign of sexism is that in the 1870s the women's cells in D Wing of Wormwood Scrubs were constructed to slightly smaller dimensions than their male counterparts. Another is that women are more likely to be jailed for non-violent minor offences. In September 1991 the British government's Inspectorate of Probation found that 2,650 women were sentenced to prison in 1989 but that, of these, over half were sent down for less than six months.

Had they been men, this group would be obvious candidates for community service or probation. But the women are regarded as unsuitable because they have young children, and thus end up in an even less suitable situation – prison, with an increased probability that their traumatised offspring will in due course follow suit.

Early female transportees fared worse. On arrival in Australia they were treated like cattle, and nowhere worse than on the hell-camp of **Norfolk Island**. As from 1800, under Major Foveaux's tenure, the new arrivals were sold off. A good specimen fetched as much as £10.

The role of auctioneer fell to the island's bellman, Potter, who held the sales in an old store. The girls had to strip and race naked round the room while Potter kept up a running commentary on his nags. On Thursday nights the women were admitted to the barrack festivities where they performed (in the words of a witness, Robert Jones) 'the dance of the Mermaids, each one being naked with numbers painted on their backs so as to be recognised by their admirers who would clap their hands on seeing their favourite perform some grotesque action'.

Women, like the Aboriginals, were the blacks of the penal colony, the prisoners of prisoners, referred to as 'drunks and scum', often degenerating into terminally alcoholic sluts. Nor did Ronnie Kray speak highly of their contribution to gangland London. 'Always it's bloody women,' he would say. 'Women's our worstest enemy. Why can't they keep their places any more? They don't want men these days. They want bloody lap dogs.' It was a valid point. Stable relationships drained away promising criminals, luring them into home life and even steady jobs.

See also **Crime Passionel, Female Offender, Rolling Pin**

Sheppard, Jack (1702–24)

Probably the single most famous highwayman, whose legendary cold genius and tragic fate continued to excite nursery tears into the nineteenth century.

In fact, Sheppard only traded as a highwayman for about a week, accumulating a total gross of thirty shillings and sixpence. He stopped a stagecoach once; a further half-crown was extracted from a lady's maid in Hampstead. The final six shillings belonged to a drunken grocer staggering out of a Hampstead pub, The Half Way House.

But as an escapee Sheppard was without equal, notching up no less than four break-outs. First he broke out from St Giles's Roundhouse, clambering out through the roof. Then on 24 May 1724 at New Prison Clerkenwell, Sheppard extricated himself from his fourteen-pound leg-irons before hacking his way through a double grille of oak and iron bars. That left the obstacle of the prison walls. With

Sheppard's first escape, from the St Giles's Roundhouse in April

a knotted rope of sheets, petticoats and a blanket, he shinned down a 25-foot drop before scaling the 22-foot wall on the other side, dragging his mistress, Edgeworth Bess, after him.

Sadly, Sheppard found it as easy to worm his way back into clink as to get out; on 3 July 1724 he was arrested and sentenced to death. But on 31 August, while awaiting execution in **Newgate**'s Condemned Hold, Bess smuggled in a file. Sheppard sawed through the barred window as she chatted to him across the grille in sight of the warders – and he was off.

Within a fortnight Sheppard was back in Newgate once more, this time thrown into the Stone Room festooned in chains: handcuffed, double irons on his legs, and shackled to the floor with a horse-lock. Now came his finest hour. On 15 September the warders tested his manacles at three in the afternoon; later that day, Sheppard freed his hands and, with a nail, opened the padlock fastening him to the floor and broke his chains. Then he wriggled up the chimney in his cell, only to discover that the way was blocked by an iron rod across the flue. But he clawed out the masonry, knocked the bar free, eased his way up to the floor above and came out through a fireplace.

On the upper floor, Sheppard forced his way onwards through four successive locked and bolted doors, each of massive iron construction, picking them like a true locksmith or tearing them off their hinges, working in pitch darkness with nothing except odd metal scraps. An additional obstacle was provided by a 12-foot internal wall surmounted with spikes. At last he came to a window and flung it wide. But there was no safe way to climb down.

So Sheppard returned to his cell and fetched a blanket. Then he scrambled away to freedom, lowering himself onto the roof of a private house before disappearing through an open window. His feat remains one of history's greatest escapes.

But by the end of the week Sheppard was captured in a drunken stupor while celebrating his achievement with a girl called Moll Frisky. Their tavern party, just outside Newgate's walls, became so rowdy that the authorities went to investigate. In a way, the lad was a transitional criminal, bright enough to master the concept of escape but unfamiliar with the ins and outs of life as a hunted man. This is not so strange; British malefactors were hardly pursued until the introduction of the Bow Street Runners, and felt reasonably safe unless under lock and key.

This last time Sheppard was encumbered with 300 pounds of chains and manacles, fetters, leg irons and padlocks. The warders watched him night and day. By now the most famous man in England, Sheppard filled pages of newsprint, inspired countless ballads, was depicted in thousands of prints (generally attached to a padlock about the size of a wheelbarrow), had his portrait painted by the fashionable Sir James Thornhill, inspired the Hogarth series 'Industry and Idleness', fathered nine stageplays in one year, enriched his Newgate jailer to the tune of £200 by his exhibition to crowds of the curious at three and sixpence a head, and went on to feature as the hero of the 1840s best-selling novel.

Sheppard's execution attracted a worshipping crowd estimated at 200,000; men fought for possession of his body, hoping to restore it to life. He did not die easy, struggling for several minutes as he choked. A riot raged outside the pub The Barley Mow in Covent Garden where his battered corpse was finally secured by his admirers. After repeatedly reading the Riot Act without effect, the frightened magistrates restored order by summoning a company of foot guards, bayonets at the ready, from the Savoy.

Sheppard was buried in a graveyard of St Martin's-in-the-Fields; building works near the National Gallery unearthed his coffin in 1866. Today, one of his Newgate handcuffs survives in Scotland Yard's Black Museum and, if truth be told, it is easy to open, with a screwdriver, a nail or any metal lever.

Shootists

The deranged Texas gunfighter Clay Allison (d. 1887) devised the word 'shootist' to describe himself. The term carries cool undertones of professional status redolent of, say, a chemist.

Allison peaked in 1870 as a spearist when he went to the aid of a damsel in distress who claimed that her husband, a rancher named Kennedy, had murdered some strangers and her own infant to boot. Allison broke into the Elizabethtown jail where Kennedy was held, dragged the man out and lynched him in a slaughterhouse. Then he cut

off the head, impaled it on a pike, and rode twenty-nine miles to exhibit the trophy in his favourite drinking den in Cimarron.

It is often said that shootists could hardly hit a barn door. But this is to exaggerate. In 1879 at the Long Branch Saloon in Dodge City, buffalo hunter Levi Richardson attempted to gun down Cockeyed Frank Loving with six shots fired from a distance close enough to pick his target's pocket. Other commentators describe their pistols as 'nearly touching'. Returning fire in self-defence, the unscathed Loving shot his assailant dead.

Serious gunfights (as opposed to the practice of taking pot-shots) were generally fought at very close range: Frank Stilwell, killed by Doc Holliday and Wyatt Earp in March 1882, was found with powder burns on his clothes. His assailants' muzzles must have been almost in contact with his body and, according to Wyatt later, Stilwell was actually holding the barrel of the gun with which he was killed. The seminal gunfight at OK Corral began at a distance of six feet, with the range gradually opening out to something more like three yards for the closing shots between Billy Clanton and the brothers Earp. Many engagements were more like brawls, with added guns.

Silence

Like any other criminal cartel, Chicago gangsters operated on a sealed-lips basis. This frequently entailed denials of reality issued to the police from the death-bed. Examples include the dying words of Frank R. Thompson to Sheriff Harry Baldwin: 'Listen Harry, I've seen everything, done everything, and got everything, and you're smart enough to know I won't talk. Go to 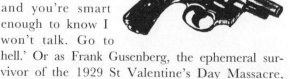 hell.' Or as Frank Gusenberg, the ephemeral survivor of the 1929 St Valentine's Day Massacre, explained to Sergeant Sweeney: 'Nobody shot me.' At the time, Gusenberg was bleeding from fourteen bullet wounds.

Interviewing gangsters *in vivo* was hardly more rewarding. At the inquest into his brother's death, witness Al Capone felt unable to contribute. Johnny Torrio, set up for a hit by Hymie Weiss on 24

January 1925, was lucky to escape with a bullet to his left arm and buckshot in his jaw and lungs after the *coup de grâce*, a shot to his brain, fell on an empty chamber. Torrio told the police, 'I know who they are and that's my business.' Likewise, on 10 August 1926 Vincent 'the Schemer' Drucci was involved in a prolonged gunfight at the junction of Michigan and Ninth Streets. After several minutes the exchange of shots was broken up by the police who, back at the station, produced one of Drucci's assailants for his inspection. Drucci took a good look at Capone gunman Louis Barko and said: 'Never seen him before. It wasn't no gang fight. It was a stick-up, that's all.'

The rule extended to wives of the deceased; Patsy Lolordo could never quite recall the names and faces of the three cronies who called round on 8 January 1929 to shoot her husband after pastries and cigars. Almost the only occasion the convention was contravened came after the St Valentine's Day Massacre when a shocked Bugs Moran let drop, 'Only the Capone gang kills like that', before clamming up.

Such 'Walls of Silence' have their roots in time immemorial and extend to the present day, binding individual interest groups in solidarity against outsiders. Doctors and solicitors are never negligent, judges never make mistakes, the police never assault suspects or fabricate evidence, drug companies never fix prices and criminals do not rat on their associates – unless they have to. A whistleblower from the professions must look to his future; an underworld grass needs eyes in the back of his head.

In Sicily, mortally wounded **vendetta** victims would respond to an invitation to identify their assailant with a muttered version of the formulaic 'If I die, may God forgive me, as I forgive the one who did this. If I manage to pull through, I know how to settle my own accounts.'

See also **Omerta**

Sinatra Connection, The

Was Frank Sinatra the decisive influence in the election of John **Kennedy**? We may never know, but we should be told that in the run up to the 1960 presidential contest, Sinatra visted Sam Giancana at the Mob's Armory Lounge headquarters in the Chicago suburbs. 'Ole Blue Eyes' lobbied for the Mob to call in their political favours on JFK's behalf.

Sinatra's pitch was that after three approaches to Kennedy's father, he felt confident of halting the FBI's investigations into Giancana. We know this because FBI Agent Bill Roemer listened on the microphone, and it was a reasonable proposition. Harry Truman regarded Kennedy Snr, who made much of his fortune from complicity in bootlegging, as 'as big a crook as we've got anywhere in the country'.

In the event, the 1960 presidential election was too close to call until Illinois came in for Kennedy; the vital West Virginia primary may also have been swayed by Mob 'donations' elicited by JFK in direct contacts with Giancana. But Sinatra's plan backfired. Whatever his father's intentions, President Kennedy appointed his brother Attorney General, and Robert made the Mob – dismissed as a quaint superstition by **Hoover** – a top priority, quadrupling the staff and budget of the Department of Justice's Organised Crime Section. In Chicago, FBI agents assigned to the Mob rocketed from five to seventy, with Giancana heading the wanted list.

Robert Kennedy rapidly established supremacy over Hoover in the 1961 Buzzer Wars. Hoover had contrived a one-on-one right to confer personally with the President, thereby enshrining his bizarre whims as governmental policy, but Kennedy insisted that the line of communication went through him, and installed a buzzer to summon Hoover as required. Hoover had the buzzer removed. So Kennedy introduced a direct telephone link. So Hoover had it answered by a secretary. Kennedy lost his temper: 'When I pick up this telephone, there's only one man I want to talk to. Get this phone on the director's desk immediately.'

All Kennedy's good work was undone by his brother's indiscretions. Whether or not Hoover was blackmailed into quiescence by the Mob for his homosexuality, he made himself an irremovable government fixture by digging up dirt on the President's indiscriminate couplings and, after JFK's 1963 assassination, swiftly reasserted his deadening influence on the Justice Department's Organised Crime Section. By 1966 Hoover had forced the crime figures down: the number of man-days in the field dropped by 50 per cent, days before a grand jury against mobsters by 72 per cent, and the issue of court briefs by 82 per cent.

See also **Executive Action**

Slave, sex

For a hitchhiker, accepting a lift from a young couple *with a baby* might seem a safe bet. Under just such a misapprehension, on 19 May 1977 20-year-old Colleen Jean Stan climbed into a blue Dodge Colt driven by a bespectacled man with his wife and child.

Somewhere outside Red Bluff, Cameron Hooker pulled off the road and put a knife to Colleen's throat. Snapping on a pair of handcuffs, he encased her head in a purpose-built plywood box which had lain on the car seat. Hooker drove in silence to his home at 114 Oak Street, where he led the terrified Colleen to the basement and removed the head-clamp box. Next, she was blindfolded, stripped naked, hung from the ceiling by her wrists and whipped. Then she heard and – through her tiny field of vision – saw her captor and his wife enjoying intercourse while she swung overhead. By their side she glimpsed an open magazine depicting a tableau like the one of which she formed a part. After climaxing, Hooker lowered Colleen to the floor, replaced the box on her head, and shovelled her into a second, larger box about three feet high. Crammed inside, Colleen felt a hand between her thighs adjusting a small, spiny object. It was designed to give electric shocks, but the device malfunctioned. All this time, hardly a word was spoken, and after twenty-four hours Colleen, still in her hutch, received her first glass of water and a bowl of potatoes *au gratin*.

So began Colleen's seven-year routine of suspension, whipping, confinement, sexual abuse and half-drowning, for which Hooker espoused the immersion technique independently developed by George Joseph Smith, raising Colleen by the knees and forcing her head under whenever he gave her a **bath**. It made a nice picture for his photograph collection.

His unassuming wife, 20-year-old Janice, had long recognised something strange about her husband. Hooker, born into a traditional, warm family, was variously regarded by neighbours as 'nice', 'courteous', 'quiet' and 'friendly', but he suspended Janice by the wrists from tree branches when courting, and she became accustomed to being trussed up and throttled into unconsciousness as they made love. When she drew the line at wearing a gas mask for sex, Hooker, his imagination fired by underground literature, talked of a girl who could not say no. In part, Janice was relieved: a real slave would deflect his attentions.

After six months Hooker removed Colleen's blindfold, and on 6 January 1978 he came across an engrossing feature in the magazine *Inside News*: 'They sell themselves body and soul when they sign THE SLAVERY CONTRACT.' On 25 January 1978 Colleen added her signature to an embellished 'Indenture'. At this stage, another player entered the scene, the fictitious 'Company' responsible for American slave management. It was they who countersigned the document. Two weeks later, Hooker showed Colleen a sealed plastic identification card, acknowledging receipt of the Company's $1,500 registration fee.

Under the deed, Colleen undertook to keep her body visually available, never wearing knickers and keeping her knees apart in Master's presence. This entitled her to menial chores upstairs or perhaps a little crochet work, which her owners sold in the San Jose market. If Hooker shouted 'Attention', Colleen stripped and stood on tip-toe with her hands above her head.

After the birth of her second child on 4 September 1978, Janice became jealous of the creature in the basement. Distressed, she took herself out of the house with a job in Silicon Valley, spending nights during the week with her sister. But this gave Hooker a free hand. In addition to scorching Colleen with a heat lamp and wiring her up to the mains, he made her fellate him, reassuring Janice that the absence of vaginal penetration betokened fidelity.

After a couple of years Colleen was rewarded with an evening off at a local dance. Divested of any will of her own, and with no understanding of her former life, she reported back at the end of the evening. Any threat to Hooker's domestic arrangements stemmed not from detection by the outside world, but from the enemy within, from disruption of the household's delicate triangular equilibrium. In one permutation, Janice took the initiative, suggesting that her husband would enjoy straight sex with Colleen. He did, first gagging the slave and then tying her spreadeagled to the bed. But watching made Janice physically sick. So it was back to the kennel for Colleen, and when Hooker bought a new mobile home off the Interstate 5 highway, he constructed a spacious new rabbit-hutch contraption under their waterbed. He stored Colleen there, letting her out for an hour every day to wash and clean, and every autumn he took her for runs in the mountains. But he still enforced the daily regimen of handcuffs, blindfolding, whipping, hanging, nipple burning and rape, stretched on a rack.

In early 1981, Hooker decided to take his slave for the weekend to her parents (who presumed her dead) in Riverside, California. Adopting a commonplace persona under which weirdos pass without comment, he posed as a computer buff, taking Colleen as his fiancée. The visit was preceded by intense security arrangements. For weeks, Hooker informed Colleen, Company operatives had mounted telephone surveillance on him, his associates and her parents, running up a bill of $30,000 before granting approval. On 20 March, the day of their trip, Hooker stopped off at the Company's headquarters in Sacramento. He disappeared into an office building, returning after a judicious interval looking relieved to report that security personnel had given clearance without the customary face-to-face briefing. They were free to go, and he handed her Company documentation authorising Colleen Stan, his slave, to bear money for the duration.

The stay passed off pleasantly, although Colleen's parents considered that their daughter looked pale. She spent one night with her father and another with her mother. When Hoooker collected her earlier than arranged, she left meekly but sulked on the drive home. So it was back to her box for another three years.

Janice and Hooker's marriage suffered from the attempt to compress three people into their relationship. They tried a new start, taking up Bible readings and asking Colleen to participate in their prayers for spiritual peace. Meanwhile Hooker started a new underground slave bunker, completing it in November 1983. But the winter rains poured in, and they gave Colleen house-room. In return, she had to earn her keep, and in May 1984 Hooker told her to be a domestic at a local motel. Each evening she returned home, but Janice disrupted their fragile tranquillity with muddled ideas about Christianity. Hooker reiterated the solid biblical precedent for his domestic arrangements. Abraham had sex with his wife's maid, so why

shouldn't he? And why not make his wife engage in lesbian love, three-in-a-bed?

To Janice, slavery conflicted with the teachings of the church that the three now attended. So much so that she asked Hooker to kill her. When he declined, she decided to tell Colleen everything. On 9 August 1984 Janice met her at work and revealed that Colleen was not really a slave: she had been born free. Hooker was a filthy pervert. After a night of tears, the two women fled. Colleen reached her parents, but Janice reverted to Hooker for another fresh start. They all kept in touch.

Still the story did not break. Colleen had sworn never to involve the law, and took refuge behind a hazy account of her seven-year absence. But Janice snapped. On 7 November 1984 she poured out her tale to a doctor's receptionist, who referred her to the local pastor. He persuaded Janice to call the police, to whom she furnished a detailed description both of Colleen's abduction and a previous murder by Hooker in 1977. The body was never found.

But there was evidence enough to arrest Hooker. Nearly a year later, he came to trial on sixteen charges including kidnapping, rape, forced oral sex and penetration with a foreign body. His lawyers conceded that Colleen was abducted, but argued that thereafter she was free to leave; she stayed voluntarily because she loved Hooker. In this version, Janice betrayed Hooker out of jealousy because he reciprocated Colleen's affections. The trial was fiercely contested and the decision a close one, but Colleen's scars carried the day, and on 22 November 1985 Hooker, characterised by Judge Clarence B. Knight as 'the most dangerous psychopath I have ever dealt with', was sentenced to 104 years. The case echoes that other miracle of brainwashing, the Patty Hearst affair, and Colleen is the subject of a book aptly entitled *The Perfect Victim*.

Smokescreen

On 1 July 1930 Jack Zuta, Chicago racketeer, was hauled in by the police. After questioning, Lieutenant George Barker agreed to escort Zuta to Lake Street in his Pontiac.

In the bustling heart of Chicago, just past Quincy Street, a blue sedan drew alongside. A gunman standing on the running board drew a .45 automatic from his shoulder holster and poured seven shots into Barker's Pontiac, aiming for Zuta. Supporting fire came from the driver and a rear-window gunner.

Lieutenant Barker slammed on the brakes and leaped out, returning fire. Since he was in plain-clothes, Barker was nearly shot by a passing police-man, but the pair joined forces and traded bullets with their assailants for some thirty sec-onds while pedestrians scattered  for cover. The assault car pulled away, Barker jumped into his Pontiac and roared off in pursuit up State Street. Suddenly the blue sedan ahead belched out clouds of black smoke and disappeared behind an impenetrable smokescreen, apparently activated by a special plunger positioned by the foot-pedals.

This fiendish device did not do much good, although the technique has an honourable record at sea. In Chicago, on the road, the intrepid Barker shot through the billowing fumes at fifty miles an hour. By the time his quarry reached Wabash Avenue, Barker was only fifty yards behind and gaining. There his engine died, the petrol tank punctured. The only fatality of the engagement was Elbert Lusader, a street-car driver hit in the neck by a stray round.

Jack Zuta survived for another month. On 1 August he was relaxing in his Lake View Hotel hide-out under the cover name of Goodman, slot-ting nickels into the electric piano. Couples were dancing, bathers swam from the beach. 'It may be Good for You, but it's So Bad for Me', played the piano. Behind Zuta's back, five of Capone's hench-men entered in single file, led by a man with tommy-gun; his four colleagues carried a rifle, two shotguns and a pistol. The silent intruders fanned out; Zuta turned and they cut him to pieces.

Soap

The final incarnation of Louise Luetgart. In 1897 her husband, Adolph Louis Luetgart, a compulsive womaniser known to chase his spouse down the street with a revolver, turned her into soap at his Chicago factory on Hermitage and Diversey. He was a prominent manufacturer of **sausages**.

Louise's disappearance was noted by her brother,

Dietrich, on 4 May. Luetgart equivocated about his wife's whereabouts, saying that she had walked out with $18 in her handbag and had not been heard of since. After a few days of fruitless enquiries with her relatives, Dietrich called in the police, and Captain Schuettler interviewed a factory employee, 'Smokehouse Frank', who described an unusual industrial process undertaken with Luetgart on 24 April. Together they had boiled up 325 pounds of caustic potash (ordered a fortnight previously) in the sausage vat to produce an excoriating brew strong enough to dissolve human flesh on contact.

A week later, on 1 May, Louise was last seen late at night in an alley near the factory with her husband. The following morning, a Saturday, the night-watchman was instructed by Luetgart, up early and fully dressed for work, to stoke the fires under the sausage vat. The watchman remarked that the meat factory floor was slimed by a gluey substance clogged with occasional pieces of bone and, after the weekend, Smokehouse Frank was told to tip the spillage down the drain and sling any residue on the nearby railway.

At the works, Captain Schuettler peered suspi-ciously into the middle vat, still two-thirds full of something very like brown soft soap. He had the sludge poured through a makeshift sacking filter and, sure enough, found two gold rings, one engraved 'L.L.' in the sediment. To make sure, on 7 August the investigators heaved another corpse into the same vat and stewed it in caustic potash for two hours. The results were suggestively similar; the new body changed into soap.

Luetgart insisted that his wife had simply left him, and claimed that he needed detergent in bulk to clean the factory. The prosecution countered that Luetgart kept a hundred boxes of soap in stock, and that more was superfluous. But the absence of Louise's body was exploited by defence allegations that she had been seen alive and well in New York, Wisconsin, here, there, and everywhere.

Today, the case would present few difficulties. But the turn-of-the-century jury distrusted experts, and felt unable to bring in a verdict despite scientif-ic testimony that the soap's principal constituent was boiled human flesh, a finding corroborated by archaeologist Professor George Dorsey's demonstra-tion that the bone fragments were human. At the second trial six weeks later, Luetgart received a life sentence, and he died in prison of a heart attack on 27 July 1899.

The widespread but misconceived view that Louise had been processed into sausages was reflected in poor seasonal sales by local butchers. But the case popularised the word 'sesamoid', hitherto a largely unknown bone.

Sodomy

In Georgia, USA, this happens whenever a person 'performs or submits to any sexual act involving the sex organs of one person and the mouth or anus of another'. The penalty is stiff (one to twenty years) and the drafting broad. Clearly heterosexual encounters are included, and – if nipples are sexual organs and kissing a sexual act – a man kissing his wife's breasts should think twice first.

On Valentine's Day 1983, GOAL (Georgian Citizens Opposed to Archaic Laws) brought a test case on behalf of a practising homosexual (Hardwick by name), alleging that the law infringed the rights of citizens wishing to engage in sodomy at home. Hardwick lost in the District Court but won on appeal. Georgia's Attorney General decided to contest the issue, and on 31 March 1986 the Supreme Court, ignoring the statute's heterosexual implications, upheld the law by a majority opinion. Justice Byron White pointed out – correctly – that Mr Hardwick 'would have us announce, as the Court of Appeals did, a fundamental right to engage in homosexual sodomy. This we are quite unwilling to do.' Today 'the abominable crime of sodomy' remains against the law in twenty-two states.

Sodomy abounded in the early Australian penal colony, where it was punishable by death. The first governor, Arthur Phillip, took a resolute line: 'I would wish to confine the criminal until the opportunity offered of delivering him to New Zealand, and let them eat him.' Convictions were rare; one Australian sodomite was hanged in 1836, but anecdotal evidence puts the number of homosexual encounters on **Norfolk Island** alone at 'fifty or sixty cases a day'. For a convict population of only 600, this may seem high, but buggery has always formed an ineradicable part of jail culture, and the Australian continent was little more than a vast prison, with sex an instrument of dominance used by the strong against the weak.

Unlike under-age homosexuality, lesbianism is not illegal. The distinction arose because Queen Victoria struck the offence from the 1861 Offences Agaist the Person Act, esteeming the practice so vile that it could only reflect the fevered imaginations of Parliamentary draftsmen.

Solution, The police's

Armchair detectives hoping to identify Jack the Ripper face a clear choice. One route is to follow hunches, attributing the means, motive and opportunity to a likely Victorian. A hundred years after the event, very few suspects can be excluded with complete confidence: hence the steady proliferation of 'final solutions'.

The alternative is to be guided by the police officers charged with the original investigation. We now know who they suspected although, tantalisingly, we do not know why. There are two pieces of evidence, the Macnaghten Memorandum and the Swanson Marginalia.

Sir Melville Macnaghten was the Assistant Chief Constable from 1889 to 1890, and in 1894 he recorded his views on the Ripper case, first setting out his reasons for believing that a man called Cutbush was not the culprit, and then discussing his three preferred suspects, now identified as Druitt, Kosminski and Ostrog. In the early 1930s Macnaghten's memorandum was copied by his youngest daughter, Lady Christabel Aberconway, who typed out seven quarto sheets, the existence of which only came to public attention in 1959.

In his memorandum, Macnaghten concludes: 'I am inclined to exonerate the last two' – Kosminski and Ostrog – 'but I have always held strong opinions about No 1' – Druitt – 'and the more I think the matter over, the stronger these opinions become. The truth, however, will never be known.' Serious historical work on Jack the Ripper's identity started with the Macnaghten Memorandum.

Of the three suspects, Druitt was a barrister who committed suicide in December 1888 shortly after the last of the murders, leaving a note to the effect that 'since Friday I felt that I was going to be like Mother, and it would be best for all concerned if I were to die'. Druitt had recently been dismissed from Valentine's school at Blackheath for an unspecified but serious offence; according to

Macnaghten he was 'sexually insane and from private information I have little doubt but that his family believed him to have been the murderer'. Macnaghten continued: 'The Whitechapel murderer in all probability put an end to himself soon after the Dorset Street affair in November 1888... Certain facts, pointing to this conclusion, were not in possession of the police till some years after I became a police officer.'

No one knows what these 'certain facts' were; the only certainty is that Macnaghten, a sensible, reliable man who knew everything about the case, believed that Druitt was his man and put his suspicions on file.

Michael Ostrog proved the most difficult suspect to track down since he operated under at least thirty aliases. Macnaghten characterised him as 'a mad Russian doctor and convict and unquestionably a homicidal maniac. This man was said to have been habitually cruel to women and carried about with him surgical knives and other instruments.' A Russian or Polish Jew born in 1833, Ostrog traded as a confidence trickster. The year before the murders, in September 1887, he appeared at the Old Bailey accused of stealing a metal tankard. Ostrog pleaded insanity, but was sentenced to six months; he was discharged from Surrey Pauper Lunatic Asylum on 10 March 1888. Thereafter he failed to report to the police and his later movements, including his whereabouts during and after the vital

period six months later, are vague, although Macnaghten notes he 'was subsequently detained in a lunatic asylum'.

Finally there is suspect Number Three: Aaron Kosminski, the Man Who Died of **Masturbation**. Kosminski was a Polish Jew, a bootmaker who arrived in Britain in 1882 at the age of seventeen. He lived at 15 Black Lion Yard in Whitechapel, and was diagnosed as syphilitic on 24 March 1888. According to the Macnaghten Memorandum, he inhabited the heart of the district where the murders were committed. He became 'insane owing to many years of indulgence in solitary vices. He had a great hatred of women with strong homicidal tendencies. He was and I believe is detained in a lunatic asylum about March 1889... There were many circumstances connected with this man which made him a strong "suspect".'

At this stage the Swanson Marginalia come into play. These are the recently discovered pencil notes made by Chief Inspector Donald Swanson in his personal copy of Sir Robert Anderson's memoirs, *The Lighter Side of my Official Life*. Anderson had early charge of the Ripper investigation; his book says: 'The conclusion we came to was that he and his people were certain low class Polish Jews; for it is remarkable that the people of that class in the East End will not give up one of their number to Gentile justice. And the result proved that our diagnosis was right on every point. I will merely add that the only person who ever had a good view of the murderer unhesitatingly identified the suspect the instant he was confronted with him, but he refused to give evidence against him. In saying that he was a Polish Jew I am merely stating a definitely ascertained fact. And my words are meant to specify race, not religion.'

For many decades these sentences were believed to refer to a suspect known as 'Leather Apron', or John Pizer. But Anderson's predecessor at the Yard, Chief Inspector Donald Swanson, owned a copy of Anderson's book, which he read and annotated. On Swanson's death, it passed to his daughter, and on her death it was inherited by his nephew who, in 1987, ninety-nine years after the murders, stumbled upon his grandfather's marginal notes.

The jottings identify Anderson's man as Kosminski, and explain the refusal of the eyewitness to confirm his identification thus: 'because the suspect was also a Jew and also because his evidence would convict the suspect'. Swanson commented that after Kosminski's identification the killings came to an end, 'and very shortly afterwards the suspect with his hands tied behind his back was sent to Stepney Workhouse and thence to Colney Hatch; poor Polish jews from Whitechapel, had a home to go to wash and people to shield him. Redischarged after three days, readmitted 4 Feb 1891. He took up a knife and threatened his sister.'

Kosminski died in confinement in 1919. Unlikely though it may be that the police allowed their prime suspect to go free from 1888 to 1891, the fact remains that the only candidates on a shortlist compiled by the handful of men versed in the full details of the police inquiry were Druitt, Osgood and Kosminski.

This trail is lukewarm at best. Macnaghten clearly knew little about Druitt, putting his age at forty-one instead of thirty-one and describing him as a doctor not a barrister; and cricket enthusiasts point out that Druitt's fixtures show him taking wickets only a few hours after the killings, turning out on Blackheath's Rectory Field on the morning of 8 September 1888. But if the the Ripper's identity is to be revealed, it is by reliance on the written record through documentary research. A cold trail is better than no trail at all, and there is no reason why the murderer should have come to public attention in any other context. Who would have heard of Ramirez, or DeSalvo, or Bianchi, but for their killings?

The 1993 'Ripper diary' designates James Maybrick as the culprit, but pre-publication doubts have focused on the handwriting, which bears no overt resemblence to Maybrick's known script.

Souvenirs

Serial killers like their trophies. A few collect whole bodies (Christie), others keep trinkets and paste jewellery (**Hansen**) or keys (**Duffy**), while some enjoy reliving their golden moments with photographs (**Glatman**), videos (**Ng**) or tape recordings (**Brady and Hindley**). Sometimes the killer takes parts home (for instance, the **kidneys**) as a keepsake or, occasionally, to eat.

For these wretched individuals the murders represent moments of significant human contact, from which stems the ordinary desire to salvage a memento of their conquest, just as a hunter lines the walls of his home with trophy heads of the creatures he has killed. Retention of these keepsakes fulfils two functions, part visual reminder and part an expression of pride.

For **Dahmer**, the people he killed represented little more than potential skulls; once they were dead, he could have their heads to remember them by. This tendency ripened into a desire to take Polaroids of his 'conquests', so that what started as a human being ended as a little piece of card a few inches square bearing a printed image. This completed the reification of the victim. Whereas a dead body belongs to the deceased, a photograph of it belongs to the photographer, as his property and his creation, and, reciprocally, to derive emotional satisfaction from arranging dismembered limbs into pleasing photogenic compositions is an activity that emanates a near-terminal quality. The body parts of Dahmer's victims fulfilled a similar function; they were to be subsumed into the grand design towards which Dahmer was groping at the time of his arrest – the 'shrine' where his skulls could be laid out in a neat row, symmetrically displayed on a magic black table flanked by a pair of plastic gryphons. Thus people would become ornaments.

The excitement over **Jack the Ripper**'s gynaecological doodlings misled Victorians into thinking they might be dealing with something familiar, namely a doctor. In fact, they were confronted by the more or less standard mutilations of something new, a serial sex killer on the prowl, hunting for souvenirs.

Sperm, frozen

In July 1978 a 13-year-old Birmingham schoolgirl, Candice Williams, was raped and then strangled. Following normal procedure, the swabs of semen from her vagina were consigned to the freezer at the West Midlands Forensic Science Laboratory.

With his record of indecent assaults, local youth Patrick Hassett was the prime suspect. But his girlfriend supplied an alibi and the blood-grouping technology of the day proved inconclusive. Hassett went free, but five years later he was jailed for ten years after kidnapping and assaulting a mental defective.

In 1986 came the discovery of **genetic finger-printing**. Another two years passed before samples of the type taken from Candice Williams could be processed. So it was not until 1988 that the bags of Hassett's semen were chemically analysed, yielding the requisite DNA fingerprint. But Hassett, still in prison, refused to supply a comparative sample.

The police waited until his 1991 release. Then they re-arrested him. He agreed to provide some hair cuttings, and these matched the 1978 spermatozoa, a one-in-12,000 chance. On 18 March 1992, Hassett was sent to prison for life.

In America, the rapist and murderer Joseph O'Dell ran a 1992 campaign from **Death Row** for the right to impregnate his girlfriend, Sheryl, with frozen sperm. As an only son, O'Dell was concerned about his family's bloodline.

See also **Romances**

Spanish Fly

An alleged aphrodisiac made from the dried beetle *Cantharis vesicatora*. It is poisonous.

A gram or so of the powder at the standard concentration of 0.6 per cent prepared insect is usually fatal; when used in Mediterranean countries as an abortifacient, it often kills both the foetus and the mother. Very possibly, smaller doses may stimulate sexual activity by irritating the mucous membranes of the mouth, intestines and vagina.

In 1954 Spanish Fly's erotic properties were put to the test in Britain by the manager of a wholesale chemists, Arthur Kendrick Ford, who was powerfully attracted to a 27-year-old typist, Betty Grant. 'We were,' he said, 'very fond of each other, but she kept putting me off.' He claimed they had intercourse together, but she went to post-mortem a virgin. Betty was no great beauty, and Ford seemed to be happily married, the father of two children for whom she often acted as a babysitter.

Ten years before, in the army, Ford overheard barrack-room gossip about an aphrodisiac which drove women wild, and in early 1954 he made the dual discovery that canthardarin was the medical term for Spanish Fly and that his firm kept some in stock. He emptied forty grains into an envelope.

The idea took hold. On 26 April, Ford talked to the firm's senior chemist, Richard Lushington. 'This is a number one poison,' he was warned.

Nevertheless, Ford purchased a bag of pink and white coconut confectionery into which he inserted quantities of the stolen drug with a pair of scissors. On Ford's reckoning, there was one piece for Betty and one for him. He offered the bag round the office. Betty ate one sweet, he downed another and – somehow – a seaside beauty queen, June Malins, also working as a typist, took a third. Other staff members guzzled up the remainder, with no ill-effects.

The two women died. Ford recovered and, lacking the intent to kill, got off with five years at the Old Bailey in a trial which he spent mostly in tears. In public his wife stood by him, writing in the press: 'Arthur Ford and I are still desperately in love with each other, and some day, somehow, we hope to regain the happiness we have known and restart our lives together.'

Spilsbury, Sir Bernard (1877–1947)

Spilsbury, the greatest medico-legal expert of his time, won his spurs for the destruction of Crippen's defence in 1910. A charismatic figure, habitually clad in a Savile Row suit with a carnation in his button-hole and a top hat from Lock's of St James's, Sir Bernard had his shirts tailor-made with detachable arms to avoid creasing his cuffs when he rolled up his sleeves for work. He conducted 25,000 post-mortems; a young barrister once courted his ire by demanding, 'When did you last examine a *live* patient, Sir Bernard?'

Few dared make such frontal assaults. Spilsbury's sway over the popular imagination and the courts was such that his word was seldom challenged. He delivered his opinions with confidence and clarity, and his cases read like a roll-call of famous British murders: Crippen, Frederick and Margaret Seddon, George Joseph Smith, Louis Voisin, Bywaters and Thompson, Herbert Armstrong, Patrick Mahon, Donald Merrett, the Brighton Trunk Murders and the like.

In his later years, Spilsbury's court appearances became increasingly erratic. He intervened on behalf of the defence in the 1943 John Barleycorn murder, contending that the four-and-a-half fingered Loughlans lacked the strength to throttle his victim. When asked how he knew, Spilsbury said that he had visited Brixton Prison and enjoined Loughans to grip his hand 'with all the strength he had'. The great pathologist had been amazed at his client's weakness. 'I do not believe,' Spilsbury said, 'that he could strangle anyone with that hand.'

Spilsbury's reputation was sufficient to secure an acquittal from a deferential jury. Twenty years later, wasted by cancer, Loughans still showed a test grip of fourteen pounds. Spilsbury was accustomed to carry the day as much by sheer force of character as by his knowledge and experience; in the 1930 Merrett case (see **ears**), one of the opposing barristers referred to him as 'Saint Bernard'.

Similar prescience prevailed at the trial of the matricide Sidney Fox. By the time the corpse was examined by defence doctors, the crucial bruising round the victim's larynx had disappeared. Not surprisingly, the defence disputed the bruises, suggesting that Spilsbury was misled by incipient putrefaction. He brushed the objection aside: 'It was a bruise and nothing else. There are no two opinions about it.' Fox was hanged in 1930.

Spilsbury was not a man to overlook an injury, and never forgave the parsimonious Southwark coroner Douglas Cowburn for paying him a single fee for examining both bodies of a pair of Siamese twins.

His declining years were marked by domestic and personal misfortune, and he committed suicide on 17 December 1947, gassing himself in his University College laboratory after dinner at his club.

Stabs

When examining stab wounds, it is best to concentrate on the cleanest slit. This indicates most clearly the type of weapon, for instance double-edged or single-edged; and the sharper the wound's outline, the sharper the instrument. Roughening or bruising round the aperture suggests something blunt, like a pair of scissors. The penetration of the deepest thrust indicates not the length of the knife but its minimum length.

Where suicide is to be weighed against murder, the corpse is studied for signs of defensive cuts. For suicides, the angulation and site of the stabs must be consistent with self-inflicted wounds. Most suicides go for the heart or thereabouts, with none of the hesitation cuts that characterise, say, self-administered throat-cutting. The murderer lands his hits wherever he can, most often on the upper chest.

What does this feel like for the the assailant? The murderer Jack Abbott, briefly the darling of New York's cocktail circuit for the literary accomplishments revealed by his *In the Belly of the Beast*, mentioned feeling the victim's 'life quivering on the end of the blade'. But there is probably no better authority than Susan Atkins of the Manson Family. Most discussions of sex crimes proceed by metaphor or analogy, drawing tentative parallels between the mutilatory and sexual processes. Atkins was more forthright. While in custody she told another inmate, Veronica Howard, about killing the pregnant Sharon Tate: 'It felt so good the first time I stabbed her, and when she screamed at me it did something to me, sent a rush through me and I stabbed her again... it was just like going into nothing, going into air... It's like a sexual release. Especially when you see the blood spurting out. It's better than a climax.'

Stalking

Technical term for the pursuit of celebrities by nonentities. Stalking can spill over into violence and even the final accolade of murder by a fan. Stalkers often subscribe to the view that their affections are reciprocated, although they may find that it needs some decisive act of armed confrontation to wring out the truth from their love-object. To date, the practice is illegal in nineteen American states.

Stalking is no new phenomenon. Roderick Maclean, incensed by Queen Victoria's refusal to read his poems, became one of her would-be assassins. A more recent pairing was of Jodie Foster and John Hinckley. Michael J. Fox, star of *Back to the Future*, received some 6,000 letters from 26-year-old Tina Ledbetter; the correspondence turned sour – 'very violent, very threatening', according to Fox – when he found a marriage partner elsewhere. Ledbetter was eventually arrested and packed off for psychiatric treatment.

In July 1992, Britain's *Sunday Times* reported an unusual case of an unnamed Hollywood actress who enjoyed a brief dalliance with an admirer, Susan Dyer; when the liaison ended, Dyer bombarded her target with telephone calls, stole her address book and then rang round the actress's friends to beg them to engineer a reconciliation. When this failed, Dyer broke into her former lover's home during a dinner party and threatened to shoot herself. A few weeks later, after Dyer's arrest, the actress called in an electrician to investigate a wiring problem and it emerged that Dyer had shared her home for months, taking up residence in a tiny space beneath the actress's bedroom floor.

Stalkers may fall prey to the delusion that their target is beaming them messages. Actress and singer Olivia Newton-John talked to Michael Perry with her eyes, and when Perry saw visions of dead bodies rising through his floor, he inferred that it was her way (as a goddess) of maintaining contact from an underground base in his home-town of Lake Arthur. Later, he killed both his parents, two cousins and a nephew, but a court found him insane and thus 'incompetent' (see **Lunette**) to be executed. To end this impasse, it was proposed to treat Perry with drugs, on the one hand making him better which would, on the other hand, qualify him for electrocution. But in October 1990 a court ruled that enforced drug therapy was 'cruel and unusual', so Perry will only be killed if he recovers by more natural means.

The full-blown stalker kills his hero. But before Mark Chapman focused his grievances on John Lennon, his resentment was directed – at lower levels of harassment – towards other targets. He telephoned a bomb threat to Hawaii's Ili Kai Hotel, and watched from the balcony opposite as the police cars arrived. He would ring a street pay-phone, visible from his window, and tell whoever picked up the receiver, 'I'm watching you. I'm going to get you. I'm going to follow you home and kill you.'

Chapman became the stalkers' prototype. He used a .38 Charter Arms Special (see **Dumdums**), and took *The Catcher in the Rye* as his Bible. John Hinckley adopted the identical combination for his attempt on Ronald Reagan, as did Robert John Bardo when he gunned down actress Rebecca Schaeffer in June 1989. Hinckley told Jodie Foster that the **assassination** of Reagan was in retaliation for Lennon's death. Underlying these similarities is an obsession with celebrity. To their fans, celebrities lead mythic lives, flickering in the limelight. But what is fame? It may not reflect any achievement apart from fame itself. The celebrity projects a fantasy of celebrity, and his admirers project fantasies onto the celebrity. Confusion and disillusion can result.

Stomach analysis

Useful in determining not only the cause (in poison cases) but also the rough time of death. As a general rule, most food stays in the stomach for a couple of hours following consumption. A really large meal may linger a further hour and a rich creamy meal tarries for even longer.

As adults know, the stomach is emotionally responsive. In pathological terms it seems that fear slows, but anger hastens, gastric movement. Severe injury will stop it completely, so both the perpetrator and the victim of an assault are likely to have erratic digestive timetables and, according to some authorities, the best tactic is simply to recognise a meal, find out when it was eaten, and then assume that death occurred subsequently. But even this broad approach would have been difficult in the case of mafioso Dominick 'Big Trin' Trinchera, gunned down in 1981 during an internecine Bonnano feud. 'You should have seen it when they shot Big Trin,' one of the killers told the undercover agent Joseph D. Pistone, 'fifty pounds of his stomach went flying.'

Given enough to work on, a conviction can be based on stomach analysis. On 10 June 1957, the body of Ontario schoolgirl Lynne Harper, missing since the previous night, was found in the undergrowth in Lawson's Bush. She had been raped and strangled. The time of death was critical, since Lynne's movements were well documented for much of her last evening.

Lynne was seen setting off on the cross-bar of a 14-year-old classmate, Stephen Truscott, at around 7.05 p.m. as he pedalled northwards down County Road. Travelling in the opposite direction were two boys returning from a dip in a local swimming hole; they started together, one on foot and the other going ahead on a bicycle. The first child crossed with Stephen and Lynne on the highway by the wood known as Lawson's Bush, but the second, a few minutes behind, did not meet them; he arrived home at 7.25 p.m. The inference was clear: the pair had struck off towards the spot where the body was discovered. A relaxed-looking Stephen arrived back in the school area around 8 p.m., when a friend asked, 'What did you do with Harper, throw her to the fishes?' Stephen replied that he had dropped her at the highway, a little north of the swimming hole and, questioned by police the next morning, he maintained that she had hitched a ride in a grey 1959 Chevrolet.

Lynne's temperature provided no assistance in determining the time of **death**; her body had lost all its natural heat. But the police knew what she had for her last meal: turkey, cranberry sauce, peas, potatoes and 'upside-down' pineapple cake. This distinctive intake remained in her stomach, and she had sat down to the fifteen-minute meal with her parents at 5.30 on the afternoon of her death.

Without realising that Stephen was a suspect, the pathologist wrote: 'I 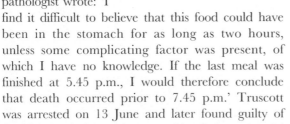 find it difficult to believe that this food could have been in the stomach for as long as two hours, unless some complicating factor was present, of which I have no knowledge. If the last meal was finished at 5.45 p.m., I would therefore conclude that death occurred prior to 7.45 p.m.' Truscott was arrested on 13 June and later found guilty of murder, incriminated by a wealth of circumstantial and forensic evidence. Eight years later the case became a *cause célèbre* when a crusading journalist, Isabel Lebourdais, heaped ill-informed scorn on the verdict, and in 1966 the case was retried, producing

a rare gathering of the world's leading authorities on stomach emptying. A pathologist arguing that Lynne 'could have died within one hour – or up to nine or ten' of her supper found no support among his peers, who believed that the stomach does have its norms. The conviction was upheld.

Straighten, to

Criminal slang meaning, roughly, to bend. Villains 'straighten out' obstacles by removing or neutralising them. Thus a burglar alarm can be straightened by being cut, or a policeman straightened by bribery, resulting in the proverbial 'bent copper'.

Strangulation

According to Professor Keith Simpson, strangulation is not particularly painful. He established this empirically in the summer of 1941 by nearly murdering himself with a ligature in London's Euston Hotel lavatories. After winding a stocking twice round his neck and knotting it before losing consciousness, Simpson came sufficiently near to death to show that self-strangulation with a ligature is both feasible and tolerable. This is no party trick; it can kill suddenly, since even momentary compression of the neck may incur a reflex vagal nerve stoppage of the heart (see **Drowning**).

As recently as 1960 defence counsel suggested that a ligature round the neck of Frances Knight (found mummified after twenty years in a Welsh cupboard) was attributable to the deceased's faith in the procedure as a folk remedy for the common cold.

It is perhaps no coincidence that strangulation is the favoured murder method of many hardened serial killers, Christie, **Nilsen** and **Dahmer** among them. The process of extinguishing life can be prolonged almost at will by the exercise of self-control, with a diminution in applied pressure producing a temporary remission. According to the prosecution in the Dahmer trial, 'It takes five minutes to strangle a man to death.' Serial killers enjoy domination, and there can be few contexts more fraught with possibilities.

Death results from oxygen deprivation of the brain and, according to anaesthetist Nigel Robson, children can survive for longer than adults and cold people for longer than those who are warm. Even with the best will in the world, it is impossible to strangle yourself manually, as the loss of consciousness relaxes the grip, although it seems that Jeanne **Weber**, the famous French babysitter, died in the attempt. Another plucky attempt was made by Amelia Dyer, the baby killer, after her arrest on 4 April 1896 (see **Pregnancy**). She failed with a ligature. Taken to Reading police station, Dyer removed her bootlaces, tied them together and, heaving with all her might, set about ending her life. Her eyes bulged, her tongue lolled and her face turned purple, but she survived, to be executed two months later. Otherwise, female stranglers are extremely rare. Simpson encountered none in a sequence of fifty-eight cases.

The hallmark of strangulation is a fracture limited to the upper horn of the thyroid cartilage. This little bone, the hyoid, is never broken on its own in any other way. As Sir Bernard **Spilsbury** pointed out with style under cross-examination, the converse is not always true. Asked if a murder victim's hyoid had been fractured, Spilsbury riposted, 'No. If it had, that would have made the strangling even more evident.' Most stranglings are ordinary domestic crimes and, after stabbing, it has long been the most popular British method of murder.

Body changes from death by asphyxia include a blueness in the face, and tiny haemorrhages in the eye membranes and the internal organs. Strangulation also diminishes bowel control, and semi-asphyxiation during masturbation heightens sexual pleasure, producing a surprising number of accidental hanging fatalities.

String

Getting the timing just right is important with electrocution. The moment to throw the switch is immediately after the condemned man empties his chest by exhaling. This prevents air from getting trapped in his lungs by the contraction of the glottis induced by the electric charge. Should this happen, the subsequent collapse of the chest when the current is switched off releases a lungful of escaping breath, engendering a highly distasteful sound and a foaming mouth (see **Allorto and Sellier**).

At the Sing Sing death house, matters were complicated by the executioner's special booth. This partitioned him from the condemned man so that he did not have to look at the prisoner while killing him. But it made the right moment impossible to judge.

It was the chief physician's job to watch the man die. So a little hole was drilled in the partition, and through it he passed a length of string with a ring attached to both ends. The executioner slipped one ring on his finger. The doctor put on the other and, when the prisoner was strapped in, he gauged the rhythm of his heaving chest and gave a tug. But stress left ample scope for misunderstanding, and the executioner's line of sight was later rearranged so the doctor was visible, allowing for visual hand-signals.

American executioners are typically called 'the electrician'. In Sing Sing the job paid $150 a head; for many years of his working life, John Hilbert used the extra income to make ends meet. He committed suicide in his cellar shortly after retirement.

Strychnine

In small doses a tonic. It comes from the orange-like fruit of the Strychnos nux-vomica tree and, after its 1817 discovery, strychnine was rapidly exploited by proprietary brands like Easton's Syrup as an aid to convalescence. It sharpened up the senses and promoted general well-being, but an overdose caused rapid or almost immediate death, an outcome demonstrated by many who forgot to shake the bottle, adequately distributing the concentrated sediment.

The poison is wholly inappropriate for discrete killing. Its use is better restricted to the random murder of strangers like the series devised by Dr Thomas Neill Cream, often believed to have made a truncated bid for immortality with his last words on the scaffold, 'I am Jack...' But this outburst can be interpreted in other ways (see **Hanging**) and, besides, the man was mad. Not only did Cream make a practice of inducing London prostitutes to swallow his pink pills just for the pleasure of watching them writhe, killing four, he wrote letters to public figures accusing them of his crimes.

Cream arrived in London in 1891 after serving ten years of a murder sentence. This charm-free man traded as an abortionist in Canada, where he once obliged a client to marry him at gunpoint, leaving her the next day. Within a month of setting foot in Britain, Cream poisoned Matilda Clover and Ellen Donworth. He tried to blackmail Lord Russell and a Dr William Broadbent for the killings, meanwhile writing to the coroner with an offer to solve the cases for £300,000. In April 1892, Cream accused a Dr Walter Harper of his next pair of murders, finally reporting him formally for the killing of Donworth and another prostitute, Louise Harvey. The police investigated, but Harvey was still very much alive; she told detectives that Cream had handed her some pills (which she did not take) for her complexion. And although Donworth was dead, her demise had been attributed to alcoholism. Exhumation detected substantial quantities of strychnine in her body, and Cream was hanged on 15 November 1892.

Title page of a contemporary account of Dr Cream's murders

Death from strychnine is attended by some of the most startling symptoms known to medicine. A fatal dose is as little as 100 milligrams, and the victim suffers horrific spasms, his back arching over so that only the heels and back of the head stay in contact with the ground, a process known as 'opisthotonos'. The face becomes fixed in a grin ('risus sardonicus'), the muscles twitch and breathing becomes first laboured and then impossible. The spasms hit in two-minute waves until extinction results from suffocation or heart failure.

It is hard to see how anyone could hope to have such manifestations ascribed to natural causes, and in 1855 Dr William **Palmer** failed in just such an enterprise. Late on 19 November, having weakened the gambler John Parsons Cook with antimony, Palmer secured three grains of strychnine from the local chemist and returned to the sickbed at the Talbot Arms. The inn's waitress reported that by midnight, 'Cook was screaming "Murder!" and was in violent pain. He said he was suffocating... His eyes looked very wild, and were standing a great way out from his head. He was beating the bed with his hands.' A chambermaid noted of Cook, 'Sometimes he would throw back his head upon the pillow, and then he would raise himself up again. This jumping and jerking was all over his body... It was difficult for him to speak, he was so short of breath... He called aloud: "Murder!"'

Cook survived this preliminary skirmish, perhaps the effects of antimony, and the following day Palmer gave him two 'ammonia pills'. The results were spectacular. According to Gordon Honeycombe's meticulous account, the patient at once 'began to scream, throwing himself back on the bed. He cried to Jones: "Raise me up – or I shall be suffocated!" Then his whole body was seized with violent convulsions, so extreme that his head and heels bent back as if they would meet. Jones, with Palmer's assistance, tried to lift or control the contorting body but failed, because of the spasms and rigidity of Cook's limbs. The convulsions lasted for about ten minutes, after which Cook's agony diminished and his heartbeat faded.' On seeing the body, Cook's step-father 'was greatly struck by the tightness of the muscles across his face', and on 14 June 1856, Palmer was hanged for murder.

Stupidity

No one knows the dumbest thing ever said by a mobster, but here is a recent crop of contenders. Gene Gotti, on being arrested for violation of the

Racketeer Influenced Corrupt Organisation Act, demanded: 'Say, who is this Mr Rico, anyway?'

An unnamed gangster, acting as a security guard during a performance of *The Nutcracker*, inquired: 'Hey, how come there's no talking in this thing?'

Perhaps the strongest candidate is the wonderful exchange between another unknown goon and a policeman, as they stood watching a robot bomb-disposal device steer itself towards a suspicious package planted outside the Gambino family New York headquarters at the Ravenite Social Club.

'I don't see no wires, so how can they make it move around like that?' the mobster asked. A deadpan policeman replied, 'There's a tiny little cop inside.'

Success

Understandably, it can make someone's day to be mistaken for a world famous desperado, a trait manifest in so-called 'motiveless' crimes where a murderer may kill just to achieve celebrity.

Thus in 1966, 18-year-old Robert Smith explained why he had blown out the brains of five women and two children in an Arizona beauty parlour: 'I wanted to get known, to get myself a name.' Kenneth Bianchi, the Hillside Strangler, wrote to the author Thomas Thomson shortly after his conviction in 1984 saying that his life would make a 'terrific movie' (see **Romances**). And Paul Knowles, finally arrested in Georgia in November 1974 after a massive manhunt following a murder spree which claimed eighteen lives, had a field day on his court outing. Crowds lined the streets, the courtroom was packed, the papers carried him all over the front pages.

Knowles had made it at last. Like royalty, he smiled graciously at everyone, reminding an interviewer that he was 'the only successful member' of his family. Jeffrey Dahmer rose further, to the coveted front cover of *Time* magazine and, after the 1991 success of the film *Silence of the Lambs*, American police were plagued with exaggerated claims from would-be serial killers. Henry Lee **Lucas**, a Texas drifter, confessed to a body count of 600, but now insists it was just his mother he killed, and Britain produced an even more pitiful example in Ian Warby. If growing into a serial killer is an expression of failure, Warby was a failed failure. At twen-

ty-six he was a worshipper of Nazism, the Devil, the Maquis de **Sade** and the fictional Hannibal Lecter, nicknaming himself The Panther and The Outsider. But, as Warby's lawyer declared in court, 'He is as physically weedy, pathetic and uncommunicative an individual as one could meet.'

On 12 October 1992, Warby went on the rampage in Essex, attacking a college boy with a hammer, a middle-aged man with a knife, hacking at two youths in a car and then going for an invalid, becoming a serial runner in the process, beaten off on every occasion. 'It doesn't say much for a serial killer when he can't even kill a victim in a wheelchair who is at his mercy,' commented his barrister. Warby was not so much a man driven to kill as a man who hoped to be driven to kill, the impetus seemingly derived from extrinsic rather than intrinsic sources, and it is rightly said that those who achieve their ambitions sometimes find the victory hollow.

Careful study of local newspaper files enables aspiring serial killers to restrict their **false confessions** to unsolved cases. Their braggardly tendency poses a temptation to police forces with an eye on clear-up rates. Critics now claim that officials used Lucas as a dustbin into which they dumped unsolved killings, taking a total of 210 murders in twenty-six states off the books, and in August 1991 officers were warily grappling with the case of ex-Marine Donald Leroy Evans. Arrested on a kidnapping charge in Mississippi, Evans confessed to 'at least sixty' killings in seventeen states.

In the first half of the twentieth century, America produced serial killers at a rate of 1.2 per annum. Between 1960 and 1980 this had risen to around a dozen a year, and it is now approaching about two a month. Nearly all are men, nearly all are white, and many are prodigious drivers, logging up to 200,000 miles a year as they scour the country for their next victim.

See also **Canonisation, Locard, Puente**

Sunday Gentleman, The

Nickname of Daniel Defoe (1660–1731) when in Bristol; Sunday was the only day he dared show his face out of doors without risking arrest for **debt**.

His real name was Daniel Foe. After issuing the immensely popular 1701 pamphlet *The True Born Englishman*, inveighing against social snobbery, he spent a brief period as D. Foe before spreading his wings as De Foe and finally Defoe. Then in 1703 he penned a satirical tract that landed him in the **pillory**. There he was feted as a popular hero; the crowds showered him with flowers crying 'Good Old Dan'. His subsequent incarceration in Newgate bore fruit twenty years later, when he described his low-life experiences through the eyes of one Moll Flanders. At about the same time he published one of the many accounts of the life and adventures of the highwayman Jack **Sheppard**, interviewing his subject in the Condemned Hold.

Defoe launched his first newspaper while in **Newgate** in 1703, and secured his release by offering to work for the Lord Treasurer Robert Harley as a spy, setting up a network of informers to keep tabs on subversives like himself. Thus he became the father of the police state and of the British Secret Service.

Sutcliffe, Peter (1946–)

The story of the Yorkshire Ripper well illustrates the point about the banality of evil. Almost the only interesting fact about Peter Sutcliffe is that between 1975 and 1980 he murdered thirteen women.

Sutcliffe was an unexceptional, inarticulate, taciturn and averagely coarse lorry driver, endowed with the normal complement of relatives, friends, workmates and drinking cronies, none of whom regarded him as anything special. Born on 2 June 1946 in Bingley, the turning point in Sutcliffe's life came in the summer of 1969 when he picked up a prostitute in Bradford's run-down Manningham Lane. She said it would cost £5. Sutcliffe became increasingly half-hearted at the prospect of back-street sex, but he handed over a £10 note; she went to a garage to change the note and then disappeared. This incident followed a row with his long-standing fiancée Sonia about a rival, an Italian with a sports car, and preceded a dressing-down the next morning for being late to work at the local Water Board, where his absence triggered an accident in which several men nearly drowned. All in all, it was a bad twenty-four hours.

Three weeks later, Sutcliffe found the woman who duped him out of his £5 drinking in another prostitutes' pub. He demanded his money back. In Sutcliffe's words: 'She thought this was a huge joke and, as luck would have it, she knew everybody else in the place and went round telling them. Before I knew what was happening, most of the people were having a good laugh.'

A week after this public humiliation, Sutcliffe assaulted a St Paul's Road whore chosen at random, cracking her on the head with a stone. Then in September 1969 he was arrested lurking behind a hedge in the red-light district armed with a heavy hammer and was – mistakenly – charged with 'going equipped for a theft'. As far as we know, that was the end of Sutcliffe's assaults for nearly six years.

In June 1975 a divorcée, Anna Rogulskyj, from the nearby town of Keighley was repeatedly accosted and followed by a strange dark-haired man with a springy beard. On the night of 4 July 1975 Sutcliffe smashed her skull with a hammer. But he was interrupted, and Anna survived after a twelve-hour operation. On 29 October 1975, Sutcliffe gave a late-night lift to prostitute Wilma McCann. She upbraided him as a slow-starter and climbed out of the car saying: 'I'm going. It's going to take you all fucking day. You're fucking useless.' Incensed, Sutcliffe caved in McCann's head and then stabbed her fourteen times. After that he was away, killing his thirteenth and final victim five years later on 17 November 1980. In the meantime he continued his ordinary social rounds of friends and family.

Sutcliffe was finally picked up almost by chance on the evening of 2 January 1981 in a car with stolen numberplates. Unaware of his true identity, the police hung on to him overnight, and the next day a conscientious Sergeant Bob Ring searched the scene of the arrest. There he found a discarded knife and hammer, which Sutcliffe had concealed in a pile of leaves while urinating before going to the police station. Next day the giant 'Ripper' manhunt, during which 250,000 people were interviewed, 32,000 statements taken, 5.2 million car numbers checked and £4 million spent, drew to its close.

'I think you are in serious trouble,' said the interrogating officer, Inspector John Boyle. Sutcliffe replied, 'I think you have been leading up to it.'

'Leading up to what?'

'The Yorkshire Ripper.'

'What about the Yorkshire Ripper?' Boyle asked.

'Well,' said Sutcliffe, 'it's me.'

Sutcliffe came from a poor area of the West Riding with its rough and ready sub-culture. Women were habitually (and often affectionately) referred to as 'fucking cunts' and wives as 'cunts'; in the bars you could buy cocktails called 'Barbarella Legspreaders' and listen to pub DJs doing commercials between records, starting off 'Worried your willie's too short?' The prostitute areas were sleazy, run-down slums where junk shops and sex shops, betting offices and minicab rooms were interspersed between the patches of broken ground left by random demolition. Here the wretched prostitutes – often abandoned wives 'on the game' to feed their children – plied their trade in the open air. Piss-ups, brawls, violence against women, broken-down cars, cars on bricks, cars with Guinness labels for tax discs, unemployment, bailiffs, rat-catching, thieving, kerb crawling and trouble with the police were not unusual.

As a baby Sutcliffe was weak, and he developed into a shy, almost listless child who clung to his mother's skirts. At school he had a 'yonderly' glaze to his eyes; he was remembered by his teachers, if at all, as passive. At home it

PETER SUTCLIFFE

One of a series of collector's cards

was not always possible to tell he was there. 'I've walked into the house many a time and he's been just sat quiet in the kitchen without me realising for ages,' recollected his sister. 'Not reading or anything; just sort of sat there staring at space.' One of Sutcliffe's few distinguishing traits was his passion for the bathroom, where he spent hours staring at himself in the mirror, occasionally snipping the odd millimetre off his hair. Most of his mid-teens were passed in his bedroom, with the door locked.

Three years after leaving school at fifteen Sutcliffe took a job as a gravedigger. To his workmates he seemed pleasant but shy, typically the one who tagged along. As girls started to feature in his mates' lives, Sutcliffe accompanied them drinking: looking, listening, and contributing nothing for hours, as though in a trance. Women found his dark and broody good looks an attraction until they tried to make conversation.

Somehow, in 1966, the young Sutcliffe hitched up with another loner, 16-year-old Sonia Szurma. She may have been an intelligent girl, even an intellectual snob by comparison with Sutcliffe; she was destined for teacher training college. But she was no more of a live wire. Uncommunicative in the extreme, she occasionally ventured into speech with remarks like 'Hello'. Sometimes she sat alone outside a pub while Sutcliffe drank inside it. She radiated disapproval, and after their 1974 wedding became obsessed with housework. Meanwhile she developed a considerable talent as a nag. For the married Sutcliffe, pubbing and cruising the red-light district provided a welcome diversion from his prim home life. In due course, one thing led to another.

Two months after his arrest, Sutcliffe pulled off a rather flashy coup. During his eighth interview with one of the Armley psychiatrists, he disclosed that his murders were at God's behest. The Almighty had ordered him to kill prostitutes. In corroboration, Sutcliffe furnished anecdotal material about voices, visions and hallucinations. The professionals trooped into line: Sutcliffe exhibited many 'first-rank signs' of mental disorder. So when he appeared in court on 29 April 1981, pleading guilty to thirteen charges not of murder, but of manslaughter, his future looked relatively rosy – the more so since the prosecution accepted his plea of diminished responsibility, guided by the evidence of three forensic psychiatrists.

The experts were unanimous in labelling Sutcliffe an 'encapsulated paranoid schizophrenic'. It was almost unheard of for three professionals to agree and, now they did, their views were dismissed. A week later the court reconvened, with the Old Bailey the improbable forum where twelve laymen spent thirteen working days deliberating the metaphysical issue of whether Sutcliffe was deranged; after all, anyone who thinks that killing people is right must be strange. The crux was whether Sutcliffe was mad or bad; his *acts* may have been 'insane', but insanity cannot be judged purely in terms of behaviour. Everyone behaves badly, but that does not prove that they suffer from a mental disorder and are entitled to disclaim responsibility for their actions. Common sense prevailed on 22 May when Sutcliffe was found guilty of murder and sentenced to life.

He took so long to catch because the police investigation, without computers, was swamped by the 151,000 reports laboriously cross-referenced by 150 officers on the case. Sutcliffe was interviewed nine times, with each report filed under a different heading. Enquiries were side-tracked for months by a 'hoaxer' who sent in an audio-cassette, beginning with the words 'I'm **Jack**', and the thousands of suspects whose voices were recognised by the public had to be individually checked.

Linguistic experts narrowed the accent on the tape to an area near Durham, but in 1980 an advisory team devised a simpler way of pinpointing the Ripper's home. There were seventeen known attack sites; clearly the murderer had to travel to each of them from home, and then return to home from each of them. So, 'What single point on the map was nearest to all the attack sites?' The answer was Heaton, between Manningham and Shipley, where Sutcliffe lived. Further corroboration came from the neat idea that the late-night attacks probably happened nearest home – he was nearly back – whereas those earlier in the evening would be further away, allowing more time to drive home. Coupled with two other 'hard' clues, the newly-minted £5 note found in Jean Jordan's handbag after her murder on 1 October 1977 and issued two days previously in one of only 5,000 wage packets, and a set of tyre tracks common to 53,000 owners in the Midlands, Sutcliffe's detection was imminent at the time of his chance arrest.

Swallowers

Customs term for smugglers who take contraband through in their stomach, normally wrapped in **condoms** or surgical gloves. The technique first came to British attention at Heathrow in 1974 when three Americans were detained for the inexplicable profusions of condoms in their luggage; if the men had flown into the Republic of Ireland, they would have been accepted as no more than illicit condom smugglers. But British Customs had

no easy explanation until it emerged *per rectum*, in the form of knotted rubbers filled with cannabis oil.

Heathrow's highest monthly tally of swallowers is a 1986 total of twenty-six. The record number of condoms secreted in a single stomach is in dispute. Gatwick has a confirmed 143; other reports claim 739 capsules of cannabis resin.

It is a good idea to take anti-diarrhoea tablets for added coagulation during transit, thereby minimising the risk of premature evacuation. Working from the far end, the opposite of a 'swallower' is a 'stuffer'.

See also **White Death**

Sweden

More Swedes are killed in collisions with elks than by unlawful assaults. It seems that Swedish criminals are a cosseted and endangered species, creating growing public resentment at the inferior treatment meted out to law-abiding citizens.

Featherbedding can disappoint. In early 1991, young offenders despatched on a six-month yacht cruise to 'find themselves' were recalled after rediscovering their identities as Viking marauders, running riot in the coastal ports, pillaging cars and shops.

Many commentators consider the Swedish machinery of justice a similar anachronism, harking back to the Dark Ages. The judiciary are not independent; judges are civil servants whose careers must progress, to some degree, according to the number of 'results'. The role of the jury is played by lay assessors; they too are political appointees. After arrest, suspects are kept in solitary, very often until they confess.

For all the faults of the adversarial system, the accused is tried before being sentenced. But in Sweden the real trial takes place before the court hearing, and consists of the pre-trial examination, for which almost anything is admissible in evidence. Specious allegations, hearsay and gossip can be accepted as fact, without the opportunity of rebuttal or cross-examination, and these pre-trial findings are presented to the court, which passes the appropriate sentence. There is no real presumption of innocence; on the contrary, the notorious 'Sanalika Skal' clause requires the prosecution not to prove that the defendant is guilty, but that he *could have* been guilty. This is hardly onerous, and only one or two per cent of defendants are discharged.

Thus the 1987 Captain Simon Hayward case is interesting not for whether Hayward 'did it' but for the light cast on Swedish justice. Hayward was arrested on 13 March 1987 in his brother's Jaguar; its door sills were crammed with cannabis. Captain Hayward did not know that the drugs were there, nor was he informed by the police. It was only after some days in prison that he learned the reason for his arrest.

Captain Hayward spent the next five months in solitary while the prosecution went through the motions of proving that he *could* have acted knowingly as a courier. *Prima facie* it was unlikely that he *had*; couriers are typically individuals on their uppers with little to lose, whereas Hayward was a rising professional soldier in a good regiment on the eve of promotion. He did not need the money, and the alleged fee was way over the odds. Why give Hayward £8,000 when a professional would do the run for a fraction of the price?

Hayward's brother Christopher, on the other hand, was a drop-out living on uncertain income in Spain, and he went to ground shortly after Hayward's arrest. His role remains open to doubt. It was he who asked Hayward to drive his car to Sweden and deliver it to a cash buyer. Hayward decided to spend his few days' leave on the trip, squeezing in a couple of day's ski-ing at the far end. But, as the Judge later pointed out, Hayward's story was a lie because... why would anyone go ski-ing in *Sweden*?

The physical evidence at the trial consisted of Captain Hayward's screwdriver. The Judge said that it was for levering open the panels and extricating the cannabis. In fact, the Swedish mechanics who dismantled the car knew that it was almost the only tool *not* needed to break into the door sills. Access required a small Phillips screwdriver, a flat-ended screwdriver, a chisel, and some wire hooks, none of which Hayward had. But there was no procedure whereby this point could be made in court.

Hayward's screwdriver was a special six-pointed Phillips, bought in Astorp to tighten the screws on the Jaguar's seat, which worked loose on the long, fast drive. Again, this explanation was ridiculed in court on the grounds that the seat was perfectly sound on arrival (after Hayward had fixed it) when

driven round the state garage at three miles an hour. Why would Hayward buy a *screwdriver* to tighten up the screws on his seat?

Another talking point was the adverse testimony given by Inspector Larsen. His evidence consisted of information which had been submitted to (and rejected by) Scotland Yard, who thought it unreliable. Larsen would not say exactly whose testimony it was. Nor would he disclose his source's address; in fact Larsen had no idea of the man's whereabouts. As the informant was a criminal, Larsen had to protect his anonymity.

The court accepted these submissions at face value, and on 10 August 1987 a warder passing Hayward's cell let him know he had been sentenced to five years in his absence.

For the equally farcical appeal, London solicitors Kingsley Napley commissioned a report from Richard New, an experienced drugs officer. He wrote: 'In my considerable experience, I have never seen a verdict reached with such blatant disregard for the facts.'

Simon Hayward was released early, in September 1989, his life broken.

Sweeney Todd

The demon barber of Fleet Street. Careful tracking through the fictional accounts suggests that he may have existed in real life.

The story of a hairdresser who cut his customers' throats, pulled a lever to catapult them into the basement and then sold their remains as meat pies, was first serialised in *The People's Periodical and Family Library* of 1846 where it appeared under the demure title *The String of Pearls* and ran for eighteen episodes. The author was a little known imitator of Edgar Allan Poe, Thomas Prest. In 1862 a journeyman writer, Frederick Hazelton, adapted Prest's serial for the stage, and it has rarely been out of production since. Before gracing the boards as a Stephen Sondheim musical, the story was filmed three times, once starring Tod Slaughter.

The cannibalistic elements of the plot are reminiscent of the Scottish legend of Sawney Beane, but an alternative inspiration is Prest's own version of the murders of the Rue de la Harpe in Paris, in which he had the victims' bodies turned into savories by a pie-maker.

Now 'though you'd have said
That head was dead
For its owner dead was he
It stood on its neck
With a smile well bred
And bowed three times to me.

'Sweet Fanny Adams'

Expression meaning 'bugger all'. It was coined by the Royal Navy, who felt their tins of chopped mutton bore a striking resemblance to the state of eight-year-old Fanny Adams on the evening of 24 August 1867.

Earlier that day Fanny's head was cut off, and at about 7 p.m. a labourer – part of a search party – discovered it balancing uneasily on two poles laid side-by-side several hours after her eyes were observed drifting down the River Wey through the Hampshire countryside. One ear had been removed, and a leg and an arm hacked from her trunk, itself disembowelled. The heart was displayed separately.

Fanny spent the last hours of her life, a warm summer's afternoon, playing in Flood Meadow about four hundred yards from her home in Alton with her sister Lizzie and their friend Minnie Warner.

But the programme notes of a 1940 New York production refer to the *Newgate Calendar* of 29 January 1802, which described in detail the career of a twisted barber called Todd. Unfortunately, no copies of this issue have survived. But the anonymous *Romance of Newgate* (1884) contains an entry seemingly derived from this source, describing a 'Sweeney Todd' who traded for seventeen months as a hairdresser in Crutched-friars before moving into larger premises in Fleet Street.

It is likely that the house in question was 186 Fleet Street, and the *Annual Register* of 1880 recorded that when it was demolished a large pit of bones was found in its cellars. But these may have come from burials in nearby St Dunstan's Church.

The delicatessen in the story, Mrs Lovett's pie shop, was said to be in Bell Yard. Charles Fox, author of an 1878 retelling of the Sweeney Todd story, includes an account of an underground tunnel linking the barber's to the meat shop and it is possible that this passage existed prior to the rebuilding of the church 1831–3.

Another outside contender for derivation from a factual basis is Poo-Bah's ditty in Gilbert and Sullivan's 1885 *Mikado*. At the time, the fringes of the medical community were preoccupied with the debate on whether decapitated **heads** survived their removal from the main body trunk. Pooh-Bah himself had no doubts, and his words afford an uncannily accurate precognition of the fate of the convict Languille:

Along came Frederick Warner, a personable 29-year-old solicitor's clerk. He helped the three children pick blackberries before presenting Minnie and Lizzie with a penny-ha'penny to buy some sweets while he stayed to look after Fanny. Then he lured her to a nearby hopfield. Then he ripped her to pieces.

Noticed in the meadow by local women, Baker was arrested with blood on his clothes and two knives in his pockets. His diary entry for the afternoon read, 'Killed a young girl today. It was fine and hot.' Baker contended that these words recorded no more than current gossip and should be construed as 'Killed today – a young girl. The weather was fine and hot.' But the jury believed the 'it' referred to his butchery-work.

Baker's family suffered from a history of mental illness, and contemporaries ascribed his crime to 'moral insanity'. With hindsight, the killing has all the hallmarks of an early sex murder.

Swordstick

The purported murder weapon in the curious case of Colin Chisam. This British trial turned on the arcane question of whether the deceased, a young man called Henderson, was killed by a bullet or a swordstick. Whatever it was had passed right through him, and thus the lawyers argued this important issue in the abstract. In 1962 the penalty for murder with a firearm was death but the legislature had, through some oversight, made no corresponding provision for death by swordstick, and the aftermath of the trial saw the first forensic application of the electron-beam probe.

Colin Chisam, a Berwick-on-Tweed garage owner and arms collector, opened fire with a .22 repeater from his front door at three passing youths on the night of 5 August 1962. They were playing their transistor radio too loudly. Infuriated, the young men ran back to Chisam's house, forced their way into the front hall and set about him and his adopted son. After a scuffle one of the intruders, Tait, died in hospital from a fatal wound which traversed his body, with an entry hole on one side and an exit hole at the other.

Except in the case of an alibi, lawyers are under no obligation to divulge their line of defence in advance. At the trial the prosecution was surprised to hear that Tait had died of a swordstick wound contracted by impaling himself on top of Chisam, and five days of expert medical evidence were insufficient to resolve the question. For the Crown, Dr H. J. Walls's half-hearted experiments with a swordstick on a laboratory corpse proved inconclusive; it was only after the trial that he realised an electron-beam probe would provide incontrovertible evidence. Too late, he discovered the tiny traces of lead from a bullet on the torn threads of the entry hole through Tait's clothing.

By then Chisam had been convicted of manslaughter, always the most likely outcome since psychiatric reports diagnosed him as subject to a condition considered exceptional by experts and near-universal by everyone else, namely 'a paranoid disorder that made him feel he was always right and everyone else was always wrong'.

T

Tapes

Few killings have shocked the British public as deeply as the Moors Murders of the 1960s, and at the heart of darkness is the 16-minute tape-recording, made by Ian **Brady** and Myra **Hindley**, of 10-year-old Lesley Ann Downey during the last minutes of her life.

Lesley was 'snatched' on 26 December 1964 while on her way home from a fair on the local Recreation Ground. Hindley made a show of dropping some parcels and asked Lesley to help, first, by taking the shopping to the car, and then by unloading the vehicle at her home. Brady was waiting in a prepared room with his lights and camera and a tape recorder. He hoped to make money by selling the pictures to child sex perverts, but this was probably the least important motivational component. His primary objective was a permanent memento (see **Souvenirs**) which would, at the same time, complete his victim's defilement, reducing her to the status of a 'performer' in his tape collection.

The tape was consigned to a Left Luggage suitcase, deposited at Manchester's Central Station, containing the pair's paraphernalia of coshes, wigs, masks and ammunition. The police came across the ticket, Number 74843, in Hindley's prayer book, *The Garden of the Soul*.

After stripping Lesley and photographing her naked apart from ankle-socks, Brady raped and killed her. The pictures do not show much, just a naked little girl in a sequence of semi-obscene poses, gagged with a man's scarf – one leg in the air, or arms outflung and the like, rather like child-ish ballet exercises. The tape was more explicit, starting with a scream and the words 'Don't... please God help me' and ending with the background recording of 'The Little Drummer Boy'.

More than twenty years later Hindley wrote to Lesley's mother from prison: 'I now want to say to you, and I implore you to believe me, because it is the truth, that your child was not physically tortured, as is widely believed.' Taking the unpopular step of giving Hindley the benefit of the doubt, and limiting interpretation of the tape to the meaning of the recorded words, then it may represent nothing particularly unspeakable. But enlarging the frame by only a few minutes, Lesley was killed for pleasure, and the mere fact that the recording could be made, almost irrespective of its contents, under overhanging homicidal intent in a suburban living room, stained British conceptions about their society and the reach of evil just as surely as the Ripper murders did for the Victorians a hundred years ago.

Hindley was convicted as an accessory to two murders in 1966 and is still in prison. She was not physically present at four of the five killings, withdrawing upstairs to the bathroom while Lesley was strangled, and otherwise busying herself parking their van as Brady guided the children across the moors to their doom. Nor did she strike their last victim, Edward Evans. Hindley has now served almost the harshest sentence of any killer since the abolition of capital punishment, and if standard parole rules were applied to her case, she would be eligible for release. But the Home Office's freedom of action is uniquely circumscribed by public opinion.

Tax havens

Tax havens attract drug dealers. The fundamentals for a narcotics syndicate laundering money are identical to the requirements of large conglomerates shifting funds offshore in a tax avoidance scheme. Both need corporate confidentiality, banking confidentiality and a stable government.

A good place to look is in the Caribbean. In 1986 the British Virgin Islands provided a home for a mere 5,000 companies. Six years later, 65,000 legal entities were registered through the competing services of forty-nine company formation agencies, advertised, in the manner of escort services, as 'Strictly Confidential' or 'Very Discreet'. Virtually no information is disclosed to the authorities: no list of shareholders, no list of directors, no annual returns, just the name and the company 'objects', typically as broad as the notorious CIA sweeper-up clause allowing the pursuit of 'any business whatsoever'. Local governments have no idea who owns the companies. Nor do the company formation agents.

Refuges like the Virgin Islands solve the drug dealers' long-standing problem of hanging on to their lucre. In a personal account, drug money is vulnerable to confiscation. Traffickers want resources on which they can draw freely which do not belong to them technically, and the ideal arrangement is as an authorised signatory for company funds. But standard national regulations for disclosure under local Companies Acts make this impracticable – except in tax havens.

Drug barons buy businesses off the shelf, thwarting investigation with a network whereby Company A is owned by Company B which in turn is owned by Company A. Thus true ownership can never be ascertained. Stratagems devised by lawyers, bankers and tax consultants representing legitimate concerns are adopted wholesale, and today the Caribbean islands are depositaries for the proceeds of the international drug business, conferring legitimate status on the cartels.

Some traffickers squander fortunes on flash consumer goods like helicopters and yachts, others on gambling; the major heroin dealer Frank Lucas dropped $15 million at blackjack in Las Vegas with apparent nonchalance. Other operators get serious, collecting skyscrapers, luxury apartments, shopping centres, hotels and even banks.

The Virgin Islands are by no means the worst offenders. Anguilla boasts a bank on the airport runway, enabling 'slush' funds to be dropped off without the depositor entering the territory, and St Martin has *no* Customs checks; you just walk your suitcases through the airport. One ton in four of the cocaine estimated to pass through the Caribbean each week enters by this route.

In 1989 the United Nations talked tough as part of its War on Drugs programme. But the Basle edict of 'Know Your Customer' encountered an insuperable obstacle: tax havens make money by not knowing their customers.

See also **World-Wide Business Centre**

Techies

FBI slang for their technical squads specialising in electronic eavesdropping. A full techie team calls on the services of locksmiths, burglars, undercover operatives, surveillance teams and electronic experts known as 'buggies' or 'Dr Bugs'. Their task is to penetrate sensitive locations – for instance a *mafioso*'s house – and plant a listening device consisting of three elements, a miniature microphone and a thin wire, leading to a battery as big as a fireplace log. Post-installation, the site is manicured so that not even a speck of dust is out of place.

The signal (scrambled to defeat scanners) is transmitted to electrical boosters maybe a quarter of a mile away and relayed to the monitoring station, where listeners are on constant alert for counter-surveillance 'sweepers'.

In the days of the **Pizza Connection**, conversations intercepted by wire-taps on public payphones were oblique in the extreme, with drug dealers rambling on about consignments of 'suits', 'shirts' or 'lemons'. By the 1992 Gotti case, the techies secured direct access to the homes of *mafiosi* like Paul Ruggiero and Paul Castellano. The underboss of the Gambino family, Aniello Dellacroce, had a bug planted right beside his sickbed, effectively his office desk during his last years. John Gotti's sidekick Angelo Ruggiero, nicknamed 'Quack-quack' for his incessant chattering rather than his ducklike waddle, provided hours of easy listening, setting up a drugs link with the Bonanno family on the telephone, prattling away about his narcotics business for hours on end, threatening to lob creditors into a swimming pool with a man-eating shark or to chop rivals into pieces. By inextricably incriminating the entire upper echelons of the Gambino clan, he set it on a course of internal warfare.

Tapped at source, the Mafia verbals were unambiguous. Thus Alphonse Sciacia arrived at the Ruggerio home saying, 'I got thirty things of heroin. That's why I'm here.' John Gotti, overheard in Dellacroce's residence, was no less forthcoming: 'I'll kick his fucking brains in', or: ' I told him, you better come and check in every week. You miss one week, and I'll kill you, you cocksucker, fucking creep.' Evidence like this is hard to shrug off.

See **Decline, Trial**

Teeth-marks

Identifying a corpse from its teeth is an obvious step when dental records are available. By the 1940s, forensic horizons extended to a study of bite-marks on the corpse. Perhaps the idea first came to Professor Keith Simpson on viewing Margery Gardner's body in Notting Hill's Pembridge Court Hotel in June 1946. Her corpse displayed seventeen lash-marks from a whip, its distinctive diamond-pattern hatched into her flesh. 'If you find that whip you've found your man,' Simpson told the police, and it was located a few days later in an attaché case belonging to Neville George Clevely Heath. He was executed on 16 October 1946 for two murders.

Scrutinising Gardner's body, Simpson's interest was also engaged by the ferocious bite-marks on her nipples. But she had not died outright from the assault, and her bruising diffused into the surrounding tissues, blurring the outline of her assailant's dentistry. Two years later, Simpson was confronted by the corpse of a Mrs Margaret Gorringe, whose exposed right breast bore a usable impression of two upper front and four lower teeth. Their uncommon spacing, irregular shape and curious angles proved sufficient to convict her husband, already under suspicion. This was the first British case, but the body of 15-year-old Linda Peacock, discovered in a Glasgow cemetery on the morning of 7 August 1957, posed a tougher test of Simpson's ingenuity.

Linda died within minutes of being bitten, and her breast showed five distinct indentations. Two

were no more than small dark rings with pale centres. The biggest measured 7mm by 13mm, the result either of two adjacent teeth or one badly compacted molar. The twenty-nine suspects were all borstal boys from a local detention centre, and plaster casts of their teeth suggested that number fourteen possessed the requisite dentistry in the form of a sharp-edged right canine. For confirmation, the cautious Simpson had the upper and lower teeth mounted on a hinged clamp and, when a suitable body arrived in the mortuary, bit it. The marks did not match.

Attention now focused on the two ring-shaped abrasions. The literature of bite-marks, mostly in Swedish and Japanese, cast no light on their origin, but Dr Warren Harvey, Scotland's leading odontologist, reasoned that they could derive from teeth with a pit in their tip, corresponding to craters in the upper and lower *right* canines of cast number 11. But the marks on Linda's breast showed the ring marks to the *left*, indicating that the killer's head was upside-down at the time. In this orientation, number eleven's broken upper left incisor and its adjacent left lateral matched the large abrasion perfectly.

Medical evidence showed that the victim was strangled from behind, and the mud on suspect number eleven's trousers intimated that he pinioned his victim from behind while kneeling, and had leaned over her shoulder to exact his bite on her breast. One thousand canines from a test sample of 342 boys of similar age revealed that only two possessed the distinctive craters, the product of hypocalcination, and no single mouth contained two pits. Simpson wrote in his report, 'A jury should have no difficulty in understanding this evidence and appreciating its strength. It is akin to tool-marking evidence or fingerprints.' Gordon Hay, aged seventeen, was arrested and found guilty of murder.

Ted **Bundy** was another killer convicted by bite marks. In 1979 Dr Richard Souviron was able to satisfy the court that his lower left incisors, sharply askew from the rest of his teeth, caused the distinctive indentations in Lisa Levy's buttock.

Teeth-snatching

A variant on **body-snatching**. During his medical career, English surgeon Astley Cooper (1768–1841) was supplied with cadavers by the proficient Tom Butler, a hard-drinking dissecting room porter. Cooper kept in touch after Butler left St Thomas's Hospital; and in 1811 Cooper sent him off to Spain with an introduction to his nephew Bransby Cooper, a surgeon serving with the Royal Artillery in the Peninsular War. 'My dear Bransby,' wrote Cooper, 'Butler will tell you the purpose of his visit.'

At that time, false teeth were made of boxwood or – preferably – someone else's molars. Those of relatively fresh origin commanded a high price. 'Oh sir,' enthused Butler to his contact in Portugal, 'only let there be a battle and there'll be no want of teeth. I'll draw them as fast as the men are knocked down.' He did, after each engagement following Bransby Cooper around the battlefield among the casualties. Pincers at the ready, Butler extracted teeth enough from the dead and dying to net £300 from their sale in England, where this practical man set up as a dentist (see **Perera**).

But drink dragged Butler into debt and serious trouble, and he was sentenced to death for passing a stolen £5 note. In prison awaiting appeal, Butler turned his hand to articulating the disassembled skeleton of the prison governor's favourite horse. His handiwork was much admired by an influential foreign visitor, an Austrian Archduke, who pulled rank to secure a pardon from the Prince Regent, and Butler is believed to have ended his days in Ireland, shipping bodies for the surgical trade into Scotland.

In 1801 Astley Cooper attracted a large crowd outside his London house in St Mary Axe by dissecting an elephant in the street.

Terminology

Mass killers must be distinguished from their counterparts, the serial killers and the spree killers. Mass murderers kill a lot of people in one place; serial murderers kill one person at a time in a lot of places.

The predominant mass killer profile is of a desolate white male in his thirties or forties overwhelmed by personal failure. For this, everyone is responsible except himself – women, workmates, teachers, bosses, entire towns and sometimes the Devil. The malevolent schemes of his tormentors infuse the killer with a festering desire for revenge, fuelled by get-even films and empowered by a fascination with guns. At this stage only a precipitating trigger is needed, like losing a job or being dumped by a girlfriend.

There are, to date, no female mass murderers, partly because they do not regard firearms as fitting objects of veneration. Further, women are more likely to admit to depression, telephone a friend, or go to therapy.

The spree killer – the next evolutionary step – takes lives without the essential 'cooling off period' which marks out the serial killer. For an official 'spree' the killings take place in different locations; a simple walk-about during a twenty-minute 'event' will qualify.

Both the spree killer and the mass killer process undifferentiated consignments of victims; anyone crossing their path is at risk, as are the killers themselves. They often commit suicide or, in America, go on killing until they have to be shot.

The serial killer is unique in desiring both to kill and to live, achieving a delicate equilibrium that imbues his psyche with a certain fascination. More discriminating, he selects his targets, limiting them to a particular type of victim. The murder itself is more controlled, representing an endeavour to extract the maximum pleasure by proceeding deliberately from one stage to the next, for example from abduction through mutilation to termination and then ritual rearrangement of the corpse. Then comes the 'cooling off period', varying anywhere between a day, several months or even years, which constitutes his inert emotional phase. The underlying pattern bears a correspondence to the process of sex or drugs, enhanced by near-infinite reverberations of self-disgust: first wanting to do it, then doing it, then regretting it, then coming to terms with having done it, and finally wanting it again. The serial killer may move on, change jobs, go to prison for something else or die, but he is unlikely to take his own life, even during the course of capture by the police.

Confusion can arise between the categories. In his final tailspin, a serial killer on the run may embark on a killing spree, like Florida's Christopher Wilder.

These seemingly academic distinctions hold great practical significance for detection, notably in the USA where the mosaic of unsolved 'incidents' are, state by state, reported back to FBI headquarters at **Quantico**, and then disentangled into distinct strands as the computer stitches together apparently unrelated homicides into the work of a single man.

The minimum FBI qualification for a serial killer is three clearly separated deaths.

See also **Sex crimes, Trolling**

Terror

Screaming can be a mistake, inciting the aggressor to shut his victim up. On his arrest in 1943, Harold Loughans, the John Barleycorn murderer, stated not untypically: 'I want to say I done a murder job in Hampshire about fourteen days ago... It's a relief to get it off my mind. I had to stop her screaming, but I didn't mean to kill the old girl, but you know what it is when a woman screams.'

Loughans led a chequered career in the courts, his tendency to confess only marginally exceeded by his verve at securing acquittals. At his first trial there was a hung jury and, at the second, the prestigious but misguided evidence of Sir Bernard **Spilsbury** got him off. Loughans was sent down for another attempted murder. On his emergence from jail in 1963 he sued the *People* for libel, but the civil courts adjudged him guilty of the murder for which he was discharged under the criminal jurisdiction. Then, learning he had cancer, Loughans confessed to everything and died.

With **sex crimes**, by the time the perpetrator has the victim safe within his lair, screaming may prolong life. The attacker's goal is not to cause death (a mere by-product) but fear and degradation. As long as the victim can yell he retains play value. As a friend of Charles **Ng**'s put it, 'The **torture**, the pure terror – Ng wanted to see terror. He wanted to see them beg, to plead. That's what he really got off on... They had to beg for it to stop... And then, once they stopped, it was no longer fun. Then it's time to put a round in their head and move on to find another one.'

In a less extreme context, running away may, like screaming, provoke a gunman to fire. Britain's Michael Peckett was given the option during the 1992 Dryden shooting (see **Planning Officer**). He reasoned: 'I'm not going to run and get it in the back. If a rabbit's running, you shoot it. If it's still, you don't.' Be that as it may, Peckett stood his ground and survived to tell the tale.

According to survivors, staring into a gun barrel is very, very frightening. In the words of Ann Bristow, a 1992 victim of a Yorkshire armed robbery, 'You don't take your eyes off the gun. It's not like you think it would be, not like on television. It's stark panic. I've never been so frightened. I can't even talk about it now without shaking.' Britain's Midland Bank retains a firm of industrial counsellors, who report that the initial post-raid reaction is uncontrollable crying coupled with endless mental replays of the incident and inability to sleep. In America, victims prefer to take in a violent film or two; apparently this consigns the trauma to the realms of fantasy. But the English Miss Bristow now leaves the room at any hint of television gunplay.

It may be worth reserving one's fear for the physical consequences of being shot rather than the pain. According to writer Auberon Waugh, who accidentally fired a machine-gun, inflicting six wounds on himself, four to the chest, the immediate experience is not unpleasant: 'To those who suffer from anxieties about being shot I can give the reassuring news that it is almost completely painless. Although the bullets caused considerable devastation on the way out, the only sensation at the time was of a mild tapping on the front of the chest. I also felt suddenly winded as they went through a lung. But there was virtually no pain for about three quarters of an hour, and then only a dull ache.'

Thiefrow

Common parlance for Heathrow, the world's busiest international airport. Terminal One is the place to go. In a single year supercrook Geoffrey Senior stole £350,000 of property from the Heathrow baggage collection-points.

Senior hardly conforms to a master criminal's stereotype. An unemployed drifter with long greasy hair and no front teeth, he pitched up in London

388

penniless at the age of twenty and was drawn to the airport because of its warmth. It provided somewhere to stand. After a while, he noticed that anyone could stroll up to the baggage carousels for domestic passengers and take a suitcase. So he did.

His first theft netted £7,000 in cash stuffed into a Jiffy bag. 'I couldn't believe it was such a doddle,' he said. 'Like any drug, I became addicted and just couldn't give it up. Sometimes I tried to keep away, but the easiness kept taking me back.' Day after day, Senior would pick up two or three bags at a time, pile them onto a trolley and wheel them to the Underground, where he rifled through the luggage in a lavatory cubicle. He found a mine of cameras, jewellery, word-processors, watches and money; after his arrest, police unearthed £15,000 in an overlooked envelope in one discarded bag.

Senior's one concession to technique was to watch from the balconies until the crowd thronging the carousels thinned out, although he varied the times of his thefts so that the security and airline staff changed with the shifts, and invested in two suits, six ties and fifteen shirts to rotate his appearance – the only tangible capital investments from a high-earning year. The rest he dissipated on premium drink, car-hire, travel and on five-star hotels, which made a change from his Hammersmith squat.

Senior estimated his profits at £80,000. Once, another passenger confronted him. 'I admitted the mistake. He smiled, and even seemed to feel sorry for me, because I had no bags,' Senior said. 'I thought I could go on forever... There was no security to penetrate.'

In September 1991 Senior was caught trundling away a set of golf clubs. Sentenced to three years, he reviewed his life contentedly: 'It were really amazing, it's hard to tell you exactly how wonderful it was.'

His story makes traditional forms of robbery, like bank raids, look old-fashioned, but the expenditure of greater ingenuity provides no guarantee of increased success – as witness the career of the miniaturised vacuum cleaner pioneered by the gem thief Julio Cesar de Monraes Barros.

A 28-year-old Brazilian in Bangkok, Barros installed a brachial implant of a long thin tube running subcutaneously from the tip of the little finger on his left hand to the wrist, where the conduit emerged to join thicker piping, in turn routed to a storage pouch in the armpit. Barros powered the system by flexing his muscles to activate a small pump.

Barros and his accomplice, Paulo dos Santos, called on a string of jewellers posing as customers. Out came the dealers' boxes of precious stones. While Santos distracted the staff's attention, Barros hoovered up loose diamonds, using his little finger as the nozzle.

But this clever ruse only solved half the thieves' problem. It is one thing for the dealer not to know *how* his baubles were stolen but quite another not to notice that they *have* been stolen. This remained a pitfall. On 12 December 1991 Barros was arrested with £7,000 of gems in his armpit. For the avoidance of incredulity, police introduced their human vacuum cleaner to journalists, still festooned with lengths of rubber hosing.

Another technological innovation brought Jenny Webb, the British eighteenth-century pickpocket, greater dividends. Supposedly the illegitimate daughter of an aristocrat and a serving girl, Jenny arrived in London in 1721, and by the age of eighteen she ran a gang of forty pickpockets. Her particular contribution involved a special dress with slits cut in either side at waist level. She became adept at rifling her neighbours' purses through these apertures, generally in church, while seated with a pair of false, law-abiding arms reassuringly folded on her lap. Webb survived a sentence of transportation, bribing her way back to England, and was hanged at **Tyburn** in 1741.

Today, more money can be made by mundane pen-pushing occupations like mortgage fraud than armed robbery, as *mafioso* John Gotti noticed in the 1980s when he graduated to the New York concrete racket, which seemed easy meat compared to his previous daily grind of narcotics distribution, loan-sharking and gambling. In the eight years before the ring was smashed, the four participating families netted an estimated $8 million, extorting a levy of 1 per cent on all construction contracts over $2 million plus $2 for every cubic yard poured. But an infuriated Gotti discovered that an Israeli émigré, Michael Markowitz, an independent operator, had devised a way of creaming off federal and state revenues to the tune of $300 million in two years simply by shuffling paper.

Markowitz targeted the tax collected by wholesale gasoline distributors for remission to the authorities, setting up a string of dummy companies which collectively syphoned off somewhere in the region of a penny a gallon. Markowitz happily split his burgeoning proceeds with college-educated Michael Franzese of the Colombo family while Gotti slugged it out with the building trade and exacted rake-offs from flea-market operators. In the event, all the participants wound up dead or in prison, but, one step further towards legality, or at least sophistication, the criminal element fades away, leaving little more than a grey smudge of suspected fraud and exponentially increased takings.

See also **High Finance**

Thompson, Edith (1894–1923)

Edith Thompson, an unhappily married book-keeper, lived with her husband Percy in the London suburb of Ilford. He beat her, but one day in June 1921 young Frederick Bywaters – a good-looking laundry steward on a P. & O. ocean liner – came to stay between voyages. He was a schoolmate of Edith's brother, and their families were longstanding friends.

The August Bank holiday of 1921 turned out fine and sunny and, while sitting in the garden, the 19-year-old Bywaters overheard Percy quarrelling with his wife. The sound of Edith being thrown across the room, where she collided with a chair, prompted him to intervene. He brought the fight to a close; angry words were exchanged, the possibility of divorce mooted, and later a tearful Edith crept up the stairs to the young man's bedroom where, for the first time, they kissed. Shortly afterwards Bywaters left to live with his mother and, as extra-marital affairs go, their romance began on a relatively honourable footing. Over the next two months the pair enjoyed assignations in teashops, parks or at *thé dansants* where they shared covert embraces; 'their tune' was *One Stolen Hour*. Percy refused to countenance a separation or a divorce and, on 9 September, the lovers finally had sexual intercourse after registering at a small hotel under false names. Bywaters sailed shortly afterwards and they consoled themselves with a passionate correspondence.

By September 1922 Bywaters was back in London. The liaison resumed, and on the afternoon of 3 October the lovers met in a London teashop. They parted to allow Edith to accompany her husband to the theatre, and that night the married couple caught the train back to Ilford and walked home down Belgrave Road.

Frederick Bywaters jumped out of the shadows. Seizing Percy by the arm, he cried, 'Why don't you get a divorce, you cad?'

'I've got her, I'll keep her and I'll shoot you,' said Percy. Bywaters pulled out his seafarer's knife. The two men struggled. 'Oh don't, don't,' Edith implored. Percy fell to the pavement, coughing blood, and Bywaters vanished into the dark while Edith rushed down the street towards a knot of distant onlookers crying, 'Oh my God, will you help me, my husband is ill; he is bleeding!' By the time a doctor arrived Percy was dead. 'Why did you not come sooner?' she sobbed.

On these unpromising facts Edith was hanged for her husband's murder. The prosecution contended that she plotted the killing with Bywaters over tea that afternoon, and in evidence – the only evidence – produced sixty-two love letters, some retrieved from Bywaters' ship's locker and others from his mother's home. In their totality Edith's letters were harmless: hundreds of pages of endearments interspersed with multitudinous schemes to break the *impasse* by elopement, divorce or even joint suicide. Among these vapourings were Edith's idiotic plans for murdering her husband. She would feed him lightbulbs – 'big pieces too – not too powdered'.

According to the written record, she tried this method three times after wearying of her labours at **poisoning**. 'I'm going to try glass again occasionally – when it's safe,' she wrote. 'I've got an electric light globe this time.' Did this work? Apparently not. 'The third time he found a piece – so I've given it up – until you come home.'

The words 'until you come home' hold the key. Edith was frantic to bolster Bywaters' interest and ensure that he did come back, whatever the marital stalemate. The only avenue for progress lay in their imaginations, and Edith's medicinal constructions embraced exotic but unspecified toxins. She entreated Bywaters to send 'something to make him ill'. Then she complained, 'You said it was enough for an elephant. Perhaps it was. But you don't allow for the taste making it possible for only a small quantity to be taken.' Her husband was becoming suspicious: 'He puts great stress on the fact of the tea tasting bitter "as if something had been put in it".'

Nothing had. No trace of poison or glass was found in Percy's body. But when the extracts from her correspondence were joined end-to-end they sounded sinister in the extreme. Other incidental material made matters worse. 'I am still willing to dare all and risk all,' wrote Edith in reference to her intended abortion. It was already an uphill task to persuade the jury of the innocence of an adulteress, and her defence dared not attempt to exculpate her from husband-murder by depicting her as an adulterous abortionist, capable of child-murder.

Edith's ambiguous phrases such as 'drastic measures' were pulled into the web, and only occasionally could her barrister, Sir Henry Curtis-Bennett, demonstrate that sentences like 'He is still well' referred to the unsurprising well-being of a bronze monkey, a gift from Bywaters. Edith tightened the noose round her neck by including news clippings of 'Poisoned chocolates' or 'Patient killed by an overdose' with her love-letters. But 'Woman the Consoler' or 'Masterful Men' were the themes of more frequent inserts, and in the dock Bywaters was asked by the prosecution: 'Did you ever believe in your own mind that she herself had given any poison to her husband?'

'No,' he replied. 'It never entered my mind at all. She had been reading books. She had a vivid way of declaring herself. She would read a book and imagine herself as the character in the book.' Perhaps the defence could have dismissed Edith's letters as the gushings of a vain and silly romantic if she had kept silent in court. But, anxious to impress, this obstinate, highly-strung woman insisted on testifying to prove her *truthfulness*, a grave tactical error compounded by the sexuality she oozed from the dock, and her cause suffered further damage from the judge, Mr Justice Shearman, who was opposed to adultery. He summed up against the defendants in a mood of strong moral indignation, ridiculing the notion (which had not been proposed) that 'the love of a husband for his wife is something improper because marriage is acknowledged by the law, and that the love of a woman for her lover – illicit and clandestine – is something great and noble'.

Both Bywaters and Thompson were sentenced to death. 'I say the verdict of the jury is wrong,' said Bywaters from the dock. 'Edith is not guilty.' The trial never addressed the issues. Had it been established that Edith did try to poison her husband (for

which attempted murder would be the appropriate charge), it remained to prove a conspiracy for the stabbing. The **Court of Appeal** dismissed the affair as 'a squalid and rather indecent case of lust and adultery'. A petition for clemency many thousands strong was submitted to the Home Secretary, and on 6 January, as the fatal day approached, Bywaters said of Edith from his cell, 'I swear she is completely innocent. She never knew that I was going to meet them that night... She didn't commit the murder. I did. She never knew about it. She is innocent, absolutely innocent. I can't believe that they will hang her'.

Bywaters' 'confession' was driven 200 miles through the night to the Home Secretary at a country house weekend. But there was no reprieve. Edith broke down when they came to fetch her on 9 January 1923 after a night of semi-consciousness, the first woman to be executed in Britain for fifteen years. Two female warders carried her to the scaffold and there, in the words of Sir Henry Curtis-Brown, 'Mrs Thompson was hanged for immorality'.

Of necessity, Percy's role in the love triangle is as reported by Edith and Frederick.

Throne Room, The

Special lavatory. Smugglers suspected of 'body-packing' do their business in the Throne Room's dry lavatory under the watchful eye of Revenue men (or women) clad in white surgical outfits. A small quantity of water is admitted to wash the suspect's faeces into a stainless steel box fronted by a glass viewing panel and a rubber-glove insert; the compartment resembles a hi-tech nuclear enclosure. Inside this box, the precious excrement undergoes a full examination: it can be washed down with water jets, subjected to probes or gently palpated by the gloved hand. The detritus is flushed away, and any contraband collected in a shiny perspex container.

The preceding generation of equipment consisted of a colander.

Throwaways

Ted **Bundy**'s term for his victims, whom he *threw away* afterwards, dumping them from his car like garbage. But in the California of the 1970s, Patrick Kearney and David Hill, the 'Trashbag Killers', developed the idea a step further, as take-aways. They put their bagged-up victims out for collection.

Bundy was fastidious in his vocabulary, posing interrogators with delicate linguistic problems in their search for inoffensive euphemisms. To Bundy, 'people' or (even worse) 'victims' was not an acceptable wording, and one interviewer hit on the euphemism 'cargo', giving rise to the following exchange.

'Is the cargo dead or alive when you put it in the vehicle?'

'I don't like to use that terminology.'

'Is the cargo *damaged* when it's in the vehicle?'

'Yes, sometimes it's damaged and sometimes it's not.'

Thugs

The term derives from the Thuggee cult, prevalent in India from at least the middle of the sixteenth century until its suppression by the British in 1853. The devotional act consisted of strangling suitable travellers (ruling out Europeans, poets, women and defective specimens lacking a hand or nose) with a yellow and white silk strip called a *rhumal*. Since many Thugs held respectable positions in society, the act of worship entailed taking a month off to form a gang to ramble on the subcontinent's roads, killing as they went. Unsuspecting prospects were enjoined to look upwards at some fascinating sight in the sky, thus exposing their necks.

To avoid distension of the corpse, leading to discovery through disinterment, the body was slit up the stomach and, what with dead men telling no tales, the hereditary cult's existence remained largely unsuspected by Europeans. Rough estimates suggest

that some 40,000 fell victim annually. A leading practitioner was one Behram, said at his trial to have 931 souls to his credit culled from the district of Oudh between 1790 and 1840. Another remarked in 1833: 'Sahib, I ceased counting when I was sure of my thousand victims.'

The sect was both discovered and ended in a few years by an English soldier-turned-magistrate, William Sleeman, who persuaded the first captured gang leader to turn Queen's evidence, betraying other gangs in return for his life. Sleeman repeated the technique, leapfrogging from gang to gang, and eventually attained the position of Superintendent for the Suppression of Thuggees.

Tichborne Claimant, The

Nineteenth-century British inheritance farce marking the outer reaches of either self-delusion or wilful cussedness.

In March 1854 the young Sir Roger Charles Tichborne set sail for South America in the hope of forgetting a blighted love affair with his cousin, Katherine Doughty. His ship, the *Bella*, foundered somewhere off Brazil; her log-book was recovered 400 miles from land.

Back in England his mother, Lady Henriette Tichborne, refused to accept that her son was dead. Said to be a woman 'of a singularly perverse, unamiable disposition', she kept a candle burning in her son's bedroom and eleven years later was still pursuing rumours of his survival with advertisements in the English and colonial press.

Over in Australia, the reading room of the Mechanics Institute in Wagga Wagga was frequented by an uncouth, semi-literate butcher, Tom Castro. There he saw the newspaper announcements, took a long hard look at the *Illustrated London News* of 1862 celebrating the enviable Tichborne estates complete with church and village in Hampshire's Itchen valley, and noted in his pocket-book: 'Some men has plenty money and no brains, and some men has plenty brains and no money. Surely men with plenty money and no brains were made for men with plenty brains and no money.'

Castro was verging on bankruptcy and so, one day in 1866, he scratched the missing baronet's initials 'RCT' on his pipe and called on his new solicitor, Mr Gibbes. At the meeting, Castro wondered aloud whether valuable property in England would be caught by any composition with his creditors. The astute Gibbes spotted the initials on the pipe-bowl and soon put two and two together, forcing Castro to admit that he was none other than the missing baronet. Then, in his new role as Sir Roger Charles Doughty Tichborne, Castro was coaxed into writing home to break the happy news of his survival.

Spelling – and grammar – were problems, but Castro requested funds by return 'has I can not get serfiance of money to come home with'. On receipt, the delighted Lady T. ascribed her long-lost son's poor showing to his expensive public school education, expressing concern that her 'poor dear Roger confuses everything in his head just as in a dream'. But neither her professional advisers nor her more conventional heirs, with whom she was already at loggerheads, were so sure.

Castro moved his family to Sydney, where he became a popular fixture, engaging a secretary, nursemaid and valet. Money flowed in, and out. Struggling to pay the bill of his hotel, he purchased it with a bouncing cheque signed 'Roger Tichborne'. By the time the draft was returned to drawer, Castro was en route to Paris, where mother and son finally met in a Paris hotel. The coarse-featured Castro, who weighed twenty-six stone and had at school been nicknamed Bullocky on account of his near-limitless extent, was immediately recognised by Lady Tichborne as the slender, delicate nine-stone Sir Roger.

Despite her son's infirmity, which obliged him to lie facing the wall in a darkened room, Lady Tichborne (possibly out of malice) was able to pick out the unmistakable family ears. Her faith overcame Castro's childhood recollections of his grandfather (who died before he was born), the memories of his schooldays at Winchester (Sir Roger was educated at Stoneyhurst) and tales of his early days as an Army trooper (Sir Roger was a commissioned officer). She arranged for Castro to receive a token allowance of £1,000 a year while the formalities were sorted out. These involved the ejection of a Colonel Lushington from Castro's ancestral seat at Tichborne House, but before matters reached this stage Lady Tichborne was dead.

Amid tremendous excitement the legal proceedings began on 10 May 1871 at the Westminster Session Court. The simple issue of whether Castro, an obvious impostor, was entitled to the Tichborne millions became obscured by so much detail that the trial ran for months. Favourable identification witnesses were called in droves; generals, colonels, JPs, clergymen, Deputy-Lieutenants, ladies and servants – over a hundred men and women of good standing swore that Castro was the long-lost baronet.

The effete Sir Roger (top left), Castro (second row, right), other principals and five prosperous lawyers

The only poor performance was put in by Castro, who displayed convincing ignorance of his former life first as a child, then as a student, and finally as an officer with the Sixth Dragoon Guards. There was much ribaldry when he alleged that Caesar was a Greek; nor did he know what 'quadrangle' meant, although Stoneyhurst boys talk of little else. Not that Castro was idle in the five years preceding the case; he studied the family's history,

Castro doffs his hat as he arrives for his first day in court. Note his bulk.

and hired two regimental servants to pad out gaps in his military career.

On the 102nd day of proceedings he withdrew his claim under a welter of inconsistencies. Then he was indicted for perjury in a hearing which ran for 188 days, notable for the weight of Lord Cockburn's summing, tipping the scales at eight-and-a-half pounds in bound volume form. The court concluded, possibly erroneously, that Castro was a former immigrant from the East End, Arthur Orton, and sentenced him to fourteen years hard labour. After remission for good conduct, he was released from Dartmoor in 1884 and died in destitution on April Fools' Day four years later.

Tobacco

Said, with minor inexactitude, to be prison currency. Until very recently tobacco was what was bought with prison currency, consisting of anything and everything.

In their impoverished environment, prisoners scavenge and swap what they can: pencil stubs, pins, bits of string, paper clips or scraps of cardboard. Give a man the striker from a gas lighter, add a scrap of wood, a twist of mop rope and a length of plug chain, and he will assemble a cigarette lighter. Matchsticks make matchstick models, rags turn into rag toys.

So bare and dead is life inside that released prisoners enthuse over mundane objects like door furniture. Paddy Hill, who spent sixteen years inside after his wrongful conviction for the Birmingham pub bombing, devoted his first morning of freedom in March 1991 to studying a doorknob as he allowed its implications to sink home. 'I stared at it for forty-five minutes,' he recalled a year later, 'I was almost paralysed.'

In the words of Ken Smith, author of *Inside Time*: 'In prison, which is all waste, nothing is wasted.' Discarded biros, for instance, can be turned into syringes, much in demand now that the traditional prison economy is under threat: tobacco has been replaced by narcotics. According to an inmate released in 1990, referred to in press reports as 'Cathy': 'I did my first stint in prison in the 1970s when cigarettes were the major currency. Now money, jewellery and clothes are bartered for cannabis and heroin.'

The 1991 British report by Professor John Gunn estimated that one in ten male convicts, and one in four women, are hooked on hard drugs. No matter how resourceful the prisoners, injection equipment tends to be shared and, given the prevalence of anal sex, there can be few more fertile hotbeds for the spread of Aids.

Tobacco smuggling remained big business with the Sicilian Mafia until the 1970s. They ran cigarettes into Italy, ultimately dealing in entire shiploads of 40,000 cases which provided gainful employment for thousands in the distribution chains. When the trade flagged towards the end of the decade, one of the old-time tobacco smugglers – the *mafioso* Nunzio La Mattina from Sicily – turned his expertise to narcotics. Thus was born the **Pizza Connection** – successor to the **French Connection** – which poured billions of dollars of heroin into America.

By 1980 La Mattina was in financial difficulties; he owed his supplier Yasar Musullu $11 million. But in the world of serious drug trafficking this is not an unimaginable sum. Musullu clocked up a career total of eight tons of **opium**, generating a profit of $57 million and, similarly, Colombia's **Escobar** cartel offered to wipe out the whole of their country's debt of $3 billion in return for legal immunity. But La Mattina was eventually murdered after reporting that one of his couriers had been taken for $1.3 million in a hold-up.

And lastly, during the Second World War, the issue of free tobacco was pressed into harness as an SS incentive scheme for shooting prisoners. Shortly after D-Day on 6 June 1944, the guards at Sylt, the most brutal of the Channel Islands' death camps, were told: 'Men, I remind you once again of the rules laid down in the sentries' orders, and I personally will give any SS man who shoots a prisoner attempting to escape three days special leave and twenty-five cigarettes.'

As there was nowhere to escape to on the tiny island of Alderney the inmates had to be encouraged. According to survivor Otto Spehr (imprisoned as a socialist), the guards 'cut down the fence of the camp and pushed the men out – the moment they stepped over the camp boundary they were shot down'. The records of British Military Intelligence describe how the Sylt guards 'competed in getting leave by shooting prisoners for the smallest offences, for example, they threw away cigarette ends and as soon as an inmate bent down to pick them up they shot them.'

Tongs

Question: when is a **Triad** not a Triad? Answer: when it is a Tong. Or perhaps not. In America, the Chinese were long the subject of institutional racism, epitomised by the Chinese Exclusion Act of 1882 banning further immigration and denying citizenship to existing Chinese residents. So they remained (and remain) an exploited inward-looking ethnic group, crammed into the hermetic ghettos of Chinatown where they established their own town halls or 'Tongs'. It has never been clear whether these tongs are merely self-help associations or straightforward overseas branches for illegal Hong Kong syndicates. Nor did it seem to matter much, as long as the Chinese kept to themselves.

Mock Duck was an early Tong leader, head of New York's 'Hip Sings' (hence, to be 'hip'). From 1900 to 1906 Duck waged a bloody war with his rival Tom Lee for Chinatown's **opium** dens, and hundreds perished before the two gangs finally signed the 1906 peace treaty at the home of Judge Warren W. Foster. Duck was an idiosyncratic marksman. On scenting trouble, he would drop to a crouching position in the streets and close his eyes tight. Then he blazed away madly in all directions, accounting for dozens of 'enemies'.

Even the so-called 'hatchet wars' of the 1920s were regarded as a private affair, and it still takes a

white corpse to flush out media attention, a trait manifested in San Francisco on 4 September 1977 after three Joe Boys raided the Golden Dragon restaurant gunning for the Wah Ching Sings in a struggle for dominion of the firework business. The attackers left four diners and one waiter dead, plus eleven wounded, all innocent bystanders, and suddenly the media were everywhere. In the words of a San Francisco cop, 'We had some fifty gang murders before the Golden Dragon, they were all Chinese-to-Chinese. The moment the violence spread beyond the Chinese, the politicians were jumping on camera.'

Certainly the Tongs are excellent in parts, fulfilling many charitable community functions. Membership is legal. But according to a Hong Kong police officer, the American Tongs are public fronts for the Triads: 'Rest assured some members are criminal and are using the Tong's apparatus to control everything from gambling to narcotics.'

Since the mid-1960s each Tong has attracted the allegiance of a particular youth gang, such as the Green Dragons or the Ghost Shadows, who terrorise the neighbourhood, driving home the doctrine of government through intimidation. The gangs extort 'protection' from local tradesmen and make examples of those (like Mon Hsiung Ting of New York's Tien Chau chop house, shot on 16 July 1989) stubborn enough to refuse. Neighbourhood restaurant openings are welcome events, triggering an inaugural payment of 'lucky money', often a multiple of the number 108 in honour of the contingent of Buddhist monks who defended the Shaolin monastery in the seventeenth century. A thousand and eighty dollars is thus a common backhander, paid in the 'red envelope' traditional among the Chinese for gifts.

At the least, the Tongs provide a tempting takeover target in the run-up to the Hong Kong criminal exodus of 1997, and the word is that the Tsung Tsin Association, one of New York's wealthiest, is now (if it was not before) a front for the Sun Yee On **triad**.

See also **Recruitment**

Torso Murders, The

In a three-year span between 1934 and 1938, someone in Cleveland, Ohio claimed the lives of a good dozen down-and-outs, some men, some women, in general mutilating or dismembering the bodies but invariably cutting off their heads, six of which were never found.

The 'Torso Murderer' is sometimes reckoned America's first serial killer and, as with **Jack the Ripper**, the phenomenon left the police floundering. The case shows detection in a transitional stage, with intensive and traditional efforts directed at establishing the victims' identities. With luck and application, this occasionally revealed who they were, but not who the killer was, and eventually a 'Torso Clinic', the forerunner of the DeSalvo seminar, was convened. The thirty-four professionals attending it included policemen, pathologists and medical consultants who agreed on seven 'points', groping their way towards a primitive profile. Otherwise, efforts concentrated on grilling those singled out by neighbours and acquaintances, including such exotic local deviants as the 'Voodoo Doctor', the 'Cave Dweller', the 'Chicken Freak', the 'Mad Russian' and the 'Crazy Greek'. Three hundred suspects were interviewed, thousands of telephone calls fielded, but for all his flair, Eliot Ness, Cleveland's Director of Public Safety, was at a loss: 'The murderer doesn't seem to leave many clues. This man seems to specialise in the sort of person nobody is likely to miss.'

When Ness made his move, it was supremely ill-judged, sullying a fine career. On 17 August, backed by eleven squad cars, two vans and three firetrucks, he cordoned off the shantytown under the Eagle Street ramp at midnight and battered his way into the down-and-outs' hovels, dragging off sixty-three derelicts to the police cells and then searching shack-to-shack to discover nothing more incriminating than two dogs and three kittens. Ness defended his actions on the grounds that he was hunting for clues or, in the alternative, bent on saving potential victims, and then had the settlements razed to the ground.

The case started on 5 September 1934 when a carpenter out for a walk noticed a curious object protruding from the sands on the Lake Erie foreshore. It was the lower half of a woman, severed at the waist and knees, and this section proved a perfect match for the upper remains discovered in North Perry by a local handyman. A fortnight later two boys playing in the Kingsbury Run, a railway cutting site of a Great Depression shantytown,

stumbled over a headless, emasculated body and, thirty feet away, in the thick brush, the police located another corpse. Both were cleanly presented and tidily arranged, legs and heels together. They had been killed elsewhere, washed, transported by car and then ferried down a steep incline to the burial site. Their genitalia lay discarded a few yards away, and ten feet beyond the detectives noticed hair growing out of the dirt. They exposed a severed head planted in the ground, and on post-mortem it emerged that decapitation was the cause of death. Although an inevitable consequence, the technique is rarely adopted by murderers.

The *Plain Dealer* reported it as 'the most bizarre double murder', and the smart money was on a perverted love triangle. The killings were not linked to the Lake Erie corpse, nor were the next three victims, all neatly dismembered. But the upper half of a headless trunk found in Kingsbury Run on 10 September 1936 ensured that twenty-five police were assigned to the case, with the perpetrator dubbed the 'Horrible Headhunter' by the press. In the absence of any promising leads, on 14 September Ness summoned a think-tank, the 'Torso Clinic', which agreed on the premise that the killer was demented but not insane and might well be leading an ostensibly normal life. It seemed that he possessed a definite knowledge of human anatomy on a par with, say, a hunter or a butcher; that he was large and strong, lived in or near Kingsbury Run and had access to a laboratory or workshop. His *modus operandi* was to befriend hobos and derelicts; the contents of their stomachs suggested that he snared them with offers of food and perhaps shelter; the lack of resistance cuts or signs of restraint implied that some were decapitated in their sleep. In today's parlance, the killings were highly **organised**, but at the time the sexual motivation was denied. Apparently, the bodies were dismembered simply to facilitate transportation, but it is hard to see how severing their genitalia helped.

Four more corpses were in the pipeline, and by the time the last two came to light on the waterfront on 16 August 1938 Cleveland was in a state of hysteria. The National Guard's 112th Observation Squadron overflew the city taking purposeless aerial photographs and, in the week starting 22 August, Ness organised a house-to-house search of the Roaring Third precinct. Six teams

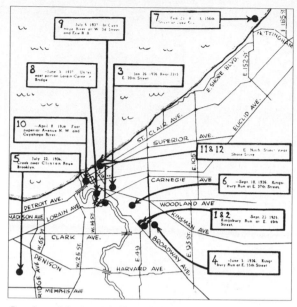

Locations of the 'torso' bodies in Cleveland

checked an area covering ten square miles, finding nothing. Perhaps they were expecting a blood-caked charnel house, but the dismembering room, its bodies flown, could have presented an innocuous aspect. Years later, Ness revealed that he had a homosexual suspect, pseudonymously known as Gaylord, under close watch. After repeated interviews, Gaylord put Ness to his proof, but before the case was fully established, he confined himself to a mental home and died the following year.

Ness made no mention of this lead at the time. Contemporary excitement centred on slaughterhouse worker Frank Dolezal, arrested on 5 July 1939. He had actually lived with the victim of 26 January 1936, Florence Portillo, and was a habitué of a run-down corner tavern on 20th Street frequented by all three identified victims. Eventually he confessed: 'I hit her with my fist. She fell into the bathroom and hit her head... Then I took a knife and cut off her head. Then I cut off her legs, then her arms...' But none of Dolezal's dates or facts tallied and, the moment he gained access to a lawyer, he recanted, claiming that his admissions had been beaten out of him. After he committed suicide in police custody on 24 August, it emerged that his interrogation had left permanent scars and six broken ribs.

Then there was the letter, perhaps from the real killer, mailed to the Chief of Police on 21 December 1938: 'You can rest easy now as I have gone out to sunny California for the winter. I felt bad operating on those people but science must advance. I shall soon astound the medical profession... What did their loss mean in comparison to all the hundreds of sick and disease-twisted bodies?' That same year a longshoreman, Emil Fronek, was almost kidnapped off his pitch by police and made to repeat a detailed story of his days as a drifter in 1935. Fronek related in convincing minutiae how a bogus doctor befriended him, inveigling him to a second floor apartment on 55th Street with the promise of a meal and a pair of shoes. Fronek was convulsed by stomach pangs as he ate and, deducing that he had been drugged, staggered out before losing consciousness. He woke up three days later barely alive. His assailant was five feet six and weighed about 150 pounds, with a light complexion and sandy hair. Fronek spent several fruitless days with the police hunting the shifting tenements for the office.

Cleveland saw its last Torso corpse in 1938, but in 1942 three more corpses with comparable mutilations were discovered in freight cars outside New Castle, Pennsylvania. A final, similar body was discovered on 22 July 1950.

See also **Heads, living, Untouchables**

Torture

Like democracy, torture can be traced directly to the Greeks and is mentioned in Aristophanes' *The Frogs* as the appropriate method for interrogating 'human-footed stock' (slaves). It descended via the Romans without adulteration to the Middle Ages and beyond, playing a role in official criminal procedure until its abolition in the 1800s throughout most of Western Europe.

The ancient and irrational dogma of the exceptional crime, so dangerous to the state that anything (for instance, torture for treason) was permissible in its prosecution, has been largely superseded. In its stead stands the modern concept of subversive crimes against an all-powerful, but strangely vulnerable, state that are so dangerous that anything is permissible in their prosecution (for instance, torture for suspected treason). Following its primary eradication in the first quarter of the nineteenth century, torture proliferated like cancer, starting in the colonies and now practised officially or otherwise in one country out of three.

From the twelfth century the history of torture was entwined with the history of **justice**, except in England where the reforms of Henry II established a legal structure that all but dispensed with it. Elsewhere, torture became a means of obtaining justice. It extracted confessions, in many cases regarded as the only reliable form of first-hand evidence.

Since the systematic infliction of agony comprised part of the legal process, its Continental exercise was finely graded according to precedent and protocol, forming the subject of thousands of pages of learned discourse on a par with, say, ecclesiastical law; presumably, ambitious mothers boasted of their sons' preferment as attorneys in torture.

The public prosecutor's first duty was to establish the truth by other means; in theory, torture was his last resort for cases where other evidence proved insufficient. A strong *prima facie* case would automatically precipitate the procedure, but the accused could lodge an interlocutory appeal, contending either that the judge had failed to satisfy the prerequisite evidential criteria for torturing, or that he was an exempted person, for instance a knight, professor, pregnant woman or king.

Even if he went down on appeal, the defendant was entitled to a properly conducted torture session. First the instruments of his **dismemberment** were ritually displayed, and their anatomical application expounded in a last-ditch endeavour to concentrate his mind. During the session, a medical expert remained in attendance, together with a notary and, of course, the judge who put the questions. Prudent prosecutors restrained their zeal for fear of provoking a civil action for improper torturing, generally espousing methods hallowed by traditional usage. Nothing new, nothing showy, was the protocol; the infliction of finely calibrated torment was a Christian undertaking. Many tortures were only administered for a specific and limited time governed by however long it took the judge to recite the Creed – a ghastly process, but still infinitely preferable to the random barbarities inflicted outside the system by, for instance, the seventeenth-century French buccaneer Montbars of Languedoc, who would slit his victim's stomach, wrench out one end of the intestines, nail them to a post, and then use a firebrand to compel the man to dance to

death as he unravelled his guts. He was particularly unpleasant to Spaniards.

Under the law, admissions counted for little until repeated in court. The defendant could recant, but his professional advisers would explain that this only courted another bout against an increased presumption of guilt, since he had already confessed. It is unlikely that hard-core enthusiasts ever observed the theoretical niceties, nor were the results entirely reliable. As the eighteenth century progressed, dispassionate observers discerned a definite tendency among tortured suspects to stake claims to murders which they could not conceivably have committed or even to admit responsibility for ones that had never happened (see **False Confessions**).

In Britain, the best remembered torturer is Charles Richardson, sentenced to twenty-five years on 6 June 1967. His implements included golf clubs, knives, lighted cigars, pliers (for ripping out teeth), electric fires (for toasting) and a hand-operated electric generator.

Torture today is the stock-in-trade of the **organised** serial killer, who deliberately controls and prolongs the process of extinguishing life. Fine distinctions must be drawn. It is not the offender's infliction of pain that produces arousal but the victim's response to it. In the words of **Quantico**'s Gregg McCrary, 'These offenders make their victims scream and beg for mercy, beg for their lives and so on. This is why **Chikatilo** stabbed them in a way which would cause a slow and painful death. It was far more gratifying for him to do so.'

Here, torture is equated with sex, but in another mutation the sadism is a prelude to sexual defilement, where the victim's degradation justifies her death. According to FBI Agent Robert Hazelwood, one killer explained to his victims, 'First I'm going to torture you in the most horrible and painful manner I can think of. Then I'm going to abuse you sexually in the most degrading way I can think of. Then I'll kill you in the slowest and most painful way I can conceive... Do you have any questions?'

Another murderer tortured a prostitute for six weeks before the kill. Robert Andrew Berdella, from Kansas, tormented his bound captives for days, beating them with boards, spiking them with needles, using bleach, drain cleaner and electricity, and sticking his fingers into their eyeballs. Interviewed in

1992 he asserted that he 'never found bondage and non-consensual sex that stimulating'. Asked to reconcile this view with his track record, he replied: 'It was done to perhaps control these individuals, to modify them, to make them controllable so they would be consensual.'

After four days of torment, his sixth and last victim was too broken to run away and only required physical restraint when Berdella went out. Otherwise, like one of Dahmer's **zombies**, the captive ambled round the house with his will broken. Asked what the process had accomplished, Berdella replied, 'A willing sex toy.' Individuals who were pre-consensual – that is, *willing* to be tied up – never became victims when they were at his mercy. They were happy to stay anyway.

See also **de Sade, Sex Crimes, Terror**

Trading justice

Term for English parish magistrates from whom a convict could secure acquittal or release in return for drink, money or sex. The practice was widespread, perhaps the most famous exponent being Thomas De Veil (d. 1746), who needed supplementary income for his army of twenty-five legitimate children and droves of bastard offspring. An avid fornicator, De Veil had a special bedchamber leading off his Bow Street office.

De Veil's early life displayed a spectacular talent for dissipation, and as a trading justice he was unusual not for his run-of-the-mill corruption but for his conscientious dedication. Not only did he think like a detective, he became one in response to approaches for outside advice, thereby anticipating the first fictional consulting sleuth – Sherlock Holmes – by more than a century.

De Veil's triumphs included having the rare acumen for the period to check a suspect's knife (with a broken-off tip) against the innards of a forced lock to a burgled house. In June 1741 he solved the mystery of the missing Mr Penny, Principal of Clement's Inn, by rational interrogation of the suspect and a thorough search for the body. These common-sense procedures were as rewarding as they were novel. Penny's body was found stuffed into an outside privy, head first, his throat slit by a disaffected servant with a fruit-knife.

See also **Fielding**

Traffic lights

Until 1930, New York traffic lights were switched off at three in the morning. This gave late-night robbers a clear run in their getaway vehicles, and the decision to keep the signals on round the clock had an appreciable impact on crime patterns. In Joe Valachi's words: 'It's getting tougher all the time... After all, if I'm being chased by one cop's car and I go through these lights, I will draw attention and have a hundred cars chasing me. Jesus!'

So Valachi decided to get out of the uncertainties of robbery and into something more secure. He joined the Mafia. But perhaps he need not have worried. According to writer John Mortimer, the late and unlamented financial fraudster Robert Maxwell gave his chauffeur standing orders to shoot red lights at seventy miles an hour during his excursions through late-night London: presumably an indication of his disrespect for rules and regulations which, at the other end of the scale, impelled him to grand larceny.

In the paranoid regimes of modern Russia (see **Torture**), the Lubianka prison incorporated a complicated system of internal passageways with red and green signal lights at every corner. A warder escorting a prisoner who happened upon a red light knew that another inmate under guard was approaching in the opposite direction, and to prevent the minimal solace of the sight of another imprisoned wretch, the prisoner was pushed face first to the wall and stood in a recess until his fellow-sufferer had passed by.

See also **Separate System**

Train Robbery, Invention of

An American invention pioneered by the Reno Brothers, preying on the state of Indiana from their Rockford headquarters. In October 1866 they stopped an eastbound train on the Ohio and Mississippi Railroad and netted $13,000 from the first small safe. Their third train robbery on 22 May 1868 did better, yielding $97,000 in gold and government bonds.

The five brothers – one of whom, like Zeppo Marx, was out of his depth and bore the distinguishing soubriquet of 'Honest' Reno – excited such fear and loathing by their brutality that after three of them (two captured by Pinkerton's men) ended up in the New Albany jail it was stormed by a specially assembled party of fifty-six vigilantes. Capped in red flannel hoods, the lynch mob pulled in by train in the early hours of 12 December 1868. Outside the jail, lawman Thomas Fullenlove stood his ground.

'I am the sheriff,' he called to the threatening crowd, 'the highest peace officer in the county and if you respect the law you will not dare shoot me.' According to Dan Walsh's contemporary account, 'a dozen revolvers belched at him'.

The three Renos and an accomplice were hanged by the mob, swinging on the pendent bodies and nearly pulling off their heads. Previously, Frank and Simon Reno had taken refuge across the border in Windsor – a sort of Canadian Dodge City – and narrowly escaped drowning during extradition when their tug was sliced in half by a steamer.

Unidentified train robbers from 1878

There are reports of train hold-ups in the American South dating to the 1850s. In a variant from this era, the outlaw John J. Moore was charged not with robbing a train but stealing it. In his endeavours to escape a frontier posse, Moore jumped a locomotive and then leaped to safety. The runaway engine ploughed up yards of track before grinding to a halt and, determined to get some satisfaction, the railroad prosecuted the outlaw with theft. With unwonted subtlety for a frontier court, Moore's attorney got his client off by arguing that a train could not be 'stolen' unless the thief first removed it from, rather than moved it along, the tracks.

Tranquilandia

The South American drugs industry was once a low-key affair, the cocaine brewed up in thousands of tiny 'kitchens', little more than ramshackle sheds producing five or ten kilos at a time. In 1982 the cartel put the business on a modern footing, appropriating an uninhabited 6.2 square-mile island in the province of Caqueta in southern Colombia, deep in the rain forests and surrounded by the Yari river. There they erected a streamlined industrial complex with a capacity of four tons a week, starting the operation by ferrying in tools and heavy materials by helicopter to build a landing strip.

Two gigantic cocaine laboratories, known as *Villa Coca* and *Coquilandia*, were constructed. Most of the site administration was handled from *Tranquilandia*, a third encampment that included executive offices, a clubhouse for the pilots, a canteen, a medical clinic and workshops. The buildings incorporated decent air-conditioning; the workers' sleeping quarters, furnished with bunk beds and mattresses, had pleasantly tiled washing and lavatory facilities. The overall workforce ran into the hundreds; there was no pension scheme, but the remuneration package included $100 a week (three times the local minimum wage), guaranteed flights home four times a year, and celebratory turkey dinners for exceeding production quotas. For leisure, staff amused themselves with videos, table games and porn magazines. Like any other industrial facility, the factory was plastered with signs like 'Please keep this place tidy' or 'Do not enter without proper authorisation from the kitchen'.

For protection, the Cartel relied on the Communist Revolutionary Armed Forces of Colombia, a guerrilla group, and the dénouement, when it came, resembled the last reel of a James Bond film – the assault on Mr Big's lair.

Tranquilandia's existence came to light through its massive appetite for ethyl ether, the surgical anaesthetic constituting the single most efficient solvent for manufacturing cocaine. The Colombian government clamped down on imports, so it had to be sought abroad.

American manufacturers were briefed to tip off the Drugs Enforcement Agency when approached by a 'suspicious' character, and characters do not come any more suspicious than the Cartel's front man Francisco Torres. He ordered a huge consignment of ethyl ether from the J. T. Baker Company in unlabelled barrels, enough to process sixty-six tons of cocaine, and proffered the $300,000 purchase price in cash.

The DEA allowed the deal to go through, fitting the first batch of barrels with electronic transmitters the size of cigarette packs, and satellite surveillance garnered photographs of a busy jungle airstrip in a theoretically deserted part of Caqueta.

On 10 March 1984 the camp was hit by an armed raid backed by two helicopters and a light plane. The communist guerrillas fought a spirited rearguard action, allowing senior management to get clear by air. Another hundred employees melted into the jungle along specially prepared escape routes. Only forty-five of the most menial workers were captured.

But the haul in material was impressive. At Tranquilandia alone police recovered 2,500 kilos of cocaine, nineteen machine guns and rifles, one mortar, four tractors, four electrical generators and seven portable radios; the other installations yielded fifteen laboratories, ten washing machines, four aeroplanes and a helicopter. The street value of the cocaine exceeded $1 billion; the river turned white when it was tipped.

The officer behind the raid, Colonel Jaime Ramirez, avoided retaliation for some time; he was not murdered until 17 November 1985. But the Justice Minister Rodrigo Lara Bonilla, who inspired the crackdown, paid for his temerity almost at once, on 30 April 1984, machine-gunned in his official Mercedes, hit eight times with an Ingram .45. His head only just stayed on.

See also **Escobar**

Treadwheel

Invented by Samuel Cubitt, one of the dynasty who built Belgravia. He devised the treadwheel in 1817 after an approach from an Ipswich magistrate concerned to suppress widespread civil disorder in East Anglia, which was prompted largely by hunger. His prison machine would now rate as an instrument of **torture**.

The treadwheel, or treadmill, consisted of a revolving cylinder of iron and wood some six feet in diameter, like a paddle wheel with a stepped outside surface. As one more refinement of the **Separate System**, convicts were prevented from fraternising with their neighbours slaving alongside by the visual barrier of individual slatted stalls.

Generally the inmates faced two daily sessions of three hours. No one was exempt, neither old men nor pregnant women. The approved rate of climb was forty-eight to fifty steps a minute, and in the course of his day a man might ascend some 10,000 feet (about two vertical miles) while remaining exactly where he was.

The treadmill was enthusiastically embraced by the public who enjoyed the ponderous spectacle, rather as audiences used to flock to the films of Tarkovsky. Magistrates too were admirers, one accurately endorsing the device as 'the most tiresome, distressing, exemplary punishment that has ever been contrived by human ingenuity'. Sometimes careless prisoners were mangled in the machinery.

Unlike the **crank,** the treadmill was not invariably pointless. The occasional prison derived some small benefit by harnessing it to pump water or grind corn. At the turn of the century, thirteen remained in operation, and their use was not suspended (as an excessive form of hard labour) until April Fools' Day 1902. Five years later the installation at York Castle prison was dismantled and sold to Madame Tussaud's.

Triads

Chinese secret societies. Their **initiation** rite was recently described by a British recruit of the Sun Lee On Triad, inducted with twenty other participants: 'There was a small shrine in the room, with a statue of an ancient Chinese warlord. We were each given a stick or two of incense, which was lit. Then we recited the thirty-six oaths, extinguishing one incense after each oath. We all stood in a circle and they pricked our middle fingers with the needle. A drop of blood from each of us was mixed with water in a bowl. The bowl was passed around and we all had to take a drink.' Then an egg with a face drawn on it was put before the group. To symbolise the fate of informers, they each knifed it.

New recruits are known as Blue Lanterns in allusion to the lamps traditionally hung on the porches of bereaved families; the ceremony represents the end of the novice's former life and his rebirth as a hood.

Today's Triads are more interested in money than ritual, now regarded as mumbo-jumbo for which an hour may suffice. In China, the rites originally lasted for up to three days, with recruits clad in silk robes, passing through the massed ranks of members, 'crossing the mountain of knives' before attaining the central altar. After the ceremonial decapitation of three dummies, demonstrating the penalty for betrayal, sharp swords were pressed into each initiate's chest. 'Which is stronger, the blade of the knife or your heart?' demanded the Master. The oath of loyalty was recited as the recruits rose to their feet; bamboo paraphernalia made it difficult to stand up without falling, and if the new member toppled forward, he could – theoretically at least – die on the sword.

In those days the Triads possessed a political purpose as Chinese nationalists. The first Triad was founded by the five surviving Foochow monks after their valiant 1674 resistance against the Manchu dynasty, and the gangs took popular root in Hong Kong following the failure of the 1851 Taiping Rebellion. It was during this period that they turned criminal and, after the 1911 revolution, General Chiang Kai-shek offered them unlimited underworld control in China and a leading role in his government.

The British kept the Triads in check in Hong Kong until the Japanese occupation of 1941, when the invaders delegated the gangs to control the colony's illegal businesses. As part of the deal, the invaders destroyed all Hong Kong police records and, after the war, in association with criminal elements from Triads in China monopolising the **opium** supply in South-east Asia, the Hong Kong syndicates were perfectly poised to play a leading role in the heroin bonanza.

Meanwhile, Triads infiltrated the Hong Kong Royal Police in strength. In the 1970s, the Independent Commission Against Corruption discovered that the five key Chinese staff sergeants inside the Triad Bureau were themselves Triads. Given advance warning, in 1974 the 'Five Dragons' fled to Vancouver where they spent staggeringly, acquiring an office building for $60 million. They paid cash.

Hong Kong today is riddled with Triads. Their traditional rackets in vice, protection, loan-sharking and gambling are themselves a billion-dollar business, permeating the minutiae of daily life, like buying a car, renting a flat or applying for a liquor licence. The dazzling **narcotics** profits of the past two decades enabled diversification into legitimate commercial operations – home decoration, wholesalers, hotels, car dealerships, casinos and banks. Meanwhile the income from narcotics continues unabated.

Comparatively, the Mafia are very small beer; their 'made' associates across the United States total perhaps 1,700 whereas Hong Kong is believed to contain some fifty gangs, with a membership between 150,000 and 300,000. Pitched gun-battles with the police are routine.

Triad control extends back to the **Golden Triangle** – where well-armed, private armies up to 15,000-strong protect the world's **opium** supply and its derivatives, morphine and heroin – and forwards to the international network of narcotics distribution.

With the expiration of the British lease on Hong Kong in 1997, Triads are searching for somewhere to settle. A vast criminal exodus looms; even the arrival of law-abiding Chinese in a host country establishes communities ripe for oppression. San Francisco is the likely first stop; advance teams have been in place since the mid-80s, when the city was awash with independent Chinese banks and big buyers paying cash for prime property. New York may be next in line. The city contains about 50 per cent of America's half-million hard-core heroin addicts, each of whom (very roughly) has a $20,000 a year habit, producing a gross revenue of $5 billion. This is a market worth going for, and the Triads have gone for it. In 1984, 5 per cent of the city's drugs came courtesy of the 'Chinese Connection' from South-east Asia; this is now closer to 80 per cent.

As ever, Britain lags behind. There are only four gangs, and police are currently investigating allegations about the stranglehold on the Chinese vegetable trade. But stories of protection, blackmail, loan sharking and credit card fraud are on the increase; in July 1992 the police raided a London brothel operated by the 14K gang. Working girls were flown in from South-east Asia, and plied their trade in conditions little better than serfdom.

There is no call for complacency. According to a Hong Kong police superintendent: 'The Triads are a totally enclosed group of criminal societies. It has taken us years to try and understand the background of these criminal groups and to develop some methods of fighting them. In Canada and the United States and in Europe, law enforcement is at least thirty years behind.'

See also **Dutch**

Trials of Life

John Gotti, the Mafia mobster, acquired a reputation as the 'Teflon Don' for his numerous non-sticking charges. But the first legal onslaught in 1986 never looked like achieving anything else.

During the early 1980s a woman prosecutor with New York's Eastern District, Diane Giacalone, decided to go it alone, mounting a case against Gotti without the help of either the FBI or the Organised Crime Task Force. Giacalone's principal information on Gotti's crimes centred on fragmentary suggestions of illegal 'tribute' skimmed from the 1980 neighbourhood robberies on IBI armoured cars.

It was Mafia custom to demand a percentage of the takings from unauthorised felonies on their patch; the payments made 'out of respect' constituted a tax on robbers. Repeated instances of such extortion could amount to 'a pattern of racketeering', and on this insubstantial basis Giacalone put in train the first Gotti case, *United States* v. *Aniello Dellacroce et al.*

Her legal colleagues were sceptical. But in 1985 she discovered that for sixteen years Willie Boy Johnson, a trusted Gotti aide, had played a double role as a deep-throat FBI informer. She charged him too, hoping to force Johnson to save his skin and talk in court.

Advice from her colleagues was unanimous: the case would merely blow Johnson's cover, jeopardising the FBI's operation against upper echelons of the Gambino clan. In any case they had Willie Boy figured as too loyal (rather than too scared) to betray Gotti.

This proved correct. Giacalone's other trump card, the informer Willie Batista, fled from his safehouse as the pressure to testify mounted. With her two main witnesses *hors de combat*, there was hardly a case to answer. Nonetheless, Gotti spent much of the trial in prison, bail refused because of a 1984 fracas when he beat up a lorry driver for hooting;

proceedings halted when the trucker saw his assailant's name in the papers and suffered an abrupt loss of memory, immortalised in the *New York Post* headline, 'I forgotti'.

The prosecution took refuge in the evidence of the hood James Cardinali, one of the original IBI robbers. But under cross-examination, Cardinali explained his prolific contradictions. 'Mr Slotnik,' he told defence counsel, 'I lie a lot.' Another prosecution witness, James Sanetore, failed to impress when asked whether his criminal career included scorching a woman's bosoms with cigarettes. 'Absolutely no,' he replied. 'All we did was tie her on the bed and throw burning matches on her breast.'

Gotti took violently against one of his more restrained attorneys, Jeffrey Hoffman. During cross-examination, Gotti sent a note saying, 'Sit down or you're dead'. Gotti preferred the ranting circus-style of Bruce Cutler, a former football player and wrestler who launched the defence by impugning the indictment as 'something to make anyone retch and vomit'. As the trial progressed, Cutler became assimilated into Mafia culture, affecting a *capo* outfit of blue socks, blue shirt and blue suit. His fellow attorneys addressed him as *Don Brucino* and interrupted him, midflow, to hand advisory notes which read: 'Fuck you'. But Cutler proved unembarrassable, man enough to assert without shame that the Gambino headquarters at the Ravenite was a social club for doddery Italian gentlemen of leisure.

Detective Michael Falciano (see **Carrier pigeons**) also achieved fame with his characterisation of mobster Angelo Ruggerio. 'How should I describe him?' Falciano pondered. 'Animal or human? He looked like a fire pump.' Asked if he still had the notes he habitually scribbled on the back of his hands, Falciano replied: 'No, I bathe a lot.'

The trial dragged on for two sombre years, concluding with the performance of bank robber Matthew Traynor, originally earmarked as a prosecution witness. Appearing for the defence, Traynor came across as another obvious liar, affirming that Giacalone had offered the inducement of a pair of her panties to sniff in return for his allegiance. The outraged Giacalone attempted to strike his testimony from the record, in effect conceding that her potential witnesses were worthless.

On 13 March 1987 all the defendants were cleared of everything. Gotti emerged from the courtroom as an immortal, a gossip-column hero: 'Nobody can touch us now.' Willie Boy Johnson survived until 29 August 1988, cut down by nineteen bullets.

Gotti remained at liberty for two more trials and the best part of five years. But on 2 April 1992, with Cutler barred from the courtroom as the Mafia's 'house lawyer', he went down on charges of racketeering and murder, convicted on overwhelming evidence in a properly structured case (see **Techies**).

Gotti is scheduled to spend the rest of his life behind bars with little to look forward to, apart from film versions of his life, and the three shirts and trousers, 65 per cent polyester, that comprise standard prison issue.

He always seemed destined for some such fate. In his words, he 'wasn't born with four fucking cents', the youngest of a construction worker's five children, and his impressionable years in New York's Italian Harlem instilled a profound sense of awe for those mysterious men who spent all day lounging outside the local Palma Boys Club. Gotti's father sweated his life away for a pittance, but these men, topped by their standard grey fedoras with a three-inch brim and clad in immaculate pinstripe suits, never worked. Yet their pockets bulged with banknotes; diamond pinky rings flashed on their fingers, and they paid likely-looking kids $5 to fetch a coffee, or $10 for a shoe shine. Their black sedans gleamed in showroom condition, beautiful women hung on their arms, and the police treated them with deference. Much as his parents might decry these potent figures of respect as 'bad men' and insist on the alternative virtues of thrift, much as his school might promote the merits of self-help and citizenship, it proved hard to ignore the realities of ghetto life.

Gotti's role model, at the age of seven, was Albert 'the Executioner' Anastasia and, after his assassination on 25 October 1957, the neighbourhood hummed with speculation on the affairs of great men. At school Gotti developed a swagger, always fighting, always in trouble, using his explosive temper to secure loyalty. Teachers called it a 'Discipline Problem', but Gotti had followers enough at school and outside, dominating his local Fulton-Rockaway gang. He ended his education at sixteen and, hoping to emulate his hero Anastasia, modelled himself on Richard Widmark's Tommy Udo in *Kiss of Death* down to the death-rasp chuckle. Gotti found his first toehold running illegal bets for former schoolmates and, out in the world – its bars, pool halls, businesses and rackets regulated by Mafia-sanctioned operations – he inevitably came to the notice of organised crime in a trial of strength, taking them on in order to be taken on by them and, later, taking them over.

See also **Decline**

Trolling

An active search for victims. Serial killers operate on a highly individual emotional cycle; 'trolling' ('Who shall I murder?') marks the compulsive stage following the so-called 'aura phase', the shadowy period when morality and taboos progressively fade away ('I might as well murder again') as the killer succumbs to obsessive **fantasising**.

For the hunt itself, each killer haunts a favoured locale, be it a department store, co-ed dormitory, playground or rural road: Gacy trolled in the demimonde of male hustlers, Bundy on Seattle campus, and Dahmer in a shopping precinct.

Once a victim is identified, the killer 'stalks' from a distance before beginning the process of 'wooing' to secure the target's confidence as a preliminary to luring him or her into the trap. Gacy disarmed his targets by offering a job; Bundy would advance a self-effacing request for assistance; and Dahmer typically suggested that his mark share a couple of beers or pose as a photographic model for a few dollars.

The ensuing 'murder phase' is said by the psychologist Joel Norris to constitute a ritual re-enactment of the disastrous experiences of the killer's childhood. One murderer who chased a young playmate with a hatchet favoured a hatchet in his adult murders. Another, Gerald Stano (see **Body language**), acquired most of his estimated thirty-six victims by specialising on those wearing blue, a colour habitually worn by his brother and childhood rival. As a child the 'co-ed killer' Edmund **Kemper** stole his sister's Christmas present, a doll, and ripped off its head; as an adult, he did the same to his female victims. Gacy recited the 23rd psalm, from his purer days, while strangling his victims slowly in his basement, and in more general terms, the killers regurgitate the abuse, and particularly the sexual abuse, vented on them as children. Thus Philadelphia's Joseph Kallinger was adopted by Austrian immigrants who flogged him with a cat-o'-nine tails, held his hand over a naked flame as a punishment for stealing, and threatened to castrate him. After being abused at knife-point, he took to masturbating while clutching a knife and, his wiring irreparably crossed, experienced orgasm on killing his son in 1975.

After the death comes the totem phase (see **Souvenirs**), where the killer messes around with the body, dismembering it, taking pictures, and burying bits in special places. Then comes the aftermath, the pit of Phase Seven – black depression.

But one inexorable day, it is time to start all over again.

Tropmann, Jean Baptiste (1848–70)

An early French serial killer (concentrating on Kincks) who inspired a genuinely festive execution. A violent homosexual loner, the young Tropmann found his niche by disposing of an entire family. He picked one with six children.

First Tropmann befriended the prosperous Mr Kinck, and on 25 August 1869 he took his new acquaintance on a rural expedition to inspect an imaginary workshop making counterfeit gold coins. Out in the country, Tropmann murdered him with a glass of wine laced with prussic acid. He cut the body up, hiding it under a heap of stones in an old moat.

Thereafter Tropmann maintained contact with the family, assuring them of father's well-being, and on 7 September he despatched his second Kinck, luring Master Gustave into the countryside and mangling rather than stabbing him to death. Next he persuaded Mrs Kinck to accompany him with her five surviving children to meet her husband, mysteriously insisting that she bring all their papers with her – birth certificates, title deeds and leases. Paying off their cab at Pantin, outside Paris, Tropmann dismounted announcing, 'Well, young-

sters, we've decided to stay here.' Then he killed them in a field, disembowelling two-year-old Hortense, butchering little Achille with a spade, strangling Emile and Henry with their mufflers, impaling Alfred, the six-year-old, on a haft, and stabbing their mother thirty times.

The bodies were found on 23 September, half-buried, and a few days later Tropmann was arrested in Le Havre with 250 francs in his pocket. Paris became obsessed with the case.

The killings heralded a new type of crime. These were not primitive murders for food and drink, or (the next step up) for shelter and domestic security. Tropmann killed for obscure personal reasons; he liked sticking things into people, so there were strong sexual undertones. But the killings were not completely without purpose, however misconceived. In a break between the murders, Tropmann remarked to his brother-in-law (he still lodged at home): 'I have a business in hand which will surprise the whole world.' His plan, or megalomaniac delusion, was to *become* Mr Kinck, although it is hard to see how this would confer realisable riches.

Tropmann's last day dawned on 19 January 1870. In the prison courtyard, coffee was served to the assembled troops, and the official pharmacist entertained fifteen friends with truffled turkey. The prison Director threw a reception (one of his most successful) with pâté de foie gras, punch and wine. Outside, the mob gathered like the crowds at a Hollywood premiere, spotting celebrities. There was Maxime Du Camp! The man of letters, Victorien Sardou! And the Russian writer, Turgenev himself, was mistaken for the executioner, the famous and affable M. Heindrecht – who showed the guests round the guillotine and scaffold for some harmless horseplay, making his visitors lie in position millimetres from the blade's path as he triggered its descent.

Turgenev landed the plum job of walking Tropmann to the scaffold, marvelling at the killer's small stature and elongated thumbs. Tropmann too entered into the spirit of the thing. True, he failed in his last-minute bid to bribe the prison pharmacist to give him poison, but after his head had been cut off it was found attached to the assistant executioner's hand, the teeth deeply embedded by a last convulsive bite.

See also **Lunette**

Trousers, spare

Those who feel excluded from high office by mere lack of ability should take heart from the career of Rayner Goddard, appointed Lord Chief Justice in 1946 at the age of sixty-nine.

Goddard's supporters conceded that he 'rarely read the papers beforehand' (Lord Denning) and that he was 'contentious, cantankerous, prejudiced' (Lady Sachs, his daughter). His detractors are less complimentary. John Parris, one of the barristers in the **Craig and Bentley** case, decried Goddard as a judge who 'ignored precedents... His knowledge of law disgraced a first year law student... He lacked every judicial quality... He would not listen and made up his mind within minutes without hearing the evidence.' In sum, Parris depicts him as 'a dishonest political fascist'.

Worse, Goddard exhibited serious personality aberrations from an early age. At school, he was a notorious bully, his party piece to recite the death sentence in dormitory. As a law student, he failed his bar exams five times. As a judge, his maiden speech in the House of Lords supported corporal punishment, and, as a pervert, he experienced emission every time he pronounced the death sentence. It was the task of the Lord Chief Justice's clerk, Arthur Harris, to take a spare pair of the standard striped trousers to court on sentencing days. When condemning a youth to be flogged or hanged, Goddard always ejaculated, and it is perhaps worth noting that, by contrast, a sex murderer is a man who kills for sexual gratification.

It is probably unfair to single Goddard out from the long tradition of Lord Chief Justices, who tend towards worthless political appointees. The first was Odo, younger brother to William the Conqueror, who attempted to buy the papacy on the death of Gregory VII. In 1350 the then incumbent, Sir William de Thorpe, was hanged for taking bribes. Robert Tresilian suffered the same fate after the Peasants' Revolt, during which he hanged the defendants without listening to the facts. He was done for a tax fiddle. The most execrated legal figure in British history held the post: Judge Jeffries, vividly described by King Charles II (who appointed him) as having 'no learning, no sense, no manners, and ten times more impudence than ten carted streetwalkers'. After sending 320 men to their deaths at the Bloody Assizes, Jeffries died in the Tower in April 1689 from a beating by the mob.

In the 1890s, the wife of John Duke Coleridge sat alongside her husband. Her duty was to nudge him awake. This century, Lord Reading whiled away the hours of courtroom drudgery by answering his correspondence; and Lord Widgery remained in office until 1980 despite his dementia.

See also **Birch**

Turpin, Dick (1705–39)

An English butcher who progressed via a career as a **highwayman** to his final status as a legend. Lack of social finesse precipitated Turpin's eventual downfall.

During life, Turpin was not so special; but after death his stature grew, fostered by ballads, prints, gossip, local history and burgeoning memorabilia – authentic 'Turpin' spurs, genuine 'Turpin' pistols and the extraordinary profusion of 'Turpin' inns where he spent the night. But what really launched his posthumous career was Harrison Ainsworth's 1824 romantic novel *Rookwood* where Turpin appeared as a secondary character. Ainsworth penned the hundred pages describing Turpin's epic but imaginary ride from Sussex to York in twenty-four hours, and the book was such a hit that seventy years later the novelist's biographer, S. M. Ellis, was shown the very hoof-marks made on five-bar gates by Turpin's mare along his way.

The son of an Essex farmer, Turpin traded as a butcher and doubled as the neighbourhood sheep-thief. After being discovered stealing oxen, Turpin moved into smuggling and joined a notorious group of burglars; soon he was leader of the Essex Gang. Their vicious exploits regularly made the columns of the *London Evening Post*, and by 1736 he and his accomplices had a price of £100 on their heads. Only by jumping out of a window did Turpin escape the hanging suffered by two other members of the gang.

Down on his luck, Turpin turned to highway robbery, operating out of a cave in Epping Forest, shooting dead a bounty hunter who cornered him in his lair. After that, killing came easy. The *Grub Street Journal* of 24 July 1736 reported that Turpin would have shot a robbery victim, Mr Omar, in cold blood had not his companion in crime 'pulled the pistol out of his hand'. Turpin became the scourge of Blackheath, and was a cool enough customer to take a short cut by riding through the middle of the City in broad daylight. Then in 1737 he shot his accomplice Tom King by accident, and by June of that year the price on his head had doubled.

The south was too hot, so Turpin headed north and set himself up as John Palmer, a country gentleman in Yorkshire where he earned his living as a horse thief. But one evening, returning home after a day's shooting, Turpin casually blasted a cockerel belonging to his landlord and threatened to kill a neighbour who remonstrated. He was arrested, imprisoned, investigated and finally identified by his old schoolmaster in Hempstead who, in his secondary capacity as postmaster, recognised his pupil's handwriting on a letter written from prison to his brother. Turpin was tried and condemned to death.

He died in style on 7 April 1739, buying a new suit for the occasion and hiring five men at ten shillings a head to act as mourners. Escorted to the gallows on what is now York racecourse, Turpin bowed to appreciative spectators with 'an air of the most astonishing indifference and intrepidity' and, it is said, chatted to his executioner for a good half hour before a carefree jump from the ladder to his death started his post-mortem career as a celebrity. No sooner was Turpin buried than ruffians made off with his body. But the mob tracked it down to a garden, and Turpin's recaptured corpse was laid on a board, covered with straw, and borne nearly naked through the city in a triumphal parade.

Tyburn

A principal place of execution from 1177 to 1783. A plaque marks the spot at the junction of London's Oxford Street and Edgware Road where some 50,000 criminals met their deaths over the centuries. Nearby was a pleasant stream popular with anglers.

From 1571 to 1759 a permanent set of triangular gallows stood there, eighteen feet high, capable of hanging eight from each beam. With a maximum capacity of twenty-four they constituted a growing threat to traffic, and in 1759 the massive installation was removed, the timber sold to a carpenter who cut it into beer-butt stands for the nearby Carpenter's Arms. A set of more modest removable gallows stood their turn until 1783, when the official

place of execution was relocated at **Newgate**, which supplied the bulk of the condemned.

It was not before time. Tyburn hangings were an affront to public decency. Execution days – and there were many – incited mob violence. The long procession across London wound its way through the teeming crowds, with the death cart, crammed with prisoners seated on a coffin, preceded by the city marshal, sheriffs, peace officers and constables. The journey took three hours, and among the street vendors lining the roadside was the occasional carriage occupied by genteel spectators partaking of hampers and wine. The cortège repeatedly stopped at public houses for liquor to ease the men's fear.

Each prisoner travelled with a noose bound to his chest, and at the gallows' foot he donned a coarse white shroud. Even then he had a quarter of an hour to live. First the condemned were transferred to another cart, positioned under the beam and built unusually wide to permit multiple executions. The prisoners crowded at its rear while the hangman fussed with the noose and the Chaplain led them in prayers and the Psalms. All around jostled a scuffling throng of rich and poor, thieves, rogues, pickpockets and pedlars, thousands strong, shouting encouragement, hurling execration, cracking jokes or launching into bawdy songs as relatives climbed up to make their farewells. Among the audience would be calm family parties of tradesmen sipping tea, and the prisoners' last moments were overlooked by a grandstand for the well-to-do, called Mother Proctor's Pews after a commercially minded farmer's widow. When the cart finally lurched forwards the men still did not die, but were left to dangle, choking slowly to death. The crowd stood awestruck by their convulsions, greeting every new contortion of the limbs with a groan or a cheer.

Many contemporary observers regarded this spectacle as counter-productive, conferring fame and recognition on the condemned. Henry **Fielding** observed in 1751: 'The day appointed by law for the thief's shame is the day of glory in his own opinion. His procession to Tyburn, and his last moments there, are all triumphant, attended with the applause, admiration and envy of all the bold and hardened. His behaviour in his present condition, not the crimes, how atrocious soever, which brought him to it, is the subject of contemplation.'

Oxford Street was formerly known as Tyburn

Road, and Park Lane used to be Tyburn Lane. 'Great Gibbet Field' was an expanse of land just off Tyburn in what is now Bayswater, and to 'dance the Tyburn jig' was to hang by the neck until dead.

Tyson, Mike (1966–)

On 26 March 1992 Mike Tyson, former world heavyweight boxing champion, was jailed for the rape of Desirée Washington in Room 606 of the Canterbury Hotel, Indianopolis. The 18-year-old beauty queen accepted a telephone invitation to visit his bedroom shortly before two a.m. on a July morning the preceding year.

During the act of carnal knowledge, Tyson asked: 'Do you want to go on top?' Desirée replied 'Yeah', and did so. After ejaculating outside her Tyson said: 'Don't you love me now?'

The champion is now convict 922335 at the Indiana Youth Correction Centre, and this bizarre outcome highlights the law's complexities. The evidence supports Tyson's assumption that he was not engaged in **rape**; the fact that Miss Washington pressed charges suggests that she thought he was.

The issue is not only a matter of who you believe, but whose belief is relevant. Criminal guilt can depend on whether the victim's or the perpetrator's point of view is paramount.

British convictions flow from the attacker's knowledge that he was committing a rape, and this produces seemingly outrageous acquittals when bone-headed dolts are convinced that the woman did not mind. American prosecutions are founded on the victim's reaction, and this means that, at its most extreme, seemingly outrageous convictions result when the accused had no idea, and received no indication, that anything was wrong.

In the Tyson case, new evidence may eventually sweep away these metaphysical considerations. Testimony barred by Judge Patricia Gifford from the first trial (because it was submitted too late) has been presented to the Indiana Court of Appeal. The sworn statements of three friends – Carla Martin, Pamela Lawrence, Renée Deal – record their impressions on watching Tyson and Miss Washington emerge from the back seat of his gold limousine and walk through the hotel foyer at 1.30 a.m. The couple were all over each other. As Carla Martin put it, 'Desirée Washington had her tongue down Mike's throat and her hands on his crotch. She was really getting it on.'

Miss Washington filed a $10 million suit against Tyson and, within two days of the hotel episode, hired a lawyer to negotiate the book and movie rights to her story. A few hours after her horrific experience in Room 606, she was videoed in an apparently ebullient mood dancing and singing for the Miss Black America pageant.

According to some of the other twenty-two beauty contestants, Miss Washington flirted with Tyson before their assignation at his hotel room. Caroline Jones overheard her comment, 'That's twenty million dollars', as the boxer arrived at the rehearsal where they first made contact. Tanya St Claire-Gills listened to her speculate about the size of his penis. And when Madeline Whittingdon asked if she intended to keep her date, Miss Washington replied, 'Of course I'm going. This is Mike Tyson. He's got a lot of money. He's dumb. You see what Robin Givens [his ex-wife] got out of him.'

Tyson's conviction was reaffirmed on appeal in August 1993, but the new testimony was not appraised, with the court ruling that it had been properly excluded from appraisal at the old hearing.

U

Ucciardone

Sicilian prison run by and for the Mafia where aged mobsters, as the saying went, 'retired into private life'. Until at least 1957 Ucciardone constituted a pleasant rest-home where the guards fell under direct Mafia control; the one governor who failed to toe the line had to pack his bags.

The cells were comfortably furnished, meals were sent in from the best Palermo restaurants, and *mafiosi* inside conducted their businesses outside with the help of warders acting as commission agents. If a prisoner's circumstances altered, as happened to Salvatore Malta (who needed a year off to run an armed band), he arranged for leave of absence while staying on the prison's books, nominally confined.

Institutional discipline for the less privileged was enforced with normal Mafia ferocity; the hospital register recorded injuries from these savage beatings as 'slipping on the stairs'. Five hundred inmates slipped on the stairs in twelve years.

Ucciardone's proudest accomplishment was a civil engineering project, tunnelling beneath the foundations to the underground pipeline running from the docks to the refinery. This the *mafiosi* tapped, syphoning off the petroleum for sale on the black market.

The vestiges of the Ucciardone tradition were not eradicated until June 1992, when the most recent anti-Mafia spasm exiled convicted mobsters from their power base to mainland 'hard' prisons.

See also **Cathedral**

Umbrellas

The existence of the most famous umbrella-gun in crime remains conjecture. Its victim, Georgi Markov, was a Bulgarian defector living in London, and on 7 September 1978 he queued for a bus on the south side of London's Waterloo Bridge. Jolted by a stab of pain in his upper thigh, he turned to notice a man picking up an umbrella as he hailed a cab. Markov continued to work, where he complained of a sore leg.

By the following morning Markov was sick. The doctor suspected 'flu, but three days later the patient was dead. In the circumstances, the bruise on the back of his right thigh was excised and forwarded to the chemical research establishment at Porton.

The tiny pellet, embedded in the inflamed tissues, consisted of a platinum and iridium sphere engineered to a diameter of 1.52mm, drilled with two 0.35mm holes. This exacting accomplishment represented the apex of a peculiarly Balkan arms race, backed by the KGB: the ammunition's manufacture entailed sophisticated micro-technology coupled with access to a defence industry high-temperature furnace. The Porton Down pathologists concluded that the cavities secreted something like 0.2 milligrams of a biotoxin, probably a first-use for ricin, an extremely potent derivative of castor-oil bean husks; hitherto, its effects were primarily known through the study of cattle. For humans, twenty-one millionths of a gram constitutes a fatal dose.

Despite the many published diagrams, the umbrella-gun hypothesis is supported only by Markov's equivocal impressions at the time of the shooting. Equally plausible variants are a straightforward gas or **airgun**, perhaps concealed in a furled umbrella. Some three months previously another Bulgarian, Kostov, survived a comparable incident on the Paris metro when he was apparently shot by a cardboard box, and the writer Alexander Solzhenitsyn weathered a similar attack .

The Bulgarian government has admitted culpability, placing the blame on their former security services, and in early 1992, the Bulgarian most closely linked to the murder, General Styoan Sanov, former deputy Interior Minister, was discovered dead in his apartment the day before his scheduled appearance in court to testify about Markov's files, which had vanished from state archives.

In America, umbrella-guns firing ordinary bullets continue in production, marketed to wealthy clients who fear violent attack, presumably in the rainy season. The weapons are indistinguishable from the genuine article except for their weight and the removable rubber tip protecting the barrel from abrasion on the pavement. On 2 June 1992 a specimen, confiscated from a John Portis by London magistrates, was destined for Scotland Yard's Black Museum.

One little-known criminal application is to poke an unopened umbrella through the ceiling from above. When unrolled, the brolly catches falling ceiling debris as the hole is enlarged, preventing any burglar-alarm wired to the floor below from detecting the incursion. This motif appeared in the film *Rififi*, and in real life was adopted by a German gang breaking into a strongroom during a 1907 hotel raid.

Unfair arrest

Unlike today, in Elizabethan times you could be thrown into **prison** for practically anything: **debt**, petty theft, assault, slander, vagrancy, suspicion of witchcraft – the list is endless. It only needed someone to swear a warrant. Prison sergeants issued them at a shilling a time, sometimes releasing the intended victim in return for a bribe, sometimes threatening him with warrants unless they received a bribe, sometimes shopping the whereabouts of a debtor to a creditor for a bribe, and sometimes all three, after insisting on being primed with a bribe.

Getting in was easy. But there was no procedure for getting out. The better-off bribed their way to the outside world, or paid off their creditors and left. But the most widespread technique of modern times (serving the sentence) did not work. There was no sentence to serve.

Prisoners were not sent to prison for any particular length of time. They were simply sent to prison. Incarceration as punishment remained an uncrystallised concept; prison was a place to stay while awaiting release, trial or death, accelerated or otherwise.

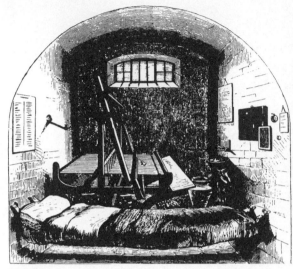

This Pentonville prisoner is lucky to have a loom rather than the dreaded crank for his task work. Note the basin with running water (right)

Obviously things are better now, but in March 1992 the National Association of Probation Officers estimated that some 550 wrongfully convicted prisoners languished in British jails. Once inside, protestations of innocence encounter almost insurmountable obstacles. One inmate had to set aside ten weeks of his prison wages to afford the photocopying of papers relevant to his case.

Other *prima facie* victims of injustice are pressurised to the limits of endurance. Bob Maynard and Reg Dudley, convicted of the 1974 Billy Moseley killing (see **Head**), learned that they had no prospect of release while they continued their protestations of innocence. This is standard practice: the Home Office informed Paul Cleeland (convicted of Terry Clarke's murder in November 1972) that he would be let out on licence if he admitted his guilt. So Cleeland – by his own account – is now jailed not despite being innocent, but because he is innocent. 'I'll rot in here,' he said in July 1992, 'rather than have anything to do with their damn licence... I'll fight them to the death. I won't give up until it comes out that I have never had a fair trial.'

Jimmy O'Connor, a civilian convicted of murder in 1941, offers a different perspective. 'It was during the war,' he says of his trial. 'No one cared whether or not people were innocent. They had more important things to think about.' Prior to his execution, the principal prosecution witness, who had been pressurised by the police, withdrew his evidence, and with one day to run, after watching the digging of his grave through his Pentonville window, O'Connor was reprieved by the King. Released ten years later, he became a scriptwriter for the BBC, but thanks to a brilliant rearguard action by the Home Office, he cannot be pardoned. The papers relating to his case are covered by the thirty-year secrecy rule, and time only started to run when his file was formally closed. Since O'Connor continued to ask to see his files, the Home Office had to open them to add his incoming letters. So his requests for disclosure have become the reason for their non-disclosure. Sadly, O'Connor did not find this out until 1971, so he has another eight years to wait.

The crime rate generally drops during wartime. Cynics say that this is because most criminals join the army.

See also **Virtual reality**

Unruth, Howard (1921–)

Howard Unruth was a 28-year-old former tank-gunner from Camden, New Jersey, who went walkabout in his home town on 9 September 1949. He killed thirteen people in twelve minutes with his 9mm Luger, but then found himself penned into his house, surrounded by armed police. During the siege, an enterprising reporter dialled his home number for a telephone interview.

Unruth took the call. In a way, this was a golden opportunity to resolve the vexed issue of what makes mass murderers tick; one cannot always obtain the opinion of the man-on-the-spot, mid-massacre. The journalist came straight to the point: 'Why are you killing people, Howard?' he inquired. 'I don't know,' Howard replied.

Unruth survived his big day, telling the police, on capture: 'I'm no psycho.' To a psychiatrist he said later: 'I'd have killed a thousand if I'd had bullets enough.'

See also **Terminology**

Untouchables, The

As a child, Eliot Ness (1903–57) was exceptionally good. He worked a paper route, helped his father deliver pastries and loved books, particularly Sherlock Holmes. As an adult, he believed in the sanctity of the law, almost a unique attribute for a **Prohibition Agent**. Perhaps surprisingly, departmental files commended his 'cool, aggressive and fearless manner' on raids, acknowledging that he made 'more than the average number of arrests' and that he never 'shirked assignments or complained'. Ness was well-dressed, well-educated, soft-spoken and clean-cut, and District Attorney George Q. Johnson, under orders to found a special Capone squad, looked no further. On 28 September 1929 he gave Ness, still residing with his parents, the assignment of crippling Capone financially.

Ness seconded nine men, four from outside Chicago, and by the end of the first year his elite cadre had captured nineteen distilleries and six breweries worth $1 million – a mere bagatelle to Capone, not one of whose men were arrested.

Ness's problem was that the bootleggers made good their escape during the minutes it took to sledgehammer his way into their illicit premises. So he commandeered a ten-ton flatbed truck, welded a giant steel ram onto its cab and, on 13 June 1930, smashed his way into a brewery at 2108 South Wabash Avenue, taking five astonished hoods prisoner. Within days a youth, 'the Kid', presented himself at Ness's office bearing a bribe of $2,000, with $2,000 to follow for each week he behaved. 'Listen,' rasped Ness, 'and don't let me ever have to repeat it: I may be a poor baker's son, but I don't need this kind of money.' A few days later two of his agents on surveillance had a package hurled into their car. When it did not go off and, as expected, kill them, they unwrapped 'a wad of bills large enough to choke an ox'. They slung the bribe back into the mobsters' vehicle and told Ness of the incident. Fired with pride, he called in the press, and a *Tribune* writer christened his squad the 'Untouchables'. From then his fame grew, with Ness often accompanied by reporters as he set off riding shotgun on his sorties.

By spring 1931 Ness had achieved ascendancy in his cat-and-mouse pursuit of the bootleggers. On 4

April, staking out a brewery, he was ringed by six armed hoods, who made another offer he could not refuse. But he did, drawling 'You haven't got enough money' before driving off. An outraged Capone assigned Michael Pitti to kill him. Ness, getting wind of the contract, drove everywhere with Pitti's mugshot at his side, eventually catching and disarming the hitman after a car chase. By mid-1931 Capone was in serious trouble, with busts at such a pitch that he could not maintain his customers in booze. Jake Guzik, a Capone henchman, was overheard on a wiretapped line telling a speakeasy that he was fresh out of liquor: the police would 'have to take a pass' on their monthly refreshers. Capone's alcohol production dropped by an estimated 80 per cent, compelling him to buy overpriced stock from out of town, and Ness staged a parade of forty-five impounded trucks past Capone's Lexington Hotel, reducing the great man to a frenzy. 'I'll kill 'im, I'll kill 'im with my own bare hands,' Capone fumed, but he delegated the job to someone else. In short order Ness survived three assassination attempts: a drive-by, a run-over and a car bomb wired to his ignition.

Although Ness secured indictments against Capone and sixty-eight confederates, citing 5,000 offences, his alcohol charges were kept in abeyance. Capone was convicted for income tax offences and, after forming his guard of honour at the station on his way to the penitentiary, the Untouchables were disbanded. Ness became Cleveland's Director of Public Safety, acquitting himself with his customary elan in the fight against civic corruption. 'Director Ness lifted fear from the hearts of honest men,' commented the press on his 1938 smashing of a union-racketeering case. But he met his match in the **Torso** serial killer, and a divorce, coupled with a drink-driving incident, tainted his squeaky-clean image. Ness resigned on 30 April 1942. After an abortive attempt at a political career he fell on hard times, once applying for a job at $60 a week, and by the 1950s eked out his life in obscurity on $150 a week as a salesman with a beaten-up car. In 1955 he ran into an old schoolfriend, Oscar Fraley, a journalist. Fraley sat up all night as Ness regaled him with half-remembered stories from his Prohibition days – about how he had gone eyeball to eyeball with 'Scarface' Capone and brought a criminal empire to its knees.

'You should write a book,' said Fraley, and Ness died on 16 December 1957, still poor, but a rightful legend in the making.

See also **Pax Capone**

Uranium

The Soviet Union's break-up led to a flurry of reports about nuclear material filtering onto the black market.

Russian inventory control of their nuclear arsenal has long been defective and their facilities woeful; newspapers commented unfavourably on warheads poking out through the windows of overloaded storage sites. Initially the nightmare spectre of unchecked nuclear proliferation went unrealised; the only corroborated reports involved conmen.

A typical incident from March 1992 culminated in the seizure of two Soviet-born Germans, one an unemployed fruit-and-veg merchant, during a car-boot sale of 1.2 kg of bomb-grade uranium (concealed in a sports bag) at an asking price of £650,000. On examination, the contents proved to be low-enriched uranium, worth about £50. Another gang arrested near Lake Como in October 1991 were hoping to shift the plutonium from a discarded heart pacemaker.

In the course of her nuclear career, Russia produced about 100 to 150 tons of weapons-grade plutonium and 1,000 tonnes of highly enriched uranium. Someone, somewhere, will want it. Worse, some 10,000 former Russian nuclear scientists are scavenging for employment. Together they comprise a 'nuclear mafia', an illicit distribution network spreading outwards from Moscow through the new Commonwealth of Independent States under the control of ex-KGB, Stassi and other assorted intelligence operatives. As from 1992, the American Senate's 'Task Force on Terrorism and Unconventional Warfare' documented increasingly serious levels of nuclear trafficking in Europe, including an abortive endeavour in October of that year by Saddam Hussein of Iraq to procure 80 kilos of Plutonium-239 (enough for twenty bombs) at $1 million a kilo. But the Reagan administration's nuclear supplies to Pakistan, which came nearer to precipitating a nuclear exchange than Cuba, somehow escaped scrutiny.

'Red mercury', that occasional feature of press

reports, is a compound of unknown composition and unknown attributes. The likelihoods are that the vendors want about £200,000 a kilo and that the purchaser obtains quicksilver dyed with cochineal. As David Kay, Secretary-General of the Uranium Institute, put it: 'A rumour started about fifteen years ago that the Soviets had found a new reactor base – something to do with mercury. Nobody knew quite what, but everybody got very excited. We thought it might be an ingredient in a hydrogen bomb, or facilitate a pressurised water reactor. It became known as 'red mercury' purely because it was Russian. People try to sell off ordinary mercury tainted with colouring.'

The illicit trade in gaseous lithium (to 'enhance' nuclear detonations) poses a more serious threat.

Usual suspects, Round up the

One of the famous last lines from *Casablanca*, where Claude Rains, who witnessed the killing of a Nazi by Humphrey Bogart, orders the arrest of 'the usual suspects'.

After the death of the Fyffe banana couple James and Marjorie Etherington on 10 June 1971, this technique was employed with telling effect on the Caribbean island of St Lucia. Foul play was obvious when an insurance investigator noticed a garden hose, smelling strongly of petrol, running into the burned-out shell of the house where firemen had discovered the Etheringtons' charred remains. Within two days the suspects were under lock and key. The local Commissioner of Police explained: 'If I get any real trouble, I bring these three in: Florius the ringleader, Faucher, and Anthony Charles, who just does what he's told. If they haven't done it, they always know who has.'

The case had two notable features. First, the length of time taken to exhume the victims' bodies. Only one of St Lucia's gravediggers attended the excavation, arriving equipped with an old spade and two enamel bowls. These had holes in them. So every time the earth was ferried out of the grave, it dribbled in again. The gravedigger himself was ancient, and tired easily. But in front of a huge crowd of onlookers eating ice cream, the old-timer felt fiercely protective of his job and status, threatening to walk out if anyone helped. Sometimes he rested and sometimes he burst into tears, but after three hours the double coffin was finally exposed. Then, when the grave-pit sides collapsed, it was dug out again.

The Etheringtons had been burgled, beaten, tied up and burned to cinders along with their house. In court, Faucher divulged that this last precaution was on the advice of Florius to prevent their victims, who were dead, from talking. Florius insisted that it was the only way to outwit Scotland Yard's posthumous electronic wizardry. 'If we burn them, ashes don't talk,' he explained. The three were hanged.

See also **Witchcrazes**

V

Vaginal devices, anti-rape

Very extreme. Theoretically, American women anticipating a **rape** can make a selection from a range of five patented intra-vaginal inserts.

All are tube-shaped. Patent number 4,167,183, registered at the US Patents Office in 1977, operates by harpooning the intruder's member with a miniature trident; number 4,508,114 encases the offending organ in a rigid sheath coated with a mixture of adhesives and acid; the 'Female Protective Device' spears it, and the creation of Joel D. Rumph administers it with a sedative injection.

All these contraptions suffer from the same drawbacks. First, they do not explain what happens next. How should the woman deal with the encumbering rapist, who would still be attached? Second,

Another bizarre innovation. A baffled strangler from the 1860s registers chagrin as an unperturbed victim strolls by, thanks to his patent Antigarotte Collar.

the 'little and large' problem is unresolved: the devices are by definition big enough to accommodate the tumescent penis. Third, conventional difficulties in predicting the exact time of a rape would compel the user either to 'dress to kill' continuously or risk counter-allegations of penile entrapment by dressing up for, and then submitting to, a particular assault.

Valfierno, Marquis Eduardo de

Turn-of-the-century Argentinian conman operating in tandem with Yves Chaudron, an accomplished forger who churned out copies of the seventeenth-century Spanish painter Murillo. Together they crackled the newly-finished canvases in front of an electric fan; sprayed on the dust of ages with a reversed vacuum cleaner; and simulated flyspecks by a scattering of coffee grains. For the period, the fakes were convincing.

The white-moustached Valfierno persuaded newly bereaved, wealthy widows to buy his Murillo for the family chapel in honour of their dear departed. But bilking widows one-by-one was time-consuming work, so the Marquis set himself up in a smart hotel in Mexico City. The capital had a genuine Murillo on public display; Valfierno's plan was to offer to steal it for gullible foreigners, mostly North Americans. Chaudron knocked up a copy, and the fake was smuggled *into* the gallery where it was slipped, a perfect fit, into the back of the original's frame, nestling unseen, face forwards behind Murillo's canvas.

Valfierno would escort his dupe into the gallery. 'That's the picture I told you about,' he would whisper, 'I can get my hands on it and arrange delivery to wherever you want.' The Marquis insisted that the buyer autograph the canvas on the back, 'so that you can be sure the painting you get is this very one.' The punter surreptitiously made his mark, sometimes snipping away a few centimetres of loose thread, while the Marquis briefly held the frame away from the wall, making a point of staring nervously out at the room.

What the punter actually signed was the concealed fake, which he later received together with a newspaper clipping reporting the theft of the original. The Marquis had these items specially printed. In a good week he could dispose of several Murillos; he hired local artists to boost production.

Word leaked out. Meanwhile the creative Chaudron grew frustrated at the limitations of his repertoire, always reworking the same masterpiece, and in 1907 the pair decamped to Paris to set up a gang, importing the talents of a monocled Englishman, a well-connected Frenchman and a socialite American, renting a villa near the Place de l'Etoile. Here they lavishly entertained selected visitors. The trap was baited by arranging some small favour for their client, perhaps a rendezvous with a Folies Bergères star, perhaps bypassing bureaucratic red tape or effecting an introduction. Then, confidence established, was there... anything else?

Valfierno's gang offered to steal to order from the Louvre. The purchaser obtained a facsimile of the designated object, along with impressive documentation on counterfeit museum stationery including a copy internal memo, marked 'confidential', stating that until the original was recovered a replica would be exhibited in its stead. All went well until, in June 1910, the gang nearly overreached themselves by 'stealing' the **Mona Lisa**. The client, bemused by the lack of international uproar, was only reassured after Valfierno persuaded amenable journalists to query the authenticity of the 'substitute' still on display.

Realising that if something was worth doing badly, it was worth doing well, the Marquis instructed Chaudron to embark on a production run of six Mona Lisas. Artists had always been permitted to set up their easels in the Louvre, provided their copy was to different dimensions. Chaudron slaved in the Salon Carré until he produced a perfect scale version, and carried it back to his studio for use as a master.

The Mona Lisa measures 30.32 by 20.86 inches, executed on close-grained Italian walnut one-and-a-half inches thick weighing eighteen pounds. For added authenticity, the Marquis sacrificed an antique Italian bed, cannibalising its wooden panels for the walnut canvas. Meanwhile a circumspect marketing campaign secured six advance orders for the 'real' Mona Lisa, and these were shipped to America, passing through customs billed as copies. There they bided their time.

According to one account, Valfierno recruited a small-time crook, Vincenzo Perruggia, to purloin the original. When the news broke worldwide on 22 August 1911, Valfierno unloaded his fakes at $300,000 apiece. In this story, a disgruntled Perruggia stole the original back and, after storing it under his bed for two years, wrote to the Florentine dealer Alfredo Geri offering to sell. His exposure and arrest followed.

Valfierno's identity is unknown, and his involvement with Perruggia is no more than a persistent rumour defying verification; its source is a *Saturday Evening Post* article of 25 June 1932 by Carl Decker, who claimed friendship with the Marquis. By their nature, stories of successful con-artists tend to lack corroborative detail. The better the scam, the less it is reported or remembered, and on inspection the facts melt away to a series of hazy impressions.

Vampire of Sacramento (1950–79)

Regarded by his family as a peaceful child. But like the classic homicidal maniac he was, Richard Chase enjoyed playing with matches and wet his bed. Later, he amused himself with cruelty to animals and, conversely, was impotent with girls (see **Pets**, **Sex crimes**).

After high school, Chase – by then an unkempt loner, generally stoned – experienced difficulty in settling down, sometimes rambling round the house with his head wrapped in a cloth to make the blood run down properly inside his skull. Soon he became seriously worried that his head was changing shape and, in a hospital emergency room, complained that someone had misappropriated his pulmonary arteries. In 1973 a neurologist concluded that Chase suffered from a 'psychiatric disturbance of major proportions'.

At first his parents would not accept that he needed treatment. But after Chase took to disembowelling rabbits and eating their entrails raw, he fell ill and was put into Sacramento's American River Hospital. He escaped, but by 19 May he was back in an extended-care mental home where staff found dead, mauled birds cluttering the corridor outside his room. Chase was often seen smeared with blood; he explained that he cut himself shaving.

Diagnosed as a paranoid schizophrenic, Chase was discharged from hospital; his mother, concerned at his zombie-like state, weaned him off medication. Left to his own devices, Chase realised that the reason that his heart had shrunk was through lack of blood.

By now he lived off a special cocktail of cola mixed in a blender with the innards of cats and dogs. In the spring of 1977 he banned his parents from his apartment, in any case too filthy for outsiders to stomach. He talked to them from his front porch, returning home just once to bring back their pet cat, which he had killed, eviscerating it and then smearing himself in its blood in his mother's presence. Neighbours saw animals aplenty entering his apartment. But none ever came out. Some were stolen, but others were bought, sometimes from the SPCA. Chase had an expensive dog habit to support and in June 1977 his mother handed over her savings from Social Security benefits, some $1,450. On 2 December 1977 Richard invested in a .22 semi-automatic pistol, firing it the day after Christmas through an open kitchen window selected at random. His bullet parted the hair on a stranger's head. Three days later he shot a passer-by dead in the street. The police investigation made no progress.

On 23 January 1978, Chase broke into the house of Theresa Wallin, three months pregnant. After shooting her, he slit her stomach open and pulled out her intestines, loop after loop. He removed her kidneys, sliced her pancreas in two, stabbed her liver, severed her lung, knifed her in the heart, liver and, repeatedly, through the left nipple. Then he defecated, wedging his faeces into her mouth. Before leaving, he scooped her blood into an empty yogurt cup and drank it.

On 27 January, Chase forced his way into Evelyn Miroth's home. This time it was worse: there were children. The police hunted the neighbourhood house-to-house and, the following afternoon, met Chase on his doorstep carrying a large cardboard box.

Portions of the second child fell out.

His apartment – walls, floors, bed, clothing, bath, furniture, kitchen – was covered in blood. The freezer housed a half-gallon container filled with animal and human organs. On the bed lay a plate of fresh child's brain, but Chase denied everything. 'It wasn't me,' he said. 'No shit, I didn't do it.' Then he admitted cutting up dogs.

A reasonably accurate police sketch of the Wallin murder suspect, with a moustache and goatee added by Detective Roberts

'Do you think it would be wrong if you ate people?' the police asked. After Chase replied, 'The Nazis ate a lot', a prolonged silence fell.

Under further questioning, Chase said that he was the victim of a conspiracy to poison him. His mother, father, Frank Sinatra, Hugh Hefner, the Mafia, Germans – they were all at it. In court, the district attorney argued that the killings were inspired by sexual sadism, and the anticipated defence of insanity did not succeed. Chase was sent to Death Row at San Quentin, where he repeatedly asked for fresh blood. Over time he stored up his medication and, on 24 December 1979, died of an overdose.

Van Meegeren, Hans (1889–1947)

Van Meegeren can be forgiven for the awful quality of his flat, soft-focus forgeries because they fooled so many experts. As a student he possessed a promising talent, taking the coveted Gold Medal at his Delft art school, and his first major one-man exhibition in the Hague in 1922 sold out. Van Meegeren prospered, but the more he painted low-brow pictures pandering to the public's taste, the better they sold. Critics, the influential Dr Abraham Bredius conspicuous among them, detested his work, and his output degenerated into commercial portraits of the nobility from London, Holland and the Riviera.

By the age of forty-three Van Meegeren was based near Roquebrune in the South of France, sufficiently embittered with the Fine Art community to devote four years to perfecting the physical technicalities of forging Old Masters. He planned to debunk his critics. Taking an unwanted seventeenth-century canvas, the *Resurrection of Lazarus*, he prepared it by rubbing down with pumice stone. He used badger-hair brushes, developed a special paint based on lilac oil hardened off with phenolformaldehyde, baked the finished work at 105 degrees centigrade, rolled the canvas in a cylinder to reproduce 'crackling', rubbed Indian ink into the cracks to simulate antique dust, nailed the painting to a stretcher with period tacks and knocked the finished work about to justify slipshod repairs. For his blue pigments he hand-ground particles of lapis-lazuli, and, were phenolformaldehyde (employed for its heat-resistant properties) not Bakelite, no scientific tests could have recognised the result as a fraud.

Whose work to forge? At first Van Meegeren considered Rembrandt and Leonardo. Then he chose a kindred spirit, the seventeenth-century Dutch artist, Jan Vermeer of Delft, whose reputation had languished for two centuries because his style failed to please a contemporary art historian.

For seven months in 1937 Van Meegeren worked up *Christ and the Disciples at Emmaus*, a hitherto unknown Vermeer measuring 1m 20cm by 1m 17cm. He added a pinch of Caravaggio to the styling, in conformity with Dr Bredius's views – previously unconfirmed – on Vermeer's Italianate inheritance. Ten years later, Van Meegeren recalled this interlude with relish. 'It was the most thrilling, the most exciting period of my whole life! There were so many things to consider, so many traps to avoid... I was happy because I felt, yes, I was positive, that good old Vermeer would be satisfied with my job. He was keeping me company. He was always with me. I sensed his presence; he encouraged me. He liked what I

Van Meegeren's signature on three of his forged Vermeers

was doing. Yes, he really did.' Van Meegeren was proud to sign his work with the monogram 'I.V.M', for his master's I.V. Meer.

Posing as an agent for an anonymous Italian family fallen on hard times, who were smuggling out an Old Master in defiance of Fascist edicts, Van Meegeren took his picture to a discerning Amsterdam lawyer in Paris. The attorney recognised a work of quality, and appreciated that Van Meegeren's source had to be protected. So he concealed the painting's illicit **provenance**, devising a cover story of his own invention: the heirs of a Dutch businessman had found a canvas gathering dust in the deceased's Parisian apartment. They did not rate it highly, but the attorney knew enough about art to catch the next train for Monte Carlo and consult the noted expert, Dr Abraham Bredius.

Over eighty and half-blind, Bredius spent two days closeted with *Christ at Emmaus* before making his triumphant attribution: 'this glorious work by Vermeer'. The *Burlington Magazine* published Bredius's rhapsodical discovery. 'It is a wonderful moment in the life of a lover of art when he finds himself suddenly confronted with a hitherto unknown painting by a great master, untouched, on the original canvas, and without any restoration, just as it left the artist's studio. Neither the beautiful signature nor the *pointillé* on the bread which Christ is blessing are necessary to convince us that we have here a – I am inclined to say *the* – masterpiece of Johannes Vermeer of Delft, and, moreover, one of his largest works, quite different from all his other works and yet *every inch a Vermeer*.'

The Netherlands seethed with excitement. Rotterdam's Boyman's Museum parted with 540,000 guilders for the canvas, popularly known as 'De Emmausgangers', and it formed the jewel in the crown of their 1938 exhibition, 'Masterpieces of Four Centuries'. Many eminent critics noted how badly underrated Vermeer had been as a religious artist, and soon millions of magazine reproductions of the Emmausgangers adorned walls throughout Europe.

So everyone was happy. Bredius had crowned his career, and Van Meegeren, something of a pragmatist, chose to omit his planned exposure of the art establishment as pompous, ignorant fools. He pocketed the money, and when friends inquired after the source of his monstrous wealth, he pointed to his regular purchases of lottery tickets. Van Meegeren returned to the Netherlands in 1939, acquiring a beautiful eighteenth-century mansion in the heart of Amsterdam, and the outbreak of World War II meant that his tranche of new Vermeers slipped onto the market without monopolising the headlines. There was a *Last Supper* (1,600,000 guilders), *The Blessing of Isaac* (1,275,000 guilders), *Christ's Ablution* and two spurious De Hoochs.

Meanwhile Van Meegeren's own reputation underwent a renaissance. But only with occupying Nazis. He specialised in black-and-white compositions of ferocious soldiers, ecstatic and libidinous nudes, Arian pianists ringed by the Ghosts of the Great Composers, torture scenes and skeletons. These visual nightmares sold strongly to the SS, and his *oeuvre* was commemorated in book form; a personally signed and dedicated copy found its way into the Führer's library. Wearing his other hat, Van Meegeren's work caught the eye of the great collector Goering. A German banker, Herr Miedl, persuaded the Reichsmarschall to hand over 1,650,000 guilders for a Vermeer, *Christ and the Adulteress*.

But Germany lost the war, and in 1945 the Allied Military Government Art Commission discovered this heritage masterpiece among Goering's plundered hoard of art treasures stored in a salt mine near Salzburg. By then Miedl had fled to Franco's Spain, but the Dutch police tracked down his associate, the dismal hack Van Meegeren. He was arrested, thrown into prison and charged as a collaborator for selling off a priceless national asset. He faced the death penalty.

By then in his late fifties, Van Meegeren was a nervous chain smoker and heavy drinker dependent on sleeping pills. After six weeks pondering his fate, Van Meegeren revealed that he had not, after all, betrayed his country by selling a Vermeer. He had duped the state's enemies by painting it.

Van Meegeren went on repeating this preposterous assertion until, under strict police supervision and watched by professors, he was released to his studio to execute another Vermeer, *Young Jesus Teaching in the Temple*, which later fetched $600 and now hangs in a Johannesburg church. Doubters were convinced when they saw his studio littered with props – dishes, weapons, clothes, furniture –

that figured in the background of previous Vermeers. In irrefutable confirmation, he sketched the underpainting of the *Resurrection of Lazarus* cloaked by his *Christ at Emmaus*. X-rays proved him correct.

Bredius was already dead. In short order Van Meegeren was bankrupted (being unable to repay what might be regarded as his well-deserved 8,000,000 guilders), and the collaboration charges reduced to 'deception'. The potential jamboree of his trial was rushed through in a few hours in 1947, and Van Meegeren died of a heart-attack six weeks into his one-year sentence before Queen Juliana could effect a pardon.

See also **Morals**

Van Schoor, Louis (1953–)

South African security guard beached on the tide of history. Until he was thirty-three, Van Schoor made very little of himself. He did badly at school, ran through four marriages, and served twelve years with the police, leaving with the same rank with which he joined – constable. But on starting work as a subcontractor for the security firms of Buffalo and Providence in 1986, Van Schoor discovered his forte. It was shooting blacks with **dumdum** bullets. His lawyer pleaded in mitigation that Van Schoor was not racially prejudiced; he would have shot whites just as happily.

In three years Van Schoor gunned his way through 101 people, killing thirty-nine. Cleared at inquest after inquest, he relied on Section 49(2) of the South African Penal Code permitting the shooting of anyone escaping from the scene of a serious crime. The word 'serious' was broadly construed to encompass petty theft while trespassing; the word 'escaping' included those hit in the chest while supposedly running away, or blown to pieces while trying to surrender, as well as those left to bleed to death.

By degrees, Van Schoor became trigger-happier. He shot Coleman Teto while he was walking to work, lured three victims to business premises to discuss job offers and then shot them, and shot another sixteen – on separate occasions – after they had surrendered. One magistrate listened patiently as Van Schoor explained a victim's frontal wound (contracted while running away) by a tale of running away backwards. 'Put it this way,' said a former client, 'I was a hell of a lot happier and I slept a lot easier when I knew Van Schoor was around.'

Detailed descriptions of the killings remove any element of ambiguity. On 11 July 1988 two youths, 13-year-old Liefe Peters and 14-year-old John Swarbooti, broke into an East London restaurant. Van Schoor found the boys hiding in the lavatories and ordered them to walk towards the shattered window. He shot Peters dead. Then he shot Swarbooti in the leg. Then he shot him in the buttock. Then he kicked him in the mouth. Then he picked him up, propped him against a table, and shot him again, in the shoulder.

Van Schoor's boss at Buffalo Security looked askance at the bodies piling up in the local morgue. So he took soundings from three senior policemen and a magistrate. Fine, they said. But the legal defence embodied in Section 49 has limitations; it only affords protection when shots are fired with intent to extinguish life.

This may sound tantamount to absolving a man of murder if he can prove that he meant to kill, but during the inquest into the January 1989 deaths of two blacks, Paliso and Bikitsha, an attentive magistrate noticed that Van Schoor had slipped up in his testimony. In attempted mitigation, Van Schoor misguidedly conceded that he only meant to wing his victims, thus laying himself open to charges of murder. But no matter. Van Schoor was acquitted because of his *constructive* intent to kill, charitably inferred by the court. 'In effect,' the magistrate concluded, 'by loosing a volley of shots he had from that moment decided to condemn them to death.'

But Section 49 has another requirement. People can only be shot if aware you are trying to arrest them – in other words, speak first, shoot later. An oversight in this department finally brought Van Schoor to book.

Apart from resigning his job, at first he did not suffer unduly. Public sentiment was reflected in the 'I love Louis' car-bumper stickers featuring a diagrammatic red heart stitched with three bullet holes. The local *Daily Dispatch* printed a letter beginning, 'I find it quite ludicrous that investigations are to be made into Mr Van Schoor, a security guard, for doing his job, and a very good job at that. In my opinion the man should be given a medal for bravery.'

But nemesis came in the wake of Nelson Mandela's release. The state needed a scapegoat as a token of its newfound good intentions, and on 10 April 1992 Van Schoor was convicted of five murders and two attempted murders. It is possible that he was not so much a luckless security guard as a blossoming serial killer suddenly presented with an endless supply of no-comeback victims. Reports depicted him as loner, of low intelligence, unable to cope with relationships and obsessed with the police and law enforcement – a perfect fit.

Vegetables

In Britain, where gun crime remains a relative rarity, it may be worth simulating a firearm with a vegetable during a robbery. The penalties on conviction are no less severe, but the chance of injury is substantially diminished, since (as a rule) the police do not carry weapons either. Shoot-outs under these conditions are risk-free. Nonetheless, most years bring a trickle of fatalities where the victim is found clasping an imitation gun.

The favoured assault vegetable is a cucumber, whether wrapped in a plastic bag or poking away menacingly in an anorak pocket. In October 1989, Ernest Coverly was sent down for robbing fourteen building societies with a cucumber; Mark Fitzpatrick from Hampshire subjected five building societies to a reign of vegetable terror before being sentenced to five years in March 1991 for his haul of £4,750 .

For his second robbery in two days at the same Shell petrol station in Old Street, London, young Carl Lancaster vacillated between cucumbers and bananas for his weapon of choice. He bought both at a local greengrocer's but, during the approach, one of the bananas was consumed by a cab-driver (Lancaster liked to rob in style) and he opted for the cucumber's superior fire-power. Lancaster relieved the cashier of £60, only to find his getaway (still by taxi) obstructed by irate customers on the forecourt. He was sentenced to three years in December 1990.

So it seems that Andrew Giles from West Yorkshire is a true innovator: in August 1991 he attempted to rob a shop assistant with a courgette.

In the 1992 British election campaign, Margaret Thatcher was attacked with a bunch of daffodils.

Her aggressor, employing subterfuge, accosted the ex-Prime Minister with the pretext that the flowers were a gift. And in November 1991 Mohammed Jabber was jailed for three years for sexual assault with a vegetable after fitting a chili pepper into the rectum of a former Bangladeshi politician living in London.

Suitably concealed, French loaves constitute occasional stand-ins for vegetables (or sawn-off shotguns) and, in a forensic variation, pathologist Professor Keith Simpson detected signs of foul play when he unearthed what looked like a badly charred human forearm from the smouldering ruins of a Bedford pub. His find was gingerly boxed up and transported to the mortuary under police escort, where the blackened French loaf went under the knife in the expectant presence of Scotland Yard and CID chiefs, the local police surgeon and the Chief Fire Officer. Professor Simpson tells this undated story against himself in his autobiography, *40 Years of Murder*.

Vendetta

The most calamitous of the Sicilian vendettas raged between 1872 and 1878 in the towns of Bagheira and Monreale. For obvious reasons, detailed eyewitness descriptions from survivors are scarce; but the bloodbath's general course is clear.

Trouble started when a member of the Fratuzzi clan, Giuseppe Lipari, denounced a rival in the Stoppaglieri family to the police. The penalty for this breach of Mafia protocol was death, and the Stoppaglieri called for Lipari's execution.

The Fratuzzi's refusal to kill their own man started the feud. Soon all the close relatives of the original antagonists were dead in tit-for-tat killings, leaving families rummaging in terror through their ancestry in case some distant kinship put them in the firing line. Keeping count was complicated by the incidence of imprisonment or emigration, and strangers might be waylayed in the street by a grieving and unfamiliar crone – head of the female line – to learn that they were the surviving head of one clan or the other and hence in a state of ritual vendetta against a remote cousin. With progressive local depopulation, whether through death or prudence, youngsters were dragged into the dispute; one lad needed his blunderbuss loaded for him.

After six years the dispute hit the buffers when another Fratuzzi, Salvatore D'Amico, wearied of life; he too went to the police, in recognition of the consequences. This time the Fratuzzi took their cue and killed him, displaying his body in atonement.

In the 1960s a similar outbreak came close to cracking the Mafia's wall of **silence**. A feud between the Riccobonos, from the village of Tommaso Natale, and their neighbours left the Cracolici one down; denied an adult male for the next sacrifical offering, they resolved to make do with 13-year-old Paolino, who was machine-gunned to death on a mountain path.

His mother, Rosa Messina, courageously reported the killers to the police; Paolino was her second son to die, and her husband too had been murdered. On 19 September 1963 expectations ran high as she was called to the witness box at Palermo Assizes, where her disclosures had landed thirty *mafiosi* in the dock. But she lost her nerve, and the prosecution fell back on the testimony of Anna Galletti, who stated: 'I live alone at Tommaso Natale. I have four children. Therefore I know nothing about everything.'

Vendettas are a throwback almost to prehistory. For economies on the fringes of subsistence, unencumbered by central authority, infringements of grazing rights or access to a spring constituted an act of war punishable by death and, to this day, many Sicilians are forced to buy their water from Mafia-owned private wells. Even in Palermo, those wanting water daily negotiate their 'surplus' requirements from the Mob, and the trickle-down theory of wealth is rigidly enforced by systematically obstructing the construction of new aqueducts or dams. In Salvatore 'the beast' Riina's native Corleone, the plans for a barrage have been successfully kept at bay since the Second World War.

As justice goes, vendettas were very rough, but preferable to the feudal courts of the Sicilian aristocracy. In this harsh school a *mafioso*'s character was formed, and his outlook travelled well to gangland America where, until long after the First World War, Chicago featured a Dead Man's Tree, a sickly poplar in the heart of Little Italy. By old Sicilian custom it was here that the names of those condemned to die were posted in advance, a tradition honoured in the 1921 aldermanic campaign when thirty men lost their lives to bombings.

See also **Anselmi and Scalise, Inquisition**

Viaducts

Viaducts form an unusual focal point for sexual gratification, and the Hungarian Sylvestre Matuscka was probably unique in obtaining fulfilment from blowing up trains on them. At first he did so in his own time, but in later years he secured a paid position for his hobby.

On 12 September 1931, Matuscka detonated eighteen sticks of dynamite under the Budapest-Ostend express as it rumbled over the Biatorbagy viaduct. Transfixed in ecstasy, he watched as five coaches plunged eighty feet over the edge, resulting in billowing clouds of steam, the screech of tearing metal, twenty-five dead, 120 injured and dozens of exciting ambulances. It was a costly means of achieving orgasm, and the alert reader will note that Matuscka was a copycat fantasist. Peter **Kürten**, the Düsseldorf Vampire who derived the same satisfaction from dreams of blood that others procure from pornography, thrived on precisely this vision of railway catastrophes. Matuscka revelled in carnage, and his confession includes the words, 'I wrecked trains because I like to see people die. I like to hear them scream. I like to see them suffer', sentiments repeated almost verbatim, excepting the first four words, half a century later by the Los Angeles Night Stalker.

As an infantry officer decorated for bravery during the First World War, Matuscka was perhaps inured to slaughter, and by 1931, aged forty, he seemed a settled and prosperous businessman, married with a teenage daughter. But he was unable to experience emission without seeing trains crash, and the deaths at Biatorbagy represented the pinnacle of an escalating campaign. Nine months before, on 31 December 1930, the engine-cab crew of the Vienna-Passau express had brought their train to a halt ahead of a damaged section of track. A month later an engine was derailed by a steel bar across the lines, but there were no casualties.

On 8 August 1931, Matuscka drew his first blood with a home-made bomb at Juterborg, when seven coaches rolled down a thirty-foot embankment, and he took such delight in the Biatorbagy disaster that his arrest was inevitable. The day afterwards, Matuscka described the spectacle to an enthralled crowd, holding court in a local café. 'I saw one woman with her arm torn off!' he cried, and executed illustrative sketches before slipping away. Then he tried to wring blood-money from the atrocity, submitting a bogus compensation claim for facial injuries and loss of baggage as a passenger in the front coach.

But no one in the front coach had survived. Investigators found a map marked with the crash sites at Matuscka's home, and he was identified as the man who bought the explosives. During the trial, he pinned the blame on 'Leo', a spirit who never left him alone, and flirted from the dock with pretty female spectators. In his defence, Matuscka maintained that he had hoped to publicise a new patent safety device cold-shouldered by the railway companies, and he was lucky to be tried in Austria (which had no death penalty), where he was sentenced to serve life imprisonment in Hungary (which had).

In the aftermath of the Second World War it transpired that Matuscka had been released, probably at the Russians' behest. Crime writer Colin Wilson relates that he surfaced again in 1953, presumably happy as a sandboy, when a group of commandos about to blow a bridge surrendered to an American patrol in the Korean War. 'I am Matuscka, the train wrecker of Biatorbagy!' proclaimed their leader. After his capture, Matuscka again disappeared, possibly in a swap for Communist secrets.

See **Fantasising, Ramirez, de Sade, Sex crimes**

Villa, Francisco 'Pancho' (d. 1923)

Revolutionary Mexican. Villa survived a firing squad in 1912 and, eleven years later, outlived most of his assassination.

Villa was an enthusiast of capital punishment for

others, executing prisoners, traitors and suspected traitors out of hand. But when Villa himself went (on a trumped-up charge) to the firing squad on 4 June 1912, he spent so long pleading for his life – demanding a priest, then bringing out trinkets, coins and his gold watch in an attempt at bribery – that a reprieve arrived after the command 'Aim' but before the order 'Fire'.

Villa was finally killed on 20 July 1923 in his 1919 Dodge touring car, dying with four of his five bodyguards. By then the revolutionary general was in retirement, a pampered landowner possessed of thousands of acres. Eight gunmen lay in ambush in the town of Parra.

Villa took sixteen hits, four in the head and twelve in his body. With his chest ripped to pieces, the intestines slid onto the Dodge's floorboards. One of his arms swung free from a couple of shreds.

'The dirty pig, we taught him,' said Ramon Guerra, one of the assassins. With his other arm, Villa drew his Colt and blew off the approaching Guerra's face. After that, they shot the general dead.

Virtual reality

In California, 'cyberspace' has reached the courtroom. Among the first cases was a pornographer who allegedly shot his brother eight times in one minute. This extended, complex incident made for descriptive problems, and in February 1992 the prosecution went to trial in San Rafael with a virtual reality animation of the shooting.

Over captions with digital time encoded, the court watched the victim get out of bed, walk to the door and get shot. With minimal reprogramming, the events could be viewed from eye-level or above the scene.

The defence appealed against the verdict, arguing that the prosecution relied on artistic merit and sound production values to sway the jury, and a similar debate preoccupied Britain after the May 1993 television screening of *Bad Company* had made it clear to millions of viewers that Michael Hickey, currently serving life for the murder of Carl Bridgewater in 1979, was innocent.

Bad Company was only a dramatisation of Hickey's story, and the British judiciary quite properly feel that prisoners should not be released sim-

ply because the audience enjoyed the show. A strictly factual documentary might carry greater weight – but the Bridgewater case received such treatment years ago. Thus the play, with its inescapable element of dramatic licence, was justified as a last recourse, adding visceral passion to what viewers already knew intellectually and, paradoxically, it is the weakness of the prosecution case that can make such convictions unassailable. There are almost no arguments to destroy, and whereas physical and forensic evidence can be reappraised with a degree of objectivity, a case founded solely on 'verbals' can only be challenged by more verbals, subject to judicial dismissal as mere verbals. Thus two truths run in companionable harness: Michael Hickey is acknowledged as innocent by a broad spectrum of the population, who despair of his release. But, judging by her determined track record, his mother may yet extricate her son from prison.

See also **Court of Appeal**

Vitiligo

Unusual clue in the recent case of John Hawkins, a Studio 54 hustler finally caught on 1 August 1991 in Sardinia, arrested in connection with Ellis Greene's murder in April 1988.

Greene's corpse served as a stand-in for the faked death of Gene Hanson, whose life was insured for a million dollars. Hawkins, the beneficiary, fled when the body-substitution came to light in June 1988, taking with him a further $240,000 of embezzled funds.

Hawkins was such a charmer that he could pull women off the street, the beach or the dance floor after a few minutes chat. As a fugitive on the Caribbean island of St Thomas, he scored 'babes' at the rate of two a day, and many more were eager to claim intimate relations. This confusing trail of contacts brought little comfort to the officer on the case, Sergeant Jon Perkins. He wanted hard evidence, like fingerprints, to enable him to sift the deluge of sightings after successful television appeals on *Unsolved Mysteries* and *America's Most Wanted*.

In 1991 a Hollywood film mogul 'serviced' by Hawkins disclosed that he suffered from vitiligo, a skin-pigmentation disease which in Hawkins's case discoloured the penis. It had a big white blemish, known as 'Spot'. So for the next year of the manhunt Sergeant Perkins weeded out attention-seekers from the women boasting of Hawkins as a conquest by insisting on a description of his genitalia.

It is true that Hawkins was eventually traced through his even more conspicuous red catamaran, moored in Sardinia's Cannigone dock, but the final identification came after the local *carabinieri* telephoned Interpol to ask if their suspect had any distinguishing features.

Vocations

Until the abolition of capital punishment in 1965, Britain carried a permanent complement of official executioners. This part-time occupation remained until the end a sought-after career. As the Royal Commission of 1953 observed: 'No doubt the ambition that prompts an average of five applicants a week for the post of hangman reveals psychological qualities of a sort no state would wish to foster in its citizens.' **Hanging** is now a bygone profession; but the vocation most missed by American serial killers remains available. Given the chance, most multiple murderers would plump for life as a cop.

In the words of FBI Agent John Douglas: 'Almost all serial killers are police buffs. When we ask them what they would do if they could start again and select another occupation, they choose law enforcement. Many of these guys in fact will have tried, but didn't make the grade. A lot end up as security guards.' A cursory glance at American periodicals like *True Police* reinforces this equation; the editorial content is mostly about sex killings ('Rape Slayer in Nunnery') and the advertisements mostly about sex ('Do You Want to Attract Women and Drive them Wild?').

Gerard **Schaefer**, sentenced to twenty years plus, actually was a policeman. He picked up female hitchhikers, took them to a remote spot, hung them by their necks, force-fed them with beer, watched them urinate and defecate, and killed them – before having sex. Schaefer's other wellspring of moral authority was as a hyper-religious member of a Christian cult subscribing to literal adherence to the Bible, with its many strictures against wanton fornication.

Jeffrey **Dahmer** is probably alone among serial killers in wishing he had been a real estate agent.

Von Bülow, Claus (1926–)

The rich may have more money, but this does not necessarily make them happy. The $75 million heiress of the Crawford fortune, Martha 'Sunny' von Bülow, was frittering her life away in semi-isolation when she succumbed to an irreversible coma at the age of fifty. Addicted to aspirin and laxatives, in a household devoid of friends and society, she teetered on the edge of divorce from an unsympathetic spouse (engaged in an affair) and had not indulged in sexual intercourse for at least five and perhaps thirteen years.

Her husband, Claus von Bülow, was born Claus Cecil Borberg, son of a Danish playwright. For the war years, his mother took refuge in Britain, sitting out hostilities in Claridges. Her son, an urbane sophisticate, evolved into a fearsome snob endowed with what writer Kirk Wilson's publishers call a 'plumy, upper-crest accent'. A capable, demanding man of great social refinement, von Bülow married into money. Sunny, unfamiliar with the world of work, reduced him to a house-husband; he complained of feeling like a gigolo. He stood to gain $14 million under her will of December 1979.

Von Bülow's lover, former soap opera actress Alexandra Isles, had issued him with an ultimatum some months before: get rid of your wife by the year's end or find another mistress. And on 27 December 1979 the obstacle to their future fell into a coma. Sunny's maid, the fiercely loyal Maria Shrallhammer, entered her employer's room to find von Bülow stretched out on one bed perusing a newspaper while her mistress lay unconscious on the other. Sunny could not be roused, but von Bülow assured Maria that there was no need for a doctor, an assertion reiterated throughout the day against Maria's deepening concern.

That evening, Sunny took an abrupt turn for the worse. Her breathing degenerated into a 'kind of rattle'. Alarmed, von Bülow telephoned for help, which arrived at the very moment his wife's heartbeats ceased and she stopped breathing. Sunny was revived by mouth-to-mouth resuscitation and rushed to hospital. Tests revealed a low blood-sugar level, 41 milligrams per 100 millilitres, outside the normal band of 70 to 110 mg. Glucose was injected, but still her blood-sugar level dropped, so five hours after admission Sunny was checked for **insulin**, which 'eats' sugar.

Her insulin reading was towards the upper end of the normal range. It gradually diminished, suggesting higher levels earlier in the day. Sunny regained consciousness twenty-four hours later with no ill effects. She suspected nothing untoward, but Maria remained on the alert, and in February 1980 Sunny succumbed to another unheralded attack, suddenly too weak to sit up in bed or speak distinctly. Von Bülow was inclined to suspect influenza. A few days later, Maria came across a black bag in one of his suitcases. Inside she saw pills, a white powder and a yellow paste. Analysed in secret by the family doctor, the first two were preparations of Valium, the last a sedative, neither available over the counter in paste or powder form.

In April, Sunny was hospitalised after another episode when her speech slurred and she lost motor-coordination. Over Thanksgiving, Maria checked von Bülow's bag and, as she testified later, found it contained a clear vial labelled 'Insulin', several needles and a syringe. On 19 December, Maria was given the weekend off. On her way out she peered into the bag: the insulin was still there. The following evening, Sunny collapsed without warning in the kitchen. Her son, Alexander, carried her to the bedroom and the following morning von Bülow discovered her unconscious in the bathroom in a pool of urine. On admission to Newport Hospital, her blood-sugar levels were extremely low (29 mg) and her insulin level extremely high (216 mg). A search of her apartment located the black bag inside a metal box in a locked cupboard. Among the bottles of pills and drugs was a used needle, which laboratory tests indicated to be encrusted with insulin, and on 16 March 1982 von Bülow was found guilty on two counts of attempted murder.

He never spent a night in prison. J. Paul Getty Jnr, an erstwhile employer, funded an appeal headed by Alan Dershowitz, the Harvard Law professor. Dershowitz mobilised his students, assigning teams to different aspects of the case, and by the time the hearing opened in April 1985, Sunny's personal habits were acknowledged as less than pristine. An unreliable witness at the first trial had intimated that Sunny recommended self-inflicted insulin injections as an aid to slimming; now writer Truman Capote assured reporters that in the 1950s Sunny had offered to show him how to inject himself, and that during the late 1970s she was 'deep into drinking' and frequently experimented with amphetamines, Demerol and Quaaludes.

In court, medical experts for the defence pointed to inconsistencies in the damning needle. They maintained that the exterior aspect of a needle is wiped clean by its removal from the body tissues. In any case, the test result could be a false positive from two other drugs detected on its tip. Sunny's count of 216 mg insulin was dismissed as one of four conflicting readings, one higher, two lower. Both of Sunny's comas could have resulted from some unspecified combination of drugs and, under cross-examination, Maria admitted that she had made no mention of the insulin bottle when first questioned in January 1981. She maintained that she had not appreciated its significance at the time, but the defence only needed to insert an element of reasonable doubt into her testimony and the surrounding evidence. On 10 June 1985, after twelve hours deliberation, von Bülow was discharged.

Perhaps the jury thought that Maria lied about the insulin. Perhaps they believed that the needle might have been dipped in insulin in order to incriminate von Bülow. Or perhaps insulin had never been present in Sunny's body.

But then why did she go into a coma? The most likely explanation for low blood-sugar which continues to drop under the impetus of a glucose injection is insulin, and the most likely reason for high test levels of insulin is… a high level of insulin. The only internal source, at anything approaching Sunny's readings, is a pancreatic tumour. But Sunny did not have a pancreatic tumour. The alternative is external administration, raising the macabre conjecture that Sunny *was* injected, and that an attempt followed to implicate von Bülow by tampering with, and embroidering, the evidence, thereby ensuring his eventual acquittal.

W

'Waldheim's disease'

A form of **amnesia** besetting war criminals. Kurt Waldheim, the Austrian President, used his affliction to avoid prison. Ernest Saunders, the former chief executive convicted of the Guinness 'share-ramping' scandal, contracted Alzheimer's disease – supposedly an irreversible form of pre-senile dementia – to get out. But after his release ten months into a five-year sentence at Britain's Ford Open Prison, Saunders rapidly underwent a miraculous recovery. By early 1992 he was in fine fettle, hosting a business seminar at Cranfield, booked to lecture £350-a-head delegates on 'the lessons of turnaround'.

In Stuttgart, Josef Franz Leo Schwammberger spent early 1992 under impressive selective amnesia. Schwammberger remembered everything up to 1939 and everything after 1945, but the years in between were blank. He could recall nothing of his four years as a labour camp commandant in Poland. Day after day, Schwammberger sat in court listening, without a flicker of recollection, to survivors' accounts of how their genitals were branded, their babies smashed against walls to save bullets, and their lives valued at twelve pfennigs a thousand, the cost of a postcard to order up another batch of Jews.

Denial is a state known to therapists, but it is not a legal defence. On 18 May 1992 the 80-year-old Schwammberger was sentenced to life imprisonment on seven specimen counts of murder.

'Dementia Americana' is another affliction occasionally produced as a defence ploy. Diseases can also feature as an unreliable **weapon**. In 1912 Frenchman Henri Giraud tried to dispose of Louis Pernotte (whose life he insured for 300,000 francs) with typhoid. But the administration of his bacterial cultures was at first very non-specific; he confined the entire *famille* Pernotte to their sickbeds. In the end the resilient Louis required individual targeting with daily injections, said by Giraud to consist of restorative doses of camomile. Six years later Giraud took his own life after falling under suspicion for the murder of a heavily insured widow.

In America, Dr Arthur Warren Waite from New York used diseases to despatch his wealthy in-laws, one by one. Waite was a bored and conscienceless society dentist who wanted to expedite his inheritance so that he could channel his energies more fully into tennis. In January 1916 he doctored his mother-in-law's rice pudding with tubes contaminated with a blunderbuss of typhoid, anthrax, diphtheria, tuberculosis and influenza. After she died, her grieving husband John E. Peck came to stay and it took Waite six weeks to polish him off. When poisoned desserts and an infected nasal spray failed to do the trick, he attempted to give his guest pneumonia; later he fell back on **arsenic** before suffocating Peck with a pillow on 12 March. In the witness box Waite related this *histoire* with such infectious good humour that the jury were reduced to sheepish giggles.

His trial was marked by that curious variant of the alibi defence, the Multiple Personality Disorder (see **MPD**). 'I believe,' Waite assured the court, 'that although my body lives in America, my soul lives in Egypt. It is the man from Egypt who has committed these foul crimes.' So Waite had really been somewhere else at the critical moment, on the banks of the Nile during the time of the Pharaohs, and accordingly the dentist was cross-examined in detail about his Egyptian period. He too remembered nothing, was found sane and guilty, and went to the electric chair on 24 May 1917, still smiling.

Walpole, Horace (1717–97)

English man of letters and a good source on eighteenth-century robberies in the centre of fashionable London. In September 1750 Walpole was comfortably ensconced in his dining room when, as he wrote, 'I heard a loud cry of "Stop, thief!"' A **highwayman** had attacked a post-chaise in Piccadilly. Walpole was later held up by a mounted robber in Hyde Park, and was lucky to escape with his life when the pistol went off (perhaps accidentally) in his face, scorching the skin with powder.

This incident was followed by a characteristic charade, played out with every appearance of courtesy. Walpole advertised, asking for the return of his property, and the reply showed 'less wit than the epistles of Voltaire, but had ten times more natural and easy politeness'. James M'Lean, the highwayman, agreed an exchange of goods through 'the same footman that was behind the Chariot when Rob'd... as We Intend Repaying him a trifle we took from him'.

M'Lean was the son of a Scottish Presbyterian minister. After wasting his inheritance, he applied himself to highway robbery with sufficient diligence to earn a smart mistress and a flat opposite White's, the London club for gentlemen. There he became a living embodiment of the highwayman myth. By day he promenaded up St James's, every inch a dandy, attired in white silk stockings, fine waistcoats and yellow Moroccan slippers; by night, he robbed.

Although some detractors averred that his lack of *true* breeding was easily discernible, at M'Lean's trial Lady Caroline Petersham testified on his behalf; while in **Newgate** he was visited (according to Walpole) by Lord Montford 'at the head of half White's', and the *Daily Journal* reported that hundreds of Ladies and Gentlemen attended his **Tyburn** execution.

Of all the acts of highwaymanly gallantry, the prize must go to Claude Duval (1643–70) for his *al fresco* dance with a lady of quality. She happened to have a flute in her pocket and, as the mounted robbers gained on her coach, she started playing to keep up her spirits. By a happy coincidence the accomplished Duval was also carrying a flute and reciprocated in kind. Drawing abreast of the carriage, he asked her to dance. 'Sir,' said she (according to Duval's 1670 biographer), 'I dare not deny anything to one of your quality and good mind. You seem a gentleman, and your request is very reasonable.'

So the couple tripped a light corranto on the heath. Duval demonstrated such consummate skill, despite his great French riding boots, that another passenger presented him with £100 in token of his esteem, and this touching scene became a favourite with Victorian narrative painters. In more robust vein, Duval is reported in the *Newgate Calendar* as snatching a silver feeding bottle from a baby, and at his arrest he would 'certainly have killed ten constables' had he not been drunk. Again, he was visited by scores of ladies in **Newgate**'s Condemned Hold; they later attended his hanging wearing masks. His tombstone can be seen in the Inigo Jones church in Covent Garden:

> Here lies Du Vall: Reader, if male thou art
> Look to thy purse; if female, to thy Heart...
> Old **Tyburn**'s Glory, England's illustrious thief,
> Du Vall, the ladies' Joy, Du Vall the ladies' grief

Watchmen

Until the eighteenth century, London was policed by a combination of constables and geriatric watchmen, the latter too aged and infirm to earn their living by real work. Known as 'charleys', they were created under Charles II by a 1663 Act of the Common Court of Council, and were soon enshrined as a popular source of derision. Writer T. A. Critchley described them as 'contemptible, dissolute and drunken buffoons who shuffled along the darkened streets after sunset with their long staves and dim lanterns, calling out the time and the state of the weather.' When a charley wanted to summon help, he sounded a wooden rattle.

Often they took their job description literally, to 'watch men' being robbed. Francis Jackson, the eighteenth-century highwayman, reported in his *Recantation*: 'Every highwayman knows that these watchmen are silly old decrepit men who will run away rather than fight. I have seen a dozen of them stand with Halberds in their Hands, yet we have robbed before their very faces, and they stand still the while, not daring to oppose us in the least.' In more energetic mode, Jackson once had a batch trussed up and then took their place for the added ease with which he could accost passers-by. In 1737 a similarly effective system of day-policing was established in the capital.

Parish constables were both more vigorous and more corrupt. Of the eighty in Westminster, **Fielding** found that only six were trustworthy. But he used these **untouchables** to found the Bow Street Runners, the forebears of the modern police force.

See also **Ratcliffe Highway**

Weapons

Murder (and attempted murder) weapons have included: a golf tee (Queripetl), a lawnmower (Whybrow), paving slabs (the Stoneman), an umbrella (Markov), a television aerial (the Goodmans), a chainsaw (Gotti), a meat grinder (Gambino), a bucket (Kidd), a bath (Smith), a pillow (Waite), a poisoned raisin (Lamson), lightbulbs (Thompson), a rattlesnake (James), a life preserver (Kipnik), a putative poisoned suppository (Monroe), an exploding purse (Orchard), a particular object (Solzhenitsyn) and, in May 1982, a cookery-book gun. Sent through the mail to a Brooklyn housewife by an anonymous donor, the *Quick and Delicious Gourmet Cookbook* shot its recipient fatally through the chest with a couple of .22 bullets.

According to the *South Wales Echo*, on 5 June 1990 a Texas Pizza delivery man, Troy Brewer, was robbed in a Balch Springs phone booth. He handed over $50 when, threatened with a turtle, he was told, 'Don't move or you're gonna get bit.' In 1991, the Californian Kao Khae Saephan opened a one-inch gash over his wife's eye with a frozen squirrel.

In 1991, 40 per cent of Britain's 708 homicides were committed with a knife or sharp instrument; seventy-one victims were strangled and eight axed to death.

Weber, Jeanne (b. 1875)

A famous French bungle from the slums of Montmartre. So addicted was Jeanne Weber to **strangulation** that she died trying to throttle herself.

The daughter of a fisherman, Jeanne arrived in Paris in 1893 and married Marcel Weber, an impoverished drunk. Together they produced three children, but two died in infancy; this may have turned her mind and she took to drink. The lure of the cradle drew Jeanne to mind her friends' children, and almost at once two of her charges died. Then on 2 March 1905 she did away with her in-laws' daughter; the killing left telltale red marks round 18-month-old Georgette's throat, shrugged off by the parents. When they invited Jeanne to babysit again, she strangled their three-year-old Suzanne.

Brother-in-law Pierre now had no children left, so Jeanne turned to the family of Leon Weber. Throughout the day of 25 March his child Germaine experienced seizures when left alone with Jeanne, who was twice observed 'massaging the infant's heart'. On the third occasion the child died. On the morning of the little girl's funeral, Jeanne moved to quell mounting rumours by suffocating her last child, Marcel. Briefly the object of sympathy, on 5 April Jeanne was asked by another sister-in-law to look after 10-month-old Maurice while she went to the shops. The mother returned just in time to find him gasping for breath. He too had red marks round his throat.

Jeanne was dragged before Inspector Coiret, who established that three years previously two more children – young Alexandre and Marcel Poyatos – in her care had died from convulsive respiratory problems. He put Jeanne under arrest and she was lucky to escape a public lynching. But when the trial opened on 29 January 1906, the eminent medical expert Dr Léon Thoinot assured the court that Maurice, Georgette, Suzanne, Germaine and Marcel had all expired naturally from ailments like bronchitis. Jeanne, he said, was the victim of a witch-hunt, and his evidence secured her discharge. Thoinot's forensic deliberations were issued as an explanatory article for the medical press.

Jeanne left Paris to work as a housekeeper for a M. Bavouzet in a run-down smallholding in the remote countryside of Indre where, on 16 April 1907, she strangled his 9-year-old son Auguste.

Noting the red marks round his neck, the local coroner diagnosed meningitis, but when the story reached Paris it exploded into scandal. Jeanne's former legal team, outraged by the new allegations, offered to defend her free of charge. At the inquest Thoinot ascribed Auguste's demise to 'intermittent fever', later denouncing the idiocy of provincial doctors to the Society of Forensic Medicine, and Jeanne found a new benefactor in Dr Georges Bonjeau, President of the Society for the Protection of Children. He gave her a job in one of the Society's homes at Orgeville.

Dismissed for attempted strangulation (which Bonjeau hushed up), Jeanne slid into the life of a prostitute and then joined forces with a lime-burner in a cheap hotel. There she throttled the inn-keeper's son and was discovered hunched over the corpse, covered in blood.

In Paris, Thoinot was asked for his comments. He conceded that this looked like murder. But it was her first. Jeanne, he said, had been 'animated by a frenzy at being accused and arraigned for crimes she did not commit'. Thoinot's influence prevented a further trial and Jeanne was sent to an island asylum off New Caledonia where she died two years later, foaming at the mouth, with her hands locked round her throat.

A recent rival was Marybeth Tinning from New York State. She killed all eight of her children between 1972 and 1985. Her special coup came in 1978 after the first six deaths, when she was taken on by an adoption agency familiar with her track record. They did not wish to increase Marybeth's problems by siding against her.

The adopted child, Michael, did well, lasting nearly three years. Despite a preliminary diagnosis of 'cot death', Marybeth's killing of four-month-old Tami Lynne in October 1985 aroused suspicions because of the blood on her pillow, and she was sentenced to life imprisonment two years later.

The practice of battering babies may be as old as time, but it first came to light in 1944, when it was mistaken for a disease. An American radiologist, Dr Caffey, noted the first cases, ascribing the disorder to a congenital fragility of the bones causing spontaneous fractures in young infants.

This puzzling skeletal anomaly, the Caffey Syndrome, was painstakingly explained to the parents, and nine years passed before another American, Dr Silverman, pointed out that victims were perfectly healthy apart from being knocked about. Only in 1955 did Doctors Wooley and Evans put the blame where it belonged, on parents and guardians.

Such was the professional and public ignorance that in Britain a grim line of cases unfolded before the condition was recognised and properly penalised. Thus in December 1963 Laurence Dean, father of 4-month-old Susan Moon, left the coroner's court a free man after explaining that his child's fractured skull, the throttling marks round her neck, extensive bruising, several fractured ribs and a broken liver were attributable to bad luck rather than retrospective birth control. Only when his second child died of similar injuries was Dean brought to book for murder.

Perhaps more disquieting, in the mid-1960s many British cases were heard in Magistrates' Courts for a maximum penalty of six months or a £25 fine.

See also **Münchausen, Pregnancy**

Weiss, Dr Carl Austin (d. 1935)

Mild-mannered **assassin** of American demagogue Huey Long, the virtual dictator of the backward state of Louisiana. No one knows why Weiss wanted Huey Long dead more than anyone else, but by 1935 the embattled Senator was speaking out against his critics from behind ranks of armed men, bayonets at the ready, with machine guns trained on his audience.

According to the generally accepted account, Weiss died immediately after mortally wounding Huey Long with a single shot to the abdomen on 9 September 1935; he hid behind a column in the state Capitol and stepped out as Long walked past. The Senator's bodyguards returned fire, filling Weiss with sixty-one bullets at close range.

In November 1991 Weiss's embalmed body was exhumed by Professor James Starrs of Scientific Sleuthing Inc. to ascertain whether Huey Long was actually shot by his own bodyguards – who turned their guns on an innocent bystander to hide their guilt. This theory calls for a reconstruction of the shooting based on the angles of Weiss's numerous entry and exit holes.

But Weiss's perforated body is badly decayed, its preservation botched by the 1935 mortician. 'He lived all these years and died a month before the dig, expressly so as to avoid my wrath,' said Professor Starrs of the undertaker. 'He promised me a decent body.' In its present condition, the corpse is almost useless.

West Midlands Serious Crime Squad *et al*

So called, according to the wags, for the serious crimes it committed in England's West Midlands. On 14 January 1992, Valentine Cooke of Birmingham became their ninth case to have his conviction quashed by the **Court of Appeal**. Cooke had been shopped by his 'partner-in-crime', supergrass Paul Jervis, who confessed to 1,510 offences.

As more than 200 of these supposed crimes occurred while Jervis was behind bars, his evidence was ruled unreliable. Two months later, Glen Lewis, serving ten years for burglary, explained why his confession proved so helpful to the prosecution. It had been made up by the police. They denied Lewis access to a solicitor, headbutted him, abused him, menaced him with a hypodermic syringe and then obtained his signature to blank sheets of statement paper. His case was sent for retrial. Delroy Hare, another West Midlands victim, said: 'My confession was totally made up by the police – they threatened to charge my mother if I didn't sign it.' His six-year sentence was quashed on 19 May 1992.

The discovery that the West Midlands Serious Crimes Squad systematically coerced suspects led to the unit's disbandment in August 1989 and the biggest-ever inquiry into police malpractice. Conducted by the police, it encountered strong internal opposition, stiffened by the fact that allegations against officers were entertained from convicted criminals. The investigation spent £1.8 million studying ninety-one complaint files against more than 226 officers, and culminated with sixteen recommendations for prosecution.

But in May 1992 the Director of Public Prosecutions found 'insufficient evidence' to bring charges – not unlikely, since it is one thing to quash a conviction because of a reasonable doubt, another to prove *beyond* doubt exactly who tampered with what and why. Similarly, the judge for the 1989 Guildford Four appeal had no doubt that their con-

viction was based on false evidence. 'The police officers must have lied,' he concluded. Twelve officers were named, three were charged and in May 1993 all were acquitted.

The case of Judith Minah Ward, convicted of the 1974 M62 bombing when twelve British servicemen lost their lives, contained more disturbing implications. As Miss Ward told the *Independent* seventeen years later: 'I was off my head at that stage. I was completely out of my tree. And after all the questioning, I would have said anything they wanted me to say.'

She did. Ward recalls: 'They would say: "I believe you are a member of the IRA," and I'd be saying "Oh yeah, sure, that's me."' But Ward's confessions went beyond the familiar domain of extorted admissions into the realms of incontrovertible mental derangement. She confessed that she was not Judith Ward, aged twenty-four, but Teresa O'Connell, aged fourteen. Her claimed marriage to Michael McVerry, the Provisional IRA chief from South Armagh, was a fantasy; she had never met him. Her tales of multitudinous bombings with supposed accomplices never matched the facts. In all, thirty-four of her forty-four police interviews were withheld. Some contained retractions, others preposterous admissions, all were contradictory and highly suggestive of a suspect with a psychiatric disorder, a diagnosis confirmed by medical reports while she awaited trial. But defence lawyers were never informed, and Ward was presented to the court as a formidable terrorist.

Nor was the forensic evidence impartial. The Greiss test for explosives by Dr Frank Skuse proved positive. But as it detects nitrates common in household cleaners, shoe polish, cigarettes, varnish, soap and so on, it is now regarded, at best, as preliminary screening; it recognises not nitroglycerine (used in explosives) but nitrocellulose (used in manufacturing). Crucially, two series of experiments before the original trial had exposed it as unreliable, but this was disclosed neither to the court, nor to the defence, nor to the prosecution. At Miss Ward's successful 1992 appeal, her original conviction was described by the judges as an 'ambush'.

This broad-brush approach to guilt raises the issue addressed head-on in 1927 by the courageous William O'Connor. As Chicago's Chief Detective, he determined to dispense with trials altogether, calling for a volunteer squad of 500 machine-gunners with war experience from the Flanders trenches.

Their assignment was to roam the Chicago streets in armoured cars and mow the prohibition gangsters down. In a ringing speech, O'Connor declared to his assembled force: 'Men, the war is on. We have got to show that society and the police department, and not a bunch of dirty rats, are running this town. It is the wish of the people of Chicago that you hunt these criminals down and kill them without mercy. Your cars are equipped with machine-guns and you will meet the enemies of society on equal terms. See to it that they do not have you pushing up daisies. Make them push up daisies. Shoot first and shoot to kill. If you kill a notorious feudist you will get a handsome reward and win promotion. If you meet a car containing bandits pursue them and fire. When I arrive on the scene my hopes will be fulfilled if you have shot off the top of their car and killed every criminal inside it.'

That very day, the detective machine-gunners raided the Candy Jobbers' Union and arrested forty-five gangsters for conscripting members by unlawful force. Then, acting on a tip-off, they proceeded to the Rex Hotel at 3142 North Ashland Avenue, where they captured the Milwaukee gunman La Mantio, thereby aborting his mission of killing Al Capone. Direct action, too, has its drawbacks.

See also **Sweden**

Westies

A particularly vicious New York **gang** of Irish-American criminals, responsible for at least thirty murders in the 1970s and 1980s. For light relief, the Westies played Russian roulette at a thousand dollars a throw. They operated as an Irish mini-Mafia, dealing in drugs, loan-sharking and labour racketeering, and their most baroque killing was the 1981 elimination of one of their own, Paddy Duggan, who defied the gang's leader James Coonan.

After cutting up Duggan's body with a machete, Coonan dropped the severed fingers into his variant of the handbag, the fingerbag, in which he habitually carried his victims' severed digits. Then he took Duggan's head out drinking to a local tavern, depositing it on the bar while he caroused with cronies, toasting his memory and stuffing a lighted cigarette – Duggan's favourite brand – into its lips.

Brutality of this order ensured that the Westies' patch along Manhattan's West Side stayed a no-go area for other gangs, and in 1977 even the Mafia negotiated terms. The Westies promised to stop roughing up *mafiosi* venturing onto their turf; instead, they would act as Gambino 'enforcers' in return for a percentage of their rake-offs.

A trouble-shooter was appointed to liaise between the two gangs and, after meeting his opposite number, Coonan remarked, 'I just met a greaseball tougher than we are.' It was John Gotti.

An earlier gang of contract killers operating out of Manhattan's Lower East Side in the 1870s was the Whyos, whose informal headquarters were a bar known as The Morgue. In 1884 Piker Ryan was arrested with a printed price list in his pocket. Fees ranged from $2 ('punching') and $15 ('ear chawed off') to $25 ('shot in leg') and $100 up for 'doing the big job'; terms were cash in advance.

See also **Murder Inc.**

Whacks *et al*

'Whack' is current Mafia jargon for 'to kill', and the New York Mafia made it a rule never to whack journalists. Until the Dios Unanue shooting of 1992 (see **Lingle**), the last murdered reporter died in 1943 for badmouthing Mussolini. According to a New York criminal pundit: 'Whacking a newspaperman, it's like the tide. You wash it out and it comes back in again. You kill a newsman, you get more coming in.'

Perhaps the first criminal laid low by the press was John Toms of Prescot, Lancashire. But this was a fluke, as was his conviction by forensic ballistics. In early 1794 Toms shot Edward Culshaw dead at close range in the head and, on examination, the deceased was found to have newspaper on the brain.

This proved to be the wadding originally rammed down Toms's pistol prior to discharge. The paper penetrated Culshaw's skull in the wake of the bullet and, when extracted, cleaned and unfolded, turned out to be a torn strip from a broadsheet which exactly matched the remainder of the page found in Toms's pocket. On 23 March 1794, he was sentenced to death.

The steady **decline** in the Mafia's fortunes has been matched by a deterioration in its whacking.

According to former undercover agent Joe Pistone: 'There was a time when a guy was supposed to get whacked, he got whacked. Now they even have trouble getting that right.' A new low was set by the hit on the unmissable Mafia *capo* Peter Chiodo in May 1991. At 547 pounds (just under a quarter of a ton), Chiodo proved a surprisingly resilient target. Left for dead at Pellicano's gas station on Staten Island after absorbing twelve gunshot wounds, he survived to turn stool pigeon.

See also **Guldensuppe, Hamilton, Lingle**

White Album

Recording by the Beatles which inspired Charles **Manson**. A long-standing fan, he interpreted their double album in the light of The Book of **Revelations** which cast the Fab Four as God's mouthpieces. Manson was riveted by the *White Album* on its December 1968 release and swiftly intuited that its tracks were prophetic. The Beatles were sending him coded messages about the end of the world, and on New Year's Eve Manson arrived in Death Valley to tell the **Family**: 'Are you hep to what the Beatles are saying? Helter Skelter is coming down. The Beatles are telling it like it is.'

On careful listening, nearly all the *White Album*'s tracks bore out his views. The lyrics of 'I will' formed a direct appeal to Manson to get into a recording studio: 'And when at last I find you, your song will fill the air, sing it loud so I can hear you.' The Beatles knew that their redeemer lived on the Pacific coast. Why else sing, 'Oh honey pie, you are driving me frantic, sail across the Atlantic, to be where you belong'?

It could only be Manson, and the time was now. In 'Blackbird', the Beatles reminded him, 'You were only waiting for this moment to arise.' The lyrics of 'Piggies' filled in the details, presaging a future where grotesque porcine couples dined out, stabbing at their food with knives and forks – which was what pigs deserved. They got it too, the following August, Rosemary LaBianca expiring from forty-one knife wounds and her husband Leno from twelve, with a fork in his stomach and 'Death to Pigs' scrawled in blood on the walls.

Then there was 'Helter Skelter', a song about a fairground ride. To Manson, it evoked the Family's dizzying descent into the 'bottomless pit' foretold in Revelations, when they would shelter from the coming bloodbath: 'Look out helter skelter, she's coming down fast.' Most of all, the extended sound-picture of 'Revolution 9' was a harbinger of the imminent carnage. In the background were machine-guns, oinking pigs and, very faintly, two minutes and thirty-four seconds into the track, the word 'Rise' repeated in a long drawn out scream, so like the same word daubed in blood on 10 August 1969 at the LaBiancas' residence, where the message 'Healther Skelter' was left on their fridge.

The killings came only a few days after Manson's humiliating musical rebuff of 5 August 1969 at the Esalen Institute, a 'personal growth' centre. He dropped by and (in the words of sidekick Paul Watkins) 'played his guitar for a bunch of people there... and they rejected his music. Some people pretended they were asleep, and others were saying, "This is too heavy for me" and "I'm not ready for that" ... and some just got up and walked out.' It so happened that a record producer, Terry Melcher, who Manson had once hoped would land him a recording deal, owned an isolated house in Benedict Canyon, and three days later Manson sent Charles 'Tex' Watson, Susan Atkins, Patricia Krenwinkel and Linda Kasabian to start Helter Skelter there, at 10050 Cielo Drive.

On the night of 8 August, Watson cut the telephone wires before climbing over the fence. A car came through the grounds towards them; Watson flagged it down and shot the driver four times. Then they broke into the house through a window, marshalled the four occupants in the living room and forced them face-down on the floor. The two women, one with child, were roped to an overhead beam by their necks, but one of the men broke free and fought his way outside to collapse from two gunshots, thirteen blows to the head and fifty-one **stab** wounds. Meanwhile one of the women ran off, escaping through the french windows. She too was caught, slashed twenty-eight times. The other man was knifed seven times and shot once, and the pregnant woman knifed sixteen times. Atkins dipped a towel in her blood, and wrote 'Pigs' on the door.

The gang withdrew, tossing their bloodstained clothes down a hill from Benedict Canyon Road. Krenwinkel's hand ached, bruised from stabbing to the bone, and the other girls' scalps smarted from having their hair pulled.

Manson was waiting at Spahn Ranch. 'What are you doing home so early?' he asked. 'Boy,' said Watson, 'it sure was Helter Skelter.' The following night, Manson led another raiding party.

Today, an audio-cassette of Manson's music survives in specialist circulation. The lyrics disclose unusually high levels of hostility, with refrains like 'You'll get yours'.

White death

A serious risk for body-packing drug runners. The contraband is sealed into perhaps a hundred grape-sized pellets of four or five grams each, wrapped in **condoms**, surgical gloves or toy balloons. These are swallowed. Nine times out of ten a punctured capsule kills; only intensive hospital care with oxygen, short-acting barbiturates, psychiatric sedatives and constant maintenance of the air passages pulls the smuggler through the onslaught of undiluted cocaine in bulk hitting the lining of his gut. This state of acute toxic psychosis, of which the most prominent symptoms are euphoria, disorientation, behavioural change and fever, is known as White Death.

Problems most often arise when a capsule gets stuck in the caecum or blind gut at the entrance of the large intestine. When a smuggler counts all the capsules in but does not count them all out, his days are generally numbered; no enema or laxative will shift the tiny cargo of death. The gastric juices rumble on, slowly eating away the rubber protective cladding until one day it ruptures.

In 1992, four of the five cases diagnosed at British airports died.

White Mischief

At 3 a.m. on the morning of 24 January 1941 the body of Josslyn Hay, Lord Erroll, was found slumped underneath the steering wheel of his Buick, plunged halfway into a deep trench by the Ngong road eight miles from Nairobi. It looked like an accident, but the bullet hole by Erroll's ear was noticed later that day in the mortuary.

Lord Erroll, aged 39 and Scotland's premier earl, was an accomplished seducer of other men's wives; he pleasured one on the billiard table of Nairobi's Norfolk Hotel. Together with his first wife Idina, the twice-divorced daughter of Earl de La Warr, he helped found Kenya's 'Happy Valley'. At their ranch, 'Clouds', Joss and Idina entertained well-bred misfits who swilled cocktails and indulged in wife-swapping and high jinks; Idina held court, bathing and dressing in front of her guests and allocating bedroom keys at will. Cocaine and heroin were flown up from Nairobi and injected with silver syringes. Golf, bridge, horse-racing, backgammon, croquet and polo provided more serious occupations.

Lord Erroll

By 1941 any number of emotional casualties might have preferred Joss dead. But the main suspect was always Sir 'Jock' Delves Broughton, the ageing husband of the desirable Diana who, in her turn, had become Erroll's very public mistress. Diana was twenty-seven. Sir Delves, thirty years her senior, suffered from an arthritic right hand and a dragging left foot. But he had money; in 1926 his spending topped £120,000. As he joylessly remarked: 'The first eighty was easy, but unless you gamble the rest is sheer extravagance.'

Sir Delves had known Diana for five years before proposing. An angelic blonde in appearance, Diana was a handsome divorcee who ran a London cocktail club, the Blue Goose. She pursued a hectic social life by private aeroplane, and if her lipstick was too red, her *penchant* for pearls too overt and her ancestry rather middlebrow, she had looks and style.

Diana's contemporaries were pairing off, and she accepted Broughton's offer. He closed the family seat, Doddington, and married her the week before they arrived in Kenya on 12 November 1940. She quickly clarified her position to her husband's old African friends: 'I'm not sharing a room with *that* dirty old man. I insist on a room to myself.' Less than three weeks later she met Lord Erroll and, the moment they were alone, he asked, 'Well, who's going to tell Jock? You or I?' Their affair ran wildfire, and on 6 January Broughton was tipped off about the romance.

Broughton had agreed to pay Diana £5,000 a year for at least five years after a divorce, making her doubly attractive to Erroll who, after the death of his second wife, an heiress, from heroin and champagne, was limping by on £300 a year. Broughton seemed to bow to the inevitable, accepting that he could not force his wife's affec-

Diana

tions. With great self-restraint he 'cut his losses', offering Diana the house at Karen while he left on a protracted trip to Ceylon.

'I am sorry it happened so soon,' she mouthed. That night Erroll, Diana, Broughton and June Carberry – an Erroll discard – sat down to a celebration supper. Broughton toasted the euphoric couple: 'I wish them every happiness and may their union be blessed with an heir.' The party broke up; Broughton and June returned to Karen where she helped him up the stairs. The maid fetched June a whisky and stayed chatting by her bedside. Erroll took Diana dancing, dropping her back at around 2.15 a.m. Still up, the maid let the young lovers in. June too remained awake. 'Please drive carefully,' said Diana as Joss left.

'Carefully but not slowly,' said the debonair Joss. Less than an hour later he was found dead two-and-a-half miles away. The murder made the headlines in wartime London, where Broughton's acquaintances at White's and Brook's laid wagers on whether he would be hanged. His motive might be clear, but the evidence was circumstantial. The prosecution could never prove *how* Broughton killed Erroll while – apparently – lying sozzled and asleep in the bedroom of a crowded and wakeful house.

Neither the maid nor June Carberry heard Broughton leave for, or return from, what would have been a five-mile round trip, and he was definitely at home at 3.30 a.m., when he called into June's bedroom 'to ask if she was all right'.

Ballistics provided the most incriminating evidence. The police recovered bullets which they claimed Broughton had fired during a practice shoot at another ranch (the 'Nanyuki' bullets). These matched the murder ammunition, and were linked to the obvious murder weapon: Broughton's registered pair of Colt .32s, reported stolen on 21 January. During a seven-hour cross-examination, the defence lawyer Harry Morris KC detailed endless tiny differences between the bullets. There always are. Then he played his trump card. 'In all these bullets was the direction uniform?' he demanded. 'Yes, it is right hand in all the bullets.'

'Is the direction in a Colt revolver right or left?'

'Left in the barrel,' admitted Harwich, the expert witness. The prosecution had not anticipated this simple point, which proved that the bullets had not come from a Colt. Their case foundered, and the explanation – that Broughton used some other make of .32 – hardly dared show its head for shame. Broughton was discharged on 1 July after withstanding twenty hours of cross-examination with *sang-froid*.

He set off for Ceylon with Diana, but their marriage soon crumbled, Diana effecting a smooth transition to the eccentric rancher Gilbert Colville, perhaps – in the words of a neighbour – 'the most boring man in the world', while Broughton left for England in September 1942 with the case still unsolved.

Kenyans discussed the crime for decades; alibis were complicated because many suspects were too drunk to remember where they were or with whom they were sleeping. Broughton remains the key. The Nanyuki bullets were charged with black powder, a propellant almost unobtainable since 1914, and black scorch marks were found on Joss's entry wound. Was Broughton's firearms certificate misleading? Were his guns really Colts? Did he have another gun? Was the gun robbery faked? Why had Broughton lit a bonfire the day after the murder in the Karen rubbish pit? A golfing stocking stained with blood smouldered in the embers, but Broughton disowned it; he never wore them.

Thirty years later Cyril Connolly and James Fox started a spirited investigation fuelled by lunches at the Savoy grill, the Connaught and the Ritz. Many 'survivors' were contacted. The Earl of Carnarvon, interviewed in Highclere Castle in May 1980, described Broughton as a weak man – vain, dishonest and a coward – who faked sunstroke to avoid war service. Behind the financial glamour, Broughton was a taciturn dullard, never known to make a joke, who allowed Lord Moyne to run off with his first wife without voicing any objection.

Despite an annual income of £80,000, Broughton dissipated his fortune in fifteen years. As money ran short he stole from the estate, appropriating £1.5 million from the sale of 32,500 acres of farmland. This too he squandered. The family found him out – hence the departure for Kenya ahead of disgrace. In June 1939 Broughton staged an insurance theft of pearls from Diana's car in the south of France, and blackmailed his accomplice, Hugh Dickinson, into stealing three over-insured pictures from Doddington, destroying two Romney portraits in the process. Broughton, in short, was bent.

In late 1942, the disconsolate Broughton was lodging alone in 'Badger's Bank', the butler's house on the estate. He ran into Alan Horn, a local horse breeder, and confessed in a Nantwich pub. Then on 30 November 1942 Broughton confided in his last remaining friend, Marie Woodhouse: 'You know I did it, I've never run so fast in my life.'

Two days later, while staying alone in Liverpool's Adelphi Hotel, he gave himself fourteen injections of Medinal and died on 5 December.

In 1980 June Carberry's stepdaughter told James Fox that Broughton had confessed to her too, at the Nyeri house the day after the murder. He arrived in a terrible state. No one else was there, and he related how everyone had mocked him and that he had shot Joss and thrown the gun into the Thika Falls.

Despite his impervious stance at the trial, Broughton was distraught at the loss of his wife, his resentment inflamed, Fox learned, by an accidental meeting with Joss and Diana glued together on the dance floor after the handover dinner. Paula Long, another old Kenya hand, said that Jock favoured golfing stockings and produced a photograph in proof.

In May 1993 the Broughton hypothesis was reinforced by the discovery of his letter to Diana of October 1942. It reveals her as more promiscuous than previously imagined, and Broughton as more deeply wounded and devious. The saga of the pearl theft reared its head anew, with Broughton blackmailing Diana. 'I have always been suspicious as to what you had inside the deed box you gave me to give to George Green [Broughton's solicitor],' he wrote. 'The penalty for this offence is fourteen years hard labour.'

Broughton catalogued Diana's infidelities. 'On board the boat you became a stranger to me. You started a fuck with Tony Morrant under my eyes and I discovered the copy of a letter you wrote to your Italian, the most violent love letter... You made such a farce of our marriage that the registrar almost refused to marry you.' Then came her affair with a man named Orle. Of his fellow-dullard and successor Colville, Broughton noted, 'You knew he was the richest settler in Kenya... and laid yourself out to ensnare him.' An interlude with Hugh Strickland followed. 'You put him in a room with no lock on the door opening straight out into your rooms... I listened to him fuck you not more than three yards away. By the way the whole bed rocked, you evidently enjoyed it, like you used to with me.'

It is of such misalliances – unworkable, unleavable, tortured and, in this case, semi-voyeuristic – that domestic murders are born.

Wild, Jonathan (1683–1725)

An underworld receiver who ran with the hare and hunted with the hounds to become 'Thief-Taker General of Great Britain and Ireland'. Wild was the first mobster, a pioneering exponent of organised crime.

After imprisonment for **debt** as a young man, Wild set up as a pimp and accumulated enough money for his own London receiver-cum-brothel, in Cock Lane.

A successful receiver could eliminate the middleman. Instead of fencing his stolen property at a discount, Wild flogged it direct to a really appreciative end-buyer: the previous owner. Both the thief and the victim went straight to Wild, who split his take with the thief, paying an unusually generous rate. There was no law against letting owners know where their goods were or in sharing in the 'reward'. Wild was careful never to take possession of the loot, but compiled a list of hot merchandise and then approached the punter to put him in touch.

A talented businessman with a bureaucratic streak, Wild invested in his market by funding crime. He organised gangs throughout England, retaining jewellers to melt plate and cannibalise jewellery. He hired out burglars' tools and exported booty to Holland in his own sloop. Meanwhile, he collected incriminating files on his burgeoning armies of crooks.

Wild laid claim to the high rewards paid to informers which, starting under the reign of William and Mary, were set at £1 for betraying a deserter, £10 for a horse thief and £40 for a highwayman. Wild kept his underlings in line by threatening to turn them in and, with every man's neck on the line, he could fabricate charges or secure acquittals at will. In a submission to the Lord Mayor petitioning for elevation as a freeman of the City, Wild noted that he had, at some personal risk, sent a good sixty criminals to the gallows. Among them was Joseph 'Blueskin' Blake, Jack **Sheppard**'s whoring companion and accomplice, brought to trial in 1724 at the Old Bailey Sessions House on Wild's evidence.

Before the hearing, Wild approached Blake and offered a swig from his flask, hoping for information to turn to advantage. Blueskin misread the gesture and asked him to put in a good word. Wild laughed: 'I can't do that. You're a dead man and will be tucked up very speedily.' Hoping to decapitate Wild and throw his head to the rabble, Blake took out a penknife and soon had Wild's throat cut to the windpipe. But the blade was blunt and further progress of the assault was impeded by Wild's thick plaited muslin stock; two surgeons standing nearby saved the informer's life. This abortive onslaught assured Blake instant nationwide popularity fanned by numerous ballads. The best of these was by John Gay, to be sung to the tune of *The Cut Purse*:

> *Attend and draw near*
> *Good news ye shall hear*
> *How Jonathan's throat was*
> *cut from Ear to Ear.*

Wild habitually dressed in lace finery, and carried a

Invitation to an execution

sword and a gold-topped cane. To the public, Wild and the law were synonymous, and his gang achieved a semi-legal, guildlike status. Parliament was not so pleased, and in 1718 the so-called 'Wild Act' created the new offence of accepting a reward without prosecuting the thief. So Wild changed tack, advising customers who wanted their goods back to abandon their money at a safe house, leaving nothing to prove that he had received payment or handled their property. Nonetheless, by a happy irony, in 1725 Wild was convicted under the Wild Act for pocketing a ten guinea finder's fee. He was hanged on 24 May of that year, pelted all the way to the **Tyburn** gallows, where the mob screamed at the hangman to hurry up. His dying act was to pick the executioner's pocket.

Wild was the eponymous hero of Henry Fielding's 1743 satirical novel *The Life of Jonathan Wild the Great* and, according to the American crime historian John Nash, inspired Conan Doyle's Moriarty, London's '**Napoleon** of Crime'. By a curious quirk of fate, for many years a publication called *Moriarty's Police Law* was the bible of the force.

Like Jonathan Wild, Scotland's Earl of Morton was hoist on his own petard. In 1565 Morton was so impressed by the **Halifax Gibbet** that he had a replica made, the Scottish Maiden, with which he himself was beheaded in 1581.

See also **Oaths**

Wind in the Willows

Kenneth Grahame was lucky to survive to write the children's classic *Wind in the Willows*. Grahame worked at the Bank of England and, in December 1903, a young man called George Frederick Robinson was ushered into his office.

Robinson handed over some papers bound up with two ribbons, one black and one white, and since Grahame chose to untie the roll with the black ribbon, Robinson drew his revolver and banged off five shots at the future author. Grahame was only hit once (see **Shootist**); Robinson ran out, shouting, 'Come on, you cowards and curs', and took refuge in another room where he was subdued with a firehose.

At his trial, it transpired that the escapade was a mad political protest; political, because of Robinson's concern about the unequal distribution of wealth, and mad because a rabid dog had bitten him. Robinson would have spared Grahame had he chosen the white ribbon.

Witchcrazes

From about 1450 to 1750, Europe – with the exception of Britain (see **Hopkins**) – was gripped by a 'witchcraze'. Witches were exterminated in huge numbers, estimated at anywhere between 200,000 and nine million. In the high period they were roped up and burned in groups of hundreds. According to Henry Charles Lea (*History of the Inquisition of the Middle Ages, 1906*): 'A bishop of Geneva is said to have burned five hundred within three months, a bishop of Bamberg six hundred, a bishop of Wurzburg, nine hundred. Eight hundred were condemned, apparently in one body, by the senate of Savoy.' It took the witch-finder Franz Buirman only five years from 1631 to incinerate half the population of a village of three hundred. Würzburg lost 757 souls, including children as young as three.

Until the thirteenth century the church clung to the old-fashioned idea that night-riding groups of devil-worshipping women were a silly superstition. But the fledgling **Inquisition** had the concept of the female heretic on a firm scientific footing by about 1430, and the 1480s saw the publication of the standard textbook, *Malleus Maleficarum* (The Hammer of the Witches), and the papal bull *Sumnis desiderantes affectibus*, which declared open season on 'heretical pravities'. As the *Malleus* noted, 'All witchcraft comes from carnal lust, which is in women insatiable... wherefore for the sake of fulfilling their lusts they consort even with devils.'

Identifying a witch was best left to the professional 'witch-prickers', common throughout Europe. Armed with long needles, they roamed from town to town, exercising their right to strip, shave, rape and stab suspects in search of the telltale W-spot insensitive to pain. This was the Devil's Mark, the sure sign of a woman given over to debauchery. The guilty were burned or strangled to protect the religious and social order, including its highly vulnerable component of the male organ.

For it was well known to readers of the *Malleus* that witches caused impotence. 'They directly prevent the erection of the member which is accommodated to fructification... they prevent the flow of the vital essences... so that it cannot be ejaculated or is fruitlessly spilled.' Countless unfortunates had their penises stolen, rounded up into early concentration camps: 'And what, then, is to be thought of those witches who in this way sometimes collect male organs in great numbers, as many as twenty or thirty members together, and put them in a bird's nest, or shut them up in a box where they move themselves like living members, and eat oats and corn, as has been seen by many and is a matter of common report?'

Indeed, as late as 1990 an outbreak of penis-snatching surfaced in Lagos, Nigeria, when a scare ran through the city that evil magicians were spiriting away citizens' willies under the pretext of shaking hands. According to the *Nation* of 30 October 1990, the missing components reappeared for sale as luxury items in the thriving witchcraft market. People lost their lives to the craze. A typical incident in the town of Enugu started when a passenger boarding a bus noticed that his member had vanished. He shouted out; the man in front was dragged down and beaten; a policeman tried to restore calm by firing warning shots which wounded a woman and her child, and killed the bus driver. Other reports claim at least four suspects were killed by lynch mobs, the mania exacerbated by hundreds of arrests for rumour-mongering after the Deputy Police Commissioner James Danbaba issued a plea for calm.

In Europe, popes, saints, theologians, scholars, and the well-known *penseur* Pascal, endorsed the only proper counter-measure of rounding up the usual suspects and burning them. Modern sociologists regard this impulse as a response to insecurity engendered by the breakdown of the medieval world in general and the emergence of a new and marginally less downtrodden role for women. Others find parallels between the witchcraze and the modern era's **sex crime**. In both, the intent is said to be gynocide; in both, the assaults are justified by manufactured categories (witch-prickers/sexual psychopath) that obscure the basic gynocidal intent. Anyone looking for a predecessor to Peter **Sutcliffe** in his mission to 'clean the place up a bit' would find the fifteenth-century witch-prickers had relevant work experience; and impotence, or the fear of impotence, is a common thread uniting the two callings. Like the witches of yore, the serial killers of today are 'down on whores' for their carnal lust, 'which is in women insatiable', and are commonly unable to respond to normal sexual

stimuli. In effect, their penises have been spirited away, and **Chikatilo**, the Russian Ripper, bared his in court for public denigration. He too regarded his underclass victims as sluts unworthy of life.

Perhaps the best-known witchcraze happened in Massachussetts at Salem Village, a settlement at the edge of the wilderness still at the mercy of scalping parties. Five witches were hanged on 19 July 1692, another five a month later, one on 19 September, and eight more three days later.

The trouble began in the kitchen of the Reverend Mr Parris, where his West Indian housewoman regaled his young class of a dozen adolescent girls with tales of palmistry, necromancy and wizards. Over the winter her impressionable charges began to see things that went bump in the night. The hysteria took root; rumours of covens proliferated, and when the girls went into fits, biting their lips until they bled, rolling on the floor and growling like animals, the local doctor diagnosed witchcraft. Their seizures, reproduced in court, may have been real, or feigned out of malice or peer-group pressure. Proof of enchantment was furnished by transference of the 'witch fluid' when a victim quietened after touching the witch – an easy courtroom stunt. Fifty-five suspects saved their lives by confessing, but the obdurate went to the gallows, among them Susanna Martin, convicted on overwhelming evidence on 29 June 1692.

Her neighbour, Robert Downer, testified that Susanna had burst into his room looking just like a cat. And when he said, 'Avoid, thou she-devil', the creature ran away. While coming back from the woods, John Kembal got lost in a cloud which made him trip over tree stumps. Afterwards he was attacked by a brown puppy which fled when he cried 'Jesus Christ'. John Pressy had crossed words

The Wonders of the Invisible World:

Being an Account of the

TRYALS

OF

Several Witches,

Lately Executed in

NEW-ENGLAND:

And of several remarkable Curiosities therein Occurring.

Together with,

I. Observations upon the Nature, the Number, and the Operations of the Devils.

II. A short Narrative of a late outrage committed by a knot of Witches in *Swede-Land*, very much resembling, and so far explaining, that under which *New-England* has laboured.

III. Some Councels directing a due Improvement of the Terrible things lately done by the unusual and amazing Range of Evil Spirits in *New-England*.

IV. A brief Discourse upon those *Temptations* which are the more ordinary Devices of Satan.

By COTTON MATHER.

Published by the Special Command of his EXCELLENCY the Governour of the Province of the *Massachusetts-Bay* in *New-England*.

Printed first, at *Boston* in *New-England*; and Reprinted at *London*, for *John Dunton*, at the *Raven* in the *Poultry*. 1693.

with Susanna twenty years before: she warned, 'That he should never have more than two cows; that 'tho' he was likely to have more, yet he should never have them.' And Pressy never did; something always cropped up.

Other witnesses told similar tales. When Susanna was asked what she had to say, 'Her chief plea was, "She had led a most virtuous and holy life."' In May 1693 the Salem episode ended with the Governor's issue of a pre-emptive group pardon, embracing both those found guilty and those awaiting trial.

There is, as yet, no sign of abatement in the American flood of satanic **ritual abuse** cases. 'In Salem,' according to psychiatrist Paul McHugh, 'the convictions depended on how judges thought the witches behaved. In our day, the conviction depends on how some therapists think a child's **memory** of trauma works.' That is, present allegations assume the reliability of 'recalled memories' stimulated under therapy.

The stories (where witches fly into bedrooms or meet in covens for human sacrifices) have not varied significantly over the centuries, unlike the status of those impeached and of their accusers. Formerly, witches were nearly all women, often misfits or outcasts; today, nearly all are men, generally of some standing and success. Research by Philadelphia's False Memory Syndrome Foundation shows that the majority of the accused had stable marriages, were college educated, on average commanding incomes in excess of $60,000, and that their families ate and vacationed together. Typically, they are denounced by their adult daughters, and those facing such charges may, with reason, evince the fashionable syndrome of white male paranoia.

Wobblies

Popular name for the anarchist wing of the revolutionary IWW group (Industrial Workers of the World) prevalent in the United States in the decade preceding the First World War. Their chief dynamiter was Harry Orchard, born Albert E. Horsley.

In 1903 Orchard blew up a mine shaft in Cripple Creek, Colorado, killing two. Next he detonated 100 pounds of explosive under a railway platform, despatching twenty-six miners – strikebreakers – and crippling fifty for life. Then Orchard singled out wealthy Fred Bradley, a member of the Mine Owners Association in San Francisco. But the taste of **strychnine** in Bradley's milk bottle made his cook throw away its contents. So Orchard blew up his target's house, completely destroying the three-storey facade as Bradley left for work, on this occasion flying across the street. He survived.

Next on Orchard's list was Luther M. Goddard, a Colorado Supreme Court judge. Planning to liquidate him with an exploding purse, Orchard deposited the device on a snow-swept path where it was picked up by another Denver citizen, Merrit W. Walley, parts of whom were found half a mile away.

Orchard was finally caught making a getaway from Caldwell, Idaho on 30 December 1905, shortly after vaporising the state's ex-Governor. He was condemned to death, but the unions exerted heavy influence to have the sentence commuted to life imprisonment.

Wolfsbane

Source of the deadly vegetable poison aconitine. Wolfsbane (*Aconitum napellus*) resembles parsley, but only in appearance; it attacks the central nervous system, causing nausea, vomiting, loss of muscle power, paralysis and death, on occasion producing death in eight minutes. A tiny dose of 1–2mg will kill, and the toxin was so fashionable among Romans that the Emperor Trajan had the plant banned. More recently, Dr George Henry Lamson was executed in April 1882 for murdering his brother-in-law Percy with an aconitine Madeira cake.

It was a tricky killing, since the crippled Percy was still at school in Wimbledon. The cake, which the prosecution argued contained a single poisoned raisin, was handed round slice by pre-cut slice in the presence of the lad's headmaster, Mr Bedbrook, while the grown-ups sipped sherry.

A misconceived diversionary ruse by Lamson accentuated suspicions. Anticipating that his nephew's abrupt demise would not pass without remark, he attempted to impress the gathering with irrefutable proof that he could not have poisoned Percy with sugar, and, calling for a bowl, spooned some into his sherry, drinking it without ill-effects. His cast-iron defence to contaminated sugar thus established, Lamson demonstrated the user-friendly qualities of a new American pill capsule to the party. Filling it from the same bowl, he said, 'Here, Percy, you are a champion pill-taker', and the lad swallowed it down.

Notwithstanding this harmless intake, Percy was dead within four hours, making it abundantly clear that he had eaten *something* that disagreed with him. That left the cake. Lamson stood to inherit through his wife; he fled to Paris, but returned to face trial. The toxicology of alkaloids was still very primitive, but Dr Thomas Stevenson, lecturer in medical jurisprudence at Guy's, processed Percy's innards for an extract of the poison. This he placed on his tongue and identified the aconitine by taste. Despite Lamson's efforts to gain a reprieve, he was executed on 28 April 1882, and during his last days hysterical women admirers sent him gifts of flowers and fruit.

See **Bobettes**

World-Wide Business Centre

In August 1980 a tiny cubicle on the tenth floor of 575 Madison Avenue, New York, was briefly the world's biggest money laundry.

Salvatore Amendolito, a former financial analyst from Milan, set up as a New York fish exporter in 1977. Two years later, three Sicilians offered to load his fish, airfreight it to Italy and then unload it themselves, paying him when the cargo completed the journey. Amendolito declined, but when he went bankrupt the following year, his business agent in Milan telephoned with a similar proposal. He explained that many New York pizzerias needed to remit **cash** to Europe. The funds were destined for the construction of a hotel in Sicily; the owners wanted to bypass the taxman. 'How much money is it anyway?' asked Amendolito. 'Nine million dollars,' he was told.

Amendolito negotiated a one per cent handling charge. He began by dividing the stash, which arrived in cardboard boxes, into bundles of just under $10,000 – the level over which cash payments are reported to the Treasury – and spent days driving round New York making deposit after

deposit at different banks. A sidekick checked the stacks as he sped along the New Jersey turnpike.

Amendolito met his punters on street corners, walking the city with $500,000 or even a million slung over his shoulder in a yellow leather bag. He picked up $3 million in three trips from the Roma Restaurant, and – after bribing a Bermudan official – flew over a metric *ton* of cash to the island.

By August, Amendolito's business was booming. He rented a proper office in the World-Wide Business Centre where he installed a money-counting machine with a safe the size of two refrigerators. The floor needed reinforcement.

In late November 1980, acting on a tip-off, an undercover FBI team photographed a delivery of one of the mysterious cardboard cartons at the entrance of 575 Madison Avenue. To their dismay, the building housed a warren of hundreds of small firms, and it was not until the autumn of 1981 that Agent Robert Paquette tracked down the intended recipient. By then Amendolito had moved on, but this lead unravelled the Sicilian Mafia's American operation, the so-called **Pizza Connection**.

The cash mountains generated by today's international drugs business are too large for standard counting machines. Sophisticated traffickers value their takings by sorting them into different denomination bills and weighing the sackloads. A million dollars in $20 notes tips the balance at 107.4 pounds.

See also **Tax havens**

Wright, Whitaker (1845–1904)

A sixteen-stone financier of modest origins who committed suicide after his disgrace in 1904. At the height of his success and influence Wright was master of Witley Park, a 2,500 acre estate in Surrey girded by an eight-foot high, fourteen-mile wall behind which lay farms, cottages, lodges, lakes and two old iron mines.

Wright spent his money with delectation and verve. He set an army of four or five hundred men to remodel his grounds and buildings, extending the old mansion until it boasted thirty-two bedrooms and a ballroom incorporating a theatre. He tacked a huge plant-house onto the east wing; the west wing culminated in an observatory with a dome and revolving roof.

After a hill had been removed, Wright's home commanded a fine view over his twenty-five acre lake, stocked with a flotilla of the latest electric motor launches to tour the grottoes and underground galleries. A huge marble dolphin was transported from Italy to form a triumphal entrance to the lake; a railway bridge had to be demolished to allow the sculpture through. Under the lake's surface lay Wright's *pièce de résistance*, a glass-roofed underwater chamber built by first draining the waters. 'On summer nights,' wrote a contemporary, 'one looks through the green water at the stars and the moon, magnified quite ten times by the curved glass and the water.'

Born in northern England, Wright made and lost his first fortune in the Wild West and returned to Britain in the high noon of Empire. He turned his first-hand knowledge of mining to good advantage in the City, setting up groups of associated companies with dummy directors. At his trial, one co-director (General Gough-Calthorpe) explained that his role was 'to sign my name many thousands of times on share certificates', while another (Mr Worters) acknowledged that his duties were 'to confirm the transactions of the managing director'. When one of the companies, Lake View Consols, ran into trouble, Wright propped up the share price with funds from his London and Globe Company, driving it into insolvency. It transpired that Consols' balance sheet had been padded by over-valued shares.

Until the Companies Act of 1901 it was not illegal to issue a fraudulent balance sheet. Wright's offences predated its provisions, and he remained beyond the reach of law. But a consortium of out-of-pocket brokers brought a prosecution under the 1861 Larceny Act. Wright lacked the requisite criminal intent, but the hostile judge encouraged the jury to a finding of guilty, and he was sentenced to seven years penal servitude. Led into the private room behind the court, the financier slipped a cyanide tablet into a glass of whisky and handed his watch to a friend, saying, 'I won't have any need of this where I'm going.' Then he fell down dead.

Wuornos, Aileen (1956–)

Dubbed 'The Damsel of Death' by the press, Aileen Wuornos (pronounced 'Warn-us') admitted to shooting seven men during 1989 and 1990 in self-defence, mostly middle-aged whites.

The Wuornos background is no fairy tale. Her father, a child molester, hanged himself in prison. Her mother abandoned her at three months. Sexually abused as a child, Wuornos attempted suicide by shooting herself in the stomach during adolescence, and was raped by her grandfather and (perhaps) her brother. After her illegitimate child was removed for adoption, she became a fourteen-year-old prostitute, maturing into an alcoholic lesbian with strong religious convictions, trawling the highways, motels and drive-ins as a hitch-hiking whore on Florida's Interstate 75.

She meant business with her .22 pistol: big business. As America's first female serial killer, Wuornos was worth serious money in movie deals, television docudramas, book rights and syndicated chat-shows to anyone delivering her to the media – provided two conditions were met. First, the public had to be convinced that she was a serial killer, and second, she needed convicting. Properly handled, Wuornos could make a fortune; and she would have no *locus standi* to jeopardise her commercial exploitation when dead.

Wuornos played the husband to her lesbian lover, Tyrea Moore, principal prosecution witness. Coming from a solid family, Moore was an object of veneration to Wuornos, perhaps the only person she ever loved. Initially, both women were wanted as suspects, and Moore cajoled Wuornos into confessing after her arrest at the 'Last Resort' bikers bar. On 17 January 1991, Wuornos began a lengthy statement: 'Well, I came here to confess to murder, I just wish I'd never done this shit. I just wish I'd never bought that **gun**...'

Wuornos earned some sympathy at her trial for the murder of television repairman Richard Mallory, an ex-convict with a ten-year prison record for attempted rape. In her words, 'He put the cord around my neck and said, "You bitch, you're going to do everything I tell you to, and if you don't, I'll kill you right afterwards, just like the others."' Mallory threatened to have intercourse with Wuornos's still-warm corpse, and started to choke her. After various assaults, he poured medical alcohol into her bleeding orifices. He laughed at her screams, and she not unreasonably inferred that he would continue playing with her. 'I gotta fight or I'm gonna die', she thought, broke free, reached her gun, and shot Mallory dead.

Wuornos might have escaped with manslaughter had the judge barred evidence of six other killings. To shoot one assailant in self-defence may be bad luck, but seven looks like deliberation, and on 27 January 1992 Wuornos responded to the jury's 'guilty' verdict by shouting: 'I was raped, I hope you get raped, scumbags of America.' But her fame as America's first female serial killer improved her lot. Arlene Pralles, a born-again Christian horse-farmer, was touched by Wuornos's plight, and adopted her. Pralles related, 'She is a beautiful woman, very kind, compassionate, with a heart of gold', and in fact, Wuornos cuts a surprisingly pleasant figure, an articulate woman with a talent for mimicry. At last someone cared for her, and she hired a new lawyer, Steven Glazer. Meanwhile, fifteen Hollywood companies competed for her story. A television film, *Overkill*, went into production, and Glazer acted as Pralle's agent; she collected 33 per cent royalties on every copy of 'On a Killing Day'.

But if Wuornos appealed against the 'similar facts' evidence of the first trial, she could overturn her conviction. Six more successes would save her life. As she said later, 'The principle is self-defence. They say it's the number. But it's still self-defence no matter how many people I shot. Two did rape me, five tried.' But Wuornos made no mention of this at the time. Instead, she deferred to the advice of her new lawyer and adoptive mother, and on 31 March 1992 pleaded 'no contest' to the next three charges. Arlene Pralles enthused, 'Our state has the death penalty, so why not go for it? I mean, Wow! She could be with Jesus in a few years.'

Importantly, this would make a better film. The police were rumoured to be turning their client investment to financial advantage. Tyrea Moore, no longer considered a suspect, was closeted with law enforcement officials, part of a witness-and-perpetrator package for the film industry. Wuornos objected to her own role, envisaged as a posthumous star. She told the court, 'I've been framed as a first-time female serial killer to make a better *title* and a bigger movie. The element of self-defence was hidden.'

The 1991 oil war precipitated Wuornos's downfall. As her 'regulars' were called up, so her earnings dwindled to $500 a month. Wuornos claimed that Tyrea Moore wanted $700 to $1,000 coming in a week and insisted that she take the risk of picking up strangers – hence the shootings. Wuornos may have been trigger-happy but, unlike her full-blown male counterparts, she never planned or stalked. Nor were her homicides recreational, and the tidy serial-killer deal was imperilled when police sergeant Brian Jervis expressed concern at departmental plans to work with Tyrea Moore in soliciting movie rights. After a month of harassment from colleagues, Jervis was transferred to patrol duties and resigned from the force. A break-in destroyed his home files on the Wuornos case and nothing else, but law enforcement agencies, up to and including the FBI, declined to investigate.

Meanwhile, a recalcitrant Wuornos had second thoughts about the wisdom of legal suicide, still promoted by her advisers, Glazer and Pralles. 'I do believe their main purpose is to see me die,' she complained from her cell. 'Arlene did not adopt me to be my mother, she adopted me to bury me and have easier visitation. Their motive was to make money... They convinced me to plead "No contest". Arlene kept on saying, "If you don't attend the sentencing the cops won't have anything for the movie."' Wuornos said that both had suggested ways of killing herself, and her suicide would make a powerful last scene which could, alternatively, come up as a scrolled caption on a black screen for the end-titles.

From prison Wuornos urged assiduous investigators to obtain a copy of the Republican Pictures movie contract, believing it could secure a retrial, and on 10 November 1992, Sheriff Moorlands announced the transfer of two policemen from his Criminal Investigation Department together with the resignation of Major Dan Henry, Chief of Staff, after a bugged conversation about film rights.

See also **Canonisation**

X

X, Operation

'Operation X' was the French Secret Service's scheme for funding the unpopular Indo-Chinese War from 1951 to 1954. Starved of official funds from home, the French army earned their keep by collecting and distributing **opium** from the **Golden Triangle**. They paid a good price to the hill tribes, ensuring their loyalty, and flew the opium out to a military school for onward trucking to Saigon. There the opium was sold to river pirates, who refined it and marketed it locally, offloading any surplus to their **Triad** connections. Huge profits were shared with the French Secret Service, enabling the financing of a mercenary counter-insurgent army.

Before 1950, opium's physical bulk tended to restrict exports, but the French Secret Service showed the potential of international narcotics trafficking by deploying an efficient transportation system based round airforce planes – a lesson not lost on American intelligence, who flew opium from Laos to South Vietnam as late as 1973 on Air America, the CIA subsidiary.

The 1954 French surrender at Dien Bien Phu stemmed from the opium middlemen creaming off too much money. The disaffected Meo clan turned a blind eye while the area was infiltrated by hostiles.

Xenophobia

The Portuguese were the supposed perpetrators of London's **Ratcliffe Highway** murders of 1811, considered far too horrible for an English killer. As the dramatist Sheridan later recounted in Parliament: 'People grew all of a sudden thoroughly persuaded that there was evidence that they were perpetrated by the Portuguese, and none but the Portuguese. "Oh, who would do it but the Portuguese ?" was the general cry.' This was during the Peninsular War, when the Portuguese were Britain's *allies*.

Soon the prejudice switched to more traditional targets. As Sheridan recounted, 'The next tribe of foreigners were the Irish and it was none but an Irish murder and could only have been done by Irishmen.' Seven were arrested almost at random and flung into jail. Sheridan continued: 'Some noise being heard, the magistrates inquired into the cause of this uproar, and they were told, "Oh! It is nothing but those horrid Irish, who can never be quiet!"... They had been confined to a hole of a room for twenty-two hours without a bed to lie upon, or a morsel of bread, or a drop of water to refresh them.' Whereupon they were released; nothing like this would happen today.

Currently occupying the racial limelight, after millennia of scant pickings in the desert, are Tuaregs. Press reports of attacks on intrepid package tourists first appeared in January 1992. A worker with an overland trekking company described the fate of two convoys ambushed in the remote Saharan border regions south of Tamanrasset. 'They lost everything except their passports, with the vehicles being driven away by the rebels into the Sahara, never to be seen again.' Tourists are held for maybe eight hours in the sands while their captors rummage through their possessions for money, cameras, personal cassette players and those puzzling coloured plastic cards. It is perhaps surprising that Toyota (see **Biggs**) have never based a publicity campaign round the desert marauders' preference for Land Cruisers, and equally surprising that Tuaregs are involved at all. For centuries they operated as peaceful traders in open markets with an innate respect for persons and property, and their popular image owes much to P.C. Wren's fiction and their stateless pedigree, making them easy scapegoats.

But at least these desert groups fared better than the British holiday-makers subjected to the spate of attacks on train journeys to the French Riviera in 1991. Overnight, their compartments were infiltrated with gas, leaving the tourists to come round with splitting headaches the following morning, still in their sleepwear, without money, luggage, ID, credit cards or clothes.

The French may have little good to say about the British. But they envied the high standards of our **highwaymen**. Abroad, the profession was all riff-raff; but visitors to England drew comfort from by the well-educated, polite bearing of the local villains, although they bridled at their sheer quantity. In the manner of a menu, roads round London were said to be 'garnis de voleurs à cheval'. One well-informed foreigner noted in early Franglais that 'les highwaymen sont, en général, d'une classe supérieure... They take a pride in carrying on their profession with distinction. One could say that they attach importance to honour, and that they think of their reputation as much as they do of their pockets.'

Not so the Chinese who, in demonstration of their sovereignty as an occupying power, prefer to execute Tibetans in public. The condemned were apt to shout 'Long live the Dalai Lama' with their dying breath. So these days their vocal cords are prophylactically slit. Alternatively, Tibetans go to execution with their throats pre-garrotted with wire, and the more obstinate cases have their tongues hooked out.

The Chinese make the relatives of the deceased pay for the bullets with which they are shot. Since the 1950 invasion, the Tibetan population has fallen by 1.2 million and overall expenditure on ammunition must have been considerable.

According to American Drug Enforcement Agency officials, the Chinese make exemplary gangsters – patient, loyal, disciplined and low-profile. Under interrogation, they would rather die than talk, perhaps because, under the **Triad** oath of silence, they will die if they do.

Mexican criminals are reputedly the keenest to blab; the Italians also talk readily, but only about making a deal.

See also **Colombia**

Y

Yakuza

Japanese Mafia. In spring 1992 the Tokyo police inaugurated a telephone hotline for mobsters anxious to quit but unsure how.

Reformed gangsters remain conspicuous, thanks to their missing little fingers snipped off in an underworld **initiation** ritual. Police from the Kanagawa prefecture tempted converts with a packaged service offering referral to a surgeon specialising in grafting toes onto hands (see **Godmothers**).

These pathetic governmental inducements are symptomatic of a battle lost long ago. The police files on 3,200 Yakuza syndicates and 88,000 gangsters were easily amassed, the task simplified by legal membership: Yakuza members display their gang's name on calling cards and office doorplates.

The Yakuza's traditional remit was to regulate prostitution, gambling and – more recently – soft drugs. Someone had to do it, and the police left well alone. But in the 1970s the Yakuza diversified into loansharking and thence construction, acquiring substantial property holdings. By the economic boom of the 1980s they had infiltrated legitimate businesses, in 1989 raking in an estimated 1,300 billion yen from commercial blackmail, takeovers and extortion. But their links with blue-chip institutions remained invisible as long as asset prices inflated and rising wealth precluded financial investigation. The stock market collapse laid bare the dealings which destroyed mainstream companies like Itoman, a business of a hundred years standing. Itoman fell into the clutches of a businessman,

Suemsitsu Ito, with Yakuza connections through a Korean, Ho Yong Chung. Ito squandered company money on buying property and paintings from Ho at vastly inflated prices, creating a debt of 1,400 billion yen, and singlehandedly drove the business into the ground.

By the time this particular fraud was exposed in September 1990 it was evident that the Yakuza were rampant throughout Japanese society. A police survey of 2,106 Tokyo businesses found that 41 per cent had been approached with offers they could hardly refuse. One third succumbed, and the bigger the company, the more enticing the target. The connections between the worlds of crime, business and politics were underlined by the discovery that the Prime Minister, Noboru Takeshita, secured his appointment by a deal with the Inagawi-kai, Tokyo's largest Yakuza gang, and when the first half-hearted anti-gang laws were passed in 1992 the Yakuza staged organised rallies and protest marches in the streets.

Yorkshire Ripper, alternative

Britain's second-ranking serial killer, arrested on 2 January 1981, was identified after a four-year manhunt as Peter **Sutcliffe**. But was he the right man? A persistent advertiser in the British satirical magazine *Private Eye* refuses to accept Sutcliffe as the real Yorkshire Ripper.

The theory is the brainchild of investigative writer Noel O'Gara, who has Sutcliffe down for a 'copy-cat' ripper, answerable only for the last four killings, as the police well knew. Supposedly, detectives were so keen for a conviction that they came to terms, offering Sutcliffe ten years in Broadmoor on diminished charges of manslaughter in exchange for his confessions, an arrangement scotched in court by an astute judge, Mr Justice Boreham. By then the true killer, William Tracey, had removed himself to Ireland.

With his beard and bushy eyebrows, Tracey is not dissimilar from Peter Sutcliffe. He fits survivors' descriptions. Like Sutcliffe, Tracey was of Irish extraction, in the forty-to-fifty age range, stocky, tattooed, a B-blood pimp with a gap tooth; and O'Gara presents evidence that Tracey had the means, motive and opportunity for the killings.

On 18 August 1983, the obsessive O'Gara extracted a written confession from his suspect: 'I William Tracey, aged 44, of 27 Kilcoursey, Clara, Co. Offaly, confess to the murders of the following women: McCann, Harrison, Jackson, Richardson, Atkinson, McDonald, Ryka, Millward, Whittaker, Leach. I have done the business on them. I have murdered them. I suppose I am unstable. I am perpetual, psychic, paranoid...'

But this admission was obtained by deception. O'Gara persuaded a friend to pose as a *News of the World* reporter and purchased two banker's drafts, one for £5 and one for £10. With a typewriter he inserted seven further noughts, and then invited Tracey to a videotaped presentation at the Prince of Wales Hotel in Athlone, offering £60,000 from the newspaper for his confession. Tracey obliged, but immediately after the formal ceremony smelt a rat and harried his tormentors round the car park with a Stanley knife. O'Gara made off with his precious confession, which he forwarded to the British police. Despite letters, telephone calls and a privately published book, he has heard no more. Doubtless he is regarded as a crank.

O'Gara's book has a frenetic 'round earth' feel that Galileo would recognise; he can prove his case time and again, but no one pays a blind bit of notice.

Young, Graham (1947–90)

A compulsive serial poisoner who assisted investigators by suggesting how his undiscovered murders were committed. When detectives checked his theory, they found it correct. So they arrested him. This happened not once, but twice.

Young's mother died of natural causes when he was a few months old, and in adolescence he developed into a loner whose heroes were Dr **Palmer**

and Hitler. In 1961, aged fourteen, Young set about **poisoning** his family with antimony. Only his stepmother Molly died, the following April, but when his father was hospitalised the doctors outraged Young by a sloppy diagnosis of arsenic poisoning. 'How ridiculous not to be able to tell the difference between antimony and arsenic,' he scoffed.

Nine years later he was released from Broadmoor bearing the endorsement of a medical certificate from consultant psychiatrist E.L. Unwin. 'He has made an extremely full recovery,' it said of Young, 'and he is now entirely fit for discharge... He would fit in well and not draw any attention to himself in any community.'

Young's neat turn-out, meticulously backswept hair and grave, precise verbal mannerisms made him attractive to employers. Years of study in the Broadmoor library on chemistry and medicine had steeped him in the lore of lesser known poisons, and the prospect of work at John Hadland's photographic works near Bovingdon held tantalising possibilities. In early 1971 Young accepted the post of assistant storeman. He laid his hands on a promising substance, thallium, a heavy metal (akin to mercury) both tasteless and easily soluble. All the auguries looked good: its curative properties on ringworm and unwanted facial hair were outweighed by serious side-effects, its medicinal use abandoned in the 1940s.

But would it kill? Young instigated a series of experiments. Each day he collected his workmates' tea from the storeroom hatch. Dosing their drinks was easy. First he tried the thallium salts on Bob Egle, the 60-year-old head warehouseman.

It made Egle throw up and, as the treatment progressed, so the symptoms increased in severity. Soon Egle evinced prolonged bouts of violent retching. Further doses engendered shooting pains in the chest and back. A touch more and he lost his balance. Finally Egle became delirious.

Young crowned these early successes on 13 July when, after weeks of agonising pain, Bob Egle died of 'peripheral neuritis' in St Alban's City Hospital. But could Young pull off the same trick on Egle's successor, 56-year-old Fred Biggs? Yes: by October, Biggs's hold on life was weakening and on 19 November he too perished. So presumably thallium would work on anyone? Yes: by then Jethro Batt and David Tilson were suffering severe stomach cramps, hair loss and attacks of numbness. And what about their four colleagues? They too fell ill.

Speculation about a 'Bovingdon Bug' encouraged the management to call in a team of toxicologists, headed by Dr Iain Anderson. He summoned a staff meeting and, hoping to quell the rumours, invited questions from the floor.

First to speak was Graham Young: didn't the doctors realise that the workers' symptoms were *obviously* consistent with thallium poisoning?

In court, the defence was handicapped by Young's diary. No special powers were required to interpret his entry for 31 October 1971: 'I have administered a fatal dose of the special compound to F... I gave him three separate doses.' Young enjoyed starring at his trial, and declared to the police, 'I could have killed them all if I wished... But I allowed them to live.' He was no less munificent towards himself. After the discovery of an 'exit dose' sewn into the lining of his jacket, Young threatened to break his own neck on the courtroom dock rail if he was found guilty. But he stayed his hand.

Young was sent back to Broadmoor, where he died of a heart attack in August 1990. His sister Winifred, who nearly perished (and suffered protracted agonies) during his 1961 rehearsal, ascribes her brother's career to his 'craving for publicity'. It seems he did love his family, but not enough.

Young, John (d. 1750)

Until 1949, the death sentence in Scotland specified both the date and the time of a hanging. In 1750 John Young, a sergeant slated to swing in Edinburgh for forgery, assumed that time was of the essence. Condemned to hang between two and four in the afternoon, Young persuaded the officials presenting themselves at the appointed hour to give him a few moments peace alone in his cell. Then he barricaded the door.

Outside, the clock ticked on while warders tried to force entry. The fateful hour of four o'clock came and went, and it was a quarter past before prison officers knocked a hole through the ceiling from the floor above.

But all Young's efforts came to nothing; the magistrates had stopped the city's clocks. So it still was between two and four in the afternoon when Young was dragged to the gallows.

Sixty-four years later Londoners were treated to the spectacle of a less grudging participant. The highwayman John Ashton went insane while awaiting his November 1814 execution at Newgate. When the moment came, Ashton dashed up the steps to the gallows as though unleashed and pranced up and down on top of the scaffold shouting to the crowds.

'Look at me!' he cried, 'I am the Lord Wellington.' They hanged him anyway and, after briefly vanishing from view beneath the trap door, Ashton miraculously rebounded onto the platform with his delusions reinforced. He continued his dance, hopping up and down next to the chaplain. 'What do you think of me? Am I not Lord Wellington now?' he shouted, between cheering and clapping. The executioner remounted the scaffold to push him to his death.

Youngstown, Ohio

A statistical microcosm of American murder. With a population of 95,000, this depressed steel town (which lost 40,000 jobs in the 1970s and 80s) recorded the country's biggest year-on-year increase in killings, up 310 per cent to a total of fifty-nine in 1991.

Part of the homicide toll was attributable to domestic and random violence, but its most striking feature was the surge in drug and gang-related deaths among young adults. Three hundred dollars is the street price for a 9mm automatic; where once grandmothers looked after children, 30-year-old grandmother addicts now buy and sell **crack**. **Gangs** confer status on the young; there is little else that will. At least twenty-five killings involved drug disputes, whether for straightforward non-payment, territorial battles, disagreements over money or executions. Seven deaths came from rows between young lovers. Forty-six perished from gunfire. There were no killings for trainers, but Jermaine Williams, aged 17, died during a row over a gold chain.

Some murders had all the refinement of gangland. Flip Williams, aged 34, masterminded the Labour Day killing of four drug-pushing rivals in their early twenties; his mob included a 16-year-old girl. Flip was captured himself in January 1992 breaking *into* jail to get at his captured lieutenants, who had turned state's evidence. When a

Colombian dealer pulled into town with nine kilos of cocaine, he was kidnapped by local teenagers and tortured for four days until he met their ransom demand of $150,000; then they killed him.

According to 14-year-old Nathan Hayes, speaking from the refuge of the Boys and Girls Club: 'Pretty soon, if I stayed, I'd be shooting my friends, one way or another. Or they'd be shooting me.' Police noted that immediately after sentence the young killers could be calmed down, like babies with a bottle, by a bag of crisps or a can of Coke.

The risk of an American teenager being murdered doubled between 1985 and 1990; it is now the third highest cause of death among all young men and the highest for young black men. The sharp reduction of the homicide rate in the early 1980s was credited by Reagan to Reagan, but it reflects the temporary population dip in teenagers and young adult males.

In 1991, the American murder total was 24,020, putting the statistical likelihood at one in 10,400 (about eight times the British rate), a figure which varies widely from area to area. Washington D.C. (pop. 605,000) accounted for 489 killings at a rate of one in 1,200; the Washington body-count is well over half the figure for the whole of Britain.

Guns are used in 64 per cent of American cases. Blacks, a 12 per cent minority, constitute nearly half of all victims. The great majority of killings are confined to victims of the murderer's racial origin.

The 1990 clear-up rate was 67 per cent, proof again that even under the most extreme circumstances murder is a risky business for the perpetrator. But in the 1960s, 90 per cent or more of the annual harvest of 8,000 homicides were solved. In New York, the percentage of drug-related killings rose from about 20 per cent of the total in the early 1980s to some 40 per cent by the close of the decade.

Yu, Wong

Inventor of hijacking. On 16 July 1947 Wong Yu and three Chinese accomplices staged a takeover of a Cathay Pacific flying boat on the Macao-Hong Kong route, planning to divert the flight and rob or ransom the passengers. But they panicked when the co-pilot set about them with an iron bar, and it was at this juncture that Wong Yu decided to shoot the pilot.

After the crash, Yu found himself the only survivor and might have escaped scot-free had he not, in hospital, related his misadventure to a fellow patient, a policeman. He was hanged.

The first American hijacking came in August 1971. Leon Bearden, an impecunious ex-convict, decided to emigrate. With his 16-year-old son, Cody, he commandeered a Continental Airlines Boeing 707 over New Mexico and demanded a passage to Cuba, but was overpowered while explaining to an FBI agent, during a pit stop in El Paso, that with 'less than twenty-five bucks to his name' he had no legitimate alternative. Bearden was sentenced to twenty years; Cody was paroled after two.

Some people nurture a sneaking admiration for the gallant D. B. Cooper, the one who got away, by parachute. On 24 November 1971, Cooper baled out of a North-West Airlines flight at 10,000 feet over the Cascade mountains south of Seattle, taking $200,000 in a rucksack, and he has never been seen since.

But a man called John List has. Or may have been. According to the police, on 9 November 1971 the 45-year-old List, a New Jersey insurance salesman, shot dead his mother, his wife and their three children with a 9mm automatic. Four were killed with a single bullet behind the ear; the fifth, their 15-year-old, was shot ten times. List disappeared, leaving a detailed account of his evening's work and a spate of press speculation about his financial double-dealing.

List was next heard of eighteen years later, featured on television as one of 'America's Most Wanted'. Visual aids for the broadcast included a computer-enhanced photograph and a sculptured bust of his head projected forwards by two decades to replicate ageing. A flood of 300 telephone calls led to the arrest of a Robert Clark, an elderly married man from Richmond, Virginia.

On 8 June 1989 the FBI announced that they were re-opening the case on Cooper, the hijacker who, it will be remembered, appeared fifteen days after List vanished. Clark materialised after the disappearance of both. Can they be related?

Yuppies

Mafia boss John Gotti was often characterised as a hoodlum's hoodlum. He was also a hoodlum's yuppie.

His takeover of the Gambino family after the murder of Big Paul Castellano on 16 December 1985 marked a pronounced change in management style. Known as the 'Dapper Don', the flashy Gotti was seldom out of the pages of *Time*, *People* and *The New York Times Magazine*. For underlings jaded by years of low-profile leaders with zero *savoir-faire*, it provided a welcome break from the endless niceties of outmoded Mafia protocol, derisively referred to as 'all this stupid *Cosa Nostra* crap'. Gotti was admired for his silk scarves and double-breasted $3,000 suits; the retail cost of his outfits was always quoted in the press, but reports did not mention that Gotti never bought a suit in his life. All were stolen.

At Gotti's trial the *Newsday* legal correspondent noted that the gangsters' courtroom benches were laden with men in 'calm stripes and turbulent ties'; younger members of the Gotti entourage were distinguished by more extreme peaked lapels and trousers with turn-ups. But Gotti's sartorial elegance was of recent origin. As a teenage punk in the 1950s, taking bets from schoolchildren, he possessed a number of striking but simple outfits. There was the all-purple look, with purple shoes. And there was the all-green look, with green shoes. He also did a number in white shoes, black trousers and an orange shirt.

Come the late 1980s and the Wall Street boom, the Mafia blossomed. Gone was the fixation with dressing as peasants in baggy trousers belted round the mid-chest. Gone were the former obsessions with courtesy and rank, symbolised by old-style godfather Tony Corallo who entered restaurants flinging his camel hair coat to one side in the absolute certainty that some fawning henchman would catch it; gone were the days of mattress cash spent on mansions with downmarket pigeon-coops on the roof.

The boomtime mobster read the financial press, sported a power haircut, invested in handmade suits and, for preference, drove a BMW. Gotti, a youthful 47, appointed comparative youngsters like Salvatore Gravano to positions of influence, and their new broom swept away the Old World pretence of not dealing in drugs, a convention long more honoured in the breach than the observance.

Likewise, the mobsters of Prohibition Chicago were paragons of fashion. After the 'Diamond Jim' excesses of the previous era, correct menswear narrowed into a pearl grey hat with black band, a dark, three-piece, double-breasted suit, handkerchief in breast pocket, white shirt, striped tie and – of course – spats; the famous photograph of 'Machine Gun' Jack McGurn's body shows that he died with his spats on (see **Names**). In his later days, Capone himself became a mite more relaxed, often photographed in a straw 'boater' with a fine watch-chain and a restrained tie.

In the late 1920s, smart mobster bodyguards were the elite of Chicago's youth: stereotypically good with *maître d's* and nightclub head waiters, at ease at the theatre or on the race track, snappy dressers with a keen eye for blondes, and good judges of diamonds. Capone's gunmen were the pick of the bunch. Said Harry Doremus, arrested in 1929: 'The Big Fellow hires nothing but gentlemen. They have to be well dressed at all times and must have cultured accents. They always say "Yes, Sir" and "No, Sir" to him.'

Physical fitness was *de rigueur*. Capone's Metropole headquarters boasted a two-room gymnasium with punch bags, horizontal bars, trapezes and rowing machines. According to Fred D. Pasley, an early Capone hagiographer, the bodyguards 'followed a schedule of training as methodical as that of college football athletes'. Their workouts included periodical trips to the Illinois outback, where the hoods practised on private machine-gun ranges. Being a mobster was a high-status, glamorous job, probably the best way the poor could make a dishonest living.

Z

Zapata, Emiliano (d. 1919)

Mexican folk-hero of the revolutionary war, elaborately liquidated by the half-breed Colonel Jesus Guajardo for $50,000 blood-money.

In 1919 the treacherous Guajardo defected to Zapata's cause, bringing 800 men as well as badly needed supplies of arms and ammunition, proving his loyalty by an attack on his own side at Jonacatepec where he executed the prisoners.

On 10 April, Zapata rode over to review Guajardo's incoming troops at the hacienda of San Juan Chinameca. As Zapata and ten aides jangled through the gates, a band began to play, and in the courtyard a guard of honour 200-strong paraded to attention. 'Present arms!' shouted Guajardo, standing slightly to one side, as Zapata halted to take the salute.

He was assassinated by volley, his blood-caked body put on display to show the Morelos peasantry that the government meant business.

Zebra Killings

A sequence of San Francisco murders claiming hundreds of lives during a 179-day period from October 1973. The zebra has alternating stripes of black and white, and the slayings were cross-racial, with blacks killing whites for religious reasons, inspired by the radical tract, 'Message to the Black Man', which embodied its precepts in question-and-answer form. Question four demanded: 'Does Allah have enemies and who are they?' The correct response was 'the white race'.

Answer ten explained the next step: 'All Muslims will murder the white devil because they know he is a snake. Each Muslim is required to kill four devils, and by bringing and presenting four at one time,

his reward is a button to wear on the lapel of his coat and free transportation to the Holy city of Mecca to see brother Mohammed.'

To beleaguered West Coast Black fanatics this constituted an attractive offer, and a squad of Death Angels formed to snatch random whites off the street, often as not raping and mutilating their victims before the kill.

The case was broken by Anthony Cornelius Harris, former prisoner B35599 of San Quentin and a judo expert. While inside, Harris was approached by Jesse Lee Cooks asking about the easiest way of killing people. In *The Zebra Killings* (1980) Cooks introduces himself with the words: 'I want to learn how to bust a heart with a punch to a chest. And how to come up behind somebody and snap their neck... See, man, in San Francisco they got what's called the Death Angels. It's a special part of the Muslims. The job of the Death Angels is to off white chumps, see? But you got to prove you can kill before they'll let you in.' Harris taught Cooks judo and kung fu.

The sect had a graded scoring system. Lukewarm devotees might have few qualms about murdering a white man, but women and children provided a tougher test of moral fibre, a distinction reflected in the 'points' for each kill. Nine adult males was the minimum qualification for admission through the pearly gates, but only five women or just four children. Elevation to the elect was signified by drawing a pair of celestial wings on the photographs of successful candidates kept at their San Francisco temple; these pictures were displayed on an easel at meetings held in the loft.

By October 1973, California had fifteen accredited Death Angels who between them killed 135 men, 75 women and 60 children, all white. Photographic evidence of the corpse *in situ* was helpful in substantiating a claim. Later, during the longest trial in Californian history, Harris turned state's evidence and testified about his participation in ten murders, including the great binge of the Night of Five. The trial started on 3 March 1975 and ended a year and six days later; the jury reached a unanimous verdict of guilty and the four defendants received life sentences.

Zlotys, Polish

Poland's privatisation programme generated unprecedented opportunities for fraud as government officers jumped the gun on what belonged to whom. First came Cigarettesgate, then Schnappsgate and finally Roublesgate, where soft Soviet roubles were converted into fairly hard Polish zlotys, which could briefly be exchanged for completely hard American dollars, bequeathing a huge loss to the national treasury.

Next came the Finance Ministry's 'Fund for Foreign Debt', specialising in the sophisticated secondary-debt market. On these high-risk deals, you win some and you lose some. Those they lost the officials debited to the state's account. Those they won they credited to their own. The scam is under investigation with an expected deficit of four hundred million dollars.

For the Poles, one of the few heartening economic events of 1990 was the phenomenal rise of the company Art-B, living proof that under capitalism a hundred million zlotys could be made overnight by giving the public what they wanted. The brainchild of two musicians, Art-B started small in sacred Catholic songs, and finished big, sponsoring music festivals, film festivals, theatre festivals and art shows; they bailed out a hospital and nearly clinched a deal to rescue the Ursus tractor factory by buying an entire year's production.

It now seems that a provincial bank clerk founded Art-B's fortune in September 1990. He issued a letter confirming that they had $300,000 on deposit in return for a $5,000 bribe, and the document became collateral for a loan at a second bank, with these monies transferred to a third bank.

In Poland, cheques are cleared by post, which can take weeks, and interest accrued while the cheques were in transit at a dollar premium rate of 60 to 80 per cent. The Art-B con consisted of devising a way of transferring funds to outpace the postal system, making deposits before the notice of withdrawal was received. This entailed ferrying suitcases of cash around the country by helicopter, raking in interest from money simultaneously in two places, and investing the proceeds in a cascade of further accounts.

After washing $18 *billion* through the banking system in little more than a year, the Art-B boys decamped to Israel with $400 million from the last bank in the chain, and – excepting the initial bribe – it is not clear if the law was contravened. No free market meant no free market regulations, and today Poland remains open to the out-dated, primitive financial swindles that had their heyday in the 1920s and 30s – 'daisy chains', 'Ponzi schemes' and the like, no longer practicable in the West. In Poland, conmen pit their wits against the combined resources of the two officials in the State Prosecutor's office with a working grasp of financial corruption.

See also **Eastern bloc, High Finance**

Zodiac Killer

An unidentified Californian murderer from the late 1960s. His continuing anonymity typifies the serial killer's insoluble dilemma in his drive for recognition: total success – evading capture – means oblivion.

Someone, somewhere may read these words knowing that the disclosure of his epic past will arouse not terror, but disgust, contempt and, perhaps, pity. There is little mileage in being a serial killer, but an unknown ex-serial killer is buried alive, a walking corpse – feckless before the murders started and a feckless murderer afterwards. It is the killings' continuance that establishes their necessity and imbues them and their author with interest and notoriety. Their cessation deprives the perpetrator of both his private justification and his public standing.

The Zodiac Killer shot courting couples: first David Faraday and Betty Lou Jensen on 20 December 1968, then Michael Mageau on 5 July 1969, then two student picnickers on 20 September, then two Pacific Union College students on 27 September 1969 and finally a San Francisco cab driver, Paul Stein, on 21 October. The murderer used the killings to elbow his way into newspapers, insisting that his letters (marked with the sign of the

Zodiac) be published to prevent further bloodshed. There are other ways of getting into print, and similarly the airtime obtained by his telephone conversation with lawyer Melvin Belli during a television chat show on 21 October was available to callers with something to say. By 1974 'Zodiac' was threatening 'to do something nasty' if he did not receive more publicity. That meant more killing. But was it worth the effort or the risk?

The police came close to catching him. The hooded attacker of 20 September was overweight, and his telephone call to the Napa police left a clear palmprint on the receiver in the public call box. Bloodstained fingerprints were found in the back of Paul Stein's cab, but to date the podgy killer with horn-rimmed spectacles remains at large.

In June 1990 a copycat 'Zodiac Killer' set out his stall on the East Coast, sending the *New York Post* a *resumé* detailing his shooting of three men on the city streets. The note began, 'This is the Zodiac the twelve sign/will die when the belts in the heaven/are seen/the first sign is dead on march 8 1990 1:45 AM/white man with cane shoot on the back in street.' Checking their records, the police found that three men *had* been shot – although not fatally – at the designated times and places, and concluded that 'Zodiac' intended to kill once for each astrological sign. With three down, nine remained to go.

The case's enduring riddle was that each victim's astrological sign matched his attribution in the *New York Post* note. Chance odds were 1,584 to one against, but none of the wounded could recall volunteering their birthdays. Mario Orozoco, shot on 8 March, reported that his assailant 'was across the street from me and crossed to meet me. He just put a gun against my back and then, bang. He shot me in the spine.'

Behavioural scientists, astrologers and computer technologists pooled resources, producing the well-thumbed profile of a loner from a broken home with a menial job. Observing that the incidents occurred at twenty-one day intervals, or multiples thereof, they deduced that the next attack was scheduled for

21 June, the first day of Cancer. That night a homeless man with a little black dog was shot at 3.52 a.m. sleeping on a Central Park bench. His star sign was Cancer, increasing the chance odds to 17,424 against, and the following day 'Zodiac' wrote to the *New York Post* correctly specifying the time of attack: 'Fourth sign dead shoot in Central Park white man sleeping on bench with little black dog shoot in chest.' That left eight to come.

At the same time 'Zodiac' asserted a pedigree as his illustrious Californian predecessor. But the New Yorker was tall (not shortish), slim (not podgy), the wrong age and the wrong colour (black not white). For the key dates of 12 July, 2 August and 23 August the streets were flooded with the officers of the Zodiac 'Operation Watchdog' Task Force, but by then, just like the original, his impetus was spent. He too languishes incognito.

See also **Jekyll and Hyde**

Zombie

A catatonic state achieved by Jeffrey **Dahmer**, the Milwaukee serial killer. During his stint as a professional soldier, Dahmer developed a serious drink problem.

On 29 December 1978, six months after his first murder, Dahmer joined the US Army at his father's insistence, hoping to become a military policeman. Reassigned as a medic, in July 1979 he was posted on exercises to Germany.

There Dahmer devised a singular way of passing the weekend. He converted his briefcase into a portable bar, and on Friday nights sat in an armchair, put his *Black Sabbath* tapes on the headphones and mixed up dry martinis from Beefeater gin. He neither moved nor spoke, and slugged shots back until he passed out. When he came round, still in the chair, he started drinking again, and continued in this manner until Monday.

Dahmer started on alcohol at the age of eleven as a counter to the objectionable ordeal of consciousness and, after his first murder in 1978, drank with ever-increasing fervour to blot out his guilt and cravings. In the process he blotted himself out, mutating into a dead zone incapable of human response. But Dahmer still needed company and, lacking the social skills to befriend the living, derived companionship from the dead.

Corpses do not make satisfactory partners for long. They decompose. In his final tailspin of 1991, Dahmer hit on the strategy of 'zombification'. As he said, 'I didn't want to keep killing people and have nothing left but the skull', and among the scant material resources in his apartment was an electric drill with two bits. Dahmer purchased a marinating syringe from 'Lecter's Kitchen Supply' and, in May 1991, after drugging Konerak Sinthasomphone, he bored a hole in the boy's cranium, angling the drill towards the frontal lobes. Then he slid the needle two inches into the skull and injected muriatic acid.

As related elsewhere (see **Edwards**), Sinthasomphone stumbled out of the apartment block while his tormentor went for a beer. Dahmer reclaimed the boy from a crowd in the streets and, safely back in his apartment, deduced that the first injection was too weak, since Sinthasomphone retained sufficient motive power and the will to leave. He administered another shot, resulting in death, and later explained the underlying rationale to Dr Wahlstrom: 'If they had their own thought processes, they might remember that they had to leave, or lived somewhere else.' This tallies with an exchange from the trial. 'What would it have taken to stop you killing?' Dahmer was asked. 'A permanent relationship.'

Zombification provided a good interim solution. As Dahmer observed of Jeremiah Weinberger, 'I wanted to find a way of keeping him with me without actually killing him.' Sinthasomphone had died from the acid, so Dahmer treated Weinberger with added circumspection, injecting him with boiling water. The patient later regained consciousness in a semi-functional state. 'He talked, it was like he was dazed,' Dahmer noted. 'I thought I would be able to keep him that way. He was walking around, going to the bathroom.'

The next evening Dahmer had to work, so he gave Weinberger 'another dose of pills and another shot of boiling water in the same hole'. Returning after the night shift, he found Weinberger dead. At the trial, this venture was discussed by prosecuting counsel and a psychiatrist, Dr Fosdal.

'Have you ever met a case of home-made lobotomy here?' Fosdal was asked.

'No, I think this is the first time internationally. Mr Dahmer is setting some precedents here.'

'It couldn't have worked, could it?'

'It's possible.'

'Did you ask him how long he was going to keep the zombie? Do you believe he would have created a zombie and never killed again?'

'Absolutely,' said Fosdal. 'That would have been the solution to his problem.' After arrest, Dahmer confided in Dr Dietz that he contemplated making a hole in the head of one of his subjects, inserting an electric cable, plugging it into the wall socket and then switching him on. Other plans included freeze-drying the dead; Dahmer's initial attempt with domestic equipment on Eddie Smith in June 1990 failed when the body retained its moisture and acidified.

By 1991 Dahmer was little more than a zombie himself. At his trial the defence presented him as an automaton who killed and partially ate his fifteen victims because he suffered from necrophilia, defined as a compulsive desire to have sex with dead bodies. The prosecution agreed, but argued that this was not officially recognised as an allowable category of madness; in their book, he still knew it was wrong, and, were Dahmer adjudged insane, he could petition for release every six months after first undergoing a year's treatment in a mental institution.

In his entire life, Dahmer only once showed interest in something other than death: an aquarium. The fish he particularly favoured was the puffer fish, certain species of which are, by coincidence, the prime source for tetrodotoxin, used by Haitian witch-doctors in the creation of voodoo zombies.

Zoo, private

As built by Pablo **Escobar**, Colombia's cocaine billionaire, on his 7,000 acre estate on the Magdalena River. One of Escobar's diversions was a private zoo stocked with elephants, hippopotami, rare birds and – apparently – a kangaroo footballer.

For many years, Escobar featured as a social benefactor. On the one hand, he put much of his profits into civic improvements for the city of **Medellin**, building swish shopping malls, gourmet restaurants, homes for the poor, sports pitches and street lighting, earning the title of 'Don Pablo'. On the other, the streets were paved with dead.

Escobar's hillside prison (see **Cathedral**) on the surrounding mountains lay above his old home town of Envigado, currently infested by banks.

Escobar controlled its civic elections with huge influxes of drug money, endowing it as the only city in Colombia able to pay adequate welfare. Such largesse bought safety during his spells as a fugitive. In the words of a senior general, 'Escobar will not abandon Envigado. Two hundred thousand eyes and ears on his side ... maybe more than 100 taxis with radios, listening and informing.' Every night the city was patrolled by a vigilante force, the 'Department of Security and Control', who took those they considered suspicious for a one-way walk, taped their mouths shut and hacked them to pieces.

Football was Escobar's great passion. He would play and referee at the same time, only blowing the final whistle when his team took the lead. In theory this should not have taken long; as an opponent from Magdalena Medio recalled, 'When Pablo kicked the ball, the other side moved away to let the ball through to the goal.' In practice, spectators recall four-hour marathons.

Zyklon B

Trade name for the Nazi concentration camps' extermination agent, hydrocyanic gas, employed today in American execution chambers.

Select Bibliography

Andrews, William *Bygone Punishments:* Andrews, 1899

Allsopp, Kenneth *The Bootleggers:* Arrow Books, London, 1970

Anspacher, Carolyn *The Acid Test:* Peter Dawnay, 1965

Arlacchi, Pino *Mafia Business:* Oxford University Press, 1988

Babington, Anthony *The English Bastille:* Macdonald, London, 1971

Bailey, Brian *Hangmen of England:* W H Allen, London, 1989

Ball, James Moores *The Body Snatchers:* Dorset Press, New York, 1989

Begg, Paul, Fido, Martin & Skinner, Keith *The Jack the Ripper A-Z:* Headline, London, 1991

Behn, Noel *Brink's!:* W H Allen, London, 1977

Berry-Dee, Christopher & Robin Odell *The Long Drop:* Viking, London, 1993

Bland, James *Crime, Strange but True:* Futura, London, 1991

Blumenthal, Ralph *The Last Days of the Sicilian Mafia:* Bloomsbury, London, 1988

Blundell, Nigel *The World's Greatest Crooks and Conmen:* Hamlyn, London, 1991

Bolitho, William *Murder for Profit:* Cape, London, 1926

Bugliosi, Vincent *Helter Skelter:* Penguin, London, 1977

Burn, Gordon *Sonebody's Husband, Somebody's Son:* Heinemann, London, 1984

Byrne, Richard *Safecracking:* Grafton, London, 1992

Bresler, Fenton *An Almanac of Murder:* Severn House, London, 1987

Brown, Peter *Marilyn, the Last Take:* Heinemann, London, 1992

Carpozi, George *Bugsy:* SPI Books, New York, 1973

Chance, John Newton *Thieves' Kitchen:* Hale, London, 1989

Clark, Sir George *The Campden Wonder:* Oxford University Press, 1959

Conradi, Peter *The Red Ripper:* Virgin, London, 1993

Cordingly, David & Falconer, John *Pirates: Fact and Fiction:* Collins & Brown, London, 1992

Cornwell, John *A Thief in the Night:* Viking, London, 1989

Cowdery, Ray *Capone's Chicago:* Northstar Maschek Books, 1987

Craig, Mary *Tears of Blood:* HarperCollins, London, 1992

Crispin, Ken *The Dingo Baby Case:* Albatross Books, Australia, 1987

Critchley, T A & James, P D *The Maul and the Pear Tree:* Constable, London, 1971

Cummings, John & Volkman, Ernest *Mobster:* Futura, London, 1991

Davis, Don *The Milwaukee Murders:* St Martin's Press, USA, 1991

De Quincey, Thomas *On Murder Considered as One of the Fine Arts*, London, 1827

Campbell, Duncan *That was Business, this is Personal:* Secker & Warburg, London, 1990

Dunstan, Keith *Saint Ned:* Methuen, Australia, 1980

Duke, Thomas *Celebrated Criminal Cases of America:* James Barry, San Francisco, 1910

Eddy, Paul *The Cocaine Wars:* Century, London, 1988

Emmons, Noel *Manson in his own Words:* Grove Press, USA, 1986

Fletcher, Tony *Memories of Murder:* Weidenfeld & Nicolson, London, 1986

Foot, Paul *Who killed Hanratty?* Cape, London, 1971

Foucault, Michel *Discipline and Punish:* Allen Lane, London, 1977

Fox, Grace *British Admirals and Chinese Pirates:* Kegan Paul, London, 1940

Fox, James *White Mischief:* Cape, London, 1982

Gamini, Salgrado *The Elizabethan Underworld:* Dent, London, 1977

Garbutt, Paul *Assassins:* Ian Allen, London, 1992

Gaute, J H H and Robin Odell *Murder 'Whatdunit':* Harrap, London, 1982

Gilbert, Michael *Fraudsters:* Constable, London, 1986

Gollmar, Robert H *Edward Gein:* Wisconsin, 1982

Goodman, Jonathan, ed. *Supernatural Murders:* Piatkus, London, 1992

Goodman, Jonathan, ed. *Trial of Ian Brady and Myra Hindley:* David & Charles, Devon, 1973

Goodman, Jonathan & Bill Waddell *The Black Museum:* Harrap, London, 1987

Green, Jonathon *Directory of Infamy:* Mills & Boon, London, 1980

Haining, Peter *The English Highwayman:* Hale, London, 1991

Harris, Robert *Selling Hitler:* Faber & Faber, London, 1986

Harrison, Fred *Brady and Hindley:* Ashgrove Press, London, 1986

Hayward, Captain Simon *Under Fire:* W H Allen, London, 1989

Hobsbawm, E J *Bandits:* Nicolson, London, 1969

Holmes, Ronald *The Legend of Sawney Beane:* Muller, London, 1975

Honeycombe, Gordon *More Murders of the Black Museum:* Hutchinson, London, 1993

Houts, Marshall *Who Killed Sir Harry Oakes?:* Hale, London, 1976

Howard, Clark *The Zebra Killings:* New English Library, London, 1980

Hughes, Robert *The Fatal Shore:* Harvill, London, 1987

Jones, Jack *Let me take you Down:* Virgin, London, 1993

Jennings, Dean *We Only Kill Each Other:* Fawcett Crest, 1967

Kennedy, Ludovic *Ten Rillington Place:* Gollancz, London, 1982

Kray, Reginald & Ronald *Our Story:* Jackson, London, 1988

Laffin, John *Anatomy of Captivity:* Abelard-Schumann, 1968

Lambourne, Gerald *The Fingerprint Story:* Harrap, London, 1984

Lane, Brian & Gregg, Wilfred *The Encyclopedia of Serial Killers:* Headline, London, 1992

Lane, Brian *The Butchers:* Virgin, London, 1992

Larsen, Richard W *Bundy: The Deliberate Stranger:* Prentice-Hall, USA, 1980

Lewis, Norman *The Honoured Society:* Eland Books, London, 1964

Lincoln, Victoria *Lizzie Borden. A Private Disgrace:* Souvenir, London, 1989

Linedecker, Clifford *Thrill Killers:* Futura, London, 1990

Markman, Ronald & Bosco, Dominic *Alone with the Devil:* Doubleday, New York, 1989

Marnham, Patrick *Trail of Havoc:* Viking, London, 1987

Marriner, Brian *A Century of Sex Killers:* Forum Press, London, 1992

Martin, Fido *Bodysnatchers:* Nicolson, London, 1988

Maas, Peter *The Valachi Papers:* London, 1970

Masters, Brian *Killing for Company:* Coronet, London, 1986

Masters, Brian *The Shrine of Jeffrey Dahmer:* Hodder & Stoughton, London, 1993

McGinniss, Joe *Fatal Vision:* André Deutsch, London, 1984

McGuire, Christine & Norton, Carla *The Perfect Victim:* Dell, New York, 1988

Mortimer, John *Famous Trials:* Penguin, London, 1984

Nash, J Robert *Compendium of World Crimes:* McGraw-Hill, New York, 1983

Neustatter, W Lindsay *The Mind of the Murderer:* Christopher Johnson, London, 1957

Nickel, Steven *Torso:* John Blair, North Carolina, 1989

Notable British Trials (A series comprising 83 titles)

Norris, Joel *Serial Killers:* Doubleday, New York, 1988

Norman, Lucas *The Sex Killers:* W H Allen, London, 1974

Parris, John *Scapegoat:* Duckworth, London, 1991

Pearson, John *The Profession of Violence:* Granada, London, 1984

Pope, Jeff & Shaps, Simon *True Crimes:* Boxtree, London, 1992

Paul, Philip *Murder under the Microscope:* Macdonald, London, 1990

Peters, Edward *Torture:* Basil Blackwell, New York, 1985

Posner, Gerald *Warlords of Crime:* Queen Anne Press, London, 1988

Rae, Simon, ed *Anthology of Drink:* Faber & Faber, London, 1992

Ritchie, Jean *Inside the Mind of Murderers:* Angus & Robertson, 1988

Rose, Andrew *Scandal at the Savoy:* Bloomsbury, London, 1988

Rule, Ann *The Stranger Beside Me:* W W Norton, New York, 1980

Rumbelow, Donald *The Triple Tree: Newgate, Tyburn and Old Bailey:* Harrap, London, 1982

Rumbelow, Donald *Jack the Ripper: The Complete Casebook:* Penguin, London, 1988

Schechter, Harold *Deviant:* Pocket Books, New York, 1989

Scott, Sir Harold *Crime and Criminals:* André Deutsch, London 1961

Scmalzbach, Oscar R *Profiles in Murder:* Hodder, London, 1971

Shears, Richard *Kingdom of Illusions:* Bandaid Publications, Australia, 1982

Simpson, Keith *Forty Years of Murder:* Harrap, London, 1978

Sondern, Frederick *The Mafia:* Panther, London, 1959

Smart, Carol *Women, Crime and Criminology:* Routledge & Kegan Paul, London, 1976

Smith, Ken *Inside Time:* Harrap, London, 1989

Smyth, Frank *Cause of Death:* Orbis, London, 1980

Sullivan, Robert *Goodbye Lizzie Borden:* Penguin, London, 1989

Summers, Anthony *The Secret Life of J Edgar Hoover:* Gollancz, London, 1993

Templewood, Viscount *The Shadow of the Gallows:* Gollancz, London, 1951

Treherne, John *Bonnie and Clyde:* Cape, London, 1984

Turkus, Burton *Murder Inc*: Gollancz, London, 1952

Whittington-Egan, R & M *The Bedside Book of Murder:* David & Charles, Devon, 1988

Williams, Emlyn *Beyond Belief:* Hamish Hamilton, London, 1967

Wilson, Colin *A Criminal History of Mankind:* Granada, London, 1984

Wilson, Colin *The Mammoth Book of True Crime:* Robinson, London, 1988

Wilson, Colin *Written in Blood:* Equation, Wellingborough, 1989

Wilson, Colin & Odell, Robert *Jack the Ripper: Summing Up and Verdict:* Transworld, London, 1987

Wilson, Kirk *Investigating Murder:* Robinson Publishing, London, 1990

Wilson, Robert *Return to Hell:* Javelin Books, 1988

Wyden, Peter *The Hired Killers:* W H Allen, London, 1964

Yallop, David *To Encourage the Others:* W H Allen, London, 1971

Yallop, David *In God's Name:* Cape, London, 1984

Sundry newspapers, crime periodicals and part works, supplemented by *Vanity Fair*, the *Fortean Times* and the *New Yorker*.

Index

Words set in **bold** designate an entry appearing in the text under that name. Numerals in **bold** indicate an entry concentrated on the designated topic or individual.

A6 murder 1
Abbott, Jack 51, 372
Acquittals 5
Adams, Dr Bodkin 314
Adams, Fanny, murder of **382**
Adipocere 6
Advertisements 7
Aeroplanes 7
Aiello Brothers 8
Airgun 9, 46
Alcatraz 111
Alcatraz, Birdman of 9
Alfano, Pietro, difficulties of 313
Aliases 9
Aliens, abduction by 256
Allison, Clay, spears and 363
Allitt, Beverley 267
Allorto and Sellier 9
Alpert, Red 269
Alphon, Peter Louis 2
Amendolito, Salvatore 439
Amis, Martin 270
Amityville Horror 141
Amnesia 10
Ananda VII, King of Siam 11
Anastasia, Albert 148, 148, 166
Anderson, Kirk 243
Animals
  assorted 12
  boa constrictor 215
  budgerigar 42
  Camels, homing 49
  canaries 9
  Carrier pigeons 53
  cats 55, 102, 275
  chickens 9
  dog 201
  Dahmer, and 76, 309
  Dingo 90
  Dolphin, sex with 93

  ducks 151
  goats, sex with 184
  homicidal triangle, and 309
  pig 93
  rabbits 42
  rat 142
  responsibility of 12
  sheep 216
  swan 216
  tilapia 9
  turkeys 16
  woodworm 12
Anselmi, Albert 13
Anthropometry 14
Antimony 266
Apalachin 15
Apollinaire 261
Apologies,
  murder, for 340
  rape, for 189
  robbery, for **16**
Appel, George, execution of 206
Arabin, William St Julian 17
Arm, false 389
Arm, James Smith's 17
Armstrong, Major Herbert 315
Arsenic 18
Arsenic and Old Lace 326
Arson 19
Art-B, takings of 450
Ashford, Mary 264
Ashton, John, execution of 446
Assassinations
  Falcone/Borsellino 145
  Franz Ferdinand, Archduke 133
  Kennedy, John F 207
  Kennedy, Robert 114, 158
  Lennon, John 101
  Lloyd George 9
  Long, Huey 428
  Markov, Georgi 409
  President Reagan 101
  Stalking 373
  Villa, Francisco 421
  Zapata, Emiliano 449

  Zog, King 133
Assassins 19
Atkins, Susan 226
  Manson and 124
  stabbing and 372
Atomite, value of 222
Attaché case, poisoned 20
Attorneys 21
Automatism 21
Axeman, 'Mad' Frank Mitchell 22

Baby farms 316
Backhouse, Graham 97
Badalamenti, Gaetano 312
Ballistics
  early days 158
  firefights, interpretation of 130
  first case 430
Bamber, Jeremy 24
Banana 419
Bardica 87
Barlow, Kenneth **190**
Barrie, J.M. 159
Barrow, Clyde **35**
Baths
  Acid in 3
  brides in 25
  court, in 115
  prevalence of 25
Beach Boys, Manson and 270
Beane, Sawney 51
Beck, Adolph 65
Becker, Charles 64
Benefit of Clergy 26
Bentham, Jeremy 303
Bentley, Derek **68**
Berdella, Robert Andrew 398
Berkowitz, David 19, 201, **355**
Berry, James 26, 108
Bertillion, Alphonse 14
Bethell, Creighton Randall, disposal of 305
Bhagwan, love and the 125
Bianchi, Kenneth
  crimes and romances of 348

psychological career **242**
Biggs, Ronald 27, 149
Bimbos, killer 212
Birch, the 28
Bismarck, Chancellor 98
Black Dahlia, the 123
Black Panther, the **276**
Black Panthers 130
Blackmail
 computer 29
 Hoover, J. Edgar, by 176
 invention of 28
 Kawaguchi, Sadamichi's 174
Blake, Joseph, achievement of 435
Blakely, David, murder of **109**
Blood, Colonel Thomas 74
Bloods 136
Bloodstains
 dingo and 92
 drops and 97
 history of **30**
 sex and 216, 372
Bodies
 absence of 5
 disposal of 101
Body language 31
Bodysnatching 32, 60
Boesky, Ivan 258, 321
Bolero, Ravel's 33
Bones, ground 34
Bonnie and Clyde 35
Bonny, Anne, life of 37
Borden, Lizzie 38, 121
Boston Globe 121
Boston Strangler 180, **188**
Bottomless pit, location of 343
Bovingdon Bug, the 446
Bow Street Runners, invention of 128
Bowden, John, case of 93
Brady, Ian 39
 Hindley, and 171
 Nonce, as 284
 Tapes 384
Brank, brake or Scold's head 40
Brazil 28
Bredius, Dr Abraham, as critic 416
Bridgewater, Carl 66, 123, 422
Brink's 40
Brinkley, Richard **2**
Broad, Mary **142**
Brodie, William 199
Broughton, Sir Jock 'Delves' **432**
Brown, Eric **15**
Browne and Kennedy **154**
Brussel, Dr
 Boston Strangler, and 189
 Mad Bomber, and 248

Brutality, Mafia and 119
Buchalter, Louis 167, 268
Buchanan, Dr Robert W **55**
Buchanon, James, friends of 114
Budgerigars 42
Buettner-Janusch, John 315
Bundy, Carol **165**
Bundy, Theodore
 Aspen escape 213
 case of **43**
 hair evidence 156
 Pick-up lines 229
 Preview 317
 References of 337
 sentencing of 183
 Throwaways 391
Bunions 133
Burke and Hare 45, 255, 256
Burmese, habits of 15
Burroughs, William 56
Butch Cassidy and the Sundance Kid, fate of 47
Butler, Robert 43
Butler, Tom, life of 387
Bywaters, Frederick **390**

Cadaveric spasm 48
Caffey Syndrome, the 428
Calabro, Carmine 111
Calcraft, William 161, 186
Calhoun, John B, experiments of 324
Calvey, Linda 175
Camargo, Daniel 48
Cambo, Judge 49
Camels, homing 49
Campden Wonder, the 49
Cannibalism 50
Cannibals
 Beane, Sawney 51
 Chikatilo, Andrei 51
 Dahmer, Jeffrey 50
 Dzhumagaliev, Nikolai 198
 Fish, A H 130
 Packer, Alferd 300
 Pearce, Alexander 306
 Sagawa, Issei 354
 Vampire of Sacramento 415
Canonisation 51
Canter, David, and profiling 100
Capone, Alphonse
 Acquittals 5
 Aiello brothers 8
 bodyguards, and 448
 Cicero 60
 Hawthorne Restaurant 163
 life of **304**
 Lingle and 230
 Lustig, and 107

Memorabilia 256
O'Bannion, and 290
 philanthropist, as 326
 Tuohy, and 272
 Untouchables and 412
Cards, collectors 52
Carrier pigeons 53
Cash 53
Cash dispensers, shortcomings of 54
Castration 188
Castro, Fidel 114, 263
Castro, Tom **392**
Cat's eyes, dead 55
Catcher in the Rye 336
Cathedral, the 54
Catholics
 celibacy, and 31
 oaths, and 290
Cats 275
Celebrity
 Canonisation 51
 Lucas, Henry Lee 237
 retrospective 200
 Stalking 372
 Success 377
Chaffers, Alexander **28**
Chamberlain, Lynne **90**
Chandler, Raymond, views of 109
Chaplin, Charles, kidnapping of 56
Chapman, Mark 20, 101, 37
Chase, Richard **415**
Chassenée, Bartholomé 12
Chater, death of 158
Cheerleaders 56
Chevalier, Yvonne **70**
Chikatilo, Andrei
 brain of 136
 cannibal, as 51
 execution of 62
 life of **57**
 masturbation, and 254
 Pick-up lines 229
China travellers 59
Chinese, the 443
Chiodo, Peter 431
Chisam, Colin **383**
Chocolates, poisoning and 315
Christianity 51, 60, 71
Christie, Harold 288
Christie, John Reginald 10, **344**
Christmas 60
Cicero 60
Clark, Douglas **165**, 200
Classroom slayings 182
Cleeland, Paul 410
Clements, Dr 80
Clown, Pogo the 52

Cocaine smuggling 282
Coconuts, effect of 11
Co-ed killer, the **206**
Coffins 60
Cohen, Ronald 10
Colander 391
Collector, The 336
Collins, William J, luck of 240
Collinson, Harry, murder of 313
Colombia, Little 61
Communist threat, and satanism 347
Compton, Veronica, romance with **348**
Concentration 61
Condemned Hold 278
Condoms 62
Cons
 Ferguson, Arthur 107
 Gray, Barry Edward 256
 Kujau, Conrad **120**
 Lucas, Henry Lee 237
 Lustig, 'Count' Victor 107
 Philips, Judith **310**
 Toft, Mary 42
 Valfierno, Marquis de 114
Conspiracies
 Craig and Bentley 68
 Kennedy, John F 207
 Kennedy, Robert 114
 Lincoln, Abraham 228
 Luciani, Albino 239
 Marlowe, Christopher 253
 Monroe, Marilyn 261
Contempt 62
Contempt of Court 63
Cook, John 301, 376
Coolidge, Valorus, 80
Cooling, rate of 83
Cooper, Alan 21
Cooper, D B 447
Corday, Charlotte, head of 168
Cornhill Burglary, the 63
Corruption 64
Costello, Frank, luck of 166
Cotton, Mary Ann 329
Courgette 419
Court of Appeal 65
Courtesy 66
Crack 62, 67
Crack kids **212**
Cracksmen, attractions of 155
Craig and Bentley 68
Crank, the 70
Cream, Dr Thomas Neill 162, **375**
Crime passionel 70, 118
Crime Without a Cause, discovery of 233
Crime, last decent 149

Criminals
 background of 71
 evolution of 128
Crippen, Cora 73
Crippen, Hawley Harvey 71, 147
Crips 136
Croswell, Edgar **15**
Crouch, Ben 32
Crown jewels 74
Cucumbers 419
Cupboards, fitted 105
Curare 9
Cussen, Desmond 110
Cuthbert, Cyril 74
Cutler, Bruce, lawyer as 403
Cutolo, Rosetta 145
Cutpurse, Moll 75

Dahmer, Jeffrey
 animals, and 76, 309
 cannibal, as 50
 Edwards, Tracy, and 105
 fantasies of 126
 Heads and 168
 life of **76**
 masturbator, as 253
 Oxford Apartments 299
 photographer as 370
 sentencing of 183
 shrine of 51
 Sinthasomphone, Konerack, and 106
 Zombie 451
Database 78
Date rape 79
Davis, Raymond, murder of 231
De Crespigny, Sir Claude 85
Dean, Laurence, case of 428
Death Angels, California's 449
Death, Certification of 80
Death, colour of 157
Death, Life after 80
Death, time of 83
Debt, effect of 83
Decomposition, rate of 83
Defoe, Daniel, life of **377**
DeFreo, Ronnie, case of 141
Dementia Americana 85
Demjanjuk, John **193**
Dempster, to 87
Derrick, origins of 87
DeSalvo, Albert **188**
Descartes, intelligence of 235
Detection, risk of 87
Detectives, inventor of 88
Diatoms 88
Dickens, Charles 88
Dillinger, John Herbert 89

Dingo 90
Diseases, as weapon 425
Dismemberment, 93
Dix, Enoch 130
Dobkin, Harry 227
Dolezal, Frank, suspect as 397
Dolphins, sex with 93
Donoghue, William **101**
Dougal, Samuel Herbert 94
Downey, Lesley Ann 384
Doyle, Sir Arthur Conan 95
Drawing and quartering 97, 114, 329
Drowning 88
Drucci, Vincent, coffin of 60
Druitt, suspect as 368
Drunk, very
 Cutpurse, Moll 75
 Dahmer, Jeffrey 76, 451
 Donoghue, William **101**
 Ellis, Ruth 110
 Hayes, John **166**
 Johns, Tommy 200
 Kidd, Captain 209
 Molloy, Mike **102**
 Parker, Annie 200
Dryden, Albert **313**
Drysdale, Alexander 140
Duck, Mock, marksmanship of 395
Dudley, Deborah, death of 286
Dudley, John, consumption of 50
Dudley, Reg 165
Duelling 98
Duffy, John Francis 99
Dumdums 101
Durability 101
Durable 102
Durand-Deacon, Olive 3
Dutch, the 102
Duval, Claude 426
Dyer, Amelia **316**, 375
Dyer, Susan, experience of 373
Dylan, Bob 163
Dzhumagaliev, Nikolai **198**

Ears, severed 104
Eastern bloc 104
Edwards, Tracy, luck of 105
Egle, Bob, death of 445
Eiffel Tower, sale of 107
Eighteenth Amendment 107, 122
Einstein, Izzy 323
Electric chair 11, **108**, 205, 375
Eliot, T S 232
Ellis, Ruth 109
Ellsome, Charles 65
Elveson, Francine 110
Emotional Maturity Instruction 275

Erroll, Lord 104, 432
Erskine, Kenneth 200
Escapes
    Alcatraz, from 111
    Aspen, from 213
    Cathedral, the 54
    Dartmoor, from 22
    diet, on 43
    Kangaroo, as 203
    mules, by 36
    Saltillo Prison, from 355
    San Quentin, from 355
    Sheppard, Jack, by 362
Escobar, Pablo
    car of 35
    life of **112**
    prison of **54**
    zoo of 452
Etherington, James and Marjorie **413**
Ethyl ether, cocaine and 400
Evans, Eddie, murder of 173
Evans, Timothy **344**
Eve, 'Teddy Bear', murder of 93
Exhibits, in court 115

Faces, identification and 182
Facial reconstruction 117
Fagin 117, 159
Fahmy, Madame 118
Fakes 120, 263, 324, 392
Falcione, Michael 53, 403
False confessions 49, **122**, 429
Family Pact, the 128
Family, the Manson 123
Fantasising 125
Fashion 88, 448
Fauntleroy, Henry 274
Feazell, Vic 238
Female Offender, the 127
Ferguson, Arthur 107
Ferrers, Lord Lawrence,
    execution of 127
Feynman, Richard, cracksman as 233
Fielding, Henry 128
Fifth Amendment, the 128
Film Extras Union 224
Finance, High
    Al Fayed 169
    Bank notes, prime 170
    Fauntleroy, Henry 274
    Maxwell, Robert 170
    Milken, Michael 258
    Sears, Richard W 170
    Vaughan, David 71
    Wright, Whitaker 439
    Zlotys 450
Finger, George Mitchell's 159

Fingerprints **129**, 341
Fink, Isidor 265
Fish, A H 130
Flanders, Moll 378
Flowers, gangsters' 131
Football 453
Footprints 132
Ford, Arthur Kendrick **371**
Forensic science
    anthropometry 14
    ballistics 130, 158
    bloodstains 30
    death, time of 83
    diatoms 88
    dingo and 92
    Doyle, Sir Arthur Conan 96
    ears and 104
    facial reconstruction 117
    fingerprints 129
    footprints 132
    genetic fingerprinting 139
    hair 156
    Metropolitan police laboratory 74
Forfarazzo 338
Forgery
    Chaudron, Yves 414
    Hebborn, Eric 263
    Hitler Diaries **120**
    Keating, Tom 264
    Provenance 324
    Van Meegeren 416
Fouqereaux, Count 'Freddie' 289
Fraden, Harlow 55
Franz Ferdinand, Archduke 133
Frasso, Contessa de 222
Frayne, Laurence 284
French Connection, the 133
French, the 443
Freud, ideas of 257
Funerals, serious 132

G-men 144
Gacy, John Wayne 53, 126
Galante, Carmine 312
Gallo, William, head of 167
Gallstones 4
Galton, Sir Francis 129
Galvanic research 136
Gangs 136
Gardner, Marge, body of 386
Garrison, Jim, deliberations of 208
Gas chamber, the 137
Gein, Edward 138, 274
Genetic fingerprinting 139
Genovese, Vito 167
George II, robbery of 258
Gerald Stano 31

Gerasimov, Mikhail 117
Getty, J. Paul III, kidnapping of 104
Giacalone, Diane 403
Giacometti, how to forge 325
Giancana, Sam 261, 364
Gibbets 142
Gilchrist, Marion, murder of **95**
Gill, Susan 175
Gilmore, Gary, eyes of 116
Giraud, Henri 425
Glasgow, identification parades in 96
Glatman, Harvey Murray 143
God, justice and 201
Goddard, Calvin, and ballistics 158
Goddard, Rayner 28, 406
Godfather, the 144
Godmothers, Mafia 145
Goebbels 223
Goering 223, 287, 418
Golden Triangle, the 65, **145**
Gordon, Lord George, imprisonment of 146
Gorringe, Margaret 386
Gotti, John
    chainsaw, and 93
    lawn of 324
    life and trial of **403**
    new broom, as 448
    philanthropist, as 326
    Westies and 430
    wiretaps and 385
Gourbin, Emil 232
Graham, Jack Gilbert 8
Grahame, Kenneth, survival of 436
Graphology 146
Gray, Barry Edward, coup of 256
Great Gatsby, inspiration for 147
Great Train Robbery 27, **149**
Gresh, Theresa 265
Griffith, D W 147
Guillotine 149
Guilt, teenagers and 150
Guldensuppe, William, case of 151
Gun control 151
Gunness, Belle 152
Gutshot 155
Gutteridge, George 154

Haarmann, Fritz **357**
Habeas Corpus 21
Haigh, John George, **3**, 231
Hair
    red, as clue 87
    red, criminality of 127
    study of **156**
Halifax Gibbet 157

Hall, Sir Edward Marshall 119
Hamilton, Dr Albert 158
Hammett, Dashiell, elegance of 147
Hanging, history of 160
Hanratty, James **1**
Hansen, Robert 162
Harding, John Wesley, life of
  163
Harper, Lynne 373
Harris, Anthony Cornelius 449
Hartevelt, Renée, murder of 354
Hartwig, Clayton **191**
Hassett, Patrick **370**
Hauptfleisch, Petrus 232
Hauptmann, Richard Bruno **219**
Hawkins, John 422
Hawthorne Restaurant, battle of
  163
Hay, Josslyn, Lord Erroll, murder of
  432
Hayes, Catherine **166**, 310
Hayward, Captain Simon **381**
Hearst, Patty 151
Hearst, William Randolph, perspi-
  cacity of 151
Heath, Neville George Clevely 386
Heathrow 388
Hebborn, Eric, views of 263
Heidnik, Gary Michael **285**
Heirens, William 199, 360
Hennard, George **235**
Henry, Edward Richard 129
Herschel, William 129
Heslin, Patrick E, murder of 226
Hickey, Michael 66
Hickman, William Edward 303
Hightower, William A 226
Highwaymen
  Apologies of 16
  Courtesy of 66
  Cutpurse, Moll 75
  Duval, Claude 426
  Horse Patrol 178
  M'Lean, James 426
  Pillory, in 311
  Sheppard, Jack 362
  story of **170**
  Turpin, Dick 406
Hijacking 447
Hill, Anita 79
Hill, Virginia 223
Hindley, Myra
  Downey, Lesley Ann and 384
  life of **171**
  Remorse of 341
  Tapes and 384
Hinman, Gary, murder of 225
Hirasawa, Sadamichi 174
Hitler, Adolph 134

Hitler Diaries **120**
Hitmen
  bogus 56
  Britain, in 87
  generally **174**
Hoffa, Jimmy, site of 256
Holland, Camille, murder of **94**
Holloway, Wanda **56**
Holmes, Sherlock 96
Homicidal triangle, the **309**
Hoodlum 137
Hooker, Cameron **365**
Hoover, J Edgar
  anti-Communism 249
  Costello, and 166
  Dillinger, and 90
  FBI, and 324
  G-men 144
  Las Vegas 224
  life of **175**
  Monroe, and 263
Horse Patrol, the 178
Horses, killing 178
Howard, John 319
Hulks 179
Hume, Donald 7
Hunter, Freedom, luck of 240
Huntley, Brian 333
Hurkos, Peter 179
Hyde, Dr Clark 296

Ideas, Gein's 138
Identification 182
In-laws **187**, 296
Infanticide 317
Inflatable dolls 182
Ingram, Paul R 183
Initiation rites 185
Injection, lethal 186
Inquisition, the 187
Insane 188
Insulin 424
Iowa 191
Irish Crown Jewels 74
Irish, the 59, 201, 442
Irving, Clifford, views of, 120
Italian-American Civil Rights
    League, composition of 144
Ivan the Terrible 192

Jack the Hat, murder of 195
Jack the Ripper
  career of **196**
  kidneys and 211
  musical, as 270
  Ripperology 344
  Solution, the police's 368
Jails, best 198
Jake 198

Jekyll and Hyde 199
Johns, Tommy, career of 200
Johnson, Dr Samuel 200
Johnson, Willie Boy 403
Jones, Cranog 138
Jonson, Ben, abilities of 99
Joyce, William, trial of 310
Judges, odd
  assorted 406
    Arabin, William St Julian 17
    Cambo 49
    Fleet 183
    Goddard 28, 183, 406
Jury 200
Justice 201
Justification 201

Kallinger, Joseph, wiring of 405
Kangaroo 203
Kaplany, Geza de **5**
Karpis, Alvin 'Creepy' 90
Kasoff, 'Muddy' 269
Kaye, Emily 268
Kelly, George 'Machine Gun' 144
Kelly, Ned 203
Kemmler, William, execution of
  205
Kemper, Edmund, 206
Kennedy, John F
  assassination of **207**
  election of 364
  indiscretions of 176
    Monroe, Marilyn, and 261
Kennedy, Robert
  death of 114
  Monroe, and 261
Kennedy Smith, William, case of
  154
Ketch, John, achievements of 209
Kidd, Captain William 209
Kidnapping
  Chaplin, Charles 56
  coffins and 61
  Getty, J. Paul III 104
  invention of 211
  Lindbergh 211, 219
  Parker, Marion 303
  Slater, Stephanie 61
  Robles, June 277
  Urschel, Charles F 144
  Whittle, Lesley **276**
Kidney, Ripper's 211
King, Harry, advice of 233
King, Rodney 6, **213**
Knowles, Paul, moment of 377
Kosminski, Aaron, suspect as 369
Kray twins
  Attaché case 20
  barmaid, and 113

Frank Mitchell, and **22**
Jack the Hat, and 195
  killing, and 196
  lives of **214**
  Ronald and matrimony 31
  Lord Boothby and 338
  military careers of **292**
Kujau, Conrad, endeavours of 120
Kürten, Peter 19, 125, **219**

Lacassagne, cadaveric spasm, and 48
Lacenaire, Pierre-François 218
Ladders 219
Lafarge, Marie 297
Lake, Leonard 279
Lamphere, Ray 153
Lamson, Dr George Henry 438
Lancelin, Madame, murder of 116
Landru, Henri Desiré 220
Lansky, Meyer 223, 224, 288
Las Vegas 222
Laughing gas 63
Lawnmower 224
Le Neve, Ethel 72
Lee, Andrew 21, 83
Lee, John 224
Leg, stabbed 225
Leopold and Loeb 320
Lepine, Marc 182
Lepke, Louis 269
Lesbianism, legality of 368
Lie detector, invention of 226
Lime, types of 227
Lincoln, Abraham 228
Lindbergh kidnapping 211, **219**
Lines, Pick-up 229
Lingle, Jake, murder of 230
List, John 447
Lividity 232
Lloyd George 88
Loaf, French 420
Locard, Edmond 232
Locks, combination 233
Loeb, case of 320
Lombroso, Cesare 127, 234
London Bridge 234
Lord Chief Justices, calibre of 406
Lottò, burial of 235
Loughlans, Harold 371, 388
Lovat, Lord, execution of 167
Love, pursuit of 125
Lubianka 399
Luby's Cafeteria, murders at 235
Lucan, Lord 236
Lucas, Henry Lee 237
Luciani, Albino, murder of 239
Luciano, Lucky 113, 275, 321
Luck, hard 240

Luetgart, Louise **367**
Lunette 240
Lustig, 'Count' Victor, life of 107
Luton sack murder 181
Lyons, Bruce 303

M'Lean, James 426
Macaronis 136
MacDonald, Dr Jeffrey 200, **244**
Macnaghten memorandum 368
Maconochie, Alexander, life of 246
Mad Bomber, the 247
Madonia family, wealth of 187
Mafia
  Apalachin 15
  Bahamas, and 288
  brutality and 119
  Commission 269
  Contempt, expressions of 62
  Courtesy of 67
  Decline of 84
  discovery of 248
  existence of 122
  Faithful, the 119
  Godfather, the 144
  Godmothers 145
  Inquisition, and 187
  Madonia family 187
  Maranzano, Salvatore 254
  Omerta 293
  Onorevole 294
  pigeons and 53
  Public relations 325
  Religion, and 339
  Stupidity, and 376
  water and 420
  Yuppies 448
Maggots 6
Magic Eraser 249
Mahai Chai prison 319
Mahon, Patrick, case of **268**
Mallory, Richard, murder of 440
Malory, Sir Thomas, life of 250
Manhattan Melodrama 90
Mannings, Frederick and Maria 88
Manson, Charles
  Atkins, Susan, and 226
  Beach Boys, and 271
  Cielo Drive, and 431
  Copycat slayings 244
  Family, the 123
  Hinman, Gary, and 225
  killing and 125
  Leg, stabbed 225
  life of 250
  musical, as 270
  sex and 124
  Revelations, Book of 342

White Album, and 431
Manton, Bertie 181
Maranzano, Salvatore 254
Marcinkus, Cardinal 240
Marine fraud 252
Markov, Georgi 409
Markowitz, Michael, idea of 389
Marlowe, Christopher 253
Martin, Susanna, witch as 437
Masochism, legality of 352
Mass murderers, definition of 387
Masturbation 253
Matson, Mark 126
Mattina, Nunzio La 394
Mattress, to go on the 254
Matuscka, Sylvestre **421**
Max Factor 356
Maxwell, Robert, 88, 170, 270, 399
Maybrick, James 345
Maynard, Bob 164
Mazzarino, monks of 339
McCummings, Bernard 243
McDougald, Dan, ideas of 275
McGurn, Machine Gun Jack 272
McKenny, H J, career move of 93
McKinney, Joyce, love of **243**
Medellin 254
Media and crime 51, 91
Medicine, first steps 32
Memorabilia 256
Memory, recalled 256
Menesclou, head of 168
Mengele, Dr Joseph 34
Mercury, red 412
Mercy 257
Merrett, Donald 104
Merrifield, Louisa 347
Messina, Rosa, testimony of 113, 420
Metesky, George **247**
Mexicans, the 443
Meyers, Billy 265
Michelle Remembers 346
Miles, Sydney 68
Milken, Michael 258
Mine, Anti-tank **15**
Miner, Bill, life of **160**
Missouri Protocol, the **186**
Mitchell, 'Mad' Frank **22**
Mitchell, George 159
Mobsters' earning power 53
Modus operandi 260
Moll, Cutpurse 75
Molloy, Mike, case of **102**
Molloy, Pat 66, 123
Mona Lisa, theft of 260, 414
Money, effect of 236, 288, 423
Monroe, Marilyn 261
Monster's Ball 146

Montesino, Zosimo 174
Montgomery, Jim 21
Mooney, Tom 263
Mortal combat 264
Morton, Jelly Roll 271
Moseley, Billy, murder of **164**
Mothers 265
Mozart, Wolfgang Amadeus 266
Münchausen syndrome by proxy 267
Müller, Franz 89
Mugging, record 243
Multiple Personality Disorder 5, **242**
Murder bag, invention of 267
Murder Inc. 248, **268**
Murderee 270
Murderesses, looks of 330
Murdrum 88
Musicals 270
Mussolini 222

Napoleon 273
Narcotics 452
  Camels, homing 49
  Colombia, Little 61
  Crack 67
  crack dealers 62
  Dutch the, and 102
  Escobar, Pablo Emilio 112
  French Connection 133
  Golden Triangle 65, 145
  Magic Eraser 249
  Medellin 254
  Nicholl and 282
  Opium, story of 294
  Pizza Connection 312
  Swallowers 380
  smuggling 274
  Tax havens 385
  Throne Room 391
  Tobacco and 394
  Tranquilandia 400
  Triads 401
  White death 432
  X, Operation 442
Necrophilia 78, 81, 206, 360, 452
Needlework 200
Neilson, Donald 276
Nelson, 'Baby Face' 89
Nesbit, Evelyn **85**
Ness, Eliot 62, 305, 396, **411**
Newgate 278
Newton-John, Olivia, eyes of 373
Ng, Charles 279
Nicholl, Charles, curious survival of 282
Nilsen, Dennis
  admission of 151

living with **80**
mirrors, and **259**
upbringing of **283**
Nonce 284
Norfolk Island 246, **284**, 361
North Marshall Street 285
Nuclear theft **412**

O'Bannion, Dion
  Coffin of 60
  Flowers and 132
  life of **290**
  narrow squeak of 6
O'Bryan, Timmy 303
O'Connor, Jimmy 411
O'Connor, William, justice and 429
O'Dell, Joseph 21, 371
Oakes, Sir Harry 288
Oaths 290
Oesterreich, Walburga 291
Officer material, Krays as 292
OK Corral, gunfight at 363
Omerta 293
One-way ride, invention of 294
Onorevole 294
Opium, story of 294
Optographs 296
Oral hygiene treatment 296
Orchard, Harry, career of 438
Orfila, Joseph Bonaventura 296
Organised crime, Hoover and 175
Organised/disorganised murderers 298
Orgeat 273
Orgies, **the Family's** 124
Orkney Islands transcripts 346
Orton, Arthur, case of **394**
Orwell, George 62
Oscar 'the Evaporator', achievement of 270
Ostrog, Michael, suspect as 369
Oxford Apartments 299

Packer, Alferd 300
Pallot, Marie, murder of 338
Palmer, Dr William 61, **301**, 376
Panopticon, the 303
Panthers, Black 130
Panty Burglar, the 303
Papin, Christiane and Lea, case of **116**
Parker, Annie, handiwork of 200
Parker, Marion 303
Parking ticket 356
Parricides 304
Parrots 42, 274
Pastrée-Beaussier 233
Pavements, allure of 303

Pawnbrokers, guillotines and 356
Payne, A D, disintegration of 305
Peace, Charlie, ladder of 220
Peacock, Linda 386
Pearce, Alexander 306
Pedigree Chum 307
Penn, Sean 336
Pepys, Samuel, hanging and 200
Perera, Dr Samuel 308
Perruggia, Vincenzo **260**, 415
Perry, John 102
Perry, Michael 373
Petiot, Dr Marcel 228
Pets 309
Petty Treason 310
Philips, Judith 310
Photography, victims of 370
Picasso 260
Pierrepoint, Albert, 287, 311
Pillory, the 311
Pino, Anthony 'Fats' 41
Pirates, heads of 167
Pittsburgh Phil, career of 269
Pizza Connection, the 312
Planning Officers 313
Plug uglies 136
Poisoning 314
Poland, opportunities in 450
Pomeroy, Jesse 316
Popp, Dr Joseph Lewis 29
Portuguese, the 442
Postmen's heads 232
Poulin, Robert 182
Precociousness 315
Pregnancy
  phantom 119
  effect of 316
Pressing 317
Price, John Giles 285
Price, Karen 34
Prisons
  best 198
  Condemned sermon 62
  Crank, the 70
  Debt, imprisonment for 83
  Gordon, Lord George 146
  history of **318**
  Hulks 179
  Lubianka 399
  Negative blocking 275
  Newgate 278
  Panopticon, the 303
  Separate System, the 358
  Tobacco 394
  Treadwheel 401
  Ucciardone 409
Privilege 320
Procession 321
Profiler 322

Profiling
  Britain, in 100
  Database 78
  DeSalvo, and 190, 322
  Elveson, Francine 110
  genesis of 248
  Iowa, and 191
  Organised and disorganised 298
  Profiler 322
  Quantico 328
Prohibition
  Acquittals in 5
  Aiello Brothers 8
  Anselmi and Scalise 13
  Corruption 64
  Cicero 60
  Eighteenth Amendment 107
  Flowers and 131
  Hawthorne Restaurant 163
  Jake 198
  Morton, Samuel 178
  O'Connor, William and 429
  Prohibition agents 323
  Smokescreen 366
  Untouchables, the 411
Prohibition agents 323
Project Artichoke 114
Proksch, Udo, case of 252
Prospects, criminal 323
Provenance 324
Provocation, and women 70
Prunier, Théotime, head of 168
Psychic detection, Hurkos and **179**
Psycho, inspiration for 138
Public relations 325
Puente, Dorothea 326

Quantico 328
Quartering, unpopularity of 329

R v. Collins 350
Racism, FBI and 177
RICO legislation, effect of 84
Rackets, origin of 137
Radford, Frederick, case of 18
Ramirez, Richard 331
Rape, aspects of 79, 250, **332**
Ratcliffe Highway murders 334
Raubal, Geli 134
Reade, Pauline, murder of 173
Reading material 336
Recalled memory **256**
Receivers 75, 159
Recruitment, hoods of 336
References 337
Reis, Professor A R 338
Reles, Abe 'Kid Twist' 9, **269**
Religion, abuse of 339
Remorse 340

Reno Brothers, lives of 399
Repsold, Herbert, escape of 355
Revelations, Book of 342
Richardson, Charles, ways of 398
Riina, Salvatore 'the beast' 67, 235, 420
Rillington Place, Number 10 344
Riots, race, causes of 214
Ripperology 344
Rivett, Sandra, murder of 236
Robberies 388
  Bank of America 233
  Brink's 40
  Cornhill Burglary, the 63
  Crown Jewels 74
  Dillinger, by 89
  gem thieves 389
  Gotti's, John 389
  Great Train 149
  Heathrow, at 388
  Mafia, and 325
  Mona Lisa 260, 414
  petrol tax 389
  Reichsbank 282
  Société Générale 281
  stagecoach 160
  take away 54
  Trains 160
  Umbrellas and 410
Robinson, George, case of 436
Robles, June, kidnapping of 277
Rodine 347
Rolling pin 348
Romances 31, 348
Ronsisvalle, Luigi, career of 174
Ross, Charlie, kidnapping of 211
Rothstein, Arnold, life of 147
Rubin, Max, head of 167
Rubinstein, Serge 274
Ruggiero, Angelo 385
Rummel, William James 349
Runyon, Damon, influence of 349
Rupolo, Ernest 167
Rust, Albert 126
Ryan, Donald, murder of 93

Sabah, Hasan bin 19
Sacco and Vanzetti 351
Sacher-Masoch, Leopold von 351
Sade, Marquis de 352
Sadism 318
Safecracking
  Locks, combination 233
  Gut/jam/ragshot 155
  how to **352**
  safety of 63

Sagawa, Issei 354
Salem 437
Salieri, Antonio 266
Sam, Son of 19, 201, 355
Sanhuber, Otto, case of **291**
Sansons, dynasty of 356
Satanic Ritual Abuse 10, 183, 227, 256, **346**
Saughton, Fishman of 9
Saunders, Ernest, recovery of 425
Sausages 99, **357**, 368
Sayre, Lincoln 187
Scalice, Frank 84
Scalise, John **13**
Schaefer, Gerard John 357, 423
Schroeder, Irene, execution of 206
Schultz, Dutch, death of 269
Schwammberger, Josef, amnesia of 425
Schwartz, Charles Henry **7**
Scotland, June **348**
Seddon, Frederick 222
Segret, Fernande 221
Selwyn, George, habits of 167
Senior, Geoffrey, robberies of 388
Separate System, the 358
Serial killers, American pre-eminence 342
  definition of 387
  missed vocations of 423
  Organised/disorganised 298
  Profiler, and 322
  Sex crimes, and 359
  Success, and 377
  Torture, and 398
  Trolling, and 404
Servants, feelings of 116
Sesamoid, popularity of, 368
Sex crimes 359
Sexism 361
Shakespeare, existence of 253
Shark, arm in 17
  guards, as 203
Shaw, Bernard 336
Sheppard, Jack, life of 362
Sherman, Lydia 329
Sheward, Martha 159
Shoes 256
Short, Elizabeth 123
Shot, getting 388
Siegel, Benjamin, life of 122, **222**
Silence, Wall of 363
Sinatra, Frank 261, 364
Singapore, thrashings in 28
Singleton, Lawrence, motivation of 201
Sinthasomphone, Konerack 106, 452
Sirhan, Sirhan 114

Skerrit, Joseph, death of 309
Slater, Oscar 95
Slave, sex 365
Smith, Francis 140
Smith, George Joseph **25**, 231
Smith, Half-hanged 156
Smith, James 17
Smith, Moe 323
Smith, William Kennedy 260
Smokescreen 366
Soap 367
Sodomy 179, **368**
Solomon, Ikey, life of 117
South African Penal Code 418
Spaggiari, Albert 281
Spahn's Ranch 124
Spanish Fly 371
Sperm 58, 370
Spilsbury, Sir Bernard 25, 73, 115, 268, **371**
Spree killers, definition of 387
Squashing, gravel mover, by 37
   rocks, by 158
   Pressing, by 317
Squirrel, frozen 427
St Louis Serial Toe Sucker, the 303
St Valentine's massacre 305
Stabs 372
Stalking 372
Stan, Colleen Jean **365**
Stano, Gerald **31**
Stanton, Edwin McMasters 228
Statistics, American murder 447
Statue of Liberty, sale of 107
Stevens, Walter, charges of 175
Stevenson, Robert Louis 109
Stielow 158
Stomach analysis 373
Stoneley, John William 201
Stoneyhurst 393
Storie, Valerie 1
Straighten, to 374
Strangulation 374
Stroud, Robert Franklin 9
Strychnine 375
Stupidity 82, **376**
Success, serial killers and 377
Suicides, posture of 12
Suits, William Calcraft's 161
Sukarno, Dewi 212
Sunset Slayer **165**
Supernatural 33, **140**
Sutcliffe, Peter 378
Swallowers 380
Swanson Marginalia 368
Swedish justice **380**
Sweeney Todd, existence of 381
Sweet Fanny Adams 382
Swope, Thomas, murder of 296

Swordstick 383

Tanet, Mustapha, record of 333
Tapes 384
Tate, Sharon, killing of 431
Tax havens 385
Taylor, William, execution of 206
Techies 385
Teeth-marks 386
Teeth-snatching 387
Terminology 387
Terrible Gennas 65
Terror 388
Thailand 33, 319
Thallium 445
Thaw, Harry **85**
Thiefcatchers 290
Thiefrow 388
Thompson, Edith 390
Thornton, Sara 361
Throwaways 391
Thugs 392
Thurber, James 336
Tichborne Claimant, the 392
Tinning, Marybeth 428
Tobacco 394
Toft, Mary 42
Tolkein, J R R 336
Toms, John 430
Tongs 395
Toole, Ottis Elwood 237
Torbet, Alex 9
Torso Murders, the 395
Torture, 201, **397**
Tracey, William 445
Trading justice 399
Traffic lights, crime and 399
Train Robbery, invention of 399
Tranquilandia 400
Treadwheel 401
Tree, to plant 309
Trevor-Roper, and forgeries 120
Triads
   Dutch, and 103
   Opium, and 295
   Recruitment 336
   story of **401**
   Tongs, and 395
Trolling 404
Tropmann, Jean Baptiste 405
Truitt, Kendall 191
Truscott, Stephen 374
Tuaregs, the 442
Tuohy, Roger 'the Terrible' 272
Turkus, Burton 269
Turpin, Dick 406
Turtle 427
Twain, Mark 336

Tyburn 407
Tyson, Mike 408

Ucciardone 409
Umbrellas 409
Unanue, Manuel de Dios 231
Unfair arrest 410
Unicorn, the 103
Unreasonable 226
Unruth, Howard 411
Untouchables, the 411
Uranium 412

Vacuum cleaner, human 389
Vaginal devices 414
Valachi, Joe 196, 399
Valfierno, Marquis Eduardo de 414
Vampire of Sacramento 415
Van Meegeren, Hans 416
Van Schoor, Louis 418
Vanzetti, Bartolomeo **351**
Vaughan, David 71
Vegetables 419
Veil, Thomas de 399
Vendetta 420
Vermeer, Jan 417
Viaducts 421
Villa, Francisco 421
Vinci, Sam, case of 6
Virtual reality 422
Vitiligo 422
Vocations, missed 423
Von Bülow, Claus 237

Waco, FBI and 329
Wagner, Waltraud, treatment of 296
Waite, Dr Arthur Warren 425
Waldheim's disease 425
Walker, Ernest 231
Walker, William, murder of 130
Walpole, Horace 426
Warby, Ian, crimes of 377
Ward, Judith 123, 429
Warner, Frederick 382
Watchmen 426
Waterloo Dummy **101**
Waugh, Auberon, sensations of 388
Weapons 427
Webb, Jenny, technique of 389
Weber, Jeanne 427
Weiss, Dr Carl Austin 428
Weiss, Hymie 163
West Midlands Serious Crime Squad 429
Westies 430
Whacks 430
Wheeldon, Mrs 9
Whitchelo, Rodney **307**

White Album 431
White death 432
White Mischief 432
White, Stanford, murder of **85**
Whittle, Lesley, kidnapping of **276**
Whybrow, Susan **224**
Whyos 430
Widow of Windy Nook 348
Wife murders, reason for 87
Wild, Jonathan 435
Wilkinson, Barbara 317
William Burroughs 56
Williams, Doyle, health of 241
Williams, John 334
Williams, Renwick 146
Williamson, Debra Sue, murder of 238
Wilson, Dennis 270
Wilson, Exxie, murder of 165

Wilson, Mary Elizabeth 347
Windsor, Duke of 288
Witchcraft, British **177**, 310
Witchcrazes 436
Wizardry, Scotland Yard's 413
Wobblies 438
Wodehouse, P G, treason of 310
Wolfsbane 438
Workman, Charles 270
World-Wide Business Centre 439
Wright, Whitaker 439
Writers, making of 292
Wuornos, Aileen 440

X, Operation 442
Xenophobia 442

Yakuza, the 444

Yorkshire Ripper, alternative 444
Young, Graham 445
Young, John, execution of 446
Youngstown, crime in 446
Yu, Wong, errors of 447
Yuppies 448

Zapata, Emiliano, assination of 449
Zebra Killings, the 449
Zeks 62
Zlotys, Polish 450
Zodiac Killers, the 450
Zog, King 133
Zombie 451
Zoo, private 452
Zuta, Jack, death of 366
Zyklon B 453